V I P
WALES
1992

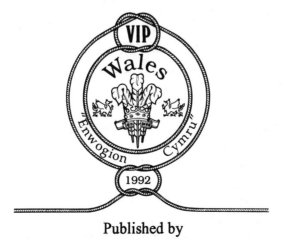

Published by
Firstspace Limited
Court Mill, Pentrecwrt, LLandysul, Dyfed SA44 5AT
Tel: (0559) 362787

Copyright © Firstspace Limited 1992
ISBN 1 871600 006

V I P WALES 1992
Published by Firstspace Limited
Court Mill, Pentrecwrt, Llandysul, Dyfed SA44 5AT

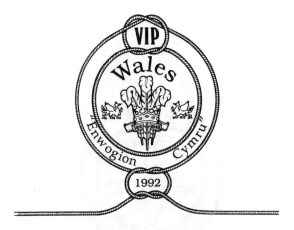

Printed in Wales. Argraffwyd yng Nghymru.

Typeset and printed by A.T. Printing, Court Mill, Pentrecwrt, Llandysul, Dyfed

This book is dedicated to

Jessica

the most important person of all.

Q.

What is probably the best way to protect your family's future?

A. Make a Will.

☐ Please send me my FREE copy of Oxfam's Will Advice Pack, a practical guide to will making.
☐ I would like my Will Advice Pack in Welsh.

Mr/Mrs/Ms/Miss_____

Address_____

_____Postcode_____

Here is my donation of £_____

Please send to Oxfam, Room BF49, FREEPOST, Oxford, OX2 7BR.
OR ring (0865) 313494

CONTENTS

INTRODUCTION by Chris Davies 7

FOREWORD by Cliff Morgan, CVO, OBE 9

ABBREVIATIONS 11

BIOGRAPHIES 39

INTRODUCTION

It is with great pleasure that I introduce this first edition of V.I.P WALES. It is an annual biographical directory for the people of Wales and is the culmination of nearly two years research and preparation. The aim of the book is to give recognition to the many thousands of Welsh people and people who are connected with Wales who have reached high office and high achievement in their particular field whether it be commerce, politics, sport, religion, the Arts or indeed charity work.

It was felt that the existing directories available did not give enough representation to Wales and its people and the wealth of ability and achievement was not represented anywhere. The superb response that we have received proves that there is a very strong demand for this publication.

There are nearly 1700 biographies in the book with less than 10% being women, in the next edition we hope to bring this level up substantially to reflect the true balance of women's contribution to the running of Wales. One other shortfall in entries has been in the entertainment business, these people have been very elusive and difficult to contact but I feel sure that we can redress this situation by the next edition also.

The process of research is a very difficult one and duplications sometimes occur, I would like to apologise to the few who were troubled by these duplications and thank them for their continued support. I would also like to thank everyone who did complete their questionaires and agreed to be included, obviously without them this book could not have been produced. Thanks also to the many letters of kind support that we have received giving encouragement and suggestions from people who feel, as I do, that this is a long overdue project and hopefully a long running one. Finally, I must thank the members of staff who worked without respite over the many months in research and production, without whom this book would not have been completed for many more months, they are namely, Sandra Grindley, Martin Flowerdew, Andrew Unett and Ray Shard.

CHRIS DAVIES

NSPCC YNG NHGYMRU IN WALES

Everyone has read about child abuse cases in the newspapers or seen reports on the TV. Behind the headlines are the Facts: an estimated 150 - 200 children die each year in England and Wales following abuse or neglect. We are the only national voluntary organisation named in statute which can take legal proceedings to protect children at risk.

The NSPCC in Wales listens to children and acts to help and protect thousands from all forms of cruelty everyday. We offer specialist childcare services according to local need - and above all we bring hope and support to those who need it most.

WAYS YOU CAN HELP

If you think a child you know is being abused, please don't hesitate. Call our free 24 hour helpline and discuss your fears. Our fully trained counsellors are there to help and can, if necessary, take immediate action to protect a child. Last year we answered 120,000 calls.

The other thing we need from you is your support. This year our work will cost us £ 35 million. Over 90% of that comes from voluntary contributions.

Whether you can spare us £ 50 or 50p we can promise you it will be put to good use. If you can make a yearly commitment, or donate tax free through our payroll giving scheme, even better.

WITH YOUR HELP WE CAN PROTECT CHILDREN

NSPCC YNG NHGYMRU, 9 BRINDLEY ROAD, CAERDYDD, CF1 7TX
FFON: 0222-230117/8

FOREWORD

By Cliff Morgan, CVO, OBE

This, the first edition of V.I.P. WALES, provides not only an invaluable reference work, but also an insight into the lives of some 1700 distinguished and successful people from, or based in, Wales. It is an extremely important new publication, and in a time of radical international change and harmonisation, recognises that Wales and it's people have a major part to play in the European Community and the world as a whole.

> *"Cofia'n Gwlad Ben-llywydd tirion,*
> *Dy gyfiawnder fyddo'i grym"*
>
> Elfed.

Invitations to appear in the book are not intended to confer distinction; rather, those entered appear on their own merits and fully justify their inclusion in this work.

I would like to take this opportunity to wish everybody involved with V.I.P. WALES every success, and look forward with great anticipation to subsequent editions.

THE GEORGE THOMAS TRUST

George Thomas Centre for Hospice Care
at 10 Ty Gwyn Road,
Penylan, Cardiff

Tel: 0222 485345

ABBREVIATIONS

A

AA	Anti-Aircraft; Automobile Association; Architectural Association; Augustinians of the Assumption
AAA	Amateur Athletic Association; American Accounting Association
AAC	Army Air Corps
AACCA	Associate, Association of Certified and Corporate Accountants
AACE	Association for Adult and Continuing Education
AAF	Auxiliary Air Force
AAFCE	Allied Air Forces in Central Europe
AAG	Assistant Adjutant-General
AAI	Associate, Chartered Auctioneers' and Estate Agents' Institute
AAIL	American Academy and Institute of Arts and Letters
AAM	Association of Assistant Mistresses in Secondary Schools
AAMC	Australian Army Medical Corps
A & AEE	Aeroplane and Armament Experimental Establishment
AASA	Associate, Australian Society of Accountants
AAUQ	Associate in Accountancy, University of Queensland
AB	Bachelor of Arts (US); able-bodied seaman; airborne
ABA	Amateur Boxing Association; Antiquarian Booksellers Association; American Bar Association
ABC	Australian Broadcasting Commission; American Broadcasting Companies
ABCA	Army Bureau of Current Affairs
ABCC	Association of British Chambers of Commerce
ABCFM	American Board of Commissioners for Foreign Missions
ABIA	Associate, Bankers' Institute of Australasia
ABINZ	Associate, Bankers' Institute of New Zealand
ABNM	American Board of Nuclear Medicine
ABP	Associated British Ports
Abp	Archbishop
ABPsS	Associate, British Psychological Society
ABRC	Advisory Board for the Research Councils
ABS	Associate, Building Societies' Institute
ABSI	Associate, Boot and Shoe Institution
ABSM	Associate, Birmingham and Midland Institute School of Music
ABTA	Association of British Travel Agents
ABTAPL	Association of British Theological and Philosophical Libraries
AC	Companion, Order of Australia; Ante Christum (before Christ)
ACA	Associate, Institute of Chartered Accountants
Acad	Academy
ACARD	Advisory Council for Applied Research and Development
ACAS	Advisory, Conciliation and Arbitration Service; Assistant Chief of Air Staff
ACBSI	Associate, Chartered Building Society Institute
ACC	Association of County Councils; Anglican Consultative Council
ACCA	Associate, Association of Certified Accountants
ACCM	Advisory Council for the Church's Ministry
ACCS	Associate, Corporation of Secretaries
ACDP	Australian Committee of Directors and Principals
ACDS	Assistant Chief of Defence Staff
ACE	Association of Consulting Engineers; Member, Association of Conference Executives
ACF	Army Cadet Force
ACFA	Army Cadet Force Association
ACFHE	Association of Colleges for Further and Higher Education
ACG	Assistant Chaplain-General
ACGI	Associate, City and Guilds of London Institute
ACGS	Assistant Chief of the General Staff
ACIArb	Associate, Chartered Institute of Arbitrators
ACIB	Associate, Chartered Institute of Bankers
ACII	Associate, Chartered Insurance Institute
ACIS	Associate, Institute of Chartered Secretaries and Administrators
ACIT	Associate, Chartered Institute of Transport
ACLS	American Council of Learned Societies
ACM	Association of Computing Machinery
ACMA	Associate, Institute of Cost and Management Accountants
ACNS	Assistant Chief of Naval Staff
ACommA	Associate, Society of Commercial Accountants
ACORD	Advisory Committee on Research and Development
ACOS	Assistant Chief of Staff
ACOST	Advisory Council on Science and Technology
ACP	Association of Clinical Pathologists; Associate, College of Preceptors; African/Caribbean/Pacific
ACPO	Association of Chief Police Officers
ACRE	Action with Rural Communities in England
ACS	American Chemical Society; Additional Curates Society
ACSEA	Allied Command South East Asia
ACSM	Associate, Cambourne School of Mines
ACT	Australian Capital Territory; Australian College of Theology; Associate, College of Technology;
ACTT	Association of Cinematograph, Television and Allied Technicians
ACTU	Australian Council of Trade Unions
ACU	Association of Commonwealth Universities
ACWA	Associate, Institute of Cost and Works Accountants
AD	Dame of the Order of Australia; Anno Domini; Air Defence
aD	ausser Dienst
ADAS	Agricultural Development and Advisory Service
ADB	Asian Development Bank; Associate of the Drama Board
ADB/F	African Development Bank/Fund
ADC	Aide-de-camp
ADCM	Archbishop of Canterbury's Diploma in Church Music
AD Corps	Army Dental Corps (now RADC)
ADC(P)	Personal Aide-de-camp to HM The Queen
ADEME	Assistant Director Electrical and Mechanical Engineering
Ad eund	Ad eundem gradum; and see under aeg
ADFManc	Art and Design Fellow, Manchester
adfw	Assistant Director of Fortification and Works
ADGB	Air Defence of Great Britian
ADGMS	Assistant Director-General of Medical Services
ADH	Assistant Director of Hygiene
Adjt	Adjutant
ADJAG	Assistant Deputy Judge Advocate General
ADK	Order of Ahli Darjah Kinabalu
Adm	Admiral
ADMS	Assistant Director of Medical Services
ADOS	Assistant Director of Ordnance Services
ADPO	Automatic Data Processing
ADPA	Associate Diploma of Public Administration
ADS&T	Assistant Director of Supplies and Transport
Adv.	Advisory; Advocate
ADVS	Assistant Director of Veterinary Services
ADWE&M	Assistant Director of Works, Electrical and Mechanical
AE	Air Efficiency Awards
AEA	Atomic Energy Authority; Air Efficiency Award
AEAF	Allied Expeditionary Air Force
AEC	Agricultural Executive Council; Army Educational Corps (now see RAEC); Atomic Energy Commission
AEF	Amalgamated Union of Engineering and Foundry Workers (now see AEU); American Expeditionary Forces
aeg	ad eundem gradum
AEGIS	Aids for the Elderly in Government Institutions
AEI	Associated Electrical Industries
AEM	Air Efficiency Medal
AER	Army Emergency Reserve
AERE	Atomic Energy Research Establishment (Harwell)
AEU	Amalgamated Engineering Union
AFA	Amateur Football Alliance
AFAIAA	Associate Fellow, American Institute of Aeronautics and Astronautics
AFBPsS	Associate Fellow, British Psychological Society
AFC	Air Force Cross; Association Football Club
AFCIA	Associate Fellow, Canadian Aeronautical Institute
AFCEA	Armed Forces Communications and Electronics Association
AFCENT	Allied Forces in Central Europe
AFD	Doctor of Fine Arts (US)
AFDS	Air Fighting Development Squadron
AFHQ	Allied Force Headquarters
AFI	American Film Institute
AFIA	Associate, Federal Institute of Accountants (Australia)
AFIAP	Artiste, Federation Internationale de l'Art Photographique
AFIAS	Associate Fellow, Institute of Aeronautical Sciences (US)
AFICD	Associate Fellow, Institute of Civil Defence
AFIMA	Associate Fellow, Institute of Mathematics and its Applications
AFM	Air Force Medal
AFOM	Associate, Faculty of Occupational Medicine
AFRAeS	Associate Fellow, Royal Aeronautical Society

AFRC	Agricultural and Food Research Council
AFV	Armoured Fighting Vehicles
AG	Attorney-General
AGAC	American Guild of Authors and Composers
AGARD	Advisory Group for Aerospace Research and Development
AGH	Australian General Hospital
GI	Artistes Graphiques Internationaux; Associate, Institute of Certificated Grocers
AGR	Advanced Gas-cooled Reactor
AGRA	Army Group Royal Artillery; Association of Genealogists and Record Agents
AGSM	Associate, Guildhall School of Music and Drama; Australian Graduate School of Management
AHA	Area Health Authority; American Hospitals Association; Associate, Institute of Health Service Administrators
AHA(T)	Area Health Authority (Teaching)
AHQ	Army Headquarters
AHSM	Associate, Institute of Health Service Management
AH-WC	Associate, Herriot-Watt College, Edinburgh
ai	ad interim
AIA	Associate, Institute of Actuaries; American Institute of Architects; Association of International Artists
AIAA	American Institute of Aeronautics and Astronautics
AIAgrE	Associate, Institution of Agricultural Engineers
AIAL	Associate Member, International Institute of Arts and Letters
AIArb	Associate, Institute of Arbitrators (now see ACIB)
AIAS	Associate Surveyor Member, Incorporated Association of Architects and Surveyors
AIB	Associate, Institute of Bankers (now see ACIB)
AIBD	Associate, Institute of British Decorators
AIBP	Associate, Institute of British Photographers
AIBScot	Associate, Institute of Bankers in Scotland
AIC	Agricultural Improvement Council; Associate of the Institute of Chemistry
AICA	Associate Member, Commonwealth Institute of Accountants; Association Internationale des Critiques d'Art
AICC	All India Congress Committee
AICE	Associate, Institution of Civil Engineers
AICPA	American Institute of Certified Public Accountants
AICS	Associate, Institute of Chartered Shipbrokers
AICTA	Associate, Imperial College of Tropical Agriculture
AIE	Associate, Institute of Education
AIEE	Associate, Institute of Electrical Engineers
AIF	Australian Imperial Forces
AIG	Adjutant-Inspector-General
AIIA	Associate, Insurance Institute of America; Associate, Indian Institute of Architects
AIInfSC	Associate, Institute of Information Scientists
AIL	Associate, Institute of Linguists
AILA	Associate, Institute of Landscape Architects
AILocoE	Associate, Institution of Locomotive Engineers
AIM	Associate, Institution of Metallurgists (now see MIM); Australian Institute of Management
AIMarE	Associate, Institute of Marine Engineers
AIME	Associate, Institute of Mechanical Engineers
AIMSW	Associate, Institute of Medical Social Workers
AInstM	Associate Member, Institute of Marketing
AInstP	Associate, Institute of Physics
AInst PI	Associate, Institute of Patentees and Inventors
AIP	Association of Independant Producers
AIPR	Associate, Institute of Public Relations
AIQS	Associate Member, Institute of Quantity Surveyors
AIRTE	Associate, Institute of Road Transport Engineers
AIRTO	Associations of Independant Research and Technology Organizations
AIS	Associate, Institute of Statisticians (now see MIS)
AISA	Associate, Incorporated Secretaries' Association
AIStructE	Associate, Institution of Structural Engineers
AITI	Associate, Institute of Translaters and Interpreters
AITP	Associate, Institute of Town Planners, India
AJAG	Assistant Judge Advocate General
AJEX	Association of Jewish Ex-Service Men and Women
AK	Knight, Order of Australia
AKC	Associate, King's College London
ALA	Associate, Library Association
Ala	Alabama (US)
ALAA	Associate, Library Association of Australia
ALAM	Associate, London Academy of Music and Dramatic Arts
ALCD	Associate, London College of Divinity
ALCM	Associate, London College of Music

ALCS	Authors Lending and Copyright Society
ALFSEA	Allied Land Forces South East Asia
ALI	Argyll Light Infantry; Associate Landscape Institute
ALICE	Autistic and Language Impaired Children's Education
ALLC	Association for Literary and Linguistic Computing
ALP	Australian Labor Party
ALPSP	Association of Learned and Professional Society Publishers
ALS	Associate, Linnean Society
Alta	Alberta
ALVA	Association of Leading Visitor Attractions
AM	Albert Medal; Member, Order of Australia; Master of Arts (US); Alpes Maritimes
AMA	Association of Metropolitan Authorities; Assistant Masters Association; Associate, Museums Association; Australian Medical Association
AMARC	Associated Marine and Related Charities
Amb.	Ambulance; Ambassador
AMBIM	Associate Member, British Institute of Management
AMBritIRE	Associate Member, British Institute of Radio Engineers
AMC	Association of Municipal Corporations
AMCT	Associate, Manchester College of Technology
AME	Association of Municipal Engineers
AMEME	Association of Mining Electrical and Mechanical Engineers
AMet	Associate of Metallurgy
AMGOT	Allied Military Government of Occupied Territories
AMIAE	Associate Member, Institution of Automobile Engineers
AMIAgrE	Associate, Institution of Agricultural Engineers
AMIBF	Associate Member, Institute of British Foundrymen
AMICE	Associate Member, Institution of Civil Engineers
AMIChemE	Associate Member, Institution of Chemical Engineers
AMIED	Associate Member, Institution of Engineering Designers
AMIEE	Associate Member, Institution of Electrical Engineers
AMIE(Ind)	Associate Member, Institution of Engineers
AMIERE	Associate Member, Institution of Electronic and Radio Engineers
AMIH	Associate Member, Institute of Housing
AMIMechE	Associate Member, Institution of Mechanical Engineers
AMIMinE	Associate Member, Institution of Mining Engineers
AMIMM	Associate Member, Institution of Mining and Metallurgy
AMInstBE	Associate Member, Institution of British Engineers
AMInstCE	Associate Member, Institution of Civil Engineering
AmInstEE	American Institute of Electrical Engineers
AMInstR	Associate Member, Institution of Refrigeration
AMInstT	Associate Member, Institute of Transport
AMInstTA	Associate Member, Institution of Traffic Administration
AMINucE	Associate Member, Institution of Nuclear Engineers
AMIRSE	Associate Member, Institute of Railway Signalling Engineers
AMIStructE	Associate Member, Institution of Structural Engineers
AMN	Ahli Mangku Negara (Malaysia)
AMP	Advanced Management Program
AMRINA	Associate Member, Royal Institution of Naval Architects
AMS	Assistant Military Secretary, Army Medical Services
AMTE	Admiralty Marine Technology Establishment
AMTRI	Advanced Manufacturing Technology Research Institute
ANA	Associate National Academician
ANAF	Arab Non-Arab Friendship
Anat.	Anatomy; Anatomical
ANC	African National Congress
ANECInst	Associate, NE Coast Institution of Engineers and Shipbuilders
ANGAU	Australia New Guinea Administrative Unit
Anon.	Anonymously
ANU	Australian National University
Anzac	Australian and New Zealand Army Corps
AO	Officer, Order of Australia; Air Officer
AOA	Air Officer in charge of Administration
AOC	Air Officer Commanding
AOC-in-C	Air Officer Commanding in Chief
AOD	Army Ordnance Department
AOER	Army Officers Emergency Reserve
APA	American Psychiatric Association
APACS	Association of Payment and Clearing Systems
APCK	Association for Promoting Christian Knowledge, Church of Ireland
APD	Army Pay Department
APEX	Association of Professional, Executive, Clerical and Computer Staff
APHA	American Public Health Association
APIS	Army Photographic Intelligence Service
APM	Assistant Provost Marshal
APMI	Associate, Pensions Management Institute
APR	Accredited Public Relations Practitioner
APS	Aborigines Protection Society; American Physics Society

APsSI	Associate, Psychological Society of Ireland
APSW	Association of Psychiatric Social Workers
APT&C	Administrative, Professional, Technical and Clerical
APTC	Army Physical Training Corps
AQ	Administration and Quartering
AQMG	Assistant Quartermaster-General
AR	Associated Rediffusion (Television)
ARA	Associate, Royal Academy
ARACI	Associate, Royal Australian Chemical Institute
ARAD	Associate, Royal Academy of Dancing
ARAeS	Associate, Royal Aeronautical Society
ARAM	Associate, Royal Academy of Music
ARAS	Associate, Royal Astronomical Society
ARBA	Associate, Royal Society of British Artists
ARBC	Associate, Royal British Colonial Society of Artists
ARBS	Associate, Royal Society of British Sculpters
ARC	Architects' Registration Council; Agricultural Research Council (now see AFRC); Aeronautical Research Council
ARCA	Associate, Royal College of Art; Associate, Royal Canadian Academy
ARCamA	Associate, Royal Cambrian Academy of Art
ARCE	Academical Rank of Civil Engineer
ARCIC	Anglo-Roman Catholic International Commission
ARCM	Associate, Royal College of Music
ARCO	Associate, Royal College of Organists
ARCPsych	Associate Member, Royal College of Psychiatrists
ARCS	Associate, Royal College of Science
ARCST	Associate, Royal College of Science and Technology (Glasgow)
ARCUK	Architect Registration Council of the United Kingdom
ARCVS	Associate, Royal College of Veterinary Surgeons
ARE	Associate, Royal Society of Painters-Etchers and Engravers; Arab Republic of Egypt; Admiralty Research Establishment
ARELS	Association of Recognised English Language Schools
ARIAS	Associate, Royal Incorporation of Architects in Scotland
ARIBA	Associate, Royal British Institute of Architects
ARIC	Associate, Royal Institute of Chemistry
ARICS	Professional Associate, Royal Institution of Chartered Surveyors
ARINA	Associate, Royal Institution of Naval Architects
Ark	Arkansas (US)
ARLT	Association for the Reform of Latin Teaching
ARMS	Associate, Royal Society of Miniature Painters
ARP	Air Raid Precautions
ARPS	Associate, Royal Photographic Society
ARR	Association of Radiation Research
ARRC	Associate, Royal Red Cross
ARSA	Associate, Royal Scottish Academy
ARSCM	Associate, Royal School of Church Music
ARSM	Associate, Royal School of Mines
ARTC	Associate, Royal Technical College (Glasgow)
ARVIA	Associate, Royal Victoria Institute of Architects
ARWA	Associate, Royal West of England Academy
ARWS	Associate, Royal Society of Painters in Water-Colours
AS	Anglo-Saxon
ASA	Associate Member, Society of Actuaries;
ASAA	Associate, Society of Incorporated Accountants and Auditors
ASAI	Associate, Society of Architectural Illustrators
ASAM	Associate, Society of Art Masters
ASBAH	Association for Spina Bifida and Hydrocephalus
ASC	Administrative Staff College, Henley
ASCA	Associate, Society of Company and Commercial Accountants
ASCAB	Armed Services Consultant Approval Board
ASCAP	American Society of Composers, Authors and Publishers
ASCE	American Society of Civil Engineers
AScW	Association of Scientific Workers (now see ASTMS)
ASD	Armament Supply Department
ASE	Amalgamated Society of Engineers (now see AUEW)
ASEAN	Association of South East Asia Nations
ASH	Action on Smoking and Health
ASIAD	Associate, Society of Industrial Artists and Designers
ASIA(Ed)	Associate, Society of Industrial Artists (Education)
ASLE	American Society of Lubrication Engineers
ASLEF	Associated Society of Locomotive Engineers and Firemen
ASM	Association of Senior Members
ASME	American Society of Mechanical Engineers; Association for the Study of Medical Education
ASO	Air Staff Officer
ASSc	Accounting Standards Steering Committee
ASSET	Association of Supervisory Staffs, Executives and Technicians
AssocISI	Associate, Iron and Steel Institute
AssocMCT	Associateship of Manchester College of Technology

AssocRINA	Associate, Royal Institution of Naval Architects
AssocSc	Associate in Science
Asst	Assistant
ASTC	Administrative Service Training Course
ASTMS	Association of Scientific Technical and Managerial Staffs
ASVU	Army Security Vetting Unit
ASWDU	Air Sea Warfare Development Unit
ASWE	Admiralty Surface Weapons Establishment
ATA	Air Transport Auxiliary
ATAE	Association of Tutors in Adult Education
ATAF	Allied Tactical Air Force
ATC	Air Training Corps; Art Teacher's Certificate
ATCDE	Association of Teachers in Colleges and Departments of Education
ATLC	Associate, Trinity College of Music, London
ATD	Art Teacher's Diploma
ATI	Associate, Textile Institute
ATII	Associate Member, Institute of Taxation
ato	Ammunition Technical Officer
ATS	Auxiliary Territorial Service (now see WRAC)
ATTI	Association of Teachers in Technical Institutions (NATFHE)
ATV	Associated TeleVision
AUA	American Urological Association
AUCAS	Association of University Clinical Academic Staff
AUEW	Amalgamated Union of Engineering Workers
AUS	Army of the United States
AUT	Association of University Teachers
AVCC	Australian Vice-Chancellors' Committee
AVCM	Associate, Victoria College of Music
AVD	Army Veterinary Department
AVLR	Audio Visual Language Association
AVR	Army Volunteer Reserve
AWA	Anglian Water Authority
AWO	Association of Water Officers

B

b	born; brother
BA	Bachelor of Arts
BAA	British Airports Authority
BAAB	British Amateur Athletic Board
BAAL	British Association of Applied Linguists
BAAS	British Association for the Advancement of Science
BAB	British Airways Board
BAC	British Aircraft Corporation
BACM	British Association of Colliery Management
BACUP	British Association of Cancer United Patients
BAe	British Aerospace
BAED	Bachelor of Arts in Environmental Design
B&FBS	British and Foreign Bible Society
BAFO	British Air Forces of Occupation
BAFPA	British Association of Fitness Promotion Agencies
BAFTA	British Academyof Film and Television Arts
BAG	Business Art Galleries
BArfSc	Bachelor of Agricultural Science
BAI	Baccalarius in Arte Ingeniaria (Bachelor of Engineering)
BAIE	British Association of Industrial Editors
BALPA	British Air Line Pilots' Association
BAO	Bachelor of Art of Obstetrics
BAOMS	British Association of Oral and Maxillo-Facial Surgeons
BAOR	British Army of the Rhine (formerly on the Rhine)
BAOS	British Association of Oral Surgeons (now see BAOMS)
BARB	Broadcasters' Audience Research Board
BARC	British Automobile Racing Club
Bart	Baronet
BAS	Bachelor in Agricultural Science
BASc	Bachelor in Applied Science
BASCA	British Academy of Songwriters, Composers and Authors
BASEEFA	British Approvals Service for Electrical Equipment in Flammable Atmospheres
BASW	British Association of Social Workers
Batt	Battery
BBA	British Bankers Association; Bachelor of Business Administration
BB&CIRly	Bombay, Baroda and Central India Railway
BBBof C	British Boxing Board of Control
BBC	British Broadcasting Corporation
BBM	Bitang Bakti Masharakat (Public Service Star) (Singapore)
BBS	Bachelor of Business Studies

BC	Before Christ; British Columbia; Borough Council
BCC	British Council of Churches
BCE	Bachelor of Civil Engineering
BCL	Bachelor of Civil Law
BCMF	British Ceramic Manufacturers' Federation
BCMS	Bible Churchmen's Missionary Society
BCOF	British Commonwealth Occupation Force
BCom	Bachelor of Commerce
BComSC	Bachelor of Commercial Science
BCS	Bengal Civil Service; British Computer Society
BCSA	British Constructional Steelwork Association
BCURA	British Coal Utilization Research Association
BCYC	British Corinthian Yacht Club
BD	Bachelor of Divinity
Bd	Board
BDA	British Dental Association
Bde	Brigade
BDS	Bachelor of Dental Surgery
BDSc	Bachelor of Dental Science
BE	Bachelor of Engineering; British Element
BEA	British East Africa; British European Airways; British Epilepsy Association
BEAMA	Federation of British Electrotechnical and Allied Manufacturers' Association (formerly British Electrical and Allied Manufacturers' Association)
BE&A	Bachelor of Engineering and Architecture (Malta)
BEAS	British Educational Administrational Society
BEC	Business Education Council (now see BTEC)
BEc	Bachelor of Economics
BEd	Bachelor of Education
Beds	Bedfordshire
BEE	Bachelor of Electrical Engineering
BEF	British Expeditionary Force; British Equestrian Federation
BEM	British Empire Medal
BEMAS	British Education Management and Administration Society
BEME	Brigade Electrical and Mechanical Engineer
BEO	Base Engineering Officer
Berks	Berkshire
BESO	British Executive Service Overseas
BFI	British Film Institute
BFMIRA	British Food Manufacturing Industries Research Association
BFPO	British Forces Post Office
BFSS	British Field Sports Society
BGS	Brigadier General Staff
Bhd	Berhad
BHRA	British Hydromechanics Research Association
BHRCA	British Hotels, Restaurants and Caterers' Association
BHS	British Horse Society
BIBA	British Insurance Brokers' Association
BIBRA	British Industrial Biological Research Association
BICC	British Insulated Callender's Cables
BICERA	British Internal Combustion Engine Research Association
BICERI	British Internal Combustion Engine Research Institute
BICSc	British Institute of Cleaning Science
BIEC	British Invisable Export Council
BIEE	British Institute of Energy Economics
BIF	British Industries Fair
BIFU	Banking Insurance and Finance Union
BIM	British Institute of Management
BIR	British Institute of Radiology
BIS	Bank for International Settlements
BISF	British Iron and Steel Federation
BISFA	British Industrial and Scientific Film Association
BISPA	British Independent Steel Producers Association
BISRA	British Iron and Steel Research Association
BJ	Bachelor of Journalism
BJSM	British Joint Service Mission
BKSTS	British Kinematograph, Sound and Television Society
BL	Bachelor of Law
BLA	British Liberation Army
BLE	Brotherhood of Locomotive Engineers; Bachelor of Land Economy
BLESMA	British Limbless Ex-Servicemen's Association
BLitt	Bachelor of Letters
BM	British Museum; Bachelor of Medicine; Brigade Major; British Monomark
BMA	British Medical Association
BMedSci	Bachelor of Medical Science
BMEO	British Middle East Office
BMet	Bachelor of Metallurgy

BMEWS	Ballistic Missile Early Warning System
BMH	British Military Hospital
BMJ	British Medical Journal
BMM	British Military Mission
BMRA	Brigade Major Royal Artillery
Bn	Battalion
BNAF	British North Africa Force
BNC	Brasenose College
BNEC	British National Export Council
BNFL	British Nuclear Fuels Ltd
BNOL	British National Oil Corporation; British National Opera Company
BNSC	British National Space Centre
BNSc	Bachelor of Nursing Science
BOAC	British Overseas Airways Corporation
BomCS	Bombay Civil Service
BomSC	Bombay Staff Corps
BoT	Board of Trade
Bot	Botany; Botanical
BOTB	British Overseas Trade Board
Bp	Bishop
BPA	British Paediatric Association
BPG	Broadcasting Press Guild
BPharm	Bachelor of Pharmacy
BPIF	British Printing Industries Federation
BPMF	British Postgraduate Medical Federation
BPsS	British Psychological Society
BR	British Rail
Br	Branch
BRA	Brigadier Royal Artillery; British Rheumatism & Arthritis Association
BRB	British Railways Board
BRCS	British Red Cross Society
BRE	Building Research Establishment
Brig	Brigadier
BritIRE	British Institution of Radio Engineers (now see IERE)
BRNC	Britannia Royal Naval College
BRS	British Road Service
BS	Bachelor of Surgery; Bachelor of Science; British Standards
BSA	Bachelor of Scientific Agriculture; Birmingham Small Arms; Building Societies' Association
BSAA	British South American Airways
BSAP	British South Africa Police
BSC	British Steel Corporation; Bengal Staff Corps
BSc	Bachelor of Science
BScA	Bachelor of Science in Agriculture
BSc(Dent)	Bachelor of Science in Dentistry
BScSoc	Bachelor of Social Science
BSE	Bachelor of Science in Engineering (US)
BSES	British Schools Exploring Society
BSF	British Salonica Force
BSFA	British Science Fiction Association
BSI	British Standards Association
BSIA	British Security Industry Association
BSJA	British Show Jumping Association
BSME	Bachelor of Science in Mechanical Engineering
BSN	Bachelor of Science in Nursing
BSNS	Bachelor of Naval Science
BSocSc	Bachelor of Social Science
BSRA	British Ship Research Association
BSS	Bachelor of Science (Social Science)
BST	Bachelor of Sacred Theology
BT	Bachelor of Teaching; British Telecommunications
Bt	Baronet; Brevet
BTA	British Tourist Authority (formerly British Travel Association)
BTC	British Transport Commission
BTCV	British Trust for Conversation Volunteers
BTDB	British Transport Docks Board (now see ABP)
BTEC	Business and Technican Education Council
BTh	Bachelor of Theology
BTP	Bachelor of Town Planning
btss	Baronetess
BUAS	British Universities Association of Slavists
BUPA	British United Provident Association
BVA	British Veterinary Association
BVM	Blessed Virgin Mary
BVMS	Bachelor of Veterinary Medicine and Surgery
Bucks	Buckinghamshire
BVetMed	Bachelor of Veterinary Medicine

BWI	British West Indies
BWM	British War Medal

C

(C)	Conservative; 100
c	child; cousin; circa (about)
CA	Central America; County Alderman; Chartered Accountant (Scotland and Canada)
CAA	Civil Aviation Authority
CAABU	Council fo the Advancement of Arab and British Understanding
CAAV	Central Association of Agricultural Valuers; also Member of the Association
CAB	Citizens' Advice Bureau; Commonwealth Agricultural Bureau
CAER	Conservative Action for Electoral Reform
CALE	Canadian Army Liaison Executive
CAM	Communications, Advertising and Marketing
Cambs	Cambridgeshire
CAMC	Canadian Army Medical Corps
CAMRA	Campaign for Real Ale
CAMS	Certificate of Advanced Musical Study
CAMW	Centraol Association for Mental Welfafe
Cantab	Cantabrigensis (of Cambridge)
Cantuar	Cantuariensis (of Canterbury)
CARD	Campaign against Racial Descrimination
CARE	Cottages and Rural Enterprises
CARICOM	Caribbean Community
CARIFTA	Caribbean Free Trade Area (now see CARICOM)
CAS	Chief of Air Staff
CASI	canadian Aeronautics and Space Institute
CAT	college of Advanced Technology
Cav	Cavalry
CAWU	Clericaol and Administrative Workers' Union
CB	Companion, Order of the Bath; County Borough
CBC	County Borough Council
CBCO	Central Board for Conscientious Objectors
CBE	Commander, Order of the British Empire
CBI	Confederation of British Industries
CBIM	Companion, British Institute of Management
CBiol	Chartered Biologist
CBNS	Commander British Navy Staff
CBS	Colombia Broadcasting System
CBSA	Clay Bird Shooting Association
CBSI	Chartered Building Societies Institute
CC	Companion, Order of Canada; City Council; County Council; Cricket Club; Cycling Club; County Court
CCAB	Consultative Committee of Accountancy Bodies
CCAHC	Central Council for Agricultural and Horticultral Co-operation
CCC	Corpus Christi College; Central Criminal Court; County Cricket Club
CCE	Chartered Civil Engineer
CCF	Combined Cadet Force
CCFM	Combined Cadet Forces Medal
CCG	Control Commissino Germany
CCH	Cacique's Crown of Honour, Order of Service of Guyana
CChem	Chartered Chemist
CCHMS	Central Committee for Hospital Medical Services
CCIA	Commission of Churches on International Affairs
CCJ	Council of Christians and Jews
CCPR	Central Council of Physical Recreation
CCRA	Commander Corps of Royal Artillery
CCRE	Commander Corps Royal Engineers
CCREME	Commander Corps of Royal Electrical and Mechanical Engineers
CCRSigs	Commander Corps of Royal Signals
CCS	Casualty Clearing Station; Celon Civil Service
CCSU	Council of Civil Service Unions
CCTS	Combat Crew Training Squadron
CD	Canadian Forces Decoration; Commander, Order of Distinction (Jamaica); Civil Defence
CDEE	Chemical Defence Experimental Establishment
CDipAF	Certified Diploma in Accounting and Finance
Cdo	Commando
CDRA	Committee of Directors of Research Associations
Cdre	Commodore
CDS	Chief of Defence Staff
CDU	Christlich-Demokratische Union
CE	Civil Engineer

CEA	Central Electricity Authority
CEED	Centre for Economic and Environmental Development
CEF	Canadian Expiditionary Force
CEGB	Central Electricity Generating Board
CEI	Council of Engineering Institutions
CEIR	Corporation for Industrial and Economic Research
CEM	Council of European Municipalities (now see CEMR)
CEMS	Church of England Men's Society
CENELEC	European Committee for Electrotechnical Standardization
CEng	Chartered Engineer
Centro	Central Treaty Organisation
CERL	Central Electricity Research Laboratories
CERT	Charities Effectiveness Review Trust
Cert Ed	Certificate of Education
CertITP	Certificate of International Teachers' Program (Harvard)
CEST	Centre for Exploitation of Science and Technology
CET	Council foe Educational Technology
CETS	Church of England Temperance Society
CF	Chaplain to the Forces
CFA	Canadian Field Artillery
CFE	Central Fighter Establishment
CFM	Cadet Forces Medal
CFR	Commander, Order of the Federal Republic of Nigeria
CFS	Central Flying School
CGA	Community of the Glorious Assension; Country Gentlemans Association
CGH	Order of the Golden Heart of Kenya (1st Class)
CGIA	Insignia Awards of City and Guilds of London Institute
CGLI	City and Guilds of London Institute
CGM	Conspicuous Gallantry Medal
CGRM	Commandant-General Royal Marines
CGS	Chief of the General Staff
CH	Companion of Honour
Chanc.	Chancellor; Chancery
Chap.	Chaplain
ChapStJ	Chaplain, Order of St John of Jerusalem (now see ChStJ)
CHAR	Campaign for the Homeless and Rootless
CHB	Champanion of Honour of Barbados
ChB	Bachelor of Surgery
CHC	Community Health Council
Ch.Ch.	Christ Church
Ch.Coll.	Christ's College
CHE	Campaign for Homosexual Equality
ChLJ	Chaplain, Order of St Lazarus of Jerusalem
HM	Chevalier of Honour and Merit (Haiti)
ChM	Master of Surgery
Chm	Chairman or Chairwoman
CHSC	Central Health Services Council
ChStJ	Chaplain, Most Venerable Order of the Hospital of St John of Jerusalem
CI	Imperial Order of the Crown of India; Channel Islands
CIA	Chemical Industries Association; Central Intelligence Agency
CIAD	Central Institute of Art and Design
CIAgrE	Companion, Institution of Agricultural Engineers
CIAL	Corresponding Member of the International Institute of Arts and Letters
CIArb	Chartered Institute of Arbitrators
CIB	Chartered Institute of Bankers
CIBS	Chartered Institution of Building Services (now see CIBSE)
CIBSE	Chartered Institution of Building Services Engineers
CIC	Chemical Institute of Canada
CICHE	Committee for International Co-operation in Higher Education
CICI	Conferration of Information Communication Industries
CID	Criminal Investigation Department
CIEx	Companion, Institute of Export
CIGasE	Companion, Institution of Gas Engineers
CIGS	Chief of the Imperial General Staff (now see CGS)
CIIA	Canadian Institute of International Affairs
CIM	China Inland Mission
CIMA	Chartered Institute of Management Accountants
CIMarE	Companion, Institute of Marine Engineers
CIMEMME	Companion, Institution of mining Electrical and Mining Mechanical Engineers
C-in-C	Commander-in-Chief
CINCHAN	Allied Commander-in-Chief Channel
CIOB	Chartered Institute of Building
CIPFA	Chartered Institute of public finance and Accountancy
CIPM	Companion, Institute of Personal Management
CIR	Commission on Industrial Relations
CIRIA	Construction Industry Research and Information Association

CIS	Institute of Chartered Secretaries and Administrators
CIT	Chartered Institue of Transport; California Institute of Technology
CIU	Club and Institute Union
CIV	City Imperial Volunteers
CJ	Chief Justice
CJM	Congregation of Jesus and Mary (Eudist Fathers)
CL	Commander, Order of Leopold
cl	cum laude
Cl.	Class
CLA	Country Landowners' Association
CLit	Companion of Literature (Royal Society of Literature Awards)
CLJ	Commander, Order of St Lazarus of Jerusalem
CLP	Constituency Labour Party
CLRAE	Conference of Local and Regional Authorities of Europe
CM	Member, Order of Canada; Congregation of the Mission (Vincentians); Master in Surgery; Certificated Master; Canadian Militia
CMA	Canadian Medical Association; Cost and Management Accountant (NZ)
CMAC	Catholic Marriage Advisory Council
CMB	Central Midwives' Board
CMF	Commonwealth Military Forces; Central Mediterranean Force
CMG	Companion, Order of St Michael and St George
CMLJ	Commander of Merit, Order of St Lazarus of Jerusalem
CMM	Commander, Order of Military Merit (Canada)
CMO	Chief Medical Officer
CMP	Corps of Military Police (now see CRMP)
CMS	Church Missionary Society; Certificate of Management Studies
CMT	Chaconia Medal of Trinidad
CNAA	Council for National Academic Awards
CND	Campaign for Nuclear Disarmament
CNI	Campanion, Nautical Institute
CNR	Canadian National Railways
CNRS	Centre National de la Recherche Scientifique
CO	Commanding oficer; Commonwealth Officer (after Aug. 1966) (now see FCO); Colonial Officer (before Aug. 1966); Conscientious Objector
Co.	County; Company
C of E	Church of England
C of S	Chief of Staff; Church of Scotland
Co.U	Coalition Unionist
COHSE	Confederation of Health Service Employees
COI	Central Office of Information
ColD	Council of Industrial Design (now Design Council)
Col	Colonel
Coll.	College; Collegiate
Colo	Colorado (US)
Col.-Sergt	Colour-Sergeant
Com	Communist
Comd	Command
Comdg	Commanding
Comdr	Commander
Comdt	Commandant
COMEC	Council of the Military Education Committees of the Universities of the UK
COMET	Committee for Middle East Trade
Commn	Commission
Commnd	Commissioned
CompICE	Companion, Institution of Civil Engineers
CompIEE	Companion, Institution of Electrical Engineers
CompIERE	Companion, Institution of Electronic and Radio Engineers
CompIGasE	Companion, Institution of Gas Engineer
CompTI	Companion of the Textile Institute
Comr	Commissioner
Comy-Gen	Commissary-General
CON	Commander, Order of the Niger
Conn	Connecticut (US)
Const	Constitutional
Co-op.	Co-operative
COPEC	Conference of Politics, Economics and Christianity
Corp.	Corporation; Corporal
COS	Chief of Staff; Charity Organization Society
COSA	Colliery Officials and Staff Association
CoSIRA	Council for Small Industries in Rural Areas
COSLA	Convention of Scottish Local Authorities
COSPAR	Committee on Space Research
COSSAC	Chief of Staff to Supreme Allied Commander
COTC	Canadian Officers' Training Corps
CP	Central Provinces; Cape Province
CPA	Commonwealth Parliamentary Association; Chartered Patent

	Agent; Certified Public Accountant (Canada) (now see CA)
CPAG	Child Poverty Action Group
CPAS	Church Pastoral Aid Society
CPC	Conservative Political Centre
CPhys	Chartered Physicist
CPL	Chief Personnel and Logistics
CPM	Colonial Police Medal
CPR	Canadian Pacific Railway
CPRE	Coincil for the Protection of Rural England
CPSA	Civil and Public Services Association
CPSU	Communist Party of the Soviet Union
CPsycol	Chartered Psychologist
CPU	Commonwealth Press Union
CQSW	Certificate of Qualification in Social Work
CR	Community of the Resurrection
cr	created or creation
CRA	Commander, Royal Artillery
CRAC	Careers Research and Advisory Centre
CRAeS	Companion, Royal Aeronautical Society
CRASC	Commander, Royal Army Service Corps
CRC	Cancer Research Campaign; Community Relations Council
CRCP(C)	Certificant, Royal College of Physicians Canada
CRE	Commander, Royal Engineers; Commission for Racial Equality; Commercial Relations and Export
Cres	Crescent
CRMP	Corps of Royal Military Police
CRNCM	Companion, Royal Northen Colege of Music
CRO	Commonwealth Relations Office (before Aug. 1966; now see FCO)
CS	Civil Service; Clerk to the Signet
CSA	Confederate States of America
CSB	Bachelor of Christian Science
CSC	Conspicuous Service Cross; Congregation of the Holy Cross
CSCA	Civil Service Clerical Association (now see CPSA)
CSCE	Conference on Security and Co-operation in Europe
CSD	Civil Service Department; Co-operative Secretaries Diploma; Chartered Society of Designers
CSEU	Confederation of Shipbuilding and Engineering Unions
CSG	Companion, Order of the Star of Ghana; Company of the Servants of God
CSI	Companion, Order of the Star of India
CSIR	Commonwealth Council for Scientific and Industrial Research (now see CSIRO)
CSO	Chief Scientific Officer; Chief Signal Officer; Chief Staff Officer
CSP	Chartered Society of Physiotherapists; Civil Service of Pakistan
CSS	Companion, Star of Sarawak; Council for Science and Society
CSSB	Civil Service Selection Service Board
CSSp	Holy Ghost Father
CSSR	Congregation of the Most Holy Redeemer (Redemptorist Order)
CSTI	Council of Science and Technology Institutes
CStJ	Commander, Most Venerable Order of the Hospital of St John of Jerusalem
CSU	Christlich-Soziale Union in Bayern
CSV	Community Service Volunteers
CTA	Chaplain Territorial Army
CTB	College of Teachers of the Blind
CTC	Cyclists' Touring Club; Commando Training Centre
CText	Chartered Textile Technologist
CU	Cambridge University
CUAC	Cambridge University Athletic Club
CUAFC	Cambridge University Association Football Club
CUBC	Cambridge University Boat Club
CUCC	Cambridge University Cricket Club
CUF	Common University Fund
CUHC	Cambridge University Hockey Club
CUMS	Cambridge University Music Society
CUNY	City University of New York
CUP	Cambridge University Press
CURUFC	Cambridge University Rugby Union Football Club
CV	Cross of Valour (Canada)
CVCP	Committee of Vice-Chancellors and Principals of the Universities of the United Kingdom
CVO	Commander, Royal Victorian Order
CVS	Council of Voluntary Service
CVSNA	Council of Voluntary Service National Association
CWA	Crime Writers Association
CWGC	Commonwealth War Graves Commission
CWS	Co-operative Wholesale Society

D

D — Duke
d — died; daughter
DA — Dame of St Andrew, Order of Barbados; Diploma in Anaesthesia; Diploma in Art
DAAG — Deputy Assistant Adjutant-General
DA&QMG — Deputy Adjutant and Quartermaster-General
DAC — Development Assistance Committee
DACG — Deputy Assistant Chaplain-General
DAD — Deputy Assistant Director
DAdmin — Doctor of Administration
DADMS — Deputy Assistant Director of Medical Services
DADOS — Deputy Assistant Director of Ordnance Services
DADQ — Deputy Assistant Director of Quartering
DADST — Deputy Assistant Director of Supplies and Quartering
DAG — Deputy Adjutant-General
DAgr — Doctor of Agriculture
DAMS — Deputy Assistant Military Secretary
D&AD — Designers and Art Directors Association
DAppSc — Doctor of Applied Science
DAQMG — Deputy Assistant Quartermaster-General
DArt — Doctor of Art
DASC — Doctor in Agricultural Sciences
DATA — Draghtsmen's and Allied Technicians' Association
DATEC — Art ,and Design Committee, Technician Education Council
DBA — Doctor of Business Administration
DBE — Dame Commander, Order of the British Empire
DC — District Council; District of Colombia (US)
DCAe — Diploma of College of Aeronautics
DCAS — Deputy Chief of the Air Staff
DCB — Dame Commander, Order of the Bath
DCC — Diploma of Chester College
DCG — Deputy Chaplain-General
DCGRM — Department of the Commandant General Royal Marines
DCGS — Deputy Chief of the General Staff
DCh — Doctor of Surgery
DCH — Diploma in Child Health
DCIGS — Deputy Chief of the Imperial General Staff (now see DCGS)
DCL — Doctor of Civil Law
DCLI — Duke of Cornwall's Light Infantry
DCLJ — Dame Commander, Order of St Lazarus of Jerusalem
DCM — Distinguished Conduct Medal
DCMG — Dame Commander, Order of St Michael and St George
DCMHE — Diploma of Contents and Methods in Health Education
DCnL — Doctor of Canon Law
DCO — Duke of Cambridge's Own
DComm — Doctor of Commerce
DCP — Diploma in Clinical Pathology; Diploma in Conservation of Paintings
DCS — Deputy Chief of Staff; Doctor of Commercial Sciences
DCSO — Deputy Chief Scientific Officer
DCT — Doctor of Christian Theology
DCVO — Dame Commander, Royal Victorian Order
DD — Doctor of Divinity
DDGAMS — Deputy Director General, Army Medical Services
DDL — Deputy Director of Labour
DDME — Deputy Director of Mechanical Engineering
DDMI — Deputy Director of Military Intelligence
DDMO — Deputy Director of Military Operations
DDMS — Deputy Director of Medical Services
DDMT — Deputy Director of Military Training
DDNI — Deputy Director of Naval Intelligence
DDO — Diploma in Dental Orthopaedics
DDPH — Diploma in Dental Public Health
DDPR — Deputy Director of Public Relations
DDPS — Deputy Director of Personal Services
DDR — Deutsche Demokratische Republik
DDRA — Deputy Director Royal Artillery
DDS — Doctor of Dental Surgery; Director of Dental Services
DDSc — Doctor of Dental Science
DDSD — Deputy Director Staff Duties
DDSM — Defence Distinguished Service Medal
DDST — Deputy Director of Supplies and Transport
DDWE&M — Deputy Director of Works, Electrical and Mechanical
DE — Doctor of Engineering
DEA — Department of Economic Affairs; Drug Enforcement Agency (US)
decd — deceased
DEconSC — Doctor of Economic Science

DEd — Doctor of Education
Del — Delaware (US)
Deleg — Delegate
DEME — Directorate of Electrical and Mechanical Engineering
DEMS — Defensively Equipped Merchant Ships
(DemU) — Democratic Unionist
DEng — Doctor of Engineering
DECVR — Duke of Edinburgh's Own Volunteer Rifles
DEP — Department of Employment and Productivity; European Progressive Democrats
Dep. — Deputy
DES — Department of Education and Science
DesRCA — Designers of the Royal College of Arts
DFA — Doctor of Fine Arts
DFC — Distinguished Flying Cross
DFH — Diploma of Faraday House
DFLS — Day Fighter's Leader School
DFM — Distinguished Flying Medal
DG — Director General; Dragoon Guards
DGAA — Distressed Gentlefolks Aid Association
DGAMS — Director-General Army Medical Services
DGEME — Director-General Electrical and Mechanical Engineering
DGLP(A) — Director-General Logistic Policy (Army)
DGMS — Director-General of Medical Services
DGMT — Director-General of Military Training
DGMW — Director-General of Military Works
DGNPS — Director-General of Naval Personal Services
DGP — Director-General of Personnel
DGPS — Director-General of Personal Services
DGS — Diploma in Graduate Studies
DGStJ — Dame of Grace, Order of St John of Jerusalem
DGU — Doctor of Griffith University
DH — Doctor of Humanities
DHA — District Health Authority
Dhc — Doctor honoris causa
DHEW — Department of Health Education and Welfare (US)
DHL — Doctor of Humane Letters
DIAS — Dublin Institute of Advanced Science
DIC — Diploma of the Imperial College
DICTA — Diploma of Imperial College of Tropical Agriculture
DIG — Deputy Inspector-General
DIH — Diploma in Industrial Health
DIMP — Darjah Indera Mahkota Pahang
Dio. — Diocese
DipAD — Diploma in Art and Design
DipAe — Diploma in Aeronautics
DipASE — Diploma in Advanced Study of Education, College of Perceptors
DipAvMed — Diploma in Aviation Medicine, Royal College of Physicians
DipBA — Diploma in Business Administration
DipBS — Diploma in Fine Art, Byam Shaw School
DipCAM — Diploma in Communications, Advertising and Marketing of CAM Foundation
DipCC — Diploma of the Central College
DipCD — Diploma in Civic Design
DipCE — Diploma in Civil Engineering
DipEcon — Diploma in Economics
DipEd — Diploma in Education
DipEl — Diploma in Electronics
DipESL — Diploma in English as a Second Language
DipEth — Diploma in Ethnology
DipFD — Diploma in Funeral Directing
DipFE — Diploma in Further Education
DipGSM — Diploma in Music, Guildhall School of Music and Drama
DipHA — Diploma in Hospital Administration
DipHum — Diploma in Humanities
DipLA — Diploma in Landscape Architecture
DipLib — Diploma in Librarianship
DipM — Diploma in Marketing
DipN — Diploma in Nursing
DipNec — Diploma of Northampton Engineering College (now City University)
DipPA — Diploma of Practitioners in Advertising (now see DipCAM)
DipREM — Diploma in Rural Estate Management
DipSoc — Diploma in Sociology
DipTA — Diploma in Tropical Agriculture
DipT&CP — Diploma in Town and Country Planning
DipTH — Diploma in Theology
DipTP — Diploma in Town Planning
Div. — Division; Divorced

DJAG	Deputy Judge Advocate General
DJPD	Dato Jasa Purba Di-Raja Negeri Sembilan (Malaysia)
DJStJ	Dame of Justice, Order of St John of Jerusalem (now see DStJ)
DJuris	Doctor Juris
DK	Most Esteemed Family Order (Brunei)
DL	Deputy Lieutenant
DLC	Diploma Loughborough College
DLES	Doctor of Letters in Economic Studies
DLI	Durham Light Infantry
DLitS	Doctor of Sacred Letters
DLJ	Dame of Grace, Order of St Lazarus of Jerusalem
DLO	Diploma in Laryngology and Otology
DM	Doctor of Medicine
DMA	Diploma in Municipal Administration
DMD	Doctor of Medical Dentistry (Australia)
DME	Director of Mechanical Engineering
DMet	Doctor of Metallurgy
DMI	Director of Military Intelligence
DMin	Doctor of Ministry
DMJ	Diploma in Medical Jurisprudence
DMJ(Path)	Diploma in Medical Jurisprudance (Pathology)
DMLJ	Dame of Merit, Order of St Lazarus of Jerusalem
DMO	Director of Military Operations
DMR	Diploma in Medical Radiology
DMRD	Diploma in Medical Radiological Diagnosis
DMRE	Diploma in Medical Radiology and Electrology
DMRT	Diploma in Medical Radio-Therapy
DMS	Director of Medical Services; Decoration for Meritorious Service (South Africa); Diploma in Management Studies
DMSSB	Direct Mail Services Standards Board
DMT	Director of Military Training
DMus	Doctor of Music
DN	Diploma in Nursing
DNB	Dictionary of National Biography
DNE	Director of Naval Equipment
DNI	Director of Naval Intelligence
DO	Diploma in Opthamology
DOAE	Defence Operational Analysis Establishment
DOC	District Officer Commanding
DocEng	Doctor of Engineering
DoE	Department of the Environment
DoH	Department of Health
DoI	Department of Industry
DOL	Doctor of Oriental Learning
Dom.	Dominus
DOMS	Diploma in Opthalmic Medicine and Surgery
DOR	Director of Operational Requirements
DOS	Director of Ordnance Services; Doctor of Ocular Science
Dow.	Dowager
DP	Data Processing
DPA	Diploma in Public Administration; Discharged Prisoners' Aid
DPD	Diploma in Public Dentistry
DPEc	Doctor of Political Economy
DPed	Doctor of Pedagogy
DPH	Diploma in Public Health
DPhysMed	Diploma in Physical Medicine
DPM	Diploma in Psychological Medicine
DPMS	Dato Paduka Mahkota Selangor (Malaysia)
DPP	Director of Public Prosecutions
DPR	Director of Public Relations
DPS	Director of Postal Services; Director of Personal Services; Doctor of Public Service
DQMG	Deputy Quartermaster-General
Dr	Doctor
DRAC	Director Royal Armoured Corps
DRC	Diploma of Royal College of Science and Technology, Glasgow
DRD	Diploma in Restorative Dentistry
Dr ing	Doctor of Engineering
Dr jur	Doctor of Laws
Dr rer. nat.	Doctor of Natural Science
DRS	Diploma in Religious Studies
DRSAMD	Diploma of the Royal Scottish Academy of Music and Drama
DS	Directing Staff; Doctor of Science
DSA	Diploma in Social Administration
DSAC	Defence Scientific Advisory Council
DSAO	Diplomatic Service Administration Office
DSC	Distinguished Service Cross
DSc	Doctor of Science
DScA	Docteur en sciences agricoles
DSCHE	Diploma in the Scottish Council for Health Education

DScMil	Doctor of Military Science
DSD	Director of Staff Duties
DSIR	Department of Scientific and Industrial Research (later SRC; now see SERC)
DSL	Doctor of Sacred Letters
DSLJ	Dato Seri Laila Jasa Brunei
DSM	Distinguished Service Medal
DSNB	Dato Setia Negara Brunei
DSNS	Dato Setia Negeri Sembilan (Malaysia)
DSO	Companion of the Distinguished Service Order
DSocSc	Doctor of Social Science
DSP	Director of Selection of Personnel; Docteur en sciences politiques (Montreal)
dsp	decessit sine prole (died without issue)
DSS	Department of Social Security; Doctor of Sacred Scriptures
Dss	Deaconess
DSSc	Doctor of Social Science
DST	Director of Supplies and Transport
DStJ	Dame of Grace, Most Venerable Order of the Hospital of St John of Jerusalem; Dame of Justice, Most Venerable Order of the Hospital of St John of Jerusalem
DTA	Diploma in Tropical Agriculture
DTD	Dekoratie voor Trouwe Dienst (Decoration for Devoted Service)
DTech	Doctor of Technology
DTH	Doctor in Tropical Hygiene
DTheol	Doctor of Theology
DThPT	Diploma in Theory and Practice of Teaching
DTI	Department of Trade and Industry
DTM&H	Diploma in Tropical Medicine and Hygiene
DU	Doctor of the University
Dunelm	Dunelmensis (of Durham)
DUniv	Doctor of the University
DUP	Democratic Unionist Party
DVA	Diploma of Veterinary Anaesthesia
DVH	Diploma in Veterinary Hygiene
DVLC	Driver Vehicle Licencing Centre
DVM	Doctor of Veterinary Medicine
DVMS	Doctor of Veterinary Medicine and Surgery
DVR	Diploma in Veterinary Radiology
DVSc	Doctor of Veterinary Science
DVSM	Diploma in Veterinary State Medicine

E

E	East; Earl; England
e	eldest
EAA	Edinburgh Architectural Association
EAHY	European Architectural Heritage Year
EAP	East Africa Protectorate
EAW	Electrical Association for Women
EBC	English Benedictine Congregation
Ebor	Eboracensis (of York)
EBU	European Broadcasting Union
EC	Etoile du Courage (Canada); European Commission; Emergency Commission
ECA	Economic Co-operation Administration; Economic Commission for Africa
ECAFE	Economic Commission for Asia and the Far East (now see ESCAP)
ECE	Economic Commission for Europe
ECGD	Exports Credits Guarantee Department
ECLA	Economic Commission for Latin America
ECOVAST	European Council for the Village and Small Town
ECSC	European Coal and Steel Community
ECU	English Church Union
ED	Efficiency Decoration; Doctor of Engineering (US); European Democrat
ed	edited
EdB	Bachelor of Education
EDC	Economic Development Committee
EdD	Doctor of Education
EDF	European Development Fund
EDG	European Democratic Group
Edin	Edinburgh
Edin	Edition
EDP	Executive Development Programme
Educ	Educated
Educn	Education
iEEC	European Economic Community; Commission of the European Communities

EEF	Engineering Employers' Federation; Egyption Expeditionary Force
EETPU	Electrical Electronic Telecommunication & Plumbing Union
EETS	Early English Text Society
EFCE	European Federation of Chemical Engineering
EFTA	European Free Trade Association
eh	ehrenhalber (honorary)
EI	East Indian; East Indies
EIA	Engineering Industries Association
EIB	European Investment Bank
EICS	East India Company's Service
E-in-C	Engineer-in-Chief
EIS	Educational Institute of Scotland
EISCAT	European Incoherent Scatter Association
EIU	Economist Intelligence Unit
ELBS	English Language Book Society
ELSE	European Life Science Editors
ELT	English Language Teaching
EM	Edward Medal; Earl Marshal
EMBL	European Molecular Biology Laboratory
EMBO	European Molecular Biology Organisation
EMP	Electro Magnetic Pulse
EMS	Emergency Medical Service
Enc.Brit.	Encyclopaedia Britannica
Eng.	England
Engr.	Engineer
ENO	English National Opera
ENSA	Entertainments National Service Association
ENT	Ear Nose and Throat
EOPH	Examined Officer of Public Health
EORTC	European Organisation for Research on Treatment of Cancer
EPP	European People's Party
er	elder
ER	Eastern Region (BR)
ERA	Electrical Research Association
ERC	Electronics Research Council
ERD	Emergency Reserve Decoration (Army)
ESA	European Space Agency
ESCAP	Economic and Social Commission for Asia and the Pacific
ESL	English as a Second Language
ESNS	Educational Sub-Normal Serious
ESRC	Economic and Social Research Council; Electricity Supply Research Council
ESRO	European Space Research Association (now see ESA)
ESU	English-Speaking Union
ETUC	European Trade Union Confederation
EUDISED	European Documentation and Information Service for Education
Euratom	European Atomic Energy Community
Eur Ing	European Engineer
EUROM	European Federation for Optics and Precision Mechanics
EUW	European Union of Women
eV	eingetragener Verein
Ext	Extinct

F

FA	Football Association
FAA	Fellow, Australian Academy of Science; Fleet Air Arm
FAAS	Fellow, American Association for the Advancement of Science
FAAO	Fellow, American Academy of Optometry
FAAP	Fellow, American Academy of Pediatrics
FAARM	Fellow, American Academy of Reproductive Medicine
FAAV	Fellow, Central Association of Agricultural Valuers
FAAVCT	Fellow, American Academy of Veterinary and Comparative Toxicology
FACC	Fellow, American Colege of Cardiology
FACCA	Fellow, Association of Certified and Corporate Accountants (now see FCCA)
FACCP	Fellow, American College of Chest Physicians
FACD	Fellow, American College of Dentistry
FACDS	Fellow, Australian College of Dental Surgeons (now see FRACDS)
FACE	Fellow, Australian College of Education
FACerS	Fellow, American Ceramic Society
FACI	Fellow, Australian Chemical Institute (now see FRACI)
FACMA	Fellow, Australian College of Medical Administrators (now see FRACMA)
FACOM	Fellow, Australian College of Occupational Medicine
FACP	Fellow, American College of Physicians
FACR	Fellow, American College of Radiology
FACRM	Fellow, Australian College of Rehabilitation Medicine
FACS	Fellow, American College of Surgeons

FACTV	Fellow, American College of Veterinary Toxicology
FAeSI	Fellow, Aeronautical Society of India
FAGO	Fellowship in Australia in Obstetrics and Gynaecology
FAGS	Fellow, American Geographical Society
FAHA	Fellow, Australian Academy of the Humanities
FAI	Fellow, Chartered Autioneers' and Estate Agents' Institute (now (after amalgamation) see FRICS);
FAIA	Fellow, American Institute of Architects
FAIAA	Fellow, American Institute of Aeronautics and Astronautics
FAIAS	Fellow, Australian Institute of Agricultural Science
FAIB	Fellow, Australian Institute of Bankers
FAIBiol	Fellow, Australian Institute of Biology
FAIE	Fellow, Australian Institute of Energy
FAIEx	Fellow, Australian Institute of Export
FAIFST	Fellow, Australian Institute of Food Science and Technology
FAII	Fellow, Australian Insurance Institute
FAIM	Fellow, Australian Institute of Management
FAIP	Fellow, Australian Institute of Physics
FAMA	Fellow, Australian Medical Association
FAMI	Fellow,Australian Marketing Institute
FAMS	Fellow, Ancient Monument Society
F and GP	Finance and General Purposes
FANY	First Aid Nursing Yeomanry
FANZCP	Fellow, Australian and New Zealand College of Psychiatrics
FAO	Food and Agricultural Organization of the United Nations
FAPA	Fellow, American Psychiatric Association
FAPHA	Fellow, American Public Health Association
FAPI	Fellow, Australian Planning Institute (now see FRAPI)
FAPS	Fellow, American Phytopathological Society
FArborA	Fellow, Arboricultural Association
FARE	Federation of Alcoholic Rehabilitation Establishments
FARELF	Far East Land Forces
FAS	Fellow, Antiquarian Society; Fellow, Nigerian Academy of Science
FASA	Fellow, Australian Society of Accountants
FASc	Fellow, Indian Academy of Science
FASCE	Fellow, American Society of Civil Engineers
FASI	Fellow, Architects' and Surveyors' Institute
FASSA	Fellow, Academy of the Social Sciences in Australia
FAusIMM	Fellow, Australasian Institute of Minning and Metallurgy
FAustCOG	Fellow, Australian College of Obstetricians and Gynaecologists
FBA	Fellow, British Academy; Federation of British Artists
FBCO	Fellow,British College of Opthalmic Opticians (Optometrists)
FBCS	Fellow, British Computer Society
FBEC(S)	Fellow, Business Education Council (Scotland)
FBHI	Fellow, British Horological Society
FBI	Federation of British Industries (now see CBI); Federal Bureau of Investigations
FBIA	Fellow, Bankers' Institute of Australia (now seeFAIB)
FBIBA	Fellow, British Insurance Brokers' Association
FBID	Fellow, British Institute of Interior Design
FBIM	Fellow, British Institute of Management
FBINZ	Fellow, Bankers' Institute of New Zealand
FBIPP	Fellow, British Institute of Professional Photographers
FBIRA	Fellow, British Institute of Regulatory Affairs
FBIS	Fellow, British Interplanetary Society
FBKS	Fellow, British Kinematograph Society (now see FBKSTS)
FBKSTS	Fellow, British Kinematograph, Sound and Television Society
FBOA	Fellow, British Optical Association
FBOU	Fellow, British Ornithologists' Union
FBPICS	Fellow, British Production and Inventory Control Society
FBPsS	Fellow, British Psychological Society
FBS	Fellow, Building Societies Institute (now seeFCBSI)
FBSI	Fellow, Boot and Shoe Society (now see FCFI)
FBSM	Fellow, Birmingham School of Music
FC	Football Club
FCA	Fellow, Institute of Chartered Accountants; Fellow, Institute of Chartered Accountants in Australia; Fellow, New Zealand Society of Accountants; Federation of Canadian Artists
FCAI	Fellow, New Zealand Institute of Cost Accountants; Fellow, Canadian Aeronautical Institute (now see FCASI)
FCAM	Fellow, CAM Foundation
FCAnaes	Fellow, College of Anaesthetists
FCASI	Fellow, Canadian Aeronautics and Space Institute
FCBSI	Fellow, Chartered Building Societies Institute
FCCA	Fellow, Association of Certified Accountants
FCCEA	Fellow, Commonwealth Council for Educational Administration
FCCS	Fellow, Corporation of Secretaries (formerly of Certified Secretaries)
FCCT	Fellow, Canadian College of Teachers
FCEC	Federation of Civil Engineering Contractors

FCFI	Fellow, Clothing and Footwear Institute
FCGI	Fellow, City and Guilds of London Institute
FCGP	Fellow, College of General Practitioners (now see FRCGP)
FCH	Fellow, Coopers Hill College
FChS	Fellow, Society of Chiropodists
FCI	Fellow, Institute of Commerce
FCIA	Fellow Corporation of Insurance Agents
FCIArb	Fellow, Chartered Institute of Arbitrators
FCIB	Fellow, Corporation of Insurance Brokers; Fellow, Chartered Institute of Bankers
FCIBS	Fellow, Chartered Institution of Building Services (now see FCIBSE)
FCIBSE	Fellow, Chartered Institution of Building Services Engineers
FCIC	Fellow, Chemical Institute of Canada (formerly Canadian Institute of Chemistry)
FCII	Fellow, Chartered Insurance Institute
FCILA	Fellow, Chartered Institute of Loss Adjusters
FCIM	Fellow, Chartered Institute of Marketing
FCIOB	Fellow, Chartered Institute of Building
FCIPA	Fellow, Chartered Institute of Patent Agents (now see CPA)
FCIS	Fellow, Institute of Chartered Secretaries and Administrators (formerly Chartered Institute of Secretaries)
FCISA	Fellow, Chartered Institute of Secretaries and Administrators (Australia)
FCIT	Fellow, Chartered Institute of Transport
FCM	Faculty of Community Medicine
FCMSA	Fellow, College of Medicine of South Africa
FCNA	Fellow, College of Nursing, Australia
FCO	Foreign and Commonwealth Office (departments merged Oct 1968)
FCollH	Fellow, College of Handicraft
FCollP	Fellow, College of Perceptors
FCommA	Fellow, Society of Commercial Accountants (now see FCSA)
FCOphth	Fellow, College of Ophthalmologists
FCP	Fellow, College of Perceptors
FCPath	Fellow, College of Pathology (now see FRCPath)
FCPS	Fellow, College of Physicians and Surgeons
FCP(SoAf)	Fellow, College of Physicians, South Africa
FCRA	Fellow, College of Radiologists of Australia (now see FRACR)
FCS	Federation of Conservative Students
FCSD	Fellow, Chartered Society of Designers
FCSP	Fellow, Chartered Society of Physiotherapy
FCSSL	Fellow, College of Surgeons of Sri Lanka
FCST	Fellow, College of Speech Therapists
FCT	Federal Capital Territory (now see ACT); Fellow, Association of Corporate Treasurers
FCTB	Fellow, College of Teachers of the Blind
FCU	Fighter Control Unit
FCWA	Fellow, Institute of Cost and Works Accountants (now see FCMA)
FDF	Food and Drink Federation
FDP	Freie Demokratische Partei
FDS	Fellow in Dental Surgery
FDSRCS	Fellow of Dental Surgery, Royal College of Surgeons of Edinburgh
FE	Far East
FEAF	Far East Air Force
FEBS	Federation of European Biochemical Societies
FECI	Fellow, Institute of Employment Consultants
FEF	Far East Fleet
FEIDCT	Fellow, Educational Institute of Design Craft and Technology
FEIS	Fellow, Educational Institute of Scotland
FEng	Fellow, Fellowship of Engineering
FES	Fellow, Educational Entomological Society; Fellow, Ethnological Society
FFA	Fellow, Faculty of Actuaries (in Scotland); Fellow, Institute of Financial Accountants
FFARACS	Fellow, Faculty of Anaesthetists, Royal Australian College of Surgeons
FFARCS	Fellow, Faculty of Anaesthetists, Royal College of Surgeons England
FFARCSI	Fellow, Faculty of Anaesthetists, Royal College of Surgeons in Ireland
FFAS	Fellow, Faculty of Architects and Surveyors, London
FFA(SA)	Fellow, Faculty of Anaesthetists (South Africa)
FFB	Fellow, Faculty of Building
FFCM	Fellow, Faculty of Community Medicine (now see FFPHM)
FFCMI	Fellow, Faculty of Community Medicine of Ireland
FFDRCSI	Fellow, Faculty of Dentistry, Royal College of Surgeons in Ireland
FFF	Free French Forces
FFHC	Freedom from Hunger Campaign
FFI	French Forces of the Interior; Finance for Industry
FFOM	Fellow, Faculty of Occupational Medicine
FFOMI	Fellow, Faculty of Occupational Medicine of Ireland
FFPHM	Fellow, Faculty of Public Health Medicine
FFPM	Fellow, Faculty of Pharmaceutical Medicine
FFPS	Fauna and Flora Preservation Society
FFR	Fellow, Faculty of Radiologists (now see FRCR)
FG	Fine Gael
FGA	Fellow, Gemmological Association
FGCM	Fellow, Guild of Church Musicians
FGGE	Fellow, Guild of Glass Engineers
FGI	Fellow, Institute of Certificated Grocers
FGS	Fellow, Geological Society
FGSM	Fellow, Guildhall School of Music and Drama
FGSM(MT)	Fellow, Guildhall School of Music and Drama (Music Therapy)
FHA	Fellow, Institute of Health Service Administrators (formerly Hospital Administrators; now see FHSM)
FHAS	Fellow, Highland and Agricultural Society of Scotland
FHCIMA	Fellow, Hotel Catering and Institutional Management Association
FHFS	Fellow, Human Factors Society
FHKIE	Fellow, Hong Kong Institute of Engineers
FHMAAAS	Foreign Honorary Member, American Academy of Arts and Sciences
FHS	Fellow, Heraldry Society; Forces Help Society and Lord Roberts Workshop
FHSM	Fellow, Institute of Health Service Management
FH-WC	Fellow, Heriot-Watt College (now University), Edinburgh
FIA	Fellow, Institute of Actuaries
FIAA	Fellow, Institute of Actuaries of Australia
FIAASA	Fellow, Institute of Australian Agricultural Science
FIAA&S	Fellow, Incorporated Association of Architects and Surveyors
FIAgrE	Fellow, Institution of Agricultural Engineers
FIAI	Fellow, Institute of Industrial and Commercial Accountants
FIAL	Fellow, International Institute of Arts and Letters
FIAM	Fellow, Institute of Administrative Management; Fellow, International Academy of Management
FIAP	Fellow, Institution of Analysts and Programmers
FIArb	Fellow, Institute of Arbitrators (now see FCIArb)
FIArbA	Fellow, Institute of Arbitrators of Australia
FIAS	Fellow, Institute of Aeronautical Sciences (US)
FIASc	Fellow, Indian Academy of Science
FIAWS	Fellow, International Association of Wood Sciences
FIB	Fellow, Institute of Bankers (FCIB)
FIBA	Fellow, Institute of Business Administration, Australia
FIBD	Fellow, Institute of British Decorators
FIBiol	Fellow, Institute of Biology
FIBiotech	Fellow, Institute of Biotechnical Studies
FIBP	Fellow, Institute of British Photographers
FIBScot	Fellow, Institute of Bankers of Scotland
FIC	Fellow, Institute of Chemistry (now see FRIC, FRSC); Fellow, Imperial College London
FICA	Fellow, Commonwealth Institute of Accountants; Fellow, Institute of Chartered Accountants in England and Wales (now see FCA)
FICAI	Fellow, Institute of Chartered Accountants in Ireland
FICD	Fellow, Institute of Civil Defence; Fellow, Indian College of Dentists
FICE	Fellow, Institution of Civil Engineers
FICeram	Fellow, Institute of Ceramics
FICFM	Fellow, Institute of Fundraising Managers
FICFor	Fellow, Institute of Chartered Foresters
FIChemE	Fellow, Institution of Chemical Engineers
FICI	Fellow, Institute of Chartered Shipbrokers; Fellow, International College of Surgeons
FICT	Fellow, Institute of Concrete Technologists
FICW	Fellow, Institute of Clerks of Works of Great Britain
FIDA	Fellow, Institute of Directors, Australia
FIDCA	Fellow, Industrial Design Council of Australia
FIE(Aust)	Fellow, Institution of Engineers, Australia
FIEC	Fellow, Institute of Employment Consultants
FIED	Fellow, Institution of Engineering Designers
FIEE	Fellow, Institute of Electrical Engineers
FIEEE	Fellow, Institute of Electrical and Electronics Engineers (NY)
FIEHK	Fellow, Institution of Engineering, Hong Kong
FIElecIE	Fellow, Institution of Electrical Incorporated Engineers
FIEI	Fellow, Institution of Engineering Inspection (now see FIQA); Fellow, Institution of Engineers of Ireland
FIERE	Fellow, Institution of Electronic and Radio Engineers
FIES	Fellow, Illuminating Engineering Society (later FIllumES;)
FIEx	Fellow, Institute of Export
FIExpE	Fellow, Institute of Explosives Engineers
FIFF	Fellow, Institute of Freight Forwarders

FIFireE	Fellow, Institution of Fire Engineers
FIFor	Fellow, Institute of Foresters (now see FICFor)
FIFST	Fellow, Institute of Food Science and Technology
FIGasE	Fellow, Institute of Gas Engineers
FIGCM	Fellow, Incorporated Guild of Church Musicians
FIGD	Fellow, Institute of Grocery Distribution
FIGO	International Federation of Gynaecology and Obstetrics
FIH	Fellow, Institute of Housing; Fellow, Insitute of the Horse
FIHE	Fellow, Institute of Health Education
FIHM	Fellow, Institute of Housing Managers (now see FIH)
FIHort	Fellow, Institute of Horticulture
FIHospE	Fellow, Institute of Hospital Engineering
FIHT	Fellow, Institute of Highways and Transportation
FIHVE	Fellow, Institute of Heating and Ventilating Engineers (later FCIBS and MCIBS; now see FCIBSE)
FIIA	Fellow, Institute of Industrial Administration (now see CBIM and FBIM); Fellow, Institute of Internal Auditors
FIIC	Fellow, International Institute for the Conservation of Historic and Artistic Works
FIIM	Fellow, Institution of Industrial Managers
FIInfSc	Fellow, Institute of Information Scientists
FIInst	Fellow, Imperial Institute
FIIP	Fellow, Institute of Incorporated Photographers (now see FBIPP)
FIIPE	Fellow, Indian Institution of Production Engineers
FIL	Fellow, Institute of Linguistics
FILA	Fellow, Institute of Landscape Architects (now see FLI)
FILDM	Fellow, Institute of Logistics and Distribution Management
FilDr	Doctor of Philosophy
Fil.Hed.	Filosofie Hedersdoktor
FIM	Fellow, Institute of Metals (formerly Institution of Metallurgists)
FIMA	Fellow, Institute of Mathematics and its Applications
FIMarE	Fellow, Institute of Marine Engineers
FIMBRA	Financial Intermediaries, Managers and Brokers Regulatory Association
FIMC	Fellow, Institute of Management Consultants
FIMCB	Fellow, International Management Centre from Buckingham
FIMechE	Fellow, Institute of Mechanical Engineers
FIMFT	Fellow, Institute of Maxillo-facial Technology
FIMH	Fellow, Institute of Materials Handling; Fellow, Institute of Military History
FIMI	Fellow, Institute of the Motor Industry
FIMinE	Fellow, Institution of Mining Engineers
FIMIT	Fellow, Institute of Musical Instrument Technology
FIMLS	Fellow, Institute of Medical Laboratory Sciences
FIMLT	Fellow, Institute of Medical Laboratory Technology
FIMM	Fellow, Institution of Mining and Metallurgy
FIMMA	Fellow, Institute of Mining and Materials Australasia
FIMS	Fellow, Institute of Mathemetical Statistics
FIMT	Fellow, Institute of the Motor Trade (now see FIMI)
FIMTA	Fellow, Institute of Municipal Treasurers and Accountants
FIMunE	Fellow, Institution of Municipal Engineers (now amalgamated with Institution of Civil Engineers)
FIN	Fellow, Institute of Navigation (now see FRIN)
FINA	Federation Internationale de Natation Amateur
FInstAM	Fellow, Institute of Administrative Management
FInstB	Fellow, Institution of Buyers
FInstBiol	Fellow, Institute of Biology (now see FIBiol)
FInstD	Fellow, Institute of Directors
FInstE	Fellow, Institute of Energy
FInstF	Fellow, Institute of Fuel (now see FInstE)
FInstFF	Fellow, Institute of Freight Forwarders Ltd
FInstHE	Fellow, Institution of Highway Engineers (now see FIHT)
FInstLEx	Fellow, Institute of Legal Executives
FinstM	Fellow, Institute of Meat; Fellow, Institute of Marketing (now see FCIM)
FInst MC	Fellow, Institute of Measurement and Control
FInstMSM	Fellow, Institute of Marketing and Sales Management (later FInstM; now see FCIM)
FInstMet	Fellow, Institute of Metals (later part of Metals Society)
FInstP	Fellow, Institute of Physics
FInstPet	Fellow, Institute of Petroleum
FInstPI	Fellow, Institute of Patentees and Inventors
FInstPS	Fellow, Institute of Purchasing and Supply
FInstSM	Fellow, Institute of Sales Management (now see FInstSMM)
FInstSMM	Fellow, Institute of Sales and Marketing Management
FInstW	Fellow, Institute of Welding (now seeFWeldI)
FINucE,	Fellow Institution of Nuclear Engineers
FIOA	Fellow, Institute of Acoustics
FIOB	Fellow, Institute of Building
FIOM	Fellow, Institute of Office Management (now see FIAM)
FIOP	Fellow, Institute of Printing
FIP	Fellow, Australian Institute of Petroleum
FIPA	Fellow, Institute of Practitioners in Advertising
FIPDM	Fellow, Institute of Physical Distribution Management
FIPENZ	Fellow, Institution of Professional Engineers, New Zealand
FIPG	Fellow, Institute of Professional Goldsmiths
FIPHE	Fellow, Institute of Public Heath Engineers (now see FIWEN)
FIPlantE	Fellow, Institution of Plant Engineers (now see FIIM)
FIPM	Fellow, Institute of Personnel Management
FIPR	Fellow, Institute of Public Relations
FIProdE	Fellow, Institution of Production Engineers
FIQ	Fellow, Institute of Quarrying
FIQA	Fellow, Institute of Quality Assurance
FIQS	Fellow, Institute of Quantity Surveyors
FIRA	Furniture Industry Research Association
FIRA(Ind)	Fellow, Institute of Railway Auditors and Accountants (India)
FIRE(Aust)	Fellow, Institution of Radio Engineers (Australia)
FIRI	Fellow, Institution of the Rubber Industry (now see FPRI)
FIRSE	Fellow, Institute of Railway Signalling Engineers
FIRTE	Fellow, Institute of Road Transport Engineers
FIS	Fellow, Institute of Statisticians
FISA	Fellow, Incorporated Secretaries' Association; Federation Internationale des Societes d'Aviron
FISE	Fellow, Institution of Sales Engineers; Fellow, Institution of Sanitary Engineers
FISP	Federation Internationale des Societes de Philosophie
FIST	Fellow, Institute of Science Technology
FISTC	Fellow, Institute of Scientific and Technical Communicators
FISTD	Fellow, Imperial Society of Teaching Of Dancing
FIStructE	Fellow, Institute of Structional Engineers
FISW	Fellow, Institute of Social Work
FITD	Fellow, Institute of Training and Development
FITE	Fellow, Institution of Electrical and Electronics Technician Engineers
FIW	Fellow, Welding Institute (now see FWeldI)
FIWE	Fellow, Institute of Water Engineers (later FIWES; now see FIWEM)
FIWEM	Fellow, Institution of Water and Environmental Management
FIWES	Fellow, Institute of Water Engineers and Scientists (now see FIWEM)
FIWM	Fellow, Institute of Works Manager (now see FIIM)
FIWPC	Fellow, Institute of Water Polution Control (now see FIWEM)
FIWSc	Fellow, Institute of Wood Science
FIWSP	Fellow, Institute of Work Study Practioners (now see FMS)
FJI	Fellow, Institute of Journalists
FJIE	Fellow, Junior Institution of Engineers (now see CIMGTechE)
FKC	Fellow, King's College London
FKCHMS	Fellow, King's College Hospital Medical School
FLA	Fellow, Library Institute
Fla	Florida (US)
FLAI	Fellow, Library Association of Ireland
FLAS	Fellow, Chartered Land Agents' Society (now (after amalgamation) see FRICS)
FLCM	Fellow, London College of Music
FLHS	Fellow, London Historical Society
FLI	Fellow, Landscape Institute
FLIA	Fellow, Life Insurance Association
FLS	Fellow, Linnean Society
Flt	Flight
FM	Field Marshal
FMA	Fellow, Museums Association
FMANZ	Fellow, Medical Association of New Zealand
FMES	Fellow, Minerals Engineering Society
FMF	Fiji Military Forces
FMS	Federated Malay States;Fellow, Medical Society; Fellow, Institute of Management Services
FMSA	Fellow, Mineralogical Society of America
FNA	Fellow, Indian National Science Academy
FNAEA	Fellow, National Association of Estate Agents
FNCO	Fleet Naval Constructor Officer
FNECInst	Fellow, North East Coast Institution of Engineers and Shipbuilders
FNI	Fellow, Nautical Institute; Fellow National Institute of Sciences in India (now see FNA)
FNIA	Fellow, Nigerian Institute of Architects
FNZEI	Fellow, New Zealand Educational Institute
FNZIA	Fellow, New Zealand Institute of Architects
FNZIAS	Fellow, New Zealand Institue of Agricultural Science
FNZIC	Fellow, New Zealand Institute of Chemistry
FNZIE	Fellow, New Zealand Institution of Engineers
FINZIM	Fellow, New Zealand Institute of Management
FNZPsS	Fellow, New Zealand Psychological Society
FONAC	Flag Officer Naval Air Command

FOR	Fellowship of Operational Research
For.	Foreign
FOREST	Freedom Organisation for the Right to Enjoy Smoking Tobacco
FOX	Futures and Options Exchange
FPA	Family Planning Association
FPC	Family Practitioner Committee
FPEA	Fellow, Physical Education Association
FPhS	Fellow, Philosophical Society of England
FPI	Fellow, Plastics Institute (now see FPRI)
FPIA	Fellow, Plastics Institute of Australia
FPMI	Fellow, Pensions Management Institute
FPRI	Fellow, Plastics and Rubber Institute
FPS	Fellow, Pharmaceutical Society (now see FRPharmS); Fauna Preservation Society (now see FFPS)
FPhysS	Fellow, Physical Society
f r	fuori ruole
FRACDS	Fellow, Royal Australian College of Dental Surgeons
FRCGP	Fellow, Royal Australian College of General Practitioners
FRICI	Fellow, Royal Australian Chemical Institute
FRCMA	Fellow, Royal Australian College of Medical Administrators
FRACO	Fellow, Royal Australian College of Ophthalmologists
FRACOG	Fellow, Royal Australian College of Obstetricians and Gynaecologists
FRACP	Fellow, Royal Australasian College of Physicians
FRACR	Fellow, Royal Australasian College of Radiologists
FRACS	Fellow, Royal Australasian College of Surgeons
FRAD	Fellow, Royal Academy of Dancing
FRAeS	Fellow, Royal Aeronautical Society
FRAgS	Fellow, Royal Agricultural Societies (ie of England, Scotland and Wales)
FRAHS	Fellow, Royal Australian Historical Society
FRAI	Fellow, Royal Anthropological Institute
FRAIA	Fellow, Royal Australian Institute of Architects
FRAIB	Fellow, Royal Australian Institute of Building
FRAIC	Fellow, Royal Architectural Institute of Canada
FRAIPA	Fellow, Royal Australian Institute of Public Administration
FRAM	Fellow, Royal Academy of Music
FRAME	Fund for the Replacement of Animals in Medical Experiments
FRANZCP	Fellow, Royal Australian and New Zealand College of Psychiatrists
FRAPI	Fellow, Royal Australian Planning Institute
FRAS	Fellow, Royal Astronomical Society; Fellow, Royal Asiatic Society
FRASB	Fellow, Royal Asiatic Society of Bengal
FRASE	Fellow, Royal Agricultural Society of England
FRBS	Fellow, Royal Society of British Sculptors; Fellow, Royal Botanic Society
FRCCO	Fellow, Royal Canadian College of Organists
FRCD(Can)	Fellow, Royal College of Dentists of Canada
FRCGP	Fellow, Royal College of General Practitioners
FRCM	Fellow, Royal College of Musicians
FRCN	Fellow, Royal College of Nursing
FRCO	Fellow, Royal College of Organists
FRCOG	Fellow, Royal College of Obstetricians and Gynaecologists
FRCP	Fellow, Royal College of Physicians, London
FRCPA	Fellow, Royal College of Pathologists of Australia
FRCPath	Fellow, Royal College of Pathologists
FRCP(C)	Fellow, Royal College of Physicians of Canada
FRCPGlas	Fellow, Royal College of Physicians and Surgeons of Glasgow
FRCSI	Fellow, Royal College of Physicians in Ireland
FRCSI	Fellow, Royal College of Surgeons in Ireland
FRCSoc	Fellow, Royal Commonwealth Society
FRCUS	Fellow, Royal College of University Surgeons (Denmark)
FRCVS	Fellow, Royal College of Veterinary Surgeons
FREconS	Fellow, Royal Economic Society
FREI	Fellow, Real Estate Institute (Australia)
FRES	Fellow, Royal Entomological Society of London
FRFPSG	Fellow, Royal Faculty of Physicians and Surgeons, Glasgow (now see FRCPGlas)
FRG	Federal Republic of Germany
FRGS	Fellow, Royal Geographical Society
FRGSA	Fellow, Royal Geographical Society of Australasia
FRHistS	Fellow, Royal Historical Society
FRHS	Fellow, Royal Horticultural Society
FRHSV	Fellow, Royal Historical Society of Victoria
FRIAS	Fellow, Royal Incorporation of Architects of Scotland; Royal Institute for the Advancement of Science
FRIBA	Fellow, Royal Institute of British Architects
FRIC	Fellow, Royal Institute of Chemistry (now see FRSC)
FRICS	Fellow, Royal Institution of Chartered Surveyors
FRIH	Fellow, Royal Institute of Horticulture
FRIN	Fellow, Royal Institute of Navigation
FRINA	Fellow, Royal Institution of Naval Architects

FRIPHH	Fellow, Royal Institute of Public Health and Hygiene
FRMCM	Fellow, Royal Manchester College of Music
FRMedSoc	Fellow, Royal Medical Society
FRMetS	Fellow, Royal Meteorological Society
FRMIA	Fellow, Retail Management Institute of Australia
FRMS	Fellow, Royal Microscopical Society
FRNCM	Fellow, Royal Northern College of Music
FRNS	Fellow, Royal Numismatic Society
FRPharmS	Fellow, Royal Pharmaceutical Society
FRPS	Fellow, Royal Photographic Society
FRPSL	Fellow, Royal Philatelic Society, London
FRS	Fellow, Royal Society
FRSA	Fellow, Royal Society of Arts
FRSAI	Fellow, Royal Society of Antiquaries of Ireland
FRSAMD	Fellow, Royal Scottish Academy of Music and Drama
FRSanI	Fellow, Royal Sanitary Institute (now see FRSH)
FRSC	Fellow, Royal Society of Canada; Fellow, Royal Society of Chemistry
FRSCM	Fellow, Royal Society of Church Music
FRSE	Fellow, Royal Society of Edinburgh
FRSGS	Fellow, Royal Scottish Geographical Society
FRSH	Fellow, Royal Society for the Promotion of Health
FRSL	Fellow, Royal Society of Literature
FRSM or	
FRSocMed	Fellow, Royal Society Medicine
FRSNZ	Fellow, Royal Society of New Zealand
FRSSAf	Fellow, Royal Society of South Africa
FRST	Fellow, Royal Society of Teachers
FRSTM&H	Fellow, Royal Society of Tropical Medicine and Hygiene
FRTPI	Fellow, Royal Town Planning Institute
FRTS	Fellow, Royal Television Society
FRVA	Fellow, Ratings and Valuation Associaton (now see IRRV)
FRVC	Fellow, Royal Veterinary College
FRVIA	Fellow, Royal Victorian Institute of Architects
FRZSScot	Fellow, Royal Zoological Society Scotland
FS	Field Security
FSA	Fellow, Society of Antiquaries
FSAA	Fellow, Society of Incorporated Accountants and Auditors
FSAE	Fellow, Society of Automotive Engineers; Fellow, Society of Art Education
FSAI	Fellow, Society of Architectural Illustrators
FSAIEE	Fellow, South African Institute of Electrical Engineers
FSAM	Fellow, Society of Art Masters
FSArc	Fellow, Society of Architects (merged with the RIBA 1952)
FSAScot	Fellow, Society of Antiquaries of Scotland
FSASM	Fellow, Australian School of Mines
FSBI	Fellow, Savings Banks Institute
fsc	Forign Staff College
FSCA	Fellow, Society of Company and Commercial Accountants
FScotvec	Fellow, Scottish Vocational Educational Council
FSDC	Fellow, Society of Dyers and Colourists
FSE	Fellow, Society of Engineers
FSG	Fellow, Society of Genealogists
FSGT	Fellow, Society of Glass Technologists
FSI	Fellow, Chartered Surveyors Institution (now see FRICS)
FSIAD	Fellow, Society of Industrial Artists and Designers (now see FCSD)
FSLAET	Fellow, Society of Licenced Aircraft Engineers and Technologists
FSLCOG	Fellow, Sri Lankan College of Obstetrics and Gynaecology
FSLTC	Fellow, Society of Leather Technologists and Chemists
FSMA	Fellow, Incorporated Sales Managers' Association (later FInstMSM; now see FInstM)
FSMC	Freeman of the Spectacle-Makers' Company
FSME	Fellow, Society of Manufacturing Engineers
FSRHE	Fellow, Society for Research intoHigher Education
FSRP	Fellow, Society for Radiological Protection
FSS	Fellow, Royal Statistical Society
FSTD	Fellow, Society of Tyographic Designers
FSVA	Fellow, Incorporated Society of Valuers and Auctioneers
FT	Finincial Times
FTAT	Furniture, Timber and Allied Trades Union
FTC	Flying Training Command; Full Technological Certificate, City and Guilds of London Institute
FTCD	Fellow, Trinity College, Dublin
FTCL	Fellow, Trinity College of Music, London
FTI	Fellow, Textile Institute
FTI	Fellow, Institute of Taxation
FTP	Fellow, Thames Polytechnic
FTS	Fellow, Australian Academy of Technological Sciences and Engineering; Flying Training School; Fellow, Tourism Society

FUCUA Federation of University Conservative and Unionist Associations (now see FCS)
FUMIST Fellow, University of Manchester Institute of Science and Technology
FVRDE Fighting Vehicles Research and Development Establishment
FWA Fellow, World Academy of Arts and Sciences
FWACP Fellow, West African College of Physicians
FWeldI Fellow, Welding Institute
FWSOM Fellow, Institute of Practitioners in Work Study, Organisation and Method (now see FMS)
FZS Fellow, Zoological Society
FZSScot Fellow, Zoological Society of Scotland (now see FRZSScot)

G

GA Geologists' Association; Gaelic Athletic (Club)
Ga Georgia (US)
GAI Guild of Architectural Ironmongers
GAP Gap Activity Projects
GAPAN Guild of Air Pilots and Air Navigators
GATT General Agreement on Tariffs and Trade
GB Great Britain
GBA Governing Bodies Association
GBE Knight or Dame Grand Cross, Order of the British Empire
GBGSA Governing Bodies of Girls' Schools Association (formerly Association of Governing Bodies of Girls' Public Schools)
GBSM Graduate of Birmingham and Midland Institute School of Music
GC George Cross
GCB Knight or Dame Grand Cross, Order of the Bath
GCBS General Council of British Shipping
GCFR Grand Commander, Order of the Federal Republic of Nigeria
GCH Knight Grand Cross, Hanoverian Order
GCHQ Government Communications Headquarters
GCIE Knight Grand Commander, Order of the Indian Empire
GCIJ Grand Cross, St Lazarus of Jerusalem
GCLM Grand Commander, Order of the Legion of Merit of Rhodesia
GCM Gold Crown of Merit (Barbados)
GCMG Knight or Dame Grand Cross, Order of St Michel and St George
GCON Grand Cross, Order of the Niger
GCSE General Certificate of Secondary Education
GCSI Knight Grand Commander, Order of the Star of India
GCSJ Knight Grand Cross of Justice, Order of St John of Jerusalem (Knights Hospitaller)
GCSL Grand Cross, Order of St Lucia
GCStJ Baliff or Dame Grand Cross, Most Venerable Order of the Hospital of St John of Jerusalem
GCVO Knight or Dame Grand Cross, Royal Victorian Order
g d grand-daughter
GDBA Guide Dogs for the Blind Association
GDS General Dental Council
Gdns Gardens
GDR German Democratic Republic
Gen. General
Ges. Gesellschaft
GFD Geophysical Fluid Dynamics
GFS Girls' Friendly Society
g g d great-grand-daughter
g g s great-grandson
GGSM Graduate in Music, Guildhall School of Music and Drama
GHQ General Headquarters
Gib. Gibraltar
GIMechE Graduate Institute of Mechanical Engineers
GL Grand Lodge
GLAA Greater London Arts Association (now see GLAB)
GLAB Greater London Arts Board
CLC Greater London Council
Glos Gloucestershire
GM George Medal; Grand Medal (Ghana)
GMB (Union for) General, Municipal, Boilermakers
BMBATU General, Municipal, Boilermakers and Allied Trades Union (now see GMB)
GMC General Medical Council; Guild of Memorial Craftsmen
GMIE Grand Master, Order of the Indian Empire
GMSI Grand Master, Order of the Star of India
GMWU General and Municipal Workers Union (later BMBATU; now see GMB)
GNC General Nursing Council
GOC General Officer Commanding
GOC-in-C General Officer Commanding-in-Chief

GOE General Ordination Examination
Gov. Governor
Govt Government
GP General Practitioner; Grand Prix
GPDST Girls' Public Day School Trust
GPO General Post Office
GQG Grand Quartier General
Gr. Greek
GRSM Graduate of the Royal Schools of Music
GS General Staff; Grammar School
gs grandson
GSA Girls' Schools Association
GSM General Service medal; (Member of) Guildhall School of Music and Drama
GSMD Guildhall School of Music and Drama
GSO General Staff Officer
GTCL Graduate Trinity College of Music
GTS General Theological Seminar (NY)
GUI Golfing Union of Ireland
GWR Great Western Railway

H

HA Historical Association; Health Authority
HAA Heavy Anti-Aircraft
HAC Honourable Artillery Company
Hants Hampshire
HARCVS Honorary Associate, Royal College of Veterinary Surgeons
Harv. Harvard
HBM His (or Her) Britannic Majesty (Majesty's); Humming Bird Gold Medal (Trinidad)
hc honaris causa
HCEG Honourable Company of Edinburgh Golfers
HCF Honorary Chaplin to the Forces
HCIMA Hotel, Catering and Institutional Management Association
HCSC Higher Command and Staff Course
HDA Hawkesbury Diploma in Agriculture (Australia)
HDD Higher Dental Diploma
HDipEd Higher Diploma in Education
HE His (or Her) Exellency; His Emminence
HEC Ecole des Hautes Etudes Commerciales; Higher Education Corporation
HEH His (or Her) Exalted Highness
HEIC Honourable East India Company
HEICS Honourable East India Company's Service
Heir-pres. Heir-presumptive
Herts Hertfordshire
HFARA Honorary Foreign Associate of the Royal Academy
HFRA Honorary Foreign Member of the Royal Academy
HG Home Guard
HGTAC Home Grown Timber Advisory Committee
HH His (or Her) Highness; His Holiness; Member, Hesketh Hubbard Art Society
HHA Historic Houses Association
HHD Doctor of Humanities (US)
HIH His (or Her) Imperial Highness
HIM His (or Her) Imperial Majesty
HJ Hilal-e-Jurat (Pakistan)
HKIA Hong Kong Institute of Architects
HKIPM Hong kong Institute of Personnel Management
HLD Doctor of Humane Letters
HLI Highland Light Infantry
HM His (or Her) Majesty or Majesty's
HMA Head Masters' Association
HMAS His (or Her) Majesty's Australian Ship
HMC Headmasters' Conference; Hospital Management Committee
HMCIC His (or Her) Majesty's Chief Inspector of Constabulary
HMCS His (or Her) Majesty's Canadian Ship
HMHS His (or Her) Majesty's Hospital Ship
HMI His (or Her) Majesty's Inspector
HMIED Honorary Member, Institute of Engineering Designers
HMOCS His (or Her) Majesty's Overseas Civil Service
HMS His (or Her) Majesty's Ship
HMSO His (or Her) Majesty's Stationery Office
HNC Higher National Certificate
HND Higher National Diploma
H of C House of Commons
H of L House of Lords

Hon.	Honorary; Honourable		ICI	Imperial Chemical Industries
HPk	Hilal-e-Pakistan		ICL	International Computers Ltd
HQ	Headquarters		ICM	International Confederation of Midwives
HQA	Hilal-i-Quaid-i-Azam (Pakistan)		ICMA	Institute of Cost and Management Accountants
(HR)	Home Rule		ICME	International Commission for Mathematical Education
HRCA	Honorary Royal Cambrian Academician		ICOM	International Council of Museums
HRGI	Honorary Member, The Royal Glasgow Institute of the Fine Arts		ICOMOS	International Council of Monuments and Sites
HRH	His (or Her) Royal Highness		ICorrST	Institution of Corrosion Science and Technology
HRHA	Honorary Member, Royal Hibernian Academy		ICPO	International Criminal Police Organization (Interpol)
HRI	Honorary Member,Royal Institute of Painters in Water Colours		ICRC	International Committee of the Red Cross
HROI	Honorary Member, Royal Institute of Oil Painters		ICRF	Imperial Cancer Research Fund
HRSA	Honorary Member, Royal Scottish Academy		ICE	Indian Civil Service
HRSW	Honorary Member, Royal Scottish Water Colour Society		ICS	Institute of Chartered Secretaries and Administrators
HSC	Health and Safety Commission		ICSID	International Council of Societies of Industrial Design; International Centre for Settlement of Investment Disputes
HSE	Health and Safety Executive			
HSH	His (or Her) Serene Highness		ICSS	International Committe for the Sociology of Sport
Hum.	Humanity, Humanities (Classics)		ICSU	International Council of Scientific Unions
Hunts	Huntingdonshire		ICT	International Computers and Tabulators Ltd (now see ICL)
HVCert	Health Visitor's Certificate		Id	Idaho (US)
Hy	Heavy		ID	Independence Decoration (Rhodesia)

I

			IDA	International Development Association
			IDS	Institute of Development Studies;Industry Department of Scotland
I	Island; Ireland		IEA	Institute of Economic Affairs
Ia	Iowa (US)		IEC	International Electrotechnical Commission
IA	Indian Army		IEE	Institution of Electrical Engineers
IAAF	International Amateur Athletic Federation		IEEE	Institute of Electrical and Electronic Engineers (NY)
IAC	Indian Armoured Corps; Institute of Amateur Cinematographers		IEEIE	Institution of Electrical and Electronics Incorporated Engineers
IACP	International Association of Chiefs of Police		IEETE	Institution of Electrical and Electronics Technician Engineers
IADR	International Association for Dental Research		IEI	Institution of Engineers of Ireland
IAEA	International Atomic Energy Agency		IEME	Inspectorate of Electrical and Mechanical Engineering
IAF	Indian Air Force; Indian Auxiliary Force		IEng	Incorporated Engineer
IAHM	Incorporated Association of Headmasters		IERE	Institution of Electronic and Radio Engineers
IAM	Institute of Advanced Motorists; Institute of Aviation Medicine		IES	Indian Education Service; Institution of Engineers and Shipbuilders in Scotland
IAMC	Indian Army Medical Corps			
IAMTACT	Institute of Advanced Machine Tool and Control Technology		IExpE	Institute of Explosives Engineers
IAO	Incorporated Association of Organists		IFAC	International Federation of Automatic Control
IAOC	Indian Army Ordnance Corps		IFAD	International Fund for Agricultural Development (UNO)
IAPS	Incorporated Association of Preparatory Schools		IFAW	International Fund for Animal Welfare
IAPSO	International Association for the Physical Sciences of the Oceans		IFC	International Finance Corporation
IARO	Indian Army Reserve of Officers		IFIAS	International Federation of Institutes of Advanced Study
IAS	Indian Administrative Service; Institute of Advanced Studies		IFIP	International Federation for Information Processing
IASS	International Association for Scandinavian Studies		IFL	International Friendship League
IATA	International Air Transport Association		IFLA	International Federation of Library Associations
IATUL	International Association of Technological University Libraries		IFORS	International Federation of Operational Research Societies
IAU	International Astronomical Union		IFPI	International Federation of the Phonographic Industry
IAWPRC	International Association on Water Pollution Research and Control		IFS	Irish Free State; Indian Forest Service
ib. or ibed.	ibedem (in the same place)		IG	Instructor in Gunnery
IBA	Independant Broadcasting Authority; International Bar Association		IGasE	Institution of Gas Engineers
IBG	Institute of British Geographers		IGPP	Institute of Geophysics and Planetary Physics
IBRD	International Bank for Reconstruction and Development (World Bank)		IGS	Independent Grammar School
			IGU	International Geographical Union; International Gas Union
IBRO	International Bank Research Organisation; International Brain Research Association		IHA	Institute of Health Service Administrators
			IHospE	Institute of Hospital Engineering
IBTE	Institution of British Telecommunication Engineers		IHVE	Institution of Heating and Ventilating Engineers
i/c	in charge; in command		IIM	Institution of Industrial Managers
ICA	Institute of Contemporary Arts; Institute of Chartered Accountants in England and Wales		IIMT	International Institute for the Management of Technology
			IInfSc	Institute of Information Scientists
ICAA	Invalid Children's Aid Association		IIS	International Institute of Sociology
ICAI	Institute of Chartered Accountants in Ireland		IISS	International Institute of Strategic Studies
ICAO	International Civil Aviation Authority		IIT	Indian Institute of Technology
ICBP	International Council for Bird Preservation		ILA	International Law Association
ICC	International Chamber of Commerce		ILEA	Inner London Education Authority
ICCROM	International Centre for Conservation at Rome		ILEC	Inner London Education Committee
ICD	Iuris Canonici Doctor; Independence Commemorative Decoration (Rhodesia)		Ill	Illinois (US)
			ILO	International Labour Office; International Labour Organistion
ICE	Institution of Civil Engineers		ILP	Independent Labour Party
ICED	International Council for Educational Development		ILR	Independent Local Radio; International Labour Review
ICEF	International Federation of Chemical, Energy and General Workers' Union		IM	Individual Merit
			IMA	International Music Association; Institute of Mathematics and its Applications
Icel	Icelandic			
ICES	International Council for the Exploration of the Sea		IMCB	International Management Centre from Buckingham
ICF	International Federation of Chemical and General Workers' Union (now see ICEF)		IMCO	Inter-Governmental Maritime Consultative Organization
			IMEA	Incorporated Municipal Electrical Association
ICFC	Industrial and Commercial Finance Corporation (later part of Investors in Industry)		IMechE	Institution of Mechanical Engineers
			IMEDE	Insitut pour l'Etude des Methodes de Direction de l'Enterprise
ICFTU	International Confederation of Free Trade Unions		IMF	International Monetary Fund
ICHCA	International Cargo Handling Co-ordination Association		IMGTechE	Institution of Mechanical and General Technician Engineers
IChemE	Institution of Chemical Engineers		IMinE	Institution of Mining Engineers
			IMM	Institution of Mining and Metallurgy
			IMMLEP	Immunology of Leprosy

IMMTS	Indian Mercantile Marine Training Ship
IMO	International Maritime Organization
Imp.	Imperial
IMRO	Investment Management Regulatory Organisation
IMS	Indian Medical Service; Institute of Management Services; International Military Staff
IMTA	Institute of Municipal Treasurers and Accountants
IMU	International Mathematical Union
IMunE	Institution of Municipal Engineers (now amalgamated with Institution of Civil Engineers)
IN	Indian Navy
Inc.	Incorporated
INCA	International Newspaper Colour Association
Incog.	Incognito
Ind.	Independent; Indiana (US)
Inf.	Infantry
INSA	Indian National Science Academy
INSEA	International Society for Education through Art
Insp.	Inspector
Inst.	Institute
InstBE	Institute of British Engineers
Instn	Institution
InstSMM	Institution of Sales and Marketing Management
InstT	Institute of Transport
INTELSAT	International Telecommunications Satellite Organisation
IOB	Institute of Building (now see CIOB)
IOC	International Olympic Committee
IOCD	International Organisation for Chemical Science in Development
IODE	Imperial Order of the Daughters of the Empire
I of M	Isle of Man
IOGT	International Order of Good Templars
IOM	Isle of Man; Indian Order of Merit
IOOF	Independent Order of Odd-fellows
IOP	Institute of Painters in Oil Colours
IoW	Isle of Wight
IPA	International Publishers' Association
IPCS	Institution of Professional Civil Servants
IPFA	Member or Associate, Chartered Institute of Public Finance and Accountancy
IPHE	Institution of Public Health Engineers (now see IWEM)
IPI	International Press Institute; Institute of Patentees and Inventors
IPlantE	Institution of Plant Engineers (now see IIM)
IPM	Institute of Personnel Management
IPPA	Independent Programme Producers' Association
IPPF	International Planned Parenthood Federation
IPPS	Institute of Physics and The Physical Society
IProdE	Institution of Production Engineers
IPS	Indian Police Service; Indian Political Service; Institute of Purchasing and Supply
IPU	Inter-Parliamentary Union
IRA	Irish Republican Army
IRAD	Institute for Research on Animal Diseases
IRC	Industrial Reorganization Corporation; Interdisciplinary Research Centre
IRCAM	Institute for Research and Co-ordination in Acoustics and Music
IRCert	Industrial Relations Certificate
IREE(Aust)	Institution of Radio and Electronics Engineers (Australia)
IRI	Institution of the Rubber Industry (now see PRI)
IRO	International Refugee Organization
IRPA	International Radiation Protection Association
IRRV	(Fellow/Member of) Institute of Revenues, Rating and Valuation
IRTE	Institute of Road Transport Engineers
IS	International Society of Sculptors, Painters and Gravers
Is	Island(s)
ISBA	Incorporated Society of British Advertisers
ISC	Imperial Service College, Hayleybury; Indian Staff Corps
ISCM	International Society for Contemporary Music
ISCO	Independent Schools Careers Organisation
ISE	Indian Service of Engineers
ISI	International Statistical Institute
ISIS	Independent Schools Information Service
ISJC	Independent Schools Joint Council
ISM	Incorporated Society of Musicians
ISME	International Society for Musical Education
ISMRC	Inter-Services Metallurgical Research Council
ISO	Imperial Service Order; International Organization for Standardization
ISSTIP	International Society for Study of Tension in Performance
ISTC	Iron and Steel Trades Confederation; Institute of Scientific and Technical Communicators
ISTD	Imperial Society of Teachers of Dancing

IStructE	Institution of Structural Engineers
IT	Information Technology; Indian Territory (US)
ITA	Independent Television Authority (now see IBA)
Ital or It.	Italian
ITB	Industry Training Board
ITC	International Trade Centre; Independent Television Commission
ITCA	Independent Television Companies Association Ltd (now Independent Television Association)
ITDG	Intermediate Technology Development Group
ITEME	Institution of Technician Engineers in Mechanical Engineering
ITF	International Transport Workers' Federation
ITN	Independent Television News
ITO	International Trade Organization
ITU	International Telecommunication Union
ITV	Independent Television
IUA	International Union of Architects
IUB	International Union of Biochemistry
IUC	Inter-University Council for Higher Education Overseas
IUCN	International Union for the Conservation of Nature and Natural Resources
IUCW	International Union for Child Welfare
IUGS	International Union of Geological Sciences
IUHPS	International Union of the History and Philosophy of Science
IULA	International Union of Local Authorities
IUP	Association of Independent Unionist Peers
IUPAC	International Union of Pure and Applied Chemistry
IUPAP	International Union of Pure and Applied Physics
IUPC	Inter-University and Polytechnic Council for Higher Education Overseas
IUPS	International Union of Physiological Sciences
IUTAM	International Union of Theoretical and Applied Mechanics
IVF	In-vitro Fertilisation
IVS	International Voluntary Service
IWA	Inland Waterways Association
IWEM	Institution of Water and Environmental Management
IWES	Institution of Water Engineers and Scientists
IWGC	Imperial War Graves Commission (now see CWGC)
IWM	Institution of Works Managers (now see IIM)
IWPC	Institute of Water Pollution Control (now see IWEM)
IWSOM	Institute of Practitioners in Work Study Organisation and Methods
IWSP	Institute of Work Study Practitioners (now see IMS)
IY	Imperial Yeomanry
IYRU	International Yacht Racing Union
IZ	I Zingari

J

JA	Judge Advocate
JACT	Joint Association of Classical Teachers
JAG	Judge Advocate General
Jas	James
JCB	Juris Canonici (or Civilis) Baccalaureus (Bachelor of Canon (or Civil) Law)
JCS	Journal of the Chemical Society
JCD	Juris Canonici (or Civilis) Doctor (Doctor of Canon (or Civil) Law)
JCI	Junior Chamber International
JCL	Juris Canonici (or Civilis) Licentiatus (Licentiate in Canon (or Civil) Law)
JCO	Joint Consultative Organisation (of AFRC, MAFF, and Department of Agriculture and Fisheries for Scotland)
JD	Doctor of Jurisprudence
JDipMA	Joint Diploma in Management Accounting Services
JG	Junior Grade
JInstE	Junior Institution of Engineers (now see IMGTechE)
jls	journal(s)
JMB	Joint Metriculation Board
JMN	Johan Mangku Negara (Malaysia)
Joh. or Jno.	John
JP	Justice of the Peace
Jr	Junior
jsc	qualified at a Juniro Staff Course, or the equivalent, 1942-46
JSD	Doctor of Jurisdic Science
JSDC	Joint Service Defence College
jsdc	completed a course at Joint Service Defence College
JSLS	Joint Services Liaison Staff
JSM	Johan Setia Mahkota (Malaysia)
JSPS	Japan Society for the Promotion of Science
JSSC	Joint Services Staff College
jssc	completed a course at Joint Services Staff College

jt, jtly	joint, jointly
JUD	Juris Utriusque Doctor, Doctor of Both Laws (Canon and Civil)
Jun.	Junior
Jun.Opt.	Junior Optime
JWS or jws	Joint Warfare Staff

K

KA	Knight of St Andrew, Order of Barbados
Kans	Kansas (US)
KAR	King's African Rifles
KBE	Knight Commander, Order of the British Empire
KC	King's Counsel
KCB	Knight Commander, Order of the Bath
KCC	Commander of Order of Crown, Belgium and Congo Free State
KCH	King's College Hospital; Knight Commander, Hanoverian Order
KCHS	Knight Commander, Order of the Holy Sepulchre
KCIE	Knight Commander, Order of the Indian Empire
KCL	King's College London
KCLJ	Knight Commander, Order of St Lazarus of Jerusalem
KCMG	Knight Commander, Order of St Michael and St George
KCSA	Knight Commander, Military Order of the Collar of St Agatha of Paterna
KCSG	Knight Commander, Order of St Gregory the Great
KCSI	Knight Commander, Order of the Star of India
KCSJ	Knight Commander, Order of St John of Jerusalem (Knights Hospitaller)
KCSS	Knight Commander, Order of St Silvester
KCVO	Knight Commander, Royal Victorian Order
KCVSA	King's Commendation for Valuable Services in the Air
KDG	King's Dragoon Guards
KEH	King Edward's Horse
KEO	King Edward's Own
KG	Knight, Order of the Garter
KGStJ	Knight of Grace, Order of St John of Jerusalem (now see KStJ)
KH	Knight, Hanoverian Order
KHC	Hon. Chaplain to the King
KHDS	Hon. Dental Surgeon to the King
KHNS	Hon. Nursing Sister to the King
KHP	Hon. Physician to the King
KHS	Hon. Surgeon to the King; Knight, Order of the Holy Sepulchre
K-i-H	Kaisar-i-Hind
KJStJ	Knight of Justice, Order of St John of Jerusalem (now see KStJ)
KLJ	Knight, Order of St Lazarus of Jerusalem
KM	Knight of Malta
KORR	King's Own Royal Regiment
KOSB	King's Own Scottish Borderers
KOYLI	King's Own Yorkshire Light Infantry
KP	Knight, Order of St Patrick
KPM	King's Police Medal
KRRC	King's Royal Rifle Corps
KS	King's Scholar
KSC	Knight of St Columba
KSG	Knight, Order of St Gregory the Great
KSJ	Knight, Order of St John of Jerusalem (Knights Hospitaller)
KSLI	King's Shropshire Light Infantry
KSS	Knight, Order of St Silvester
KStJ	Knight, Most Venerable Order of the Hospital of St John of Jerusalem
KStJ(A)	Associate Knight of Justice, Most Venerable Order of the Hospital of St John of Jerusalem
KT	Knight, Order of the Thistle
Kt	Knight
Ky	Kentucky (US

L

(L)	Liberal
LA	Los Angeles; Liberal Association; Literate in Arts; Liverpool Academy
La	Louisiana (US)
LAA	Light Anti-Aircraft
(Lab)	Labour
LAC	London Athletic Club
LACSAB	Local Authorities Conditions of Service Advisory Board
LAMDA	London Academy of Music and Dramatic Art
LAMSAC	Local Authorities' Management Services and Computer Committee
LAMTPI	Legal Associate Member, Town Planning Institute
L-Corp.	Lance-Corporal

Lancs.	Lancashire
LARSP	Language Assessment, Remediation and Screening Procedure
Lautro	Life Assurance and Unit Trust Regulatory Organisation
LBC	London Broadcasting Company
LC	Cross of Leo
LCAD	London Certificate in Art and Design (University of London)
LCC	London County Council (later GLC)
LCh	Licentiate in Surgery
LCJ	Lord Chief Justice
LCL	Licentiate in Surgery
LCP	Licentiate, College of Preceptors
LCSP	London and Counties Society of Physiologists
LCST	Licentiate, College of Speech Therapists
LD	Liberal and Democratic; Licentiate in Divinty
LDDC	London Docklands Development Corporation
LDiv	Licentiate in Divinity
LDS	Licentiate in Dental Surgery
LDV	Local Defense Volunteers
LEA	Local Education Authority
LEPRA	British Leprosy Relief Association
LG	Lady Companion, Order of the Garter
LGSM	Licentiate, Guildhall School of Music and Drama
LGTB	Local Government Training Board
LH	Light Horse
LHD	Literarum Humaniorum Doctor (Doctor of Literature)
LHSM	Licentiate, Institute of Health Services Management
LI	Light Infantry; Long Island
LIBA	Lloyd's Insurance Brokers' Association
Lib Dem	Liberal Democrat
LIBER	Ligue des Bibliotheques Europeennes de Recherche
Lic Med	Licentiate in Medicine
Lieut	Lieutenant
LIFFE	London International Financial Futures Exchange
Lincs	Lincolnshire
LIOB	Licentiate, Institute of Building
Lit.	Literature; Literary
LitD	Doctor of Literature; Doctor of Letters
Lit.Hum.	Literae Humaniores (Classics)
LittD	Doctor of Literature; Doctor of Letters
LJ	Lord Justice
LLA	Lady Literate in Arts
LLB	Bachelor of Laws
LLCM	Licentiate, London College of Music
LLD	Doctor of Laws
LLL	Licentiate in Laws
LLM	Master of Laws
LM	Licentiate in Midwifery
LMBC	Lady Margaret Boat Club
LMC	Local Medical Committee
LMCC	Licentiate, Medical Council of Canada
LMed	Licentiate in Medicine
LMH	Lady Margaret Hall, Oxford
LMR	London Midland Region (BR)
LMS	London, Midland and Scottish Railway; London Missionary Society
LMSSA	Licentiate in Medicine and Surgery, Society of Apothecaries
LMRTPI	Legal Member, Royal Town Planning Institute
(LNat)	Liberal National
LNER	London and North Eastern Railway
LOB	Location of Offices Bureau
L of C	Library of Congress; Lines of Communication
LP	Limited Partnership
LPH	Licentiate in Philosophy
LPO	London Philharmonic Orchestra
LPTB	London Passenger Transport Board (later LTE; now see LRT)
LRAD	Licentiate, Royal Academy of Dancing
LRAM	Licentiate, Royal Academy of Music
LRCP	Licentiate, Royal College of Physicians, London
LRCPE	Licentiate, Royal College of Physicians, Edinburgh
LRCPI	Licentiate, Royal College of Physicians of Ireland
LRCPSGlas	Licentiate, Royal College of Physicians and Surgeons of Glasgow
LRCS	Licentiate, Royal College of Surgeons of England
LRCSE	Licentiate, Royal College of Surgeons, Edinburgh
LRCSI	Licentiate, Royal College of Surgeons in Ireland
LRFPS(G)	Licentiate, Royal Faculty of Physicians and Surgeons, Glasgow
LRIBA	Licentiate, Royal Institute of British Architects
LRPS	Licentiate, Royal Photographic Society
LRT	London Regional Transport
LSA	Licentiate, Society of Apothecaries; Licence in Agricultural Sciences
LSE	London School of Economics and Political Science
LSHTM	London School of Hygiene and Tropical Medicine

LSO	London Symphony Orchestra
Lt	Lieutenant; Light
LT	London Transport (now see LRT); Licentiate in Teaching
LTA	Lawn Tennis Association
LTB	London Transport Board (later LTE; now see LRT)
LTCL	Licentiate of Trinity College of Music, London
Lt-Col	Lieutenant-Colonel
LTE	London Transport Executive (now see LRT)
Lt-Gen.	Lieutenant-General
LTh	Licentiate in Theology
(LU)	Liberal Unionist
LUOTC	London University Officers' Training Corps
LVO	Lieutenant, Royal Victorian Order (formerly MVO (Fourth Class))
LWT	London Weekend Television
LXX	Septuagint

M

M	Marquess; Member; Monsieur
m	married
MA	Master of Arts; Military Assistant
MAA	Manufacturers' Agents Association of Great Britain
MAAF	Mediterranean Allied Air Forces
MAAT	Member, Association of Accounting Technicians
MACE	Member, Australian College of Education; Member, Association of Conference Executives
MACI	Member, American Concrete Institute
MACM	Member, Association of Computing Machines
MACS	Member, American Chemical Society
MADO	Member, Association of Dispensing Opticians
MAEE	Marine Aircraft Experimental Establishment
MAF	Ministry of Agriculture and Fisheries
MAFF	Ministry of Agriculture, Fisheries and Food
MAI	Magister in Arte Ingeniaria (Master of Engineering)
MAIAA	Member, American Institute of Aeronautics and Astronautics
MAICE	Member, American Institute of Consulting Engineers
MAIChE	Member, American Institute of Chemical Engineers
Maj.-Gen.	Major-General
Man	Manitoba (Canada)
MAO	Master of Obstetric Art
MAOT	Member, Association of Occupational Therapists
MAOU	Member, American Ornithologists' Union
MAP	Ministry of Aircraft Production
MAPsS	Member, Australian Psychological Society
MARAC	Member, Australasian Register of Agricultural Consultants
MArch	Master of Architecture
Marq.	Marquess
MASAE	Member, American Society of Agricultural Engineers
MASC	Member, Australian Society of Calligraphers
MASCE	Member, American Society of Civil Engineers
MASME	Member, American Society of Mechanical Engineers
Mass	Massachusetts (US)
MATh	Master of Arts in Theology
Math.	Mathematics; Mathematical
MATSA	Managerial Administrative Technical Staff Association
MAusIMM	Member, Australasian Institute of Mining and Metallurgy
MB	Medal of Bravery (Canada); Bachelor of Medicine
MBA	Master of Business Administration
MBASW	Member, British Association of Social Workers
MBC	Metropolitan/Municipal Borough Council
MBCS	Member British Computer Society
MBE	Member, Order of the British Empire
MBFR	Mutual and Balanced Force Reductions (negotiations)
MBHI	Member, British Horological Institute
MBIFD	Member, British Institute of Funeral Directors
MBIM	Member, British Institute of Management (now see FBIM)
MBKS	Member, British Kinematograph Society (now see MBKSTS)
MBKSTS	Member, British Kinematograph, Sound and Television Society
MBOU	Member, British Ornithologists' Union
MBPICS	Member, British Production and Inventory Control Society
MBPS	Member, British Computer Society
MBritIRE	Member, British Institution of Radio Engineers
MBS	Member, Building Societies Institute
MBSc	Master of Business Science
MC	Military Cross; Missionaries of Charity
MCAM	Member, CAM Foundation
MCB	Master in Clinical Biochemistry
MCBSI	Member, Chartered Building Societies Institute

MCC	Marylebone Cricket Club; Metropolitan County Council
MCCDRCS	Member in Clinical Community Dentistry, Royal College of Surgeons
MCD	Master of Civic Design
MCE	Master of Civil Engineering
MCFP	Member, College of Family Physicians (Canada)
MCh	Master of Surgery
MChE	Master of Chemical Engineering
MChemA	Master in Chemical Analysis
MChOrth	Master of Orthopaedic Surgery
MCIBS	Member, Chartered Institution of Building Services
MCIBSE	Member, Chartered Institution of Building Services Engineers
MCIM	Member, Chartered Institute of Marketing
MCIOB	Member, Chartered Institute of Building
MCIS	Member, Institute of Chartered Secretaries and Administrators
MCIT	Member, Chartered Institute of Transport
MCL	Master in Civil Law
MCMES	Member, Civil and Mechanical Engineers' Society
MCom	Master of Commerce
MConsE	Member, Association of Consulting Engineers
MCOphth	Member, College of Opthalmologists
MCP	Member of Colonial Parliment; Master of City Planning (US)
MCPA	Member, College of Pathologists of Australia
MCPath	Member, College of Pathologists (now see MRCPath)
MCPP	Member, College of Pharmacy Practice
MCPS	Member, College of Physicians and Surgeons
MCS	Malayan Civil Service; Madras Civil Service
MCSEE	Member, Canadian Society of Electrical Engineers
MCSP	Member, Chartered Society of Physiotherapy
MCST	Member, College of Speech Therapists
MCT	Member, Association of Corporate Treasurers
MD	Doctor of Medicine; Military District
Md	Maryland (US)
MDC	Metropolitan District Council
MDes	Master of Design
MDS	Master of Dental Surgery
MDSc	Master of Dental Science
Me	Maine (US)
ME	Minning Engineer; Middle East; Master of Engineering
MEAF	Middle East Air Force
MEC	Member of Executive Council; Middle East Command
MEc	Master of Economics
MECAS	Middle East Centre for Arab Studies
Mech.	Mechanics; Mechanical
MECI	Member, Institute of Employment Consultants
Med.	Medical
MEd	Master of Education
MEF	Middle East Force
MEIC	Member, Engineering Institute of Canada
MELF	Middle East Land Forces
Mencap	Royal Society for Mentally Handicapped Children and Adults
MEng	Master of Engineering
MEO	Marine Engineering Officer
MEP	Member of the European Parliment
MetR	Metropolitan Railway
MetSoc	Metals Society (formed by amalgamation of Institute of Metals and Iron and Steel Institute; now merged with Institution of Metallurgists to form Institute of Metals
MEXE	Military Engineering Experimental Establishment
MF	Master of Forestry
MFA	Master of Fine Arts
MFC	Mastership of Food Control
MFCM	Member Faculty of Community Medicine
MFGB	Miners' Federation of Great Britain (now see NUM)
MFH	Master of Foxhounds
MFHom	Member, Faculty of Homeopathy
MFOM	Member, Faculty of Occupational Medicine
MGA	Major-General in charge of Administration
MGC	Machine Gun Corps
MGDS RCS	Member in General Dental Surgery, Royal College of Surgeons
MGGS	Major-General, General Staff
MGI	Member, Institute of Certificated Grocers
MGO	Master General of the Ordnance; Master of Gynaecology and Obstetrics
Mgr	Monsigor
MHA	Member of House of Assembly
MHCIMA	Member, Hotel Catering and Institutional Management Association
MHK	Member of the House of Keys
MHR	Member of the House of Representatives
MHRA	Modern Humanities Research Association
MHRF	Mental Health Research Fund

MI	Military Intelligence
MIAeE	Member, Institute of Aeronautical Engineers
MIAgrE	Member, Institution of Agricultural Engineers
MIAM	Member, Institute of Administrative Management
MIAS	Member, Institute of Aeronautical Science (US) (now see MAIAA)
MIBF	Member, Institute of British Foundrymen
MIBritE	Member, Institution of British Engineers
MIB(Scot)	Member, Institute of Bankers in Scotland
MICE	Member, Institution of Civil Engineers
MICEI	Member, Institution of Civil Engineers of Ireland
MICFor	Member, Institute of Chartered Foresters
Mich	Michigan (US)
MIChemE	Member, Institution of Chemical Engineers
MICorrST	Member, Institution of Corrosion Science and Technology
MICS	Member, Institute of Chartered Shipbrokers
MIDPM	Member, Institute of Data Processing Management
MIE(Aust)	Member, Institute of Engineers
MIED	Member, Institute of Engineering Designers
MIEE	Member, Institute of Electrical Engineers
MIEEE	Member, Institute of Electrical and Electronic Engineers (NY)
MIEI	Member, Institution of Engineering Inspection
MIE(Ind)	Member, Institution of Engineers, India
MIERE	Member, Institution of Electronic and Radio Engineers
MIES	Member, Institution of Engineers and Shipbuilders, Scotland
MIEx	Member, Institute of Export
MIExpE	Member, Institute Explosive Engineers
MIFA	Member, Institute of Field Archaeologists
MIFF	Member, Institute of Freight Forwarders
MIFireE	Member, Institute of Fire Engineers
MIFor	Member, Institute of Foresters
MIGasE	Member, Institution of Gas Engineers
MIGeol	Member, Institute of Geologists
MIH	Member, Institute of Housing
MIHM	Member, Institute of Housing Managers (now see MIH)
MIHort	Member, Institute of Horticulture
MIHT	Member, Institution of Highways and Transport
MIHVE	Member, Institution of Heating and Ventilation Engineers
MIIA	Member, Institute of Industrial Administration (now see FBIM)
MIIM	Member, Institute of Industrial Managers
MIInfSc	Member, Institute of Information Science
MIL	Member, Institute of Linguists
Mil.	Military
MILGA	Member, Institute of Local Government Administrators
MILocoE	Member, Institution of Locomotive Engineers
MIM	Member, Institute of Metals (formerly Institution of Metallurgists)
MIMarE	Member, Institute of Marine Engineers
MIMC	Member, Institute of Management Consultants
MIMechE	Member, Institution of Mechanical Engineers
MIMI	Member, Institute of the Motor Industry
MIMinE	Member, Institution of Mining Engineers
MIMM	Member, Institute of Mining and Metallurgy
MIMunE	Member, Institution of Muncipical Engineers (now amalgamated with Institution of Civil Engineers)
Min.	Ministry
MIN	Member, Institute of Navigation (now see MRIN)
Minn	Minnesota (US)
MInstAM	Member, Institute of Administrative Management
MInstBE	Member, Institution of British Engineers
MInstCE	Member, Institution of Civil Engineers (now see FICE)
MInstD	Member, Institute of Directors
MInstE	Member, Institute of Energy
MInstF	Member, Institute of Fuel (now see MInstE)
MInstHE	Member, Institution of Highway Engineers (now see MIHT)
MInstM	Member, Institute of Marketing (now see MCIM)
MInstMC	Member, Institute of Measurement and Control
MInstME	Member, Institution of Mining Engineers
MInstMet	Member, Institute of Metals (later part of Metals Society, now see MIM)
MInstP	Member, Institute of Physics
MInstPet	Member, Institute of Petroleum
MInstPI	Member, Institute of Patentees and Inventors
MInstPkg	Member, Institute of Packaging
MInstPS	Member, Institute of Purchasing and Supply
MInstR	Member, Institute of Refrigeration
MInstRA	Member, Institute of Registered Architects
MInstT	Member, Institute of Transport
MInstTM	Member, Institute of Travel Managers in Industry and Commerce
MInstW	Member, Institute of Welding (now see MWeldI)
MInstWM	Member, Institute of Wastes Management
MINucE	Member, Institution of Nuclear Engineers
MIOB	Member, Institute of Building (now see MCIOB)
MIOM	Member, Institute of Office Management (now see MIAM)
MIOSH	Member, Institution of Occupational Safety and Health
MIPA	Member, Institute of Practitioners in Advertising
MIPlantE	Member, Institution of Plant Engineers (now see MIIM)
MIPM	Member, Institute of Personnel Management
MIPR	Member, Institute of Public Relations
MIProdE	Member, Institute of Production Engineers
MIQ	Member, Institute of Quarrying
MIRE	Member, Institution of Radio Engineers (now see MIERE)
MIRT	Member, Institute of Reprographic Technicians
MIRTE	Member, Institute of Road Transport Engineers
MIS	Member, Institute of Statisticians
MISI	Member, Iron and Steel Institute (later part of Metals Society)
MIS(India)	Member, Institution of Surveyors of India
Miss	Mississippi (US)
MIStructE	Member, Institution of Structural Engineers
MIT	Massachusetts Institute of Technology
MITA	Member, Industrial Transport Association
MITD	Member, Institute of Training and Development
MITE	Member, Institution of Electrical and Electronics Technician Engineers
MITT	Member, Institute of Travel and Tourism
MIWES	Member, Institution of Water Engineers and Scientists
MIWM	Member, Institution of Works Managers (now see MIIM)
MIWPC	Member, Institute of Water Pollution Control (now see MIWEM)
MIWSP	Member, Institute of Work Study Practitioners (now see MMS)
MJI	Member, Institute of Journalists
MJIE	Member, Junior Institution of Engineers (now see MIGTechE)
MJS	Member, Japan Society
MJur	Magister Juris
ML	Licentiate in Medicine; Master of Laws
MLA	Member of Legislative Assembly; Modern Language Association; Master in Landscape Architecture
MLC	Member of Legislative Council
MLCOM	Member, London College of Osteopathic Medicine
MLitt	Master of Letters
Mlle	Mademoiselle (Miss)
MLM	Member, Order of the Legion of Merit (Rhodesia)
MLO	Military Liaison Officer
MLR	Modern Language Review
MM	Military Medal
MMA	Metropolitan Museum of Art
MMB	Milk Marketing Board
MME	Master of Mining Engineering
Mme	Madame
MMechE	Master of Mechanical Engineering
MMet	Master of Metallurgy
MMGI	Member, Mining, Geological and Metallurgical Institute of India
MMin	Master of Ministry
MMM	Member, Order of Military Merit (Canada)
MMS	Member, Institute of Management Services
MMSA	Master of Midwifery, Society of Apothecaries
MN	Merchant Navy
MNAS	Member, National Academy of Sciences (US)
MNECInst	Member, North East Coast Institution of Engineers and Shipbuilders
MNI	Member, Nautical Institute
MNSE	Member, Nigerian Society of Engineers
MO	Medical Officer; Military Operations
Mo	Missouri (US)
MoD	Ministry of Defence
Mods	Moderations (Oxford)
MOF	Ministry of Food
MOH	Medical Officer(s) of Health
MOI	Ministry of Information
MOMI	Museum of the Moving Image
Mon	Monmouthshire
Mont	Montana (US); Montgomeryshire
MOP	Ministry of Power
MoS	Ministry of Supply
Most Rev.	Most Reverend
MoT	Ministry of Transport
MP	Member of Parliament
MPA	Master of Public Administration; Member, Parliamentary Assembly, Northern Ireland
MPBW	Ministry of Public Building and Works
MPH	Master of Public Health
MPIA	Master of Public and International Affairs
MPO	Management and Personnel Office
MPP	Member, Provincial Parliament

MPRISA	Member, Public Relations Institute of South Africa
MPS	Member, Pharmaceutical Society (now see MRPharmS)
MR	Master of the Rolls; Municipal Reform
MRAC	Member, Royal Agricultural College
MRACP	Member, Royal Australasian College of Physicians
MRACS	Member, Royal Australasian College of Surgeons
MRAeS	Member, Royal Aeronautical Society
MRAIC	Member, Royal Architectural Institute of Canada
MRAS	Member, Royal Asiatic Society
MRC	Medical Research Council
MRCA	Multi-Role Combat Aircraft
MRCGP	Member, Royal College of General Practitioners
MRC-LMB	Medical Research Council Laboratory of Molecular Biology
MRCOG	Member, Royal College of Obstetricians and Gynaecologists
MRCP	Member, Royal College of Physicians, London
MRCPA	Member, Royal College of Pathologists of Australia
MRCPE	Member, Royal College of Physicians, Edinburgh
MRCPGlas	Member, Royal College of Physicians and Surgeons of Glasgow
MRCPI	Member, Royal College of Physicians of Ireland
MRCPsych	Member, Royal College of Psychiatrists
MRCS	Member, Royal College of Surgeons of England
MRCSE	Member, Royal College of Surgeons of Edinburgh
MRCSI	Member, Royal College of Surgeons in Ireland
MRCVS	Member, Royal College of Veterinary Surgeons
MRE	Master of Religious Education
MRI	Member, Royal Institution
MRIA	Member, Royal Irish Academy
MRIAI	Member, Royal Institute of the Architects of Ireland
MRIC	Member, Royal Institute of Chemistry (now see MRSC)
MRIN	Member, Royal Institute of Navigation
MRINA	Member, Royal Institution of Naval Architects
MRPharmS	Member, Royal Pharmaceutical Society
MRSanI	Member, Royal Sanitary Institute (now see MRSC)
MRSC	Member, Royal Society of Chemistry
MRSH	Member, Royal Society for the Promotion of Health
MRSL	Member, Order of the Republic of Sierra Leone
MRSM or	
MRSocMed	Member, Royal Society of Medicine
MRST	Member, Royal Society of Teachers
MRTPI	Member, Royal Town Planning Institute
MRUSI	Member, Royal United Service Institution
MRVA	Member, Rating and Valuation Association
MS	Master of Surgery; Master of Science (US)
MS, MSS	Manuscript, Manuscripts
MSA	Master of Science, Agriculture (US); Mineralogical Society of America
MSAE	Member, Society of Automotive Engineers (US)
MSAICE	Member, South African Institution of Civil Engineers
MS&R	Merchant Shipbuilding and Repairs
MSAutE	Member, Society of Automobile Engineers
MSC	Manpower Services Commission; Missionaries of the Sacred heart; Madras Staff Corps
MSc	Master of Science
MScD	Master of Dental Science
MSD	Meritorious Service Decoration (Fiji)
MSE	Master of Science in Engineering (US)
MSF	(Union for) Manufacturing, Science, Finance
MSH	Master of Stag Hounds
MSIAD	Member, Society of Industrial Artists and Designers
MSINZ	Member, Surveyors' Institute of New Zealand
MSIT	Member, Society of Instrument Technology (now see MInstMC)
MSM	Meritorious Service Medal; Madras Sappers and Miners
MSN	Master of Science in Nursing
MSocIS	Member, Societe des Ingenieurs et Scientifiques de France
MSocSc	Master of Social Sciences
MSR	Member, Society of Radiographers
MSTD	Member, Society of Typographic Designers
Mt	Mount, Mountain
MT	Mechanical Transport
MTA	Music Trades Association
MTAI	Member, Institute of Travel Agents
MTB	Motor Torpedo Boat
MTCA	Ministry of Transport and Civil Aviation
MTD	Midwife Teachers' Diploma
MTEFL	Master in the Teaching of English as a Foreign or Second Language
MTh	Master of Theology
MTIRA	Machine Tool Industry Research Association (now see AMRTI)
MTPI	Member, Town Planning Institute (now see MRTPI)
MTS	Master of Theological Studies

MUniv	Master of the University
MusB	Bachelor of Music
MusD	Doctor of Music
MusM	Master of Music
MV	Merchant Vessel, Motor Vessel (naval)
MVEE	Military Vehicles and Engineering Establishment
MVO	Member, Royal Victorian Order
MVSc	Master of Veterinary Science
MW	Master of Wine
MWA	Mystery Writers of America
MWeldI	Member, Welding Institute
MWSOM	Member, Institute of Practitioners in Work Study Organisation and Methods (now see MMS)

N

(N)	Nationalist; Navigating Duties
N	North
n	nephew
NA	National Academician (America)
NAACP	National Association for the Advancement of Colored People
NAAFI	Navy, Army and Air Force Institutes
NAAS	National Agricultural Advisory Service
NAB	National Advisory Body for Public Sector Higher Education
NABC	National Association of Boy' Clubs
NAC	National Agriculture Centre
NACCB	National Accreditation Council for Certification Bodies
NACRO	National Association for the Care and Resettlement of Offenders
NADFAS	National Association of Decorative and Fine Arts Societies
NAE	National Academy of Engineering
NAEW	Nato Airborn Early Warning
NAHA	National Association of Health Authorities (now see NAHAT)
NAHAT	National Association of Health Authorities and Trusts
NALGO or	
Nalgo	National and Local Government Officers' Association
NAMAS	National Measurement and Accreditation service
NAMCW	National Association for Maternal and Child Welfare
NAMH	MIND (National Association for Mental Health)
NAMMA	NATO MRCA Management Agency
NAPT	National Association for the Prevention of Tuberculosis
NASA	National Aeronautics and Space Administration (US)
NASDIM	National Association of Security Dealers and Investment Managers (now see FIMBRA)
NAS/UWT	National Association of Schoolmasters/Union of Women Teachers
NATCS	National Air Traffic Services (now see NATS)
NATFHE	National Association of Teachers in Further and Higher Education (combining ATCDE and ATTI)
NATLAS	National Testing Laboratory Accreditation Scheme
NATO	North Atlantic Treaty Organisation
NATS	National Air Traffic Services
Nat. Sci.	Natural Sciences
NATSOPA	National Society of Operative Printers, Graphical and Media Personnel (formerly of Operative Printers and Assistants
NAYC	Youth Clubs UK (formerly National Association of Youth Clubs)
NB	New Brunswick
NBA	North British Academy
NBC	National Book Council (later NBL); National Broadcasting Company (US)
NBL	National Book League
NBPI	National Board for Prices and Incomes
NC	National Certificate; North Carolina (US)
NCA	National Certificate of Agriculture
NCARB	National Council of Architectural Registration Boards
NCB	National Coal Boards
NCC	National Computing Centre; Nature Conservancy Council
NCCI	National Committee for Commonwealth Immigrants
NCCL	National Council for Civil Liberties
NCDAD	National Council for Diplomas in Art and Design
NCET	National Council for Educational Technology
NCLC	National Council for Labour Colleges
NCSE	National Council for Special Education
NCTA	National Community Television Association (US)
NCU	National Cyclists' Union
NCVCCO	National Council of Voluntary Child Care Organisations
NCVO	National Council for Voluntary Organisations
NCVQ	National Council for Vocational Qualifications

NDA	National Diploma in Agriculture
NDak	North Dakota (US)
ndc	National Defence College
NDD	National Diploma in Dairying; National Diploma in Design
NDH	National Diploma in Horticulture
NDIC	National Defence Industries Council
NDTA	National Defence Transportation Association (US)
NE	North-east
NEAC	New English Art Club
NEAF	Near East Air Force
NEARELF	Near East Land Forces
NEB	National Enterprise Board
Neb	Nebraska (US)
NEBSS	National Examinations Board for Supervisory Studies
NEC	National Executive Committee
NECCTA	National Educational Closed Circuit Television Association
NECInst	North East Coast Institution of Engineers and Shipbuilders
NEDC	National Economic Development Council; North East Development Council
NEDO	National Economic Development Office
NEH	National Endowment for the Humanities
NEL	National Engineering Laboratory
NERC	National Environment Research Council
Nev	Nevada (US)
New M	New Mexico (US)
NFC	National Freight Consortium (formerly Corporation, then Company)
NFER	National Foundation for Educational Research
NFMS	National Federation of Music Societies
NFS	National Fire Service
NFT	National Film Theatre
NFU	National Farmers' Union
NFWI	National Federation of Womens' Institutes
NGO	Non-Governmental Organisation(s)
NGTE	National Gas Turbine Establishment
NH	New Hampshire (US)
NHBC	National House-Building Council
NHS	National Health Service
NI	Northern Ireland; Native Infantry
NIAB	National Institute of Agricultural Botany
NIACRO	Northern Ireland Association for the Care and Resettlement of Offenders
NIAE	National Institute of Agricultural Engineering
NIAID	National Institute of Allergy and Infectious Diseases
NICEC	National Institute for Careers and Education Counselling
NICG	Nationalised Industries Chairman's Group
NICS	Northern Ireland Civil Service
NID	Naval Intelligence Division; National Institute for the Deaf; Northern Ireland District; National Institute of Design (India)
NIESR	National Institute of Economic and Social Research
NIH	National Institutes of Health (US)
NIHCA	Northern Ireland Hotels and Caterers Association
NII	Nuclear Installations Inspectorate
NILP	Northern Ireland Labour Party
NISTRO	Northern Ireland Science and Technology Regional Organisation
NJ	New Jersey (US)
NL	National Liberal; No Liability
NLCS	North London Collegiate School
NLF	National Liberal Federation
NLYL	National League of Young Liberals
NMR	Nuclear Magnetic Resonance
NNMA	Nigerian National Merit Award
NNOM	Nigerian National Order of Merit
Northants	Northamptonshire
NOTB	National Ophthalmic Treatment Board
Notts	Nottinghamshire
NP	Notary Public
NPA	Newspaper Publishers' Association
NPFA	National Playing Fields Association
NPk	Nishan-e-Pakistan
NPL	National Physical Laboratory
NRA	National Rifle Association; National Recovery Administration (US)
NRAO	National Radio Astronomy Observatory
NRCC	National Research Council of Canada
NRD	National Registered Designer
NRDC	National Research Development Corporation
NRPB	National Radiological Protection Board
NRR	Northern Rhodesia Regiment
NS	Nova Scotia; New Style in the Calendar (in Great Britain since 1752); National Society; National Service
ns	Graduate of Royal Naval Staf College, Greenwich
NSA	National Skating Association

NSAIV	Distinguished Order of Shaheed Ali (Maldives)
NSF	National Science Foundation
NSM	Non-Stipendiary Minister
NSMHC	National Society for Mentally Handicapped Children
NSPCC	National Society for Prevention of Cruelty to Children
NSRA	National Small-bore Rifle Association
N/SSF	Novice, Society of St. Francis
NSTC	Nova Scotia Technical College
NSW	New South Wales
NT	New Testament; Northern Territory (Australia); National Theatre; National Trust
NT&SA	National Trust & Savings Association
NTDA	National Trade Development Association
NUAAW	National Union of Agricultural and Allied Workers
NUBE	National Union of Bank Employees (now see Bifu)
NUFLAT	National Union of Footwear Leather and Allied Trades
NUGMW	National Union of General and Municipal Workers
NUHKW	National Union of Hosiery and Knitwear Workers
NUI	National University of Ireland
NUJ	National Union of Journalists
NUJMB	Northern Universities Joint Matriculation Board
NUM	National Union of Mineworkers
NUMAST	National Union of Marine, Aviation and Shipping Transport Officers
NUPE	National Transport of Public Employees
NUR	National Union of Railwaymen
NUT	National Union of Teachers
NUTG	National Union of Townswomen's Guilds
NUTN	National Union of Trained Teachers
NUU	New Univrsity of Ulster
NW	North-West
NWFP	North-West Frontier Province
NWP	North-Western Province
NWT	North-Western Territories
NY	New York
NYC	New York City
NYO	National Youth Orchestra
NZ	New Zealand
NZEF	New Zealand Expeditionary Force
NZIA	New Zealand Institute of Architects

O

O	Ohio (US)
o	only
OA	Officier d'Academic
O & E	Operations and Engineers (US)
O & M	organisation and method
O & O	Oriental and Occidental Steamship Co.
OAS	Organisation of American States; On Active Service
OAU	Organisation for African Unity
OB	Order of Barbados
ob	obiit (died)
OBE	Officer, Order of the British Empire
OBI	Order of British India
OC	Officer, Order of Canada (equivalent to former award SM)
oc	only child
OC or o/c	Officer Commanding
OCA	Old Comrades Association
OCDS or ocds Can	Overseas College of Defence Studies
OCF	Officiating Chaplain to the Forces
OCSS	Oxford and Cambridge Shakespeare Society
OCTU	Officer Cadet Training Unit
OCU	Operational Conversion Unit
OD	Officer, Order of Distinction (Jamaica)
ODA	Overseas Development Administration
ODI	Overseas Development Institute
ODM	Ministry of Overseas Development
ODSM	Order of Diplomatic Service Merit (Lesotho)
OE	Order of Excellence
OEA	Overseas Education Association
OECD	Organization for Economic Co-operation and Development
OED	Oxford English Dictionary
OEEC	Organization for European Economic Co-operation
OF	Order of the Founder, Salvation Army
OFEMA	Office Francaise d'Exportation de Materiel Aeronautique
OFM	Order of Friars Minor (Franciscans)

OFMCap	Order of Friars Minor Capuchin (Franciscans)
OFMConv	Order of Friars Minor Conventual (Franciscans)
OFR	Order of the Federal Republic of Nigeria
OFS	Orange Free State
OFT	Office of Fair Trading
Oftel	Office of Telecommunications
OGS	Oratory of the Good Shepherd
OHMS	On His (or Her) Majesty's Service
O i/c	Officer in charge
OJ	Order of Jamaica
OL	Officer, Order of Leopold; Order of the Leopard (Lesotho)
OLM	Officer, Legion of Merit (Rhodesia)
OM	Order of Merit
OMCS	Office of the Minister for the Civil Service
OMI	Oblate of Mary Immaculate
OMM	Officer, Order of Military Merit (Canada)
ON	Order of the Nation (Jamaica)
OND	Ordinary National Diploma
Ont	Ontario
ONZ	Order of New Zealand
OON	Officer, Order of the Niger
OP	Ordinis Praedicatorum (of the Order of Preachers (Dominican)); Observation Post
OPCON	Operational Control
OPCS	Office of Population Censuses and Surveys
OQ	Officer, National Order of Quebec
OR	Order of Rorima (Guyana); Operational Research
ORC	Orange River Colony
Ore	Oregon (US)
ORGA-LIME	Organisme de Liaison des Industries Metalliques Europeennes
ORL	Otorhinolaryngology
ORS	Operational Research Society
ORSL	Order of the Republic of Sierra Leone
ORT	Organization for Rehabilitation by Training
ORTF	Office de la Radiodiffusion et Television Francaise
o s	only son
OSA	Order of St Augustine (Augustinian); Ontario Society of Artists
OSB	Order of St Benedict (Benedictine)
osc	Graduate of Overseas Staff College
OSFC	Franciscan (Capuchin) Order
O/Sig	Ordinary Signalman
OSNC	Oriental Steam Navigation Co.
o s p	obiit sine prole (died without issue)
OSRD	Office of Scientific Research and Development
OSS	Office of Strategic Services
OstJ	Officer, Most Venerable Order of the Hospital of St John of Jerusalem
OSUK	Ophthalmological Society of the United Kingdom
OT	Old Testament
OTC	Officers' Training Corps
OTL	Officer, Order of Toussaint L'Ouverture (Haiti)
OTU	Operational Training Unit
OTWSA	Ou-Testamentiese Werkgemeenskap in Suider-Afrika
OU	Oxford University; Open University
OUAC	Oxford University Athletic Club
OUAFC	Oxford University Association Football Club
OUBC	Oxford University Boat Club
OUCC	Oxford University Cricket Club
OUDS	Oxford University Dramatic Society
OUP	Oxford University Press; Official Unionist Party
OURC	Oxford University Rifle Club
OURFC	Oxford University Rugby Football Club
OURT	Order of the United Republic of Tanzania
Oxon	Oxfordshire; Oxoniensis (of Oxford)

P

PA	Pakistan Army; Personal Assistant
Pa	Pennsylvania (US)
PAA	President, Australian Academy of Science
pac	passed the final examination of the Advanced Class, The Military College of Science
PACE	Protestant and Catholic Encounter
PAg	Professional Agronomist
P&O	Peninsular and Oriental Steamship Co.
P&OSNCo.	Peninsular and Oriental Steam Navigation Co.
PAO	Prince Albert's Own
PASI	Professional Associate, Chartered Surveyors' Institution

PBS	Public Broadcasting Service
PC	Privy Counsellor; Police Constable; Perpetual Curate; Peace Commissioner (Ireland); Progressive Conservative (Canada)
pc	per centum (in the hundred)
PCC	Parochial Church Council
PCE	Postgraduate Certificate of Education
PCFC	Polytechnics and Colleges Funding Council
PCMO	Principal Colonial Medical Officer
PdD	Doctor of Pedagogy (US)
PDG	President Directeur General
PDR	People's Democratic Republic
PDRA	post doctoral research assistant
PDSA	People's Dispensary for Sick Animals
PDTC	Professional Dancer's Training Course Diploma
PE	Procurement Executive
PEI	Prince Edward Island
PEN	Poets, Playwrights, Editors, Essayists, Novelists (Club)
PEng	Registered Professional Engineer (Canada); Member, Society of Professional Engineers
Penn	Pennsylvania
PEP	Political and Economic Planning (now see PSI)
PER	Professional and Executive Recruitment
PEST	Pressure for Economic and Social Toryism
PETRAS	Polytechnic Educational Technology Resources Advisory Service
PF	Procurator-Fiscal
PFA	Professional Footballers' Association
pfc	Graduate of RAF Flying College
PFE	Program for Executives
PGA	Professional Golfers' Association
PGCE	Post Graduate Certificate of Education
PH	Presidential Order of Honour (Botswana)
PHAB	Physically Handicapped & Able-bodied
PhB	Bachelor of Philosophy
PhC	Pharmaceutical Chemist
PhD	Doctor of Philosophy
Phil.	Philology, Philological; Philosophy, Philosophical
PhL	Licentiate of Philosophy
PHLS	Public Health Laboratory Service
PhM	Master of Philosophy
PhmB	Bachelor of Pharmacy
Phys.	Physical
PIARC	Permanent International Association of Road Congress
PIB	Prices and Incomes Board (later NBPI)
PICAO	Provisional International Civil Aviation Organization
pinx.	pinxit (he painted it)
PIRA	Paper Industries Research Association
PITCOM	Parliamentary Information Technology Committee
PJG	Pingat Jasa Gemilang (Singapore)
PJK	Pingkat Jasa Kebaktian (Malaysia)
Pl.	Place; Plural
PLA	Port of London Authority
PLC or plc	public limited company
Plen.	Plenipotentiary
PLI	President, Landscape Institute
PLP	Parliamentary Labour Party
PMA	Personal Military Assistant
PMC	Personnel Management Centre
PMD	Program for Management Development
PMG	Postmaster-General
PMN	Panglima Mangku Negara (Malaysia)
PMO	Principal Medical Officer
PMRAFNS	Princess Mary's Royal Air Force Nursing Service
PMS	Presidential Order of Meritorious Service (Botswana); President, Miniature Society
PNBS	Panglima Negara Bintang Sarawak
PNEU	Parents' National Educational Union
PNG	Papua New Guinea
PNP	People's National Party
PO	Post Office
POB	Presidential Order of Botswana
POMEF	Political Office Middle East Force
Pop.	Population
POUNC	Post Office Users' National Council
POW	Prisoner of War; Prince of Wales's
PP	Parish Priest; Past President
PPA	Periodical Publishers Association
PPCLI	Princess Patricia's Canadian Light Infantry
PPE	Philosophy, Politics and Economics
PPInstHE	Past President, Institution of Highway Engineers
PPIStructE	Past President, Institution of Structural Engineers

PPITB	Printing and Publishing Industry Training Board
PPP	Private Patients Plan
PPRA	Past President, Royal Academy
PPRBA	Past President, Royal Society of British Artists
PPRBS	Past President, Royal Society of British Sculptors
PPRE	Past President, Royal Society of Painter-Etchers and Engravers
PPROI	Past President, Royal Institute of Oil Painter
PPRTPI	Past President, Royal Town Planning Institute
PPS	Parliamentary Private Secretary
PPSIAD	Past President, Society of Industrial Artists and Designers
PQ	Province of Quebec
PR	Public Relations
PRA	President, Royal Academy
PRBS	President, Royal Society of British Sculptors
PRCS	President, Royal College of Surgeons
PRE	President, Royal College of Painter-Etchers and Engravers
Preb.	Prebendary
Pres.	President
PRHA	President, Royal Hibernian Academy
PRI	President, Royal Institute of Painters in Water Colours; Plastics and Rubber Institute
PRIA	President, Royal Irish Academy
PRIAS	President, Royal Incorporation of Architects in Scotland
Prin.	Principal
PRISA	Public Relations Institute of South Africa
PRO	Public Relations Officer; Public Records Office
Proc.	Proctor; Proceedings
Prof.	Professor; Professional
PROI	President, Royal Institute of Oil Painters
PRONED	Promotion of Non-Executive Directors
PRORM	Pay and Records Office, Royal Marines
Pro tem.	Pro tempore (for the time being)
Prov.	Provost; Provincial
Prox.	Proximo (next)
Prox.acc.	Proxime accessit (next in order of merit to the winner)
PRS	President, Royal Society; Performing Right Society Ltd
PRSA	President, Royal Scottish Academy
PRSE	President, Royal Society of Edinburgh
PRSH	President, Royal Society for the Promotion of Health
PRSW	President, Royal Scottish Water Colour Society
PRUAA	President, Royal Ulster Academy of Arts
PRWA	President, Royal West of England Academy
PRWS	President, Royal Society of Painters in Water Colours
PS	Pastel Society; Paddle Steamer
ps	passed School of Instruction (of Officers)
PSA	Property Services Agency; Petty Sessions Area
psa	Graduate of RAF Staff College
PSD	Petty Sessional Division
PSGB	Pharmaceutical Society of Great Britain (now see RPSGB)
PSI	Policy Studies Institute
PSIAD	President, Society of Industrial Artists and Designers
PSM	Panglima Setia Mahkota (Malaysia)
psm	Certificate of Royal Military School of Music
PSMA	President, Society of Marine Artists
PSNC	Pacific Steam Navigation Co.
PSO	Principal Scientific Officer; Personal Staff Officer
PSSC	Personal Social Services Council
PTA	Passenger Transport Authority Parent Teacher Association
PTE	Passenger Transport Executive
Pte	Private
ptsc	passed Technical Staff College
Pty	Propietary
PUP	People's United Party
PVSM	Param Vishishc Seva Medal (India)
PWD	Public Works Department
PWE	Political Welfare Executive
PWO	Prince of Wales's Own
PWR	Pressurized Water Reactor

Q

Q	Queen
QAIMNS	Queen Alexandra's Imperial Military Nursing Service
QALAS	Qualified Associate, Chartered Land Agents' Society (now (after amalgamation) see ARICS)
QARANC	Queen Alexandra's Royal Army Nursing Corps
QARNNS	Queen Alexandra's Royal Naval Nursing Service
QBD	Queen's Bench Division

QC	Queen's Counsel
QCVSA	Queen's Commendation for Valuable Service in the Air
QEH	Queen Elizabeth Hall
QEO	Queen Elizabeth's Own
QFSM	Queen's Fire Service Medal for Distinguished Service
QGM	Queen's Gallantry Medal
QHC	Queen's Honorary Chaplain
QHDS	Queen's Honorary Dental Surgeon
QHNS	Queen's Honorary Nursing Sister
QHP	Queen's Honorary Physician
QHS	Queen's Honorary Surgeon
Qld	Queensland
Qly	Quarterly
QMAAC	Queen Mary's Army Auxiliary Corps
QMC	Queen Mary College, London (now see QMW)
QMG	Quartermaster-General

R

(R)	Reserve
RA	Royal Academician; Royal Artillery
RAA	Regional Arts Association
RAAF	Royal Australian Air Force
RAAMC	Royal Australian Army Medical Corps
RABI	Royal Agricultural Benevolent Institution
RAC	Royal Automobile Club; Royal Agricultural College; Royal Armoured Corps
RACGP	Royal Australian College of General Practitioners
RAChD	Royal Army Chaplains' Department
RACI	Royal Australian Chemical Institute
RACO	Royal Australian College of Ophthalmologists
RACOG	Royal Australian College of Obstetricians and Gynaecologists
RACP	Royal Australasian College of Physicians
RACS	Royal Australasian College of Surgeons; Royal Arsenal Co-operative Society
RADA	Royal Academy of Dramatic Art
RADAR	Royal Association for Disability and Rehabilitation
RADC	Royal Army Dental Corps
RADIUS	Religious Drama Society of Great Britain
RAE	Royal Australian Engineers; Royal Aerospace Establishment (formerly Royal Aircraft Establishment)
RAEC	Royal Army Educational Corps
RAeS	Royal Aeronautical Society
RAF	Royal Air Force
RAFA	Royal Air Force Association
RAFO	Reserve of Air Force Officers (now see RAFRO)
RAFRO	Royal Air Force Reserve of Officers
RAFVR	Royal Air Force Volunteer Reserve
RAI	Royal Anthropological Institute; Radio Audizioni Italiane
RAIA	Royal Australian Institute of Architects
RAIC	Royal Architectural Institute of Canada
RAM	(Member of) Royal Academy of Music
RAMC	Royal Army Medical Corps
RAN	Royal Australian Navy
R&D	Research and Development
RANR	Royal Australian Naval Research
RANVR	Royal Australian Naval Vounteer Reserve
RAOC	Royal Army Ordnance Corps
RAPC	Royal Army Pay Corps
RARDE	Royal Armament Research and Development Establishment
RARO	Regular Army Reserve of Officers
RAS	Royal Astronomical Society; Royal Asiatic Society
RASC	Royal Army Service Corps (now see RCT)
RASE	Royal Agricultural Society of England
RAuxAF	Royal Auxiliary Air Force
RAVC	Royal Army Veterinary Corps
RB	Rifle Brigade
RBA	Member, Royal Society of British Artists
RBC	Royal British Colonial Society of Artists
RBK&C	Royal Borough of Kensington and Chelsea
RBS	Royal Society of British Sculptures
RBSA	(Member of) Royal Birmingham Society of Artists
RBY	Royal Bucks Yeomanry
RC	Roman Catholic
RCA	Member, Royal Canadian Academy of Arts; Royal College of Art; (Member of) Royal Cambrian Academy
RCAC	Royal Canadian Armoured Corps
RCAF	Royal Canadian Air Force

RCamA	Member, Royal Cambrian Academy
RCAS	Royal Central Asian Society (now see RSAA)
RCDS	Royal College of Defence Studies
RCGP	Royal College of General Practitioners
RCHA	Royal Canadian Horse Artillery
RCHM	Royal Commission on Historical Monuments
RCM	(Member of) Royal College of Music
RCN	Royal Canadian Navy; Royal College of Nursing
RCNC	Royal Corps of Naval Constructors
RCNR	Royal Canadian Naval Reserve
RCNVR	Royal Canadian Naval Voluteer Reserve
RCO	Royal College of Organists
RCOG	Royal College of Obstetricians and Gynaecologists
RCP	Royal College of Physicians, London
RCPath	Royal College of Pathologists
RCPSG	Royal College of Physicians and Surgeons of Glasgow
RCPsych	Royal College of Psychiatrists
RCR	Royal College of Radiologists
RCS	Royal College of Surgeons of England; Royal Corps of Signals; Royal College of Silence
RCSI	Royal College of Surgeons in Ireland
RCT	Royal Corps of Transport
RCVS	Royal College of Veterinary Surgeons
RD	Rural Dean; Royal Naval and Royal Marine Forces Reserve Decoration
Rd	Road
RDA	Royal Defence Academy
RDC	Rural District Council
RDF	Rural Dublin Fusiliers
RDI	Royal Designer for Industry (Royal Society of Arts)
RDS	Royal Dublin Society
RE	Royal Engineers; Fellow, Royal Society of Painter-Etchers and Engravers; Religious Education
REACH	Retired Executives Action Clearing House
react	Research Education and Aid for Children with potentially Terminal illness
Rear-Adm.	Rear-Admiral
REconS	Royal Economic Society
Regt	Regiment
REME	Royal Electrical and Mechanical Engineers
REngDes	Registered Engineering Designer
REPC	Regional Economic Planning Council
RERO	Royal Engineers Reserve of Officers
RES	Royal Empire Society (now Royal Commonwealth Society)
Res.	Resigned; Reserve; Resident; Research
RETI	Association of Traditional Industrial Regions
Rev.	Reverend; Review
RFA	Royal Field Artillery
RFC	Royal Flying Corps (now RAF); Rugby Football Club
RFH	Royal Festival Hall
RFN	Registered Fever Nurse
RFPS(G)	Royal Faculty of Physicians and Surgeons, Glasgow
RFU	Rugby Football Union
RGA	Royal Garrison Artillery
RGI	Royal Glasgow Institute of the Fine Arts
RGJ	Royal Green Jackets
RGN	Registered General Nurse
RGS	Royal Geographical Society
RGSA	Royal Geographical Society of Australasia
RHA	Royal Hibernian Academy; Royal Horse Artillery; Regional Health Authority
RHAS	Royal Highland and Agricultural Society of Scotland
RHB	Regional Hospital Board
RHBNC	Royal Holloway and Bedford New College, London
RHC	Royal Holloway College, London (now see RHBNC)
RHF	Royal Highland Fusiliers
RHG	Royal Horse Guards
RHistS	Royal Historical Society
RHR	Royal Highland Regiment
RHS	Royal Horticultural Society; Royal Humane Society; Member, Royal Institute of Painters in Water Colours; Rhode Island
RIA	Royal Irish Academy
RIAI	Royal Institute of the Architects of Ireland
RIAM	Royal Irish Academy of Music
RIAS	Royal Incorporation of Architects in Scotland
RIASC	Royal Indian Army Service Corps
RIBA	(Member of) Royal Institute of British Architects
RIBI	Rotary International in Great Britain and Ireland
RIC	Royal Irish Constabulary; Royal Institute of Chemistry
RICS	Royal Institute of Chartered Surveyors

RIE	Royal Indian Engineering (College)
RIF	Royal Inniskilling Fusiliers
RIIA	Royal Institute of International Affairs
RIM	Royal Indian Marines
RIN	Royal Indian Navy
RINA	Royal Institution of Naval Architects
RINVR	Royal Indian Naval Volunteer Reserve
RIPA	Royal Institute of Public Administration
RIPH&H	Royal Instititue of Public Health and Hygiene
RIrF	Royal Irish Fusiliers
RLSS	Royal Life Saving Society
RM	Royal Marines; Resident Magistrate; Registered Midwife
RMA	Royal Marine Artillery; Royal Military Academy Sandhurst
RMB	Rural Mail Base
RMC	Royal Military College Sandhurst (now see RMA)
RMCM	(Member of) Royal Manchester College of Music
RMCS	Royal Military College of Science
RMedSoc	Royal Medical Society, Edinburgh
RMetS	Royal Meterological Society
RMFVR	Royal Marine Forces Volunteer Reserve
RMIT	Royal Melbourne Institute of Technology
RMLI	Royal Marine Light Infantry
RMN	Registered Mental Nurse
RMO	Resident Medical Officer(s)
RMP	Royal Military Police
RMPA	Royal Medico-Psychological Association
RMS	Royal Microscopical Society; Royal Mail Steamer; Royal Society of Miniature Painters
RN	Royal Navy; Royal Naval
RNAS	Royal Naval Air Force
RNAY	Royal Naval Aircraft Yard
RNC	Royal Naval College
RNCM	(Member of) Royal Northern College of Music
RNEC	Royal Naval Engineering College
RNIB	Royal National Institute for the Blind
RNID	Royal National Institute for the Deaf
RNLI	Royal National Life-boat Institution
RNLO	Royal Naval Liaison Officer
RNR	Royal Naval Reserve
RNS	Royal Numismatic Society
RNSA	Royal Naval Sailing Association
RNSC	Royal Naval Staff College
RNT	Registered Nurse Tutor
RNTNEH	Royal National Throat, Nose and Ear Hospital
RNVR	Royal Naval Volunteer Reserve
RNVSR	Royal Naval Volunteer Supplementary Reserve
RNXS	Royal Naval Auxiliary Service
RNZAC	Royal New Zealand Armoured Corps
RNZAF	Royal New Zealand Air Force
RNZIR	Royal New Zealand Infantry Regiment
RNZN	Royal New Zealand Navy
RNZNVR	Royal New Zealand Navy Volunteer Reserve
ROC	Royal Observer Corps
ROF	Royal Ordnance Factories
R of O	Reserve of Officers
ROI	Member, Royal Institute of Oil Painters
RoSPA	Royal Society for the Prevention of Accidents
(Rot.)	Rotunda Hospital, Dublin (after degree)
RP	Member, Royal Society of Portrait Painters
RPC	Royal Pioneer Corps
RPMS	Royal Postgraduate Medical School
RPO	Royal Philharmonic Orchestra
RPR	Rassemblement pour la Republique
RPS	Royal Photographic Society
RPSGB	Royal Pharmaceutical Society of Great Britain
RRC	Royal Red Cross
RRE	Royal Radar Establishment (now see RSRE)
RRF	Royal Regiment of Fusiliers
RRS	Royal Research Ship
RSA	Royal Scottish Academician; Royal Society of Arts; Republic of South Africa
RSAA	Royal Society for Asian Affairs
RSAD	Royal Surgical Aid Society
RSAF	Royal Small Arms Factory
RSAI	Royal Society of Antiquaries of Ireland
RSAMD	Royal Scottish Academy of Music and Drama
RSanI	Royal Sanitary Institute (now see RSH)
RSC	Royal Society of Canada; Royal Society of Chemistry; Royal Shakespeare Company
RSCM	Royal School of Church Music

RSCN	Registered Sick Childrens Nurse
RSE	Royal Society of Edinburgh
RSF	Royal Scots Fusiliers
RSFSR	Russian Socialist Federated Soviet Republic
RSGS	Royal Scottish Geographical Society
RSH	Royal Society for the Promotion of Health
RSL	Royal Society of Literature; Returned Services League of Australia
RSM	Royal Schools of Mines
RSM or	
RSocMed	Royal Society of Medicine
RSMA	Royal Society of Marine Artists
RSME	Royal School of Military Engineering
RSMHCA	Royal Society for Mentally Handicapped Children and Adults (see Mencap)
RSNC	Royal Society for Nature Conservation
RSO	Rural Sub-Office; Railway Sub-Office; Resident Surgical Officer
RSPB	Royal Society for Protection of Birds
RSPCA	Royal Society for Prevention of Cruelty to Animals
RSRE	Royal Signals and Radar Establishment
RSSAILA	Returned Sailors, Soldiers and Airmen's Imperial League of Australia (now see RSL)
RSSPCC	Royal Scottish Society for Prevention of Cruelty to Children
RSTM&H	Royal Society of Tropical Medicine and Hygiene
RSUA	Royal Society of Ulster Architects
RSV	Revised Standard Version
RSW	Member, Royal Scottish Society of Painters in Water Colours
RTE	Radio Telefis Eireann
Rt. Hon.	Right Honourable
RTO	Railway Transport Officer
RTPI	Royal Town Planning Institute
RTR	Royal Tank Regiment
Rt. Rev.	Right Reverend
RTS	Religious Tract Society; Royal Toxophilite Society; Royal Television Society
RTYC	Royal Thames Yacht Club
RU	Rugby Union
RUC	Royal Ulster Constabulary
RUI	Royal University of Ireland
RUKBA	Royal United Kingdom Beneficent Association
RUR	Royal Ulster Regiment
RURAL	Society for the Responsible Use of Resources in Agriculture and on the Land
RUSI	Royal United Services Institute for Defence Studies (formerly Royal United Service Institution)
RVC	Royal Veterinary College
RWA or	
RWEA	Member, Royal West of England Academy
RWAFF	Royal West African Frontier Force
RWF	Royal Welch Fusiliers
RWS	(Member of) Royal Society of Painters in Water Colours
RYA	Royal Yachting Association
RYS	Royal Yacht Squadron
RZSScot	Royal Zoological Society of Scotland

S

(S)	(in Navy) Paymaster; Scotland
S	Succeeded; South; Saint
s	son
SA	South Australia; South Africa; Societe Anonyme
SAAF	South African Air Force
SABC	South African Broadcasting Corporation
SAC	Scientific Advisory Committee
sac	qualified at small arms technical long course
SACEUR	Supreme Allied Commander Europe
SACLANT	Supreme Allied Commander Atlantic
SACSEA	Supreme Allied Command, SE Asia
SA de CV	sociedad anomonia de capital variable
SADF	Sudanese Auxiliary Defence Force
SAE	Society of Automobile Engineers (US)
SAMC	South African Medical Corps
Sarum	Salisbury
SAS	Special Air Service
Sask	Saskatchewan
SASO	Senior Air Staff Officer
SAT	Senior Member, Association of Accounting Technicians

SATRO	Science and Technology Regional Organisation
SB	Bachelor of Science (US)
SBAA	Sovereign Base Areas Administration
SBAC	Society of British Aerospace Companies (formerly Society of British Aircraft Constructors)
SBS	Special Boat Service
SBStJ	Serving Brother, Most Venerable Order of the Hospital of St John of Jerusalem
SC	Star of Courage (Canada); Senior Counsel (Eire, Guyana, South Africa); South Carolina (US)
sc	student at the Staff College
SCAO	Senior Civil Affairs Officer
SCAPA	Society for Checking the Abuses of Public Advertising
SCAR	Scientific Committee for Antartic
ScD	Doctor of Science
SCDC	Schools Curriculum Development Committee
SCF	Senior Chaplain to the Forces; Save the Children Fund
Sch.	School
SCI	Society of Chemical Industry
SCL	Student in Civil Law
SCM	State Certified Midwife; Student Christian Movement
SCONUL	Standing Conference of National and University Libraries
Scot.	Scotland
ScotBIC	Scottish Business in the Community
SCOTVEC	Scottish Vocational Education Council
SD	Staff Duties
SDA	Social Democratic Alliance; Scottish Diploma in Agriculture; Scottish Development Agency
SDak	South Dakota (US)
SDB	Salesian of Don Bosco
SDF	Sudan Defence Force; Social Democratic Federation
SDI	Strategic Defense Initiative
SDLP	Social Democratic and Labour Party
SDP	Social Democratic Party
SE	South-east
SEAC	South-East Asia Command
SEALF	South-East Asia Land Forces
SEATO	South-East Asia Treaty Organization
SEC	Security Exchange Commission
Sec.	Secretary
SEE	Society of Environmental Engineers
SEN	State Enrolled Nurse
SEPM	Society of Economic Palaeontologists and Mineralogists
SERC	Science and Engineering Research Council
SERT	Society of Electronic and Radio Technicians
SESO	Senior Equipment Staff Officer
SFInstE	Senior Fellow, Institute of Energy
SFInstF	Senior Fellow, Institute of Fuel (now see SFInstE)
SFTA	Society of Film and Television Arts (now see BAFTA)
SFTCD	Senior Fellow, Trinity College Dublin
SG	Solicitor-General
SGBI	Schoolmistresses' and Governesses' Benevolent Institution
Sgt	Sergeant
SHA	Secondary Heads Association; Special Health Authority
SHAC	London Housing Aid Centre
SHAEF	Supreme Headquarters, Allied Expeditionary Force
SH&MA	Scottish Horse and Motormen's Association
SHAPE	Supreme Headquarters, Allied Powers,Europe
SHHD	Scottish Home and Health Department
SIAD	Society of Industrial Artists and Designers (now see CSD)
SIAM	Society of Industrial and Applied Mathematics (US)
SIB	Shipbuilding Industry Board; Securities and Investments Board
SID	Society for International Development
SIESO	Society of Industrial and Emerergency Services Officers
SIMA	Scientific Instrument Manufacturers' Association of Great Britain
SIME	Security Intelligence Middle East
SIMG	Societas Internationalis Medicinae Generalis
SinDrs	Doctor of Chinese
SITA	Societe Internationale de Telecommunications Aeronautiques
SITPRO	Simpler Trade Procedures Board (formerly Simplification of International Trade Procedures)
SJ	Society of Jesus (Jesuits)
SJAB	St John Ambulance Brigade
SJD	Doctor of Jurisdic Science
SL	Serjeant-at-Law
SLA	Special Libraries Association
SLAC	Stanford Linear Accelerator Centre

SLAET	Society of Licensed Aircraft Engineers and Technologists
SLAS	Society for Latin-American Studies
SLD	Social and Liberal Democrats
SLP	Scottish Labour Party
SM	Medal of Service (Canada) (now see OC); Master of Science; Officer qualified for Submarine Duties
SMA	Society of Marine Artists (now see RSME)
SMB	Setia Mahkota Brunei
SME	School of Military Engineering (now see RSME)
SMHO	Sovereign Military Hospitaller Order (Malta)
SMIEEE	Senior Member, Institute of Electrical and Electronics Engineers (New York)
SMIRE	Senior Member, Institute of Radio Engineers (New York)
SMMT	Society of Motor Manufacturers and Traders Ltd
SMN	Seri Maharaja Mangku Negara (Malaysia)
SMO	Senior Medical Officer; Sovereign Military Order
SMP	Senior Managers' Program
SMPTE	Society of Motion Picture and Television Engineers (US)
SMRTB	Ship and Marine Requirements Technology Board
SNAME	Society of Naval Architects and Marine Engineers (US)
SND	Sisters of Notre Dame
SNP	Scottish National Party
SNTS	Society for New Testament Studies
SO	Staff Officer; Scientific Officer
SOAS	School of Oriental and African Studies
Soc.	Society
Soc & Lib Dem	Social and Liberal Democrats (now see Lib Dem)
SODEPAX	Committee on Society, Development and Peace
SOE	Special Operations Executive
SOGAT	Society of Graphical and Allied Trades
SOLACE	Society of Local Authority Chief Executives
SOM	Society of Occupational Medicine
SOSc	Society of Ordained Scientists
SOTS	Society for Old Testament Study
sowc	Senior Officers' War Course
sp	sine prole (without issue)
SP	Self-Propelled (Anti-Tank Regiment)
SPAB	Society for the Protection of Ancient Buildings
SPCA	Society for the Prevention of Cruelty to Animals
SPCK	Society for Promoting Christian Knowledge
SPCM	Darjah Seri Paduka Cura Si Manja Kini (Malaysia)
SPD	Salisbury Plain District
SPDK	Seri Panglima Darjal Kinabula
SPG	Society for the Propagation of the Gospel (now see USPG)
SPk	Sitara-e-Pakistan
SPMB	Seri Paduka Makhota Brunei
SPMO	Senior Principal Medical Officer
SPNC	Society for the Promotion of Nature Conservation
SPNM	Society for the Promotion of New Music
SPR	Society for Psychical Research
SPRC	Society for Prevention and Relief of Cancer
sprl	societe de personnes a responsabilite limitee
SPSO	Senior Principal Scientific Officer
SPTL	Society of Public Teachers of Law
SPUC	Society for the Protection of the Unborn Child
Sq.	Square
sq	staff qualified
SQA	Sitara-i-Quaid-i-Azam(Pakistan)
Sqdn or Sqn	Squadron
SR	Special Reserve; Southern Railway; Southern Region (BR)
SRC	Science Research Council (now see SERC); Students' Representative Council
SRHE	Society for Research into Higher Education
SRIS	Science Reference Information Service
SRN	State Registered Nurse
SRNA	Shipbuilders and Repairers National Association
SRO	Supplementary Reserve of Officers
SRP	State Registered Physiotherapist
SRY	Sherwood Rangers Yeomanry
SS	Saints; Straits Settlements; Steamship
SSA	Society of Scottish Artists
SSAC	Social Security Advisory Committee
SSBN	Nuclear Submarine, Ballistic
SSC	Solicitor before Supreme Court (Scotland); Sculptors Society of Canada; Societas Sanctae Crucis (Society of the Holy Cross); Short Service Commission
SSEB	South of Scotland Electricity Board
SSEES	School of Slavonic and East European Studies
SSF	Society of St Francis

SSJE	Society of St John the Evangelist
SSM	Society of the Sacred Mission; Seri Setia Mahkota (Malaysia)
SSO	Senior Supply Officer; Senior Scientific Officer
SSRC	Social Science Research Council (now see ESRC)
SSStJ	Serving Sister, Most Venerable Order of the Hospital of St John of Jerusalem
STA	Sail Training Association
St	Street; Saint
STB	Sacrae Theologiae Baccalaurues (Bachelor of Sacred Theology)
STC	Senior Training Corps
STD	Sacrae Theologiae Doctor (Doctor of Sacred Theology)
STh	Scholar in Theology
Stip.	Stipend; Stipendiary
STL	Sacrae Theologiae Lector (Reader or a Professor of Sacred Theology)
STM	Sacrae Theologiae Magister (Master of Sacred Theology)
STP	Sacrae Theologiae Professor (professor of Divinity, old form of DD)
STRIVE	Society for Preservation of Rural Industries and Village Enterprises
STSO	Senior Technical Staff Office
STV	Scottish Television
SUNY	State University of New York
Supp. Res.	Supplementary Reserve (of Officers)
Supt	Superintendent
Surg.	Surgeon
Surv.	Surviving
SW	South-west
SWET	Society of West End Theatre
SWIA	Society of Wildlife Artists
SWPA	South West Pacific Area
SWRB	Sadler's Wells Royal Ballet
Syd.	Sydney

T

T	Telephone; Territorial
TA	Telegraphic Address; Territorial Army
TAA	Territorial Army Association
TA&VRA	Territorial Auxiliary and Volunteer Reserve Association
TAF	Tactical Air Force
T&AFA	Territorial and Auxiliary Forces Association
T&AVR	Territorial and Army Volunteer Reserve
TANS	Territorial Army Nursing Service
TANU	Tanganyika African National Union
TARO	Territorial Army Reserve of Officers
TAS	Torpedo and Anti Submarine Course
TASS	Technical, Administrative and Supervisory Section of AUEW (now part of MSF)
TAVRA	Territorial Auxiliary and Volunteer Reserve Association
TC	Order of the Trinity Cross (Trinidad and Tobago)
TCCB	Test and County Cricket Board
TCD	Trinity College, Dublin (University of Dublin, Trinity College)
TCF	Temporary Chaplain to the Forces
TCPA	Town and Country Planning Association
TD	Territorial Efficiency Decoration; Efficiency Decoration (T&AVR) (since April1967); Teachta Dala (Member of the Dail, Eire)
TDD	Tubercular Diseases Diploma
TEAC	Technical Education Advisory Council
TEC	Technician Education Council (now see BTEC); Training and Enterprise Council
Tech(CEI)	Technician
TEFL	Teaching English as a Foreign Language
TEM	Territorial Efficiency Medal
TEMA	Telecommunication Engineering and Manufacturing Association
Temp.	Temperature; Temporary
TEng(CEI)	Technician Engineer (now see IEng)
Tenn	Tennessee (US)
TeoID	Doctor of Theology
TES	Times Education Supplement
TET	Teacher of Electrotherapy
Tex	Texas (US)
TF	Territorial Force
TFR	Territorial Force Reserve
TGEW	Timber Growers, England and Wales Ltd
TGO	Timber Growers' Organisation (now see TGEW)
TGWU	Transport and General Workers' Union
ThD	Doctor of Theology
THED	Transvaal Higher Education Diploma
THELEP	Therapy of Leprosy
THES	Times Higher Education Supplement

ThL	Thoelogical Licentiate
ThSchool	Scholar in Theology
TIMS	The Institute of Management Sciences
TLS	Times Literary Supplement
TMMG	Teacher of Massage and Medical Gymnastics
TNC	Theatres National Committee
TOSD	Tertiary Order of St Dominic
TP	Transvaal Province
TPI	Town Planning Institute (now see RTPI)
Trans.	Translation; Translated
Transf.	Transferred
TRC	Thames Rowing Club
TRE	Telecommunications Research Establishment (now see RRE)
TRH	Their Royal Highnesses
TRIC	Television and Radio Industries Club
Trin.	Trinity
TRRL	Transport and Road Research Laboratory
TS	Training Ship
TSB	Trustee Savings Bank
tsc	passed a Territorial Army Course in Staff Duties
TSD	Tertiary of St Dominic
TSSA	Transport Salaried Staffs' Association
TUC	Trades Union Congress
TULV	Trade Unions for a Labour Victory
TUS	Trade Union Side
TV	Television
TVEI	Technical and Vocational Education Initiative
TWA	Thames Water Authority
TYC	Thames Yacht Club (now see RTYC)

U

(U)	Unionist
u	uncle
UAE	United Arab Emirates
UAR	United Arab Republic
UAU	Universities Athletic Union
UBC	University of British Columbia
UBI	Understanding British Industry
UC	University College
UCCA	Universities Central Council on Admissions
UCET	Universities Council for Education of Teachers
UCH	University College Hospital (London)
UCL	University College London
UCLA	University of California at Los Angeles
UCMSM	University College and Middlesex School of Medicine
UCNS	Universities' Council for Non-academic Staff
UCNW	University College of North Wales
UCRN	University College of Rhodesia and Nyasaland
UCS	University College School
UCSD	University of California at San Diego
UCW	University College of Wales; Union of Communication Workers
UDC	Urban District Council; Urban Development Corporation
UDF	Union Defence Force; Union Democratique Francaise
UDR	Ulster Defence Regiment; Union des Democrates pour la Veme Republique (now see RFR)
UDSR	Union Democratique et Socialiste de la Resistance
UEA	University of East Anglia
UED	University Education Diploma
UEFA	Union of European Football Associations
UF	United Free Church
UFAW	Universities Federation of Animal Welfare
UFC	Universities' Funding Council
UGC	University Grants Committee (now see UFC)
UIAA	Union Internationale des Associations d'Alpinisme
UICC	Union Internationale contre le Cancer
UIE	Union Internationale des Etudiants
UISPP	Union Internationale des Sciences Prehistoriques et Protohistoriques
UJD	Ultriusque Juris Doctor (Doctor of both Laws, Doctor of Canon and Civil Law)
UK	United Kingdom
UKAC	United Kingdom Automation Council
UKAEA	United Kingdom Atomic Energy Authority
UKCC	United Kingdom Central Council for Nursing, Midwifery and Health Visiting
UKCIS	United Kingdom Chemical Information Service
UKIAS	United Kingdom Immigrants' Advisory Service
UKISC	United Kingdom Industrial Space Committee
UKLF	United Kingdom Land Forces

UKMF(L)	United Kingdom Military Forces (Land)
UKMIS	United Kingdom Mission
UKOOA	United Kingdom Offshore Operators Association
UKPIA	United Kingdom Petroleum Industry Association Ltd
UKSLS	United Kingdom Services Liaison Staff
ULCI	Union of Lancashire and Cheshire Institutes
UMDS	United Medical and Dental Schools
UMIST	University of Manchester Institute of Science and Technology
UN	United Nations
UNA	United Nations Association
UNCAST	United Nations Conference on the Applications of Science and Technology
UNCIO	United Nations Conference on International Organisation
UNCITRAL	United Nations Commission on International Trade Law
UNCSTD	United Nations Conference on Science and Technology for Development
UNCTAD or	
Unctad	United Nations Commissions for Trade and Development
UNDP	United Nations Development Programme
UNDRO	United Nations Disaster Relief Organisation
UNECA	United Nations Economic Commission for Asia
UNEP	United Nations Environment Programme
UNESCO or	
Unesco	United Nations Educational, Scientific and Cultural Organisation
UNFAO	United Nations Food and Agriculture Organisation
UNFICYP	United Nations Force in Cyprus
UNHCR	United Nations High Commissioner for Refugees
UNICE	Union des Industries de la Communaute Europeenne
UNICEF or	
Unicef	United Nations Children's Fund (formerly United Nations International Children's Emergency Fund)
UNIDO	United Nations Industrial Development Organisation
UNIDROIT	Institut International pour l'Unification du Droit Prive
UNIFIL	United Nations Interim Force in Lebanon
UNIPEDE	Union Internationale des Producteurs et Distributeurs d'Energie Electrique
UNISIST	Universal System for Information in Science and Technology
UNITAR	United Nations Institute of Training and Research
Univ.	University
UNO	United Nations Organisation
UNRRA	United Nations Relief and Rehabilitation Administration
UNRWA	United Nations Relief and Works Agency
UNSCOB	United Nations Special Commission on the Balkans
UPGC	University and Polytechnic Grants Committee
UPNI	Unionist Party of Northern Ireland
UPU	Universal Postal Union
(UPUP)	Ulster Popular Unionist Party
URC	United Reformed Church
US	United States
USA	United States of America
USAAF	United States Army Air Force
USAF	United States Air Force
USAID	United States Agency for International Development
USAR	United States Army Reserve
USC	University of Southern California
USDAW	Union of Shop Distributive and Allied Workers
USM	Unlisted Securities Market
USMA	United States Military Academy
USN	United States Navy
USNR	United States Naval Reserve
USPG	United Society for the Propagation of the Gospel
USPHS	United States Public Health Service
USS	United States Ship
USSR	Union of Soviet Socialist Republics
USVI	United States Virgin Island
UTC	University Training Corps
(UU)	Ulster Unionist
(UUUC)	United Ulster Unionist Coalition
(UUU)	United Ulster Unionist Party
UWIST	University of Wales Institute of Science and Technology
UWT	Union of Women Teachers

V

V	Five (Roman numerals); Version; Vicar; Viscount; Vice
v	versus (against)
v or vid.	vide
V&A	Victoria and Albert
VAT	Value Added Tax
VC	Victoria Cross

VD	Royal Naval Volunteer Reserve Officers' Decoration (now VRD); Volunteer Officers' Decoration; Victorian Decoration
VDC	Volunteer Defence Corps
Ven.	Venerable
Vet.	Veterinary
VIC	Victoria Institute of Colleges
Vice-Adm.	Vice-Admiral
Visc.	Viscount
VM	Victory Medal
Vol.	Volume; Volunteers
VP	Vice-President
VQMG	Vice-Quartermaster-General
VR	Victoria Regina (Queen Victoria); Volunteer Reserve
VRD	Royal Naval Volunteer Reserve Officers' Decoration
VSO	Voluntary Service Overseas
(VUP)	Vanguard Unionist Party

W

W	West
WA	Western Australia
WAAF	Women's Auxiliary Air Force (now see WRAF)
Wash	Washington State (US)
WCC	World Council of Churches
W/Cdr	Wing Commander
WEA	Workers' Educational Association; Royal West of England Academy
WEU	Western European Union
WFTU	World Federation of Trade Unions
WHO	World Health Organization
WhSch	Whitworth Scholar
WI	West Indies; Women's Institute
Wilts	Wiltshire
WJEC	Welsh Joint Education Committee
WLA	Women's Land Army
Wm	William
WMO	World Meteorological Organization
WNO	Welsh National Opera
WO	War Office; Warrant Officer

Worcs	Worcestershire
WOSB	War Office Selection Board
WR	West Riding; Western Region (BR)
WRAC	Women's Royal Army Corps
WRAF	Women's Royal Air Force
WRNS	Women's Royal Naval Service
WRVS	Women's Royal Voluntary Service
WUS	World University Service
WVS	Women's Voluntary Services (now see WRVS)
WWF	World Wide Fund for Nature

X

X	Ten (Roman numerals)
XO	Executive Officer

Y

y	youngest
YC	Young Conservative
Yeo.	Yeomanry
YES	Youth Enterprise Scheme
YHA	Youth Hostels Association
YMCA	Young Men's Christian Association
Yorks	Yorkshire
yr	younger
yrs	years
YTS	Youth Training Scheme
YVFF	Youth Volunteer Force Foundation
YWCA	Young Women's Christian Association

Z

ZANU	Zimbabwe African National Union
ZAPU	Zimbabwe African People's Union

ABEL, Prof. Edward William, BSc.,PhD. *Currently:* Deputy Vice-Chancellor, University of Exeter, 1991- . *Born on* 3 Dec 1931 at Kenfig Hill. *Son of* the late Sydney John and the late Donna Maria (neeGrabham). *Marriage:* to Margaret Rosina, da of Glyndwr Vivian Edwards (d 1974). *Children:* Christopher and Julia. *Educated at* Bridgend GS Glamorgan; Univ. Coll., Cardiff; Northern Poly, London. *Career:* Nat. Serv. 1953-55; res fell Imp Coll 1957-79; lectr and reader Univ of Bristol, 1959-71; prof of inorganic chemistry Univ of Exeter, 1972; visiting prof: Univ. of Br. Columbia 1970, Japan 1971, Tech Univ of Braunschweig 1973, Australian Nat Univ Canberra 1990; int. sec Int Confs on Organometallic Chemistry 1972-88; Royal Soc of Chemistry: membr Cncl 1978-82 and 1983-89, chm Local Affairs Bd 1983-87, chm Divnl Affairs Bd 1990- , memb Dalton Divnl Cncl 1977-83 and 1987-91, vice pres 1989-91, (pres 1987-89), sec and treas 1977-82; Univ Grants Ctee: memb 1986-89, chm Physical Sci Sub Ctee 1986-89; Cncl for Nat Academic Awards, 1991-: chm Physical Sci Ctee 1987-91, memb Academic Affairs Ctee 1987-91; nat advsr for chemistry to exec Univ Funding Cncl 1989- ; assessor to Res Ctee Poly and Coil Funding Cncl; Royal Soc of Chemistry: Main Gp Chemistry award 1976, Tilden medal and lectr 1981. *Publications:* Royal Soc Chemistry Specialist Periodical Reports on Organometallic Chemistry Vols 1-20 (jt ed, 1970-) Comprehensive Organometallic Chemistry 9 Vols (exec ed, 1984). *Recreation:* gardening and cycling *Address:* 1a Rosebarn Avenue, Exeter, Devon, EX4 6DY. Dept. Of Chemistry, University Of Exeter, Exeter, Devon, EX4 4QD Tel: 039 226 3489

ABERCONWAY, Lord Charles Melville Mclaren, 3rd Baron, cr 1911, of Bodnant, Bt 1902; JP. *Born on* 16 April 1913 at London. *Son of* 2nd Baron Aberconway, CBE, LLD and the late Christabel y d of Sir Melville Macnaghten, CB. *Marriage:* 1). to Deirdre Knewstub 1941 (marr.diss. 1949); 2). to Ann Lindsay Bullard, o d of Mrs A.L.Aymer, New York City 1949. *Children:* 1st marriage one s, 2 d; 2nd marriage one s. *Educated at* Eton; New Coll., Oxford. *Career:* Barrister, Middle Temple 1937; Served War of 1939-45, 2nd Lieut RA; Deputy Chairman: Sun Alliance & London Insurance 1976-85 (Dir, London Assurance 1953); Westland Aircraft 1979-84 (Dir, 1947-85); Dir, National Westminster Bank (formerly National Provincial Bank), 1953-83; President, Royal Horticultural Society 1961-84; President Emeritus 1984- .JP Denbighshire 1946; High Sheriff of Denbighshire 1950. *Recreations:* Gardening, travel. *Address:* 25 Egerton Terrace, London SW3. Bodnant, Tal-Y-Cafn, Colwyn Bay, Clwyd.

ABERDARE, The Rt. Hon Lord Morys George Lyndhurst, K.B.E.,D.L., LL.D. (Hon) *Currently:* Chairman of Committees, House of Lords; Chairman Metlife (UK) Ltd.; Albany Life Assurance; The Football Trust. *Born on* 16 June 1919 in London. *Son of* 3rd Lord and Lady Aberdare. *Marriage:* to Sarah Dashwood, 1946. Children: Alastair, James Adam and Charles Bruce. *Educated at* Wincheser New College *Career:* Welsh Guards, 1939-46; BBC, 1949-55; Minister of State D.H.S.S., Deputy Leader House of Lords, 1970-74; Minister without Portfolio, Privy Councillor, 1974- . *Publications:* The Story of Tennis; The Willis Faber Book of Tennis and Rackets Recreation: Sport and gardening *Clubs:* Cardiff and County; MCC; The Queen's Club; Lansdowne Club. *Address:* 32 Elthiron Road, London SW6 4BW. House Of Lords,London SW1

ABSE, Dr Dannie, MRCS.,LR.,CP.,DLit(Wales).,FRSL. *Currently:* Author. *Born on* 22 Sept 1923 at Cardiff. *Son of* Rudy Abse and Kate Shepherd. *Marriage:* to Joan Mercer. *Children:* Keren, Susanna and David *Educated at* St. Illtyd's Coll., Cardiff; Univ. of Wales, Cardiff; Kings Coll. London; Westminster Hospital,London. *Career:* No career - only a destiny! *Publications:* include White Coat, Purple Coat (Hutchinson 1989); There was a young man from Cardiff (Hutchinson 1991). *Recreation:* Football and chess *Address:* C/o Sheil Land Associates Ltd, 43 Doughty St, London WC1 2LF

ABSE, Mr Leo, *Born on* 22 April 1917 *Son of* Rudolph and Kate Abse. *Marriage:* to Marjorie Davies, 1955. *Children:* one s one d. *Educated at* Howard Gardens High School; LSE. *Career:* Served RAFD 1940-45 (arrest for political activities in ME, 1944, precipitated parly debate). Solicitor; sen. partner in Cardiff Law firm; First solicitor permitted to appear before the High Court 1986.Chrmn. Cardiff City Lab. Party 1951-53; Mbr., Cardiff CC 1953-58; Contested (Lab) Cardiff N, 1955 (MP (Lab): Pontypool, Nov. 1958-83; Torfaen, 1983-87. Chmn., Welsh Parly Party, 1976-87; Mbr., Home Office Adv. Cttees on the Penal System, 1968, on adoption, 1972; first Chmn., Select Cttee on Welsh Affairs, 1980; Mbr., Select Cttee on Abortion, 1975-76; Sec., British-Taiwan Parly Gp, 1983-87; Sponsor or co-sponsor of Private Mem's Acts relating to divorce, homosexuality, family planning, legitimacy, widows' damages, industrial injuries, congenital disabilities and relief from forfeiture; sponsored Children's Bill 1973, later taken over by Govt to become Children's Act, 1975; sponsored Divorce Bill, 1983, later taken over by Govt to become Matrimonial and Family Proceedings Act, 1985; initiated first Commons debates on genetic engineering, Windscale, in vitro pregnancies. Led Labour anti-devolution campaign in Wales, 1979. Mbr. Council, Inst. for Study and Treatment of Delinquency, 1964- ; Chm. Parly Friends of WNO, 1985-87. Mbr. of Court: Univ. of Wales 1981-87; UWIST Regents' Lectr. Univ. of Calif. 1984. Received best dressed man award of Clothing Fedn, 1962; Order of Brilliant Star (China) 1988. Chairman, Winnicott Clinic of

Psychotherapy 1988- (Trustee 1980-). *Publications:* Private Member: a psychoanalytically orientated study of contemporary politics, 1973; (contrib) In Vitro Fertilisation: past, present and future, 1986; Margaret, daughter of Beatrice: a psychobiography of Margaret Thatcher 1989. *Recreation:* Italian wines, psycho-biography. *Address:* 54 Strand-On-The-Green, London W4 3PD. Via Poggio Di Mezzo, Nugola Vecchia, Livorno, Italy. Tel: 081 994 1166

ACKLAND, Mrs Dorothy Janet, NDD, ATD *Born on* 19 Dec 1938 at Ystrad Mynach. *Daughter of* Lionel and Irene Palmer. *Marriage:* to Robert William Ackl. *Children:* Christopher and Michael *Educated at* Lewis' Grammar for Girls; Cardiff College of Art. *Career:* Schoolteacher, Art and Craft 1960-80. 2 Bronze medals at World Championships Worthing 1977; Gold Medal Singles, World, New Zealand 1988; represented Wales at 1982, 86 and 90 Commonwealth Games; Member of British Isles Team in New Zealand 1990; National Singles winner twice, also triples and fours; British Isles fours winner 1989 and 1990. Recreation: Bowling and organising bowls tournaments. *Clubs:* Belle Vue Bowling, Penarth. *Address:* 62 Dochdwy Road, Llandough, Penarth, S.Glam CF6 1PD.

ADAMS, Mr Hervey Cadwallader, RBA., FRSA *Currently:* Retired. *Born on* 15 Feb 1903 at London. *Son of* the late Cadwallader Edmund Adams and the late Dorothy Jane Knight. *Marriage:* to Iris Gabrielle Bruce 1929. *Children:* Bruce Hervey Adams and John Francis Julian Adams. *Educated at* Private Schools and Charterhouse *Career:* Worked and taught privately as artist; elected to Royal Society of British Artists 1932; Art Master Berhamsted School 1937-40; Art Master Tonbridge School 1940-63; Elected to Royal Society of Arts for services to education; lectured widely for Foyles lecture agency; continued work as artist. *Publications:* An Approach to Landscape Painting (Pitman); 18th & 19th Century painting in Europe (Medici); The Adventure of Looking (Bell). *Recreation:* Art. *Address:* Pummel, Houndscroft, near Stroud, Glos., GL5 5DG.

ADAMS, Honourable Marjorie Heather, JP *Currently:* retired. *Born on* 27 Oct 1923 at Blackburn, Lancs. *Daughter of* the late John Percival Davies, 1st Baron Darwen and the late Mary Kathleen. *Marriage:* to Frederick Joseph Adams, CBE, MA(Cantab), formerly Director of Education, South Glamorgan. *Children:* Christopher Stephen. *Educated at* Queen Mary School, Lytham St.Annes; Friends School, Great Ayton, Nr Middlesbrough; The Mount School, York; Rachel McMillan Training College. *Career:* Teacher and Magistrate. *Recreation:* painting, dressmaking, walking. *Address:* 5 Wordsworth Close, Llantwit Major, South Glamorgan, CF6 9WZ.

ADLER, Eur Ing George Fritz Werner, OBE, FEng, BSc(Eng), DIC, FICE, FIMechE, FBIM, FInstD. *Currently:* Self-employed Consultant. *Born on* 12 Jan 1926 at Stettin. *Son of* Fritz Jacob Sigismund Adler and Hildegard Julie (nee Lippmann). *Marriage:* to June Moonaheim Margaret (nee Nash). *Children:* Helen Margaret Suzanne, Fiona Ruth and Caroline Francesca Mathilde. *Educated at* County Grammar Penarth; Cardiff University & Technical College; Imperial College. *Career:* Graduate Apprentice, English Electric Co., Rugby 1945-47; Chief Development Engineer Rugby 1956-58; Chief Mechanical Engineer, Marconi Co, Chelmsford 1958-62; Manager, Mechanical Products Division Marconi 1962-66; Manager, Hydraulics Divisions, English Electric Co 1966-71; Director of Research, British Hydromechanics Research Assoc 1971-86; Secretary Association of Independent Research & Technology Organisations 1986-89; President, Institution of Mechanical Engineers 1983-84; Liveryman, Worshipful Company of Engineers and Freeman of City of London 1984; Fellow, University of Wales College of Cardiff; member, Governing Body of Imperial College 1985- ; member, Engineering Council 1986-89; Chairman, British National Committee for International Engineering Affairs 1986-89; Vice-President, European Federation of National Engineering Associations (FEANI) 1987-89; Treasurer and member of Council, Fellowship of Engineering 1988-91. *Publications:* Kempe's Engineers Yearbook (contributor 1956 onwards). *Recreation:* crafts, gardening, music, golf. *Clubs:* Carlton *Address:* The Haining, Orchard Close, Longburton, Sherborne, Dorset DT9 5PP.

AINSLEY, Mr David Edwin, B.Arch(Hons); RIBA; FFAS. *Currently:* partner in Ainsley Gommon Wood, Architects and Landscape Architects, Birkenhead, Clwyd and London, formerly titled Innes Wilkin Partnership, later Innes Wilkin Ainsley Gommon, since 1979. Practice has won several National Design awards including: Welsh National Eisteddfod Architecture Prize, Royal Town Planning Institute Commendation, Housing Centre Trust Award, Liverpool International Garden Festival Best Home Garden, twice winner of Times/RIBA Community Enterprise Scheme Award, Civic Trust Commendation. *Born on* 13 Sept 1944 at Ripon, Yorkshire. *Son of* Edwin Ainsley and the late Gertrude Mary. *Marriage:* 1st to Pauline Elisabeth, 1970 (diss 1984); 2nd to Beatrix Parry. *Children:* Sam and Christian; Nathan and Ben (step sons). *Educated at* Portsmouth Grammar School; University of Liverpool. *Career:* Liverpool City Architects Dept., 1969-72; Birkenhead Borough Architects Dept., 1972-74; Wirral Borough Council Architects 1975-79. Founder member and chairman Oxton Society 1981; Governor, Christchurch C.E. Primary School, Birkenhead 1990; Hon Secretary, Liverpool Architecture Society. *Recreation:* music, keyboard in Low Flier. *Address:* 24 Village Road, Oxton, Birkenhead, Wirral, L43 5SR Tel: 051 652 4064. Ainsley Gommon Wood, Techbase, 3, Newtech Square, Deeside Industrial Estate, Clwyd, CH5 2NU. Tel: 0244 280033.

AINSWORTH, Mr John Edward, C.C. *Currently:* Director. *Born on* 30 May 1941 at St. Asaph. *Recreation:* Local Government and British stamps *Address:* 14 Llys Idris, Elwy Park, St. Asaph, Clwyd LL17 OAJ.

ALEXANDER, Professor Robert Mcneill, PhD, DSc, FRS. *Currently:* Professor of Zoology, University of Leeds, since 1969. *Born on* 7 July 1934 at Lisburn, N.Ireland. *Son of* Robert Priestley Alexander and Janet (nee McNeipp). *Marriage:* to Ann Elizabeth Coulton, 1961. *Children:* Jane Coulton Alexander (now Mrs Dearden) and Robert Gordon Alexander. *Educated at* Tonbridge School; Trinity Hall Cambridge. *Career:* University College of North Wales Bangor: Assistant Lecturer 1958; Lecturer 1961; Senior Lecturer 1968. *Publications:* Animal Mechanics, 1968; Elastic Mechanisms in Animal Movement, 1988; Dynamics of Dinosaurs and other Giants, 1989; various other books and numerous papers in scientific journals, mainly on biomechanics. *Recreation:* Local history, history of natural history. *Address:* Dept Of Pure & Applied

Biology,University Of Leeds,Leeds, LS2 9JT. 14 Moor Park Mount,Leeds LS6 4BU Tel: 0532 332911

ALLISON, Mr John,CBE.,JP.,DL *Currently:* Director, Municipal Mutual Inst. Ltd., Swansea Sound Ltd. *Born on* 4 Oct 1919 at Morriston, Swansea. *Son of* Thomas William Allison and Margaret Grey. Marriage: to Elvira Gwendoline Lewis, 1948. Children: Susan Margaret, Jillian and Richard *Educated at* Elementary Glanmore Sec. School; Swansea Technical Coll. *Career:* Local Govt: Elected Swansea City Council, 1957; Deputy Major, 1967-68 and 1971-72; Leader of City Council, 1967-74; Elected West Glam C.C., 1974; Leader 1977-89; Chrmn. of Assoc. of County Councils, 1986-88; Deputy Chrmn. of Dev. Corp. of Wales, 1971-85; Chrmn. of S.Wales Police Authority, 1987-89; commercial interests: Mainly small companies including family music business: Picton Music Ltd. Recreation: Rugby, golf and fishing *Clubs:* Morriston Golf *Address:* Penbryn,155 Vicarage Road,Morriston,Swansea. W. Glam,SA6 6DT.

ALLEN, Mr John Derek,CBE, BA. *Currently:* Chairman of Housing for Wales since 1988; Deputy Chairman Land Authority For Wales since 1976. *Born on* 6 Nov 1928 at Cardiff. *Son of* the late William Henry Allen and the late Lalla (nee Bowen). Marriage: to Jean Hooper, 1951. Children: Nicholas John Allen (b.1961). *Educated at* Cardiff High School; Cardiff College of Technology. *Career:* Civil Engineer then Chairman and M.D., of John Morgan Group Cardiff 1949-77; subsequently non executive director of several other companies. President of National Federation of Building Trade Employers U.K., 1979-80; then Treasurer, 1981-83. Deputy Chairman then Chairman Cwmbran Development Corporation 1979-88; Freeman City of London 1980; FCIOB 1980; FBIM 1980. Recreation: golf, fly fishing. *Clubs:* Cardiff & County, Cardiff Golf. *Address:* 6 Egremont Road,Penylan,Cardiff,,CF2 5LN.

ALLEN,Mr Peter Dobson,CBE (1988), DL, BSc, C.Eng, FIM. *Currently:* Chairman, West Glamorgan Health Authority; Non-Exec Board member, British Rail. *Born on* 4 Jan 1931 at Dewsbury, Yorks. *Son of* the late Frederick Allen and the late Ethel Allen (nee Dobson). Marriage: to Janet Thurman, 1956. Children: Timothy Dobson, Christopher Thurman and Nicholas John. *Educated at* Wheelwright GS; University of Birmingham. *Career:* Steel Industry, British Steel 1948-90: Managing Director, Welsh Division Strip Products 1976-90, Director, Port Talbot Works 1972-76, various managerial posts in Steel Industry in Sheffield and Midlands 1960-72. National Service Lt. Royal Artillery 1955-57. *Publications:* none in recent years. Recreation: rugby, music, racing (horse), Welsh culture. *Address:* 82 Merthyr Mawr Road,Bridgend,Mid Glam., CF31 3NS.

ALLFREY, Major (Henry) John, OBE *Born on* 30 Dec 1924. *Son of* the late Maj Henry Sydney Allfrey, JP, DL, of The Grange, How Caple, Hereford and the late Vera. Marriage: 1st to Jocelyn, 1957 (ma dis 1980), da of Cdr The Maurice Fitzroy-Newdegate; 2nd to Sonia Elisabeth,1980, da of Col Juan Beresford Hobbs. Children: from 1st marriage, David, Charles and Lucia. *Educated at* Winchester. *Career:* cmmnd RHA 1944, World War II 1945-46 India, Malaya and Java, Staff Capt SE Asia Land Forces HQ 1946-48; regtl serv: airborne RHA, Jr Ldrs Regt and Berks Yeomanry 1948-59, staff coll 1956, GSO II HQ 4 Infantry Div 1957-59, GSO II Brig Author MOD 1959-61; dir: Harp Lager

(Southern) 1965-70, Courage (Central) 1967-69, Courage (Eastern) 1969-70, Courage (Brewing) 1973-80; MD Courage (Central) 1971-79; dir Research into Ageing (registered charity) 1980-89, vice chairman and chairman Wokingham Cons Assoc 1966-72, governor Elstree Sch 1975-88, founder and patron Berks Retirement Assoc 1976-89; member Exec Council: Assoc of Med Res Charities, Br Soc for Res into Ageing; FInstl, MInstMktg, member Inst Fund Raising Managers. *Publications:* from 1959-61: The Nuclear Land, Battle, Keeping the Peace, Training For War. Recreation: fishing, shooting, gardening. *Clubs:* Boodle's *Address:* The Dower House,Castle Hedingham,Nr Halstead,Essex,CO9 3DG. 25b Wilton Row,London SW1X 7NS

ALLISON,Mr John,CBE., JP., DL. *Currently:* Company Director. *Born on* 4 Oct 1919 at Morriston, Swansea. *Son of* Thomas William Allison and Margaret Grey. Marriage: to Elvira Gwendoline Lewis, 1948. Children: Susan Margaret, Jillian and Richard *Educated at* Morriston Junior; Glanmore Secondary; Swansea Technical College. *Career:* Livelihood: various business interests; Political & Local Government; President: Swansea Labour Assoc., 1962-63; Contested Barry Constituency, General Election, 1970; Leader of Swansea City Council, 1967-73 and leader West Glamorgan CC, 1977-89; Chairman of West Glam 1976-77; Chairman of Assoc. of County Councils, 1986-87. Recreation: Fishing, golf and rugby *Clubs:* Morriston Golf *Address:* Penbryn, 155 Vicarage Road, Morriston, Swansea. SA6 6DT.

ANDERSON,Dr Arthur John Ritchie,CBE, MA. *Currently:* Senior Partner, General Medical Practice. *Born on* 19 July 1933 at Pontrhydygroes, Cardigan. *Son of* the late Dr John Anderson, of Pontrhydygroes and the late Dorothy Mary Anderson. Marriage: to Janet Edith Norrish, 1959. Children: John Richard (b.1963), Margaret Hazel (b.1965) and Alan James (b.1971). *Educated at* Bromsgrove School; Downing College Cambridge (MA,MB,Bchir); St.Mary's Hospital Medical School. *Career:* Gen Med and hospital practitioner; member Regional Planning Council for S.E. 1977-79; member NW Thames Regional Health Authority 1978-85; Vice Chairman Herts CC 1985-87 (ldr 1977-83); chairman Crouchfield Trust 1989- , chairman Herts Police Authority 1983-86, chief whip Conservative Group Herts CC 1989- President British Medical Association Hertfordshire Branch 1970; MRCGP, MRCS, LRCP, DCH, DRCOG, FRSM. *Publications:* various. *Clubs:* Herts 100 (chairman). *Address:* Leaside,Rucklers Lane,Kings Langley,Herts,WD4 9NQ. Tel: 0923 262884

ANDERSON,Mr Donald,Hon Fellow, Univ. Coll. Swansea. *Currently:* M.P. *Born on* 17 June 1939 at Swansea. *Son of* David Robert and Eva (nee Mathias). Marriage: to Dorothy Trotman. PhD. Wales. *Children:* Robert John, Hugh Jenkin David and Geraint Frank Christian. *Educated at* Swansea Grammar School (Bishop Gore); Univ. Coll., Swansea, *Career:* Member Senior Branch HM Foreign Service, 1960-64; Lecturer Politics Dept. Univ. College, Swansea, 1964-66; MP Monmouth, 1966-70; Barrister called 1969- . President Boys Brigade of Wales, Board of Directors, World Vision. MP Swansea East 1974- ; Commanders Cross Order of Merit from German Federal Republic for contribution to British German Relations 1986. *Address:* 88 Ladbroke Road, London W11 3ND. 8 Marine Walk, Swansea

ANDERSON, John Elwyn, Police Long Service Medal; Service Cross RLSS *Currently:* retired. *Born on* 21 Dec 1929 at Maesteg. *Son of* David John Anderson and Gwladys May (nee Jones). Marriage: to Patricia Margaret Bush. Children: Paul and Janet. *Educated at* Plasnewydd School; Llwynderw Senior, Maesteg. *Career:* NCB 1946; Coygnant Colliery "Norths Navigator", Caerau, Maesteg, 1944-47; Welsh Guards 1947-53. Glamorgan Police, 1953, to amalgamation in 1965; South Wales Contabulary 1965 to retirement in 1983.Has been an active member of the East Wales branch of the Royal Life Saving Society since 1953, of which he is the present Chairman. As the Wales Lifeguard Delegate in 1967 he formed the South Wales Lifeguard Corps, being Executive Officer for Wales on the National Committee until 1972. He was on the instructional staff of the No. 8 District Police Training Centre at Bridgend from January 1964 to January 1972, as P.E., swimming and drill instructor. He holds the Police Long Service and Good Conduct Medal, The Recognition Badge and Bar and the Service Cross of the R.L.S.S. He has represented Glamorgan, Welsh and British Police at rugger and played for Maesteg, London Welsh, Bridgend and Glamorgan County R.F.C. Recreation: gardening, walking, swimming. *Clubs:* Royal British Legion, United Services and Welsh Guards, w/o & Sgts Association, South Wales Police Ath. and former Players Association. *Address:* 4 Cefn Coed,Bridgend,Mid Glam,S.Wales,CF31 4PH.

ANDERSON,Professor Michael John,BA(Bristol). *Currently:* Professor of Drama, University of Kent at Canterbury, since 1990.*Born on* 4 June 1937 at Cardiff.*Son of* the late Ronald Arthur Anderson and Dorothy Alma (nee Daniel). *Marriage:* to Alessandra Pierangela Lucia Di Gregorio, 1973. *Children:* 2 daughters, Silvia and Marina. *Educated at* Taunton School; University of Bristol. *Career:* The Welch Regiment 1956-58; Manager, New Theatre, Cardiff 1963-64; lecturer in Drama, University of Bristol 1964-78; Professor of Drama, University College of North Wales, Bangor 1978-90. Chairman, Standing Committee of University Drama Departments 1979-82; member, Welsh Arts Council 1985-90 (Chairman, Drama Committee); Joint Secretary General, International Federation for Theatre Research 1989- . *Publications:* Classical Drama and its Influence (ed., 1965); Anger and Detachment, a Study of Osborne, Arden and Pinter 1976. *Recreation:* books, travel films. *Clubs:* Royal Commonwealth Society, Circolo Unione Bisceglie (Italy). *Address:* 28 Nunnery Fields, Canterbury, Kent CT1 3JT

ANDREW, Mrs Elizabeth Honora,LL.B. *Currently:* Barrister, Assistant Recorder. *Born on* 6 March 1946 at Pontypridd. *Daughter of* Dilwyn and Morfydd Thomas. *Marriage:* 1967. *Children:* two s. *Educated at* Pontypridd Girls Grammar School; University, London. *Career:* prior to the Bar, buyer Retail/Wholesale fashion industry. *Publications:* articles in various legal journals. *Recreation:* travel, reading, music. *Address:* Devereux Chambers, Devereux Court, Temple, London, WC2.

ANDREW, Dr Kenneth,D.Phil, M.Phil, MSc, DIC, B.Eng, FRS, FIOD, MIB, M.BIM *Currently:* Chief Executive Officer, Aetna Financial Management International Ltd. *Born on* 21 Dec 1944 at Darlington. *Son of* Arthur James and Emily Sarah. *Marriage:* Elizabeth Honora Andrew. *Children:* two sons *Educated at* Doctorate in Marketing, Masters in Operational Research, Batchelor (1st) in Engineering (Wales). *Career:* Various posts in National Westminster Bank plc 1969-84; Group Director, Good Relations Group plc 1984-85; European Consumer Marketing Director, Chase Manhattan 1985-87; Group Director National & Provincial Building Society 1987-90; Independent Management Consultant 1990-91. *Publications:* Bank Marketing in A Changing World; The Bank Marketing Handbook; The Financial Public Relations Handbook. *Recreation:* travel, swimming, reading, writing. *Clubs:* Royal Society of Arts, MCC *Address:* Aetna U.K., Aetna House, 2-12 Pentonville Road, London, N1 9XG.

ANDREWS,Professor John,JP, MA, BCL, Barrister-at-Law. *Currently:* Professor of Law, since 1967 and Head of Department of Law, since 1970,University College of Wales, Aberystwyth. *Born on* 29 Jan 1935 at Newport, Gwent. *Son of* the late Arthur George Andrews and the late Hilda May Andrews. *Marriage:* to Elizabeth Ann Mary (nee Wilkes), 1960. *Children:* Carolyn Elizabeth (b.1963) and Susan Rebecca (b.1966). *Educated at* Newport High School; Wadham College, Oxford. *Career:* Barrister, Gray's Inn 1960, Bencher 1991; Assistant Lecturer, Univ of Manchester 1957-58; Lecturer Univ of Birmingham 1958-67; Vice Principal UCW Aberystwyth 1985-88. Visiting Professor Univ of Thessaloniki 1974 and 1990, Univ of Cracow 1978, Univ of Maryland 1983; Editor, Legal Studies 1981- ; Chairman Council of Validating Univs 1987-90; Member, Lord Chancellor's Committee on Legal Education 1987-90; Chairman Police Promotion Examinations Board 1987- ; member, Police Training Council 1987- ; President Society of Public Teachers of Law 1988-89; Trustee, Hamlyn Trust 1969- ; Wales Advisory Body, Chairman Standing Working Group 1990-92; member Court of Governors, National Library of Wales 1978- ; Law Adviser UFC 1989- ; *Publications:* Welsh Studies in Public Law (ed.1970) Human Rights in Criminal Procedure (ed.1982); Welsh Language in the Courts (with L.G.Henshaw 1984); The International Protection of Human Rights (with W.Hines 1987); Criminal Evidence (with M.Hirst 1987 and 1992); Criminal Evidence, Statutes and Materials (1990). *Recreation:* walking, theatre, food. *Clubs:* Brynamlwg. *Address:* 7 Maeshendre, Aberystwyth, Dyfed, SY23 3PR. Faculty Of Law, University College Of Wales, Aberystwyth, SY23 3DY Tel: 0970 622712

ANGLESEY,7th Marquess of Anglesey George Charles Henry Victor Paget,FSA; FRHists; FRSL; Hon. FRIBA; Hon.D.Litt. *Currently:* Peer of the Realm; Chairman, Historic Buildings Council for Wales; member, National Heritage Memorial Fund. *Born on* 8 Oct 1922 in London. *Son of* 6th Marquess of Anglesey; Marjorie, Marchioness of Anglesey. *Marriage:* to Eliz Shirley Vaughan, Marchioness of Anglesey, 1948. *Children:* Alexander, Earl of Uxbridge; Lord Rupert Paget; Ladies Henrietta, Sophia and Amelia Paget. *Educated at* Wixenford, Wokingham; Eton College, Windsor. *Career:* Major, RHG, 1946; Div Dir. of Wales, Nationwide Building Soc., 1973-89; President: Anglesey Conservative Assoc., 1948-83; Nat. Museum of Wales, 1962-68; Friends of Friendless Churches, 1966-84; Ancient Monuments Soc., 1979-84; Treasurer, Danilo Dolci Trust (Britain), 1964-86; Vice-Chm., Welsh Cttee, Nat. Trust, 1975-85; Member: Historic Buildings Council for

Wales, 1953- ; (Chm., 1977-); Royal Fine Art Commn, 1965-71; Redundant Churches Fund, 1969-78; Royal Commn on Historical Manuscripts, 1984- ; Council, Soc. of Army Historical Research; Trustee: Nat. Portrait Gall., 1979-90; Nat. Heritage Memorial Fund, 1980- ; Hon. Prof., UCW, 1986; FSA 1952; FRSL 1969; Hon.FRIBA, 1971; FRHistS, 1975; Anglesey: CC, 1951-67; JP, 1959-68,1983-89; DL, 1960; Vice-Lieut, 1960; Hon.Fellow, Royal Cambrian Acad. Freeman of the City of London, Hon. DLitt Wales 1984; CStJ 1984. *Publications:* (ed) The Capel Letters, 1814-1817, 1955; One-Leg: the Life and Letters of 1st Marquess of Anglesey, 1961; (ed) Sergeant Pearman's Memoirs, 1968; (ed) Little Hodge, 1971; A History of the British Cavalry, 1816-1919, vol I, 1973, vol II, 1975, vol. III, 1982, vol. IV, 1986. *Recreation:* Music, gardening *Address:* Plas-Newydd, Llanfairpwll, Anglesey, Gwynedd, LL61 6DZ.

ANGLESEY,Marchioness (Elizabeth) Shirley Vaughan Paget,DBE 1983 (CBE 1977). *Currently:* Vice-Chairman: Museums and Galleries Commn 1989- , (member since 1981). *Born on* 4 Dec 1924. *Daughter of* the late Charles Morgan and Hilda Vaughan (both novelists). *Marriage:* to Marquess of Anglesey, qv, 1948. *Children:* two s three d *Educated at* Francis Holland School, London; St James', West Malvern; Kent Place School, USA. *Career:* Personal Secretary to Gladwyn Jebb, FO, until marriage. Dep. Chairman, Prince of Wales Committee 1970-80. Member: Civic Trust for Wales 1967-76; Arts Council 1972-81 (Chairman, Welsh Arts Council 1975-81); Royal Commn on Environmental Pollution 1973-79; IBA 1976-82; Radioactive Waste Managment Advisory Committee 1981-91. Chairman, Drama and Dance Advisory Committee 1981-81, (member of Board since 1985), British Council; Chairman, Broadcasting Complaints Commission, 1987-91. Government Working Party on Methods of Sewage Disposal 1969-70. Chairman, NFWI 1966-69. Trustee, Pilgrim Trust 1982- . Hon.LLD Wales, Hon. Fellow Bangor UNW 1977. *Recreation:* theatre, Russia. *Address:* Plas-Newydd,Llanfairpwll,Gwynedd.

ANWYL-DAVIES, His Honour Judge Marcus John, Queen's Counsel *Currently:* One of Her Majesty's Circuit Judges. *Born on* 11 Jul, 1923 at London. *Son of* the late Thomas Anwyl-Davies MD, FRCP, and the late Kathleen Beryl (nee Oakshott). *Marriage:* 1st to Eva Paulson, 1954, one d, one s, (marriage dissolved); 2nd to Myrna Ruth Dashoff, 1983. *Children:* Eva Alexandra Cornel and Nicholas Thomas Gustav. *Educated at* Harrow School; Christ Church, Oxford. Career: Captain, Royal Artillery, including service with Hong Kong and Singapore RA, 1942-47, Mentioned in Despatches (World War II 1945). Called to the Bar, Inner Temple 1949. Queen's Counsel 1967. Legal Assessor Disciplinary Committees of the General Medical Council and General Dental Council 1969-72. Appointed Circuit Judge January 1972, Resident Judge St.Albans Crown Court 1977-82 and Liaison Judge to Herts Magistrates. Vice-President Herts Magistrates Association. President Council of H.M. Circuit Judges 1989. Associate Member Chartered Institute of Arbitrators 1992. *Publications:* Recreation: photography. *Clubs:* Reform. *Address:* 7 Pheasantry House, Jubilee Place, London SW3 3TQ.

ap EVANS,Capt. Humphrey,MC *Currently:* Author, Magazine Contributor, Farmer. *Born on* 18 Sept 1922 at Lovesgrove, Aberystwyth. *Son of* Major J.J.P. Evans, MBE, MC and Viola M. Robinson. *Marriage:* to Cherry Drummond of Megginch, 16th Baroness Strange, 1952. *Children:* Adam, Charlotte, Humphrey, Amelie, John and Catherine. *Educated at* Eton; Trinity College Cambridge. *Career:* Carmarthen LDV and Home Guard 1939, 1st mountain Regt 1941-46; General Secretary CPRW (Cymdeithas Diogelu Harddwch Cymru) 1947-50; Welsh Representative National Trust 1949-54; Chairman Society of Authors (Scotland) 1975-81; Founder and Master Kilspindie Basset Hounds 1953-66; Founder and Proprietor The Historical Press; Proprietor The Scottish Salmon Fisheries. Photo journalist. *Publications:* Hist. Biog: The Queen's Man; Our Man in Scotland; The King's Enemy; Falconry; Falconry For You; Falconry in the East etc. Recreation: Pre-Raphaelitism, mechanical musical instruments, heavy horses. *Clubs:* Garrick. *Address:* Megginch Castle, Errol, Perthshire, PH2 7SW. 160 Kennington Road, Lambeth, London, SE11 6QR

ap ROBERT,His Hon. Judge Hywel Wyn Jones,MA Oxon. *Currently:* County Court Judge (Circuit Judge). *Born on* 19 Nov 1923 at Pontyberem. *Son of* Y Parch. Robert John Jones, B.A., B.D. and Mrs Jeanette Jones, B.Sc. (nee Evans). *Marriage:* to Elizabeth Davies, 1956. *Children:* Catrin Elisabeth Maelor and Lowri Elisabeth Maelor Carling. *Educated at* Cardiff High School; Corpus Christi College, Oxford; Middle Temple; Indian Military Academy. *Career:* Cardiff Bar, 1950-72; Stipendiary Magistrate, (Cardiff, then South Glamorgan), 1972-75; Circuit Judge, 1975- ; County Court Judge, Mid Glam, West Glam and Powys, 1984- ; War Service, Intelligence Corps (Britain and India)and Foreign Office. *Recreation:* Welsh and classical literature, languages. *Clubs:* Cardiff and County *Address:* Law Courts, Cardiff.

ap THOMAS,Mrs Gwyneth, *Currently:* self-employed. *Born on* 29 Oct 1937 at Bangor. *Daughter of* the late Ifan and the late Jane Jones. *Marriage:* to Dafydd ap Tomos, 1971 (qv). *Children:* Barry, Lynda, Joseff, Gwyn and Carrog. *Educated at* Caernarfon Grammar School. *Career:* Artist and Gallery owner. since 1979, together with husband Dafydd ap Tomos, devoted time and energy to restore and reinstate 'Plas Glyn-y-Weddw', Llanbedrog as a major art venue which is now open to the public. *Recreation:* any form of art. *Clubs:* Soroptomist International (South Caernarfonshire). *Address:* Plas Glyn-Y-Weddw, Llanbedrog, Pwllheli, Gwynedd, LL53 7TT. Tel: 0758 740 763

Ap TOMOS,Mr Dafydd, *Currently:* Art Gallery proprietor (self-employed). *Born on* 2 Nov 1938 at Bangor. *Son of* David Thomas and the late Mary Thomas. *Marriage:* 1971. *Children:* Barry, Lynda, Joseff, Gwyn and Carrog. *Educated at* Ysgol Dyffryn Nantlle. *Career:* Devoted time since 1979 to restore and reinstate Plas Glyn-y-Weddw, Llanbedrog, as a major Art Centre which is now open to the public. *Recreation:* rugby, music, reading. *Clubs:* Pwllheli Rugby. *Address:* Plas Glyn-Y-Weddw, Llanbedrog, Pwllheli, Gwynedd, LL53 7TT. Tel: 0758 740763

ARCH, Charles John,FRAg.S. Churchill Fellow. *Currently:* Director, Wales Agricultural Training Board, since 1990. Comentator at Agricultural Events. *Born on* 3 March 1935 at Strata, Florida. *Son of* the late Thomas and Margaret Arch. *Marriage:* to Mari Osborne Jones. *Children:*

Mererid Osborne and Ifer Osborne. *Educated at* Tregaron Grammar School. *Career:* Farming at Strata, Florida to 1963; YFC Organiser for Montgomeryshire 1963-69; NFU Area Secretary, Tregaron Area 1969-70; Agricultural Trainer Adviser 1970-90. *Publications:* A Study of The Hill Farming Problems in Scandinavia and Europe (part of Churchill Fellowship). *Recreation:* play writing, sheepdog training. *Address:* ATB Wales Office, Rwas Showground, Llanelwedd, Builth Wells, LD2 3SY. Fflur, Pennal, Machynlleth, Powys, SY20 9JT

ARMFIELD, Miss Diana Maxwell, RA(Elect)., RWS., RWA., NEAC, RCA. *Currently:* Painter. *Born on* 11 June 1920 at Ringwood, Hants. *Daughter of* Joseph J. Armfield and Gertrude Mary (nee Uttley). *Marriage:* to Bernard Dunstan RA. *Children:* Andrew Joseph, David James and Robert Maxwell. *Educated at* Bedales School; Bournemouth Art School; Slade School; Central School of Arts & Crafts. *Career:* Textile Designer 1949-65; Taught Central School & Byam Shaw Art School; Lectured, Artist in Residence, Perth, Australia; Jackson Hole, Wyoming, USA; Commissions from HRH Prince of Wales, National Trust, Reuters and others; work in V & A Permanent collection (Textiles); Nat. Trust; Govt: Picture Collection; Yale Centre for British Art; Lancaster County Museum; Contemporary Art Soc. for Wales; and many collections at home and abroad; British Museum; selected exhibitions: Tegfryn Art Gall, Anglesey 1965 & 78; Browse & Darby (Lond) 1979, 81; Stremmel Gallery Reno, Nevada 1981; Bruton Gallery, Somerset; Royal West of England Academy, Bristol 1982; Eisteddfod Swansea 'Invited artist' 1982; Browse & Darby (Lond) 1984; Perth, Western Australia 1985; NEAC Centenary Exhib., Sotherby 1986; Browse & Darby (Lond); Albany Gall; Nat. Trust, The Long Perspective 1987; Oriel 31 Gall. in Newtown & Welshpool (combined retrospective with Bernard Dunstan) 1988; Browse & Darby (Lond) 1990; Featured artist Jonleigh Gall., Guildford, 1991. *Publications:* written for Art mags (Editorial Board) contributed to many Art Publications, Studio Vista, Phaidon, Collins, Quarto etc. *Recreation:* Gardening and music. *Clubs:* Arts Club (Dover St) *Address:* Llwynhir, Parc Bala, Gwynedd, North Wales. LL23 7YU. 10 High Park Road, Kew Gardens, Richmond, Surrey, TW9 4BH

ARMSTRONG, Dr. David Alun, BSc (Wales) PhD (Liverpool) *Currently:* Staff Tutor - Technology at The Open University in Wales. *Born on* 14 Mar 1943 at London. *Son of* the late Rev Trefor H. Armstrong and Mrs Doreen Armstrong. *Marriage:* to Gwendoline Mary Robbins 1971. *Children:* Ruth, Sian and Steffan. *Educated at* Bishop Gore Grammar School, Swansea; University College of North Wales; University of Liverpool *Career:* University Scholarship, 'Steel Company of Wales, 1961; Welsh Laboratories, British Steel, 1968-81. *Publications:* Several in the field of work roll metrology for the metal rolling and paper industries. *Recreation:* Carving Welsh Love Spoons, music and swimming. *Address:* The Open University, 24 Cathedral Road, Cardiff CF1 9SA. 21 Bessant Close, Cowbridge, S. Wales CF7 7HP

ARNOLD, Malcolm, *Currently:* British Athletic Federation National Coach Wales, since 1974. *Born on* 4 April 1940 at Northwich, Cheshire. *Son of* the late Colin William Arnold and Jane Arnold. *Marriage:* Madelyn Morrissey. *Children:* Helen (b.1964) and Andrew (b.1966). *Educated at*

Loughborough University 1958-61. *Career:* Teacher of Physical Education: Marple Hall Grammar School, Stockport 1961-64; Rodway School, Bristol 1964-68; Director of Athletics Coaching, Uganda 1968-72; Hessle High School 1973. *Publications:* Six titles on Athletics *Recreation:* rally driving *Address:* 56 Rolls Avenue, Penpedairheol, Hengoed, Mid Glamorgan, CF8 8HQ.

ARTHUR, Professor Geoffrey Herbert, DVSc., FRCVS *Currently:* Regional Postgraduate Veterinary Dean for West and S.West England and South Wales. *Born on* 6 March 1916 at Llangibby, Nr Usk. *Son of* William Gwyn and Ethel Jesse. *Marriage:* to Lorna Isabel Simpson, 1948. *Children:* Angela, Richard, Hugh, Charles and James. *Educated at* Abersychan Secondary and Liverpool University. *Career:* Lecturer in Veterinary Medicine, Liverpool Univ. 1941; Professor of Veterinary Obstetrics, London University 1976; Professor of Veterinary Surgery, Bristol University 1973; Clinical Veterinary Professor, King Faisal University, Saudi Arabia 1980. *Publications:* Veterinary Reproduction and Obstetrics *Recreation:* Animal welfare in North Africa *Clubs:* Royal College of Veterinary Surgeons *Address:* Fallodene, Stone, Allerton, Axbridge Som., BS26 2NH. Tel: 0934 712 077

ARTHUR, His Hon. Judge John Rhys, DFC., MA., JP. *Currently:* H.M. Circuit Judge since 1975. *Born on* 29 April 1923 at London. *Son of* John Morgan Arthur and Eleanor Arthur (nee Rees). *Marriage:* to Joan Tremearne Pickering, 1951. *Children:* 2 sons, 1 daughter *Educated at* Mill Hill School; Christ's College, Cambridge *Career:* RAF 1942-46; Cambridge 1946-48; Called to Bar Inner Temple 1949; Ass. Recorder Blackburn Q.S. 1970; Dep. Chairman, Lancs Q.S. 1970-71; Recorder 1972-75. *Clubs:* MCC; Old Millhillians; Athenaeum (Liverpool); Cardiff Athletic Club. *Address:* Orovales, Caldy Road, Caldy, Wirral, L48 1LP.

ARTHUR, Roland William, MA (Cantab). *Currently:* Solicitor, Partner in Harding Evans, Newport. *Born on* 21 Dec 1938 at Redwick. *Son of* C.W. Arthur and E.O. Arthur. *Marriage:* to Margot. *Children:* Justine, Robin and Sarah. *Educated at* Monmouth School; St.Catharines, College, Cambridge. *Career:* Director/Secretary St.Davids Investment Trust plc. *Recreation:* golf, rugby. *Address:* Queens Chambers, North Street, Newport, Gwent, NP9 1TE. Tel: 0633 244233

ASHLEY, Mr Nick, *Currently:* Laura Ashley PLC since 1982. *Born on* 15 Jan 1957. at Limpsfield. *Son of* Laura Ashley and Bernard Ashley. *Marriage:* to Ari. *Children:* *Educated at* Machynlleth Primary School; Caersws School; Newtown High School. *Career:* St.Martin's School of Art, London 1979; Academi Julian School of Art, Paris 1980; Vogue Magazine London 1981; Tommy Nutter tailors, Savile Road, London 1982. *Recreation:* dirt bike racing. *Clubs:* Hafren Dirt Bike. *Address:* Tyn Y Cwm, Beulah, Powys. SY20 9LB. Tel: 0654 791 253

ASHTON, Mr Anthony Southcliffe, MA *Currently:* Retired *Born on* 5 July 1916 at Sheffield. *Son of* Professor T.S. Ashton FBA and Marion Hague Slater. *Marriage:* to Katharine Marion Louise Vivian. *Children:* Theresa Marion and Vivien Lucy. *Educated at* Manchester Grammar School; Hertford College, Oxford. *Career:* Civil Servant 1937-39; Army 1939-45; Asst. Financial Edit. Manchester Guardian 1945-47; NCB 1947-49; Oil Ind. (ended Finance Director, Esso Petroleum Co) 1949-69; Finance Mbr, Post Office

Corp 1969-74; Director, Provincial Ins. Co 1974-86; Chairman, Exeter Trust Ltd 1982-86; Mbr, Shipbuilding Ind. Board 1967-71; Director, Tyzack Ltd 1974-84; Course Director, Oxford Univ. Business School 1974; Mbr of Council, Manchester Business School 1968-81; Trustee, Post Office Pension Fund 1975-83; Vice-President, Hertford College Society 1977- . *Recreation:* Walking mountains and natural philosophy *Clubs:* Army & Navy; Campaign for the Protection of Rural Wales. *Address:* Quarry Field, Stonewall Hill, Presteigne, Powys LD8 2HB.

ASTALL, Mr John, F.C.A. *Born on* 25 Dec 1950 *Marriage:* yes. *Children:* 2 *Address:* Finance Director, Manweb plc, Sealand Road, Chester CH1 4LR

ASTOR, Bronwen Viscountess Astor Janet Bronwen Alun, *Currently:* Analytical Psychotherapist. *Born on* 6 June 1930 at London. *Daughter* of Sir Alun and Lady Pugh. *Marriage:* to Third Viscount Astor, 1960. *Children:* Janet March (Countess) and The Hon Pauline Case. *Educated at* Dr.Williams School, Dolgellau, Merioneth. *Career:* Elocution teacher (trained at Central School of Speech and Drama). Model Girl at Balmain Paris. *Recreation:* windsurfing, tennis, fishing. *Address:* Tuesley Manor, Godalming, Surrey, GU7 1UD.

ATKINS, Professor Anthony George, BSc, MA, PhD, ScD, FIMechE, FIM, CEng. *Currently:* Professor of Engineering, University of Reading. *Born on* 10 Oct 1939 at Cardiff. *Son of* the late Walter George Atkins and Emily Irene (nee Aldridge). *Marriage:* to Margaret Ann Proud. *Children:* Philip George, Richard James and Margaret Ruth. *Educated at* Canton High School, Cardiff; University College Cardiff; Trinity College Cambridge. *Career:* Research Fellow and Exeter College Lecturer, University of Oxford; Research Engineer, US Steel Corporation, Pittsburgh; Associate Professor of Engineering, University of Michigan, Ann Arbor, USA; Research Manager, Delta Group. *Publications:* over 100 papers in Learned journals; 'Strength and Fracture of Engineering Solids'; 'Elastic and Plastic Fracture'; 'Manufacturing Engineering'; A history of GWR Goods Wagons. *Recreation:* music, skiing, GWR history, carpentry. *Address:* White House, Heads Lane, Inkpen Common, Newbury, Berks RG15 OQS.

AULD, Margaret Gibson, RGN RM., MPhil., Hon.DSC., FRCN., CBIM *Currently:* Retired. *Born on* 11 July 1932 at Cardiff. *Daughter of* the late Eleanor Margaret Ingram and the late Alexander John Auld. *Educated at* Glasgow, Cardiff High School for Girls; Edinburgh University. *Career:* Student nurse Radcliffe Infirmary, Oxford; Midwifery, Cardiff and Blackburn; Midwifery Sister,

Cardiff Hosp; Matron, Simpson Memorial Maternity Pavillion; Chief Area Nursing Officer Borders Health Board; Chief Nursing Officer, Scottish Office Home & Health Dept., *Publications:* How Many Nurses-Kent Publications; many articles in Nursing and latest Health Publications, Quality, Who Says What?; Midwives Chronicle, to be published "early 1992". *Recreation:* Reading and cooking *Address:* Staddlestones, Neidpath Road, Peebles. EH45 8NN.

AXWORTHY, Mr Geoffrey John, M.A. Oxon *Currently:* Retired Theatre Director; Board member Sherman Theatre. *Born on* 10 Aug 1923 at Plymouth, Devon. *Son of* William Henry Axworthy and Gladys Elizabeth Kingcombe. *Marriage:* 1) Irene Dickinson (d1975) 2) Caroline Ann Griffiths. Children: Carole, Timothy, Nigel, Eliza and Christopher. *Educated at* Sutton High School, Plymouth; Exeter College, Oxford. *Career:* WWII RAFVR, 1942-47; Tutor Oxford Delegacy for Extra-Mural Studies, 1950-51; Lecturer, College of Arts and Sciences, Bagdad, 1951-56; Lecturer, Univ. Coll., Ibadan, Nigeria, 1956-60; Appointed Director of Drama, 1960; Founder Director of Univ. of Ibadan School of Drama and Travelling Theatre; Principal, Central School of Speech and Drama, London, 1967-70; Dir., of Drama, Univ. Coll., Cardiff, 1970-88; First Artistic Dir., Sherman Theatre, 1973-88. *Recreation:* Travel and meeting people; anything to do with the Arts; directing plays, particularly new ones. *Address:* 22 The Walk, West Grove, Roath, Cardiff CF2 3AF. C/o Sherman Theatre, Senghennydd Road, Cardiff CF2 4YE

B

BACK, Dr Paul Adrian Auchmuty,BSc, DPhil, FICE, FEng *Currently:* Director, Sir Alexander Gibb & Partners, responsible for design and site supervision of Cardiff Bay Barrage. *Born on* 30 May 1930 at Grahamstown, S.Africa. *Son of* Adv and Mrs A.W.Back, Q.C. Marriage: to Jacqueline Sarah (nee Hide). *Children:* Jonathan, Rupert and Nicholas *Educated at* St.Andrew's College; Captetown University; Oxford (Trinity). *Career:* joined Sir Alexander Gibb from Oxford in 1955. Worked on the design of thermal power stations joined the hydro department to work on the design of the Kariba Dam in Central Africa. He spent three years at site during its construction. Since then he has devoted his professional life to major hydro electric projects around the World, including the Victoria and Samanalawewa hydro electric projects in Sri Lanka. He has acted on Panels for both the World Bank and the Kuwait Fund and is a member of Panel I under the U.K. Reservoir Safety Act (1930) and its successor (1975). He was appointed by the U.K. Overseas Development Administration to investigate the failure of Kantalai Dam in Sri Lank and was recently in charge of a major review of all large dams in the country. He has served on the British National Cttee on Large Dams (BNCOLD) for a total of 9 years and was the Fellowship of Engineering representative on the SERC Cttee dealing with joint industrial/university research projects. He is a member of the Advisory Board to the Engineering Faculty of Bradford University and an external examiner.He was elected to the Council of the Institution of Civil Engineers in 1989. He has been the keynote speaker at the A.G.M. of the British National Cttee on Large Dams. He was invited to give the first Geoffrey Binnie lecture to the British Dam Society and was also the Guest Speaker at the Sri Lanka Association for the Advancement of Science in 1989. Member of an advisory panel for the Katse Dam and transfer tunnel in Lesotho and the geotechnical and prefeasibility studies for the proposed Batoka Gorge hydro scheme. *Publications:* contributed a number of papers to learned societies; Leisure Design Study of a Double Curvature Arch Dam, ICE 1969; The Victorian Project Sri Lank, ICE 1991. *Recreation:* sailing *Clubs:* RAF, Piccadilly, London *Address:* Parsonage Farm,How Lane,White Waltham,Berks,SL6 3JP. C/o Sir Alexander Gibb & Ptnrs,Earley House,London Road,Reading, Berks,RG6 1BL

BADHAM, Mr Douglas George,CBE., JP., KStJ., FCA. *Currently:* Retired. *Born on* 1 Dec 1914 at Aberdare. *Son of* David Badham JP & Edith Badham. *Marriage:* to Doreen Spencer Phillips, 1939. *Children:* Edith Anne and Mary Victoria *Educated at* Leys School, Cambridge *Career:* Lord Lt. for Mid Glam 1985-89; Mer Majesty's Lt. for Mid Glam, 1982-85; Deputy Lt. for Mid Glam, 1975-82; Magistrate County of Glamorgan, 1962; High Sheriff for Mid Glamorgan, 1976; Director: World Trade Centre Wales Ltd., Hamill (West) Ltd.,(Chairman); Past Directorships: Dev. Copr for Wales, 1965-83 (Chmn 1971-80); Powell Duffryn Group (Exec Dir), 1938-69; Telecomm. Board Wales & The Marches, 1973-80; Welsh Council (Chmn Ind. & Planning Panel), 1971-80; Welsh Dev. Agency, 1978-85, (deputy chmn 1980-85); Nat. Health Serv., staff adv. cmmt for Wales, 1974-77; Btsh Conservancy Council Adv. Cmmt for Wales, 1974-77; Btsh Gas Corp, 1974-83; Btsh Railways (Western) Brd, 1977-82; Economic Forestry Group PLC, 1978-88 (Chmn 1981-88); Forestry Comm., S. Wales Adv. Cmmt, 1946-76 (Chmn 1973-76); UWIST Council Mbr, 1975-80. *Recreation:* Forestry *Clubs:* Cardiff & County Club *Address:* Swyn-Y-Coed, Watford Road, Caerphilly, Mid Glamorgan CF8 1NE.

BAELZ,The Very Reverend Peter Richard,D.D. *Currently:* Retired. *Born on* 27 July 1923 at London. *Son of* the late Eberhard Baelz and the late Dora Baelz (nee Focke). *Marriage:* to Anne Thelma Cleall-Harding, 1950. *Children:* Simon Richard Alec, Nicholas Charles and Timothy Francis. *Educated at* Dulwich College; Christ's College, Cambridge. *Career:* Asst. Curate of Bournville, 1947-50; Asst. Curate of Sherborne, 1950-52; Asst. Chaplain of Ripon Hall, 1952-53; Rector of Wishaw, Birmingham, 1953-56; Vicar of Bournville, 1956-60; Dean of Jesus College, Cambridge, 1960-72; Canon of Christ Church, Oxford and Regius Professor of moral and pastoral theology in the University of Oxford, 1972-79; Dean of Durham Cathedral, 1980-88. *Publications:* Prayer and Providence, 1968; The Forgotten Dream, 1975. *Recreations:* Cycling, reading and watching my wife gardening. *Address:* 36 Brynteg, Llandrindod Wells, Powys. LD1 5NB. Tel: 0597 825404

BAGOT, 9th Baron and 14th Baronet (1627) Heneage Charles, *Born on* 11 June 1914 at Rochford House, Tenbury, Worcs. *Son of* Charles Heneage and Lorina Bagot. *Marriage:* to Patricia Moore-Boyle. *Children:* Caroline Patricia and Charles Hugh Shaun. *Educated at* Harrow *Career:* Ex-Indian Army (Gurkhas); Plantation interests (Ceylon). Documents in Latin relating to familys' connection with Wales date back to 1243. *Publications:* Skis in India. *Recreation:* Sailing, shooting, skiing. *Clubs:* Himalayan Club; Alpine Ski Club. *Address:* Tyn-Y-Mynydd, Llithfaen, Gwynedd, LL53 6PD. 16 Barclay Road, London, SW6

BAGULEY,Mr Frank Sidney Sudbury,LDS (Bristol) *Currently:* Retired Dental Surgeon. *Born on* 20 Nov 1915 at Dowlais. *Son of* the late Frank Sudbury Baguley and Mabel Baguley (nee Hughes). *Marriage:* to Ella Watson, 1945. *Children:* Douglas Ronald Frank *Educated at* Neath Grammar School; Bristol University *Career:* Principal/

Senior School & Community Dental Officer with Aberdare UDC, 1938; Glamorgan C.C., 1946; Merthyr Tydfil County Borough, 1952; Mid Glamorgan Health Auth., 1972; Major in the Army Dental Corp during World War II; Hon. Sec. of Cambrian Caving Council since 1972; Hon. Sec. of National Caving Assoc., since 1982; Chairman Outdoor Pursuits Group of the Welsh Sports Assoc., since 1978; Mbr of several commtts. of the Sports Council for Wales. *Publications:* Cambrian Caving Council journals Nos. 1-18. *Recreation:* Motor engineering, gardening, DIY, caving and outdoor pursuits, conservation. *Address:* White Lion House, Ynys Uchaf, Ystradgynlais, Swansea, SA9 1RW. Tel: 0639 849519

BAILEY, Mrs Gwendoline Ridgeway, *Currently:* Managing Director of: Golley Slater Recruitment Ltd; Group Recruitment Services; Golley Slater Telephone Marketing; Golley Slater Training. *Born on* 3 April 1937 at Blundellsands, Lancs. *Daughter of* the late Arthur Ridgeway-Ball and Sarah Gladys (nee Balmer). *Marriage:* to Graham Whitney Bailey, son of the late Capt. Charles Bailey, O.B.E. *Children:* Mark Henry Arthur (Barrister, MA Oxon) and Joanna Tracy (decd). *Educated at* Merchant Taylor's School for Girls; Liverpool College of Art. *Career:* Television Wales & West, Granada TV 1960-62; Thomson Regional Newspapers 1964-70; Director Golley Slater Group 1971-; Board member Ogwr Partnership Trust; Board member Mid Glamorgan Training and Enterprise Council. *Recreation:* boating, painting, piano, singing, food and wine. *Clubs:* Mid-Thames Motor Boat and Yacht; River Thames Society. *Address:* 9-11 The Hayes, Cardiff, CF1 1NU.

BAKER, Professor Colin, MBE, BA, LLB, M Phil, DPA, PhD, FRGS. *Currently:* Professor and Head of Department of Business and Administrative Studies, The Polytechnic of Wales 1974- , and Professor of Business Studies, The Institute of Education, Business College, Dublin. *Born on* 3 Aug 1929 at Beccles, England. *Son of* Arthur Walter Baker and Doris Kathleen Baker (nee Ward). *Marriage:* to Shirley Foale 1956. *Children:* Daryll Marc, Lynette Elizabeth (and one son deceased). *Educated at* Sir John Leman School; Universities of Birmingham and London. *Career:* Colonial Administrative Service, Malawi, Under Secretary, Cabinet Office, 1954-62; Principal, Institute of Public Administration, University of Malawi, 1962-71; Director, Institute of Administration, University of Ife, Nigeria, 1971-74. *Publications:* Over 70 Articles in learned journals; Training for Public Administration, The English Press 1969, xi pp134 (Editor); Johnston's Administration: A History of the British Central Africa Administration, The Zomba Press, 1971, pp134; Education and Research in Public Administration in Africa, ed with A. Adedeji, Hutchinsons, 1974, pp425; The Evolution of Local Government in Malawi, University of Ife Press, 1975, pp60; Essays in Public Administration, ed with M.J. Balogun, University of Ife Press, 1975, pp187. *Recreation:* Research - African Administrative History. *Clubs:* Corona. *Address:* Mpemba, 55a Lon Y Deri, Rhiwbina, Cardiff CF4 6JP

BAKER, Dr (John) Harry Edmund, BSc, MB BS, MRCP. *Born on* 8 Jan 1949. *Son of* the late Joseph Elmer Grieff Baker, and Mary Irene Elizabeth. *Educated at* Epsom College, The Middx Hospital Medical School Univ of London. *Career:* Major RAMC TA, specialist pool HQ AMS, British Army Trauma Life Support Team, chief medical adviser ACFA/CCFA, lately DADMS (TA) HQ W Mid Dist; lecturer University of Nottingham Medical School 1976-77, registrar Nat Hospital for Nervous Diseases 1977-80, senior registrar Nat Spinal Injuries Centre Stoke Manderville 1980-83, Midland Spinal Injury Centre Oswestry 1983-85, consultant in spinal injuries and rehabilitation med S Glamorgan Health Authority and Welsh Health Common Services Authority 1985-, consultant adviser in rehabilitation Dept of Social Security Nat Pensions Office, pubns in med jnls on immediate care and emergency handling of spinal co injury, mgmnt of spinal injuries at accident sites, accident and disaster med; asst. surgeon in chief St John Ambulance Bde, chm Professional Panel St John Aero Med Servc, vice chm Wales and member Exec Board (UK) British Assoc of Socs of Immediate C member Med Bd of St. John Ambulance (Priory for Wales); Member Joint Royal Colleges Committee Panel for Trauma. med adviser Nat Rescue Trg Cncl; member Cncl: Int Soc of Aeromedical Servs, Int Med Soc of Paraplegia, World Assoc of Emergency and Disaster Med; conslt advsr to Conjoint Ctee of the Voluntary Aid Socs; advsr and lectr in mngmnt of spinal cord injury to: Fire Servs, NHS Trg Authy, Ambulance Serv, Med Equestrian Assoc, Various Equestrian bodies, RAC, MSA, various other motor sports orgns, Mountain Rescue Team, RLSS; CStJ 1988; Fell NY Acad Sci (USA) 1988. *Publications:* Management of Mass Casualties (contrib 1980). *Address:* 56 Bridge St, Llandaff, Cardiff CF5 2EN. Rookwood Hospital, Fairwater Road, Cardiff CF5 2YN

BAKER, Sir (Thomas) Scott (Gillespie), *Currently:* Judge of the High Court, since 1988. *Born on* 10 Dec 1937 at London. *Son of* the late, The Rt Hon Sir George Baker and Lady Baker (nee Findlay). *Marriage:* to (Margaret) Joy Strange, 1973. *Children:* Ross, Katrina and Gordon. *Educated at* Haileybury; Brasenase, Oxford. *Career:* Barrister 1961; Q.C. 1978; Bencher, Middle Temple 1985; Presiding Judge Wales and Chester Circuit 1991-. Member of the Warnock Committee on Human Fertilisation 1982-84. *Recreation:* golf, fishing, shooting. *Clubs:* M.C.C. *Address:* Royal Courts Of Justice, Strand, London WC2A 2LL.

BALCHIN, Emeritus Professor William George Victor, MA(Cantab); PhD.(London); FKC *Currently:* Theoretically retired but continuing in active geographical work - writing, consultation etc. *Born on* 20 June 1916 at Aldershot, Hampshire. *Son of* Victor Balchin and Ellen Winifred Gertrude Chapple. *Marriage:* to Lily Kettlewood, 1939. *Children:* Peter Malcolm, Joan Margaret (deceased) and Anne Catharine. *Educated at* Aldershot County High School (State & County Major Scholar); St. Catharine's College, Cambridge; Kings College London. *Career:* Junior Demonstrator in Geography, Univ. of Cambridge, 1937-39; Hydrographic Officer, Hydrographic Dept., Admiralty, 1939-45; Lecturer in Geography, King's College, London, 1945-54; Prof. & Head of Dept., of Geography, Univ. Coll., of Swansea, 1954-78, (Foundation Professor); Dean Faculty of Pure & Applied Science, Swansea, 1959-61; Vice Principal Univ. Coll., Swansea, 1964-66 & 1970-73; Emeritus Prof. of Geography, Swansea, 1978; Fellow of King's Coll., London, 1984. *Publications:* Geography & Man (3 vols) 1947 - Editor; Climatic & Weather Exercises (with A.W.

Richards) 1952; Cornwall, making of the English Landscape. 1954; Geography, outline for the Intending Student, 1970; Swansea and its Region, Editor and Contributor, 1971; Living History of Britain, Editor and Contributor, 1981; Concern for Geography, 1981; The Cornish Landscape, 1983; together with over 200 research papers, articles and contributions in the fields of geomorphology, climatology, hydrology, economic geography and cartography in learned journals. *Recreation:* Travel and writing *Clubs:* Royal Commonwealth and Geographical *Address:* 10 Low Wood Rise, Ben Rhydding, Ilkley, West Yorks., LS29 8AZ.

BALFOUR, Mr Robert Peter, MB, ChB, FRCOG, DTMIH *Currently:* Consultant Obstetrician & Gynaecologist, Princess of Wales Hospital, Bridgend. *Born on* 5 Nov 1942 at Liverpool, UK. *Son of* the late Peter Balfour and Evelyn (nee Murgatroyd). *Marriage:* to Jean Margaret (nee Faram), 1965. *Children:* Sharon, David and Jonathan *Educated at* Liverpool Institute; Liverpool University. *Career:* Junior medical posts in Liverpool; Vom Christian Hospital Nigeria; Bangor and Cardiff. Chairman, Federation of Pro-Life Doctors; Member, Parliamentary Pro-Life Scientific Committee. *Address:* Heddfan, Marine Walk, Ogmore-By-Sea, Bridgend, CF32 OPQ.

BALL, Anthony George (Tony), MBE (1986). *Born on* 14 Nov 1934. *Son of* Harry Clifford Ball, of Bridgwater, Somerset and Mary Irene Ball. *Marriage:* to Ruth, 1957, da of Ivor Parry Davies (d.1976) of Mountain Ash, S.Wales. *Children:* Kevin, Michael and Katherine. *Educated at* Bridgwater GS; Bromsgrove Coll of Further Education. *Career:* indentured engineering apprentice Austin Motor Co 1951, responsible for launch of Mini 1959, sales manager Austin Motor Co 1962-66, sales and marketing exec BMC 1966-67, chairman Barlow Rand UK Motor Group 1967-68 (MD Barlow Rand Ford S.Africa 1971-73 and Barlow Rand Euro Ops 1973-78), MD Br Leyland Overseas Trading Ops 1978-82; dir: BL Cars, BL International, Rover Triumph, Austin Morris, Jaguar Cars, Jaguar Rover Triumph Inc (USA) and BL overseas subsidiaries; chairman Nuffield Press 1978-80, chairman and MD BL Europe and Overseas 1979-82, World Sales Chief BL Cars 1979-82 (responsible for BL's Buy British campaign and launch of Austin Metro 1980); chief exec Henlys plc 1982-84; chairman: Tony Ball Assocs plc (marketing, product launch and sales promotion agency). Tony Ball Consultants; dep chm Lumley Insurance; dir: Customer Concern Ltd, Jetmaster UK, Jetmaster Int Ltd; Billy Marsh Associates Ltd; Billy Marsh Organisation; Freeman City of London 1980; Liveryman: Worshipful Co of Coach Makers and Coach Harness Makers 1980, Worshipful Co of Carmen 1983; hon.FCIM 1981 (for launch of Metro and servs to British motor industry); hon mem City & Guilds of London (for educational and vocational servs 1982), 1984 Prince Philip Medal for Mktg Achievement and Servs to Br Motor Indust; mktg advsr to Sec of State for Energy 1983-87; responsible for UK dealer launch of Vauxhall Astra for Gen Motors; launches for: Mercedes-Benz, Fiat, Proton, Lada, Leyland DAF, Bedford, GM Europe; mktg adviser to Sec of State for Wales 1987-91; Responsible for creating 'Wales-Land of Quality' theme and logo for Welsh Office; responsible for arranging WRU International sponsorship 1983-1992; Responsible for staging launch and opening ceremonies Rugby World Cup 1991; Appointed by SMMT for marketing, presenting and

promoting British International Motor Show 1992; *Publications:* Contributions to "Tales out of School", 1984, "Better Business Presentations", 1986. A Study of the Marketing of the Welsh Craft Industry, 1988. *Recreation:* military history, theatre, after-dinner speaking, sharing humour. *Clubs:* Oriental *Address:* Blythe House, Bidford-On-Avon, Warwicks B50 4BY. 249 Grove End Gardens, Grove End Road, St John's Wood, London, NW8 Tel: 0712 860899

BALL, Michael Ashley, *Currently:* Actor/Singer. *Born on* 27 July 1962 at Bromsgrove, Worcs. *Son of* Tony and Ruth Ball (nee Parry Davies) of Mountain Ash, Glam. *Educated at* Plymouth College; Farnham 6th Form College. *Career:* Surrey Youth Theatre "Undermilk Wood" and "The Boy Friend" 1980-81; Graduated with Diploma, Guildford School of Drama 1981-84; First professional appearance as John The Baptist/Judas in "Godspell" at Arts Theatre, Aberystwyth, N.Wales 1984. Frederick in "Pirates of Penzance", Opera House Manchester 1985. Coronation Street for Granada TV 1985. West End debut created the role of Marius in original production of "Les Miserables"at Barbican and Palace Theatre 1985-87; Royal Shakespeare Player 1985. Record, original London Cast album of "Les Miserables" awarded Platinum Disc for record sales. UK Tour "The Music of Andrew Lloyd Webber" with Sarah Brightman 1987; Raoul in "Phantom of The Opera", Her Majesty's Theatre London 1987-88; Created the role of Alex in original London production of "Aspects of Love" 1988-90 and Broadway 1990. Records: Original London Cast album of Aspects of Love. Solo recording "Love Changes Everything", awarded silver disc for record sales. Also recorded "The First Man you Remember" with Diana Morrison and "Rage of the Heart" album. Signed recording contract with Polydor Records 1991. Solo recording "Its Still You". Countless TV and Radio broadcasts include "Wogan", "Top of the Pops", Aspel, Gloria Hunniford Show, Save the Children Xmas Spectacular and awarded "Most Promising Artiste 1991", by Variety Club of Gt.Britain. Appeared in 2 Royal Variety Command Performances and also children Royal Variety Performance. International concerts in LA., "A tribute to Andrew Lloyd Webber", as well as appearances in Moscow, Hawaii and Royal Fesitval Hall London with the RPO. Chosen to represent Britain in Eurovision Song Contest 1992. *Recreation:* music, charity work, unwinding in the countryside. *Address:* C/o James Sharkey Associates, Golden Square, London.

BALL, Rev. George Raymond, B.A. *Currently:* Vice Chairman Dyfed County Council; Officiating Chaplain to Castlemartin RAC Ranges. *Born on* 24 Jan 1915 at Llandyssul, Cards. *Son of* Frederick Henry Ball and Rachel Ball. *Marriage:* to Pauline Cunniffe, 1950. *Children:* Christopher; Stephen; David and Anthony *Educated at* Llandyssul Grammar School; Llandrindod County Sch; Lampeter College. *Career:* Curate at Llansamlet, 1942-46; Townhill, Swansea, 1946-50; Rector of Bosherston & Vicar of St. Twynnels, Pembroke 1950-85; H.M. Chaplain's Department O.C.F. Castlemartin 1951-65 and 1990 to date; also attached to Pembroke Yeomanry, 1952-63; Boy Scout movement 1925-80 ending as District Scout Leader, Pembroke. *Recreation:* Crosswords, all sports and psychology *Clubs:* Pembroke Yeomanry Dinner Club

Address: 1 Meadowbank, St. Twynnells, Pembroke, Dyfed, SA71 5HZ.

BANKS, Philip Francis, BSc *Currently:* A.T.Kearney Inc, Chicago, Illinois, USA. *Born on* 27 Aug, 1933 at Harrow. *Son of* William and Winifred Banks. *Marriage:* to Judith Monica (nee Marren). *Children:* Jessica Sarah Bridget Webster. *Educated at* Finchley Grammar; London University. *Career:* Vice President International at Kearney Inc; Managing Director at Kearney Ltd; Marketing Director, James Wilkes Ltd; Management Trainee, Unilever. Prospective Parliamentary Candidate, Wrekin Const.1972. Chairman UK Management Consultants Assoc. *Recreation:* reading, music. *Clubs:* Les Ambassadeors, London, Landsdowne, London, Metropolitan, Chicago. *Address:* Kearney's, Lon Edynfed, Criccieth, Gwynedd Luxborough House, Luxborough Street, London W1M 3LE

BANTON, Professor Michael Parker, JP., PhD., DSc. *Currently:* Professor of Sociology, University of Bristol, 1965-92. *Born on* 8 Sept 1926 at Birmingham. *Son of* Francis Clive and Kathleen Blanche (nee Parkes). *Marriage:* to Rut Marianne (nee Jacobson), of Lulea, Sweden. *Children:* Sven Christopher, Ragnhild Cecilia, Lars Nicholas Clive and Dagmar Hulda. *Educated at* King Edward's School, Birmingham; London School of Economics. *Career:* Pro-Vice-Chancellor, Univ. of Bristol, 1985-88; Pres., Royal Anthropological Inst., 1987-89; Mbr, Royal Commsn on Criminal Procedure, 1978-80; Mbr, Royal Commsn on Bermuda, 1978; Mbr UN Commt on the Elimination of Racial Discrimination, 1986-94. *Publications:* include West African City, 1957; The Policeman in the Community, 1964; Roles, 1965; Racial and Ethnic Competition, 1983; Promoting Racial Harmony, 1985; Investigating Robbery, 1985; Racial Theories, 1987; Racial Consciousness,1988. *Address:* The Court House, Llanvair Discoed, Gwent. NP6 6LX.

BARKER,Professor, Dr, Mr Geoffrey Ronald,MSc, BSc, MB, BS, BDS, FDS, FRCS, LRCP *Currently:* Medical Director, Astra Pharmaceuticals Ltd. *Born on* 4 April 1943 at Coventry. *Marriage:* divorced. *Children:* Peter, Jacqueline, Simon and Matthew. *Educated at* Bishop Veseys Grammar School Sutton Coldfield; Guy's Hospital Medical & Dental Schools 1963-73. *Career:* Principal medical practitioner, medical adviser and part-time dental practitioner for the Channel Islands of Alderney and Guernsey. Lecturer/ Senior Lecturer in Oral & Maxillofacial Surgery and Oral Medicine: University of Birmingham; University of Manchester Medical & Dental Schools; Professor and Honorary Consultant in Oral & Maxillofacial Surgery, University of Wales College of Medicine. *Publications:* refereed journals over 40. Abstracts over 30. Invited lectures (overseas Hong Kong, Scandinavia, Germany, Canada, Spain, Hungary, Cyprus) 20. U.K. 20. *Recreation:* golf, travel, walking, gardening. *Clubs:* Army & Navy, CO 372 MFS T (RAMC(V). *Address:* 14 The Grove, Chesham Bois,Bucks, HP6 5LJ. 87 Green Pastures, Heaton Mersey, Stockport, Cheshire, SK4 3RB.

BARNES, Mr James Frederick,CB, MA. *Currently:* Stewardship Adviser, Diocese of Monmouth, since May 1989. *Born on* 8 March 1932 at Calverley, Yorkshire. *Son of* the late Wilfred Barnes and the late Doris Martha Barnes. *Marriage:* to Dorothy Jean Drew, 1957. *Children:* Amanda, Richard and Elizabeth. *Educated at* Almondbury Grammar School; Taunton's School, Southampton; The Queen's College Oxford. *Career:* Engine Division, Bristol Aeroplance Company 1953-54; National Gas Turbine Establishment, Farnborough 1955-70; Ministry of Aviation Supply 1970-72; Counsellor (Scientific), British Embassy Washington 1972-74; Ministry of Defence 1974-78; Royal Aircraft Establishment, Farnborough 1978-79; Deputy Secretary, Ministry of Defence 1979-89. Governor, Yateley Manor School 1980- ; Trustee, Roger Williams & Queen Victoria Almshouses 1990- ; Member, Monmouth & Llandaff Housing Association 1991-. *Publications:* Scientific papers in learned journals and books. "Christian Stewardship-Principles & Practice", 1992. *Recreation:* making things, gardening, local history. *Address:* Monmouth Diocesan Office, 64 Caerau Road, Newport, Gwent, NP9 4HJ.

BARNETT, Kenneth Thomas,CB (1979) *Currently:* Director, Abbey Data Systems Ltd., since 1984. *Born on* 12 Jan 1921 at Cardiff. *Younger son* of the late Frederick Charles and the late Ethel Barnett (nee Powell). *Marriage:* to Emily May Lovering, 1943. *Children:* Lynne Carole. *Educated at* Howard Gardens High School, Cardiff. *Career:* Deputy Secretary, Department of The Environment 1976-80. Entered Ministry of Transport 1937; Service in RAF 1941-46; Executive Officer, Sea Transport 1946-51; Accountant Officer and Secretary to Divisional Sea Transport Officer, Middle East, Port Said 1951-54; Higher Executive and Senior Executive posts, Roads Divisions 1954-61; Principal, Finance Division 1961-65; Assistant Secretary, then Under Secretary, Ports 1965-71; Under Secretary Cabinet Office (on secondment) 1971-73; Housing Department of the Environment 1973-76, Deputy Secretary Housing 1976-80. *Recreation:* rugby, gardening, property upkeep, crosswords, reading. *Address:* The Stone House, Frith End, Nr. Bordon, Hampshire, GU35 ORA. Tel: 0420 472856

BARNIE,Dr John Edward,MA., PhD. *Currently:* Co-Editor of Planet - The Welsh Internationalist since 1990. *Born on* 27 March 1941 at Abegavenny, Gwent. *Son of* the late Edward Charles Barnie and the late Melva Jean Barnie. *Marriage:* to Helle Michelsen. *Children:* Talfan Donald Barnie. *Educated at* King Henry VIII's Grammar School, Abergavenny; Birmingham & Nottingham Universities. *Career:* Lecturer in English and American Literature, Univ. of Copenhagen, 1969-82; Hon. Fellow, Center for Southern Folklore, Memphis, Tennessee, 1979; Assistant Editor, Planet, 1985. *Publications:* War in Medieval Society, 1975; Lightning Country, 1987; The King of Ashes, 1989; The Confirmation, 1992. *Recreation:* Natural history; blues and gospel music and gardening *Societies:* Mbr of Yr Academi Gymreig and Harry Martinson-Sallskap *Address:* Greenfields, Comins Coch, Aberystwyth, Dyfed.

BARNISH, Mr Alan Joseph, B.Comm; IPFA. *Currently:* Chief Executive & County Treasurer, Powys County Council. *Born on* 13 Oct 1949 at Preston,Lancashire. *Son of* Sydney and Dora. *Marriage:* to Elizabeth Sanders, 1972. *Children:* Ian and Clare. *Educated at* Hutton Grammar School, Lancs; Leeds University. *Career:* Accountant, London Borough of Sutton 1971-73; Accountant, City of Swansea 1973-75; Accountant, West Glamorgan County Council 1975; Deputy County Treasurer, Mid Glamorgan County Council 1975-90. *Address:* 'Great House', Newbridge On Wye, Powys LD1 6HT. Tel: N.O.W. 350

BARNSLEY, Mr Thomas Edward, OBE(1975)., FCA., ACMA *Currently:* Retired *Born on* 10 Sept 1919 at Wednesbury. *Son of* Alfred E Barnsley and Ada F. (nee Nightingale). *Marriage:* to Margaret Gwyneth Llewellin, 1947. *Children:* Thomas Malcolm and Victoria *Educated at* Wednesbury Boys High School *Career:* Ch., Raleigh Industries, 1968-74; MD, Tube Investments, 1974-82; Dir, H.P. Bulmer Holdings, 1980-87; Ch. Industrial National Savings Committee, 1972-76. *Recreation:* Gardening, music and listening *Clubs:* Sloane *Address:* The Old Rectory, Llanelidan, near Ruthin, Clwyd, LL15 2PT.

BARON COHEN, Gerald,BA, FCA. *Currently:* Chartered Accountant; Director Calders of Cardiff; Jothams Ltd; Morris Cowan (Baron Suits) Ltd. *Born on* 13 July 1932 at London. *Son of* the late Morris Baron Cohen and Miriam. *Marriage:* to Daniella Naomi,Dip Soc, 1962, da of Dr.H.I. Weiser, Tel Aviv. *Children:* Jonathon Ammon (b.1964), Erran Boaz (b.1968) and Sacha Noam (b. 1971). *Educated at* Radyr Elementary School; Whitchurch Grammar; Canton High School; University of Wales, Cardiff. *Career:* Co. Director ed Mosaic 1960-62; Dep ed New Middle East 1967-68; past president Bnai Brith First Lodge 1979-80 (nat treasurer 1984); Vice Chairman Hillel Foundation 1970- ; past vice chairman Union Jewish Students; chairman Bamah Forum for Jewish Dialogue; FCA 1954. *Publications:* Editor ''The Cantonian''; editor ''Outrage'' (University of Wales ''Rag'' mag) 1950-51. *Address:* C/o 760 Finchley Road, London NW11 7TH.

BARRETT, Mr David Neil, BAHons (Wales) 1968. *Currently:* District Manager for South Wales, Post Office Counters Ltd, 1986-. *Born on* 30 June 1947 at Chelmsford, Essex. *Son of* Lionel Wilson Barrett and Eva Maud Barrett. *Marriage:* to Linda Peregrine, 1972. *Children:* Graham and Kevin. *Educated at* Doncaster Grammar School, 1958-65; Univ. Coll., Swansea, 1965-69. *Career:* Joined Post Office 1969; Assist. Head Postmaster, Swansea 1978-83; Assist. Head Postmaster, Cardiff, 1983-85; Head Postmaster, Newport, 1985-86. *Recreation:* Sport, playing cricket, music and theatre. *Clubs:* Newport Fugitives Cricket Club. *Address:* 4 Vanbrugh Close, Rogerstone, Newport, Gwent, NP1 ODF.

BARRIT, Mr Desmond, *Currently:* Playing Toad in ''Wind In The Willows'' at National Theatre. *Born on* 19th Oct 1944 at Swansea. *Son of* Gwyneth and Islwyn Brown.Marriage: .Children: *Educated at* Garw Grammar School *Career:* Olivier Award Best Comedy for ''3 Men On A Horse''; Clarence Derwent Award for Trinculo in ''The Tempest'' at the RSC; West End appearances in ''The Scarlet Pimpernel'', ''The Respectable Wedding'', ''The Liar''; National Theatre appearances in ''The Magistrate'', ''Jacabowsky and the Colonel'', ''3 Men On A Horse'', ''Wind In The Willows'', and ''The Recruiting Officer''; with the Royal Shakespeare Company ''Macbeth'', ''The Tempest'', ''Twelfth Night'', ''King Lear'', ''Comedy of Errors'', ''Constant Couple'', ''The Man Who Came To Dinner'' *Publications:* Included in numerous books including ''Conversations with Jonathan Miller'', ''Faces of British Theatre'' *Recreation:* Antiques and Gardening, Charity Work including Macmillan Nurses, Samaritans, Lighthouse, Children in Need; Started the ''Richard Haines Charitable Trust'' *Address:* 114 Mapledene Road, Hackney, London E8 3LL. 18 Heol Llan, North Cornelly, Pye, Glamorgan,

BARTLETT, Keith, *Currently:* Consultant radiotherapist, ARI Aberdeen, since 1979. *Born on* 10 June 1944. *Son of* the late Charles Windsor Bartlett and Olive May Bartlett. *Marriage:* to Lilian Mary, 1968, da of Alan Oakley Davis (d.1988). *Children:* Paul Andrew (b.1974), Nicola Ann (b.1969) and Andria Louise (b.1970). *Educated at* Pontllanfraith GS; Welsh Nat School of Medicine (MB.BCh). *Career:* Consultant radiotherapist, University Hospital Saskatoon Saskatchewan 1976-78, Wolverhampton 1978; Locum GP Wordsley W Midlands 1978-79. Winner of Zworykin Prize for paper on Bioengineering (Inst of Electrical Engineers) 1989; member: Panel of Specialists in Radiotherapy, Scot Breast Trials Steering Committee Edinburgh; director Radiotherapy Res Group Aberdeen; initiated Radio-Frequency Hyperthermia Scotland 1980, immuno modulation for breast cancer 1990; DMRT 1972, FRCR 1976. *Recreation:* music, live recording, car maintenance, target shooting, electronics. *Address:* Granville, 58 Victoria St, Dyce, Aberdeen, AB2 OEE. Radiotherapy & Oncology Dept, Aberdeen Royal Infirmary Tel: 0224 681818

BARTON, Martin, FCA *Currently:* Partner in Bartons, Chartered Accountants. *Born on* 7 May 1944 at Merthyr Tydfil. *Son of* Walter Barton and the late Sadie (nee Shipman). *Marriage:* to Jeanette, 1969, da of Arran Lermon (d.1988). *Children:* David (b.1970) and Susannah (b.1972). *Educated at* Quakers Yard GS, nr Cardiff; County G.S., Merthyr Tydfil. *Career:* Articled Clerk, Leyshon & Lewis CA's, Merthyr Tydfil 1963-68; Partner Curitz Berg & Co 1971 (joined 1970); formed own practice Barton Felman & Co 1979 (Barton Felman & Cotsen 1981, Barton Cotsen & Co 1983, Bartons 1990) *Recreation:* bridge, ice hockey, badminton. *Clubs:* Cardiff Bridge Club. *Address:* 15 Ty Gwyn Crescent, Penylan, Cardiff CF2 5JL. Bartons, Chartered Accountants, Lermon Court, Fairway House, Links Business Park, St.Mellons, Cardiff CF3 OLT Tel: 0222 777756

BARWICK, Stephen Royston, *Currently:* Professional Cricketer. *Born on* 6 Sept 1960 at Neath. *Son of* Margaret and Roy. *Marriage:* to Margaret Ann. *Children:* Michael Warren *Educated at* Cwrt Sart Comprehensive; Dwr-y-Felin Comprehensive. *Recreation:* watching football, rugby. *Clubs:* Glamorgan CCC.*Address:* C/o Glamorgan C.C.C., Sophia Gardens, Cardiff.

BASSETT,Dr Douglas Anthony,BSc; PhD; FMA. *Currently:* retired. *Born on* 11 Aug 1927 at Llanelli. *Son of* Hugh Bassett and Annie Jane Bassett. *Marriage:* to Elizabeth Menna Roberts 1954. *Children:* Sara, Sian and Lynne. *Educated at* Llanelli G.S. for Boys; Univ. Coll. of Wales, Aberystwyth. *Career:* Lecturer, University of Glasgow 1954-59; Keeper of Geology, National Museum of Wales 1959-77 (Director 1977-85); Chairman, Committee for Wales, Water Resources Board 1968-73; Chairman, Advisory Committee for Wales, Nature Conservancy Council 1973-85; Founder Chairman 1967; Association of Teachers of Geology; Founder Member and Director, National Welsh-American Foundation 1980-87, 1990- ; Member, Ordnance Survey Committee 1978-80; Hon. Professorial Fellow, University of Wales College of Cardiff 1977- ; Hon. Research Fellow, National Museum of Wales 1986- ; Honours: Officer de L'Ordre des Art et des Lettres 1984; Silver Medal, Czechoslovak Society for International Relations

1985; Aberconway Medal, Institute of Geologists 1985. *Publications:* Articles in various scientific periodicals on geology and the history of geology and on museums. *Recreation:* music. *Address:* 4 Romilly Road, Canton, Cardiff, CF5 1FH.

BAXTER,Mr Keith,Bronze Medal (RADA) *Currently:* Actor/Playwright. *Born on* 29 April 1933 at Newport, Gwent. *Son of* Stanley Baxter Wright and Emily Marian Howell. *Educated at* Newport High School; Barry Grammar School; Royal Academy Dramatic Art. *Career:* After repertory work at the Oxford Playhouse, his first appearance in London was at the Comedy Theatre in "Tea And Sympathy". Further London appearances were in "Phedre"; "Change of Tune"; "Time and Yellow Roses". He played Prince Hal in Belfast and in Dublin, with Orson Welles as Falstaff, in Welles's production of Shakespeare's "King Henry IV" Histories. He won the New York "Theatre World" Award as Most Promising Actor for his first appearance on Broadway as King Henry VIII in "A Man For All Seasons" with Paul Scofield. He remained in New York to play in "The Affair". Returning to England he played Gino in E.M. Forster's "Where Angels Fear To Tread". He joined Ralph Richardson's company at the Haymarket Theatre to play Valentine in "You Never Can Tell" and Bob Acres in "The Rivals". At Chichester he was Horner in "The Country Wife" with Maggie Smith, and Octavius Caesar in "Antony And Cleopatra" with Margaret Leighton and John Clements. He created the role of Milo in "Sleuth" with Anthony Quayle, both in London and New York where he won the Drama Desk Award and the Outer Circle Critics' Award. In England he was "Macbeth" at Birmingham and Benedick in "Much Ado About Nothing" at the 90th Anniversary of the Royal Lyceum Theatre in Edinburgh. He was Vershinin in "Three Sisters" at Greenwich. At Chichester he was Rico in Pirandello's "Tonight We Improvise". He directed and played the lead in Tennessee Williams's "Red Devil Battery Sign" at the Phoenix Theatre. At Stratford, Ontario he played opposite Maggie Smith in "Antony And Cleopatra"; as Witwoud in "The Way Of The World" and as Vershinin in "Three Sisters". At Chichester he was Lord Illingworth in Wilde's "A Woman of No Importance" and Dorante in Marivaux's "The Inconstant Couple"; on Broadway was in Christopher Isherwood's "A Meeting by the River"; at the Kennedy Centre he played in Maughams's "Home and Beauty" with Rosemary Harris and Jose Ferer; returned to Canada to play "Hamlet"; in New York was seen as Holmes in "The Penultimate Case of Sherlock Holmes and in Bernard Slade's "Romantic Comedy"; with the Hartford Stage Company was Friedrich in "Undiscovered Country", and Edmund Kean in Sartre's "Kean", both directed by Mark Lamos; was the Narrator in Stsrvinsky's opera "Oedipus Rex" with Jessye Normanat the Philadelphia Opera House; played the twin brothers in the thriller "Corpse!" in London, on Broadway and in Australia; was in "Light up the Sky!" at the Globe Theatre; directed Priestley's "Time and the Conways"; was Elyot in Coward's "Private Lives" at the Aldwych Theatre; with the Hartford Stage he was Cassius in Mark Lamos's production of "Julius Caesar"; played in his own first play "56 Duncan Terrace" in Canada; second play "Cavell" was seen at Chichester with Joan Plowright; appeared in his third play "Barnaby and the Old Boys" at the

Vaudeville Theatre; has appeared many times on television and his films include Orson Welles's "Chimes at Midnight"; "La Regenta"; "Ash Wednesday" with Elizabeth Taylor; "Golden Rendezvous"; and "Berlin Blues" with Julia Migenes. *Publications:*"Barnaby and The Old Boys". *Recreation:* The Sea. *Address:* ICM, 388/396 Oxford St, London, W1N 9HE. ICM, 40 West 57th Street, New York, New York 10019

BAYNES,Lt.Col. Sir John Christopher Malcolm (7th Baronet),M.Sc. *Currently:* Author; Partner Lake Vyrnwy Hotel. *Born on* 24 April 1928 at Bath. *Son of* Lt.Col. Sir Rory Baynes, Bt and the late Mrs Bayns. *Marriage:* to Miss S.M. Dodds, 1955. *Children:* Christopher, Timothy, Simon and William. *Educated at* Sedbergh School; RMA Sandhurst; Edinbugh Univ. *Career:* Regular Army 1946-72; Joint owner Lake Vyrnwy Hotel 1972-87. *Publications:* Seven books of Military & General History. *Recreation:* Shooting, walking and reading *Clubs:* Army and Navy, London *Address:* Talwrn Bach, Llanfyllin, Powys, Mid Wales, SY22 5LQ. Tel: (069 184) 576

BEALE, Mr John, MA.,MEd.,DipEd.,FRSA.,FIL. *Currently:* Director of Education, West Glam County Council. *Born on* 26 Aug 1930 at Swansea. *Son of* the late Elizabeth Anne and Wilfred. *Marriage:* to Joan Mary Beale (nee Godsall), 1952. *Children:* Janet, Andrew and Judith *Educated at* Dynevor Grammar School; Leeds University *Career:* Teacher, 1952-62; Deputy Ed. Officer, 1962-64; Director of Education, Merthyr Tydfil, 1964-74; Past mbr of Equal Opportunities Commission, Sports Council for Wales, 1974- *Recreation:* Sport, walking and reading *Address:* 4 Clos Bryn Dafydd, Penllergaer, Swansea, W. Glam., SA1 3SN. West Glamorgan County Hall, Swansea SA1 3SN

BEALES, Mr Ian Michael, *Currently:* Editor of the Western Daily Press. *Born on* 16 July 1944 at Writtle, Essex.. *Educated at* The Sweyne School, Rayleigh, Essex. *Career:* Deputy Editor of the Western Daily Press 1970-80; Vice Chairman of Parliamentary and Legal Committee of the Guild of British Newspaper Editors. *Recreation:* gardening *Address:* The Knapp, Nympsfield, Stroud, Gloucestershire

BEARDMORE, Professor John Alec, Univ. of Helsinki Medal 1980; PhD.,CI.Biol.,FI.Biol *Currently:* Professor of Genetics and Head of School of Biological Sciences, Univ. Coll. of Swansea. *Born on* 1 May 1930 at Burton on Trent. *Son of* George Edward Beardmore and Anne Jean (nee Warrington).Marriage: to Anne Patricia Wallace 1953.Children: Anne Virginia, James Wallace, Hugo John and Charles Edward. *Educated at* Burton-on-Trent Grammar School; Birmingham Central Technical College; Univ of Sheffield (1st class Honours 1953) *Career:* Research Demonstrator Univ. of Sheffield, 1954-56; Harkness Fellow, Columbia Univ. N.Y.,USA, 1956-58; Visiting Assist. Prof. Cornell Univ.,USA, 1958;Lctr in Genetics, Univ. of Sheffield 1958-61; Rsrch Assoc., Rochester Univ.,USA, 1961; Prof. of Genetics, Univ. Groningen, Netherlands, 1961-66; NSF Fellow Pa.State Univ, USA 1966; Univ. Coll.Swansea: Prof. of Genetics 1966- , Head Genetics Dept. 1966-87; Dir. Inst. Marine Studies, 1983-87; Head School of Biol. Sciences 1988- ; Dean of Science 1974-76; Vice Principal 1977-80; Mbr of Council 1971-74, 1986-89, 1991- ; Univ. of Wales: Chrmn Biological Sciences subject panel 1991- ; Mbr Joint

Planning & Resources Commt 1991- ; Manager ODA Fish Genetics research programme 1990- ; Mbr: NERC Aquatic Life Scis. Cmmt., 1982-87 (Chm 1984-87). CNAA: Life Scis Cmmt, 1979-85; Cmmt for Science, 1985-87 Res. Cmmt A 1986- ; Bd. Council of Sci. & Technology Insts., 1983-85; (Chm 1984-85); Cncl, Galton Inst. 1980- ; (Chm Res. Cmmt., 1979-87); Cncl, Linnean Soc., 1989- ; MAFF CFRD Fish Genetics Group 1987- ; Btsh Nat. Cmmt for Bioogy, 1983-87; Inst. of Biology: Council, (Vice Pres. 1986-89; Hon.Sec. 1980-85); Council of European Commtts Biologists Assoc. 1980-87. *Publications:* Ed. with B. Battaglia Marine Organisms: Genetics, Ecology, Evolution; Plenum 1977. Many papers in Scientific journals on Evolutionary genetics, human genetics and fish genetics. *Recreation:* Bridge, walking and treasurer Swansea Abbeyfield Society *Clubs:* Athenaeum *Address:* 153 Derwen Fawr Road, Swansea SA2 8ED

BEAUMONT, William Anderson,CBE 1986; OBE (mil) 1961; AE 1953. *Born on* 30 Oct 1924 *Son of* the late William Lionel Beaumont and Mrs E.Taverner. *Marriage:* 1st to Kythe, 1946 (d 1988), d of the late Major K.G.Mackenzie, Victoria, BC; 2nd to Rosalie, 1989,widow of Judge Michael Underhill, QC. *Children:* one d (from 1st marriage). *Educated at* Terrington Hall, York; Cranleigh School (Entrance Exhibitioner); Christ Church, Oxford (MA, DipEd). *Career:* Speaker's Secretary, House of Commons 1982-86. Served RAF, Navigator, 1942-47, 355 Sqdn, 232 Sqdn, SEAC (Flt Lt); RAuxAF 3507 (Co. of Somerset) FCU, 1948-54; 3609 (W.Riding) FCU, 1954-61 (Wing Commander CO, 1958-61); Observer Commander, No.18 (Leeds) Group, Royal Observer Corps 1962-75 (ROC Medal 1975). Assistant Master, Bristol Grammar School 1951-54; Beaumont and Smith Ltd, Pudsey 1954-66 (Managing Director 1958-66); Henry Mason (Shipley) Ltd (Managing Director 1966-76); Principal, Welsh Office 1976-79; Asst.Secretary, Welsh Office 1979-82. Director, St.David's Forum 1986- ; Secretary, Prince of Wales Award Group 1987-90. FRSA 1977. *Recreation:* inland waterways, reluctant gardening, walking. *Clubs:* Royal Air Force; Civil Service; United Services Mess (Cardiff). *Address:* 28 Halford Road, Richmond, Surrey TW10 6AP. Tel: 081 940 2390

BEAUMONT, Mr Christopher Hubert, MA., Barrister *Currently:* Barrister; Recorder of the Crown Court since 1981; Chairman Agricultural Land Tribunal, Eastern Area since 1985. *Born on* 10 Feb 1926 at London. *Son of* Hubert Beaumont, M.P., and Beatrix Beaumont. *Marriage:* 1) to Catherine Clark (d.1971), 2) Sara Patricia Magee. *Children:* Simon, Guy and Justine. *Educated at* West Monmouth School, Pontypool; Balliol College,Oxford, *Career:* Served RN, 1944-47 (Sub-Lt.RNVR); Called to Bar, Middle Temple, 1950; Asst. Dep. Coroner, Inner West London, 1963-81; Dept.Chmn.,Agric. Land Tribunal, Eastern Area, 1979-85. *Publications:* Law Relating to Sheriffs, 1968; Town and Country Planning Act, 1968 (1969); Town and Country Planning Acts 1971 and 1972, (1972); Land Compensation Act, 1973 (with W.G. Nutley, 1973); Community Land Act, 1975 (with W.G. Nutley, 1976); Planning Appeal Decisions (jt.ed.with W.G. Nutley, in series from 1986-) *Address:* Rose Cottage, Lower Eashing, Godalming, Surrey. GU7 2QG. 2 Harcourt Buildings,Temple,London EC4Y 9DB Tel: 071 353 8415

BEAVEN,Mr John Lewis,CMG.,CVO. *Currently:* Retired. Part-time United States representative, Save the Children Fund. *Born on* 7 July 1930 at Newport, Gwent. *Son of* Charles Beaven and Doris Margaret Beaven (nee Lewis). *Marriage:* 1st to Jane Leigh Beeson, 1960 (diss. 1975); 2nd to Jane McComb Campbell, 1975. *Children:* Jacqueline Leigh and Christopher Gerard. *Educated at* Durham Road Elementary School, Newport; Newport High School. *Career:* Board of Trade 1947; RAF 1948-90; Second Secretary Pakistan 1956-60; Sierra Leone 1961-64; First Secretary Cyprus 1964-67; Kenya 1967-69; Foreign & Commonwealth Office 1969-72; Head of Chancery Jakarta 1972-74; Economic Counsellor Lagos 1975-78; Deputy Consul General New York 1978-82; Consul General San Francisco 1982-86; Ambassador to Sudan 1986-90. *Recreation:* Computing, walking, music, tennis. *Clubs:* Reform; The Brook, New York. *Address:* Scannell Road,Ghent, NY 12075,USA, Tel: 05183922152

BEDINGFIELD,Mr Christopher Ohl Macredie,TD., QC., MA. *Currently:* Queen's Counsel; Recorder. *Born on* 2 June 1935 *Son of* the late Norman Macredie Bedingfield and Mrs Peggy Macredie Bedingfield.*Educated at* Rugby School, Univ. Coll., Oxford *Career:* Admitted Gray's Inn 1948; Recorder 1972; Queen's Counsel 1976; Bencher of Gray's Inn 1986; Shaw Scholar and Lee Prizeman; T.A. Officer, 2 Monmouthshire Regt. and Royal Welch Fusiliers; County Commandant and Lt.Col. Denbigh and Flint/Clwyd ACF 1973-76. *Clubs:* Bristol Channel Yacht Club; Reform. *Address:* 21 Whitefriars, Chester. CH1 1NZ. Nantygroes, Knighton, Powys LD7 1NP

BEER, Professor Stafford,MBA., LL.D., FRSA *Currently:* Research Professor in Managerial Cybernetics, European Business Management School, University of Wales, Swansea; Visiting Professor Manchester & Durham Business Schools; Adjunct Professor of Education, University of Toronto; Hon.Professor of Organizational Transformation, Liverpool Business School. *Born on* 25 Sept 1926 at London. *Son of* Doris Ethel and the late William John Beer. *Marriage:* 1). to Cynthia Margaret Hannaway, 2). to Christine Sallie Steadman (nee Child). *Children:* 1st marriage: Jane Francesca, Simon St. John, Mark Dominic, Stephen Leo and Matthew Giles; 2nd marriage: Kate, Polly Persephone and Harry Cosmo. *Educated at* Whitgift Sch; University Coll., London. MBA Manchester. *Career:* Lieut, 9th Gurka Rifles 1945; Captain Royal Fusiliers 1947; Man. of Operational Res. and Prodn Controller, S.Fox & Co., 1949-56; Head of Op. Res. and Cybernetics, United Steel, 1956-61; Man. Dir, SIGMA Science in General Management Ltd and Dir. Metra International 1961-66; Develt Dir, International Publishing Corp., Dir, International Data Highways Ltd; Chm, Computaprint Ltd 1966-69; Advisor in Cybernetics to Ernst and Whinney (Canada) 1970-87; Dir, Metapraxis Ltd (UK) 1984-87; Chm, Viable Systems Internat (USA) 1987-88; Vis.Prof. of Gen. Systems, Open Univ., 1970-71; Scientific Dir, Profect Cybersyn Chile 1971-73; Co-Dir, Project Urucib, Uruguay 1986-87; Ex-Pres., Operational Res.Soc., Ex-Pres., Soc for Gen. Systems Res (USA); Pres., World Orgn of Systems and Cybernetics (formerly of Gen.Systems and Cybernetics), 1981- ; Mem.UK Automation Council 1957-69; Mem. Gen. Adv. Council of BBC 1961-69; Governor, Internat. Council for Computer Communication 1973- ; Hon. Chm, The Stafford Beer

Foundn 1986- ; FWA 1986; Hon. Fellow, St.David's UC, Wales 1989, also Chairman of the Advisory Board for Continuing Education; Hon. LLD Concordia, Montreal 1988; Silver Medal, Royal Swedish Acad. for Engrn Scis 1958; Lanchester Prize (USA) for Ops Res., 1966; McCulloch Award (USA) for Cybernetics 1970; Wiener Meml Gold Medal for Cybernetics, World Orgn of Gen. Systems and Cybernetics 1984. *Publications:* Cybernetics and Management 1959; Decision and Control 1966; Management Science 1967; Brain of the Firm 1972 (new edn. 1981); Designing Freedon 1974; Platform for Change 1975; Transit (poems) 1977, extended edn 1983; The Heart of Enterprise 1979; Diagnosing the System for Organizations 1985; Pebbles to Computers: the thread 1986; To Someone or Other (paintings) 1988; chapters in numerous other books. *Recreation:* spinning, yoga, classics, staying put. *Clubs:* Athenaeum. *Address:* Cwarel Isaf, Pont Creuddyn, Llanbedr Pont Steffan Dyfed. 34 Palmerston Square, Toronto, Ontario, Canada, M6G 2S7 Tel: 416 535 0396

BELLI,Dr Anna-Maria,MBBS, FRCR. *Currently:* Senior Lecturer and Consultant Radiologist, The Royal Postgraduate Medical School, since 1990. *Born on* 5 Aug 1957 at Swansea. *Daughter of* Bartolomeo Belli and Carmen Belli (nee Lumbardelli). *Marriage:* to Mr Baird Michael John Pugsley. *Educated at* Glanmor Grammar School, Swansea; Bishopgore Secondary Comprehensive School, Swansea; Middlesex Hospital Medical School, London. *Career:* Medical training, The Middlesex Hospital Medical School, University of London 1975-80; Consultant/Senior lecturer in Radiology, The University of Sheffield 1987-90. *Publications:* contributions to text books: Laser-Assisted Angioplasty in "Pros and Cons in PTA and Auxiliary Methods", ed. Zeitter and Seyferth 3rd edition 1989; Laser - assisted Angioplasty using the Thermal Hybrid Laser Probe: Techniques, Results and Indications in "Endovascular Surgery", ed. Moore and Ahn, 1st edition 1989; numerous review articles and oriiginal scientific papers on percutaneous transluminal angioplasty techniques. *Recreation:* fly fishing, reading, travel. *Address:* Dept Of Radiology, Royal Postgraduate Medical Sch, Hammersmith Hospital, Du Cane Road, London W12 ONN.

BELLIS,Mr John Herbert,LL.B. *Currently:* Chairman, Industrial Tribunals, Manchester, 1984- . *Born on* 11 April 1930 at Bangor. *Son of* Thomas and Jane Bellis. *Marriage:* to Sheila McNeil Ford, 1961. *Children:* Nicholas, Mark and Linda *Educated at* Friars Grammar School, Bangor; Liverpool Univ. *Career:* National Service, 1953-55, 2/Lt. The Welch Regt; Liberal Parliamentary Candidate, Conwy, 1959; Solicitor, Private Practice, John Bellis & Co, Penmaenmawr, Llanfairfechan, Llandudno, 1958-84. *Recreation:* Golf; walking; gardening and horse racing. *Address:* Heron Watch, 148 Grove Lane, Cheadle Hulme, Cheadle, Cheshire SK8 7NH. Alexandra House, Parsonage, Manchester.

BENNETT,Mr Phillip,O.B.E. *Currently:* Sports Development Officer, Llanelli Borough Council. *Born on* 24 Oct 1948 at Llanelli. *Son of* Robert and Mary. *Marriage:* to Pat. *Children:* Steven John and James John *Educated at* Felinfoel C.P., Coleshill Secondary Modern. *Career:* (Sport) Llanelli Schoolboys, Llanelli, Wales, Barbarians, British Lions.DuPort Steel, Llanelli Radiators, Courage Brewers and Dimex Chemicals. *Publications:*Everywhere for Wales

(Sports Autobiography) *Recreation:* Following my sons in their sport. *Clubs:* Felinfoel Cricket, Llanelli RFC and Felinfoel FRC *Address:* Villa Lago,Swiss Valley,Llanelli,Dyfed SA14 8EJ. Llanelli Borough Council, Town Hall,Llanelli,Dyfed

BENNETT,Rt.Hon Sir Frederic (Mackarness),Kt.1964; P.C. 1985; MP. *Currently:* Retired Member of Parliament/ Barrister. *Born on* 2nd Dec 1918 at London. *Son of* Sir Ernest Bennett, (M.P.Cardiff Central 1929-45)and Lady (Marguerite Bennett, nee Kleinwort). *Marriage:* to Marion Patricia Burnham 1945, e d of Cecil Burnham, OBE, FRCSE. *Educated at* Westminster *Career:* Served War of 1939-45, enlisted Middx Yeo., 1939; Commissioned RA 1940; Commended for gallantry 1941; Military Experimental Officer in Petroleum Warfare Dept 1943-46. Lt.Col. TA&VRA, 1973-83. Called to English Bar, Lincoln's Inn, 1946, Southern Rhodesian Bar, 1947. Military Observer, Greek Communist War, 1947-49; Diplomatic Correspondent, Birmingham Post, 1950-52. Contested (C) Burslem, 1945; Ladywood Div. of Birmingham, 1950; MP (C) Torbay, 1955-87 (Reading N. 1951-55. PPS to Under-Sec of State, Home Office, 1953-55; to Minister of Supply, 1956-57, to Paymaster-General, 1957-59, and to Pres. Bd of Trade, 1959-61. Hon. Treas, Chm. Exec. Cttee, CPA Gen. Council 1958-73. Leader UK Delegation and Vice President Council of Europe and WEU Assembly, 1979-87; Chm. Europ, Democratic Political Group, Council of Europe and CD, ED&RPR Federated group, WEU. Former Director: Kleinwort, Benson (Europe) SA. Director: Bristol-Myers, Squibb; Commercial Union Assurance (London West End Board); Gibraltar Building Society. Hon. Vice-President R.H.B. Trust Co Ltd., (Grand Cayman). Lord of the Manor of Mawddwy; Freeman - City of London, 1984; Hon. Doctor of Law, Istanbul, 1984. Commander, Polonia Restituta, Poland, 1977, Grand Commander's Cross, 1984, Ordr. of Polonia Restituta (First Class (1990); Cmdr. Order of Phoenix, Greece, 1963; Star of Pakistan (Sithari), First Class, 1964; Order of Al-Istiqlal, First Class (Jordan) 1980; Order of Isabell-la-Catolica, (Spain), 1982; Order of Hilali-Quaide-i-Azam, (Pakistan), 1983; Grand Cross - Order of Merit, (Germany) 1989; Deputy Lord Lieutenant of Greater London, 1990; Knightly Order of Vitez (Hungary), 1990. Founder Chmn.,Anglo-Pakistan Society *Publications:* Speaking Frankly, 1960; Detente and Security in Europe, 1976; China and European Security, 1978; The Near and Middle East and Western European Security, 1979, 2nd end 1980; Impact of Individual and Corporate Incentives on Productivity and Standard of Living, 1980; Fear is the Key (Northern Ireland); Reds under the Bed - or The Enemy at the Gate - and Within, 1979, 3rd edn 1982. *Recreation:* Shooting, fishing, yachting. *Clubs:* Carlton, Beefsteak, Anglo-Belgian, Royal Torbay Y.C.Member, CLA (Powys), Member, Montgomeryshire Society. *Address:* No. 2 Stone Buildings, Lincoln's Inn, London WC2A 3XB. Plas Cwmllecoediog, Aberangell, Nr. Machynlleth, Powys SY20 9PQ

BERNSTEIN, Ronald,DFC,QC. *Currently:* Arbitrator and Author. *Born on* 18 Aug 1918 at Pontypridd. *Son of* Mark and Fanny Bernstein. *Marriage:* to Dr. Judy Levi, MB, BS, DPH. *Children:* Mark, John, Sarah and Daniel. *Educated at* Swansea GS; UC of Swansea; Balliol Coll Oxford. *Career:* Commanded 654 Air O.P. Squadron RAF 1945; 661 Air

O.P. Squadron RAuxAF 1948-54; Barrister 1948- ; Q.C., 1969- ; Bencher, Middle Temple 1975- ; Vice-President, Chartered Institute of Arbitrators 1987-91; Vice President, Emeritus Chartered Inst. of Arbitrators 1991- ; Hon ARICS 1985; Hon.FSVA 1986;President, The Highgate Society 1985- . *Publications:* (joint) FOA, Landlord & Tenant; Handbook of Rent Review; Handbook of Arbitration Practice. *Recreation:* music, travel, computers. *Clubs:* Athenaeum *Address:* Falcon Chambers, Falcon Court, London EC4Y 1AA. Highgate Village, London N6 6BG

BEST,Dr Alfred Charles,CBE, DSc. *Currently:* retired, Director Met. Office Services 1966. *Born on* 7 March 1904 at Finchley, Middlesex.. *Son of* Charles William Best and Cecilia Best. *Marriage:* to Renee Margaret Parry 1932. *Children:* Brian Charles and Peter John. *Educated at* Barry Grammar School; Univercity College Cardiff. *Career:* Professional Assistant, Meteorological Office 1926, Shoeburyness 1926,Porton 1928, Air Min. 1933, Malta 1936, Larkhill 1939, Air Min.1940, Wing Comdr RAFVR, ACSEA 1945; Air Min 1945; Research 1945-54; Met. Office Services 1955-66. *Publications:* Physics in Meteorology 1957; Meteorological papers in journals. *Recreation:* photography.*Address:* 10 Flintgrove, Bracknell, Berks. RG12 2JN.

BEST,Mr Keith Lander,TD.,MA(Oxon) *Currently:* Director of Prisoners abroad.*Born on* 10 June 1949 at Brighton.*Son of* Peter Edwin Wilson Best and Margaret Louisa Best. *Marriage:* to Elizabeth Margaret Gibson, 1990. *Children*: Phoebe (daughter) b. 1991. *Educated at* Brighton College; Keble College, Oxford. *Career:* Barrister; Major 289 Parachute Battery, Royal Horse Artillery (Volunteers) and 289 Commando Battery (TA); Mbr of Parliament Anglesey (Ynys Mon) 1979-87; Parliamentary Private Sec. to Sec. of State for Wales. Chairman of the World Federalist Movement. Vice-Chairman, Conservative Action for Electoral Reform. *Publications:*Write your own Will; Probate - The Right Way to Prove a Will; various political articles *Recreation:* Being useful *Clubs:* St. Stephen's Constitutional club; Holyhead Conservative *Address:* 15 St Stephen'sTerr, London. SW8 1DJ.7 Alderley Terrace, Holyhead, Anglesey, Gwynedd, LL65 1NL

BETTINSON,Dr Christopher David, PhD, Chevalier des palmes academiques. *Currently:* Sen. Lecturer French, University of Wales College of Cardiff. *Born on* 5 Nov 1943 at Sudbury, Suffolk. *Son of* William Harold and Joan Leslie Bettinson. *Marriage:* 1). to Susan Minifie 1963; 2). to Emma James 1992. *Children:* Timothy, Nicholas and Jonathan. *Educated at* Sudbury Grammar School; University of Reading. *Career:* University of Glasgow 1966-74; University College,Cardiff 1974-89; University of Wales College of Cardiff 1989- . Elected South Glamorgan CC, Ty Glas Ward 1989. *Publications:* Gide: Les Caves du Vatican 1972, Andre Gide 1976; A Guide to European Studies Courses 1988. *Recreation:* Rugby, cricket, theatre, travel. *Clubs:* London Welsh Rugby Club, Glamorgan CCC. *Address:* Preswylfa, 17 Blenheim Road, Penylan, Cardiff, CF2 5DS.

BEVAN,County Councillor David Franklyn,CBE; FRSH *Currently:* County Councillor, Vice Chairman of West Glam County Council; Chairman of Council May 1992. *Born on* 17 June 1913 at Swansea. *Son of* Thomas Bevan and Mary Annie Bevan (nee Lewis). *Marriage:* to Annie Muriel Williams, 1942. *Children:* Lynne, Christine and Moira. (one s. two d). *Educated at* Waunarlwydd School; Swansea Technical College. *Career:* Member Sardis Welsh Chapel, Waunarlwydd; Engineering Tookmaker, 1930-55; Own Motor Business, 1955-78; became Councillor, Swansea Council, 1945; Chairman: Public Health & Welfare Serv.Cttee, 1960-75; Chmn: Swansea Port Health Auth., 1965-75; First City Mayor, Investiture, Prince of Wales, 1969; CBE in honours list, 1970; Hon. Fellow, Royal Soc. of Health (FRSH), 1970; Nat.Pres. (Nat. Assoc. of Port Health Auth. G.B.), 1968 and 1974; Hon.Fellow (Nat.Assoc.Port Health & Airport Assoc), 1978; West Glam C.Councillor, 1974; Vice-Chmn and Chmn, Social Servs, 1978-90; Chairman, West Glam (Blind Welfare Assoc), Vice Chmn of W.Glam County Council, Blind Workshops Chairman; Delegate: Wales Council for the Blind; Chmn; FPC 1974-84; Past mem. Glantawe Hospitals Management & Area Health & Dist.Health Auth; Active in the Trade Union and Labour Party, being Branch Chmn AM,EN, Union; Pres: Rhumatism & Athritis research Council, Swansea, Cor Plant Waunarlwydd, Waunarlwydd Senior Citizens; Chairman: Governors Dillwyn Llewellyn Comprehensive, Waunarlwydd Primary School, Login Fach Bilingual School. *Recreation:* Politics, Community work. *Address:* Highridge, 41 Swansea Road, Waunarlwydd, Swansea, SA5 4TQ.

BEVAN, Dr. Daniel,MB.,BCh.,DCH.,DPH.,FFPHM., FRSM. *Currently:* Chief Executive, Powys Health Authority, 1990- *Born on* 9 March 1933 at Blaendulais, W.Glamorgan. *Son of* Thomas Bevan and Hetty (nee Evans). *Marriage:* to Catherine Buddug Morgan, 1957. *Children:* Marc and Sian. *Educated at* Univ. of Wales; Coll. of Medicine & Bristol Univ. *Career:* Post graduate training, Univ. of Wales; Royal Air Force, 1960-76; General Practitioner, 1976-84; Chief Admin. Medical Officer, District General Manager, Powys Health, 1984-90. Health Management Consultant World Bank 1991- . *Publications:* Major Disaster Planning 1968. *Recreation:* Gardening and travel *Clubs:* *Address:* Stoneacre, Knucklas, Powys LD7 1PF. Mansion House, Bronllys, Brecon LD3 OL5

BEVAN,Mr Richard Thomas,M.D. FRCP, FFCM, Q.H.P. *Currently:* Retired. *Born on* 13 Jan 1914 at Ogmore Vale, Glamorgan..*Son of* Mr & Mrs T Bevan. *Marriage*: to Beryl Badham, 1940. *Children:* David, John and Catherine. *Educated at* Bridgend County School, Welsh National School of Medicine. *Career:* War Service R.A.F. (Wing Commander), Lecturer Welsh National School of Medicine, Deputy County Medical Officer, Glamorgan 1948-62; Civil Service Welsh Office (Chief Medical Officer) 1962-77. *Recreation:* Carpentry and Painting *Address:* 47 Chelveston Cres., Solihull, W. Midlands. B91 3YH.

BEVAN,Mr Robert William,MA *Currently:* Director of Education, Powys since 1974. *Born on* 14 April 1938 at Swansea. *Son of* Leslie Bevan and Vera (nee Grove). *Marriage:* to Adele Anne Roberts. *Children:* Nicola, Penelope and Lucinda. *Educated at* Dynevor Grammar School, Swansea; London Universities. *Career:* Director of Education, Radnorshire 1968-74; Assistant Director, Swansea 1964-66; Teacher, Hereford 1962-64; Education Officer, Nigeria 1960-62. *Publications:* articles in 'Times Educational Supplement'; 'Education'; 'Country Quest'. *Recreation:* Church architecture, music, drama. *Address:*

Upperby, Llandrindod Wells, Powys LD1 5NL

BEVAN,Rev. Canon Richard Justin William, PhD. *Currently:* Canon Emeritus of Carlisle Cathedral since 1989; Chaplain to The Queen since 1986. *Born on* 21 April 1922 at St.Harmon, Radnor (Powys). *Son of* Rev. Richard and Margaret Mabel Bevan (nee Pugh). *Marriage:* to Sheila Rosemary, 1949, da of Thomas Barrow of Fazakerley, Liverpool. *Children:* Roderick, Nicholas, Timothy, Christopher (decd) and Rosemary *Educated at* Rhayader School; St.Edmund's School, Canterbury; St.Augustine's College, Canterbury; University of Durham. *Career:* Asst Curate, Stoke-on-Trent 1945-49; Chaplain, Aberlour Orphanage, Scotland 1949-51; Asst. Master, Burnley Tech High School 1951-60; Rector of St.Mary-le-Bow, Durham 1961-64; Chaplain, University of Durham 1961-74; Chaplain St.Cuthbert's Society, University of Durham 1961-74; St.Mary's College 1961-72; St.Aidan's College 1960-66; Durham Girls' High School 1966-74; Trevelyan College 1966-72; examining Chaplain to Bishop of Carlisle from1969; vicar of United Benefice of St.Oswald with St.Mary-le-Bow, Durham 1964-74; Governor St. Chad's College Durham 1969-89; Rector of Grasmere 1974-82; President and founder member of Grasmere Village Society 1976-80; Theol consultant Churchman Publishing Ltd 1986-90; Canon residentiary, Carlisle Cathedral 1982-89; Treasurer and Librarian 1982-89; Vice Dean 1986-89; Acting Dean 1987-88; Hon. Th.D.Geneva Theol Coll 1972; PhD Columbia Pacific University 1980; Hon. Th.D. Greenwich University, USA 1990; member: Dove Cottage Committee (Dove Cottage, Grasmere, the home of Wm. Wordsworth), 1974-82. *Publications:* Steps to Christian Understanding (ed), 1959; The Churches and Christian Unity (ed), 1964; Durham Sermons (ed), 1966; Unfurl The Flame (poems), 1980; A Twig of Evidence: Does Belief in God Make Sense?. 1986. *Recreation:* train travel and spotting; poetry reading (especially Henry Vaughan, Dylan Thomas and R.S.Thomas), musical appreciation. *Clubs:* Victory Services, London. *Address:* Beck Cottage, Burgh-By-Sands, Carlisle, Cumbria, CA5 6BT. The Diocesan Resources Centre, West Walls, Carlisle CA3 8UE

BEYNON,Dr John David Emrys,PhD, FEng, FKC *Currently:* Principal, King's College, London, since Sept 1990. *Born on* 11 March 1939 at Risca, Gwent. *Son of* John Emrys Beynon and Elvira Beynon. *Marriage:* to Hazel Jane Hurley, 1964. *Children:* Sarah, Graham and Nigel. *Educated at* University of Wales; University of Southampton. *Career:* Scientific Officer, Radio Research Station, Slough 1962-64; Lecturer, Sr. Lecturer, then Reader, University of Southampton 1964-67; Professor of Electronics, University of Wales Institute of Science and Technology, Cardiff 1977-79; Head, Dept of Electronic and Electrical Engineering, University of Surrey 1979-83; Pro-Vice-Chancellor 1983-87; Senior Pro-Vice-Chancellor 1987-90, University of Surrey; Hon Fellow University College of Swansea 1990; Fellow of King's College 1990. *Publications:* Charge-Coupled Devices and Their Applications (with D.R.Lamb), 1980; papers on plasma physics, semi-conductor devices and integrated circuits and engineering education. *Recreation:* music, photography, travel. *Clubs:* Athenaeum. *Address:* King's College London, Strand, London WC2R 2LS. Tel: 071 873 2027

BEYNON,Mr Timothy George, MA.,FRGS. *Born on* 13 Jan 1939 at Mumbles. *Son of* the late George and Fona Inanda (nee Smith). *Marriage:* to Sally Jane Wilson, 1973. *Children:* Sorrel and Polly. *Educated at* Swansea Grammar School; Kings College, Cambridge. *Career:* Asst. Master, City of London School, 1962-63, Merchant Taylor's School joined 1963, Housemaster 1970-78, Senior Master 1977-78; Denstone College, Headmaster, 1978-86; The Leys School, Headmaster, 1986-90; expdns: Petra (overland) 1961, Spain, Hungary, Austria, Romania (ornithological); Denstone Expdn to Inaccessible Island 1982-83, sci advsr on wetland reserves to Glamorgan Co Naturalists Tst; mem: Eng Cncl 1986-89, Oxford and Cambridge Sch Examination Syndicate Appts Ctee; FRGS 1973, HMC 1978. *Recreation:* Ornithology; fishing; shooting sport; music and expeditions. *Address:* The Croft, College Road, Denstone, Uttoxeter Staffs. ST14 5HR.

BEYNON, Professor Sir William John Granville,CBE., Ph.D., D.Sc., F.R.S. *Currently:* Retired. *Born on* 24 May 1914 at Dunvant, Swansea. *Son of* William Beynon and Mary Beynon (nee Thomas). *Marriage:* to Megan (d. of Arthur James and Megan Glantawe),1942. *Children:* Margaret Elinor, William Meurig and Granville James *Educated at* Gowerton County; University College of Swansea. *Career:* Senior Scientific Officer, Radio Division, National PhysicalLaboratory, 1938-46; Senior Lecturer in Physics, University College of Swansea, 1946-58; Professor and Head of Department of Physics, 1958-81; University College of Wales, Abersytwyth. *Publications:* Numerous publications in national and international scientific journals. *Recreation:* Music, gardening, rugby, cricket and snooker. *Address:* 'Caebryn', Caergog, Aberystwyth SY23 1ET. Bryneithin, 103 Dunvant Road, Swansea SA27 NN Tel: 0792 03585

BICHAN,Dr Herbert Roy,BSc, PhD, FEng, FIMM *Currently:* Consultant to Simon Engineering plc and Deputy Chairman (non-executive), Simon-Robertson,since 1991. *Born on* 5 Nov 1941 at Orkney Is., Scotland. *Son of* Peter and Jesse Bichan. *Marriage:* to Fiona Keay. *Children:* Inga, Michael and Susie. *Educated at* Kirkwall Grammar School; Aberdeen University; Leeds University. *Career:* The Robertson Group plc, initially as junior geologist and finally as Chairman and Chief Executive 1967-91. Chairman CBI North Wales 1990-92 and member of CBI Welsh and National Councils. Past President Institution of Mining and Metallurgy 1988-89. Chairman, Welsh Industrial Development Advisory Board 1992-95. *Publications:* The Igneous and Metamorphic Rocks of Socotra, 1968; Origin of Chromite Seams in the Hartley Complex of the Great Dyke, Rhodesia, in 'Magmatic, Ore Deposits', 1969; The Evolution and Structural Setting of the Great Dyke, Rhodesia, 'African Magmatism and Tectonism', 1970; Economic Geological Appraisal of British Carbonate Deposits, 1970; The Geology of Socotra Island, Gulf of Aden. Quarterly Journal of the Geological Society, 1970; Future Sources of Tin and Tungsten, 1979; Geothermal Energy: Fuel for the Future, 1988; The Southwest Pacific: Current and Future Mining, 1990. *Recreation:* gardening, golf. *Address:* 33 Allanson Road, Rhos-On-Sea, Colwyn Bay, Clwyd, LL28 4HL.

BIDDLE, Neville Leslie, *Currently:* Barrister, Criminal Practice, Liverpool and North Wales Chambers, Peel House Harrington Str, Liverpool, L2 9QA. *Born on* 24 April 1951

at West Kirby. *Son of* Walter Alan Biddle and Beryl Mary Biddle (nee Meadows). *Marriage:* to Sheila Ruth Biddle (nee Sen), 1976. *Children:* Caroline, Josephine, Rebecca and Charlotte. *Educated at* Wrekin College Wellington Shropshire; U.C.W. Aberystwyth. *Career:* BSc Econ 1972; Called to Bar 1974. *Recreation:* sailing, gliding. *Clubs:* West Kirby Sailing. *Address:* Peel House, Harrington St, Liverpool L2 9QA.

BIRCH,Mr Tom Svend, *Currently:* Area Manager, Welsh Freight, British Railways Board (Trainload Freight). *Born on* 23 July 1955 at Manchester. *Educated at* Burnage Grammar School, Manchester. *Career:* Area Terminals Manager, Watford Midland Region, 1982-84; Area Operations Manager, Orpington Southern Region, 1984-88; Area Manager, St. Pancras Midland Region, 1988-89; Current Operations Manager, Western Region, 1989-91. *Recreation:* Travel; current affairs; walking and reading *Address:* British Railways Brd, CP90 2nd Floor, Brunel House, 2 Fitzalan Rd. Cdf, CF2 1SA. Tel: 0222 499811

BOARD,Professor Kenneth,BSc, PhD, DSc, CEng. *Currently:* Full-time Professor, Dept Electrical and Electronic Engineering, Univ Coll, Swansea. *Born on* 15 April 1941 at Llanelli. *Son of* George Herbert Board and Beryl Board (nee Roberts). *Marriage:* to Meriel Board (nee Jones). *Children:* Meirion James (b.1973) and Alun Rhys (b.1975). *Educated at* Llanelli Boys Grammar; University College Swansea; UCNW Bangor (PhD). *Career:* Apprentice, Richard Thomas & Baldwins 1956-59; Research Engineer, GEC Hirst Research Centre 1968-69; Research Engineer, Philips Research Labs Redhill 1969-75; Lecturer, Dept Electrical Engineering, University College Swansea 1975- . *Publications:* 60 scientific papers, 1 text book, editor 2 conference proceedings. *Recreation:* golf, woodwork, gardening. *Clubs:* Clyne Golf. *Address:* University Of Wales, Singleton Park, Swansea Tel: 0792 295415

BODDINGTON,Mr Lewis,CBE; MoF(USA); CEng; FIME; FRAeS. *Currently:* retired 1972. *Born on* 13 Nov 1907 at Brithdir, Mid Glam. *Son of* James and Anne Boddington. *Marriage:* to Morfydd Anne (nee Murray) 1936. *Children:* *Educated at* Lewis School, Pengam; City of Cardiff Tech. College; UCSW, Cardiff. *Career:* Pupil Engineer, Fraser & Chalmers Engineering Works (G.E.C.) 1928-31; Assistant to Major H.N.Wylie 1931-36; Royal Aircraft Establishment 1936-51; Head of Naval Aircraft Dept, Ministry of Supply, Aviation 1951-60 Assistant Director R & D Naval, Director Aircraft R & D (Naval), Director General R & D (RAF), Director, Assistant Managing Director, Westland Aircraft, Yeovil 1961-72. *Address:* Flat 6, Penarth House, 28 Stanwell Road, Penarth, S.Glam. CF6 2EY Tel: 0222 701832

BODEN,Mr Thomas Bennion,O.B.E. *Currently:* Farming, Agricultural Politics. *Born on* 23 Oct 1915 at Denstone Hall. *Son of* Harry, Florence (nee Boden). *Marriage:* to Dorothy Eileen Ball, 1939. *Children:* June Sylvia, David Thomas and Mary Christine. *Educated at* Alleynes Grammar School, Uttoxeter, Nottingham University. *Career:* Teaching Farming; Lecturing European Commission Chairman. *Publications:* Works on Milk Quotas, Agricultural Farm Size Structure. *Recreation:* Sport, Bell Ringing *Clubs:* Farmers, N.F.U., President Tennis, Bowls and Cricket clubs. *Address:* Denstone Hall, Denstone, Uttoxeter, Staffs. ST14 5HF.

BONE,Mr Peter William,F.C.A. *Currently:* Palm Travel (West) Limited, Florida House, 7/9A Baneswell Road, Newport, Managing Director. Prospective Conservative Parliamentary Candidate for Islwyn. *Born on* 19 Oct 1952 at Billericay, Essex. *Son of* Wiliam and Marjorie Bone. *Marriage:* to Jeanette Beatrice Bone (nee Sweeney) 1981. *Children:* Alexander John William and Helen Louise *Educated at* Westcliff Grammar School for boys, 1968-71 *Career:* Columbia Precision Products Ltd., Financial Director, 1978-81; Varitext Displays Ltd., Chief Executive, 1981-90. *Recreation:* Keen sportsman, completed 3 London Marathons *Clubs:* Newport Fugitives Cricket Club and Newport Golf Club *Address:* 11 Stow Park Circle, Newport, Gwent NP9 4HF.

BONNELL,Dr John Aubrey Luther,MB, BS, FRCP, FFOM *Currently:* retired, Consultant Occupational Health Physician. *Born on* 2 March 1924 at Cymmer, Glam. *Son of* the late Thomas Luther Bonnell and the late Ruth Bonnell. *Marriage:* to Gillian Mathias, 1991. *Children:* two d (by previous marriage), Sian and Mandy. *Educated at* Llanelli Grammar School; Kings College Hospital. *Career:* Hospital Appointments, Metropolitan Hospital & Romford Hospital 1948-50; Medical Research Council, Dept for Research in Industrial Medicine 1950-58; Deputy Chief Nuclear Health & Safety Officer CEGB 1958-76; Chief Medical Officer CEGB 1976-86; Medical Adviser Electricity Council and Elec. Association 1976-91; member: Society of Occupational Medicine, president 1976; Royal Soc of Medicine, president Section of Occ. Med, 1981-82; Society for Radiological Protection, president 1972-74; Board member International Commission on Occ. Health 1982-87; Liveryman, of "Worshipful Society of Apothecaries of London" 1971; chairman Livery Committee 1986-88. *Publications:* co author "Aspects of Occ. Health", Faber & Faber 1984; co author "Current Approaches to Occ. Heath", 3rd edition 1987; co author Recent Advances in Occ. Health, Oxford University Press 1987; various publications on Industrial Toxicology, Radiological Protection, Environmental Health and Occupational Medicine. *Recreation:* gardening, music, bowls. *Clubs:* Royal Society of Medicine. *Address:* 71 The Green, Ewell, Surrey KT17 3JX. Tel: 081 393 1461

BONNOR-MAURIE, Major Edward Arthur Trevor,DL, MFH *Currently:* self-employed. Chairman: British Horse Society, since 1990; Master, Tanatside Foxhounds since, 1971. *Born on* 24 April 1928 at Berkshire. *Son of* Trevor and Mary Bonner-Maurie. *Marriage:* to Lavinia Ann Leighton, 1958, eldest dau of Sir Richard Leighton Bart. *Children:* Emma Mary (Fane) and Frances Flavia. *Educated at* Winchester College 1941-46. *Career:* Coldstream Guards 1946-61; Montgomeryshire CC 1962-75; High Sheriff Powys 1975-76. *Recreation:* filed sports, music, gardens. *Clubs:* Cavalry & Guards, M.C.C. *Address:* Bodynfoel Hall, Llanfechain, Powys SY22 6XD.

BOSTON, William John, *Currently:* Licencee. *Born on* 6 Aug 1934 at Cardiff. *Son of* John and Ellen. *Marriage:* to Joan (nee Rudd), 1956. *Children:* Christine, Lisa, Karen, Angela and Stephen. *Educated at* South Church St School. *Career:* National Service, Royal Signals 1952-54; former Rugby Union and Rugby League player: Cardiff Schoolboys 1948, Welsh Assoc Boys Clubs 1950, Welsh Youth Team 1951, Cardiff Int. Rugby 1951, Cardiff R.W., 1952. Joined

Wigan RLFC 1953-68, debut 1953, 564 appearances, 571 tries, International R.L., 31 caps for G.Britain, toured Australia 1954 and 1962. Second highest try scorer in rugby league history, installed in Whitbread Hall of Fame, Leeds and Welsh Sporting Hall of Fame Cardiff. Honours 3 Challenge Cup Winners medals, 3 runner up medals. *Publications:* Who's Who in Sport, Debretts People of Today. *Recreation:* all sports. *Address:* Griffin Hotel, 94 Standish Gate, Wigan, WN1 1XA.

BOULTON, Mr George, Dip. in Health Serv. Admin, Assoc. Inst. of Health Svce Mngmnt *Currently:* National Health Service; District General Manager, Mid Glamorgan Health Authority. *Born on* 28 Dec 1946. at Burton-on-Trent. *Son of* Herbert Charles and Joyce (nee Hinsley). *Marriage:* to Carole Ann Holford 1968. *Children:* Faye, Christopher and Sarah. *Educated at* Burton-on-Trent Grammar School; Aston University. *Career:* Administrator, Queen Elizabeth Medical Centre; Hospital Secretary, Birmingham General, Dental & Jaffray Hospitals; Deputy Area Administrator, Salop Area Health Authority; Deputy Regional Administrator, South Western Regional Health Authority; District General Manager, Mid Glamorgan Health Authority; Governor, Polytechnic of Wales; member, Welsh National Board for Nursing and Midwifery; representative, European Erasmus Consortium on Nurse Education; member, all-Wales NHS Working Groups on Information, Manpower, Cervical Cytology Services and Nursing. *Publications:* (recent) - Energy Conservation in NHS; Information Technology; Social Deprivation. *Recreation:* all sports, literature. *Clubs:* Ogmore, Bridgend, Bridgend RFC. *Address:* 3 Swn-Y-Mor, Southerdown, Nr.Bridgend, CF32 0RN.

BOWDEN, Mr Geoffrey Anthony, MinstM, FInstD, FBIM. *Currently:* Management Consultant since 1990. *Born on* 5 June 1939 at Southampton. *Son of* Irene Queenie and the late James Benjamin Phillip. *Marriage:* 1st, 1960; 2nd to Wendy Elizabeth, 1973. *Children:* Alison, Matthew, Katie and Alex. *Educated at* Farnborough; Guildford; Wimbledon. *Career:* MD Siebe Gorman & Co 1977-82; Dep Chairman: Merryweather & Sons 1979-82, John Morris & Sons 1979-82; Chairman and MD Glossmark Ltd 1982-84; Chairman Mainstay Computer Cover Ltd 1983-85, chairman and MD RJT 40 Ltd 1985-89 (business consultant), chief executive Mainstay Computer Cover NV and BV 1986-88, chief exec Accord Engineering Services Ltd 1988-90. *Publications:* Deep Diving, eighth edition. *Recreation:* golf, skiing, community sports, leader, toastmaster. *Clubs:* St.Pierre, Roehampton. *Address:* Belair, Llanfechfa, Gwent, NP44 8BU. 42a Chilton Road, Richmond, Surrey.

BOWEN, Mr Anthony James George, KstJ, JP, DLC, FIMI. *Currently:* Chairman and Managing Director, Green Bower Garages Ltd since 1966, joining family business in 1963; Chairman Pembrokeshire N.H.S. Trust; Partner Slebech Finance Co. *Born on* 29 Jan 1941 at Llawhaden, Dyfed. *Son of* the late Howard James Bowen and Georgina Ann Bowen. *Marriage:* to Mrs Patricia Ann Barrett (nee Hutchinson), 1973. *Children:* (step) Simon Barrett and Lisa Barrett. *Educated at* Narberth Grammar School; Loughborough College of Advanced Technology. *Career:* J.Bowen & Sons (Llawhaden) Ltd., Director (resigned 1987); Bowens of Carmarthen, Partner 1975-88. Voluntary work 'The Princes Trust'; Area chairman, Mid, West Wales;

member, Management Board (London); chairman, Princes Youth Business Trust (Dyfed); Order of St.John, Sub Prior, Priory for Wales. *Recreation:* golf, skiing, travel. *Address:* St Giles, Uzmaston Road, Haverfordwest, Dyfed, SA61 1TZ. Flat 8, Berners Mansions, 34-36 Berner St, London, W1P 3DA.

BOWEN, Professor David Aubrey Llewellyn, MA, MB, BChi, FRCP, FRCP(Edin) ,FRCP.Path. DMJ, D.Path. *Currently:* Emeritis Professor of Forensic Medicine, University of London. *Born on* 31 Jan 1924 at Pontycymmer, Glamorgan. *Son of* the late Dr. Rufus Bowen J.P. and the late Catherine (nee Llewellyn). *Marriage:* 1st to Joan Rosemary (nee Davis), 1950, (d 1973) 2nd to Helen Rosamund. *Children:* Mark Roderick and Diana, from 1st marriage. *Educated at* Garw Secondary School, Pontycymmer and Caterham School, Surrey. *Career:* House Officer, West Middlesex Hospital, 1947; RAMC 1947-49. London Chest Hospital, 1949-50; Bristol Royal Infirmary, 1950-51; Registrar London Chest Hospital, 1951-52; National Hospital for nervous diseases, 1952-55, (Pathology); Royal Marsden Hospital, 1955-56; Forensic Medicine Lecturer, St. Georges Hospital, London, 1956-66; Senior lecturer Forensic Medicine, Charing Cross Hospital, London, 1966-73; (Reader 1973-77; Professor, 1977-90; Lecturer in Forensic Medicine University Oxford, 1974-90. *Publications:* Numerous articles on forensic pathology and medicine. *Recreation:* Hockey and road running. *Clubs:* London Welsh RFC and West Herts Hockey Club. *Address:* 19 Letchmore Road, Radlett, Herts., WD7 8HU.

BOWEN, Professor David Quentin, BSc., Ph.D. *Currently:* Professsor and Director of the Institute of Earth Studies, UCW, Aberystwyth since 1988. *Born on* 14 Feb 1938 at Llanelli. *Son of* the late William Esmond Bowen and Jane (nee Williams). *Marriage:* to Elizabeth Nia Williams, 1965. *Children:* Huw Quentin Bowen and Wyn Quentin Bowen. *Educated at* Llanelli Grammar School; Univ. Coll. London. *Career:* Professor of Geography, London University (RHBNC) 1985-88, Professor of Physical Geography, UCW Aberystwyth 1983-85. Deputy Chairman, Countryside Council for Wales since 1991; Member of the Nature Conservancy Council 1986-91; President of the Quaternary Research Association 1979-81; President of the Stratigraphy Commission of the International Union for Quaternary Research and International Union of Geological Sciences since 1991; Chairman, NERC Radiocarbon Cttee 1983-87; Chairman, NERC Expert Group on Quaternary Research 1987; Member of NERC Research Grant and Research Studentship Training Cttees 1976-80; Editor-in-Chief of Quaternary Science Reviews, the International Research and Review Journal; Fellow of the Geological Society of London; Fellow of the Royal Geographical Society; Member of the American Geophysical Union; Member of the Geological Society of America; Member of the Quaternary Research Association. *Publications:* Quaternary Geology (Pergamon Press) 1978, Russian edition 1981; The Llanelli Landscape (Llanelli Borough) 1980; Glaciations of the Northern Hemisphere (Pergamon Press) 1986; The Past Three Million Years (Royal Society) 1988; Quaternary of Wales (Nature Conservancy Council) 1989; 70 articles in journals including Nature, Geological Magazine, Geologists Association, Geological Journal, Geological Society of London etc. *Recreation:* Rugby football; cricket; travel and music *Clubs:* Athenaeum *Address:* 5 Castell Brychan, Aberystwyth, Dyfed, SY24 2JD. Tel: 0970 622631

BOWEN, Professor Ivor Delme,BSc, PhD, DSc, FRMS. *Currently:* Professor of Cell Biology. *Born on* 20 March 1944 at Glanaman. *Son of* Benjamin Ivor Bowen and Sara Eirwen Bowen. *Marriage:* to Dr Sandra Maureen Bowen. *Children:* Dewi Rhys, Gareth, Rhian Angharad and Rhodri Ifor. *Educated at* Amman Valley Grammar; University College Cardiff. *Career:* Research Demonstrator in Zoology 1967-68; Assistant Lecturer in Zoology 1968-69; Lecturer in Zoology 1969-76; Senior Lecturer 1976-80; Reader in Cell Biology, University of Wales, 1980-86; Personal Research Chair in Cell Biology 1986- . *Publications:* a total of 85 scientific papers including 2 books, the latest being "Cell Death in Tumours & Tissues", 1990. *Recreation:* politics, Plaid Cymru County Councillor, Mid Glam; Parliamentary candidate for Pontypridd. *Clubs:* Pontyclun Athletic, Pontyclun Rugby. *Address:* 12 Rhyd-y-Nant, Pontyclun, Mid Glam.,CF7 9HE. University Of Wales College, Cardiff, P.O. Box 915, Cardiff, CF1 3TL.

BOWEN, John Griffith *Currently:* Writer. *Born on* 5 Nov 1924 at Calcutta, India. *Son of* Hugh Griffith Bowen and Ethel May Cooke. *Educated at* Queen Elizabeth's Grammar School, Crediton, Devon; Pembroke College, Oxford; St.Antony's College, Oxford. *Career:* Novels: The Truth Will Not Help Us, 1956; After the Rain, 1958; The Centre of the Green, 1959; Storyboard, 1960; The Birdcage, 1962; A World Elsewhere, 1965; Squeak, 1983; The MacGuffin, 1984; The Girls, 1986; Fighting Back, 1988; The Precious Gift, 1992 (most of these novels have also been published in paperback, in the USA and various European countries). Plays: I Love you, Mrs Patterson, 1964; After the Rain, 1966; Little Boxes, 1968; Fall and Redemption, 1969; The Disorderly Women, 1970; The Waiting Room, 1970; The Corsican Brothers, 1970; Robin Redbreast, 1974; Heil, Caesar, 1974; Florence Nightingale, 1975; Which Way Are You Facing?, 1976; Singles, 1977; Bondage, 1978; The Inconstant Couple, 1978; Spot The Lady, 1981 The Geordie Gentleman, 1987; The Oak Tree Tea Room Siege. 1990. (most of these plays have been published, and many have been staged in the USA and various other countries). Many television plays, including: A Holiday Abroad, 1960; The Candidate, 1961; Nuncle, 1962; Finders Keepers, 1967; Robin Redbreast, 1970; Miss Nightingale, 1974; Brief Encounter, 1976; A Dog's Ransom, 1978; The Ice House, 1978; Dying Day, 1980; Dark Secret, 1981; Honeymoon, 1983; also episodes of Front Page Story, The Power Game, The Wylde Alliance, The Villains and seven of the thirteen episodes of The Guardians. Radio Plays: Varieties of Love, 1968; The False Diaghilev, 1987. Producer of TV Drama: for Thames TV, London Weekend TV and the BBC. Director of Stage Plays: for the Stables Theatre, Manchester, the Hampstead Theatre Club, the Pitlochry Festival Theatre and the Soho Poly. *Clubs:* P.E.N. *Address:* Old Farm Lodge, Sugarswell Lane, Edgehill, Banbury, OX15 6HP.

BOWEN, Mr Kenneth John, MA, Mus.B.Hon RAM, FRSA, ARCM. *Currently:* Professor of Singing, Royal Academy of Music, since 1967; Conductor, London Welsh Chorale since, 1983. *Born on* 3 Aug 1932 at Llanelli. *Son of* Hector John Bowen and Sarah Ann (Sally) Davies. *Marriage:* to Angela Mary Evenden. *Children:* Geraint and Meurig. *Educated at* Llanelli Grammar School; University College of Wales, Aberystwyth; St.John's College, Cambridge; Institute of Education, University of London. *Career:* Flying Officer, Education Branch, RAF 1958-60; Head of Vocal Studies, Royal Academy of Music 1987-91; Former concert and operatic tenor (retired 1988), debut Tom Rakewell, New Opera Company Saddlers Wells 1957; appeared: Promenade Concerts, Three Choirs Festival, Aldeburgh, Bath, Fishguard, Llandaff, St.Asaph, Swansea festivals; performance at Royal Opera House, ENO, WNO, Glyndebourne Touring Opera, English Opera Group, English Music Theatre, Kent Opera, Handel opera; numerous recordings and appearances in Europe, Israel, Hong Kong, Singapore, Canada and USA. Winner First Prize Munich International Competition and Queens prize. Member of Gorsedd of Bards, National Eisteddfod of Wales (Cennydd o Ddyfed); member of Council British Youth Opera; Voce president Guild for the Promotion of Welsh Music; President RAM Club 1990; Chairman AOTOS 1990-91; member I.S.M. Royal Society of Musicians. *Publications:* The Handel Opera Repertory (Tenor) with Geoffrey Pratley. *Recreation:* golf, fell-walking, cinema, wine. *Address:* 12 Steele's Road, London, NW3 4SE.

BOWEN, The Very Reverend (BA) Lawrence, (Finals) Economics, Welsh, History, Philosophy, European Hist. *Currently:* Retired. *Born on* 9 Sept 1914 at Llanelli. *Son of* William and Elizabeth Ann. *Marriage:* to Hilary Myrtle Bowen, 1941. *Children:* Celia Mary Fanstone and Ruth Margaret Bayley. *Educated at* Intermediate Boys Grammar School, Llanelli; UCW Aberystwyth; St. Michaels Theological College, Llandaff, Senior Student awarded Crossley Exhibition. *Career:* Ordination St. Davids Cathedral, 1938, (Deacon) Priest 1939;Curate of Pembrey 1939-40; Minor Canon St. Davids Cathedral 1940-46; Vicar of St.Clears with Llangynin 1946-64; Rector of Tenby with Gumfreston & New Hedges 1966; Rector of Rectorial Parish of Tenby with Gumfreston New Hedges and Penally, Canon of St. Davids Cathedral 1972; Dean, 1972; Precentor & Vicar of St. Davids, 1972-84. *Recreation:* Rugby, golf, cricket and welsh poetry. *Clubs:* Rotary; Probus *Address:* Saddle Point, Slade Way, Fishguard, Dyfed. SA65 9NY.

BOWEN, Mark Rossllyn *Currently:* Professional footballer for Norwich City F.C.. *Born on* 7 Dec 1963 at Neath. *Son of* Rossllyn Llewelyn and Mary. *Marriage:* to Kare Rose Hollingdale. *Children:* Daniella Rose and Joshua Thomas. *Educated at* St. Josephs RC Comprehensive, Port Talbot. *Career:* signed apprentice for Tottenham Hotspur F.C., July 1979 - Professional July 1981. 20 league div. 1 and cup games. represented English league v Italian league, Jan 1991. Welsh schoolboy, youth, under 21 and 16 full caps. Norwich player of Year 1989-90. *Recreation:* horse racing, golf. *Address:* 5 Prince Rupert Way, Camellia Court, Thorpe St Andrew, Norwich.

BOWEN-SIMPKINS, Mr. Peter, MA, MB, B.Chir, LRCP, MRCS, FRCOG. *Currently:* Consultant Obstetrician & Gynaecologist, Singleton Hospital, Swansea, since 1979. *Son of* the late Horace John and Christine (nee Clarke). *Marriage:* to Kathrin (nee Ganguin), 1967. *Children:* Emma Jane (b.1969) and Philippa (b.1971). *Educated at* St.John's, Porthcawl; Malvern College; Selwyn College, Cambridge; Guy's Hospital Med. School. *Career:* Resident Medical Officer, Queen Charlottes Maternity Hospital 1971; Res. Surgical Officer, Samaritan Hospital for Women 1972;

Senior Registrar & Lecturer, Middlesex Hospital and Hospital for Women, Soho Sq, 1972-78; Lecturer in Family Planning, Margaret Pyke Centre, London; Lecturer & Broadcaster; Inspector of Nullity for Wales; Handcock Prize for Surgery, Royal College of Surgeons. Leader Cambridge Expedition to Eritrea 1963. Co founder and past chairman of Victor Bonney Society; Liveryman, Worshipful Company of Apothecaries, Freeman City of London. Member: British Medical Assoc., British Fertility Soc., Gynaecology Travellers; Welsh Obstetrics & Gynaecology Soc., London Obstetric & Gynaecology Soc. Examiner: General Medical Council, Royal College of Obst. & Gynae; University of Wales. *Publications:* ''Pocket Examiner in Obstetrics & Gynaecology''; contributions, chapters in various books in obstetrics and gynaecology; papers in B.M.J., B.J.O.G., Fertility & Sterility etc. *Recreation:* fly fishing, golf, tennis, skiing, sailing. *Clubs:* Royal Overseas League, Pennard Golf. *Address:* Bosco's Knoll, 73 Pennard Road, Southgate, Swansea, SA3 2AJ. Consulting Rooms: Walter Road, Swansea, SA1 5NW Tel: 0792 655600

BOWERS, Dr Eric Anthony, BSc., PhD., DipEd., M.Ed.(Wales), M.I.Biol. *Currently:* Staff Tutor in Science, The Open Univ. in Wales, 1971- . *Born on* 8 Aug 1939 at Port Talbot. *Son of* the late William Bowers and Betty Bowers (nee Woods). *Marriage:* to Glenys Evans, 1965. *Children:* Ceri and David. *Educated at* Trefelin Primary; Duffryn Grammar, Port Talbot; Univ. Coll., Swansea. *Career:* Lecturer/Senior Lecturer in Zoology, The Polytechnic of Central London, 1966-70. *Publications:* A number of papers on Marine Parasitology in various refereed journals. *Recreation:* All sports, reading and local politics. *Clubs:* Aberavon RFC; Glamorgan CCC; Bridgend LTSC. *Address:* The Open University In Wales, 24 Cathedral Road, Cardiff. CF1 9SA.

BOWN, Mr Philip Arnold, MBE. *Born on* 1 Sept 1934 at Bridgewater, Somerset. *Son of* the late Ernest Bown and Gladys Bown. *Marriage:* to Diana (nee Richards), 1962. *Children:* one s Damian; three d Olivia, Tiffany and Coralie. *Educated at* King Edwards Bath; Newport HS. *Career:* Lt RA 1957-59; CA; Peat Marwick 1951-56, United Transport plc and subsids 1959-85 (dir 1977-85), chm and chief exec Brushes International 1979- ; High Sheriff Co of Gwent 1989-90; gen cmmr of Income Tax; FCA, CBIM. *Recreation:* sailing. *Clubs:* Royal Yacht Sqdn, Royal Thames Yacht. *Address:* Uplands, Chepstow, Gwent, NP6 6BQ. Brushes Int. Ltd, Lower Church St, Chepstow, Gwent, NP6 5XT. Tel: 0291 629022

BOX, Mr Donald Stewart. *Currently:* Member International Stock Exchange; partner Margaret Box Relocations; non exec. director N.M. Rothschild & Sons (Wales) Ltd. *Born on* 22 Nov 1917 at Llandaff. *Son of* the late Stanley Carter Box and the late Elizabeth Mary Stewart (nee Bassett). *Marriage:* to Margaret Rose Davies, 1973. *Children:* Clarissa Lyda Stewart Box. *Educated at* Llandaff Cathedral; St John's, Pinner; Harrow County School. *Career:* RAF ranks, 1939, commissioned 1941; overseas service Egypt, Palestine, Transjordan 1941-44; demobbed with rank of Flt-Lieut 1945; Partner, Henry J Thomas & Co, stockbrokers 1945-66. MP (C) Cardiff North 1959-66; Member Stock Exchange and partner Lyddon & Co., 1966-86; Senior partner 1978-86. *Recreation:* rugby, racing. *Clubs:* Cardiff & County *Address:* Laburnum Cottage, Sully Road, Penarth, S.

Glamorgan CF6 2TX. 14 - 15, Douglas Buildings, Royal Stuart Lane, Cardiff, CF1 6EL. Tel: 0222 494822

BOYCE, Mr Michael David, D.M.A. *Currently:* Chief Executive, South Glamorgan County Council and Clerk to the Lieutenancy, since 1987. *Born on* 27 May 1937 at Torquay, Devon. *Son of* Clifford and Vera Boyce. *Marriage:* to Audrey May Gregory, 1962. *Children:* Andrea and Adrian. *Educated at* Queen Elizabeth's School, Credition. *Career:* Admitted Solicitor 1968; Asst. Solicitor 1968-69; Senior Asst. Solicitor, and Asst. Clerk of the Peace 1969-71; Exeter CC; Dep. Town Clerk 1971-73; Dep. Chief Executive 1973-74; Newport, Gwent. County Solicitor, South Glam 1974-87; Sec. Lord Chancellor's Adv. Cttee 1987. Member of the Boards of Cardiff-Wales Airport; Welsh College of Music and Drama; South Glamorgan Training and Enterprise Council; Cardiff Marketing Limited; Council Member of University of Wales College of Cardiff; Cardiff Chamber of Commerce. *Recreation:* France and French, Association Football, music, railways and travel. *Address:* 1 White Oaks Drive, Old St. Mellons, Cardiff. CF3 9EX.

BRADLEY, Charles Stuart, CBE, Master Mariner, FCIT. *Currently:* Director ABPH; Managing Director ABP, since 1988; Chairman Red Funnel Group. *Born on* 11 Jan 1936 at Penarth Glam. *Son of* Charles and Amelia Jane Bradley. *Marriage:* to Kathleen Marina (nee Loraine), 1959. *Children:* Philip and Bridget. *Educated at* Penarth County School; University College, Southampton. *Career:* Deck Officer, P&OSN Co 1952-64; Joined British Transport Docks Board, subseq ABP, Ass. Dock Master, S.Wales Ports 1964; Dock and Harbour Master, Silloth 1968-70; Dock Master 1970-74; Dock and Marine Superintendent 1974-76, Plymouth; Docks Manager Lowestoft 1976-78; Port Manager, Barry 1978-80; Dep Port Manager 1980-85, Port Manager 1985-87, Hull; Assistant Managing Director (Resources) 1987-88. *Recreation:* Welsh rugby football, cycling, theatre. *Clubs:* Honourable Company of Master Mariners; Cardiff Athletic. *Address:* C/o Associated British Ports, Holdings Plc, 150 Holborn, London, EC1N 2LR.

BRADLEY, Mr David Rice, MA *Currently:* Chief Executive, London Borough of Havering, since 1990. *Born on* 9 Jan 1938 at Llandrindod Wells. *Son of* George Leonard and Evelyn Annie Bradley (nee Rice). *Marriage:* Josephine Elizabeth Turnbull Fricker, (nee Harries). *Children:* David Joel Turnbull and Tristan James Rice. *Educated at* Christ College Brecon; St.Catharine's College Cambridge (MA English); Edinburgh University (Postgraduate). *Career:* National Service (commission), South Wales Borderers 1956-58; British Council Officer 1961-73; Civil Servant, Dept of the Environment 1973-90 (Gwilym Gibbon Senior Research Fellow, Nuffield College Oxford-on special leave from DOE 1982-83); Director, Merseyside Task Force (DOE) 1988-90. *Recreation:* gardening *Address:* 27 Clare Lawn Avenue, London SW14 8BE. Tel: 071 876 2232

BRADSHAW, Professor Anthony David, MA; PhD; MIEEM; FIBiol; FLS; FRS. *Currently:* Emeritus Professor and Honorary Research Fellow, University of Liverpool. *Born on* 17 Jan 1926 at Richmond, Surrey. *Son of* the late Harold Chalton Bradshaw and the late Mary Bradshaw (nee Taylor). *Marriage:* to Betty Margaret Alliston 1955. *Children:* Jane, Penelope and Sarah. *Educated at* St.Pauls School, Hammerswmith; Jesus College, Cambridge. *Career:* PhD on plant evolution, University of Wales, Aberystwyth and Bangor 1958; Lecturer/Senior lecturer/Reader, Department of Agricultural Botany, Bangor 1950-68; Holbrook Gaskell Professor of Botany, University of Liverpool 1968-88; also Nature Conservancy Council 1958-73; Natural Environment Research Council 1969-74; Sports Turf Research Institute Board of Management 1960- ; Vice-President 1982- ; Institute of Ecology and Environmental Management President 1991- ; British Ecological Society, President 1982-84; Honorary Member 1988- ; Prince of Wales Award for land reclamation 1973; Honorary Fellow Indian National Academy of Science 1989. *Publications:* over 200 scientific papers and books on plant evolution and land reclamation and urban ecology, much in relation to Wales. *Recreation:* sailing, gardening, walking. *Address:* 60 Knowsley Road, Liverpool L19 OPG. Dept. Environmental and Evolutionary Biology, University Of Liverpool, Liverpool, L69 3BX

BRAHAM,Mr Charles James, *Currently:* Managing Director, Swansea Sound Limited, appointed May 1974, having been founder member of original consortium. *Born on* 25 Sept 1931 at London. *Son of* the late Charles and the late Violet Alice (nee Bain). *Marriage:* to Maureen Evans 1954. *Children:* Alison and Mark Richard. *Educated at* Haverfordwest Grammar School; Millfield, Street, Somerset. *Career:* Journalist, national magazine sub-editor, newspaper editor; Managing Director Llanelli Star Ltd., 1957-73; Member of Council of Association of Independent Contractors 1974-85; Chairman Independent Radio News Network Cttee 1980-82; Trustee AIRC Pension Fund since 1974; Chairman Cardigan & Tivyside Advertiser Ltd., weekly newspaper publishers, 1966-88; President, South Wales Newspaper Society 1963-64 and 1987-88; President, Llanelli Rotary Club 1970-71. *Address:* Winscott, 172 Felinfoel Road, Llanelli, Dyfed, SA15 3NJ.

BRAIN,Professor Paul Fredric,BSc, PhD, CBiol, FIBiol. *Currently:* Personal Chair in Zoology, University of Wales, Swansea, since 1987. *Born on* 1 July 1945 at Manchester. *Son of* Frederick Ernest Brain and Ada Squirell. *Marriage:* to Sonja Strijbos, 1975. *Children:* Fulke (s), Ilka (d), Vincent (s) and Daniel (s). *Educated at* University of Hull, Yorkshire; University of Sheffield. *Career:* Lecturer in Zoology, University College of Swansea 1971-78; Senior Lecturer, Univ Coll of Swansea 1978-83; Visiting Professor in Psychology, Univ of Hawaii, USA 1982; Reader in Zoology, Univ College of Swansea 1983-87; Visiting Professor in Biology and Psychology, Univ of Hawaii, USA 1986; 1990; Visiting Professor in Zoology, Univ Kebangsaan, Malaysia 1989. *Publications:* 13 books, some 50 book chapters and 140 papers in the area of Physiology and Behaviour. *Recreation:* travel, photography, road running, (up to marathon distance). *Clubs:* Glynneath Joggers, Sospan Road Runners. *Address:* Biological Sciences, University Coll Of Swansea, Swansea SA2 8PP.

BRAMMER,Mr Leonard Griffiths,RE; ARCA; FRSA. *Currently:* retired, formerly Head of Longton, Stoke on Trent School of Art and then Supervisor of Art Education for the City of Stoke on Trent. *Born on* 4 July 1906 at Burslem, N.Staffordshire. *Son of* F.W. & M. Brammer of Burslem, N. Staffordshire. *Marriage:* to Florence M. Barnett of Smallthorne, N.Staffs. *Children:* Patricia Margaret. *Educated at* Park Road School, Burslem; School of Arts, Burslem; Royal College of Art, London. *Career:* Painter and etcher, ARCA Painting 1929; Travelling Scholar, School of Engraving, Royal College of Art 1930 - Prints exhibited in exhibitions all over the world, organised by the British Council. Represented by exmaples of my work in the Tate Gallery, The Victoria and Albert Museum, London, The British Museum, London, The Ashmoleum Museum, Oxford, City of Carlisle Art Gallery, Cith of Stoke of Stoke-on-Trent, The Wedwood Museum, Stoke-on-Trent, Birmingham Art Gallery and other important private Collections, including the University of Keele, N.Staffs, the Gladstone Pottery Museum, Longton, Stoke-on-Trent. *Publications:* work reproduced in 'Fine Prints of the Year', 'The Studio', 'Artists Country'. *Recreation:* reading, collecting prints. *Address:* Swn-y-Wylan, Beach Road, Morfa Bychan, Porthmadog. LL49 9YA.

BRENCH,Mrs Marion Ilyd, *Currently:* Constituency Manager for Alex Carlile esq., Q.C., M.P., since 1988. *Born on* 4 Dec 1943 at Ffestiniog, Gwynedd. *Daughter of* Robert Emrys and Doris Francis Jones. *Marriage:* 1965, divorced 1990. *Children:* Laura Kathryn and Huw Gareth Robert. *Educated at* Ysgol Sir Ffestiniog. *Career:* Civil Servant to 1978; Accountant 1978-88; County Councillor (Powys) 1988- . *Recreation:* pre-school education, history of 1st World War and India. *Address:* Haulfryn, Stepaside, Newtown, Powys. SY16 4JQ.

BREWSTER,Mr Richard David,F.C.A. *Currently:* Chief Executive, Jarvis Porter Group plc; Director of Welsh Development Agency, David S Smith (Hldgs) plc, Bankers Investment Trust plc. *Born on* 5 Jan 1946 at London. *Son of* David Edward Brewster and Nancy Winter. *Marriage:* to Susan Ann Jones, daughter of Stanley Boscawenones, born at Steynton, Milford, Pembroke. *Children:* Edward, William, Emily and Rachel *Educated at* Highgate School, London. *Career:* Chartered Accountants, Pridie Brewster, 1963-69; Consultant, 1969-70; Giltspur plc, 1970-83; David S.Smith (Holdings) plc, Neath West Glam, 1983-91; Vice President of Inst. of Packaging. *Publications:*The Livery Lecture, 1991 at the Worshipfull Company of Stationers. *Recreation:* National Committee of Royal National Inst. of Blind ''Looking Glass Appeal''; local history and photography. *Clubs:* Island Cruising Club; Richmond Cricket and Tennis club *Address:* C/o Jarvis Porter, 131 Beddington Lane, Croydon CRO 4TD. Tel: 081 683 0770

BRIDGEMAN, John Stuart,DL (Oxon 1989) *Born on* 5 Oct 1944 *Son of* the late James George Bridgeman of Whitchurch, Cardiff and Edith Celia (nee Watkins). *Marriage:* to Lindy Jane, 1967 da of Sidney Fillmore, of Gidea Park, Essex. *Children:* Victoria (b.1972), Philippa (b.1974) and Annabel (b.1980). *Educated at* Whitchurch School, Cardiff; University College Swansea (BSc). *Career:* Alcan Industries 1966, Aluminium Co of Canada 1969, Alcan Australia 1970, Commercial Dir Alcan (UK) Ltd 1977-80, Vice President (Europe) Alcan Basic Raw Materials 1978-82, Director Saguenay Shipping 1979-82, Divisional MD Alcan Aluminium (UK) Ltd 1981-82, MD Extrusion Division British Alcan Aluminium plc 1983-87, MD British Alcan Enterprises 1987- , Chairman Alcan Building Products Ltd, Alcan Ekco Packaging Ltd, Alcan Extrusions and Tubes Ltd, Aluminium Corporation Ltd, British Alcan Wire & Conductor Ltd, British Alcan Consumer Products Ltd, Luxfer UK Ltd, Luxfer USA, Superform Metals; Trustee Magnesium Industry Council 1976-80, Member Bauxite

Advisory Group Aluminium Federation 1977-81, Council Aluminium Extruders Assoc 1982-91 (Chairman 1987-88), US Aluminium Association Prize Winner 1988, British Airways Consumer Council 1978- , Chairman North Oxon Business Group 1984- , TAVRA Oxon and E Wessex 1985- , Governor North Oxon College 1985- (Chairman 1989, Vice Chairman 1990-), Chairman Enterprise Cherwell Ltd 1985- , Chairman Banbury and District Appeal for Katherine House Hospice 1986- , Vice Chairman Heart of England Training and Enterprise Council 1989- , Member Monopolies & Mergers Commission 1989- ; FBIM; FRGS; AMIPM. Territorial Army and Reserve Forces, commnd TA 1978, QOY 1981-84, Maj REME (V) 1985- , Staff College 1986, Defence Science Adv Council 1991-. *Recreation:* education, gardening, public affairs, shooting, skiing. *Clubs:* Glamorgan County Cricket. *Address:* British Alcan Aluminium Plc, Enterprises Division, Southam Road, Banbury, Oxfordshire OX16 7SN. Tel: 0295 264444

BRIDGES, Rt. Revd. Dewi Morris, MA *Currently:* The Bishop of Swansea & Brecon: Elected on Tuesday 26th January 1988, by the Electorial College of The Church in Wales assembled in the Cathedral Church at Brecon; Election confirmed by the Synod of Bishops of The Church in Wales at Bangor Cathedral on 8th March, 1988; Consecrated in the Metropolitical Cathedral of St.Davids on Lady Day, 25th March 1988, by the Archbishop of Wales and the Bishops of St.Asaph, Bangor, Llandaff, Monmouth, Aberdeen and Orkney, Wyoming, Bishop Eric M.Roberts, Bishop J.J.A. Thomas, Bishop Mark Wood and Bishop R.W.Woods; Enthroned in Brecon Cathedral on 23rd April 1988. *Born on* 18 Nov 1933 at Beaufort. *Son of* Harold Davies Bridges and Elsie Margaret Bridges. *Marriage:* to Rhiannon (nee Williams). *Children:* (Mrs) Sian Rhian Cammack and Jonathan Huw Bridges. *Educated at* SDC, Lampeter 1951-54; Trahern Schol: BA(Hist.Hons 1) 1954; Corpus Christi Coll. Cambridge 1954-56 Purvis Prize & Exhib: BA(Theol.,Hons 2.1) 1956; MA 1960. Westcott Hse.,Cambridge 1957. *Career:* D: 1957; P: 1958. Mon. Crawley Prize, 1958. C: Rhymney 1957-60. C: Chepstow 1960-63. V: Tredegar St.James 1963-65. Lecturer, Sommerfield Coll. of Education, Kidderminster, 1965-68; Senior Lecturer, 1968-69; Gen Lic.Dio. Worcester 1965-69 V; Kempsey (Dio.Worcester) 1969-79 R.D. of Upton on Severn, 1974-79. R: Tenby W. Gumfreston 1979-85 R: Rectorial Benef. of Tenby W. Penally & Gumfreston 1985-88. R.D. of Narberth 1980-82; Archdeacon of St. Davids 1982-88. *Recreation:* music, walking, gardening. *Address:* Ely Tower, Brecon, Powys. LD3 9DE. The Bishop's Flat, Church And House Of The Good, Shepherd, Eastmoor, Clyn Common, Swansea SA3 3JA

BRIDLE, Prof. (Hon Univ. Wales, Cdf) Ronald Jarman, BSc.,FEng.,FICE.,FIHT *Currently:* Consultant & visiting Professor, Cardiff; Inventor - patents ceded to Cardiff Univ.Industry Centre, currently being exploited. *Born on* 27 Jan 1930 at Abersychan, S.Wales. *Son of* Raymond & Dorothy Bridle. *Marriage:* to Beryl Eunice (nee Doe). *Children:* Rachel and Sian. *Educated at* West Monmouth School for Boys; Bristol Univ. *Career:* Engineering posts in West Africa and local Government; Director Midland Road Construction Unit, 1967; Under Secretary Department of Transport, 1972; Chief Highway Engineer, 1976; Controller of R & D and Director Transport & Road Research

Laboratory, 1980; Director of Technology Mitchell Cotts plc, 1983; Retired S.Wales, Consultant, 1987- ; Chairman, Bldg and Civil Eng Council of BSI, and mbr of board, 1977-83; Mbr EDC for Civil Eng, 1976-80; Mbr OECD Commt.Transport Research, 1980-83; Pres.Inst.of Highways & Transportation, 1981; Chrmn Brtsh Nat.Commt, Permanent Int. Assoc. of Road Congresses,1984-88; Mbr Cnl Inst. of Civil Eng., 3 terms. *Publications:* Technical papers in Professional Journals and International Conferences. *Recreation:* Golf, painting and reading. *Address:* Parsonage Farm, Kemeys Commander, Usk, Gwent. NP5 1SU. Tel: 0873 880 929

BRIERLEY, Sir Zachry, CBE.,CBIM. *Currently:* Retired. *Born on* 16 April 1920 at Llandudno. *Son of* Zachry Brierley and Nelli (nee Ashworth). *Marriage:* to Iris Macara, 1946. *Children:* one daughter. *Educated at* Rydal School, Colwyn Bay. *Career:* Joined family business (founded 1920), 1938; RAFVR (T) Flying Officer, 1941-44; Dir. of Z.Brierley Ltd.,1952; Man.Dir.of Z.Brierley Ltd.,1957; M.B.E.,1969; Pres.Z.Brierley (USA)Inc N.Y., 1972; C.B.E.,1978; Knight Bachelor,1987; Companion of British Inst.of Management, 1989; Mbr,Brd of Civic Trust for Wales, 1976- ; Pres.,Conwy Cons.Assoc.,1982- ; Governor,Penrhos Coll.Colwyn Bay, 1980- ; Chrmn of N.Wales Bus.Club,1984- ; Mbr,Welsh Ind.Dev.Brd,Welsh Office; Mbr Brd of Governors,Llandrillo Tech.Coll; Mbr Wilson Commt.(Review of Financial Insts)1977-80; Chrmn CBI Wales Reg.Cncl,1975-77; Chrmn Small & Medium Firms Commsn,UNICE,1975-77; Past Vice-Chrmn N.Wales Med.Trust; Past Chrmn: 'Industry Year', CBI N.Wales Commt, CBI N.Wales Commt,N.Western Export Club; Mbr: Overseas Commt CBI, Smaller Firms Cncl CBI, Central Cncl CBI, Europe Commt CBI, Companies Commt CBI, Wales Reg.Cncl CBI, Smaller Firms Europe Commt CBI, President Commt CBI, Finance & General Purposes Commt CBI, Economic & Financial Policy Commt CBI; Welsh Cncl, Welsh Office; Welsh Cncl Ind.Panel, Celtic Sea Advisory Commt, Welsh Dev. Agency,1975-86, Design Cncl,BBC Advisory Cncl,Wales, 1981-85; Dist.Vice Chrmn (110) Rotary; Past Chrmn & Vice Chrmn Conwy Cons.Assoc; Chrmn Wales Advisory Commt, Design Cncl, 1976-86; Chrmn Wales Cons.Assoc,1982-86; Past Pres.Cons.Political Centre Wales,1981-89; Pres.Wales Area Cons.Assoc.1986-88; led overseas trade missions to the USA and Australasia. *Publications:* 'Following in Footsteps' *Recreation:* Current Affairs, reading and sketching *Clubs:* Carlton *Address:* West Point, Gloddaeth Avenue, Llandudno, Gwynedd. LL30 2AN.

BRISTOW, Professor Stephen Leigh, BSc(Econ); MA; PhD; MBCS; FBIM; FCIS; FCollP; FRSA; FRSH. *Currently:* Assistant Director (Academic Affairs), The Polytechnic of Wales. *Born on* 25 Dec 1948. at Slough, Bucks. *Son of* Donald Eric Bristow and Betty Irene Bristow (nee Hathaway). *Marriage:* to Kathleen Mae Bloomfield 1970. *Children:* Jennie Kathryn and Anna Elizabeth. *Educated at* Sir William Borlase's School; University of London(LSE); University of Kent at Canterbury; University of Reading; University of Salford. *Career:* Lecturer and Senior Lecturer, Manchester Polytechnic 1971-78; Principal Lecturer, Head of Social & Health Studies and Dean of Modular Studies, Wolverhampton Polytechnic, 1978-89; Partner, Network Intelligence (Social and Market Research Consultancy),

1982-88; Director (non-executive), The West Midlands Examinations Bd, 1988-89; ICSA Distance Learning Ltd., 1988-89; Polytechnics Central Admissions System 1989- ; ICSA Publishing Ltd., 1990- ; Student Training and Admissions Registry Ltd., 1991- ; Personal Chairs at Wolverhampton Polytechnic, 1987-89, and the Polytechnic of Wales, 1990- ; Hon.Treasurer, Inst. of Chartered Secretaries and Administrators, 1991, Vice President 1992, and Chairman, Education Cttee, 1988-92; Vice-Pres., College of Preceptors 1989-90; Member, Admin. Lead Body, Dept. of Employment 1991- ; and Final Selection Bd, 1991- ; Chairman of Governors, Wolgarston High School, Penkridge, Staffs, 1985-89.Court of Governors, University College, Swansea 1990- . *Publications:* The Redundant Counties, 1984; many articles on local government and politics, policy studies and education, including: Parents, Power and Participation; 'To Know Ourselves: A Profile of Preceptors'; 'Access and Success: Mature Students' Perceptions of FE and HE'; Reporting to Parents: The Implementation of the 1986 Education Act; Rates and Votes - the 1980 District Council Elections; The Criteria for Local Government Reorganisation and Local Authority Autonomy; Women Councillors. *Recreation:* music, wine and food, travel, photography. *Clubs:* Royal Commonwealth Society, LSE. *Address:* 29 Clos Caradog, Llantwit Fardre, Mid Glamorgan CF38 2DQ.

BROOKE,Mr Arthur Caffin,CB 1972, MA *Currently:* Retired, Chairman Arts Council of Northern Ireland, 1982-86. *Born on* 11 March 1919 *Son of* the late Rev. J.M.Wilmot Brooke and the late Constance. *Marriage:* to the late Margaret Florence Thompson, 1942. *Children:* Michael A.C.Brooke, JP and Dr.Peter E.C.Brooke. *Educated at* Abbotsholme School Derbyshire and Peterhouse, Cambridge. *Career:* Served War 1939-46, Royal Corps of Signals; Joined Ministry of Commerce, Northern Ireland, 1946; Head of Ind.Development, 1955; Permanent Sec.,1969-73; Permanent Secretary, Dept.ofEducation, Northern Ireland, 1973-79. *Recreation:* Walking; touring; history; the arts. *Address:* 4 Camden Court, Brecon, Powys. LD3 7RP.

BROOKE OF YSTRADFELLTE, Baroness Barbara Brooke, D.B.E. *Born on* 14 Jan 1908 at Swansea. *Daughter of* the late Canon A.A. Mathews and the late Ethel Frances (nee Evans). *Marriage:* to the late Henry Brooke PC.CH., (later Baron Brooke of Cumnor), 1933. *Children:* 2 sons, 2 daughters. *Educated at* Queen Anne's School, Caversham. *Career:* Joint Vice-Chairman, Conservative Party Organisation, 1954-64; Member Hampstead Borough Council, 1948-65; North West Metropolitan Regional Hospital Board, 1954-66; Management Committee, King Edwards Hospital Fund for London, 1966-71; Chairman Exec. Cmmt Queen's Institute of District Nursing 1961-71; Governing Body of Godolphin and Latymen School, Hammersmith Chairman 1960-78; Hon. Fellow, Westfield College. *Recreation:* Lacrosse. *Clubs:* University Women's Club - Hon. member. *Address:* Romans Halt, Mildenhall, Marlborough, Wilts. SN8 2LX.

BROOKS,Mr Douglas,DipSoc Sci. CIPM. *Currently:* Independent Management Consultant. *Born on* 3 Sept 1928 at Abercarn. *Son of* Oliver James Brooks and Olive (nee Davies). *Marriage:* to June Anne (nee Branch), 1952. *Children:* Jonathan and Sarah. *Educated at* Newbridge Grammar School; University College Cardiff. *Career:* Employment Officer, Girling Ltd., 1953-56; Personnel Officer to Personnel Director, Hoover Ltd., 1956-78; Chief Personnel Executive, Tarmac PLC 1979-80; Director, Walker Brooks & Partners 1980-90; Director, Flexello PLC 1987-91. Vice President Inst. of Personnel Management 1972-74; Visiting Research Fellow, Policy Studies Institute 1982-84; Council Member ESRC 1976-82; Member BBC Consult Group on Social Effects of Television 1978-80; Chairman Wooburn Festival Society Ltd., 1978-86. *Publications:* various articles in professional journals. With Prof. Michael Fogarty - Trade Unions and British Indust. Development. *Recreation:* talking, reading, music, cooking, gardening. *Clubs:* Reform. *Address:* Old Court, Winforton, Hereford HR3 6EA. 29 Dolphin Court, Kingsmead Road, Loudwater, High Wycombe HP11 1XE

BROOM,Air Marshal Sir Ivor Gordon, KCB, CBE, DSO, DFC & 2 Bars, AFC. *Currently:* International Aerospace Consultant, since 1977; Chairman, Gatwick Handling Ltd., since 1982; Chairman Farnborough Aerospace Development Corporation plc, since 1985; Chairman Carroll Aircraft Corporation plc, since 1987. *Born on* 2 June 1920 at Cardiff. *Son of* the late Alfred Godfrey and the late Janet. *Marriage:* to Jessica Irene, 1942. *Children:* David, Diane and Ian. *Educated at* West Mon School, Pontypool; Pontypridd County School. *Career:* Joined Royal Air Force 1940, retired 1977. Wartime Bomber pilot, appointments included, OC No. 163 Sqn, 1945, OC No.28 Sqn, 1946, OC No. 57 Sqn, 1953, OC Bomber Command Development Unit 1956; OC RAF Bruggen 1962; Commandant Central Flying School 1968; A.O.C., No.11 (Fighter) Group 1970; Controller National Air Traffic Services and member Board of Civil Aviation Authority 1974. *Recreation:* President, Royal Air Forces Assoc (Wales area); President Moor Park Golf Club (captain 1977). *Clubs:* Royal Air Force, Pathfinder, Moor Park. *Address:* Cherry Lawn, Bridle Lane, Loudwater, Rickmansworth, Herts. WD3 4JB. Tel: 0923 778878

BRUCE-GARDNER, Sir Douglas, Bt., M.A. *Currently:* retired. *Born on* 27 Jan 1917 at Chester. *Son of* Sir Charles & Lady Bruce-Gardner (nee Shill). *Marriage:* 1st to Monica Jefferson; 2nd to Sheila Stilliard. *Children:* (from 1st marriage) Judith, Robert and Tanis; (from 2nd marriage) Joanna and Graham. *Educated at* Uppingham & Trinity, Cambridge *Career:* Ch. GKN Steel 1965-67; GKN Rolled & Bright Steel 1968-72; Director GKN Group 1960-82; Dep.Ch. 1974-77; Director Iron Trade Employers Insurance Assoc 1977-87; Primewarden, The Worshipful Company of Blacksmiths 1983-84. Pres. Iron & Steel Institute 1966-67; Pres. British Independent Steel Producers Assoc 1972. *Recreation:* fishing & photography *Address:* Stocklands, Lewstone, Ganarew, Nr. Monmouth NP5 3SS.

BRUNSKILL,Mr Ronald William,OBE 1990; MA, PhD; FSA *Currently:* Architect, lecturer and author; Hon Fellow, School of Architecture, University of Manchester, since 1989 (Lecturer 1960-73, Senior Lecturer 1973-84, Reader in Architecture 1984-89). *Born on* 3 Jan 1929 *Son of* William Brunskill and Elizabeth Hannah Brunskill. *Marriage:* to Miriam Allsopp, 1960. *Children:* two d. *Educated at* Bury High School; Univ. of Manchester (BA Hons Arch 1951, MA 1952, PhD 1963). *Career:* Registered Architect and ARIBA 1951; FSA 1975. National Service,

2nd Lieut RE 1953-55. Studio Asst. in Arch., Univ of Manchester 1951-53; Architectural Asst, LCC 1955; Asst in Arch, Univ of Manchester 1955-56; Commonwealth Fund Fellow (arch and town planning) MIT 1956-57; Architect to Williams Deacon's Bank, 1957-60; Architect in private practice 1960-66; Partner, Carter, Brunskill & Associates, chartered architects 1966-69; Consultant 1969-73. Vis Prof. Univ of Florida, Gainesville 1969-70. President: Vernacular Arch Gp 1974-77; Cumberland and Westmorland Antiquarian and Archael Soc., 1990- ; Vice-Pres Weald and Downland Museum Trust 1980- ; Member: Historic Bldgs Council for England 1978-84; Royal Commn on Ancient and Historical Monuments of Wales 1983- ; Historic Buildings and Monuments Commn (English Heritage) 1989- (Mem Historic Buildings Adv. Cttee and Ancient Monuments Adv Cttee of Historic Buildings and Monuments Commn 1984-90); Chairman Ancient Monuments Soc 1990- .(Hon.Architect 1983-88, Vice- Chm 1988-90); Cathedrals Adv. Commn for England 1981- ; Manchester Diocesan Adv Cttee for Care of Churches 1973-79 and 1987- ; Manchester Cathedral Fabric Cttee 1987- ; Blackburn Cathedral Fabric Cttee 1989- ; Council Soc for Folk Life Studies 1969-72 and 1980-83. Trustee, British Historic Buildings Trust 1985-; Neale Bursar, RIBA 1962; President's Award, Manchester Soc of Architects 1977. *Publications:* Illustrated Handbook of Vernacular Architecture 1971, 3rd edn (enlarged) 1987; Vernacular Architecture of the Lake Counties 1974; (with Alec Clifton-Taylor) English Brickwork 1977; Traditional Buildings of Britain 1981, 2nd ed.(enlarged), 1992; Houses (in series, Collins Archaeology) 1982; Traditional Farm Buildings of Britain 1982, 2nd edn (enlarged) 1987; Timber Building in Britain 1985; Brick Building in Britain 1990l articles and reviews in archaeol and architectural journals. *Recreation:* enjoying the countryside *Clubs:* Athenaeum. *Address:* 159 Glan Gors, Harlech, Gwynedd LL46 2SA. Three Trees, 8 Overhill Road, Wilmslow SK9 2BEA

BRUTON, Professor Michael John, BA, MSc(Eng)DIC, DipTP, MCIT, FRTPI, MIHT. *Currently:* Professor of Town Planning, since 1977; Registrar University of Wales Cardiff, since 1988. *Born on* 28 March 1938 *Son of* the late Patrick John Bruton and Louise Bruton (nee Roberts). *Marriage:* to Sheila G.Harrison, 1963. *Children:* Suzanne C Bruton and Catherine J Bruton. *Educated at* Richard Hale School; University College London; Imperial College London. *Career:* Planning Practice London County Council, Lanarkshire County Council, Buckingham County Council, 1961-67; Principal Lecturer Oxford Polytechnic, 1967-72; Head School Planning & Landscape Birmingham Polytechnic, 1972-77; Vice Principal UWIST, 1982-85; Deputy Principal UWIST, 1985-88. Fellow Royal Town Planning Institute; Fellow Chartered Institute Transport; Member Institute Highways and Transport. *Publications:* Books: Introduction ot Transportation Planning (3 eds); Spirit & Purpose of Planning (2 eds); Local Planning in Practice; numerous articles in learned journals. *Recreation:* watching rugby, cricket. *Clubs:* Commonwealth. *Address:* University Of Wales Cardiff, P.O. Box 920, Cardiff CF1 3XP.17 Coedydafarn, Lisvane, Cardiff CF4 5RQ

BRYANT, David John, BA (Hons). *Currently:* Medical representative. *Born on* 21 Feb 1967 at Bridgend. *Son of* John Martin Bryant and Andrea Irene Bryant. *Marriage:* to

Sera Jane. *Educated at* Bryntyrion Comprehensive; Swansea University; South Glamorgan Institute. *Career:* Rugby: Captained: Welsh Secondary Schools, Welsh Universities, Welsh Colleges, Welsh Students, Wales 'B', Wales 7's, Bridgend RFC. Other *Clubs:* Crawshays, Welsh Accies, Steep Holme. Vice captain - Wales, 8 caps. *Recreation:* golf, rugby, food and wine. *Address:* 17 Long Close, Bradley Stoke South, Bristol BS12 8BG.

BUCKLEY, Major William Kemmis, MBE; KStJ; MA; DL *Currently:* Director, Felinfoel Brewery Co. *Born on* 18 Oct 1921 at York. *Son of* Lt.Col William Howell Buckley and Karolie Kathleen(nee Kemmis). *Educated at* Radley College; New College, Oxford. *Career:* Commissioned into Welsh Guards, served N.Africa, Italy, Cyprus, Suez; Director, Rhymney Brewery, Whitbread (Wales); Chairman, later President, Buckley's Brewery; Lay member of Press Council and Chairman of S.Wales Brewers Assn; Vice Lord Lieutenant of Dyfed; High Sherrif of Carmarthenshire 1967. *Publications:* in local hisotry journals. *Recreation:* gardening, tapestry. *Clubs:* Brooks's, Cardiff and County. *Address:* Briar Cottage, Ferryside, Dyfed. SA17 5UB.

BUFTON, Air Vice-Marshal Sydney Osborne, CB 1945; DFC 1940. *Born on* 12 Jan 1908 at Llandrindod Wells, Radnor. *Son of* the late J.O. Bufton JP. *Marriage:* to Susan Maureen, 1943, d of Colonel E.M.Browne, DSO, Chelsea. *Children:* two d. *Educated at* Dean Close School, Cheltenham. *Career:* Commissioned RAF 1927; psa 1939; idc, 1946. Served War of 1939-45, Bomber Comd., Nos 10 and 76 sqdns, RAF Station, Pocklington 1940-41; Dep. Dir Bomber Ops, Air Min, 1941-43, ; Dir of Bomber Ops, 1943-45; AOC Egypt, 1945-46; Central Bomber Establishment, RAF, Marham, Norfolk, 1947-48; Dep. Chief of Staff (Ops/ Plans). Air Forces Western Europe 1948-51; Dir of Weapons, Air Min., 1951-52; AOA Bomber Command, 1952-53; AOC Brit. Forces, Aden, 1953-55; Senior Air Staff Officer, Bomber Comd, 1955-58; Assistant Chief of Air Staff (Intelligence), 1958-61; retired Oct 1961. Invented radio and electronic construction system (Radionic), 1961-62; Man. Dir, Radionic Products Ltd, 1962-70. FRAeS 1970. High Sheriff of Radnorshire, 1967. Comdr Legion of Merit (US); Comdr of Orange Nassau (with swords), Netherlands. *Recreation:* hockey (Welsh International 1931-37, Combined Services, RAF), golf, squash. *Clubs:* Royal Air Force *Address:* 1 Castle Keep, Reigate, Surrey RH2 9PU. Tel: (0737) 243707

BULLOCK Aka Bulloch, Mr John Angel, *Currently:* Author and Freelance Journalist. *Born on* 15 April 1928 at Penarth. *Son of* Capt. W.P.G. Bullock and Mrs Dorothy Bullock. *Marriage:* 1st to Hazel Campbell; 2nd to Susan Birkett; 3rd to Jill Brown. *Children:* Nicholas, Adam Jill, Oya and James. *Educated at* Penarth County School; HMS Conway. *Career:* Cadet, Merchant Navy; local papers in S.Wales and N.E.England; P.A.,Foreign Cor; Daily Telegraph; Diplomatic Corr; BBC World Service; Middle East Editor, The Independent 1986-89; Diplomatic Correspondent, Independent on Sunday 1989-91. *Publications:* Spy Ring; Akin to Reason; The Making of a War; Death of a Country; The Gulf; The Gulf War; Saddam's War. *Recreation:* Growing vegetables, brewing and wine making. *Address:* 71 Bainton Road, Oxford OX2 7AD.

BURGE, Professor Ronald Edgar, B.Sc.Ph.D.D.Sc.C.Phys. FKC.F.Inst.P. *Currently:* Wheatstone Professor of Physics and Head of Department of Physics, King's College, London. *Born on* 3 Oct 1932 at Cardiff. *Son of* the late John Burge and Edith (nee Thompson). *Marriage:* to Janet Mary Pitts, 1953. *Children:* Andrew John and Peter Ronald. *Educated at* Canton High School, Cardiff; King's College, London. *Career:* Assistant Lecturer in Physics, King's College, University of London, 1954-58; Lecturer in Physics, King's College, 1958-62; Reader in Biophysics, King's College, 1962-63; Professor of Physics & Head of Department, Queen Elizabeth College, University of London, 1963-84; Member: Swinnerton-Dyer Cttee concerning Academic Governance of University of London, 1979-82; Computer Board for Universities & Research Councils (responsible for Computer development in Universities in Scotland and, latterly, SW England, 1978-82; Professor of Physics & Head of Department, King's College, 1984-89; Vice-Principal, King's College, University of London, 1987-91. *Publications:* In fields of electron-microscopy, X-ray physics, optical physics, synthetic aperture radar, imaging, scattering theory. *Recreation:* Gardening and music. *Clubs:* Member of The Royal Institution of Great Britain (1988). *Address:* 60 Sutherland Avenue, Orpington, Kent. BR5 1RB. Physics Department, King's College, Strand, London, WC2R 2LS

BURGESS (nee Evans),Mrs Dilys (Averil),BA Hons, FRSA. *Currently:* Headmistress, South Hampstead High School, London, since 1975. *Born on* 8 July 1938 at Liverpool. *Daughter of* the late David Llewellyn Evans and Dorothy (nee Owen). *Marriage:* to Clifford Burgess, 1959 (marr diss. 1973). *Educated at* Ashby-de-la-Zouch Girls' Grammar School, Leics; Queen Mary College, University of London. *Career:* member: Girls' Schools Association Education Sub committee 1983-87; Girls Public Day School Trust Bursaries Management Ctee 1979-84; Governor, Central School of Speech and Drama 1981- ; President, Girls' Schools Association 1988-89; Chairman, Independent Schools Joint Council Policy Group 1990-92; Member: Council for Accreditation of Teacher Education 1990- ; Member: National Commission on Education 1991- . *Recreation:* walking in Wales, learning Welsh, books, theatre, film. *Clubs: Address:* South Hampstead High School, 3 Maresfield Gardens, London NW3 5SS. 123 North Hill, Highgate, London N6 4DP

BURGOYNE,The Reverend Edward Geoffrey,BA (Wales). *Currently:* retired Priest - Schoolmaster. *Born on* 18 Nov 1927 at Bridgend, Glam. *Son of* Edward Godfrey Burgoyne and Florence Mildred (neeLloyd) *Educated at* Cowbridge; UCW Aberystwyth; St Michael's College Llandaff. *Career:* Deacon 1951, Priest 1952 Diocese of Llandaff; Curate Aberavon 1951-55; Ynyshir 1955-63; Vicar Bockleton W.Leysters & P.i.C. Hatfield 1963-70; Head of House, The Bishop of Hereford's Bluecoat School 1970-91. Licenced under Seal, Diocese of Hereford 1970- ; attached as Honorary Assistant Priest at All Saints' & St.Barnabas, Hereford; Clinical Pastoral Counsellor 1965. *Recreation:* gardening, pottery, painting, fly fishing. *Address:* Lawnswood, Tupsley, Hereford HR1 1UT. Tel: 0423 268860

BURN, Mr Michael Clive, MC *Currently:* Author. *Born on* 11 Dec 1912 in London. *Son of* Sir Clive Burn and Phyllis Stoneham. *Marriage:* to Mary Booker (nee Walter) 1947. *Educated at* Winchester New Coll., Oxford (open scholar)

Hons. Degree in Soc., Scis., Oxford with distinction in all subjects (awarded whilst POW at Colditz) *Career:* Journalist, The Times 1936-39; Lieut 1st Bn Queens Westminsters, KRRC 1939-40; Officer in Independent Companies, Norwegian Campaign 1940, subseq. Captain No. 2 Commando, taken prisoner in raid on St. Nazaire 1942, prisoner in Germany 1942-45; Foreign Correspondent for The Times in Vienna, Jugoslavia and Hungary 1946-49; Keats Poetry First Prize, 1973; Plays: The Modern Everyman (Prod. Birmingham Rep., 1947); Beyond the Storm (Midland Arts Co., and Vienna 1947); The Night of the Ball (prod. New Theatre 1956). *Publications:* Yes Farewell 1946, repr. 1975; Childhood at Oriol 1951; The Midnight Diary 1952; The Trouble with Jake 1967; sociological: Mr Lyward's Answer 1956; The Debatable Land 1970; poems: Poems to Mary 1953; The Flying Castle 1954; Out On A Limb 1973; Open Day And Night 1978; play: The Modern Everyman 1948; non-fiction: Mary & Richard 1988. *Address:* Beudy Gwyn, Penrhyndeudraeth, Gwynedd, North Wales. LL48 6EN.

BURR, Michael Rodney,Solicitor, Recorder. *Currently:* Senior Partner, Peter Williams & Company, Solicitors, 93 Walter Road, Swansea, SA1 5QA, since 1972. *Born on* 31 Aug 1941 at Machynlleth. *Son of* Frank Edward Burr and Aileen Maud Burr. *Marriage:* to Rhoda (nee Rule), 1963. *Children:* David, Richard, Andrew, Elizabeth and Edwin. *Educated at* Brecon County Grammar School; King Edward VI School; Chelmsford College of Law. *Career:* Admitted Solicitor 1964; Assistant Solicitor Hilliard & Ward Chelmsford 1964-69; Assistant Recorder 1983, Recorder 1988; Secretary Incorporated Law Society of Swansea and District 1980-83; non council member of Law Society Committees: Professional Purposes Committee 1985-86, Adjudication Committee 1986-89; Member Law Society. *Recreation:* flying, reading. *Address:* 93 Walter Road, Swansea SA1 5QA.Tel: 0792 465597

BURTON, Archimandrite Ian Hamilton (in Religion-Barnabas), *Currently:* Priest-Monk of Greek Orthodox Church, Archdiocese Thyateira and Great Britain. *Born on* 3 Sept 1915 at Pennal, Nr.Machynlleth, Powys. *Son of* Peter Jones and Margaret Burton (nee Latham) *Educated at* Pennal Primary School; Towyn Grammar School; St.David's College, Lampeter; Ely Theological College; Seminary of Three Holy Doctors, Villemoisson, Sur-Orge, Seine et Oise. *Career:* Curacies in Anglican Church 1938-60; Colwyn Bay, Buckley Bangor Cathedral, Landore Wantage, St.Michael's College, Tenbury,St.Asaph Cathedral; Monk at Seminary of Three Holy Doctors, Villemoisson-Sur Orge SetO, France 1960-65; St. Elias Monastery Willand Devon 1965- ; New Mills Newtown Powys 1973. *Publications:* "Strange Pilgrimage" (autobiography). *Recreation:* gardening, music. *Address:* Mynachdy Sant Elias, New Mills, Newtown, Powys SY16 3NQ. Metochion Of St. Tydfil, 12 Bridge Street, Aberfan, Merthyr Tydfil CF48 4RB Tel: 0686 650424

BUTLER,Mr Christopher John,MA (Cantab) *Currently:* Member of Parliament (Con) for Warrington South, since 1987. *Born on* 12 Aug 1950 at Cardiff. *Son of* Dr. John Butler and the late Eileen (nee O'Neil). *Marriage:* to Jacqueline Clair Harper. *Educated at* Cardiff H.S. for Boys; Emmanuel College Cambridge. *Career:* Market Research Executive 1972-75; Market Research Consultant 1975-77;

Conservative Research Department covering Wales area 1977-80; Political Office, 10 Downing Street, London SW1, 1980-83; Special Adviser to Secretary of State for Wales 1983-85; Market Research Consultant 1985-86; Special Adviser to Minister for the Arts 1986-87. *Publications:*''Cymraeg: Iaith Ein Plant?''; ''A Conservative Approach to The Welsh Language; "Aids - A Darkness Over Africa''. *Recreation:* reading, writing. *Address:* House Of Commons, London SW1A OAA.

BUTLER,Mr John Michael, IPFA FCCA IRRV FBIM *Currently:* City Treasurer, Swansea City Council since 1979; Clerk and Treasurer, Swansea Bay Port Health Authority. *Born on* 12 Sep 1943 at Bromley, Kent. *Son of* Reginald Butler and the late Kathleen (nee Garside). *Marriage:* to Daphne Ann 1964. *Children:* David Michael and Michael Alan. *Educated at* Beckenham and Penge Grammar School *Career:* Audit Asst. Croydon and King, 1960; Audit Asst. Beckenham BC, 1960-61; Accountancy Asst., Sevenoaks UDC, 1961-63; Accountant, Caterham UDC, 1963-64; Senior Accountant, Dorking UDC, 1964-66; Asst. Treasurer, Esher UDC, 1966-70; Asst. Borough Treasurer, Greenwich LBC, 1970-74; Chief Finance Officer, Lambeth LBC, 1974-79; Principal Financial Adviser to the ADC Council of Welsh Districts; Finance Director, Swansea City Development Company; Exec. Cttee. Memb. Assoc. of District Council Treasurers; Past Pres. Inst. of Revenues Rating & Valuation; Past Pres. CIPFA in South Wales & West of England; Past Chmn. CIPFA West Wales Students Soc.; Past Treasurer, CIPFA South East Region; Past Sec., CIPFA Joint Cttee. of Members' Sections; Past Examiner - Inst. of Chartered Secretaries & Administrators, Business Education Council- Assoc. of Accounting Technicians; *Publications:* Rate Support Grant, 1968; Capital Financing Budget, 1971; Manpower Planning, 1976; Swansea Enterprize Zone, 1981; Welsh RSG Settlement, 1983; Local Authority Approaches to EEC Aid, 1983; Manager Welsh Senior Orienteering Team; Chmn. Welsh Orienteering Assoc.; Chmn., Swansea Bay Orienteering Club. *Recreation:* Orienteering, skiing and sailing *Clubs:* Swansea Bay Orienteering (Chmn.); Mumbles Yacht; South Wales Ski; *Address:* The Guildhall, Swansea SA1 4PE. Tel: 0792 301301

BUTTON, Mr John Haddon, OBE., FHSM., ACIS. *Currently:* Management Consultant. *Born on* 17 April 1931 at Neath. *Son of* the late Charles Haddon Button and the late Mary Louise Button (nee Davies). *Marriage:* to Morfydd Rees 1952. *Children:* Mark Christopher and Gillian Mary. *Educated at* Neath Grammar School *Career:* Hospital Secretary, Aberystwyth Hospitals, 1958-61; Hospital Sec., Broadgreen Hospital, Liverpool, 1961-63; Dep. Group Sec., Rotherham & Mexborough Hospital Management Commt., 1963-67; Asst. Sec., (Planning), Liverpool Regional Hospital Board, 1968-70; Group Sec., North Mon. Hospital Management Commt, 1970-73; Chief Exec. Dir., W.Glamorgan Health Authority, 1973-91; W.Wales Training & Enterprise Council, Brd Mbr & Chairman of Health/Care Sub board, 1990-91; Nat. Health Service Training Auth.- Welsh Management mbr, 1985-91 and Chairman of its Ambulance Staff Commt. Assoc of Chief Admin. of Health Authorities (Eng & Wales) Council mbr, Chairman, 1983-84; Inst of Health Service Mgt, Nat. Council mbr, 1976-83; V.Chairman, Wales Training & Dev. Commt to 1991. *Publications:* World Hospitals (1986); Health Service Review, 1979; Health Manpower Management 1989; Health Services Review 1989, ''Wales Today''. *Recreation:* Golf, music and rugby football *Clubs:* Swansea Rotary Club *Address:* 27, Derwyn Fawr, Swansea, SA2 9LY.

BUTTRESS,Mr Donald Reeve, MA., Dip Arch., RIBA., FSA. *Currently:* Surveyor of the Fabric of Westminster Abbey, 1988; Chichester Cathedral, 1985; Architect to Llandaff Cathedral. *Born on* 27 April 1932 at Manchester, UK. *Son of* Edward Crossley Buttress and Evelyn Edna Reeve-Whaley. *Marriage:* to Elsa M. Bardsley, 1956. *Children:* Helen, Richard,Fiona, John and Lucy. *Educated at* Stockport School and University of Manchester. *Career:* RAF Flying Officer, 1958-61; Lecturer University of Manchester, 1964-78; Vis. Professor & Fulbright Travelling Fellow, University of Florida, 1987-88; Partner Buttress Fuller Alsop, Architects, Manchester and London. *Clubs:* Royal Air Force *Address:* 2b Little Cloister, Westminster Abbey, London. SW1 3PA.

C

CADOGAN,Colonel Henry Michael Edward,OBE *Currently:* Army Schools Liai *Son of* ficer for N.W. of England (and for North Wales from August 1992). *Born on* 18 Jan 1935 at Hadnall, Salop..*Son of* Col.E.H.Cadogan CBE(late Royal Welch Fusiliers)andthe late Lady Veronica Cadogan(d of Earl Cavan). *Marriage:* to Daphnie Jane Richards Mason, 1966. *Children:* Camilla (.1968) and Edward (b. 1970). *Educated at* Winchester College; RMA Sandhurst; StaffCollege Camberley. *Career:* Commissioned Royal Welch Fusiliers 1955. Served Germany, Malaya, Cyprus (ADC to Director of Operations), Hong Kong and Kenya. Instructor RMA Sandhurst 1963-65; ADC to Lord Lieutenant of Caernarfon in 1969, over period of investiture of HRH The Prince of Wales. Commanded 3rd (Volunteer) Bn RWF 1978-80. Defence, Naval, Military and Air Attache Damascus and Beirus 1983-85. Military Adviser to Minister of Defence U.A.E. (H.H.Sheikh Mohammed at Maktouu) 1985-87. Hon. Col. 3rd (V) Bn RWF since 1989. Chairman N.Wales Committee of Army Benevolent Fund. *Recreation:* sailing, shooting, gardening. *Clubs:* Army and Navy. *Address:* Fronisaf, Pentrecelyn, Ruthin, Clwyd, LL15 2HR.

CADOGAN,Professor Sir John (Ivan George),CBE; PhD; DSc; CChem; FRSC; FRSE; FRS. *Currently:* Director of Research, British Petroleum Co since 1981. *Born on* 8 Oct 1930 at Pembrey, Carms. *Son of* Alfred and Dilys Cadogan. *Marriage:* to Margaret Jeanne Evans, Swansea. *Children:* Richard and Jane. *Educated at* Swansea Grammar School; Kings College, London. *Career:* Lecturer in Chemistry, Kings College, London, 1956-63; Purdie Professor of Chemistry, Univ. St.Andrews 1963-69; Forbes Professor of Chemistry, Univ. Edinburgh 1969-79; Chief Scientist BP 1979-81; President Roy Soc. Chemistry 1982-84; Member Roy Commission Criminal Justice 1991- ; Hon.DSC: Leicester, Durham, London, Wales, Edinburgh, St.Andrews, Stirling, Aberdeen, Aix Marseille. *Publications:* over 250 scientific papers.*Clubs:* Athenaeum *Address:* British Petroleum Co. Plc, Britannic House, 1 Finsbury Circus, London,EC2M 7BA.

CALDWELL,Dr. Neil Edward,PhD *Currently:* Director CPRW, 1988- . *Born on* 17 April 1952 at London. *Son of* Robert A Caldwell and Kathleen C Caldwell (nee Barnard). *Marriage:* to Betsan Charles Jones, 1977. *Children:* Catrin Lowri Iorwerth and Owain Rhys Iorwerth (notCaldwell). *Educated at* Dr Challoners Grammar School, Amersham; Univ. Coll. Aberystwyth; Polytechnic of Wales. *Career:* President, NUS Wales, 1975-77; Research Assistant Polytechnic of Wales, 1977-82; The National Trust, 1982-88; Fellow of the Royal Soc. for the Arts Council; Mbr of the Inst. of Welsh Affairs; Vice Chrmn of Wales Wildlife & Countryside Link; Mbr of National Rivers Auth.Welsh Regional Rivers Advisory Commt; Mbr of Wales Council for Voluntary Action's, North and West Wales Advisory Commt; Mbr of Council for National Parks; Mbr of Green Alliance. *Publications:* N E Caldwell,A T Williams and L F Gulbrandsen, Storm induced beach morphological changes 1978; NE Caldwell, AT Williams and AP Yule, Beach morphology changes at Ynyslas Spit, Wales, 1981; NE Caldwell and AT Williams, Sediment disturbance by "beach paddlers",along the Glamorgan Heritage Coast, Shore & Beach, 1981; NE Caldwell,AT Williams and P.Davies, The Glamorgan Heritage Coast:A Guide to its Landforms, Glamorgan Heritage Coast Pubs,1981; Relationship between tracers & background beach materials, 1981; NE Caldwell and AT Williams, Coastal Research in Bulgaria, 1981; with AT Williams and GT Roberts, the swash-force transducer, 1982; Using tracers to assess size and shape sorting processes on a pebble beach, 1982; with AT Williams, Instability in the glacial tills of western Llyn, N.Wales, indicating the balance between natural processes, human intervention and *Recreation:* walking, cycling, travel. *Address:* Campaign For The Protection Of Rural Wales, Ty Gwyn 31 High St., Welshpool, Powys SY21 7JP. Bryn Rhosyn, Llanfair Caereinion, Powys SY21 OBS

CALLAGHAN OF CARDIFF,The Rt. Hon Lord Leonard James,KG., PC *Born on* 27 Mar 1912 *Son of* James Callaghan, Chief Petty Officer RN. *Marriage:* to Audrey Elizabeth Moulton 1938. *Children:* one s, two d. *Educated at* Elementary & Portsmouth Northern Sec. Schls. *Career:* Entered Civil Serv. as a Tax Officer, 1929; Asst.Sec., Inland Rev. Staff Fed., 1936-47 (with an interval during the War of 1939-45 when served in Royal Navy); Joined Labour Party, 1931, MP (Lab): S.Cardiff 1945-50; SE Cardiff 1950-83; Cardiff S and Penarth, 1983-87; Parly. Sec.,Min. of Transport 1947-50; Chm Cmmt on Road Safety, 1948-50; Parliamentary & Financial Sec., Admiralty, 1950-51; Opposition Spokesman: Transport, 1951-53; Fuel & Power, 1953-55; Colonial Affairs, 1956-61; Shadow Chancellor, 1961-64; Chancellor of the Exchequer, 1964-67; Home Sec. 1967-70; Shadow Home Sec. 1970-71; Opposition Spokesman on Employment, 1971-72; Shadow Foreign Sec., 1972-74; Sec. of State for Foreign & Commonwealth Affairs, 1974-76; Min of Overseas Develt, 1975-76; Prime Minister and First Lord of the Treasury. 1976-79; Leader, Labour Party 1976-80; Leader of the Opposition, 1979-80; Father, House of Commons, 1983-87; Deleg to Council of Europe, Strasburg, 1948-50 and 1954; Mbr., Labour Party NEC, 1957-80; Treasurer, Labour Party, 1967-76, Vice-Chm, 1973, Chm 1974; Consultant to Police Fedn of England and Wales and to Scottish Police Fedn, 1955-64; Pres: Adv. Cttee on Pollution of the Sea, 1963- ; (Chm., 1952-63); U.K. Pilots Assoc, 1963-76; Jt. Pres., RIIA.Hon.Pres., Internat. Maritime Pilots Assoc., 1971-76;

Pres., UC Swansea, 1986- ; Visiting Fellow, Nuffield Coll. Oxford, 1959-67; Hon.Life Fellow, 1967; Hon.Fellow: UC Cardiff, 1978; Portsmouth Polytechnic, 1981; Hon. Fellow Cardiff Institute of Higher Education, 1991; Hon.LLD: Univ. of Wales, 1976; Sardar Patel Univ., India, 1978; Univ. of Birmingham, 1981; Univ. of Sussex, 1989; Hon.Bencher, Inner Temple, 1976; Hon.Freeman: City of Cardiff, City of Portsmouth, City of Sheffield, Honorary degrees University of Wales, Birmingham University, Sardar Patel University (Gujarat), Sussex University, Mesei University (Japan); 1978 awarded the first Hubert Humphrey Award for International Statesmanship, New York; awarded the Grand Cross First Class of the Order of Merit of the Federal Republic of Germany, 1979: *Publications:* A House Divided: the dilemma of Northern Ireland, 1973; Time and Chance (autobiog), 1987. *Address:* House Of Lords, Westminster, London. SW1.

CALVIN, Mr Wyn (alias: Wyndham Calvin-Thomas), MBE (Birthday Honours 1989) *Born on* 27 Aug 1927 at Narberth, Pembrokeshire. *Son of* the late John Calvin-Thomas and the late Ethel (nee Griffiths). *Marriage:* to Carole Tarvin-Jones, 1975. *Educated at* Canton High School, Cardiff. *Career:* A lifetime of involvement in Theatre, Radio and television since leaving school in 1945. National Chairman: Wales Committee Variety Club of Great Britain 1980-84; 'King Rat' Grand Order of Water Rats 1991; Vice-President, London Welsh Male Choir; Vice President, Cor Meibion De Cymru. Governor: Monkton House Educational Trust. Vice-Chairman: Stars Organisation for Spastics, etc. *Publications:* occasional newspaper columnist. *Recreation:* reading, writing, world travel. *Address:* 121 Cathedral Road, Cardiff CF1 9PH.

CAMERON, Dr Keith Colwyn, BA, LesL, Doct.de l'Univ. *Currently:* Reader in French and Renaissance Studies, University of Exeter, since 1988. *Born on* 1 April 1939 at Cwmbran, Gwent. *Son of* the late Leonard George Cameron and Ethel Cameron(nee Booth). *Marriage:* to Marie-Edith Francoise Briens, 1962. *Children:* Anne, Cecilia and Virginia. *Educated at* Jones' West Monmouth School, Pontypool; Universities of Exeter, Cambridge, Rennes. *Career:* Lecturer, Rennes 1962-64; Asst. Lecturer, Aberdeen 1964-66; Lecturer, Exeter 1966-76; Senior Lecturer 1976-88; Dean of the Faculty of Arts, Exeter 1991-94. Director: Exeter Tapes, Elm Bank Publications. Chairman: Devon Branch of the European Movement, 1985- . *Publications:* Montaigne et l'humour, 1966; Agrippa d'Aubigne, 1977; Henri III - a maligned or malignant king?, 1978; Rene Maran, 1985; B.Palissy: Recepte veritable, 1988; Concordance des OEuvres poetiques de J. du Bellay, 1988; From Valois to Bourbon, 1989; Computer Assisted Language Learning, 1989; Louise Labe. Feminist and Poet of the Renaissance, 1990. Editor: Exeter Tapes 1972- ; Exeter Textes litteraires 1970- ; Computer Assisted language Learning 1990- . *Recreation:* travel, walking, theatre. *Address:* Department Of French, Queen's Building, The University, Exeter EX4 4QH.

CAMPBELL, Mr Bryn, FRPS, FBIPP. *Currently:* Consultant picture editor and photographer. *Born on* 20 May 1933 at Penrhiwceiber, Glam. *Son of* the late Mr Brinley Campbell and Mrs Dorothy Irene Campbell. *Marriage:* to Audrey Campbell (nee Berryman), 1960. *Educated at* Mountain Ash Grammar School; Manchester University. *Career:*

National Service, RAF, photographer; Asst Ed. Practical Photography also Photo News Weekly, 1959-60; Ed. Cameras 1960-61; Assoc ed. British Jnl of Photography 1962-63, redesigned and picture edited 1964 B.J.Annual; picture ed The Observer, also helped to launch The Observer Colour Magazine 1964-66; Freelance photographer retained by The Observer 1966-72, travelled widely at home and abroad covering hard news, sport and features; Awarded 1st Prize (News), British Press Pictures of the Year, 1969 Awarded fellowhsip of the British Institute of Professional Photographers; Awarded fellowship of Royal Photographic Soc, 1971; Official photographer of British Headless Valley Expedition which carried out the first-ever North-South transnavigation of Canada by water, 1972; worked through Magnum Photos as a 'named' photographer 1972-73; Awarded one of first Kodak Bursaries for 'Photography of social importance', 1973; Awarded photography grant by Arts Council 1974; Awarded hon., assoc. lectureship in photographic arts by Polytechnic of Central London, the first photographer to receive this honour, 1974-77; External examiner in photography to eight polytechnics and art colls 1974- ; first foreign photographer invited to give week-long series of lectures at Univ of Vaasa to the Guild of Finnish Professional Photographers; Tstee, The Photographers' Gallery, London 1974-84; photographed final stages of Vietnam War 1975; travelled widely on assignment for major magazines 1975-77; mem, Photography Bd, Cncl for Nat. Academic Awards 1977-78; mem. Photography Ctee, Arts Cncl of G.B., 1978-80; wrote and presented six-part BBC TV series Exploring Photography, 1978, wrote and edited accompanying book; 1979-82, official photographer of the Transglobe Expedition that carried out the first ever transnavigation of the world's surface on it's polar axis; 1981, edited World Photography, published in U.K., U.S.A., and Japan; 1980-83 Member of the Arts Panel, the Arts Council of G.B.; 1984-85, Consultant picture editor Sunday Express Magazine; 1984-88 Chairman, Sports Pictures of the Year judging panel; 1985, British judge, World Press Photo competition; 1985-86 interviewed Richard Avedon and Alfred Eisenstaedt for BBC TV; occasional appearances on Saturday Review, BBBC TV arts programme; 1985-87, consultant picture editor The Illustrated London News; 1985- , consultant picture editor Orient-Express Magazine; 1987-88 consultant picture editor Daily Telegraph Magazine; 1988- , consultant picture editor the Illustrated London News; 1989 British Judge International Centre for Photography Annual Awards, New York; 8 major individual exhibitions from 1973 to 1981; 6 group exhibitions from 1975 to 1983: *Publications:* The British Journal of Photography Annual, pic ed, 1963; The British Journal of Photography Annual, designer and pic ed, 1964; Lonliness (photographs), with text by Jeremy Seabrook, 1973; The Headless Valley (photographs), with others: with text by Sir Ranulph Fiennes, 1973; The Experience of Sport (photographs), with various texts, 1975; Children and Language (photographs), with various texts, 1976; The Facts About A Football Club (photographs), with text by Alan Road, 1976; Newspaper Dragon, (photographs), with text by Alan Road, 1977; Goalkeepers Are Crazy (photographs), with text by Brian Glanville, 1977; Expioring Photography, ed. book to accompany BBC TV series, 1978; World Photography, ed. 1981; I Grandi Fotografi (for Fabbri, Milan), co-ed with Romeo Martinez, 1982; The

Great Photographer, consult ed; Great Action Photography, ed. 1983. *Recreation:* reading, studying art. *Address:* 11 Belsize Park Mews, London NW3 5BL.

CAMPION, Mr David Bardsley (Barry), *Currently:* Director, Bensons Crips PLC; Director West Trust PLC; Chairman Meridian Foods Ltd; Chairman Wilsons of Holyhead Ltd. *Born on* 20 March 1938 at Southport, Lancs. *Son of* the late Norman Campion and the late Enid Mary Campion (nee Bardsley). *Marriage:* 1st marriage dissolved, 2nd to Sally Manning (nee Arkle), 1979. *Children:* Andrew Mark and Sarah Louise. *Educated at* Shrewsbury School 1951-55. *Career:* Co-operative Wholesale Society Ltd., 1982-87, Chairman Food Division; Dee Corporation PLC 1965-81, Director responsible for all UK operations and subsequently overseas acquisitions and subsidiaries; Proctor & Gamble Ltd., 1958-65, District Sales Manager. *Recreation:* collecting old maps of Anglesey, golf, tennis, sailing. *Clubs:* MCC, Royal Birkdale, Delamere Forest & Holyhead Golf, Inst. of Directors, Fellow Marketing Society; Fellow Institute of Grocery Distribution. *Address:* Monarchy Hall Farm, Utkinton, Tarporley, Cheshire CW6 OJZ. Ty Camp, Ravenspoint Road, Trearddur Bay, Anglesey, Gwynedd.

CANTLAY, Mr George Thomson, CBE Knight of St. John. *Currently:* Retired Stockbroker, Chairman and Company Director. *Born on* 2 July 1907 at Aberdeen, Scotland. *Son of* George and Anabel Cantlay. *Marriage:* to Sibyl Stoker, 1934. *Children:* Duncan and Fiona. *Educated at* H.S. Glasgow. *Career:* Founder Member of the board of WNOC and was on the board for thirty five years. *Recreation:* Opera, travel, music, gardening. *Address:* 9 Park Road, Penarth. S. Glam CF6 2BD.

CAREY-JONES, Mr Norman Stewart, CMG., MA. *Born on* 11 Dec 1911 at Swansea. *Son of* S. Carey Jones and Jessie Isabella (nee Stewart). *Marriage:* 1946. *Children:* Thomas David and Owen Myles. *Educated at* Monmouth School; Merton College, Oxford. *Career:* Colonial Audit Service (Gold Coast, Northern Rhodesia, British Honduras, Kenya), 1935-54; Colonial Admin. Serv. (Kenya), 1954-65; Assist Financial Sec., Treasury, 1954-56; Deputy Sec. Min of Agric & Water, 1956-62; Perm. Sec. Min. of Lands & Settlement, 1962-65; Price Controller, 1955-56; Editor, East African Economics Review, 1957-61; Pres. European Civil Servants' Assoc., 1951-54; Mbr of Sundry Statutory Boards, 1956-62; Director in Dev. Admin, Leeds Univ., 1965-77. *Publications:* The Pattern of a Dependent Economy, 1952; The Anatomy of Uhuru 1966; Politics, Public Enterprise and The Industrial Development Agency, 1974; contributions to Journal of Rhodes Livingstone Institute East African Economics Review, Geographical Journals, Journal of Administration Overseas, Political Studies, African Quarterly. *Clubs:* Commonwealth Trust. *Address:* Mawingo, Welsh St. Donats, near Cowbridge, S. Glam. CF7 7SS.

CARLILE, Mr Alexander Charles, QC., MP., LL.B., AKC *Currently:* Member of Parliament and Queen's Council. *Born on* 12 Feb 1948 at Rossett, Denbighshire. *Son of* Erwen Falik M.D., and Sabina Falik. *Marriage:* to Frances Carlile (nee Soley). *Children:* Anna, Eve and Ruth *Educated at* Epsom College, Univ. of London (Kings College), Council of Legal Education *Career:* Called to the Bar by Gray's Inn, 1980; Q.C., 1984; Chrmn Welsh Liberal Party, 1980-82; M.P. for Montgomery (Lib. Dem), 1983- ; Liberal Democrat

spokesman on Trade and Industry; Lay Mbr of General Medical Council; Mbr of Advisory Council on Public Records; Fellow of the Industry & Parliament Trust; Vice-Chrmn of G.B. East Europe Centre; Council mbr of the Howard League for Penal Reform; campaigner for individual freedoms and liberties; Recorder of the Crown Court, 1985- *Publications:* Many articles and broadcasts *Recreation:* Reading, theatre, music and sport (spectator) *Clubs:* Reform, National Liberal, Bristol Channel Yacht (Swansea) *Address:* Cil y Wennol, Berriew, Welshpool SY21 8AZ. 1 Dr. Johnson's Buildings, Temple, London EC4Y 7AX

CARNEY, Mr Michael, *Currently:* Secretary, The Water Services Association, 1 Queen Anne's Gate, London, SW1H 9BT. *Born on* 19 Oct 1937 at Holywell, Clwyd. *Son of* the late Bernard Patrick Carney and Gwyneth Carney (nee Ellis). Children: Owen Gerallt, Bethan Mair and Gwyn Emyr. *Educated at* The Grammar School, Holywell; UCNW Bangor, University of Wales. *Career:* NCB, staff officer to Deputy Chairman 1963-67; Electricity Council, Admin officer 1968-70, Assistant Secretary (Establishments) 1970-74; CEGB, Secretary, South Western Region 1974-80, Personnel Manager, Midlands Region 1980-82; Oxfam, Personnel Director 1982-87. *Recreation:* book collecting, reading. *Address:* 16 Brodrick Road, London SW17 7DZ.

CARR, Mr Edward Arthur John, M.A. *Currently:* Chief Executive, CADW Welsh Historic Monuments Executive Agency, 1985- . *Born on* 31 Aug 1938 at Nottingham. *Son of* the late E.A. Carr, CMG, and the late Margaret Alys (nee Willson). *Marriage:* to 1) Verity Martin (dislvd), 1960, 2) Patrice Metro, 1980. *Children:* Tess Amanda, Emma Lucy, Katelin and Edward Willson. *Educated at* The Leys School, Cambridge; Christ's College, Cambridge. *Career:* Journalist, Thomson Newspapers, 1960-69; General Management, Times Newspapers, 1970-80; Director, Neath Devel. Partnership, 1981-84. *Publications:* Various: Academic Collections; Newspaper and Magazine articles. *Recreation:* Walking, gardening, rugby football and old buildings. *Clubs:* Civil Service Club *Address:* 2 Eastcliff, Southgate, Swansea SA3 2AS.

CARTER, Mr Alan Owen, BA(Hons History), DipEd. *Currently:* retired since 1991. *Born on* 28 July 1932 at Cardiff. *Son of* the late Arthur Henry Carter and the late Lily May Carter (nee Jones). *Marriage:* to Wendy Barbara Page, 1962. *Children:* Matthew Christian (b.1967) and Emma Sian (b.1971). *Educated at* Penarth Grammar School; University of Wales, Cardiff. *Career:* Commissioned Officer, Royal Air Force 1955-58; appointed to Penarth Grammar School, Stanwell School, Penarth, Head of history, Head of careers, Head of sixth form, School Governor 1989-91. Member South Glamorgan Young Enterprise Board 1991- . member, University of Wales, Glamorgan, South Wales Hockey Squads 1953-64; captain, secretary, player. Chairman Penarth Hockey Club 1950- ; secretary, University College Cardiff Athletic Board 1954-55; chairman, Welsh Schoolboys Hockey Association 1973-75; president, Welsh Hockey Assoc., 1986-91; president, Welsh Hockey Umpires Assoc., 1985- ; Hon Life member, Welsh Hockey Assoc; chairman, Welsh Hockey Umpires Selection Committee 1986- ; Vice-chairman, Welsh hockey Assoc., 1991; member, International Hockey Federation as an international umpire for indoor and outdoor hockey 1971-81; member European Hockey Federation committee for the European Club and

Cup Winners competitions; appointed, Technical Delegate and/or Judge to European tournaments, Moscow 1987, Finland 1988, Sardinia 1989, Sweden 1990, Gibralter 1991, Denmark 1991, Swansea 1992. President, Penarth Hockey Club 1991- . *Recreations:* music, theatre, writing, reading, public speaking, sport, cricket, hockey. *Clubs:* Penarth Hockey, Penarth Athletic. *Address:* 48 Minehead Avenue, Sully, Penarth, S.Glam CF6 2TJ.

CARTER-JONES,Mr Lewis,BA.Hons,Wales; Master of Open Univ,MSc., Salford Univ. *Currently:* Retired Member of Parliament. *Born on* 17 Nov 1920 at Gilfach Goch. *Son of* Thomas Jones and Elizabeth (nee Carter). *Marriage:* to Patricia Bastiman, 1945. *Children:* Susan Elizabeth and Dianne Jennifer. *Educated at* Bridgend County, 1935-39; Univ. Coll. of Wales, Aberystwyth, 1946-50. *Career:* Vol. for Royal Air Force, served as a Navigator from 1940-46; Bachelor of Arts Honours Degree in Economics & Statistics, as well as Diploma in Education; Captain of College, Univ. and County Hockey Teams; Chairman of Student Finance Commt; Rugby Referee to 1972, 1946; Head of Bus. Studies Dept at Wrexham Tech High Sch, and lectured extensively for the University of N.Wales Extra-mural Department 1950- ;Member of Parliament for Eccles, parliamentary career from 1964 to retirement in 1987; Chairman Brtsh Commt of Rehabilitation International, 1982-; Mbr of Sec. of State for Transport's Disabled Persons Advisory Commt, Chairman of Aviation Sub-Commt of DIPTAC, 1988; Chairman of''Access to the Skies'', 1984- ; Vice Pres. Wales Council for Disabled People, 1981- ; Vice Pres of RADAR, 1987- ; Mbr Disablement Services Authority, 1987- ; Trustee of the Granada Region of Telethon, 1987- ; Harding Award for campaigning on behalf of disabled people, 1986; Hon.Degree of Master of the Open University for diables, 1987; Hon Degree of Master if Arts by Salford University, 1990; Parliamentary career from 1964 to 1987; Hon.Parliamentary Adviser to BLESMA; Sec. & Vice chairman All-Party Aviation Group; newly appointed to Advisory Group on Rehabilitation to the Secretary of State for Health; Actively associated either directly or indirectly for over 20 years with nearly all the legislation concerning disabled, chronically sick and elderly people; Also deeply involved with the preservation of all aspects of the British Aviation Industry; Successfully promoted the Spastics Society peri-natal mortality and handicapped campaign for over 7 years. *Publications:* ''Compassion and Chips'' (Technology for Disabled) *Recreation:* Independent living for disabled and elderly persons. Use of advanced technology and alternative site advanced medical and rehab, based on Home & Community and gardening. *Address:* Cader Idris, 5 Cefn Road, Rhosnesni, Wrexham. LL13 9NF.

CARTWRIGHT, Mr William Frederick,CBE *Currently:* Retired. *Born on* 13 Nov 1906 at Aynhoe. *Son of* Rev. W.D. Cartwright *Marriage:* to Sally Chrystobel. *Children:* Nigel, Peter and Lucy *Educated at* Dragon, Oxford; Rugby; G.W.R. Swindon *Career:* G.K.N. London Dowlais enquiries; Steel Co._of Wales, director - chairman; British Steel Corp.,S.Wales div., deputy chairman. *Publications:* Numerous papers on iron and steel. *Recreation:* Sailing, ocean racing *Clubs:* Royal Yacht Squadron; Royal Ocean Racing *Address:* Castle-upon-Alun, St. Brides Major, near Bridgend, Mid Glam. CF32 OTN.

CASE, Mrs Janet Ruth,LLB Dunelm *Currently:* Barrister at Law. *Born on* 29 June 1943 at Ashby de la Zouch. *Daughter of* James and Kathleen Simpson (nee King). *Marriage:* to Jeremy David Case, 1965 (dissolved 1981). *Children:* Charlotte and Edwin. *Educated at* Bishop Blackall School; Durham University. *Career:* Called to Bar, Inner Temple 1975. Chairman Medical Appeals Tribunals 1988- *Recreation:* gardening, friends. *Clubs:* Lansdowne *Address:* Croeswylan, Oswestry, Shropshire SY11 2AN. 40 King Street, Chester CH1 2AH

CATFORD, Professor John Charles, MA, MSc, MB, BChir, DCH, FFPHM, FRCP, DM. *Currently:* Executive Director (Chief Executive), Health Promotion Authority for Wales since 1987; Professor of Health Promotion and Health Education University of Wales College of Medicine since 1984, Director, Institute for Health Promtion; Director of World Health Organisation Collaborating Centre for Health Promotion and Health Education Development, since 1992. *Born on* 10 Dec, 1949 at Sutton Coldfield, Warwickshire. *Son of* John Robin CBE, and Daphne Georgina (nee Darby). (Society of Public Health), 1988; Wales Communicator of the Year (Institute of Public Relations), 1990; H.M. Queen Elizabeth Queen Mother Lecturer (UK Faculty of Public Health Medicine), 1992. Publications: a number of scientific papers and two books on health promotion and disease prevention, Editor in Chief of ''Health Promotion International'' quarterly scientific journal published by Oxford University Press. Recreation: sailing, swimming, guitar, housebuilding, avoiding gardening. Clubs: Barry Yacht; Chairman South Wales Relate (marriage guidance). Address: Health Promotion Authority For,Wales, Brunel House,8th Floor, 2 Fitzalan Road,Cardiff Tel:0222 472472,CF2 1EB.Rectory House,Peterston Super Ely,Cardiff Tel: 0446 760093

CAVE, Mr Henry Joseph,F.R.I.C.S. *Currently:* County Land Agent & Valuer, Powys County Council, 1978- . *Born on* 17 Dec 1932 at Mitcham, Surrey. *Son of* the late Joseph Cave and the late Nelly Kate Cave (nee Woodward). *Marriage:* to Grace Mary Caldecourt, 1954. *Children:* Virginia, Kim, Gwyneth (dec'd), Richard and Hilary *Educated at* Sutton County Grammar School, Sutton, Surrey *Career:* Branch Manager, J.F.Gwyther & Co.,Milford Haven, 1957-64; Branch Manager, Adkin Belcher & Bowen, Abingdon, 1964-65; Asst. Valuer, Carmarthen C.C., 1965-74; Dept.CLA & V, Powys, 1974-77; Acting CLA & V, 1977-78. *Recreation:* Sec. Llandrindod Wells Baptist Church, reading, walking and languages *Address:* Estates Dept. County Hall, Llandrindod Wells, Powys LD1 5LG.

CELLAN-JONES, Allan James Gwynne, *Currently:* Film & Television Producer/Director. *Born on* 13 July 1931 at Swansea. *Son of* the late C.J.Cellan-Jones OBE, FRCS and the late Lavinia (nee Johnson-Dailey). *Marriage:* to Margaret, d of Ernest Eavis, 1959. *Children:* Rory, Simon, Deinol and Lavinia. *Educated at* Dragon School Oxford; Charterhouse; Lycee Jaccard Lausanne; St.Johns Coll, Cambridge (MA). *Career:* Nat Service commnd RE 1953, Troop Cdr Korea later Airborne;Call-boy BBC 1956, worked to be Freelance Director 1963, prods include: The Forsyte Saga, Portrait of a Lady, Jennie, Caesar and Cleopatra; The Kingfisher, Bequest to the Nation,Much Ado About Nothing, The Adams Chronicles NY 1976; Head of plays BBC TV 1976-79; dir: School Play, The Day Christ Died, A Fine Romance, Oxbridge Blues, Comedy of Errors, Fortunes of

War, A Perfect Hero; DGA award 1976, Cable award 1985; BAFTA (vice-chairman 1981-82,chairman 1983-85); US Acad TV Arts & Sci 1975; mem. Directors Guild of America; Directors Guild of GB (Founder member), Vice Chairman 1988, Chairman 1991- . W.D. Thomas memorial feature, U.C. of Swansea, 1992. *Publications:* several songs (words and music) for television, films *Recreations:* scuba diving, home made wine. *Clubs:* Garrick *Address:* 19 Cumberland Road, Kew, Surrey TW9 3HJ. Worthy Cottage, Pilton, Nr Shepton Mallet, Som.

CHADWICK, Julian William Mark, *Currently:* Solicitor, partner in Penningtons, 69 Old Broad Street, London EC2 and Phoenix House, London Road, Newbury, RG13, 1985-90. *Born on* 3 Jan 1957 at Datchet, Bucks. *Son of* Douglas Herbert Chadwick and Elizabeth Mary (nee Evans). *Educated at* R.G.S. High Wycombe; Christ Church Oxford. *Career:* Solicitor, Gamlens, Lincoln's Inn 1982-85. *Publications:* various professional journals. *Recreation:* Master, Christ Church and Farley Hill Beagles. *Clubs:* Oxford & Cambridge. *Address:* Lime Tree Cottage, Bletchingdon, Oxon,,OX5 3BH. Bryntawel, Drefach, Llanybydder, Dyfed

CHALFONT, The Rt. Hon The Lord. Alun Arthur Gwynne, OBE., MC., PC. *Currently:* Chairman, VSEL Consortium plc, 1987- ; Chairman, Radio Authority, 1991- ; Chairman, All Party Defence Group, House of Lords, 1980- . *Born on* 5 Dec 1919 at Llantarnam. *Son of* Arthur Gwynne Jones and Eliza Alice Hardman. *Marriage:* to Dr. Mona Mitchell. *Educated at* West Monmouth School. *Career:* Commissioned South Wales Borderers, 1940-61; Defence Correspondent, The Times, 1961-64; Minister of State, Foreign & Commonwealth Office, 1964-70. *Publications:* Montgomery of Alamein; The Great Commanders 9ed); Star Wars; Defence of the Realm; By God's Will. *Recreation:* Rugby, cricket, music and theatre. *Clubs:* Garrick, MCC, Lord's Taverners, City Livery. *Address:* 65 Ashley Gardens, Ambrosden Avenue, London SW1P 1QS. House Of Lords, London SW1A OPW

CHAMBERLAIN, Professor Geoffrey Victor Price, RD.,MD.,FRCS.,FRCOG.,FACOG(hon) *Currently:* Professor of Obstetrics & Gynaecology, Univ. of London at St. George's Hospital Medical School, London. *Born on* 21 April 1930 at Hove, Sussex. *Son of* the late Albert Victor Chamberlain MBE and Irene May (nee Price) MBE. *Marriage:* to Jocelyn Olivia Peter, da of Sir Peter Kerley KCVO, 1956. *Children:* Christopher, Mark, Patrick, Hilary and Virginia. *Educated at* Llandaff Cathedral School; Cowbridge Grammar School; Cardiff High School. *Career:* RNVR 1955-57; RNR,1957-70 (Surg.Lt.Cmdr 1961-70; Surg Cdr, 1970-74) ret 1974; Demonstrator in Anatomy, Royal Univ of Malta, 1956-57; Res: Royal Postgraduate Med.Sch.Hosp for Sick Children, Great Ormond St (and others), 1958-62; Sr.Registrar, King's Coll.Hospital, 1962-69; Visiting Research Fell.George Washington Univ, USA, 1966-67; Consultant Obstetrician & Gynaecologist, Queen Charlotte's Hosp. for Women, 1970-82; Visiting Prof. USA 1984, Hong Kong 1985, Brisbane 1987, SA 1988; Medical Examiner: London Univ. 1972- , Liverpool Univ. 1973-75, Manchester Univ. 1979-83, Birmingham Univ.1979-82, Cambridge Univ.1981-86, Glasgow Univ.1985-87, Kuala Lumpar Univ. 1986-87, Nottingham Univ. 1987- , Wales 1988- , Malta 1988- , Examiner RCOG 1972- ; Chrmn Med.Commt, Nat.Birthday Trust; former Chrmn Blair Bell

Research Soc; Hon. Gynaecologist British Airways,; Fellow Univ.Coll. London; former Vice Pres. Royal Coll. of Obstetricians & Gynaecologists; Treasurer Royal Soc. of Med; Insp. of Nullity; Freeman City of London, 1982. *Publications:* Lecture Notes in Obstetrics, 1984; Practice of Obstetrics and Gyaencology, 1985; Pregnancy Survival Manual, 1986; Birthplace, 1987; Lecture Notes in Gynaecology, 1988; Manual of Obstetrics, 1988; Obstetrics, 1989; Ten Teachers in Obstetrics, 1990; Ten Teachers in Gynaecology, 1990' Preparing for Pregnancy, 1990; Illustrated Obstetrics, 1991; Clinical Physiology in Obstetrics, 1991. *Recreation:* Opera, gardening, writing and travel *Clubs:* Perinatal; Blair Bell Society; McDonald *Address:* Groose Cottage, Cwm Ivy, Llanmadoc, Gower Glam. SA3 1DJ. 10 Burghley Road, Wimbledon, London SW19 5BH

CHAMBERT, Paul Dennis, *Currently:* Editor, Herald of Wales, Series of Free Newspapers, Swansea 1986- . *Born on* 27 Oct 1936 at Swansea. *Son of* Louis and Margaret Chambert. *Marriage:* to Gaynor Hughes 1958. *Children:* Anne. *Educated at* Mumbles Junior; Dynevor Grammar, Swansea. *Career:* Assist. News Editor, S.Wales Evening Post 1976-86. *Recreation:* Swansea City AFC, reading, music. *Clubs:* Vice-President, Mumbles Rangers Boys' Club *Address:* 46 Fairwood Road, West Cross, Swansea. W.Glam SA3 5JP.

CHANCE, Sir (George) Jeremy (Ffolliott), BT (Barnet), MA. *Currently:* retired. *Born on* 24 Feb 1926 at Blackheath, Middlesex. *Son of* Sir Roger James Ferguson Chance, BT and Mary Georgina Chance (nee Rowney). *Marriage:* to Cecilia Mary Elizabeth Chance, 1950. *Children:* Victoria, Sebastian, Helena and Tobias. *Educated at* Gordonstoun School, Morayshire; Christ Church, Oxford. *Career:* Sub-Lt, RNVR 1944-47; Harry Ferguson Ltd., 1950-53; Massey-Ferguson (UK) Ltd., 1953-78; Director, Administration, European Region 1973-75; Director Public Affairs, UK 1975-78; farming in Wales 1978-86. *Recreation:* wildlife, music, painting. *Address:* Rhosgyll Fawr, Chwilog, Pwllheli, Gwynedd LL53 6TQ.

CHAPMAN, Kenneth James, BSc(Hons), DipT.P.(dist), MRTPI, MBIM. *Currently:* Chairman, Chapman Warren, Town Planning and Development Consultants, since 1981. *Born on* 14 Sept 1950 at London. *Son of* Kenneth Roland Chapman and Marie Elizabeth (nee Robinson). *Marriage:* to Pamela Margaret Sertin, 1970. *Children:* Mark Alan James and Daniel Kenneth. *Educated at* Hornchurch Grammar School; Rayleigh Sweyne School' University of Wales, under graduate and post graduate. *Career:* Glamorgan County Council 1972; Mid Glamorgan County Council 1974; Monmouth District Council 1975; Bradley Planning Services Ltd 1979. member Royal Town Planning Institute Branch Committees; member Council of Swindon Chamber of Commerce; Chairman of Swindon Town Football Club (Barclays League Division 2) 1990-91. *Recreation:* football, power boats. *Address:* Fairwater House,1 High Street, Wroughton, Swindon, Wilts SN4 7ER. 6 Museum Place, Cardiff CF1 3BG

CHAPMAN, Mr Leslie Charles, *Currently:* Lecturer & Writer; Farmer. *Born on* 14 Sept 1919 at Windsor. *Son of* Charles Richard and Lilian Elizabeth Chapman. *Marriage:* to Beryl Edith, 1947, y.d. of Bertram George England of Leighton Buzzard, Beds. *Children:* Robin Leslie Charles.

Educated at Bishopshalt School Hillingdon. *Career:* Civil Service, 1939-45-73; Army 1939-45, commissioned R.A. 1939; Regional Director S. Region D.O.E. memb. Executive London Transport memb Nat Council of Freedom Assoc, and Nat Council of Freedom of Information Assoc; Chmn Campaign against waste in Public Expenditure. *Publications:* "Your Disobedient Servant", 1979, 2nd revised ed. 1981; "Waste Away", 1982. *Recreation:* Countryside conservation, reading and music. *Address:* Caradog, Ffarmers, Llanwrda, Dyfed. SA19 8NQ

CHATTERTON, (Charles) Robert, *Born on* 30 Sept 1913 *Son of* the late Charles Chatterton, of Penarth, Glamorgan and the late Lilian (nee Saunders). *Marriage:* to Lilian May, 1937 (d 1990), da of Howard Henry Sladen (d 1959), of Cardiff. *Children:* Peter (b.1939) and Susan (b.1947). *Educated at* Cardiff GS; Cardiff Tech Coll; Bloggs Coll. Cardiff. *Career:* TA 1937-45, Welsh Regt 1939, commnd Queen's Own Royal West Kents 1940, A/Maj, served overseas (despatches twice); Territorial Efficiency Medal; chairman: Reardon Smith Group of Cos. 1970-85 (jr accountant 1929, asst Co.Sec 1961, Dir and Co Sec. 1963), Cardiff Ship Management & Services Ltd., 1985- (and Dir); Dir. Bank of Wales plc 1974-88; Member of Committee General Council of British Shipping 1970-85; Chairman: Horton and Port Eynon Lifeboat Committee; The Missions to Seamen (Cardiff Station); Liveryman Worshipful Company of Shipwrights; Queens Silver Jubilee Medal, F.Inst.D. *Recreation:* ornithology, walking, fishing. *Clubs:* Cardiff Business. *Address:* Green Meadow, Ger Y Llan, St.Nicholas, Cardiff CF5 6SY. 2 White Rocks "The Boarlands, Port Eynon SA3 1NX Tel: 0446 760723

CHESTERS, Professor Graham, MA *Currently:* Professor of French, University of Hull, since 1988. Pro-Vice-Chancellor, University of Hull, since 1991. *Born on* 10 Oct 1944 at Crewe, Cheshire. *Son of* Thomas Leslie and Nelly Chesters. *Marriage:* 1968. *Children:* Timothy Graham and Anna Sian. *Educated at* Crewe County Grammar; University College of Swansea 1963-69. *Career:* Tutor in French, University College Swansea 1969-70; Lecturer in French, Queen's University Belfast 1970-72; Lecturer in French, University of Hull 1972-80; Senior Lecturer in French 1980-88. *Publications:* Some Functions of Sound Repetition in Baudelaire's Les Fleurs Du Mal, 1975; An Anthology of Modern French Poetry (with P.Broome),1976; The Appreciation of Modern French Poetry (with P.Broome), 1976; Baudelaire & The Poetics of Craft, 1988. *Recreation:* chess *Address:* 35 Newland Park, Hull, Humberside HU5 2DN.

CHEUNG, Professor Yau-Kai, Hon.Fellow, Univ, Swansea; DSc;DE;FEng. *Currently:* Pro Vice-Chancellor and Professor and Head of Department of Civil and Structural Engineering, University of Hong Kong, since 1977. *Born on* 18 Sept 1934 at Hong Kong. *Son of* Cheung Tze-Shiu and the late Yip Lai-King. *Marriage:* to Chu Yuk-Baw, 1961. *Children:* Cheun Ngai-Wah, Cheung Ngai-Tseung and Cheung Ngai-Fung. *Career:* Structural Engineer, Chengchow Honan China 1958-61; University of Wales, Research Assistant 1961-64; Senior Research Fellow 1964-65; Lecturer in Civil Engineering 1965-67; Professor of Civil Engineering, University of Calgary, Canada 1970-74 (Associate Professor 1967-70); Professor of Civil Engineering and Chairman of Department, University of Adelaide

Australia 1974-77; Director of High Building Research Centre 1977-81; Dean of Engineering and Architecture, Feb-June 1978; Dean of Engineering 1978-87; Pro-Vice Chancellor, University of Hong Kong 1988- . *Publications:* Many books on Civil Engineering and papers accepted for Publication. *Address:* C/o Department Of Civil & Structural Engineering, University Of Hong Kong, Hong Kong

CHUBB, The Hon Mrs Barbara, *Currently:* retired. *Born on* 14 Dec 1931 at Pontypridd. *Daughter of* Baron Champion and Lady Emma Champion. *Marriage:* to Trevor Chubb, 1957. *Children:* Alison, Judith and Claire. *Educated at* Pontypridd Girls' GS; Rachel McMillan Training Coll. *Career:* Teaching for many years. *Recreation:* painting and other arts. *Address:* 160 Redland Road, Redland, Bristol BS6 6YG.

CHURCHHOUSE, Professor Robert Francis, CBE., BSc.,MA., PhD. *Currently:* Professor of Computing Mathematics, Univ. of Wales Coll. of Cardiff, 1971- . *Born on* 30 Dec 1927 at Manchester. *Son of* Robert Francis and the late Agnes (nee Howard) Churchhouse. *Marriage:* to Julia McCarthy 1954. *Children:* Gerard Martin, Robert Andrew and John Patrick *Educated at* St.Bede's Coll. Manchester; Manchester Univ; Cambridge Univ. *Career:* Royal Naval Scientific Service 1952-63; Head of Programming, Atlas Computer Labs.,SERC 1963-71; Chrmn, Computer Bd for Universities 1979-82; President, Inst. of Mathematics 1986-88; Mbr. Welsh Commt.Univ. Funding Council 1989- . *Publications:* Numerous papers in mathematical computing journals *Recreation:* Astronomy, cricket, history *Clubs:* Challenor, Royal Commonwealth *Address:* 15 Holly Grove, Lisvane, Cardiff. CF4 5UJ.

CLANCY, Mr Michael John, MA (Cantab) *Currently:* Director, Employment Department Office for Wales.. *Born on* 31 March 1949 at Tredegar, Gwent..*Son of* the late William John Clancy and the late Chrissie Melinda (nee Clarke). *Marriage:* separated. *Children:* Carys and Brett. *Educated at* Lewis School Pengam; Trinity College, Cambridge. *Career:* Welsh Office graduate trainee 1972-74; Assistant Private Secretary to Secretary of State for Wales 1974-76; Principal, Welsh Office Health Department 1976-81; Principal Assistant Secretary of Transport, Hong Kong Government 1981-86; Head of Personnel Management, Welsh Office 1986-89; Senior Consultant, Hay Management Consultants 1989-91. *Recreation:* cinema, hiking, cycling. *Clubs:* Civil Service. *Address:* Companies House, Crown Way, Cardiff CF4 3UT. 7 Duffryn Avenue, Lakeside, Cardiff CF2 6LE

CLARIDGE, Professor Michael Frederick, MA; D.Phil *Currently:* Professor of Entomology and Head, School of Pure and Applied Biology, University of Wales, Cardiff since 1988. *Born on* 2 June 1934 at Dunchurch, Warwickshire. *Son of* the late Frederick William Claridge and the late Eva Alice (nee Jeffrey). *Marriage:* to Lindsey Clare Hellings, 1967. *Children:* John Bleddyn, Robert Iwan and Elin Mary. *Educated at* Lawrence Sheriff School, Rugby; Keble College, Oxford. *Career:* Lecturer, Senior Lecturer, Reader and Professor at University College, Cardiff 1959-88; President Linnean Society of London 1988-91; President Systematics Association 1991- ; Scientific Adviser to House of Lords Select Committee on Science and Technology 1991. *Publications:* more than 80 papers in scientific journals; Chapters in The Leafhoppers and

Planthoppers 1985, John Wiley; Organisation of Communities Past and Present 1987, Blackwell; Prospects in Systematics, 1988 Oxford. Co-Author of Handbook for the Identificationof Leafhopper and Planthopper Pests of Rice, 1991, CABI. *Recreation:* Natural History, music, cricket. *Address:* School Of Pure & Applied Biology, University Of Wales College Of Cardiff, P.O.Box 915, Cardiff CF1 3TL. Tel: 0222 874 147

CLARKE,Mr Michael John Marshal,MA *Currently:* retired. *Born on* 3 Feb 1927 at Surrey, England. *Son of* Admiral Sir Marshal Clarke, KBE, CB, DSC and Ina Leonora (nee Edwards). *Marriage:* to Flavia Dorothea Coryton, 1954. *Children:* Julian Marshal (b.1958) and Emily Sarah (b.1960). *Educated at* Sir Edward's School, Oxford; Trinity College, Oxford. *Career:* Imperial Chemical Industries Ltd., 1951-64; The Industrial Society 1964-67; British Steel Corporation 1967-84; member, Central Arbitration Committee, Industrial Court and Industrial Arbitration Board 1970-; Police Arbitration Tribunal 1980-; Welsh Arts Council (Vice Chairman), Arts Council of Great Britain 1983-91; High Sheriff of Gwent 1985-86; member of Council, National Museums of Wales 1985-.Chairman, Haberdashers Monmouth Schools Governors 1989-. *Recreation:* growing vines, landscape painting. *Address:* Osbaston House, Monmouth, Gwent NP5 4BB.

CLARKE,Professor Patricia Hannah,FRS.,BA(Cantab)., DSc(London).,Hon.D.Sc.Kent),Hon.DSc(CNAA).*Born on* 29 July 1919 at Pontypridd. *Daughter of* the late David Samuel Green and the late Daisy Lilian Amy (nee Willoughby). *Marriage:* to Michael Clarke 1940. *Children:* Francis Willoughby and David John. *Educated at* Coedpenmaen Elementary; Howells School Llandaff; Girton College Cambridge. *Career:* Armament Research Dept.Min. of Supply 1940-44; Wellcome Research Labs 1944-47; Nat.Collection of Type Cultures, Public Health Labs, Colindale, 1951-53; Dept.of Biochemistry, Univ. Coll. London 1953-84; Prof. of Microbial Biochemistry 1974-84; Hon. Prof. Fellow,Univ.of Wales 1984-89; Leverhulme Emeritus Fellow 1984-87; Kan Tong-Po Prof.Chinese Univ.of Hong Kong 1986; Mbr. Council of The Royal Soc.and Vice-Pres. 1981-82; Mbr. Council of Soc. for General Microbiology 1960-70, Hon.Gen.Sec. 1965-70; Mbr. Cncl for Nat. Academic Awards 1967-77; Mbr. Commt The Biochemical Soc.1978-81; Mbr. Science Bd Science & Eng.Research Cncl 1979-83; Mbr. The Biotechnology Mangmnt.Commt.,1980-84; Mbr. Cncl Freshwater Biol. Assoc.1980-84; Mbr. Govng. Body of Wye Coll.1980-85; Mbr.ofCncl London Sch of Hygiene & Tropical Med. 1982-87; Mbr. Advisory Cncl British Library 1983-88; Mbr. Health & Safety Exec. Advisory Commt. on Genetic Manipulation 1984-86; Mbr. Bd of Management Inst. for Biotechnological Studies 1984-89, Chrmn.1986-87. Mbr. Cncl University of Bath, Mbr. Advisory Commt. Palm Oil Research Inst. Malaysia. Mbr.Cncl Cheltenham Ladies Coll.1984-90; Emeritus Prof. Biochemistry Univ. London; Hon.Research Fellow Dept. of Chemical and Biochemical Eng; Biological Editor Science Progress (Blackwell Scientific Publications); Governor Cirencester Deer Park Comp. School. *Publications:* Genetics and Biochemistry of Pseudomonas (with M.R.Richmond); 120 papers in scientific journals on microbial biochemistry and genetics and enzyme evolution. *Recreation:* Walking, gardening, reading,

dressmaking *Address:* 7 Corinium Gate, Cirencester, Glos GL7 2PX.

CLARKSON, Prof. Brian Leonard, DSc., FEng. *Currently:* Principal, University College, Swansea, 1982- *Born on* 28 July 1930 at Driffield, Yorks. *Son of* the late Leonard Clarkson and the late Irene (neeShouler). *Marriage:* to Margaret Elaine Wilby 1953. *Children:* Stephen Anthony, John Michael, Carol Margaret andPaul Richard. *Educated at* Beverley Grammar School, Yorks; University of Leeds. *Career:* de Havilland Aircraft Co., 1953-57; University of Southampton 1957-82; Prof. Vibration Studies 1966-82; Director Inst. of Sound & Vibration Studies 1967-78; Dean of Engineering 1978-80; Deputy Vice Chancellor 1980-82; Vice Chancellor University of Wales 1987-89; Vice Chairman Association of Commonwealth Universities 1991- *Publications:* Technical papers on Jet Noise and its effect on aircraft structures; ed. Stochastic Problems in Dynamics 1977. *Recreation:* Travelling, walking, gardening. *Clubs:* Athenaeum. *Address:* University College, Singleton Park, Swansea SA2 8PP. 236 Gower Road, Swansea SA2 9JJ

CLATWORTHY, Robert Ernest, RA *Currently:* Sculptor. *Born on* 31 Jan 1928. at Bridgwater. *Son of* the late Ernest William Clatworthy and Gladys (neeChanning). *Marriage:* 1st to Pamela (nee Gordon, 1954 (diss 1966); 2nd to Jane (nee Illingworth Stubbs), 1989. *Children:* Benn (b.1955), Thomas (b.1959) and Sarah Alexandra (b.1957). *Educated at* Dr. Morgan's GS Bridwater; W. of England Coll of Art; Chelsea School of Art; Slade School of Fine Art. *Career:* National Service, head of Fine Art wing E Formation Coll 1949; lecturer W of England Coll of Art 1967-71; visiting tutor RCA 1960-72, member Fine Art Panel Nat Council for Dips in Art and Design 1961-72; governor St.Martin's School of Art 1970-71; head of Dept of Fine Art Central School of Art and Design 1971-75; exhibitions: Hanover Gallery, Waddington Galleries, Holland Park Open Air Sculpture, Battersea Park Open Air Sculpture, Br Sculpture in the Sixties Tate Gallery, Br Sculptors Burlington House 1972, Basil Jacobs Fine Art Ltd., Diploma Galleries Burlington House, Photographer's Gallery, Quinton Green Gallery, Chapman Gallery, Keith Chapman 1990, Austin/ Desmond Fine Art Keith Chapman 1991; Putney Bridge Gallery 1992; work in the collections of: Art Council, Contemporary Art Soc, Tate Gallery, V & A, GLC, Nat Portrait Gallery, Monumental Horse and Rider; ARA 1968, RA 1973. *Recreation:* music *Clubs:* Chelsea Arts *Address:* Moelfre, Cynghordy, Llandovery, Dyfed SA20 OUW.Tel: 0550 20201

CLEAVER, Mr William Benjamin, C.Eng.,FIMinE.,OStJ, JP. *Currently:* Retired. *Born on* 15 Sept 1921 at Treorchy, Rhondda. *Son of* the late David John Cleaver and the late Blodwen (nee Miles). *Marriage:* to Mary Watkin 1943. *Children:* John, Pamela and Patricia. *Educated at* Pentre GS Rhondda; Univ. of Wales (BSc) *Career:* Mining engineer, NCB: Area Gen.Mangr. 1958-67; Dep.Dir. (Mining) 1967-83; Welsh Rugby Int. 1947-50 14 caps; Brtsh Lion NZ and Aust. 1950; Fndr chm Welsh Youth Rugby Union 1949-57; Vice-chm Welsh Arts Cncl 1977-83; Mbr.Arts Cncl GB 1980-83; Sec.Contemporary Art Soc.for Wales 1973- 91; mbr.Cncl Nat. Museum Wales 1977-; Chm.Cncl Museums in Wales 1986-. *Recreation:* Rugby football, fine arts, wine appreciation. *Clubs:* Cardiff & County, Saville. *Address:* 29 Lon-y-Deri, Rhiwbina, Cardiff CF4 6JN Tel: 0222

693242

CLEDWYN OF PENRHOS, Lord, P.C., C.H., LL.D.
Currently: Leader of the Opposition, House of Lords. *Born on* 14 Sept 1916 at Holyhead, Anglesey. *Son of* Rev. Henry David Hughes and Mrs Emily Hughes. *Marriage:* to Jean Beatrice Hughes d. of Captain and Mrs Jesse Hughes. *Children:* Emily Ann and Harri Cledwyn. *Educated at* Holyhead Grammar School; University Coll. of Wales. *Career:* Solicitor-Practising in Anglesey from 1946 after war service in RAF; Member of Parliament for Anglesey, 1951-79; Shadow Minister for Housing and Local Government, 1959-64; Minister for Commonwealth Relations, 1964-66, Secretary of State for Wales, 1966-68; Minister for Agriculture, Fisheries and Food, 1968-70. Chairman, Parliamentary Labour Party 1974-79. President, University College of Wales 1975-85. Pro-Chancellor, University of Wales 1984- . *Publications:* Conditions in St. Helena, 1959. *Recreation:* Eisteddfodau; sport generally and reading. *Clubs:* Travellers and RAF Clubs *Address:* House Of Lords, London SW1. Penmorfa, Trearddur, Anglesey

CLEMENT, Mr Anthony, *Currently:* Leasing Executive,
Days Contract Hire (subsidiary of C.E.M. Day Group). *Born on* 8 Feb 1967 at Swansea. *Son of* Mr Malcolm David Clement and Mrs Dorothy May Clement. *Marriage:* to Mrs Debra Clement. *Educated at* Llansamlet Junior Comp; Morriston Senior Comp; Neath College. *Career:* Rugby: Swansea Schools under 13, under 14, under 15. Morriston Youth/Swansea & District Youth. Wales Youth, 6 caps 1984-86; Wales under 20 (Captain) Wales under 21; Swansea RFC/Wales B, 2 caps; Wales Senior side 19 caps. Barbarians/ British Lions (tour to Australia 1989) World XV. *Recreation:* football, sport in general, gardening. *Clubs:* Swansea RFC *Address:* 5 Cae Eithin, Llangyfelach, Swansea, W.Glam SA6 6EZ

CLEMITS, Mr John Henry, RIBA: (Dist in Thesis) FRSA.
Currently: Managing Director, PSA Projects, Cardiff. *Born on* 16 Feb 1934 at Plymouth. *Son of* the late Cyril Clemits and the late Minnie (nee Simmons). *Marriage:* to Elizabeth Angela Moon, 1958. *Children:* Elizabeth Jane Clemits and Roger John Clemits. *Educated at* Sutton High School, Plymouth; Plymouth College of Art. *Career:* Plymouth City Architects Department 1954-59; National Service RAF 1959-61; Watkins Gray & Partners, Architects, Bristol 1961-63; South West Regional Hospital Board 1963-65; Captain RE (TA) 43 Wessex Division and Royal Monmouthshire RE (Militia) 1964-69; Architect, Ministry of Public Building & Works (MPBW) 1965-69; Senior Architect MPBW Regional HQ Rheindahlen, Germany 1969-71; Naval Base Planning Officer MPBW, Portsmouth 1971-73; Superintending Architect PSA Directorate of Building Development 1973-75; Superintending Planning Officer PSA Rheindahlen 1975-79; Director of Works (Army) Chessington 1979-85; Director for Wales Property Services Agency (PSA) 1985-91. *Recreation:* golf, choral singing, DIY, committee member Dewi Sant Housing Association. *Clubs:* Naval. *Address:* "The Lodge", Hendrescythan, Creigiau, Nr Cardiff CF4 8NN. PSA Projects Cardiff, St Agnes Road, Gabalfa, Cardiff CF4 4YF Tel: 0222 586760

COHEN, Professor Samuel Isaac, BSc, MD, FRCP,
FRCPsych. *Currently:* Emeritus Professor of Psychiatry, University of London, formerly Professor of Psychiatry, The London Hospital Medical College, retired 1991. *Born on* 22 Nov 1925 at Cardiff. *Son of* the late Gershon Cohen and the late Ada (nee Samuel). *Marriage:* to Dr. Vivienne Wolfson, 1955. *Children:* Michael and Elizabeth. *Educated at* Cardiff High School; Welsh National School of Medicine, Univ of Wales; University of London; Inst of Psychiatry and Maudsley Hospital. *Career:* formerly: Lecturer in Medicine, University of Wales, Medical Unit, Cardiff; Consultant Psychiatrist, The London Hospital; Hon. Consultant Psychiatrist, The Brompton Hospital. former offices held: Chairman of the Medical Council, The London Hospital; Royal College of Psychiatrists: member of Council, member of Public Policy Committee, member Appeals Committee, member Court of Electors, Chairman: E.Anglian Division, Regional Adviser, N.E. Thames Regional Health Authority; Adviser, Special Hospitals Authority; Medical Examiner for General Medical Council; Examiner University of London, Royal College of Psychiatrists, Royal College of Physicians. *Publications:* papers and chapters in books on Diagnosis of Physical Symptoms, Asthma and generally on the borderland between Medicine and Psychiatry. *Recreation:* hill-walking, music, Jewish studies. *Address:* 8 Linnell Drive, London NW11 7LT Tel: 081 455 4781

COHEN, Professor Sydney, CBE., MD., PhD., FRS
Currently: Emeritus Professor of Chemical Pathology, London University. *Born on* 18 Sept 1921 at South Africa. *Son of* Morris and Pauline Cohen. *Marriage:* to June Bernice Adler 1950. *Children:* Roger and Jennifer. *Educated at* King Edward VIII School; Witwatersrand & London Universities *Career:* Emergency Medical Serv. U.K., 1944-46; Lec. Dept Physiology, Witwatersrand Univ. 1948-53; Nuffield Dominion Fellow in Medicine 1953; Scientific Staff, Nat. Inst. for Med. Research, London 1955-60; Reader in Immunology, St. Mary's Hosp. Med. Sch, London 1960-65; Prof. of Chemical Pathology, Guy's Hosp., London 1965-86; Medical Research Council 1974-76; Council of Royal Soc. 1981-83. *Publications:* Papers and books on Immunology and Tropical Infections *Recreation:* Golf, gardening, walking and carpentry *Clubs:* Royal & Ancient, St. Andrews. *Address:* Hafodfraith, Llangurig, Powys SY18 6QG.

COLEMAN, Talbot Pascoe Hilbut, *Currently:* Managing
Director, Assi Pulp & Paper UK) Ltd., since 1977. *Born on* 10 Oct 1934 at Cardiff. *Son of* the late Jack Coleman and Marjorie (nee Butt). *Marriage:* to Ann MacDougal, 1958. *Children:* Nial Talbot and Charlotte Ann. *Educated at* Cardiff High School. *Career:* RAF 1952-54; RAFVR 1959-65, Flg Officer. Thames Bd Mills Ltd 1956-66; Assi Pulp & Paper 1966- ; President UK Paper Agents Assoc 1984-86; Chairman Croydon Central Conservative Assoc 1985-88, Vice-President 1988- ; Member: Worshipful Co of Gold & Silver Wyre Drawers 1979- ; Brixton Prison B.O.V. 1985- ; Craft Lodge No. 3817, P.A.G. St.B. *Recreation:* rugby, golf, cricket, reading. *Clubs:* Carlton, MCC. *Address:* Prudential House, Wellesley Road, Croydon CR9 2DQ.

COLES, Professor Bryan Randell, BSc(Wales),
D.Phil(Oxon), FRS *Currently:* Professor of Solid State Physics, Imperial College, London; Chairman, Taylor & Francis (Scientific Publishers). *Born on* 9 June 1926 at Cardiff. *Son of* Charles Frederick and Olive Irene Coles (nee Randell). *Marriage:* to Merivan Robinson, 1955.

Children: Matthew Frederick and Jonathan Robert *Educated at* Canton High School, Cardiff; University of Wales (Cardiff); University of Oxford (Jesus College). *Career:* Lecturer, Reader, Professor, Imperial College 1950- ; Dean of Royal College of Science 1984-86; Pro-Rector, Imperial College 1986-91; Chairman Physics Committee, Science & Engineering Research Council 1973-76; Chairman Neutron Beam Committee, Science Engineering Research Council 1984-88; Vice-President, Inst of Physics 1968-72; Visiting Professor: California (UCSD), 1969, University of Minnesota, 1983, University of Michigan, 1991. *Publications:* Atomic Theory for Students of Metallurgy (with W.Hume-Rothery); Electronic Structures of Solids (with A.D.Caplin); 120 papers in scientific journals. *Recreation:* Natural History, Mediaeval architecture, opera. *Address:* 61 Courtfield Gardens, London SW5 0NQ. Shoe Cottage, Vines Cross, Heathfield, E.Sussex TN21 2EN

COLLINS, John Hardie, OBE, BSc, DL *Currently:* Leader, Cheshire County Council. *Born on* 26 Feb 1923 at Rhiwbina, Cardiff. *Son of* William S and Hannah. *Marriage:* 1st to Dorothy Archibald, 1947 (decd); 2nd to Rona 1981. *Children:* Jean. *Educated at* Cowbridge GS; University College Cardiff. *Career:* Industrial Chemist 1943-81; Member Widnes & Halton District Councils 1945-91; Cheshire CC 1981- ; Chairman Cheshire Police Authority 1984- . *Recreation:* golf, music. *Address:* 5 Shelley Road, Widnes WA8 7DE

COLWYN, Rt.Hon.The Lord Ian Anthony, CBE.,BDS., LDS.,RCS. *Currently:* Dental Surgeon; Band Leader; Company Director. *Born on* 1 Jan 1942 at Cheltenham. *Son of* the late Ian Hamilton-Smith and Miriam Ferguson. *Marriage:* 1st to Sonia Morgan (d.1975); 2nd to M.Nicola Tyres, 1976. *Children:* Craig Peter, Jaqueline, Kirsten and Tanya. *Educated at* Cheltenham College; Univ. of London; St. Bartholomews Hospital; Royal Dental Hospital. *Career:* Cheltenham Rugby XV, 1970-74; Dental Practice, 1967- ; House of Lords, 1967; Jt.Pres. All Party Gp. for Alternative & Complementary Medicine; President Natural Medicine Society; Director Jazz FM - Lord Colwyn Orchestra; Patron, Research Council for Complementary Medicine; Patron, Blackie Foundation; Patron, Cancer First Aid; Director: Three B.Consultants Ltd, Dental Protection Ltd., Scout Projects Ltd *Publications:* various, in Dental Press *Recreation:* Music and broadcasting *Clubs:* Royal Society of Medicine; Seaview Yacht Club. *Address:* 53 Wimpole Street, London W1M 7DF. House Of Lords, London SW1

CONWAY, Mr William Elwyn, Queens Jubilee Medal 1977 *Currently:* General Secretary, Rhyl Labour Club Ltd. *Born on* 12 July 1925 at Rhyl. *Son of* the late Aneurin Conway and Elizabeth Mary (nee Roberts). *Marriage:* to the late Miss Betty Carroll 1970. *Children:* Elizabeth and Faye. *Educated at* Emmanuel School, Rhyl *Career:* Royal Marines 1943-46; 33 years Local Govt Councillor; 1st Mayor Rhyddlan B.C., 1973; Chmn Clwyd C.C., 1986; Chmn Welsh C.Counties 1985-86; 1st Leader Clwyd C.C.1989; Govt appointed mbr. N.H.S. Past chmn Denbighshire & Flint Exec. Cncl of N.H.S. 1959-90; Mbr. Welsh Water Authority 1985-90; Justice of Peace 1965, Chmn. of Rhuddlan Div. Bench of Magistrates 1985-90; 44 yrs mbr. of TGWU, past Branch Sec. Branch Chrmn; Cert. of Merit for outstanding Voluntary service to the Labour Party 1976; mbr. Vice-Chmn. N.Wales Police Auth. *Recreation:* Snooker, swimming, walking, music. *Address:*

71 Vale Road, Rhyl, Clwyd LL18 2PF. 13-15 Bodfor Street, Rhyl, Clwyd LL18 1AS

COOKE, Professor Emeritus Brian Ernest Dudley, MDS.,FDS.,FRC Path.,MRCS.,LRCP *Currently:* Retired. *Born on* 12 Jan 1920 at Woodford, Essex. *Son of* Charles Ernest Cooke and Margaret Beatrice Wood. *Marriage:* to Marion Neill Orkney Hope, 1948. *Children:* Nigel Trevor and Susan Margaret. *Educated at* Merchants Taylor's School; The London Hospital Medical and Dental Schools. *Career:* RNVR (Dental Branch), 1943-46; Nuffield Dental Fellow, 1950-52; Travelling Nuffield Fellowhsip Australia and New Zealand, 1964; Lecturer, 1952-57; Reader in Dental Medicine, Guys Hospital Dental School, 1958-62; Professor of Oral Medicine and Oral Pathology, Founder Dean of Welsh National School of Medicine Dental School and Consultant Dental Surgeon to University Hospital of Wales, 1962-82; Hon. Coll. Fellow of Univ. of Wales Coll. of Medicine; Visiting Prof. to Univ. of Sydney, 1986-87; Representative of Univ. of Wales on General Dental Council, 1964-82; Civilian Consultant in Dental Surgery to the Royal Navy, 1967- ; Mbr of Board of Faculty of Dental Surgery, RCS.Eng., 1964-72; Vice-Dean, 1971-72; Mbr of S.Glam AHA, 1974-76; Mbr of Board of Governors of United Cardiff Hospitals, 1965-71; Vice Provost, of Welsh Nat. School of Medicine, 1974-76; Charles Tomes Lecturer RCS, 1963; Guest Lctr. to Univ. of Witwatersraand Univ, 1967; Pres. of Section of Odontology Royal Soc. of Medicine, 1975; Founder Pres. of Btsh Soc of Oral Medicine, 1981; Founder Vice-Pres. of Head & Neck oncologists of G.B.,1967; Cartwright Prize and Medal R.C.S., 1955; Chesterfield Prize and Medal St.John Hospital for diseases of the skin 1955. *Publications:* (jointly) Oral Histopathology, 1959; Scientific Contributions to Medical and Dental Journals. *Recreation:* Various - literature, poetry, medical history and carpentry. *Clubs:* Royal Society of Medicine, London, W1. *Address:* 38 St. Aidan Cres., Heath, Cardiff CF4 4AU.

COOMBE-TENNANT, Mr Alexander John Serocold, BA *Born on* 20 Nov 1909 at Neath. *Son of* the late Charles Coombe Tennant, JP, and the late Winifred Margaret (nee Serocold), JP.late. *Marriage:* to Jenifer Margaret, da of Frederic Luttman-Johnson, JP, 1954. *Children:* Charles (b.1955), John (b.1957), Mark (b.1958), Rosalie (b.1960) and Susanna (b.1964). *Educated at* Sherborne, Trinity College Cambridge (BA). *Career:* Min of Econ Warfare 1940-45, Army Gen List 2/Lt A/Major 1944; stockbroker, member LSE; partner Cazenove & Co 1952-79; director Societe Generale Merchant Bank plc 1979- ; GT Japan Investment plc 1979-89, Monterey Trust SA Luxembourge; chairman Port Tennant Co Ltd; Freeman City of London. Liveryman Worshipful Co of Clothworkers (1955); Member of the Gorsedd of Wales, title Gwas Catwg; Member Lloyds of London. *Recreation:* skiing, golf, travel. *Clubs:* Naval and Military. *Address:* Gostirode Farm, Chiddingfold, Godalming, Surrey, GU8 4SR.

COOPER, Professor John Philip, CBE(1983), DSc, FRS(1977), FIBiol. *Currently:* Emeritus Professor of Agricultural Botany, University of Wales; Hon.Fellow, Institute of Grassland and Environmental Research, Aberystwyth. *Born on* 16 Dec 1923 at Buxton, Derbyshire. *Son of* Frank Edward and Nora Goodwin Cooper (nee Stubbs). *Marriage:* to Christine Mary Palmer, 1951, daughter of Robertand Enid Palmer of Swansea. *Children:* David Martin, Caroline Mary, Jennifer Ann and Elizabeth Gillian. *Educated at* Stockport Grammar School; University of Reading, BSc.(Agric); University of Cambridge, Dip.Agric.Sci. *Career:* Scientific Officer, Welsh Plant Breeding Station 1946-50; Lecturer (Agric.Botany) University of Reading 1950-54; Plant Geneticist, Welsh Plant Breeding Station 1954-59; Head, Dept. Devel. Genetics, Plant Breeding Station 1959-75; Director, Welsh Plant Breeding Station and Professor of Agricultural Botany, University College of Wales, Aberystwyth 1975-83; Consultant, F.A.O. Rome 1956; Nuffield/Royal Society Bursary, CSIRO, Canberra 1962; Visiting Professor, University of Kentucky 1965; Visiting Professor, University of Khartoum 1975; Visiting Professor, University of Reading 1983-89; member, Intern. Board for Plant Genetic Resources. *Publications:*(ed with P.F.Wareing) Potential Crop Production, 1971; (ed) Photosynthesis and Productivity in Different Environments, 1975; over 100 papers on crop physiology and genetics. *Recreation:* walking, field archaeology. *Clubs:* Farmers. *Address:* 31 West End, Minchinhampton, Stroud, Glos. GL6 9JA.

COPPACK,Mrs Mair Hafina Clwyd (Hafina Clwyd), *Currently:* Editor: Y Faner. *Born on* 1 July 1936 at Gwyddelwern, nr. Corwen. *Daughter of* Alun and Morfydd Jones. *Marriage:* to Clifford Coppack. *Educated at* Gwyddelwern Primary Sch; Bala Girls' Grammar Sch; Brynhyfryd Sch, Ruthin; Normal Coll., Bangor. *Career:* School Teacher, London 1957-79; Vice-Pres. Hon. Soc. of Cymmrodorion; Fnd.Mbr. Clwyd Family History Soc; Mbr. Gorsedd of Bards; Ed. Y Bedol - commn. paper for Ruthin & Dist. 1981-89, Consultant ed; Cncl.Mbr. Denbighshire Historical Soc. *Publications:*Shwrwd; Clychau yn y Glaw; Defaid yn Chwerthin; Perfedd Hen Nain Llewelyn; Buwch ar y Lein; Cwis a Phos; Merch Morfydd. *Recreation:* Family history, crosswords.*Address:* Tafwys,36 Erw Goch, Ruthin, Clwyd, LL15 1RR.

COPPOCK, Professor John Terence,CBE, FBA, FRSE, MA, PhD. *Currently:* Secretary and Treasurer Carnegie Trust for the Universities of Scotland (1986-); Also Professor Emeritus, University of Edinburgh 1986-. *Born on* 2 June 1921 at Cardiff.*Son of* Arthur Leslie Coppock and Margaret Valerie Coppock(nee Phillips). *Marriage:* to Sheila Mary Burnett 1953,(Decd 1990). *Children:* Helena Margaret (now Baillie) and John David. *Educated at* Victoria Elementary School, Penarth 1926-32; Penarth County School 1932-37; Queen's College Cambridge 1947-50; (Exhibitioner 1948, Scholar 1949). *Career:* Civil Servant, Lord Chancellor's Dept, Ministry of Works, Board of Customs and Excise, 1938-47; Army Service, 1939-46, Welch Regiment 1939-41, Royal Artillery 1941-46; Assistant Lecturer, Lecturer, Reader, Dept. of Geography, Univ. College London 1950-65; Ogilvie Professor of Geography, Univ. of Edinburgh 1965-86; Vis.Sen Lec, Univ. of Ibadan 1963-64; Vis. Prof of Geography, Univ. of Waterloo 1971; vis. Prof of Recreation and Leisure Studies, Loughborough Univ. 1986-89; Vis. Prof of Geography, Birkbeck College, London 1986- ; mbr: England Cttee, Nature Conservancy 1965-71; Chmn, Land Use Panel, Nature Conservancy 1967-70; mbr, Land Use Data Sub-Cttee, Natural Resource Advs Cttee 1965-66; mbr Land Use Research Grants Cttee, Natural Environment Research Cncl, 1967-73; Specialist

Advisor, Select Cttee on Scottish Affairs 1971-72; mbr: Dept. Cttee on Tourism, Scottish Dev. Dept. 1966-67; Dept. Cttee on Educn in the Countryside 1969-74; Scottish Educ. Dept; Scottish Joint Cttee on Information Systems for Planning 1968-72; Scottish Dev. Dept; Ordnance Survey Review Cttee, Dept. of the Environment 1978-79; Scottish Sports Cncl 1976-87; Chmn: Facilities Planning Cttee 1984-87; Chmn Review Panel on Information Needs in the Humanities, British Library/British Academy 1990-92; mbr: Cncl of the Inst. of British Geographers 1966-74; Pres. 1973-74; mbr: Cncl, Royal Scottish Geographical Soc 1966, Vice-Pres, 1976- ; mbr: Exec.Cttee, Scottish Field Studies Assoc 1966- ; Chmn. 1977-80; mbr: Scottish Environmental Educ.Cncl 1978- ; Vice Pres. Scottish Recreational Land Assoc 1972- ; Vice Pres Scottish Inland Waterways Assoc.1976- ; mbr. British Nat. Cttee for Geography 1968-87, Chmn, 1979-84; Mbr. Royal Society Ordnance Survey Scientific Committee, 1980- ; Mbr. Council of the Royal Society of Edinburgh, 1978-81;Mbr. Council British Academy, 1984-87, Vice Pres., 1985-87; Mbr. Sport and Recreation Studies Board, Council for National Academic Awards, 1983-87; Mbr. Council, International Union for the Conservation of Nature, 1976-84; Chmn. Commission on Agriculture and Food Production, International Geographical Union, 1976-80; Chmn. working Group on environmental maps, International Geographical Union, 1984-88; Editor, International Journal of Geographical Information Systems, 1986- : *Publications:* The Changing Use of Land in Britain (with R.H.Best) 1962; An Agricultural Atlas of England and Wales 1964, 2nd edn 1976; Greater London (ed. with H.C.Prince) 1964; An Agricultural Geography of Great Britain 1971; Recreation in the Countryside: a Spatial Analysis (with B.S. Duffield) 1975; Spatial Dimensions of Public Policy (ed.with W.R.D.Sewell) 1976; An Agricultural Atlas of Scotland 1976; Second Homes: Curse or Blessing? (ed) 1977; Public Participation in Planning (ed. with W.R.D.Sewell) 1977; Land Use and Town and Country Planning (with L.F.Gebbett) 1978; Land Assessment in Scotland (ed. with M.F. Thomas) 1980; Agriculture in Developed Countries 1984; Innovation in Water Management (with W.R.D.Sewell and A.Pitkethly) 1986; Geography, Planning and Policy Making (ed.with P.T.Kivell) 1986; numerous papers: mainly in geographical journals. *Recreation:* Badminton, walking, nature study, listening to music. *Address:* 57 Braid Avenue, Edinburgh EH10 6EB.

CORY,Mr Charles (Raymond),CBE *Born on* 20 Oct 1922 at Peterston-Super-Ely. *Son of* the late Charles Cory and the late Ethel Cory (neeCottam). *Marriage:* 1st to Vivienne Mary Roberts 1946 (d.1988); 2nd to Mrs Betty Horley, widow of Lt.Col. Roy Horley. *Children:* Mrs Elizabeth Larby, Mrs Rosemary Allen and Mrs Charlotte Dunseath. *Educated at* Harrow; Christ Church, Oxford. *Career:* served WW II Lt RNVR N Atlantic, Channel, North Sea; CinC commendation 1944; chm: John Cory and Sons Ltd 1965-91; Mountstuart Dry Docks 1962-66, vice-chm: Br Transport Docks Bd 1970-80 (memb 1966),AB Electronic Products GR Ltd 1978- , chm: South Glamorgan Health Authy 1974-84; Milford Haven Conservancy Bd 1982- ; memb ctee of management RNLI 1954- ,(vice-pres 1969- dep chm 1985-), chm Finance Ctee Church in Wales 1975- , dep chm Rep Body 1985; chm: Welsh Cncl Mission to Seamen 1984-. *Recreation:* skiing, countryside. *Clubs:*

Cardiff and County. *Address:* The Coach House, Llanblethian, Cowbridge, South Glam. CF7 7JF. The Ridge, Wotton-Under-Edge, Glos. GL12 7PT

CORY, Mr John, JP, DL. *Currently:* Farmer. *Born on* 30 June 1928 at St.Brides-Super-Ely. *Son of* John and Cecil Cory. *Marriage:* to Sarah Meade 1965. *Children:* Anna and Clare. *Educated at* Eton; Trinity College Cambridge. *Career:* JP 1961; DL 1968; Glamorgan High Sheriff 1959-60; Vice Lord Lieutenant 1990, South Glamorgan. Chairman: Cardiff R.D.C., 1971-72; member: Representative Body of Church in Wales; KStJ. *Clubs:* Cardiff & County. *Address:* The Grange, St.Brides-Super-Ely, Cardiff CF5 6XA. Tel: 0446 760211

CORY (Cory Of Coryton, Whitchurch), Sir (Baronet) (Clinton Charles) Donald, *Born on* 13 Sept 1937 at Derby. *Son of* Sir Clinton James Donald Cory, Bart., Lady Mabel Mary Cory (nee Hunt). *Educated at* Brighton College and abroad. *Recreation:* Collecting Greek and Roman antiquities; student of classical studies.*Address:* 18 Cloisters Road, Letchworth, Herts. SG6 3JS.Tel: 0462 677206

COUPE,Professor Peter Stephen, BSc(Eng).,ACGI., PhD(Cantab).,CEng.,MICE.,Pr.Eng.,MSAICE. *Currently:* Head of Department of Civil Engineering and Building, The Polytechnic of Wales 1988- . *Born on* 10 Jan 1946 at Stockton-on-Tees, Co.Durham. *Son of* Stephen and Freda (nee Reay). *Educated at* Grangefield Grammar School, Stockton-on-Tees; Imperial Coll. Univ. of London; Fitzwilliam Coll. Univ. of Cambridge. *Career:* Engineering Trainee, Imp. Chem Ind. Billingham 1965; Structual Design Eng. 1971-73, Resident Site Eng. 1974-77, Assoc. Partner with Hawkins Hawkins & Osborn 1978-80; Consulting Civil Eng. in S.Africa, Botswana and Namibia. Sen.Lec. 1980-84, Principal Lec. 1984-88, Dept. of Civil Eng. Sunderland Polytechnic. Examiner for Engineer Council 1981-91. *Publications:* in Geotechnics *Recreation:* Photography, environmental conservation *Address:* Dept.of Civil Eng & Building, Polytechnic of Wales, Pontypridd Mid Glam CF37 1DL. Tel: 0443 480480

COUPER, Professor. Alastair Dougal, MA.,DipEd., PhD., Master Mariner. *Currently:* Professor of Maritime Studies, UWCC, 1989- . *Born on* 4 June 1931 at Aberdeen. *Son of* F. Daniel Alexander Couper and M. Davina (nee Rilley). *Marriage:* to Norma Milton 1958. *Children:* Callum, Rona, Katrina and Roderick. *Educated at* Robert-Gordons School of Navigation; University of Aberdeen; Australian National University. *Career:* Merchant Navy 1947-57; Student, University of Aberdeen 1958-62; Research Scholar Australian National University 1963-66; Lecturer University of Durham 1966-70; Professor UWCC 1970- ; (World Maritime Univ. Sweden 1987-89); Chairman Editorial Board Jnl Maritime Policy and Management; Member Executive Board Law of the Sea Institute; Consultant to UN agencies; Research work Pacific Ocean Region; Editor Times Atlas and Encyclopaedia of the Sea. *Publications:* Several books, atlases and over 70 papers on Maritime subjects, plus UN Reports. *Recreation:* Hill walking, organic gardening, wine and music. *Address:* 112 Ely Road, Llandaff, Cardiff CF5 2DA. Dept. Of Maritime Studies & International Transport, UWCC, P.O. Box 907, Cardiff. CF1 3YP

COWELL, Mr Richard Wynn, LL.B.(Liverpool) D.P.A.(Oxon) *Currently:* Secretary for Wales, Professional

Assoc. of Teachers. *Born on* 30 March 1931 at Pwllheli, N.Wales. *Son of* the late Alderman Thomas Robert Cowell and Nesta (nee Wynne-Griffith). *Marriage:* to Jean Furlong-Richards 1960. *Children:* Bethan and Owain. *Educated at* Pwllheli Grammar School; Univs. Liverpool and Oxford *Career:* Careers Adviser U.C.W. Aberystwyth 1962-86; Mbr. Dyfed C.C., 1977- ; former Chrmn county Road Safety Commt., Public Protection Commt., Highways & Transportation Commt; Governor, Penglais Comp., and other schools; Mbr. Court of Governors U.C.W; Chmn. Day Centre Aberystwyth; Former Chmn. Aberystwyth Citizens Advice Bureau Management Commt. *Publications:* Handbook on Careers; various articles on education and employment *Recreation:* Gardening, golf, RNLI fund raising and welfare of the elderly *Clubs:* 41 Club *Address:* Bodnant, Borth, Dyfed SY24 5NL. Tel: 0970 871401

COX, County Councillor Ronald Tom Cooper,JP *Currently:* retired, Industrial Civil Servant. *Born on* 17 Dec 1912 at Penygraig. *Son of* Alfred and Annie Cox. *Marriage:* to Hannah Davies of Llandysul, 1939. *Children:* Mary Elizabeth of Kimberley B.C. Canada. *Educated at* Tonypandy. *Career:* served for over 42 years in local government, Community, Rural Borough; Past-chairman and Mayor of Taff Ely Borough, at present Community and County Councillor; Governor of Tonyrefail Welsh, Tonyrefail Primary and Tonyrefail High School. *Recreation:* rugby, local government. *Address:* 8 Parkland Cres., Tonyrefail, Porth., Mid Glam, CF39 8PF. 25 Esplanade Avenue, Porthcawl, Mid Glam

CRADICK, Mr Christopher (Roger), *Currently:* Partner, Morgan Bruce, Solicitors. *Born on* 6 Nov 1932 at Goole, Yorks. *Son of* the late Henry Cyril Cradick and Rita Cradick. *Marriage:* 1st to Mary Elizabeth Stephenson, 1957; 2nd to Gillian Susan Whetter, 1968. *Children:* Simon John, Sian Elizabeth, Neil Henry and Richard Paul. *Educated at* Penarth Grammar; Llandovery College. *Career:* Solicitor 1954; Partner in Hardwickes 1963, merged with Morgan Bruce and Nichols 1987; appointed Deputy District Registrar of High Court and County Court 1976. Deputy Judge 1991. Chairman of Social Security Appeal Tribunal 1978, Chairman of Medical Appeal Tribunal 1986. President Cardiff & District Law Society 1985. *Recreation:* rugby (ex referee), cricket, gardening. *Clubs:* Old Penarthians RFC (Vice-President). *Address:* Bradley Court, Park Place, Cardiff, CF1 3DP. '' De Novo '', St.Andrew's Road, Dinas Powis, S.Glam, CF6 4HB

CRAIG, Mr George Charles Graham, BA *Currently:* Principal Establishment Officer Welsh Office. *Born on* 8 May 1946 *Son of* the late George Craig and E.S.Craig (nee Milne). *Marriage:* to (Ethne) Marian, 1968, er d of late H.H.A. Gallagher and of E.F. Gallagher. *Children:* two s one d. *Educated at* Brockley County Grammar School; Nottingham Univ.; *Career:* Assistant Principal, Ministry of Transport 1967; Welsh Office Private Secretary to Minister of State 1970-72; Principal 1972; Private Parliamentary Secretary to Secretary of State for Wales 1978-80; Assistant Secretary 1980; Under Secretary 1986; *Address:* Welsh Office, Cathays Park, Cardiff CF1 3NQ

CRAWSHAY,Sir William (Robert),Kt 1972;DSO 1945; ERD; TD; VL *Currently:* Retired. *Born on* 27 May 1920 at London. *Son of* Jack William Leslie Crawshay, MC, Caversham Park,Oxon and the late Hon Mrs Clare Egerton.

Marriage: to Elizabeth Mary Boyd Reynolds, 1950. *Educated at* Eton *Career:* Vice Lord Lieutenant of Gwent, since 1979. Served Royal Welch Fus (SR), 1939-46; SOE 1944 (DSO, despatches twice); TA, 1947-62, Parachute Regt. Welch Regt, SW Brigade, ADC to HM the Queen 1976-81. Hon.Colonel: 3rd RRW (V) Bn, 1970-82; Cardiff Univ. OTC, 1977-85. Mem., Arts Council of GB, 1962-74; Chairman: Welsh Arts Council, 1968-74; Council, University Coll. of Cardiff, 1966-87; Member: Council and Court, Univ. of Wales, 1967; Welsh Council, 1966-69, 1970- ; Council and Court, Nat. Museum of Wales, 1966- (Pres., 1977-82). Pres., Royal British Legion, Wales Area, 1974-88. Mem., Crafts Adv. Council, 1974-78. Hon. LLD, Univ. of Wales, 1975. DL Glamorgan, 1964, Monmouthshire, 1970, Gwent, 1974. Chevalier, Legion d'honneur, 1956l Croix de Guerre (France) with Palms twice, 1944, 1945. KStJ (formerly KJStJ) 1969. *Clubs:* Whites, Cardiff & County. *Address:* Llanfair Court, Abergavenny, Gwent NP7 9BB

CROWLEY-MILLING, Michael Crowley,CMG, MA, CEng, FIEE. *Currently:* Free Lance Consultant Engineer to a number of Nuclear Physics Laboratory, since 1985. *Born on* 7 May 1917 at Rhyl, Flintshire. *Son of* the late Thomas William and the late Gillian May (nee Chinnery). *Marriage:* to Gee Dickson, 1958. *Educated at* Kingsland Grange, Shrewsbury; Radley College, St.Johns Cambridge. *Career:* Research Engineer 1938-63, Metropolitan-Vickers Elec Co. Ltd., Manchester, Development of Radar, then Electron Linacs for treatment of cancer etc; Directorate member of The Daresbury Nuclear Physics Laboratory, Nr Warrington 1963-71. Construction of elecxtron synchrotron "NINA2. European Organization for Nuclear Research (CERN) Geneva, Switzerland 1971-75, Group Leader for Control System for Proton Synchrotron "S.P.S"; S.P.S., Division leader 1976-78; Director for the Accelerator Programme 1978-80; Consultant to CERN (full time) 1980-83; Stanford University - visiting scientist 1983-85. *Publications:* Many publications in Scientific Journals. Books: "Accelerator Control Systems" (ed) North Holland 1986; "Accelerator and Large Experimental Physics Control Systems (ed) North Holland 1990. *Recreation:* vintage cars, sailing (yacht "SPS"). *Clubs:* Vintage Sports Car; Llanbedr & Pensarn Yacht. *Address:* C/o Barclays Bank Plc, 84 Mostyn St, Llandudno, Gwynedd, LL30 2SH.

CROWTHER, His Honour Judge Thomas Rowland, Q.C. *Currently:* Circuit Judge, since 1985. *Born on* 11 Sept 1937 *Son of* Dr. and Mrs K.V. Crowther. *Marriage:* to Gillian Jane (nee Prince), 1969. *Children:* Thomas and Lucy. *Educated at* Newport High School; Keble College, Oxford (MA). *Career:* President, Oxford Univ. Liberal Club, 1957; Editor, Oxford Guardian, 1957. Called to the Bar, Inner Temple, 1961; Junior and Wine Steward, Wales and Chester Circuit, 1974. A Recorder, 1980-85. Contested (L) General Elections: Oswestry, 1964 and 1966; Hereford, 1970. Founder Mem., Gwent Area Broadcasting, 1981. *Recreation:* garden. *Clubs:* Cardiff and County; Newport Golf. *Address:* Lansor, Caerleon, Gwent NP6 1LS.

CROWTHER, Mr Peter Hayden,CEng *Currently:* retired. *Born on* 1 June 1926 at Barry, Glam. *Son of* the late Charles Crowther and the late Gwendoline (nee Matthews). *Marriage:* to Anne Marie Costain, 1955, y da of Sir Richard Costain, CBE. *Children:* Hugh Hayden (b.1958) and

Penelope Anne (b.1960). *Educated at* Barry County School; Manchester Col. of Technology. *Career:* Commissioned Royal Engineers 1945-48. joined Babcock & Wilcox Ltd., 1948; Managing Director, Bailey Meters & Controls Ltd., 1963-74; dir Babcock & Wilcox (UK Investments) Ltd., 1968-72; dir Babcock & Wilcox (Management) Ltd., 1972-74; joined Vickers plc 1975; chairman local Board Vickers Eng Group, Newcastle 1975-80; dir Vickers Eng Group 1975-80. Chairman and MD, BAJ Ltd., 1984-86; Deputy Chairman, BAJ Holdings 1985-87; Chairman, Board of Governors EITB Training Centre, Croydon 1967-74; member: Northern Industrial Development Board 1978-80; member: Herefordshire Health Authority 1989-90. *Recreation:* reading, farming. *Clubs:* Army & Navy. *Address:* Highbridge Farm, Dymock Road, Ledbury, Herefordshire, HR8 2HT Tel: 0531 2798

CRUMPLIN, Mr Michael Kenneth Hugh, MB, BS(Lond), MRCS, LRCP(Eng), FRCS(Eng). *Currently:* Consultant General Surgeon, Clwyd Health Authority, since 1977. *Born on* 12 Aug 1942 at Glasgow. *Son of* Col. W.C.D. Crumplin and Mrs. M.E.K. Crumplin. *Marriage:* to Elizabeth Ann Bunting. *Children:* Iain Douglas, Patrick Gordon and Fiona Jane *Educated at* Wellington College; Middlesex Hospital. *Career:* House Surgeon, Middlesex Hospital; House Physician, Central Middlesex Hospital 1965, SHO Colchester 1966-67; Registrar, Swindon and Middlesex Hospital 1968-72; Hon. Research Fellow West Midlands 1972-73; Senior Registrar, West Midlands 1973-77; Member (ex council member), Association of Surgeons of Great Britain and N.Ireland. Member of Welsh Board (RCS); Regional Adviser for Surgery N.Wales (RCS); Chairman Court of Examiners RCS (Eng); Member Editorial Board British Journal Surgery. *Publications:* numerous medical articles, articles on Military surgery; 3 chapters in Medical textbooks. *Recreation:* Military medical history (Battle of Waterloo), shooting, sailing. *Clubs:* East India. *Address:* 57 Wynnsay Lane, Marford, Nr Wrexham, Clwyd, LL12 8LH. Maelor General Hospital, Watery Road, Wrexham, Clwyd.

CRWYS-WILLIAMS,Air Vice-Marshal David Owen,CB, FIPM, RAF. *Currently:* Director General of RAF Personal Services. *Born on* 24 Dec 1940 at Llangollen, Clwyd. *Son of* Gareth Crwys-Williams and Francis Ellen Crwys-Williams (nee Strange). *Marriage:* 1st to Jennifer Jean (nee Pearce) 1963; 2nd to Irene Thompson (Suzie) (nee Whan), 1973. *Children:* Jacqueline Lara and Geraint Miles from 1st marriage; Huw David, Kirsty Jane and Claire Elizabeth from 2nd marriage. *Educated at* Oakham School; RAF College, Cranwell. *Career:* No. 30 Sqn, Kenya 1961-63; No. 47 Sqn, RAF Abingdon 1964-65; ADC to C in C, RAF Training Command 1966-68; OC No. 46 Sqn, RAF Abingdon (Sqn Leader) 1969-71; OC, RAF Masirah, Oman 1972; Army Staff College 1973; Personal Staff Officer to C in C Near East Air Force, Cyprus 1974-75; Wing Commander 1975; OC No. 230 Sqn, RAF Odiham 1976-77; Personnel Officer, MoD 1977-79; Deputy Director, Air Plans, MoD (Gp Captain) 1979-81; OC RAF Shawbury, Salop 1983-85; Royal College of Defence Studies 1985; Director of Air Support/Air Staff Duties, MoD (Air Commodore) 1985-87; Commander British Forces, Falkland Islands (Air Vice-Marshal) 1988-89. *Recreation:* fly fishing, furniture restoration, building. *Clubs:* Royal Air Force. *Address:*

C/o Barclays Bank Ltd, Marcham Road, Abingdon, Oxon OX14 1UB.

CRYSTAL,Professor David,BA.,PhD.,FRSA.,FCST *Currently:* Author, lecturer and broadcaster on language and linguistics; author and editor of general reference books. *Born on* 6 July 1941 at Lisburn, N.Ireland. *Son of* Samuel Cyril Crystal and Mary Agnes Morris. *Marriage:* 1) to Molly Irene Stack (d1976), 1964; 2) to Hilary Frances Norman, 1976. *Children:* Steven David; Susan Mary; Timothy Joseph, Lucy Alexandra and Benjamin Peter. *Educated at* St. Mary's Coll., Liverpool; Univ. Coll., London (ECL) *Career:* Research Assist. UCL, 1962-63; Assist.Lecturer, Univ. Coll., of North Wales, 1963-65; Lecturer, 1965-69; Reader, 1969-75; Professor, Reading Univ., 1975-85; Independent Scholar, 1985- . *Publications:* Systems of prosodic & paralinguistic features in English (with R.Quirk),1964;Linguistics language and religion, 1965; What is linguistics?, 1968, 5th ed. 1985; Prosodic systems & intonation in English, 1969; Investigating English style (with D.Davy), 1969; The English language, Vol.2.(with W.F.Bolton), 1969,2nd ed.1987; Linguistics,1971,2nd ed.1985; The English tone of voice,1975; Advanced conversational English (with D.Davy),1975; Skylarks (with J.Bevington),1975; The grammatical analysis of language disability (with P.Fletcher,M.Garman), 1976,2nd ed.1989; Child language,learning and linguistics,1976,2nd ed.1988; Working with LARSP,1979; Intro. to language pathology, 1980,2nd.ed.1988; A dictionary of linguistics and phonetics,1980,3rd ed.1991; (ed) Eric Partridge: in his own words,1980; Clinical linguistics,1981; Directions in applied linguistics,1981: Profiling Linguistics Disability, 1982, 2nd edn 1992: (ed) Linguistic Controversies, 1982: Who Cares About English Usage?, 1984: Linguistic Encounters with Language Handicap, 1984: Listen to Your Child, 1986: Yhe Cambridge Encyclopedia of Language, 1987: Rediscover Grammar, 1988: The English Language, 1988: Pilgrimage, 1988: Convent: the Bon Sauver Community in Holyhead (with J.C. Davies), 1989: Databank (with J.L. Foster, 1979-85: (ed) The Cambridge Encyclopedia, 1990:Datasearch (with J.L. Foster), 1991: Language A-Z, 1991: Making Sense of English Usage, 1991: *Recreation:* Cinema, music, bibliophily, the development of Holyhead.*Address:* P.O.Box 5, Holyhead, Gwynedd LL65 1RG.

CUDLIPP, Baron created 1974 (Life Peer) Hugh,Knight 1973; OBE 1945. *Born on* 28 Aug 1913 at Cardiff.. *Son of* William and Bessie Cudlipp of Cardiff. *Marriage:* 2nd to Eileen Ascroft 1945 (d 1962); 3rd to Jodi,da of late John L. Hyland of Florida,USA, 1963. *Educated at* Howard Gardens School, Cardiff. *Career:* Journalist, Provincial newspapers in Cardiff and Manchester, 1927-32; Features Editor, Sunday Chronicle, London, 1932-35; Features Editor, Daily Mirror, 1935-37; Editor, Sunday Pictorial, 1937-40; Military Service, 1940-46; after Desert War, Commanding Officer, British Army Newspaper Unit, CMF, Editor-in-Chief of official Services newspapers ('Union Jack') in Algeria, Tunisia, Italy, Greece, Austria; Editor Sunday Pictorial 1946-49; Managing Editor Sunday Express, 1950-52; Editorial Director Daily Mirror and Sunday Pictorial 1952-63; Joint Managing Director, Daily Mirror and Sunday Pictorial, 1959-63; Chairman Odhams Press Ltd., 1961-63; Chairman, Daily Mirror Newspapers Ltd., 1963-68; Chairman, International Publishing Corporation Ltd., 1968-73 (Deputy Chairman, 1964-68); IPC Newspaper Division 1970-73; Deputy Chairman (editorial), Reed International Board 1970-73; Director, Associated Television Ltd., 1956-73; Member Royal Commission on Standards of Conduct in Public Life; Founder Executive Chairman, Chichester Festivities 1975; Member Chichester Festival Theatre Productions Company 1980-87; Vice President Chichester Festival Theatre Trust 1987- : *Publications:* Publish and be Damned 1955; At Your Peril 1962; Walking on the Water 1976; The Prerogative of the Harlot 1980. *Recreation:* Music. *Clubs:* Garrick; Chichester City Club *Address:* House Of Lords, London SW1A OPW

CUDLIPP, Mr Reginald, Order of Sacred Treasure, Japan 1982. *Currently:* retired. *Born on* 11 Dec 1910 at Cardiff. *Son of* William and Mrs B.A. Cudlipp. *Marriage:* to Rachel Braham 1945 *Educated at* Gladstone School, Cardiff, Cardiff Technical College. *Career:* Began journalistic career on Penarth News, 1926; Sub-Editor Western Mail 1931-38; joined News of The World sub-editorial staff 1938; served war 1940-46; rejoined News of The World and became special correspondent in USA 1946-47; features editor 1948-50, deputy editor 1950-53; editor 1953-59; Director News of The World Ltd., 1955-60; Specialised on Japan and became director Anglo-Japanese Economic Institute 1961-86; Editor ''Japan'' (quarterly review and monthly survey) and special publications on the Japan scene 1961-86; extensive industrial tours and on-the-spot economic study of Japan regularly 1962-86; Lecturer and writer on Japan's Past, Present and Future; also first-hand research on developing nations and economic co-operation, especially in Asia and Africa; Life member National Union of Journalists 1929- ; completed 60 years in active journalism 1926-86. *Publications:* numerous contributions to newspapers and periodicals on Japan and Anglo-Japanese affairs. *Recreation:* Music, travel and reading, writing and talking about Japan. *Address:* 14 Walberton Park, Walberton, Arundel, West Sussex. BN18 OPJ.

CURTIS, David, *Currently:* Sole Proprieter, Sportfix, Stanley Street, Cwmfellinfach, est 1981. *Born on* 16 Feb 1948 at Ynysddu. *Son of* Gwyn and Eileen. *Marriage:* to Marian. *Children:* Lisa (21 years) and Paul (18 years). *Educated at* Pontllanfraith Junior Mixed; Oakdale Comprehensive. *Career:* Involved in sport for many years, participating at International Level as a Trampolinist, British Champion, World Champion, Synchronised runner up. *Recreation:* golf *Clubs:* Pontllanfraith Rotary. *Address:* 16 High Field Road, Pontllanfraith, Blackwood, Gwent NP1 7AR.

D

DANIEL, Lady Valerie Davidia,BA. *Born on* 14 Feb 1918 at Pwllheli. *Daughter of* Richard and Roberta Lloyd George. *Marriage:* to Goronwy Daniel, 1940. *Children:* Anne, Gwyneth and David. *Educated at* St.Felix School, Southwold; St.Hilda's College Oxford. *Career:* Statistical Assistant to Sir William Beveridge 1939-40. Teaching-Queens College, Harley Street, London. *Recreation:* gardening, reading, studying. *Address:* Cae Ffynnon, 67 St. Michaels Road, Cardiff CF5 2AN.

DANIEL, Mr Afan Bowen, MA(Cantab) *Currently:* retired. *Born on* 7 May 1928 at Port Talbot. *Son of* Richard David Daniel and Mary Catherine Daniel (nee Bowen). *Marriage:* 1st to Beatrice Mary Dobson, 1952; 2nd to MargaretRose Roberts, 1981. *Children:* by 1st marriage, Adrian Richard Huw and Beverley Mair. *Educated at* Port Talbot Grammar School; Trinity College Cambridge. *Career:* RAF Flying Officer 1948-50; Assistant Master, King Edward VI School Stafford 1950-52; Assistant Master St.Benedict's School 1952-55; Assistant Education Officer Norfolk CC 1955-56; Head of History Cheshunt Grammar School 1956-63; Headmaster Ystalyfera Gr. School 1963-69; Headmaster Gowerton Boys' Gr. School 1969-73; Headmaster Gowerton School 1973-90. Chairman: Headmasters Association - Wales 1978-80; President: Welsh Secondary Schools Assoc 1986; Member: Secondary Exams Council 1983-86; Admiralty Interview Board since 1966; Secretary: Gowerton Cricket Club 1975-89; Secretary: Welsh Cricket Assoc, since 1990; Trustee: Cummins Engine Co Ltd Educational Fund, since 1976. *Recreation:* sport of all kind, especially cricket; bridge; gardening. *Clubs:* Swansea Bridge, Swansea Sports, All White Former Players; Life Patron-Gowerton Cricket. *Address:* 33 Hendrefoilan Avenue, Sketty, Swansea SA2 7NA. Tel: 0792 290075

DANIEL, Mr Emyr,MA *Currently:* Managing Director since 1991, and Director of Programmes since 1989, HTV Cymru/Wales. *Born on* 30 Aug 1948 at Maenclochog, Dyfed. *Son of* Rev.Moguwyn and the late Mrs H.E. Daniel. *Marriage:* to Catrin Gerallt 1982. *Children:* Mathew Rhys and Hannah Fflur. *Educated at* Queen Elizabeth G.S, Carmarthen; Jesus College, Oxford. *Career:* Reporter/interviewer, Report Wales (HTV), 1970; Editor "Outlook" 1971-74; Contract presenter BBC Wales 1974-81; Producer/Presenter HTV 1981-85; Head of Current Affairs 1985-87; Assistant Controller of Programmes 1987-89. *Recreation:* very occasional golf. *Address:* 12 The Parade, Whitchurch, Cardiff CF4 2EF.

DANIEL, Sir Goronwy Hopkin, KCVO.,CB.,D.Phil. *Currently:* Retired. *Born on* 21 March 1914 at Ystradgynlais. *Son of* David Daniel and Annie Daniel. *Marriage:* to Lady Valerie Daniel 1940. *Children:* Anne, Gwyneth and David *Educated at* Pontardawe Sec. and Amman Valley Co.

Schools; UCW Aberystwyth; Jesus College Oxford. *Career:* Lecturer Dept. Economics, Bristol Univ. 1940-41; Clerk House of Commons (attached to Select. Comm. on National Expenditure) 1941-43; Ministry of Town and Country Planning 1943-47; Chief Statistician, Assistant Secretary and then Under Secretary, Ministry of Fuel and Power 1947-64; Permanent Sec. Welsh Office 1964-69; Principal UCW Aberystwyth (and Vice-Chancellor Univ. of Wales 1977-79), 1969-79; Director and Deputy Chairman (1984-90) Bank of Wales, 1972-90; H.M. Lieutenant for Dyfed 1979-89; Dep. Chairman Prince of Wales Committee 1980-86; Chairman of Welsh Fourth Channel Auth. 1981-86; Chairman or member of various other committees; Hon. Freeman, City of London; Hon. LLD Wales; Hon. Fellow, Jesus Coll. Oxford. *Publications:* Articles on energy, administrative, population and other subjects. *Recreation:* Country persuits. *Clubs:* Travellers. *Address:* Cae Ffynnon, 67 Saint Michaels Road, Llandaff, Cardiff, CF5 2AN. Ridge Farm, Letterston, Haverfordwest, Dyfed, SA62 5TT

DARBY, Sir (Henry) Clifford, CBE; LittD; PhD *Currently:* retired. *Born on* 7 Feb 1909 at Resolven, Glamorgan. *Son of* Evan and Janet Darby (nee Thomas). *Marriage:* to Eva Constance Thomson, 1941. *Children:* Jennifer Elizabeth and Sarah Caroline. *Educated at* Neath County School; St.Catharine's College, Cambridge. *Career:* Professor of Geography, Liverpool 1945-49; University College London 1949-66; Cambridge 1966-76; Admiralty 1941-45; Member, Royal Commission Historical Monuments 1953-77; Water Resources Board 1964-68. *Publications:* Domesday Geography of England (gen.ed.) 1952-77; other works on Historical Geography. *Address:* 60 Storey's Way, Cambridge CB3 ODX. King's College, Cambridge CB2 1ST

DAVEY, Mr Idris Wyn,BSc. *Currently:* retired, Under Secretary Welsh Office 1972-77. *Born on* 8 July 1917 at Blaina, Gwent. *Son of* the late Samuel and Margaret Davey. *Marriage:* to Lilian Lloyd-Bowen 1943. *Children:* Jocelyn and Celia. *Educated at* Nantyglo Grammar School; Cardiff Technical College. *Career:* Admiralty Scientist 1940-47; Assistant Principal Welsh Board of Health 1948; Principal 1951; Secretary Local Govt. Commission for Wales 1959-62; Welsh Office Asst Sec. (in Ministry of Housing & Local Govt) 1962; Establishment Officer 1966-72; Under Sec 1972, Seconded as Secretary and Member Local Govt. Staff Commission for Wales and NHS Staff Commission for Wales 1972-73; Member Sports Council for Wales 1978-88; Deputy Chairman Local Govt. Boundary Commission for Wales 1979-89. *Recreation:* gardening, golf, University of the Third Age (U3A). *Address:* 4a Southgate Road, Southgate, Swansea SA3 2BT.

DAVID, Mr Brian Rhodri,TD *Currently:* retired. *Born on* 20 Sept 1917 at Cardiff. *Son of* the late H.Cyril David and the late Enid Mary David (nee Rees). *Marriage:* to Joan Margaret Kemp, 1939. *Children:* Nicholas Brian and Sally Margaret (married name Ellis). *Educated at* Llandaff Cathedral School; Mill Hill School. *Career:* Timber trade, Robinson David & Co. Ltd, Assistant Managing Director; Chairman, Principality Building Society 1981-91 (Director 1958-91); Member of Council, Timber Trades Federation of U.K; Deputy Chairman of Softwood Section, now retired. Chairman, Wales & West Building Societies Association (retired); Chairman, Port of Cardiff Employers Association 1958; President, Cardiff Chamber of Commerce 1963; President, Newport & Gwent Chamber of Commerce 1975. *Recreation:* rugby football, reading. *Clubs:* Cardiff & County, Glamorgan Wanderers, Old Millhilians *Address:* 20 Mill Road, Llanishen, Cardiff CF4 5XB.

DAVID, Mr Joseph,OBE, FTI, FIWSc. *Currently:* retired. Non-executive Chairman, Catomance Ltd; Governor Hatfield Polytechnic. *Born on* 22 March 1928 at Treforest, Glam. *Son of* the late Morris David and Goldie David (nee Freedman). *Marriage:* to Shirley Selbey, 1959. *Children:* Keren Sarah, Alun Morris and Deborah Judith. *Educated at* Pontypridd Intermediate Boys School; Manchester University. *Career:* Chemist/Dyer 1948-53, BDA Ltd; Catomance Ltd 1953-90, Technical Service Manager 1953-68, Director 1968- , Managing Director and Chairman 1977-90, Chairman 1977-. Served on various BSI committees 1953- ; President British Pest Control Association 1976-78; Vice President Textile Institute 1972-74; President British Wood Preserving Association 1987-89; Treasurer British Wood Preserving and Damp-proofing Association 1990- . *Recreation:* music, gardening, higher education. *Address:* 16 Guessens Road, Welwyn Garden City, Herts AL8 6QR.

DAVID, Mr Tudor,OBE *Currently:* Freelance Journalist; Editor, "Oil and Gas Finance & Accounting" (quarterly). *Born on* 25 April 1921 at Barry, Wales. *Son of* the late Thomas David and the late Blodwen David (nee Jones). *Marriage:* 1st to Nancy Ramsay 1943, (deceased 1984); 2nd to Margaret Dix 1987. *Children:* (from 1st marriage) Martyn and Glenwyn. *Educated at* Barry Grammar School; Univ. of Manchester; Univ. of Oxford. *Career:* Royal Air Force (Squadron leader) 1942-47; Extra Mural Lecturer, Univ. of Newcastle upon Tyne 1947-50; Careers Officer, Lincolnshire 1950-55; Assistant Editor, "Education" 1955-65; Editor "The Teacher" 1965-70; Editor "Education" 1971-86; Member Council of the Cymmrodorion Vice-President, London Welsh Assoc; Editor "London Welshman" 1960-73; Editorial Board "Planet". *Publications:*"Church and School"; Scunthorpe and its Families"; "Perspectives in Geographical Education" (part); Education - the wasted years? (part),1973-86; *Recreation:* Wales; The Isle of Dogs, opera..*Clubs:* London Welsh Association. *Address:* 21 Pointers Close, Isle of Dogs, London. E14 9EP.

DAVID, Mr Wayne,BA (Hons) PGCE(FE) *Currently:* Member of the European Parliament for South Wales (Labour). *Born on* 1 Jul 1957 at Bridgend. *Son of* D. Haydn David and Edna A. David. *Marriage:* to Catherine (nee Thomas). *Educated at* Univ. College, Cardiff and Univ. College, Swansea. *Career:* History Teacher, Brynteg Comp. School 1983-85; Mid Glam. Tutor Organiser for W.E.A. 1985-89; Elected M.E.P. in JUne 1989; Treasurer of European Parliamentary Labour Party 1989-91; Labour Spokesperson on European Regional Policy 1989- ;

Publications: Contrib. to The Oxford Companion to Literature of Wales; Various Pamphlets and Articles in Newspapers; *Recreation:* Music and Reading *Address:* Ty Cathway, 8 Bryn Rhedyn, (off The Rise), Tonteg Pontypridd Mid Glam. CF38 1UY. South Wales European Office, 199 Newport Road, Cardiff, South Glam CF32 1AJ Tel: 0222 490215

DAVID, Mr William Nigel, MA, FCA. *Currently:* Director, Corporate Finance, Hoare Govett, since 1983. *Born on* 13 May 1951 at Bristol. *Son of* Idris Thomas David and Joan David (nee Morgan). *Marriage:* to Karen Susan Phipps, 1975. *Children:* Thomas Morgan and Sarah Louise. *Educated at* Kent College Canterbury; St. Edmund Hall Oxford. *Career:* Simon & Coates, trainee investment analyst 1973-74; Touche Ross & Co, left as audit manager 1975-80; Manager, Company Supervision, The Stock Exchange 1980-83. *Recreation:* golf, cricket, rugby, gardening, travel. *Clubs:* Vincents (Oxford). *Address:* Harrow Cottage, Old London Road, Knockholt, Nr Sevenoaks, Kent. TN14 7JW.

DAVIE,Mr Henry Moyes,FCIB *Currently:* Regional Executive Director, Lloyds Bank PLC, South Wales and Severnside Regional Executive Office, Cardiff. *Born on* 16 May 1941 at Dunfermline, Scotland. *Marriage:* to Jean. *Children:* 2 daughters *Educated at* Park High School, Birkenhead *Career:* Joined Lloyd's Bank in Liverpool and has held various managerial appointments; Chief Manager, Gloucester. *Recreation:* Rugby (spectator), golf and music. *Address:* Lloyds Bank plc, Severnside House, St Mellons Bus.Park, Cardiff CF3 OYY.

DAVIES,Mr (Anthony) Roger,LL.B(Hons), A.K.C., Barrister-at-Law *Currently:* Metropolitan Stipendiary Magistrate, Horseferry Road Magistrates Court, London SW1. *Born on* 1 Sept 1940 at Pengam, Glam. *Son of* the late R.George Davies and Mrs Megan Davies. *Marriage:* to Clare Cameron Walters, daughter of Commander W.A. Walters R.N., 1967. *Children:* Antonia, George and Hugo (twins). *Educated at* Pontypridd and Bridgend Grammar Schools; King's College,London; Grays Inn. *Career:* Called to Bar Grays Inn, 1965, Lord Justice Holker Senior Scholarship; Practised at the Bar in London and South Eastern Circuit 1965-85; Appointed Stipendiary Magistrate 1985; Chairman of London Juvenile Courts since 1986; Asst. Recorder of Crown Court since 1988. Governor of Welsh Girls' School, Ashford since 1979. *Recreation:* Reading (history and Biography) music (esp.opera); travel and Wales; family life. *Clubs:* Travellers; Cardiff and County. *Address:* c/o Horseferry Road, Magistrates Court, London SW1.

DAVIES, (Norah) Olwen, MA (Edin) Dip.Ed (Oxon) *Currently:* retired. *Born on* 21 March 1926 at Liverpool. *Daughter of* the late Revd. E.A. Davies and the late Norah A.M.Parry. *Educated at* Tregaron County School; Walthamstow Hall, Sevenoaks; Edinburgh University. *Career:* Teacher, Girls' Remand Home, Essex; Woodford House, New Zealand (Deputy Head); Westonbirt School, Glos; Headmistress: St. Mary's Hall, Brighton 1965-73, St. Swithun's School, Winchester 1973-86; President, G.S.A. 1982-83; Governor of St.John's Special School (Ch.Mn), Brighton; Lord Mayor Treloar College, Alton; Tormead School, Guildford; Godolphin School, Salisbury; St.Christopher's School, Farnham. *Recreation:*Education, gardening, travel. *Address:* 28 Arle Gardens, Alresford,

Hants SO24 9BA.

DAVIES, Adrian Leigh, *Currently:* Professional Squash player. *Born on* 6 Jan 1966 at Carmarthen. *Son of* David Wyndham and Pamela Davies. *Children:* Hannah Elizabeth and Lewis Cerryg Leigh Davies. *Educated at* Ysgol Gyfun Y Graig; Rugby Public School. *Career:* Youngest ever Welsh Senior Int at 15 years old; Past winner of: European Champion of Champions, Welsh Open, Dutch Open, Marbella Open, Irish Open, 110 Welsh junior caps, 86 senior caps, Welshmens National Captain, Leekes Wizards Captain (British Team Champion) 89/90, Llanelli Sportsman of Year 89/90/91; World ranked 10 (Nov 1991). *Recreation:* all sports. *Clubs:* Leekes Wizards, Strings Squash. *Address:* 7 Llyswestfa, Swiss Valley, Llanelli, Dyfed Tel: 0554 778025

DAVIES, Mr Alan Barry Clive, B.Ed. *Currently:* Company Director Rugby Clothing. *Born on* 22 Aug 1944 at Ynysybwl. *Son of* the late Thomas George Davies and Sarah Anne Davies (nee Page). *Marriage:* to Dorothy Anne Davies (nee Cartwright). *Children:* Sarah Louise and Alison Mary. *Educated at* Carlton-Le-Willows GS, Nottingham; Loughborough University. *Career:* Royal Air Force Electronics Technician 1961-71; Loughborough University 1971-75; Director of Physical Education Trent College 1977-89; ABC Direction Proprietor, P.R. and Marketing. Coaching Rugby Football: Nottingham, Midlands, England B, 1986-88; England to Australia and Fiji 1988. National Coach of Wales 1992- . *Recreation:* golf, music, wine. *Clubs:* Breadsall Priory Golf, Nottingham RFC, Wine Society. *Address:* 248a Breedon Street, Long Eaton, Nottingham NG10 4FD. A.B.C Direction, 13 Plant Lane, Sawley, Long Eaton, Notts, NG10 38

DAVIES, Mr Albert John, BSc (Hons) FI Biol *Currently:* Retired. *Born on* 21 Jan 1919 at Pontardulais. *Son of* David Daniel Davies and Annie Hilda Davies. *Marriage:* Winnifred Ivy Caroline (nee Emberton). *Children:* Peter John and Susan Caroline (Ellen) *Educated at* Amman Valley Grammar School; Univ. College Wales Aberystwyth. *Career:* Ad. Staff Univ. College Wales Aberystwyth 1940-41; Montgomery WAEC 1941-44; Welsh Plant Breeding Station 1944-47; Crop Husbandry and Grassland Adviser National Agricultural Advisory Service 1947-59; Deputy Director NAAS Wales 1959-64 and Director South West Region 1964. Senior Agicultural Adviser 1966-68. Deputy Director NAAS 1968-71; Chief Agricultural Officer Agricultural Development and Advisory Service MAFF 1971-79. *Publications:* Articles in learned societies and agricultural press. *Recreation:* Gardening and golf *Clubs:* Farmers *Address:* Cefncoed, 38a Ewell Downs Road, Ewell, Epsom Surrey KT17 3BW. Tel: 081 393 0069

DAVIES, Dr Alun Grier, CBE(1980), LLD Wales, 1991. *Born on* 16 Sept 1914 at Llanelli. *Son of* Thomas Davies and Sarah Ann Davies. *Marriage:* to Claudia Eleanor Davies, 1940. *Children:* Gareth ap Alun Grier Davies (b.1945). *Educated at* Amman Valley Grammar School; University College of Wales Aberystwyth BA; Grays Inn, Barrister-at-Law. *Career:* called to the Bar Gray's Inn 1945, HM Inspector of taxes Inland Revenue 1936-47, taxation controller Consolidated Zinc Corp 1947-65, executive director RTZ Corp plc 1965-79, int consultant 1979-87; member Audit Committee UCW 1990- (member Ct 1973 and 1980- , hon treasurer 1980-91), member Audit Committee, Univ. of Wales 1991- ; member of Central Fin Bd Methodist Church 1960-88; pres: Christian Assoc of Business Execs 1977-82, Int Fiscal Assoc 1979-83; council member: IOD 1966-84, CBI 1970-73; chairman of Tax Committees: IOD 1965-78, CBI 1970-73; Freeman City of Londonb 1975, Liveryman Worshipful Co of Lriners 1975; FInstD, FTII. *Publications:* Man the World Over 1947; Render unto Caesar 1966. *Recreation:* wine tasting, freelance journalism. *Clubs:* Caledonian, RAC. *Address:* 7 Craigleith, Grove Road, Beaconsfield, Bucks HP9 1PT. The Toft, Aberdyfi, Gwynedd LL35 OPY

DAVIES, Sir Alun Talfan, Q.C., kt 1976; QC; MA; LLB. *Born on* 22 July 1913 at Gorseinon. *Son of* the late Rev. W. Talfan Davies, Presbyterian Minister, Gorseinon. *Marriage:* to Eiluned Christopher 1942. *Children:* one s three d. *Educated at* Gowerton Grammar School; Aberystwyth University College of Wales (LLB) *Career:* Hon.Professorial Fellow 1971; Gonville and Caius Coll.,Cambridge (MA,LLB); Called to the Bar, Gray's Inn 1939, Bencher 1969; Contested (Ind) University of Wales (by-elec) 1943; contested (L): Carmarthen Div., 1959 and 1964; Denbigh 1966. Mem. Court of University of Wales and of Courts and Councils of Aberystwyth and Swansea University Colls; Recorder: of Merthyr Tydfil 1963-68; of Swansea 1968-69; of Cardiff 1969-71; of the Crown Court 1972-85; Hon. Recorder of Cardiff 1972-86; Dep.Chm., Cardiganshire QS 1963-71; Judge of the Courts of Appeal, Jersey and Gurnsey 1969-84; Member: Commn on the Constitution 1969-73; Criminal Injuries Compensation Bd, 1977-85; Founder of Llyfrau's Dryw (1940), Welsh magazine Bary (1962).President: Court of Nat. Eisteddfod of Wales 1977-80; Court, Welsh Nat. Opera 1978-80; Welsh Centre of Internat. Affairs 1985-89; Dir. Cardiff World Trade Centre Ltd 1985- ; Dep. Chm., Bank of Wales 1973- (Dir. 1971-); Dir, HTV Ltd, 1967-83 (Vice-Chm., and Chm. Welsh Board 1978-83); Vice-Chm., HTV (Group) Ltd 1978-83. Chm. Trustees, Aberfan Fund (formerly Aberfan Disaster Fund) 1969-88; Hon. LLD Wales: Aberystwyth 1973; Chmn. Bank of Wales. *Clubs:* Cardiff and County (Cardiff). *Address:* 10 Park Road, Penarth, South Glam., CF6 2BD. Tel: 0222 701341

DAVIES, The Very Reverend Alun Radcliffe, M.A. *Currently:* Dean of Llandaff and Vicar of Llandaff with Capel Llanilterne. *Born on* 6 May 1923 at Pontyclun. *Son of* the late Reverend Rhys Davies and the late Jane (nee Radcliffe). *Marriage:* to Winifred Margaret Pullen 1952. *Children:* Dyfrig, Michael and Katharine. *Educated at* Cowbridge Grammar School; University College of South Wales and Monmouthsire; Keble College, Oxford. *Career:* Ordained Deacon 1948; Priest 1949; Curate of Roath 1948-49; Lecturer St. Michael's College, Llandaff 1949-53; Warden of Ordinands 1950-71; Domestic Chaplain to Bishop of Llandaff 1952-59; Chaplain RNR 1953-60; Vicar of Ystrad Mynach 1959-75; Chancellor of Llandaff Cathedral 1959-71; Archdeacon of Llandaff 1971-77; Chairman Liturgical Commission of the Church in Wales 1971-85; Dean of Llandaff 1977; Fellow Univ. of Wales College of Cardiff 1983; Judge of the Provincial Court of the Church of Wales 1986. *Recreation:* Ecclesiastical Architecture and Liturgica *Address:* The Deanery, The Cathedral Green, Llandaff, Cardiff. CF5 2YF. 13 Maes Y Crochan, St. Mellons, Cardiff. CF3 OEL Tel: 0222 561545

DAVIES, Ashwynne, *Currently:* retired Consulting Engineer. *Born on* 16 June 1931 at BrynIwan, Dyfed. *Son of* Iwan and Margaretta Davies. *Marriage:* to Valmai (nee Jones) of Ystradgynlais. *Children:* Bethan Wyn Evans and Stephen Wyn Davies. *Educated at* Queen Elizabeth Grammar School Carmarthen; University of Cardiff. *Career:* Partner, CDC Braine & Partners, Freeman Fox Braine & P. Director Freeman Fox Wales Ltd (chairman); Freeman Fox Ltd Acer Freeman Fox Wales. *Recreation:* computers, building, travelling, reading. *Address:* 77 Heol Briwnant, Rhiwbina, Cardiff CF4 6QH. Tel: 0222 620583

DAVIES, Mr Bryn,C.B.E. *Currently:* Chairman, Mid Glam Health Authority. *Born on* 22 Jan 1932 at Tonyrefail. *Son of* the late Gomer and the late Annie. *Marriage:* 1st to the late Esme Irene; 2nd to Katherine (nee Lewis-Williams), 27th December 1991. *Children:* Nigel Rhys and Gareth Wayne *Educated at* Elementary School *Career:* South Wales Organiser, National Union of Agricultural Workers Union, 1956; Chairman Mid Glamorgan Health appointed 1978. Board Member South Wales Electricity; Member Welsh Water Authority; Development Commissioner; Member Forestry Commission, Welsh Committee; Member Wales TUC & former Chairman; Chairman, Welsh Association of Health Authorities and Trusts; Executive Committee Member of National Association of Health Authorities and Trusts. *Recreation:* Jogging, gardening, rugby, golf. *Clubs:* St.Mary's Golf, Tonyrefail, Bridgend and Pyle Rugby. *Address:* 3 Lias Cottages, Porthcawl, Mid Glamorgan

DAVIES, Lord David,MA, MBA, MICE *Currently:* Managing Director, Evans & Owen (Builders) Ltd., since 1974. Chairman, Welsh National Opera, since 1975. *Born on* 2 Oct 1940 *Son of* David Davies, 2nd Baron and Eldrydd Davies. *Marriage:* to Beryl Christine, 1972. *Children:* Eldrydd Jane, David Daniel, Lucy Medina and Benjamin Michael Graham *Educated at* Eton; Kings College Cambridge *Address:* Plas Dinam, Llandinam, Powys SY17 5DQ.

DAVIES, Mr David,BA(Econ), FCA, Chartered Accountant. *Currently:* Self-employed, David Davies & Co., Chartered Accountants; Consultant Touche Ross Chartered Accountants. *Born on* 8 March 1936 at Crickhowell, Brecnock. *Son of* the late Counsillor David Sidney Davies and the late Mrs Annie Elizabeth Davies. *Marriage:* 7th August 1972. *Children:* Justin Alexander Davies and Juliet Susannah Eliz Davies. *Educated at* Boys Grammar School, Brecon; University of Wales Cardiff. *Career:* Partner Alban & Lamb 1966, after two year career in London & Rotterdam with Coopers & Lybrand, in charge of Staff and major audits; Insolvency Partner and later Managing Partner Spicer and Pegler Welsh Region 1978-90; Partner Touche Ross, until retirement January 1991. Member for three years Parochial Church Council All Saints Penarth, two years on Committee Cardiff and District Chartered Accountants, two years member of Prince of Wales Finance Committee, Treasurer 2 years People Versus Handicapped, Board member Taff Ely Enterprize Trust, and member Cardiff Bay Liason Committee. *Publications:* Times, Accountancy, Financial Times. *Recreation:* Vice Pres Glamorgan Cricket Club, reading, music. *Clubs:* Cardiff & County, Penarth Yacht. *Address:* Highcliff, 157 Plymouth Road, Penarth, South Glam, CF6 2DG.

DAVIES, Mr David Garfield, *Currently:* General Secretary of Union of Shop, Distributive and Allied Workers (Usdaw). *Born on* 24 June 1935 at Bridgend, Glam. *Son of* David John Davies and Lizzie Anne Davies. *Marriage:* to Marian (nnee Jones), 1960. *Children:* Helen Claire, Susan Karen, Karen Jane and Rachel Louise. *Educated at* Secondary Modern, Technical. *Career:* Junior Operative, Electrical Apprentice and Electrician, British Steel Corporation, Port Talbot 1950-69; National Service RAF 1956-58; Area Organiser - Usdaw, Ipswich, 1969-73; Deputy Divisional Officer, Usdaw, London/Ipswich 1973-78; National Officer, Usdaw, Manchester 1978-85. Elected General Secretary of Usdaw 1985. Re-elected unopposed 1989. JP 1972-79. Currently member of TUC General Council and Economic Committee, Employment Policy & Organisation Committee, Chairman of the International Committee; Women's Committee; Special Review Body; Finance & General Purposes Ctee. International - Vice President of EURO-FIET; Exec Ctee mem World-FIET; Chmn Commercial Section EURO-FIET. Director Unity Trust Bank; Vice Pres Industrial Participation Assoc; member Employment Appeal Tribunal; member Governing Body Salford College of Technology; Trustee National Museum of Labour History. *Recreation:* reading, sport (cricket, soccer rugby), currently playing golf. *Address:* Usdaw, 188 Wilmslow Road, Fallowfield, Manchester, M14 6LJ. 64 Dairyground Road, Bramhall, Stockport, Cheshire, SK7 2QW

DAVIES, Mr David Gwilym Evans,JP., MRCVS *Currently:* Chairman, Dyfed County Council. *Born on* 30 Sept 1920 at Ponshaen, Llandysul. *Son of* William and Annie Helena Davies. *Marriage:* to Mary Noeline Davies. *Children:* Ann Elaine Davies. *Educated at* Llandysul Primary; Llandysul Grammar; Royal Veterinary College, London. *Career:* Partner in Veterinary Practice 1943-73; Mbr. of Dyfed County Council 1943- ; Chairman Cardiganshire Federation of Young Farmers Clubs 1945-48; Federation of Young Farmer's Clubs 1970-72. Past Chairman of Education Commt., 1979-81; First Chairman Economic Development Commt., 1983-87; First Chairman of Antur Teifi 1978-83; Chairman Cymdeithas Tai Teifi 1979-85. *Recreation:* Local history, walking *Address:* Brynawelon, Prengwyn, Llandysul SA44 4LX.

DAVIES, Dr David Hedydd,BSc, MEd, PhD. *Currently:* Carmarthen Area Education Officer, since 1979. *Born on* 17 June 1940 at Carmarthen. *Son of* the late Stephen John and the late Emily (nee Jones). *Marriage:* to Margaret Eiddwen Jenkins, 1968. *Educated at* Queen Elizabeth GS, Carmarthen; Birmingham University; Oxford University; London University. *Career:* Lecturer, Kilburn Polytechnic 1965-71; lecturer, Mid Cheshire College of Further Education 1971-73; Assistant Education Officer in London Borough of Hillingdon 1973-79. Hon. Treasurer Welsh AAA 1983- ; represented Wales in 1970 Commonwealth Games; Vice President, Athletics Association of Wales; Chairman Dyfed AAA; Chairman Carmarthen Harriers. *Recreation:* Athletics. *Address:* Frynhir, Capel Dewi Road, Carmarthen, Dyfed

DAVIES, Sir David Henry, *Currently:* Retired. *Born on* 1 Dec 1909 at Beaufort, Gwent. *Son of* David Henry Davies and Ann (nee Millard). *Marriage:* to Elsie May Battrick. *Children:* 1 s, 1 d (1 d dec'd) *Educated at* Briery Hill, Ebbw Vale, Gwent. *Career:* Mbr. Ebbw Vale U.D.C. 1945-50;

Gen.Sec.Iron & Steel Trades Confederation 1967-75 (Assist. Gen.Sec. 1953-66) Organiser 1950; Chmn.Joint Adv. Commt. Safety & Health in Iron & Steel Ind. 1965-67; Vice-Chmn.Nat.Dock Labour Bd. 1966-68; Hon.Treasurer WEA 1962-69; Mbr. Central Council & Exec. Commt. 1954-69; Hon. Treasurer British Labour party 1965-67; Mbr. Nat. Exec. 1954-67; Chmn. 1963; Hon. Sec. British Sect. Int. Metalworkers Fed. 1960-75; Royal Inst. Int. Affairs 1954-75; Iron & Steel Operatives Course Adv.Commt. City & Guilds of London Inst. Dept. of Tech. 1954-68; Iron & Steel Ind. Training Bd. 1964-75; Constructional Materials Group, Economic Dev. Commt. Building & Civil Eng. Ind. 1965-68; Iron & Steel Adv.Commt. 1967; English Ind. Estates Corp. 1971-76; First Btsh Pres. European Coal & Steel Commn.Consultative Commt 1973-74,Vice Pres. 1975; Governor Ruskin Coll. Oxford 1954-68; Iron & Steel Ind. Management Training Coll. Ashorne Hill, Leamington Spa 1966-75; Mbr. T.U.C. General Council 1967-75; First Chmn. Welsh Dev. Agency 1976-79. *Recreation:* Gardening, current affairs *Address:* 82 New House Park, St. Albans, Herts AL1 1UP.

DAVIES, Brigadier David Hugh,MC *Currently:* retired. *Born on* 17 Aug 1918 at Carmarthen, Dyfed. *Son of* David John Davies and Catherine Jane Davies (neePhilipps). *Marriage:* to Audrey Smith of Tenterden, Kent, 1943. *Children:* Jane Caroline. *Educated at* QE School Carmarthen; Cathedral School Hereford; RMC Sandhurst. *Career:* cmmnd KORR 1938, active service Palestine 1938-39 (wounded), World War II serv 107 Regt RAC (Adj, Sqdn Leader, Acting CO), Holland (wounded 1944), Staff Coll Haifa Palestine 1945, GS02 1 Div and Acting GS01 Palestine 1946-48, transferred 7 QOH, Adj 1948-49 (despatches 1949), DAAG AG 17 WO 1949-51, Sqdn Leader and 2 i/c 7 Hussars 1951-53, Instrictor Staff College Camberley 1956-58, CO 1958-61 asst director plans Joint Planning Staff MOD 1961-63, Cdr 5 Inf Bde Gp 1963-65, Col QOH 1964-72, Brig RAC HQ Western Cmd 1966-68; chairman Rose Smith & Co (Fuel) Ltd 1978-84 (non executive director 1968-75), Kent Royal British Legion; president Ashford Valley Foxhounds, Rolvenden and Tenterden branches Royal British Legion; treasurer Rolvenden Cons Assoc; Hon Freeman Carmarthen 1950. *Recreation:* hunting, fishing. *Clubs:* Cavalry and Guards, Army and Navy. *Address:* Barton Wood, Rolvenden, Cranbrook, Kent TN17 4ND. Tel: 0580 241294

DAVIES, Dr David Hywel, MA Phd FEng FIEE *Currently:* Consultant. *Born on* 28 Mar 1929 at Cardiff. *Son of* John and Maggie Davies. *Marriage:* to Valerie Elizabeth Nott 1961. *Children:* Virginia, Katherine and Christopher *Educated at* Cardiff High School; Christs College, Cambridge; *Career:* Radar Research Establishment 1956; Head of Airborne Radar Grp. RRE 1970; Head of Weapons Dept. Admiralty Surface Weapons Estab. 1972; Assistant Chief Scientific Adviser (Projects) Min. of Defence 1976; Director Royal Armament Research and Development Estab. 1979; Deputy Controller Research Programmes 1980; European Commission, Deputy Director General for Science Research and Development 1982-86; Managing Director Topexpress Ltd. 1988-89; *Publications:* Papers on Radar, Electron Optics, Remote Sensing. *Recreation:* Europe, Computing, Knots *Clubs:* Civil Service *Address:* 52 Brittains Lane, Sevenoaks, Kent.TN13 2JP.

DAVIES, Mr David Levric, CB;OBE;LL.B (Hons)Wales; Barrister-at-Law (Middle Temple) *Currently:* Retired. *Born on* 11 May 1925 at Brynmenyn. *Son of* the late Ben Davies and the late Elizabeth (nee Jones). *Marriage:* to Beryl Justine Hammond 1955. *Educated at* Llanrwst Grammar School, Head Boy 1941-42; University of Wales Aberystwyth, President Univ. Law Society 1947-48. *Career:* War Service, Sub-Lieutenant RNVR 1943-46;Colonial Legal Service 1950-64; Crown Counsel Aden 1950-55; Assistant to the Law Officers Tanganyika 1955-58; Parliamentary Draftsman Tanganyika 1958-61; Solicitor General Tanganyika 1961-64; Home Civil Service 1964-82; Office of the Parliamentary Counsel 1964-72; Seconded Jamaica as Senior Parliamentary Counsel 1965-69; Seconded Seychelles as Attorney General 1970-72; Senior Legal Assistant Treasury Solicitors Dept. 1972-73; Assistant Treasury Solicitor 1973-77; Under-Secretary (Legal) Treasury Solicitors Dept. 1977-82. *Publications:* Co-Revisioner, Revised Laws of Aden 1955. *Recreation:* Reading, gardening, travel. *Address:* Greystones, Breach Lane, Shaftesbury, Dorset SP7 8LF.

DAVIES, Prof. David Roy,B.Sc., Ph.D. *Currently:* Deputy Director John Innes Institute and Professor of Applied Genetics, Univ. of East Anglia. *Born on* 10 June 1932. *Son of* the late J.O. and A.E. Davies. *Marriage:* to Winefred Frances Davies (nee Wills) J.P.,B.A.,1957. *Children:* Mark, Sian, Anna and Andrew. *Educated at* Llandyssul and Grove Park, Wrexham Grammar Schools, Univ. of Wales. *Career:* UK Atomic Energy Authority 1956-62 and 1963-68; U.S. Atomic Energy Commission 1962-63; Univ. of East Anglia and John Innes Institute 1963-present; Dean of Biological Sciences, Univ of East Anglia 1985-1991. *Publications:* Scientific papers on radiobiology, plant genetics and molecular biology; edited book on these topics; Editor of Heredity 1975-82. *Recreation:* Sailing, D.I.Y., Music and various local activities. *Address:* 57 Church Lane, Eaton, Norwich. NR4 6NY.

DAVIES, Professor David Protheroe,MA, BD. *Currently:* Deputy Principal, since 1988 and John James Professor of Theology,since 1986, St.David's University College Lampeter. *Born on* 19 July 1939 at Bronllys, Brecon. *Son of* William John and Maureen Davies. *Marriage:* to Brenda Lloyd Owen, 1963 (divorced 1991). *Children:* Siwan Eleri (b.1972). *Educated at* Christ College Brecon; Corpus Christi College Cambridge; Corpus Christi College Oxford; Ripon Hall Oxford. *Career:* Curate St Mary's Swansea 1964-67; Lecturer 1967-76; Senior Lecturer 1976-86, St.David's University Lampeter; Dean of Arts 1977-81; Dean of Theology 1975-77,1981-91; Chairman & Director Cwmni'r Gannwyll 1989- ; Chairman & Director Cwmni Creuddyn 1990- ; Member University of Wales Court and Council; Member of Central Religious Advisory Council, BBC & ITV, Academic Board. *Publications:* Yr Efengylau A'r Actau,1978; Gwir Dduw o Wir Dduw, 1981; Diwinyddiaeth Ar Waith, 1984. *Recreation:* sport *Address:* Dept Of Theology & Religious Studies, St.David's University College, Lampeter, Dyfed SA48 7ED. Tel: 0570 424708

DAVIES, Mr Donald,OBE (1973) CBE (1978) B.Sc. *Currently:* Consultant Mining Engineer. *Born on* 13 Feb 1924 at Ebbw Vale. *Son of* Wilfred Lawson and Alwyn (nee Feebury). *Marriage:* to Mabel Hellyar 1948. *Children:* Gaynor and Shelagh *Educated at* Ebbw Vale Grammar

School; University College Cardiff. *Career:* Colliery Manager, N.C.B. 1951-55; Area General Manager NCB 1961-67; Area Director NCB 1967-73; Exec. Mbr. NCB 1973-84; Chairman NCB Opencast Executive 1973-83; Chairman NCB Ancillaries 1976-86. *Recreation:* Golf, walking, gardening, reading *Address:* Wendy Cottage, Dukes Wood Avenue, Gerrards Cross, Bucks SL9 7LA.

DAVIES, Vice-Chmn of the County Councl Edwin James *Currently:* Retired, Mechanical Engineer, now member Mid-Glamorgan County Council. *Born on* 30 Dec 1912 at Pontardawe, Swansea. *Son of* Mr & Mrs J.T.Davies. *Marriage:* September 14th, 1940. *Children:* Derek James Davies. *Educated at* Elementary School. *Career:* Kenfig Parish and Town Council - served 32 years, Chairman of Parish Council on 4 occasions; Mayor of the Borough of Kenfig; served 20 years Penybont Rural District Council; Chairman of the Council 1966-67; Chmn of Staff Cttee until the re-organisation of the Council; Past Pres. Glamorgan Assoc. of Local Councils; Chmn of its Exec.Cttee; Pres. of Mid Glam Assoc of Local Councils; Mbr Mid Glam C.C. since 1973; Vice-Chmn of Estab Cttee for 8 years; Chmn Econ Dev and Emp Cttee since 1980; Past-Chmn of Governors: Cefncribwr Primary School; Mynydd Cynffig Junior and Infants Scl; Pyle Primary Scl; Brynteg Comp Scl; Chmn of Governors: Ysgol y Ferch O'r Sger Primary Scl (Welsh); Corneli Jnr Scl; Marlas Infants Scl; Afon-y-Felin Prim Scl; Mbr Kenfig Hill Comp Scl Governors; Mbr. Cardiff Wales Airport Consortium; Chmn 1983,84 and 85; Dir Cardiff Wales Airport PLC; Mbr Govrn Body Univ. Court (Wales) Dir: Science Park, Bridgend; Mbr.Assoc. of County Councils; Dir. Ogwr Partnership Trust (now merged with Taff Ely Enterprise); Dir. Merthyr & Aberdare Ent.(now merged with Rhymney Econ.Dev.Partnership Ltd); Dir.Rhondda Dev.Assoc; Mbr of the Gorsedd of Bards, Nat. Eisteddfod of Wales; Current Exec. and former Pres. of Bridgend Const. Labour Party; mbr. of Labour party for 54 years; past Exec.Mbr. & Pres. Aberabon Const. Labour party; Trade Union Movement: Swansea Branch AEU, Sec; served on Dist.Cttees & Tribunals, etc; Pres. Horticultural Soc; Pres.Wildfowling & Conservation Soc; Pres. Sker Riding Club; Vice-Pres.Porthcawl Dist.Art Soc. Past Chmn Bridgend & Dist. Co-operative Mngmnt Bd; Justice of the Peace. *Recreation:* gardening, local government, local history. *Clubs:* local sports. *Address:* "Lamborough", 11 Heol Ton, Ton Kenfig, Pyle Bridgend. CF33 4PS. Chairmans Parlour, Mid Glam County Hall, Cathays Park, Cardiff. CF1 3NE

DAVIES,Mr Emlyn Glyndwr,M.Sc. *Currently:* Retired (1976) Home Office Forensic Adviser & Controller HO Forensic Science Laboratory Service. *Born on* 20 March 1916 at Penrhiwfer. *Son of* the late William and Elizabeth (nee Evans).Marriage: to Edwina Rees Morgan (Blaengarw) 1940.Children: Roger Michael and Richard Alan. *Educated at* Maesycwmmer & Bargoed Sec. Schools; U.C.W. Aberystwyth. *Career:* Biology Master, Arwyn School Aberystwyth 1939-42; Ministry of Supply and Scottish Seaweed Research Assoc., 1942-44; Forensic Science Lab., Cardiff 1944-58; Director For Sc. Lab., Nottingham 1958-59; Director For Sc. Lab., Preston 1959-63; Home Office Forensic Science Adviser 1963-74.President of Forensic Science Society 1975-77. *Publications:* Contributions to Scientific Journals. *Recreation:* Watching Rugby Football.

Address: 14 Church Hill Close, Llanblethian, Cowbridge, S. Glamorgan. CF7 7JH.

DAVIES, Mr Emrys Thomas,C.M.G. *Currently:* Diplomatic Service. *Born on* 8 Oct 1934 at London. *Son of* Evan William Davies and Dinah Davies (nee Jones). *Marriage:* to Angela May. *Children:* Robert, Victoria and Elizabeth. *Educated at* Parmiters Foundation School, London; various periods at Univs. of Cambridge, London, Oxford, Tours, Grenoble. *Career:* Diplomatic Service: Peking 1956-59; FCO 1959-60; Bahrain 1960-62; FCO 1962-63; Hong Kong 1963-68; Ottawa 1968-71; FCO 1972-76; Peking 1976-78; Nato Defense College 1979; Ottawa 1979-82; FCO Inspectorate 1982-84; UKDEL OECD Paris 1984-87; Ambassador Hanoi 1987-90; High Commissioner to Barbados, Grenada, St. Vincent, St.Lucia, Dominica, Antigua, St. Kitts & Nevis 1991- . *Recreation:* Theatre, cinema, walking, reading, golf, tennis. *Clubs:* Commonwealth Trust, London; Cambridge University Centre. *Address:* c/o Foreign & Commonwealth Office, (Bridgetown), King Charles St, London. SW1A 2AH.

DAVIES, Professor Eurfil Rhys,CBE; MA; MB; BChir;FRCPE;FRCR;FFR(RCSI);FDSRCS. *Currently:* Professor of Clinical Radiology, University of Bristol; Hon. Consultant United Bristol Hospitals, NHS Trust. *Born on* 18 April 1929 at Maerdy, Rhondda. *Son of* the late Daniel Haydn Davies and the late Mary (nee Jenkins). *Marriage:* to Zoe Doreen Chamberlain. *Children:* 3 sons. *Educated at* Rhondda Grammar School; Llandovery College; Clare College, Cambridge; St. Mary's Hospital. *Career:* President British Nuclear Medicine Society 1972-74; Member: Administration of Radioactive Substances Advisory Ctee., 1976-80; Bristol and Weston Health Authority 1984-86; General Medical Council 1989- ; Working Group on Ionising Radiation Health & Safety Executive 1988- ; Court University of Bath 1989- ; Clinical Standards Advisory Group 1991- ; Registrar Royal College of Radiologists 1976-81; Warden Royal Coll. of Radiologists 1984-86; President Royal Coll. of Radiologists 1986-89; Civilian Advisor in Clinical Radiology to the Royal Navy 1989- . *Recreation:* Theatre, travel, music. *Address:* 19 Hyland Grove, Westbury-On-Trym, Bristol BS9 3NR.

DAVIES, Mr Gareth,FCA.,CBIM *Currently:* Group Chairman and Chief Executive Clynwed In. PLC, Birmingham. *Born on* 13 Feb 1930 at Aberdare. *Son of* the late Lewis Davies and Margaret Ann Davies (nee Jones). *Marriage:* to Joan Patricia Prosser 1953. *Children:* Mark Lyndon *Educated at* King Edward VI Grammar School, Aston, Birmingham *Career:* various promotions from Company Accountant in 1957 to Chairman in 1984; also - non-executive director of: Midlands Electricity PLC, Raglan Property Trust PLC, Barclays Regional Board *Recreation:* Opera, gardening and athletics *Address:* 4 Beechgate, Roman Road, Little Aston Park, West Midlands. B74 3AR.

DAVIES, Mr Geraint Talfan, *Currently:* Controller, BBC Wales, Broadcasting House, Llandaff, Cardiff, CF5 2YQ. *Born on* 30 Dec 1943 at Carmarthen. *Son of* the late Aneirin Talfan Davies OBE and the late Mary Anne (nee Evans). *Marriage:* to Elizabeth Shan (nee Yorath) 1967. *Children:* Mathew, Rhodri and Edward. *Educated at* Cardiff High School; Jesus College Oxford. *Career:* Welsh Affairs Correspondent, Western Mail, Cardiff 1966-71; The Journal, Newcastle-upon-Tyne 1971-73; The Times, London 1973;

Assistant Editor, Western Mail, Cardiff 1974-78; Head of News and Current Affairs, HTV Wales 1978-82; Assistant Controller of Programmes, HTV Wales 1982-87; Director of Programmes, Tyne Tees Television 1987-90. *Recreation:* Theatre, music, architecture. *Address:* 15 The Parade, Whitchurch, Cardiff CF4 2EF.

DAVIES, Gilli, cordon blue certificate *Currently:* FOOD Editor, Thomson Regional Newspapers, Freelance journalist, author, broadcaster, TV presenter and cook, specialist in Welsh food. *Born on* 18 Oct 1950 at Sleaford, Lincs. *Daughter of* Douglas Arthur & Barbara Peacock. *Marriage:* to Alun James Davies, 1973. *Children:* Max, Augusta and Bonnie. *Educated at* Winceby House School, Bexhill; Secretarial and Cookery Diplomas. *Career:* 1970 Opened a Bistro in the Buttery Bar of St. Anthony's College for Graduates in Oxford. 1972 Chalet girl in Switzerland. Head Cook at the Open Air Theatre in Regent's Park. 1973 Ran courses of Cookery Demonstrations for the Royal Army Education Corps in Osnabruck, West Germany. 1974 Appointed Catering Manager in a country hotel in Northern Ireland. 1978 Managed two restaurants for the Army in Berlin. Broadcast on British Forces Broadcasting Services in Berlin and Cologne with a 'live' cookery spot. Produced an accompanying cook book. Wrote cookery columns for the Forces magazines The Berlin Bulletin and Sixth Sense. Took part in the Ski Leaders Course with the Ski Club of Great Britain, and subsequently lead annual parties in the Alps for members of the Ski Club. Set up a Directors Dining Room for Alan Mann's Aviation Company in Surrey. 1985 Returned to Cardiff after 10 years abroad. Broadcast on Red Dragon Radio. Wrote for Western Mail and had weekly page in Echo about food in Wales. Took a business course. Appeared as guest on BBC Wales and HTV in various chat shows. Broadcast regularly on 'The Food Show' on BBC Wales, Radio. Gave 'microwave' cookery demonstrations. Became 'Welsh' correspondant for TASTE magazine. Contributed to various national magazines and travel and ski books. Commissioned by Grafton (Collins) to write cook book on Welsh food, LAMB LEEKS and LAVERBREAD, published Spring 1989. 1987 Moved to Cyprus with British Forces, broadcast and wrote regularly for British and Cypriot media. Wrote and published 'A TASTE OF CYPRUS' by Interworld Publications in 1990. Wrote GOOD FOOD GUIDE TO CYPRUS for Cyprus Consumer Council. 1989 Returned *Recreation:* sport - skiing, swimming, food. *Clubs:* Guild of Food Writers. *Address:* Glebe Farm, St. Andrew's Major, S. Glamorgan CF6 4HD. Tel: 0222 514141

DAVIES, Emeritus Principal Revd. Dr. Gwynne Henton, MA., BD (Wales), M. Litt(Oxon) DD(Glasgow) *Currently:* Retired. *Born on* 19 Feb 1906 at Aberdare, Glam. *Son of* John and Myfanwy Davies. *Marriage:* Sept 3rd 1935. *Children:* Yona (Mrs Yona Pusey B.A.) and Elaine (Mrs E. Mason) *Educated at* County School, Aberdare; Perse Grammar School, Cambridge; South Wales Baptist College; Univ. Coll. of S. Wales, Cardiff, First class Hons (Hebrew) MA(Distinc)BD(Distinc) Regent's Park Coll & St. Catherine's Coll Oxford *Career:* 1991 Honorary Moderator Penuel Baptist Church, Manorbier Pembs. Pastor West End Baptist Church London, 1935-38; Tutor Bristol Baptist College and Special Lecturer University of Bristol 1938-51; First Professor of O.T. Studies University of

Durham 1951-58; Eleventh President and Principal of Regent's Park College, University of Oxford 1958-72; President of The Baptist Union of Great Britain and Eire 1972; Dean of Faculty of Theology, Univ. of Durham 1957; Visiting Professor Rochester: Colgate Rochester, School of Divinity 1958; Vancouver School of Theology B.C. 1973-74; Pacific School of Religion, Berkerley, Calif. 1975; South Eastern Seminary, Wake Forest, N.C., USA; Meredith Coll, Raleigh N.C., USA 1978-79; New Zealand Baptist College Auckland NZ; Whitley Coll. Melbourne, Australia; William Jewell Coll. Libery, Miss; Select Preacher: Univ. of Oxford, Univ. of Cambridge; Lecturer in Oriental Languages Faculty and in Faculty of Theology; Visiting Professor: Southern Baptist Seminary, Louisville Kent; Mid Western Seminary, Kansas; New Orleans Seminary; South Western Seminary, Forth Worth; all of the Southern Baptist Convention; Univ. of Uppsala Faculty of Theology; *Publications:* Exodus in Torch Bible Commentary; Deuteronomy in Peake's Commentary on the Bible (second edition); Genesis in Broadman's Biblical Commentaries, U.S.A. *Recreation:* growing orchids and chrysanthemums. *Address:* Headlands, Broad Haven, Haverfordwest, Dyfed. SA62 3JP Tel: 0437 781339

DAVIES, Mr Handel, CB., FEng., MSc., Hon. FRAeS., FAIAA *Currently:* Aerospace Technology Consultant. *Born on* 2 June 1912 at Aberdare. *Son of* Henry John and Elisabeth Davies. *Marriage:* to Mary Graham Davies (nee Harris). *Educated at* Aberdare Grammar School; Univ. of Wales, Cardiff *Career:* Chief Sup. Aeroplane & Armament Experimental Estb., Boscome Down 1952-55; Scientific Adviser, Air Ministry 1955-56; Dir. Gen. Scientific Research (Air) Min. of Supply 1957-59; Dep. Dir. Royal Aircraft Estb. Farnborough 1959-63; Dep. Cont. Research & Development, Min. of Aviation 1963-69; Technical Dir. Btsh Aircraft Cor., 1969-77; Adviser to the Chrmn of British Aerospace 1977-79; Chmn Inter-Govnt Man. Commt for Comcorde 1963-66; Chmn. Anglo/German/Italian organising Commt. for Tornado 1966-69; Chmn. Technical Bd. Soc. of British Aircraft Constructors 1974-77; Pres. Royal Aeronautical Soc. 1977-78; Chmn. Standing Conference on Schools Science & Technology 1978-81. *Publications:* Barriers to Progress in Aerospace - Past, Present and Future, 1979; European Collaboration in Aerospace, 1967. *Recreation:* Sailing, skiing, music *Clubs:* Royal Air Force Yacht *Address:* Keel Cottage, Woodham Road, Horsell Woking, Surrey. GU21 4DL.

DAVIES, Right Reverend Howell Haydn, Dip. Arch. (Birm); ARIBA *Currently:* Vicar of St. Jude's Parish Church, Wolverhampton. *Born on* 18 Sept 1927 at Barry, Glamorgan. *Son of* Ivor Thomas Davies and Sarah Gladys Davies (nee Thomas). *Marriage:* to Jean Wylam Davies (nee King) 1958. *Children:* Caryl, Jenifer, Philip, Stephen, Timothy and Bethan. *Educated at* George Dixon Grammar School, Birmingham; Bridgnorth Grammar School, Shropshire; Birmingham School of Architecture; Tyndale Hall, Bristol. *Career:* RAF Med/Me 1945-48, Corporal Clerk/GD; Assistant Architect 1952-56, Worcester CC, Middlesex CC, Private Practice; Assistant Curate 1959-61: St. Peter's Church, Hereford; Missionary, (BSCMS) Kenya, 1961-79, with the Bible Churchmen's Missionary Society (BCMS); Vicar of St. Peter's Church, Woking 1979-81; Missionary, (BCMS), Uganda, 1981-87, with BCMS;

Archdeacon of North Masero 1971-74; Provost of Nairobi Cathedral 1974-79; Bishop of Karamoja 1981-87; Buildings designed and completed in Kenya: Church Training Centre, Kapsabet; Teachers' College Chapel, Mosoriot; St Andrew's Parish Church Centre, Kapenguria; Cathedral Church of the Good Shepherd, Nakuru; Three-storey Administration block and bookshop, Kakamega; various mission and church staff housing in Kenya and Uganda. *Recreation:* DIY and building design, walking, reading. *Address:* St Jude's Vicarage, St Jude's Road, Wolverhampton, West Midlands., WV6 OEB.

DAVIES, Mr. Hugh Llewelyn, *Currently:* Head of Far Eastern Department, Foreign and Commonwealth Office since 1990. *Born on* 8 Nov 1941 at Cuttack, India. *Son of* Vincent Ellis Davies OBE and Rose Trench Davies (nee Temple). *Marriage:* to Virginia Ann Lucius 1968. *Children:* Charlotte Rhiannon and Jonathan Henry. *Educated at* Rugby School, Churchill College Cambridge. *Career:* Diplomatic Service, Foreign Office 1965; Chinese language studies, Hong Kong 1966-68; Second Sec. and HM Consul, Peking 1969-71; China Desk FCO 1971-74; First Sec (econ) British Embassy, Bonn 1974-77; Head of Chancery, British High Commission, Singapore 1977-79; Assistant Head Far Eastern Dept. FCO 1979-82; Secondment, Barclays Bank International 1982-83; Commercial Cllr, Peking 1984-87; Deputy UK Permanent Rep OECD 1987-90. *Recreation:* Sports, art and gardens *Address:* Bentley Lodge, Dormans Park, East Grinstead, West Sussex RH19 2NB.

DAVIES, Mr Huw Humphreys, M.A. (Oxon) *Currently:* HTV Group Director of Television. *Born on* 4 Aug 1940 at Llangynog, Powys. *Son of* Mrs Harriet Davies and the late Mr. William Davies. *Marriage:* to Shân (nee Harries). *Children:* Elin Mari and Catrin Humphreys *Educated at* Llandovery College; Pembroke College, Oxford *Career:* Director/Producer: Television Wales and West 1964; HTV 1968; HTV Cymru/Wales: Asst. Controller of Programmes 1978; Controller of Programmes 1979-81; Dir. of Programmes 1981-87; Produced and directed many programmes and series in English and Welsh; latterly numerous plays and drama-documentaries; Chmn. Regional Controllers, ITV 1987-88; Mbr. Gorsedd of Bards; Governor, Welsh Coll. of Music and Drama. *Recreation:* Reading, swimming *Clubs:* Groucho *Address:* 2 Walston Close, Wenvoe, Cardiff. CF5 6AS. H.T.V., The Television Centre, Culverhouse Cross, Cardiff CF5 6XJ

DAVIES, Mr Ian Leonard, CB.,MA.,CEng.,FIEE. *Currently:* Retired. *Born on* 2 June 1924 at Barry, Glamorgan. *Son of* the late Harry L. Davies and the late Janet Doris(nee Hellings). *Marriage:* to Hilary Dawson 1951. *Children:* Roger L., James O. Davies, Siriol M. Hinchliffe and Barbara M.I. du Preez. *Educated at* Barry County School; University College, Cardiff; St. John's College, Cambridge. *Career:* Ministry of Supply etc., TRE 1944-46; BLEU 1946-47; RRE 1949-69; Head of Quantum & Microwave Electronics 1960-63; Head of Airborne Radar Dept. 1963-69; IDC 1970; MOD, Assistant Chief Scientific Adviser (Projects) 1971-72; Dep. Controller Electronics 1973; Dep. Controller Air Systems (D) 1973-75; Director, Admiralty Underwater Weapons Establishment 1975-84; IEE. Member Council 1974-77; Chairman Electronics Divisional Board 1975-76; Temp. Advisor MMC 1986 & Min. of Defence 1985-88. *Publications:* Various papers on

Information Theory, Radar & Lasers. *Recreation:* Music, walking, DIY. *Clubs:* Athenaeum *Address:* 37 Bowleaze Coveway, Preston, Weymouth, Dorset DT3 6PL.

DAVIES, Dr Ivor John (neu Ifor)., NDD, ATD, PhD. *Currently:* Arlunydd. *Born on* 9 Nov 1935 at Treharris, Glam. *Son of* David Howell Davies and the late Gwenllian (nee Phillips). *Educated at* Penarth County Sch; Cardiff Coll of Art; Swansea Coll of Art; University of Lausanne; University of Edinburgh. *Career:* Arlunydd; Hanesydd Celf; Darlithydd. Teaching experience: Little Ealing SMB School 1957-59, Univ of Lausanne 1959-61, Univ of Wales, Cardiff 1961-63 part time extra-mural, personal research and painting, Univ of Edinburgh 1963-78, Gwent Coll of Higher Educ 1978-88. Many one man exhibitions incl: Traverse Theatre Edinburgh 1968, Welsh Arts Council Gallery, Cardiff 1974, Talbot Rice Art Centre, Univ of Edinburgh 1972-74 and 77, Holsworthy Gallery New King's Road, London 1980-81, Newport Museum and Art Gallery 1987, Max Rutherston, London 1989, Jedda, Saudi Arabia 1990, West Wharf Gallery Cardiff 1991. Wrexham library arts centre touring to 1993. Public collections: Welsh Arts Council, including 1975 National Eisteddfod Purchase Prize, Scottish Arts Council, National Museum of Wales, Arts Council of G.B. purchase for collection 1984, Newport Museum and Art Gallery Collection 1987, The Deal collection of drawings, Dallas 1989, private collections all over the world. Multi-Media and Experimental Theatre: International Destruction in Art Symposium, London 1966, reviewed in Time, Life, Studio International, Structure and various national newspapers. Group Exhibitions include: Nat Museum of Wales, Cardiff 1953-59, Young Contemporaries, RBA Galleries, London 1953-59, 'Wales Now' Welsh Arts Council Travelling Exhibition 1968, 'Wales and the Modern Movement', Univ Coll Aberystwyth 1973, National Eisteddfod Exhibitions, 'Artists in Cardiff', 1980, 'Arts and the Sea' 1980-81, 'Celtic Vision', international Touring Exhibition, 'The States of Wales' a 'Becca' 1988, Glynebourne Opera Gallery 1989, 'The Proberty of Virtue', open exhibition 1990, Irish-Welsh Exchange Exhibition, 1991, Mostyn Gallery , Llandudno, 1992, Breton Gallery, Bath: *Publications:* many articles and reviews, and contributions to books in English and Welsh. *Recreation:* hynafiaeth, iaeth a'r iaeth Gymraeg. *Clubs:* Les amis du vin. *Address:* 99 Windsor Road, Penarth, De Morganwg

DAVIES, Dr James Brian Meredith, MD (hons); FFPHM; DPH. *Currently:* Retired from full-time work but working in industry running Pre-retirement Courses and speaking on Health Topics. *Born on* 27 Jan 1920 at Stockport. *Son of* Dr Goronwy Meredith Davies and Mrs Caroline Davies. *Marriage:* to Charlotte (nee Pillar), 1944. *Children:* James, Thomas and Richard. *Educated at* Bedford School; London University; Bristol University. *Career:* After a period in the RAMC, 1943-47, specialised in Preventive Medicine; worked in Lancs, Oxford and then for 28 years in Liverpool; became first Director of Social Services, Liverpool 1971-82; Lecturer (part-time) at Liverpool University 1953-85, in Preventive Medicine and in Preventive Paediatrics. *Publications:* Community Health and Social Services, 5th edition, 1991; The Disabled Child & Adult 1982; Community Health, Preventive Medicine and Social Services 6th edition, due early 1992. *Recreation:* fishing, skiing, gardening, music.

Address: Tree Tops, Church Road, Thornton Hough, Wirral Merseyside. L63 1JN.

DAVIES, Mr John Brent,MCIT *Currently:* Manager Wales Regional Railways. *Born on* 7 Jul 1943 at Neath, West Glamorgan. *Son of* Frank Kenneth Davies and Mabel Irene (nee Powis). *Educated at* Neath Grammar School *Career:* British Rail 1961- ; Sales and Marketing Executive, 1971-79; Sales Manager (E.Anglia), 1979-82; Passenger Manager (S.Wales), Services Manager (S.Wales); *Recreation:* Scouting, Travel, Photography and Hill Walking. *Address:* 7 Pinetree Court, Sketty, Swansea, West Glamorgan

DAVIES,Professor John Christopher Hughes (Christie), MA(Cantab) 1st class hons. *Currently:* Professor of Sociology, University of Reading, since 1984. *Born on* 25 Nov 1941 at Sutton. *Son of* the late Christopher George Davies and the late Marian Eileen (nee Johns) *Educated at* Dynevor Grammar School, Swansea; Emmanuel College Cambridge University. *Career:* Tutor in Economics, University of Adelaide 1964; Radio Producer, BBC Third Programme 1967-69; Lecturer in Sociology University of Leeds 1969-72; Lecturer, Senior Lecturer, Reader in Sociology University of Reading 1972-84; Visiting Professor Universities of Baroda, Bombay, Punjab and Centre for Advanced Study, Delhi University 1973-74; Distinguished Scholars Interdisciplinary Lecturer, Institute for Humane Studies, George Mason University, Virginia 1986, Visiting Lecturer, Jagiellonian University, Krakow, Poland 1991. *Publications:* Wrongful Imprisonment (London 1973); Permissive Britain (London 1975); Censorship and Obscenity (London 1978); Welsh Jokes (Cardiff 1978); Ethnic Humour Around the World, A Comparative Analysis (University of Indiana Press, Bloomington 1990 and Open Univ Press, Buckingham). *Recreation:* travel, walking, art galleries. *Clubs:* Union Society, Cambridge (President 1964). *Address:* C/o Dept Of Sociology, University Of Reading, Whiteknights, Reading RG6 2AA.

DAVIES, Dr John Duncan,OBE.,MSc.,PhD.,DSc. *Currently:* Director, Polytechnic of Wales. since 1978. *Born on* 19 March 1929 at Swansea. *Son of* the late John and the late Gertrude Davies. *Marriage:* to Barbara Davies. *Children:* Heatherlee, Denise and Sheree *Educated at* Treforest School of Mines; Univ. of London *Career:* Engineer with contractors, consultants, local authorities; Military Service Royal Engineers; Lec. UMIST; Snr.Lec., Reader, Professor, Dean Univ. Coll. Swansea; Principal, West Glam. Inst. of Higher Education. *Publications:* 60 books/papers on structural mechanics *Recreation:* helping animals *Address:* Polytechnic of Wales, Treforest, Pontypridd, Mid Glamorgan. CF37 1DL.

DAVIES, John Howard,CBE, BA, DipEd, FRSA, DL(Clwyd). *Currently:* Chairman S4C.. *Born on* 6 May 1926 at Chittagong. *Son of* Rev. W.H. Davies and Mary Eunice (nee Thomas). *Marriage:* to Elizabeth Jenkins, 1954. *Children:* Jonathan, Mark and Timothy. *Educated at* Holyhead County School; Bangor University; Potiers University. *Career:* Indian Military Academy, Captain RWF, 1944-48, served India, Burma, Malaya, Sumatra. Colonial Education Officer N.Nigeria 1952-56. District Education Officer Notts, Deputy Director ED, Flints, Director ED Flints and Clwyd 1974-85. Ex chairman Duke of Edinburgh's Award Scheme, Wales, School Broadcast Council (Wales), Urdd Nat. Eisteddfodau Rhyl and Mold

since 1985 Chairman Council UCNW, Bangor, Member of Univ Wales, Council & Court, Univ Coll of Medicine, N.Wales Arts Council. *Recreation:* gardening, golf. *Address:* Staddle Stones, Hendy Road, Mold, Clwyd CH7 1QR.

DAVIES, Wg. Cdr. John Irfon, MBE. *Born on* 8 June 1930 at Penclawdd. *Son of* T.M. Davies and M.M.Davies (nee Harris). *Marriage:* to Jean Marion Anderson. *Children:* Jane Elizabeth Rhonwen *Educated at Career:* Retired Wing Commander Royal Air Force, 1974. Retired Under Secretary, Welsh Office, 1990. *Recreation:* Golf, piano and books *Clubs:* Farmers; RAF; Radyr Golf. *Address:* Friston, 15 Windsor Road, Radyr, Cardiff. CF4 8BQ.

DAVIES, John Simon (Sim),FRICS Principal: Kemp & Hawley, Chartered Valuation Surveyors. *Born on* 12 March 1937 at Newcastle-Emlyn. *Son of* the late Arthur and the late Elizabeth (nee Jones). *Marriage:* to Sheila. *Children:* Michael (decd) and Kathleen. *Educated at* Cardigan Grammar; College of Estate Management; President Students Union. Former Chairman London Welsh Trust; Hon Member Gorsedd; Freeman City of London; former President: London Cardiganshire Society, Cardigan Eisteddfod, Newcastle Emlyn RFC & Agricultural Show. Winner National & Urdd National Eisteddfods. *Recreation:* rugby, opera. *Address:* 13 Monmouth Street, London WC2H 9DA. Tel: 071 405 8161

DAVIES, Mr Jonathan, *Currently:* Widnes RLFC; Sunday Mirror Newspaper; ARC Northern, Chester. Captain of Great Britain RL v France, Feb 1992. *Born on* 24 Oct 1962 at Trimsaran. *Son of* Len and Diana Davies. *Marriage:* to Karen Marie. *Children:* Matthew Scott Davies. *Educated at* Gwendraeth Grammar School. *Career:* Trimsaran RFC; Neath RFC; Llanelli RFC; Barbarians, Wales (Captain 4 times); Widnes RLFC, Canterbury Bankstown RLFC (Australia) Great Britain. *Publications:*"Jonathan" book, The Jonathan Davies story video. *Recreation:* spending time with family, golf, any sport. *Clubs:* Widnes Golf. *Address:* Widnes R.L.F.C., Naughton Park, Lowerhouse Lane, Widnes, Cheshire. WD8 7DZ.

DAVIES, Mr Lewis Mervyn,CMG; CBE; Commandeur de L'Ordre National du Merite. *Currently:* retired. *Born on* 5 Dec 1922 at Crewe, Cheshire. *Son of* the late Rev. Canon L.C. Davies and the late Mrs Phyllis Davies. *Marriage:* 1st to Betty Ione Davies, died 1973; 2nd to Mona Agnes Davies. *Children:* Simon Lewis Davies and 2 stepsons James Birley and Hugh Birley. *Educated at* St.Edwards School, Oxford. *Career:* Fleet Air Arm Pilot, Lt. 'A' RNVR 1941-46; Colonial Service 1946; Gold Coast, Asst.District Commissioner 1948; Western Pacific High Commission, Senior Assistant Secretary 1956, Financial Secretary 1962, Chief Secretary 1965; Bahamas 1970, Deputy Governor; Hong Kong 1973, Secretary for Security, Secretary General Duties: involved in negotiations on Hong Kongs future between China and the U.K. *Recreation:* Sailing, tennis, walking. *Clubs:* Oriental; Commonwealth Trust; Royal Hong Kong Yacht. *Address:* Apartado 123, Felanitx 07200, Mallorca, Spain

DAVIES (Lloyd), Mr Henri *Currently:* Managing Director, Bryneithin Estates Limited. *Born on* 12 Dec 1946 at Cardiff. *Son of* the late Henry George and the late Emmeline Mary (nee Thomas). *Marriage:* to Norma Yvonne (nee Davies), 1977. *Children:* Henry James, William Meirion and Charlotte Emmeline. *Educated at* Rugby; Bath University. *Career:* T I Group 1969- 71; M.D. Cleglen Publishing Ltd 1971-87; Governor University College Cardiff 1978-99; Life Vice-President Royal Welsh Agricultural Society, Chairman Wales Conservative Political Centre 1991- ; Conservative Parliamentary Candidate Swansea East 1992. *Recreation:* sailing. *Clubs:* Naval. *Address:* Bryneithin, New Inn, Llandeilo, Dyfed, SA19 7LL. 16 Dunraven House, Westgate Street, Cardiff, CF1 1DL

DAVIES, Maldwyn Thomas,B.Mus *Currently:* Freelance Opera/Concert singer. Now works with most of the major orchestras in this country and records extensively for the BBC. He sings regularly with the Bach Choir and the Huddersfield Choral Society and has given concerts with the Academy of St.Martin-in-the-Fields, the BBC Welsh Symphony, London Symphony, Scottish Symphony, Scottish National, BBC Philharmonic and Philharmonia Orchestras. *Born on* 24 Oct 1950 at Rhigos, Nr.Aberdare, Mid Glam. *Son of* Mervyn Davies and Ceinwen Davies. *Marriage:* to Christine Margaret (nee Powell), 1978. *Children:* Bethan Catherine Davies and Elin Angharad Davies. *Educated at* Merthyr Tydfil Grammar School; Welsh College of Music and Drama; University College Cardiff. *Career:* Was runner-up in the 1980 Richard Tauber Competition and was subsequently awarded an Arts Council Grant to study in Vienna and Salzburg. His concert work has included appearances at the Edinburgh, Leeds, Bath,Cheltenham, Fishguard, Windsor, Hong Kong, Florence, Bergen and Vienna Festivals and also in Zurich, Paris, Stuttgart, Strasbourg and Frankfurt.He made his Canadian debut in 1989 with the National Arts Centre Orchestra and his American debut, also in 1989, with the Saint Louis Symphony Orchestra. Under contract to the Royal Opera House, Covent Garden 1980-82, singing many small roles. He made his debut with the English National Opera as Jack in the new production of ''A Midsummer Marriage'' to celebrate Sir Michael Tippett's 80th birthday. Recordings include Handel's 'Alcina' (EMI) and 'The Messiah (Hyperion). Last season he performed with the BBC Welsh Symphony Orchestra in Amsterdam, London and the Flanders Festival, the Huddersfield Choral Society and the Royal Liverpool Philharmonic and Scottish National Orchestras. He has toured Germany and appeared in concert in Spain and Scandinavia. This season has included performances of Beethoven's 'Ninth Symphony' in Antwerp, Beethoven's 'Miss Solemnis' in Switzerland, Britten's ''War Reqiem'', in Jerusalem, a recording of Mozart's 'Requiem' with Jane Glover and the London Mozart Players for ASV Records. He has also sung with the Salzburg Mozarteum Orchestra, the Israel Philharmonic Orchestra and with the National Orchestra of Belgium, and Mozart's 'Requiem' in Canterbury Cathedral and St.Paul's Cathedral. *Recreation:* reading *Address:* 43 Frobisher, Haversham Park, Bracknell, Berks, RG12 7WQ.

DAVIES, Melvyn John (Mel), *Currently:* Founder and Managing Director South Wales Shower Supplies Ltd. *Born on* 27 Aug 1948 at Newport, Gwent. *Son of* William John Davies and Ruby Rosalia Davies. *Marriage:* to Rosalie Rhonda James, 1980. *Children:* Gregory James (b.1987) and Jonathan William (b.1990). *Educated at* Duffryn Comp School. *Career:* Racehorse owner; total 25 race wins, 17 by Barnbrook Again: Queen Mother Champion 2m chase (twice), Arlington Premier Final, Gerry Fielden Hurdle, Ladbroke Hurdle Leopardstown, Comton Brothers Chase, Hurst Park Chase, 5 times winner Newbury, 5 times winner Cheltenham incl South Wales Showers Caradon Mira Silver Trophy; records held by Barnbrook Again: 2m course Newbury, 2 1/2m course Cheltenham; sponsor of 5 races Cheltenham and 3 races Chepstow, presenter Channel 4 racing Newmarket 1990; apprentice plumber then plumber. Raised money towards res into children's cancer illnesses and for Spinal Injuries Assoc; nominated for S.Wales Young Business award 1988. *Recreation:* horse racing. former Newport County FC devotee, various charities. *Address:* 4/5 Court Road Ind Estate, Cwmbran, Gwent NP44 3AS.

DAVIES, Reverend Noel Anthony, BSc(Wales); BA(Oxford). *Currently:* General Secretary, CYTUN: Churches Together in Wales. *Born on* 26 Dec 1942 at Dowlais. *Son of* the late Reverend R.Anthony Davies and Mrs Anne Da. *Marriage:* to Patricia, 1968. *Educated at* Garw Grammar School; UCNW Bangor; Mansfield College, Oxford. *Career:* Minister, Bryn Seion Congregational Church, Glanaman, 1968-77; General Secretary, The Council of Churches for Wales and the Commission of the Covenated Churches, 1977-90; Chairman, Union of Welsh Independents Council, 1990- ; Moderator, Churches Commission on Mission, 1991-; *Publications:* numerous articles in religious newspapers and magazines; Gweddio 1975; O Ddydd i Ddydd, Maj. 1990. *Recreation:* Classical music and Hi-fi; gardening; Westhighland white terriers, Oriental cookery. *Address:* 16 Maple Crescent, Uplands, Swansea. SA2 OQD.

DAVIES, Colonel Norman Thomas,MBE 1970; BA 1979; JP 1984. *Currently:* Registrar General Dental Council, 37 Wimpole Street, London, W1M 8DQ, since 1981. *Born on* 2 May 1933 at Southport, Lancs. *Son of* the late Edward Ernest Davies and Elsie Davies (nee Scott). *Marriage:* to Penelope Mary Agnew d of Peter Graeme Agnew, 1961. *Children:* Captain Edward Peter Davies, The Light Infantry and Clare Mary Davies. *Educated at* Holywell CS; RMA Sandhurst; Open University (BA 1979). *Career:* Commissioned RA 1954; Regimental and Staff Appointments Malaya (during Emergency), Germany and UK 1954-64; ptsc 1966; psc 1967; Mil. Asst. to Chief of Staff Northern Army Group 1968-69; Commander C BTY and 2IC 3RHA 1970-72; GSOI (DS) Staff College Camberley and Canadian Land Forces Command and Staff College 1972-74; Commanded 4 Field Regiment RA 1975-77; Military Director of studies RMCS Shrivenham 1977-80; retired from Army 1980; Appointed Registrar General Dental Council 1981; Member EC Advisory Ctee on the Training of Dental Practitioners 1983- ; JP (Hants) 1984; Hon. Member British Dental Association 1990. *Recreation:* rugby, gardening, wine. *Clubs:* Royal Society of Medicine. *Address:* Lowfields Cottage, London Road, Hartley Wintney, Hants. RG27 8HY.

DAVIES, Owen Mansel, Eur. Ing, MA, FEng, FInst.Pet, FIChemE. *Currently:* General Manager, Business Services, BP Engineering, since 1988. *Born on* 3 June 1934 at Dinas Powis, South Glam. *Son of* D.Mansel Davies and the late Margaret Phyllis Davies. *Marriage:* to Elisabeth Jean (nee Leedham), 1960. *Children:* Catherine, Timothy and Susan. *Educated at* Swansea Grammar School; Clifton College; Peterhouse Cambridge University. *Career:* Degree in

Chemical Engineering, Cambridge University 1959. Worked on plant operations and development at BP's refinery in Aden, South Yemen 1960-64; Process Engineer in BP's London Engineering Department mainly concerned with distillation and heat transfer 1964-68; Project Engineer in Italy for new refinery at Volpiano 1968-69; Manager of catalytic process branch in BP's London Engineering Department 1969-72; Manager of BP refinery projects based in London 1972-75; Managing Director of BP marketing and refining companies in South East Asia based in Singapore 1975-78; General Manager, Projects Department, BP International Limited, based in London 1980-88. Director of: British Pipeline Agency Limited, BP Venezuela. *Publications:* Recent Advances in Oil Industry Project Management (N.E.Coast Inst. of Engineers & Shipbuilders) 1991. *Recreation:* sailing, gardening, photography. *Address:* B P Engineering, Uxbridge One, 1 Harefield Road, Uxbridge, Middx. UB8 1PD.(home) 63 High Street, Braunston, Daventry, Northants NN11 7HS

DAVIES, Mr Peter Lewis Morgan,OBE, 1978; FBIM 1973. *Born on* 19 Feb 1927 at Whitland. *Son of* the late David Morgan Davies (d 1962) and the late Annie Lee (nee Jones). *Marriage:* to Gwenith, 1953, da of Thomas Devonald Thomas Cilgerran (d 1969) of Cilgerran.*Educated at* Fishguard Co School. *Career:* Lt Welch Regiment and Royal Welch Fusiliers 1944-48; Midland Bank plc 1943-51; Barclays Bank Int. Ltd: Bahamas 1952-55, Nigeria 1955-67, Libya 1968-70, Zambia 1970-79, manager Kaunda Square Kitwe (northern area manager), alternate dir Barclays Zambia Ltd; team leader World Bank Mission to Indonesia 1979-80. MD Pembrokeshire Business Initiative 1983-86. Business councellor Welsh Development Agency 1986-89, Br Exec Service Overseas Fiji 1990 (Turks and Ciacos Is 1982-83); member: TAVRA Wales regional committee and association, Nat Employers Liason Committee Wales; county treasurer Royal British Legion Pembrokeshire, Hon patron 4 Bn Royal Regiment of Wales, board member Fishguard Music Festival. *Recreation:* photography, philately. *Address:* Court House, Tower Hill, Fishguard, Pembrokeshire SA65 9LA.

DAVIES, Major General Peter Ronald, FBIM., FITD *Currently:* GOC Wales (to Nov. 1991) then Chief Executive RSPCA. *Born on* 10 May 1938 at Gibralter. *Son of* Lt.Col. C.H. Davies (Harry) and Mrs Joy (nee Moore). *Marriage:* to Rosemary Julia (nee Felice) 1960. *Children:* Tristan D.H. and Cecily H. Eaton. *Educated at* Llandovery College; Welbeck College; R.M.A. Sandhurst *Career:* Commander Communications BAOR 1987-89; Dir. of Studies, Army Staff College 1986-87; Royal Coll. of Defence Studies 1985; Commander 12th Armoured Brigade 1983-84; Appointed: Colonel The King's Regiment (8th,63rd,96th) 1986- ; Chmn. Regimental Council and King's Regimental Assoc. 1986- ; Colonel Commandant Royal Corps of Signals 1990- ; Governor Welbeck College 1980-81; Mbr. Int. Strategic Planning Advisory Board,Andrew Corporation (USA) 1991- . *Recreation:* Rugby football, wine, music, dog walking *Clubs:* Army & Navy; Royal Overseas League; London Rugby; Cardiff & County. *Address:* C/o National Westminster Bank, Market Square, Llandovery, Dyfed SA20 OAE.

DAVIES, Mr Philip Thomas (Phil)., *Currently:* City Industrial Supplies, Neath, Sales Director. *Born on* 19 Oct, 1963 at Seven Sisters. *Son of* Mr Tudor Davies and Mrs Kay Davies. *Marriage:* to Caroline. *Children:* Dannika Louise and Rebecca Emma. *Educated at* Llangatwg Comprehensive, Neath. *Career:* Llanelli Captain five years; Welsh Palyer of the Year, 1989; Forward of the year 1989-91; 29 Full Welsh Caps, Llanellis most Capped Forward. *Publications:* none as yet. *Recreation:* golf, reading, my family. *Clubs:* Llanelli, Seven Sisters, Baba's RFC; Glynneath RFC. *Address:* 38 Llys Westfa, Swiss Valley, Llanelli, Dyfed SA14 2RR.

DAVIES, Dr Rachel Bryan, *Currently:* Commercial Law Reporter, Financial Times since 1981; Chairman, Industrial Tribunals, London South, since 1986. *Born on* 6 Oct 1935 *Daughter of* John Edwards and Gweno Davies Bryan. *Marriage:* to Geraint Tim Davies. *Children:* Angharad, Crisiant, Manon, Sion and Rhianon.*Education:* LLB Wales, LLM London; PhD London. *Career:* Barrister 1965- ; Law Reporter The Times 1974-81; De Lancey De la Hantey Prize for Medico-Legal Journalism 1981; Chairman, Rent Tribunals 1981-86; Consultative Editor, Executive Editor,Kluwer Law Publishing 1984-89. *Clubs:* Fellow of the Royal Society of Arts. *Address:* Gelli Eblyg, Llangynwyd, Maesteg, Mid Glam, CF34 ODT.

DAVIES, His Honour Judge Rhys Everson, Q.C., LL.B. *Currently:* Judge, The Honorary Recorder of Manchester 1990- . *Born on* 13 Jan 1941 at Hengoed, Glam. *Son of* the late Evan Davies MA. and the late Nancy Caroline Davies BA. *Marriage:* to Katherine Anne Yeates 1963. *Children:* Mark Davies MA. and Carolyn Davies BA. *Educated at* Cowbridge G.S; Neath G.S; Univ. of Manchester. *Career:* LLB 1961; Called to Bar Gray's Inn 1964; Barrister Northern Circuit 1964-90; Junior of the Northern Circuit 1967; Q.C. 1981. *Recreation:* Music, travel *Address:* Crown Court, Crown Square, Manchester. M3 3FL.

DAVIES, Sir Richard Harries,KCVO; CBE; CEng; FIEE. *Born on* 28 June 1916 at Rhondda. *Son of* Thomas Henry Davies and Minnie Oakley (nee Morgan). *Marriage:* to 1) Hon. Nan Macpherson 1944; 2) Patricia P. Ogier, 1979. *Children:* Gregory, Richard, Lucy and Nancy. *Educated at* Porth County School; Cardiff Technical College. *Career:* Scientific Civil Service 1939-46; Vice President Ferranti Electric Inc 1948-63; New York, Dir. Ferranti Ltd 1970-76; Duke of Edinburgh's Household 1977-84. *Recreation:* Gardening, sailing, amateur radio. *Clubs:* Athenaeum, Pratts.*Address:* Haven House, Thorpeness, Leiston, Suffolk, IP16 4NR.

DAVIES, Professor Robert, MSc, PhD, CEng, MIMechE, MIM. *Currently:* Professor of Mechanical Engineering, University of Birmingham, since 1982. *Born on* 5 Jan 1935 at Mountain Ash, Glamorgan. *Son of* the late Thomas Stephen and the late Winifred Gertrude (nee Taylor). *Marriage:* to Sylvia Meriel, 1959. *Children:* Sylvia Anne. *Educated at* Mountain Ash Grammar School; University of Birmingham. *Career:* Technical Officer, ICI Metals Division 1957-60; Deputy Ch.Eng. Allied Ironfounders Ltd 1960-61; ICI Research Fellow, University of Birmingham 1963-65; Lecturer in Mechanical Engineering, University of Birmingham 1965-71; Senior Lecturer in Mechanical Engineering 1971-78; Reader in Engineering Plasticity, University of Birmingham 1978-82. *Publications:* Developments in High Speed Metal Forming, Machinery Publishing Co. 1971; 70 papers on research into metal forming, adhesive technology, powder metallurgy and lasers. *Recreation:* Antiques, ornithology. *Address:* School Of Manufacturing & Mechanical Engineering, The University Of Birmingham, Edgbaston, Birmingham B15 2TT.

DAVIES, Mr Robert Leighton, MA(Oxon), BCL. *Currently:* Barrister. *Born on* 7 Sept 1949 at Cardiff. *Son of* the late Robert Brinley Davies and Elizabeth Nesta Davies. *Marriage:* to Linda Fox, 1979. *Children:* Rhoss, Rhia and Greg. *Educated at* Rhondda County Grammar School, Porth Rhondda; Corpus Christi College, Oxford. *Career:* Open exhibition to Corpus Christi College, Oxford to Read Law; called to Bar, Gray's Inn, London 1975; practising as Barrister in Cardiff 1975- ; appointed Crown Court Recorder 1990. *Recreation:* reading, gardening, fly-fishing. *Clubs:* Treorchy Rugby Football. *Address:* 'Bryn Corun', Glyncoli Road, Treorchy, Mid Glam CF42 6SA. 34 Park Place, Cardiff CF1 3BA Tel: 0222 382731

DAVIES, Professor Robert Rees, DPhil, FBA 1987. *Currently:* Professor of History, since 1976; Vice-Principal 1988-91, University College of Wales, Aberystwyth. *Born on* 6 Aug 1938 *Son of* William Edward Davies and Sarah Margaret Davies. *Marriage:* to Carys Lloyd Wynne, 1966. *Children:* one s one d. *Educated at* University College London (BA); Merton College Oxford (DPhil). FRHistS 1968. *Career:* Assistant Lecturer, UC Swansea 1961-63; Lecturer, UCL 1963-76. Wiles Lecturer, QUB 1988; James Ford Special Lecturer, University of Oxford 1988. Chairman Nat Curriculum History Committee for Wales 1989-90; Convenor, History at Universities Defence Group 1991- ; Member: Ancient Monuments Board for Wales 1977- ; Council, Nat. Museum of Wales 1987-90; Council, Historical Assoc., 1991- . Vice Pres., RHistS 1988- (Member Council 1979-82). President Elect, Royal Historical Society 1992-96. Wolfson Literary Award for History 1987. Assistant Editor and Review Editor, History 1963-73. *Publications:* Lordship and Society in the March of Wales 1282-1400, 1978; (ed) Welsh Society and Nationhood, 1984; Conquest, Co-existence and Change; Wales 1063-1415, 1987; (ed) The British Isles 1100-1500, 1988; Domination and Conquest: the experience of Ireland, Scotland and Wales 1100-1300, 1990; numerous contributions to learned journals. *Recreation:* walking, music. *Address:* Maeshyfryd, Ffordd Llanbadarn, Aberystwyth, Dyfed. Tel: 0970 617113

DAVIES, Mr Robert Stephen, FCA *Currently:* Finance Director, Gulf Oil, since 1980. *Born on* 23 Feb 1945 at Cardiff. *Son of* the late Richard George Davies and Megan Davies (nee Matthews). *Marriage:* to Philippa Mary Woodley, 1970. *Children:* Charles George Woodley, Nicholas Edward Robert, Lucy Louis and Katy Clare. *Educated at* Bridgend Grammar School *Career:* R.H.March Son & Co, Chartered Accountants, Cardiff, Articled Clerk/ Audit Senior 1965-70; Mann Judd & Co, Chartered Accountants London, Assistant Audit Manager 1970-71; Management Consultant 1971-72; Gulf Oil International London, Financial Analyst/Supervisor Budgets and Planning 1972-76; Gulf Oil Refining Ltd, Milford Haven, Manager Finance and Services 1976-78; Gulf Oil Switzerland, Zurich, Finance Director 1978-80. *Recreation:* antiques, vintage cars, music, tennis *Clubs:* Bentley Drivers *Address:* C/o Gulf Oil, The Quadrangle, Imperial Square, Cheltenham, Glos GL50 1TF.

DAVIES, Mr Ron, *Currently:* M.P. *Born on* 6 Aug 1946 at Machen. *Son of* the late Francis Ronald and Beryl. *Marriage:* to Christina (nee Rees) 1987. *Children:* Angharad *Educated at* Bassaleg G.S; Polytechnic Portsmouth; UCW Cardiff *Career:* Former WEA Tutor/Organiser, Mid Glam; FE Organiser; Ex-Opposition Whip; New Opposition Spokesman, Food and Agriculture & Animal Welfare. *Recreation:* Walking, gardening *Clubs:* Machen CIU Life Member *Address:* House of Commons, London SW1A 0AA.

DAVIES, Right Reverend Roy Thomas, BA, B.Litt. *Currently:* Bishop of Llandaff since November 1985. *Born on* 31 Jan 1934 at Llangennech, Llanelli. *Son of* Hubert and Dilys Davies. *Marriage:* . *Children:* *Educated at* St.David's College, Lampeter; Jesus College; St.Stephen's House Oxford. *Career:* Assistant Curate, St.Paul's Llanelli 1959-64; Vicar of Llanfan and Gwnnws, Cardiganshire 1964-67; Chaplain to Anglican Students at Aberystwyth 1967-73; Sec of Provincial Council for Mission and Unity of The Church in Wales 1973-79; Vicar of St.David's Carmarthen 1979-83; Archdeacon of Carmarthen 1982-85; Clerical Sec of Governing Body of Church in Wales 1983-85. *Recreation:* reading, walking. *Clubs:* Cardiff & County *Address:* Llys Esgob, Cathedral Green, Llandaff, Cardiff, CF5 2YE.,

DAVIES, Mr. Ryland, FRMCM. *Currently:* Opera/Concert singer; also since 1987 Teacher of singing privately and at Royal Northern College Music. *Born on* 9 Feb 1943 at Cwm, Ebbw Vale, Gwent *Son of* Richard Gethin Davies and Joan Davies. *Marriage:* to Deborah Jane Rees, 1983. *Children:* Emily Sian. *Educated at* Tre Uchaf Sec.Mod. Loughor, Glam; Royal Manchester Coll. Music. *Career:* Entered Royal Manchester College of Music at age seventeen to study singing with Frederic Cox OBE, continuing until the influential teacher's death; awarded two major prizes and was made a Fellow of the College in 1971; mbr of Glyndebourne chorus 1964,65,66. Won Boyce and Mendelssohn Foundation Scholarship in 1964 and 65, was first recipient of John Christie Award; studying in Italy, firstly with Ettore Campogagliani in Mantova and then with Luigi Ricci in Rome; operatic debut in major role for the Welsh National Opera Autumn 1964, this production was repeated in 1965 leading to an engagement with Saddler's Wells Opera; debut with Scottish Opera in 1966 and in 1967 sang first Ferrando in the famous Besch production of Cosi Fan Tutte; made his Glyndebourne major role debut as 'Belmonte' in "Die Entfurung Aus dem Serai" under the baton of Sir John Pritchard in 1968, that summer he was engaged by Sir Georg Solti to sing Fenton-Falstaff, Ottavio-Don Giovanni Alfredo-Traviata and Hylas in the Trojans which was in fact his debut role in the R.O.H. house in September 1969; he was invited by Herbert non Karajan to sing at the Salzburg Festival in 1970 and for 2 subsequent years; 1970 marked his U.S. debut as 'Ferrando' in "Cosi Fan Tutte" at San Francisco, leading to an engagement and debut in the same role at Chicago Lyric Opera 1972, Metropolitan Opera 1975,76 ; made many apperances in opera houses in many parts of the world including Geneva, Paris Munich, Madrid, Buenos Aires, Holland, Lyons, Salzburg, Brussels, Nice, Milan, Palermo and Hong Kong; sung frequently with most of the major orchestras, the English Chamber Orchestra, the Chicago Symphony Orchestra, the Philadelphia Orchestra, the Vienna Symphony and the Bavarian Radio Orchestras; broadcasts regularly with the BBC; has made numerous recordings for Decca, Phillips, R.C.A. and Deutche Gramaphone, most of which have been re-issued on Compact Disc - these were made under the musical direction of the following maestri: Colin Davis, John Pritchard, Richard Bonyge, Daniel Barenbouime, Subin Meta, Carlo Maria Giulini, Nello Santi, George Solti, Charles Maccheras, Raymond Leppard, and Fausto Cleva; future plans include two seasons for the Netherlands Opera Company in Amsterdam, plus various concerts and recitals. *Recreation:* Sports, theatre and paintings   *Address:* 71 Fairmile Lane, Cobham, Surrey. KT11 2DG.

DAVIES, Mr Thomas Gerald Reames, DLC (Loughborough College); MA(Cantab). *Currently:* Rugby Writer (The Times); Non Exec. Director HTV plc, since 1978. *Born on* 7 Feb 1945 at Llansaint. *Son of* Tudor and Mary Davies. *Marriage:* to Priscilla Elizabeth. *Children:* Emily and Ben. *Educated at* Queen Elizabeth Grammar School, Carmarthen. *Career:* Teacher: Llanrumney High School 1966-68, Christ Hospital, Horsham, Sussex 1971-74; Tech.Officer: Sports Council for Wales 1974-80; Member Prince of Wales Committee 1986- ; ABSA (Business Sponsorship of the Arts 1988- ; Member Sports Council for Wales 1990- ; Member of Welsh Adv. Committee of British Council 1991-. *Publications:* Autobiography; Welsh Rugby Scrapbook; Tries; Sidesteps (with John Morgan). *Recreation:* Reading, music, cooking, running, travelling, sometimes gardening. *Clubs:* Wig & Pen; Cardiff Athletic. *Address:* C/o HTV Cymru Wales, Television Centre, Culverhouse Cross, Cardiff CF5 6XJ.

DAVIES, Mr Thomas Glyn, CBE 1966 *Currently:* retired. *Born on* 16 Aug 1905 at Gwaelod Y Garth. *Son of* Thomas and Mary Davies. *Marriage:* to Margaret Berry 1934. *Children:* Mary. *Educated at* Pontypridd Grammar School; Univ. Coll.Cardiff, MA, Fellow. *Career:* Assistant Master Howard Gardens High School, 1927-37; Warden, Pontypridd Dist. Educ. Settlement 1937-43; Dir. of Educ. Mongomeryshire 1943-58; Dir. of Educ. Denbighshire 1958-70; Dist. Governor Wrexham 1965-66; Chmn.BBC Schools Council 1960-70; Mbr. g.B.A. 1970-75; Pres. CEM Wales (Christian Ed. Movement) 1970- ; Mbr. Court & Council Univ. Coll., Bangor 1960- ; Mbr. of Court Univ. of Wales 1960- ; Past mbr. Court. Univ. Cardiff 1960-80; past mbr. Court. Univ. Aberystwyth; past Chmn. CCPR Welsh Commt. 1960-80; past Vice Chmn. of Sports Council Wales. *Recreation:* Travel, music, drama *Clubs:* Rotary club, Wrexham *Address:* 42 Park Avenue, Wrexham, Clwyd. LL12 7AH.

DAVIES, County Councillor Thomas Graham, F.R.T.P.I. *Currently:* Town Planning & Development Consultant. *Born on* 27 March 1934 at Briton Ferry. *Son of* the late William Samuel and the late Edith Anne (nee Edwards). *Marriage:* to Mary Myrtle (nee Williams) 1962. *Children:* Mark Lloyd, Nigel Spencer and Jane Elizabeth Victo *Educated at* Neath Technical College; Welsh School of Architecture (p/t) *Career:* Chief Planning Assist. Merthyr Tydfil County Borough 1970-74; Planning Officer Monmouth Borough Council 1974-90; Chmn. S.East Wales Arts Assoc. 1985-86; Vice-Chmn. Economic Dev. & Emp. Commt. Mid Glamorgan C.C., 1989; Vice-Chmn. Glamorgan Joint Archives Commt 1990. *Recreation:* Travel, looking at buildings *Clubs:* 41 Club *Address:* Llys Pendarren, Penydarren Park, Merthyr Tydfil CF47 8YW. 4

Beach Court, The Strand, Saundersfoot, Dyfed

DAVIES, County Councillor Thomas Isaiah William Arthur, *Currently:* retired - started work at Abercynon Colliery in 1926 and remained there until 1972 when he retired. *Born on* 2 April 191006 at Ynysybwl. *Son of* Evan and Mary Hannah Davies. *Marriage:* 1937. *Children:* Eirlys. *Educated at* Abercynon Secondary Modern School. *Career:* Became a member of the Labour Party 60 years ago; Chairman of the Mountain Ash Trades and Labour Council, also chairman of the Industrial Section 1964-66; Chairman of the Aberdare and Mountain Ash Education Divisional Executive Committee 1969-71; member of the old Mountain Ash District Council in 1964; as a representative for the Abercynon Ward in 1968 became Chairman of the Housing also chairman of the Industrial Committee until 1973, when he became Vice Chairman of the Authority; County Councillor for Ynysybwl and Abercynon Ward, 1974; Chairman and Vice Chairman of the Construction and Civil Engineering Units for Mid Glam C.C. 1974-92; Chairman and Vice-Chairman of Residential Blind School at Bridgend for the past 17 years; member of South Wales Police Authority 1974-92; member of the W.J.E.C. 1983-92; Chairman Aberdare College of F.E. 1977-79; Chairman of 4 Primary Schools; Chairman of Mountain Ash Comprehensive School 1974-92; Chairman of Mid Glam County Council 1984-85. *Recreation:* Played Rugby for Abercynon from 1926-32; played for Pontypridd, 1932-39; reading, walking, watching all types of sport. *Address:* 15 Gwendoline Terrace, Abercynon, Mountain Ash CF45 4TE.

DAVIES, Mr Thomas Peter Lloyd, ACIB *Currently:* County Executive Officer, Farmer's Union of Wales. *Born on* 6 Apr, 1956 at Aberystwyth. *Son of* Thomas John Lloyd Davies and Ellen Davies. *Marriage:* to Barbara Elizabeth Davies. *Children:* Anna Kate Henshall, Robert John Lloyd Davies and Owen Michael Lloyd Davies. *Educated at* Llandysul Grammar School. *Career:* Midland Bank plc, 1972-91; Farmers' Union of Wales 1991- . Treasurer, Ceredigion and Pembroke North Conservative Assoc; Treasurer, Dyfed Commonwealth Games ; Chairman & Manager Llandysul Town Football Club; member: Cymdeithas Tai Cantref (Tai Cantref Housing Association) Finance and Development Committee. Dyfed Co-Ordinator, Peace through NATO: *Interests:* politics, sport.*Address:* Hafan Hedd, Aberbanc, Penrhiwllan, Llandysul, Dyfed SA44 5NP. Tel:0559 371281

DAVIES, Dr William Edmund Vincent John, B.Sc(Maths & Physics), B.Sc.(1st class Physics). *Currently:* Lecturer at Afan Tertiary College, Port Talbot 1971- . *Born on* 14 March 1939 at Gothic Villa, St Clears. *Son of* William and Sybil Davies. *Marriage:* to Brenda (nee Howell) 1980. *Children:* Diana and Delia. *Educated at* St. Clears Nat. School; Whitland Grammar School; Univ. Coll. Swansea. *Career:* Senior Research Officer (sponsored by the CEGB) 1964-66; Senior Scientific Officer (British Iron & Steel Research Assn), Sketty Hall, Swansea 1966-71; last ever elected County Councillor for Carmarthenshire County Council prior to re-organisation 1973; Dyfed County Councillor 1974- ; Mayor of St. Clears Town 1975-76 and 1984-85; Chairman of Schools and Schools Services (Dyfed) 1976-78; Chairman of Dyfed Agric. Ctee 1987-89; Mbr. of the: Univ. Council of Wales 1975- ; Investment (Univ of Wales) 1975- ; Univ. Coll. Council Swansea; Univ. Coll

Council Lampeter; Gregynog Committee; Member of many sub-committees of the University of Wales; Chairman of the last Grammar school in Wales (Whitland Grammar School) which closed in 1990; Member of: Dyfed Educ. Ctee 1974- Dyfed Devel. & Finance Educ. Ctee; Mbr of the Welsh Joint Educ. Ctee 1973- ; Schools Council for Curriculum & Examinations (Science Panel) W.J.E.C; Technical Educ. Ctee W.J.E.C; Technical Examinations Ctee W.J.E.C; Awarding Ctee for General Courses W.J.E.C; Mbr Governing Body (Univ. of Swansea) 1973- ; Mbr of the Court of Governors (Univ. of Wales) 1973- . Member of the Daniel Committee reporting the Future of the University of Wales, 1989- . *Publications:* Ph.D. (Thesis: "The Mechanism of Electrical Breakdown of Gases at High Voltages"); "Electrical Breakdown of Air at High Voltages", "Nature" Vol. 205, 1965; "The Mechanism of Electrical Breakdown of Gases at High Voltages", VII International Conference (Belgrade), 1966; An Apparatus for the Investigation of Pre-Breakdown Ionization, J. Sci. Inst. Vol. 43, July 1966. *Recreation:* Bridge, sport (rugby, soccer, cricket), stock markets. *Clubs:* Member of a number of local sporting clubs. *Address:* Gothic Villa, St. Clears, Dyfed SA33 4DY. Tel: 0994 230772

DAVIES, Mr William John (Jack), MBE, 1975; FHA; ACIS; MBIM. *Currently:* retired. *Born on* 20 June 1918 at Brynaman, West Glam. *Son of* the late David William Davies and the late Ann (nee Davies). *Marriage:* to Ruth (nee Williams), 12 August 1948. *Children:* Janet Ruth and John Kendal. *Educated at* Ystalyfera County School, Glamorgan; Swansea Technical College. *Career:* Admin. Officer, Glamorgan C.C., 1948-74; Admin Officer West Glam Area Health Auth., 1974-82; Trade Union: Member Nalgo Nat. Exec. Cttee 1970-82; Founder mbr Wales TUC 1973-82; Chmn. Wales TUC's Loc. Govt, Housing and Educ. Cttee 1977-78; Mbr. SW Provincial Council (APT&C staff) 1952-82; Local Government appoints: mbr Cwmaman Urban Dist.Cncl (Chmn 1966), 1960-74; Clerk, Cwmaman Town Council 1974-77; Mbr. Dyfed C.C. 1977-; Mbr. S.W. Provincial Council (Manual Workers), 1964-74. Govnmnt appoints: mbr. Welsh Hospitals Bd 1969-74; mbr. Industrial Tribunal 1974-86; mbr. War Pensions Cttee 1986- ; mbr. Court of Governors UC Aberystwyth and Swansea 1963-74. Political: mbr. Labour Party 1931-86; Parliamentary Agent - Rt.Hon.James Griffiths MP 1966-70; Parly Agent - Rt.Hon Denzil Davies MP,QC 1970-77; Voluntary Organisations: Pres. AV Hospital League of Friends 1970- ; Pres. Clwb Godrer's Mynydd Du- Fishing and Shooting Club 1979- ; Pres. Royal British Legion (Garnant Branch) 1984- ; Chmn. Cwmaman Meals on Wheels Assocn 1984- . *Publications:* various newspaper articles only. *Recreation:* music, reading. *Address:* 17 Cwmamman Road, Glanamman, Ammanford. SA18 1DQ.

DAVIES, Mr William Vivian, MA., FSA (1980) *Currently:* Keeper of Egyptian Antiquities, British Museum. *Born on* 14 Oct 1947 at Gorseinon. *Son of* Walter Percival Davies and Gwenllian Davies (nee Evans). *Marriage:* to Janet Olwen May Foat, 1970. *Children:* Elen Mai and Thomas Dafydd Robert. *Educated at* Llanelli Grammar School, 1959-66; Jesus College, Oxford 1967-73; Queen's College, Oxford 1973-74. *Career:* Assistant Keeper, British Museum, Dept of Egyptian Antiquities, 1974-81; Deputy Keeper, British Museum, Dept of Egyptian Antiquities, 1981-88; Visiting Professor of Egyptology, University of Heidelberg, 1984-85; Keeper of Egyptian Antiquities, British Museum, 1988- ; Honorary Librarian, Egypt Exploration Society, 1975-85; General Editor of Publications of the Egypt Exploration Society, 1989- ; Reviews Editor of the Journal of Egyptian Archaeology, 1975-85; Member of Council of the British Institute in Eastern Africa, 1989- ; Chairman of the Sudan Archaeological Research Society, 1991- . *Publications:* Egyptian Sculpture (with T.G.H. James), 1983; Saggara Tombs 1 (with A.B. Lloyd and A.J. Spencer), 1984; Problems and Priorities in Egyptian Archaeology, (ed with J. Assmann and G. Burkard), 1987; Egyptian Hieroglyphs, 1987; Catalogue of Egyptian Antiquities in the British Museum, V11,1, Axes, 1987; Egypt and Africa. Nubia from Prehistory to Islam (ed), 1991; Reviews and articles in learned journals. *Recreation:* Chess, art, music, theatre, reading and real ale. *Address:* Dept. of Egyptian, Antiquities, British Museum, London. WC1B 3DG.

DAVIES-COOKE, Mr Richard Lyndon, M.Inst P.S. *Currently:* County Supplies Officer, Gwent County Council (formerly Monmouthshire C.C.), since 1969 progressing - Buyer/Senior Buyer/Assistant County Supplies Officer/ C.S.O. (Jan 1984). *Born on* 9 Dec 1932 at Pantyrawel, Nr Bridgend, Glam. *Son of* George and Rosalind (nee Phillips). *Marriage:* to Mary Elizabeth Lloyd, 1960. *Educated at* Ogmore Grammar School; Cardiff Coll. of Technology. *Career:* former Glamorgan County Council, Clerk/Assistant Buyer 1956-69. *Publications:* short stories, poems. *Recreation:* fishing, gardening *Address:* " Kathyra ", The Oaks, Royal Oak, Machen, NP1 8SN. Central Supplies Dept., Gwent C.Council, The Polo Ground, New Inn, Pontypool, NP4 OYA

DAWSON, Mr Joseph Peter, B.Sc; Dip.Ed. *Currently:* Assistant Secretary (Pensions and Membership Services) National Association of Teachers in Further and Higher Education and General Secretary European Trade Union Ctee for Education. *Born on* 18 March 1940 at Swansea. *Son of* Joseph Glyn Dawson and Winifred Olwen Dawson. *Marriage:* to Yvonne Anne Charlton (Smith) 1964. *Children:* Jo-Anne Michelle and Alex Martin. *Educated at* Bishop Gore Grammar, Swansea 1951-58; University College Swansea. *Career:* Assistant Master in Physics, Chiswick Grammar School 1962-65; Vice President National Union of Students 1962-64; Senior Field Officer, National Union of Teachers 1965-68; Assistant Secretary and Negotiating Secretary, ATTI and NATFHE 1969-79; General Secretary, NATFHE 1979-89. *Recreation:* Cricket, football, theatre. *Clubs:* Surrey County Cricket. *Address:* NATFHE, 27 Britannia Street, London. WC1X 9JP. ETUCE, 33 Rue De Treves, 1040 Brussels, Belgium

de WINTON, Mr Michael Geoffrey, CBE, OBE, MC *Currently:* Retired. *Born on* 17 Oct 1916 at Hay on Wye. *Son of* John Jeffreys de Winton (Son of William de Winton DLJP, Llanfrynach, Brecon) and Ida de Winton. *Marriage:* to Ursula Lightwood in 1948. *Children:* Anthony Charles, Amanda Fawcett, William Michael. *Educated at* Monmouth School *Career:* Solicitor 1939; War Service 1939-46; Commissioned South Wales Borderers 1940; Company Commander Indian Army in India, Middle East and Burma 1942-45 (despatches twice); Administrative Officer in the Colonial Service in Nigeria 1946-48; Crown Counsel 1948-53; Called to the Bar Grays Inn 1953; Principal legal draftsman 1954; Solicitor General and Permanent Secretary, Ministry of Justice, W Nigeria 1957-61; Retired from Colonial Service and re-admitted as Solicitor 1961; Assistant legal adviser Colonial Office 1961-66; H.M. Diplomatic Service 1966-70; Assistant legal adviser CRO 1967; FCO 1968; Law Officers department 1969-70; Assistant Solicitor 1970; Under Secretary 1974; Assistant Legal Secretary to the Law Offices 1972-80; responsible for international and constitutional matters and deputy head of department. Retired from Crown Service 1980; Legal consultant to overseas governments and international organisation 1980-86; Principal Legal Adviser to British Indian Ocean Territories 1982-83. *Recreation:* Music and painting pictures. *Address:* Stable Cottage, Church Walk, Stalbridge, Dorset. DT10 2LR.

DEAKINS, Mr Joseph Clifford *Currently:* Farmer - started life as a ploughboy. *Born on* 6 Sept 1917 at Whitton. *Son of* Richard and Elenor Thedoska Deakins. *Marriage:* 1936. *Children:* Raymond, Audrey Jean, Ruth, Roy, Christine, Angelaand John. *Educated at* Llangunllo School, until 14 years old. *Career:* Presteign Town council member for 35 years; Mayor 6 times; County Councillor, Radnorshire, then Powys, for 31 years; Chairman of John Beddoes School Governors for 21 years; Chairman of Sites and Buildings Committee for Powys, former Vice-Chairman of Agricultural Cttee; Former chairman Powys Valuation Panel, former Presteigne Y.F.C. President; Chairman of Prestemede Old Folks Home; Member of N.F.U. and Member of Agricultural Lands Tribunal.Chairman, Presteigne Primary School for 30 years as a Governor. *Publications:* featured in "The Book of John Beddoes School". *Recreation:* working horses *Clubs:* Treasurer Presteigne Methodist Church for many years. *Address:* Lower Dolley, Ackhill, Presteigne, Powys. LD8 2EE.

DEINIOL, Very Reverend Abbot Father ,B.D., M.TH. *Currently:* Rector of The Russian Orthodox Church of The Holy Protection, Blaenau Ffestiniog. *Born on* 29 April 1950 at Bangor. *Son of* Meirion Davies and the late Nesta (nee Williams) *Educated at* Grove Park Grammar School, Wrexham; King's College London *Career:* Divinity Master, Archbishop Whitgift Grammar School, South Croydon 1972; Head of Religious Education Ysgol Ardudwy, Harlech 1973-85; Supply teaching, Gwynedd School 1985- ; Tonsured Monk by Archimandrite Barnabas at St. Elias Monastery, New Mills, Powys 1977; Professed Monk, ordained Deacon, ordained Priest by Metropolitan Anthony of Sourozh 1979; established the Russian Orthodox Church's Community in Wales 1979; with the blessing of His Holiness, the late Patriarch Pimen of Moscow and all Russia, awarded The Gold Cross and elevated to the rank of Igoumen (Abbot) by Metropolitan Philaret of Minsk and Byelorussia in the Holy Trinity - St. Sergei Lavra, Zagorsk (U.S.S.R.) 1987; with the blessing of His Holiness, Patriarch Alexii II of Moscow and all Russia, awarded the Palitsa and Jewelled Cross (Patriarchal Awards) by Bishop Anastasii of Kazan and Mari in the St.Nicholas Cathedral, Kazan (U.S.S.R.) 1990; Orthodox Church representative on "Cytun" (The Welsh Ecumenical Body). *Publications:* established "Manod Orthodox Publications", 1987, to produce material pertaining to The Russian Orthodox Church; completed translation of, and published, as a cassette The Divine Liturgy of St.John Chrysostom ("Offeren Ddwyfol"), 1989;

published various articles in journals, mainly about The Life of The Russian Orthodox Church; frequent broadcasts (mainly in Welsh). *Recreation:* gardening, railways *Address:* Church Of The Holy Protection, 11 Manod Road, Blaenau Ffestiniog, Gwynedd, LL41 4DE.

DERRICK, John, *Currently:* Professional Cricketer, Cricket Development Officer, Bleanau Gwent. *Born on* 15 Jan 1963 at Cwmaman, Aberdare. *Son of* John Raymond and Megan Irene. *Marriage:* to Anne Irene. *Children:* Liam Kyle and Joanna Louise *Educated at* Bleangwawr Comprehensive School. *Career:* Junior Pro Lords Groundstaff 1978-80; playing and coaching in Brisbane Australia winters of 1982/83/84; playing and coaching in Bay of Plenty New Zealand winters of 1985/86/87/88. Joined G.C.C.C. in 1981 finished Sept 1991. Captained Welsh School under 11, took 9 wickets for 9 runs first game, clean bowled everyone and second game 6 for 6. Capped by Glamorgan 1988. *Recreation:* all sports *Clubs:* Glamorgan, Pontardulais, Maesteg Celtic and Aberdare. *Address:* 27 Broniestyn Terrace, Trecynon, Aberdare, Mid Glam, CF44 8EG.

DEWAR, Mr. Ian Stewart, JP; MA (Oxon) *Currently:* South Glamorgan County Councillor (Lab) (Vice Chairman 1990-91) Civil Servant (retired). *Born on* 29 Jan 1929 at Cogan, Penarth. *Son of* William S. Dewar and Eileen Dewar (nee Godfrey). *Marriage:* to Nora Dewar (nee House). *Children:* Jane and David. *Educated at* Cogan School; Penarth Grammar; Cardiff Univ. Coll; Oxford Univ. *Career:* Asst. Archivist, Glamorgan County Council 1952-53; Civil Servant, Ministry of Labour, Dept. of Employment, Civil Service Commission, Commission on Industrial Relations 1953-70; Welsh Office 1970-83 (Under Secretary 1973-83); South Glamorgan County Council 1985- ; Member Governing Bodies of Univ. of Wales and Cardiff Univ. Coll; Chairman of National Museum of Wales Schools Service Ctee. *Recreation:* Politics, history, languages, Yr Iaith Gymraeg. *Clubs:* United Services Mess, Cardiff; Civil Service Club; Penarth Labour Club. *Address:* 59 Stanwell Road, Penarth, South Glam. CF6 2LR.

DICKINSON, Mr Neil *Currently:* Managing Editor of the 'Tenby Observer', post held since 1989. *Born on* 26 Jan 1955. at Tenby. *Son of* Ronald and Olwen Myfanwy Dickinson (nee Jones). *Marriage:* to Alison Muriel Smith 1988. *Educated at* Greenhill School, Tenby. *Career:* began as a Junior Reporter with the 'Tenby Observer' in 1972, and has remained with the paper ever since, rising through the ranks as reporter, chief reporter and assistant editor to his my present position. *Recreation:* All sports, photography, music, reading and gardening. *Address:* Newspaper House, Warren Street, Tenby, Pembrokeshire, SA70 7JY.

DIMOND, Professor Bridgit Carolyn, MA., LL.B., DSA., AHSM., Barrister-at-Law *Currently:* Assistant Director and Dean of Faculty of Professional Studies, Polytechnic of Wales. *Born on* 7 Dec 1941 at Gwent. *Daughter of* Alfred & Phyllis Price. *Marriage:* to Stuart John Dimond 1968. *Children:* Clare and Rebecca *Educated at* Oxford Univ. (St.Hugh's College); Middle Temple. *Career:* Health Service Manager/Barrister/lecturer/reader Mental Health Act Commissioner; Non-executive mbr. of Mid. Glamorgan F.H.S.A; Professional Practice Commt. Welsh National Board. *Publications:* Legal aspects of Nursing 1990; many articles on legal aspects of health care, professional liability, mental health law. *Recreation:* Elgar, walking and travelling *Clubs:* Elgar Society *Address:* Faculty Of Professional Studies, Polytechnic of Wales, Pontypridd, Mid Glam, CF37 1DL.

DISLEY, Mr John Ifor, CBE; DLc *Currently:* Director Reebok UK Limited; Director London Marathon Limited. *Born on* 20 Nov 1928 at Corris, Merionedd. *Son of* Harold Disley and Marie Hughes. *Marriage:* to Sylvia Cheeseman 1957. *Children:* Emma Sian and Kate Elunid. *Educated at* Oswestry H.S., Loughborough University. *Career:* Former British Steeplechase Record holder; Welsh mile record holder; Bronze medal 1952 Olympics; Sportsman of Year 1955; Welsh Empire Games Captain 1954; Vice-Chairman Sports Council 1974-82; Director Silva UK 1973-81; Chairman Plas Y Brenin Nat. Mountaineering Centre 1975-82; Member Royal Commission on Gambling. *Publications:* Tackle Climbing; Orienteering; Guide to Athletics; Duke of Edinburgh's Award Expedition Guide. *Recreation:* Mountaineering, National Parks. *Clubs:* Climbers' Club; Ranelagh Harriers. *Address:* Hampton House, Upper Sunbury Road, Hampton, Middx., TW12 2DW. Llidiart Y Gwynt, Nant B.H., Llanrwst, Gwynedd.

DIVERRES, Emeritus Professor Armel Hugh, MA(Wales), L-es-L (Rennes) D. de l' Univ (Paris). *Currently:* Retired since 1981. *Born on* 4 Sept 1914 at Liverpool. *Son of* Paul Diverres and Elizabeth Jones. *Marriage:* to Ann Dilys Williams 1945. *Children:* Branwen, Catrin and Paul. *Educated at* Swansea Grammar School; U.C. Swansea; Univ. of Rennes; Sorbonne, Paris. MA(Wales), LesL (Rennes), Docteur de l'Universite de Paris. Fellow of Univ of Wales 1938-40. *Career:* Served in RA and Int Corps, 1940-46, Captain; Asst. Lecr in French 1946-49; Lecturer 1949-54, Univ. of Manchester; Sen.Lecturer in French 1954-57, Carnegie Prof., 1958-74, Dean, Faculty of Arts 1967-70, Univ. of Aberdeen. Governor: Nat. Mus. of Wales 1978-81; Centre for Information on Language Teaching and Res., 1977-82; Aberdeen Coll. of Education 1971-74. Member: CNAA Lang. Board 1965-78, Cttee for Res., 1975-82, Humanities Bd 1978-81; Welsh Jt Educn Cttee 1975-81. Pres. British Br., Internat. Arthurian Soc., 1978-80, Internat. Pres 1979-81; Pres., Soc. French Stud., 1976-78. Officer des Palmes Academiques 1971; Chevalier de l'Ordre National du Merite 1986. *Publications:* Voyage en Bearn by Froissart (ed) 1953; La Chronique metrique attribuee a Geffroy de Paris (ed) 1956; Chatterton by A. de Vigny (ed) 1967; articles and reviews in learned journals. *Recreation:* Walking, travelling *Address:* 23 Whiteshell Drive, Langland, Swansea, W. Glam., SA3 4SY.

DIX, Mr Bernard, S.O.B. *Born on* 30 March 1925 at Woolwich. *Son of* Gertrude Turner and Thomas Dix. *Marriage:* to' Eileen V.Smith, 1979. *Children:* Matthew, Simon and Jacob; by previous marriage: Alan, Janice and Justin. *Educated at* LCC Elementary; L.S.E. (TUC Scholar) 1952-53. *Career:* Engineering 1939-41; Army 1941-47; Engineering 1947-55; TUC Press & Publications Office 1955-63; NUPE Research Officer 1963-75; NUPE Asst. Gen. Secretary 1975-82; TUC Delegate 1968-81; TUC Local Govt. Cttee 1971-82; TUC Hotel & Catering Cttee 1975-79; Local Govt. Training Board 1972-79; Hotel & Catering E.D.C. 1975-79; Health Service Board 1976-80; Labour Party Nat. Exec. Cttee 1981; Labour Party NEC Social Policy Sub-cttee 1975-81; Governor Ruskin College,

Oxford 1970-81; Associate Fellow Warwick University 1981-82. London Correspondent Labour Action (New York) 1955-58; Asst. Editor Labour-The TUC Magazine 1955-83; Editor, Public Employees Journal 1963-80; Director, Tribune 1977-82; Llanddarog Community Council 1987-; (Chairman 1991-92); Member Cymdeithas Yr Iaith Gymraeg. *Publications:* Local Government Enterprize (with others) 1964; Low Pay and How to End It (with Alan Fisher) 1974; The Forward March of Labour Halted? (with others) 1981; Serving The Public-Building The Union (with Stephen Williams) 1987. *Recreation:* Socio Linguistics of the Geographically extended family. *Clubs:* Mynydd Cerrig Workingmens Club. *Address:* Pant Tawel, Mynydd Cerrig, Pontyberem, Dyfed, SA15 5BD.

DIXON, Dr John Richard, BSc; PhD; C.Chem; FRSC. *Currently:* Head of Department, Science & Chemical Engineering, Polytechnic of Wales, since 1988. *Born on* 5 May 1939 at Wolverhampton. *Son of* Richard and Mary Gladys Dixon. *Marriage:* to Mari Lloyd Davies. *Children:* Helen Sian and Ruth Elin. *Educated at* Wolverhampton Grammar School; University College of Wales, Aberystwyth. *Career:* Assistant Lecturer, University of Newcastle-upon-Tyne 1963-66; Lecturer, Glamorgan Polytechnic 1966-70; Senior Lecturer, Polytechnic of Wales 1970-78; Principal Lecturer, Polytechnic of Wales 1978-88 (Deputy Head of Science Dept., 1984-88). *Publications:* numerous in various journals. *Recreation:* Secretary Diocesan Association of Readers; Provincial Committee for Readers. *Address:* 11 Sycamore Close, Bridgend, Mid Glamorgan, CF31 1QS.

DOBB, Major Erlam Stanley, CB, TD, FRICS, FRAgS. *Currently:* retired. *Born on* 16 Aug 1910 at Bardsley, Lancs. *Son of* Arthur Erlam and Ann, resided Old Colwyn 1921-1957/58. *Marriage:* to Margaret Williams of Colwyn Bay, 1937. *Educated at* Ruthin School; University College North Wales Bangor. *Career:* Land Management in Anglesey and Merioneth to 1935; Assistant Land Commissioner in Wales 1935-39; Royal Welch Fusiliers (Major) 1939-45; Regional Land Commissioner Wales 1948-52; Director Agricultural Land Service 1959-70; Director General ADAS 1973-75; Governor Royal Agriculture College 1960-75; Chairman of Trusties Thomas Philip Price Trust 1970-75; Member, Agricultural Research Council 1973-75; Member, Council Royal Welsh Agricultural Society. *Publications:* various papers on land management and rural matters. *Recreation:* gardening, golf. *Clubs:* Farmers. *Address:* Churchgate, Westerham, Kent, TN16 1AS.

DODDS, Denis George, CBE, LLB, CompIEE *Currently:* Chairman, British Approval Service for Cable. *Born on* 25 May 1913 at Newcastle-upon-tyne. *Son of* Herbert Yeaman Dodds and Violet Katherine Bewick. *Marriage:* to Muriel Reynolds Smith, 1937. *Children:* Michael, Gareth, Philippa, Jaqueline and Stephanie. *Educated at* Rutherford College, Newcastle; Kings College, Durham University. *Career:* Solicitor Gateshead Corporation 1936-41; Royal Navy, Lt.RNVR 1941-46; Deputy Town Clerk and Deputy Clerk of the Peace, Cardiff 1946-48; Secretary, South Wales Electricity Board 1948-56; Chief Industrial Relations Adviser Electricity Council 1957-60; Deputy Chairman 1960-62, Chairman 1962-77 Merseyside and North Wales Electricity Board; Chairman, Merseyside Chamber of Commerce 1976-78; Port of Preston Advisory Board 1978-80; Assoc Members of State Industry Boards 1976-85; Member: CBI Council for Wales 1960-78; NW Economic Planning Council 1971-79; National Advisory Council for Employment of Disabled People 1978-91. *Recreation:* music, gardening. *Clubs:* Commonwealth Society. *Address:* " Corners ", 28 Grange Park, Westbury-On-Trym, Bristol, BS9 4BP.

DONALD, Professor Kenneth William, OBE., DSC., MA., MD.Cantab., DSc B'ham., FRSE., FRCP., FRCPE. *Currently:* Emeritus Professor of Medicine, Edinburgh University. *Born on* 25 Nov 1911 at Harrismith O.F.S. *Son of* Col. Wm. Donald, M.C.R.A., and Julia Jane Donal. *Marriage:* to Rethe Pearl Evans, sister of the late Clifford Evans, Welsh actor, producer and writer. *Educated at* Dover Grammar School; Emmanual Coll., Cambridge (Senior Scholar), 1st Class Hons.; St. Bartholomews Hospital, London. *Career:* Resident Posts: Bath R.U.H., & Addenbrooke Hospital, Cambridge 1938-39; Flotilla Med. Off. 2nd & 5th Flotilla Destroyers 1939-41; Senior M.O., Admiralty Experimental Diving Unit 1942-45; Chief Assistant Medical Professorial Unit, St. Bartholomews Hospital 1945-47; Rockefellow Fellowship Bellevue Hospital New York 1947-48; Senior Lecturer, London Univ, Brompton Hospital 1949; Reader in Medicine, Birmingham Univ., and Cons. Physician, Queen Elizabeth Hospital 1950-59; Professor of Medicine, Edinburgh University, Senior Consultant Physician, Royal Informary 1959-76; Dean and Chairman, Medical Faculty, Ed.Univ. 1967-70; Chairman Royal Naval Personnel Ctee (Med. Res. Council) 1966-89; Chairman Under Water Physiology Ctee (R.N.P.R.C.) 1960-89; Chairman Advisory Ctee to Sec. of State for Scotland on Safety of workers in North Sea Industry 1974- ; Member Medical Ctee, Univ. Grants Ctee 1966-76; Commissioner Commonwealth Scholarship Commission 1962-77; Scientific Consultant to Royal Navy 1946- ; Chairman Physiology Ctee National Coal Board on Safety in Mines 1956-76; Secretary, Advisory Ctee on Industrial Safety, Med. Res. Council 1952-59; Physician to the Queen in Scotland 1963. *Publications:* On the heart and the lungs in health and disease, on resuscitation and drowning, on hyperbaric physiology including diving, oxygen poisoning and submarine escape. book (in press) Oxygen Poisoning in Divers. *Recreation:* fishing, theatre. *Clubs:* Rotary, Athenaeum. *Address:* Nant-y-Celyn, Cloddiau, Welshpool, Powys. SY21 9JE.

DONALDSON, Mr Alistair, OBE., B.Sc.(Eng)., CEng., Eur.Ing. *Currently:* Retired (Director of Highways and Transportation, Clwyd County Council, until January 1991). *Born on* 3 Dec 1932 at Aberdeen. *Son of* the late William Donaldson and the late Rose Ritchie (nee Hay). *Marriage:* to Isobel Middleton, 1959. *Children:* Carol, Andrew and Nigel. *Educated at* Robert Gordon's College, Aberdeen; University of Aberdeen. *Career:* Banff County Council, Asst. Engineer, 1955-57; James Leith, Jnr Ltd., Site Agent/ Engineer, 1957-58; Ross & Cromarty County Council, Assistant District Surveyor, 1958-59; Peebleshire County Council, Senior Assistant, 1959-62; Cumberland County Council, Senior Assistant Engineer, 1962-65; Cumberland County Council, Assistant County Surveyor, 1965-71; Fife County Council, County Surveyor & Engineer, 1971-75. Fellow Inst. of Chartered Secretaries & Administrators 1974; Fellow Inst. of Civil Engineers 1960; Fellow Inst. of Water & Environment Management 1974; Fellow Inst. of

Highways & Transportation 1957; Fellow British Inst. of Management 1970; Fellow Inst. of Lighting Engineers 1966; Associate Mbr. Inst of Directors 1986. *Publications:* several Reports and Articles on Highway and Traffic Engineering. *Recreation:* Rotary woodworking and stock market. *Address:* 14 Acton Gate, Wrexham, Clwyd, LL11 2PN. Tel: 0978 356596

DONNELLY, Dr. Peter Duncan, MBA; MPH; MBChB; DA; MFPHM; MHSM. *Currently:* Acting Assistant Director, Breast Test Wales; various responsibilities as Registrar, Senior Registrar and then Locum Consultant in Public Health Medicine, South Glamorgan Health Authority, since 1989. *Born on* 27 Jan 1963 at Bangor, N.Wales. *Son of* Dr.James Donnelly and Mrs Gwyneth Donnelly (nee Gittins). *Marriage:* to Joan Donnelly (nee Dymock) 1988. *Educated at* Perth Academy; Edinburgh University Medical School. *Career:* Medical Training in Edinburgh 1980-85; Clinical Medical jobs in various specialities 1985-88; NHS MDG Scholar Stirling University, graduated MBA (with distinction) 1988-89; elected Cardiff City Councillor for Heath Ward 1991- ; selected as prospective Parliamentary Candidate (Conservative) for the Pontypridd Constituency 1991- ; School Governor Birchgrove Primary 1991- . *Publications:* various, on matters of professional and political interest. *Recreation:* hillwalking, ski-ing, gardening. *Clubs:* County Conservative. *Address:* 42 St. Benedict Crescent, Heath, Cardiff, CF4 4DQ.

DOWN, Mr Graham Lindsay, MIPA; ATT; MSPI *Currently:* Insolvency Practitoner with Robson Rhodes, chartered accountants. *Born on* 28 June 1956 at Cardiff. *Son of* the late Gordon H.Down and the late Jean Down (neeTrew). *Marriage:* to Julia Alyson (nee Evans) 1981. *Children:* Alexander and Rebecca. *Educated at* Bridgend Boys Grammar School; Polytechnic of Wales *Career:* Gordon H. Down & Co., chartered accountants, 1976-90, Principal Partner, 1987-90; Mbr., Mid Glam Health Authority, 1986-90; Adopted as Conservative prospective Parliamentary candidate for Llanelli, 1990. *Recreation:* Reading, swimming and family life. *Address:* 7 Wyelands View, Mathern, Nr. Chepstow, Gwent, NP6 6HN. Tel: 0291 621 846

DOWNING, John Cottrill Ralph, DL, MA (Cantab). *Currently:* Financial Consultant, adviser on Financial PR, Corporate Communications and Investor Relations, and a non executive director of a number of companies. *Born on* 22 May 1931 at Cardiff. *Son of* the late Dr. Ralph Downing MD and the late Ruby (nee Elliot). *Marriage:* to Muriel Maureen Webb, 1959. *Children:* Caroline (married A.D.S. Liddle 1986) and Nicola. *Educated at* Felsted and Pembroke College, Cambridge. *Career:* Formerly a Stockbroker and Merchant Banker. *Recreation:* golf, watching cricket, gardening, reading. *Clubs:* Brooks's Constitutional (Windsor), Cardiff & County, MCC, Royal Porthcawl. *Address:* North Lodge, Court Colman, Pen-Y-Fai, Nr Bridgend, Mid Glam, CF31 4NG. P.O. Box 5, Bridgend, Mid Glamorgan, CF31 4YS

DRAKE, Mr Robert (Geoffrey), BA; DipEd. *Currently:* Chairman and Managing Director, Drake Group of Companies, Founder Drake Group of Companies 1971. *Born on* 6 April 1937 at Tonypandy, Rhondda. *Son of* the late Robert Ronald and the late Alice (nee Simcox). *Marriage:* to Marion Elaine, 1959. *Children:* Heather,

Alison and Jonathan. *Educated at* Tonypandy Grammar School; UCW Swansea (BA,DipEd). *Career:* Parl. Candidate for Labour 1966 General Election for Walsall South Constituency; Member: SDP National Committee 1987-89, CBI and CBI Smaller Firms Council; Chairman SDP Council for Wales 1987-90, Parliamentary Candidate SDP Alliance Cardiff West 1987; Former Executive Member British Educational Equipment Association; Vice President Welsh Centre for International Affairs. *Publications:* Educational materials. *Recreation:* tennis, writing. *Clubs:* Commonwealth Trust. *Address:* 4 Llwyn Drysgol, Radyr, Cardiff, CF4 8DN. 89 St.Fagans Road, Fairwater, Cardiff, CF5 3AE

DRAY, Mr Mike, *Currently:* County Emergency Planning Officer for Powys. Address: County Hall, Llandrindod Wells, Powys LD1 51G.

DRENNAN, Mr Ronald Francis Peter. *Currently:* retired local government officer 1982. *Born on* 25 July 1932 at Liverpool. *Son of* Harold Sinclair and Ana Mary Drennan. *Educated at* Universities of Oxford and Liverpool and Leicester Polytechnic. *Career:* served in Royal Air Force 1950-53; Assistant Governor in H.M.Prison Service 1966-68; Full-time official of Labour Party; Professional social worker in various local authorities; principal training officer with Cheshire County Council Social Services Department; member Clwyd Health Authority 1975-90; elected member Clwyd County Council 1980; elected member Alyn & Deeside District Council 1983; Vice-Chairman, Chester Blind Welfare Society; Chairman, Clwyd Drugs Advisory service; Chairman, North Wales School of Radiography training committee. *Recreation:* Labour Party politics, reading. *Address:* 81 Victoria Road, Saltney, Chester, CH4 8SY.

DRISCOLL, Mr James, FREconS., FRSA. *Currently:* Chairman, Lifecare NHS Trust; Senior Partner, Woodcote Consultancy Services; Policy Adviser to Nationalised Industries' Chairmen's Group; member, Investigation Committee, Institute of Chartered Accountants of E & W; *Born on* 24 April 1925 at Cardiff. *Son of* Henry James Driscoll and Honorah Driscoll. *Marriage:* to Jeanne Lawrence Williams 1955. *Children:* Fiona Elizabeth and Jonathan James Lawrence. *Educated at* Coleg Saint Illtyd, Cardiff; Univ. Coll. of Wales, Cardiff. *Career:* Assistant Lecturer, Univ. Coll., Cardiff, 1951-53; British Iron & Steel Fed., 1953-67, Latterly as Economic Director; Btsh Steel Corp 1967-80 (MD Corp. Strategy, then Policy Adviser to the Board; Nat. Industries' Chairmen's Group 1980-90, Director; Parliamentary Candidate, (Cons) Rhondda West, 1950; Chrmn, Welsh Young Cons. 1949; Nat. Vice Chairman, Young Cons. 1950; Deputy Chrmn, Nat. Union of Students, 1951-53; Mbr CBI Council since 1970; Observer Mbr, Nat. Economic Dev. Council since 1975; Chrmn, Economic Commt, Int. Iron & Steel Inst., 1972-74; Fellow of Univ. of Wales Coll., of Cardiff; Mbr. Court of Governors, Univ. Coll., Cardiff 1970-88; Mbr. Court of Governors, Univ. of Wales Coll., of Cardiff 1990- . *Recreation:* Travel, reading and bridge. *Address:* Foxley Hatch, Birch Lane, Purley, Surrey, CR8 3LH.

DUCKER, Elizabeth Alice, A.L.A. *Currently:* County Librarian, Powys County Library, 1983- . *Born on* 20 May 1934 at London. *Daughter of* Francis, Leonard Ducker and Pedrazinni, Ida EP *Educated at* Stroud High School for

Girls. *Career:* Deputy County Librarian, Mongomeryshire, 1969-74; Deputy County Librarian, Powys, 1974-83. *Recreation:* reading, walking, gardening. *Address:* Bwlch Yr Adwy Wynt, Llanafan Fawr, Builth Wells, Powys, LD2 3PE.

DUERDEN, Professor Brian Ion, BSc, MD, FRCPath. *Currently:* Professor of Medical Microbiology, University of Wales College of Medicine since 1991; Director Public Health Laboratory Cardiff; Manager, Microbiology Services of South Glamorgan Health Authority. *Born on* 21 June 1948 at Nelson, Lancs. *Son of* the late Cyril Duerden and Mildred (nee Ion). *Marriage:* to Marjorie Hudson, 1972. *Educated at* Nelson Grammar School, Nelson, Lancs; University of Edinburgh Medical School. *Career:* House Surgeon and Physician, Thoracic Surgery & Infectious Diseases Units, City Hospital, Edinburgh 1972-73; Lecturer, Department of Bacteriology, University of Edinburgh Medical School 1972-76; Lecturer and Hon Sen. Registrar, Department of Medical Microbiology, University of Sheffield Medical School 1976-79; Sen.Lecturer, Department of Medical Microbiol, Sheffield and Hon Consultant, Children's Hospital, Sheffield 1979-83; Professor of Medical Microbiology and Hon Consultant (Children's Hospital), Sheffield 1983-90. *Publications:* Research papers and reports on: Anaerobic microbiology and anaerobic infections; use of antibiotics, especially in immunocompromised patients and children; genito-urinary infections. (with T.M.S.Reid, J.M.Jewsbury and D.C.Turk) A new short textbook of microbial and parasitic infection, 1987. Topley and Wilson's Principles of Becteriology, Virology and Immunity, 8th edition, 1990; volume editor, vol 2, author: ''The Bacteriodaceae: Bacteroides, Fusobacterium and Leptotrichia'', Chapter 29, vol 2 and ''Infections due to gram-negative non-sporing anaerobic bacilli'', Chapter 15, vol 3. (with B.S.Drasar) (eds). Anaerobes in Human Disease, 1991; Author/co-author of chapters on: Introduction to anaerobes; Anaerobes in the normal flora; Genitourinary infections; Superficial necrotizing infections; Antibacterial therapy. *Recreation:* cricket, travel, photography, music. *Address:* Pendle, Welsh Street, Crossway Green, Chepstow, Gwent, NP6 5LU.

DUNFORD, Cynthia Mary, Justice of The Peace. *Born on* 8 March 1929 at Cardiff. *Daughter of* Leonard Douglas Rumbelow and Phyllis Mary (nee Perkins). *Marriage:* to Daniel Francis Dunford, 1957. *Children:* Celia Mary and Jonathan Paul Francis. *Educated at* University College Cardiff (University of Wales). *Career:* Deputy Centre Organiser Cwmbran W.R.V.S. 1958-63; Chairman Cwmbran N.S.P.C.C. 1958-63; Member and subsequent Chairman, Cwmbran Family Planning Association 1960-71; Founder President, Soroptimist International of Cwmbran and district 1980; appointed: Justice of The Peace 1967; Chairman Cwmbran Juvenille Panel 1983-90; Chairman Cwmbran Magistrates 1988-90; Member Gwent Magistrates' Court Committee 1987-90; Member Gwent County Probation Committee 1987- ; Deputy Chairman East Gwent Magistrates 1990- ; Chairman East Gwent Juvenille Panel 1990- . *Recreation:* social history, theatre, opera, food. *Address:* Stow House, Isca Road, Caerleon, Gwent, NP6 1QG.

DUNFORD, Daniel Francis, OBE *Currently:* District Judge. *Born on* 22 Sept 1926 at Newbridge. *Son of* Frank Hoskins

Dunford and Winifred Mary (nee West). *Marriage:* to Cynthia Mary Rumbelow of Cardiff, 1957. *Children:* Celia Mary and Jonathan Paul Francis *Career:* Admitted a Solicitor 1951; Partner in Granville-West, Chivers and Dunford Solicitors, Pontypool and Newbridge 1951-62; Honorary Solicitor to the Monmouthshire Baptist Association 1956-62; Appointed a District Registrar of the High Court and a Registrar of County Courts, later re-styled District Judge 1962- ; National President, The Association of District Judges 1986-87; Sometime member of the Supreme Court Procedure Committee; Member of Cwmbran Urban District Council 1960-62; Board Member Cwmbran New Town Development Corporation 1966-69; Founder Member Gwent Marriage Guidance Council 1969; Founder Vice President of The Rotary Club of Cwmbran 1961; Member of Newport and East Monmouthshire Hospitals Management Committee 1969-74; Chairman, Newport and East Monmouthshire Hospitals Mental Health Committee 1970-74; Assistant County Commissioner for Scouts for Gwent 1967-70; Deputy Chief Commissioner of Wales, The Scout Association 1975-81; Chief Commissioner of Wales, The Scout Association 1981-89; Life Vice President, The Welsh Scout Council 1989-; Vice-President, Gwent County Scout Council 1990- . *Recreation:* history, religions, wildlife. *Address:* Stow House, Isca Road, Caerleon, Gwent, NP6 1QG.

DUNLEAVY, Mr Philip, C.B.E., J.P. *Currently:* Retired. *Born on* 5 Oct 1915 at Cardiff. *Children:* Ann, Michael, Paul and Jane *Educated at* St. Cuthberts School, Butetown, Cardiff. *Career:* Executive Officer, Post office. *Recreation:* Local History; Hafod Housing Assoc; CAB and Butetown Railway Soc. *Address:* 35 Merches Gardens, Grangetown, Cardiff. CF1 7RF.

DUTHIE, Professor Sir Herbert Livingston, MD HonLLD FRCS FRCSEd *Currently:* Provost of the University of Wales College of Medicine 1979- . *Born on* 9 Oct 1929 at Glasgow. *Son of* Herbert William Duthie and Margaret Mcfarlane Livingston. *Children:* 3 sons & 1 daughter *Educated at* Whitehall School, Glasgow; University of Glasgow *Career:* Registrar & Lecturer in Surgery, Western Infirmary Glasgow 1956-59; Rockefeller Travelling Fellow, Mayo Clinic, Rochester Minn. USA 1959-60; Lecturer in Surgery, University of Glasgow 1960-61; Senior Lecturer University of Leeds 1961-63; Reader, Department of Surgery 1964; Professor of Surgery, University of Sheffield 1964-79. *Publications:* Author and papers on Gastroenterological Subjects. *Clubs:* Army and Navy Club *Address:* University Of Wales College Of Medicine, Heath Park, Cardiff, CF4 4XN. 'St Curig', 29 Windsor Road, Radyr, Cardiff, CF4 8BQ

DUTTON, Dr. Peter Leslie, FRS *Currently:* Director, Johnson Research Foundation for Molecular Biophysics. *Born on* 12 March 1941 at Ashton-U-Lyne, Lancs. *Son of* Arthur Bramwell and Mary. *Marriage:* to Julia R (nee Dwyer) 1965. *Children:* Michael James, Sara Catherine and Simon Nicholas. *Educated at* University of Wales BSc 1963, PhD 1967. *Career:* Post Doctoral Fellow, Univ. of Wales 1967; Post Doctoral Fellow Univ. of Pennsylvania 1968; Asst. Prof. Univ. of Pennsylvania 1976; Prof. Univ. of Pennsylvania 1981; *Honours:* U.S. Nat. Inst. of Health Research Career Dev. Award 1974; Hon. MA,Univ of Pennsylvania 1976; US Nat.Inst. of Health MERIT Award 1989; Fellow of Royal Soc., 1990; Eldridge Reeves Johnson

Professor 1991. Advisory Board, Reg. Laser & Biotechnology Labs. Univ. of Pennsylvania; *Consultancies:* Bell Research Labs. 1975-78; Xerox Research of Canada 1981-86; DIFCO 1988- ; E.I. Dupont De Nemours 1988- ; Enzymatics Inc. 1989- ; *Editorial Positions:* Archives of Biochemistry 1976-79; FEBS Letters 1981-89; Managing Ed. Bioenergetics Reviews Section 1981- ; Man. Ed. Biochimica et Biophysica Acta 1989- . NIH Advisory Ctee 1986-90, 1990-94; *Research Funding:* NSF, NIH, DOE. *Research interests:* Photosynthesis and respiration. Mechanisms of biological electron and proton transfer, charge separation and enery coupling. *Recreation:* Painting, sailing. *Clubs:* Mantoloking Yacht Club; Corinthian Y.C. (Philadelphia) *Address:* 654 West Rose Tree Road Media, PA 19063, U.S.A.

DYKES, Dr David Wilmer, C.St.J., M.A., Ph.D., F.S.A., F.R.Hist.S. *Currently:* Voluntary - Chancellor, Priory for Wales, Order of St. John of Jerusalem 1991- . Hon. Lecturer in History, Univ. Coll., Cardiff, later Univ. of Wales Coll. of Cardiff, 1975- . *Born on* 18 Dec 1933 at Swansea. *Son of* the late Captain David Dykes, OBE., and Jenny Myfanwy Dykes. *Marriage:* to Margaret Anne George 1967. *Children:* Elizabeth Anne and Rosemary Louise. *Educated at* Swansea Grammar School; Corpus Christi College. *Career:* Commissioned Service, Royal Navy 1955-58; Civil Servant, Board of Inland Revenue 1958-59; Administrative appointments, University of Bristol and Univ. Coll. of Swansea 1959-63; Dep. Registrar, Univ. Coll of Swansea 1963-69; Registrar, Univ. of Warwick 1969-72; Secretary, Nat. Museum of Wales 1972-86; Acting Director 1985-86; Director 1986-89; Awarded Parkes-Weber Prize of the Royal Numismatic Society 1954; Elected F.R.S.A. 1990; Liveryman, Worshipful Co. of Tin Plate Workers 1985; Freeman of the City of London 1985. *Publications:* Anglo-Saxon Coins in the National Museum of Wales, 1977; Alan Sorrell: Early Wales Recreated (edit & contrib) 1980; Wales in Vanity Fair 1989; articles and reviews in numismatic, historical and other journals. *Recreation:* Writing, numismatics, gardening. *Clubs:* Athenaeum; Cardiff and County (Cardiff); Bristol Channel Yacht (Swansea). *Address:* Cherry Grove, Welsh St. Donats, near Cowbridge, S. Glam. CF7 7SS.

E

EABORN, Prof. Colin, PhD, DSc(Wales), Hon.DSc (Sussex), FRS. *Currently:* Regional Editor, Journal of Organometallic Chemistry; Emeritus Professor, Univ. of Sussex. *Born on* 15 March 1923 at Churton, Cheshire. *Son of* the late Tom Stanley Eaborn and the late Caroline (nee Cooper). *Marriage:* to Joyce Thomas, Newcastle Emlyn, 1949. *Educated at* Holt Endowed School, Clwyd; Ruabon Grammar School; Univ College of N.Wales, Bangor. *Career:* Asst. Lecturer, 1947; Lecturer 1950; Reader 1954-62, in Chemistry, Univ. of Leicester; Prof. of Chemistry, Univ of Sussex 1962-88; Dean of School of Molecular Sciences 1964-68, 1978-79; Pro-Vice Chancellor (Science) 1968-73; Research Associate (Rotary Foundation Fellow), Univ of California at Los Angeles 1950-51; Robert A.Welch Visiting Scholar, Rice Univ, Texas 1961-62; Erskine Fellow, Univ of Canterbury (NZ) 1965; Distinguished Prof. New Mexico State Univ 1973; Canadian Commonwealth Fellow and Visiting Prof., Univ of Victoria (BC) 1976; Riccoboni Memorial Lecturer, Univ of Padua 1977; Gilman Memorial Lecturer, Iowa State Univ 1978; Hon-Sec Chemical Society 1964-71; Vice President, Dalton Division 1971-75; member: Italy/UK Mixed Cultural Commission 1972-78; Chairman, Brit.Committee on Chemical Education 1967-69; F.S.Kipping Award for Organosilicon Chemistry (American Chemical Society) 1964; Ingold Medal (Royal Society of Chemistry) 1976; Organometallic Chemistry Award (Royal Society of Chemistry) 1975; Main Group Chemistry Award (Royal Society of Chemistry) 1988; Elected FRS 1970; Hon DSc., Univ of Sussex 1990. *Publications:* 'Organosilicon Compounds', 1960; approx 460 research papers, mainly in Journal of the Chemical Society or Journal of Orgametallic Chemistry. *Recreation:* Alpine walking. *Address:* School Of Chemistry And Molecular Sciences, University Of Sussex, Brighton BN1 9QJ.

EAGERS, Mr Derek, *Currently:* retired, Under Secretary, Department of Trade & Industry, 1984. *Born on* 13 Sept 1924 at Sheffield. *Son of* the late Horace and the late Florence (nee Green). *Marriage:* to Hazel Maureen Henson. *Children:* Nigel and Mark. *Educated at* King Edward VIII School, Sheffield; Brasenose College, Oxford. *Career:* RNVR 1943-47; joined Civil Service (Ministry of Fuel and Power) as Assistant Principal, 1949. *Recreation:* cricket, gardening, railway history. *Address:* Bryniau Golau, Llangower, Bala, Gwynedd. LL23 7BT.

EATON, Philip Bromley, B.Arch, RIBA. *Currently:* Consultant, Eaton Manning Wilson. *Born on* 3 June 1925 at Malpas, Cheshire. *Son of* Percy Eaton of N.Wales and Ethel Mary Eaton, BA, (nee Swindell). *Marriage:* to Joan, 1953, da of William Frederick Welch, MBE. *Children:* Mark (b.1956). *Educated at* Sir John Talbot's School, Whitchurch; Liverpool University School of Architecture.

Career: Capt. K.S.L.I., served Egypt, Palestine, Cyprus. Founder Architectural Practice Eaton Manning Wilson, Shrewsbury, Welshpool and Newcastle-under-Lyne 1961. Chm. Shropshire Soc. of Architects 1986-88; Chm. Ludlow, Constituency Lib. Party 1982-87, Pres. 1987- . *Recreation:* travel, gardening, music. *Address:* Scotsmansfield, Burway, Church Stretton, Shropshire SY6 6DP. 31 Severn Street, Welshpool, Powys.

EBDON, Howard Tom, DSc, AALPA(Agric), RTD. *Currently:* retired. *Born on* 1st June 1919 at Newport. *Son of* the late Tom Ebdon, Dorset and the late Ellen (nee Tidball), Somerset.). *Marriage:* to Grace, 1961, dau of William Thomas Bond, (d. 1951). *Educated at* College of Estate Management in Agricultural Estate Management. *Career:* Ministry of Agriculture; Lecturer in Valuations and the Law of Dilapidations. Member Art Collection Fund; Assoc of Croquet Assoc of London, sidesman St Woolos Cathedral, Newport, Gwent, Friend of RA. *Recreation:* arts, music, reading. *Clubs:* Royal Overseas, St.James's London. *Address:* Harlyn, 56 Bryngwyn Road, Newport, Gwent, NP9 4JT.

EDMUND, Mr John Humphrey, MA (Oxon). *Currently:* Senior partner, Beor, Wilson & Lloyd, Solicitors, Swansea, since 1963. *Born on* 6 March 1935 at Swansea. *Son of* Charles Henry Humphrey Edmund and Vera May Edmund (nee Warmington). *Marriage:* to (Elizabeth Ann) Myfanwy (nee Williams), 1965. *Educated at* Swansea Grammar School; Jesus College Oxford. *Career:* admitted Solicitor 1961; Undersheriff of West Glamorgan 1983- ; Clerk to General Commissioners of Taxes (Swansea Division) 1986- *Clubs:* Vincents (Oxford), Bristol Channel Yacht (Swansea). *Address:* 84 Pennard Road, Pennard, Swansea SA3 2AA. Calvert House, Calvert Terrace, Swansea SA1 6AP.

EDWARDS, Professor Anthony Davies, MA, MPhil, PhD. *Currently:* Professor of Education and Dean of the Faculty of Education, University of Newcastle upon Tyne, since 1979. *Born on* 4 June 1936 at Swansea. *Son of* Gwilym Morgan Edwards and Beryl Eileen (nee Davies). *Marriage:* to Ann Hopkins Griffiths, 1960. *Children:* Kathryn Jane (b.1964), Ceri David (b.1966) and Megan Ruth (b.1967). *Educated at* Swansea Grammar School; Corpus Christi College, Cambridge. *Career:* School teaching 1957-58, 1959-66; Lecturer in Education, Exeter University 1966-71; Lecturer/Senior Lecturer in Education, Manchester University 1971-79. Chairman, Universities Council for the Education of Teachers 1991- ; Education Adviser, Universities Funding Council 1988- ; Curriculum Review Committee, National Curriculum Council 1988-91. Human Behavious and Development Group, Economic and Social Research Council 1986-90. *Publications:* Language in Culture and Class, 1976; The Language of Teaching (with

J.Furlong), 1979; Analysing Classroom Talk (with D.Westgate), 1987; The State and Private Education (with J.Fitz and G.Whitty), 1990. *Recreation:* cinema, opera, photography, hill walking. *Address:* 2 Hollin Hill Terrace, Riding Mill, Northumberland NE44 6HR.

EDWARDS, Mr David Graham, HND *Currently:* Principal, Marketing and Public Relations Agency. *Born at* Shrewsbury. *Son of* John Arthur and Enid Anne (nee Fernyhough). *Educated at* Harper Adams Agricultural College, Shropshire. *Career:* Consultant with Shrewsbury based PR Agency, Agrafax; prospective Conservative Parliamentary candidate for Ogmore; Conservative Group Leader on Montgomeryshire District Council; member of Planning and Recreation Committees; Chairman of Housing Letting Panel, Newtown Area; member of Newtown Town Council. *Recreation:* fly fishing, biographies, history, after dinner speaking. *Address:* Nevaddfraith Hall, Newtown, Powys SY16 3AW. Tel: 0686 630253.

EDWARDS, Professor Gwynne, BA, PhD. *Currently:* Professor of Spanish, University College of Wales, Aberystwyth. *Born on* 14 April 1937 at Tonypandy, Rhondda. *Son of* the late William Edwards and the late Rachel Mary Edwards. *Marriage:* to Gillian Marilyn Davies, 1964. *Children:* Eleri Wynne and Gareth Wynne. *Educated at* Porth County Grammar School; University College Cardiff; King's College London. *Career:* Lecturer, University of Liverpool 1962-67; Lecturer, Senior Lecturer, Reader, Professor, University College of Wales, Aberystwyth 1967-. Theatre Translator: Professional Productions include: Lorca's Blood Wedding, at Contact Theatre, Manchester; Lorca's Dona Rosita, at Bristol Old Vic; Lorca's When Five Years Pass, at The Edinburgh Festival; Calderon's Three Judgements in One, at the Gate Theatre, London. *Publications:* many articles and books on Spanish Theatre of the Seventeenth and Twentieth Centuries and Spanish Cinema including: Lorca: The Theatre Beneath The Sand, 1980; The Discreet Art of Luis Bunuel, 1982; Dramatists in Perspective: Spanish Theatre in The Twentieth Century, 1985. Translations include: Lorca Plays: One, 1987; Lorca Plays: Two, 1989; Calderon Plays: One, 1991. *Recreation:* theatre, cinema, music, sport. *Address:* 66 Maeshendre, Waun Fawr, Aberystwyth, Dyfed. Dept of European Languages, University College Of Wales, Aberystwyth, Dyfed.

EDWARDS, Dr Huw, MB, BS, DPM, FRCPsych, JP. *Currently:* Consultant Psychiatrist, St.David's Hospital, W.Wales General Hospital Carmarthen and Bronglais General Hospital Aberystwyth. *Born on* 22 Dec 1938 at Carmarthen. *Son of* Evan Dewi and Doris Edwards. *Marriage:* to Brenda, 1963. *Children:* Siwan Angharad, Catrin Sioned and Manon Heledd. *Educated at* Queen Elizabeth Grammar School, Carmarthen; Medical College of St. Bartholomew's Hospital London. *Career:* formerly Registrar, Whitchurch Hospital Cardiff and Senior Registrar, Dept of Psychological Medicine, Welsh National School of Medicine Cardiff. Chairman 'Y Gymdeithas Feddygol' (Welsh Medical Society), 1988-91. *Publications:* Wynebu Bywyd (essays on Psychiatric topics); Gwasg Gee, 1979; Y Pryfyn Yn Yr Afal (essays on Psychiatric topics and medical history), Gwasg Gee, 1981. *Recreation:* Collecting old books, medical history, archaeology, natural history. *Address:* Garth Martin, Ffordd Henfwlch, Caerfyrddin,

Dyfed, SA33 5EG. St.David's Hospital, Carmarthen, Dyfed SA31 3HB.

EDWARDS, Mr Ifan Prys, DipArch (Wales), RIBA. *Currently:* Chairman, Wales Tourist Board, since 1984. *Born on* 11 Feb 1942 at Aberystwyth. *Son of* Sir Ifan Ab Owen and Lady Edwards. *Marriage:* to Catherine Edwards. *Children:* Lisa Mair Edwards and Sion ab Ifan Edwards. *Educated at* Yr Ysgol Gymraeg, Lluest, Aberystwyth; Abermad Preparatory School, Nr Aberystwyth; Leighton Park School, Reading; The Welsh School of Architecture, Cardiff. *Career:* Member of Staff: E.Francis-Jones (Architect) Aberystwyth; Partner: E.Francis-Jones, Prys Edwards and Associates (Architects), Aberystwyth; Director, Aberystwyth Sports Centre; Partner, Prys Edwards Architects Unit, Aberystwyth; Senior Partner, Prys Edwards Partnership (Architects), Aberystwyth 1976-89; Director, Prys Edwards Consultancy. Development Board for Rural Wales, Newtown, Board Member, 1977-85; Chairman of Development Committee D.B.R.W. 1981-August 1984; Wales and the Marches Postal Board 1982-83; Member British Tourist Authority 1984- ; Urdd Gobaith Cymru (Welsh League of Youth): National President (9 years), Honorary Secretary (5 years), Treasurer (6 years), Director Cwmni'r Brig.Chairman (6 years). National Eisteddfod of Wales: Member of Eisteddfod Court, Past Member Eisteddfod Council, Past Member of Arts & Crafts Panel, Hon. Member of the Gorsedd of Bards. Past Chairman and Founder of the Welsh Society, UWIST, Cardiff; Former Member of EEC U.K. Committee on Lesser Used Languages; Member of Secretary of State for Wales' Working Party on the Welsh Language; Vice-President Cardiff Business Club; Vice-President Llangollen International Musical Eisteddfod. Chairman, Radio Ceredigion. *Recreation:* golf, sailing (participating), rugby and most sports (spectator). *Address:* Bryn Aberoedd, Caemelyn, Aberystwyth, Dyfed SY23 2HA.

EDWARDS, Dr Iorweth Eiddon Stephen, CMG 1973; CBE 1968; MA, LittD; FBA 1962; *Born on* 21 Jul 1909. *Son of* the late Edward Edwards, Orientalist and Ellen Jane (nee Higgs). *Marriage:* Elizabeth 1938 daughter of the late Charles Edwards Lisle. *Children:* one daughter and one son (decd) *Educated at* Merchant Taylors'; Gonville and Caius College, Cambridge (Major Scholar); Merchant Taylors' School Exhibitioner and John Stewart of Rannoch Univ. Scholar, 1st Class Oriental Languages Tripos (Arabic and Hebrew), Parts I and II, 1930-31: Mason Prize (Hebrew), Tyrwhitt Scholarship (Hebrew and Syriac), Wright Studentship (Arabic), 1932, Cambridge. *Career:* Entered Dept. of Egyptian and Assyrian Antiquities, British Museum 1934, Keeper of Egyptian Antiquities, 1955-74; retired 1974. Seconded to British Embassies, Cairo and Bagdad and to Secretariat, Jerusalem 1942-45; T.E. Peet Prize, Liverpool Univ, 1947; Visiting Professor Brown Univ. Providence, RI, USA, 1953-54; Glanville Meml. Lecturer, Cambridge Univ. 1980; Foreign Guest Lecturer College de France, 1982; Pioneered and chose objects for Tutankhamun Exhibition, London, 1972; Member Unesco-Egyptian Ministry of Culture Archaeological Cttees. for Saving Monuments of Philae, 1973-80, for Planning National Museum, Cairo, 1982; Member of Egyptian Ministry of Culture Cttees. for reorganizing Egyptian Museum, Cairo, 1985, for protection of monuments of Giza, 1990; Vice-

President Egypt Exploration Society, 1962-88; Member Austrian Archaeological Institute; Mem. of German Archaeol. Inst; Assoc. Mem.Inst. of Egypt; Mem. Cttee of Visitors to Metropolitan Museum of Art, NY; Corres. Mem. Fondation Egyptologique Reine Elisabeth; Foreign Corrs. Mem. Academie des Inscriptions et Belles-Lettres. *Publications:* Hieroglyphic Texts in the British Museum, Vol. VIII, 1939; The Pyramids of Egypt, 1947, (4th edn. 1991, amny translations); Hieratic Papyri in the British Museum, 4th Series (Oracular Amuletic Decrees of the Late New Kingdom), 1960; The Early Dynastic Period in Egypt, 1964; Joint Editor of the Cambridge Ancient History (3rd edn), vols. I-III, 1970-91; Treasures of Tutankhamun (Catalogue of London exhibn), 1972; Treasures of Tutankhamun (Catalogue of US exhibn.), 1976; Tutankhamun's Jewelry, 1976; Tutankhamun: his tomb and its treasures, 1976; Articles in Journal of Egyptian Archaeology and other scientific periodicals *Recreation:* Watching cricket and gardening *Clubs:* Athenaeum *Address:* Dragon House, The Bullring, Deddington, Oxon.OX15 0TT.

EDWARDS, Sir John (Clive) Leighton, BT *Currently:* retired. *Born on* 11 Oct 1916 at Sketty. *Son of* Sir John Bryn Edwards and Lady Kathleen Edwards. *Educated at* Horris Hill, Winchester College, various Cramers and The Army. *Career:* joined Army 1940 as driver RASC. Demobilised as Captain RPC (Royal Pioneer Corp). Light engineering on own account. *Recreation:* gardening, motoring, reading, cyling. *Clubs:* Bugatti Owners, Midland A.C. (Hon Life member), Brooklands Society, Brooklands Museum. *Address:* Milnstown, Ramsey, Isle Of Man.

EDWARDS, John Daniel, FNCP, FCIM. *Currently:* Psychologist - self-employed private practice, since 1973. *Born on* 23 June 1922 at London. *Son of* the late David Daniel Edwards and the late Margaret (nee Jenkins). *Marriage:* to Patricia Margaret Gibson, 1969. *Educated at* Central School London; St.Martins School of Art; The Architectural Association. *Career:* R.A.F.V.R. 1941-46; Assistant Publicity Manager, Crittall Mfg Co.Ltd., 1947-61; Marketing Services Manager, Ingersoll-Rand Co.Ltd., 1962-72. Member Executive Committee London Welsh Association; Freeman City of London 1976; Liveryman Worshipful Company of Marketors 1977; F.InstM 1972, FNCP 1983, FCIM 1989. *Recreation:* travel, photography, motoring, flying, swimming, walking. *Address:* Ridgedale, Allison Gardens, Purley On Thames, Pangbourne, RG8 8DF. Tel: 0734 422955.

EDWARDS, Rear Admiral John Phillip, CB., LVO., MA., C.Eng., FI.Mech.E., FBIM. *Currently:* Fellow and Bursar of Wadham College, Oxford, 1983-. *Born on* 13 Feb 1927 at Ruthin, Clwyd. *Son of* Robert Edwards and Dilys (nee Phillips). *Marriage:* to Gwen (nee Bonner), 1951. *Children:* Susan, Lynn and Sian. *Educated at* Ysgol Brynhyfryd, Ruthin; HMS Conway; RN Engineering College, Plymouth. *Career:* Served Royal Navy 1944-83; Served in HM ships, King George V, Vengeance, Mauritius, Torquay, Lion, Diamond, Defender and HMY Britannia; Appointments ashore, both in UK and Canada chiefly concerned with ship building and repair, and also personnel management and training; Senior appointments included Deputy Director RN Staff College, Asst. Director Enginering, Captain of HM Naval Base Portland, and as Rear Admiral,

Director General Fleet Support Policy and Services: Mbr. of Health Policy Board for Wales 1985-90; President, Midland Naval Officers' Assoc. 1965- ; Vice- President, SSAFA (Oxon): *Publications:* Various papers to Institutions on logistic matters in the RN; The Soviet Merchant Fleet 1977. *Recreation:* Golf, Naval and Maritime affairs; Welsh affairs. *Clubs:* Frilford Heath *Address:* Wadham College, Parks Road, Oxford, OX1 3PN.

EDWARDS, Keith Harrap, *Currently:* Consultant, Edwards Geldard Solicitors, Cardiff. *Born on* 17 Oct 1940 at Cardiff. *Son of* the late Sir Martin Edwards and the late Lady Edwards (nee Harrap). *Marriage:* to Susan Eleanore Walker, 1964. *Children:* Juliet, Elizabeth and Caroline *Career:* joined C & M Edwards Shepherd & Co 1961; partner 1969; parter Edwards, Geldard and Shepherd (later changed to Edwards Geldard) 1971-91: Administration Partner 1972, Managing Partner 1983, Senior Partner 1985 *Recreation:* industrial archaeology, walking, local history. *Clubs:* Cardiff Athletic, Glamorgan Wanderers RFC, Cardiff & County *Address:* Ivydene, Aberthin, Cowbridge, S.Glam, CF7 7HB.

EDWARDS, Mrs Noreen Louisa, CBE, TD, JP, DL, SRN, SCM. *Currently:* Chairman, Gwynedd Health Authority. *Born on* 20 March 1926 at Pentir, Nr. Bangor. *Daughter of* the late Reverend Daniel Thomas and the late Margaret (nee Newton). *Marriage:* to David Geoffrey Edward, MBE., LL.B. 1973. *Educated at* Gloddaeth Hall College, Llandudno; Qualified at Queen Elizabeth Hospital, Birmingham; Queen Charlotte's Maternity Hospital, London; St. David's Hospital, Bangor. *Career:* Matron, Colwyn Bay & West Denbighshire Hospital and Abergele Hospital, North Wales, 1962-73. First Chairman of the Welsh Board of the Royal College of Nursing, established in 1962: held office until 1969. Mbr of Council of the Royal College of Nursing of the U.K. 1957-73; Chairman of U.K. Council 1969-71; Deputy President 1971-73. OBE 1970. CBE 1988. Territorial Decoration 1970. First lady Deputy Lieutenant of County of Clwyd 1980. High Sheriff, County of Clwyd 1985-86. Mbr of Queen Alexandra's Royal Army Nursing Corps, retired with rank of Lieutenant-Colonel. JP County of Clwyd 1977- . Past President (twice) Colwyn Bay & District Soroptomist Club. Past Chairman Management Cttee of Cheshire Home, Colwyn Bay. Past President North Wales Centre, National Trust. Governor Rydal School, Colwyn Bay since 1974; Vice-Chairman Governing Body 1986- . Nurse Mbr Gwynedd Health Authority 1973-79; Deputy Chairman 1979-82; Chairman 1982- . Member of Government Cttee of Inquiry into Human Fertilisation and Embryology (Warnock Cttee) 1982-84. Mbr of Council for Professions Supplementary to Medicine (appt by Privy Council) 1984- Chairman of Welsh Office Cttee appointed to conduct a Review of Community Nursing in Wales and to report (The Edwards Report 1987). Member of Council of University of Wales College of Medicine 1990- . University of Wales founded the "Noreen Edwards Chair in Health Care Studies", 1991. *Recreation:* Gardening. *Address:* Pine Trees, Llanrwst Road, Upper Colwyn Bay, Clwyd, LL28 5YS. Gwynedd Health Authority, Coed Mawr, Bangor, Gwynedd

EDWARDS, Professor Richard Humphrey Tudor, BSc; MB; BS; PhD; FRCP. *Currently:* Professor of Medicine, Head of Department of Medicine, University of Liverpool. *Born on* 28 Jan 1939. *Son of* Hywel Iswyn Edwards and

Menna Tudor Edwards (nee Davies). *Marriage:* to Eleri Wyn Edwards (nee Roberts). *Children:* Rhiannon Tudor Edwards and Tomos Tudor Edwards (d.1982). *Educated at* Llangollen Grammar School. *Career:* Medical Education at Middlesex Hospital, Medical School, London; Resident appointments at the Middlesex, National Heart and Hammersmith Hospitals, London; Wellcome Swedish Research Fellow at Karolinska Institute, Stockholm, Sweden; Wellcome Senior Clinical Research Fellow; sometime visiting Professor at McGill University, Montreal and Northwestern University, Chicago; Co-director of the Jerry Lewis Muscle Research Centre at the Royal Postgraduate Medical School, Honorary Consultant Respiratory Physician at the Hammersmith Hospital and subsequently Professor of Human Metabolism at University College Hospital Medical School and Head of the Department of Medicine, University College, London; past President of the European Society of Clinical Investigation; Awarded the Robert Bing Prize of the Swiss Academy of Medical Sciences for development of new techniques for analyzing human muscle weakness and fatigue; Honorary Consultant Physician to the Royal Liverpool University Hospital and also to the Robert Jones and Agnes Hunt Orthopaedic Hospital, Oswestry; Currently chairs the Faculty of Medicine Curriculum Strategy Cttee concerned with improving educational standards in medical education; He is currently engaged in scientific and operational research projects aimed at improving patient care. *Publications:* Clinical Exercise Test, 1975; Muscle Weakness & Fatigue, 1980; sci. papers on human muscle in health and disease in Journal of Physiology, Clinical Sci., Clinical Physiol., Muscle and Nerve, etc. *Recreation:* planting trees, dry stone walling, mountain walking, Welsh Literature, music. *Address:* 85B South Parade, West Kirby, Wirral L48 ORR.

EDWARDS, Mr Richard Ieuan, BA., ALA., MBIM., FRSA. *Currently:* Director, Libraries and Arts, South Glamorgan County Council, 1982- . *Born on* 28 Feb 1945 at Pontrhydygroes. *Son of* Thomas Caradog and Margaret Edwards (nee Evans). *Marriage:* to Hilary (nee Thomas). *Children:* Gareth and Geraint Ifor. *Educated at* Tregaron County School; Welsh Library College. *Career:* Cardiganshire Joint Library 1963-69; Area Librarian, Hertfordshire County Council 1969-77; Senior Assistant County Librarian, South Glamorgan 1977-82. *Publications:* Professional articles *Recreation:* Rugby, food and drink. *Clubs:* Royal Society of Arts. *Address:* 1 Holyhead Court, Hendredenny, Caerphilly CF8 2UH.

EDWARDS, County Cllr. Richard John, CC., MICFM., Cert.Ed. *Currently:* Regional Public Affairs Manager - Wales/West Midlands, NSPCC. *Born on* 15 Aug 1952 at Prestatyn, Clwyd. *Son of* Evan John and the late Joan Edwards. *Marriage:* to Hilary Evans 1985. *Children:* Sion Owain and Rhys. *Educated at* St. Asaph Grammar School; Coleg Normal, Bangor, Gwynedd. *Career:* Member Prestatyn Town Council 1973-85; Rhuddlan Borough Council 1974- ; Clwyd County Council 1980- ; Chairman Rhuddlan Economic Development Ctee 1984- ; Leader of Radical Group Clwyd County Council 1990- ; Member of Welsh Joint Education 1980-85 and 1990- ; Ctee. Member Clwyd Health Authority 1985-90; Member Association of District Councils in Wales; President Prestatyn Community Hospital Support Group; Member Welsh Language Educational

Development Ctee 1990- ; Exec. Member North Wales Blind Society. *Recreation:* Hillwalking, local government *Clubs:* Round Table *Address:* Llys Tegid, Sandy Lane, Prestatyn, Clwyd. LL19 7SH. Drws-Y-Coed, Bryn Eithin, Prestatyn, Clwyd LL19 9LS Tel: 0745 854758 Fax:0745 889106.

EDWARDS, Robert Wynne, MBE *Currently:* Farmer, 450 acres at Llangedwyn. *Born on* 12 Sept 1917 at Liverpool. *Son of* the late Edward Thomas Edwards and the late Angelina Louise (nee Morris). *Marriage:* to Joan Gretton, formally Knowles, 1948. *Children:* Mary, Kenneth, Janet and Jean. *Educated at* Llangedwyn and Llansilin Church Schools; Oswestry Boys High School-school Certificate with honours in eight subjects; Shrewsbury Technical College-evening school for three years. *Career:* Bank clerk 1936-47. Army Service 6 years. Trained as a Vickers machine gunner in Channel Islands and involved with Coastal Defence in Kent and Sussex. Later the Regiment was issued with anti-tank artillery and landed on the Normandy beaches with self-propelled anti-tank guns. Member of Ceiriog R.D.C. 1969-74; Member Denbighshire County Council 1971-74; Member of Clwyd County Council 1973-89; Chairman Clwyd County Council 1988-89. Agricultural Training Board: Chairman Clwyd Training Cttee 1978-88; former member, Wales Consultative Cttee and member Welsh Training Cttee from inception; Chairman, Dyffryn Tanat Training Group 1975-87; President, Dyffryn Tanat Training Group 1987- . National Farmers Union: Former Chairman Llanrhaeadr Branch; Chairman Oswestry Branch 1968-70; President, Oswestry Branch 1982-84; Former Chairman, Shropshire NFU Hill Farming Cttee; Ex-member, NFU Welsh Council and former Chairman, Education and Training Panel; Former Chairman, Land Use Panel. Member, Welsh Joint Education Cttee until 1989; Member, WJEC Agricultural Advisory Panel until 1989; Member, WJEC Further Education Panel until 1989. Agricultural Education: Chairman, Llysfasi College Governors until 1989; Chairman, Clwyd Rural Enterprise Unit (CREU) until 1989; Member, Agricultural and Forestry Liaison Cttee, UCNW Bangor until 1989. Member, Governors of Welsh Agric College since inception; Chairman, Joint Cttee Welsh Agric College; Former Chairman, Llanfyllin High School Governors; Former Chairman, Dinas Bran School, Llangollen, Governors. Welsh Water Authority: Member, Dee and Clwyd Land Drainage Cttee 1974-89; Member, Regional Land Drainage Cttee 1985-89. *Address:* Garther, Llangedwyn, Oswestry SY10 9LQ.

EDWARDS, Prof. Ronald Walter, DSc; FIBiol, FIWEM, FIFM. *Currently:* Retired Professor, School of Pure and Applied Biology, Univ. of Wales, Cardiff (formerly Professor and Head of Department of Applied Biology, University of Wales Institute of Science and Technology). *Born on* 7 June 1930. *Son of* Walter and Violet Edwards. *Educated at* Solihull School; Warwicks; Univ. of Birmingham (BSc, DSc), FIBiol 1965; FIWEM (FIWPC 1981) *Career:* Biologist, Freshwater Biol. Assoc., 1953-58; Senior Principal, and Senior Principal Scientific Officer, Water Pollution Res. Lab., 1958-68; Chairman, Nat. Parks Rev. Panel 1989- ; Dep. Chairman, Welsh Water Authority 1983- (Mem. 1974-); Member: Natural Environment Res. Council 1970-73 and 1982-85; Nat. Committee European Year of the Environment 1987-88; Council, RSPB, 1988- ; Nat. Rivers Authority 1988- . *Publications:* (co-ed) Ecology and the Industrial Society 1968; (co-ed) Conservation and Productivity of Natural Waters 1975; (with Dr M Brooker) The Ecology of the River Wye 1982; Acid Waters in Wales 1990; about 90 papers in learned journals. *Recreation:* music, collecting Staffordshire pottery. *Address:* NRA Welsh Region, Rivers House, St.Mellons Business Park, Cardiff CF3 OLT.

EDWARDS, Sir Sam(uel Frederick), FRS, membre de L'Institut *Currently:* Cavendish Professor of Physics, Cambridge University. *Born on* 1 Feb 1928 at Swansea. *Son of* Richard and Mary Jane Edwards. *Marriage:* to Merriell E.M. Bland, 1953. *Children:* Ruth, Margery, Richard and Alison. *Educated at* Swansea Grammar School; Caius College, Cambridge; Havard. *Career:* Member of Institute for Advanced Study, Princeton 1952-53; Birmingham Univ., 1953-58; Manchester Univ., 1958-72, Cambridge 1972- ; Chief Sci Adviser, Dept of Energy, 1983-88. Chm., SRC, 1973-77. UK Deleg to NATO Sci Cttee, 1974-79; Mem., Planning Cttee, Max-Planck Gesellschaft, 1974-77. Vice-Pres., Inst. of Physics, 1970-73 (mem. Council, 1967-73); Mem. Council, Inst of Mathematics and its Applications, 1976- (Vice-Pres., 1979, Pres., 1980-81). Member: Physics Cttee, SRC, 1968-73 (Chm 1970-73); Polymer Cttee, SRC 1968-73; Science Bd, SRC 1970-73; Council, European Physical Soc., 1969-71 (Chm Condensed Matter Div. 1969-71); UGC, 1971-73; Defence Scientific Adv.Council, 1973- (Chm. 1977-80); Metrology and Standards Req.Bd, Dept of Industry, 1974-77; Chm., Adv. Council on R&D, Dept of Energy, 1983-88 (Mem., 1974-77); Mem., Council: European R&D (EEC) 1976-80; Royal Soc., 1982-83 (a Vice-Pres. 1982-83); Pres., BAAS 1988-89 (Chm, Council 1977-82); Foreign Mem., Academie Des Sciences, France 1989. Non-exec. Director: Lucas Industries, 1981- ; Steetley plc, 1985- .FInstP; FIMA; FRSC.Hon.DTech Loughborough, 1975; Hon, DSs: Salford, Edinburgh 1976; Bath, 1978; Birmingham, 1986; Wales 1987; Sheffield 1989; Dublin 1991; DUniv Strasbourg 1986. Maxwell Medal and Prize, Inst of Physics 1974; High Polymer Physics Prize, Amer. Phys Soc, 1982; Davy Medal, Royal Soc., 1984; Gold Medal Inst of Maths 1986; Guthrie Medal and Prize Inst of Physics, 1987; Gold Medal Rheological Soc. 1990. *Publications:* Technological Risk, 1980; (with M.Doi) Theory of PolymerDynamics 1986; contribs to learned journals. *Clubs:* Athenaeum *Address:* 7 Penarth Place, Cambridge. CB3 9LU. Cavendish Laboratory, Cambridge CB3 OHE.

EDWARDS, Very Reverend Thomas Erwyd Pryse, BA *Currently:* Dean of Bangor Cathedral, since 1988. *Born on* 26 Jan 1933 at Aberystwyth. *Son of* Richard Humphreys and Gwladys. *Marriage:* to Mair (nee Roberts), 1961. *Children:* Sion Erwyd (b.1965) and Huw Thomas (b.1969). *Educated at* Machynlleth GS; St.David's University College Lampeter; St.Michaels College Llandaff. *Career:* Ordination, Deacon 1958; Priest (Bangor), 1959; Curate Caernarfon 1958-63; Assistant Chaplain, St.George's Hospital London 1963-66; Senior Chaplain King's College Hospital London 1966-72; Vicar: Penmon & Llangoed, Ynys Mon 1972-75, Menai Bridge 1975-81, St.Davids Bangor 1981-86, St.Davids & St.James Bangor 1986-88. Canon of Bangor Cathedral 1988. *Recreation:* DIY, music. *Address:* The Deanery, Cathedral Close, Bangor, Gwynedd.

Tel: 0248 370693, Cathedral Office, Diocesan Centre, Cathedral Close, Bangor, Gwynedd. Tel: 0248 353983

EDWARDS-JONES, Miss Diana Elizabeth, OBE *Currently:* T.V. Consultant. *Born on* 13 Dec 1932 at Swansea. *Daughter of* Dr. J.C. Edwards-Jones and Nancy (nee Davies). *Educated at* Battle Abbey School, Sussex; Nat. Coll Music & Drama, Cardiff; Bristol Old Vic Theatre School. *Career:* Stage Manager, Swansea Rep 1953-55; ITN 1955-89; Director General Election Results Progs 1974, 79, 83, 87, for ITV; U.S. Election Progs - coverage Space Exploration - Apollo programmes, helped create News at Ten 1967; Director All Main ITN News Progs. Head of Programme Directors ITN 1980. Director numerous Royal occasions, The Popes visit, Royal Television Society Award for coverage of 1974 Elections (2). *Recreation:* theatre, music, travel, horse racing, reading. *Clubs:* Chairman London Welsh Publicity Society, BAFTA. *Address:* 2 Parkview, 87 Part Road, Chiswick, London W4 3ER.

EGDELL, Dr. John Duncan, MB, ChB, FFPHM, Dip.Soc.Med. *Currently:* Consultant in Public Health Medicine, Clwyd Health Authority since 1986. *Born on* 5 March 1938 at Bristol. *Son of* the late John William Egdell and Nellie (nee Thompson). *Marriage:* to Dr. Linda Mary Flint, 1963. *Children:* Brian, Robin and Ann. *Educated at* Clifton College, Bristol; University of Bristol. *Career:* General Practice 1962-65; Medical Administrative appointments, Newcastle Regional Hospital Board 1966-69; South Western Regional Hospital Board 1969-74; Regional Specialist in Community Medicine, South Western Regional Health Authority 1974-76; Regional Medical Postgraduate Co-ordinator, University of Bristol 1973-76; Regional Medical Officer, Mersey Regional Health Authority 1977-86. *Recreation:* nature conservation, delving into the past. *Address:* Gelli Gynan Lodge, Llanarmon-yn-Ial, Nr Mold, Clwyd. CH7 4QX. Tel: 08243 345.

EILLEDGE, Mr Elwyn Owen Morris, MA, FCA. *Currently:* Senior Partner, Ernst & Young, Chartered Accountants, since 1986; Co-Chairman, Ernst & Young International (previously Ernst & Whinney International), since 1988. *Born on* 20 July 1935 at Welshpool, Montgomeryshire. *Son of* the late Owen Eilledge and the late Mary Elizabeth. *Marriage:* to Audrey Ann Faulkner Ellis, 1962. *Children:* Amanda Gail Caroline (b.1968) and Julian Alexander Stephen (b.1970). *Educated at* Oswestry Boys High School; Merton College, Oxford. *Career:* Articles with Farrow Bersey Gain Vincent & Co (now Binder Hamlyn) 1959-66; Whinney Murray & Co., (now Ernst & Young), Liberia, 1966-68; Hamburg 1968-71; Partner London 1972; Managing Partner, London Office 1983-86. Council member of the Institute of Chartered Accountants in England & Wales, member of the Financial Reporting Council and Accounting Standards Board, Fellow of the University College of Wales, Aberystywth. *Recreation:* gardening, opera, swimming, tennis. *Clubs:* Brooks's *Address:* Whitethorn House, Long Grove, Seer Green, Beaconsfield, Bucks. HP9 2QH. Becket House, 1 Lambeth Palace Road, London SE1 7EU.

ELIAS, Mr Gerard, Q.C. *Currently:* Barrister. *Born on* 19 Nov 1944 at Cardiff. *Son of* Leonard and Patricia Elias. *Marriage:* to Elisabeth Kenyon, 1970. *Children:* David, Robert and James. *Educated at* Cardiff High School; Exeter University (LL.B) *Career:* Called to the Bar, Inner Temple,

1968; Queen's Counsel, 1984 Recorder of the Crown Court 1984- ; Assistant Boundary Commissioner for Wales 1983- ; Treasurer of the Wales & Chester Circuit 1990- . *Recreation:* cricket (member of executive committe of Glamorgan County Cricket Club 1985), music, sailing. *Clubs:* Cardiff and County, Bristol Channel Yacht, Tresaith Mariners. *Address:* 13 The Cathedral Green, Llandaff, Cardiff, S.Glam CF5 2EB.

ELIAS-JONES, Mr Peter John, B.A.; Dip. *Currently:* Independent TV producer, consultant.*Born on* 29th May 1943 at .*Son of* the late William Peter Jones of Llangefni, Anglesey, and Margaret, nee Elias.*Marriage:* to Elinor Mair, daughter of the late Cyril Owens of Ammanford, Dyfed, on 10th April 1971.*Children:* Elen 1973, Mari Wyn 1976 *Educated at* Llangefni; Ysgol Gyfun; University of Leeds (BA); University of Manchester (Dip) *Career:* Teacher of music and drama, Wallasey 1966; Studio Manager TWW Ltd Cardiff 1967; HTV Ltd Cardiff: director news 1968, producer and director children's programmes 1971, head of children's programmes 1974, assistant programme controller 1981, programme controller entertainment 1988; Independent TV producer, consultant 1992; editor books for young people, numerous articles; international guest speaker; member, ITV network committee; board of appointments consultant, RTE, Dublin *Address:* Rhiw Goed, Westra, Dinas Powys, Caerdydd, De Morg., CF6 4HA. Tel: 0222 512405.

ELLIS, Alice Thomas, *Currently:* Writer. *Born on* 9 Sept 1932 *Daughter of* John Lindholm and Alexandra Lindholm. *Marriage:* to Colin Haycraft, 1956. *Children:* 4 s, 1 da (and 1 s, 1 da decd) *Educated at* Bangor County GS for Girls; Liverpool Sch of Art. *Career:* Yorkshire Post: Novel of the Year award 1985; Unexplained Laughter Writers Guild Award 1991; Best Fiction: The Inn at the Edge of the World; Columnists: The Spectator: The Universe. *Publications:* (as Anna Haycraft): Natural Baby Food 1977; Darling you Shouldn't Have Gone to so much Trouble (with Caroline Blackwood) 1980; (as Alice Thomas Ellis: The Sin Eater 1977; The Birds of the Air 1980; The Twenty-Seventh Kingdom 1982; The Other Side of the Fire 1983; Unexplained Laughter 1985, Secrets of Strangers (with Tom Pitt-Aikens) 1986; Home Life 1986; More Home Life 1987; The Clothes in the Wardrobe 1987; The Skeleton in the Cupboard 1988; Home Life Three 1988; Home Life Four 1989; The Loss of the Good Authority (with Tom Pitt-Aikens) 1989; The Fly in the Ointment 1989; The Inn at the Edge of the World 1990; A Welsh Childhood 1990. Editor and compiler ''A Welsh Anthology'', 1989. *Address:* 22 Gloucester Cres., London. NW1 7DY. Tel: 071 485 7408

ELLIS, Professor Haydon Douglas, BA, PhD, DSc, C.Psychol, FBPsS. *Currently:* Head, School of Psychology, University of Wales, Cardiff since 1988. *Born on* 25 Oct 1945 at Newport, Gwent. *Son of* A.D. Ellis and M.L.Ellis (nee Oliver). *Marriage:* to Diane Margaret Newton. *Children:* Stephen, Robert and Jack. *Educated at* St. Julians HS, Newport; Reading Univ; Aberdeen Univ. *Career:* Lecturer/Senior Lecturer Univ of Aberdeen 1970-86; Professor UWIST 1986-88. *Publications:* Four books and more than 100 scientific papers. *Recreation:* golf, beekeeping.*Address:* Llwynarthen House, Castleton, Cardiff CF3 8UN.

ELLIS, Mair Helena, *Currently:* Gwynedd County Councillor since 1981. *Born on* 25 April 1943 at Caernarfon. *Daughter of* the late Ellis Griffith Ellis and the late Daisy Cross Ellis. *Educated at* Local schools. *Career:* Vice-Chairman of the Gwynedd County Council full Social Services Committee; Deputise on All Wales Association for Social Service; Chairman Social Services Finance and Priorities Sub Committee; represented Gwynedd County Council on the Gwynedd Health Authority for one year but the Authority ceased due to National Health's Reorganisation. mem North Western and North Wales Sea Fisheries ctee; Vice Chairman Fisheries Finance Ctee; Court mem Univ of Wales; Court mem Univ College of Bangor; mem North Wales Police Authority Consultative Ctee; mem North Wales Provincial Councils; former mem Caernarfon Royal Town Council; (former Major and Deputy Constable for Caernarfon Castle 1985-86); former Chairman North Wales Assoc of Town Councils; former mem area Citizens Advise Bureau Management Ctee (for 10 years); founder and first secretary (a) Caernarfon and Dist British Heart Foundation; founder and first Secretary (b) Caernarfon and Dist Tourist Assoc; founder and first Chairman and still hold its position for Plas Maesincla Home for the Elderly League of Friends; President for number of local voluntary organisations; Faithfull member of Caersalem Baptist Chapel. *Recreation:* operas, National Trust, reading *Address:* 38 William Street, Caernarfon, Gwynedd LL55 1ND.

ELLIS, Miss Margaret Anne, M.B.E. *Currently:* Head of Physical Education, Gowerton School. Coach Swansea Ladies (Welsh Cup holders 5 times) since 1987. *Born on* 21 Sept 1940 at Swansea. *Daughter of* Mr E.M. and the late Mrs G.Ellis. *Educated at* Gowerton Girls' Grammar School; Glamorgan Training College, Barry. *Career:* Hockey playing represented Wales 1963-80; 136 consecutive Caps (most Capped Welsh player); Captain of Wales 1973-80; Captain of first G.M. Olympic team 1977; Captain from 1977-80 - team chosen for Moscow Olympics but withdrawn because of political situation. World Conferences: Baltimore, USA 1963; Cologne, Germany 1967; Auckland, N.Z., 1971. World Championships: Edinburgh, Scotland: Wales runners-up to England 1975; Vancouver, Canada: Wales placed 5th, 1979. Tours: USA 1963; South Africa 1969; Sri Lanka, Hong Kong, Thailand, Australia, New Zealand, Fiji, Canada, USA 1971; West Indies - Barbados, Jamaica, Trinidad 1973; USA 1974; Canada 1979. retired fron International Hockey 1980. *Career:* Advanced Coaching Award W W H A; Coach to G.B. Olympic team 1980-84, tours to USA, Germany and Holland; Coach to Welsh team, 1983-85; Inter-Continental Cup in Argentina, Wales placed 6th 1985. Captain/Coach Swansea Ladies (1985 B Division Club Champions), 1984. Sports Council for Wales Medal of Honour for services to Welsh Hockey 1979; awarded M B E for services to Hockey 1980; Vice-President, Welsh Women's Hockey Association 1987-present; member Working Party set up for formation of British Institute of Sports Coaches 1989; received British Coach of the Year Award for contribution to coaching Women's Hockey 1989; member, European Hockey Federation Development Committee 1990; member of International Hockey Coaching Development Committee 1990. *Recreation:* travel, music. *Clubs:* Penarth Ladies 1960-75. Swansea Ladies since 1975. *Address:* 1 Heol Gwili, Frampton Park, Gorseinon, Swansea, SA4 2GE. Gowerton School, Cecil Road,

Gowerton, Swansea SA4 3DL.

ELLIS, Professor Richard Salisbury, B.Sc., Ph.D., F.R.A.S. *Currently:* Professor of Astronomy, Durham 1985-SERC Senior Research Fellow (1989-). *Born on* 25th May 1950 at Colwyn Bay. *Son of* late Captain Arthur Ellis M.E.E. and Marion Ellis(nee Davies). *Marriage:* to Barbara (nee Williams), 1972. *Children:* Hilary Rhona (1976) and Thomas Marc (1978) *Educated at* University College London 1968-71; Oxford University 1971-74 *Career:* Senior Demonstrator in Physics, University of Durham 1974-77; Senior Research Assistant, University of Durham 1977-81; Lecturer in Astronomy, University of Durham 1981-83; Principal Research Associate, Royal Greenwich Observatory 1983-85; Senior Visiting Fellow, Space Telescope Science Institute, Baltimore, USA; Professor of Astronomy, University of Durham 1985-present; SERC Senior Research Fellow 1989-present; Senior Visiting Fellow, Anglo-Australian Observatory, Sydney, Australia 1991 *Publications:* The Epoch of Galaxy Formation; Observational Tests of Cosmological Inflation *Recreation:* Travel, music, photography *Address:* Physics Department, South Road, University Of Durham, Durham DH1 3LE.

ELLIS, Mr Robert Thomas, *Currently:* Retired. *Born on* 15 March 1924 at Rhosllanerchrugog. *Son of* Robert and Edith Ann Ellis. *Marriage:* to Nona Harcourt Williams. *Children:* Susan Lucy, Charles Thomas, Mark Harcourt and Graham Jonathan. *Educated at* Ruabon Grammar School; Universities of Wales and Nottingham. *Career:* Works Chemist 1944-47; Coal Miner 1947-51; Mining Engineer 1954-70; M.P. 1970-83. *Publications:* Miners and Men 1971, Educational Publishers. *Recreation:* Music, reading, gardening. *Address:* 3 Old Vicarage, Ruabon, Clwyd. LL14 6LG.

ELMES, Dr. Peter Cardwell, BM, BCh, BSc, MA, FRCP, FFOM, MD (Western Reserve Univ.USA) *Currently:* retired Physician. *Born on* 12 Oct 1921 at Hemyock, Devon. *Son of* Florence Romaine Elmes and Lilian Bryham (nee Cardwell). *Marriage:* to Dr. Margaret Elizabeth (nee Staley). *Children:* Ann Elizabeth, John Peter Henry and David Antony. *Educated at* Rugby School; Christ Church Oxford. *Career:* Postgraduate training at the Radcliffe Infirmary Oxford and Royal Postgraduate Medical School Hammersmith London; Senior Lecturer, Reader and Professor in Dept. of Therapeutics and Pharmacology and consultant Physician Queens University Belfast, 1959-76; Director Medical Research Council Pneumoconiosis Unit Llandough Penarth 1976-81; Consultant in Occupational Lung Disease. *Publications:* numerous papers in professional journals and chapters in textbooks concerning chronic lung disorders. *Recreation:* DIY, preserving the environment. *Address:* Dawros House, St. Andrews Rd, Dinas Powys, S. Glam., CF6 4HB. Tel: 0222 512102. Fax: 0222 515975.

ELY, Mr Sydney (Keith), BA *Currently:* Editor, Daily Post, since 1989. *Born on* 17 April 1949 at Liverpool, England. *Son of* Charles Rodenhurst Ely and Dorothy Mary Ely (nee Rowlands). *Marriage:* to Patricia Davies, 1970. *Children:* Leah, Gillian Louise and Elizabeth Ruth. *Educated at* Maghull Grammar; Kirkby College; Open University. *Career:* Assistant News Ed, Daily Post 1972; Chief Sub-editor, Reuters 1979; Business editor, Daily Post 1981; Deputy editor, Daily Post 1987; Director, Corporate Culture Ltd., 1989, Liverpool Daily Post & Echo Ltd., 1989.

Recreation: music, computing. *Address:* 6 Harrington Close, Formby, Merseyside L37 1XP.

ELYSTAN-MORGAN, His Hon.Lord Dafydd Elystan, LLB (Hons) *Currently:* Circuit Judge on Wales & Chester Circuit, since 1987. *Born on* 7 Dec 1932 at Aberystwyth. *Son of* the late Dewi Morgan and the late Olwen Morgan. *Marriage:* to Alwen (nee Roberts) 1959. *Children:* Eleri Elystan and Owain Elystan. *Educated at* Ardwyn Grammar School; Law Department UCW Aberystwyth. *Career:* Solicitor (1957 qualified) Partner in North Wales firm 1958-68; Member of Parliament for Cardiganshire 1966-74; Under Secretary of State Home Office 1968-70; Front Bench Opposition Spokesman 1970-74; Barrister 1971; Recorder Wales and Chester Circuit 1983-87; Life Peer (Baron) 1981. *Address:* Carreg Afon, Dolau, Bow Street, Dyfed.

EMANUEL, Mr David, FCSD., MA. *Currently:* David Emanuel Couture. *Born on* 17 Nov 1952 at Wales. *Son of* John Lawrence Morris Emanuel and the late Elizabeth Emanuel. *Marriage:* to Elizabeth Weiner 1975, seperated 1990. *Children:* Oliver and Eloise. *Educated at* Cardiff College of Art; Harrow School of Art; Royal College of Art. *Career:* Won various design prizes/scholarships/bursaries while at College; Made Fellow of The Society of Industrial Artists and Designers; Two 'Student' vacations in the design room at Hardy Amies working with Ken Fleetwood - Design Director - Couture and RTW; worked in Design room for 'Cojana' RTW; worked in the Design room with the Designer Roland Klein at Marcel Fenez; formed 'Emanuel' 1977-90; apart from Ready-To-Wear and Couture Collections worked for stage, screen and television; working with Lady Diana Spencer - H.R.H. The Princess of Wales from - Pre-Engagement - Wedding - Private and Public Engagements 1981- ; Only British Designer to participate in 'Night of 100 Stars' Radio City Hall, New York 1984; Gala Fashion Show 'Section' - Finale spot with Actress Ann-Margaret and Rockettes; Fashion Aid 1985 with Bob Geldof; Fashion Aid Japan, Tokoyo 1986; Appearing with H.R.H. The Princess of Wales in the ITV Documentary Film and Book 'In Private In Public' 1986; Invited back as former old student to participate in 150th Anniversary Celebration of The Royal College of Art Gala Fashion Show - Finale spot 1987. Artistic Director 'Queen Charlotte Ban', 1991, David Emmanuel 'Ready-to-Wear', 1991. *Publications:* 'Style for all Seasons' Pavillion Books 1983. *Recreation:* My two children, horse-riding, jet-skiing, tennis, good conversation, Pre-Raphaelite paintings, snow-skiing, cooking, photography, live theatre. *Clubs:* White Elephant; Royal Ascot Tennis (Berks). *Address:* 13 Regent's Park, Terrace, London. NW1 7ED.

EMMETT, Mrs Angela Ann, *Currently:* Salary & Benefits Adviser, BAT Industries plc. *Born on* 24 Aug 1952 at London. *Daughter of* the late Patrick and Mary Lynchehaun (nee Gavaghan). *Marriage:* divorced. *Children:* none. *Educated at* Slough College (now Thames Valley Polytechnic), Post Grad in General Management. *Career:* In personnel management, covering various employment issues, including pay and equal opportunity. *Publications:* none. *Recreation:* theatre, opera, SCUBA diving. *Clubs:* St.Stephen's Constitutional, SW1. *Address:* 276 Corporation Road, Newport, Gwent NP9 0DZX.

EMMS, Mrs Judith Mary Ann, BSc; MSc; MBCS; CEng. *Currently:* Staff Tutor in Mathematics and lecturer in Computing, Open University, 1991. *Born on* 28 May 1944 at Taunton. *Daughter of* the late Arthur William Pearse and the late Kathleen (nee Nott). *Marriage:* 1st to Roy David Chapman, 1967 (divorced 1985); 2nd to Stephen John Emms, 1986. *Children:* Alan Seth Chapman and Kirsty Chapman. *Educated at* Weston-Super-Mare Girls Grammar; University of Sussex. *Career:* Programmer/Analyst University of London, 1965; Senior Programmer/Analyst, Hatfield Polytechnic, 1966; Lecturer in Computer Science, Hatfield Polytechnic, 1971; lecturer in computing, Open University, 1978-86; Staff Tutor, East Midlands Region, OU, 1987-91; Chair Open University, Myalgic Encephalomyelitis Society 1989- . *Publications:* Abstract Data Types OUP, 1988 with Thomas and Robinson; various papers on Database systems and Women in Computing. *Recreation:* Literature, art, plants, ornithology, Alexander Technique. *Address:* The Open University In Wales, 24 Cathedral Road, Cardiff. CF1 9SA. Tel 0222 397911

ENGLAND, Dr Glyn, FEng, CBIM, DSc(Hon Bath), JP, Freeman City of London. *Currently:* Chairman, Windcluster Ltd., Woodlands Initiatives Ltd and Silvanus Trust; Consultant to World Bank; Director UK Centre for Economic and Environmental Development; Adviser Centre for Sustainable Industry. *Born on* 19 April 1921 at Tonyrefail, Glam. *Son of* Charles Thomas, headmaster Cwmlai Council School and Alice. *Marriage:* to Tania Reichenbach, 1942. *Children:* Gillian and Janet. *Educated at* Cwmlai Council School; Penarth County; Queen Mary College, London University; London School of Economics; Manchester Business School. *Career:* Industrial Research 1939-40; War Service REME 1942-47; Director General S.W.Region CEGB 1971-73; Chairman, South Western Electricity Board 1973-77; Chairman, Central Electricity Generating Board 1977-82; Chairman Environmental Council 1983-88; Director F.H.Lloyd (Holdings) 1982-87; Director Triplex Lloyd plc 1987-90; Vice-President International Union of Producers and Distributors of Electrical Energy; member Hertfordshire County Council. *Publications:* various papers on Electricity Supply Industry; Planning for Uncertainty; Railway and Power: the linked Networks (Tritton Lecture); Efficiency Audit and Public Enterprise; Landscape in the Making (jointly); Understanding the Civil Service - a view from Industry. *Recreation:* actively enjoying the countryside. *Address:* Woodbridge Farm, Ubley, Bristol BS18 6PX. Tel: 0761 462479.

ENSOR, Mr George Anthony, LL.B. Solicitor. *Currently:* Senior Partner, Weightman Rutherfords Solicitors; Recorder of The Crown Court since 1983. *Born on* 4 Nov 1936 at Porthmadog. *Son of* George Ensor and Phyllis Ensor of Pwllheli. *Marriage:* to Dr. Jennifer Caile. *Children:* Elizabeth and Jane. *Educated at* Troed-yr-Allt, Pwllheli; Malvern College; Liverpool University. *Career:* Deputy Coroner, City of Liverpool 1966- ; Part-time Chairman Industrial Tribunal 1975- ; Director Liverpool Football Club 1985- ; Trustee Empire Theatre Liverpool 1986- . *Recreation:* sport, theatre. *Clubs:* Pwllheli Golf, Formby Golf, Artists Liverpool, Waterloo R.U.F.C. *Address:* Weightman Rutherfords, Richmond House, Rumford Place, Liverpool, L3 9QW. Tel: 051 227 2601.

ERICKSON, Raymond John, Management Accountant, FBIM, FInstD. *Currently:* Retired, but some financial consultancy, John Curran Ltd. *Born on* 2 Aug 1926 *Son of* the late Lawrence Erickson, of Penarth and the late Olive Annie. *Marriage:* to Mary Frances, 1964, dau of Thomas Brian (d 1981), of Barry. *Children:* Lisa (b.1964). *Educated at* Penarth Co.School. *Career:* Chief Accountant, John Curran Ltd., 1966-76; Finance Director 1976-84; Chairman 1984-89. *Recreation:* motoring, music. *Address:* 5 Minehead Avenue, Sully, Penarth, CF6 2TH. John Curran Ltd, P.O. Box 72, Curran Road, Cardiff, CF1 1TE.

EVANS, The Very Reverend (Thomas) Eric, *Currently:* Dean of St.Paul's, since 1988. *Born on* 1928. *Son of* the late Eric John Rhys Evans and Florence May Rogers. *Marriage:* to Linda Kathleen Budge, 1957. *Children:* two d. *Educated at* St.David's College, Lampeter (BA); St.Catherine's College Oxford (MA); St.Stephen's House Oxford. *Career:* Ordained, 1954; Curate, Margate Parish Church 1954-58; Sen. Curate, St.Peter's, Bournemouth 1958-62; first Director, Bournemouth Samaritans; Diocesan Youth Chaplain, dio. Gloucester 1962-69; Residentiary Canon of Gloucester Cathedral 1969-88; Archdeacon of Cheltenham 1975-88. Wing Chaplain, ATC 1963-69; Hon. Chaplain: Gloucester College of Education 1968-75; Gloucestershire Constabulary 1977-88, Chairman, Glos Training Committee 1967-69; Proctor in Convocation and Member Gen. Synod of C of E 1970- ; a Church Comr 1978- (member Board of Governors 1978- , Assets Committee 1985-88). Canon Missioner, dio Gloucester 1969-75; Chairman: House of Clergy, dio. Gloucester 1979-82; Board of Social Responsibility, dio. Gloucester 1982-83; Glos Assoc. for Mental Health 1983-85 (Vice-Chairman 1965-78); Glos Diocesan Adv. Committee 1984-88. Member Exec Committee 1975-88, Chairman 1981-88, Council for the Care of Churches (formerly Council for Places of Worship). Dean, Order of St.Michael and St.George 1988- ; Dean, Order of the British Empire 1988- ; Chaplain to Guild of Freemen of City of London 1988- . Dir, Ecclesiastical Insurance Office Ltd 1979- . Member Council, Cheltenham Ladies' College 1982- . Freeman of the City of London 1988. Sub-Prelate of the Order of St.John of Jerusalem 1991. Hon. Freeman of the Gardeners Company 1992. *Recreation:* travel, esp. Middle East. *Address:* The Deanery, 9 Amen Court, London EC4M 7BU.

EVANS, Mr Alun, O.B.E., F.R.AgS *Currently:* Farmer. *Born on* 13 May 1934 at Tywyn, Gwynedd. *Son of* the late Lewis and Catherine Evans. *Marriage:* to Janet Sylvia, 1958. *Children:* Richard, Dylan and Elspeth *Educated at* Tywyn Grammar School; Nuffield Scholar. *Career:* Chairman, British Wool Marketing Board 1985- ; Chairman NFU Mutual Insurance Group 1990- ; Chairman Welsh Food Promotions Ltd 1991- ; Chairman Secretary of State, Welsh Advisory Sub Committee for Hills and Uplands 1986- ; Member of Council Food from Britain 1986- ; School Governor; V. Chairman U.K. Federation of Agric Co-operatives 1991- ; *Recreation:* Reading, current affairs and sport. *Clubs:* Farmers. *Address:* Caerffynnon, Bryncrug Tywyn, Gwynedd LL36 9RE.

EVANS, Hon. Sir Anthony Howell Meurig, LLM RD *Currently:* a Judge of the High Court of Justice. *Born on* 11 June 1934 at Cardiff. *Son of* the late David Meurig Evans (County Court Judge) and the late Joy (nee Sander). *Marriage:* in 1963 to Caroline Mary Fyffe Mackie. *Children:*

1 son 2 daughters. *Educated at* Bassaleg Grammar School, Mon.; Shrewsbury School; St.John's College, Cambridge; *Career:* Called to Bar, Gray's Inn 1958; Bencher 1979; QC 1971; High Court Judge 1984- ; Presiding Judge of Wales and Chester Circuit 1986-88; Judge of the Commercial Court 1984- ; Dep.Chmn. Boundary Commission for Wales 1989- ; *Publications:* (Jt. Editor) The Law of the Air (Lord McNair) 1964 *Recreation:* Sailing, Music *Clubs:* Royal Lymington Yacht *Address:* c/o Royal Courts of Justice, Strand, London. WC2A 2LL.

EVANS, Mr Arthur Mostyn, *Currently:* Retired, Elected May 1991 Labour Councillor West Nor. *Born on* 13 July 1925 at Merthyr Tydfil. *Son of* Frederick & Hannah Evans. *Marriage:* to Laura, 1947. *Children:* Adrian, Royston, Kevin (d), Yvonne, Vivienne and Dianne. *Educated at* Cefn Coed Primary; Birmingham Sec. Modern. *Career:* Dist. Off., Birmingham Chem & Eng Ind., 1956; Reg. Off. Midlands, 1960; Nat. Officer Eng., 1966; Nat. Sec. Chem Rubber & Oil Ind., 1969; Eng In., 1969; TGWU, 1967-73; Nat. Organiser TGWU, 1973-78; P/Time Mem. Nat. Bus Co., 1976-78; Mbr BOTB 1978-79; NEPC 1978-84; Exec. ITF, 1980- ; Council ACAS, 1982- ; Pres. ICEF, 1982- ; Vice Pres, 1980-82. Gen.Sec. T.G.W.U. 1978-85. *Publications:* Ford Wage Claim 1971. *Recreation:* Music and horse racing. *Address:* Cheney House, Cheney Hill, Heacham, King's Lynn. PE31 7BX.

EVANS, Mr Charles Winstone (Win), FIPM *Currently:* Director, ACAS Wales 1988- . *Born on* 12 Jan 1936 at Swansea. *Son of* the late Thomas Henry Evans and the late Florence Mabel (nee Medwell). *Marriage:* to Betty Belsey 1966. *Children:* Carolyn Andrews. *Educated at* Swansea Grammar School. *Career:* Administrative Officer, Admiralty 1953-59; Customs Officer, HM Customs and Excise 1959-72; Senior Officer, Value Added Tax Office (Swansea) 1972-77; Senior Industrial Relations Officer, ACAS London 1977-82; Deputy Director, ACAS Wales 1983-88; Chairman Joint Industrial Relations Forum 1988; Member WJEC Management Studies Advisory Panel 1988; Fellow of Swansea and West Wales Branch Institute of Personnel Management 1990- ; Member, Institute of Welsh Affairs 1990- . *Recreation:* Reading, walking. *Address:* ACAS Wales, Phase 1 Building, Ty Glas Rd., Llanishen, Cardiff. CF4 5PH. Tel: 0222 762636.

EVANS, The Reverend Charles Wyndham, MA(Oxon), BA(Wales). *Currently:* Vicar of Llanrhaeadr since 1979 and Prion, Rural Dean of Denbigh, since 1984. *Born on* 16 Oct 1928 at Bala. *Son of* William Lloyd Evans and Ada Henrietta Evans. *Marriage:* to Sheila Huw Jones, 1961. *Children:* Helen (b.1965) and Jonathan (b.1966). *Educated at* Bala Grammar School; UCNW, Bangor; St.Catherine's College, Oxford. *Career:* Curate, Denbigh 1952-55; Chaplain and Housemaster, Llandovery College 1955-67; Chaplain and Senior Lecturer in Education, Trinity College, Carmarthen 1967-79; Chaplain of Ruthin School 1979-86; Trustee, St. Mary's Trust; Member, Welsh National Religious Education Centre, Bangor; Diocesan Advisor in Religious Education, 1982; Tutor in Philosophy and Ethics, N.S.H. Course, St. Deiniol's Library, 1984-87; Chaplain to the High Sheriff of Clwyd, 1992-93. *Publications:* Bible Families, 1965. *Recreation:* gardening. *Address:* The Vicarage, Llanrhaeadr, Denbigh, Clwyd LL16 4NN. Tel: 074 578 250.

EVANS, Mr Clifford John , MA(Cantab), FEng, FICE, FIStructE, FCIARB, FIHT, FASCE, FIWEM, *Currently:* Chairman, Wallace Evans Ltd., Also Director of Wallace Evans (Jamaica) Ltd., P & T Wallace Evans Ltd., (Hong Kong) and UNIECO SA, Spain; also Registered Arbitrator (registered in UK., Hong Kong and Paris). *Born on* 9 Oct 1928 at Cardiff. *Son of* Wallace, Consulting Eng., and Elsie. *Marriage:* to Molly Walker, 1953. *Children:* Christopher and Robert. *Educated at* Cardiff High School; Gonville & Caius College, Cambridge University. *Career:* Wallace Evans & Partners, 1951-53; Chief Engineer, Caribbean Construction Co. Ltd., (Jamaica), 1954-60; Since 1962 with Wallace Evans & Partners, Consulting Engineers; Partner Resident in Jamaica until 1966; Partner in UK, from 1961; Senior Partner from 1971-90 when name was changed to Wallace Evans Ltd; President Institution of Structural Engineers, 1981-82; Fellow of the Fellowship of Engineering; Mbr. Court Univ. of Wales Coll.Cardiff; Cncl Mbr. Cardiff Chamber of Commerce; Former Cncl Mbr. CBI Wales; Former Chrmn Wales Branches of I.Struc.E, Inst.Civil Eng, Inst.Highways & Transportation, Chartered Inst. of Arbitrators; Liveryman of Worshipful Co.of Engineers, Worshipful Co.of Arbitrators & Worshipful Co.of Constructors; Mbr. Cncl of Inst. of Civil Engrs; Mbr. Cncl of Chartered Inst. of Arbitrators. *Publications:* Numerous papers on Civil Engineering, Ports and Maritime Works; Transportation, construction contracts. *Recreation:* Sport (Attache for Wales Team, Commonwealth Games Jamaica 1966) Swimming (Welsh Int. & Cpt. of Cambridge Univ. Swim Club 1950-51) Sailing and off shore racing, skiing. *Clubs:* Cardiff & County, Hawks, Royal Ocean Racing, Royal Thames Yacht, Penarth Yacht. *Address:* Wallace Evans Ltd., Plymouth House, Plymouth Road, Penarth. S.Glam. CF6 2YF.

EVANS, Prof. David Alan Price, MD., DSc., PhD., FRCP., BSc., MBChB., MRCP., MSc. *Currently:* Director of Medicine, Riyadh Armed Forces Hospital, P.O.Box 7897, Riyadh 11159, Kingdom of Saudi Arabia. *Born on* 6 March 1927 at Birkenhead. *Son of* Owen Evans and Ellen Evans (nee Jones). *Educated at* University of Liverpool; Johns Hopkins Univ., Balto, MD, USA. *Career:* Hon. Professor of Medicine, King Saud University, Riyadh.Henry Briggs Memorial Medal (Obst. & Gynaec), Sir Robert Kelly Mem. Medal (Surgery), J.Hill Abram Prize, N.E. Roberts Prize, Samuels Prize - Univ. of Liverpool; House Physician & House Surgeon, Liverpool Royal Infirmary 1951-52; Holt Fellow in Physiology Univ. of Liverpool, 1952-53; Nat. Service Capt. RAMC 1953-55; Active service in Japan, Korea, Singapore and Malaya, UN Korea and GS Malaya medals; Snr. Hse. Office Broadgreen Hospital Liverpool 1955-56; Medical Registrar Stanley Hosp. Liverpool 1956-58; Research Fellow Dept Med. Johns Hopkins Univ. 1958-59; Med. Registrar David Lewis Northern Hosp. Liverpool 1959-60; Lec. Dept. Med. Univ Liverpool 1960-62; Snr. Lec. Univ. Liverpool 1962-68; Personal Chair Univ. Liverpool 1969-72; Chrmn.Dept. of Med. Univ.Liverpool & Director Nuffield Unit of Medical Genetics 1972-83; Dir. of Med. Rugarh Armed Forces Hosp. 1983- ; Ext.Examiner: Univs. Sheffield, London; Visiting Prof: Johns Hopkins Univ, Kasolinska Univ. Stockholm, Helsinki Univ; Mbr.Commt. on Safety of Med. & Adverse Reactions subcommittee; Examiner for mbrshp of Royal Coll. of Physicians; Chrmn. Specialist Advisory Commt. on General

Int. Med. of the Royal Colleges of Physicians. *Publications:* Numerous medical and scientific, principally concerned with The Genetic Factors Governing the Responses to Drug Therapy. *Recreation:* Country pursuits *Address:* 28 Montclair Drive, Liverpool, L18 OHA. Pen Yr Allt, Llangristiolus, Bodorgan, Gwynedd, LL62 5PD

EVANS, Mr David Anthony, Q.C. *Currently:* Barrister. *Born on* 15 March 1939 at Swansea. *Son of* the late T.J.Evans M.D., and the late May Evans. *Marriage:* to Angela Bewley, 1974. *Children:* Serena Evans and Tessa Evans. *Educated at* Clifton College, Bristol; Corpus Christi College, Cambridge. *Career:* Called to the Bar by Grays Inn 1965; practised at the Bar 1965- ; Recorder of the Crown Court 1980- ; Queens Counsel 1983; D.T.I. Inspector 1988. *Recreation:* Rugby football and most other sports. *Clubs:* Turf, MCC, Cardiff & County, Swansea Cricket and Football. *Address:* Carey Hall, Rhyddings, Neath, West Glamorgan, SA10 7AU. 4 Paper Buildings, Temple, London EC4Y 7EX. 55 The Marlborough, 61, Walton Street, London, SW3.

EVANS, Mr David Anthony Mainwaring, *Currently:* Editor, Western Telegraph, Haverfordwest; Director, Pembrokeshire Business Initiative. *Born on* 18 July 1943 *Son of* the late David Louis Mainwaring, publisher and Anne (nee Bratherton). *Marriage:* to Carole Newnham Barker 1973. *Children:* Katie (b 1975) and Jennie (b 1977). *Career:* Westminster Press Group, London 1960; Hotel Business, Spain 1964; Sub-editor, Kent Messenger 1966; Sub-editor, Western Daily Press, Bristol 1967; later features Editor, Western Daily Press 1972; News Editor, Western Telegraph, Pembrokeshire 1977; Deputy Editor, Western Telegraph 1978-88; 1981 Welsh feature Writer of Year; Member of Royal Naval Auxiliary Service (Navigator); President, Pembrokeshire Branch Cystic Fibrosis Research Trust; Friend of Little Actors Factory; Friend of Pembrokeshire College; Founder Member Cleddau Rowing Club; President, Pembrokeshire Short-oared Rowing Federation; Adviser to Pembrokeshire Schools Young Enterprise Groups. *Publications:* Pembrokeshire Then and Now, Volumes I & II (1988/89) as editor. *Recreation:* sailing and the sea, cliff walking, wining and dining. *Address:* Western Telegraph, Merlins Bridge, Haverfordwest, Dyfed. SA61 1XF. Tel: 0437 763133

EVANS, Venerable David Eifion, BA, 1932; MA, 1951. *Currently:* retired Archdeacon of Cardigan, 1967-79. *Born on* 22 Jan 1911 at Borth, Dyfed. *Son of* John Morris Evans and Sarah Pryce Evans. *Marriage:* 1st to Iris Elizabeth Gravelle (d.1973); 2nd to Madeleine Kirby, 1979. *Children:* John Wyn Evans. *Educated at* Ardyn, Aberystwyth; U.C.W., Aberystwyth; S.Michael's, Llandaff. *Career:* Deacon 1934; Priest 1935; Curate: Llanfihangel-ar-Arth 1934-36, Llanbadarn Fawr 1936-40, C.F., 1940-45; Vicar, Llandeloy W.Llanrheithan 1945-48; Penrhyncoch 1948; W.Elerch 1952-57; S.Michael, Aberystwyth 1957-67; Rural Dean, Llanbadarn Fawr 1957-67; Chaplain, Anglican Students 1966-67; Canon, St.Davids Cathedral (Caerfai) 1963-67; vicar, Llanafan Llanwnnws 1967-69; Chaplain, Earl of Lisburne 1967-69; vicar, Newcastle Emlyn 1969-79; mem., Governing Body and Liturgical Com. C in W 1956-79; mem., Court and Council, U.C.W. Aberystwyth 1958-67; Sub-visitor, S.D.U.C., Lampeter 1972-79. *Publications:* contributions to Llen Cymru yn y Bedwaredd Ganrifar

Bymtheg, 1968; Journal of Hist. Soc., Church in Wales and other Welsh Church periodicals and papers. *Recreation:* soccer, athletics, reading. *Address:* 31 Bryncastell, Bow Street, Dyfed. SY24 5DE.

EVANS, Professor David John, DSc, PhD, MSc, BSc, FIMA, C.Math, FBCS, C.Eng. *Born on* 30 Sept 1928 *Son of* the late Stanley Evans, of Llanelli, Dyfed, Wales and the late Margaret Ann (nee King). *Marriage:* to Naldera (nee Derry), 1955, da of Michael Owen (Late of Aberystwyth). *Children:* Neil Wyn (b.1961), Tracy Susanne (b.1962 (d.1990))and Clare Joanne (b.1963). *Educated at* Llanelli GS, Univ Coll Wales Aberystwyth (BSc), Univ of Southampton (MSc), Univ of Manchester (PhD), Univ of Wales (DSc). *Career:* Nat Service RAF 1950-52; Senior mathematician Rolls Royce Ltd Derby 1955-58; res fellow Univ of Manchester 1958-64; dir Computing Laboratory Univ of Sheffield 1964-71; professor of computing Loughborough Univ of Technology 1971- (dir Parallel Algorithms Res Centre 1988-_ FBCS, FIMA. *Publications:* Preconditioning Methods Theory and Applications, 1983; Parallel Processing Systems, 1983; Sparsity and its Applications, 1985. *Recreation:* music. *Address:* Croeso, 3 Milldale Close, Clifton Village, Nottingham NG11 8NU.

EVANS, Mr David Mervyn, MB, BS, FRCS. *Currently:* Hand Surgeon, Guy's Hospital and the Hand Clinic, Windsor. *Born on* 18 Sept 1942 at London. *Son of* E. Mervyn Evans FRCS and Muriel H.Evans (nee Amison). *Marriage:* to Dr.Elizabeth C.Hornung, 1971. *Children:* Daniel and Kate. *Educated at* Clifton College, Bristol; Middlesex Hospital Medical School. *Career:* previously Honorary Secretary, British Society for Surgery of the Hand; Council Member, British Association of Plastic Surgeons. Editor, The Journal of Hand Surgery (British Volume); Chairman, Medical Commission on Accident Prevention. Previously Consultant Plastic Surgeon, Wexham Park Hospital, Slough. *Publications:* papers and book chapters on Hand Surgery and Plastic Surgery. *Recreation:* piano, windsurfing, cycling, skiing. *Address:* The Hand Clinic, Oakley Green, Windsor SL4 4LH. Crossways, Hawthorn Lane, Farnham Common, Slough, SL2 3SW. Tel: 0753 831333.

EVANS, Mr David Milne, MA. *Currently:* Retired. *Born on* 8 Aug 1917 at Wallington, Surrey. *Son of* Walter Herbert Evans MSc and Florence Mary Evans (nee Milne). *Marriage:* to Gwynneth May (nee Griffiths) BA. *Educated at* Charterhouse (Scholar) Gonville & Caius College, Cambridge (Scholar, Warden, Maths Tripos). *Career:* Admin. Class Home Civil Service (War Office) 1939; Served Army, Major R.A. 1940-45; Assistant Secretary 1954; Imperial Defence College 1954; Under-Secretary of State, Ministry of Defence 1967-77; (Civil Service Department 1972); Cabinet Office 1977-81. *Recreation:* Reading, music, gardening. *Address:* 1 Church Rise, Walston Road, Wenvoe, Cardiff. CF5 6DE. Tel: 0222 597129.

EVANS, Dr David Philip, CBE, M.Sc., PhD., FRSC. *Currently:* Retired 1972. *Born on* 28 Feb 1908 at Taibach, Port Talbot. *Son of* David Charles Evans and Jennet (nee Thomas). *Marriage:* to Vura Helena Harcombe. *Children:* Dr David Harcombe Evans MB., BS.(London), FRCS(C), FACS. *Educated at* Port Talbot Grammar School; University College Cardiff. *Career:* Lecturer in Chemistry, Cardiff Technical College 1934; Principal Bridgend Technical College 1944; Principal Glamorgan Technical College

1952; Principal Glamorgan College of Technology 1958; Principal Glamorgan Polytechnic (later The Polytechnic of Wales) 1972; Hon. Fellow University of Wales College, Cardiff 1981; Hon. Fellow Polytechnic of Wales 1984. *Publications:* Various papers in the Journal of the Chemical Society; The Journal of the Faraday Society; The Journal of the Pharmaceutical Society; The Journal of the Society of Chemical Industry. *Recreation:* Gardening and music. *Address:* Tree Tops, St. Bride's Road, Ewenny Cross, Ewenny Bridgend. CF35 5RG.

EVANS, Mr David Roderick, QC., LL.M. *Currently:* Barrister. *Born on* 22 Oct 1946 at Gorseinon. *Son of* Thomas James Evans and Dorothy Evans (nee Carpenter). *Marriage:* to Kathryn Rebecca (nee Lewis) 1971. *Children:* Ioan, Gwion, Saran and Gruffudd. *Educated at* Bishop Gore Grammar School, Swansea 1957-64; University College, London 1964-68. *Career:* Called to the Bar of Gray's Inn 1970; Recorder of Crown Court assigned to Wales & Chester Circuit 1987; Appointed Queen's Counsel 1989. *Recreation:* Walking, reading, welsh ceramics. *Address:* Sycharth, 221 Clasemont Road, Morriston, Swansea, SA6 6BT. Angel Chambers, 94 Walter Road, Swansea SA1 5QA.

EVANS, Mr David Wyn, BSc (Hons); DipSoc Stud (Oxon). *Currently:* Development Officer for The Sports Council for Wales. *Born on* 1 Nov 1965 at Wootten Bassett. *Son of* Mr Gareth Norman Evans and Mrs Wendy Maureen Evans. *Marriage:* to Mrs Roberta King-Evans (nee King). *Children: Educated at* BSc (Jons) Management Science, Swansea University 1985-88; Diploma in Social Studies, Oxford University 1988-89. *Career:* Under 18 Welsh Schoolboys (3 caps), under 21 Welsh Captain, under 23 Welsh Captain, Wales B, Wales (11 caps), Oxford Blue, 1988-89, Barbarians, Public School Wanderers, Glamorgan County Captain, Crawshays, British Students, Welsh Students (12 caps and captain), Cardiff RFC Captain 1990-91 and 1991-92, Welsh Academicals, Swansea University 1985-88. *Recreation:* playing the guitar, learning to speak Welsh, bungy jumping. *Clubs:* Cardiff RFC. *Address:* 13 Maes-Y-Sarn, Pentyrch, Mid Glamorgan, S.Wales. CF4 8QQ.

EVANS, Sir Geraint Llewellyn, CBE., OSt.J. *Currently:* Retired. *Born on* 16 Feb. 1922 at Cilfynydd, Pontypridd. *Son of* the late Williams John Evans and the late Charlotte May Evans. *Marriage:* to Brenda Evans Davies, 1948. *Children:* Alun Grant Evans and Huw Grant Evans *Educated at* Guildhall School of Music and Drama *Career:* International Opera Singer; Founder Director HTV; C.B.E., 1959; Knighthood, 1969; Fellow of: Guildhall School of Music, 1960, Univ. Coll.Cardiff, 1976, Royal Northern Coll. of Music, 1978, Jesus Coll. Oxford, 1979, Royal Coll. of Music, 1981, Royal Soc. of Arts, 1984, Trinity Coll. of Music, London, 1987, University College, Aberystwyth, 1988, Univ. Coll. Swansea, 1990; Hon.D.Mus: Univ. Coll.of Wales, 1965, Univ.of Leics, 1969, Council for Nat. Academic Awards, 1980, Univ. of London, 1982, Oxford University, 1985; Hon.Mbr.Royal Academy of Music, 1969; Mbr Royal Soc. of Musicians, 1981; Mbr.of Gorsedd of Bards, Nat. Eisteddfod Wales; Vice-Pres. Hon.Soc. of Cymmrodorion, 1984; Offcr. of the Order of St. John, 1986; Freeman of City of London, 1984; Sir Charles Santley Memorial Award, 1963; Harriet Cohen Int. Music Award, Opera Medal, 1967; San Francisco Opera Medal, 1980; Fidelio Medal (Int.

Assoc. of Opera Directors), 1980; High Sheriff of Dyfed, 1991-92. *Publications:* Sir Geraint Evans, a Knight at the Opera (with Noel Goodwin), 1985. *Recreation:* Sailing and rugby *Clubs:* Athenaeum, Cardiff and County. *Address:* Trelawney, Aberaeron, Dyfed. SA46 OBD.

EVANS, Glyn, *Currently:* Editor Y Cymro since 1979. *Born* at Anglesey. *Marriage:* to Sandy White (died December 1988). *Children:* Catrin, Bethan and Dyfan. *Educated at* Ysgol David Hughes, Beaumaris; College for 1 year. *Career:* Labourer, Railway Worker, Local Government Officer Glamorgan Education Dept; Joined Y Cymro 1967, Herald Newspapers News Editor 1976, Arfon Borough Council Translator 1979. *Publications:* Minafon, Pigion am y gyfres deledu (Hughes 1989); various articles. *Recreation:* gardening, reading, writing. *Address:* Swyddfa'r Cymro, Parc Busnes, Yr Wyddgrug, Clwyd, CH7 1XY. Tel: 0352 700022.

EVANS, Mr Gwynfor, MA., Ll.B., D.Litt. *Currently:* Retired. *Born on* 1 Sept 1912 at Barry. *Son of* Dan and Catherine Evans. *Marriage:* to Rhiannon Prys, 1941. *Children:* Alcwyn Deiniol, Dafydd Prys, Meleri Mair, Guto Prys, Meinir Ceridwen, Branwen Eluned and Rhys Dyrfal. *Educated at* Barry County School; Univ. Coll. of Wales, Aberystwyth; St. John's Coll. Oxford. *Career:* Market Gardener; Hon.Sec.Heddychwyr Cymru, 1939-45; Plaid Cymru Exec. since 1937; Vice-Pres.Plaid Cymru, 1943-45; Pres. 1945-81; Currently Hon.Pres; Carmarthen C.C., 1949-74; Pres. Union of Welsh Independents, 1954; M.P. for Carmarthen, 1966-70, 1974-79; Univ. of Wales Court, 1946-71, Council, 1970-78; Council and Court UCW Aberystwyth, 1946-91; Welsh Advisory Commt.Brtsh Council, 1947-91; Undeb Cymru Fydd Cncl, 1940-60; Welsh Broadcasting Cncl, 1957-60; Chrmn, Celtic League, 1964-74; Vice-Pres.CND Cymru, 1982-87. *Publications:* Plaid Cymru & Wales; Rhagom I Ryddid; Wales Can Win; Aros Mae; Land of My Fathers; Nonviolent Nationalism; A National Future for Wales; Diwedd Prydeindod' Seiri Cenedl; Welsh Nation Builders; Pe Bai Cymru'n Rhydd; Fighting for Wales; Heddychiaeth Gristnogol yng Nghymru. *Address:* Talar Wen, Pencarreg, Llanybydder, Dyfed.

EVANS, Mr Haydn Keith, BA., Dip.Ed., MA., FRSA. *Currently:* Director of Education, Clwyd County Council 1984- . *Born on* 21 Jan 1931 at Gorseinon, Glam. *Son of* the late D.B. Evans and the late A.O. Evans. *Marriage:* to Dorothy Cyrene Llewellyn 1956. *Children:* Ceri Llewellyn and Elizabeth Anne. *Educated at* Port Talbot Secondary Grammar School; University College, Cardiff. *Career:* Royal Army Educational Corps. 1952-54; Teacher/Lecturer Secondary Modern School, College of F.E., Comprehensive School (Port Talbot) 1955-62; Lecturer in Education University College, Swansea 1962-68; Education Officer/ Producer HTV (Cardiff and Bristol) 1968-70; Deputy Director of Education (Flintshire) 1970-74; Deputy Director Clwyd 1974-84; Board Member of Training & Enterprise (N.E.Wales Tec) 1990- . *Recreation:* Walking, theatre, cinema, snooker. *Clubs:* Mold Ex Servicemens *Address:* 4 Maes Yr Haf, Mold, Clwyd CH7 1TR. Tel: 0352 753743 Department Of Education, Shire Hall, Mold, Clwyd CH7 6TR.

EVANS, Prof. Henry John, BSc; PhD; F.I.Biol; FRCPE; FRSE *Currently:* Director, MRC Human Genetics Unit, Edinburgh. *Born on* 24 Dec 1930 at Llanelli. *Son of* David

Evans and Gwladys Evans. *Marriage:* 1st to Gwenda R (nee Thomas) (d.1974); 2nd to Roslyn R.(nee Angell), 1976. *Children:* Paul D, W.Hugh. John K and Owen J. *Educated at* Llanelli Boys Grammar; Univ. of Wales, Aberystwyth. *Career:* Research Scientist MRC Radiobiological Research unit, Harwell, 1955-65; Research Fellow, Brookhaven Nat. Lab., NY, USA 1960-61; Prof. Genetics Univ. Aberdeen 1965-69; Hon.Prof., Univ Edinburgh 1970; Chmn.Assoc. Radiation Research 1970-72; member, MRC Biol Res.Bd., 1968-72; MRC Council 1978-82; DHSS Cttee on Mutagenesis 1978- ; on medical aspects of radiation exposure 1985- ; board of Governors, Lister Inst. Med. Res., 1982- ; National Radiological Protection Board 1982- ; Caledonian Res. Found. 1989- ; Alberta Heritage Found. for Medical Res., 1986- ; Imp. Cancer Res. Found., 1985-90; Cancer Res. Campaign 1990- ; Beatson Inst. for Cancer Res., 1987- ; Chairman, Int. Agency Res. in Cancer, Lyon 1982-86; Scientific Cttee Cancer Research Campaign 1990- ; visiting professor, Rome Italy 1967; Kyoto, Japan 1981; Calgary, Vancouver, Canada 1983; Adelaide, Australia 1986; various eponymous lectures, prizes. *Publications:* some 300 research publications on genetics and in particular on radiation genetics, mutation and cancer; editor of various journals and books on mutagenesis and human genetics. *Recreation:* golf, fishing and despairing at current Welsh rugby. *Clubs:* New, Edinburgh. *Address:* M R C Human Genetics Unit, Western General Hospital, Crew Road, Edinburgh, EH4 2XU. 45 Lauder Road, Edinburgh EH9 1UE.

EVANS, Mr Huw Prideaux, MA., MSc. *Currently:* Deputy Secretary (Overseas Finance) H.M. Treasury. *Born on* 21 Aug 1941 at Carmarthen. *Son of* Richard Hubert Evans and Kathleen (nee Collins). *Marriage:* to Anne (nee Bray). *Children:* Richard and Lewis. *Educated at* Cardiff High School; King's College, Cambridge; L.S.E. *Career:* Economist, H.M. Treasury 1964-73; Economic Adviser, Hong Kong Government 1973-75; Senior Economic Adviser, H.M. Treasury 1976-79; Under Secretary in charge of economic forestry 1980-86; International finance 1986-89. *Recreation:* Walking, opera, Edwardian topography. *Clubs:* Oxford and Cambridge. *Address:* c/o HM Treasury, Parliament Street, London. SW1.

EVANS, Dr. Ian Philip, MA PLd MRSC C.Chem *Currently:* Headmaster, Bedford School. *Born on* 2 MAy 1948 at Wrexham, Clwyd. *Son of* Joseph Emlyn Evans and Beryl Evans. *Marriage:* Sandra Veronica Waggett 1972. *Children:* Benjamin Joseph and Roland Mathonwy *Educated at* Ruabon Boys' Grammar School; Churchill College, Cambridge; Imperial College, London; BA 1970 1st Class Honours Nat. Scis. Tripos; MA 1973; Phd 1973: *Career:* Post Doctoral Fellowship, Australian National Univ. 1973-5; Assistant Master, St. Paul's School 1975-90; (Head of Chemistry Dept. 1984-80); Chief Examiner A-Level Chemistry, Univ. London School Examination Board 1987-90; *Publications:* Papers in Learned Journals. *Recreation:* Cricket, music and poetry. *Address:* Bedford School, Burnaby Road, Bedford. MK40 2TU. Tel: 0234 353436.

EVANS, Colonel James Ellis, CBE, TD, JP. *Currently:* Retired. *Born on* 6 Aug 1910 at Manchester. *Son of* James William and Eleanor Evans. *Educated at* Epworth College, Rhyl, Chartered Accountant. *Career:* Lord Lieutenant of Clwyd 1979-85; Joined TA 1937; served War of 1939-45, RA: France, 1940; N.Africa 1941-44; Italy 1944-45; comd.

384 Light Regt RA (RWF), TA 1947-52; Dep. CRA 53 (Welsh) Div., 1953-57; Chm. Denbigh and Flint TA Assoc., 1961-58; Chm. Wales and Mon TA&VRA, 1971-74 (Vice-Chm., 1968-71); Pres., Wales TA&VRA 1981-85; Mem., Prestatyn UDC, 1939-74 (Chm 1947); Member, Prestatyn Town Council 1974-75; Clwyd, formerly Flintshire: JP 1951; DL 1953; High Sheriff 1970-71; Vice-Lieut 1970-74; Vice Lord-Lieut 1977-79; Chm. North Wales Police Authority 1976-78. *Publications:* none *Recreation:* lawn tennis (played for Wales and Lancashire 1936-48), gardening, watching sporting events. *Clubs:* City (Chester). *Address:* Trafford Mount, Gronant Road, Prestatyn, Clwyd. LL19 9DT.

EVANS, The Venerable John Barrie, MA *Currently:* Archdeacon of Newport, since 1986. *Born on* 14 July 1923 at Caerleon. *Son of* the late John B.Evans and the late Maude (nee Holland). *Marriage:* to Joan Morton, 1951 (decsd). *Children:* Christopher and Martin. *Educated at* S.D.C. Lampeter, BA; St.Edmund Hall Oxford MA. *Career:* Ordained 1951; Curate of Trevethin 1951-57; Vicar of Caerwent and Llanfair Discoed 1957-64; Vicar of Chepstow 1964-79; Canon of Monmouth 1971; Archdeacon of Monmouth 1977; Rector of Llanmartin and Langstone 1979-86. *Recreation:* gardening, travel. *Clubs:* St.Pierre. *Address:* 16 Stow Park Crescent, Newport, Gwent NP9 4HD. Tel: 0633 264919.

EVANS, His Honour Judge John Field, Q.C., M.A. *Currently:* Circuit Judge since 1978 (Resident Judge, Wolverhampton Crown Court). *Born on* 27 Sept 1928 at Llandaff. *Son of* John David Evans and Lucy May Evans (nee Field). *Educated at* Cardiff High School; Exeter College Oxford. *Career:* National Service 1947-49, Royal Air Force. Commissioned Pilot Officer 1948. Called to the Bar Inner Temple, 1953, Q.C., 1972. Formerly: a Deputy Chairman Worcestershire Quarter Sessions and a Recorder of the Crown Court. *Recreation:* golf. *Clubs:* Vincents (Oxford), Edgbaston and Royal St.David's Golf. *Address:* Wolverhampton Combined Court, Centre, Pipers Row, Wolverhampton.

EVANS, Lieutenant Colonel John Roberts, TD** (1954) DL (1973). *Currently:* Solicitor. *Born on* 16 Jan 1917 at Pontypridd, Glamorgan. *Son of* the late David James Haydn Evans and the late Bronwen Evans (nee Roberts). *Marriage:* to Sheila Rita Ball, 1945. *Children:* Laraine Joy and David Roderic Brennan. *Educated at* Llandovery College; Exeter University. *Career:* BA (Hons 1939); served in World War II with H.A.C. and Royal Artillery (UK, India, Far East), 1939-46; with Welch Regiment (TA), 1947-66; Lieut-Colonel 6th (Glam) Battalion The Welch Regiment (TA) 1963-66. Admitted a Solicitor of the Supreme Court 1952; President Cardiff and District Law Society (formerly Vice-Pres) 1981-82; Honorary Solicitor, Welsh Rugby Union 1968- ; Trustee: Welsh Rugby Union Charitable Fund 1972- ; Trustee: Welsh Sports Trust 1978- ; Governor, Welsh Sports Aid Foundation 1982- ; Trustee of Llandovery College, 1972- (Chairman of Trustees of Llandovery College 1981-92); member Court of Governors, University College, Cardiff 1975-81. *Recreation:* music, reading, rugby football. *Clubs:* Cardiff & County. *Address:* Greenbanks, 20 Highfields, Llandaff, Cardiff, CF5 2QA. Tel: 0222 562480

EVANS, Mr John Wynford, MA, FBCS, F.Inst.D, FRSA, CBIM, Comp.IEE. *Currently:* Chairman, South Wales

Electricity Plc. since 1984. *Born on* 3 Nov 1934 at Llanelli. *Son of* the late Gwilym Everton and Margaret Mary Elfreda Evans. *Marriage:* to Sigrun Brethfield 1957. *Children:* three s. *Educated at* Llanelli Grammar School; St. John's Coll., Cambridge. *Career:* Served RAF (Flying Officer) 1955-57; IBM 1957-58; NAAFI, W.Germany 1959-62; Kayser Bondor 1962-63; various posts. inc. Computer and Management Services Manager S.Wales Electricity Board 1963-76; ASC, Henley 1968; Dep. Chm. London Electricity Board 1977-84; Member: Hon.Soc. of Cymmrodorion 1978; Dep.Chmn. Court, Cranfield Inst. of Tech. 1980-88; Milton Keynes IT Adv. Panel 1982-84; CBI Wales, Reg.Council 1984- , Chmn. 1991-; Nat.Trust Cttee for Wales 1985-90; Chmn, SE Wales Cttee, Industry Year 1986; Govnr, Polytechnic of Wales 1987-88; Dir, 1992 Nat.Garden Festival Ltd., 1987-88; Welsh Language Board 1988-89; Dir, Welsh Nat.Opera Ltd., 1988-; Dir, Bank of Wales 1989-; Dep.Chmn, Prince of Wales Cttee 1989-. *Recreation:* Fishing, cross-country ski-ing, golf. *Clubs:* Flyfishers', London Welsh; Cardiff and Country, Radyr Golf. *Address:* South Wales Electricity Plc, Newport Road, St.Mellons, Cardiff CF3 9XW.

EVANS, Mrs Linda, *Currently:* Bowls coach p/t, Swansea Leisure Centre. *Born on* 14 March 1942 at Briton Ferry. *Daughter of* Eileen and Ritchie Thomas. *Marriage:* to Keith, 1971. *Educated at* Neath Girls Grammar School. *Career:* International 1982- ; Commonwealth Games Gold Medalist in Fours, Edinburgh 1986; represented Wales in Commonwealth Games Fours in New Zealand 1990; represented British Isles in Australia, Bi Centennial Tournament 1988; Welsh Pairs winner 1986; Welsh Triples winner 1980-81; Welsh Fours winner 1979. County 2 wood singles winner 1990; County 4 wood singles winner 1989; County pairs winner 1982/86; County triples winner 1979/80/82/83 and 90; County fours winner 1985/87. Qualified Bowls Coach and Umpire. First lady to umpire in Granada Television's 'Superbowl' Tournament. *Recreation:* television, knitting, live theatre. *Clubs:* Outdoor Bowls, Port Talbot; Indoor Bowls, Swansea. *Address:* 278 Old Road, Briton Ferry, Neath, West Glamorgan SA11 2ET.

EVANS, Mr Mark, LLB *Currently:* Barrister. *Born on* 21 March 1946 at Carmarthen. *Son of* Rev. Clifford Evans and Mary Evans (nee Jones) of Brynamman. *Marriage:* to Dr.Barbara Skew, 1971. *Children:* John Clifford Evans and Claire Elizabeth Evans. *Educated at* Christ College, Brecon; Kings College, London (LLB). *Career:* Called to Bar, Grays Inn, 1971; practised London and Bristol; formed St. Johns Chambers, Bristol 1978; Head of Chambers 1987; Trustee Youth and Community Help Trust 1984; Director Avon Motor Project 1984; Chairman South Glamorgan Child Abuse Enquiry 1989. *Recreation:* music, vintage motor engineering. *Clubs:* Bristol Savages *Address:* 6 Cotham Road, Bristol BS6 6DR.

EVANS, Mr Myrddin, *Currently:* Retired, Prudential Ass.Co. Ltd., Agent. *Born on* 14 Nov 1919 at Ammanford. *Son of* the late William Arthur Evans and Mary Ann Evans. *Children:* Delyth Ann Evans *Educated at* Ammanford Technical College. *Career:* Chairman, Prudential Ass.Co.Ltd., Staff Union; Chairman, Ammanford UDC 1962 & 1972; Chairman Dyfed CC 1990-91; Chairman of Finance; Chairman Development Finance Education; Chairman of Investment Panel Dyfed Superanuation Fund;

Vice-Chairman of Policy Resources; Governor of Swansea University; Life President of Ammanford Boys Scouts, one of the founders. *Recreation:* fishing, music. *Clubs:* Trustee of Babtist Ebenezer, Ammanford. *Address:* 43 High Street, Ammanford, Dyfed SA18 2NB.

EVANS, Mr Nigel Martin, BA, *Currently:* Retail in Swansea; Research in political matters in Clitheroe. *Born on* 10 Nov 1957 at Swansea. *Son of* Albert and Betty Evans. *Educated at* Dynevor School, Swansea; Swansea University. *Career:* former Vice-Chairman of Wales Young Conservatives; former Chairman of Welsh Conservative Parliamentary Candidates; West Glamorgan County Councillor 1985-91; Contested Swansea West for Conservative (Gen.Elec), 1987; Deputy leader of Conservative W.G.County Council 1989; contested Pontypridd for Conservatives at by-election 1989; contested Ribble Valley for Conservatives at by-election 1991; President of A.W.Conservative candidates. *Recreation:* tennis, cinema, travel, int. politics, charity work. *Clubs:* Royal Commonwealth Society, Royal Overseas League, National Trust. *Address:* 6 Crumpax Avenue, Longridge, Nr Preston PR3 3JQ. 5 Graiglwyd Square, Cockett, Swansea SA2 OUY.

EVANS, Dr. Noel John Bebbington, CB., MA., MB., BChir., DPH., FRCP., FFPHM., Barrister at Law *Currently:* Chairman, National Biological Standards Bd' Chmn, U.K. Transplant Support Serv (special Health Auth); Consultant in Health Serv. Management; Mbr. of Chairmen's Panel Recruitment and Assessment Serv; Privy Council nominee on Council of Royal Pharmaceutical Society of G.B. *Born on* 26 Dec 1933 at Cardiff. *Son of* William John and Gladys Ellen (nee Bebbington). *Marriage:* to 1) Elizabeth Mary Garbutt, 1960 (dissolved); 2)Eileen Jane McMullan 1974. *Children:* David, Sarah and Hugh. *Educated at* Hymers College, Hull; Christ's College, Cambridge; Grays Inn. *Career:* Deputy CMO, and subsequently administrative Deputy Sec.DHSS 1977-84; Mbr.Countryside Commission Commt. for Wales 1985-90; Chmn.Welsh Commt. on Drug Misuse 1986-91; *Publications:* Reports to Welsh Office on Health Services Research 1986; Microbiology Services in S.Glamorgan 1988; Postgraduate and continuing Medical Education in Wales 1991; Reports to Dept. of Health on Control of Medicines with P. Cunliffe 1987; United Kingdom Transplant Service 1990; Report to Isle of Man Government on Health Services Inquiry with P. Benner 1986; Various studies for Cabinet Office Top Management Programme 1985-89; Report on Organisation and Planning of Health Services in Yugoslavia 1967. *Recreation:* Photography (trading as John Evans Photographic, Grosmont). *Address:* Athelstan, Grosmont, Abergavenny, Gwent NP7 8LW. Tel: 0981 240616

EVANS, Emeritus Professor Rhydwyn Harding, CBE 1958; MSc, DSc, PhD; FICE, FIMechE, MSocCE, Hon. MIPlantE. *Currently:* formerly Professor of Civil Engineering and Administrative Head of Engineering Departments, University of Leeds 1946-68. *Born on* 9 Oct 1900 *Son of* the late David Evans, Tygwyn, Pontardulais, Glam. *Marriage:* to Dilys Elizabeth, 1929, o c of late George Reespoet and Hymnologist, and Kate Ann Rees, London. *Children:* one s. *Educated at* Llanelly Grammar School; University of Manchester. *Career:* Mercantile Marine 1918-20. BSc top 1st class Graduate Prizeman 1923; MSc 1928; PhD 1932; DSc 1943. Demonstrator, Asst.

Lecturer, Lecturer, Senior Lecturer and later Reader in Civil Engineering, University of Leeds 1926-46; Dean, Faculty of Tech, University of Leeds 1948-51; Pro-Vice-Chancellor, Univ. of Leeds 1961-65; Lectures: Unwin Meml ICE 1960; first George Hondros Meml, WA 1970. IStructE: Vice-Pres., 1948-49; Chm Yorks Br., 1940-41, 1955-56 and 1958-59 (Yotkshire Br. Prize 1946-47 and 1950-51); ICE: Chm. Yorks Assoc., 1942-43 and 1952-53; Mem. Council, 1949-52; Mem., Joint Matriculation Bd, Manchester 1949-68; Chm Leeds Univ Min of Labour and NS Bd 1949-60; first Chm Trng Consultative Cttee, Cement and Concrete Assoc 1966-73; Consulting Editor in Civil Engineering: McGraw-Hill Book Co. (UK) Ltd 1975- ; Pitman Ltd 1978- ; Longmans Group 1986; Routledge Chapman Hall 1987; Hon.Mem. Concrete Soc 1970. Hon DesSc Ghent 1953. Hon DTech Bradford 1971. Rugby Engrg Soc Student's Prize 1925; Telford Premiums 1942-43-44; Medal, Ghent Univ 1949, 1953; George Stephenson Gold Medal 1956; Institution of Water Engineers, Instn Premium 1953; Reinforced Concrete Assoc Medal 1961; Instn of Struct Engrs, Research Diploma 1965; Certif. of Commendation 1970; Henry Adams Award 1971. *Publications:* Prestressed Concrete (with E.W.Bennett) 1962; Concrete Plain, Reinforced Prestressed, Shell (with C.B. Wilby) 1963; Reinforced and Prestressed Concrete (with F.K. Kong) 1975 (3 edn 1988); papers on elasticity and plasticity of concrete and other building materials, strain and stress distribution in reinforced concrete beams and arches; prestressed concrete; extensibility, cracking and tensile stress-strain of concrete; bond stresses; shear stresses; combined bending and shear stresses; torsional stresses; preflexed pre-stressed concrete beams; lightweight aggregate concrete; vibration and pressure moulding of concrete in Journals of Institutions of Civil, Struct and Water Engineers, Concrete Soc., Philosophical Magazine, Engineer, Engineering, Civil Engineering and Public Works. *Recreation:* motoring, travel, gardening. *Address:* 23 Christopher Rise, Pontlliw, Swansea, West Glam. SA4 1EN. Tel: 0792 891961.

EVANS, Rev. Robert Alun, B.A. *Currently:* Head of Production Centre, BBC Bangor. *Born on* 7 Sept 1936 at Llanbryn-Mair, Powys. *Son of* the late Robert and the late Ada Evans. *Marriage:* to D. Rhiannon Morris. *Children:* Rhys Powys and Betsan Powys. *Educated at* Univ. Coll. of N. Wales and Bala-Bangor Theological Coll. *Career:* Minister of Religion (Seion Congregational Church, Llandysul, 1961-64; BBC TV Producer, 1964-69; Freelance Broadcaster, 1969-79. *Publications:* Editor Eight Vols. Rhwng Gwyl a Gwaith *Recreation:* Fly Fishing, sport in general *Address:* Nant Yr Eira, 35 Tal Y Cae, Tregarth, Bangor, Gwynedd, LL57 4AE. Bryn Meirion, Bangor, Gwynedd LL57 2BY.

EVANS, Mr Roger Kenneth, MA (Cantab). *Currently:* Barrister. *Born on* 18 March 1947 at Cardiff. *Son of* Gerald Raymond Evans and Dr. Annie Margaret Evans. *Marriage:* to June Rodgers 1973. *Children:* Edward and Henry. *Educated at* The Grammar School, Bristol; Trinity Hall, Cambridge. *Career:* Chairman of Cambridge University Conservative Association (Lent 1969); President of Cambridge Union (Lent 1970); Parliamentary Candidate for Conservatives, Warley West 1974-79; Ynys Mon 1987; Monmouth Bye-Election 1991; PPC for Monmouth. *Clubs:*

Carlton, Cumphry (Chairman 1976-77, Treasurer 1983-87. *Address:* Cae Coed, Great Oak, Nr Raglan, Gwent NP5 2BN. 2 Harcourt Buildings, Temple, London EC49 9DB.

EVANS, Mr Roy Lyon, *Currently:* General Secretary, Iron & Steel Trades Confederation, since 1985. *Born on* 13 Aug 1931 at Pontardulais, W.Glam. *Son of* the late David Lewis Evans and Saray (nee Lyon). *Marriage:* to Brenda Yvonne Jones, 1960. *Children:* Julie, Ian and Lisa. *Educated at* Gowerton Grammar School; Rutgers Coll., USA. *Career:* Divisional Organiser ISTC, Mancehster, 1964; Divisional Organiser ISTC, Swansea, 1969; Asst. General Secretary ISTC, London 1973; Chairman TUC Steel Committee 1985- ; Hon.Sec., IMF (British Section), 1985- ; Pres. Iron & Steel Dept IMF 1985- ; member of ECSC Conservative Committee 1985- ; President ECSC Cons, Comm., 1986-88, (Vice Pres. 1989-90); Chairman Committee General Objectives, ECSC Cons, Comm., 1990- ; member, Executive Comm, Labour Party 1981-84; TUC General Council 1985- ; member, F&GP, TUC, Comm, 1990- ; President, Industrial Orphopaedic Society Manor House Hospital 1987-88; Board member, BS plc (Industry) Ltd., 1986- ; Employee Secretary Slag JIC, 1973-85; Employees Secretary, Sheet/Strip Trade Board BS plc, 1985- . *Recreation:* opera, music, walking, reading (non fiction). *Address:* 26 Crecy Gardens, Redbourn, Nr. St Albans, Herts AL3 7BQD.

EVANS, Professor Trevor, FRS 1988, BSc, PhD, DSc (Bristol Univ 1948-55), FInstP. *Currently:* Professor of Physics, University of Reading. *Born on* 26 April 1927 at Tondu, Glamorgan. *Son of* Henry Evans and Margaret Evans. *Marriage:* to Patricia Margaret Booth (nee Johnson). *Children:* Martin David Evans and Jonathan Michael Evans. *Educated at* Tondu School; Bridgend Grammar; University of Bristol. *Career:* RAF 1945-48; British Nylon Spinners 1955-56; Tube Investments Research Laboratory 1956-58; Physics Department, University of Reading 1958- ; Warden, Wantage Hall, Univesity of Reading 1971-84; Head of Physics Department, Reading University 1984-88. *Publications:* Scientific papers in Phil. Mag., and Proc. Roy Soc., mostly concerning synthetic and natural diamonds. *Recreation:* gardening, opera. *Address:* Aston, Tutts Clump, Reading, Berks. RG7 6JZ. J.J.Thomson Physical Lab., Whiteknights University, P.O. Box 220, Reading, RG6 2AF.

EVANS, Mr Trevor Mills, ACIS, ATII (Solicitor). *Born on* 28 Sept 1924 at Swansea, Glamorgan. *Son of* the late William Arthur Evans and the late Alma Evans (nee Mills). *Marriage:* to Margaret (nee Jones), 1952. *Children:* Eifrion Mills Evans, Adrian Mills Evans, Meirion Mills Evans and Susan Alma Evans. *Educated at* Swansea Grammar School. *Career:* until June 1988 Senior Partner in Sydney G.Thomas & Co., Solicitors, Builth Wells and thereafter Consultant with same firm; H.M.Coroner for South Powys 1966-89. *Recreation:* dogs (Chairman of Welsh Kennel Club), photography, male voice choirs, sport. *Clubs:* Kennel Club *Address:* Plasnewydd, Broadway, Builth Wells, Powys, LD2 3DB. Tel: 0982 553688.

EVANS, Dr William Anthony Lloyd, MSc, PhD. *Currently:* retired. *Born on* 4 Feb 1924 at Aberdare. .*Marriage:* to Kathleen Bullock, 1949 (now K.Evans OBE, JP, BSc.). *Children:* Dr Paul Evans *Educated at* University of Birmingham; University of London. *Career:* Senior Lecturer in Zoology, Cardiff University 1946-86; Dean of

Science 1979-82; Chief Examiner for W.J.E.C., 1964-72; President Cardiff Scientific Society 1976-78; Hon Secretary Welsh AAA 1974-91; Chairman, British Amateur Athletic Board 1980-84; Chairman AAA 1989-91; Chairman BAF (British Athletic Federation), 1991- (formed in 1991); member, Sports Council for Wales 1984-90; Chairman, Welsh Sports Aid Grants Committee 1983- ; member, Sports Aid Foundation, Grants Committee 1983- . *Publications:* articles in various scientific journals *Recreation:* athletics *Clubs:* Cardiff AAC, Glamorganshire GC *Address:* "Winterbourne", Greenway Close, Llandough, Penarth, CF6 1LZ.

EVANS, Professor William Desmond, BSc, DPhil. *Currently:* Professor of Pure Maths, University of Wales, College of Cardiff, since 1977. *Born on* 7 March 1940 at Brynaman. *Son of* Bryngwyn and the late Evelyn (nee Jones). *Marriage:* to Mari (nee Richards), 1966. *Children:* Dyfed Wyn and Owain Prys. *Educated at* Ystalyfera Grammar School; University of Wales, Swansea; Jesus College, Oxford University. *Career:* Lecturer and Senior lecturer, University College, Cardiff 1964-75; Reader, University of Wales, Cardiff 1975-77. *Publications:* book: Spectral Theory and Differential Operators (with D.E.Edmunds) OUP, 1987 and 1990; about 70 papers in Mathematical journals; Editor (with J.Wiegold) of The Proceedings Of The London Mathematical Society, 1986- . *Recreation:* tennis, walking, reading, music. *Address:* 9 The Lettons Way, Dinas Powys, South Glamorgan, CF6 4BY.

EVANS, Mr William Emrys, CBE 1981. *Born on* 4 April 1924 at Bwlch-y-Pentre, Llangadfan, Welshpool, Powys. *Son of* the late Richard and Mary Elizabeth Evans. *Marriage:* to Mair Thomas 1946. *Children:* one d. *Educated at* Llanfair Caereinion Country School, FCIB. *Career:* Senior Regional Director, Wales, Midland Bank PLC 1976-84; Served War, RN 1942-46 (despatches 1944); Entered Midland Bank Ltd 1941; Asst. Gen. Manager (Agric), 1967-72; Reg. Dir. S.Wales 1972-74; Reg. Dir. Wales 1974-76; Director: Executive Secondment Ltd 1983-90 (Vice Chm., 1983-90); Align-Rite Ltd 1984- ; National Welsh Omnibus Services Ltd 1989-92 ; Chm. Menter a Busnes 1988- ; Chmn: Welsh Cttee for Economic and Industrial Affairs 1984-91; Midland Bank adv. Council for Wales, 1984- ; Director: Develt Corp for Wales 1973-77; Welsh Ind. Develt Adv. Bd, 1975-86; Develt Bd for Rural Wales 1976-89; Royal Welsh Agricl Soc., 1973- ; Mem. Council CBI, Wales 1975-86 (Chm. 1979-81); Pres., Royal Nat. Eisteddfod of Wales Foundn 1980- ; Chm. Dr Barnardo's Centenary in Wales Appeal 1988; Trustee: Catherine and Lady Grace James Foundn 1973- ; John and Rhys Thomas James Foundn, 1973- ; Welsh Sports Aid Trust 1980- ; (Vice Chm 1988-); Llandovery Coll., 1982- ; Chm. Welsh Sports Aid Foundn 1988 - (Gov. 1980-); Member: Council for the Welsh Lang., 1973-78; Design Council Wales Adv.Cttee 1981-86; Prince of Wales Cttee 1975-87; Dairy Produce Quota Tribunal 1984-92; Pres. Welsh Congregational Church in Wales 1989; Treasurer: Congregational Church in Wales 1975-86; Mansfield Coll. Oxford 1977-89 (Trustee 1989-); Mem of Court and Council, UC Cardiff 1981-84; Mem. Court and Council, Univ. of Wales 1972- ; Hon. LLD Wales 1983; FRSA 1982; High Sheriff, S Glamorgan 1985-86. *Recreation:* golf, gardening, music. *Clubs:* Cardiff and

County (Cardiff). *Address:* Maesglas, Pen-y-turnpike, Dinas Powis, S. Glam., CF6 4HH. Tel: 0222 512985

EVANS, Mr William Lloyd, *Currently:* Retired Headmaster. *Born on* 27 Nov 1927 at St. Nicholas, Pembrokeshire. *Son of* the late John Evans and Dinah (nee Vittle). *Children:* Julia. *Educated at* Fishguard Secondary and Trinity College. *Career:* Army Service with the Indian Army in the Far East; Sports Master Nuneaton followed by various posts in Primary and Secondary Schools in Dyfed; Headmaster; County, District and Town Councillor; Past Chairman District Council and Mayor of Fishguard & Goodwick; Past Chairman Dyfed Schools Committee; Present Chairman of Preseli Planning Committee. *Recreation:* Participation in sport in younger days now interested in following rugby, soccer and cricket. *Address:* Cabrini, Church Road, Goodwick, Fishguard. SA64 OEH.

EVANS OF CLAUGHTON, Baron David Thomas Gruffydd, LL.B., J.P., D.L. *Currently:* Senior Partner of Solicitors on Merseyside. *Born on* 9 Feb 1928 at Claughton, Wirral. *Son of* John Cynlais Evans and Neni Evans. *Marriage:* to Moira Elizabeth Rankin. *Children:* Elizabeth, David, Sarah and Jane. *Educated at* Birkenhead School; Friars School Bangor; University of Liverpool. *Career:* Former President of Welsh Liberal Party; Former Chairman of Liberal Party Organisation 1966-69; Former President of Liberal Party Organisation 1978; Chairman of National League of Young Liberals 1962; Councillor in Merseyside 1957-81; Chairman Marcher Sound Radio Wrexham, Granada T.V. *Recreation:* Reading politics and media. *Clubs:* MCC; National Liberal; Ceredigion Antiquarian Society. *Address:* 69 Bidston Road, Claughton, Birkenhead, L43 6TR.3 Upton Road, Claughton, Birkenhead, L41 ODE

EWARD, Paul Anthony, *Currently:* Solicitor. *Born on* 22 Dec 1942 at Colchester. *Son of* the late The Reverend Harvey Kennedy Eward and Delphine Eugenie Louise Eward (nee Pain). *Marriage:* to Dene Kathleen Bartrip, 1966. *Children:* Sarah Elizabeth Eward and Lucy Catharine Eward. *Educated at* Radley College, Abingdon. *Career:* admitted Solicitor January 1967; Partner: Slades (Newent, Gloucestershire) and Orme Dykes & Yates (Ledbury, Herefordshire); chairman Newent Business and Professional Association 1981-83; Secretary Ross-on-Wye PCC 1972-88; Hon.Treasurer Ross and Archenfield Deanery Synod 1980-88; Lay co-chairman Ross & Archenfield Deanery Synod 1988- . member: Hereford Diocesan Synod; Hereford Diocesan Board of Finance, Vacancy in See committee 1985- ; Board of Patronage 1988- ; Vice-chairman Hereford Diocesan Revenue Committee 1991- . Committee of Gloucestershire & Wiltshire Incorporated Law Society 1990- ; member: Herefordshire, Breconshire and Radnorshire Law Society. member: Transport Users Consultative Committee for Western England 1991- . *Recreation:* Anglican church matters, rail transport, railways, model railways. *Clubs:* E.M. Gauge Society, Gloucester Model Railway, Ross-on-Wye Conservative *Address:* Oakleigh, Gloucester Road, Ross-On-Wye, Herefordshire, HR9 5NA. 5 Broad Street, Newent, Gloucestershire, GL18 1AX.

EYTON-JONES, Colonel Philip, TD, DL, RIBA, MRTPI, FRSA. *Currently:* Director of Architecture, Planning and Estates, Clwyd County Council, since 1987. *Born on* 6 Aug 1940 at Ruabon, Clwyd. *Son of* the late John Arthur Eyton-Jones and Myfanwy (nee Owen). *Marriage:* to Doreen (nee

Whitley). *Children:* Jane Alexandra *Educated at* Ruthin School; Architectural Assn. *Career:* Denbighshire County Council 1958-60; Flintshire County Council, Architectural/ Planning Assistant 1962-74; Principal Architect, Clwyd CC 1974-81; Assistant County Architect 1981-85; Deputy Director of Architecture, Planning and Estates 1985-87. *Recreation:* Territorial Army 1960-89, walking, building conservation. *Address:* Mathrafal, Bodfari, Denbigh, Clwyd, LL16 4BS.

EZRA, Lord Derek, *Currently:* Company Chairman; Voluntary Activities; Liberal Democrat; spokesman on Economic Affairs in House of Lords. *Born on* 23 Feb 1919 at Hobart, Tasmania. *Son of* David and Lillie Ezra. *Marriage:* to Julia Elizabeth Wilkins, 1950. *Educated at* Monmouth School, Magdalene College, Cambridge *Career:* Wartime Army Service 1939-47; National Coal Board 1947-82, Chairman 1971-82. *Publications:* Coal and Energy 1979; The Energy Debate 1983. *Clubs:* National Liberal Club, Whitehall Place, London SW1 *Address:* House of Lords, Westminster, London, SW1. Tel: 071 219 3180.

F

FAGE, Professor John Donnelly, MA., PhD., FRHist.S. *Currently:* Emeritus. *Born on* 3 June 1921 at Teddington. *Son of* the late Arthur Fage, CBE, FRS and the late Winifred Eliza(nee Donnelly). *Marriage:* to Jean Banister 1949. *Children:* Michael Donnelly Fage and Mrs Julia Elizabeth Moore-Kelly. *Educated at* Tonbridge School; Magdalene College, Cambridge. *Career:* Royal Air Force 1941-45; Bye-Fellow, Magdalene Coll. 1947-49; Lecturer, Senior Lecturer, Profesor, Univ. Coll. of the Gold Coast 1949-59; Deputy Principal 1957-59; Lecturer in African History, School of Oriental & African Studies, Univ. of London 1959-63; Visiting Professor, Univ. of Wisconsin, Madison, 1957, and Smith College, Northampton, Mass. 1962; Univ. of Birmingham: Director, Centre of West African Studies, 1963-81; Professor of African History 1963-84; Dean, Faculty of Arts 1975-78; Pro-Vice Chancellor 1979-84; Vice Principal 1981-84; founding Hon.Sec. African Studies Assoc. of U.K., 1963-66; President, 1968-69; Council of Int. African Inst., 1965-75; Consultative Director 1975-80; UNESCO Scientific Cttee for General History of Africa 1971-80; Culture Advisory Cttee of U.K. Nat. Commission for UNESCO 1967-85; Chairman 1978-85; Co-ordinating Council of Area Studies Assoc., 1980-86; Chairman 1984-86; Editor (with Roland Oliver) The Journal of African History, 1960-73; General Editor (with Roland Oliver), The Cambridge History of Africa, 8 vols, 1975-86; Meirionnydd Executive Cttee of Campaign for the Protection of Rural Wales, 1991- ; Hon. Fellow, S.O.A.S. *Publications:* An introduction to the History of West Africa, 1955, 3rd ed. 1962; An Atlas of African History 1958, 2nd ed. 1978; Ghana, a Historical Interpretation 1959; A Short History of Africa (with Roland Oliver), 1962, 6th ed. 1987; A History of West Africa, 1969; (ed) Africa Discovers Her Past, 1969; (ed.with Roland Oliver) Papers on African Prehistory, 1970; A History of Africa, 1978, 2nd ed. 1988; A Guide to Published Sources for Precolonial Western Africa, 1987; contributions to historical and Africanist journals and collections. *Recreation:* Doing things to gardens and houses. *Clubs:* Athenaeum. *Address:* Hafod Awel, Pennal, Machynlleth, Powys SY20 9DP.

FAIRFIELD, Mr Ian McLeod, C.B.E. *Currently:* retired Chairman December 1991, appointed Dep. Chairman. *Born on* 5 Dec 1919 at Cardiff. *Son of* the late Geoffrey Fairfield and the late Inez Helen Thorneycroft Fairfield. *Marriage:* to Joyce Ethel, 1941, da of Cdr Percy Fletcher RN (5). *Children:* Clive and Julian. *Educated at* Monkton House School Cardiff; Manchester College of Technology. *Career:* cmmnd RNVR Electrical Branch 1940-45; engineering trainee Callenders Cables & Construction Co Ltd (now BICC plc), area sales manager St.Helens Cable & Rubber Co 1945-51, group chairman Chemring Group plc 1985- (sales dir 1951, MD 1952, dep chairman, chairman and group chief exec 1980, chairman 1984, chairman and group chief exec 1985). *Recreation:* motor boat cruising. *Clubs:* Athenaeum, Royal Naval Sailing Assoc. *Address:* Chemring Group Plc, Fratton Trading Estate, Portsmouth, PO4 8SX.

FARQUHAR, Mr Denis, Dip.EE; C.Eng; FIEE. *Currently:* Director, Network Services Division, Manweb plc. *Born on* 15 June 1931 at Helmsdale. *Son of* Ronald Bain Farquhar and Anna. *Marriage:* to Anne Mary Williams, 1961. *Children:* Robin Richard and David Ronald Bain. *Educated at* Helmsdale H.G.School; Liverpool Technical College. *Career:* Electrician, 1948-54; joined Manweb 1955, held commercial and engineering posts. *Recreation:* DIY, sailing, fishing. *Address:* The Crest, 21 Howey Lane, Frodsham, Cheshire, WA6 6DD. Manweb Plc, Sealand Road, Chester, CH1 4LR.

FARRER, Judge Brian Ainsworth, LLB(London). *Currently:* Circuit Judge, Midland and Oxford Circuit, appointed 1985. *Born on* 7 April 1930 at London. *Son of* the late Albert A Farrer and the late Gertrude Farrer (nee Hall). *Marriage:* to Gwendoline Valerie (nee Waddoup J.P.), 1960. *Children:* Julie Valerie, Paul Ainsworth and Adam Ainsworth. *Educated at* Kings College Taunton; London University, (University College). *Career:* Called to the Bar by Grays Inn 1957; Member of Midland Oxford Circuit 1957-85; Recorder 1973; Queens Counsel 1976. *Recreation:* music, bridge, chess, golf. *Clubs:* Aberdovey Golf. *Address:* C/o Aberdovey Golf Club, Aberdovey & Queen Elizabeth II, Law Courts, Birmingham.

FAZAKERLEY, Andrew Neil, BA *Currently:* Joint Creative Director, Fox, Parrack, Fox, London. *Born on* 22 March 1950 at Ormskirk. *Son of* George Fazakerley and Muriel Boyd Magrady. *Marriage:* to Vibeke Lunn 1976. *Children:* Sam, Jack and Pip. *Educated at* Abergele G.S; Manchester Poly (BA). *Career:* Creative Director and Board Director, Davidson Pearce Ltd., 1982-87; Creative Director, Boase Massimi Pollitt Ltd., 1988-89. *Recreation:* computing, genealogy, conservation. *Address:* 42 Nelson Road, Harrow On The Hill, Middlx., HA1 3ET.

FELDMAN, Mr Maurice Avrom, MB., ChB., FRCS.Ed., FRCS. *Currently:* Consultant Surgeon, Dudley Road Hospital, Birmingham. *Born on* 7 Aug 1927 at Cardiff. *Son of* the late Lewis Feldman and the late Leah (nee Voloshen). *Marriage:* to Vera Cohen, 1959. *Children:* Leah Rivka and Adam. *Educated at* Cardiff High School for Boys; Bristol University Medical School. *Career:* Junior Doctor posts at N.H.S. hospitals in Bristol, Sheffield, Nottingham etc; National Service, R.A.M.C., Captain, served in Singapore and Malaya 1953-55; Malaya Medal 1955. Sir Ernest Finch Research Price 1965. Senior Clinical Lecturer in Surgery, Birmingham Medical School. *Publications:* Professional papers in various medical and surgical journals. *Recreation:* walking, gardening, toy making. *Address:* 90 Knightlow Road, Harborne, Birmingham B17 8QA.

FERRIS, Mr Paul, *Currently:* Writer. *Born on* 15 Feb 1929 at Swansea. *Educated at* Swansea Grammar School. *Career:* Writing. *Publications:* Fiction, biography, reportage. Novels include 'The Detective', 'Talk to me about England', 'Children of Dust'; Biography includes: 'Dylan Thomas', 'The House of Northcliffe', 'Sir Huge: The Life of Huw Wheldon'. *Address:* c/o Curtis Brown Ltd, 162-168 Regent St, London W1R 5TB.

FESSEY, Mr Mereth Cecil, CB., MSc(Econ)., FSS., FIS., FLA. *Currently:* Retired. *Born on* 19 May 1917 at Clwer Windsor, Berks. *Son of* Morton Frederick Fessey and Ethel (nee Blake). *Marriage:* to Grace Lilian Bray 1945. *Children:* Marion, Judith and Paul Mereth. *Educated at* Retired. *Career:* HM Forces WW II 1940-46; Civil Service 1946-77: Board of Trade, now Department of Trade and Industry; Chief Statistician 1965-68; Director, Business Statistics Office 1968-77; Expert Adviser to the Statistical Office of the European Cttees 1978 and 1990-; Adviser to governments of Syria, Mexico and Ecuador 1978-80; Adviser to the Statistical Office of the United Nations 1980-81; Lecturer at the EEC School for Advanced Studies, Munich 1981; Chairman of the Institute of Statisticians 1970-73; Vice President of the Royal Statistical Society 1975-76; Hon. Fellow of the Library Assoc. 1983; Chairman of the Cttee of Librarians and Statisticians 1976- ; Governor of Gwent College of Higher Education 1972-77; Governor, Nash College of Further Education 1972-77; Vice Chairman of Governors, Undy Primary and Junior School 1989- . *Publications:* Dev. of statistical expert systems, London 1990; Report of a seminar on the development of statistical expert systems, London 1990; Business censuses and surveys in developing countries in The Statistician Volume 30, London 1981; A decade of centralisation in Journal Series A Volume 141, London 1978; The Business Statistics Office, London 1973; The statistical unit in business inquiries in Statistical News HMSO, London 1971; Dev. in economic statistics since 1934, London 1968; Short term forecasting of United Kingdom exports in Economic Trends, HMSO, London 1967; The Librarian and financial analysis, London 1967; Statistiques des finances au Royaume-uni, Louvain 1964. *Recreation:* Chess, walking, gardening. *Clubs:* Civil Service. *Address:* Undy House, Undy, Gwent. NP6 3BX.

FINE, Dr Jeffrey Howard, MB, BS, MRCPsych. *Currently:* Private Medical Practice. *Born on* 5 Oct 1955 at Cardiff. *Son of* Nathan Fine and Rebecca (nee Levi). *Marriage:* partner Kirsty Elizabeth. *Children:* Alexander (b.1990). *Educated at* The Howardian High School, Cardiff; The Medical College of St.Bartholomew's Hospital, London. *Career:* Professorial Registrar Academic Unit of Psychiatry, Royal Free Hospital London 1981; Registrar Psychological Medicine, National Hospital for Nervous Diseases, Queen Square, London 1982-83; Med. Officer Home Officer 1981-89; Gen. Medical practice, London 1985; European Neuroendocrine Adviser, Eli Lilly Pharmaceuticals 1986-87; MRCPsych 1984; FRSM 1987; BMA 1980; British Assoc of Neuropsychiatry 1988; Assoc of Independent Drs 1989. *Publications:* author of papers on Depression, Light and Obesity (journal of Affective Disorder 1987). *Recreation:* jazz, tennis, painting. *Clubs:* Ronnie Scott's,

West Heath Lawn Tennis. *Address:* 68 Harley Street, London, W1N 1AE. 3 Denning Road, Hampstead, London, NW3. Tel: 071 935 3980.

FISHER, Miss Doris Gwenllian, BAHons Eng & French. *Currently:* Retired. *Born on* 22 March 1907 at Pontypool. *Daughter of* Mabel Fisher (nee Harmston) and Garthorne John Fisher. *Educated at* Pontypool County Girls' Grammar School; Farringtons, Chislehurst; University of London; Sorbonne. *Career:* Urmston Grammar School 1932-34; Maidenhead Co. Grammar School (Senior English Mistress) 1934-39; Dover Girls Grammar School (Snr. English & Deputy Head 1939-46; Head Mistress Farringtons School, Chiselhurst 1939-46; Lecturer in French and English, Westminster, Avery Hill Training Colleges 1957-62; President of Kent Secondary Heads' Association 1950-57; Chairman Chislehurst and Mottingham Girls Club 1950-53; Govoernor St. Margarets School for Spastics, Croydon 1948-57; Member of The Samaritans London Branch 1963-77 and Newport Branch 1986-91; Member of The Women's Institute, Westbourne Canterbury 1977-85. *Recreation:* Drama, various charities, education. *Address:* 9 The Ridgeway, Newport, Gwent. NP9 5AF.

FISHER, Mr Dudley Henry, CBE *Currently:* former Regional Chairmanm British Gas Wales. *.Marriage:* first wife died in 1984, remarried 1985. *Children:* one s, two d. *Educated at* City of Norwich School. *Career:* Joined Norwich County Borough Council as a Junior Audit Assistant in 1938; Served in RAF as a Pilot from 1941-46, flying various aircraft from Tiger Moths to Lancasters and Ansons to DC3 Dakotas, this included two years as a flying instructor; entered gas industry in 1953 as Principal Accountancy Assistant with the Northern Gas Bd; Joined Wales Gas Bd in 1956 as Assistant Chief Accountant in 1974, retiring 1987; served as Chairman of CBI Welsh Council 1987-89; Hon. Treasurer British Nat. Cttee of World Energy Conference and chairman of its International Admin. Cttee until 1989; member of Council of University College, Cardiff, and Treasurer and Chairman of Finance Cttee 1987-88; member of Exec. Commission formed to oversee the merger of U.C.C. and UWIST; mbr. of Council of the Univ. of Wales Coll. of Cardiff; mbr. of Audit Cttee of Univ. of Wales; National Trustee of Help the Aged charity and mbr. of HelpAge International; served on Audit Commission for Local Authorities in England and Wales 1983-88; mbr of Broadcasting Cncl for Wales for five years and Pres. of Cardiff Branch British Inst. of Management until 1989; Governor of Atlantic Coll. and a Deputy Chmn of Inst. of Welsh Affairs; High Sheriff for S.Glam 1988-89, awarded CBE in 1990. *Recreation:* Reading, gardening, golf, music. *Clubs:* Cardiff and County (Cardiff), Royal Air Force (London). *Address:* Norwood Edge, 8 Cyncoed Avenue, Cardiff. CF2 6SU.

FITTON, Mr Arthur Martin Hervey, B.A.; M.A. *Currently:* National Park Officer for the Brecon Beacons Park. *Born on* 8th May 1942 at Huddersfield. *Son of* the late Arthur and the late Betty Fitton. *Marriage:* to Judith Wilburn 1966. *Children:* Charlotte and Thomas *Educated at* King James School, Almondsbury, Manchester University, Syracuse University *Career:* Academic Appointments at the Universities of Manchester, Ibadan, Nigeria, and Aberystwyth; Chief Officer for Wales, Countryside Commission; Member, Wales Board:

Agricultural Training Board; Council Member Wales Rural Forum. *Recreation: Address:* 7 Glamorgan Street, Brecon, Powys.

FITZGERALD, Mr Bryan, *Currently:* Secretary, Aberaman Ex-servicemens Club since 1974. *Born on* 25 Jan 1933 at Cwmdare. *Son of* Thomas Emlyn and Phyllis May Fitzgerald. *Marriage:* To Verina (nee Cates). *Children:* Karen *Educated at* Mardy House Secondary Modern *Career:* Chairman Highways and Transportation Ctee. Mid Glamorgan County Council; Chairman, Transportation Joint Sub-Ctee, Chmn. Rights of Way Ctee.; Vice Chairman Road Safety Council for Wales; Gvnr. Univ. College, Cardiff; Gvnr. Univ. of Wales; Memb. South Wales Police Authority; Memb. Standing Conference on Regional Policy; Memb. Assembly of Welsh Counties; Memb. County Joint Liaison Ctee.; Memb. Standing Conference of Severnside Local Authorities; Memb. Wales Council for the Deaf; Memb. Mid Glam. Health Authority (1983-89); Mental Health Manager; Chmn. of Governors Blaengwawr, Oaklands and Ysgol Gynradd Gymraeg Aberdare Primary Schools; Vice Chmn. Blaengwawr Comprehensive School; Vice Pres. Abercwmboi Rugby Club; Vice Pres. Aberdare Referees Society; Pres. Aberaman Ex-servicemens F.C. Member Aberaman Ex-servicements Club, Aberaman Royal British Legion. *Recreation:* Association Football *Clubs:* Aberaman Ex-servicemens, Aberaman Royal British Legion. *Address:* 7 Holford Street, Aberaman, Aberdare Mid Glamorgan, CF44 6UG. Mid Glamorgan County Hall, Cathays Park, Cardiff, CF1 3NE. Tel: 0685 874587.

FLOWERS, The Lord Brian Hilton Flowers, Baron Flowers of Queen's Gate in the City of Westminster cr. 1979 (Life Peer), Kt 1969; FRS 1961. Vice-Chancellor, University of London 1985-90; Chairman, Nuffield Foundation, since 1987 (a Managing Trustee, since 1982). *Born on* 13 Sept 1924. *Son of* the late Rev. Harold J. Flowers, Swansea. *Marriage:* to Mary Frances, er d of the late Sir Leonard Behrens, CBE. *Children:* two step s. *Educated at* Bishop Gore Grammar School, Swansea; Gonville and Caius College (Exhibitioner), Cambridge (MA); Hon Fellow 1974; University of Birmingham (DSc). *Career:* Anglo-Canadian Atomic Energy Project 1944-46; Research in nuclear physics and atomic energy at Atomic Energy Project Research Establishment, Harwell, 1946-50; Dept of Mathematical Physics, University of Birmingham 1950-52; Head of Theoretical Physics Division, AERE, Harwell 1952-58; Professor of Theoretical Physics 1958-61; Langworthy Professor of Physics 1961-72, Univ. of Manchester; Rector of Imperial Coll. of Science and Technology 1973-85. Chairman: Science Research Council 1967-73; Royal Commn on Environmental Pollution 1973-76; Standing Commn on Energy and the Environment 1978-81; Univ. of London Working Party on future of med. and dent. teaching resources 1979-80; Cttee of Vice-Chancellors and Principals 1983-85; Select Cttee on Science and Technology, H of L 1989- (member 1980-). President: Inst of Physics 1972-74; European Science Foundation 1974-80; Nat. Soc. for Clean Air 1977-79. Chairman: Computer Board for Univs and Research Councils 1966-70. Founding Member and Member Exec Council, Academia Europaea 1988. Founder Member SDP 1981. FInstP 1961. Hon FCGI 1975; Hon. MRIA (Science Section) 1976; Hon. FIEE 1975; Sen. Fellow, RCA 1983; Hon Fellow, UMIST 1985; Corresp. Member Swiss

Acad. of Engineering Sciences 1986. MA Oxon 1956; Hon. DSc: Sussex 1968; Wales 1972; Manchester 1973; Leicester 1973; Liverpool 1974; Bristol 1982; Oxford 1985; NUI; Hon. DEng Nova Scotia 1983; Hon ScD Dublin 1984; Hon LLD: Dundee 1985, Glasgow 1987. Rutherford Medal and Prize 1968, Glazebrook Medal and Prize 1987, IPPS; Chalmers Medal, Chalmers Univ. of Technology, Sweden 1980. Officier de la Legion d'Honneur 1981 (Chevalier 1975). *Publications:* (with E. Mendoza) Properties of Matter, 1970; contributions to scientific periodicals on structure of the atomic nucleus, nuclear reactions, science policy, energy and the environment. *Recreation:* music, walking, computing, painting, gardening. *Address:* 53 Athenaeum Road, London, N20 9AL. Tel: 081 446 5993.

FLYNN, Mr Paul Philip, *Currently:* M.P. Labour, 1987- . *Born on* 9 Feb 1935 at Cardiff. *Son of* James Flynn and Kathleen Flynn (nee Williams). *Marriage:* to 1) Ann Harvey (dissolved), 1962; 2) Samantha Morgan, 1985. *Children:* James, Alex, Natalie and Rachel (Dec'd) *Educated at* St. Iltyds High School, Cardiff; Univ. Coll. Cardiff. *Career:* Industrial Chemist until 1982 with B.S.C; Broadcaster on local radio, 1982-84; Researcher for Llew Smith MEP, 1984-87; Spokesman on Wales, 1988 then on Social Security, 1988-90. *Recreation:* Celtic history and languages *Address:* House of Commons, London, SW1A OAA.

FOGG, Prof. Gordon Elliott, C.B.E., Sc.D., Hon. LL.D., F.I.Biol., F.R.S *Currently:* Retired (Emeritus Professor of Marine Biology in the University of Wales). *Born on* 26 Apr 1919 at Langar, Notts, England. *Son of* Rev. Leslie Charles & Doris Mary Fogg (nee Elliott). *Marriage:* to Elizabeth Beryl Llechid-Jones, 1945. *Children:* Elizabeth Helen and Timothy Dolben. *Educated at* Dulwich College, London; Queen Mary College, London; St. John's College Cambridge. *Career:* Plant Physiologist, Pest Control Ltd., Cambridge 1943-45; Successively Ass. Lecturer, Lecturer, Reader, Dept of Botany, University College London 1945-60; Professor of Botany, Westfield College, London 1960-71; Professor of Marine Biology, University College of North Wales 1971-85. Subsidiary appointments: Chairman of Council, Freshwater Biological Association 1974-85; Trustee of the British Museum (Natural History) 1976-85; Member of Royal Commission on Environmental Pollution 1979-85; Trustee of the Royal Botanic Gardens, Kew 1983-89. *Publications:* Numerous papers in scientific journals. The Metabolism of Algae 1953; The Growth of Plants 1963; Photosynthesis 1968; The Blue-green Algae (with W.D.P. Stewart, P Fay & A.E. Walsby) 1973; Algae Cultures and Phytoplankton Ecology (with B. Thake) 1987; The Explorations of Antarctica (with D. Smith) 1990. *Recreation:* Walking, Photography and Antarctic History. *Clubs:* Athenaeum. *Address:* School Of Ocean Sciences, (U.C.N.W.) Marine Science Laboratories, Menai Bridge, Anglesey, Gwynedd., LL59 5EY. Bodolben, Llandegfan, Anglesey, Gwynedd, LL59 5TA.

FOLEY, Mr John Patrick Thomas, M.B.E. *Currently:* Division Office, South Wales/West of England area, Iron & Steel Trades Confederation. *Born on* 20 March 1930 at Port Talbot. *Son of* Patrick Foley and Mary Foley (nee Hancorn). *Marriage:* to Pauline Foley (nee Cosker). *Children:* Gareth, Sharon and Patrice. *Educated at* Aberavon Boys School. *Career:* Previous membership: Art Council (Wales), Technical Education Council (Tec) UK; West Wales

Training Enterprise Council; Current: Director, South Wales Electricity plc; Board Member Welsh Development Agency, General Council - Wales T.U.C., Member S.Wales Panel, Industrial Tribunals. *Recreation:* Rugby football. *Address:* 25 Ascot Drive, Baglan, Port Talbot, West Glam.

FONSECA, Jose Maria, *Currently:* Director of Models One Agency, opened in the Kings Road 1988. *Born on* 9 Jan 1944 at Crickhowell. *Daughter of* Kathleen and Amador Fonseca. *Marriage:* to Richard Kries (Dutch). *Educated at* Sacred Heart Convent,Highgate; Ursuline Convent Sansebastian Spain; Ursuline Convent St. Pol De Leon, Brittany. *Career:* Ran first Boutique in Kings Road 1965; ran English Boy Model Agency 1966-68. *Recreation:* walking, theatre, reading, travel *Clubs:* Tramps, Freds *Address:* Omega House, 471-473 Kings Road, London, SW10.

FORD, Dr Sydney John, PhD; BSc. *Currently:* Christian Salvesen PLC, 50 East Fettes Avenue, Edinburgh, EH4 1EQ, since 1988. *Born on* 23 Aug 1936 at Swansea. *Son of* the late Sidney and the late Barbara Ford. *Marriage:* to Morag Ann (nee Munro), 1990. *Children:* Gareth and Rhodri. *Educated at* Bishop Gore School Swansea; University College Swansea. *Career:* The British Aluminium Company, Managing Director 1966-82; British Alcan Aluminium, Deputy Managing Director 1982-85; Williams Holdings PLC, Operations Director 1985-88. *Recreation:* rugby football, (qualified referee & coach), art, photography. *Address:* Glanmor, 37 Ross Avenue, Dalgety Bay, Dunfermline, Fife, KY11 5YN. C/o Christian Salvesen Gmbh, Rondenbarg 25, 2000 Hamburg 54, Germany, Tel: 040 853 1190.

FORD, Mr Trevor, *Currently:* Semi-Retired. *Born on* 1 Oct 1923 at Swansea. *Son of* Trevor and Daisy Ford. *Marriage:* to Louise Ford. *Children:* David and Martyn *Educated at* Townhill School *Career:* Professional Sportsman (Football) *Publications:* "I Lead The Attack" (Stanley Paul & Co. Ltd) *Recreation:* All sport *Clubs:* Swansea, Aston Villa, Sunderland, Cardiff City, P.S.V. Eindhoven, Wales. *Address:* 14 Alderwood Road, West Cross, Swansea, W.Glam., SA3 5JD.

FORSE, Mr Thomas Richard, President F/A Wales 1989-92. *Currently:* Retired Company Director. *Born on* 19 Oct 1916 at Cardiff. *Son of* Edward Richard Forse and Florence Forse. *Marriage:* 1939. *Children:* Elizabeth Mary *Educated at* Canton High School,Cardiff. *Career:* Business man *Recreation:* Football, golf. *Clubs:* Cardiff Corinthians AFC (gained International Honours 1937-39); Creigiau Golf, Cardiff, Cardiff City F.C. *Address:* 309 Western Avenue, Llandaff, Cardiff, CF5 2BA.

FORSTER, Mr Robert Anthony, FCMA *Currently:* Managing Director,Biomet Limited, Bridgend, since 1974. *Born on* 26 July 1945 at Sully, Glam. *Son of* Henry Knight Forster and Margaret Rutherford Forster (nee Metcalf). *Marriage:* to Christine Elizabeth Forster (nee Milward), 1970. *Children:* Annabel Jane Forster (b.1973). *Educated at* Llandaff Cathedral School; Dean Close School, Cheltenham. *Career:* E.M.Manufacturing Co.Ltd., 1964-68; Western Mail & South Wales Echo Ltd., 1968-69; Standard Telephones & Cables Ltd., 1969-70; Aeroquip Ltd.,1970-74. Past Secretary and President, currently Committee Member, South Wales Branch Chartered Institute of Management Accountants; Past Secretary, currently

Committee Member, Wales Division Institute of Directors; Treasurer, Peterston-Super-Ely Parochial Church Council; Past President, Cardiff Chamber of Commerce and Industry; Board Member, South Glamorgan Training and Enterprise Council. *Address:* 7 Duffryn Crescent, Peterston-Super-Ely, South Glam, CF5 6NF.

FRANCE-HAYHURST, Mrs Jeannie, Barrister-at-Law *Currently:* Consultant; Prospective Parliamentary Candidate (Conservative). *Born on* 20 Jan 1950 in the U.K. *Daughter of* Mair Davies and William Smith. *Marriage:* to Anthony Jamieson 1978-83; to James France-Hayhurst 1983. *Children:* Camilla, Charles, Lucinda and Serena. *Educated at* Towyn Grammar School; Univ. of Wales, Aberystwyth; Inn of Court, School of Law. *Career:* Barrister; Law Lecturer; Consultant. *Publications:* Various legal, political and business journals. *Recreation:* Art, theatre, the countryside, charity work, swimming, tennis, skiing, friends, children, animals. *Clubs:* Women's Enterprise Network; 300 Group; Association of Women Barristers; The Polite Society; Mensa; Tory Reform Group; Tory Green Initiatives; Future of Europe Group. *Address:* C/o Conservative Association, 20 High Street, Welshpool SY21 7JP.

FRANCIS, His Honour Judge (William) Norman, MA, BCL (Oxon). *Currently:* Circuit Judge. *Born on* 19 March 1921 at Cardiff. *Son of* Llewellyn Francis and Margaret Ceridwen Francis (nee Davies). *Marriage:* to Anthea Constance (nee Kerry),1951. *Children:* William Stephen Francis and Nicola Mary Thomas *Educated at* Bradfield College; Lincoln College Oxford. *Career:* War Service 1941-45, Royal Artillery. Called to Bar 1946, appointed County Court Judge 1969. Deputy Chairman,Brecknock Quarter Sessions 1962-71. Chancellor, Diocese of Llandaff *Address:* 2 The Woodlands, Lisvane, Cardiff, CF4 5SW.

FRANCIS, Professor Edward Howel, DSc., FRSE., C.Geol., FGS. *Currently:* Retired, Emeritus Professor of Earth Sciences University of Leeds. *Born on* 31 May 1924 at Cwmavon, Glam. *Son of* Thomas Howel Francis and Gwendoline Amelia (nee Richards). *Marriage:* to Cynthia Mary (nee Williams). *Children:* Susan Mary. *Educated at* Port Talbot County School; Univ. of Wales Swansea. *Career:* Served Army 1944-47; British Geological Survey (Geologist 1949 to Assistant Director 1977); Professor of Earth Sciences,University of Leeds 1977-89; President, Geological Society 1980-82 and Coke Medal 1989; Edinburgh Geological Society Clough Medal 1983 and Honorary Fellow 1984; Yorkshire Geological Society Sorby Medal 1983; Hon. Fellow University College Swansea 1989. *Publications:* Papers and book chapters on Palaeovolcanism (especially dolerite sills) and coalfield geology. *Recreation:* golf, music (especially opera). *Clubs:* Sand Moor G.C. *Address:* Michaelston, 11 Millbeck Green, Collingham, near Wetherby. LS22 5AJ.

FRANCIS, Mr Gwyn Jones, CB; BSc; MSc; FIC For. *Currently:* retired. *Born on* 17 Sept 1930 at Llanelli. *Son of* the late Daniel Brynmor Francis and Margaret (nee Jones). *Marriage:* 1st to Margaretta Meryl (nee Jeremy) (d 1985); 2nd to Audrey Gertrude (nee Gill). *Children:* two s one d. (one s. decd). *Educated at* Llanelli Grammar School; University College of North Wales, Bangor; University of Toronto. *Career:* Director General and Deputy Chairman, Forestry Commission 1986-90; Forestry Commissioner 1983-86; Director Marketing 1976-83; Assistant Conservator

1969-76; Principal Forester Training School 1962-69; District Officer 1954-62. *Recreation:* ornithology, gardening, walking. *Clubs:* New Club, Edinburgh. *Address:* 21 Campbell Road, Edinburgh. EH12 6DT.

FRANCIS, Captain John Lionel, OBE, OStJ, DL, FRICS, FAAV *Currently:* retired, Chartered Surveyor and Land Agent; Chairman Carmarthen Journal Newspaper Co. *Born on* 4 July 1921 in Carmarthenshire. *Son of* Major John Francis DSO, TD, DL and Margurite Francis (nee Thomas) of Trehale, Pembs. *Marriage:* to Susan Mary Francis (nee Macleod Clarke) (d.1986). *Children:* Mrs S.P.M. Boggis-Rolffe and Mrs T.J.M. Bromley-Davenport. *Educated at* Cheltenham College; RAC Cirencester. *Career:* Commissioned 17/21st Lancers 1941, served World War II in N.Africa and Italy, wounded twice. Capt R.A.R.O; High Sheriff of Carmarthenshire 1969; Deputy Lieutenant of Dyfed 1971- ; Chairman Carmarthen Conservative Assoc 1973-76; Mid & West Wales Euro Conservative Council 1983-88; President of Carmarthen Conservative Assoc and Mid & West Wales Council. Vice President Dyfed Country Landowners Assoc (chairman 1957-60). Commissioner of Taxes, member of Panel Agricultural Arbitrators; Under writing member of Lloyds. *Publications:* The Thunderer of South Wales; History of Carmarthen Journal, 1810-1990. *Clubs:* Cavalry and Guards *Address:* Llwynhelig, Llandeilo, Carmarthenshire SA19 6AZ.

FRANCIS, Dr. John Michael, Phd (Lond.) FRSE *Currently:* Chief Executive, Nature Conservancy Council for Scotland. *Born on* 1 May 1939 at London. *Son of* the late William Winston Francis, of Haverfordwest, Pembs, and Beryl Margaret Francis (nee Savage). *Marriage:* to Eileen Sykes, Cyncoed, Cardiff 1963. *Children:* Sarah Katherine and Rachel Victoria. *Educated at* Gowerton Grammar School; Imperial College of Science, Technology and Medicine (University of London) *Career:* CEGB Research and Development Dept. 1963-70; Director, Society, Religion and Technology Project, Church of Scotland 1970-74; Senior Research Fellow, Heriot Watt Univ. 1974-76; Assistant Secretary, The Scottish Office 1976-84; Director Scotland, Nature Conservancy Council 1984-90; Consultant on Science, Technology and Social Ethics, World Council of Churches, Geneva 1971-83; Chmn. Church of Scotland Ctee. on Society, Religion and Technology 1980- ; Chmn., Edinburgh Forum 1984- ; Member of Council, National Trust for Scotland 1985- ; Member, Advisory Ctee. on Marine Fish Farming, Crown Estate 1989- ; Fellow, Institute for Advanced Studies in the Humanities, University of Edinburgh 1988- ; Elected Honorary Fellow of the Royal Scottish Geographical Society 1990- ; Visiting Fellow, Centre for Values and Social Policy, Univ. of Colorado at Boulder 1991- ; *Publications:* Scotland in Turmoil 1973; (jtly) Changing Directions 1974; (jtly) The Future as an Academic Discipline 1975; Facing up to Nuclear Power 1976; (jtly) The Future of Scotland 1977; Contributions to scientific and professional journals and periodicals. *Clubs:* University of Edinburgh *Address:* Nature Conservancy, Council for Scotland, 12 Hope Terrace, Edinburgh. EH9 2AS.

FRASER, Professor William Irvine, M.D. (comned); FRCPsych; D.P.M. *Currently:* Professor of Mental Handicap University of Wales College of Medicine. *Born on* 3rd Feb 1940 at Greenock. *Son of* late Duncan Fraser late Muriel (nee MaCrae). *Marriage:* Joyce Carrol Gilchrist. *Children:* Alan Ewen *Educated at* Greenock Academy Glasgow University *Career:* Director Mental Handicap Services, Fife 1974-78; Senior Lecturer Dept. of Psychology, University of St. Andrews 1974-87; Senior Lecturer Dept. of Rehabilitation, Edinburgh University 1974-87; Consultant Psychiatrist, Lothian 1974-87; Editor, Journal of Intellectual Disability Research 1982-; Medical Advisor to Royal Society of Mentally Handicapped Children and Adults (MENCAP); Burden Neurological Institute Prize; Prize Medallist for Research into Mental Handicap 1989. *Publications:* Communicating with Mentally Retarded Children and Adults 1981; Care of People with Mental Handicaps 1991; over 60 scientific papers *Clubs:* R.S.M. *Address:* 146 Wenallt Road, Cardiff CF4 6TQ. Academic Unit, 55 Park Place, Cardiff Tel: 0222 645347

FRENCH, Professor Edward Alexander, BSc(Econ), LLB, PhD, FCCA, FRSA, Barrister. *Currently:* Professor of Accounting, University of Wales, College of Cardiff, since 1987. *Born on* 17 Oct 1935 at Birmingham, England. *Son of* Edward Francis French and Clara Baldwin. *Marriage:* to Lillias Margaret Riddoch, 1967. *Children:* Daniel Edward, Gregory Niall and Steven Ainsley Martin. *Educated at* Bemrose School, Derby; London School of Economics; Lincolns Inn. *Career:* Audit Examiner, District Audit Service 1955-59; National Service, RAF 1955-57; Principal (former Assistant Principal) Home Civil Service, GPO 1963-67; Lecturer in Accounting, L.S.E., 1967-77; Prof and Head of Department of Accounting and Financial Control, University College, Cardiff 1977-87. President, South Wales Society of Certified Accountant 1982-83; Member, National Council Chartered Society of Certified Accountants 1983-86. *Publications:* various. *Recreation:* golf, swimming, reading. *Clubs:* Radyr Golf, Cullen Golf (Morayshire, Scotland). *Address:* 112 Pencisley Road, Llandaff, Cardiff CF5 1DQ.

FULLARD, Hon Glenys, *Currently:* retired. *Born on* 26 March 1923 at Ashton-in-Makerfield. *Daughter of* the 1st Baron Rt. Hon Lord MacDonald and Lady MacDonald of Gwaesysgor. *Marriage:* to Mr Robert Fullard, 1949. *Children:* Judith Mary and Cathryn Elisabeth. *Educated at* Upholland Grammar School; Darlington Training College. *Career:* Teacher of Physical Education, Manchester; Teacher in Special Education, Oldham; Head of Service of Visually Impaired, Oldham; Magistrate, Westriding 1964-72, and Oldham 1972- . Held numerous positions in Girl Guide Movement. *Recreation:* walking, music, art. *Address:* 2 Thornley Lane, Grotton, Oldham, Lancs OL4 5RP.

G

GAFFNEY, Dr James Anthony, CBE; F.Eng; BSc(Eng); DSc; FICE. *Currently:* retired Civil Engineer; Vice President, Fellowship of Engineering. *Born on* 9 Aug 1928 at Bargoed, Glam. *Son of* James F.Gaffney and V.M.Gaffney (nee Vestey). *Marriage:* to Margaret M. Evans, Pontypridd. *Children:* James Edward, Joanna and Claire. *Educated at* De La Salle; St. Illtyd's Cardiff; Cardiff Tech; Univ.Coll, Cardiff. *Career:* Highway Engineer, Glamorgan C.C; Asst. County Surveyor, Somerset C.C; Dep. County Surveyor, Nottinghamshire C.C; County Engineer & Surveyor, West Riding Yorkshire; Director Eng. Services, West Yorkshire M.C.C; President Inst. Civil Engineers; President,Inst. Highway Engineers; President, County Surveyors Soc; National & International Adviser & Consultant. *Recreation:* golf, watching rugby, travel, family. *Clubs:* Royal Automobile, Alwoodley Golf. *Address:* Drovers Cottage, 3 Boston Road, Wetherby, W. Yorks. LS22 5HA. Tel: 0937 583960.

GAIT, Mr Robert Charles Campbell, MA(Cantab) *Currently:* Partner, McKenna & Co., Solicitors, Mitre House, 160 Aldersgate Street, London, EC1A 4DD, since 1985. *Born on* 16 June 1955 at Tenby. *Son of* the late Robert William and the late Jean (nee Campbell). *Marriage:* to Anne Rose Nicolson,1978. *Children:* Michael, Jonathan and Nicholas. *Educated at* Pembroke Grammar School; Jesus College Cambridge 1974-77. *Career:* articles, McKenna & Co.,1978-80; Assistant Solicitor, McKenna & Co.,1980-85. *Recreation:* rugby football (as player and spectator), skiing. *Clubs:* London Welsh RFC. *Address:* 95 Drakefield Road, London SW17 8RS.

GAMES, Professor David Edgar, BSc, PhD, DSc, CChem, FRCS. *Currently:* Professor of Mass Spectrometry and Director of Mass Spectrometry Research Unit, University College of Swansea since 1989. *Born on* 7 April 1938 at Ynysddu. *Son of* Alfred William Games and Frances Elizabeth Bell Games (nee Evans). *Marriage:* to Marguerite Patricia Lee. *Children:* Gwilym John Games and Evan William Games. *Educated at* Lewis School Pengam; King's College University of London. *Career:* Lecturer, Senior Lecturer, Reader, Personal Chair, University College Cardiff 1965-89; Chairman British Mass Spectrometry Society 1981-83; Member Horserace Scientific Advisory Committee 1991- ; Chairman SERC Chemistry Committee Panel on Instrumentation 1989- ; Royal Society of Chemistry Award in Analytical Separation Methods 1987; The Chromatographic Society Martin Medal 1991. *Publications:* Editor-in-Chief Biomedical & Environmental Mass Spectrometry 1980-90; over 180 publications in Scientific Journals. *Recreation:* swimming, reading, walking. *Address:* 12 Brunel Avenue, Rogerstone, Newport, Gwent NP1 ODN. Mass Spectrometry Research Unit, University College Of Swansea, Singleton Park, Swansea SA2 8PP.

GARDINER, Professor John MacDonald, BSc, PhD, FBPsS. *Currently:* Professor of Psychology, City University London,since 1986. *Born on* 15 Sept 1941 at Swansea. *Son of* the late Kenneth MacDonald Gardiner and the late Marjorie Gardiner (nee Taylor). *Educated at* Wycliffe College, Glos; Bognor Regis College of Education; University of London. *Career:* Schoolteacher 1964-69; Lecturer in Psychology, City University 1972, Senior Lecturer 1978, Reader 1981; Associate Editor, British Journal of Psychology 1982-84; Consultant Editor, Journal of Experimental Psychology: Learning, Memory and Cognition 1984- ; Memory 1992- . *Publications:* various articles on psychology of memory. *Recreation:* jaunts, walks, occasional lunch. *Address:* Department Of Social Sciences, City University, Northampton Square, London EC1V OHB.

GARDNER, Dr David Colyn, BA., MSc., PhD., FCIB. *Currently:* Chairman,Capelfield Ltd; Director,Welsh Development Agency. *Born on* 6 April 1949. *Son of* the late Brynley Gardner and Esme Gardner (nee Daniel). *Marriage:* to Gillian Mary Small 1977. *Children:* Huw Samuel Gardner. *Educated at* Aberdare Boys' Grammar School. *Career:* Formerly Chairman, D.C.Gardner Group plc; Vice President, Barkers Trust Company, New York; Assistant Vice President, Chemical Bank. *Recreation:* Sport, music, travelling. *Clubs:* Colchester Garrison Officers' Club, Essex. *Address:* Blue Bridge House, Halstead, Essex CO9 1QG.

GEE, Mr Robert George, MA, FBIM *Currently:* retired from full time employment. *Born on* 16 Oct 1931 at London. *Son of* the late George Gee and Dulcie Gee. *Marriage:* to Loveday Elisabeth Talbot Lewes, d of Captain J.Hert Lewes, OBE, RN. *Children:* Matthew (b.1960), Emma (b.1962) and Patrick (b.1963). *Educated at* Rugby School; Oriel College, Oxford. *Career:* National Service 1950-51; T.A. The Argyll & Sutherland Highlanders 1951-64; Qualified as a Solicitor 1958; Secretary and Director The Rugby Portland Cement Co. Ltd.,1968-78; Secretary and Director Norcros plc 1978-88; member Development Board for Rural Wales 1989- ; member Council, Executive Committee and Audit Committee of St.Davids University College, Lampeter; Deputy President Dyfed Red Cross Society. *Recreation:* gardening. *Address:* Llanllyr, Talsarn, Lampeter, Dyfed SA48 8QB.

GEORGE, Mr Hywel, CMG, OBE, BA(Wales), MA(Cantab), JMN, PDK (Malaysia) *Currently:* retired. *Born on* 10 May 1924 at Holyhead. *Son of* the late Rev. W.M.George and Catherine Margaret (nee Lloyd). *Marriage:* to Edith Pirchl, 1955. *Children:* Carol,Tamara and Frances. *Educated at* Llanelli Grammar School; University College of Wales, Aberystwyth; Pembroke College Cambridge;

SOAS London. *Career:* Navigator RAF 1943-46; Colonial Administrative Service North Borneo 1949-62; Resident Sabah Malaysia 1963-66; Administrator 1967-69, Governor 1969-70, St.Vincent; Administrator British Virgin Islands 1971; Fellow and Bursar Churchill College Cambridge 1971-90; Life Fellow 1991-. *Recreation:* walking, watching rugby. *Address:* Tu Hwnt I'r Afon, The Close, Llanfairfechan LL33 OAG. 46 St Margarets Road, Girton, Cambridge CB3 OLT.

GEORGE, Mr Llewellyn Norman Havard, *Currently:* Solicitor. *Born on* 13 Nov 1925 at Newport, Pembs. *Son of* Capt B.W. George, DSO, RNR and Mrs A.J. George. *Marriage:* to M.E.M. Davies 1980. *Children:* Sarah Lee Nichols *Educated at* Cardiff H.S.; Fishguard G.S. *Career: Recreation:* golf, reading *Clubs:* Pembroke; Newport, Pembs Golf. *Address:* Four Winds, Tower Hill, Fishguard, Dyfed SA65 9LA.

GEORGE, Mr Thomas Rees, OBE *Currently:* retired. *Born on* 3 June 1919 at Cilgwyn, Boncath. *Son of* Thomas George and Margaret George. *Marriage:* to Dilys Mair Davies. *Children:* Eurig Meirion and Bethan. *Career:* Farmer; member Cemaes RDC 1952-74; member Pembs C.C., 1961-74; member Dyfed C.C., since 1974, was chairman Dyfed C.C.,1980-81; sitting on Highways and Transportation Social Services and Education Committees; member Dyfed Powys Police Authority since 1974, chairman 1988-89. *Address:* Maes-Y-Meillion, Newchapel, Boncath, Dyfed SA37 OEH.

GEORGE, Professor William Owen, BSc; PhD; DSc; FRSC; CHEM; FRSA. *Currently:* Assistant Director and Dean of Faculty, Polytechnic of Wales, since 1975. *Born on* 26 Aug 1933 at Swansea. *Son of* the late Mr W.J.George and Mrs G.George (nee Bishop). *Marriage:* to Joan (nee Duffield),1958. *Children:* Vernon, Karen and Timothy. *Educated at* Dynevor Sec. Grammar School; Swansea Technical College; Univ. Coll. Swansea. *Career:* United Kingdon Chemicals,Swansea,1950-53; The Distiller Company,Epsom,1960-62; Kingston Polytechnic, Kingston 1962-75; Committees of CNAA, SERC, RSC. *Publications:* over 80 publications in journals or books. *Recreation:* sailing, music, walking. *Clubs:* Mumbles Yacht; Swansea Sports; Cardiff Athletic. *Address:* Ynysgarw, Groesfaen, Pontyclun, Mid Glam CF7 8NF.

GEORGE, Dr William Richard Philip, D.Litt. *Currently:* Solicitor. *Born on* 20 Oct 1912 at Criccieth. *Son of* Anita and Wiliam George. *Marriage:* to Margarete (Greta) 1953. *Children:* Philip, Anita, Elisabeth and Gwen *Educated at* Friars School,Bangor; Wreckin College,Wellington,Salop. *Career:* Qualified as Solicitor 1934; pt. time Clerk to Barmouth Justice 1948-75; dep. Circuit Judge 1975-80; County Councillor representing Criccieth Ward since 1967; Member ACC; Current chairman Assembly Welsh Counties; Archdderngdd Cymru 1990-93; Hon. D.Litt (University of Wales) 1988; Won poetry Crown National Eisteddfod, Bromyrddin 1974. *Publications:* 5 Volumes Welsh verse; Gyfaith Hoff (letters of Eluned Morgan); The Making of Lloyd George 1976; Lloyd George Backbenches 1983. *Recreation:* Golf; boating; walong. *Clubs:* Criccieth Golf *Address:* Garth Celyn, Criccieth., Gwynedd LL52 OAH.

GIARDELLI, Mr (Vincent Charles) Arthur, M.B.E., M.A. *Currently:* Artist. *Born on* 11th Apr 1911 at London. *Son of* Vincent Giardelli Annie Giardelli (nee Lutman).

Marriage: Phillis Evelyn Berry, Beryl Mary Butler. *Children:* Judith Lawrence *Educated at* Alleyn's, Dulwich Hertford College,Oxford *Career:* Fireman 1939-45; Music Teacher,Gyfarthfa Castle School,Merthyr Tydfil 1941-45; Tutor, then Senior Tutor University College of Wales, Aberystwyth 1958-78; Artist attached to Grosvenor Gallery, London 1962- ; One man exhibitions include Nat. Library of Wales 1963, Manchester Coll. of Art 1964, Welsh Arts Council 1975, Univ. of Wales 1977 and 1978, Gallerie Convergence Nantes 1980, Grosvenor Gallery 1987; collections include: Nat. Library Wales, Nat. Museum Wales, Gallery Modern Art Dublin, Arts Council G.B., Welsh Arts Council, Musee des Beaux Arts Nantes, Nat. Gallery Slovakia,Nat. Gallery Prague,Tate Gallery; British Council Award 1979; Chairman 56 Group Wales 1958-92; Nat. Chairman Assoc. of Tutors in Adult Education 1964-67; memb. Calouste Gulbeukian Enquiry into economic situation of the visual artist 1977. Hon fellow Univ. Coll. Wales 1979-85; member Artists and Designers Wales; Silver Medal Czechoslovak Soc. for International Relations 1985 *Publications:* Up with the Lark (O.U.P) 1939; The Grosvenor Gallery 1960-1971; The Delight of Painting (University College of Swansea), 1976. *Recreation:* Viola *Address:* The Golden Plover, Warren, Pembroke, Dyfed SA71 5HR.

GIBBARD, Mr David Ronald, MBE *Currently:* Commercial Director, South Wales Electricity plc. *Born on* 27 Dec 1942. at Sevenoaks, Kent. *Son of* Arthur Gibbard and the late Grace (nee Simmons). *Marriage:* to Janet Mary Stickland, 1963. *Children:* Rachel, Sophie and Charlotte. *Educated at* Sevenoaks School; Sidney Sussex College, Cambridge. *Career:* Administrative Assistant, National Coal Board,1964-66; Administrative Officer,Electricity Council,1966-70; MSC Programme,London Business School,1970-72; Tariffs Manager, Eastern Electricity, 1972-90. *Recreation:* gardening, music, reading. *Address:* Furnace Farm, Tintern, Chepstow, Gwent, NP6 6TU.

GIBBON, His Honour Judge Michael, Q.C.,M.A.(Oxon) *Currently:* Circuit Judge; Honorary Recorder of the City of Cardiff. *Born on* 15 Sept 1930 at Cardiff. *Son of* Frank Gibbon and Jenny Gibbon (nee Leake). *Marriage:* to Malveen Elliot Seager,1956. *Children:* Nigel Elliot, David Frank and Juliet Rebecca. *Educated at* Brightlands,Charterhouse and Pembroke College,Oxford. *Career:* Commissioned in Royal Artillery (National Service 1949); T.A.,1950-57; Called to Bar,1954; Queen's Counsel,1974; Deputy Chairman/Chairman Local Government Boundary Commission for Wales,1974-79; Appointed to Bench,1979; Member of Parole Board for England and Wales,1986-88; Honorary Recorder,City of Cardiff,1986- ; Chairman Lord Chancellors Advisory Committee for South Glamorgan,1990- . *Recreation:* Golf and music. *Clubs:* Cardiff and County, Royal Porthcawl G.C., Cardiff G.C., Arkaves. *Address:* C/o Cardiff Crown Court, Cathays Park, Cardiff.

GIBBS, Stephen, Dip. Sp.Educ. *Currently:* Assistant Manager, Abersychan Leisure Centre,Pontypool. *Born on* 2 May 1946 at Cwmbran. *Son of* Morgan Gibbs and Joan Mary Gibbs. *Marriage:* to June Roynon,1968. *Children:* David (b.1974) and Jonathan (b.1974). *Educated at* Abersychan Grammar School; Culham College Education, Oxon. *Career:* Secretary Pontypool Assoc NASUWT 1971-

78,1985-91; Secretary Eastern Valley Table Tennis League 1971-91; Secretary Gwent Table Tennis Assoc 1974- ; Secretary Table Tennis Assoc of Wales 1989- ; member British League Committee of English Table Tennis Assoc 1991- ; British League Administrator of The Year 1989. *Recreation:* table tennis, music. *Clubs:* Pontypool L.C., Colley Toyota, Gwent. *Address:* 31 Maes-Y-Celyn, Griffithstown, Pontypool, Gwent NP4 5DG.

GIBSON, Major (William) David, *Currently:* Chairman, W.J.Tatem Ltd., since 1970; Chairman,Waverley Components & Products Ltd., since 1990. *Born on* 26 Feb 1925 at Dinas Powis. *Son of* the late George C.Gibson OBE and Angela Madelaine (nee Llewellin-Evans). *Marriage:* 1st to Charlotte Henrietta Pryor,1959 (d.1973); 2nd to Jane Marion Rhodes, 1975. *Children:* Anna Dalrymple, Martin, George and Edward. *Educated at* Harrow; Cambridge. *Career:* Welsh Guards 1944-57; Major; Director W.J.Tatem Ltd., 1957, chmn 1970- ; dir. Atlantic Shipping & Trading Co.Ltd.,1957, Chmn 1970-77; Dir. West of England Ship Owners Mutual Protection & Indemnity Assoc., London 1959-86, Luxembourg 1970-83; dir. International Shipowners Investment Co.,1970-83, chmn 1977-83; National Hunt Committee Steward 1963-66; Senior Steward 1966,deputy Senior Steward Jockey Club 1969-71; member, Tattersalls Committee 1963-69, chmn 1967-69; Master Worshipful Company of Farriers 1979. *Recreation:* racing and sailing (boat Klaxton). *Clubs:* Cavalry & Guards, Jockey Club, Royal Yacht Squadron, Royal Thames Yacht. *Address:* Bishopswood Grange, Ross-On-Wye, Herefordshire HR9 5QX. W.J.Tatem Ltd., C/o Blenheim House, Fitzalan Court, Newport Road, Cardiff. CF2 1TS.

GIBSON, Sir Donald (Evelyn Edward), KT 1962; CBE 1951; DCL; MA, FRIBA, FRTPI. *Currently:* Controller General, Ministry of Public Building and Works, 1967-69, now Consultant. *Born on* 11 Oct 1908 *Son of* the late Prof. Arnold Hartley Gibson. *Marriage:* 1st to Winifred Mary (nee McGowan), 1936 (decd); 2nd to Grace Haines, 1978. *Children:* three s one d, from 1st marriage. *Educated at* Manchester Gram School; Manchester Univ. BA Hons Architecture; MA. *Career:* Work in USA,1931; private practice,1933; professional Civil Service (Building Research),1935; Dep. County Architect,Isle of Ely,1937; City Architect and Town Planning Officer,County and City of Coventry,1939; County Architect, Notts, 1955; Dir-Gen. of Works,War Office,1958-62; Dir-Gen., R&D, MPBW, 1962-67; Hoffmann Wood Prof. of Architecture,University of Leeds,1967-68. Mem. Central Housing Advisory Cttee,1951,1953 and 1954. President: RIBA,1964-65; Dist Heating Assoc.,1971-. Hon. FLI 1968. *Publications:* various publications dealing with housing, planning and architecture in RIBA and RTPI Journals. *Recreation:* model railways. *Address:* Bryn Castell, Llanddona, Beaumaris, Gwynedd. LL58 8TR. Tel: 0248 810399.

GIBSON-WATT, Rt. Hon Lord James David, MC, DL, FRAGS *Currently:* retired. *Born on* 11 Sept 1918 at Llandrindod Wells, Powys. *Son of* Major James Miller (G.W.) and Marjorie Adela. *Marriage:* to Diana Hambro,1942. *Children:* Julian, Robin, Claerwen and Sian. *Educated at* Eton; Trinity College Cambridge: *Career:* Welsh Guards 1939-46, served in North African and Italian campaigns. MC & 2 Bars. Fought Brecon and Radnor constituency as a Conservative in 1950 and 1951 - not

successful. M.P. for Hereford 1956-74. Forestry Commissioner for 10 years. Hon Pres Timber Growers UK. Chairman of Council on Tribunals for 6 years. Chairman of Council of Royal Welsh Agricultural Society. *Recreation:* Forestry *Clubs:* Boodle's *Address:* Doldowlod, Llandrindod Wells, Powys LD1 6HF.

GIDDEN, Clr. Captain Richard Malcolm, BSc (Hons). *Currently:* Retired. *Born on* 18 March 1940 at Cardiff. *Son of* Richard Graham Gidden and Irene Alice Gidden. *Marriage:* to Wendy Pauline Parker 1967. *Children:* Richard Andrew and Jeremy Alexander. *Educated at* Cardiff High School for Boys 1951-55; WCAT,various 1956-66; UWIST,Cardiff 1967-71. *Career:* Apprentice Deck Officer Sir William Rerdon Smith & Sons 1956-64; Shaw Savill & Albion 1965-71; Lecturer 1 Llandaff College Technology, Senior Lecturer 1971-86; Newport Borough Council 1976; Gwent County Council 1984; National Examiner B.Tech 1987-88. *Publications:* Distance Learning Courses, ONC, OND, NAUT, Class III, Class IV. *Recreation:* Philately; Chairman Marsh Field JXI Governors. *Clubs:* Honourable Company of Master Mariners. *Address:* Malwenan, 4 Pentrepoeth Close, Bassaleg, Newport, Gwent NP1 9LX.

GIDDINGS, Roy Llewellyn, *Currently:* Employed by British Steel since 1962, currently Cashier, British Steel Strip Products, P.O. Box 10, Newport, Gwent NP9 OXN. *Born on* 16 April 1936 at Pencoed. *Son of* the late Robert Richard Giddings and the late Beryl Marjorie (nee Morris). *Marriage:* to Pauline Lavinia Mackenzie, 1967. *Children:* Nichola Sian and Sara Louise. *Educated at* Cowbridge Grammar School. *Career:* Pencoed R.F.C., Hon Secretary 1962-88; East District Rugby Union, Hon Secretary since 1976; Welsh Rugby Union, member of the General Committee elected as District Representative (District 'B'), November 1988 *Recreation:* rugby *Clubs:* Pencoed RFC *Address:* 4 Orchard Close, Pencoed, Mid Glamorgan, CF35 6YZ.

GIDDINS, Mr John Dudley, FRICS, IRRV *Currently:* Self-employed Chartered Surveyor, since 1989. *Born on* 25 May 1915 at Dovercourt. *Son of* Gladys Dudley May Bury and Jack Giddins. *Marriage:* 1939. *Children:* Edward John, David (deceased) and Julie Lesley. *Educated at* Hanley High School, Stoke on Trent; Grove Park School, Wrexham. *Career:* Articled to K.Hugh Dodd, Auctioneer and Estate Agent, Wrexham 1933-37; Passed final exam, Chartered Auctioneers & Estate Agents Inst, FAI 1939; On unification with RICS, became a Fellow, 1970; Manager, Mold Branch of K.Hugh Dodd 1937; Manager, Mold & Chester branches 1939; returned to former employment after War Service 1946; Purchased, with two others, Mold, Chester and Colwyn Bay offices from K.Hugh Dodd 1952; became Senior Partner 1955; retired after having opened further offices at Shotton, Buckley, Ruthin, Denbigh and Bala 1983; consultant to the firm 1983 to termination in 1988. Member of the Chartered Surveyors Panel of Arbitrators and Independent Experts for about fifteen years. Main areas of practice are the sale and valuation of residential and commercial property; planning applications and occasional appeals; hotel and public house valuations and transfer valuation; furniture, antiques and fine art. Mold Cricket Club Patron; Flintshire and District Cricket League President; North Wales Cricket Association President; Welsh Cricket Association: Member of the Board of Control, Member of the Cricket Committee, Member of the Minor Counties, Member of the Selection Committee. Life Member, Flintshire County Cricket Club. *Publications:* At present compiling a history of Mold Cricket Club. *Recreation:* watching cricket, gardening. *Clubs:* Mold Round Table, founder member; Mold 41 Club, founder member and twice President; Mold Rotary, past President; Chester Assoc of Auctioneers, Valuers, Estate Agents and Surveyors, past Chairman. *Address:* 41 Greenside, Mold, Clwyd, CH7 1TN. 102 High Street, Mold, Clwyd, CH7 1BH.

GILBERTSON, Mr Cecil Edward Mark, *Currently:* Director, Bell Lawrie White & Co. Ltd., (Member of Stock Exchange). *Born on* 2 June 1949. *Son of* Elizabeth (nee Dawson) and Mark Gilbertson. *Marriage:* to Nicola Leslie Bellairs Lloyd Phillips, 1986. *Children:* Georgina Charlotte Bellairs and Harry Edward Bellairs. *Educated at* Maidwell Hall Prep; Eton, Public. *Career:* Lyddon & Co 1975-89; elected Member of Stock Exchange 1976; Director Pembroke Fund 1986; member, Investment Sub Committee of the Rep. Body of The Church in Wales 1990. *Recreation:* cricket, tennis, squash, golf, shooting. *Clubs:* MCC, Cardiff and County, Royal Porthcawl Golf. *Address:* Cathedine Hill, Bwlch, Nr Brecon, Powys, LD3 7SX. Llangwarren Estate, Letterston, Haverfordwest, Dyfed, SA62 5UL.

GILL, Mr Peter, OBE *Currently:* Associate Director, National Theatre since 1980. *Born on* 7 Sept 1939 at Cardiff. *Son of* George John Gill and Margaret Mary (nee Browne). *Educated at Career:* Dramatic Actor and Director. Assistant Director, Royal Court Theatre 1964-65; Associate Director, Royal Court Theatre 1970-72; Founder Director, Riverside Studios 1976-80; Founder Director, National Theatre Studio 1984-90. *Publications:* Plays: The Sleepers' Dew, Overgardens Out, Small Change, Kick For Touch, Mean, Tears in the Blue. *Address:* c/o Margaret Ramsay, 14a Goodwin's Court, St Martin's Lane, London. WC2N 4LL.

GILLARD, Miss Isabelle, LL.B. Barrister-at-Law *Currently:* Practising Barrister, Barrister and Company Secretary Anglo-Scandinavian Trading Co. *Born on* 17 Dec 1959 at Oxford. *Daughter of* Professor Robert Gillard and Diana (nee Laslett). *Educated at* Howell's School, Llandaff; University of Birmingham. *Recreation:* films *Address:* 1 Crown Office Row, Temple, London, EC4Y 7HH.

GILLHAM, Rev. Christopher Leon, MA. *Currently:* Minister Tabernacle Congregational Church Haverfordwest & Middle Hill Congregational Church Freystrop. *Born on* 9 Aug 1948 *Son of* Leonard George Gillham and Audrey Youens Gillham (nee Cutter). *Educated at* Private; University College Cardiff (BA 1970, MA 1971); Congregational College Manchester; University of Manchester. *Career:* Congregational Minister since 1973. Assistant Secretary Congregational Federation Welsh Province 1971-75; Chairman Congregational Federation Northern Area 1977-78; Chairman Cong. Fed., Peak Area Association 1975-82; member Charlesworth Parish Council 1977-82, Chairman Cong. Fed. South West Area 1984-85; member Crediton Town Council (Liberal) 1983-85; Founder Chairman Crediton Area Museum & Historical Society 1983-85; Chairman Crediton Arts Festival Committee 1983-84; Chairman Congregational Federation Welsh Province 1988-89; member Spittal Community Council 1988-91; Cong. Fed Christian Education Officer 1985-91. Free Church

Chaplain to Withybush Hospital since 1990; British Sailors Society Hon Chaplain for Pembroke Dock, Milford and Fishguard since 1987; Cong. Fed. Representative on the Steering Cttee of Cytun since 1990; Cong. Fed. Representative on the Assembly of Churches together in Britain & Ireland since 1990; member: Cong. Fed. Christian Education Board, Inter Church Board, Free Church Federal Council Education Cttee; member of the Board of the National Christian Education Council; member Pilot Panel (childrens organisation of Cong. Fed. & URC); member Dyfed Sacre; Vice-Chairman Pembrokeshire Historical Society. Represented the Congregational Federation in talks with Churches and Church bodies in Western Samoa and Czechoslovakia, 1990, Geneva 1991. *Publications:* various articles, mainly in "Congregational Quarterly"; contributions to "When You Pray With Young People", (NCEC, 1988); editor "A Fact File on Congregationalism" (Cong. Fed. 1989). *Recreation:* travel, history, fine art, children, trains. *Clubs:* Rotary, Haverfordwest. *Address:* Crosslyn, Spittal, Haverfordwest, Dyfed, SA62 5QT.

GIMBLETT, Mr (Frederick) Gareth Robert, OBE, DL. *Born on* 20 Dec 1931 at Cardiff. *Son of* the late Dan William Davies Gimblett of Tonyrefail, Mid Glam and the late Annie (nee Flook). *Marriage:* to (Moreen) Margaret, da of Charles Cornford (d 1970). *Children:* Richard (b.1959), Michael (b.1960), Jonathan (b.1965) and Briony (b.1966). *Educated at* Tonyrefail GS, University Coll of Wales Aberystwyth (BSc, MSc), Univ of Manchester. *Career:* Scientific offr Royal Aircraft Establishment Farnborough Hants 1955-58; hon. sr. res. fellow Brunel University 1989-90 (lecturer physical chemistry 1958-82, senior res. fellow 1982-89); freelance sci ed and writer 1989- ; executive council member ACC 1983- ; chmn sub-committee Manpower 1985-87, Berks CC 1986-89 (member 1977- , ldr 1981-86,1991-), LAMSAC 1988-89 (member 1986-89), Local Government Training Board 1989-90 (member 1983-90), Care Sector Consortium 1988- ,(member 1988-); vice chairman Central Council for Education and Training in Social Work 1990- ,(member 1989-), Joint Local Authority Associations' Working Party on Social Services Training and Staff Development 1990-, Local Government Management Board 1990- (member 1990-); FRSC 1989; cdr Royal Order of Merit Norway 1988. *Publications:* Inorganic Polymer Chemistry (1962); Introduction to Kinetics of Chemical Chain Reactions (1970). *Recreation:* walking, rugby football (spectator). *Address:* 6 Park View Drive South, Charvil, Reading, Berks, RG10 9QX.

GLADSTONE, Sir (Erskine) William, 7th Bt cr 1846; JP. *Currently:* Lord-Lieutenant of Clwyd, since 1985. *Born on* 29 Oct 1925. *Son of* Charles Andrew Gladstone (6th Bt), and the late Isla Margaret. *Marriage:* to Rosamund Anne 1962. *Children:* two s one d. Heir:s Charles Angus Gladstone (b 1964; m Caroline o d of Sir Derek Thomas, qv; 1988, one s. *Educated at* Eton; Christ Church, Oxford (MA History). *Career:* Served RNVR 1943-46; Asst Master at Shrewsbury 1949-50, and at Eton 1951-61; Head Master of Lancing Coll., 1961-69, Chief Scout of UK and Overseas Branches 1972-82; Mem., World Scout Cttee 1977-83 (Chm. 1979-81) DL Flintshire 1969, Clwyd 1974, Vice Lord-Lieut, 1984; Alderman, Flintshire CC 1970-74; Chm. Rep. Body of Church in Wales 1977-92; Chm. Council of Glenalmond Coll. (formerly Trinity Coll., Glenalmond) 1982-86; JP

Clwyd 1982. *Publications:* various school textbooks. *Recreation:* reading history, watercolours, shooting, gardening. *Address:* Hawarden Castle, Clwyd, CH5 3PB. Fasque, Laurencekirk, Kincardineshire AB3 1DJ Tel: 0244 520210.

GLANUSK, The Rt. Hon. Lord. David Russell 5th Baronet (1855) 4th Baron, *Currently:* retired. *Born on* 19 Nov 1917 at Llandaff. *Son of* the late Hon. H.C. Bailey and Kathleen (nee Salt). *Marriage:* to Lorna Dorothy (nee Andrews), 1941. *Children:* Christopher Russell (b 1942) and Susan Mary James(b 1944). *Educated at* Eton College. *Career:* joined Royal Navy 1935, invalided 1951. Mullard Equipment Ltd.,1954-64; Elliott Bros Ltd.,1964-66. Man Dir. Wandel & Goltermann (UK) Ltd.,1966-81 (Chairman 1981-87). Liveryman Worshipful Co. Scientific Instrument Makers, Liveryman Worshipful Co. Clockmakers. *Recreation:* gardening, clock repairing. *Clubs:* Army & Navy, Pall Mall. *Address:* Apartado 62, Correos, Pollenca Mallorca, Spain.

GLAZEBROOK, Mr William Field, MA (Cantab). *Currently:* Solicitor, Partner Lace Mawer, Liverpool and Manchester, 1960-92, and Farmer. *Born on* 18 June 1929 at Willaston,Wirral. *Son of* the late Reginald Field and Daisy Isabel (nee Broad). *Marriage:* to Sara Elizabeth (nee Boumphrey),1959. *Children:* Charles Field,William Jonathan and David Neil (d.1989). *Educated at* The Leas, Hoylake, Eton, Pembroke College Cambridge. *Career:* 2 Lt. South Wales Borderers 1948-49; Capt. Cheshire Yeomanry TA 1952-59; Admitted Solicitor 1956; Former Chairman Liverpool Merchants Guild; Former Legal Adviser to British Association for Shooting and Conservation (England and Wales). *Recreation:* tennis, golf, fishing, shooting, gardening. *Clubs:* Liverpool Racquet. *Address:* Pontruffydd Hall, Bodfari, Denbigh, Clwyd, LL16 4BP.

GLEDHILL, Ms Ruth, *Currently:* Religion Correspondent, The Times, since 1990. *Born on* 15 Dec 1959 at Loughton, Essex. *Daughter of* Rev Peter Gledhill and Mrs Bridget Gledhill (nee Rathbone). *Marriage:* to John Edward Stammers,1989. *Educated at* Thomas Alleyne's GS, Uttoxeter. HND London College of Printing. *Career:* Birmingham Post & Mail 1982-84; Daily Mail 1984-87; The Times 1987- . *Clubs:* Reform. *Address:* 1 Pennington Street, London, E1 9XN. Yr Hen Felin, Pwllfanogl, Llanfairpg, Gwynedd, LL61 6PD Tel: 071 782 5001.

GODDING, Alan, *Currently:* Editor, Mid Wales Journal, Shrewsbury Chronicle, S.Shropshire Journal, Ludlow Journal, Hereford & Leominster Journal, Mid-Week Chronicle,Shropshire Farmer, Staffs Farmer. *Born on* 6 Feb 1942 at Ipswich. *Son of* the late H.W. and Mrs M.M. Godding. *Marriage:* to Susan Elizabeth Godding. *Children:* Ian and Joanne. *Educated at* Market Harborough Grammar School, Leics. *Career:* Reporter with Northamptonshire Evening Telegraph, sub-editor with Nottingham Evening News,Nottingham Evening Post, sub-editor then chief-sub-editor, Shropshire Star, now Group Editor, Chronicle-Journal Weekly series of Shropshire Newspapers Ltd. Seconded to China Daily in Peking 1982. *Recreation:* music, hi-fi, cycling, squash. *Clubs:* Racing Sec. Midland Division BCF, Organiser National Professional Road Race Championship 1986/7/9. *Address:* 6 Haygate Drive, Wellington, Telford, Shropshire.

GOLDING, Mrs Llinos, *Currently:* Member of Parliament for Newcastle Under Lyme. *Born on* 21 March 1933 at Hengoed. *Daughter of* Ness Edwards (formerly M.P. for Caerphilly) and Elina Victoria Edwards. *Marriage:* 1).to Dr. John Lewis (divorced); 2). John Golding (former M.P. Newcastle Under Lyme). *Children:* John Stephen, Caroline Anne and Janet Margaret. *Educated at* Caerphilly Girls Grammar School of Radiography, Cardiff Royal Infirmary. *Career:* Former: Radiographer; Secretary/Agent to Member of Parliament; Present: Member of Parliament since July 1986, appointed Labour West Midlands Whip 1987; Vice Chairman P.L.P. Committee on Home Affairs; Parliamentary Affairs and Vice Chairman all party Parliamentary Group on children; former member; North Staffs District Health Authority; former member District Manpower Services Board; former president Constituency Labour Party; former secretary Newcastle & District Trades Council; former NUPE branch secretary. *Recreation:* Fishing. *Clubs:* Halmerend Working mens club. *Address:* 6 Lancaster Ave, Newcastle-under-Lyme, Staffs., ST5 1DR.

GOLDSTONE, Mr David Joseph, LLB *Currently:* Chairman and Chief Executive Regalian Properties PLC. *Born on* 21 Feb 1929 at Swansea. *Son of* Solomon and Rebecca Goldstone. *Marriage:* to Cynthia Easton 1957. *Children:* Jonathan Lee, Debra Ann and Karen Ella. *Educated at* Dynevor, Swansea, to 1948; London School of Economics & Political Science 1949-52; LLB Honours Degree 1952; Admitted as a Solicitor of the Supreme Court 1955. *Career:* Legal Practioner specialising in property, corporate affairs and taxation 1955-62; Director of property development & Investment Co 1962-67; Managing Director of Group of Companies 1968; Chief Executive Officer Regalian Group of Companies 1971. Member of the Court of Governors London School of Economics and Atlantic College. Director of London City Airport Ltd and Swansea Sound Commercial Radio Ltd. Former Director of Welsh National Opera 1984-89 and Member of the Football Assoc. of Wales 1970-72. *Recreation:* family, reading, farming, sport. *Clubs:* RAC, Bath & Raquets, Riverside Raquet Centre. *Address:* Regalian Properties Plc, 44 Grosvenor Hill, London, W1A 4NR.

GOODRIDGE, Councillor Richard John, Sheriff of Carmarthen *Currently:* Royal Mail letters. *Born on* 5 Oct 1960 at Carmarthen. *Son of* Stanley Hubert Charles Goodridge and Mary Goodridge (nee Mayhook). *Educated at* Pentrepoeth Infants & Junior School; Ystrad Tywi; Queen Elizabeth Boys Grammar school. *Career:* Elected to Carmarthen Town Council 1987; Dyfed County Council 1989; Member of Court of Governors Swansea University; elected Sheriff of Carmarthen 1991. *Publications:* Numerous Journals and magazines. *Recreation:* Military & Local history (member of OMRS) *Clubs:* Victory Services Club, London. *Address:* Sarn Villa, Pensarn, Carmarthen, SA31 2DJ. Tel: 0267 232343.

GOSS, Professor Richard Oliver, PhD. *Currently:* Professor, Department of Maritime Studies, University of Wales Institute of Science and Technology, since 1980. *Born on* 4 Oct 1929. *Son of* the late Leonard Arthur Goss and Hilda Nellie Goss (nee Casson). *Marriage:* to Lesley Elizabeth Thurbon (marr. diss. 1983). *Children:* two s one d. *Educated at* Christ's Coll., Finchley; HMS Worcester; King's Coll., Cambridge. Master Mariner 1956; BA 1958; MA 1961; PhD 1979. FCIT 1970; MNI (Founder) 1972; FNI

1977. *Career:* Merchant Navy (apprentice and executive officer), 1947-55; NZ Shipping Co. Ltd, 1958-63; Economic Consultant (Shipping, Shipbuilding and Ports), MoT, 1963-64; Econ. Adviser,BoT (Shipping), 1964-67; Sen. Econ. Adviser (Shipping, Civil Aviation, etc), 1967-74; Econ. Adviser to Cttee of Inquiry into Shipping (Rochdale Cttee), 1967-70; Under-Sec., Dept of Industry and Trade, 1974-80. Nuffield/Leverhulme Travelling Fellow,1977-78. Governor, Plymouth Polytechnic, 1973-84; Mem.,Council: RINA, 1969- ; Nautical Inst. (from foundn until 1976); Member: CNAA Nautical Studies Bd, 1971-81; CNAA Transport Bd, 1976-78. Editor and Editor-in-Chief, Maritime Policy and Management, 1985- . *Publications:* Studies in Maritime Economics, 1968; (with C.D.Jones) The Economics of Size in Dry Bulk Carriers, 1971; (with M.C. Mann, et al) The Cost of Ships' Time, 1974; Advances in Maritime Economics, 1977; A Comparative Study of Seaport Management and Administration, 1979; Politics for Canadian Seaports, 1984; Port Authorities in Australia, 1987; numerous papers in various journals, translations and to conferences. *Recreation:* cruising inland waterways, travel. *Address:* 8 Dunraven House, Castle Court, Westgate Street, Cardiff, CF1 1DL. Tel: 0222 344338.

GRAESSER, Mr Norman Rhidian, *Currently:* retired. *Born on* 21 Oct 1924 at Overton on Dee, Flintshire. *Son of* Norman Hugo and Annette Stewart (nee Durward). *Marriage:* to Stella Aimley Hoyle, 1952. *Children:* Jonathan Hugo, Max Ainley and Fern. *Educated at* Oundle School; Royal Naval College Dartmouth. *Career:* Joined Royal Navy as Cadet 1942. Served Mediterranean, North Atlantic, East Indies, West Indies and S.America in Battleships and cruisers, invalided out of RN 1948 at Lieutenant (S). Joined James Lithgow (UK) Ltd, Buckley, Clwyd, 1953 as commercial director and worked for company through its name changes of Ensecote Lithgow to Lithgow Saekaphen until 1986 when ill health brought early retirement. *Publications:* Family History. *Recreation:* Countryside, gardening, conversation, rugby football, bridge, crossword puzzles. *Clubs:* Lansdowne, London. *Address:* Fron Fanadl, Llandyrnog, Denbigh, Clwyd, LL16 4HR.

GRAVELL, Mr Raymond William Robert, *Currently:* Broadcaster, BBC; Actor. *Born on* 12 Sept 1951 at Cydweli. *Son of* the late Thomas John and Nina Eileen (nee Johns). *Marriage:* to Mari Roberts 1991. *Educated at* Queen Elizabeth Grammar School, Carmarthen. *Career:* Llanelli RFC (Capt 1980-82),1969-85; Wales XV 1975-82; British Lions 1980. *Publications:* "Grav", 1986. *Recreation:* Rugby, walking, fishing on Gwenllian Farm. *Clubs:* Llanelli RFC, Life Member Mynyddgarreg RFC. *Address:* 2 Brynhyfryd, Mynyddygarreg, Cydweli, Dyfed, SA17 4PA.

GRAY, Mr John Walton David, CMG., MA *Currently:* Ambassador, UK Permanent Representative to Organisation for Economic Co-operation & Development, Paris. *Born on* 1 Oct 1936 at Burry Port,Carms. *Son of* Myrddin and Elsie Gray (nee Jones). *Marriage:* Anthoula Yerasimou. *Children:* Helen Irene, Clare Marian and Nicholas Myrddin Christopher *Educated at* Blundell's School, Tiverton, Devon; Christ's College, Cambridge; Middle East Centre, Oxford; American University, Cairo. *Career:* Diplomatic posts in Lebanon, Bahrain, London, Geneva and Sofia, 1962-77; Counsellor (Commercial), Jedda, 1978-79; Deputy Head of Mission, Jedda, 1980-81; Head of Maritime, Aviation & Environment

Dept., FCO, 1982-85; HM Ambassador to the Lebanon, 1985-88. *Recreation:* History, travel, drama, spectator sports and Wales *Clubs:* Athenaeum; Commonwealth Trust; Inst. of Welsh Affairs. *Address:* UK Delegation To OECD, 19 Rue De Franqueville, 75116 Paris. C/o F.C.O., King Charles St, London, SW1A 2AH

GREENAWAY, Dr Frank, MA(Oxford)., MSc., PhD., FRSC., FMA., FSA *Currently:* Retired, Research Fellow, The Science Museum, South Kensington, London, entered 1949 as Assistant Keeper, retired 1980 as Keeper (Head of Department). *Born on* 9 July 1917 at Cardiff. *Son of* the late Henry James and the late Louisa Kate Greenaway. *Marriage:* to Margaret May (Miranda) Brumfit (nee Warner). *Children:* 2 sons, 3 daughters. *Educated at* Cardiff High School; Jesus Coll. Oxford; Univ. College London. *Career:* Royal Army Ordnance Corp. 1940-41; Science Master (Bournemouth, Epsom), 1941-43; Research Laboratories, Kodak Ltd., 1944-49; Department of Chemistry, (Honorary) Reader in History of Science, Royal Inst. of G.B., 1970-85; Regents' Fellow, Smithsonian Inst., Washington, 1985; served as mbr of governing bodies of: British Soc. for the History of Science 1958-68, 1974-78, Vice Pres. 1962-65; Museums Assoc. 1961-70, 1973-76, Hon.Editor 1965-70; Royal Inst. of G.B. 1963-65, 1990- ; British Nat. Commt. International Council of Museums (variously 1967-83, British Nat. Commt. for the History of Science 1972-81; British Nat. Commt for Int. Council of Scientific Unions 1972-77; Int. Union of the History and Philisophy of Science 1972-81, Sec-Gen. 1972-77; Commonwealth Assoc. of Museums (President 1979-83, Royal Philharmonic Soc. 1980-84, 1986-88; President Nonsuch Antiquarian Soc. 1990- . *Publications:* Science Museums in Developing Countries (UNESCO) 1962; John Dalton and the Atom 1966; Science in the Early Roman Empire ed. 1986; Lavoisier's Essays, Physical and Chemical ed. 1971; Royal Inst. Archives ed. 1971-85; official publications of Science Museum, London. *Recreation:* Music and travel *Clubs:* Athenaeum *Address:* 135 London Road, Ewell, Epsom, Surrey, KT17 2BS.

GREENER, Mr Michael John, BA, FCA, BA(Open). *Currently:* Managing Director of small retail booksellers, since 1973. *Born on* 28 Nov 1931 at Barry. *Son of* Gabriel William and Morfydd (nee Morgan). *Marriage:* to Heather Georgina Balshaw, 1964 (divorced 1974). *Children:* Matthew Dominic. *Educated at* Douai School, Woolhampton; University of Wales, Cardiff. *Career:* Articled with Deloitte, Plender, Griffiths & Co., Cardiff; qualified as Chartered Accountant 1956; Assistant to Secretary, Western Mail & Echo, Cardiff 1957-59; Assistant then Lecturer, College of Commerce, Wednesbury 1959-62; Director then Managing Director family jewellery business 1962-87. *Publications:* Between the Lines of the Balance Sheet (Pergamon Press), 1968, revised edition 1980; Problems for Discussion in Mercantile Law (Butterworth) 1970; Penguin Dictionary of Commerce, 1970, revised 1980, revised and reissued as Penguin Business Dictionary 1987; many articles in Business and Accounting journals. *Recreation:* creative writing, reading, bridge. *Address:* 33 Glan Hafren, The Knap, Barry, S.Glam., CF6 8TA. Tel:0446 732867

GREENWALD, Ms Michelle Ruth, *Currently:* Regional Manager for Wales BTCV/Gwarchodwyr Cefn Gwlad 1989- *Born on* 14 Aug 1948 at New Jersey, U.S.A. *Daughter of*

Edwin D. Greenwald and Margaret (nee Kreps). *Educated at* A.B. Vassar College; M.A. Univ. of Michigan *Career:* Researcher, National Heritage Ltd., 1972; Historian, North Pickering Community Dev. Proj., 1973; Proj. Historian, Min.of Natural Resources (Ontario,Canada) 1974-76; Conservation Officer, Min. of Citizenship & Culture (Ontario, Canada) 1976-86; East Midlands Regional Officer, BTCV 1986-89; Mbr. Nottingham Civic Society Environment Commt., 1988-89; head Building Recording Unit Nottingham Civic Society 1988-89. *Publications:* The 'Rehab' Wave - Re-Using Old Buildings in Cipher, Vol. VII, No. 11, 1980; Townsend Traces with J. Bucovetsky, Toronto, 1978; The Welland Canals: Historical Resource Analysis and Preservation Alternatives, with A.Levitt and E.Peebles, Toronto: Ministry of Culture and Recreation, 1976; The Historical Complexities of Pickering - Markham-Scarborough-Uxbridge. Toronto, 1973. *Recreation:* Dance, theatre, cinema, reading, industrial archaeology. *Clubs:* Vassar of London. *Address:* BTCV Wales, Frolic House, Frolic Street, Newtown, Powys SY16 1AP Tel:0686 628600.

GREY - MORGAN, Professor Colyn, BSc (Hons), MSc, PhD, F. Inst.P., C.Phys., FIEE, C.Eng., *Currently:* Professor of Physics and Head of Department, University College of Swansea, Dean of International Affairs. *Born on* 23 Mar 1925 at Pontypridd. *Son of* the late Edwin John Morgan and the late Margaret (nee Williams). *Marriage to* Menna Hopkins, 1951. *Children:* Timothy Grey-Morgan (qv) *Educated at* Amman Valley Grammar School, University College of Swansea. *Career:* Royal Society Warren Research Fund Fellowship, University College Swansea; Principal Scientific Officer, UKAEA, Risley Lancs. 1956; AERE Harwell 1958; Lecturer in Ionisation Physics, Univ. College Swansea, 1961; Visiting Scientist, European Centre for Nuclear Research 1963-1970; Served as Chairman of SERC Central Laser Faculty; Member of Science Board of SERC, and Chairman Physics Committee 1972-74; Governor HOST; British Council Committee for International Collaboration in Higher Education; Consultant to Ministry of Defence 1951- ; Academic Assessor and External Examiner to - Universiti of Malaya, Universiti Kebangsaan, Malaysia, Universiti Teknologi Malaysia, Universiti Sains Malaysia, National University of Singapore, Nan Yang Technical University, Universiti Brunei Darussalam; Editor, Journal of Applied Physics (Phys.D) Published by Institute of Physics *Publications:* Two books and several papers on Nuclear and Atomic Physics, Laser Physics and Spectroscopy. *Recreation:* Yachting *Clubs:* Royal Overseas, St. James', London. *Address:* 6 Westport Avenue, Ridgewood Park, Mayals, Swansea SA3 5EA   Dept. of Physics, University College of Swansea, Singleton Park, Swansea SA2 8PP.

GREY - MORGAN, Dr. Timothy, BSc, PhD, M.Inst.P. C.Phys. *Currently:* Manager, Cyclotron Division, Amersham International, Bucks. *Born on* 28 Sept 1960 *Son of* Professor Colyn Grey-Morgan (qv) and Menna Grey Morgan *Educated at* Ecole International De Geneve, Geneva, Switzerland; St.Faiths School, Cambridge; The Leys School, Cambridge; University College of Swansea 1978-81; 1st Class Honours Degree in Physics, 1981; Awarded Science and Engineering Research Council Studentship, 1981-84; Royal Society Research Unit, University College Swansea, awarded PhD for thesis on

Controlled Exitation and Reactions of Ions; *Career:* Senior Physicist, Special Products division Amersham International, Bucks. 1984-89; Group Leader, Research Division Applied Materials Inc.(UK) at Horsham, Sussex, 1989-91; Manager, Cyclotron Div. Amersham International, 1991- ; *Publications:* 15 papers and several patents in Atomic, Ionic Physics, Mass Spectrometry and Isotope Separation.. *Recreations:* Yachting and Skiing. *Address:* 23 Carter Walk, Tyler Green, Penn, Bucks. HP10 8ER Tel: 0494 815019. Cyclotron Division, Amersham International Ltd., White Lion Rd., Amersham, Bucks. Tel: 0494 543 550.

GRIFFIN, Dr. John Parry, BSc, PhD, MB, BS, FRCP, FRCPath *Currently:* Director of The Association of The British Pharmaceutical Industry since 1984; Hon.Consultant, Lister Hospital, Stevenage. *Born on* 21 May 1938 at Cardiff. *Son of* David J.Griffin and the late Phyllis M.Griffin. *Marriage:* to Margaret (nee Cooper), 1962. *Children:* Jane Rachel,Ruth Catherine and Timothy David. *Educated at* Howardian High School, Cardiff; London Hospital Medical College, Lethby and Buxton Prizes, 1958BSc (1st Cl.Hons) 1959; PhD 1961: George Riddoch Price in Neurology 1962; MB, BS 1964; LRCP, MRCS 1964;MRCP 1980. FRCP 1990; FRCPath 1986 (MRCPath 1982) *Career:* House Phys., London Hospital, Med Unit; House Surgeon, London Hospital, Accident and Orthopaedic Dept 1964-75; Lecturer, Kings College London 1965-67; Head of Clinical Research, Riker 3M Laboratories 1967-71; Professional Head of Medicines Division (now Medicines Control Agency), Dept of Health 1971-84; Medical Assessor, Medicines Commission 1977-84. Member: Joint Formulary Committee for British Nat. Formulary 1978-84; UK Representative EEC Committee on Proprietary Med. Products: Chairman, Committee on Prop. Med Products Working Party on Safety Requirements 1977-84. FRSM. *Publications:* (jointly) Iatrogenic Diseases, 1972, 3rd edition 1985; (jointly) Manual of Adverse Drug Interactions, 1975, 4th edition 1988; (jointly) Drug Induced Emergencies,1980; Medicines: research, regulation and risk, 1989; (jointly) International Medicines Regulations, 1989; numerous articles in science and medical journals, mainly on aspects of neurophysiology and clinical pharmacology and toxicology. *Recreation:* local history, gardening. *Clubs:* Athenaeum *Address:* 12 Whitehall, London, SW1 2DY.

GRIFFIN, Mr Kenneth James, OBE 1970. *Currently:* a Deputy Chairman, British Shipbuilders,1977-83. *Born on* 1 Aug 1928. *Son of* the late Albert Griffin and the late Catherine (nee Sullivan). *Marriage:* to Doreen Cicely Simon,1951. *Children:* one s one d (and one s decd). *Educated at* Dynevor Grammar School, Swansea; Swansea Technical College. *Career:* Area Sec., ETU, 1960; Dist Sec., Confederation of Ship Building Engrg Unions, 1961; Sec., Craftsmen Cttee (Steel), 1961; Mem., Welsh Council 1968; Mem., Crowther Commn on Constitution (Wales), 1969; Joint Sec., No. 6 joint Industrial Council Electrical Supply Industry, 1969; Industrial Adviser, DTI, 1971-72; Co-ordinator of Industrial Advisers, DTI 1972-74; Special Adviser, Sec. of State for Industry, 1974; part-time Mem., NCB, 1973-82; Chm., Blackwall Engrg, 1983-85 Member: Suppl. Benefits Commn, 1968-80; Solicitors Disciplinary Tribunal 1982- . Chm., Castleton Retirement Homes, 1989- ; Vice-Chm., UK Housing Trust 1989- ; Exec. Advr, Mobile Training, 1989. *Recreation:* golf, music, reading. *Clubs:*

Reform. *Address:* 214 Cyncoed Road, Cyncoed, Cardiff, CF2 6RS. Tel: 0222 752184

GRIFFITH, Mr Edward Michael Wynne, CBE DL *Currently:* Vice Lord Lt. Clwyd; Chmn. Countryside Council for Wales; Chmn Postgrad Medical & Dental Education Council. *Born on* 28 Aug 1933 at Daresbury, Cheshire. *Son of* the late Major H.W.Griffith MBE and the late Mrs P.L.Griffith. *Marriage:* to Jill Grange Moseley daughter of Major D.P.G.Mosey. *Children:* James and Anthony. *Educated at* Eton, Royal Agricultural College, Cirencester. *Career:* Agric Research Council 1972-82; Chmn Clwyd Health Authority 1980-90; Chmn Nat Trust in Wales 1984-91; Member Nat Trust Council; Dir. National Westminster Bank Advisory board 1974-92. Ch. Council for Postgrad Medical & Dental Education; Ch.Clwyd Health Authority 1980-90; Vice Lt.,Clwyd. U.F.C. Committee for Wales 1990- . *Recreation:* Countryside, Horses *Clubs:* Boodles *Address:* Greenfield, Trefnant, Denbigh, Clwyd, LL16 5UE.

GRIFFITH, Mr Kenneth, *Currently:* Writing script for BBC on Life of Roger Casement and writing second history book on 2nd Anglo-Boer War, plus various film projects. About to film in West Africa for "Heart of Darkness: a life of Roger Casement". Involved in a B.B.C. film about himself: only mildly embarrassed. . .; Also researching a proposed film about Croatia. *Born on* 12 Oct 1921 at Tenby, Pembs. *Marriage:* to (1) Joan, (2) Doria, (3) Carole. *Children:* David, Eva, Jonathan, Polly and Huw. *Educated at* Tenby Council and Tenby Grammar schools *Career:* Actor at age 16; Films, television and Old Vic before war-service; R.A.F; Probably 100 films, mostly rubbish, but not all. Many television plays, little rubbish. Protege of Tyrone Guthrie, Shapespeare: played Hamlet, Iago, Shylock and Oberon. For last 20 years made films, very proud of these. *Publications:* "Thank God We Kept the Flag Flying" (Boer War); "Curious Journey" (with Timothy O'Grady); "The Discovery of Nehru" (experiences in India) *Recreation:* Collecting Anglo-Boer War letters etc. *Clubs:* Try to avoid joining anything. Bad team man. *Address:* Michael Collins House, 110 Englefield Road, Islington, London, N1 3LQ.

GRIFFITH, Mr Owen Glyn, CBE., MVO. *Currently:* Diplomatic Service (retired). *Born on* 19 Jan 1922 at Neath. *Son of* the late William Glyn Griffith MBE and the late Glwndys May (nee Picton Davies). *Marriage:* to Rosemary Elizabeth Cecil (nee Earl), 1949. *Children:* David and Michael *Educated at* Friars School, Bangor, Oundle Schhol, Trinity Hall, Cambridge. *Career:* Cmmnd. Welsh Guards, 1941-43 (wounded twice in Tunisia)., H.M. Overseas Service, Uganda, 1944-63; District Officer, 1944-51; Private Secretary to Governor, 1952-54; District Commissioner 1954-61; Permanent Secretary, 1961-63; H.M. Diplomatic Service, 1963-82; Principal CRO, 1963; First Secretary and Head of Chancery Khartoum,1965,First Secretary (commercial) Stockholm, 1969; Deputy High Commission, Malawi, 1973; Inspectorate 1976; High Commissioner, Lesotho, 1978. *Recreation:* Golf and fishing *Clubs:* Denham Golf.*Address:* The Sundial, Marsham Way, Gerrards Cross, Bucks., SL9 8AD. Blaengwilym, Rhydwilym, Clynderwen, Dyfed, SA66 7QH.

GRIFFITH WILLIAMS, Mr John, QC MA *Currently:* Barrister. *Born on* 20 Dec 1944 at Teignmouth, Devon. *Son of* Griffith John Williams TD, Alison Rundle nee Bennett. *Marriage:* to Mair Tasker Watkins, 3 Apr 1971.*Children:* Joanna Kate and Sarah Jane. *Educated at* King's School,Bruton; The Queen's Collage,Oxford; *Career:* Called to Bar,Gray's Inn 1968; Recorder of the Crown Court 1984; QC 1985; Commissioned Royal Welch Fusiliers (TA) 1964; Welsh Volunteers 1967; Lieutenant 1966; *Recreation:* Golf, Reading *Clubs:* Army and Navy, Cardiff and County, Royal Porthcawl Golf *Address:* Goldsmith Building, Temple, London, EC4Y 7BL.

GRIFFITHS, (John) Hywel, BA, DipEd. *Currently:* MD, CRM Consultants Ltd, since 1989. *Born on* 9 Oct 1933 at Ystrad Mynach. *Son of* Hopkin and Gwendoline Margaret Griffiths. *Marriage:* to Joan Ethel (nee Morton), 1960. *Children:* Meurig, Charlotte, Sarah and Louisa. *Educated at* Caerphilly GS; UCNW Bangor; Trinity Hall Cambridge. *Career:* Provincial Community Development Officer, HMOCS Northern Rhodesia 1957-63; Director British Council Port Harcourt Nigeria 1963-65; Lecturer in Community Development Manchester University 1965-70; Director Northern Ireland Community Relations Commission 1970-72; Professor of Social Administration New University of Ulster 1972-79; Consultant to VSU Home Office 1979-82; Director Wales Council for Voluntary Action 1982-89; trustee Nat Aids Tst, HTV Telethon Tst, Welsh Voluntary Tst; Chm Neighbourhood Energy Action. *Publications:* Community Work and Social Change (jointly) 1969; Current Issues in Community Work (jointly) 1973; The Development of Local Voluntary Action 1981. *Recreation:* music, walking, gardening, bee-keeping. *Clubs:* Royal Commonwealth Trust *Address:* Plymouth House, Caerphilly, CF8 2RL.

GRIFFITHS, Mr (William) Robert, MA, BCL(Oxon), Barrister. *Currently:* Barrister in private practice. *Born on* 24 Sept 1948 at Swansea. *Son of* (William) John Griffiths and (Marjorie) Megan Griffiths (nee Green). *Marriage:* to Angela May (nee Crawford), 1984. *Children:* Anna-Victoria Sophia, Helena Elizabeth Rose and Charles William Alexander. *Educated at* Haverfordwest GS; St.Edmund Hall, Oxford. *Career:* Open Scholarship (History) to St.Edmund Hall, Oxford 1968; Called to the Bar 1974; Junior Counsel to the Crown (Common Law) 1989- . *Recreation:* collecting modern first editions, reading, cricket. *Clubs:* MCC, Honourable Society of the Cymmrodorion; Honourable Society of Middle Temple. *Address:* 4/5 Gray's Inn Square, London, WC1R 5AY.

GRIFFITHS, Prof. A.P., BA.(Wales), BPhil (Oxon). *Currently:* Professor of Philosophy, University of Warwick, since 1964; Director, Royal Institute of Philosophy, since 1979. *Born on* 11 June 1927. *Son of* John Phillips Griffiths and Elsie Maud (nee Jones). *Marriage:* 1st to Margaret Lock, 1948 (d.1974); 2nd to Vera Clare, 1984 (diss 1990). *Children:* one s one d, from 1st marriage. *Educated at* University College Cardiff,Hon.Fellow 1984; University College Oxford. *Career:* Sgt. Intelligence Corps 1945-48 (despatches), Assistant Lecturer University of Wales 1955-57; Lecturer Birkbeck College Univ of London 1957-64; Pro-Vice-Chancellor, University of Warwick 1970-77. Visiting Professor: Swarthmore Coll., Pa,1963; Univ of California, 1967; Univ of Wisconsin 1965 and 1970; Carleton College Minnesota 1985. Silver Jubilee Medal 1977. *Publications:* (ed) Knowledge & Belief 1967; (ed) Of

Liberty 1983; (ed) Philosophy and Literature 1984; Philosophy and Practice 1985; (ed) Contemporary French Philosophy 1988; (ed) Key Themes in Philosophy 1989; (ed) Wittgenstein Centenary Essays 1991; (ed) A.J.Ayer: Memorial Essays 1992; articles in learned philosophical journals. *Clubs:* Conservative (Kenilworth). *Address:* Dept. of Philosophy, University Of Warwick, Coventry, CV4 7AL. Tel: 0203 523320.

GRIFFITHS, His Honour Bruce (Fletcher), Q.C., LL.B. *Currently:* Retired. *Born on* 28 April 1924 at Barry, Glam. *Son of* Edward Griffiths and Nancy Olga Griffiths. *Marriage:* to Mary Kirkhouse Griffiths (nee Fuell, nee Jenkins), 1952. *Children:* David, Richard and Branwen. *Educated at* Whitchurch Grammar School; Kings College, London. *Career:* RAF, 1942-47; Barrister (Gray's Inn), 1952; Queen's Councel, 1970; Circuit Judge, 1972-86. *Clubs:* Naval & Military Club, London, Cardiff and Country Club. *Address:* 15 Heol Don, Whitchurch, Cardiff, CF4 2AR. Estraves No. 15, 07108 Port De Soller, Mallorca, Spain.

GRIFFITHS, David Vaughan, MA *Currently:* Managing Director, Aitken Hyme Bank, London. *Born on* 14 April 1947 at Rugby. *Son of* Arthur Griffith and Josephine (nee East). *Marriage:* to Tina Frost, 1977. *Children:* one s five d. *Educated at* Cardiff High School; Balliol College, Oxford. *Career:* S.G.Warburg & Co.Ltd., 1970-73; Edward Bates & Sons 1973-75; Orion Bank Ltd., 1975-76; Saudi International Bank 1976-86, (seconded Ministry of Finance, Riyadh 1978-80). Banque Paribas, Executive Director, London 1986-91. *Recreation:* hill walking, railways. *Clubs:* Reform. *Address:* 30 City Road, London, EC1Y 2AY. Tel: 071 638 6070.

GRIFFITHS, Mr Gareth Lloyd, MA(Oxon), Barrister-at-Law *Currently:* Corporate Communications Adviser. *Born on* 28 March 1954 at Rhondda. *Son of* the late Curwen Lloyd Griffiths and Doris Ceinwen Griffiths (nee Hughes). *Educated at* Penarth Grammar School; Jesus College, Oxford; City University, Council of Legal Education. *Career:* Thomson Regional Newspapers 1975-78; Liverpool Daily Post 1978-79; Financial Times 1979-84, Journalist. Director, Shandwick Consultants 1986-90; International Director, Shandwick Consultants 1989-90; Called to the Bar of England and Wales, June 1986; Member, Gray's Inn; Independent Corporate Affairs Adviser 1991- ; mem. Paddington and N Kensington Community Health Cncl 1984-86; mem. Bodleian Library Appeal Ctee, Hon Soc of Cymroddorion; mem: Royal Inst of PA, Royal Inst of Int. Affairs. *Publications:* Opticians and Competition Policy, 1987; Brunei in Profile (8 editions), 1988. *Recreation:* Church history, 19th century history, charitable fund raising. *Clubs:* Reform, London Welsh. *Address:* 2 St Donats House, Seaview Court, Kymin Road, Penarth, S.Glam., CF6 1AS.

GRIFFITHS, Mr Harold Morris, *Currently:* retired. *Born on* 17 March 1926 at Burry Port. *Son of* the late Rt.Hon James Griffiths, CH and the late Winifred (nee Rutley). *Marriage:* 1st to Gwyneth Lethby, 1951 (d.1966); 2nd to Elaine Burge 1966. *Children:* 5 sons, 1 daughter. *Educated at* Llanelli County School; London School of Economics. *Career:* Editorial Staff, Glasgow Herald, 1949-55; Editorial staff (Manchester) Guardian 1955-67; H.M.Treasury 1967-75 and 1978-86; Economic Councellor UK Embassy, Washington 1975-78. *Recreation:* National Parks,

birdwatching. *Address:* 32 Teddington Park, Teddington, Middx., TW11 8DA. Penwaundwr, Crai, Brecon, Powys.

GRIFFITHS, Mr John Charles, JP *Currently:* Chairman: Rodhales Ltd, since 1978; Minerva Arts Channel; Minerva Vision. *Born on* 19 April 1934. *Son of* Sir Percival Griffiths. *Marriage:* 1st to Ann Timms, 1956 (marr diss); 2nd to Carole Jane Mellor, 1983 (marr.diss). *Children:* four s from 1st marriage; 1 d from 2nd marriage. *Educated at* Uppingham; Peterhouse, Cambridge (MA). *Career:* Dep. Manager, Press Association, 1968-70; PR adviser, British Gas, 1970-74; Chm., MSG Public Relations, 1974-78; Chmn., and founder, The Arts Channel, 1983-89. Chairman: National Legue of Young Liberals, 1962-64 (Mem., Nat.Exec., 1964-66); Assoc. of Liberals in Small Business and Self Employed, 1980; Pres., Liberal Party, 1982-83. Contested (L): Ludlow, 1964; Wanstead and Woodford, 1966; Bedford, Feb 1974, Oct 1974. JP Cardiff, 1960. *Publications:* The Survivors, 1964; Afghanistan, 1967; Modern Iceland, 1969; Three Tomorrows, 1980; The Science of Winning Squash, 1981; Afghanistan: key to a Continent, 1981; The Queen of Spades, 1983; Flashpoint Afghanistan, 1986; The Third Man (biography of William Murdoch), 1992. *Recreation:* walking, conversation, reading, music. *Clubs:* Royal Automobile. *Address:* 1 Crossoak Cottages, Talybony-On-Usk, Brecon, Powys, LD3 7UQ. Tel: 0874 730164.

GRIFFITHS, Professor Keith, BSc, PhD, DSc. *Currently:* Professor of Cancer Research, Univ of Wales College of Medicine since 1971; Director of Research, Tenovus Inst. for Cancer Research since 1966. *Born on* 1 April 1935 at Middlesborough, Yorkshire. *Son of* the late Richard and Lilian Griffiths (nee Ebbs). *Marriage:* to Veronica, 1958, Da of Robert Henry Williams, Llandaff Close, Penarth. *Children:* David James (b.1960) and Timothy Richard (b.1962). *Educated at* Sir William Turners School, Coatham, North Yorks; University of Edinburgh (BSc, PhD, DSc). *Career:* Research Associate, University of Minnesota, USA 1960-61; Lecturer, Dept of Steroid Biochemistry, Glasgow University 1961-66; Chairman, Welsh Office, Welsh Scientific Advisory Committee 1975-84; Chairman, Society for Endocrinology 1987-90. *Recreation:* cricket, motoring, gardening. *Address:* Tenovus Institute For Cancer, Research, Univ Of Wales Coll Of Medicine, Heath Park, Cardiff, CF4 4XX.

GRIFFITHS, Mr Lawrence, MA(Cantab). *Currently:* Recorder of the Crown Court, Barrister at Law. *Born on* 16 Aug 1933 at Swansea. *Son of* Bernard and Olive Griffiths. *Marriage:* to Josephine Ann Cook 1959. *Children:* Isobel, Julia and Nicholas. *Educated at* Gowerton Grammar School; Christ's Coll., Cambridge. *Career:* Called to the Bar (Inner Temple) 1957; practise Iscoed Chambers, Swansea; Member Mental Health Review Tribunal 1971-91; Prosecuting Counsel for Wales and Chester Circuit to Inland Revenue, 1969 to date and HM Customs and Excise, 1990 to date. Recorder of the Crown Court since 1972. *Recreation:* Wine and food, snooker, ships and the sea. *Clubs:* Bristol Channel Yacht, Mumbles. *Address:* Peverell, 26 Hillside Crescent, Uplands, Swansea, SA2 ORD.

GRIFFITHS, Rev. Dr. Leslie John, MA, PhD. *Currently:* Methodist Minister, Superintendent of the Finchley and Hendon Circuit, 1991- . *Born on* 15 Feb 1942 at Burry Port, Dyfed. *Son of* the late Sidney J. Griffiths and the late Olwen (nee Thomas). *Marriage:* to Margaret (nee Rhodes), 1969. *Children:* Timothy, Jonathan and Ruth *Educated at* LLanelli Boys' Grammar School 1953-60; Univ. College of South Wales and Monmouthshire, Cardiff 1960-64; Cambridge University 1967-70; School of Oriental and African Studies, London Univ. 1984-87; *Career:* Assistant lecturer, St.David's College Lampeter 1964-67; Methodist Minister in Cambridge 1969-70; Reading 1974-77; Loughton 1980-86; Superindendent of the West London Mission 1986-91; Missionary in Haiti 1970-74 and 1977-80; worked in education, political education, community development. Governor of several schools. Board of Christian Aid 1991-; Trustee of Addiction Recovery Council 1987- ; Religious and news broadcasting; articles for a variety of journals and newspapers. Chairman of the Methodist Church's Caribbean and Latin America Advisory Group 1983-89. *Publications:* The history of Methodism in Haiti: Port-au-Prince 1991 *Recreation:* Rugby; Cricket; Reading; Writing; Talking. *Clubs:* The Graduate Club, Cambridge. *Address:* 24 Monkville Avenue, Temple Fortune, London, NW11 0AH. Tel: 081 455 8063.

GRIFFITHS, Mr Peter Anthony, *Currently:* Chief Executive, Guy's & Lewisham Trust. *Born on* 19 May 1945 at Newport, Gwent. *Son of* the late Albert Griffiths and the late Grace Griffiths. *Marriage:* to Margaret Harris, 1966. *Children:* 2 sons. *Educated at* Swansea Technical College *Career:* Deputy Chief Executive, NHS Management Executive, Dept of Health, 1989-91; Regional General Manager, South East Thames Regional Health Authority, 1988-89; District General Manager, Lewisham & North Southwark Health Authority, 1984-88; District Administrator, Lewisham & North Southwark Health Authority, 1982-84; Acting Area Administrator, Kent Area Health Authority, 1976-81; District Administrator, Medway Health Authority, 1976-81; Associate Member of Institute of Health Service Managers; Association Member of British Institute of Management; Member of the Royal Society of Arts. *Recreation:* Golf, reading and gardening. *Address:* Longlands, 38 Holmewood Ridge, Langton Green, Tunbridge Wells, Kent, TN3 OED.

GRIFFITHS, Peter Kevin, BA(Hons), 1st Wales. *Currently:* Senior Producer, BBC Radio (Network) Features, Arts and Education Department, London, since 1990. *Born on* 15 Oct 1956 at Cardiff. *Son of* Denis Griffiths and E.Joyce (nee Linck). *Educated at* Llanishen High School (comp); Univ Coll Cardiff. *Career:* Studio Manager, BBC Radio 1978-81; Producer 'Womans Hour', Radio 4, 1981-82; Radio 4 Features Department 1982-83; Radio 4, Presentation 1983-85; Network Features Dept., Manchester 1985; Senior Producer Sport and Outside Broadcasts, Radio 1985-90. *Recreation:* music, celtic history, books, friends. *Clubs:* Member Radio Academy. *Address:* BBC Broadcasting House, Portland Place, London, W1A 1AA. 3 Lancaster Cottages, Lancaster Park, Richmond, Surrey, TW10 6AE.

GRIFFITHS, Mr William John, *Currently:* retired. *Born on* 19 Jan 1922 at Swansea. *Son of* the late Evan William Griffiths and Ann Griffiths (nee Ley). *Marriage:* to Marjorie Megan Green, 1944. *Children:* W.R.Griffiths (Barrister) and J.A.Griffiths (Solicitor). *Educated at* Grammar School, Glanmor, Swansea. *Career:* Swansea County Treasurers Dept 1946-51; Chief Auditor, Pembrokeshire County Council 1951-73; Assistant County Treasurer, Dyfed County

Council 1974-87; Hon Treasurer Pembs National Playing Fields Assoc 1968 to dissolution 1980; Pembroke County Cricket Executive member 1965- ; Vice Chairman 1974; Chairman 1977-89; Hon Treasurer 1991- ; Welsh Cricket Assoc Executive member for approx 20 years; Finance Chairman 10 years, Vice Chairman 10 years; Johnston Pembrokeshire Community Hall Management Chairman 1966- . *Recreation:* cricket, theatre, reading. *Clubs:* numerous Cricket Clubs *Address:* Crestalyn, 6 Park Road, Queensway, Haverfordwest, SA61 2PD. Tel: 0437 768693

GRIFFITHS OF FFORESTFACH, Lord Brian, MSc (Econ). *Currently:* International Adviser. *Born on* 27 Dec 1941 at Swansea. *Son of* Ivor Winston and Phyllis Mary. *Marriage:* to Rachel Jane Jones. *Children:* Aeronwen, James and Owenna. *Educated at* Dynevor Grammar School, Swansea; London School of Economics. *Career:* Lecturer, London School of Economics 1965-76; Professor of Banking, City University 1977-85; Dean of City University Business School 1981-85; Director, Bank of England 1983-85; Head of Prime Ministers Policy Unit 1985-90. *Recreation:* *Address:* House Of Lords, London, SW1.

GRIST, Mr Ian, MA MP *Currently:* MP (Cons.) Cardiff Central since 1983 (Cardiff North. Feb 1974-83). *Born on* 5 Dec. 1938 at Southhampton. *Son of* Basil William Grist MBE and Leila Helen Grist (both decd). *Marriage:* 24.3.66 Wendy Ann (nee White), JP, BSc. *Children:* Julian and Toby. *Educated at* Repton School, Jesus College, Oxford (Open Scholar Hons. PPE) *Career:* Colonial Officer Southern Cameroon Plebiscite 1960-61; Sales Manager, Kingsway Stores, United Africa Co. Nigeria 1961-63; Conservative Central Office Information Officer Wales 1963-74; Conservative Research Dept. 1970-74; *Recreation:* Music, Poetry. *Address:* 126 Penylan Road, Cardiff, CF2 5RD.

GRONHAUG, Mr Arnold Conrad, CEng., FIEE., HonFCIBSE *Currently:* Retired (except for various voluntary works). *Born on* 26 March 1921 at Barry, Glam. *Son of* the late James Gronhaug MBE and the late BeatriceMay Gronhaug. *Marriage:* to Patricia Grace Smith, 1945. *Children:* Patricia Anne and Jennifer Elizabeth. *Educated at* Barry Grammar School; Cardiff Technical College. *Career:* Electrical Officer RNVR, 1941-46; Air Ministry Works Directorate, 1946-63: Area Mechanical & Electrical Engineer, Singapore and Malaya, 1950-52; Air Ministry Headquarters, 1952-60; Deputy Chief Engineer (AMWD), RAF Germany, 1960-63; Ministry of Public Building & Works, 1963-73: Senior Engineer, Portsmouth Area, 1963-67; Joint Services Staff College, (jssc), 1964-65; Superintending Engineer, Headquarters, 1967-71; Director, Defence Works (Overseas), 1971-73; Property Services Agency, Department of the Environment, 1973-81: Director, Social & Research Services, 1973-75; Director Mechanical & Electrical Engineering Services (Under Secretary), 1975-81; Professional Institutions etc. Engineering Council, Nominations Committee, 1983- ; IEE Interviewer since 1968; IEE Membership Committee, 1975-82, (Chairman 1979-82); IEE Membership Adviser, Surrey, 1984-91; CIBSE Technology Board, 1979-81; CIBSE Qualifications Board, 1981-87; Admitted to the Freedom of the City of London 1979, Worshipful Company of Engineers 1984, Admitted to the Livery 1984. *Publications:* Various technical papers. *Recreation:* Photography and music

Address: 6 Pine Hill, Epsom, Surrey, KT18 7BG.

GRONOW, Dr David Gwilym Colin, MSc., PhD. *Currently:* Retired. *Born on* 13 Jan 1929 at Leigh-on-Sea, Essex. *Son of* the late David Morgan and the late Harriet Hannah(nee Simpson). *Marriage:* 1). to Joan Andrew Bowen 1953 (divorced) and 2). to Rosemary Freda Iris Keys 1970. *Children:* Adrian David Gronow and Beverly Clare Tayler.(both by first marriage). *Educated at* Grammar School, Swansea and University College, London. *Career:* Scientific Officer/Senior Scientific Officer RAF Institute of Aviation Medicine, Farnborough, Hants., 1951-57; Second Engineer/Senior Engineer, Central Electricity Generating Board, London 1957-64; Assistant Chief Commercial Officer/Chief Commercial Officer, South of Scotland Electricity Board, Glasgow 1964-79; Marketing Adviser/ Commercial Adviser/Member for Engineering, Marketing and Research, Electricity Council, London 1979-90. *Recreation:* Travel, theatre, golf, horseracing, birdwatching. *Address:* 8 Arundel Way, Highcliffe, Christchurch, Dorset, BH23 5DX.

GRONOW, John, *Born on* 16 March 1942 at Cardiff. *Son of* Thomas Gronow and Gladys Gronow (nee Isgar). *Marriage:* divorced. *Children:* David Gronow. *Educated at* Windsor Clive Secondary Modern. *Career:* Accident in 1959 left him paralysed; been involved in Sport for the Disabled since 1963, competed both Nationally and Internationally at European Championships, World Championships and Olympic Games, also Commonwealth Games. Main sport is bowls. *Recreation:* fly fishing, table tennis. *Clubs:* Rookwood Paraplegic Sports; Welsh Para & Tetra Sports Assoc. *Address:* 10 Fern Place, Fairwater, Cardiff, CF5 3HG.

GRONOW, Dr Michael, BSc(Wales), PhD(Cantab). *Born on* 26 July 1937 at Cardiff, S.Wales. *Son of* Vivian and Mary Amelia (nee Chappell). *Marriage:* to Janet Ruth Tompkins, 1968 (divorced 1991). *Children:* Simon Richard (b.1972) and Kathryn Louise (b.1973). *Educated at* Cardiff HS; University College of S.Wales (BSc); Trinity College Cambridge (PhD). *Career:* University of Cambridge: MRC res assistant Dept of Radiotherapeutics 1963-65, demonstrator Dept of Chem 1962-65; Res assoc Dept of Pharmacology Baylor University Houston Texas USA 1965-66, Res assoc and demonstrator Dept of Biochem University of Oxford 1966-69, lecturer Dept of Experimental Pathology and Cancer Res University of Leeds 1969-75, permanent senior res fellow Cancer Res Unit University of York 1975-79; consultant PA Tech Centre Int 1979-80, head of biosciences PA Centre for Advanced Studies 1980-81, jt MD and founder Cambridge Life Science plc 1981-88, MD CRL Ltd 1989, director Aquamarine Sciences and Cambridge Phenomenon Promotions 1989; trustee and founder Cambridge Cancer Research Fund 1988. member: Biochemical Soc 1967, British Assoc Cancer Res 1969. *Publications:* author of 50 publications. *Recreation:* music, photography, hockey, chess, wine. *Address:* Thornton House, 131 Waterbeach Road, Landbeach, Cambridge, CB4 4EA.

GRONOW, County Councillor Sylvia Enid, *Currently:* Insurance Rep. *Born on* 3 Jan 1938 at Bridgend. *Daughter of* the late George and Sarah Cox. *Marriage:* to Griffith 1957 (divorced 1980). *Children:* David, Phillip and Paul. *Educated at* Heol-Gam Sec. & Bridgend College of Technology. *Career:* Civil Service 1953-56; Assistant Accountant 1956-58; Civil Service 1965-73; Insurance Advisor 1974; Branch Sec. M.S.F. Trade Union, Member Mid Glam C.C. from 1985; Member Community Health Council; Chairman 4 school governors; member Appeals Panel and Medical Board for D.H.S.S. *Recreation:* Music, history, reading, theatre, charities, politics. *Address:* 9 Oak Terrace, Coyrahen, Bridgend, CF32 ODY.

GROSVENOR, Hon Hugh Richard, A.I.A.G.E., SAWMA *Currently:* retired. *Born on* 25 Nov 1919 at Rickmansworth, Herts. *Son of* the late Lord & Lady Ebury. *Marriage:* 1st to Margaret Neilsen; 2nd to Victoria Wright. *Children:* Elizabeth, from 1st marriage and William Alexander and Rebecca from 2nd marriage. *Educated at* Radley College; Sandhurst. *Career:* Army 1937-45, 2nd Lt, Capt, Major. Ministry of Agriculture 1946-83. Chairman Shropshire Lands Committee; Vice President Heart of England Wildfowlers; Vice President Carmarthen Wildfowlers. *Publications:* articles in sporting magazines; pamphlets on Gundog training. *Recreation:* fishing, shooting, sailing, conservation, ornithology, ufology, archaeology. *Clubs:* Carmarthen Businessmens. *Address:* River Ridge, Courtland Park, Carmarthen, Dyfed.

GROVE, Mr William Dennis, BSc (Mathematics) *Currently:* Chairman, North West Water Group PLC. *Born on* 23 Jul 1927 at Gower. *Son of* the late William Grove and the late Elizabeth Charlotte. *Marriage:* Audrey I. Saxel, 1953. *Children:* Christopher J.B. and Sally D. *Educated at* Gowerton School; King's College, London; *Career:* Army, Lieutenant, South Wales Borderers and RWAFF, 1945-48; University 1948-51; Dunlop Group, finally Overseas General Manager 1951-70; Chairman and Chief Executive TPT Group and SONOCO Europe (Paperboard Packaging Worldwide) 1970-85; Member, Paper Industry Council 1975-85; Chairman North West Water Authority 1985-89; Member, Water Industry (WAA and WSA) Council 1985-; *Recreation:* Travel, golf and watching sports. *Clubs:* Bramall Park Golf, Mottram Hall Golf. *Address:* Larkrise, Meadow Brow, Alderley Edge, Cheshire SK9 7XD. Dawson House, Great Sankey, Warrington, WA5 3LW Tel: 0925 234000.

GROVE-WHITE, Mr Robin Bernard, BA(Oxon). *Currently:* Director, Centre for the Study of Environmental Change, Lancaster University, since 1990; Forestry Commissioner since 1991. *Born on* 17 Feb 1941 at Dublin. *Son of* C.W.Grove-White and Mrs C.M. Rabbiage. *Marriage:* 1st to Virginia Ironside 1970-74; 2nd to Helen Elizabeth Smith, 1979. *Children:* William (b.1973), Ruth (B.1980), Simon (b.1982) and Francis (b.1986). *Educated at* Uppingham School, 1954-59; Worcester College, Oxford, 1960-63. *Career:* Freelance Writer, 1963-71; Asst.Secretary, Council for the Protection of Rural England (CPRE) 1972-80; Director, CPRE 1981-87; Research Fellow, Imperial College, London 1987-89; Vice-Chairman, Council for National Parks 1985-87; Vice Chairman European Environmental Bureau 1985-87. *Publications:* numerous articles and papers in journals and other periodicals. *Recreation:* walking, cricket, theatre *Address:* Conaer Mill Cottage, Quernmore, Lancaster, LA2 9EE. Brynaau, Llanfechell, Amlwch, Gwynedd, LL68 ORT.

GUEST, Dr George Howell, CBE., MA., Mus.D., FRCSM., FRCO., FRCCO., Hon.RAM. *Currently:* Freelance musician. *Born on* 9 Feb 1924 at Bangor, Gwynedd. *Son of* the late Mr E.J. Guest and the late Mrs G Guest. *Marriage:* to Nancy Mary Talbot, 1959. *Children:* David Stephen Benedict and Elizabeth Mary Helen. *Educated at* Friars School, Bangor; Kings School, Chester; St. John's College, Cambridge. *Career:* Asst. Organist, Chester Cathedral, 1946; Org. Scholar, St. Johns Coll., Cambridge, 1947; Org. St. Johns Coll, John Stewart of Rannoch Scholar in Sacred Music, 1951-91; Univ. Asst. Lecturer in Music, 1953; Univ. Lecturer in Music, 1956-82; University Org., Camb. Univ., 1973-91; Aelod er Awrhydedd Gorsedd y Beirdd Eistedd. Gen, 1977; Director Cor Cenedlaethol Cymru, concerts with St. Johns Coll. Choir in Australia, Japan, USA, Canada, Brazil, Hong Kong and most European countries, Choral seminars in South Africa and the Phillippines, 1984. *Publications:* Some 110 records, cassettes and C.D's of sacred music with St. Johns Coll. Choir. *Recreation:* Yr Iaith Gymraeg, Assn. football. *Clubs:* United University, London and Clwb Ifor Bach, Caerdydd. *Address:* St Johns College, Cambridge, CB2 1TP. Ty Canol, Cwmystwyth, Aberystwyth, Dyfed.

GUNN, Dr. Roderick Walter, BSc., PhD., PGDip(EdMan)., MBA., DipM., MCIM, MBIM. *Currently:* Head of Management Studies, Polytechnic of Wales, 1990- . *Born on* 9 Nov 1947 at Glasgow. *Son of* George and Elizabeth Gunn (nee Collins). *Marriage:* to Pauline Anne Gunn (nee Brown), 1973. *Children:* James Daniel and Christopher *Educated at* Clevedon College, Swansea; UCW, Swansea; UCW, Aberystwyth. *Career:* Lecturer (part-time) College of Further Education Aberystwyth), 1970-71; Tutor, UCW, Aberystwyth, 1971-72; Assist. Teacher, Chatham House Grammar School for Boys, Ramsgate, Kent, 1973-75; Head of Department of Mathematics and Statistics, Heolddu Comp., Bargoed, 1975-84; Senior Lecturer, The Polytechnic of Wales, 1984-89; Principal Lecturer, Curriculum Development Manager, Enterprise Unit, The Polytechnic of Wales; Course Supervisor, HNC Public Admin., 1984-86; Course Supervisor, HNC Business & Finance, 1985-88; Admissions Tutor, HND Business & Finance, HND Public Admin., HNC Business & Finance, 1985-87; Course Supervisor, HND Business & Finance, HND Public Admin., 1987-89; Mbr of Faculty Bd for Professional Studies; Mbr of Validation & Review Commt; Mbr of Working Party on Overseas Policy; Mbr of Working Party on Flexible Learning; Mbr of Faculty Research Sub-Commt; Faculty Validation team for the Business Studies Degree; Mbr of: MBA/DMS submission team, MSc(Health Care) sub. team, MSc/DipEdM sub team, HND/C Bus. & Finance, Public Admin. re-submission team. Chmn: MBA Exam & Course Bd of Studies, M.Sc. in Management studs (Health Care) Exam & Course Bd of Studies, Diploma in Ed. Mangmt/Msc. (Educ Management) Exam & Course Bd of Studies, Diploma in Management Studies (Gen.full time) Exam & Course Bd of Studies, Diploma in Mangmnt Studs (Public Sector, p/t) Exam & Course Bd of Studies, Dip in Mngmnt Studies (Health Service, p/t) Exam & Course Bd of Studies, Dip. in Mngmnt Studies (General p/t) Exam & Course Bd of Studies, Cert. in Mngmnt Studies Exam & Course Bd of Studies, Inst. of Personnel Mngmnt (f/t) Exam & Course Bd of St *Publications:* On Newtonian and Non-Newtonian Flow in a Rotating Pipe. ZAMP, Vol 25, 1974; (with Morris & Pringle) National Numeracy Test, Used for 1st Year Business Studies students in HE, BETA, 1986; (with Saunders) The Assessment and Evaluation of Communication Skills Associated with Simulation/Gaming, 1990 To be published: Organising a Students' Conference 1990; Workshadowing for Management Students' 1990. *Recreation:* Running, weight training, music, travelling *Clubs:* Cardiff High School old boys, Radyr Turning Assoc. *Address:* Dept.of Management, Studies, Polytechnic of Wales, Pontypridd Mid Glam., CF37 1DL. 20 Maes Yr Awel, Radyr, Cardiff, CF4 8AN.

GWILLIAM, Mr John Albert, MA *Currently:* retired. *Born on* 28 Feb 1923 at Pontypridd. *Son of* T A and A M Gwilliam. *Marriage:* to Pegi Lloyd George, 1949. *Children:* Catherine, David, Peter, Philip and Rhiannon. *Educated at* Monmouth School 1934-41; Trinity College, Cambridge. *Career:* Assistant Master, Trinity College, Glenalmond 1949-52; Bromsgrove School, 1952-56; Head of Lower School, Dulwich College SE21, 1956-63; Head of Birkenhead School, 1963-88. *Recreation:* Golf, walking. *Clubs:* Hawks. *Address:* Araulfan, 13 The Close, Llanfairfechan, Gwynedd., LL33 OAG.

H

HABAKKUK, Sir John Hrothgar, MA., FBA, Hon.D.Litt. *Currently:* Retired. *Born on* 13 May 1915 at Barry, Glam. *Son of* Evan Guest Habakkuk and Anne (nee Bowen). *Marriage:* to Mary Elizabeth Richards, 1948. *Children:* David, Alison (Hoddell) Kate and Lucy (Gilchrist) *Educated at* Romilly Road Elementary; Barry County School; U.C. Cardiff; St. John's College, Cambridge. *Career:* Fellow Pembroke College, Cambridge 1938-50; Lecturer Faculty Economics, Cambridge 1946-50; Chichele Professor of Economic History, Oxford 1950-67; Principal, Jesus College Oxford 1967-84; Vice-Chancellor, Univ. of Oxford 1973-77; Chairman Commt. of V-Cs and Principals 1976-77; President: University College, Swansea, 1975-84 (Hon.Fellow, 1991); Fellow of All Souls College Oxford 1950-67, 1988- . *Publications:* American & British Technology in 19th Century (1962); Population & Economic Growth (1971) *Address:* 28 Cunliffe Close, Oxford, OX2 7BL. All Souls College, Oxford, OX1 LAL.

HACKET PAIN, Major Wyndham Jermyn, JP (Surrey 1964), DL (Surrey 1986). *Born on* 27 Dec 1921. *Son of* the late Lt Col Michell Wyndham Hacket Pain, of Surey and Audrey Ernestine Jermyn (nee Ford). *Marriage:* to Wenllian Kennard, 1949, o da of Sir Godfrey Llewellyn, 1 Bt, CB, CBE, MC, JP, DL (d 1986). *Children:* Nicholas Wyndham Llewellyn Hacket Pain (b.1953) and Simon Michell Hacket Pain (b.1956). *Educated at* Harrow, RMA Sandhurst. *Career:* served Grenedier Guards: Western Desert, Italy (Salerno landing), Palestine (despatches), Malaya 1941-52; director: Lloyds brokers, Laurence Philipps and Co, Anderson Finch Villiers and Co 1953-67; chairman Michell and Jermyn Co Ltd 1968- ; chairman Woking Cons Assoc 1965-68, serv SE Area Executive Committee, area assistant treasurer and serv on Central Board of Finance 1973-74, elected SE Area rep Council of Nat Union 1969-74; chairman: Woking Bench 1979-87. Surrey Magistrates' Courts Committee 1984-87; appointed member Court Univ of Surrey 1986- ; High Sheriff of Surrey 1988-89. *Recreation:* shooting. *Clubs:* Boodle's, Pratt's, MCC. *Address:* Dixton Lodge, Hadnock, Monmouth. Tel: 0600 716702.

HACKNEY, Dr Roderick Peter, PPRIBA, MA, BA Arch, ACIArb, PhD, DLitt, ASAI, MCIOB, FFB. *Currently:* Managing Director, Rod Hackney & Associates Limited, established practice in 1972, additional practices established Birmingham, Leicester, Belfast, Cleator Moor, Workington, Carlisle, Millom, Clitheroe, Manchester, Stirling, Burnley, Chesterfield, Stoke-on-Trent, 1975-88. Director, Castward Limited, established firm 1983. *Born on* 3 March 1942 at Liverpool, England. *Son of* William Hackney and Rose (nee Morris). *Marriage:* to Christine (nee Thornton). *Children:* one s Roan Challoner. *Educated at* Ysgol Dyffryn Ogwen, Bethesda; John Bright's Grammar School, Llandudno;

Manchester University. *Career:* Job Architect, Expo'67, Montreal Canada for the monorail stations 1967; Housing Arch. for Libyan Govt in Tripoli 1967-68; Asst. to Arne Jacobsen in Copenhagen working on Kuwait Central Bank 1968-71; Council Mem Royal Inst of British Architects (RIBA), incl Vice Pres for Public Affairs & Vice Pres for Overseas Affairs 1978-84; Pres Royal Inst of British Architects 1987-89; Cncl mem Union of Int Architects (UIA) 1981-85; First Vice Pres UIA 1986-88; Pres, UIA 1988-91; Jury mem Cembureau Award for Low Rise Housing in France 1982-83, chmn of Jury for Herouville Town Centre Competition, France; Jury mem Prix Int. d'Architecture de l'Institut National du Logement 1983; mem Cultural Deleg. to USSR under Anglo/Soviet Cultural Exchange Agreement 1984; Vis Prof UP6 Paris 1984; Chmn The Times/RIBA Comm.Enterprise Scheme 1985-89; Pres. Young Architects' Forum, Sofia 1985; Pres, Building Communities (Int Community Architecture Conference), London 1986; Presentation of the case for Int. Year of Shelter for the Homeless to all four Party Conferences 1986; Chmn Trustees of the Inner City Trust 1986- ; Pres Snowdonia Nat. Park Soc 1987- ; Special Prof in Architecture, The Univ of Nottingham 1987-90; mem Chartered Inst of Building 1987- ; Patron Llandudno Museum & Art Gall 1988, Editorial Bd UIA Jnl of Architectural Theory & Criticism; mem Council, Nat Hist. Building Crafts Inst 1989- Pres, N.Wales Centre of the Nat Trust 1990- ; Musical play based on Rod Hackney's work, Good Golly Miss Molly, opens in London 1991; Lec. tour of India sponsored by British Council. Hon Fellow American Inst of Architects; Federacion de Colegios de Arquitectos de la Republica Mexicana - 1988; United Architects of the Philippines; 1990, Royal Architectural Institute of Canada Hon. Fellow; 1990, Indian Institute of Architects, Hon. Fellow; Hon Member Consejo Superior de los Colegios de Arquitectos de Espana 1987; Awards: DoE Good Design in Housing Award, 1975, 1980; 1st Prize St. Ann's Hospice, Manchester1976; Prix International d'Architecture l'Institute National du Logement 1979-80; RICS / TIMES Conservation Award 1980; Civic Trust Award of Commendation 1980, 1981, 1984; Sir Robert Mathew's Award (Hon. Mention) 1981; Manchester Society of Architects' President's Award 1982; Otis Award Commendation for Architecture 1982; Gold Medal, Bulgarian Inst. of Architects 1983; Gold Medal, Young Architect of the Year, Sofia 1983; Grand Medal of the Federacion de Colegios de Architectos de la Republica Mexicana 1986; Award for work and leadr of Community Architecture movement from City of Charleston, USA *Publications:* 'Highfield Hall: a community project', 1974; 'The Good the Bad and the Ugly' 1990; articles in UK and foreign journals; also TV features incl. 'Build Yourself a House', 1974; Community Architecture, 1977; BBC

Omnibus: The Hackney Way, 1987. *Recreation:* outdoor pursuits, walking, butterflies, fossils, travelling, ballooning, looking at buildings, speaking at conferences. *Clubs:* Royal Commonwealth. *Address:* St Peter's House, Windmill Street, Macclesfield, Cheshire, SK11 7HS.

HAINES, Professor Michael, BSc, PhD, FCIM, FRSA. *Currently:* UCW Aberystwyth, Professor of Agricultural Marketing and Business, since 1981. *Born on* 13 Aug 1939 at Kettering. *Son of* the late Arthur and Winifred (nee Wright). *Marriage:* to Barbara Ann. *Educated at* Kettering Grammar School; University of Leeds; Purdue University, USA. *Career:* Ass. Agricultural Adviser, MAFF Newtown (Montg) 1963; Agricultural Adviser, MAFF Carmarthen 1966; Kellogg Fellow, Purdue University, USA 1969; Cooperation Adviser, MAFF Cambridge 1970; Lecturer, Agricultural Marketing, UCW Aberystwyth 1971; William Evans Fellow, University of Otago, New Zealand 1985; Visiting Professor, University of Otago, NZ 1987; Adviser, Dyfed County Council Economic Development Committee 1983-90; Member, Secretary of State for Wales's Agriculture Advisory Panel 1984-90; Fellow, Chartered Institute of Marketing 1988; Senior Partner, Beresford Haines Associates Agricultural Marketing Consultants 1985- ; Independent Board Member, Seafish Industry Authority 1987- . *Publications:* An introduction to Farming Systems, Longmans 1982 (rp 1985); Diversifying the Farm Business, Blackwell 1987; plus many papers. *Recreation:* history, reading, gardening. *Clubs:* Farmers. *Address:* Pen-Y-Figyn, Talybont, Dyfed, SY24 5EQ. U.C.W. Aberystwyth SY23 3DD

HALL, Dr Derek Gordon, BSc; PhD. *Currently:* Managing Director, J.P.Morgan GmbH, since 1991. *Born on* 17 April 1944 at Cardiff. *Son of* the late Gordon Ivor and May Magretta (nee Horsey). *Marriage:* to Susan (nee Eaton). *Children:* Guy Sebastian, Samantha Kate and Daniel Gordon. *Educated at* Penarth County Grammar School; University College, London. *Career:* Andersen Consulting 1970-76; J.P. Morgan, London 1976-91. *Address:* J P Morgan Gmbh, Mainzer Landstrasse 46, 6000 Frankfurt/main 17.

HALL, Mr Michael Robert, BSc (Hons)., BA(Cantab) *Currently:* Cooke & Arkwright, Chartered Surveyors. *Born on* 13 Oct 1965 at Bryncethin. *Son of* Anthony David Hall and Julia Hall. *Educated at* Wolfson College, Cambridge; Cardiff Univ; Brynteg Comprehensive. *Career:* Wales- 17 Full Caps; British Lion - Australia, 1989- ; 1st Test, World XV v South Africa (2 tests); Wales 'B'; Wales U20 and U21 (Captain); Barbarians; Two Blues, Cambridge University 1988-89; Welsh Tours - New Zealand/Australia *Recreation:* Golf, swimming and football. *Clubs:* Cardiff, Cambridge University, Maesteg. *Address:* 72 Llanfair Rd., Pontcanna, Cardiff CF1 9QA

HALL, Professor Emeritus Reginald, CBE (1979)., BSc., MD (Dunelm), FRCP. *Currently:* Retired Professor of Medicine, University of Wales College of Medicine, Heath Park, Cardiff. *Born on* 1 Oct 1931 at Belmont, Durham. *Son of* R.P. Hall and M.W. Hall. *Marriage:* to Dr. Molly Hall, FRCP Consultant Physician. *Children:* Susan M, Amanda M, John R, Andrew J, Stephanie C. *Educated at* Alderman Wraith, Spennymoor Grammar School, Univ. of Durham. *Career:* Harkness Fellow of the Commonwealth Fund, Harvard University, 1960-62; Professor of Medicine

University of Newcastle Upon Tyne, 1970-80; Professor of Medicine and Head of Department, University of Wales College of Medicine, 1980-89. *Publications:* Fundamentals of Clinical Endocrinology 4th ed, 1989; Atlas of Endocrinology, 1990, 2nd ed. *Recreation:* Bryology, modern literature and cookery. *Address:* 37 Palace Road, Llandaff, Cardiff. CF5 2AG.

HALL, Wayne Hopkin, *Currently:* Wood Machinist. *Born on* 29 Jan 1958 at Bridgend. *Son of* Gerwyn & Violet (nee Worgan). *Marriage:* to Gail Elizabeth (nee Hooper). *Children:* Grant Gerwyn (10) and Lydia Gail (4). *Educated at* Pencoed Comprehensive *Recreation:* all types of field sports, ie gun dogs/clay shooting. *Clubs:* Pencoed RFC, Maesteg RFC, Bridgend RFC. *Address:* 66 Penprisk Road, Pencoed, Bridgend CF35 6RH.

HALL WILLIAMS, Professor John Eryl., LL.M (Wales; Hon LL.D; Barrister-at-Law. *Currently:* Retired, Law Dept., L.S.E. *Born on* 21 Sept. 1921 at Cardiff. *Son of* Edward Hall Williams and Kitty Hughes of Barry. *Marriage:* to Constance Mary Evans 1951. *Educated at* Barry County School; UCW Aberystwyth; Hon. LL.D., John F. Kennedy University, California; of The Middle Temple, Barrister-at-Law. *Career:* Reader in Criminology, LSE 1959; Lecturer in Law, LSE 1950; University of Hull 1946-50. *Publications:* Criminology and Criminal Justice 1982; (with Huw Rees) Punishment, Custody and the Community (edited papers) 1989; Changing Prisons 1975; The English Penal System in Transition 1970; (with L.H.Leigh) The Management of The Prosecution Process in Denmark, Sweden and The Netherlands 1981. *Recreation:* Landscape painting. *Address:* Law Dept., L.S.E., Houghton St, Aldwych, London, WC2A 2AE.

HALLAM, Chris Alexander, MBE *Currently:* Athlete. *Born on* 31 Dec 1962 at Derby. *Son of* John James and Anne Hallam. *Educated at* Llantarnam Comprehensive; Crosskeys College. *Career:* Paraplegic since a motorcycle accident in 1980, two days before his Welsh trials in swimming. Swimming was his only sport up until the 1984 Olympics, where he struck gold in the 50 metre breaststroke event. In 1986 he struck gold again in the World Championship with a World Record that still stands of 48.36 seconds in the same event, but by then Wheelchair Racing was his predominate sport with his last swim being the 50 metre Breaststroke in the Seoul Olympics where he took silver - losing by 0.3 seconds. Since then has won many road racing titles including: London Marathon 1985 and 1987, third in 1986, 1988 and 1989. British Marathon Champion held at various venues 1984, 86-90. British half Marathon Champion held at the Great North Run 1986-90, excluding 1988 when he was second. Won the British Road Racing Grand Prix, 1990-91, a 12 race series, consisting 4 Marathons, 4 Half-Marathons and 4 shorter road races. Personal Records: Road - Marathon 1.45.07 Switzerland 1990; Half Marathon 56.31 Great North Run 1990; 15kms, 37.11 U.S.A., 1989; 10kms, 23.55 Australia 1991. Track - 100m, 16.23 Cwmbran, Wales 1991-W.R; 200m, 29.20 Cwmbran, 1991-W.R; 400m, 57.1 Dublin 1991; 800m, 2.03.52 Switzerland 1990; 1500m, 3.30.92 Australia 1991; 5000m, 12.39.8 Dublin 1991; 10,000m, 27.45.5 Cwmbran 1991. In the 1991 B.W.R.A. National Track Championships held at Cwmbran Stadium on May 11th/12th he set two new World Records over 100m and 200m. Chairman: British Wheelchair Racing Assoc;

Secretary: PvsH (People versus Handicap) to build the Wales Sports Cente for the Disabled; Awarded the MBE for services to sport in 1988. *Recreation:* television, travel *Address:* 61 Perthy Close, Hollybush, Cwmbran, Gwent, NP44 7LP.

HALLIDAY, Mrs John (Mary) Elizabeth, MBE 1980, JP 1958. *Born on* 20 Feb 1909. *Daughter of* the late Maj William Edmond Stewart, DSO, DL, JP and the late Mary Adela Morland (nee Rice). *Marriage:* to Ruthven John Wyllie Halliday, 1935 (d.1973). *Children:* David Ruthven Stewart (b.1939) (d. 1983). *Educated at* St.Mary and St.Anne's Abbots Bromley, Harcombe House; Hoster's Sec.Training College. *Career:* Army Welfare Officer and W.V.S. Canteen Organiser World War II; Borough Councillor 1957-62; General Commissioner of Income Tax 1959-84; Ministers' Rep Carms Executive Council and FPC (NHS) 1958-82; member, Council and Executive, Trinity College, Carmarthen 1971-80; member, Governing Body of Church in Wales 1969-74; Foundation member of Council of Coleg Elidyr Camphill College for Special Education 1973-88; President, Llandovery Royal British Legion, Womens Section since 1958. *Recreation:* gardening, music. *Address:* Llanfair House, Llandovery, Dyfed SA20 OYF.

HAMILTON, Mr Mostyn Neil, M.Sc., Econ., LL.B. *Currently:* M.P. & Government Whip. *Born on* 9 Mar 1949 at Fleur De Lis, Monmouthshire. *Son of* Ronald Hamilton and Norma (nee Jones). *Marriage:* 1983. *Educated at* Amman Valley Grammar School, Ammanford; UCW Aberystwyth & Corpus Christi College, Cambridge. *Career:* Called to the Bar (Middle Temple) 1978; Conservative candidate, Abertillery 1974; Bradford North 1979; Elected M.P. for Talton (Cheshire) 1983; PPS to Minister for Public Transport 1986-87; Member Treasury Select Committee 1987-90; Government Whip 1990-present. *Publications:* US/UK Double Taxation (1980) Various political pamphlets. *Recreation:* Gardening, music and architecture. *Address:* House of Commons, London. SW1A 0AA.

HANSEN, Mr Jorgen, B.Sc. Econ. *Currently:* Head of European Commission Office in Wales, 1988- . *Born on* 18 April 1951 at Aarhus, Denmark. *Son of* Axel and the late Ruth Hansen. *Marriage:* to Enid Roberts. *Children:* Lisbet Rhiannon. *Educated at* United World College of The Atlantic, St. Donats 1968-70; University College of Wales, Aberystywth 1971-74. *Career:* Commission of the European Communities, Brussels 1974-88. *Clubs:* Danish Club, Knightsbridge, London. *Address:* Commission Of The European Communities Office In Wales, 4 Cathedral Road, Cardiff. CF1 9SE.

HARDEN, Major James Richard Edwards, DSO., OBE., MC., DL., JP. *Currently:* Retired. *Born on* 12 Dec 1916 at Tandragee, Northern Ireland. *Son of* the late James Edwards Harden and the late Letitia Grace Campell Connal. *Marriage:* to Ursula Joyce, 1948, d. of Gerald Murray Strutt. *Children:* David, Theresa and Carolyn. *Educated at* Bedford Sch., RMC Sandhurst. *Career:* commissioned Royal Tank Regiment 1937, retired Agricultural release 1947, MP (UU) Armagh 1948-54, JP Armagh 1956, Caernarvonshire later Gwynedd 1971-82, DL Armagh 1946, Caernarvonshire 1968. High Sheriff Caernarvonshire 1971-72. Chairman Regional Land Drainage Committee Welsh Water Authority 1973-83. Landowner (5000 acres) and Farmer. *Recreation:* Shooting. *Address:* Hendy, Nanhoran, Pwllheli,

Gwynedd., LL53 8DL. Tel: 07883432 .

HARDY, Professor Barbara Gladys, MA(Lond) Hon D.Univ.(Open) *Currently:* Professor Emeritus, Univ. of London; Honorary Professor, Univ. Coll., Swansea. *Born on* 27 June 1924 at Swansea. *Daughter of* Gladys Emily Ann Nathan (nee Abraham) and Maurice Nathan. *Marriage:* to the late Ernest Dawson Hardy. *Children:* Julia and Kate. *Educated at* Swansea High School; Univ. Coll., London *Career:* On staff of English Dept. of Birkbeck Coll., London; Prof. of English, Royal Holloway Coll., Univ. of London, 1965-70; Prof. of English Birkbeck College 1970-89. Mbr. Welsh Acad.Pres., Dickens Soc., 1987-88; Hon. Mbr. MLA DUniv. Open, 1981. *Publications:* The Novels of George Eliot, 1959; The Appropriate Form, 1964; (ed) George Eliot: Daniel Deronda, 1967; (ed) Middlemarch: Critical Approaches to the Novel, 1967; The Moral Art of Dickens, 1970; (ed) Critical Essays on George Eliot, 1970; The Exposure of Luxury: radical themes in Thackeray, 1972; (ed) Thomas Hardy: The Trumpet-Major, 1974; Tellers and Listeners: the narrative imagination, 1975; (ed)Thomas Hardy: A Laeodicean, 1975; A Reading of Jane Austen, 1975; The Advantage of Lyric, 1977; Particularities: readings in George Eliot, 1982; Forms of Feeling in Victorian Fiction, 1985; Narrators and Novelists, collected essays. vol. 1, 1987. *Recreation:* Acting and walking *Address:* C/o Birkbeck College, Malet Street, London. WC1E 7HX.

HARDY, Mr Graham John, B.Arch (Hons) Wales, RIBA. *Currently:* Chartered Architect, Graham J.Hardy & Associates. *Born on* 5 March 1938. at Cardiff. *Son of* the late William A.Hardy and the late Lettie M. (nee Lovell). *Marriage:* to Sara Maureen (nee Morgan), 1963. *Children:* Keiron (b.1972), Bridget (b.1966) and Elise (b.1968). *Educated at* Llandaff Cathedral School; Cathays H.S; University of Wales, Welsh School of Achitecture. *Career:* Ecclesiastical Architect & Surveyor: Prince of Wales Award 1984 St.John Ev.Church, Cardiff; Prince of Wales Award 1984 Eglwysilian Church, Mid Glam; Catnic UK Restoration Award 1981; First Prize-Competition for Inner Areas Prince of Wales' Ctee 1982; Civic Trust Commendation-Victoria Place, Newport 1980; Lord Mayors' Civic Award, Cardiff 1990; Architect & Surveyor to the Fabric-Margam Abbey, Old Priory Caldey Abbey, St. Illtuds Church, Llantwit Major, St.Germans Church, Cardiff etc. Architect to The Cathedral Parish of Llandaff. *Recreation:* Conservation, Rotary International. *Clubs:* Past President, Rotary Club of Cardiff East. *Address:* 'Timbers', 6 Cefn Coed Road, Cyncoed, Cardiff, CF2 6AQ. Tel: 0222 752960.

HARPER, The Hon. Mrs Hazel Eleanor, J.P. *Currently:* Farmer, sheep farming full time. *Born on* 11 Dec 1938 at Cheshire. *Daughter of* The Right Hon The Lord Woolley and Lady Woolley. *Marriage:* to Dr David Harper, MA, MB, B.Chir(Cantab), Jan 21, 1961. *Children:* Andrew, Katherine and James. *Educated at* Malvern Girls College *Career:* Nursing Degree 1957-60 - Nursing Sister. Part-time night sister (handicapped children). Magistrate 1979-90. *Recreation:* farming & farming! *Address:* Clogwyn Y Gwin, Rhyd Ddu, Caernarfon, Gwynedd.

HARPER, Prof. John Lander, CBE., FRS. *Currently:* Retired. *Born on* 27 May 1925 at Rugby. *Son of* John Hindley Harper and Harriet Mary (nee Archer). *Marriage:* to Borgny Lero, 1954. *Children:* Belinda Solveig Jane, Claire Catherine Elise and Jonathan Tor *Educated at*

Magdalen College, Oxford, BA., MA., D.Phil. *Career:* Demonstrator, Dept. of Agric., Univ. of Oxford, 1951-52; Lecturer, Dept. of Agric., Univ. of Oxford, 1953-59; Rockefeller Foundation Fellow, Univ. of California, Davis, California, 1959-60; Prof. of Agric. Botany, Univ.Coll. of N.Wales, Bangor, 1960-67; Head of the School of Plant Biology, Univ.Coll. N.Wales, 1967-78; Prof. of Botany & Head of School of Plant Biology, Univ.Coll., N.Wales, 1978-82; Dir.of the Unit of Plant Population Biology, Univ.Coll. of N.Wales, 1982-90; Emeritus Prof. Univ. of Wales, 1982- ; Fellow of Inst.Biol., 1982; British Ecological Soc., (Pres.) 1966-68; American Soc.of Agronomy, 1965-77; American Soc. of Naturalists, 1960- ; Soil Science Soc. of America, 1965-77; Soc.of Experimental Biology, 1982; European Soc. Evolutionary Biology, 1989- ; President, 1993; Fellow of the Royal Soc., elected 1978; Mbr. of Council, 1987-89; Hon. Assoc. of the Swedish Soc. for Phytogeography, elected 1981; Corresponding mbr. of the Botanical Soc.of America, 1982; Foreign Assoc.of the Nat. Academy of Sciences, USA, elected 1984; Dist.Ecologist Award, Ecological Soc.of America, 1984; Hon.D.Sc., Univ.of Sussex, 1984; Commnd of the British Empire; Queen's Birthday Honours, 1989; Darwin Medal of the Royal Soc., 1990; Nat.Env.Research Council, 1971-81, Roy.Soc.Assessor, 1988-90; Agric.& Food Research Council, 1980-90; Comite du Direction, CEPE (CNRS) France, 1984-90; Joint Nature Cons.Commt, 1990- ; Trustee Btsh Museum of Natural History, 1990- . Scientific Interest: Plant demography, Grassland ecology, The Role of predation in population dynamics of plants, The demography of plants parts, Resource allocation, Reproductive strategies, Ecological signf.of sex. *Publications:* Editorial: Editor in Chief Agroecosystems, 1974-81; Co-Editor, Oecologia, 1982- ; Assist.Ed. Proceedings of the Royal Society, 1980-82; Assit.Ed. Philisophical Transactions of the Royal Soc., 1990- ; Ed. Board Acta Oecologica, 1989- ; Pubs: The Biology of Weeds, 1960 (Ed) Blackwell; Population Biology of Plants, 1977 Academic Press; Ecology: Individuals, Populations and Communities, 1986 (with M.Begon and C.R.Townsend). Blackwell, 2nd Ed. 1990. *Recreation:* Gardening *Clubs:* The Farmer's Club, Whitehall Court, London. *Address:* Cae Groes, Glan y Coed Park, Dwygyfylchi, Penmaenmawr, Gwynedd, LL34 6TL.

HARPER, Professor John Martin, MA., PhD., FRCO(CHM) *Currently:* Professor of Music, University of Wales at Bangor 1991- . *Born on* 11 July 1947 at Wednesbury, West Midlands. *Son of* Geoffrey Martin Harper, RIBA and Kathleen Birks. *Marriage:* 1st to Cynthia Margaret Dean 1970 (divorced 1991); 2nd to Sally Elizabeth Roper 1991. *Children:* Edward John Harper, William George Harper and Joseph Martin Harper. *Educated at* King's College School, Cambridge 1956-61; Clifton College, Bristol 1961-66; Selwyn College, Cambridge 1966-70; University of Birmingham 1970-74. *Career:* Music Tutor Ingestre Hall 1970-71; Lecturer in music Birmingham Univ., 1974-75, 1976-81; Director, Edington Music Festival 1971-78; Director of music St. Chad's Cathedral, Birmingham 1972-78; Fellow, Organist, Informator Choristarum, tutor in music, Magdalen College, Oxford 1981-90. *Publications:* Orlando Gibbons: Consort Music (Musica Britannica 48) 1982; The Forms and Orders of Western Liturgy 1991. *Recreation:* Walking, Ecclesiastical

architecture. *Address:* Dept of Music, University Of Wales, Bangor, Gwynedd, LL57 2DG.

HARRHY, Mr Gordon Leslie, MMS *Currently:* General Manager/ Chief Executive, South Glamorgan Health Authority. *Born on* 26 Sept 1933 at Newport. *Son of* Thomas William and the late Doris Evelyn (nee Wallace). *Marriage:* to Constance Ann. *Children:* Stephen Mark and Ruth Elizabeth. *Educated at* Newport High School. *Career:* member of The Court, University of Wales, 1989- ; member of Council, University of Wales College of Medicine, 1986- ; Governor, Cardiff Institute of Higher Education 1989- ; President, Association of Football League Referees and Linesmen 1985-86; member, South Glamorgan Health Authority, 1990- ; President, Monmouthshire Referees Association, 1985- . *Recreation:* Golf, Association Football. *Address:* 52 Beechwood Road, Newport, Gwent NP9 8AH.

HARRIES, Mr Gruffydd John, BA Hons (Geography). *Currently:* Self-employed Musician and Broadcaster. *Born on* 29 Aug 1954 at Pontypridd. *Son of* Norman and Eryl (nee Pugh). *Marriage:* to Julie Barbara, 1981. *Children:* Rhian, Owain and Eleri. *Educated at* Neath Boys' Grammar School; Cambridge College of Arts and Technology. *Career:* Arts Producer and English and Welsh Presenter for Swansea Sound Radio, Professional Musician with Welsh Chamber Orchestra and National Symphony Orchestra and Loose Tubes Jazz Orchestra; Founder and Director of W.C.O., and Welsh Philharmonic Orchestra, Swansea Sound Sinfonia and Swansea Sound Showband. Director of Captain Q Music and Pin Sharp Productions, Musical Associate/ Contractor with numerous T.V. companies. Music Tutor at University College, Swansea and Trinity College, Carmarthen. *Recreation:* swimming, reading, rugby, music. *Address:* 40 Tudor Court, Murton, Swansea SA3 3BB.

HARRIES, Mr John Arthur Jones, CBE; JP; MRCVS *Currently:* Retired Veterinary Surgeon. *Born on* 24 Nov 1923 at Llangain. *Son of* Tom Llewellyn Harries and Muriel. *Marriage:* 1st to Hazel 1950 (d 1982); 2nd to Margaret Mair 1983. *Children:* Ieuan, Wendy, Gwyn and Julie/ Paul, Martin and Annea. *Educated at* QEG Carmarthen; RV College London. *Career:* Veterinary Surgeon; qualified 1946; self employed practice Carmarthen 1946-82; memb: Calvanistic and Deacon Moriah Chapel Llanstephan 1935- ; cncl S.Wales div. Br.Vet Assoc 1985- ; cncl Br Vet Assoc 1966-86; cncl Trinity Coll Carmarthen 1973- ; Welsh Counties Cttee 1973- (ldr ind gp), cncl OU 1973, cncl Nat Eisteddfod 1975-84, Member of Welsh Joint Education Committee 1970- , Chairman 1977-85. Assoc of CCs 1976- (ind spokesman on educn and policy), nat steering gp Tech Vocational Educnl Initiative 1980-89, cncl Int Union of Local Authorities 1981- ; cncl of Euro Municipalities 1981- ; Welsh Adsvy Body 1984-89; ct and cncl Univ of Wales; Cncl member Univ. of Wales College of Medicine, Cardiff; Chmn Carmarthenshire College of Technology & Art; chmn Cttee for the Accreditation of Teacher Educn (sw Wales) 1990- ; fndr (later sec, then pres) W Wales Vet Clinical Club 1950- ; ldr Carmarthenshire CC 1969-73, (memb 1966-73), vice chmn Welsh Coll of Music and Drama, Cardiff 1976-89; dir: WNO Co 1981-87, Business and Technician Educn Cnl 1986- ; pres Carmarthen Rotary Club 1982-83, admitted to the Druidical order of Gorsedd 1985, chm cttee Local Educn Authorities 1986-87; MRCVS 1946, member BVA 1947. *Recreation:* sailing, gardening.

Clubs: Rivertywi Yacht, Nat Liveral. *Address:* Pilroath, Llangain, Carmarthen SA33 5AJ.

HARRIES-JENKINS, Professor Gwyn, LL.B, MA, M.Phil, PhD. *Currently:* Director of Adult Education, University of Hull, since 1983. *Born on* 13 July 1931 at Risca. *Son of* the late Gwyn Charles Jenkins and Olwen James. *Marriage:* to Ina Mitchell Millar, 1956. *Children:* 3 d. Siona, Morag and Elaine. *Educated at* West Monmouth School; University of Wales; University of East Anglia. *Career:* Regular Officer Royal Air Force 1953-69, Fg.Off., 1953, Flt.Lt 1956, Sqn.Ldr 1963. University of Hull 1969-: Staff Tutor 1969; Lecturer 1973; Senior Lecturer 1977. Dean of School of Adult & Continuing Education 1986-90. *Publications:* The Army in Victorian Society; Demise of Liberal Adult Education; Armed Forces and Society. *Recreation:* reading, geneology. *Address:* 6 The Ridings, Beverley, N.Humberside HU17 7ER. The University Of Hull, Hull HU6 7RX.

HARRINGTON, Mr Illtyd, JP; DL *Currently:* Restlessly retired. *Born on* 14 July 1931 at Methyr Tydfil. *Son of* Timothy and Sarah Burchell. *Educated at* St.Illtyd's, Dowlais; Merthyr County Grammar; Trinity College, Carmarthen. *Career:* Member: Paddington Borough Council 1959-64; Westminster City Council 1964-68 and 1971-78. Leader, Lab Gp 1972-74; GLC 1964-67 and for Brent S 1973-86; Alderman 1970-73; Chairman, Policy and Resources Cttee 1973-77, Special Cttee 1985-86; Dep.Leader 1973-77, 1981-84; Dep Leader of the Opposition 1977-81; Chm of the Council 1984-85; Special Advr to Chm. and Leader of ILEA 1988-90. JP Willesden 1968. First Chairman, Inland Waterways Amenity Adv Council 1968-71; Chm, London Canals Consultative Cttee 1965-67, 1981-; Member: British Waterways Bd 1974-82; BTA 1976-80. Member: Bd Theatre Royal, Stratford E 1978- ; Bd Wiltons Music Hall 1979- ; Nat.Theatre Bd 1975-77; Bd Nat Youth Theatre 1976-; Globe Theatre Trust 1986-; Chm Half Moon Theatre 1978- ;Director: Soho Poly Theatre 1981- ; The Young Vic 1981- ; President: Grand Union Canal Soc 1974- ; Islington Boat Club 1985-; SE Region, IWA 1986-; Immunity (Legal aid facility for AIDS victims) 1986-; Chmn: Kilburn Skills 1977- ; Battersea Park Peace Pagoda 1984- ; Limehouse Basin Users Gp 1986- ; Vice Pres., Coventry Canal Soc., 1970-. Patron, Westminster Cathedral Appeal 1977-; Gov., London Marathon 1980- ; Trustee, Kew Bridge Pumping Mus., 1976- ; Chiswick Family Rescue 1978- ; Queen's Jubilee Walkway 1986- ; Arthur Koestler Awards for Prisoners 1987-; CARE 1987-; Dominica Overseas Student Fund 1987- ; Mem. Montgomery Coral Trust 1988- ; Managing Trustee, Mutual Municipal Ins. Co.1985-. Govnr Brunel Univ., 1981-87; DL Greater London 1986; Vice-President Inland Waterways Association of U.K. *Publications:* Too much journalism in Tribune, New Statesman and both Telegraphs, Guardian. *Recreation:* travel, theatre, selective malice. *Clubs:* N.Paddington Labour. *Address:* 16 Lea House, Salisbury Street, London NW8 8BJ.

HARRIS, Glyn, M.C.T. *Currently:* Finance Director and Company Secretary Graig Shipping PLC, since 1984. *Born on* 11 Sept 1950 at Cardiff. *Son of* Ivor Kenneth and Ivy Margaret. *Marriage:* to Jill Rosalind Sudbury, 1974. *Children:* Stephen Neil, Sally Elizabeth and Amy Rebecca. *Educated at* Whitchurch Grammar School; Bristol Polytechnic. *Career:* Graig Shipping PLC 1967-91; made Managing Director of seperate PLC Coal Mining Company called Europe Energy Group PLC in April 1991. *Recreation:* sailing, badminton. *Address:* Ty-Gwyn, 95 Boverton Road, Llantwit Major, South Glam, CF6 9YA.

HARRIS, Dr Kenneth Morgan, C.B.E., LLD (Hon)., F.C.I.B. *Currently:* Retired 1974. *Born on* 16 Jan 1909 at Whitchurch, Cardiff. *Son of* the late Thomas Harris and the late Martha Ellen (nee Llewellyn). *Marriage:* to Margaret McLean, 1937. *Children:* Christopher John, Timothy Richard, Anna Elizabeth, Adam and Sian Ellen Howitt. *Educated at* Penarth County School and Cardiff Technical College *Career:* Joined Barclays Bank, Pontypridd, 1926; Assistant Manager, St. Mary St., Cardiff, 1949; District Manager, 1951; Local Director, 1955-74; Hon. Treasurer Welsh Rugby Union, 1952-84; President, 1970-71; Life Member 1971; Represented Wales International Rugby Board, 1966-79; Life Member, 1971; Hon. Treasurer & Trustee Welsh Rugby Union Charitable Fund, 1972-; Hon. Treasurer University College, Cardiff, 1965-75; Hon. Treasurer Welsh National School of Medicine (now University of Wales College of Medicine), 1965-79; Member of Court of Governors University of Wales, 1965-75; Governor and Trustee Welsh Sports Aid Foundation, 1980- *Recreation:* Gardening, walking and reading. *Clubs:* Cardiff Athletic Club *Address:* Blair Athol, Lisvane Road, Llanishen, Cardiff, CF4 5SE.

HARRIS, Mr Maldwin John, *Currently:* Retired, County Councillor, Gwent. *Born on* 2 Feb 1932 at Aberdare, Glam. *Son of* the late D.J. and M. Harris. *Educated at* Aberdare Secondary School. *Career:* G.W.Railway 1947-60; RAF National Service, 1949-52; Richard Thomas Baldwin 1959-64; British Steel Corp., 1964-87; Union Works Rep., BISAKTA and ISTC, 1960-87; H.N.C. Iron & Steel making 1978; Chairman, CAB Caldicot and member 1979- ; Community Councillor Portskewett and Sudbrook, Gwent 1961-82; Caldicot Community Aid; Gwent F.P.C. member; Wye local flood defence committee 1981- ; member local Community charge tribunal, Gwent; Chairman Caldicot Comp. School; Chairman Rogiet Primary School; Chairman Undy Primary School. *Recreation:* golf, rugby, cricket. *Address:* 8 Manor Way, Portskewett, Newport., Gwent, NP6 4TQ. Gwent County Council, County Hall, Cwmbran, Gwent.

HARRIS, Mrs Patricia Ann, Teaching Diploma, Distinction. *Currently:* Central President of the Mothers' Union. *Born on* 29 May 1939 at Newport Monmouthshire. *Marriage:* to Revd. James Nigel Kingsley Harris 1963. *Children:* Sarah and Michael. *Educated at* St. Julian's High Newport Mon; Trinity College, Carmarthen. *Career:* Teaching. Mem. Diocesan Houses Board (Goucs) 1975- ; Synod 1980- ; Pastoral Cttee 1984- ; Education Ctee 1986-89; Mothers' Unions Dioc. Pres. 1980-85; Mem. General Synod (House of Laity) 1985- ; Central President Mothers' Union 1989- ; Mem. Council of Churches for Britain & Ireland 1990- ; Exec. Mem. General Synod Board of Mission 1991- . *Recreation:* Watching Gloucester XV play Rugby Union, swimming, embroidery. *Address:* The Vicarage, Elm Road, Stonehouse, Glos., GL10 2NP. Mary Sumner House, 24 Tufton Street, London SW1P 3RB.

HARRISON, Mr Thomas Gwyn (known As Gwyn), BA., B.Arch.(Hons), RIBA., FBIM *Currently:* County

Architect, Gwynedd County Council. *Born on* 26 Jan 1948 at Mountain Ash, Glamorgan. *Son of* the late Thomas Frederick Charles and Marjorie (nee Hyslop). *Marriage:* to Lynne (nee Williams) 1972. *Children:* Heledd Wyn (daughter). *Educated at* Mountain Ash Grammar School; Bristol University. *Career:* Chairman, Society of Chief Architects in Local Authorities Wales (SCALA Wales) 1987-89; Chairman of Chief Officers Group Consortium Local Authorities Wales (CLAW) 1987-89; Member of Society of Chief Architects in local authorities sub-group on future of local government 1991- . *Recreation:* Mountaineering, photography and music *Address:* 19 Gwel Eryri, Llandegfan, Porthaethwy, Gwynedd, LL59 5PY.

HART, Mr Kenneth Mortimer, ARICS, MRTPI. *Currently:* Author. *Born on* 24 March 1914 *Son of* the late Frank Mortimer Hart of Bristol and the late Minnie Anna (nee Houlson) da of Robert Isaac. *Marriage:* to Shirley Burkinshaw, 1946. *Children:* Catherine (b.1955). *Educated at* Redland Hill House, Bristol. *Career:* Second War, RAFVR and IAFVR 1939-45, Star Burma Star, War Medal, Defence Medal. Senior Housing and Planning Inspector, Ministry of Housing and Local Government and Welsh Office 1962; Town Planning Consultant 1974; Chairman Conwy Valley Civic Society 1975-81. *Publications:* The Conwy Valley and The Lands of History etc. *Recreation:* History of Gwynedd and Wales, formerly swimming. *Clubs:* Royal Commonwealth. *Address:* Pen Rhiw, Ro Wen, Conwy, Gwynedd, LL32 8TR. Tel: 0492 650 343

HARTLEY EDWARDS, Capt. Elwyn, MC and Bar. *Currently:* Author, Publishing Consultant, Saddlery Consultant etc. *Born on* 17 April 1927 at Dehra Dun, India. *Son of* the late Lt. Col Edward Hugh Hartley Edwards and May Florence Vaughan. *Marriage:* to Mary Purnell Hodgson, 1955. *Children:* Sarah Elizabeth and Louise Mary. *Educated at* Doon School, U.P. India; I.M.A. *Career:* Commissioned 2nd KEO VIII Goorkha Rifles - Cap. act: Major. Seconded 1951 Army of Pakistan. Editor Riding Magazine 1965-81; Consultant Editor Horse and Hound 1981-85; Governor Coleg Glynllifon, Caernarfon 1989. Chairman N.W. Wales Region British Horse Society 1988. British Council member (Wales) 1991. *Publications:* Saddlery; The Horseman's Manual; Horse Training and Management; Training Aids; The Saddle; Bitting; The Complete Book of the Horse; The Encyclopaedia of the Horse; Owning a Pony; Buying Horses and Ponies; Horses-Their Role in the History of Man; The Country Life Book of Saddlery; The Foot and Shoeing; Standard Guide to Horse and Pony Breeds; The Ultimate Horse Book; Horses and Ponies of the World; Riding; All About Horses and Ponies; Know Your Horse; Bridleways of Britain; From Paddock to Saddle; The Kingdom of the Horse; Lucinda Green-A Biography. etc. etc. *Recreation:* Teaching horses/riders - Equestrian history etc. *Clubs:* Willingdon, Bombay, Gymkhana, Delhi. *Address:* Tyn Rhos, Chwilog, Pwllheli, Gwynedd, LL53 6SG.

HARTNACK, Mr Paul Richard Samuel, *Currently:* Controller General and Chief Executive, The Patent Office since 1989. MP. *Born on* 17 Nov 1942 at Livingstone. *Son of* Carl Samuel and Maud Godden Hartnack (nee Griffiths). *Marriage:* to Marion Quirk 1964. *Children:* Christopher Stephen and Michael David. *Educated at* Hastings Grammar School. *Career:* Board of Trade 1961-67; Second Secretary (Civil Aviation) British Embassy Paris 1968-72; Department of Trade and Industry, Export Division 1973-78; Secretary of National Enterprise Board and subsequently British Technology Group 1978-85; Department of Trade and Industry, Finance Division 1985-89. *Recreation:* gardening, watching rugby. *Address:* The Patent Office, Cardiff Road, Newport, Gwent NP9 1RH. Tel: 0633 814500.

HARWOOD, Professor John Leander, PhD, DSc. *Currently:* Professor of Biochemistry, since 1984. *Born on* 5 Feb 1946 at Epsom, Surrey. *Son of* Leslie James and Beatrice Harwood. *Marriage:* to Gail (nee Burgess), 1967 (widowed 1991). *Children:* Nicholas James. *Educated at* King Edwards Grammar School, Aston; University of Birmingham. *Career:* Post doctoral research fellow, University of California at Davis 1969-71; M.R.C., research fellow University of Leeds 1971-73; appointed lecturer in Dept of Biochemistry, University College Cardiff 1973, Reader in 1980. *Publications:* over 250 papers, 2 books and 4 books edited. *Recreation:* rock climbing, have edited 3 rock climbing guides, over 500 first ascents. *Clubs:* Biochemical Society, Society for Experimental Biology, Phytochemical Society, Midland Association of Mountaineers, Climbers. *Address:* Department Of Biochemistry, University Of Wales Cardiff, P.O.Box 903, Cardiff, CF1 1ST.

HASKELL, Professor Peter Thomas, C.M.G., B.Sc., Ph.D., DIC., FRES., FI.Biol. *Currently:* Research Co-ordinator, School of Pure & Applied Biology, University of Wales College of Cardiff. *Born on* 21 Feb 1923 at Portsmouth UK. *Son of* the late Herbert James and Mary Ann Haskell. *Marriage:* to Aileen Mary Scott. *Children:* one s. *Educated at* Portsmouth Grammar School; Imperial College, London. *Career:* Asst. Lectr, Zoology Dept., Imperial Coll., London, 1951-53; Lectr, 1953-55; Sen. Sci. Officer, Anti-Locust Research Centre, Colonial Office, 1955-57; Principal Sci. Officer, 1957-59; Dep. Dir, 1959-62; Dir, Anti-Locust Research Centre, ODM, 1962-71; Dir, Centre for Overseas Pest Res. and Chief Advr on Pest Control, ODA, 1971-83; Consultant: FAO, UN, 1962- ; UNDP, 1970- ; WHO, 1973-92; OECD, 1975- ; UNEP, 1976- ; Agricl and Vet. Adv. Cttee, British Council, 1976- ; AFRC Plants and Envnt Res. Cttee, 1988- ; Vice-Pres., Inst. of Biology, 1982. Professorial Res. Fellow, University Coll., Cardiff, 1971-83; Mem., Bd of Governors, Internat. Centre for Insect Physiology and Ecology, Kenya, 1972- ; (Vice-Chm., 1978; Chm., 1979) Vis. Prof., Univ. of Newcastle, 1977; Thamisk Lectr, Royal Swedish Acad. of Scis, 1979; Van Den Brande Internat. Prize, 1982; Chief Editor, Tropical Pest Management. 1985- ; Mem., Editorial Bd, Review of Applied Entomol, 1988-92; *Publications:* Insect Sounds, 1962; The Language of Insects, 1962; Pesticide Application: principles and practice, 1985; many papers and articles in scientific and literary jls. *Recreation:* Gardening, reading and talking. *Address:* School Of Biology, P.O. Box 915, University Of Wales College, Cardiff, CF1 3TL.

HASSALL, Dr. Cedric Herbert, FRS., PhD., DSc(Hon)., ScD. *Currently:* Consultant to Pharmaceutical Industry and for overseas development (notable: Indonesia, China, India, New Zealand). *Born on* 6 Dec 1919 at Auckland, New Zealand. *Son of* the late L & H Hassall, Auckland, N.Z. *Marriage:* 1st to H.E. Cotti, 1946; 2nd to J.A. Mitchelmore, 1984. *Children:* Maureen and Peter (deceased) *Educated at* Auckland Grammar Sch., Auckland Univ., Univ of

Cambridge. *Career:* Lectr., Univ. of Otago, N.Z., 1943-45; Sen. Studenship Royal Commn for 1851, Cambridge, 1946-48; Foundn. Prof. of Chemistry, U of W.I., 1948-56; Carnegie & Rockefeller Flps in USA., 1950-56; Head Department of Chemistry, Univ. College of Swansea, 1957-71; D. of Research, Roche Products Ltd., 1971-84; Planning Adviser, Univ. of Jordan, 1965-71; Univ. of Aleppo, 1965; Adbul Aziz Univ, Jedda, 1966-68; Vis. Prof. Univ. of Kuwait, 1969-79; Aligarh Univ., India (Roy.Soc.) 1969-70, Univ. of Liverpool, 1971-79; U.C. London, 1979-85; Imp. College, 1989- ; Warwick Univ. 1985- . *Publications:* Over 200 publications in journals of Chemistry and Biochemistry. *Recreation:* International travel, nature studies and rugby. *Address:* 2 Chestnut Close, Westoning, Beds. MK45 5LR. Riverdale, R.D. Route 309, Whitianga, New Zealand.

HAVARD-WILLIAMS, Professor Peter, MA.PhD. DipEd. Hon PhD. Hon FLA.FRSA. FLAI. FBIM.Finst Inf.Sc. *Currently:* Professor and Head of Dept of Library & Information Studies, Univ. of Botswana 1988- ; and educational and library consultant. *Born on* 11 July 1922 at Dinas Powys, nr Cardiff. *Son of* Graham Havard-Williams and Elizabeth James. *Marriage:* 1) to the late Rosine Cousin; 2) Eileen Cumming. *Children:* Vanessa, Lucy and Elizabeth. *Educated at* Swansea Grammar School; Univ. Coll. Swansea; Oxford Univ. *Career:* Chief Librarian & consultant, Council of Europe, Strasburg, 1986-87; Foundation Prof. and Head of Dept. of Library & information studies, Loughborough Univ, 1972-87, (Emeritus 1987-); Dean and Professor of Library Science Ottawa Univ. 1971-72; Librarian Queen's Univ. Belfast, 1961-71; Founder and Director School of Library and Information Studies, 1964-71; Deputy Librarian, Brotherton Library, Univ. of Leeds, 1960-61; Librarian and Keeper of the Hocken Collection Univ. of Otago, 1956-60; Sub-Librarian Faculty of Arts Univ of Liverpool, 1951-56; Asst. Librarian Univ. Coll., of Swansea, 1949-50; Lecturer in Music and French Endsleigh Coll. of Education Kingston upon Hull, 1945-47. Consultant to Unesco, EEC, Council of Europe and foreign governments. Vice-President, Internat, Feder. of Library Associations 1970-78. Vice-President, Library Association 1968-70, 1974-82. *Publications:* Reports for international bodies and foreign governments, articles in learned and professional journals. *Recreation:* Music (harpsichord, organ, piano), collecting Bloomsbury first editions, planning buildings, idling. *Clubs:* Athenaeum, Commonwealth Trust, Gaborne. *Address:* University Of Botswana, PB0022, Gaborone, Botswana. 31 Westfield Drive, Loughborough, Leics, LE11 3QJ.

HAWKES, Professor Donald Durston, BSc(Lond); MSc; PhD(Birm); C.Geol; FGS; FRSA. *Currently:* Head of School of Earth Sciences, The University of Birmingham, Birmingham, since 1988. *Born on* 18 July 1934 at Cardiff. *Son of* the late Clifford George Durston Hawkes and the late Mabel Sophia (nee Stephens). *Marriage:* to Janet Beatrice Davies, 1958. *Children:* Jane Elizabeth and David John. *Educated at* Canton Grammar School; University College, Exeter; Birmingham University. *Career:* British Antarctic Survey 1956-59; Overseas Geological Survey 1959-62; University of Sierra Leone 1963-72; Professor and Head of Earth Sciences, University of Aston 1972-88. *Publications:* Scientific papers in learned journals. *Recreation:* motor boat cruising, herb gardening, fishing. *Address:* School of Earth Sciences, The University Of Birmingham, Edgbaston, Birmingham, B15 2TT.

HAWKSLEY, Mr Philip Warren, *Currently:* Hotelier - owner with wife of Country House Hotel, Nr Welshpool, Powys, which in 2 years from being a derelict Georgian manor, has become an award-winning Restaurant. *Born on* 10 March 1943 at Oswestry. *Son of* Mr Warren and Mrs Monica Hawksley. *Marriage:* to Evelyn Giles-Gash, 1987. *Children:* Emma and Charlotte *Educated at* Millmead School, Shrewsbury; Denstone College, Uttoxeter. *Career:* Employed by Lloyds Bank in various positions up to Sub Manager At Shrewsbury, 1960-79; Conservative Member of Parliament for The Wrekin, 1979-87. *Publications:* Co-author, Adam Smith Institute "Review of the Home Office". *Recreation:* mainly involved in politics as a voluntary worker and County Councillor in Shropshire. *Clubs:* Restaurants Association. *Address:* Edderton Hall, Forden, Nr.Welshpool, Powys SY21 8RZ. 22 Blaenwern Drive, Halesowen, West Midlands.

HAYCRAFT, Anna Margaret (also Known As Alice Thomas Ellis), *Currently:* Writer/Author/Journalist. *Born on* 9 Sept 1932 at Liverpool. *Son of* John and Alexandra Lindholm (nee Griffiths). *Marriage:* to Colin Haycraft, 1956. *Children:* William and Joshua (d.1978), Thomas, Oliver and Arthur, Rosalind (d.1970) and Sarah. *Educated at* Bangor Grammar School for Girls; Liverpool Art College *Career:* Fiction Editor: Duckworth; Columnists: The Spectator, The Universe. *Publications:* Novels as Alice Thomas Ellis: The Sin Eater, 1977; The Birds of The Air, 1980; The 27th Kingdom, 1982; The Other Side of the Fire, 1983; Unexplained Laughter, 1985; The Clothes in the Wardrobe, 1987; The Skeleton in the Cupboard, 1988; The Fly in the Ointment, 1989; The Inn at the Edge of the World, 1990; Pillars of Gold, 1992. Columns published as books: Home Life, 1986; More Home Life, 1987; Home Life III, 1988; Home Life IV, 1989. Cookery Books: Natural Baby Food, 1977; Darling, You Shouldn't Have Gone to So Much Trouble (with Caroline Blackwood), 1979. (with Tom Pitt-Aikens) Secrets of Strangers, 1986; The Loss of The Good Authority, 1989. Autobiography: A Welsh Childhood, 1990. Anthology: Wales-An Anthology, 1991. *Address:* 22 Gloucester Crescent, Camden Town, London, NW1 7DY.

HAYES, Mr (George) Forbes, CEng, FIMechE, FRHS, FRAS, CStJ. *Born on* 22 April 1917 at Porthcawl. *Son of* the late Raymond Stanley Hayes JP, of Bryngarw, Bridgend and the late Gladys Vera (nee Keating). *Marriage:* to Jean, 1942, da of Charles Cory. *Children:* John Forbes Raymond (b.1948) and Ann Caroline Milne (b. 1945). *Educated at* Wycliffe Coll Stonehouse Glos; Trinity Coll Cambridge (MA). *Career:* 2 Lieut 81 Field Regiment RA (TA) 1938-39, Maj REME WWII 1943-46; apprentice engineer TH & J Daniels Stroud 1934-38, director and chairman Sheppard & Sons (later Hayes Industries) 1946-66; Director Hill Samuel & Co Ltd 1966-76; chairman Henley Forklift 1973-75; High Sheriff Glamorgan Co 1972-73; pres: Engineering and Employers Federation S Wales 1960-61, Indust Assoc of Wales & Mon 1964; founder chairman CBI Council Wales 1965; UWIST: member Council 1973, chairman Council 1974-82, vice president 1982-88; vie president Univ of Wales Coll of Cardiff 1988- , (member Council 1988); Freeman City of London 1951, member of Court of Assts Worshipful Co of Tin Plate Workers 1961- (member

1951, Master 1975-76), governor RAS, Bath and West Soc. CEng, FI *Recreation:* music, garden, golf, travel. *Clubs:* Farmers, City Livery, Cardiff and County, Royal (Porthcawl). *Address:* Brocastle, Bridgend, Mid Glam CF35 5AU. Tel: 0656 660600.

HAYES, Professor John Desmond, BSc, MS, PhD, FI.Biol. *Currently:* Professor of Agriculture, since 1979. *Born on* 27 July 1931 at Narberth. *Son of* William John Hayes and Annie Matilda (nee Butler). *Marriage:* 1959. *Children:* Sharon, John, Michael and Timothy. *Educated at* Narberth GS; University College of Wales (BSc, PhD); University of Wisconsin (MS). *Career:* King George VI Memorial Fellow 1954-55; Head of Arable Crops Breeding Department Welsh Plant Breeding Station 1955-77; Sci Adviser to Agric Res. Council 1977-79. Membership Governing Bodies NSDO; SCRI; NVRS; AGRS. member of UK Seeds executive. Fellow Indian Society of Genetics and Plant Breeding. *Publications:* various scientific publications concerned with Plant Breeding. *Recreation:* family, rugby, travel, exploring villages. *Clubs:* Farmers. *Address:* Dunstall, Borth, Dyfed SY24 5NN. Dept Of Agricultural Sciences, University College Of Wales, Aberystwyth, Dyfed, SY23 3DD.

HAZELL, Quinton, CBE, DL. *Currently:* Chairman, E.Quinton Hazell Ltd. *Born on* 14 Dec 1920 at Manchester. *Son of* Thomas and Ada Kathleen Hazell. *Marriage:* to Morwenna Parry-Jones, 1942. *Children:* Morris. *Educated at* Manchester Grammar School. *Career:* Royal Artillery 1939-46; Dir, Hawker Siddeley Gp PLC 1979-91; Snr Steward, Manchester Gramm Sch 1984; Deputy Chmn & Chmn Appeal Cttee, Warwick Private Charitable Hosp 1978- ; Gnr, Lord Leycester Hosp, Warwick 1971- ; Chmn, Arnold Lodge Sch Cncl, Leamington Spa 1981- ; Chmn, Arnold Lodge Sch Jubilee Appeal for the Joe Homan Int. Boys' Towns 1984; Pres, Colwyn Bay Eventide Homes 1972-84; Dep Chmn, Warwick NSPCC Centenary Appeal 1983-84; Hon Vice-Pres, Warwick & Leamington Conservative Assoc; Chmn, Offa Retreat House, Coventry Diocese, Church Rebuilding Appeal; Chmn, Warwick & Leamington Conservative Assoc Patrons' Club 1984- ; Mem. Steering Cttee for Private Health Sector under Dame Jill Knight, DBE, MP 1983-84; Chmn, Rugby Means Business Panel 1982-83; Vice-Pres, Rydal Sch Centenary Appeal 1982; Fndr, Chmn & M.D., Quinton Hazell PLC 1946-73 (Obtained Queen's Award to Industry 1972); Dir, Burmah Oil plc 1972-73; Dir, Foreign & Colonial Investment Trust PLC 1978-90; Chmn, & M.D., Supra Gp plc 1973-87; Chmn, Aerospace Eng plc 1986-90; Chmn, F & C Enterprise plc 1981-86; Dir, Banro Ind.plc 1985-88; Dir, Union Marine Ins.Co.Ltd 1958-68; Dir, Phoenix Assurance plc 1968-85; Dir, Winterbottom Energy Trust plc 1978-82; Dir, English & Caledonian Invest.Trust 1976-78; Chmn, West Midlands Economic Planning Council 1971-77; Mem.Welsh Advis Cttee for Civil Aviation 1961-67; Dir, Wales Gas Bd 1961-65; Cncl Mem, Univ Coll of Bangor 1966-68;Mem Welsh Bd of Ind (N.Wales) 1952-57; Cncl Mem, Univ of Birmingham 1977-82;Freeman City of London; Dep.Lieut Warwick.Mem Worshipful Co of Coachmakers and Coach Harness Makers.Hon Testimonial Royal Humane Soc 1950- saving a child's life. *Recreation:* metalwork, woodwork, antiques, gardening. *Address:* Wootton Paddox, Leek, Wootton, Nr Warwick, CV35 7QX.

HEAL, Sylvia Lloyd, JP., MP., BSc.(Econ). *Currently:* Member of Parliament since 1990. *Born on* 20 July 1942 at Clwyd, N. Wales. *Daughter of* the late John Lloyd Fox and Ruby Fox. *Marriage:* to W. Keith Heal 1965. *Children:* Joanne Sian Lloyd and Gareth Aneurin. *Educated at* Elfed Sec. Mod. School, Buckley, Clwyd; Coleg Harlech N. Wales; Univ. College Swansea. *Career:* Medical Records Clerk; Social Worker; Dept of Employment and the Health Service. *Recreation:* Male voice choirs, walking; theatre. *Address:* House of Commons, London SW1A OAA.

HEATON, Major Basil Hugh Philipse, MBE *Currently:* Landowner and farmer. *Born on* 23 Dec 1923 at Mold. *Son of* Commander and Mrs H.E.Heaton. *Marriage:* 1st to Bronwyn Poole (d.1978); 2nd to Jennifer Williams. *Children:* Sara Margaret (b.1956), Julia Mary (b.1959) and Victoria Bronwyn (b.1971, d.1979). *Educated at* Shrewsbury School. *Career:* Royal Artillery 1942-65, landed on D.Day, service in Korea (MBE), Malaya, retired 1965. *Publications:* A Short History of Rhual. *Recreation:* shooting, fishing. *Address:* Rhual, Mold, Clwyd CH7 5DB. Tel: 0352 700457.

HEDGER, Dr. Merylyn Anne, BSc., MCD., PhD., MRTPI DIC. *Currently:* Environmental Planning Consultant 1990- ; Mbr. Countryside Council for Wales 1991- . *Born on* 2 June 1947 at London. *Daughter of* Alexander McKenzie and Wendy Morgan. *Marriage:* to John Hedger 1969. *Children:* Anwen Fflur and Alasdair Kenneth *Educated at* Horsham High School for Girls; London School of Economics; University of Liverpool; Imperial College. *Career:* Senior Planning Officer, Carmarthenshire C.C., 1970-73; Deputy Director of Planning Ceredigion D.C., 1974-81; Research Officer, (in Ecuador) ODA., 1982-84; Research student, Imperial College 1985-86; W.S. Atkins Planning Consultants 1987-88; Mbr. Countryside Commission 1988-91; Mbr. Commt. for Wales, Countryside Commission 1988-91; Lecturer, Department of Geography, University of Papua, New Guinea 1990-91. *Recreation:* Travelling, walking, photography *Address:* Inst of Earth Studies, University College of Wales, Aberystwyth, Dyfed, SY23 3DB.

HEDGES, Mr Michael John, B.Sc., (Hons) PGCE *Currently:* Lecturer, Pontypridd Technical College; W.Glam County Councillor and Secretary, Swansea East Labour Party. *Born on* 8 July 1956 at Swansea. *Son of* William John and Rosemarie June. *Educated at* Penlan Comprehensive; Swansea University; Cardiff University. *Career:* Research Officer BSC, 1978-81; Computer Consultant, 1981-83; County Councillor, 1989- ; Vice Chairman Finance, 1989- ; Vice Chairman Roadforce Board, 1989-90; Chairman Roadforce Board, 1990- ; Vice Chairman Grants Committee, 1991- ; Secretary Swansea East CLP, 1987- ; Wales LP Executive, 1991- . *Publications:* Letters in South Wales Evening Post, Herald of Wales Tribune. *Recreation:* Cricket and soccer *Clubs:* Ynystawe Cricket, Morriston Soccer and Morriston Working Mens. *Address:* 4 Glyncollen Drive, Ynysforgan, Swansea SA6 6RR.

HENDERSON, James Ronald, BA Law, Durham. *Currently:* Royal Mail District Head Postmaster for Chester & North Wales, since 1989. *Born on* 4 May 1951 at Newcastle Upon Tyne. *Son of* Robert and Edith Henderson. *Marriage:* to Sandra. *Children:* Robert and Matthew *Educated at* Dame Allens School, Newcastle Upon Tyne; Durham University. *Career:* Joined Post Office, 1972;

Managerial Appointments in Personnel and Operations in Brighton, Manchester & London. *Recreation:* Theatre, Cinema and music *Address:* Royal Mail District Office, Chester & N. Wales, Station Road, Chester CH1 3AA.

HENDERSON, Mr John Stuart Wilmot, *Currently:* Retired 1976. *Born on* 31 March 1919 at Levenshulme, Manchester. *Son of* Bruce Wilmot Henderson and Sarah Henderson (nee Marchant). *Marriage:* 1st to Elsie Kathleen (nee Rose, 1941 (d1981); 2nd to Yvonne Crawley (nee Smith), 1984. *Children:* Elizabeth Anne, Jill Frances, John Graham Wilmot and Felicity June. *Educated at* Wade Deacon Grammar School, Widnes. *Career:* Executive Officer, Royal Ordnance Factories, Royal Arsenal, Woolwich, 1938-39; Royal Fusiliers, 1939-43; Intelligence Corps, 1944-47; Staff Captain, Adjutant General's Department, War Office, 1946-47; various appointments in Ministries of Supply, Aviation, Technology and Defence, 1947-76 including Secretary of the Transport Aircraft Requirements Committee and Secretary of the Shipbuilding Industry Board, on Secondment; Under Secretary, Ministry of Defence and Director General of Ordnance Factories. *Recreation:* Enjoying music, gardening, reading and world affairs. *Address:* Tregaron, Llantrissent, near Usk, Gwent NP5 1LG.

HENRI, Mr Adrian Maurice, D.Litt(Hons); Hons B.A. Fine Art (Dunelm) *Currently:* Freelance poet and painter and occasional critic, playwright and songwriter. *Born on* 10 April 1932 at Birkenhead. *Son of* Arthur Maurice Henri and Emma (nee Johnson). *Marriage:* to Joyce (nee Wilson) 1959, div. 1974, d. 1987. *Educated at* St.Asaph Grammar School; Dept. Fine Art, King's College, Newcastle. *Career:* Lecturer, Manchester College of Art 1961-64; Lecturer, Liverpool College of Art 1964-67; led poetry/rock group 'Liverpool Scene' 1967-70; writer in residence, The Tattenhall Centre, Cheshire 1981-82; Dept. of Education, Univ. of Liverpool 1989; President, Merseyside Arts Assoc. 1978-80; President, Liverpool Academy of Arts 1972-81; exhibitions: Major One-man; ICA London 1968; Art Net.London 1975; Williamson Art Gallery 1976; Demarco Gallery Edinburgh 1978; 'The Art of Adrian Henri' touring retrospective 1986-87; John Moores Liverpool Exhibitions 1962, 64, 67, 72 (second Prizewinner), 1974, 78, 80, 89. *Publications:* Collected Poems 1986; Wish You Were Here (poems) 1990; The Phantom Lollipop Lady (poems for children) 1987; Rhinestone Rhino (poems for children) 1989; Eric The Punk Cat (for children) 1980; Eric and Frankie in Las Vegas (for children) 1987; The Postman's Palace (for children) 1990; Box and other Poems (for teenagers) 1990; The Wakefield Mysteries (playscript) 1991. *Recreation:* travel, food and wine, Liverpool F.C. *Clubs:* Chelsea Arts. *Address:* 21 Mount Street, Liverpool., L1 9HD.

HERBERT, Reginald, *Currently:* Editor, Evening Leader, 1985- ; Editor in Chief, North Wales Newspapers, 1986- . *Born on* 11 Oct 1936 at Liverpool. *Son of* the late Mr James Herbert and the late Gertrude Molyneaux. *Marriage:* to Jean Maureen Roberts. *Children:* Mark, Jason, Justin and Dominic. *Educated at* St.Michael's in the Hamlet; Rose Lane Schools, Liverpool. *Career:* Liverpool Evening Express, 1954-58; North Wales Newspapers since 1958: Reporter, Wrexham Leader; Chief Reporter, Wrexham Leader. *Recreation:* music, sport, reading. *Clubs:* Erddig

Rotary of Wrexham. *Address:* Tintagel, 28 Edinburgh Road, Wrexham, Clwyd, LL11 2RS.

HERBERT, Dr. Trevor, BA; PhD; Cert.Ed; ARCM; LGSM *Currently:* Staff Tutor and Senior Lecturer in Music, Open University, since 1976 academic with Open University (variously Sub-Dean of Arts Faculty and Acting Deputy Welsh Director). *Born on* 18 Oct 1945 at Cwmparc, Rhondda. *Son of* Megan Herbert (nee Pearce) and Trevor John Herbert. *Educated at* Tonypandy Grammar School; St.Lukes Coll, Exeter; Royal College of Music. *Career:* Musician (Trombone player) with various London Orchestras, 1970-76; freelance musician. *Publications:* six books in The Welsh History and its Sources series (Ed. with G.E.Jones), Univ. of Wales Press 1988. Bands: Open Univ. Press 1991. Composed the theme music for many TV programmes including: 'The Divided Kingdom', 'Saer Doliau', 'Wales, Wales', Under Milk Wood'. *Recreation:* music, rugby. *Clubs:* Cardiff RFC, BBC. *Address:* The Open University In Wales, 24 Cathedral Road, Cardiff CF1 9SA. Tel: 0222 397911.

HERBERT-JONES, Mr Hugh Jarrett, CMG; OBE; MA *Currently:* Retired. *Born on* 11th Mar 1922 at London. *Son of* late Capt. H. Herbert-Jones, RWF and late Mrs Dora Herbert-Jones, MBE. *Marriage:* to Margaret, daughter of Rev.J.P. Veall. *Children:* Sarah, Nicholas and Sian. *Educated at* Bryanston and Worcester College, Oxford *Career:* Welsh Guards 1941-46; HM Foreign Service 1947-79: served in Berlin, Hong Kong, SE Asia, East Africa, Cape Town, and Paris; Director of International Affairs, Confederation of British Industry 1979-87 *Recreation:* Sailing, golf, shooting, music *Clubs:* London Welsh RFC; MCC; Garrick Club *Address:* Prior's Hill, Park Road, Aldeburgh, Suffolk, IP15 5ET. 408 Nelson House, Dolphin Square, London SW4 3NZ.

HESELTINE, The Rt. Hon. Michael Ray Dibbin, PC., MP. *Currently:* Secretary of State for the Environment since 1990. *Born on* 21 March 1933 at Swansea. *Son of* the late Col. Rupert Heseltine and Eileen (nee Pridmore). *Marriage:* to Anne Williams, 1962. *Children:* Annabel, Alexandra and Rupert. *Educated at* Shrewsbury & Pembroke College, Oxford. *Career:* Nat. Service, 1959, commissioned into Welsh Guards; Publisher & Chairman, Haymarket Publishing Group; fought Gower, 1959, Coventry North, 1964; elected for Tavistock, Devon, 1966, represented Henley since 1974; appointed Parliamentary Under-Sec., of State at Dept. of Environment, 1970; Minister for Aerospace, 1972; Opposition spokesman on Industry, 1974-76; Opposition spokesman on the environment, 1976; Sec. of State for the Environment, 1979-83; Mbr. of Privy Council; appointed Sec.of State, Min. of Defence, 1983, resigning, 1986; Hon. Degree, Liverpool University, 1990; Hon. Fellow Leeds Polytechnic, 1988; Hon. Fellow, Pembroke College, Oxford, 1986; Hon. Fellow, RIBA, 1991; *Publications:* Where There's a Will, 1987; The Challenge of Europe: Can Britain Win?, 1989. *Recreation:* Planting trees *Address:* c/o House of Commons, London., SW1A OAA.

HEYCOCK, Clayton Rees, MA (Master of Arts), Leic; MSc (Master of Science), Wales. *Currently:* Secretary and Chief Officer, Welsh Joint Education Committee, since 1990. *Born on* 19 Sept 1941 at Port Talbot. *Son of* the late Lord Heycock of Taibach and Lady Heycock. *Marriage:* to Lynda (nee Williams), 1964. *Children:* Alyson Sian (b.1970) and Rebecca Louise (b.1973). *Educated at* Central Infants and Junior School, Port Talbot; Glanafan Grammar School, Port Talbot; Univ Coll., of Swansea; University of Leicester. *Career:* various teaching posts, 1965-71, Sandfields Comprehensive School, Port Talbot; Senior Adviser in Secondary Education, Glamorgan County Council 1972-74; Deputy Director of Education, West Glamorgan County Council 1974-90; Association of Education Committees European Trust Fellow 1982- ; Secondment (part-time) Audit Commission 1988-89. *Publications:* Comprehensive School Study, 1971; plus numerous articles in various education journals. *Recreation:* travel, rugby football (spectator). *Clubs:* Rotary Club of Port Talbot (President 1987-88). *Address:* 6 Tanygroes Place, Port Talbot, West Glamorgan SA13 2TU.

HEYES, Mr John Graham, FDS, DOrth, DDO. *Currently:* Consultant Orthodontist. *Born on* 11 March 1945 at Edinburgh. *Address:* Maelor Hospital, Wrexham LL13 7TD.

HIBBARD, Professor Bryan Montague, MD., PhD., FRCOG *Currently:* Emeritus Professor, University of Wales College of Medicine. *Born on* 24 April 1926 at England. *Son of* the late Montague Reginald Hibbard and the late Muriel (nee Wilson). *Marriage:* to Elizabeth Donald Grassie 1955. *Educated at* Queen Elizabeths School, Barnet; St. Bartholomews Hospital Medical College. *Career:* Principal Central Government appointments: Medicines Commsn 1986-89; Ctee Safety of Medicines 1980-84; Admin. of Radioactive substances advisory ctee 1975-77; Maternity services advisory ctee 1980-85; Confidential enquiries into maternal deaths in England & Wales (Regional & Central Assessor) 1980-88, Confidential Enquiries into Maternal Death for U.K., Central Assessor and mbr of Editorial Bd 1988- ; Chairman, Clinical Sub Group 1991- . Ctee on Gynaecological Cytology 1983-89; Health Educ. Cnl antenatal working party 1979-84; Joint colleges and ambulance services ctee 1989- ; Welsh Office: Welsh Med. ctee 1981-83; Perinatal working party (chairman) 1981; Wales Perinatal Initiative 1983-87; Welsh ctee for Hospital Med. Serv. 1974-76; Advisory Sub ctee in Obstetrics and gynaecology 1974- (chairman 1989- ; S.Glam Health Auth: mbr. 1983-88; Chrmn Executive ctee 1975-80; Maternity Serv. Liason ctee 1984 - ; Chairman 1984-87; Ethics Ctee 1978-81; Royal Coll. of Obstetricians & Gynaecologist: Council 1984-88, 89- ; RCOG Finance & Exec.ctee 1986-88; Scientific Advisory ctee 1973-76; Fellowship selection ctee 1979-83; Welsh Exec. ctee 1974- (Chairman 1989-); Joint Standing Advisory ctee on Obstetric Anaesthesia & Analgesia 1985-91 (Chairman 1988-); Jnt standing ctee of RCOG/RCM 1988-91 (Chairman); Central Congress ctee 1975-80 and 1986-88; Chmn 24th British Congress of Obstetrics and Gynaecology 1986; Curator of Instruments 1986- ; of Museum 1990- ; Library ctee 1986- (Chairman 1987-); mbr. of Birthright Council 1987-91; Gynaecological Visiting Society of Great Britain and Ireland Convenor 1980-87. Welsh Obstetric & Gynaecological Society, President 1985-86. *Publications:* Principles of Obstetrics 1988; The Obstetric Forceps 1988; numerous publications in obstetric journals etc. *Recreation:* Collecting 18th C drinking glasses; history of obstetrics; fell walking; coarse gardening. *Clubs:* Royal Society of Medicine. *Address:* The Clock House, Cathedral Close, Llandaff, Cardiff CF5 2ED

HIBBERD, Professor Peter Richard, MSc., FRICS., ACI.Arb. *Currently:* Head of Department, Department of Property and Development Studies. *Born on* 9 June 1944 at Oxford. *Son of* Reginald Victor William and Mary Gwenllan (nee Jones). *Marriage:* to Jean Bernice Himbury 1971. *Children:* Caroline and Catherine. *Educated at* Adcroft School, Trowbridge; College of Estate Management, London; UMIST. *Career:* Quantity Surveyor, Local government 1966-72; Partner, Madlin & Maddison 1973-76; Senior Lecturer/ Principal Lecturer, Bristol Polytechnic 1976-80; Director, CH Building (Martley) Ltd 1979-85; Director, Amber Developments 1982-85; Head, Polytechnic of Wales 1989; Director, WPE Hibberd Ltd 1988-90. *Publications:* Variations in Construction Contracts 1986; Sub-Contracts under the JCT Intermediate Form 1989; Key Factors in Contractual Relationships 1991. *Recreation:* Horse riding, sport, countryside. *Address:* Polytechnics Of Wales, Pontypridd, Mid Glam CF37 1DL.

HIBBERT, Sir Reginald Alfred, G.C.M.G. *Currently:* Retired diplomat. *Born on* 21 Feb 1922 *Son of* Alfred Hibbert and the late Kathleen (nee Rann). *Marriage:* to Ann Alun Pugh, 1949, daughter of Sir Alun Pugh. *Children:* 2s and 1d; *Educated at* Queen Elizabeth's School, Barnet and Worcester College, Oxford *Career:* War service- with Special Operations Executive in Albania, and with 4th Queen's Own Hussars in Italy; H.M. Diplomatic Service in Romania, Austria, Guatemala, Turkey, Belgium; Charge D'Affaires at Ulan Bator, Mongolia, 1964-66; Political Adviser to C-in-C Fareast at Singapore, 1968-71; Minister at Embassy, Bonn, 1972-75; Political Director Foreign Office, 1977-79; Ambassador at Paris, 1979-82; Director, Ditchley Foundation, 1982-87. Hon. Fellow, Worcester College, Oxford, 1991- ; Hon. Research Fellow, Swansea University Coll. 1987- . *Publications:* The Albanian National Liberation Struggle, The Bitter Victory, Pinter, 1991. *Recreation:* Gardening, books and writing. *Clubs:* Reform *Address:* Frondeg, Pennal, Machynlleth, Powys. SY20 9JX. Tel: 0654 791220.

HIGGIN, Captain William Bendyshe, *Currently:* Landowner/ Farmer Cheshire, Shropshire and North Wales. *Born on* 14 Feb 1922 at Puddington, Cheshire. *Son of* Major Walter Wynnefield Higgin DL and Olive (nee Earle). *Marriage:* to Mary Patricia, 1947, da of Capt. G.Lee-Morris RNVR. *Children:* Mark (b.1954), Jonathan b.1956) and Rosemary Gail(b.1947). *Educated at* Greshams School, Holt, Royal AG College Cirencester. *Career:* W.W.II Coy Cmdr 5/10 Baluch Regt. 1.A 1941; ADC to Goc-inC n.India 1943-44; invalided out 1946; Life member CPRW; CLA; BASC. *Recreation:* game shooting, gardening, restoration of old buildings. *Clubs:* SIND, Shropshire. *Address:* Melus Manaw, Bodedern, Anglesey, Gwynedd, LL65 3UN. Oror, Gwydellwern, Corwen, Clwyd LL21 .

HILL, Mrs Audrey Winifred Louise, *Currently:* retired. *Born on* 2 May 1919 at Hampshire. *Daughter of* the late Charles Lockyer and the late Maria (nee Stride). *Marriage:* to Sidney George Hill, 1937. *Children:* d. Lesley, b.1941 and s. Ronald, b.1944. *Educated at* Sarisbury Grammar School. *Career:* Area Manager, subsidiary J.Walter Thompson Advertising Agency, 1960-79; County Councillor 1983- ; Counsellor N.C.H. Careline 1979-90; Conservative Party Worker 1959- . *Recreation:* reading, travel, Conservative Party Worker. *Address:* 26 Castle Drive,

Dinas Powys, S.Glam CF6 4NP.

HINDS, William James, MBE, JP, FRAGS. *Currently:* retired. *Born on* 9 Sept 1910 at Carmarthen. *Son of* Ben Hinds and Bariah Hinds. *Marriage:* to Gwendolen Harries, 1938. *Educated at* Queen Elizabeth Grammar School; Pibwrlwyd Farm Inst; UCW. *Career:* mem (S.Wales Milk Marketing Board 1952-62 and 1965-83, Cncl Royal Welsh Agric Soc 1983-91 (pres 1987), Ct of Governors UCW Aberystwyth; former mem S W Wales River Authority, hon life member Carmarthenshire NFU 1984; High Sheriff Dyfed 1981-82; FRAGS 1988. *Recreation:* fishing, Rugby football. *Clubs:* Patron of Scarlets, Llanelli *Address:* Danyyrallt, Abergorlech Road, Carmarthen, Dyfed, SA32 7AY.

HINSON, Mr Kenneth Jack, FCA, FAAI. *Currently:* Self-employed Chartered Accountant. *Born on* 19 Sept 1943 at Isleworth, UK. *Son of* Thomas W.Hinson and Doris E.Hinson. *Marriage:* 1st dissolved; 2nd to Christina P.Holt, 1989. *Children:* Gary T.Hinson, Lorna E.Bland and Deon A.Holt. *Educated at* Wandsworth Grammar. *Career:* Harvey Preen & Co 1962-76, Articled, Audit Manager, Partner; Managing Director Bottcher UK Ltd., 1977-91; Partner, Ash Financial Services, 1992. *Publications:* Professional Magazines. *Recreation:* shooting, vintage cars. *Address:* Onen House, The Onen, Monmouth, Gwent, NP5 4EN.

HIORNS, Dr Brennan Martin, PhD *Currently:* Deputy Managing Director, Kleinwort Benson Securities and Head of Research, since 1987. *Born on* 21 Sept 1943 at Cardiff. *Son of* Hubert and Catherine Hiorns (nee Brennan). *Marriage:* to Mary Diana (nee Long). *Children:* Catherine Victoria and Christopher Brennan. *Educated at* Lewis School, Pengam; Birmingham University. *Career:* Research Engineer, ICI Plastics Division 1970-74; Stockbroker, Grieveson Grant 1974-85, Partner 1983; In 1985 Grieveson Grant taken over by Kleinwort Benson. *Publications:* various in journals. *Recreation:* archaeology, reading, military history. *Address:* 16 Prospect Lane, Harpenden, Herts. AL5 2PL.

HOARE, Mr Kenneth Ninian, MBE, MA(Oxon), F.Inst.D. *Born on* 4 March 1916 at Cardiff. *Son of* the late Capt. F.E.Hoare RAOC and the late Mrs M.E. Hoare. *Marriage:* 1st to Marion G.Spencer, 1940 (dissolved 1971); 2nd to Daphne J.Lubbock, 1971. *Children:* Gillian Sheila and Celia Jennifer. *Educated at* Cardiff High School; Jesus College, Oxford; Middle Temple, Inns of Court. *Career:* Commissioned Royal Artillery 1938, invalided 1940, followed by service in the Admiralty. Director of Administration, PIRA International 1945-79; Member of Council and Honorary Secretary-General, International Association of Research Institutes for the Graphic Arts Industry 1965-. *Publications:*, Graphic Arts Research, 1973, 1978, 1983 and 1992. *Recreation:* travel, antiques, gardening, reading. *Clubs:* Oxford Union, Institute of Directors. *Address:* Lanterns, 18 The Ridgeway, Fetcham Park, Leatherhead, Surrey, KT22 9AZ. Old Bell Cottage, Ferring-By-Sea, West Sussex BN12 5QS.

HODDINOTT, Emeritus Professor Alun, CBE, DMus, *Born on* 11 Aug 1929 at Bargoed, Glamorgan. *Son of* Thomas Ivor and Gertrude (nee Jones). *Marriage:* to Beti Rhiannon Huws 1953. *Children:* Huw Ceri 1957. *Educated at* Gowerton Grammar School; Univ. College Cardiff; *Career:* Lecturer Welsh College Music & Drama 1951-59;

Lecturer Univ. College Cardiff, 1959-65; Reader, Univ. of Wales, 1965-67; Professor & Head of Dept. of Music, U.C.Cardiff, 1967-87; Founder & Artistic Director, Cardiff Festival of Music, 1967-89; Hon. Member, Royal Academy of Music; Fellow, Royal Northern College of Music; Fellow, Welsh College of Music & Drama; Fellow, U.C.Cardiff; Hopkins Medal, St.David's Society of New York; Bax Medal; Walford Davies Prize, Univ. of Wales; Member, BBC Music Advisory Cttee.; Member, British Council; Member, Welsh Arts Council; Governor, St.John's College, Cardiff; President, Cardiff Festival of Music; *Publications:* Operas- The Beach of Falesa, The Magician, What the Old Man Does is Always Right, The Rajah's Diamond, The Trumpet Major;Orchestral Music- Symphonies 1-6, Symphony for Organ & Orchestra, Sinfoniettas 1-4, Fioriture, Passaggio, Landscapes, Star Children, Rhapsody on Welsh Tunes, Improvisation on an Old Welsh Tune, Welsh Dances (Suites 1-4), Lanterne des Mortes, Scena for String Orchestra, Concertos for Clarint, Horn, Oboe, Harp, Violin, Viola, Piano (3), Nocturnes & Cadenzas for Cello & Orchestra, Noctis Equi for Cello & Orchestra, Doubles for Oboe, Strings & Harpsichord, Scenes for Strings trumpet & Harpsichord; The heaventree of stars for violin & orchestra; Ritornelli for trombone, wind & percussion. Instrumental music- sonata for organ; sonatas for piano 1-10; sonatas for violin & piano 1-4; 2 sonatas for cello & piano; sonata for harp, clarinet & piano, horn & piano *Address:* Maesawelon, 86 Mill Road, Lisvane, Cardiff ,CF4 5UG.

HODGE, Sir Julian Stephen, K.St.G., K.St.J., FCCA., FTII. LLd *Currently:* Retired Banker. *Born on* 15 Oct 1904 *Son of* Alfred and Jane. *Marriage:* to Moira. *Children:* Jane, Robert and Jonathan. *Educated at* Cardiff Technical College *Career:* Certified Accountant, 1930, Fellow Inst. of Taxation 1941- ; Founded Hodge & Co. Accountants and Auditors: Man. Dir 1963-75. Exec. Chm., 1975-78. Hodge Group Ltd: former Chairman: Julian S Hodge & Co Ltd: Gwent Enterprises Ltd: Hodge Finance Ltd: Hodge Life Assurance Co Ltd: Carlyle Trust Ltd 1962-85; Dir.Standard Chartered Bank 1973-75; Founded: The Jane Hodge Foundation 1962 and (Chairman); Sir Julian Hodge Charitable Trust 1964; Chairman: Aberfan Disaster Fund Industrial Project Sub-Cttee; Member: Welsh Economic Council 1965-68; Welsh Council 1968-79; Council, Univ of Wales Inst of Science and Technology (Treasurer 1968-76, Dep Pres. 1976-81, Pres 1981-85); Foundation Fund Committee Unif of Surrey Duke of Edinburgh Conf 1974; Prince of Wales Committee; Pres S.Glam Dist St.John Ambulance Bds; Trustee, Welsh Sports Trust. Former Governor All Hallows (Cranmore Hall) School. Trust Ltd; Treas. Welsh Centre for Int. Affairs 1973-84. Founder & Chairman Bank of Wales 1971-85. FTII 1941. FRSA Hon LLD Univ of Wales 1971. KStJ 1977 (CStJ 1972); KSG 1978. *Publications:* Paradox of Financial Preservation, 1959. *Recreation:* golf, walking, reading, gardening. *Clubs:* Victoria (St.Helier, Jersey); La Moye Golf (Jersey). *Address:* Clos des Seux, Mont du Coin, St. Aubin, St. Brelade, Jersey JE3 8BE.

HOLDEN, Lady Mabel, *Born on* 14 Nov 1914 at Cefn Henllan, Nr Usk, Gwent. *Daughter of* Harry Horace Morgan and Ethel Morgan. *Marriage:* to Michael Herbert Frank Holden, KT, CBE. *Children:* John Michael, Susan Mary and Peter Holden. *Educated at* Penarth County School;

Secretarial Schools and 2 years in France. *Career:* Lived in West Africa, apart from annual leave, for 30 years and assumed the usual duties of a judges wife. During the war worked in Homegrow Timber dept, Ministry of Supply. *Recreation:* music, history, travel. *Clubs:* Northern Nigerian Dining *Address:* 3 Rushton Road, Wilbarston, Nr Market Harborough, Leics, LE16 8GL.

HOLLAND, Mr Robert Einion, BSc., FIA. *Currently:* Retired *Born on* 23 April 1927 at Dolwyddelan, Gwynedd. *Son of* Robert Ellis Holland and Bene (nee Williams). *Marriage:* to Eryl Haf (nee Roberts) d.1988. *Children:* Sian, Eluned and Gareth. *Educated at* Llanrwst Grammar School; Univ. College of North Wales *Career:* Pearl Assurance 1953-89; Asst. Actuary 1961; Asst. General Manager 1967; General Manager 1972-83; (Retitled Chief General Manager 1977); Executive Chairman 1983-89; Pearl Group PLC Chairman 1986-89; Directorships: Aviation & General Insurance Co. 1973-89 (Chairman 1976-78, 1984-85); British Rail Property Bd., 1987-90; Crawley Warran Group PLC 1987-; Community Reinsurance Corpn., 1973-89; Mbr. Welsh Development Agency 1976-86; Civil Service Pay Research Unit Bd., 1980-81; Mbr. Council University of Wales 1990- . *Recreation:* golf, crosswords. *Clubs:* Langley Park. *Address:* 55 Corkscrew Hill, West Wickham, Kent BR4 9BA.

HOLLINS, Rear-Adm. (1974) Hubert Walter Elphinstone, CB,,FBIM, MNI. *Currently:* Marine Consultant. *Born on* 8 June 1923 at Gillingham, Kent. *Son of* the late Lieutenant Colonel and Mrs W.T.Hollins. *Marriage:* to Jillian Mary daughter of D.L. McAlpin of Victoria, Australia 1963. *Children:* Rupert Patrick (1964) and Rachel Jane (1965) *Educated at* Stubbington House; Royal Naval College, Dartmouth; *Career:* Commander 1957; Captain 1963; Rear Admiral 1972; In Command of HM ships Petard, Dundas, Caesar and Antrim; Flag Officer, Gibraltar, 1972-74: Com. Gib. Med. & Port Admiral Gibraltar 1972-74; Admiral Commanding Reserves 1974-76; Gen. Man. ME Navigation Aids Service, Bahrain 1977-84; Younger Brother of Trinity House; Dir. Trinity House Lighthouse Board; Associate Memb. of the Corporation of Trinity House 1985-91; Commodore, Bahrain Yacht Club, 1981-83; Master Mariner. Member RNVR Yacht Club; Trustee, Royal Merchant Navy School, Bearwood 1984-; President Newbury and District Royal Naval Assoc. 1985-90; President Newbury and District Sea Cadet Corps, 1985-91; MNI, FBIM; *Recreation:* Fishing, golf and sailing *Clubs:* RNVR Yacht; Naval; *Address:* Waunllan, Llandyfriog, Newcastle Emlyn, Dyfed SA38 9HB. Tel: 0239 710456.

HOLLINSON, Peter James, *Currently:* Editor, Wales on Sunday, Thomson House, Havelock Street, Cardiff, CF1 1WR. *Born on* 24 May 1945 at Haddington, East Lothian. *Son of* Brenda (nee Lythgoe) and the late George Henry (Flt.Lt.RAF, DFC). *Marriage:* 1st to Lynn Barbara Corbyn, 1971 (divorced 1977). 2nd to Candice Lynn Mycock, 1983. *Children:* Lee (deceased) and Grace Lynn (from 1st marriage); Sarah Elizabeth and Adam Peter from 2nd marriage. *Educated at* Clarendon Road Juniors, Eccles, Manchester; Eccles Grammar School. *Career:* Tillotson's Newspapers (Bolton) Ltd., 1962-67; Daily Mail Manchester 1967-68; The Sun (IPC) Manchester 1968-69; The Sun (News International) London 1969-72; West of England

Newspapers Plymouth 1972-74; Daily Mail Manchester 1974; Sunday Mirror Manchester (Chief Sub-Editor) 1974-88; North West Times Manchester (Night Editor and Systems Manager) 1988; Joined Wales on Sunday pre-launch January 1989 as Assistant Editor. *Recreation:* Newspapers, computers, reading. *Address:* -. Wales on Sunday, Thomson House, Havelock Street, Cardiff, CF1 1WR .

HOLMES, Professor George Arthur, FBA *Currently:* Chichele Professor of Medieval History; Fellow of All Souls College, Oxford. *Born on* 22 April 1927 at Aberystwyth. *Son of* the late John Holmes and the late Margaret (nee Thomas). *Marriage:* to Evelyn Anne Klein, 1953. *Children:* Susan, Catherine and Nicholas. *Educated at* Ardwyn Cty.Sch, Aberystwyth; UC.Aberystwyth; St. John's College, Cambridge (MA;PhD). *Career:* Fellow, St. John's College, Cambridge 1951-54; Tutor, St. Catherine's Society, Oxford 1954-62; Fellow, St. Catherine's College, Oxford 1962-89; Vice-Master, St. Catherine's College 1969-71; Member, Institute for Advanced Study, Princeton 1967-68; Jt.Editor, English Historical Review 1974-81. *Publications:* The Estates of the Higher Nobility in Fourteenth Century England 1957; The Later Middle Ages 1962; The Florentine Enlightenment 1400-1450, 1969; Europe Hierarchy and Revolt 1320-1450, 1975; The Good Parliament 1975; Dante 1980; Florence, Rome and the Origins of the Renaissance 1986; Editor of: The Oxford Illustrated History of Medieval Europe 1988; The First Age of the Western City 1300-1500, 1990; articles in periodicals. *Address:* Highmoor House, Bampton, Oxon OX18 2HY.

HOLMES, Mr. George Dennis, CB., D.Sc., FRSE., FICFor. *Currently:* Board Member, Scottish Legal Aid Board; Director, Bank of Scotland, East Board. Chairman, Scottish Council for Spastics. *Born on* 9 Nov 1926 at Conwy. *Son of* Henry and Florence Holmes, Ty Gwyn Gardens, Conwy. *Marriage:* to Sheila Rosemary Woodger, September, 1953. *Children:* Carolyn, Deborah and Nicola. *Educated at* John Bright's School, Llandudno; UCNW, Bangor. *Career:* Professional Forester, - mainly with the Forestry Commission; retired as Director General, November, 1986. *Recreation:* golf, fishing. *Address:* 7 Cammo Road, Edinburgh EH4 8EF.

HOLMES, Professor Patrick, B.Sc., PhD., M.I.C.E., C.Eng. *Currently:* Professor of Hydraulics, Dept. of Civil Engineering, Imperial College London and Consulting Engineer, 1983- . *Born on* 23 Feb 1939 at Hawarden, Clwyd. *Son of* Normand and Irene Holmes. *Marriage:* to Olive Holmes (nee Towning). *Children:* Katie Elizabeth and Christopher Peter. *Educated at* Hawarden Grammar; Univ. College, Swansea. *Career:* PhD., U.C. Swansea, 1963; Research Engineer, U.S. Navy, California, U.S.A., 1963-66; Lecturer then Professor, Univ. of Liverpool, 1966-83. *Publications:* Published widely on topics in civil engineering, hydraulics, estuary and coastal engineering; offshore engineering; environmental impact. *Recreation:* Choral singing, yachting and walking *Address:* West Winds, The Green, Steeple Morden, near Royston Herts. SG8 OND. Dept. Of Civil Engineering, Imperial College, South Kensington, London, SW7 2BU.

HOOSON, The Rt Hon The Lord. Hugh Emlyn, *Currently:* (Life Peer), of Montgomery in the County of Powys and of Colomendy in the County of Clwyd. QC 1960; a recorder of the Crown Court, since 1972 (Recorder of

Swansea 1971). *Born on* 26 March 1925 at Colomendy. *Son of* the late Hugh and Elsie Hooson, Colomendy, Denbigh. *Marriage:* to Shirley Margaret Wynne, 1950, da of late Sir George Hamer, CBE. *Children:* two d. *Educated at* Denbigh Grammar School; University College of Wales, Aberystwyth. *Career:* Royal Navy. Gray's Inn, Bencher 1968; Vice-Treasurer 1985; Treasurer 1986. Called to Bar 1949; Wales and Chester Circuit (Leader 1971-74); Dep. Chairman Flint QS 1960-71; Dep Chairman Merioneth QS 1960-67, Chairman 1967-71; Recorder of Merthyr Tydfil 1971. MP (L) Montgomery 1962-79. Leader 1966-79, Pres., 1983-86, Welsh Liberal Party. Vice-Chairman Political Committee, North Atlantic Assembly 1975-79. Dir (non-exec) Laura Ashley (Holdings) Ltd 1985-. Pres., Llangollen Internat. Eisteddfod, 1987- . Hon. Professional Fellow, University College of Wales 1971. Director Institute of Grassland and Environmental Research (IGER). Chairman (Non Executive) Severn River Crossing plc. Farms Pen-Rhiw farm, Llanidloes. White Bard of the Gorsedd of Beirdd of the Royal National Eisteddford since 1966. *Publications:* Pamphlet "the New Radical"; "The Heartland"; "A Bill of Rights". *Recreation:* reading, music. *Address:* Summerfield, Llanidloes, Powys 1 Dr Johnson's Buildings, Temple, London EC4Y 7AX.

HOPKIN, Sir William Aylsham Bryan, CBE 1961. *Currently:* Honorary Professorial Fellow, University College of Swansea. *Born on* 7 Dec 1914 at St-Brides-Ely, S. Glam. *Son of* William Hopkin and Lillian Hopkin (nee Cottelle). *Marriage:* to Renee Ricour, 1938. *Children:* John Edward and Richard Douglas. *Educated at* Barry, Glam County School; St. Johns College, Cambridge; Manchester University. *Career:* Min. of Health, 1938-41; Prime Minister's Statistical Branch, 1941-45; Royal Commission on Population, 1945-48; Economic Sect., Cabinet Office, 1948-50; Central Statistical Office, 1950-52; Dir. Nat. Inst. of Econ. & Soc. Research, 1952-57; Sec., Council on Prices, Productivity and Incomes, 1957-58; Dep. Dir., Econ. Sect. H.M. Treasury, 1958-65; Econ. Planning Unit, Mauritius, 1965; Min. of Overseas Dev., 1966-67; Dir. Gen of Economic Planning ODM., 1967-69; Dir. Gen. DEA., 1969; Chief Economic Adviser, HM Treasury, 1974-77; Mem. Commonwealth Devt. Corp., 1972-74; Chm. Manpower Services Committee for Wales, 1978-79. *Publications:* articles on Economic subjects. *Address:* Aberthin House, Aberthin, near Cowbridge, Sth. Glam. CF7 7HB. Tel: 0446 772303.

HOPKINS, Professor Colin Russell, BSc, PhD. *Currently:* Director, MRC Laboratory for Molecular Biology, University College London. *Born on* 4 June 1939 at Cardiff. *Son of* the late Bleddyn Hopkins and Vivienne Russell. *Marriage:* to Hilary (nee Floyd). *Children:* Sally (b.1970) and Laurence (b.1973). *Educated at* Pontypridd Boys Grammar School; University of Wales. *Career:* Rank Professor of Physiological Chemistry, Imperial College London 1985-90; Professor Medical Cell Biology, University of Liverpool Medical School 1974-85; Furbright Scholar, visiting Professor, Rockefeller University, New York 1971-72. *Publications:* over 60 in scientific literature. *Recreation:* music *Address:* MRC Laboratory For Molecular Cell Biology, University College, London, WC1E 6BT. 86 Bedford Court Mansions, Bedford Avenue, Bloomsbury, London, WC1B 3AE.

HOPKINS, Mr Russell, OBE, BDS, LRCP, MRCS, RCS, FDS. *Currently:* Consultant in Oral and Maxillo Facial Surgery; Director Medical/Dental Audit South Glamorgan Health Authority. *Born on* 30 April 1932 at Sunderland. *Son of* the late Charles A. Hopkins and the late Frances Doris Hopkins (nee Baldwin). *Marriage:* to Jill Margaret Hopkins (nee Pexton), 1970. *Children:* Richard J, Claire L. and Robert G.R. *Educated at* Barnard Castle School; Durham University, London University. *Career:* Chairman BMA Council for Wales 1991-; Chairman Welsh Consultants and Specialist Committee 1990- ; Chairman Welsh sub-committee of Joint Consultants Committee 1985-; President British Association of Oral & Maxillo Facial Surgeons 1992-93; Chairman Medical Board South Glamorgan 1980-82; member Joint Consultants Committee 1980- . *Publications:* Oral Preprosthetic Surgery, Wolfes Medical 1986, in Fractures Facial Skeleton, Rowe/Williams Livingstone, in Surgery Face and Jaws, Moore Blackwells, in Clinical Dentisty, Rowe Blackwells. *Recreation:* golf, photography, walking, shooting, sea fishing. *Clubs:* Cardiff Golf, Newport Boat, Newport Golf, Dyfed. *Address:* 179 Cyncoed Road, Cardiff CF2 6AH. Glamorgan House, BUPA Hospital, Pentwyn, Cardiff, CF2 7XL.

HOPPER, Mr Andrew Christopher Graham, *Currently:* Solicitor; Consultant to Cartwright Adams and Black of Cardiff. *Born on* 1 Oct 1948 at Swansea. *Son of* the late Christopher Hopper and the late Adele Hopper (nee Harper). *Marriage:* to Rosamund Heather Towers, 1980. *Educated at* Monkton Combe School, Bath. *Career:* admitted as Solicitor 1972; Senior partner of the former firm of Adams & Black, Cardiff 1982-88; HM Deputy Coroner for South Glamorgan 1979-86; Principal of specialist legal practice concerned with aspects of the professional conduct of Solicitors 1988; Principal member of panel of Solicitors retained by the Law Society to advise and act on behalf of the Society on matters of professional conduct. *Publications:* articles in legal press. *Recreation:* Burgundy, sloth. *Clubs:* East India. *Address:* Talygarn House, Talygarn, Pontyclun, Mid Glam, CF7 9JT.

HORNBY, Mr Raymond Peter, BSc., C.Eng., MICE. *Currently:* Wallace Evans Ltd, Division Director, 1990. *Born on* 10 Aug 1946 at Southall, Middx. *Son of* the late Edwin and the late Alice. *Marriage:* to Janette Margaret (nee Taylor) 1970. *Children:* Rachel, Katherine and Daniel. *Educated at* Spring Grove School, Isleworth; Westminster Technical College; University College Swansea. *Career:* Sir William Halcrow & Partners: Dams Department, London 1963; Marine Department, London 1970; Area Office, Dubai 1971; Port Qaboos, Muscat, Oman 1974; Port of Jubail, Saudi Arabia 1976; Wallace Evans: St.Kitts Deepwater Port, West Indies 1978; Port & Marine Department, Penarth 1981; Associate Partner, Penarth 1987. *Recreation:* Sport, travel, reading, music. *Clubs:* Dale Yacht Club. *Address:* 113 Plymouth Road, Penarth, South Glamorgan CF6 2DF.

HORNE, Mr Anthony John, NCA NEBSS Dip *Currently:* Ground Manager with Welsh Rugby Union. *Born on* 15 Jan 1952 at Bridgend. *Son of* the late Robert Charles and Joan Horne. *Marriage:* Carol Ann Fehrs (nee Godfrey) 1982. *Children:* 2 step daughters Sian Elizabeth and Anna Jane Fehrs *Educated at* Llantwit Major Secondary Modern; Gelli Aur Farm Inst.; Royal Agricultural College, Cirencester; Pengoed College of Horticultural; Llandaff College of

Technology; *Career:* Groundsman with Glamorgan Education Cttee., 1972; Deputy Superintendant School Playing Fields South Glamorgan Educ. Cttee., 1978; Ground Manager Welsh Rugby Union, 1985; Chmn. South Wales Branch Institute of Groundsmanship, 1986; Scout Master / District Commissioner 1972; *Recreation:* Golf, sports, music, fishing and boy scouts *Clubs:* St.Athan Golf; Various Rugby; *Address:* 8 Castle Court, Llantwit Major, South Glamorgan CF6 9SX.

HOSELITZ, Mr Steve, *Currently:* Editor, South Wales Argus. *Born on* 12 March 1947 *Address:* South Wales Argus, Cardiff Road, Newport, Gwent, NP9 1QW.

HOWARD, Rt.Hon. Michael, PC; QC. *Currently:* British politician and barrister. *Born on* 7 July 1941 *Son of* Bernard Howard and Hilda Howard. *Marriage:* to Sandra Clare Paul, 1975. *Children:* one s. one d. one step-s. *Educated at* Llanelli Grammar School; Peterhouse Cambridge. *Career:* President Cambridge Union 1962; called to Bar, Inner Temple 1964; Junior Counsel to the Crown (Common Law) 1980-82; a Recorder 1986- ; Conservative parl. candidate, Liverpool (Edge Hill) 1966, 1970; Chair, Bow Group 1970-71; M.P. for Folkstone and Hythe 1983- ; Parl Private Secretary to Solicitor-General 1984-85; Under Secretary of State, Dept of Trade and Industry, Minister for Corporate and Consumer Affairs 1985-87; Under-Secretary Dept of the Environment 1987; Minister of State, Dept of the Environment 1987-88, Minister of Water and Planning 1988-90; Sec of State for Employment 1990- ; Chair Soc. of Conservative Lawyers 1985. *Recreation:* watching football and baseball. *Address:* House of Commons, London SW1A OAA. Tel: 071 219 5493.

HOWE, The Rt Hon Sir (Richard Edward) Geoffrey, QC *Currently:* MP (C) Surrey East, since 1974 (Reigate, 1970-74); Lord President of the Council, Leader of the House of Commons, and Deputy Prime Minister, since 1989. *Born on* 20 Dec 1926 at Port Talbot. *Son of* the late B.E.Howe and Mrs E.F.Howe (nee Thomson), Port Talbot, Glamorgan. *Marriage:* to Elspeth Rosamund Morton Shand, 1953. *Children:* Caroline (b.1955) and Amanda and Alexander (b.1959). *Educated at* Winchester Coll. (Exhibitioner); Trinity Hall, Cambridge (Scholar, MA, LLB). *Career:* Pres., Trinity Hall Assoc., 1977-78; Lieut Royal Signals 1945-48. Chm. Cambridge University Conservative Assoc., 1951; Chm Bow Group 1955; Managing Director, Crossbow 1957-60, Editor 1960-62. Called to the Bar, Middle Temple 1952; Bencher, 1969; Member General Council of the Bar 1957-61; Member Council of Justice 1963-70. Dep Chm., Glamorgan QS 1966-70. Contested (C) Aberavon 1955, 1959; MP (C) Bebington 1964-66. Sec. Conservative Parliamentary Health and Social Security Cttee 1964-65; an Opposition Front Bench spokesman on labour and social services 1965-66; Solicitor-General 1970-72; Minister for Trade and Consumer Affairs, DTI 1972-74; opposition fron bench spokesman on social services 1974-75, on Treasury and economic affairs 1975-79; Chancellor of the Exchequer 1979-83; Sec. of State for Foreign and Commonwealth Affairs 1983-89. Chm., Interim Cttee, IMF 1982-83. Director: Sun Alliance & London Insce Co. Ltd 1974-79; AGB Research Ltd 1974-79; EMI Ltd 1976-79. Member: (Latey) Interdeptl Cttee on Age of Majority 1965-67; (Street) Cttee on Racial Discrimination 1967; (Cripps) Cons. Cttee on Discrimination

against Women 1968-69; Chm Ely Hospital, Cardiff, Inquiry 1969. President: Cons.Political Centre Nat.Adv.Cttee 1977-79; Nat Union of Cons. and Unionist Assoc 1983-84. Member Council of Management, Private Patients' Plan 1969-70; an Hon Vice-Pres., Consumers Assoc., 1974- . Hon LLD Wales 1988. *Publications:* various political pamphlets for Bow Group and Conservative Political Centre. *Recreation:* photography *Clubs:* Garrick, Athenaeum. *Address:* C/o House Of Commons, London SW1.

HOWE, Mr Allen, Barrister-at-Law *Currently:* Chairman, Medical Appeal Tribunals, Wales, since 1982. *Born on* 6 June 1918 at Barnsley, Yorks. *Son of* the late Frank and Dora Howe. *Marriage:* to Katherine Davies of Pontypridd, 1952. *Children:* Eryl and Elizabeth. *Educated at* Holgate Grammar School, Barnsley. *Career:* Served E.Yorks Regt. and R.W.A.F.G., 1939-46, France, Africa, India and Burma (Major); H.M.Colonial Administrative Service 1946-55, Senior District Commissioner; called to Bar, Middle Temple 1953; Judicial Adviser, Ashanti 1954-55; practised Wales and Chester Circuit 1955-59; Legal Dept., Welsh Board of Health 1959-65; Legal Dept., Welsh Office 1965-74; Circuit Administrator, Wales and Chester Circuit, Lord Chancellor's Dept., 1974-82. *Recreation:* golf, gardening, walking. *Clubs:* Radyr golf, Cardiff and County. *Address:* 2 Orchard Drive, Whitchurch, Cardiff CF4 2AE.

HOWE, Professor George Melvyn, BSc., MSc., PhD., DSc, FRSE. *Currently:* Retired Emeritus Professor of Geography, University of Strathclyde. *Born on* 7 April 1920 at Abercynon, Glam. *Son of* Reuben and Edith Howe. *Marriage:* to Patricia Graham Fennell 1947. *Children:* Gillian, Lise and Clare. *Educated at* Boys' Grammar School, Caerphilly; University College of Wales, Aberystwyth. *Career:* Served with R.A.F. 1940-46; Meteorological Branch 1940-42; Commissioned Intelligence (Air Photographic Interpretation) Branch 1942-46; Middle East Command. Lectr, later Senior Lectr. in Geography, University College of Wales, Aberystwyth 1948; University of Wales, Reader in Geography 1964; Foundation Professor of Geography, University of Strathclyde, Glasgow 1967-85; Visiting Professor, (Health & Welfare, Canada) 1977; Mem. Council Inst. of British Geographers (Pres. 1985);Mem. Medical Geography Cttee R.G.S., 1960- ; British Rep. on Medical Geography Commission of Intern. Geographical Union 1970- ; Mem. British National Ctee for Geography, Roy.Soc. 1978-83; Gill Memorial Award, Roy Geog. Soc., 1964. *Publications:* Wales from the Air 1957, 2nd edn. 1966;(with P. Thomas) Welsh Landforms and Scenery 1963; National Atlas of Disease Mortality in the United Kingdom 1963, 2nd. edn. 1970; The Soviet Union, 1968, 2nd edn. 1983; The U.S.S.R., 1971; Man, Environment and Disease in Britain 1972, wnd. edn. 1976; (ed.and contrib) Atlas of Glasgow and the West of Scotland 1972; (contrib.) Wales (ed.E.G. Bowen) 1958; (contrib.) Modern Methods in the History of Medicine (ed.E. Clark) 1970; (ed. with J.A. Loraine, and contrib.) Environmental Medicine 1973, 2nd. edn. 1980; (contrib.) Environment and Man (eds. J.Lenihan and W.W. Fletcher) 1976; (ed. and contrib.) A World Geography of Human Diseases 1977; (ed and contrib.) Global Geocancerology 1986; articles in geographical, meteorological, hydrological and medical journals. *Recreation:* Foreign travel. *Clubs:* Royal Air Force. *Address:* Hendre, 50 Heol Croes Faen, Nottage, Porthcawl CF36

3SW.

HOWELL, Mr Gwynne Richard, BSc Wales; Dip TP (Manchester) RMTPI. *Currently:* Opera Singer. *Born on* 13 June 1938 at Gorseinon, nr Swansea. *Son of* the late Gilbert and the late Ella Howell. *Marriage:* to Mary Morris. *Children:* Richard and Peter. *Educated at* Pontardawe Grammar; Swansea Art College; Swansea University, (Hon. Fellow); Manchester University. *Career:* Studies singing with Redvers Llewellyn while at UCW; pt time student, Manchester RCM, with Gwilym Jones, during DipTP trng at Manchester Univ; studies with Otakar Kraus 1968-72. Planning Asst, Kent CC, 1961-63; Sen.Planning Officer, Manchester Corp., 1965-68, meanwhile continuing to study music pt-time and giving public operatic performances which incl. the role of Pogner, in Die Meistersinger; as a result of this role, apptd Principal Bass at Sadler's Wells, 1968; also reached final of BBC Opera Singers competition for Nof Eng., 1967. In first season at Sadler's Wells, sang 8 roles, incl. Monterone and the Commendatore; appearances with Halle Orch., 1968 and 69; Arkel in Pelleas and Melisande, Glyndebourne and Covent Garden, 1969; Goffredo, in Il Pirato, 1969. Royal Opera House, Covent Garden: debut as First Nazarene, Salome 1969-70 season; the King, in Aida; Timur, in Turandot; Mephisto, in Damnation of Faust; Prince Gremin, in Onegin; High Priest, in Nabucco; Reinmar, in Tannhauser, 1973-74; (later role, Landgraf); Colline, in La Boheme; Pimen, in Boris Godunov; Ribbing, Un ballo in maschera; Padre Guardiano, in La forza del destino; Hobson, in Peter Grimes, 1975; Sparafucile, in Rigoletto, 1975-76 season; Ramfis in Aida, 1977; Tristan and Isolde, 1978, 1982; Luisa Miller 1978; Samson et Delilah 1981; Fiesco in Simon Boccanegra 1981; Pogner in Die Meistersinger 1982; Arkell in Pelleas et Melisande 1982; Dossifei in Khovanshchina 1982; Semel 1982; Die Zauberflote 1983; English National Opera: Don Carlos, Die Meistersinger 1974-75; The Magic Flute, Don Carlos 1975-76; Duke Bluebeard's Castle 1978; The Barber of Seville 1980 *Recreation:* Golf, good wine, walking, gardening, tennis. *Clubs:* MCC *Address:* 197 Fox Lane, London N13 4BB.

HOWELL, Professor John, *Currently:* Director, (O.D.I.)., since 1987. *Born on* 16 July 1941 at Welwyn Garden City. *Son of* Frederick Howell and the late Glenys Griffiths (deceased 1990). *Marriage:* divorced. *Educated at* University College, Swansea; University of Manchester. *Career:* Lecturer, University of Khartoum 1966-73; Senior Lecturer, University of Zambia 1974-77; Research Fellow, O.D.I. 1977-87; adviser: All Party Parliamentary Group on overseas development, HRH The Princess Royal's Africa Review Group; Member, National Executive Council, Voluntary Service Overseas (VSO); visiting professor, University of London (Wye College). *Publications:* Borrowers and Lenders, 1980; Agricultural Extension in Practice, 1988; Structural Adjustment and the African Farmer, 1991. *Clubs:* Royal Commonwealth Society. *Address:* Overseas Dev.Inst (O.D.I.), Regents College, Inner Circle, London., NW1 4NS. 11 St Marys Grove, London N1 2NT.

HOWELL, Professor John Bernard Lloyd, CBE; BSc; MBBS; PhD; FACP(Hon; FRCP. *Currently:* Retired, Emeritus Professor of Medicine; Chairman, Soton & S.W.Hants DHA; Chairman, Board of Science & Education,

BMA. *Born on* 1 Aug 1926 at Swansea. *Son of* David J and Hilda M. *Marriage:* to Heather Joan Rolfe, 1952. *Children:* Gillian, David and Peter. *Educated at* Swansea Grammar School; Middlesex Hospital Medical School, London. *Career:* Junior Medical posts at Middx and Brompton Hospitals, 1950- 51; RAMC, 1952-54; Senior Lecturer, Phys., Manchester Royal Infirmary, 1960-69; Foundation Prof. of Medicine, Southampton University 1969- ; Dean, Faculty of Med., Univ. of Soton 1978-83. President, British Thoracie Soc., 1988-89. President, B.M.A., 1989-90. *Publications:* On Respiratory physiology and medicine. *Recreation:* wine, France, DIY. *Address:* The Coach House, Bassett Wood Drive, Southampton SO2 3PT.

HOWELL, Major-General Lloyd, CBE., MA., BSc., CEng. *Currently:* Director, Building Trades Exhibitions Ltd., 1980- . *Born on* 28 Dec 1923 at Barry, Glam. *Son of* the late Thomas Idris Howell and the late Nancy Howell. *Marriage:* to 1).Hazel Barker (dec'd) 1945; 2). ElizabethBuchanan Husband (nee Atkinson) 1975. *Children:* Rhodri (dec'd) Geraint, Carys, Eirlys, Ceri, Dewi, Sara and Alwyn. *Educated at* Barry Grammar School; University College Cardiff; Royal Military College of Science. *Career:* Regimental & Staff Appointments Royal Artillery 1943-47; Instructor RMA Sandhurst 1949-53; Trials Officer, GW Ranges 1954-57; S02 (Education) Div.Hq., 1957-59; D.S. Royal Military Coll. of Science 1959-64; SEO Army Apprentices College 1964-67; Headmaster & Commandant, Duke of York's RM School 1967-72; Colonel (Ed) MOD 1972-74; Chief Education Officer, UKLF 1974-76; Director, Army Education 1976-80; Colonel Commandant RAEC 1982-86; Hon. Member City & Guilds of London Institute 1977- ; Consultant, Technical Education Development, Univ. Coll. Cardiff 1980-86; Fellow UCC 1980- ; Court of Governors UCC 1980- . *Recreation:* Gardening, golf, music, school governor. *Clubs:* Army & Navy. *Address:* c/o Midland Bank, The Forum, Old Town, Swindon Wilts., SN4 OAA.

HOWELL, Mr Michael Edward, CMG, 1989; OBE 1980. *Currently:* British High Commissioner, Mauritius, since 1989. *Born on* 2 May 1933 at Dinas Powis. *Son of* Edward and Fanny Howell. *Marriage:* to Joan Little 1958. *Children:* Christopher (b 1962) and Frances (b 1965). *Educated at* Newport High School. *Career:* HM Diplomatic Service; RAF 1951-53. Colonial Office 1953; CRO, 1958; Karachi 1959, 2nd Secretary: Bombay 1962. UK Delegation to Disarmament Cttee, Geneva 1966: 1st Secretary (Parly Cler), FCO, 1969; Consul (Comm) New York, 1973; NDC 1975; FCO, 1976; Head of Chancery, later Charge, Kabul, 1978; Consul-General: Berlin 1981;l Frankfurt, 1983; High Commissioner Papua New Guinea, 1986. *Recreation:* Tennis. *Address:* (Port Louis) C/o Foreign & Commonwealth Office, King Charles St, London, SW1A 2AH. Brisco Hill, 17 The Hills, Reedham, Norfolk, NR13 3TN.

HOWELL, Mr Peter Adrian, MA, M.Phil. *Currently:* Lecturer, Department of Classics, Royal Holloway and Bedford New College (University of London). *Born on* 29 July 1941 at Valletta, Malta. *Son of* Lt. Col. Harry Alfred Adrian Howell, MBE and Madge Maud Mary (nee Thompson). *Educated at* Downside School; Balliol College, Oxford. *Career:* Assistant Lecturer, then Lecturer, Department of Latin, Bedford College, (University of

London) 1964-85. *Publications:* Victorian Churches, 1968; Companion Guide to North Wales (with Elisabeth Beazley), 1975; Companion Guide to SouthWales (with Elisabreth Beazley), 1977; A Commentary on Book I of the Epigrams of Martial, 1980; (edited with Ian Sutton), The Faber Guide to Victorian Churches, 1989. *Recreation:* Art, Architecture, music. *Address:* Flat 1, 127 Banbury Road, Oxford OX2 6JX. 27 Ruskin House, Erasmus Street, London SW1P 4HU

HOWELL, Dr. Raymond C., PhD *Currently:* Senior Lecturer, Gwent College, 1981- . *Born on* 13 Dec 1947 *Son of* the late Dr. R.C. Howell and Marjorie (nee Hill). *Marriage:* to Jadwiga Szczuka 1977. *Children:* David. *Educated at* King's College, University of London. *Career:* Editor, Cymro Llundain 1979- ; Director, Archaeological excavations, Trelech, Gwent 1987- . *Publications:* Fedw Villages: A Lower Wye Valley History 1985; The Royal Navy & the Slave Trade 1987; A History of Gwent 1988, re-printed 1989; Early Peoples in Wales (forthcoming); Monographs, Teachers Guides: The Kingdom of Gwent 1986; Norman Gwent 1988; Yr Hen Iaith 1989; National Trust - The Romans 1991; Articles: numerous, including "Gwent-Bro Yr Hen Iaith", Cymro Llwndain 1988; "A report of excavations in Trelech 1987-89", Monmouth Archaelogy 1989; "A Prehistoric Assemblage from Trelech", Monmouth Archaeology 1989; "A report of the excavation of a medieval industrial site in Trelech", Medieval & Later Pottery in Wales 1989; Scripts: BBC series "Every Brooch Tells a Story" 1991. *Recreation:* Rugby, opera, stonework. *Clubs:* London Welsh R.F.C. *Address:* Bwthyn Y Ffynnon, St. Arvans, Nr. Chepstow, Gwent, NP6 6EZ.

HOWELL, Dr Tudor Morgan, M.B. B.Chir (Cantab). *Currently:* retired General Medical Practitioner, at Caersws 1960-90. *Born on* 24 May 1924 at Seven Sisters. *Son of* David John Howell and Annie (nee Morgan). *Marriage:* to Sara Margaret Janey Raven, 1953. *Children:* James Emlyn, Charlotte Janey and William Geoffrey *Educated at* West Monmouth School; Gonville & Caius College, Cambridge; St.Thomas's Hospital Medical School. *Career:* Royal Navy 1942-46. Past member Powys Health Authority; Past Vice-Chairman Powys Family Practitioner Committee; Past Vice-Chairman Powys Local Medical Committee. High Sheriff of Powys 1980-81. *Address:* Ynyswen, Trefeglwys, Newtown, Powys, SY17 5PH.

HOWELLS, Col. (William) Peter, CBE (1988), OBE (Mil, 1976), TD (1964, 2 clasps 1970 and 1976) DL. *Born on* 17 Oct 1931 *Son of* the late Lt-Col Percy Rotherham Howells and MaggieMay (nee Jones), MBE, JP. *Marriage:* to Marlene Jane, 1956, da of Richard Stanley Scourfield (d.1966). *Children:* Paul (b.1958) and Philip (b.1960) *Educated at* Ellesmere Coll Shropshire. *Career:* 1 Bn The Welch Regt,1950-52, 4 (V) Bn The Welch Regt 1952-69 (Hon Col 1982-); Pembroke Yeomanry 1967-69, 224 Sqdn RCT(V) 1969-71; CO 157 (Transport) Regt RCT (V) 1973-76; Col TA Wales 1977-80, Hon Col 4 (V) Bn Royal Regt of Wales 1982- ; MD and chairman Howells (Jewellers) Ltd., 1961- ; ADC to HM The Queen 1978-82, High Sheriff of Dyfed 1980-81, OstJ (1988, SUBStJ 1980); Wales Territorial Army Assoc: member West Wales Committee 1969- , member 1973- , chairman 1985, member Council Reserve Forces 1985- ; vice chairman Tax Cmmrs for Haverfordwest Dist 1984- (tax cmmr 1977- ; Nat Assoc of Round Tables: chairman Tenby Branch 1955 (founder vice chairman 1954), pres Haverfordwest Branch 1979 (founder chairman 1957); pres: Haverfordwest Rotary Club 1969, Little and Broad Haven Lifeboat Committee RNLI 1978- , St.John Ambulance Brigade Haverfordwest 1980- , Boys Brigade Co Haverfordwest 1982-83, Dyfed Committee Duke of Edinburgh Award Scheme 1988- ; Broad and Little Haven Branch Royal British Legion: member 1977- , vice president 1978-81, president 1981- , member Committee 1981- ; chairman Pembroke Yeomanry Dinner Club 1979- ; Royal British Legion: patron of Pembrokeshire Co.Branch 1980- , elected Vice President for Wales 1988, elected President for Wales 1992. Freeman Haverfordwest 1975. *Recreation:* motoring, shooting, walking, music. *Clubs:* Cardiff and County, Naval and Military. *Address:* 2 Quay Street, Haverfordwest, Pembrokeshire, Dyfed, SA61 1BG. Tel: 0437 762050.

HOWELLS, David John, BDS; MScD (Wales); LDS; D.Orth; M.Orth; FDSRCS, Eng. *Currently:* Consultant in Orthodontics to South Glamorgan and East Dyfed Health Authorities, and in private practice. *Born on* 14 March 1953 at Crws Oswallt. *Son of* Ivor Mervyn and Veronica Carey Howells. *Marriage:* to Lisa Pauline Noble, 1979. *Children:* Lowri Elisabeth and Ffion Angharad. *Educated at* Abraham Darby School, Telford, Shropshire. *Career:* London Hospital Medical College, Dental School 1972-77; Surgical training in London, Shrewsbury and Cardiff 1978-80; Postgraduate Student of Orthodontics at Welsh Nat. School of Medicine 1980-82; Registrar Queen Alexandra Hospital, Portsmouth 1982-84; Senior Registrar Birmingham Dental Hospital 1984-87; Consultant appointment 1987; Clinical Director Morriston Hospital 1989- ; and Prince Phillip Hospital, Llanelli 1991-; Chairman: W.Glam District Dental Advisory Committee and S.W.Wales section British Dental Association. *Publications:* several publications in specialist journals. *Recreation:* hill walking, SCUBA diving, conservation, photography. *Address:* Maxillofacial Department, Morriston Hospital, Swansea SA6 6NL. Tel: 0792 703101.

HOWELLS, Mr Geraint Wyn, *Currently:* M.P. Liberal, elected 1974. *Born on* 15 April 1925 at Ponterwyd. *Son of* David John and Mary Blodwen Howells. *Marriage:* yes. *Children:* Gaenor and Mari *Educated at* Ponterwyd P. School; Ardwyn Grammar School, Abersytwyth *Career:* Farmer; Vice Chairman, British Wool Board, 1972-83; Pres. of the Royal Welsh Show, 1983; Mbr.Cardiganshire C.C., 1952-73; mbr.of the Gorsedd, National Eisteddfod of Wales, Sec. Ponterwyd Eisteddfod since 1944; *Publications:* Rural Wales in Crisis *Recreation:* Walking, rugby and football *Address:* Glennydd, Ponterwyd, Cardiganshire, Dyfed.

HOWELLS, Dr Kim Scott, BA (Jt.Hons); PhD. *Currently:* MP Pontypridd, 1989- . *Born on* 27 Nov 1946 at Merthyr. *Son of* Glanville James and Joan Glenys (nee Edwards). *Marriage:* to Eirlys Davies 1983. *Children:* Seren, Cai and Scott. *Educated at* Penywaun Primary; Mountain Ash Grammar; Hornsey Coll. Art London; Cambridge CAT; Warwick University. *Career:* Steelworker 1969-70; Coalminer 1970-71; Lecturer 1975-79; Research Officer Swansea University 1979-82; Research Officer/Editor NUM S. Wales area 1982-89; various Radio, TV and newspaper wirting/presentation 1986-89. *Publications:* Various: mainly

Energy, Labour history and journalism. *Recreation:* Mountaineering, jazz, film and literature. *Clubs:* Llantwit Fadre CC; Hopkinstown CC; Pontypridd RFC. *Address:* 30 Berw Road, Pontypridd, Mid Glamorgan., , CF37 2AA. House Of Commons, London SW1 1AA.

HOWELLS, Michael Sandbrook, *Born on* 29 May 1939 at Pembroke Dock. *Son of* the late Benjamin George Howells and the late Blodwen (nee Francis). *Marriage:* to Pamela Vivian, da of the late Gordon Harry Francis of West Clandon, Surrey, 1966. *Children:* Luke (b.1970) and Toby (b.1972). *Educated at* Bryntirion School, Bridgend; Dean Close School, Cheltenham; University College London. *Career:* Solicitor 1966, partner, Price & Kelway, solicitors, 1971 (senior partner, 1980); Chairman, Milford Haven Round Table, 1971-72; HM Coroner for Pembrokeshire, 1980; member, Council of The Law Society of England & Wales, 1983; member, Supreme Court Rules Committee, 1985-90; member, Council of Coroners' Society of England & Wales, 1986; President, Milford Haven Civic Society, 1990; member, Milford Haven Rotary Club, 1991. *Recreation:* theatre, bee-keeping, messing about in boats. *Clubs:* RAC; Waterloo, Milford Haven; Neyland Yacht. *Address:* Glenowen, Mastlebridge, Milford Haven, Pembrokeshire, SA73 1QS Tel: 0646 600208 Price & Kelway, 17 Hamilton Terrace, Milford Haven, Pembrokeshire, SA73 31A. Tel: 0646 695311 Fax: 0646 695848.

HOWELLS, Roger Godfrey, ACA *Currently:* Partner in Cavells Chartered Accountants since 1985; Partner FGS Cavells Insolvency Services. *Born on* 21 Oct 1954 at Bridgend. *Son of* Hilda and Godfrey Frank Howells. *Marriage:* divorced. *Educated at* Bridgend Boys Grammar School; Polytechnic of Wales. *Career:* Gordon H. Down and Partners, Cardiff 1974; Burton Sweet & Co., Bristol 1978; Bruce N. Simmonds & Associates, Bristol 1980. Director of Mutual Accountants Professional Indemnity Club 1987. *Recreation:* golf, motor racing, music, travel *Clubs:* Dewstow Golf. *Address:* Ross Cottage, Northwick Road, Pilning, Bristol, BS12 3HB.

HOWKINS, Dr John, MD gold medal, MS, FRCS, FRCOG *Currently:* Retired. *Born on* 17 Dec 1907 at Hartlepool. *Son of* John Drysdale and Helen Louise. *Marriage:* to Lena Brown 1940. *Children:* William, Sarah and Jane. *Educated at* Shrewsbury & London University, Arts Scholar, Middx. Hospital, 1926. *Career:* Gynaecological Surgeon to St Bartholomew's Hospital 1946-69 (Hon. Consultant Gynaecologist since 1969) to Hampstead General Hospital 1946-67 (Hon. Consultant Gynaecologist since 1968) and to Royal Masonic Hospital, 1948-73; House Surgeon and Casualty Surgeon Middx. Hospital 1932-34; RMO Chelsea Hosp. for Women 1936; Gynaecological Registrar, Middx. Hosp., 1937-38; Resident Obstetric Surg., st Bartholomew's Hosp., 1938 and 1945; Temp. Wing-Comdr, RAFVR Med. Br., 1939-45; Hunterian Prof. RCS 1947; William Meredith Fletcher Shaw Lectr, RCOG 1975; Sometime Examiner in Midwifery to Univs of Cambridge and London, RCOG, Conjoint Bd of England. Chm., Council Ski Club of Great Britain 1964-67 (Hon. Life Member 1968, Trustee 1969-); Mem., Gynaecological Traveller's Club. *Publications:* Shaw's Textbook of Gynaecological Surgery, 7th edn 1964, 8th edn 1974. *Recreation:* gardening, building and fishing. *Clubs:* Ski Club of Great Britain; Gynaecological Travellers.

Address: Caen Hen, Abercegir, Machynlleth, Powys, SY20 8NR.

HUBBARD, William Victor, JP retired 1985. *Born on* 20 June 1925 at Aberaeron. *Son of* the late John Aeron William and the late Jennie (nee Evans). *Marriage:* 1st to Valmai, 1953 (decd); 2nd to Joan, 1980. *Children:* Avril, Jeffrey and Neil from 1st marriage. *Educated at* National and County Schools, Aberaeron. *Career:* Wm Hubbard & Sons 1939-43; Services A.P.T.C., 1944-48; South Wales Elec. Board 1948-55; P.D. J.D. Lloyd 1955-85; Company Director R.G. Purser Limited, Glynneath 1964-67; Company Director PTD Lloyd 1969-82; Fellow Inst. of Builders Merchants 1970-85; member Dyfed/Powys Police Authority. Chairman Dyfed Magistrates Courts Committee 1991-92. Sport: President Welsh Bowling Association 1983; Manager of Welsh Bowling Team 1985-88; President, British Isles Bowling Council 1991. *Recreation:* bowls, football. *Clubs:* Sports. *Address:* Gorsaf Dawel, Aberaeron, Dyfed, SA46 ODU.

HUBBARD-MILES, Mr Peter Charles, C.B.E. *Currently:* Retired. *Born on* 9 May 1927 at Mynyddislwyn. *Son of* Charles Hubbard and Ruth Agnes (nee Lewis). *Marriage:* to Pamela Wilkinson 1948. *Children:* Penelope Anne, Piers, Philippa Jane, Pamela Jane and Peter St. John. *Educated at* Lewis' School Pengam. *Career:* R.A.F., 1945-48; Member for Bridgend 1983-87; Contested Aberavon 1974; Committees: Member, Inter Parliamentary Union; Member B.A.P.G.; Committees: Member Select Ctee for Welsh Affairs; Political *Career:* Member Mid-Glamorgan County Council 1967-89 and leader of its group of Conservative Councillors since 1974; Member Porthcawl Urban District Council 1970-74; Chairman South Wales Group of Conservative Associations 1973-76; Member Ogwr Borough Council 1974-87; leader of the opposition 1974-83; President Aberavon Conservative Association 1976-83; first Conservative Mayor of Ogwr Borough 1979-80; Chairman Wales Area Local Government Advisory Committee 1979-82; PPS to Secretary of State for Wales 1985-87; Special political interest: Health, Education Self-employed businessman; Awarded CBE 1981; Member Ogwr Borough Council 1991- . *Recreation:* Theatre. *Address:* 18 Lougher Gardens, Porthcawl, CF36 3BJ.

HUDSON-WILLIAMS, Prof. Harri Llwyd, M.A. Emeritus Professor of Greek, Univ. of Newcastle upon Tyne (formerly King's Coll. Newcastle upon Tyne, Univ. of Durham). *Born on* 16 Feb 1911 at Bangor. *Son of* the late Prof. T. Hudson-Williams and the late Gwladys (nee Williams). *Marriage:* to Joan (nee Fisher), 1946. *Children:* Sarah Charis and Catherine. *Educated at* Friars School Bangor; Univ. Coll., of N. Wales; King's Coll., Cambridge; Univ. of Munich. *Career:* Assist. Lect. in Greek, Liverpool Univ. 1937-40; Intelligence Corps. 1940-41; Foreign Office, 1941-45; Reader in Greek, King's Coll., Newcastle upon Tyne, 1950-52; Professor of Greek, King's Coll., Newcastle upon Tyne, 1952-76; Head of Dept. of Classics, 1969-76; Dean of Faculty of Arts, 1963-66. *Publications:* Contributions to various classical journals etc. *Recreation:* Gardening *Address:* The Pound, Mill Street, Islip, Oxon, OX5 2SZ. Tel: 08675 5893.

HUGGINS, The Hon Jean Audrey, *Currently:* Charitable works. *Born on* 2 Feb 1932 at Canterbury. *Daughter of* the late Lord and Lady Wigg. *Marriage:* to Andrew Henry

Huggins, 1955. *Children:* Cecilia Ann, Sally Edwina and Sara Minette *Educated at* St.Dominic's High School, Stoke-on-Trent. *Recreation:* gardening, reading, travel *Address:* Ty Eiddew, Garndolbenmaen, Gwynedd, N Wales, LL51 9TZ.

HUGH-JONES, Sir Wynn Normington, LVO, MA, FBIM. *Currently:* (Voluntary) Govr Queen Elizabeth Foundation for the Disabled. Vice Chairman Euro-Atlantic Group. Trustee Wilts Community Foundation. *Born on* 1 Nov 1923 at Llangollen. *Son of* the late Huw Hugh-Jones and the late May Hugh-Jones (nee Normington). *Marriage:* 1st to Ann (nee Purkiss), 1958, one s two d.; 2nd to Oswynne (nee Buchanan). *Children:* Julia, Robert and Katherine. *Educated at* Llangollen CS; Ludlow GS; Selwyn College, Cambridge. *Career:* RAF 1943-46; Foreign Service (Diplomatic Service) 1947-73. Served FO., Jeddah, Paris, Conakry, Rome (head of Chancery), F.C.O., Elizabethville (now Lubumbaski), Ottawa (Counsellor and Head of Chancery), F.C.O., Lord President's Office, Cabinet Office. English Speaking Union:- Director-General 1973-77; Liberal Party: Secretary-General 1977-83, Hon.joint Treasurer 1984-87. *Recreation:* golf, gardening *Address:* Fosse House, Avebury, Nr Marlborough, Wilts, SN8 1RF.

HUGHES, Mr Aneurin Rhys, BA *Currently:* Ambassador and head of Delegation. of the European Commission. Oslo, Norway 1987- . *Born on* 11 Feb 1937 *Son of* William Hughes of Swansea and Hilda Hughes. *Marriage:* to Jill Salisbury 1964. *Children:* Elis and Sion. *Educated at* Swansea GS; Oregon City HS, USA; UCW Aberystwyth. *Career:* Pres. NUS 1962-64, res. on Higher Education in South America; HM Dip Dip Serv FO London 1966-68; First sec: Political Advsrs's Office (later Br.High Cmmn) Singapore 1968-70; Br. Embassy Rome 1971-73; Secretariat General of the Euro Community: head Div for International Co-ordination 1973-76, advsr to Spokesman and DG for Infor 1977-80, chef de cabinet of Ivor Richard (memb Euro Cmmn) 1981-85; chm. Selection Bd. for Candidates from Spain and Portugal 1985-87. *Recreation:* Squash, golf, music, hashing. *Clubs:* Travellers'. *Address:* European Commission Delegation, Haakon VII's Gate 6, P.O.Box 1643 Vika, 0119 Oslo 1 Norway.

HUGHES, Dr. Antony Elwyn, MA., DPhil., FInst.P. *Currently:* Director Programmes and Deputy Chairman, Science and Engineering Research Council. *Born on* 9 Sept 1941 at Glan Conway, Clwyd. *Son of* Ifor Elwyn and Anna Betty Hughes (nee Ambler). *Marriage:* to Margaret Mary Lewis 1963. *Children:* Stephen Antony, Sarah Margaret, James Elyn and Joanna Mary *Educated at* Newport H.S. Gwent and Jesus College, Oxford *Career:* Harkness Fellow, Cornell Univ. USA, 1967-69; Scientist, Ukaea Harwell Laboratory 1969-75; Individual Merit Appointment, Harwell 1975-81; Senior Personal Appointment, Harwell 1981-83; Head, Materials Physics and Metallurgy Division, Harwell 1983-86; Director Underlying and Non-Nuclear Energy Research 1986-87; Chief Scientist, Ukaea 1987-88; Director Laboratories Serc. 1988-91. *Publications:* Real Solids and Radiation (1975); Defects and Their Structure in Non-Metallic Solids (ed 1976) *Recreation:* Walking, cycling watching rugby and cricket, music and gardening. *Address:* Science & Eng Research Council, Polaris House, North Star Avenue, Swindon, Wilts, SN2 1ET. Kingswood, King's Lane, Harwell, Didcot, Oxon, OX11 OEJ.

HUGHES, His Hon. Judge David Morgan, LL.B. (Hons) London *Currently:* H.M. Circuit Judge, Wales & Chester Circuit, 1972- . *Born on* 20 Jan 1956 at Brynsiencyn. *Son of* the late Rev. John Edward Hughes, BA., BD., and the Mrs M.E. Hughes, M.B.E. *Marriage:* to Elizabeth Jane Roberts, 1956. *Children:* Janet Mary, Karen Elizabeth and David Richard. *Educated at* Beaumaris Grammar School; UCNW Bangor; London Univ; McGill Univ.Montreal (Post Graduate) *Career:* Army, Captain 2nd Welch Regt. Burma, 1944-47; Univ. of London L.S.E., LL.B.(Hons), 1948-51; Institute of International Airlaw, McGill Univ, Rockefeller Foundation Fellowship, 1951-52; Called to the Bar, Middle Temple, 1953; Practised at the Bar, Wales & Chester Circuit, 1953-72; Dep. Chairman Caernarfon Quarter Sessions, 1970-72; Recorder Crown Courts, 1972; Mbr Mental Health Review Tribunal; Mbr Council of H.M. Circuit Judges; Past Dep.Chairman Agric. Lands Tribunal Wales. *Recreation:* Gardening, tennis, cricket, travelling and reading. *Address:* Chester Crown Court, The Castle, Chester.

HUGHES, Dr Glyn Tegai, MA., PhD. *Born on* 18 Jan 1923 at Chester. *Son of* the late Rev. John Hughes and the late Ketura (nee Evans). *Marriage:* to Margaret Vera Herbert of Brisbane, Queensland 1957. *Children:* Alun Tegai and David Tegai. *Educated at* Newtown and Towyn Co. School; Liverpool Institute; Manchester Grammar; Corpus Christi College, Cambridge. *Career:* RWF 1942-46, temp Major DAAG HQ ALFSEA; Lektor in English, University of Basel 1951-53; Lecturer in Comparative Literary Studies 1953-64 and Tutor to the Faculty of Arts 1961-64, University of Manchester; Warden of Gregynog, University of Wales 1964-89; BBC National Governor for Wales and Chairman Broadcasting Council for Wales 1971-79; Member Board of Channel 4 TV 1980-87, and Authority of S4C 1981-87; Liberal candidate West Denbigh 1950, 1955, 1959; Member Welsh Arts Council 1976-76; Chairman Undeb Cymru Fydd 1968-70; Vice President North Wales Arts Association 1977- ; Chairman Welsh Broadcasting Trust 1988- ; Member Yr Academi Gymreig; Methodist Local Preacher; Chairman Relate Mid-Wales. *Publications:* Eichendorff's Taugenichts 1961; Romantic German Literature 1979; Thomas Olivers (ed.1979); Williams Pantycelyn 1983; Gwasg Gregynog 1970-90 (ed. with David Esslemont 1990). *Recreation:* Book collecting, shrub propagation. *Address:* Rhyd-y-Gro, Tregynon, Newtown, Powys. SY16 3PR. Tel: 0686 650609.

HUGHES, Dr Graham Robert Vivian, MD (Lond), FRCP. *Currently:* Consultant Rheumatologist, St.Thomas' Hospital, London; Head of Lupus Arthritis Research Unit, Rayne Institute, St.Thomas' Hospital, since 1987. *Born on* 26 Nov 1940 *Son of* the late Robert Arthur Gwylfor and the late EmilyElizabeth. *Marriage:* to Monica Ann, 1966. *Children:* Sarah Imogen and Richard John Vivian. *Educated at* Ardwyn Grammar School, Aberystwyth; Cardiff High School for Boys; University of Wales, Cardiff; The London Hospital Medical College. *Career:* Posts in London Hospital; Visiting fellow Columbia University, New York 1969-70; Head of Rheumatology and Reader, Royal Postgraduate Medical School, Hammersmith Hospital London 1975-85. *Publications:* 6 books including "Connective Tissue Diseases" and "Lupus-a guide for patients"; 600 publications, largely in Rheumatology research. *Recreation:*

piano (classical and jazz), tennis, sailing. *Address:* Dept. Of Rheumatology, St.Thomas Hospital, London SE1.

HUGHES, Mr Harold Victor, CBE; BSc; FRAgS; Hon. Assoc. RICS. *Currently:* retired 1990, Principal Emeritus Royal Agric. College. *Born on* 2 Feb 1926 at Waters Hill, Kilgetty, Pembrokeshire. *Son of* Thomas Brindley and Hilda Hughes. *Educated at* Redberten N.P. School; Greenhill Grammar School Tenby; University College of Wales, Aberystwyth. *Career:* Lecturer, Pencoed Training School for Ex-Servicement, 1947-50; National Agricultural Advisory Service, 1950- ; Lecturer, Royal Agricultural College, Cirencester, 1950-54; Vice-Principal, Brooksby Agric. College, Leics, 1954–60; Farms Director, Royal Agric. College, 1960-78; Vice Principal, Royal Agric. College, 1976-78; Principal, Royal Agric. College, 1978-90. *Publications:* numerous articles in Farming Journals. *Recreation:* Shooting, travelling. *Address:* 17 Quakers Row, Coates, Cirencester, Glos., GL7 6JX.

HUGHES, Professor Ieuan Arwel, MD., FRCP(C)., FRCP., MA(Cantab) *Currently:* Professor of Paediatrics and Head of Dept., Univ. of Cambridge; Honorary Consultant Paediatrician to Cambridge Health Authority. *Born on* 9 Nov 1944 at Cardiff. *Son of* the late Arwel Hughes and Enid (nee Phillips). *Marriage:* to Margaret Maureen Davies, 1969. *Children:* Mari Arwel, Gareth Arwel and Wiliam Arwel *Educated at* Howardian High School, Cardiff; Univ. Of Wales Coll.of Medicine, Cardiff. *Career:* Senior House Officer in Paediatrics, Hammersmith Hospital, London 1969; Medical Registrar, Univ. Coll.Hospital, London 1970-72; Senior Resident in Paediatrics, Dalhousie Univ. Canada, 1972-74; Paediatric Research Fellow, Tenovus Inst. Cardiff 1976-79; Senior Lec. later reader, Dept. of Child Health, Univ. of Wales Coll. of Medicine, Cardiff 1979-89; Sec.European Society for Paediatric Endocrinology 1987-92, President 1993: *Publications:* Scientific papers on paediatric endocrine diseases; Handbook of Endocrine Tests in Children, Butterworths. *Recreation:* Music, walking, travel, squash and cycling. *Clubs:* British Paediatric Association; Royal College of Physicians of London. *Address:* 4 Latham Road, Cambridge CB2 2EQ. Dept. Of Paediatrics, Addenbrooke's Hospital, Hills Road, Cambridge, CB2 2QQ.

HUGHES, Dr John Bowen, MSc, PhD, FSS, *Currently:* Lecturer in Mathematics, UCNW Bangor since 1961; Chairman Finance Committee Gwynedd C.C. since 1987; Member, University of Wales Council, since 1986. *Born on* 30 July 1929 at Llanrwst. *Son of* the late Edward John Hughes and the late Margaret (nee Williams). *Marriage:* to Blodwen Eluned Evans, 1957. *Children:* Sian Bowen, Ceri Bowen, Geraint Bowen and Rhys Bowen. *Educated at* Llanrwst Grammar School *Career:* Plessey Nucleonic Northampton, 1957-58; AEI-John Thompson Nuclear Power Co., Knutsford, 1958-59; Salford College of Advanced Technology, 1959-61; Ynys Mon Plaid Cymru Election Agent, 1969, 74, 83 and 87. *Publications:* various papers on Mathematics (especially Operations Research), in learned journals. *Recreation:* walking, climbing, music. *Address:* Goyllwyn, Benllech., Gwynedd LL74 8SG. School Of Mathematics, UCNW, Bangor, Gwynedd Tel: 0248 351151

HUGHES, Professor Leslie Ernest, DS., FRCS., FRACS. *Currently:* Professor of Surgery, University of Wales College of Medicine, 1971-. *Born on* 12 August 1932 at Parramatta, N.S.W. Australia. *Son of* the late Charles Joseph Hughes and the late Vera Dorothy (nee Raines). *Marriage:* to Marian Castle 1955. *Children:* Bronwyn, Gillian, Graeme and Stephen. *Educated at* Parramatta High School; University of Sydney. *Career:* Surgical Training, Sydney Hospitals 1955-59; Surgical Registrar Derby and West Middlesex Hospitals 1959-71; BECC Cancer Research Fellow, King's College Hospital, London 1962-63; Reader in Surgery, University of Queensland 1964-71; Eleanor Roosevelt International Scholar, Roswell Park Memorial Institute, Buffalo NY, 1969-70; Hon. Consultant Surgeon, Cardiff Royal Infirmary, University Hospital of Wales, 1971-; Examiner FRCS England 1974-80, 1985-91; External examiner, Universities of London, Edinburgh, Aberdeen, Sheffield, Liverpool, Bristol; President, Melanoma Study Group 1985-87; President Welsh Surgical Society 1991-92; President Surgical Research Society 1992-94. *Publications:* Benign Disorders of the Breast, Bailliere 1989; numerous papers on surgery of cancer, colon, immunology etc. *Recreation:* Music, gardening. *Address:* Dept of Surgery, University Of Wales College of Medicine, Cardiff CF4 4XN.

HUGHES, Dr Louis, *Born on* 10 March 1932 *Son of* the late Richard Hughes and the late Anne (nee Green). *Marriage:* to Margaret Caroline Mary, 1959, da of Thomas Cyril Wootton, of Newport, Gwent. *Children:* Christopher (b.1964) and Deborah (b.1960) *Educated at* Holyhead County School; Univ Coll Cardiff; Welsh Nat School of Med. (MB,BCh,DObst). *Career:* Capt RAMC (TA) 1964; pt/t MO (infertility) Queen Charlotte and Chelsea Hospital 1979- conslt. (infertility) Margaret Pyke Centre 1979- ; mem management committee Int Wine and Food Soc (chm 1982-86), chm Childless Trust 1980-83; Freeman City of London 1975, mem Worshipful Soc of Apothecaries 1974; RCOG, FRSM, MBMA, mem Br Fertility Soc, Br Andrology Soc, mem American Fertility Soc. *Publications:* numerous papers on infertility, Monographs on Wine. *Recreation:* golf, wine and food, cricket, book collecting. *Clubs:* MCC, Savile, Saintsbury, Denham GC. *Address:* Beechwood, Burton's Lane, Chalfon St Giles, Bucks, HP8 4BA. 99 Harley Street, London W1.

HUGHES, Councillor Mark James, *Currently:* Chairman, Lightning Skills Ltd; Executive, Vendridge Limited. *Born on* 23 Sept 1961 at Enfield, Middlx. *Son of* the late Kenneth James and the late Diane Margaret (nee Bennett). *Marriage:* to Hazel Jean Pleasance 1986. *Educated at* Sheredes School, Herts; Kingsway Princeton College, London. *Career:* Communications Manager, GKN Stern Osmat Ltd., 1980-85; Computer Operations Controller, E.Herts D.C., 1985- ; Freelance work with Hughes Computer Serv., 1989- ; Joined Conservative Party, 1979; Political Officer Broxbourne Young Cons., 1983-84; Const.Chrmn Broxbourne Young Cons., 1984-85; Eastern Area Young Const., Management Commt. 1984-86; Vice-Chrmn. Broxbourne Const.Cons.Assoc., 1984-86; Broxbourne Const. Cons.Assoc.CTU Chrmn., 1985-87; North Herts. Const. Cons.Assoc.Rep. on Eastern Earea CPC., 1985- ; Founder N.Herts. Young Cons., 1986-; Const.Chrmn N.Herts Young Cons., 1987-88; Sec. and Vice Chrmn. Royston Cons.Assoc., 1987-88; Vice-Chrmn.N.Herts Const.Cons.Assoc., 1987-88; Chrmn. Royston Campaigning Commt. 1988-89; Treasurer & mbr. Union Exec. Nat.Assoc. of Local Govrn.Officer,

1986-88; Vice-Chrmn: Royston Town Council Planning Commt, 1987- ,North Herts D.C.Planning Commt, 1988- , N.Herts D.C. Transport Commt, 1988- ; School Governor Roysia Middle School, 1988- ; Former mbr National Youth Theatre; qualified Football referee; mbr. Sports Council; mbr. Town Twinning Assoc; Mayor of Royston, 1990-91; Prospective Parliamentary candidate for Merthyr Tydfil & Rhymney, 1990; Chrmn. Public Transport Commt, N.Herts D.C., 1991. *Recreation:* Travel; Association football and Historical studies *Address:* 'Little Acorns', 9 Betony Vale, Royston, Herts.

HUGHES, Michael,BA(Econ), MSc(Econ), AMSIA. *Currently:* Managing Director, BZW Economics & Strategy; Director BZW Securities Ltd. *Born on* 26 Feb 1951. at St.Asaph. *Son of* Leonard and Gwyneth Mair Hughes. *Marriage:* 11th February 1978. *Children:* Sophie Charlotte and Harriet Rose. *Educated at* Manchester University; London School of Economics. *Career:* Executive Director, BZW Gilts Ltd., 1986-89; Partner, de Zoete & Bevan 1982-96; Associate member and Chief Economist de Zoete & Bevan 1980-82; Senior Economist, de Zoete & Bevan 1976-80; Economist, Capel-Cure Myers 1975-76; Economist, BP Pension Fund 1973-75. *Publications:* Journal of Investment Analysts; regular contributions to "The Times". *Recreation:* horse riding, music. *Clubs:* Gresham, National Liberal. *Address:* Ebbgate House, 2 Swan Lane, London EC2R 3TS. Tel: 071 623 2323.

HUGHES, Owen Gareth,BA, Dip.Social Admin. *Currently:* Director, Wales Regional Co-ordinator NFHA then Director Welsh Federation of Housing Association, since 1987. *Born on* 26 Nov 1942 at Bangor, Gwynedd. *Son of* Owen Hughes and Gwendoline (nee Roberts). *Marriage:* to Christine Mary O'Meara, 1980. *Children:* Aneurin, Robert, Bethan and Rhian. *Educated at* Friars Grammar School; Coleg Harlech; London School of Economics. *Career:* Compositor (apprentice) Printer, North Wales Chronicle 1959-64; Field Worker/Agent Conwy Constituency Labour Party 1964-65; Full time Education 1965-68/9; Tutor organiser WEA East Midlands, part-time Lecturer Extra Mural Dept., Nottingham University 1969-71; Deputy then Head Intelligence Dept., Nat Council of Social Service 1971-75; Deputy Director NFHA 1975-87. *Publications:* numerous housing publications *Recreation:* sport, music, politics. *Address:* 23 St.Martins Road, Caerffili, Mid Glamorganshire CF8 1EF.

HUGHES, MP Royston John, *Currently:* M.P. *Born on* 9 June 1925 at Pontllanfraith, Gwent. *Son of* John Hughes (miner) and Alice. *Marriage:* 1957. *Children:* Rosemary Eluned, Pamela Hilda and Meriel Ann. *Educated at* Pontllanfraith Grammar School *Career:* Elected MP Newport 1966; Newport East since 1983; Front bench spokesman Welsh Affairs 1984-88; Member of Speakers Panel 1990; Chairman Welsh Grand Cttee 1990; Member of Council of Europe 1990; WEV Treasurer later Parliamentary Union (British Group) 1990. *Recreation:* Rugby - Life member Newport RFC; Vice President Crawshay; RFC Wales. *Clubs:* United Service Mens, Cardiff - Life Member; Caldicot Labour Club, Pontllanfraith Workingmens Club. *Address:* Chapel Field,Chapel Lane, Abergavenny, Gwent, NP7 7BT. 68 Vanbrugh Court, Kensington, London SE11

HUGHES, Mr Thomas Merfyn, LL.B. *Currently:* Barrister-at-Law and Recorder, since 1991, of the Crown Court. *Born* on 8 April 1949 at Rhuddlan, Clwyd. *Son of* John Medwyn Hughes and Jane Blodwen (nee Roberts). *Marriage:* to Patricia Joan Talbot, 1977. *Children:* Caitlin Mary, Thomas Jenkin Edmund and Joshua Edward Talbot. *Educated at* Rydal School, Colwyn Bay; Liverpool University; Inns of Court, School of Law. *Career:* Called to the Bar 1971; member Honourable Society of Inner Temple; practising Wales and Chester Circuit 1971- ; Assistant Recorder 1986. Labour Parliamentary Candidate, Arfon, 1979. *Recreation:* sailing rugby, squash. *Clubs:* Royal Anglesey Yacht, Bangor Rugby. *Address:* Plas Llanfaes, Beaumaris, Gwynedd LL58 8RH. 40 King Street, Chester CH1 2AH Tel: 0244 323886.

HUGHES, Sir Trevor Poulton, KCB 1982 (CB 1974); C.Eng; FICE;Hon FIWES;Hon Fellow Poly Wales *Currently:* Chairman B. & C.E.H.M. Co.Ltd.; B. & C.E. Benefits Scheme Trustee Ltd since 1987. *Born on* 28th Sept 1925 at Ffynnongroyw. *Son of* the late Rev. John Evan Hughes and the late Mary Grace Hughes. *Marriage:* 1st to Mary Ruth Walwyn, 1950 (marr.diss);2nd to Barbara June Davison, 1978. *Children:* Michael Hywel and Anthony David (from 1st marriage). *Educated at* Ruthin School *Career:* R.E. 1945-48 Captain 13 Fld. Svy. Co.; Municipal engineering 1948-61; Min. of Transport 1961-62; Min. of Housing and Local Government Engineering Inspectorate 1962-70; Dep. Chief Engineer 1970-71; Dir. 1971-72 and Dir. Gen. 1972-74 Water Engineering DoE; Dep. Sec. Environmental Protection DoE 1974-77; Dep. Sec. Dept. of Transport 1977-80; Permanent Secretary Welsh Office 1980-85; Vice Chairman Public Works Congress 1975-89; Chairman 1989-90; Member British Waterways Board 1985-88; Vice-President, I.C.E. 1984-86; Chief Govt. Delegate PIANC 1985-91. *Recreation:* Gardening; reading; music *Address:* Clearwell,13 Brambleton Ave, Farnham, Surrey GU9 8RA.

HUGHES - PARRY, Thomas Antony,FCA *Currently:* Partner, Beer Aplin, Chartered Accountants, Exeter, since 1979. *Born on* 9 Feb 1949 at Port Dickson, Malaysia. *Son of* the late Thomas Hughes-Parry and Rachael (nee Roger). *Marriage:* to Rosemary Constance Foster, 1976. *Children:* Thomas David and Philip John. *Educated at* Canford School; Exeter University. *Career:* Articled with Harmood Banner 1969-73; Deloitte Haskins & Sells, Investigation Department 1974-78; member, South West Society of Chartered Accountants Technical Advisory Committee 1979-90; Chairman, Exeter and District Society of Chartered Accountants 1990-91; SWESCA General practitioner board representative 1990- . *Recreation:* squash, fishing, yoga, reading, classical music. *Address:* Tregenna, 14 Longlands, Dawlish, Devon EX7 9NF. Cam O'r Fechan, Maesmawr Road, Llangollen, Clwyd.

HUGHES DAVIES, Mr Colin, BA., M.Litt., FCIS., DL *Currently:* Chmn. Colchester Estates (Holdings); Director, Inst. of Welsh Affairs. *Born on* 23 May 1928 at London. *Son of* the late John Davies and the late Mary Elizabeth (nee Hughes). *Marriage:* to Helena Mary 1947. *Children:* Philip Anthony and Susan Elizabeth. *Educated at* Clifton, Bristol University and Magdalen Coll. Oxford. *Career:* National Service, Royal Navy, Fleet Air Arm. pilot, 1948-50; Director, Western Plant & Equipt. Ltd., 1950-65; Director,Colchester Estates (Holdings) 1950- ; In. motor racing driver, mbr British Racing Drivers' Club, 1955-58; Amateur Nat. Hunt Jockey, 1958-64; Nat. Hunt Trainer, 1964-78; Derby Award as N.H. Trainer of the Year, 1969; Trained the N.H. Horse of the Year, 1968, 1969 and 1970; Mbr. of Council, The Sail Training Assoc, 1977- ; Deputy Chairman Schooner Commt. 1978-86; Chairman, National Advisory Commt. 1980-82; National Commt, Boys Clubs of Wales, 1965- ; Vice President 1981- ; Freeman of the City of London, 1967; Freeman of the Guild of Air Pilots and Navigators, 1967; D.T.I. Yachtmaster, 1978; Fellow, Royal Society of Arts, 1982; Fellow, British Inst. of Management, 1984; Governor, St. John's School, Chepstow, 1985; H.M. High Sheriff of Gwent, 1986; HM Deputy Lieutenant, Gwent, 1990. *Recreation:* Sailing, reading and music. *Clubs:* Royal Yacht Squadron; Royal Thames Yacht Club; Cardiff and County Club. *Address:* Oakgrove, Chepstow, Gwent NP6 6EH. Tel: 0291 622876.

HUGHES-MORGAN, His Honour Judge Sir David (John), Bt, CB 1983, CBE 1973 (MBE 1959). *Currently:* Circuit Judge, Croydon Combined Court Centre. *Born on* 11 Oct 1925 at Teddington. *Son of* Sir John Hughes-Morgan Bt and Lady (Lucy Margaret) Hughes-Morgan. *Marriage:* to Isabel Jean, 1959, da of W.M.Lindsay of Annan. *Children:* Parry, Jonathan and Mark. *Educated at* R.N.C. Dartmouth. *Career:* Royal Navy 1943-46. Admitted solicitor 1950. Commissioned Army Legal Services 1955; Brig., Legal Staff, HQ UKLF 1976-78; Dir, Army Legal Services, BAOR 1978-80, MOD, Maj.Gen, 1980-84; a Recorder 1983-86. *Address:* C/o National Westminster Bank Plc., Bromley South, 1 High Street, Bromley, Kent BR1 1LL.

HUMPHREYS, Mr Emyr Owen, *Currently:* Author. *Born on* 15 April 1919 *Son of* William and Sarah Rosina Humphreys, Prestatyn, Flints. *Marriage:* to Elinor Myfanwy, 1946, d. of Rev. Griffith Jones, Bintnewyddm Caerns. *Children:* three s one d. *Educated at* Univeristy Coll., Aberystwyth; University Coll., Bangor (Hon.Fellow, Univ of Wales, 1987) *Career:* Gregynog Arts Fellow, 1974-75; Hon. Prof., English Dept, Univ. Coll of N.Wales, Bangor 1988. Hon. DLitt Wales 1990. *Publications:* The Little Kingdom, 1946; The Voice of a Stranger, 1949; A Change of Heart, 1951; Hear and Forgive, 1952 (Somerset Maugham Award, 1953); A Man's Estate, 1955; The Italian Wife, 1957; Y Tri Llais, 1958; A Toy Epic, 1958 (Hawthornden Prize, 1959); The Gift, 1963; Outside the House of Baal, 1965; Natives, 1968; Ancestor Worship, 1970; National Winner, 1971 (Welsh Arts Council Prize, 1972); Flesh and Blood, 1974; Landscapes, 1976; The Best of Friends, 1978; Penguin Modern Poets No 27, 1978 (Soc.of Authors Travelling Award, 1979); The Kingdom of Bran, 1979; The Anchor Tree, 1980; Pwyll a Riannon, 1980; Miscellany Two, 1981; The Taliesin Tradition, 1983 (Welsh Arts Council Non-Fiction Prize 1984); Jones: a novel, 1984; Salt of the Earth, 1985; An Absolute Hero, 1986; Darn o Dir, 1986; Open Secrets, 1988; The Triple Net, 1988; Bonds of Attachment, 1991; Outside Times, 1991. *Recreation:* rural pursuits. *Address:* Llinon, Penyberth, Llanfairpwll, Ynys Mon, Gwynedd LL61 5YT.

HUMPHREYS, Gareth, BA (Hons), Dip.Ed. *Currently:* retired school teacher, former Head of Department of Geography, Barry Boys Comprehensive School. *Born on* 15 Nov,1935 at Tylorstown, Rhondda. *Son of* the late Trevor, and Catherine (nee Hopkins). *Marriage:* to Audrey Jenkins, 1958. *Children:* Stephen and Andrew. *Educated at* Ferndale Grammar School; University College of Wales

Aberystwyth. *Career:* International bowler and Bowls Administrator, 90 Welsh Caps between 1963-84, Commonwealth Games 1974, World Championships 1972 (Bronze Medalist), numerous Welsh and British Titles. Hon. Secretary Barry Athletic Bowls Club 1966-78, member Council of Welsh Bowling Association 1969-92, President 1979. President, British Isles Bowling Council 1987, Hon Development Officer, Welsh Indoor Bowls Association 1975-90. President Welsh Indoor Bowls Association 1991-92. President Barbarians B.A., 1976; Welsh Team Manager 1988-92; British Team Manager 1988. Founder Chairman Welsh Bowls Umpires Association; Founder Chairman Welsh Bowls Coaching Association; Life member: Vale of Glamorgan County Bowling Association; South Vale Bowling Association; Welsh Bowls Umpires Association. Rhondda Recognition Award, National Sports Council for Wales Gold Medal of Honour for outstanding contribution to Welsh Sport. *Publications:* Editor Welsh Bowls Coaching Handbook. *Recreation:* rugby football (W.R.U. coach), reading (biographical), classical music, concert going, current affairs, travel. *Clubs:* Barry Athletic, Cardiff Athletic. *Address:* 'Alston', Romilly Park Road, Barry, South Glamorgan, CF6 8RN.

HUMPHREYS, Mr Gwilym Esmor, BSc., DipEd., C.Chem.,FRSC. *Currently:* Director of Education, Gwynedd County Council since 1983. *Born on* 27 Sept 1931 at Wallasey, England. *Son of* the late James and Rachel Humphreys. *Marriage:* to Elizabeth Carys (nee Williams) 1955. *Children:* Nia Mererid and Gareth Wyn. *Educated at* Ruabon Grammar School; University College of North Wales, Bangor. *Career:* Head of Chemistry, Llangefni Comp. School, Anglesey 1954-60; Head of Physical Sciences, Caerleon College 1960-62; Headmaster, Ysgol Gyfun Rhydfelen (Bilingual Comp. School) 1962-75; H.M.I. (of Schools) Welsh Office 1975-83; Chairman of Governors Normal College, Bangor; Member of: Court & Council, University of Wales; Court & Council U.C.N.W. Bangor; Welsh Language Development Committee; Welsh Joint Educ. Ctee; Vice-Chairman Council of the National Eisteddfod of Wales. *Recreation:* Walking, gardening, snooker, watching rugby, music (esp. Choral). *Address:* *(office)* Education Office, Castle Street, Caernarfon., Gwynedd LL55 1SH. *(Home)* 1 Bodlondeb, Ffordd Y Borth, Bangor, Gwynedd LL57 2HX Tel: 0286 679160.

HUMPHRIES, Mr. John Charles Freeman, *Currently:* Editor, Western Mail, Cardiff, since 1988. *Born on* 2 Jan 1937 at Newport, Gwent. *Son of* Lillian and Charles Humphries. *Marriage:* to Eliana. *Children:* Owen, Mark and Rachel. *Educated at* St.Julian's High School, Newport, Gwent. *Career:* News Editor, Western Mail 1967-74; Deputy Editor, Western Mail 1974-81; European Correspondent, Thomson Regional Newspapers 1981-85; London City Editor, Thomson Regional Newspapers 1985-87; Launch Editor, Wales on Sunday 1988-89. *Recreation:* Walking, theatre, opera, reading, rugby. *Address:* Plas Cwm Coed, Usk Road, Tredunnock NP5 1BE.

HUMPHRYS, John, *Currently:* BBC Broadcaster, Today Programme and TV News. *Born on* 17 Aug 1943 at Cardiff. *Son of* the late George and the late Winifred. *Marriage:* divorced 1991. *Children:* Christopher and Catherine. *Educated at* Cardiff High School *Career:* Penarth Times; Merthyr Express; Western Mail; TWW/HTV; BBC Foreign

Correspondent. *Recreation:* farming, music, cello. *Address:* B.B.C., Broadcasting House, Room 4062, London W1.

HUNT, Rt. Hon. David James Fletcher, MBE, MP, LLB *Currently:* the Secretety of State for Wales and MP for Wirral West,(Cons.) 1976-83. *Born on* 21 May 1942 at Glyn Ceiriog. *Son of* the late Alan Nathaniel Hunt OBE and Jessie Edna Northrop Hunt. *Marriage:* to Patricia Margery (nee Orchard) 1973. *Children:* 2 sons and 2 daughters. *Educated at* Liverpool College; Montpellier Univ.; Bristol Univ.; Guilford College of Law; *Career:* Solicitor of Supreme Court of Judicature, Admitted 1968; Ptnr, Stanleys & Simpson North 1977-88;Beachcroft Stanleys 1988- ;Ptnr, Consultant, Stanley Wasbrough & Co., 1965-85; Dir, BET Omnibus Services Ltd,1980-81;Chmn. Conservative Shipping and Shipbuilding Ctee.,1977-79;Vice Chmn. Parliamentary Youth Lobby, 1978-80; Vice Pres. Conservative Group for Europe, 1984- (Vice Chmn. 1978-81, Chmn. 1981-82); a Vice Chmn. of the Conservative Party 1983-85; Parliamentary Private Secretary to Sec. of State for Trade, 1979-81; PPS to Sec. State for Defence, 1981; Asstnt. Govt. Whip 1981-83;Lord Commissioner of HM Treasury, 1983-84; Parliamentary Under-Sec. of State, DOE 1984-87; Treasurer of HM Household & Deputy Chief Whip, 1987-89; Minister for Local Govn. & Inner Cities, DOE, 1989-90; Chmn. Bristol Univ. Conservatives, 1964-65;Winner of Observer Mace for British Universities Debating Comp. 1965-66; Nat. Vice Chmn. FUCUA 1965-66;Chmn. Bristol City CPC, 1965-68; Nat Vice Chmn. YCNAC 1967-69;Chmn. Bristol Fed. of YCS 1970-71; Vice Chmn. Nat. Union of Conservative & Unionist Assocs., 1974-76;Vice Pres. Nat. Playbus Assoc., 198Í- ; Contested (C) Bristol South 1970, Kingswood 1974, member for Wirral 1976-83; member: South Western Planning Council 1972-76; Advisory Committee on Pop Festivals 1972-75.; *Publications:* Europe Right Ahead, 1978; A Time for Youth 1978; *Recreation:* Cricket and Walking *Clubs:* Hurlingham *Address:* Hoylake Conservative Club, Meols Drive, Hoylake, Wirral.

HUNT, Emeritus Professor Hugh Sydney,CBE, MA(Oxon & Manchester). *Currently:* Retired. *Born on* 25 Sept 1911 at Camberley, Surrey. *Son of* the late Capt C.E. Hunt and the late Ethel Helen (nee Crookshank). *Marriage:* to Janet Mary (nee Gordon). *Children:* Caroline and Simon. *Educated at* Marlborough College, Sorbonne University, Heidelberg University, Magdalen College Oxford. *Career:* Pres. of OUDS 1933-34; Producer: Maddermarket Theatre, Norwich 1934; Croydon Repertory & Westminster Theatres 1934-35; Producer, Abbey Theatre, Dublin 1935-38;; produced The White Steed, Cort Theatre, NY; Entered HM Forces 1939, served War of 1939-45; with Scots Guards, King's Royal Rifle Corps, and Intelligence Service; demobilised 1945; Director of Bristol Old Vic Company, 1945-49; Director Old Vic Company, London 1949-53; Adjudicator Canadian Drama Festival Finals 1954; Executive Officer, Elizabethan Theatre Trust, Australia 1955-60; Artistic Dir, Abbey Theatre, Dublin 1969-71; Mem. Welsh Arts Council 1979-85; (Chm Drama Cttee 1982-85); Produced: The Cherry Orchard 1948, Love's Labour's Lost 1949, Hamlet 1950, New Theatre; Old Vic Seasons, 1951-53: Twelfth Night, Merry Wives of Windsor, Romeo and Juliet, Merchant of Venice, Julius Ceasar; The Living Room, New York 1954; in Australia, Medea 1955,

Twelfth Night, 1956, Hamlet 1957, Julius Ceasar 1959; The Shaughraun, World Theatre Season, Dublin, 1968; Abbey Theatre Productions include: The Well of the Saints 1969; The Hostage 1970; The Morning after Optimism 1971; Arrah-na-Pogue 1972; The Silver Tassie 1972; The Three Sisters 1973; The Vicar of Wakefield 1974; Red Roses for Me 1980; Sydney Opera House: Peer Gynt 1975; The Plough and the Stars 1977. *Publications:* Old Vic Prefaces 1954; The Director in the Theatre 1954; The Making of Australian Theatre 1960; The Live Theatre 1962; The Revels History of Drama in the English Language, vol Vii section 1 and 2, 1978; The Abbey, Ireland's National Theatre 1979; Sean O'Casey 1980; author or co-author of several Irish plays including The Invincibles and In The Train. *Address:* Cae Terfyn, Criccieth, Gwynedd LL52 OSA.

HUNT, Jack, *Currently:* retired. *Born on* 8 July 1936 at Winsford, Cheshire. *Son of* Mary and Jack Hunt. *Marriage:* to Elizabeth. *Children:* Michael and Steven. *Educated at* Winsford Grammar; Mid-Cheshire College; Alsager College. *Career:* Civil Engineer; Lecturer; School-teacher; teacher, adviser for Technology in Clwyd. Curling: won ten Welsh Championships, captain of the Welsh Team in ten European Curling Championships. President of the Welsh Curling Association, 1991-92. Bowling: Won the individual British Championships in1980. The Welsh individual champion on two occasions. The Crown King Champion on two occasions at the Waterloo in Blackpool, and many more major tournament wins. Manager of the Welsh Crown Green Senior Bowling Team for the last two years. *Recreation:* curling, bowling (Crown Green). *Clubs:* Kinnerton Vikings (curling), Sychdyn (bowling). *Address:* Llys-Ifor, Lixwm, Nr Holywell, Clwyd CH8 8NQ. Tel: 0352 780421.

HUNTER, Dr Charles Christopher, MB, BS, MRCS, LRCP, MRCPsych, DPM. *Currently:* Consultant Forensic Psychiatrist to South Glam and Mid Glam Health Authorities; Co-ordinator of the All-Wales Forensic Psychiatric Service; Advisor in Forensic Psychiatry to The Welsh Office; Clinical Director, South Wales Forensic Psychatric Service, Caswell Clinic, Glanrhyd Hospital, Bridgend. *Born on* 2 Feb 1950 at Nottingham, England. *Son of* the late Charles William and Dorothy Mary (nee Ward). *Educated at* High Pavement Grammar' School, Nottingham; Guys Hospital Medical School, University of London. *Career:* Surgeon-Lieutenant Royal Navy 1974-79 (Medical Officer HMS Glamorgan 1974-76); Specialist in Neuropsychiatry, Royal Navy 1978-79; Senior Registrar Forensic Psychiatry, Southampton 1979-82; Consultant Forensic Psychiatrist and Deputy Medical Director, Park Lane Special Hospital 1982-89. *Recreation:* reading, travel, theatre. *Address:* South Wales Forensic & Psychiatric Service, Caswel Clinic, Glanrhyd Hospital, Bridgend CF31 4LN. Tel: 0656 662179.

HUNTER, Mr Philip Brown,T.D., LL.B. *Born on* 30 May 1909 at Birkenhead. *Son of* Charles Edward and Marion Hunter. *Marriage:* to Joyce Mary Holt 1937. *Children:* Philippa, Charles, James and Katharine. *Educated at* Birkenhead School; London University. *Career:* Solicitor 1933; Commissioned Royal Artillery TA 1939, served with Royal Artillery UK, India, Burmah 1939-45, Captain 1941, Major 1942; Partner Laces & Co solicitors 1946-60; Director Cammel Laird & Co 1949-70 (chm 1966-70); Director John Holt & Co (Liverpool) Ltd 1952-71 (chm 1967-71); Director

Guardian Assurance 1967-69; Director Guardian Royal Exchange Assurance 1969-79. *Recreation:* Sailing, gardening. *Clubs:* Law Society, Caledonion. *Address:* Bryn Hyfryd, Lixum, Holywell, Clwyd CH8 8LT. Greystones, Trearddur Bay, Anglesey.

HUTTON, John Christopher, M.A.; F.S.S.; A.M.S. *Currently:* Finance, Housing, and Marketing Consultant; Director, The Wildscreen Trust 1987; Director, Bristol Buildings Preservation Trust 1984; Member, Financial Advertising Committee, Advertising Standards Authority 1982; ConsultantMoney Which? 1971. *Born on* 7th June 1937 at Cardiff. *Son of* John Francis Hutton and Elizabeth Margery Ethel (nee Pugh). *Marriage:* to Elizabeth Ann, daughter of the late Professor Eric Evans, on 5th Aug 1963. *Children:* Catrin Margaret Clare 1965, and Bethan Margery Jane 1968. *Educated at* Monmouth School; Kingswood School, Bath; Christ Church, Oxford; University of Aston. *Career:* National Service: Royal Artillery, Cyprus 1956-58; Tube Investments: Graduate Trainee 1961, Methods Engineer 1963-64. Bristol & West Building Society: P.A. to General Manager 1964, Research Manager 1967; Assistant General Manager (Marketing & Research 1976-86, Corporate Information & Analysis 1986-88). Director, Bristol & West Personal Pensions Ltd. 1988-89. Building Societies Association: Chairman, Housing Finance Panel 1973-84 (Member 1967-); Leader, Netherlands Research Group 1979; Member Council Sub-Committee on Reserves & Liquidity 1981. National Economic Development Office: Member, Housing Strategy Committee 1975-77; Member Construction Industries Joint Forecasting Committee 1978-89; Joint Advisory Committee on Mortgage Finance: Co-Chairman of Technical Sub-Committee 1973-82. *Publications:* many articles in National Press *Recreation:* Journalism, Antiques, Countryside *Address:* Ferns Hill, Kingsweston Road, Bristol BS11 0UX. Wyevern, Aberedw, Builth Wells, Powys LD2 2UN.

I

INGRAM, Allison Gaynor, B.A. *Currently:* Regional Railways Service Group Manager for South and West Wales since 1990. *Born on* 19 August 1964 at Aberdare. *Daughter of* Evan Raymond Ingram and Doreen (nee Davis). *Educated at* Aberdare Girls Grammar School; Southampton University. *Career:* Joined BR September 1986, Station Manager, Grove Park, 1987; Station Manager, Bromley South, 1988; Area Performance Manager, Brighton, 1989. *Recreation:* Riding, reading and travelling. *Address:* Regional Railways, Brunel House, 2 Fitzalan Road, Cardiff CF2 1SA. Tel: 0222 499811.

INGRAM EVANS, Mr Graeme, F.R.I.C.S. *Currently:* Partner, Ingram Evans Care & Co. FRICS, 55 Penlline Road, Whitchurch, Cardiff. *Born on* 10 June 1940 at Cardiff. *Son of* Charles and Dorothy (nee Cooper Trill). *Marriage:* to Jennifer (nee Bickerton). *Children:* Mitzi Philippa and Charles. *Educated at* Taunton School; College of Estate Management. *Career:* Articled Lucas & Madley, Cardiff 1958-62; District Valuer & V.O. 1962-64; New Zealand 1964; Graeme Ingram Evans & Co. 1967-87; Catholic Housing Aid Society & Family Housing Assoc. 1967-73; Chairman CHAS 1968-69; FHA 1969-70; United Kingdom Housing Assoc. 1984-89; inc. Kingdomwide Housing; present United Welsh Housing Assoc. Vice-Chairman, Chairman Development sub commitee 1990-92; Whitchurch Chamber of Trade, Chairman 1985. Chmn., UWHA, 1992- ; *Recreation:* Golf, fishing, voluntary housing, Lloyds underwriter. *Clubs:* Catenians, Boshers, Old Tauntonians, various angling clubs. *Address:* 5 Orchard Drive, Whitchurch, Cardiff CF4 2AE. Tel: 0222 614411.

J

JACKSON, Grenville William, MA (Econ), Dip URP. *Currently:* Marketing Director, Development Board for Rural Wales. *Born on* 15 May 1949 at Nottingham. *Son of* the late Edwin Jackson and Florence (nee Mills). *Marriage:* to Anne-Marie Winstanley, 1972. *Children:* Rory Daniel and Corin Craig. *Educated at* High Pavement, Nottingham; Oxford Polytechnic; Lancaster University. *Career:* Lanarkshire County Council 1971-73; Greater Manchester Council 1974-77; Development Board for Rural Wales 1977- ; Director, Wales Co-operative Development and Training Centre 1986- ; Director, Mid Wales Training Ltd 1986- . *Recreation:* football, badminton, gardening. *Address:* Development Board For Rural Wales, Ladywell House, Newtown, Montgomeryshire SY16 1JB.

JACKSON, Major Howard Robert, HND; NSch; MID. *Currently:* Farmer, M.D. Land Reclamation (Wales) Ltd; Dep. Chairman, Wallace Evans Ltd. *Born on* 1 Aug 1920 at Treforest, Glam. *Son of* the late Robert Harry Jackson and the late Elizabeth Mary (nee Smith). *Marriage:* to Eileen Marjorie Watkin Jones, 1946; *Children:* Michael Robert and Pamela Frances. *Educated at* Cardiff High School; Cardiff Technical College. *Career:* H.M.Forces, Royal Engineer, 1938-49; Farming since 1950; Pres. Glam NFU 1965; NFU Council Mem., 1967-71; Mem. Glam Riv. Auth., 1963-73; Mem. Welsh Water RLDC and Chmn, Glam LLDC 1974-83; Board member Welsh Water and Chmn, RLDC 1983-89; NRA Welsh Reg, Chmn RFDC, 1989-90; Mem. Ind. Tribs., 1967-87; Mem. Glam C.C. Lands Cttee, 1963-71; Nuffield Scholar U.S., 1960; Mem. Glam COA,Ex.Ct., 1961-75; Mem. S.W. Army Benev. Cttee since 1983. *Recreation:* gardening, rugby football, horse racing, travel. *Clubs:* Cardiff & County, Army Navy, Farmers, Assoc. RAF. *Address:* Little Parc, Thornhill, Cardiff CF4 5UA.

JACOBS, Professor John Arthur, PhD (London); DSc (London) Hon. DSc Univ. British Columbia, 1987; Fellow Royal Soc. Canada, 1958. *Currently:* Honorary Professor, Univ. Coll., of Wales, Aberystwyth. *Born on* 13 April 1916 at London. *Son of* Arthur George Jacobs and Elfrida Malvine Jacobs (nee Boeck). *Marriage:* 1st to the late Daisy Sarah Ann Montgomerie, 1941. 2nd to Margaret Jones, 1974 (diss,1981); 3rd to Ann Grace Wintle, 1982. *Children:*

Coral Elizabeth and Margaret Ann (d 1990). *Educated at* Dorking High School, Surrey, 1927-34 *Career:* Lieut. Commander R.N.V.R. 1941-46; Sn. Lecturer Applied Math., Royal Naval Engn. Coll., Devonport (Also Depy. Training Cdc), 1944-46; Lecturer Applied Math, Univ. London, 1946-51; Assoc. Prof. Applied Maths, Univ. Toronto, 1951-54; Assoc.Prof Geophysics, Univ. Toronto, 1954-57; Prof. Geophysics, Univ. British Columbia, 1957-61. Director, Inst. of Earth Sciences, Univ British Columbia 1961-67, Killam Memorial Professor of Science, Univ of Alberta 1967-74, Director Inst Earth & Planetery Physics, Univ of Alberta 1970-74, Professor of Geophysics, Univ of Cambridge 1974-83, (Emeritus Professor 1983-). Cent. Medal Canada, 1967; Gold Medal Can. Assoc. Phys., 1975; g.Tuzo Wilson Medal Can. Geophys. Un., 1982. *Publications:* More than 160 papers in Technical Journals and 7 books. *Recreation:* Walking and music. *Clubs:* Royal Astronomical Society. *Address:* 4 Castell Brychan, Aberystywth, Dyfed SY23 2JD. Inst. of Earth Studies, Univ. Coll. of Wales, Aberystywth, Dyfed, SY23 3DB.

JAMES, Professor Alan Morien, *Currently:* Research Professor of International Relations, Keele University, Keele, Staffs, ST5 5BG. *Born on* 20 Jan 1933 at Newport, Gwent. *Son of* the late Willie James and the late Martha (nee John). *Marriage:* 1st to Jean Valerie Hancox, 1956 (dissolved 1980); to Lorna Lloyd, 1981. *Children:* from 1st marriage: Morien, Helen (decd), Nesta, Gwyn, Gareth, David and Ceri. *Educated at* Newport High School; London School of Economics and Political Science. *Career:* Civil Service 1955-57; London School of Economics and Political Science: Assistant Lecturer, Lecturer, Senior Lecturer, Reader in International Relations 1957-73; Columbia University, New York, USA: Rockefeller Research Fellow, Institute of War and Peace Studies 1968; Keele University: Professor and Head of Department of International Relations 1974-91; Ife University, Ife, Nigeria: Visiting Professor, Department of International Relations 1981; Jawaharlal Nehru University, New Delhi, India: Visiting Professor, School of International Studies 1983; Chairman, British International Studies Assoc 1979-83; Member, University Grants Committee, Social Studies Sub-Committee 1983-89; Advisor in Politics and International Studies, Universities Funding Council 1989- ; Vice-Chairman, International Law Section, International Studies Association (USA), 1991- . *Publications:* The Politics of Peacekeeping, 1969; The Bases of International Order (ed), 1973; Sovereign Statehood: The Basis of International Society, 1986; Peacekeeping in International Politics, 1990. *Recreation:* hill and coast walking, supporting Port Vale Football Club. *Clubs:* Royal Commonwealth Society. *Address:* 23 Park Lane, Congleton, Cheshire, CW12 3DG. Tel: 0260 271801.

JAMES, Sir Cynlais Morgan, KCMG. *Currently:* Director General of Canning House. *Born on* 29 April 1926 at Resolven. *Son of* Thomas James and Lydia James (nee Morgan). *Marriage:* to Teresa Girouard, da of R.D.Girouard and Lady Blanche Girouard. *Children:* Emma Galloway and Sarah James. *Educated at* St. Marylebone Grammar School; Trinity CollegeCambridge, (MA). *Career:* Diplomatic Service: entered Senior Branch 1951, posts at Tokyo, Rio de Janeiro, Moscow, Paris, Saigon, Minister (Paris), H.M. Ambassador at Warsaw, Assistant Under-Secretary of State, F.C.O., H.M. Ambassador to Mexico

1983-86. Director of various companies, including Thomas Cook and Foreign & Colonial. Various decorations: Order of Aztec (Mexico); Order of Andres Bello (Venezuela); Order of Merit (Chile). *Recreation:* walking, music. *Clubs:* Brooks's, Beefsteak, Pratt's, Travellers (Paris), M.C.C. *Address:* 20 Greville Road, London, NW6. The Old Forge, Lower Oddington, Moreton-In-Marsh, Glos.

JAMES, David (Keith) Marlais, MA *Currently:* Partner, Phillips & Buck, Solicitors, Chairman of the Board. *Born on* 10 Aug 1944 at Carmarthen, Wales. *Son of* James Lewis James and Margaret Evelyn (nee Thomas). *Marriage:* to Kathleen Linda James, 1973. *Children:* Alys, Elizabeth and Thomas. *Educated at* Cowbridge Grammar School; Cardiff High School; West Monmouth School; Queens' College Cambridge. *Career:* Member of the Board of the Welsh Common Services Authority 1991- ; Member of the General Advisory Council BBC 1991- ; Vice Chairman Eversheds Group 1989- ; Member of the Representative Body of the Church in Wales 1989- ; Member of the Editorial Board Welsh Economic Review 1989- ; Director of the Bank of Wales plc 1988- ; Member of the Court and Council of the University of Wales College of Cardiff 1988- ; Deputy Chairman of the Institute of Welsh Affairs 1987- ; Vice President of the Cardiff Business Club 1987- ; Member of the Advisory Panel, Cardiff Business School 1986- ; Member of the Court and Council of UWIST 1985-88; Member Welsh Management Committee of Institute of Directors 1985- ; Chairman Welsh Centre for International Affairs 1979-84; Member UK Management Committee, Freedon from Hunger Campaign 1978-87; Chairman Welsh Executive United Nations Association 1977-80. *Recreation:* golf *Clubs:* Cardiff & County, Royal Porthcawl Golf. *Address:* Fitzalan House, Fitzalan Road, Cardiff, CF2 1XZ.

JAMES, Dr David Geraint, MA, MD (Cantab), FRCP (Lond), LlD (Hons. Wales), FACP(Hon. USA) *Currently:* Visiting Professor of Medicine, Royal Free Hospital, Universities of London and Miami. *Born on* 2 Jan 1922 at Treherbert, Wales. *Son of* David James (Defynnog) and Sarah (Aeronia). *Marriage:* to Professor Dame Sheila Sherlock, 1951. *Children:* Amanda Melys and Auriole Zara. *Educated at* Porth and Pontypridd County Schools; Jesus College, Cambridge; Columbia University, New York. *Career:* Dean and Consultant Physician Royal Northern Hospital, London. Consultant Ophthalmic Physician, St.Thomas' Hospital, London; Consulting Physician, Royal Navy. Editor-in-Chief, Journal Sarcoidosis. President, World Association of Sarcoidosis. Past President London Glamorgan Society; Medical Society of London; Harveian Society, Osler Club. *Publications:* numerous scientific articles and medical textbooks. *Recreation:* The Internationalism of Wales, rugby football. *Clubs:* The Athenaeum. *Address:* 149 Harley Street, London, W1N 1HG.

JAMES, Dr. David William Francis, OBE., BSc., PhD., F.I.Ceram., FRSA, FIM. *Currently:* Consultant. *Born on* 20 March 1929 at Merthyr Tydfil. *Son of* the late Thomas Martin James and Margaret Anne. *Marriage:* to Elain Maureen Hewett 1953. *Children:* Rosalind (1955) and Heather (1958). *Educated at* Cyfarthfa Grammar School; University of Wales (Swansea); University London. *Career:* Flying Officer RAF 1954-56 (Education Branch); Research Officer I.C.I.Ltd 1956-60; Lecturer and Senior lecturer

Univ. of Wales (Bangor) 1960-71; Deputy Principal Glamorgan Polytechnic 1971-72; Director Polytechnic of Wales 1972-78; Chief Executive, British Ceramic Research Ltd 1978-91; Council for National Academic Awards (CNAA): Council Member 1975-82; Chairman Ctee for Research Degrees 1980-86; Member Research Degrees 1976-86; Committee for Institutions 1978-86; Member SERC Polytechnic ctee 1975-78; Training ctee, Wales Council for Disabled 1974-78; Consultant to several Industrial Companies and Govt. Res. Establishments; Hon Fellowship Polytechnic of Wales 1986; F.R.S.A. 1976- ; President Institute of Ceramics 1989; Vice-President Institute of Materials 1992. *Publications:* Numerous in various scientific and technical journals. *Recreation:* Photography, travel, church work. *Clubs:* Royal Commonwealth; Federation, Stoke on Trent. *Address:* Fairways, Birchall, Leek, Staffs., ST13 5RD.

JAMES, Councillor Dewi Llewellyn, *Currently:* Managing Director - Dewi James & Sons; Civil/Residential Bldg Developer, Plant Hire Contractor, Pine Furniture Manufacturer. *Born on* 3 Oct 1932 at Castle Rag., Wolfscastle, Dyfed. *Son of* Rees Jones James and Doris Anna (nee Evans). *Marriage:* to Joyce Edna Hart 1954. *Children:* Haydn David James and Nigel Stanley James. *Educated at* Hayscastle School (Pembs. C.C. School); Joinery Apprenticeship. *Career:* Nat. Service, Royal Artilary Regiment, drafted to the Middle East to serve in the Suez Crisis and in Jordon; Self Employed Builder; Formed Dewi Janes & Sons; further companies created - Hayguard Plant Hire, small furniture manufacturing and retail business; Joined N.F.B.T.E. (now B.E.C.) 1976, Pres. for 3 years 1981-83 & 1987-88; Mbr of N.H.B.C., C.I.T.B., Nat. Fed. of Self Employed; Elected to Haverfordwest Town Council 1983, Mayor of Haverfordwest and Admiral of the Port 1986-87; Town Sheriff 1989-90; re-elected for a further term 1991; Deacon of Tabernacle Congregational Church, Haverfordwest; elected to be a County Councillor in 1989 representing The Camrose Div; Company Dir. for Tourism for S. Wales; Chrm, Community Sports Commt; Vice-Chrm Community Educ. Commt; Mbr: Public Protection Commt, Further Education Cmmt, Culture Services Commt, Education Commt, Economical & Ind. Commt, Wintern Day Centre Commt; Chrm of The Long Boats Competition; as Mayor raised money and erected a Hart Beat Wales Trim Trail for Haverfordwest; Pres. of Solva A.F.C. 1985-88; commt mbr The Sail Training Assoc. *Recreation:* Arts, travel (pilgrimage to Israel & Egypt), general sports enthusiast - RFC and AFC suporter. *Address:* Llygad-yr-Haul, 32 City Road, Haverfordwest, Dyfed, SA61 2ST. Hafod-Y-Garreg, 7 Anchor Down, Solva, Pembs. SA62 2TQ.

JAMES, Air Vice Marshal Edgar, CBE., DFC., AFC & Bar; F.R. Ae.S. *Currently:* Retired 1985. *Born on* 19 Oct 1915 at Rochdale (Subsequently Briton Ferry, Glam). *Son of* Richard Geo. James and Gertrude James (nee Barnes). *Marriage:* to Josephine Moscrop Steel, B.A., 1941. *Children:* Stephen John Barnes and David Steel Barnes. *Educated at* Neath Grammar School, RAF Staff College. *Career:* Glamorgan County Surveyor's Dept., 1933-39; Royal Air Force, 1939, Commissioned 1940; Flying instructor, U.K. and Canada, 1940-43; Operational duties 1944, with Nos. 305 and 107 Squadrons; Kings Commendation for Valuable

Service in the air, 1943, 1944, 1956; Empire Central Flying School, 1945-48; Fighter Command Operations Staff, 1948-49; RAF Staff College, 1950; Air Ministry, Operational Reqt, 1951-52; 2nd Tactical Air Force, Germany, 1953-55; Command of No. 68 Squadron - night fighters, Central Fighter Establishment, 1956; Commanded All-Weather Development Wing. HQ, Fighter Command Air Staff, 1958-59; Central Flying School, Assistant Commandant and Chief Instructor, 1959-60; RAF, Leeming, Comm. Officer, 1961-62; Ministry of Defence (Air Force Dept), Director, Operational Reqt., 1962-66; Commander, British Forces, Zambia, 1966; Deputy Controller, Ministry of Aviation (then Ministry of Technology, 1966-69; Wing Commander, 1953; Group Captain, 1959; Air Commodore, 1963; Air Vice Marshal, 1967; Aviation Consultant, 1970-85. *Recreation:* Golf and sailing *Clubs:* Royal Air Force; Royal Western Yacht Club. *Address:* Lowmead, Traine Paddock, Modbury, Ivybridge, Devon, PL21 ORN.

JAMES, Dr Ian Meurig, MB, PhD, FRCP, FRSA *Currently:* Consultant Physician; Reader in Clinical Pharmacology at the Royal Free Hospital and Medical School. *Born on* 15 Feb 1937 at Swansea. *Son of* Thomas John James and Margery James, Gowerton. *Marriage:* to Jane Elizabeth Faulkner. *Children:* Alice Margery, Emily Angela and Jeremy Rhidian. *Educated at* Gowerton GS; University College London; Gonville & Caius Cambridge. *Career:* Founder and Chairman British Performing Arts Medicine Trust; Founder of British Association for Performing Arts Medicine. *Publications:* many publications on, Clinical Pharmacology/ Hypertension, performing arts, medicine. *Recreation:* music and the arts. *Address:* 12 Dawes Lane, Sarratt, Rickmansworth, Herts, WD3 6BB. Dept Medicine, Royal Free Hospital, Pond Street, Hampstead, London, NW3 2QG.

JAMES, John Christopher Urmston, *Currently:* Secretary The Lawn Tennis Association. *Born on* 22 un 1937 at LLanelli. *Son of* John Urmaston James and Ellen Irene James *Marriage* to 1st 1959 Gillian Mary Davies (diss. 1982) 2nd Patricia Mary White 1982. *Children:* David James and Christopher James. *Educated at* St. Michael's School, Llanelli and Hereford Cathedral School. *Career:* Harrods, London 1959; Jaeger, 1961; Pringle, 1972; *Recreation:* Tennis, Rugby Football, Architecture, Countryside. *Clubs:* The Queen's Club, London Welsh, International Club of GB, Llandeilo RFC, Quesdrs. *Address:* 77 Devonshire Road, Ealing, London W5 4TS.

JAMES, Mrs Sian Catherine, BA *Currently:* S. Wales Area organiser Save The Children Fund. *Born on* 24 June 1959 at Morriston. *Daughter of* Martha Griffiths (nee Morgan) and Melbourne Griffiths. *Marriage:* to Martin Raymond James 1976. *Children:* Rhodri and Rowena. *Educated at* Cefn Saeson Comp. Neath; Swansea University. *Career:* After raising my two children and gaining a great deal of confidence during the 1984-85 miners strike, decided to attend University full time. Was accepted on a degree course at Swansea University and graduated in 1989 in Welsh. Gained employment as a trainer with West Glam Video Workshop on a Welsh Arts funded project in W. Glam schools. Video training and media studies through the medium of Welsh. From there was appointed (1990) field officer for the Young Farmers Clubs in Wales. Main brief being staff development and training for members and staff.

In 1991 was appointed S.Wales area organiser for the Save the Children Fund and responsible for development of the funds work in shcools, colleges and businesses through the medium of welsh in S.Wales. *Recreation:* Antiques, interior design, politics, current affairs and good conversation. *Address:* 10 Is Y Rhos, Caterbont, Abercraf, Cwmtawe, LA9 1SS.

JAMES, Thomas Garnet Henry, CBE 1984, FBA 1976 *Currently:* retired. Keeper of Egyptian Antiquities, The British Museum, 1974-88. *Born on* 8 May 1923 at Neath. *Son of* the late Thomas Garnet James and Edith (nee Griffiths). *Marriage:* to Diana Margaret Vavasseur Durell, 1956. *Children:* Stephen Garnet Vavasseur. *Educated at* Neath Grammar School; Exeter College Oxford, MA in Literae Humaniores (Classics) and Oriental Studies (Eqyptian and Coptic). *Career:* War Service: Royal Artillery 1942-45; active service in North-West Europe. Entered British Museum in 1951 and remained there until retirement in 1988. Laycock Student of Egyptology, Worcester College, Oxford 1954-60; Wilbour Fellow, The Brooklyn Museum 1964-65; Visiting Professor, College de France, Paris 1983; Visiting Professor Memphis State University 1990; Chairman, Egypt Exploration Society 1983-89; Vice-President, Egypt Exploration Society 1990; Chairman Advisory (London) committee of the Freud Museum 1987-. Member German Archaeological Institute 1974; Fellow British Academy 1976; Commander of the Order of the British Empire (C.B.E.) 1984. Excavations at Saqqara 1953; Epigraphic projects at Saqqara 1951; Thebes 1952; Gebel es-Silsila 1955. Many lectures given in universities, museums and other institutions in Europe, North America and Australia. *Publications:* (selected): The Mastaba of Khentika called Ikhekhi, 1953; Hieroglyphic Texts in the British Museum, 1, 1961; The Hekanakhte Papers and other Early Middle Kingdom Documents, 1962; (with R.A.Caminos) Gebel es-Silsilah, i, 1963; Hieroglyphic Texts in the British Museum, 9, 1970; Archaeology of Ancient Egypt, 1972; Corpus of Hieroglyphic Inscriptions in The Brooklyn Museum, i, 1974; Pharaoh's People, 1984; Egyptian Painting, 1985; Ancient Egypt. The Land and its Legacy, 1988. forthcoming: Egypt. The Living Past; Howard Carter. The Path to Tutankhamun; articles in learned journals, many contributions to archaeological reports etc. Further popular publications. Editor of many publications. *Recreation:* music, reading, food and wine. *Clubs:* United Oxford and Cambridge Universities. *Address:* 14 Turner Close, London, NW11 6TU.

JAMES, Mr Thomas Geraint Illtyd, B.Sc. M.B. (Wales), M.Ch (Wales), FRCS (Eng), FRCS (Edin) *Currently:* Retired Senior Surgeon, Central Middlesex Hospital, Teacher of Surgery Middlesex Hospital, Consultant Neurosurgeon N.W. Met. Reg. Board. *Born on* 12 Jul 1900 at Barry, Glamorgan. *Son of* Evan Thomas James and Elizabeth James. *Marriage:* to Dorothy John 1932. *Children:* Hugh Geraint (decd) and Peter David *Educated at* Barry County School; Univ. College Cardiff; Welsh National School of Medicine; St.Mary's, Guys. *Career:* Surgeon C.M. Hospital 1935-65; Clinical Assistant St.Peter's Hospital, St.Mark's Hospital; Assistant Dept. Neurosurgery, London Hospital; Member BMA; Fellow Royal Society of Medicine; Member, British Neurosurgery Society; Corresponding Member, Spanish-Portuguese Neurological Society; Member Society of Apothecaries; Freeman City of London; Fellow, Associatio of Surgeons of Great Britain; *Publications:* Articles to Surgical Journals and Chapters in Surgical Text Books *Recreation:* Gardening, Travel and Classical Literature *Address:* 1 Freeland Road, Ealing, London, W5 3HR.

JAMES, Professor Vivian Hector Thomas, BSc; PhD; DSc; Hon MRCP; FRC.Path. *Currently:* Scientific Consultant (Private). *Born on* 29 Dec 1924 at London. *Son of* the late William P.James and the late Alice James (nee Holdsworth). *Marriage:* to Betty Pike, 1952. *Educated at* Latymer's School, London; University of London. *Career:* Served as Pilot on flying duties, RAFVR 1942-46; Scientific Staff,Medical Research Council 1952-56; Dept. of Chemical Pathology, St.Mary's Hospital Medical School; Lecturer 1956; Reader 1962; Prof. of Chemical Endocrinology 1967; Prof. of Chemical Pathology 1973; Emeritus Prof. of Chemical Pathology, Univ. of London 1991; Leverhulme Research Fellow 1992- Secretary/ President, Endocrine Section, Royal Society of Medicine 1972-78, Secretary, Treasurer, Society for Endocrinology 1979-91; Sec.Gen. European Fedn Endocrine Societies 1986- ; Chairman, Clinical Endocrinology Cttee 1976-82; Chairman, DHSS National Quality Control Cttee 1986-91. Freeman, Haverfordwest, 1946. *Publications:* over 300 in medical and scientific journals; Ed: Hormones in Blood, The Adrenal Gland. *Recreation:* languages. *Clubs:* Royal Society of Medicine *Address:* Dept of Metabolic Medicine, St Mary's Hospital Medical Sch, London, W2 1PG.

JARMAN, Mr Roger Whitney, B.Soc.Sc.Hons; Cert in Education. *Currently:* Under Secretary: Housing, Health and Social work services since 1988. *Born on* 16 Feb 1935 at Bargoed, Mid-Glamorgan. *Son of* Reginald Cecil Jarman and Marjorie Dix Jarman. *Marriage:* to Patricia Dorothy Odwell 1959. *Children:* Christopher. *Educated at* Cathays High School, Cardiff; Univ. of Birmingham. *Career:* Recruitment and Selection Officer, Vauxhall Motors Ltd 1960-64; Assistant Secretary, Univ. of Bristol appointments board 1964-68; Assistant Director of Recruitment, CSD 1968-72; Welsh Office: Principal, European Division 1972-74; Assistant Secretary, Devolution division 1974-78; Assistant Secretary, Permanent Secretary's Div. 1978-80; Under Secretary: Land Use & Planning Group 1980-83; Transport, Highways and Planning Group 1983-88; Transport, Planning, Water and Environment group 1988. *Recreation:* Walking, reading, cooking. *Clubs:* Civil Service *Address:* Welsh Office, Cathays Park,Cardiff. CF1 3NQ. Tel: 0222 825257.

JARVIE, Mr Thomas Hunter, LL.B(Hons); Solicitor. *Currently:* Self employed Solicitor in partnership, with offices in Cardiff, Cowbridge and Bridgend since 1971. *Born on* 22 March 1944 at Glasgow. *Son of* Thomas Jarvie and Doreen Jarvie (nee Swaithes). *Marriage:* to Christina (nee Minoprio), 1971. *Children:* Nicholas Hunter Jarvie b.1974 and Emma Rhiannon Jarvie b.1977. *Educated at* Ifield Grammar School, Sussex; University of Birmingham. *Career:* George Wimpey and Company Limited, as assistant solicitor; assistant solicitor and assistant company secretary with Performing Right Society; Is Deputy Chairman of Vale of Glamorgan Conservative Association; Past Chairman of Cowbridge Branch of the Association; acted as Clerk in Charge for 1983 General Election Campaign for local area; member of Vale of Glamorgan B.C. since 1982 and is now

Chairman of the Council's Economic Development Cttee; also of the Council's Finance and Policy, Environmental Health, Housing and Leisure Services Cttees; At the invitation of the Wales Area Office contested Llanrumney North Electoral Div (a safe Labour seat) in the May 1985 South Glamorgan C.C. Election; elected President of Bridgend Dist. Law Society, 1986; elected Mayor of the Vale of Glamorgan B.C., 1988; has been Chairman of the former Bridgend Branch of Torch Trust for the Blind, Treasurer of local PCC and representative on Diocesan Conference; Was adopted as Prospective Parliamentary Candidate for Cardiff South and Penarth May 1990; Appointed by the Secretary of State for Wales to the Board of Cardiff Bay Development Corporation, 1991 *Recreation:* family, gardening, travel, music, squash, steam engines. *Clubs:* National, St.James, London; Ogmore, Bridgend. *Address:* The Old Vicarage, Llanblethian, Cowbridge, South Glamorgan, CF7 7JL.

JEFFERS, Mr Raymond Jackson, LLB, BCL. *Currently:* Self-employed Lawyer. *Born on* 5 Aug 1954 in Britain. *Son of* George Jeffers and Janine (nee Jacquier). *Marriage:* to Carol Elizabeth Awty, 1982. *Educated at* Stanwell Comprehensive School, Penarth; University College of Wales, Aberystwyth. *Career:* Solicitor 1980; Partner, Linklaters & Paines 1986; Senior Employment Partner 1989; Member City of London Solicitors' Company; Employment Law Committee 1987. *Publications:* contributor to books on "Joint Ventures" and "Doing Business in the UK", as well as articles on corporate law topics. *Recreation:* golf, badminton, field ornithology. *Address:* Barrington House, 59-67 Gresham Street, London, EC2V 7JA. Tel: 071 606 7080.

JENKINS, Miss Catrin Mary, LIB *Currently:* Partner Francis & Buck solicitors, Fitzalan House, Fitzalan Road, Cardiff, 1989-90. *Born on* 22 Dec 1958 at Carmarthen. *Daughter of* Charles Bryan and Anne Jenkins (nee Davies-Jones). *Educated at* Girls Grammar School, Llanelli; UCW Cardiff. *Career:* Articled R.L.Edwards & Partners, Bridgend; qualified and joined Philips and Buck as solicitor December 1983. *Recreation:* horse riding. *Address:* 15 Hollybush Rise, Cyncoed, Cardiff CF2 6TG. Tel: 0222 733695.

JENKINS, Clive Ferguson, Dip Arch (Wales) ARIBA *Currently:* Principal of Clive F.Jenkins & Associates, Chartered Architects, since 1973. *Born on* 19 Oct 1936 at Swansea. *Son of* the late Merlyn Jenkins and the late Annie Elizabeth Jenkins (nee Davies). *Marriage:* to Pauline Helen Jenkins (nee Sutton), 1962. *Children:* Kimberley Sian (BA Oxon) and Craig Warren. *Educated at* Dynevor Grammar School; Swansea Technical College; Welsh School of Architecture. *Career:* Qualified 1961; Assistant architect to Peter D.Howell 1961-62; to Morgan Harries 1962-63; to Swansea Town Council 1963-67; to Percy Thomas Partnership 1967-73. Founded Mumbles Water Ski Club 1960, Hon Sec for 11 years. founder member and secretary of Welsh Water Ski Committee 1964. past Figures, Jumping & Overall water ski champion of Wales; past figures and runner-up National Veteran water ski champion 1969. *Recreation:* water sports, snow skiing, golf, water colour painting. *Address:* (home) Pine Lodge, 8 Northway, Bishopston, Swansea, SA3 SJN. (business) 42 Newton Road, Oystermouth, Swansea, SA3 4BQ.

JENKINS, Mr David, BA (Hon); Teaching Cert, Further Education. *Currently:* General Secretary, Wales TUC Cardiff since 1983, during his twelve years with the Wales TUC, has sought to concentrate the resources and the activities of the Wales TUC on job creation and employment growth; Welsh Industrial Development Board member since 1988; Community Industry Board member since 1986; Wales Cttee for Econ and Industrial Affairs member since 1983; Wales Co-operative Centre Bd member since 1983, founded by the Wales TUC in 1983, remains unique in the UK as a trade union initiated employment creating agency; South Glamorgan TEC Director since 1989. *Born on* 21 Sept 1948 *Marriage:* to Felicity, 1976. *Children:* Ruth, Gareth and Sam. *Educated at* Canton High School, Cardiff; Liverpool University; Garnett College London. *Career:* Industrial Sales Organiser, ITT Distributors Cardiff 1970-74; Maintenance Worker, GKN Steel Ltd Cardiff 1974; Lecturer, Peterborough Technical College Peterborough 1975-78; Research and Admin Officer, Wales TUC Cardiff 1978-83; MSC Committee for Wales member 1983-88; Welsh Arts Council member 1983-89. David Jenkins has visited Norway, Finalnd, Denmark, Japan and Korea to meet potential inward investing companies and he is currently involved in discussions with European regional trade union organisations with the aim of improving and developing the role which trade unions can undertake at regional and local level in employment and enterprise creating initiatives. *Clubs:* Member and currently Treasurer of Llandaff Rowing. *Address:* 12 Bruton Place, Llandaff, Cardiff, CF5 2ER. 1 Cathedral Road, Cardiff, CF1 9SD.

JENKINS, Dr David, CBE; MA; D.Litt (Hon.Wales) *Currently:* retired. *Born on* 29 May 1912 at Blaenclydach, Rhondda. *Son of* Evan and Mary Jenkins. *Marriage:* to Menna Rhys (nee Williams), 1948. *Children:* (Mrs) Nia Mair (Lewis) and Emyr Wyn Jenkins. *Educated at* Ardwyn Grammar School, Aberystwyth; U.C.W. Aberystwyth, BA (Hons 1936). *Career:* Librarian National Library of Wales 1969-79; W.P.Thomas (Rhondda) Schol., 1936; Sir John Williams Research Student 1937-38; Served War of 1939-45, Army: Major 1943 N.Europe; Nat.Lib. Wales, Asst. Dep. Mss 1939-48; Asst. Keeper, Dept of Printed Books 1949; Keeper 1957; Sen.Keeper 1962; Professorial Fellow U.C.W., Aberystwyth 1971; J.P., 1959-72; Gen.Comr. of Income Tax 1968-77; Chm. Mid Wales HMC 1969-70; Chm Welsh Books Council 1974-80; Member: Court, UCW Aberystwyth; British Records Assoc, 1970-79; BBC Archives Adv.Cttee 1976; Hon.Soc. Cymmrodorion; Catherine & Lady Grace Trust 1969- ; Editor, NLW Jl., 1968-79; Jl. Welsh Bibliog.Soc; Ceredigion 1973-83. *Publications:* articles in numerous journals; Cofiant T Gwynn Jones, 1973 (biog. Welsh Arts Council Prize, 1974); Bro a Bywyd Thomas Gwynn Jones; ed. Ysqrifau ac Erthyglau Kate Roberts, 1978; Bro Dafydd ap Gwilym, 1992. *Recreation:* walking. *Address:* Maesaleg, Cae Mawr, Penrhyn-Coch, Aberystwyth, SY23 3EH.

JENKINS, Mr David Gerald, BSc; MIFM *Currently:* Director, Coed Cymru, since 1988. *Born* at Rhondda. *Children:* 2 children *Educated at* Tonysguboriau CPS; Cowbridge GS; Reading Univ. *Career:* After graduating from Reading University joined Dwr Cymru in 1974 and Thames Water in 1976 as Senior Fisheries Officer for Oxford Area. *Recreation:* Wildlife and Conservation, woodcraft. *Address:* Coed Cymru, Frolic Street, Newtown, Powys, SY16 1AP.

JENKINS, David Lewis, DGS; CEng; FICE; FIHT; MCIT. *Currently:* County Engineer, County of South Glamorgan, since 1985. *Born on* 5 July 1938 at Markham, Mon. *Son of* the late David Emrys and Phyllis May (nee Edwards). *Marriage:* to Eluned Read Brown, 1963. *Children:* Simon David and Mark Lewis. *Educated at* Pontllanfraith County Grammar; Birmingham University. *Career:* Engineer Learner to County Surveyor, Monmouthshire County Council, 1958-68; joined Cardiff City Council as Transportation Officer until April 1985. Chaired South Wales Counties Transportation Group 1974-85; Chairman Welsh County Surveyor's Society 1990-91; Vice-President National County Surveyor's Society 1990-91; present Chairman of Glamorgan Surveyors Association. *Recreation:* classic cars; house designs. *Address:* Tudor Lodge, Bonvilston, Cardiff, CF5 6TR. Tel: 0446 781330.

JENKINS, Very Reverend Frank Graham, M.A. *Currently:* Retired Priest. Chairman (Voluntary) Gwent Assoc. of Voluntary organisations; Chairman (Voluntary) Welsh Assoc. of County Voluntary Bodies. *Born on* 24 Feb 1923 at Merthyr Tydfil. *Son of* Edward and Miriam Jenkins. *Marriage:* to Ena Doraine Parry 1950. *Children:* Caroline, Timothy and Peter. *Educated at* Cyfarthfa Castle Secondary School, Merthyr Tydfil; Port Talbot Secondary School; St. David's College, Lampeter; Jesus College, Oxford; St. Michael's College, Llandaff, Cardiff. *Career:* Ordained Deacon 1950; Priest 1951; Curate of Llangeinor 1950-53; Minor Canon Llandaff Cathedral 1953-60; CF (TA) 1956-62; Vicar of Abertillery 1960-64; Vicar of Risca 1964-75; Vicar of Caerleon 1975-76; Dean of Monmouth 1976-90; Chairman Church in Wales Division for social responsibility 1983-90. *Recreation:* Voluntary sector social concerns; study of history; family and grandchildren; travel. *Address:* Rivendell, 209 Christchurch Rd, Newport, Gwent, NP9 7QL.

JENKINS, County Councillor Garth, JP., FRSA. *Currently:* Retired Technical Officer, British Telecom. *Born on* 1 Jan 1936 at Pengam. *Son of* the late Hugh R.H. and the late A. Elisabeth (neeEdmunds). *Marriage:* to Jennet Rose (nee Tancock), 1959. *Children:* Helen, Ann and Carol. *Educated at* Lewis School, Pengam; City & Guilds. *Career:* Elected member for Pengam and Maesycwmmer, Monmouthshire C.C. 1967-74; Chm. Tech. Ed. Sub committee and FE Colleges 1969-74; elected member for Pengam (+ Cefn Fforest fr. 1989), Gwent C.C. 1973- ; Chm. Gwent Educ. Cttee 1977-80; Chm. Gwent College of HE Governors 1979-86, 1989-92; Chm. Assoc. of Colleges for F and HE 1982, 1990; Chm. Gwent County Council 1986-87; Chm. S.E. Wales Arts Assoc. 1988-90; Chm. FE Sub Cttee and Ebbw Vale, Newport, Pontypool Colleges 1989-91, Cross Keys Coll. 1989- ; Chm. Welsh Joint Educ. Cttee 1989- ; Vice-Chm. The Staff College, Blagdon 1990- ; Governor, Blackwood Comprehensive and local primary schools, University of Wales, Nat. Library of Wales; Member UWCC Council, Wales Advisory Body for L.A.H.E. Gwent College of Higher Education Corporation. *Recreation:* Welsh history, opera, driving (member of Inst. of Advanced Motorists), Hon. Sec. Islwyn Diabetic Branch of BDA. *Address:* Gwaun y Borfa, 24 High Street, Pengam, Blackwood, NP2 1SZ.

JENKINS, Mr Gwyn, M.A. *Currently:* Assistant Keeper, Department of Manuscripts and Records, The National Library of Wales, with special responsibility for the Welsh Political Archive. *Born on* 7 July 1949 at Aberystwyth. *Son of* D.H. and Lilian Jenkins. *Marriage:* to Valerie Vaughan Griffith 1974. *Children:* 1d, 1s. *Address:* The National Library Of Wales, Aberystwyth, Dyfed, SY23 3BU.

JENKINS, Mr Hugh Royston, FRICS, FPMI. *Currently:* Chief Executive, Prudential Portfolio Managers and Director, Prudential Corporation since 1989; Chairman of The Property Advisory Group. Department of the Environment. *Born on* 9 Nov 1933. *Marriage:* to Mrs Beryl Kirk 1988. *Educated at* Llanelli Grammar School. *Career:* National Service, Royal Artillery 1954-56; Valuer, London County Council 1956-62; Assistant Controller 1962-68; Managing Director, 1968-72, Coal Industry (Nominees) Ltd; Dir. Gen. of Investments, NCB 1972-85; Vice Chm. National Assoc. of Pensions Fund 1979-80; Chief Exec. Officer, Heron Financial Corp. 1985-86; Group Investment Dir, Allied Dunbar Assce, 1986-89; Dep. Chm. and Chief Exec. Allied Dunbar Asset Management 1987-89; Director: Unilever Pensions Ltd 1985-89; IBM Pensions Trust PLC 1985-89; Heron International 1985-89; Member: Property Adv. Group DoE 1976-85, 1988- ; The City Capital Markets Cttee 1982; Lay Mem. of the Stock Exchange 1984-85. *Recreation:* golf. *Clubs:* Garrick *Address:* (office) 1 Stephen Street, London. W1P 2AP.

JENKINS, Dr. Ivor, CBE, 1970, BSc., MSc., DSc., FEng., FIM *Currently:* Consultant, Metallurgy. *Born on* 25 July 1913 at Gorseinon, Swansea. *Son of* the late Thomas and Mary Jenkins (nee Evans). *Marriage:* to Caroline Wijnanda James 1941. *Children:* Brian James and Peter Anthony *Educated at* Gowerton County School; Univ. Coll., Swansea *Career:* Bursar, GEC Research Labs, Wembley 1934; Scientific Staff, GEC 1935; Dep. Chief Metallurgist, Whitehead Iron & Steel Co., Newport 1944; Head of Metallurgy Dept. 1946; Chief Metallurgist 1952; GEC Wembley, Director of Research and Director, Manganese Bronze Holdings Ltd., 1961-69; Director of Research Delta Metal Co Ltd., and Director Delta Metal (B.W.) Ltd., 1969-73; Managing Director Delta Materials Research Ltd., 1973-78; F.I.M. 1948 (Pres. 1965-66); Fellow Amer. Soc. Materials 1974; Mbr. Inst. of Metals 1932 (Pres. 1968-69) and Platinum Medallist 1978; Mbr. Iron & Steel Inst. 1937 (Williams Prize 1946). *Publications:* Controlled Atmospheres for the Heat Treatment of Metals 1946; Contributions to learned journals at home and abroad on Metallurgical and related topics; Editor book series on Powder Metallurgy. *Recreation:* Music, gardening, swimming *Clubs:* Anglo Belgian *Address:* 31 Trotyn Croft, Aldwick Felds, Aldwick, Bognor Regis., PO21 3TX. 11 Kings Cottages, Tombs Of The Kings Road, Paphos, Cyprus.

JENKINS, Lt. Col. Michael Vaughan, RM., MIDPM., MBIM. *Currently:* General Manager, Mid Glamorgan FHSA. *Born on* 1 Oct 1941 at Caerleon. *Son of* the late Clifford Hayden and Zelda (nee Moses). *Marriage:* to Judith Mary Teresa (nee Coulter) 1965. *Children:* Paul and Robey. *Educated at* Jones West Monmouth, and Prince of Wales, Nairobi, Canadian Command & Staff College. *Career:* Commissioned 2/Lt Royal Marines 1960; Qualified pilot 1964; Military assistant to commandant general 1973; Corps promotions and drafting officer 1977; Instructor RN staff college 1980; Chief training officer 1984; Bursar, Monkton Combe school 1986. *Publications:* Stress and

Leadership; The Underwater and Air Threat to Atlantic Reinforcement. *Recreation:* Royal Marines Reserve, orienteering, paragliding. *Address:* Mid Glamorgan Family Health, Services Authority, 5th Floor, Churchill House, Churchill Way, Cardiff, CF1 4TW.

JENKINS, Mr Peter White, IPFA *Currently:* Financial Consultancy. *Born on* 12 Oct 1937 at Streetly, Staffs. *Son of* the late John White Jenkins and Dorothy (nee Humphreys). *Marriage:* to Joyce Christine Muter, 1961. *Children:* Tim and Emily. *Educated at* St. Mary's G.S., Walsall; King Edward VI G.S., Nuneaton. *Career:* Deputy Treasurer, Birkenhead County Borough Council, 1969-73; County Treasurer, Merseyside C.C., 1973-84; Director of Finance, Welsh Water Authority, 1984-87. *Recreation:* Cooking, gardening, walking and trying to be agreeable. *Address:* 9 Camden Crescent, Brecon, Powys. LD3 7BY.

JENKINS, His Honour Judge Richard Peter Vellacott, MA (Cantab) *Currently:* Circuit Judge, 1989. *Born on* 10 May 1943 at Radlett, Herts. *Son of* the late Gwynne Jenkins and Irene (nee Vellacott). *Marriage:* to Agnes Anna Margaret Mullan 1975. *Children:* Daniel Gwynne and Isobel Sarah. *Educated at* Radley; Trinity Hall, Cambridge. *Career:* Barrister, called 1966; Member of Midland Circuit 1968-71; Member of Midland & Oxford circuit 1972-89; (Rememberancer & Asst. Treasurer 1985-89); Recorder of the Crown Court 1988-89. *Clubs:* MCC; London Welsh R.F.C. *Address:* Hall Barn, Far End, Boothby, Graffoe Lincoln, LN5 OLG.

JENKINS, Mr Stanley Kenneth, *Currently:* retired, 1978. *Born on* 25 Nov 1920 at Brecon, Powys. *Son of* Benjamin and Ethel (nee Edwards). *Marriage:* to Barbara Mary Marshall (nee Webb) 1957. *Children:* Nicola Jane, Caroline Mary, Nina Anna and Alison Fay. *Educated at* Cardiff Technical College 1946-50. *Career:* Served Royal Artillery and Royal Engineers 1942-46; President Welsh Universities and Colleges Student Council and President National Union of Students 1949-51; Foreign (subsq) Diplomatic Service 1951; Served Singapore, Malaya, Burma and Cyprus. *Recreation:* Gardening, sport. *Clubs:* Commonwealth Trust. *Address:* 1 Beehive Lane, Ferring, Worthing, West Sussex, BN12 5NL.

JENKINS, Mr Vivian Evan, MBE(Military)., BA. *Currently:* Retired 1976. *Born on* 12 Sept 1918 at Pontypridd. *Son of* the late Arthur Evan and the late Blodwen. *Marriage:* to Megan Myfanwy Evans, 1946. *Children:* John David Jenkins and Mari Elizabeth Brewer. *Educated at* Pontypridd Grammar School' Univ. Coll., Cardiff. *Career:* Commissioned 1943 RCOS; served in 1st and 6th Airborne Divisions 1942-46 in Europe, India and Palestine; awarded M.B.E. for distinguished services 1945, parachutist; Inspector Home Officer Childrens Department in Cardiff and Leeds 1952-71; Appointed Director of Social Services Dept, Cardiff City Council in 1971; after retirement served as member and later chairman of Civil Service selection boards, Executive Officer appointments; Welsh rugby schoolboy caps in 1933 and 1937; Captain Univ. XV and Pontypridd R.F.C. *Recreation:* Golf, rugby, cricket *Clubs:* Radyr Golf Club; Cardiff West Probus Club. *Address:* 24 Windsor Road, Radyr, Cardiff. CF4 8BQ.

JENKINS (nee McDougall), Doctor Rachel, MA, MB, B.Chir, MD (Cantab), MR.C.Psych. *Currently:* Principal Medical Officer, Department of Health. *Born on* 17 April 1949 at Manchester. *Daughter of* Peter Osborne McDougall and Beryl McDougall (nee Braddock). *Marriage:* to Keith Jenkins, 1974. *Children:* Ruth Gudrun and Benjamin Dougal. *Educated at* Monmouth School for Girls', 1960-65; St.Paul's Girls' School, London, 1965-67. *Career:* Mandsley registrar rotation 1975-77; Researcher, Welcome Fellow, Lecturer and Senior Lecturer at The Institute of Psychiatry 1978-85; Consultant and Senior Lecturer, St.Bartholomew's Hospital 1985-88; Principal Medical Officer, Mental Health Division, Department of Health 1988- . *Publications:* 50 published papers and several books. *Recreation:* Wild orchids. *Address:* 68 Clapham Common, Northside, London, SW4 9SB.

JENKINS OF HILLHEAD,The Rt Hon. Lord Roy Harris, Life Peer UK, Cr. 1987; P.C. 1964. *Currently:* Chancellor, University of Oxford since 1987, President of the Royal Society of Literature since 1988, Leader, Liberal Democratic Peers since 1988, First Leader, Social Democratic Party 1982-83 (Member of Joint Leadership 1981-8), President of the Commission of the European Communities 1977-81. *Born on* 11 Nov 1920 *Son of* the late Arthur Jenkins MP, and Hattie Jenkins. *Marriage:* to Jennifer Morris (Dame Jennifer Jenkins), 1945. *Children:* two s one d. *Educated at* Abersychan Grammar School; University Coll., Cardiff (Hon. Fellow 1982); Balliol Coll., Oxford (Hon.Fellow 1969) Career: Sec and Librarian, Oxford Union Soc; Chmn, Oxford Univ. Democratic Socialist Club; First Class in Hon.Sch. of Philosophy, Politics and Economics, 1941; DCL by diploma Oxford 1987. Served War of 1939-45, in RA 1942-46; Captain 1944-46. Contested (Lab) Solihull Div. of Warwicks at Gen Election 1945. Mem. of Staff of Industrial and Commercial Finance Corp.Ltd 1946-48; Mem. Exec Ctee of Fabian Soc 1949-61; Chm. Fabian Soc 1957-58; Mem. Ctee of Management Soc of Authors 1956-60; Governor, British Film Inst 1955-58; Adviser John Lewis Partnership 1954-62; Dir of Financial Operations 1962-64; Dir.Morgan Grenfell Hldgs Ltd 1981-82; MP (Lab): Central Southwark 1948-50; Stechford, Birmingham 1950-76; PPS to Sec. of State for Commonwealth Relations 1949-50; Minister of Avaiation 1964-65; Home Sec 1965-67, 1974-76; Chancellor of the Exchequer 1967-70; Dep leader, Labour Party 1970-72. Contested: Warrington bye-election as first Social Democratic candidate, July 1981; Glasgow Hillhead (SDP/ Alliance) 1987. MP (SDP) Glasgow, Hillhead 1982-87. UK Deleg to Council of Europe 1955-57; Vice-Pres Inst of Fiscal Studies 1970- ; Formerly: Dep Chm Federal Union; Pres. Britain in Europe, Referendum Campaign 1975;Chm Labour European Ctee. A President of UK Council of the European Movement. Pres UWIST 1975-81. Trustee Pilgrim Trust 1973- . Dimbleby Lecture 1979. Liveryman, Goldsmiths' Co; Freeman, City of London 1965. Freeman, City of Brussels 1980. Hon Foreign Mem Amer.Acad. Arts and Sciences 1973. Hon. Fellow Berkeley Coll., Yale 1972. Hon. degrees: Leeds 1971; Havard 1972; Pennsylvania 1973; Dundee 1973; Loughborough 1975; Bath 1978; Michigan 1978; Wales 1979; Bristol 1980; Glasgow, 1972; Oxford 1973; City 1976; Aston 1977; Keele 1977; Essex 1978; Open 1979; Kent 1992; *Publications:* (ed) Purpose and Policy (a vol. of the Prime Minister's Speeches), 1947; Mr Attlee: An Interim Biography, 1948; Pursuit of Progress 1953; Mr. Balfour's Poodle, 1954; Sir Charles Dilke: A Victorian Tragedy, 1958; The Labour Case (Penguin

Special), 1959; Asquith, 1964; Essays and Speeches, 1967 Afternoon on the Potomac?, 1972; What Matters Now, 1972; Nine Men of Power, 1975; Partnership of Principle, 1985; Truman 1986; Baldwin 1987; A Gallery of Twentieth Century Portraits, 1988; European Diary, 1977-81, 1989; A Life at the Centre, 1991; Contrib to New Fabian Essays, 1952; contrib to Hugh Gaitskell, A Memoir, 1964; *Clubs:* Beefsteak, Brook's, Oxford and Cambridge University. *Address:* 2 Kensington Park Gardens, London W11 3HB St. Amamd's House , East Hendred, Oxon. OX12 8LA.

JENNETT, Frederick Stuart, CBE, Dip.Arch, FRIBA, MRTPI, FRSA. Currently: Consultant Architect and Town Planner since 1st Jan, 1990; Consultant to Studio BAAD Architects, Hebden Bridge since Mar 1990 and Mouchel Management LTD, West Byfleet *Born on* 22 April 1924 at Rhiwbina, Cardiff. *Son of* Horace Frederick Jennett and Jenny Sophia Jennett (nee Hall). *Marriage:* to Nada Eusebia Jennett (nee Phillips), 1948. *Children:* Sara Elizabeth and Claire Katy Bauer. *Educated at* Whitchurch Grammar School; Scholarship to Welsh School of Architecture; Diploma with distinction (UWIST) and external exam of Town Planning Institute. *Career:* Lieut Royal Signals, 1942-46; Chairman & Senior Partner, Percy Thomas Partnership, 1971-89; Partner Percy Thomas Partnership, Bristol, 1964-71; Associate Percy Thomas Partnership, Bristol, 1962-64; Associate S. Colwyn Foulkes & Partners, Colwyn Bay, 1956-62; Senior Architect/Planner Loius De Soissons & Partners, Welwyn Garden City, 1955-56; Architect Planner Cwmbran Development Corporation, 1951-55; Architect T. Alwyn Lloyd & Gordon, Cardiff, 1949-51; Experience ranges over New Town Neighbourhood Planning, Public & Private sector housing, Ecclesiastical (Clifton Cathedral, Bristol), University and Hospital projects in U.K. and Middle East & Far East, and refurbishment of historic buildings. *Publications:* include papers in: "World Hospitals" and to Advanced Architectural Studies York; Arab Bankers Association UAE; Nucleus Hospitals to Malaysian Government Dept; Regional Hospital Architects Conference at Bristol. *Recreation:* Water colour painting, hill walking and running. *Clubs:* Reform and Royal Overseas league. *Address:* Portland Lodge, Lower Almondsbury, Bristol. BS12 4EJ. Studio BAAD, Linden Mill, Hebden Bridge, West Yorks, HX7 7DN.

JEWITT, County Councillor Ronald William, *Currently:* Chief Chemist, London Underground Ltd., 55 Lots Road, Chelsea. *Born on* 25 Jan 1942 at Newport, Mon. *Son of* the late Cyril George and the late Hilda Laura. *Marriage:* to June Rose Barley, 1963. *Children:* Peter Ronald (b.1964), David Charles (b.1965) and Penelope Anne (b.1967). *Educated at* Newport Grammar School; Newport & Mon Coll of Technology; Brunel. *Career:* Monsanto Chemicals 1958-62; Expandite Ltd., NW10 1962-64; Burt Boulton & Haywood 1964-66; London Transport 1966- . Political: member, Reading Borough Council 1973-91, (Housing Chairman 1979-84, Mayor 1984-85, Dep-Mayor 1985-86). member, Berkshire County Council 1977-, (Leader of The Council 1986-90). President, Reading Midweek Cricket League; President, Berkshire Sports Club; President, Caversham Royal British Legion. *Recreation:* hillwalking, swimming, cycling, photography. *Address:* 98 Chiltern Road, Caversham, Reading, Berks, RG4 OJD. Tel: 0734 481147.

JOHN, (Richard) Alun, *Born on* 7 April 1948 at Llandaff. *Son of* the late Thomas Guy John and the late Edith. *Marriage:* to (Elizabeth) Sara, 1980, da of Denis W.Kent, Beaconsfield, Bucks. *Children:* Guy (b.1985) and Lucy (b.1989). *Educated at* Whitchurch Grammar School Cardiff; Ashridge Managment College; USW Cologne. *Career:* Photographer, South Wales Echo and Western Mail 1966; photographer The Press Association 1977; editor The Associated Press; deputy Picture Editor The Evening Standard 1981; deputy Picture Editor The Mail on Sunday 1982; Picture Editor The Independent 1986; Group Picture Editor Mirror Group Newspapers 1989; Deputy Chairman Syndication International 1989; Managing Director Alun John Communications Ltd 1991. External examiner Univ. of Sheffield; selector RPS Exhibitions 1988-89; Consultant Picture Editor the Thomson Foundation. The Gerald Barry Award, Granada Television 1987. *Publications:* author Newspaper Photography, 1988. *Recreation:* shooting, writing. *Address:* 7 Randall Mead, Binfield, Berkshire, RG12 5EL. Tel: 0344 411746. Fax: 0344 360760.

JOHN, Dr. David Dilwyn, CBE., TD., DSc., LL.D. *Currently:* Retired. *Born on* 20 Nov 1901 at Llangan, S. Glam. *Son of* Thomas & Julia John. *Marriage:* to Marjorie Emily Page, 1929. *Children:* Mary Elizabeth and David Dilwyn. *Educated at* Bridgend County School; University College of Wales, Aberystwyth. *Career:* Research Zoologist, Discovery Investigations in Antarctic seas, 1925-35, for which awarded Polar Medal, 1942; Assistant Keeper Zoology British Museum (Natural History), 1935, made Deputy Keeper, 1948; Captain, promoted Major, 1942; 99th London Welsh Heavy Anti-Aircraft Regt., 1939-45; Secretary Challenger Society, 1945-48; Director National Museum of Wales, 1948-68; President Cardiff Naturalists Society, 1952-53 and Museums Association, 1963-64. *Publications:* Papers on zoological subjects, chiefly on Echinoderms, in scientific periodicals etc. *Recreation:* Natural history and the countryside and English literature. *Address:* 7 Cyncoed Avenue, Cardiff. CF2 6ST.

JOHN, Mr Maldwyn Noel, FEng 1979, FIEE, FIEEE, MConsE. *Currently:* Chairman of Kennedy & Donkin Group Ltd, since 1987. *Born on* 25 Dec 1929 at Pontypridd, Glamorgan. *Son of* Thomas Daniel John and Beatrice May John. *Marriage:* to Margaret Cannell, 1953. *Children:* Steven Thomas (b.1959) and Paul David (b.1962). *Educated at* University College Cardiff, BSc 1st Class Honours, Electrical Eng. *Career:* Metropolitan Vickers Electrical Co Manchester 1950-59; Atomic Energy Estab UKAEA Winfrith 1959-63; AEI/GEC Manchester, chief engineer and divisional manager 1963-69; Kennedy & Donkin Consulting Engineers, chief electrical engineer 1969-72, partner 1972-87. President Institution of Electrical Engineers 1983-84, Chairman IEE Wiring Regulations Committee 1985-87; Member Court of the University of Wales Institute of Science and Techn 1984-88 (UWIST); Overseas Projects Board 1987-90, Director NICEIC 1988-91; Member: Executive Committee; British National CIGRE Committee 1989- ; Freeman: City of London 1987, Worshipful Co of Engineers 1987. *Publications:* Practical Diakoptics for Electrical Networks (jointly), 1969; Power Circuit Breakers Theory & Design (jointly) 1st edition 1975, 2nd edition 1982. *Recreation:* golf. *Clubs:* Bramley Golf (Surrey). *Address:* Kennedy & Donkin Group Ltd, Westbrook Mills,

Godalming, Surrey, GU7 2AZ. Tel: 0483 425900.

JOHN, County Councillor Thomas David Melvin, City Guild Cert. Steel Process *Currently:* Member West Glamorgan County Council. *Born on* 24 Sept 1931 at Cwmafan. *Son of* David Llewellyn and Kate John (nee David). *Marriage:* 1953. *Children:* David Llewellyn and Susan Anne *Educated at* Elementary, Secondary, TUC courses, capt. Cwm school: soccer, rugby and cricket *Career:* S.Co. Wales later British Steel Corp, 1948-1982; Stocktaker, Port Talbot; Supervisor, Abbey works; Trade Union Official, Bisakta (ISTC) holder of highest awards plaque and scroll; Member Port Talbot borough council, 1959-74; Mayor, 1971-72; Member W. Glam county council, 1974- ; Chairman, 1986-87; Chair Governors, Cwmafan, Bryn, Rhos, Afan Welsh, 1974- ; Chair Governors, Afan Tertiary College, Dyfryn Comp 1977; Chair Margam Parc Board, 1977- ; President: Cwmafan Snr Cit.; Cwm Garden Club; Cwm Senior Soccer; Cwm Youth Rugby. President W. Glam V.C.C.T., 1988- ; Director, W.Glam Employment Agency, 1987; Director, Sculpture at Margam, 1989; Past President Aberafan Constituency Labour Party, Port Talbot Borough Labour Party; Executive member Swansea Festival; member of Swansea Bay Chamber of Trade; Member South Wales Police Authority; Member Glamorgan Archives. *Address:* 119 Cwmclais Road, Cwmafan, Port Talbot. SA12 9NA.

JOHNSON, Colonel Neil Anthony, OBE(Mil) (1989), TD (1985), ADC, FIMI, MInstM, MBIM. *Currently:* Main Board Director Rover Group plc (Executive Director BAe). *Born on* 13 April 1949 at Cardiff. *Son of* Anthony Johnson and Dilys Mabel Vera (nee Smith). *Marriage:* to Gail, 1971, daughter of Drs Ian and Sybil Ferguson of Llandaff, Cardiff. *Children:* Sarah Anne (b.1973), Amanda Jane (b.1975) and Victoria Rhiannon (b.1977). *Educated at* Canton High School, Cardiff; Royal Military Academy, Sandhurst. *Career:* various Exec Director appointments within British Motor Corporation 1973-81; Sales & Marketing Director Jaguar Cars Ltd., 1981-86; On Secondment to MoD (Army) Commanded 4th Bn The Royal Green Jackets 1986-89; British Aerospace, Director of European Operations for Rover Group plc 1989-92; (Military) Deputy Commander 160 (Welsh) Brigade 1989-92; Foreign Honours etc: Palme De Vermielle Avec Coronne (France 1987); Freeman of City of London (1983); Liveryman Worshipful Company of Coachmaker & Coach Harness Makers. *Recreation:* farming, shooting, skiing, reading, music. *Clubs:* Army & Navy, Royal Automobile, Cardiff & County, 'Fadeaways'. *Address:* Hillhampton Farm, Great Witley, Worcester, WR6 6JJ. Castle Court, Westgate Street, Cardiff, CF1 1DJ.

JONES, Mr (Gwilym) Wyn, CBE, BA. *Currently:* Retired, Assoc member Gwynedd H.A. *Born on* 12 July 1926 at Llanrwst. *Son of* Rev. John Jones, MA, BD and Elizabeth (nee Roberts). *Marriage:* to Ruth (nee Thomas), 1951. *Children:* Nerys Wyn (b 1956) and Gareth Wyn (b.1964). *Educated at* Llanrwst Primary and Grammar Schools; UCNW; London Univ. *Career:* Served RN 1944-47, Cadet, Colonial Admin Service, Gilbert and Ellice Islands 1950; DO, DC and Secretariat in Tarawa, Line Islands, Phoenix Islands and Ocean Island 1950-61; Solomon Islands 1961; Asst. Sec., 1961-67; Sen. Asst Sec., 1967-74; Dep. Chief Sec., 1974; Sec to Chief Minister and Council of Ministers, 1974-77; Governor, Montserrat 1977-80. Administrator,

Cwmni Theatr Cymru (Welsh Nat. Theatre) 1982-84; Mem. Court, UCNW Bangor 1980-83. *Recreation:* walking alone. *Address:* 13 Warren Drive, Deganwy, Gwynedd, LL31 9ST. Tel: 0429 583377.

JONES, Mr (Robert) Gerallt Hamlet, *Born on* 11 Sept 1934 at Nefyn. *Son of* the late Rev. Richard Emrys Jones, of Ynys Mon and the late Elizabeth Ellen. *Marriage:* to Susan Lloyd da of Richard Heber Lloyd Griffith(d 1975), of Borth-y-Gest. *Children:* two s Rh⁻⁻ Gerallt b. 1969, Dafydd Gerallt b.1972; 1 da Ceri Rhiannon b. 1964. *Educated at* Deonstone and UCNW Bangor, BA 1954, MA 1956. *Career:* Lecturer in educn Univ of Wales 1960-65; princ. Mandeville Teachers Coll Jamaica 1965-67; warden and headmaster Llandovery Coll 1967-76; sr tutor Extra-Mural Dept UW 1979-88; warden Gregynog Hall UW 1988- ; author of TV documentaries and series incl Joni Jones; winner: Prose Medal Nat Eisteddfod 1977 and 1979. Hugh Mcdiarmid Trophy 1987, Welsh Arts Cncl Poetry Award 1990; ed. Taliesin 1986- ; mem., Broadcasting Cncl Wales 1967-72; chm Welsh Acad 1982-87, dir Aberystwyth Devpt Studies Courses 1986- ; mem., Welsh Arts Cncl 1987- ; mem., Welsh Fourth Channel Authority, 1991-; mem., Yr Academi Cymreig (the Welsh Acad), 1964. *Publications:* author of 35 vols in Welsh language incl Ymysg y Drain, 1959; Cwlwm, 1962; Y Foel Fawr, 1962; Poetry of Wales 1930-70, 1972; Jamaican Landscape, 1969; Jamaican Interlude, 1972; Triptych, 1977; Cafflogion, 1979; Tair Drama, 1988; Seicoleg Cardota, 1989; Cerddi 1959-89, 1989. *Recreation:* cricket, hill-walking. *Address:* Gregynog, University Of Wales, Newtown, Powys.

JONES, Sir (Thomas) Philip, CB., MA. *Currently:* Chairman: Total Oil Holdings Ltd., Total Oil Marine plc. *Born on* 13 July 1931 at Erith, Kent. *Son of* William Ernest and Mary Elizabeth. *Marriage:* to Mary (nee Phillips) 1955. *Children:* Christopher Philip and David Gareth. *Educated at* Cowbridge Grammar School; Jesus College Oxford (Hon Fellow). *Career:* 2nd Lieut, Royal Artillery 1953-55; Asst. Principal Min of Supply 1955; Principal Min. of Aviation 1959; on loan to HM Treasury 1964-66; Principal Private Secretary to Minister of Aviation 1966-67; Asst. Secretary Min. of Technology, subseq. Min. of Aviation Supply 1967-71; Under Secretary, DTI 1971; Under Secretary 1974; Dep. Secretary 1976-83; Dept. of Energy; Chm. Electricity Council 1983-90; Member: BNOC 1980-82; BOTB 1985-88; Chm., Nationalized Industries' Chairmen's Group 1986-87; Gov., Henley Management Coll., 1986- ; Freeman, City of London 1986; CBIM 1983; CompIEE 1987; FRSA 1987. *Recreation:* Reading, walking, watching Rugby football. *Clubs:* Traveller's, Royal Overseas League. *Address:* 16 Herald's Place, Kennington, London, SE11 4NP. The Grange, Collingbourne, Kingston, Nr Marlborough, Wilts.

JONES, Mr Alan, BSc *Currently:* Managing Director, Welsh Water Enterprises Limited. *Born on* 3 Sept 1943 at Berkeley. *Son of* Frank and Annie Jones (nee Stephens). *Marriage:* to Barbara Hancock, 1965. *Children:* Philip Graham and Jacqueline Margaret. *Educated at* Dursley Grammar School; Southampton University. *Career:* Rio Tinto Zinc, 1965; PA Management Consultants 1969; Danver Management Services, 1974; Cape Industries, 1977; Urwick, Orr and Partners 1979; Braithwaite Engineers, Managing Director, 1984; Price Waterhouse, 1986; Welsh Development Capital Management, Managing Director, 1987. *Recreation:*

sporting and cerebral *Address:* 'Long Drive', Wellfield Court, Marshfield, Cardiff, CF3 8TJ. Tel:0633 680379.

JONES, Mr Allan Victor, Grad.I Fire E *Currently:* Chief Fire Officer - Gwynedd Fire Service. *Born on* 26 Feb 1942 at Caernarfon. *Son of* the late Samuel Morgan Jones and Gwennie Jones. *Marriage:* to Margaret Doris Lees 1963. *Children:* 2 daughters Wendy and Gaynor. *Educated at* Sir Hugh Owen Grammar School, Caernarfon. *Career:* Gwynedd Constabulary 1958-61; Caernarfon County Fire Brigade 1961-74; Gwynedd Fire Service 1974; District Commander 1976; Deputy Senior Fire Prevention Officer 1977; Deputy Senior Staff Officer 1977; Principal Staff Officer 1981; Senior Staff Officer 1983; Deputy Chief Fire Officer 1983; Chief Fire Officer 1989; Chmn. CACFOA Communications Working Group (Wales). Council Member of Commonwealth and Overseas Fire Services Association (COFSA). Assessor, Fire Service Examination Board. *Recreation:* Motorcycling and DIY *Address:* Fire Service Headquarters, Llanberis Road, Caernarfon, Gwynedd, LL55 2DF. Tel: 0286 3811.

JONES, Mr Alun, LL.B.(Wales) Solicitor *Currently:* Managing Partner, Gwyn and Gwyn, Solicitors, Cowbridge since 1968. *Born on* 21 Dec 1937 at Gorseinon, W.Glam. *Son of* David and Catherine Mary Jones. *Marriage:* to Jeanette Ferrier, 1966. *Children:* Three children. *Educated at* Gowerton School; Univ. Coll. of Wales, Aberystwyth; College of Law, Guildford. *Career:* Solicitor, E.T.Ray, 1960-65; Lecturer in Law, 1963-65 (part-time); Solicitor: Glam.C.C., 1966-67, Gwyn & Gwyn, 1967-68; Partner, Gwyn & Gwyn, 1968- ; Pres., Bridgend Dist.Law Soc., 1985; Sec: Glam.Local Med.Commt, 1968-74, Welsh Assoc. of Local Med.Commt, 1969-74, Mid Glam Local Med.Commt, 1974- ; mbr: S.Glam Health Auth., 1980-84, Chrmn Disciplinary Appeals & Grievance Procedure Hearings; Des.Mbr. Whitchurch, Velindre & Ely Hospitals; Chrmn.Auth.Inquiry into TB outbreak at Whitchurch Hospital 1981; Chrmn: S.Glam. Health Auth. 1984-, Training and Dev.Grp of NHS Wales, 1988-91, Welsh Health Auth.Chrmns Commt, 1989-91; Mbr: NHS Reg.Chrmns Pay & Personnel Grp, 1990-; NHS Wales Manpower Strategy Grp, 1987-91; NHS Wales Manpower Resource Grp, 1991- ; Brd of Welsh Health Tech.Serv.Orgn, 1984-86; Brd.of Welsh Health Common Serv.Auth., 1986-87; Cncl of Univ.of Wales Coll.of Med., 1984- ; Planning and Resources Commt, of UWCM, 1987- ; C Merit Awards Advisory Commt for NHS Med.Consultants in Wales, 1990- ; Cncl of Inst.of Welsh Affairs, 1989- . Chrmn, Llantwit Major RFC, 1968-74; President, Llantwit Major RFC, 1974-76. *Recreation:* Singing in Opera and Oratorio; playing in Chamber Music groups and orchestras; watching rugby and hill walking. *Clubs:* Crawshays Welsh RFC. *Address:* Bryn-Y-Fro, Llanblethian, South Glamorgan, CF7 7EY. C/o South Glamorgan Health Auth., Temple Of Peace & Health, Cathays Park, Cardiff, CF1 3NR Tel: 0222 231021.

JONES, Dr Alun Denry Wynn, CPhys, FInstP. *Currently:* Chief Executive, Institute of Physics, since 1990. *Born on* 13 Nov 1939. *Son of* Thomas D. Jones and Ray Jones. *Marriage:* to Ann, 1964, da of Brinley Edwards (d 1955), of Betws, Dyfed. *Children:* Helen (b. 1966) and Ingrid (b.1969). *Educated at* Amman Valley GS Ammanford; Christ Church, Oxford (MA, DPhil). CPhys, FInstP. 1973 *Career:* Senior Student Commission for Exhib. of 1851, 1964-66, Sen.

Research Fellow UKAEA, 1966-67, Lockheed Missiles and Space Co., California 1967-70, Tutor, Open Univ., 1971-82; joined Macmillan and Co., Publishers, 1971; Dep. Editor, Nature, 1972-73; British Steel Corp., 1974-77; British Steel Overseas Services, 1977-81; Asst Dir, Technical Change Centre, 1982-85; Dep. Dir, 1986-87, Dir, 1987-90, Wolfson Foundn. Sec. of working party on social concern and biological advances, 1972-74, Mem., Section X Cttee, 1981- , BAAS. British Library: Adv. Council, 1983-85; Document Supply Centre Adv. Cttee, 1986-89; Mem: Council, Nat. Library of Wales, 1987- (Gov., 1986-). Gov., UCW, Aberystwyth, 1990- ; Gov., City University, 1991. *Publications:* (with W.F. Bodmer) Our Future Inheritance: choice or chance, 1974. *Recreation:* gardening, theatre, cricket. *Clubs:* Athenaeum *Address:* Institute Of Physics, 47 Belgrave Square, London, SW1X 8QX 4 Whatsheaf Close, Woking, Surrey, GU21 4BP Tel: 071 235 6111.

JONES, Alun Ellis, *Currently:* retired. *Born on* 16 May 1931 at Taffs Well. *Son of* the late Edward and the late Winnifred. *Marriage:* to Miriam Thomas-Owen, 1961. *Children:* Geraint Huw and Delyth Mary Wyn. *Educated at* Caerfilli Grammar: RSA Certificates English/Maths. *Career:* Royal Air Force 1949-51; Claims/Ledger Dept British Rail 1951-54; Statistics Dept CWS Ltd 1954-58; Area Sales Executive representing Elida Gibbs Ltd/Unilever Ltd 1958-86. Hon Secretary Taffs Well RFC 1961-81 and 1986-87; Chairman East District Rugby Union 1972-88; District B Representative Welsh Rugby Union Committee 1988- . *Recreation:* rugby, music, reading. *Clubs:* Taffs Well RFC; United Services Mess Cardiff. *Address:* 'Islwyn', 20 Heol-Y-Pentre, Pentyrch, Cardiff, CF4 8QE.

JONES, Rt. Hon. Aubrey, BSc(Econ), Hon DSc(Bath). *Born on* 20 Nov 1911 at Merthyr Tydfil. *Son of* Evan Jones and Margaret Aubrey. *Marriage:* to Joan Godfrey-Isaacs 1948. *Children:* David Andrew Aubrey and Simon Rodney Aubrey. *Educated at* Cyfarthfa Castle Secondary School, Merthyr Tydfil; London School of Economics. *Career:* Visiting Fellow, Science Policy Research Unit, Univ. of Sussex 1986. Editorial Staff, Western Mail 1937; Foreign and editorial staff of The Times 1937-39 and 1947-48; Army Intelligence Staff, War Office and Mediterranean Theatre 1940-46; Staff of British Iron & Steel Fed, Economic Director, General Director 1949-55; M.P. (C) Birmingham, Hall Green 1950-65; Minister of Fuel and Power 1955-57; Minister of Supply 1957-59; Chairman, Nat. Board for Prices and Incomes 1965-70; Leading consultant to Nigerian Govt. on organisation of government 1973-74; Adviser to Iranian Government on application of oil revenues to the national plan 1974-78; Dir.Guest Keen & Nettlefolds Steel Co.Ltd 1960-65; Dir. Courtaulds Ltd 1960-63; Chmn: Staveley Ind. Ltd (Dir. 1962-65) 1964-65; Chmn Laporte Ind. (Holdings)Ltd 1970-72; Dir.Thomas Tilling Ltd 1970-82; Dir.Cornhill Ins.Gp (Chmn 1971-74) 1970-82; Consultant, Plessey Ltd 1978-80; Mbr.Panel of Conciliators, Int. Centre for Settlement of Investment Disputes, Washington DC 1974-81; Fellow Commoner, Churchill Coll. Cambridge 1972-74; Visiting Fellow, New College Oxford 1978; Snr Research Associate, St. Antony's Coll.Oxford 1979-82; Fellow Commoner Churchill Coll. Cambridge 1982-86; Regent Lectr. Univ. of California at Berkeley 1968; Hon.Fellow London School of Economics 1959; Mbr.Plowden Cttee of Enquiry into Aircraft Industry

1965-66; Mbr.Court of Governors, London School of Economics 1964-86; Chmn, Oxford Energy Policy Club 1976-86. *Publications:* The Pendulum of Politics 1946; Industrial Order 1950; The New Inflation: the politics of prices and incomes 1973; Economics and Equality (ed) 1975; My LSE (contributor) 1977; Oil: The Missed Opportunity 1981; Britain's Economy: The Roots of Stagnation 1985. *Address:* Arnen, 120 Limmer Lane, Felpham, Bognor Regis, West Sussex. PO22 7LP.

JONES, Barry, *Currently:* Member of Parliament.*Born at* Mancot, Deeside, Clwyd. *Son of* the late Stephen and Grace Jones. *Marriage:* to Janet, daughter of the late Mr & Mrs F.W.Davies. *Children:* Stephen. *Clubs:* Connahs Quay Labour Club.*Address:* House Of Commons, London SW1A OAA.

JONES, Mr Clive Lawson, BSc *Currently:* Commission of the European Communities, Deputy Director-General for Energy, since 1986. *Born on* 16 March 1937 at London.*Son of* the late John Lawson Jones and Gladys Irene (nee Daines). *Marriage:* to Susan Brenda McLeod 1961. *Children:* 1 son, Robin; 1 daughter, Tracy. *Educated at* Cranleigh School; University of Wales. *Career:* Principal, UK Ministry of Power (DTI), 1968-72; Principal, UK Dept of Trade and Industry, 1972-74; Assistant Secretary, UK Dept of Energy, 1974-77; Counsellor, British Embassy, Washington D.C., 1977-81; Under Secretary, UK Dept of Energy, 1981-82; Director for Energy Policy, Commission of the European Communities 1982-86. *Recreation:* Art, Antiques. *Address:* Rue De La Loi, 200, 1049 Brussels, Belgium.

JONES, Mr Clive William, BSc(Econ) Honours. *Currently:* Managing Director and Editor in Chief, London News Company (News and transmission company jointly owned by LWT and Coulton Television). *Born on* 10 Oct 1949 at Llanfrechfa, Gwent. *Son of* Kenneth Jones and Joan (nee Withers). *Marriage:* 1st to Frances, 1971 (marr.dissolved); 2nd to Fern, 1989. *Children:* Paul Dafydd, Samuel Alun and Angharad (from 1st marriage). *Educated at* Newbridge Grammar School; London School of Economics. *Career:* Yorkshire Post Group 1970-73; Morning Telegraph, Sheffield, Assistant Editor 1973-78; Yorkshire Television, Senior Producer 1978-82; TV-AM Managing Editor and then Editor 1982-84; Television South Ltd., Deputy Managing Director and Director of Regional Programmes 1984-91. Vice-Chairman, Artswork (Britain's largest Youth Arts Charity). *Recreation:* rugby, cinema books. *Clubs:* Winchester RFC, LSE. *Address:* 6 Hereford Road, Southsea, Hampshire, PO5 2DM.

JONES, Dr Cyril Gareth, MA, PhD *Currently:* Chairman "Wales 2010", Institute of Welsh Affairs; Director Welsh National Opera; Vice Chairman Shaw Homes; Non-Executive Director, Gwent Health Authority; Governor Polytechnic of Wales. *Born on* 28 May 1933 at Blaina, Gwent. *Son of* the late Lyell Jones and Ceridwen Jones. *Marriage:* 1st to Anne Pickard 1958; 2nd to Helen Rahming 1989. *Children:* Christopher, Katy and Rebecca. *Educated at* Nantyglo Grammar School; Christ's College Cambridge; Birkbeck College London. *Career:* Dulwich College, Assistant Master 1959-63; Esso Petroleum Co., 1963-69; Booz Allen & Hamilton 1969-85; Director Booz Allen and Hamilton Inc 1981-84; Managing Partner Ernst & Whinney Management Consultants 1985-89; Member, Welsh Water Authority 1981-85. *Recreation:* music, travel, walking. *Clubs:* Reform, Institute of Directors, Cardiff and County, C.G.90. *Address:* Tre Graig House, Bwlch, Powys, LD3 7SJ. Tel: 0874-730-650.

JONES, Mr David, OBE, SRN, RMN, RNT, Cert.Ed, B.Ed(Hons). *Currently:* Principal, Sheffield and North Trent College of Nursing and Midwifery. *Born on* 27 July 1940 at Corwen, Meirionydd. *Son of* the late John Evan and the late Edith Jones. *Marriage:* to Janet Mary Ambler, 1962. *Children:* Jonathan, Susan, Stephen and Carolyn. *Educated at* Boys Grammar School, Bala. *Career:* formerly: Chief Executive Officer, English National Board for Nursing Midwifery and Health visiting 1987-89; Chief Administrative Nursing Officer Gwynedd Health Authority 1978-87; Chairman of the Welsh National Board 1979-86. *Publications:* Development of Comprehensive Counselling Service for Nurse Leaners: Journal of Advanced Nursing 1978; various articles of a general nature in the Nursing Press. *Recreation:* Welsh affairs. *Address:* 60 Whirlowdale Road, Sheffield, S7 2NH. Sheffield And North Trent Coll, of Nursing and Midwifery, 22 Collegiate Crescent, Sheffield, S10 2BA.

JONES, David Elwyn (known As D.Elwyn Jones)., *Currently:* Conservative Party Agent. *Born on* 3 July 1945 at Tremadog.*Son of* Elwyn Jones and Margaret Jones (late of Blaenau Ffestiniog). *Marriage:* divorced.*Educated at* Ysgol Glanypwll, Blaenau Ffestiniog Primary; Ysgol Sir Ffestiniog Secondary; UCNW Bangor; UCC Cardiff. *Career:* Trainee Agent, Anglesey Constituency 1970; Trainee Agent, City of Cardiff and Denbigh Constituencies 1970; Appointed Acting Agent Conwy Constituency Conservative Association, January 1971; Full Time Agent and Secretary to Conwy Conservative Assoc and Rt.Hon Sir Wyn Roberts, M.P., 1971; Freelance Journalist writing for Welsh Language Magazine "Y Faner" and Scripts (Welsh) and General Broadcasting 1982; Consultant Agent to Caernarfon Constituency Conservative Assoc 1977-91; Agent and Secretary to Clwyd South West Conservative Assoc, 1983-, and to Robert Harvey 1983-87; Sub-Agent North Wales Constituency European Parliament Elections 1979 & 1984; Personal Assist to Miss Beata Brookes MP in European Parliamentary Election North Wales 1989; Member Wales Branch, Nat Soc of Conservative and Unionist Agents 1971-; Wales Branch Chairman 1977 & 1985; Wales Branch Hon.Sec: involving attending quarterly meetings at Central Office and discussions with Ministers of Cabinet Rank, etc., 1987-90; Hon.Sec of N.Wales Gp Conservative Women's Cttee 1985- ; Hon Sec N.Wales European Constituency Conservative Council 1989- ; Agent and Secretary to nine Parliamentary Candidates in N.Wales 1970-90; Sec to Gwynedd Conservative Gp of Councillors 1971-81; Election Agent to over thirty Conservative Councillors on Gwynedd, Aberconwy and Llandudno Town Councils 1971-82; Leader of Gwynedd "No Assembly" campaign 1979; Member, and latterly (1990) Hon Sec of Clwyd Constituencies County Co-ordinating Cttee 1983- ; Organised or helped to organise innumerable Ministerial visits and tours including for Secretaries of State For Wales, Thomas, Edwards, Walker and Hunt, etc. *Publications:* Monthly Political Columnist on Welsh Weekly Current Affairs Magazine "Y Faner". Now occasional guest columnist. Frequent contributor to: Welsh Magazine "Golwg", "Cymro", and Women's Magazine "Mela", contributing articles on Non-Political matters. "Y Rebel Mwyaf?", political autobiography. Poem in "Winter Bouquet", Dec 1991. *Recreation:* American football (watching only), broadcasting and writing, cats, (active member of Colwyn Cats Protection League). *Clubs:* Honorary Life Member: Caernarfon Conservative *Address:* "Highmoor", 14 Park Drive, Deganwy, Gwynedd, LL13 9YB.

JONES, Mr David Evan Alun, CBE; DL; LL.B. *Currently:* retired: Treasurer of UCNW, Bangor; holds other offices in voluntary organisations. *Born on* 9 Aug 1925 at Aberaeron, Dyfed. *Son of* Capt. David Jacob Jones, O.B.E. and Margaret

Jane Jones. *Marriage:* to Joan Margaret Erica (nee Davies), 1952. *Children:* Jonathan E.Jones and David Mark Jones. *Educated at* Aberaeron County School; U.C.W., Aberystwyth. *Career:* Assistant Solicitor, posts in Exeter, Ilford, Southampton, Berkshire and Surrey; Deputy Clerk of Denbighshire County Council, subsequently Clerk of County Council and Clerk of the Peace, 1961-74; Chief Executive, Gwynedd County Council, 1974-80; Commissioner for Local Administration in Wales, 1981-85; BBC Welsh Council, 1981-85; member, Local Government Boundary Commission for Wales, 1985-88; Chairman, All-Wales Advisory Panel on development of Services for mentally handicapped people, 1985-89. member, Prince of Wales Committee, 1985- . *Recreation:* golf, gardening, reading, travel. *Clubs:* National Liberal; Baron Hill Golf. *Address:* Min-y-Don, West End, Beaumaris, Gwynedd., LL58 8BG.

JONES, Mr David Harold, BSc (Elec Eng), MSc (Eng). *Currently:* Managing Director, South Wales Electricity plc, since 1990. *Born on* 14 May 1942 at Sutton Coldfield, Warks. *Son of* Harold and Irene Jones. *Marriage:* to Betty Marie Anne Ashford. *Children:* Julie Rebecca and Ashley David. *Educated at* Bishop Vesey's Grammar School; University of Aston. *Career:* With the Midlands Electricity Board: Student Engineer 1960-65, Assistant Engineer 1965-75, Senior Engineer 1975-77, District Commercial Engineer 1977-78, Supplies Systems Manager, Head Office 1978-80; With the South Western Electricity Board: Management Services & Development Officer 1980-82, Computer & Information Systems Controller 1982-85, Engineering Director 1985-88; Deputy Chairman, South Wales Electricity 1988-90. Chairman, Teeside Power Limited 1990- ; Director: The National Grid Holding Company 1990- ; Director, South Wales Electricity Generating Limited 1990- ; Director: South Wales TPL Investments Limited 1990- ; Director: Celtic Contracting Services Limited 1991- ; Director: B.E.I. Lighting Limited 1991- ; Director: Electra Brands Limited 1991- . *Recreation:* opera, tennis. *Address:* Elm Lodge, Whitelye, Catbrook, Nr Chepstow, Gwent, NP6 6NP.

JONES, Mr David Michael, *Currently:* Farmer. *Born on* 18 July 1935 at Solihull. *Son of* Iorwerth Maurice Jones and the late Margaret Winifred Jones. *Marriage:* to Berenice Doreen Arthur 1960. *Children:* David Arthur and Helen Anne. *Educated at* Caersws Primary; Newtown Boys Grammar. *Career:* County Chairman Y.F.C., 1956; Council member Council of Wales N.F.U., 1965; County Chairman N.F.U., 1972; Chairman Governors Newtown High School 1980-88; Chairman N.F.U. Hill Farming Committee 1985- ; Council Member N.F.U., 1985- ; Council member Royal Welsh Agricultural Society 1972- ; County Councillor Powys 1989- . *Recreation:* music, reading, equine activities. *Clubs:* Farmers. *Address:* Cwm Derw, Aberhafesp, Newtown, Powys, SY16 3JD.

JONES, Mr David Morris, *Currently:* Controller News & Current Affairs, TVS Television; Executive Producer "Coast to Coast", Director, NewsNet UK Ltd; Consultant Editor Regional News, Oracle Teletext Ltd.; *Born at* Beaumaris, Anglesey. *Son of* Captain Morris Jones (M.N.) and Mrs Menna Lloyd Jones. *Marriage:* to Mrs Patricia Jones. *Children:* Sian Morris Jones and Eira Morris Jones. *Educated at* Beaumaris Grammar School; University of Wales. *Career:* formerly editor Wales News & Current Affairs, BBC Wales 1985-89; Managing editor News Current Affairs BBC Wales 1982-85. *Recreation:* sailing. *Clubs:* Royal Television Society; Radio Television News Directors Association of USA. *Address:* 21 Uppercliff Close, Penarth, South Glamorgan, CF6 1BE. T.V.S. Television, Southampton. Tel: 0703 834050.

JONES, Professor David Thomas, FFCM., FRCGP., FRSH *Currently:* Consultant, Strategic Health Studios. *Born on* 25 June 1931 at Maenan, Nr Llanrwst. *Son of* the late Thomas Jones and the late Eleanor (nee Pearson). *Marriage:* to Dr. M.M. Tannahill, 1985. *Children:* Owen, Daniel and Huw (from prev.marriage). *Educated at* Llanrwst Grammar; Univ. of Leeds. *Career:* Assist. Lecturer, Leeds School of Medicine, 1958-60; Principal in G.P.Harrogate, 1960-71; Asst.Senior Med.Officer., Welsh Hosp.Board., 1971-74; Specialist in Comm.Med., Clwyd Health Authority, 1975-78; Chief Medical Officer., Clwyd Health Auth., 1978-87.Dist. Gen. Manager, Clwyd Health Auth., 1987-91. *Publications:* Numerous publications on organisation and delivery of health care. *Recreation:* Gardening, travelling, antiques, modern Welsh and Scottish art. *Address:* 12 The Wigdale, Hawarden, Clwyd CH5 3LL. Dept. of Psychology, Univ. Of Wales Bangor, Bangor, Gwynedd, LL57 2DG

JONES, Della Louise Gething, GRSM. LRAM. ARCM. Currently: Opera/Concert Singer.*Born* at Neath, Glamorgan. *Daughter of* Eileen Gething Jones and the late Cyril Vincent Jones. *Marriage:* to Paul Vigars. *Children:* Raphael Anthony Gething. *Educated at* Neath Girls Grammar; Royal College of Music, London, Centre Lyrique, Geneva. *Career:* Won the Kathleen Ferrier Memorial Scholarship. Member of English National Opera, 1977-82, and remains a regular guest artist. Sung with all the major British opera companies. Extensive concert and operatic appearances throughout Europe, Russia, U.S.A. and Japan. Appears regularly on Radio and T.V. and has prolific recordings with all the major recording companies. Her wide repertoire encompasses the Baroque period up to contemporary music but, is best known for her interpretations of Handel and the Bel Canto style. *Recreation:* animals, art appreciation, writing cadenzas, T.V. soap operas. *Address:* C/o Music International, 13 Ardilaun Road, London, N5 2QR. Tel: 071 359 5183.

JONES, Mr Edgar Stafford, C.B.E. *Currently:* Retired as Head of Finance Dept. H.M. Diplomatic Service. *Born on* 11 June 1909 at Liverpool. *Son of* Theophilus and Florence (nee Edwards). *Marriage:* to Margaret Aldis Askew 1938. *Children:* Richard Stafford and Penelope Stafford *Educated at* Liverpool Institute High School. *Career:* over 50 years in Public Service. *Recreation:* Interest in all sports. *Clubs:* Vice President London Welsh RFC; Vice President Richmond Cricket Club; Member Rugby Club of London. *Address:* 30 Wingfield Road, Kingston-upon-Thames, Surrey KT2 5LR.

JONES, Mr Edward Bartley, BA(Hons) Oxon. *Currently:* Barrister. *Born on* 24 Dec 1952 at Oswestry. *Son of* Meurig Bartley Jones and the late Ruby Jones (neeMorris). *Educated at* Cardiff High School for Boys; Balliol College, Oxford. *Career:* BA(Hons) Modern History (Oxon) 1973; called to the Bar Lincoln's Inn 1975; Chancery/Commercial Barrister C in Liverpool since 1976; part-time Lecturer, Liverpool University 1977-81. *Recreation:* horse riding, hunting, opera, skiing. *Clubs:* Oxford & Cambridge, Pall Mall London. *Address:* Church Farmhouse, Dodleston, Cheshire, CH4 9NN. 7 Stone Buildings, Lincoln's Inn, London WC2

JONES, Mr Eleri Wynne, BA *Currently:* Member: Independent Television Commission 1990- ; Practitioner and Trainer in Psychotherapy and Counselling 1978- . *Born on* 9 Aug 1933 at Llangwnnadl. *Daughter of* the late Ellis Edgar Griffith and Ellen Mary (neeJones). *Marriage:* to (Professor) Bedwyr Lewis Jones, 1960. *Children:* Nia b.1964, Gronw b.1966 and Huw b.1970. *Educated at* Howell's School Denbigh (Foundation Scholar); UCW, Aberystwyth (BA Hons); UC of S.Wales, Cardiff (Diploma in Personnel Management). *Career:* Member Sianel Pedwar Cymru Authority 1984-90; Director Channel Four Television

1986-90; Lecturer Gwynedd Technical College, Bangor 1980-85; Supervisor and Counsellor N.Wales Marriage Guidance (Relate) 1975-87; Careers Officer Meirionnydd & Mon 1958-64; Teaching, Itchen Grammar School 1957-58; Journalism, Hamilton, Ontario, Canada 1956-57. *Recreation:* walking, film and television, eisteddfod. *Address:* Bodafon, Sili-wen, Bangor, Gwynedd LL57 2BH.

JONES, Mr Emlyn Bartley, MBE., FBIM. *Currently:* Consultant, Sport and Leisure Projects 1983- . *Born on* 9 Dec 1920 at Buckley, Clwyd. *Son of* the late Ernest Jones and Sarah (nee Bartley). *Marriage:* to Constance Inez (nee Jones). *Children:* Madeleine Bartley (nee Jones) and Ward *Educated at* Alun County School, Mold; Bangor Normal College; Loughborough College of Physical Education. *Career:* F/Lt. Radar Branch, RAF 1941-46; Teacher, Hist/Phys. Education, Flint Mod. Sec. Sch, 1946; Technical Representative, Central Council of Physical Recreation in N. Wales, 1947-51; Tech. Advisor, C.C.P.R., London HQ, 1951-62; Director, Crystal Palace Nat. Sports Centre, 1962-78; Director General, The Sports Council, 1978-83; TV Commentator ITV, 1955-85; President, British Assoc. of National Sports Admins; Vice Pres., Nat., Assoc. of Boy's Clubs; Governor, Dulwich College; Individual Mbr, C.C.P.R. *Publications:* Learning Lawn Tennis (1960); Sport in Space (1985) *Recreation:* Golf, skiing, watching sport, reading and walking. *Clubs:* RAF Club *Address:* Chwarae Teg, 1B Allison Grove, Dulwich, London, SE21 7ER.

JONES, Professor Emrys, M.Sc;PhD;D.Sc (Hon); D.Univ (Hon); Hon.Fellow, UC Wales. *Currently:* Retired. *Born on* 17 Aug 1920 at Aberdare, Glam. *Son of* Samuel Garfield and Annie Jones. *Marriage:* to Iona Vivien (nee Hughes), 1948. *Children:* Catrin Prydderch and Rhianon Elen (d). *Educated at* Aberdare Boys' Grammar School; Univ. College of Wales, Aberystwyth. *Career:* Ass.Lect., Univ. College, London, 1947-50; Rockefeller Fellow, N.Y., 1948-49; Lect./ Sen.Lec., in Geography, Queens Univ., Belfast, 1950-59; Reader, 1959-61, Professor, 1961-85, London School of Economics Visiting scholar - Australia, 1968; Berkley Ca., 1981; Tel Aviv, 1987; Sometime planning consultant; Chairman Regional Studies Ass., 1968-70; Victoria Medal, Royal Geographical Society; Council Univ Coll. Wales, 1972-86. *Publications:* Co-author Welsh Rural Communities, 1960; Social Geography of Belfast, 1960; Introduction to Human Geography, 1964; Towns and Cities, 1965; with D.J. Sinclair, Atlas of London, 1970; with E. Van Zaudt, Cities, 1974; Ed. Readings in Social Geography, 1975; with J. Eyles, Introduction to Social Geography, 1977; Editor: The World and its Peoples, 1979; Metropolis, 1990; Numerous chapters and papers on geographical, sociological and planning topics. *Recreation:* President Hon. Society of Cymmrodorion, 1989- ; music and books. *Clubs:* Athenaeum *Address:* 2 Pine Close, North Road, Berkhamsted, Herts., HP4 3BZ.

JONES, Professor Emrys Lloyd, F.B.A. *Currently:* Goldsmiths' Professor of English Literature, University of Oxford and Fellow of New College, Oxford. *Born on* 30 March 1931 at London. *Son of* Peter and Elizabeth Jane Jones. *Marriage:* to Barbara Everett 1965. *Children:* Susannah Hester. *Educated at* Neath Grammar School, Glamorgan; Magdalen College, Oxford. *Career:* Tutorial Fellow in English, Magdalen College 1955-77; Reader in English 1977-84; Goldsmiths' Professor 1984- ; Fellow of the British Academy 1982. *Publications:* Scenic Form in Shakespeare 1971; The Origins of Shakespeare 1977; (ed) The New Oxford Book of Sixteenth-Century Verse 1991; articles on Thomas More, Ben Jonson, Dryden, Pope, Johnson, Byron etc. *Recreation:* Opera, looking at buildings, travel. *Address:* New College, Oxford OX1 3BN.

JONES, Councillor Francis, JP *Currently:* retired. *Born on* 11 Nov 1926 at Askern, Doncaster. *Son of* the late John William Jones and the late Ellen Ann Jones (nee Thomas). *Marriage:* to Jennie May Humphreys, 1949. *Children:* John Gwynedd Jones. *Educated at* Brynrefail County School. *Career:* Engineering Dept., Electricity Board (MANWEB) for 39 years, 1948-87; elected on the old Gwyrfai District Council, 1972, on re-organisation in 1974, the Arfon Borough Council, served until May 1991; Vice Chairman Housing Comm. 1975-76; Chairman, Development & Ammenities Comm., 1978-80; Chairman, Housing Comm., 1987-89; Chairman, Finance Comm., 1990-91; elected Mayor of The Borough of Arfon 1982-83; elected to Gwynedd County Council 1977-92. Member of the Statutory Consultative Comm 1977-84 and the Liaison Comm 1977-82 with CEGB members during the construction period of the Dinorwic Power Station. Member of the Padarn Park Comm 1977-92, Chairman 1985-92. Member of the National Park Comm 1981-92. Vice-Chairman 1985-92. Member of the Snowdon Comm 1981-92. Chairman 1983-92. Member of School Governors, Brynrefail Secondary School 1977-92, Chairman 1981-84. Dolbadarn Primary School Llanberis 1977-92, Chairman 1982-92. Cwmyglo Primary School 1977-92, Chairman 1989-92. Llanrug Primary School 1989-92. Member of the Llanberis Community Council 1975-87, Chairman 1982-83. Due to wife's illness and severe disability resigned from the Gwynedd County Council February 1992. Appointed Justice of the Peace 1980. *Recreation:* photography, landscape painting, music, reading. *Clubs:* Sailing, Caernarfon. *Address:* 3 Maes Padarn, Llanberis., Gwynedd LL55 4TE.

JONES, Professor Gareth (Hywel), QC, FBA, LLD. *Currently:* Fellow and Vice-Master Trinity College Cambridge, Downing Professor of the Laws of England, Cambridge University since 1975. *Born on* 10 Nov 1930 at Tylorstown. *Son of* the late Benjamin and the late Mabel Jones (nee Griffiths. *Marriage:* to Vivienne Joy (nee Puckridge). *Children:* Christopher, Steven and Alison. *Educated at* Rhondda County G.S; University Coll. London; St. Catherines Coll. Cambridge; Harvard Univ. *Career:* Choate Fellow, Harvard 1953; Yorke Prize 1960; Called to Bar, Lincoln's Inn 1955 (Scholar); Hon. Bencher 1975; Lecturer: Oriel and Exeter Colls, Oxford 1956-58; KCL 1958-61; Trinity College, Cambridge: Lectr, 1961-74; Tutor, 1967; Sen. Tutor 1972; Vice-Master 1986- ; Univ. Lecturer Cambridge 1961-74; Chm. Faculty of Law 1978-81; Vis. Professor: Harvard 1966 and 1975; Chicago 1976-90; California at Berkeley 1967 and 1971; Indiana 1971, 1975; Michigan 1983; Georgia 1983; Lectures: Harris, Indiana 1981; Wright, Toronto 1984; Lionel Cohen, Hebrew Univ., 1985; Butterworth, QMC 1987; Mem. American Law Inst. *Publications:* (with Lord Goff of Chieveley) The Law of Restitution 1966, 3rd edn 1986; The History of the Law of Charity 1532-1827, 1969; The Sovereignty of the Law 1973; (with Sir William Goodhart) Specific Performance 1986; various articles. *Clubs:* Beefsteak. *Address:* 9B Cranmer Road, Cambridge CB3 9BL. Clay Street, Thornham, Magna, Eye, Suffolk, IP23 8HE.

JONES, Mr Gareth Lloyd, MA Barrister at Law *Currently:* Retired. *Born on* 3 May 1927 at Cardiff. *Son of* the late John Martin Jones and the late Anne Ceridwen (nee Evans). *Marriage:* to Ann Parry Williams 1960. *Children:* Ruth, Ceri and Rhiannon. *Educated at* Cardiff High School 1937-44; Jesus College Oxford 1944-48; Inner Temple 1950-52. *Career:* Assistant Master, Merchant Taylor's School 1952-58; Headmaster Alun Grammar School, Mold 1958-65; HM Inspector of Schools 1965-84; Staff Inspector 1974-84; Secretary Welsh Joint Education Committee 1984-90;

Member of Schools Council, School Curriculum Development Committee; Curriculum Council for Wales; Coleg Harlech Council, Governors of Welsh College of Music and Drama, Museum Schools Service Committee, University of Wales Court, Welsh Language Education Development Committee. *Recreation:* Music, walking, reading, sports. *Address:* 24 Marionville Gardens, Llandaff, Cardiff CF5 2LR.

JONES, Mr Geraint, MIPM *Currently:* BT National Manager Wales; Chairman BBC Radio Gloucestershire; Member BBC South and West Advisory Panel. *Born on* 9 June 1938 at Holyhead, Anglesey. *Son of* Gwilym Idwal and Alice Jones. *Marriage:* Jennifer Mary Weetman. *Children:* Robin Alexander, Victoria Louise and Richard Owen. *Educated at* Holyhead Grammar School. *Career: Recreation:* golf, tennis, music. *Address:* 25 Pendwyallt Road, Coryton, Cardiff CF4 7YR.

JONES, Mr Geraint Iwan, F.R.A.M. *Born on* 16 May 1917 at Porth, Glam. *Son of* the late (Rev) Evan and Caroline Jones (nee Davies). *Marriage:* 1st to M.A.Kemp, 1940, one d Isobel; 2nd to Winifred Roberts, 1949. *Children:* Isobel *Educated at* Bargoed Secondary; Caterham School; Royal Academy of Music. *Career:* Conductor, organist, harpsichordist; Organ recitals at National Gallery Concerts 1940-44; Conductor, Mermaid Theatre, Perfs of Purcell Dido and Aensas with Kirsten Flagstad 1950-53; founded Geraint Jones Singers and Orchestra 1951, with whom many recordings; frequent tours in Europe and America since 1948 as organist, conductor and as harpsichordist with violinist wife Winifred Roberts; many recordings of Historic organs in Europe for HMV, many recordings for HMV, Decca & DGG and numerous series of recitals for BBC, many of which broadcast in U.S. and Canada; series of complete organ works of Bach in London 1945-46; and twelve Bach concerts with own choir and orchestra, Royal Festival Hall 1955; Grand Prix du Disque 1959 and 1966; Soloist at promenade concerts for many years and at many British and Continental festivals; Prof. Royal Academy of Music 1961-87; Artistic director, Lake District Festival 1960-78; Salisbury Festival 1972-77; Manchester International Festival 1977-87; Kirckman Concert Society (promoting young artists in London) 1963- ; as organ consultant has designed many instruments including those at Royal Northern Coll. of Music, Manchester; St.Andrews Univ; Royal Academy of Music; Academy for Performing Arts, Hong Kong; Tsim Sha Tsui Cultural Centre, Hong Kong. *Publications:* Translations of Clicquot's Theorie-Pratique de la Facture de L'Orgue (1789) and Les Grandes Orgues De L'Abbatiale St.Etienne De Caen by Robert Davy; articles in musical journals. *Recreation:* antique furniture, architecture, wine, photography. *Address:* The Long House, Arkley Lane, Barnet, Herts., EN5 3JR.

JONES, Mr Geraint Stanley, BA, Dip.Ed *Currently:* Chief Executive S4C since 1989. *Born on* 26 April 1936 *Son of* Rev David Stanley Jones and Mrs Olwen Jones. *Marriage:* to Rhiannon, 1961. *Children:* Sioned and Siwan *Educated at* Pontypridd Grammar School, UCNW Bangor. *Career:* Served RAEC, Sgt.; BBC Wales: studio manager 1960-62, production assistant Current Affairs (TV) 1962-65, TV producer Current Affairs 1965-69, producer Features and Documentaries 1969-73, Assistant Head of Programmes Wales 1973-74, Head of Programmes, Wales 1974-81, Controller BBC Wales 1981-85, Director Public Affairs 1986-87; Managing Director Regional Broadcasting BBC 1987-89; hon fell UCNW, member Court and Council University College of Wales, Aberystwyth; Chairman: Welsh College of Music and Drama, Euro Broadcasting Union TB Programme Committee; Ryan Davies Trust;

member UK Freedom from Hunger Committee; FRSA. *Recreation:* music, painting and horse riding. *Clubs:* Cardiff and County. *Address:* c/o S4C, Parc Busnes Ty Glas, Llanishen, Cardiff, CF4 5DU.

JONES, Professor Glanville Rees Jeffreys, MA, FSA. *Currently:* Emeritus Professor of Historical Geography, University of Leeds (retired 1989). *Born on* 12 Dec 1923 at Felindre, Llangyfelach. *Son of* the late Benjamin and the late Sarah (nee Jeffreys). *Marriage:* 1st to Margaret Rosina Ann Stevens, 1949, (dissolved 1958), no issue; 2nd to Pamela Winship, 1959. *Children:* Sarah Catryn and David Emrys Jeffreys. *Educated at* Neath Grammar School; University College of Wales, Aberystwyth. *Career:* Army 1943-46 (Royal Engineers; Royal Welch Fusiliers, commissioned 1944). Successively Assistant Lecturer, Lecturer and Senior Lecturer in Geography, University of Leeds 1949-69; Reader in Historical Geography, University of Leeds 1969-74; Professor of Historical Geography, University of Leeds 1974-89; Hywel Dda Prize, University of Wales 1974; O'Donnell Lecturer, University of Wales 1975; Chairman, Area Advisory Committee (Dept of Environment) for Rescue Archaeology in Yorkshire - Humberside 1975-79; Pres. Anthropology and Archaeology Section, British Assoc for the Advancement of Science 1982-83. *Publications:* Geography as Human Ecology (author and ed. with S.R.Eyre), 1966; Leeds and its Region (author and ed. with M.W.Beresford), 1967; Post Roman Wales in The Agrarian History of England and Wales, 1972. *Recreation:* gardening, military history, observing politics. *Address:* 26 Lee Lane East, Horsforth, Leeds LS18 5RE. Department of Geography, The University of Leeds, Leeds, LS2 9JT Tel: 0532 582968.

JONES, The Revd. Canon. Glyndwr, Dip.Th. *Currently:* General Secretary, The Missions to Seamen, since 1990. *Born on* 25 Nov 1935 at Seven Sisters, Neath. *Son of* Bertie Samuel Jones and Elizabeth Ellen Jones. *Marriage:* 1st to Cynthia Elaine Jenkins, 1961 (d.1964); 2nd to (Marion) Anita Morris, 1966. *Children:* Susan (b.1968) and Robert (b.1970). *Educated at* Dynevor School, Swansea; St.Michael's Theological College, Llandaff; University of Wales. *Career:* Ordained Deacon, Brecon Cathedral 1962; Ordained priest, Brecon Cathedral 1963; Curate of Clydach, Diocese of Swansea and Brecon 1962-64; Curate of Llangyfelach with Morriston, Diocese of Swansea and Brecon 1964-67; Curate of Sketty, Swansea, Diocese of Swansea and Brecon 1967-70; Rector of Bryngwyn with Newchurch & Llanbedr, Painscastle with Llandewi Fach, Diocese of Swansea and Brecon 1970-72; Missions to Seamen Port Chaplain at Swansea and Port Talbot 1972-76; Missions to Seamen Senior Chaplain to the Port of London 1976-81; Auxiliary Ministries Secretary, Central Office, The Missions to Seamen 1981-85; Assistant General Secretary, Central Office, The Missions to Seamen 1985-90; Appointed member of Royal College of Chaplains, 9th November 1990. Honorary Chaplain, The Royal Alfred Seafarers Society 1987; Honorary Canon of St.Michael's Cathedral, Kobe, Japan 1988; Chaplain to the Company of Information Technologists 1989; Chaplain to the Worshipful Company of Innholders 1990; Chaplain to the Worshipful Company of Farriers 1990; Chaplain to the Worshipful Company of Carmen 1990; Honorary Member of the Honourable Company of Master Mariners 1990; Freeman of the City of London 1990; Member of the Council of: The Marine Society, Partnership for World Mission, International Christian Maritime Association, Merchant Navy Welfare Board. *Recreation:* sport, reading, music, theatre, travelling. *Clubs:* Royal Commonwealth Society. *Address:* The Missions To Seamen, St.Michael Paternoster Royal, College

Hill, London, EC4R 2RL.

JONES, Reverend Godfrey Caine, B.A., M.Ed. *Currently:* Rector of Clocaenog, Cyffylliog and Llanfwrog. *Born on* 28 Feb 1936 at Brymbo. *Son of* Glyn Idwal Jones and Elsie Jane Jones (nee Caine), of Corris. *Marriage:* to Dorothy Edith Huntley, 1968. *Children:* Gareth Michael and Matthew Caine. *Educated at* Grove Park Boys Grammar Wrexham; Durham, London, Birmingham and Aston Univs. *Career:* Head of Religious Education Oswestry Boys High School, 1960-65; Vice-Principal Jesus College Otukpo, Nigeria, 1966-69; Lecturer in Religious Studies Westhill College Selly Oak Birmingham, 1970-73; Deputy Principal The Hill Adult Education College Abergavenny, 1974-75; Head of Humanities Denbigh High School, 1975-81; Senior Lecturer Matlock College Derbyshire, 1981-83; Ordained by Bishop of St. Asaph, 1978; Curate of St. Peter's Ruthin, 1983-84; Rector of Clocaenog, Cyffylliog and Llanfwrog, 1984- ; Glyndwr District Councillor, 1987-91; Clwyd County Councillor, 1989- ; Chairman of Clwyd PTA, 1987-89; Chairman of Governors of Borthyn School and of Brynhyfryd High School Ruthin, 1988- ; Tutor on St. Asaph Diocesan Ministerial Training Course, 1991- ; Chairman of Clwyd SACRE, 1991-92; Member of Court of Governors of National Museum of Wales, 1990- ; Member of Court of Liverpool University 1991-; Member of W.J.E.C. 1991-. *Recreation:* Music, squash and photography. *Address:* Llanfwrog Rectory, Ruthin, Clwyd LL15 1LE. Tel: 08242 4866.

JONES, Sir Gordon Pearce, Bsc., CBIM., FIWEM. *Currently:* Chairman, Yorkshire Water PLC, since 1983; Chairman Hicksons International PLC, 1991-. *Born on* 17 Feb. 1927 at Morriston, W.Glam. *Son of* Alun Pearce and Miriam Jones. *Marriage:* to Gloria Stuart Melville, 1951. *Children:* Elspeth, Huw and Hywel. *Educated at* Swansea Grammar School, Univ. Coll., Swansea. *Career:* Royal Navy, 1947-51; British Iron & Steel Res. Assn., 1951-56; Raw Material & Energy Planning, BISF Iron & Steel Board, 1956-60; Fuel Oil Manager, Esso Petroleum, 1960-64; various Management appointments in Steel Industry, ending as Man.Dir., Firth Vickers, 1974-79; Director, Thos W. Ward plc, 1979-82; Chairman, Water Authorities Assn., 1986-89; Mbr Presidents advisory commt, CBI, 1986-89; Hon.Fellow Univ.Coll. Swansea, 1991. *Publications:* Many newspaper articles and journals. *Recreation:* Railway history, opera, music, travel and reading *Clubs:* Naval & Military *Address:* Bryngower, Sitwell Grove, Rotherham, S. Yorks. S60 3AY.

JONES, His Honour Judge Graham Julian, MA., LL.M.(Cantab). *Currently:* Circuit Judge. *Born on* 17 July 1936 at Ystrad Rhondda. *Son of* the late D.J. Jones esq., C.B.E., (Town Clerk Rhondda), and Mrs Jones (nee Marshall). *Marriage:* to Dorothy Tickle 1961. *Children:* Nicholas David Julian, Sarah Elizabeth and Timothy James Julian. *Educated at* Porth County Grammar School; St. John's College, Cambridge. *Career:* Solicitor 1961; Partner Morgan Bruce & Nicholas 1961-85; Deputy Circuit Judge 1975-78; Recorder 1978-85; Circuit Judge 1985; Past President of Associated Law Societies of Wales of and Pontypridd, Rhondda & District Law Society; Member Council Cardiff Law Society; Member Law Society Bye Laws Revision Committee 1984-85; Member Lord Chancellor's Legal Aid Advisory Committee 1980-85. *Recreation:* Golf, boats. *Clubs:* Cardiff & County, Royal Porthcawl & Radyr golf clubs. *Address:* Cardiff Crown Court, Cathays Park, Cardiff.

JONES, Assistant Commissioner Graham Wyn, Q.P.M. 1987 *Currently:* Assistant Commissioner of Police of the Metropolis. *Born on* 12 Oct 1943 at Ystradgynlais. *Son of* Thomas James and Mary Elizabeth (nee Almrott). *Marriage:* 1970. *Educated at* Thornbury Grammar School; Univ. of Exeter (LL.B.Hons) *Career:* Gloucestershire Constabulary 1963-79; Inspector 1968; Chief Inspector 1973; Superintendent 1976; Thames Valley Police 1979-84; Chief Superintendent, Oxford 1979; Assist. Chief Constable 1982; Metropolitan Police 1984- ; Deputy Assist. Commissioner 1984; Assistant Commissioner 1989. *Publications:* Various articles on Police and the Media, Public Order and Equal Opportunities. *Recreation:* Rugby football, theatre and golf *Clubs:* The Unnamed *Address:* New Scotland Yard, Broadway, London SW1 0BG.

JONES, Mr Griffith Winston Guthrie, Q.C., M.A. (Cambridge) LL.B.(Wales) *Currently:* Retired. *Born on* 24 Sept 1914 at Dolgellau. *Son of* Rowland Guthrie Jones and Mari Elizabeth Griffith. *Marriage:* to 1).Anna McCarthy 1959 (died 1969) 2). Janet L'Estrange 1978. *Educated at* Bootham School, York; University College of Wales, Aberystwyth; St. John's College, Cambridge. *Career:* Called to the Bar by Gray's Inn 1939; War Service as Capt. R.A. in Egypt, French North Africa, Italy, Yugoslavia and Germany 1940-46; Queen's Counsel 1963; Deputy Chairman of Cumberland Quarter Sessions 1963-68; Recorder of Bolton 1968-73. *Publications:* 'The Family of Wynne of Hazelwood' *Recreation:* Local history, gardening. *Address:* Culleenamore, Sligo, Ireland.

JONES, Mr Gwilym Haydn, M.P. *Currently:* Member of Parliament for Cardiff North 1983- . *Son of* Evan Haydn Jones and Mary Elizabeth Gwenhwyfar Jones (nee Moseley). *Marriage:* to Linda Margaret Jones (nee John). *Children:* Grant Hilary Jones and Fay Alicia Jones. *Educated at Career:* Parliamentary Private Secretary, Dept. of Transport 1991-; Director, Bowring Wales Limited 1980-; Councillor, Gabalfa, Cardiff 1969-72; Councillor, Rhiwbina, Cardiff 1973-83; Vice Chairman Wales Area Young Conservatives 1968-70; Chairman Federation of Public Passenger Transport Operators, S. Wales 1976-79; Conservative election agent Cardiff South East 1974; Chairman, Cardiff North West Conservative Assoc. 1981-83; Secretary Welsh Conservative backbenchers group 1985- ; Secretary All Party group Replacement of Animals in Medical Experiments 1986- . *Publications:* Contributed forewords to: 'Your Phone Bill - Fact or Fiction?' by Nathaniel Ramanaden, 'Phantoms, Poltergeists and Rogues' by Nathaniel Ramanaden. *Recreation:* Golf, model railways, watching Wales win at rugby. *Clubs:* County Conservative, Cardiff and County, United Services Mess, Whitchurch Bowls (President) Tongwynlais Football (Vice President), Rhiwbina Rugby Club. *Address:* House of Commons, London SW1A 0AA.

JONES, Professor Gwilym Henry, BA, PhD, DD (Wales), MA(Oxon) *Currently:* Professor of Religious Studies, University of Wales, Bangor, since 1987. *Born on* 16 July 1930 at Caernarvonshire. *Son of* John Lloyd Jones and Jennie (nee Roberts). *Marriage:* to Mary Christabel Williams, 1959. *Children:* Rhys (b.1966), Huw (b.1969) and Ruth (b.1975). *Educated at* Pwllheli Grammar School; University College of North Wales, Bangor; Jesus College Oxford. *Career:* Minister Presbyterian Church of Wales 1956-61; Professor of Hebrew, Theological College, Abersytwyth 1961-66; Lecturer, University of Wales, Bangor 1966, Senior Lecturer 1979, Reader 1984; Dean of Divinity, University of Wales 1987-90; Dean of Arts, University of Wales, Bangor 1988-91. *Publications:* Arweiniad i'r Hen Destament, 1966; Gwirionedd y Gair, 1974; Cerddi Seion, 1975; Gramadeg Hebraeg y Beibl, 1976; Diwinyddiaeth yr Hen Destament, 1979; 1 and 2 Kings (New Century Bible) 2 vols, 1984; Y Gair Ddoe a Heddiw: Eseia o Jerwsalem, 1988; The Nathan Narratives, 1990. *Recreation:* walking, music. *Address:* Coed Gadlys, Llansadwrn, Menai Bridge,

Gwynedd, LL59 5SE. Dept of Religious Studies, University of Wales, Bangor, Gwynedd LL57 2DG. Tel: 0248 351151.

JONES, Professor Gwyn, *Currently:* retired. *Born on* 24 May 1907 at Blackwood, Gwent. *Son of* George Henry Jones and Lilian Florence (nee Nethercott). *Marriage:* 1st to Alice (nee Rees), 1928, (d.1979); 2nd to Mair (nee Sivele), widow of Prof. Thomas Jones. *Educated at* Tredegar County School; University of Wales, Cardiff College. *Career:* Schoolmaster 1929-35; Lecturer in English, U.C., Cardiff 1935-40; Professor of English UCW, Aberystwyth 1940-64 (Fellow 1987), Professor at UC Cardiff 1965-75 (Fellow 1980); Pres. Viking Society for Northern Research 1950-52 (Hon. Life member 1979); Mem. Arts Council of G.B., 1957-67, and Chairman of the Welsh A.C; Director Penmark Press 1939- ; Honours: CBE 1965; Commander's Cross of the Icelandic Order of the Falcon 1987 (Chevalier 1963); The Phi Beta Kappa Christian Sauss Award 1972; The Annual Gwyn Jones Lecture 1978- ; Hon.D.Litt. (Wales 1977, Nottingham 1978, Southampton 1983); Hon. Freeman of Islwyn 1988; Cymmrodorion Medal 1991. *Publications:* Novels: Richard Savage 1935; Times Like these 1936; repr.1979; Garland of Bays 1938; The Green Island 1946; The Flowers Beneath the Scythe 1952; The Walk Home 1962; Short Stories: The Buttercup Field 1945; The Still Waters 1948; Shepherd's Hey 1953; Translations: The Vatnsdalers' Saga 1942; with Thomas Jones The Mabinogion 1948; Egil's Saga 1960; Eirik the Red 1961; Non-Fiction includes: (ed) The Welsh Review, 1939-49; A Prospect of Wales 1948; Welsh Legends and Folk-Tales 1955; Scandinavian Legends and Dyfed Folk-tales; Kings, Beasts and Heroes 1972; Being and Belonging (BBC Wales Annual Radio Lecture), 1977; (ed with I.Ff.Elis) Twenty-Five Welsh Short Stories, 1971 (re-issued as Classic Welsh Stories 1992); Oxford Book of Welsh Verse in English, 1977; Fountains of Praise 1983; A History of the Vikings (rev), 1984; The Norse Atlantic Saga, new edition, 1986; Background to Dylan Thomas and Othe Explorations, 1992; contrib. to numerous learned and literary journals. *Address:* Castle Cottage, Sea View Place, Aberystwyth SY23 1DZ.

JONES, Dr. Gwyn (Miah Gwynfor), BSc., PhD., FBCS. *Currently:* Chairman, Welsh Development Agency 1988- . *Born on* 2 Dec 1948 at Porthmadog. *Son of* Robert Jones and Jane Irene Jones. *Marriage:* to Maria Linda Johnson. *Children:* Victoria and Holly. *Educated at* Ysgol Eifionydd, Porthmadog; University of Manchester; University of Essex. *Career:* British Steel 1975-77; ICL 1977-81; Corporate Technology plc Chairman and Chief Executive 1981-87; Director: ACT Group plc 1989- ; Welsh Water Enterprises Ltd 1990- ; Council Member University of Wales; Member Prince's Youth Business Trust; Member Board European Business School, Swansea; Hon Fellow Polytechnic of Wales. *Recreation:* Travel, golf, tennis, skiing. *Address:* Welsh Dev. Agency, Pearl House, Greyfriars Road, Cardiff., CF1 3XX.

JONES, Dame Gwyneth, CBE., DBE Hon.D.M. *Currently:* Soprano. *Born on* 7 Nov 1936 at Pontnewydd, Wales. *Daughter of* the late Edward George Jones and the late Violet (nee Webster). *Marriage:* to Till Haberfeld. *Children:* 1 daughter *Educated at* Royal Coll. of Music, with Arnold Smith & Ruth Packer; Accademia Chigiana, Siena; Int. Opera Centre, Zurich, with Maria Carpi in Geneva. *Career:* Debut: Zurich Opera: as a mezzo-soprano, 1962-63, a soprano, Amelia, Un Ballo in Maschera; Principal Dramatic Soprano: since 1963, Covent Garden since 1966, Deutsche oper Berlin since 1966; Vienna State Opera since 1967, Bavarian State Opera, Munich, roles include: Leonore, Fidelio; Leonora, Il Trovatore; Senta, Der Fliegende Hollander; Sieglinde, Die Walkure; Brunnhilde,

Gotterdammerung; Desdemona; Otello; Lady Macbeth, Macbeth; Elisabeth de Valois, Don Carlos; Kundry, Parsifal; Isolde, Tristan and Isolde; Ortrud, Minnie, Erwartung, La Voir Hirmaine; Marschallin, Der Rosenkavalier; Elisabeth, Tannhauser; Dyer's Wife, Die Frau ohne Schatten; title roles: Aida, Tosca, Medee, Salome, Elektra, Turandot. Major operatic deputs include: Covent Garden: 1964: Leonore, Fidelio; Leonora, Il Trovatore; 1965, Sieglinde, Die Walkure; 1966, Leonore, Fidelio: Bavarian State Opera, Munich; Vienna State Opera; Geneva Opera, Desdemona, Otello; Deutsche Oper, Berlin, Leonora, Il Trovatore; Dallas Civic Opera, Lady Macbeth, Macbeth; 1967, La Scala, Milan, Leonora, Il Trovatore; 1970, Hamburg State Opera, title role, Salome: 1972, Metropolitan Opera, New York, Sieglinde, Die Walkure; 1978, Paris Opera, title role, L'Incoronazione di Poppea; Bayreuth Festival: 1966, Sieglinde, Die Walkure; 1968, Eva, Die Meistersinger von Nurnberg; 1969: Kundry, Parsifal; Senta, Der Fliegende Hollander; 1972, Elisabeth/Venus, Tannhauser; 1974, Brunnhilde, Gotterdammerung; 1975 and 1976 (centenary production), Brunnhilde, Der Ring des Nibelungen; Recent roles in the U.K. include: Since 1990, Covent Garden: Brunnhilde, Der Ring des Nibelungen; title role, Turandot; Recording include: Beethoven, Fidelio (DG); R.Strauss, Der Rosenkavalier (CBS); Verdi, Otello (EMI); Wagner: Der Fliegende Hollander, Lohengrin, Parsifal (all DG); Der Rimg des Nibelungen (PHIL); Famous Operatic Scenes (DG), Wagner Recital (Chandos); Films, Television and Video include: numerous appearances in Wagner, Der Ring des Nibelungen (Bayreuth Festival); The Life of Richard Wagner (directed by Tony Palmer); Awards and Honours include: 1976, Commander, Order of the British Empire (CBE); 1977, Kammersangerin, Austria and Bavaria; 1986, Dame Commander, Order of the British Empire (DBE); 1987, Shakespeare Prize, Hamburg; 1988, Commander's Cross of the Order of Merit, Federal Republic of Germany; Fellow Royal College of Music, University of Wales; Honorary Member Vienna State Opera, 1989. *Address:* P.O. Box 8037, Zurich, Switzerland.

JONES, Ms Gwyneth Ann, *Currently:* writer/novelist. *Born on* 14 Feb 1952 at Manchester. *Daughter of* D.T.Jones and M.R.Dugdale. *Marriage:* to M.Peter Wilson Gwilliam, 1976. *Children:* one s: Gabriel Jimi Jones. *Educated at* Notre Dame High School; Manchester University, of Sussex Falmer BA Hons 2: 2 History of Ideas with latin. *Career:* Writer of 12 novels for children, eight under the Nom de Plume Ann Halam, the latest Dinosaur Junction appears June 1992, (Orchard Books), plus four adult science fiction novels: Divine Endurance, 1984; Escape Plans, 1986; Kairos, 1988; White Queen, 1991. White Queen has won the James Tiptree Memorial Award 1992 and is short listed for the Arthur C.Clarke Award. Numerous short stories reviews critical articles. *Publications:* Orchard Books, London Gollancz, London. *Recreation:* gardening, weight training, travel. *Clubs:* The Zap, The Reform (Brighton), Shape. *Address:* 30 Roundhill Crescent, Brighton, E.Sussex BN2 3FR.

JONES, Mr Hywel Francis, MA (Cantab)., IPFA *Currently:* Retired. *Born on* 28 Dec 1928 at Morriston, Swansea. *Son of* the late Brynmor and the late Maggie Beatrice Jones. *Marriage:* to Marian Rosser Craven 1959. *Children:* Sharon Elisabeth (Fraser). *Educated at* Swansea Grammar School; St.John's College Cambridge. *Career:* Nat. Service RAPC 1953-55; Deputy County Treasurer, Breconshire C.C. 1956-59; Assistant County Treasurer Carmarthenshire C.C. 1959-66; Borough Treasurer Port Talbot B.C. 1966-75; Secretary Commission for Local Admin. in Wales 1975-85; Local Commissioner (Ombudsman) for Wales 1985-91; Member

1972-74; Treasurer National Eisteddfod of Wales since 1975; Member Gorsedd of Bards 1977. *Recreation:* Music, reading, gardening. *Address:* Godre'r Rhiw, 1 Lon Heulog, Baglan, Port Talbot SA12 8SY.

JONES, Rt.Rev. Hywel James, D.D. *Currently:* Retired. *Born on* 4 March 1918 at Porthcawl, Glamorgan. *Son of* Ivor James Jones and Annie Jones (nee Twiss). *Marriage:* to Margaret Wilcox. *Children:* Margaret Lindsay and Peter Hywel. *Educated at* Emmanuel College; Univ. of Saskatchewan *Career:* Deacon 1942; Priest 1942; Travelling Priest 1942-44; Incumbent Parksville Qualicum Beach 1944-47; Colwood & Langford 1947-56; Rector St. Mary The Virgin, Oak Bay 1956-59; Hon. Canon BC 1959-68; Archdeacon Quatniho 1968-71; of Victoria 1971-77; Emeritus 1977-80; Bishop of British Columbia 1980-84. *Recreation:* Reading, music, gardening *Clubs:* Union, Victoria BC *Address:* 2028 Frederick, Norris Road, Victoria, Bc Canada, V8P 2B2.

JONES, Mr Iddon Lloyd, JP, BSc, CEng, FICE, FIHT, M.ConsE. *Currently:* Consulting Civil Engineer, Mott MacDonald Ltd (previously James Williamson & Partners), since 1957. Worked on Ffestiniog and Rheidol Hydro Electric Projects, Wylfa Nuclear Power Station, North Sea Oil related work offshore Shetlands. Partner in charge of site of Dinorwig Power Station project. Magistrate since 1979. *Born on* 1 Nov 1933 at Harlech, Gwynedd. *Son of* the late Morris Jones and the late Dorothy Lloyd Jones. *Marriage:* to Ann Trefor (Jones), 1968. *Children:* Nia Lloyd Jones and Huw Lloyd Jones. *Educated at* Barmouth Grammar School; University College Swansea. *Career:* National Service Commission, Airfield Construction Branch, RAF, Middle East. Managing Director Merz Rendel Williamson Ltd; Divisional Director of Mott McDonald Group's Wales Region and Power Division. *Recreation:* golf. *Clubs:* Penmaenmawr Golf. *Address:* Treflys, Conwy Old Road, Penmaenmawr, Gwynedd, LL34 6RD.

JONES, Ieuan, ARCM *Currently:* Solo Concert Harpist. *Born on* 24 Jan 1963 at Oswestry. *Son of* Mr & Mrs David Jones. *Educated at* Royal College of Music, London. *Career:* harpist; appointed harpist to the House of Commons 1984, London debut Purcell Room 1985, Wigmore Hall debut 1987; recitals: Dusseldorf 1986 and 1990, Amsterdam 1987, Ireland 1987, Vienna 1987, Holland 1987, Valencia Spain 1987, 1988 and 1991; Mid West tour USA 1989, Wigmore Hall 1990, Paris 1990, St.David's Hall Cardiff 1988, 1990 and 1991; tours with: Bournemouth Sinfonietta 1986, 1987 and 1988, Welsh Chamber Orch 1988, London Festival Orch 1989 and 1990; TV and radio appearances incl: Wogan 1986, Daytime Live 1988, AVRO TV Holland 1987, Billy Butler Show 1988 and 1990, Derek Jameson 1988, Gloria Hunniford 1988 and 1990; appearances at many festivals in the UK and abroad; private appearances before HRH Queen Elizabeth the Queen Mother at the Royal Lodge Windsor 1986, guest appearances St.James' Palace 1988 and Holyrood House 1989; recordings: The Uncommon ·Harp (1987), The Two Sides of Ieuan Jones (1988). In the French Style (1990), Mozart in Paris (1990); ARCM 1981. *Recreation:* health and fitness, travel. *Address:* 26 Orville Road, London, SW11 3LR. Mathrafal, Meifod, Powys, SY22 6HT.

JONES, Mr Ieuan Llewelyn, BA(Hons), Wales. *Currently:* Councillor on Afton Borough Council and also Gwynedd County Council. Prior to retirement, Head of History Department, Ysgol Dyffryn Ogwen, Bethesda. *Born on* 24 March 1921 at Llanfairfechan, Gwynedd. *Son of* Thomas Llewelyn Jones and Jane Jones. *Marriage:* to Eurwen Kathlyn Roberts, 1951. *Children:* Owain Llewelyn and Sian Llewelyn *Educated at* Friars School, Bangor;

University College of N.Wales, Bangor, graduated BA(Hons) in History. *Career:* Served with the RAF in Sicily, Italy and Greece, 1942-46; Councillor, Arfon Borough Council since 1976, representing Bethesda; Mayor of Arfon 1988; Chairman, Finance Committee, 1986; current Chairman of Policy and Resources Committee; current Vice-Chairman, Planning Committee; member of Council and Court, University College of North Wales, also college representative on Court University of Wales; member, North Wales Tourism Board, Theatr Gwynedd Management committee; member for Llandygai Ward, Gwynedd County Council, since 1985, current Vice-Chairman, Finance Committee. Chairman, Governing Body of Gwynedd Technical College, Bangor. Chairman, Governing Body of Ysgol Dyffryn Ogwen. member, Governing Body of Coleg Normal, Bangor; present Chairman, Bethesda Community Council, organist and deacon, Jerusalem Chapel, Bethesda, at one time accompanist to Penrhyn Male Voice Choir. *Recreation:* music, drama and the Arts in general, sport, *Clubs:* Founder member, Clwb Rygbi, Bethesda. *Address:* Hafod y Coed, Bethesda, Gwynedd, LL57 3LU. Tel: Bethesda 600498.

JONES, Mr Ieuan Wyn, LL.B, MP *Currently:* Member of Parliament, Ynys Mon 1987- . *Born on* 22 May 1949 at Dinbych, Clwyd. *Son of* the late John Jones and Mair Elizabeth (nee Pritchard). *Marriage:* to Eirian Llwyd, 1974. *Children:* Gerallt, Gwenllian and Owain. *Educated at* Pontardawe Grammar; Ysgol-y-Berwyn, Y Bala; Liverpool Polytechnic. *Career:* Solicitor, partner 1974-87, William Jones & Talog Davies Ruthin, Denbigh and Llangefni; National Chair Plaid Cymru 1978-80 and 1990- ; Senior Vice Chair 1987-90; Deputy Treasurer 1984-87; President North Wales Relate 1990- . *Recreation:* sport, local history, walking. *Address:* Ty Newydd, Rhosmeirch, Llangefni Ynys Mon, , Gwynedd., LL77 7RZ. House Of Commons, London SW1A OAA.

JONES, Mr Ivor Graham, *Currently:* retired due to ill health. *Born on* 2 July 1932 at Rassau, Ebbw Vale. *Son of* the late Tom Jones and the late Evelyn (nee Jenkins). *Educated at* Ebbw Vale Grammar School; Crumlin Technical College. *Career:* Junior Trainee Accountant Mon County Council 1950-55; Cost Clerk and Senior Clerk Ebbw Vale UDC 1956-69; Chief Administrative Officer Risca UDC 1969-74; Chief Clerk and Administrative Officer Blaenau Gwent Borough Council 1974-84; Town Clerk Tredegar T.C., 1984-86; National Service Royal Army Pay Corps 1951-52. President Welsh Bowling Assoc 1991; member Welsh Bowling Council 1957-60, 1970-77, 1984-; National Selector 1973-77; Pres of Monmouthshire Bowling Assoc 1976; Match Secretary 1983- ; Chairman of Selectors since 1981; member Management Ctee 1955- ; Pres West Mon Bowling Assoc 1990-; Chairman West Mon Bowling Assoc 1965-67 and 1988; Pres Beaufort Bowling Club 1990- ; Secretary Beaufort Bowling Club 1955-74 (two periods). Drama: Over fifty productions for Ebbw Vale Municipal Theatre Group and other local societies, as an actor in a wide spectrum of plays from Ibsen to Priestley. Past Chairman and Secretary of Ebbw Vale and Risca Branches of NALGO. *Publications:* Sixty Years of Monmouthshire Bowling 1924-1984; History of Beaufort Bowls Club 1976. *Recreation:* sport (bowls, cricket, rugby football), drama, music (particularly opera), reading, keen railway enthusiast. *Clubs:* Beaufort Bowls, Ebbw Vale Rugby Football. *Address:* Glan-Y-Nant, Rassau Road, Rassau, Ebbw Vale, Gwent, NP3 5BJ.

JONES, Janet Eveline, J.P. *Currently:* retired, Head teacher 1971-81. *Born on* 27 June 1930 at Connah's Quay. *Daughter of* Edward Leslie Coppack and Agnes Jamieson (nee McRae).

Marriage: to Thomas Mathias Jones, 1954. *Children:* Helen Lesley (Mrs Byrne), Christopher Thomas and David Edward. *Educated at* Hawarden Grammar School; The Froebel Education Institute. *Career:* President, Nat Assoc of Head Teachers, Halton South 1975-76; President Runcorn and Dist Soroptomists 1985-86 and 1990-91; National Chairman British Assoc for Early Childhood Education 1986-89; Co-Chairman The Womens National Commission 1987-89; Patron Prix De Femmes D'Europe; Borough Councillor (Lib-Dem) Halton 1990; member Standing Committee Social Sciences (S.E.A.C.); member 300 Group. *Publications:* Report to Select Committees on Education; Reports for Womens Nat. Commission. *Recreation:* Reading, swimming, photography. *Clubs:* Soroptomist, 63 Bayswater Road. *Address:* 8 Kenilworth Avenue, Runcorn, Cheshire, WA7 4XQ.

JONES, Hon. Jeffrey Richard, CBE., MA (Oxon). *Currently:* Retired. *Born on* 18 Nov. 1921 at Newtown, Mongommery. *Son of* Rev. Thomas Jones and Winifred (nee Williams). *Marriage:* to Ann Rosaleen Jones. *Children:* Thomas Etienne Jones and Philippa Marie Pascale Jones. *Educated at* Nat. School Wrexham; Grove Park Wrexham; Denstone College Staffs; Keeble College, Oxford; Council of Legal Education. *Career:* School Master (Art and general) Mountgrace Comprehensive, Middlx; Called to Bar, Middle Temple, 1954; Barrister & Solicitor Nigeria 1955-57; Magistrate N.Nigeria 1957-65; High Court Judge, N.Nigerian 1965-75; Chief Justice Kano State (N) 1975-80; Chief Justice of Republic of Kiribati 1980-85; Member of Appeal Courts of Vanuatu and Solomon Islands 1983-85. *Publications:* Law Reports of Northern Nigeria 1966-72 (editor); some cases on Criminal Procedure & Evidence 1968 and 1969; Criminal Procedure in Northern States of Nigeria 1975, rep. 1978. *Recreation:* Gardening, painting, DIY, travel, nature study. *Clubs:* Bath & County club, N.T., RSPB. *Address:* Bradley Cottage, Bradley Lane, Holt, near Trowbridge, BA14 6QE.

JONES, His Honour John Edward, B.Com., LLB. *Born on* 23 Dec 1914 at Liverpool. *Son of* Thomas Robert and Elizabeth Jane Jones. *Marriage:* to Katherine Elizabeth SRN daughter of Ezekiel Richard and Ellen Edwards. *Children:* Glenys Wyn and Michael Wyn. *Educated at* Sefton Park Council School, Liverpool Inst. High School *Career:* Circuit Judge (formerly County Court Judge) 1969-84; ACIS 1939-70; Called to the Bar by Gray's Inn 1945; Mbr. Northern Circuit 1946; Deputy Chrmn. Lancashire Quarter Sessions 1966-69; Deputy Chrmn. Workmen's Compensation (Supplementation) and Pneumoconiosis and Byssonosis Benefit Brds 1968-69; Director Chatham Building Society 1955-59; Dir. Welsh Calvinistic Methodist Assurance Trust 1953-59; Vice-Pres. Merseyside Branch Magistrates Assoc. 1974-84; Vice-Pres. Liverpool Welsh Choral Union 1973, then President 1987- ; Life Mbr. Welsh National Eisteddfod Court, Mbr. of Gorsedd of Bards with Bardic Title Ioan Maesgrug 1987; Governor of Aigburth Vale Comprehensive School 1976-85; and of Calderstones Community Comprehensive School 1985-88, both in Liverpool; Dir. World Friendship 1986 and its Chairman 1990- ; Mbr. of Exec. Commt. of Liverpool Free Church Federal Council 1988- ; Deacon Bethel, Heathfield Road, Welsh Presbyterian Church, Liverpool, 1947, Moderator of its Liverpool Presbytery 1971; and mbr. of its North Wales Synod 1989- ; Justice of the Peace for Liverpool and Lancashire. *Publications:* Antur a Menter Cymry Lerpwl 1987. *Recreation:* Calligraphy, word-processing and bowling *Clubs:* Athenaeum, Liverpool *Address:* 45 Sinclair Drive, Liverpool L18 OHW.

JONES, Mr John Emrys, CBE 1979. *Currently:* Retired.

Born on 12 March 1913 at Penrhiwceiber, S.Wales. *Son of* the late William Jones and the late Elizabeth Susan (nee Davis). *Marriage:* to Stella (nee Davies) 1935. *Children:* Glenys Maureen Mullin (nee Jones). *Educated at* Mountain Ash Secondary School, South Wales. *Career:* Shop Assistant 1928-29; Railwayman, and youngest representative of N.U.R. 1929-33; Clerk at Rootes Motor Factory, Luton 1933-36; Regular contributor to 'Railway Review' under pen-name 'Jay' 1934-40; Railwayman, S. Wales 1936-49; Labour councillor, Cardiff Central 1945; Secretary and organiser, Labour Party South West Region 1949-60; Secretary and Organiser, Labour Party West Midlands 1960-65; Labour Party Organiser and Secretary of Welsh Council of Labour/TUC/Co-operative party 1965-79; Referendum Campaign Committee 1977-79. *Publications:* Pamphlet: 'Evidence of the Labour Party in Wales to the Commission on the Constitution', pub. Jan 1970. *Recreation:* Reading, gardening. *Address:* 51b High Street, Hanham, Bristol, BS15 3DQ.

JONES, His Honour Judge John Geoffrey, LLB., LLM. *Currently:* Circuit Judge, Midland & Oxford Circuit. *Born* 14 Sept 1928 at Burry Port. *Son of* the late Wyndham Jones and Lilias Jones (nee Johns). *Marriage:* to Shelia Gregory 1954. *Children:* 3 sons. *Educated at* Brighton & Hove Grammar School; St. Michael's School Bryn, Llanelli; St. David's College, Lampeter; University College, London. *Career:* Army: Commissioned into R.A.S.C., 1946-48; Co. Director in electrical wholesale merchants, Llanelli 1948-52; Holker Junior scholar Gray's Inn 1952; Called to The Bar by Gray's Inn 1956; practised on The Midland and Oxford Circuit, at first from Leicester and then from London Chambers 1958-75; Appointed Circuit Judge April, 1975; President of Mental Health Review Tribunals from 1986; Hon. Academic Fellow, Leicester Polytechnic 1989. *Recreation:* Golf. *Address:* Leicester County Court, Lower Hill Street, Leicester LE1 3SJ.

JONES, Dr John Howel, MA; MD; FRCP. *Currently:* Non-Executive member Coventry Health Authority. *Born on* 4 March 1928 at Aberystwyth. *Son of* the late John Emrys Jones and the late Mary (nee Edwards). *Marriage:* to Sheila Mary Forster, 1953. *Children:* one d two s. Elizabeth, Hugh and David. *Educated at* Ardwyn Grammar School, Aberystwyth; Wrekin College, Wellington; Sidney Sussex College, Cambridge; St Georges Hospital, London. *Career:* Hospital posts St.Georges Hospital, London; Brompton Hospital London, Queen Elizabeth Hospital, Birmingham 1952-66; RAMC 1954-56; Consultant Physician West Midlands Regional Health Authority (Coventry & Rugby) 1966-91; Medical Officer Great Britain Olympic Team 1976-84; England Commonwealth Games Team 1976-84; Hon.Medical Advisor, Commonwealth Games Federation 1982-90. *Publications:* Research papers in professional journals. *Recreation:* gardening, history. *Address:* 41 Hillmorton Road, Rugby, Warwicks CV22 5AB.

JONES, Professor John Richards, PhD, DSc, FRSC, CChem. *Currently:* Head of Chemistry Department, University of Surrey, since 1991. *Born on* 27 Dec 1937 at London. *Son of* Mary Ann and the late William Jones. *Marriage:* to Eirlys Williams Thomas. *Children:* Carys Mair and Sian Eleri. *Educated at* Tregaron County School; UCW Aberystwyth. *Career:* Assistant lecturer, Battersea College of Technology 1961; lecturer 1963; Reader 1982, University of Surrey; Acting Head of Chemistry Department 1984-85; Professor of Radiochemistry 1988- ; Deputy Dean (Faculty of Science) 1989-91. *Publications:* The Ionisation of Carbon Acids, Academic Press, 1973; Handbook of Tritium NWR Spectrscopy (with E.A.Evans, J.A.Elvidge and D.C.Warrell), Wiley 1985. *Recreation:* cricket, gardening. *Address:* Chemistry Department, University Of Surrey, Guildford, Surrey, GU2 5XH. Heatherdale, New Park Road, Cranleigh, Surrey, GU6 7HJ

JONES, Mr Joseph Patrick, *Currently:* Professional Footballer at Wrexham Football Club, since 1987 (2 Welsh cup runners up medals). *Born on* 4 March 1955 at Bangor, North Wales. *Son of* Harry Humphrey Jones and Eileen Bernadette (nee Burns). *Marriage:* to Janice (nee Griffiths), 1976. *Children:* Darren Joseph. *Educated at* Mostyn Secondary School, Llandudno. *Career:* Wrexham F.C. (Welsh Cup Winners 1975), 1970-75; Liverpool F.C. 1975-78, (2 league division one champions 1975-76, 76-77, 2 European champions cup winners, 1977 and 78, i U.E.F.A. cup winners 1976, 1 European super cup 1977, 2 charity shields 1976 and 77, 1 F.A. Cup runners up 1977); Wrexham F.C., 1978-82; Chelsea F.C., 1982-84 (2nd division champions 1983-84); Huddersfield Town F.C., 1985-87; 72 Welsh Caps, 4 under 23 caps, 7 youth caps. *Publications:* autobiography published soon. *Recreation:* walking the dogs, watching boxing. *Address:* 30 Ffordd Glyn, Coed-Y-Gyln, Erddig, Wrexham, Clwyd LL13 7QN. Wrexham Football Club, Mold Road, Wrexham, Clwyd.

JONES, Councillor Kelvin, DML *Currently:* Deputy Clerk to the Justices, employed within the magistrates' court service since 1976; member of Association of Magisterial Officers, since 1976. *Born on* 28 Oct 1956 at Llwynypia, S.Wales. *Son of* Alfred Glenville and Mary Bronwen Jones. *Marriage:* to Diane Maureen (nee Pearce), 1976. *Children:* Louise Maureen and Rhian. *Education:* Diploma in Magisterial Law (Bristol); Common Professional Exam (Manchester). *Career:* member of National Council & Joint Negotiating Committee and appeals tribunal, 1982-4; law lecturer for W.M. Club & Institute Union 1980- ; member of Newtown & Llanllwchaiarn Town Council 1986- , Mayor 1990-91; Chairman of its Xmas lights committee; member Powys County Council 1988- ; legal editor of 'Club Secretary' magazine, 1988- ; legal adviser to the Recreational Managers' Association of Great Britain, 1988- ; Treasurer, Montgomeryshire Conservative Association and Vice Chairman of Newtown Branch, 1987-89; member of Wales Council for the Deaf Governing Bodies of Newtown High School, 1988- ; Penygloddfa CP School and Chairman Hafren CP School. *Publications:* editor of 500 points in Club Law. *Recreation:* tennis *Clubs:* Newtown Royal British Legion. *Address:* 12 Glandulas Drive, Newtown, Powys SY16 4JB. Tel: 0686 624984

JONES, Sir Kenneth, CBE, QC. *Currently:* retired 1980. *Born on* 11 July 1910 at Abergavenny. *Son of* John Jones and Agnes Powell. *Marriage:* to Menna Jones, 1940. *Children:* tw s. *Educated at* King Henry VIII Grammar School, Abergavenny; University College of Wales, Aberystwyth; St.John's College, Cambridge, BA, LLB. *Career:* Barrister, Lincoln's Inn 1937; In practice 1937-39; Served Royal Artillery 1939-45, Major; entered Home Office as Legal Assistant 1945, CBE 1956. Legal Adviser to Home Office 1956-77; Member of the Criminal Law Revision Committee 1959-80. QC 1976. *Clubs:* Athenaeum *Address:* 7 Chilton Court, Walton On Thames, Surrey, KT12 1NG.

JONES, Hon Sir Kenneth (George Illtyd), KT 1974 *Currently:* retired. *Born on* 26 May 1921 at Griffithstown. *Son of* the late Richard Arthur Jones and Olive Jane Jones. *Marriage:* 1st to Dulcie (d 1977); 2nd to June Patricia Doxey 1978. *Children:* Penelope b 1949, Christopher b 1951 and Philippa b 1956. *Educated at* Briggs Grammar School; University College Oxford MA. *Career:* Treasurer Oxford Union Society 1941; Shropshire Yeomanry (76 Med Regt. RA) 1942-45; Staff Captain H.Q. 13 corps 1945 (despatches); Called to Bar Grays Inn 1946; Practised

Oxford Circuit 1947-72; Q.C. 1962; Mem. General Council of Bar 1961-65, 1968-69; Bencher Grays Inn 1969; Treasurer 1987; Judge of the High Court of Justice Queens Bench Division 1974-89; Recorder Shrewsbury 1964-66; Wolverhampton 1966-71; Crown Court 1972; Circuit Judge 1972-73; Dep. Chmn. Boundary Comm. for Wales 1984-89. *Recreation:* Theatre, opera, fishing, gardening. *Address:* C/o Royal Courts of Justice, Strand, London.

JONES, Mr Martyn David, MI.Biol. *Currently:* Member of Parliament, Clwyd S.W. *Born on* 1 March 1947 at Britain. *Son of* Vernon Pritchard and Violet Gwendoline. *Marriage:* 1974, diss. 1991. *Children:* Linzi Ruth and Nicholas Pritchard. *Educated at* Grove Park Grammar Wrexham; various Polytechnics. *Career:* Microbiologist Brewing Industry 1969-87; Clwyd County Councillor 1981-89. *Recreation:* Backpacking, target shooting, tennis, sailing. *Clubs:* Wrexham Lager Sports and Social. *Address:* 20 High Street, Johnstown, Wrexham LL14 2SN.

JONES, Mr Medwyn, LLB (Hons). *Currently:* Partner, Walker Martineau, since 1983. *Born on* 13 Sept 1955 at Bangor, N.Wales. *Son of* Ieuan Glyn Du Platt Jones and Margaret Jones (nee Owen) (divorced). *Marriage:* to Rita (nee Bailey), 1990. *Educated at* Scorton School; Chester Grammar School; Sheffield University; College of Law. *Career:* Articled Clerk, Messrs Theodore Goddard 1978-80; Solicitor Messrs Theodore Goddard 1980-81; Solicitor Messrs Walker Martineau, 1981-83. *Recreation:* skiing, music, regular exersise *Clubs:* Law Society, Worshipful Company of Solicitors, Freeman of the City of London. *Address:* 26 Queens Road, London SW14 8PJ. C/o Walker Martineau, 64 Queen Street, London EC4R 1AD

JONES, Michael Lynn Norman, MA, ACIArb. *Currently:* Senior Partner, Hugh James, Jones & Jenkins, Solicitors, Cardiff, since 1970. *Born on* 14 Jan 1943 at Maesteg. *Son of* Lynn Daniel Jones and Mary Hannah Jones (nee Edwards). *Marriage:* to Ethni Daniel, 1974. *Children:* Garmon ap Michael, Mererid, Gwenfair and Rhiannon Michael. *Educated at* Neath Boys' CGS; Jesus College, Oxford. *Career:* Partner, Hugh James, Jones & Jenkins 1966; Asst. Secretary, Cardiff Law Soc., 1968-91, Vice President 1991- ; member, Wales & Chester Circuit Advisory Committee 1971-77; member Curriculum Cl for Wales 1988-91, Govr 1985- ; chmn 1989- ; Coed-y-Gof Welsh Primary School Governor Glantaf Welsh HS 1988- , Chairman Rhieni Dros Addysg Gymraeg 1991- . *Recreation:* gardening, walking. *Clubs:* Oxford Union, Cardiff & County. *Address:* Allt-Y-Wennol, Llanbedr-Y-Fro, Caerdydd CF5 6NE.

JONES, The Right Reverend Noel Debroy, BA, CB. *Currently:* Lord Bishop of Sodor and Man, since 1989. *Born on* 25 Dec 1932 at Pontypool. *Son of* Brinley and Gwendoline Jones. *Marriage:* to Joyce Barbara Leelavathy, 1969. *Children:* Vanessa and Benjamin. *Educated at* Jones West Monmouth; St.David's College, Lampeter; Wells Theological Coll. *Career:* Vicar of Kano, N Nigeria 1960-62; Chaplain, RN 1962; GSM Brunei 1962, Borneo 1963; RM Commando Course prior to service in Aden with 42 Cdo, 1967; GSM S Arabia 1967; Mid Service Clergy Course at St.George's House, Windsor Castle 1974; Staff Chaplain MoD 1974-77; Chaplain of the Fleet and Archdeacon for the Royal Navy 1984-89. QHC 1983-89. CB 1986. *Recreation:* rugby, music, family. *Clubs:* Sion College, London, Army and Navy, Pall Mall. *Address:* Bishop's House, Quarterbridge Road, Douglas, Isle Of Man. 111 Belgrave Road, London, SW1.

JONES, Dr Norman Fielding, MA, MD, FRCP. *Currently:* Physician St Thomas' Hospital London since 1967. *Born on* 3 May 1931 at Rhymney, Gwent. *Son of* William John and Winifred Jones. *Marriage:* to Ann Pye Chavasse. *Children:*

Christopher, Richard and Michael. *Educated at* Christ College, Brecon; King's College Cambridge; St.Thomas' Hospital London. *Career:* Rockefeller Fellowship Univ N.Carolina 1963-64; Physician King Edward VII's Hospital for Officer 1977- ; Chairman District Management Team St.Thomas' Hospital 1977-78; Consulting Physician to Metropolitan Police 1980- ; Hon.Consulting Physician to Army 1980- ; Chief Medical Officer, Equitable Life Assurance Soc., 1980- .Chairman of Committees, Royal Coll of Physicians on Renal Disease, Legal Aspects of Medicine; Senior Censor 1989-90; Treasurer 1991- . *Publications:* editor of text books on Renal Disease; author of papers on Renal Disease & General Medicine. *Recreation:* Iconology, modern eng. lit. *Address:* St.Thomas' Hospital, London. SE1 7EH.

JONES, Mr Peter George Edward Fitzgerald, CB; BSc; ChP; FInst Physics. *Currently:* Retired 1987, Part time Consultant to Ministry of Defence. *Born on* 7 June 1925 at Truro, Cornwall. *Son of* the late Christopher Jones and the late Isobel (nee Howell). *Marriage:* 1). to Gwendoline Iris Humphreys (d 1964) 2). to Jaqueline Angela Gilbert. *Children:* 1st marriage one s (and one s decd) 2nd marriage two s one da. Graham, Christopher, Tracey and Jason. *Educated at* Fairfield School Birmingham; Dulwich College; Croydon Tech; Battersea Polytechnic; London University. *Career:* Pilot RAF 1943-47; Senior Scientist GEC Wembley 1951-54; UKAEA 1954-73 and MOD 1973-87; Senior Scientific Officer 1954-58; Principal 1958-63; Asst. Director London Communications Security Agency 1964; Supt. Electronics Research 1964-66; Senior Supt. Warhead Electronics 1966-68; Senior Supt. Special Systems 1968-74; Chief Warhead Devt. 1974-76; Deputy Director 1976-80; Princ.Dep. Director 1980-82; Director AWRE 1982-87. *Recreation:* motoring, flying. *Clubs:* Rolls-Royce Enthusiasts; Reliant Sabre and Scimiter Owners. *Address:* Rhyd-Y-Felin, Upper Llanover, Abergavenny, Gwent, NP7 9DD.

JONES, Peter Henry Francis, MA Hons(Oxon). *Currently:* Solicitor (admitted July 1977), Partner: John Howell & Co., Solicitors, Sheffield, since 1987. *Born on* 25 Feb 1952 at Swansea. *Son of* Eric R.Jones, MBE, of Swansea and the late Betty I.Jones (nee Longhurst). *Marriage:* to Anne Elizabeth Jones, 1978. *Children:* Clare (b.1980) and Eleanor (b.1982). *Educated at* Brynmill Junior Mixed School, Swansea; Bishop Gore G.S., Swansea; Newport H.S., Gwent; Balliol College Oxford. *Career:* articled Clerk and Solicitor, Coward Chance London 1974-78; Solicitor and Partner Darlington & Parkinson, London 1978-87; Member Lord Chancellors Legal Aid Advisory Committee 1983- ; Chairman Legal Services Conference 1986-90; member Children Act Procedure Advisory Group 1990; member Law Society Family Law Committee 1986- ; Consultant to NAO Review of Legal Aid 1991; Lecturer on Child Care Law to Legal Profession, Social Workers and other groups. *Publications:* various articles on Child Care Law and Legal Aid. *Recreation:* rugby, tennis, cricket, reading, quizes. *Clubs:* Dethreau Boat, Scorpions CC, Rustlings L.T.C. *Address:* C/o John Howell & Co, 427/431 London Road, Sheffield S2 4HJ. Tel: 0742 501000.

JONES, Rita, *Currently:* Housewife. *Born on* 28 Sept 1937 at Bargoed, Mid Glam. *Daughter of* the late Naiomi and the late Albert Pritchard. *Marriage:* to Kenneth James Jones. *Children:* Craig. *Educated at* Bargoed Secondary Modern School. *Career:* Achievements in Bowls: total of seventy eight Welsh caps, includes indoor and outdoor Internationals. Outdoors: Won Gold Medal Commonwealth Games Scotland 1986 (Four Plays); Won Bronze Medal World Bowls Australia 1985 (Triples Play); Welsh Singles Champion

1989; 2 Wood Champion 1990; Fours 1991. Indoors: National Singles Champion 1979, 1984, 1986, 1991; Triples 1989; Fours 1991; British Isles Triples Winner 1989; Singles Finalist 1984-91. *Recreation:* bowls, walking, knitting. *Clubs:* Gilfach Bargoed Bowls. *Address:* 23 Maesygraig Street, Gilfach, Bargoed, Mid Glam CF8 8JE.

JONES, Mr Robert, BSc, FInstSMM. *Currently:* Director of Relaxations Ltd; Director of The Curlew Partnership. *Born on* 8 Dec 1946 at Tredegar. *Son of* John Idris Jones and Eleanor Myfanwy Jones. *Marriage:* to Elsa Jones, 1976. *Children:* Timothy Robert Jones (b.1978). *Educated at* Rhymney Grammar; Tredegar Grammar; Sir John Cass College, London University. *Career:* graduate trainee Unilever 1969-70; account manager: S.H.Benson & Co 1970-71; Young & Rubicam 1971-73; account director McCann Erickson 1973-75; Counter Products Marketing 1975-79; MD Imbibers Wines 1979-87; business development dir VAP Group 1987-91. Accomplishments: Compagnon Confrerie St.Etienne Alsace 1979; member Circle of Winewriters 1984; developed Tagcards (the mountaineering safety scheme) 1988; fellow Institute of Sales and Marketing Management 1991. *Publications:* The Imbibers Guide to Wine Pronunciation, 1980; European Rulers, 1981; Snowdon - Yr Wyddfa, 1992. *Recreation:* mountaineering, photography, cylcing, wine, music. *Clubs:* Royal Photographic Society. *Address:* P.O. Box 333, Aylesbury, Bucks HP18 9XG.

JONES, Dr. Robert Brinley, MA; D.Phil; FSA; *Currently:* Member Broadcasting Standards Council, 1988-91; Board of British Council, 1987-. *Born* at Penygraig, Rhondda. *Son of* Mary Ann and John Elias Jones. *Marriage:* to Stephanie Avril Hall. *Children:* Aron Rhys. *Educated at* Dinas Boys School; Tonypandy Grammar; Univ. Coll., Cardiff; Jesus Coll. Oxford. *Career:* Schoolmaster Penarth Grm Sch 1958-60; Lec. Univ. Coll., Swansea 1960-66; Assist. Registrar Univ. of Wales 1966-69; Dir. of Univ. of Wales Press 1969-76; Warden of Llandovery Coll., 1976-88; Fellow of Univ. of Wales, Coll. of Cardiff 1984; Hon. Fellow Saint David's Univ. Coll., Lampeter 1987; Governor: Saint David's Univ.Coll., Lampeter, Trinity Coll.Carmarthen, Saint Michael's Theological Coll. Llandaff; Chmn of Provincial Validating Bd. of Theological Educ. in the Church of Wales; mbr. of Episocopal Coll. of Electors (Church of Wales); Chmn. Dinefwr Tourism gp; Mbr. Welsh Academy; Vice-Pres. International Eisteddfod; Hon. Mbr. Druidic Order (National Eisteddfod). *Publications:* The Old British Tongue 1970; Introducing Wales 1978, 82, 88; Certain Scholars of Wales 1986; Songs of Praises 1991; ed. and contributor to Anatomy of Wales 1972; Co-ed. with Meic Stephens, Writers of Wales series 1970- ; Co-ed. with Rachel Bromwich, Astudiaethau o'r Hengerdd (Studies in Old Welsh Poetry) 1978; Co-ed. with D.Ellis Evans, Cofio'r Dafydd 1987; and articles and reviews in learned journals. *Recreation:* Music, family, walking *Clubs:* Royal Commonwealth (London) *Address:* Drovers Farm, Porthyrhyd, Llanwrda, Dyfed SA19 8DF. Tel: 05585 649.

JONES, Robert Gerallt, MA *Currently:* Warden of Gregynog since 1989. *Born on* 11 Sept 1934 at Nefyn. *Son of* the late Rev.Richard Emrys Jones and Elizabeth Ellen Jones. *Marriage:* to Susan Lloyd Griffith, 1962. *Children:* Ceri, Rhys and Dafydd. *Educated at* Denstone College; UCNW Bangor. *Career:* Senior English Master, Sir Thomas Jones School, Amlwch 1957-60; Lecturer in Education, UCW Aberystwyth 1960-65; Principal, Mandeville Teachers College, Jamaica 1965-67; Warden, Llandovery College 1967-76; Creative Writing Fellow, UCW 1976-79; Senior Lecturer, Extra-Mural Dept., UCW 1979-89; Lay Reader, Ch in Wales 1958- ; Member Ch in Wales Governing Body

1959-64; Member Welsh Arts Council 1969-72, 1987- ; Member Broadcasting Co., for Wales 1967-72; Member Welsh Academy 1960- , Vice Chairman 1981-82, Chairman 1982-87; Ch.Welsh National Films Video Archive 1988- ; Member S4C Authority 1991- ; Editor 'Taliesin' 1987- ; Director Aberystwyth Third World Dev Course 1986- . *Publications:* Cafflogion (Nofel), 1979; Tair Drama, 1988; Seicoleg Cardota (Crit), 1989; Cerddi 1959-89 (Sel.Poems), 1990. *Recreation:* cricket, walking, conversation *Address:* Gregynog, University of Wales, Newtown, Powys SY16 3PW.

JONES, Professor Robert Maynard, MA, PhD, DLitt. *Currently:* Professor Emeritus. *Born on* 20 May 1929 at Cardiff. *Son of* Sydney and Edith Jones. *Marriage:* to Beti (nee James). *Children:* Lowri Dole and Rhodri Sion. *Educated at* Cathays High School, Cardiff; Universities of Wales and Ireland. *Career:* Teaching in Llanidloes and Llangefni; Lecturer, Trinity College, Carmarthen; Lecturer in Education, UCW Aberystwyth; Lecturer, Senior Lecturer, Reader; Professor and Head of Department of Welsh Language and Literature, UCW Aberystwyth 1980-89. Former Chairman Yr Academi Gymreig; Vice President, UCCF; Editorial Board of Geiriadur Prifysgol Cymru. *Publications:* poetry, novels, short stories, literary criticism, linguistics. *Recreation:* walking. *Club:* Y Bedol. *Address:* Tandderwen, Heol Llanbadarn, Aberystwyth, Dyfed SY23 1HB. Tel: 0970 623603.

JONES, Mr Robert Nicholas, *Currently:* Business Development Executive, Swansea Building Society. *Born on* 10 Nov 1965 at Glanamman. *Son of* Mr Cliff and Mrs Marion Jones. *Marriage:* to Megan. *Educated at* Trebanos Primary; Cwmtawe C.S. *Career:* Welsh Schools Rugby, 12 caps (under 15, 16 and 18's); Welsh Schools Cricket, under 11, 13, 15 and 18's); Welsh Rugby caps-42, (Deput v England 1986); Captained Welsh Team in 1989/90 season. British Lions 1986, Australia 1989, 3 tests Barbarians. Swansea RFC since 1983, captain 1989-91. *Recreation:* golf, cricket. *Clubs:* Swansea and Trebanos RFC. *Address:* 215 Swansea Road, Trebanos, Swansea, W Glam, SA8 4BT

JONES, Professor Ronald Samuel, MVSc, Dr.Med.Vet, DVSc, DVA, FIBiol, FRCVS. *Currently:* Professor of Veterinary Anaesthesia, University of Liverpool since 1990. *Born on* 29 Oct 1937 at Oswestry. *Son of* Samuel and Gladys Jane (nee Philips). *Marriage:* to Pamela (nee Evans). *Children:* Rachel Mary Patricia and Alison Jane. *Educated at* High School For Boys Oswestry; Liverpool University. *Career:* House Surgeon, University of Glasgow 1960-61; Assistant in Veterinary Pharmacology, University of Glasgow 1961-62; Lecturer, University of Liverpool 1962-77, Senior Lecturer 1977-87, Reader 1987-90. Dean of the Faculty of Veterinary Science 1987-91. *Publications:* numerous in the field of Veterinary Anaesthesia. *Recreation:* gardening, horse-racing, philately. *Address:* 7 Birch Road, Oxton, Birkenhead, Merseyside, L43 5UF.

JONES, Mr Terence Graham Parry (Terry), *Born on* 1 Feb 1942 at Colwyn Bay. *Son of* the late Alick George Parry Jones and Dilys Luoise (nee Newnes). *Marriage:* to Alison Telfer, 1970. *Children:* William and Sally. *Educated at* Royal GS Guildford; St.Edmund Hall, Oxford. *Career:* Played the Condemned Man in "Hang Down Your Head and Die" 1964; worked for BBC Light Entertainment Scrip Dept., "Late Night Line-up", BBC2. started writing with Michael Palin for Ken Dodd, Lance Percival, Billy Cotton, Kathy Kirby, Roy Hudd, Marty Feldman, Two Ronnies etc., 1965-67; "The Late Show", 1966; Script editor for "A Series of Birds", 1967, wrote and appeared in short films for "Twice A Fortnight", "Do Not Adjust YourSet"; Wrote "Aladdin" pantomie for Watford Civic Theatre Rep.,

1968; Wrote and appeared in "The Complete and Utter History of Britain", wrote "Beauty and The Beast" pantomime for Watford Rep., 1969; "Monty Python's Flying Circus", 1969-74; "And Now For Something Completely Different", 1970-71; Wrote (with Michael Palin) "Secrets" 1973; Co-directed (with Terry Gilliam) "Month Python and The Holy Grail", 1975; Wrote "Their Finest Hours" (with Michael Palin) 1976; "Bert Fegg's Nasty Book for Boys and Girls" (written with Michael Palin), re-titled "Dr Fegg's Nasty Book of Knowledge" in US, 1976; Worte (with Michael Palin) "Ripping Yarns", 1977-78; Directed "Monty Python Live at the Hollywood Bowl", "Chaucer's Knight", 1980; "Chaucer's Knight" reprinted, "Fairy Tales", hosted TV series "Paperback" for BBC, 1981; "Chaucer's Knight" pub. in p/back, "Fairy Tales" released in U.S., dir. and presented "The Rupert Bear Story", 1982; Directed Month Python's 'Meaning of Life' 1983, "The Saga of Erik the Viking" published, "Fairy Tales" pub. in p/back 1983; "Dr.Fegg's Encyclopeadia (sic) of All World Knowledge" (co-written with Michael Palin), wrote screenplay of "Labyrinth" 1984; "Nicobobinus" published 1985; Directed 'Personal Services' with Julie Walters, 1986; wrote "Goblins of the Labyrinth" with illustrator Brian Froud, published by Pavilion, 1986; "Labyrinth" released USA, Summer 1986; Screenplay of "Eric The Viking", based (loosely) on the book, Autumn 1986; Winter 1986, "Labyrinth" released in UK; January 1987, "Personal Services" released; 1987, wrote regular "Input" column for Young Guardian; collected articles, published as a book "Attacks of Opinion" in autumn 1988 by Penguin; wrote book of children's verse, "The Curse of the Vampire's Socks and other doggerel", published by Pavilion, Autumn 1988; 1987/88, wrote screenplay for "Gullivar's Travels" for 20th Centuy Fox; 1988/89, Erik the Viking filmed in Malta, Britain and Norway, released Sept. 1989, book of the film, published by Methuen Nov. 1989; 1990, Curse of the Vampire's Socks issued in paperback by Puffin, working on new film script in Autumn 1990; 1991, writing and presenting TV Pilot documentary "So This Is Progress?" (formerly "Turning Circles: The Myth of Progress") for BBC TV; Further work on new film script; April 1991, Melbourne Comedy Festival, guest of honour; Summer 1991, directing episode in Young Indiana Jones series for Lucasfilm. *Note:* Although working on filmscripts has kept him very busy, he is still reportedly available for odd jobs, party catering and lunchtime recitals. He also sells ladies' underwear in his spare time. *Address:* 68a Delancey Street, London, NW1 7RY.

JONES, Mr Thomas Glanville, LLB(Lon). *Currently:* Barrister at Law. *Born on* 10 May 1931 at London. *Son of* the late Evan James Jones and the late Margaret Olive (nee Evans). *Marriage:* to Valma Shirley (nee Jones), da of Ivor Jones and Muriel Eugenie Jones (nee Morris), Swansea. *Children:* Aled Prydderch b 1966, Dyfan Rhodri b 1968 and Geraint Islwyn b 1971. *Educated at* University College London(LLB); Inns of Court School of Law; Called to the Bar 1956. *Career:* Recorder of the Crown Court; Commissioner Boundary Commission for Wales; Committee Member Wales Medico-Legal Society. *Recreation:* Chairman Guild for the Promotion of Welsh Music. *Address:* Gelligron, 12 Eastcliff, Southgate, West Glamorgan, SA3 2AS. Angel Chambers, 94 Walter Road, Swansea SA1 5QA

JONES, Mr Thomas Henry, BA ARAGS *Currently:* Agriculture. *Born on* 8 Feb 1950 at Machynlleth. *Son of* Cadwaladar and Olwen Jones. *Marriage:* to Dr.Margaret Jones. *Children:* Owain Cadwalader, Siwan Wyn and Steffan Harri. *Educated at* Llanerfyl Primary; Tywyn Secondary; Univ. College Wales Aberystwyth; *Career:* Former Vice

President Farmers' Union of Wales; Member Agricultural Training Board; Member National Parks Review Panel; Member Countryside Council for Wales; Member S4C Authority; President Wales Young Farmers Movement; *Publications:* Brain yn y Brwyn; Dyddiadur Ffarmwr; *Address:* Plas Coch, Dolanog, Welshpool, Powys, SY21 OLA.

JONES, The Venerable Thomas Hughie, BA., BD., MA., FRSA., FBIM. *Currently:* Archdeacon of Loughborough, since 1986. *Born on* 15 Aug 1927 at Manchester, England. *Son of* F.(Edward) Teifi Jones and M. Ellen Jones. *Marriage:* to Beryl Joan Henderson, 1949. *Children:* Susan Beryl and Christine Anne. *Educated at* William Hulme's Grammar School Manchester; Universities of Wales, London and Leicester. *Career:* Warden and Lectr, Bible Trng Inst., Glasgow, 1949-54; Minister, John Street Baptist Church, Glasgow, 1951-54; RE specialist, Leicester and Leics schs, 1955-63; Sen.Lectr in RE, Leicester Coll. of Educn, 1964-70; Vice-Principal, Bosworth Coll., 1970-75; Principal, Hind Leys College, Leics, 1975-81; Rector, The Langtons and Stronton Wyville, 1981-86; Hon. Canon of Leicester Cathedral, 1983. Vice-Chairman, Ecclesiastical Law Society. *Publications:* (contrb. OT articles) New Bible Dictionary, 1962, 2nd edn 1980; Old Testament and religious and canon law education articles in relevant jls. *Recreation:* Entomology, geneaology, Welsh interests, *Clubs:* Carlton; Leicestershire (Leicester); Leicestershire County Cricket, Leicester Sporting. *Address:* The Archdeaconry, 21 Church Road, Glenfield, Leicester LE3 8DP. Tel: 0533-311632.

JONES, Mr Thomas William, *Currently:* British Gas Wales. *Born on* 20 Feb 1938 at Colwyn Bay. *Son of* the late Robert Edwin and Mary (nee Pritchard). *Marriage:* to Sheila Mary Bagnall. *Children:* Della Wyn Austin and Lisa Davies, both married. *Educated at* Colwyn Bay Grammar School *Career:* Clwyd County Councillor 1989- ; Branch Secretary GMB 1973-; Mbr DHSS Tribunals 1975-89; Mbr N.Wales Manpower Commt 1975-79; Governor Bryn Elian Comprehensive School Colwyn Bay 1989; Managment Council Coleg Harlech 1989-; Governor Llanrillo Technical College 1975- ; Mbr Clwyd North Community Health Council 1990- . *Recreation:* Reading and gardening *Clubs:* Chairman C.Bay British Legion *Address:* 8 York Road, Colwyn Bay, Clwyd LL29 7ED.

JONES, Professor Tudor Bowden, BSc, PhD, DSc, F.InstP, CEng, FIEE. *Currently:* Professor of Physics, University of Leicester. *Born on* 8 Nov 1934 at Ystradgynlais. *Son of* Idris and Tydfeil-Ann Jones. *Marriage:* to Patricia (nee Brown), 1960. *Children:* Owen Bowden Jones and Hywel Bowden Jones. *Educated at* University of Wales; University College of Swansea. *Career:* Lecturer, m senior lecturer, reader, at Leicester University. Senior Resident Research Associate, NOAA, Boulder, Colorado, USA; Senior Research Associate, Communications Research Committee, Ottawa, Canada. Consultant to various Government Agencies in UK, USA and Canada. member of various Serc and Nerc Committees, former Chairman of the Eiscat Council. *Publications:* more than 100 published papers in the field of Ionospheric Physics and Radio Wave Propagation. *Recreation:* Classical music, former member of the National Youth Orchestra. *Address:* 4 Covert Close, Oadby, Leicester LE2 4HB. Dept of Physics & Astronomy, The University, University Road, Leicester, LE1 7RH

JONES, Professor Walton Glyn, MA, PhD. *Currently:* Professor of Scandinavian Studies, University of East Anglia, since 1986. *Born on* 29 Oct 1928 at Manchester. *Son of* the late Emrys and Dorothy Ada (nee North). *Marriage:* 1st to Karen Ruth Fleischer, 1954 (diss 1981); 2ndto Kirsten Gade, 1981. *Children:* by 1st marriage, Stephen Francis,

Olaf Emrys Robert, Catherine Monica and Anna Elizabeth. *Educated at* Manchester Grammar School; Pembroke College Cambridge. *Career:* Assistant Lecturer in Danish, University College London 1956; Lecturer in Danish, University College London 1958; Reader in Danish, University College London 1966; Professor of Scandinavian Studies, University of Newcastle-upon-Tyne 1973; Professor of Literature, Faroese Academy 1979-81; Visiting Professor of Danish, University of Iceland. Honorary Member: Swedish Literature Society in Finland 1985; Corresponding Member: Danish Society of Authors 1987; Fellow of Royal Norwegian Academy of Sciences 1988. Guest lecturer at universities throughout Europe and USA. *Publications:* Johannes Jorgensens modne ar, Copenhagen 1963; Johannes Jorgensen, New York 1969; Denmark, London, New York 1970; William Heinesen, New York 1974; Faero og kosmos, Copenhagen 1974; Danish. A Grammar, Copenhagen 1981 (in collaboration with Kirsten Gade), 2nd ed. 1985, 3rd ed. 1988, 4th ed. 1990, 5th ed. 1992; Tove Jansson, Boston 1984; Vagen fran Mumindalen, Helsinki, Stockholm 1984; Denmark. A Modern History, London 1986; Georg Brandes. Selected Letters, Norwich 1990; Blue Guide. Denmark, London 1992 (in collaboration with Kirsten Gade). *Recreation:* music, medieval Danish church architecture, translating. *Address:* School of Modern Languages &, European History, Univ of East Anglia, Norwich NR4 7TJ. Tel: 0603 56161

JONES, William David, *Currently:* Director of Mission of The Church in Wales. *Born on:* 13th June 1928 at Llanelli *Son of:* David Edward Jones and Olwen Margaret (nee Morgan). *Marriage:* to Sheila Mary Dedman 1957. *Children:* 1 son, 2 daughters *Educated at* Scholar SDC Lampeter, BA 1948; St.Michael's College Llandaff 1948-50; Crossley Exhibition and Senior Student; UC Cardiff 1950-51; WCC Scholar 1951; King's College, University of London 1955-57; University of Leeds. *Career:* Monmouth C of Risca 1951-54, Chepstow with St Arvans and Penterry 54-55, St George in the East, Stepney 1955-59, Farnham Royal Diocese of Oxford 1959-65; Lecturer in Divinity, Culham College Oxon 1965-67; Head of Dept of Religious Studies, Doncaster College of Education and L to officiate Diocese of Sheffield 1967-74; Vice-Principal of Bede College, Univ of Durham 1974; Vice-Principal of College of St.Hild and St.Bede, Lecturer in Theology, University of Durham 1975-89; L to Officiate in Diocese of Durham; Proctor in Convocation and Member of General Synod for the Universities of Durham and Newcastle 1980-85; Chairman of Durham Diocese Council of Education 1984-89; Director of Mission for Church in Wales since 1989; Member of Board of Education, General Synod, Member of ACC Ecumenical Research Group; Treasurer of British and Irish Assoc for Mission Studies; Metropolitical and Honorary Canon of St. Davids 1990. *Publications:* various articles. *Recreation:* cooking, DIY and fishing. *Address:* Church In Wales Centre, Woodland Place, Penarth, S.Glam CF6 3EX. Tel: 0222 705278.

JONES, Professor William Jeremy, BSc, MSc, PhD. *Currently:* Professor of Chemistry, University College of Swansea, since 1988. *Born on* 15 Aug 1935 at Llandeilo (Dyfed). *Son of* Thomas John Jones and Margaret Jeremy. *Marriage:* to Margaret Ann Robertson, Cobourg, Ontario. *Children:* John Jeremy (d.1987), Michael Greystock and Suzanne Victoria. *Educated at* Llandeilo G.School; Univ Coll of Wales, Aberystwyth; Trinity Coll Cambridge. *Career:* Post.Doc.Res.Fellow National Res.Council, Ottawa, Canada 1962-64; Title A Fellow, Trinity College, Cambridge 1960-64; Title C Fellow, Trinity College, Cambridge 1964-78; Demonstrator & Lecturer, University of Cambridge 1965-

78; Professor and Head of Chem. Dept., University College of Wales 1978-88. *Publications:* Extensive scientific publications in the field of chemical physics in general and in spectroscopy and lasers in particular. *Recreation:* walking, gardening, golf. *Address:* Department of Chemistry, University College of Swansea, Singleton Park, Swansea, SA2 8PP. Tel: 0792 295507.

JONES, Wynn Rees, A.C.I.B. *Currently:* Regional Director Barclays Bank, Shrewsbury Regional Office, since 1988. *Born on* 18 Feb 1941 at Machynlleth, Powys. *Son of* Iorwerth and Catherine Jane Jones. *Marriage:* to Eira, 1963. *Children:* Karen Wynn Jones (BA.Hons) and Nia Wynn Jones (BA.Hons). *Educated at* Machynlleth Grammar School. *Career:* Barclays throughout Wales since 1958, Manager Port Talbot 1980-82, General Managers Assistant, Lombard St 1982-84; Local Director, South Wales 1984-88. *Recreation:* Vintage cars, antiques, reading, all sports. *Clubs:* Council member, Nat.Museum of Wales. *Address:* South Lodge, Norton, Shifnal, Shropshire TF11 9EE.

JONES (Bishop Of St.Asaph), The Right Reverend Alwyn Rice, MA (Cantab). *Currently:* Bishop of St.Asaph, 1982; Archbishop of Wales 1991. *Born on* 25 March 1934 at Capel Curig, Caernarvonshire. *Son of* John Griffith and Annie Jones. *Marriage:* to Meriel Ann Thomas 1968. *Children:* Nia Rice Jones. *Educated at* Llanrwst Grammar School; St.David's Univ. Coll., Lampeter BA 1955; Fitzwilliam Coll., Cambridge, BA 1957, MA 1961. *Career:* Ordained deacon 1958; priest 1959; Curate of Llanfair-is-gaer 1958; SCM Staff Secretary in North Wales College 1962-65; Chaplain St.Winifreds School, Llanfairfechan 1965-67; Director of Education - Bangor Diocese; Vicar of Porthmadog 1975-79; Dean of Brecon and Vicar of St. Mary's, Brecon 1979-82. *Recreation:* music, walking. *Address:* Esgobty, St. Asaph, Clwyd LL17 OTW.

JONES-HUMPHREYS, County Councillor Tudwal, *Currently:* retired, but still a County Councillor and since 1945, local Community Council; Lay Preacher for 40 years. *Born on* 5 Oct 1909 at Caerau, Maesteg, S.Wales. *Son of* Robert Rolant Humphreys and Kate Lily Humphreys. *Educated at* Pwllheli Grammar School. *Career:* Elected with large majority to Caernarvonshire County Council 1955; elected alto to Gwynedd County Council (3 corner) with a large majority and unopposed ever since; teaching piano to local pupils; organist of my church for 22 years; accepted as Lay Preacher in Lleyn Eifionydd in 1950; was President of Lleyn Presbytery; Voluntary Social Worker and official hospital visitor in the County Hospitals for nearly 60 years. *Publications:* contributed to local press, the Presbytery Publications, poems and hymns. *Recreation:* music, poetry, local and national Eisteddfodau, climbing Lleyn cliffs from an early age. *Address:* Bwlch-Y-Clawdd Uchaf, Cilan, Abersoch, Pwllheli, Gwynedd, LL53 7DD.

JONES-PARRY, Sir Ernest, MA., PhD., FR Hist.S. *Born on* 16 July 1908 at Rhyl. *Son of* John Parry and Charlotte Jones. *Marriage:* to Mary Powell 1938. *Children:* Rupert and Tristram. *Educated at* St. Asaph; University of Wales; University of London. *Career:* Lecturer in History, University College of Wales 1935-40; Ministry of Food 1941; Treasury 1946-47; Asst. Sec. Ministry of Food 1948-57; Under-Secretary 1957; Director of establishments, Ministry of Agriculture, Fisheries and Food 1957-61; Executive Director International Sugar Council 1965-68; International Sugar Organisation 1969-78. *Publications:* The Spanish Marriages 1841-1846; The Correspondence of Lord Aberdeen and Princess Lieven 1832-54 (2 vols); articles and reviews. *Recreation:* Reading, watching cricket. *Clubs:* Athenaeum. *Address:* Flat 3, 34 Sussex Square, Brighton, Sussex BN2 5AD.

JONES-WILLIAMS, Mr Dafydd Wyn, OBE., MC., TD., DL., LLB. *Currently:* Retired. *Born on* 13 July 1916 at Dolgellau. *Son of* John and Lowry Jones-Williams (nee Griffith). *Marriage:* to Rosemary Sally Councell 1945. *Children:* Susan Mary and Sarah Elizabeth. *Educated at* Dolgellau Grammar School; UCW Aberystwyth. *Career:* Solicitor 1939; Clerk of County Council, Clerk of Peace, and Clerk to Lieutenancy, Merioneth 1954-70; Circuit Administrator, Wales and Chester Circuit 1970-74; Commissioner for Local Administration for Wales (Local Ombudsman) 1974-79; Served 1939-45 with HAC and X Royal Hussars (Western Desert), formerly comdg 446 (Royal Welch) AB, LAA Regt, RA (TA); Member Hughes-Parry Committee on Legal Status of Welsh Language 1963-65; Lord Chancellor's Advisory Committee on Training of Magistrates; Council on Tribunals 1980-86; formerly - BBC General Advisory Council, Broadcasting Council for Wales; Member Nature Conservancy (Chm. Committee for Wales) Chairman Merioneth and Montgomeryshire T & AFA. *Recreation:* Golf, reading, motoring and playing snooker. *Clubs:* Royal St. David's and Dolgellau Golf clubs. *Address:* Bryncoedifor, Rhydymain, near Dolgellau, Gwynedd LL40 2AN.

JOSEPH, Sir Herbert Leslie, D.L. *Currently:* Retired. *Born on* 4 Jan 1908 at Swansea. *Son of* Ernest and Florence Joseph (nee Hill). *Marriage:* to 1) Emily Irene Murphy (dec'd) 1934; 2)to Christine Jones 1989. *Children:* Mary and Christine *Educated at* The Kings School, Canterbury; Swansea Tech. Coll; Wimbledon Tech. Coll. *Career:* Major Royal Engineers 1940-45; Managing Director, Porthcawl Recreations Ltd., 1930-51; M.D. Belle Vue Zoological Gardens 1955-65; M.D. Festival Gardens Battersea Park London 1951-71; Chrmn & M.D. Trust Houses Forte Leisure Ltd. 1970-80; Director First Leisure Corp., 1980-91; Director Sir Leslie Joseph Properties Ltd, Entam Ltd., Talk of the Town Ltd., British Automatic Co. Ltd. and others; Chrmn. Housing Production Bd Wales 1952-53; High Sheriff Mid Glamorgan 1975-76; Governor The Kings School Canterbury; Mbr. Council of Swansea Univ; Art Commt. Nat. Museum of Wales; Chrmn. Assoc. of Amusement Park Propprietors of G.B., 1949-51; Chrmn.Nat. Amusements Council 1950-51; Amusement Caters Assoc. 1953-54; Contribution to "William Billingsley". *Publications:* Swansea Porcelain *Recreation:* Rugby, 19th Century Swansea painters antiques generally. *Clubs:* Naval & Military *Address:* Coedargraig, Newton, Porthcawl, Mid Glamorgan, CF36 5SS.

JOYNSON, Dr David Huw Malcolm, MB, BCh, MRCP, FIBiol, Dip.Bact. *Currently:* Director, Public Health Laboratory and Toxoplasma Reference Laboratory, Swansea, since 1985. *Born on* 4 Oct 1943 at Cardiff. *Son of* David Cyril Joynson and Rosetta (nee Gough). *Marriage:* to Menna Bennett Joynson (nee Bennett Owen), 15 July 1967. *Children:* Nia, Owain and Heledd. *Educated at* Bassaleg Grammar School, Gwent; Welsh National School of Medicine. *Career:* Registrar in Chest Diseases, Sully Hospital Penarth 1969-71; Senior Microbiologist, Public Health Laboratory, University Hospital of Wales 1971-75; Consultant Microbiologist, West Glamorgan Health Authority 1975-85. *Publications:* Scientific publications re: Clinical Pathology, Medical Microbiology and Toxoplasmosis. *Recreation:* golf, skiing, rugby, antique maps, Welsh culture and language. *Address:* Public Health Laboratory, Singleton Hospital, Sgeti, Abertawe, SA2 8QA.

KAYE, William, *Born on* 26 Feb 1914 *Son of* the late Henry Kaye of Wakefield and the late Alice Kay. *Marriage:* 1st to Emma May (d 1947) dau of Rowland Harrison of Wakefield; 2nd to Elizabeth Branwen Elwy (d.1982) dau of the Rev. Thomas Elwy Williams of Trefriw, N.Wales. *Children: Educated at* Thornes House School. *Career:* served R.A.F. 1942-44; Civil Servant retired 1970; member of the Governing Council Federation of Environment Societies 1968-70; Patron Natl Domesday Celebrations 1986; Landowner, Lord of the Manor of Hulland, Derbyshire, member of the Manorial Society of G.B. *Recreation:* travel, music, golf, studies in medieval history. *Clubs:* Civil Service, Betws-y-Coed Golf. *Address:* Minffordd, Capel Garmon, Llanrwst, Gwynedd Tel: 0690 710483

KEAR, Mr Graham Francis, BA(Oxon). *Currently:* Assistant Secretary, The Abbeyfield Richmond Society, Richmond, Surrey. *Born on* 9 Oct 1928 at Cwmfelinfach, Mon. *Son of* the late Richard Kear and the late Eva (nee Davies). *Marriage:* to Joyce Eileen Parks, 1978. *Children: Educated at* St.Julians High School for Boys, Newport, Mon; Balliol College, Oxford. *Career:* joined Senior Civil Service 1951; Ministry of Supply-Ministry of Aviation 1951-72, with secondments to Foreign Office 1953-54, Delegation to European Coal and Steel Community; NATO 1959-61; Ministry of Defence 1962-65; and The Cabinet Office 1968-71. Associate Fellow, Harvard University 1972-73; Department of Energy 1973-80. *Recreation:* reading, music, working for my local church. *Address:* 28 Eastbourne Road, Brentford, Middlesex, TW8 9PE.

KELLAWAY, Professor Ian Walter, B.Pharm, PhD, DSc, FRPharmS. *Currently:* Professor of Pharmaceutics, Welsh School of Pharmacy, UWCC, since 1979. *Born on* 10 March 1944 at Plympton. *Son of* the late Leslie William and Margaret Seaton (nee Webber). *Marriage:* to Kay Elizabeth Downey, 1969. *Children:* Robert Ian and Jane Elizabeth *Educated at* King Edward VI Grammar School, Totnes; University of London, School of Pharmacy. *Career:* Lecturer, Leicester Polytechnic 1968-69; Lecturer University of Nottingham 1969-79; SERC, Chemistry Com 1986-90; Chemistry Pharmacy and Standard Committee 1987-90; Welsh Scheme for the Development of Health and Social Research Committee 1986- ; Welsh Committee for Postgraduate Pharmaceutical Education 1985-. *Recreation:* gardening, travel *Address:* 9 Dan-Y-Bryn Avenue, Radyr, Cardiff, CF4 8DB.

KELLY, Dr David Roy, BSc, PhD(Salford), MRSC, CChem. *Currently:* Lecturer. *Born on* 16 April 1955 at London. *Son of* Roy and Marie Kelly (nee Kirby). *Marriage:* to Judith Wendy Hadfield, 1980. *Children:* Lauren. *Educated at* Dartford Technical High School, Wilmington, Kent. *Career:* Postdoctoral fellow University of Waterloo, Canada, Univesity of Maryland 1979-81; University of Oxford 1981-84. *Publications:* Biotransformations in Preparative Organic Chemistry (with R.H.Green, G.Davies, S.M.Roberts). *Recreation:* cabinet maker *Address:* School Of Chemistry and Applied Chemistry, University Of Wales College of Cardiff, P.O.Box 912, CF1 3TB.

KELSALL, Professor Malcolm Miles, MA, B.Litt *Currently:* Professor of English, University of Wales, Cardiff, since 1975. *Born on* 27 Feb 1938 at Twickenham, England. *Son of* the late Alec James and Hetty May (nee Miles). *Marriage:* to Mary Emily (nee Ives), 1961. *Educated at* William Hulme's Grammar School, Manchester; Brasenose College Oxford. *Career:* Staff Reporter, The Guardian newspaper 1961; Assistant Lecturer, Exeter University 1963; Lecturer, Reading University 1964; Visiting Professor University of Paris 1978; visiting professor University of Hiroshima 1979. *Publications:* Editor: S.Fielding, David Simple 1969; ed. T.Otway, Venice Preserved 1969; ed. W.Congreve, Love for Love 1969; ed. J.Trapp, Lectures on Poetry 1973; ed. J.M.Synge, The Playboy of the Western World 1975; Christopher Marlowe 1981; Congreve 1981; ed. J.Trapp, The Preface to the Aeneis 1982; ed. J.C.Hobhouse, A Trifling Mistake 1984; Studying Drama 1985; Byron's Politics 1987; awarded the Elma Dangerfield Prize 1991; joint ed. Encyclopedia of Literature and Criticism 1990; The Great Good Place: The Country House and English Literature 1992; the Warton Lecture 1992 and part author of sixteen further books. *Recreation:* theatre, long distance running. *Address:* School Of English, University Of Wales, P.O. Box 94, Cardiff, CF1 3XE.

KEMP, Hubert Bond Stafford, MS, FRCS, FRCSE *Currently:* Consultant Orthopaedic Surgeon: Royal National Orthopaedic Hospital, London and Stanmore, 1974-90; The Middlesex Hospital, 1984-90; Hon. Consultant Orthopaedic Surgeon, St.Luke's Hospital for the Clergy, 1975-90; University Tacher in Orthopaedics. *Born on* 25 March 1925 at Cardiff. *Son of* John Stafford Kemp and Cecilia Isabel (nee Bond). *Marriage:* to Moyra Ann Margaret Odgers, 1947. *Children:* three d. *Educated at* Cardiff High School; University of South Wales; St.Thomas' Hospital; University of London (MB, BS 1949; MS 1969); MRCS, LRCP 1947; FRCSE 1960; FRCS 1970. *Career:* Robert Jones Gold Medal and Assoc. Prize 1969 (Proxime Accessit, 1964); Hunterian Prof., RCS, 1969; Hon. Consultant, Royal Nat. Orthopaedic Hospital, London and Stanmore, 1965-74; Sen. Lecturer, Inst of Orthopaedics 1965-74, Hon. Sen. Lecturer 1974-90. Visiting Professor, VII Congress of Soc. Latino Amer. de Orthopedia y Traumatologica 1971. Member: MRC Working Party on Tuberculosis of the Spine, 1974-; MRC Working Party on Osteosarcoma, 1985-. Fellow, Brit. Orthopaedic Assoc., 1972- ; Chairman, London Bone Tumour Unit, 1985-91; Member: Brit. Orthopaedic Research Soc., 1967- ; Internat Skeletal Soc., 1977-. *Publications:* (jointly) Orthopaedic Diagnosis, 1984; chapter in: A Postgraduate Textbook of Clinical Orthopaedics, 1983, 1992 awaiting publication; Bailliere's Clinical Oncology, Bone Tumours, 1987; papers on diseases of the spine, the hip, metal sensitivity, bone scanning and haemophilia. *Recreation:* fishing, painting. *Address:* 55 Loom Lane, Radlett, Herts., WD7 8NX. Tel: 0923 854265. 107 Harley Street, London, W1N 1DG. Tel:071 935 2776.

Fax: 071 935 5187.

KEMP, Dr Michael Alan Reginald, BSc; PhD (Liverpool). *Currently:* Registrar, University of Wales. *Born on* 1 Oct 1935 at Barry. *Son of* Reginald William & Millicent Kemp. *Marriage:* to Alwen Gwyneth (nee Parry), 1961. *Children:* Lowri Alane and Siwan Heledd. *Educated at* Barry Grammar School; University of Liverpool. *Career:* ICI Research Fellow, University of Liverpool 1959-60. Guest Physicist, Brookhaven National Laboratory, USA 1961-62; Scientific Officer/Senior Scientific Officer, Rutherford Laboratory, Serc, UK 1962-65; Principal Scientific Officer/University Lecturer, Rutherford Lab/Bristol University 1966-68; Principal Scientific Officer, Serc, Daresbury Laboratory 1968-75; Visiting Scientist, CERN, Geneva 1970-72; P.S.O. Rutherford Lab 1976-79; Visiting Scientist, CERN 1976-79; Scientific Spokesman British-French-German Collaboration 1978-79; Head of Science Group, Astronomy Radio Space Division, Serc 1979-84. *Recreation:* travel, art and architecture, music, sailing, photography, skiing, motor cars. *Address:* University of Wales, University Registry, Cathays Park, Cardiff, CF1 3NS. Llawenog, 51 Cherry Orchard Road, Llysfaen, Caerdydd, CF4 5UE.

KEMP, Dr Richard Bernard, BSc, PhD, CBiol, FIBiol. *Currently:* Reader in Zoology in the Department of Biological Sciences, since 1986. *Born on* 19 Oct 1941 at Enfield. *Son of* William Cecil Norman Kemp and Lillian Maud Kemp (nee Davies). *Marriage:* single. *Educated at* Enfield Grammar School (1953-60); The University College of Wales, Aberystwyth (1960-67). *Career:* Senior Research Associate, 1967-71; Lecturer, 1971-83; Senior Lecturer, 1983-86 all at The University College of Wales, Aberystwyth. *Publications:* Two books; 5 reviews and 70 original papers. *Recreation:* cricket, aviation, chess, Bruckner and George Bernard Shaw. *Clubs:* Brynamlwg *Address:* Neuadd Cwrt Mawr, Waunfawr, Aberystwyth, Dyfed, SY23 3AN.

KENNY, Mr Arthur William, CBE, 1977; CChem, FRSC. *Formerly:* Director in the Directorate General of Environmental Protection of the Department of the Environment, 1974-79. *Born on* 31 May 1918. *Son of* Ernest James Kenny and Gladys Margaret Kenn. *Marriage:* to Olive Edna West, 1947. *Children:* one s two d. *Educated at* Canton High School, Cardiff; Jesus Coll., Oxford (schol.) BA (1st Cl.Hons Natural Sci.), MA, BSc, Oxon. *Career:* Min. of Supply, 1941; Min. of Health, 1950; Min. of Housing and Local Govt, 1951; DoE, 1971. *Publications:* papers on disposal of radioactive and toxic wastes and on quality of drinking water. *Address:* 134 Manor Green Road, Epsom, Surrey, KT19 8LL. Tel: 0372 724850.

KERSHAW, Mr W.H. (Bill), MA(Cantab)., MICE. *Currently:* Retired. Director of Environmental Services, Newport B.C. 1986-90. *Born on* 6 April 1925 at Birmingham. *Son of* the late Bert Kershaw and the late Alice (nee Royal). *Marriage:* to Ellen Dwyllis Morgan 1955. *Children:* Jane and Tracey (one son Simon dec'd). *Educated at* K.E.G.S. Five Ways, Birmingham; Emmanuel Coll., Cambridge. *Career:* Royal Navy 1947-49; Civil Engineering Contracting; New Town Development; Deputy Borough Eng. Newport CBC 1972; Commt. Mbr. S.Wales Assoc. of Inst. Civil Engineers 1971-73, 1981-84, 1986-89;(Hon Sec. Transportation Group 1960-73); Chrmn. Welsh Trail Riders Assoc. 1979- ; Founder Mbr. Motoring Organisations' Land Access & Recreation Assoc. 1986; Chrmn. Countryside Commt. Cambrian Council of Welsh M/C Clubs 1988- ; Chrmn. Forum for Motorised Sport in Wales 1991- ; Pres. East South Wales Centre of ACU 1992-93; Pres. Rotary Club of Newport 1992-93. *Recreation:* Motorcycling, gardening. *Clubs:* Rotary, WTRA, TRF. *Address:* 20 High Cross Drive, Newport, Gwent, NP1 9AB.

KILPATRICK, Professor George Stewart, OBE, MD, FRCP(Lond & Edin). *Currently:* retired. *Born on* 26 June 1925 at Edinburgh. *Son of* Hugh and Annie Kilpatrick. *Marriage:* to Joan Askew. *Educated at* George Watsons College Edinburgh; Edinburgh University. *Career:* various medical posts in Edinburgh, London and Wales since 1947. David Davies Professor of Tuberculosis and Chest Diseases, University of Wales College of Medicine 1963-90. Honorary Consultant Physician to S.Glam Health Authority 1963-90; Vice Provost, College of Medicine 1988-90. *Publications:* many on medical and medical education matters. *Recreation:* travel, photography, bird watching. *Address:* 14 Millbrook Road, Dinas Powis, CF6 4DA. Tel: 0222 513149.

KING, Hilary, *Born on* 15 Sept 1931 at Treherbert. *Daughter of* Olwen and Wilfred Pomeroy. *Marriage:* to Mr S.F.King at St.Peter's Church, Pentre, 1955. *Children:* Andrew and Louise. *Educated at* Porth County Girls Grammar School. *Career:* Secretary, Treherbert Ladies Bowls Club 1977-92; Hon. Sec Glamorgan County Women's Bowling Association 1984-89; Hon Sec Welsh Ladies Indoor Bowling Association 1988-92; Member, British Isles Women's Indoor Bowling Association 1988-92; Bowling Umpire; Bowling Coach. *Publications:* Welsh Ladies Indoor Bowling Association Yearly Handbook 1990-92. *Recreation:* bowls, grandchildren, music. *Clubs:* Treherbert Outdoor Bowls, Rhondda Indoor Bowls. *Address:* Hillcrest Villa, Mountain View, Tynewydd, Treorchy, Mid Glamorgan, CF42 5LU.

KING, Mr John Edwards, *Currently:* Retired. *Born on* 30 May 1922 at Aberystwyth. *Son of* the late Captain Albert Edward King and the late Margaret (Peggy) (nee Edwards). *Marriage:* to 1) Pamela (nee White) 1948, (dissolved) to 2) Mary Margaret (nee Beaton) 1956. *Children:* Melanie Pamela, from 1st marriage; Fiona Margaret and Amanda Mary Elizabeth, from 2nd marriage. *Educated at* Penarth County School; School of Oriental & African Studies, London Univ. *Career:* WWII 1941-45: Rifle Brigade, Royal Welch Fusiliers, Royal West African Frontier Force; Captain, served with Special Force - Chindit campaign, Burma (despatches); Staff Captain, Basic O.C.T.U., Aldershot 1946-47: Cadet, Colonial Administrative Service, Northern Nigeria, 1947; Local Authority and Magistrate, Zaria 1951; Permanent Sec., Fed. Government of Nigeria 1960; Member of Council, Univ. of Lagos, 1962; retired 1963; Commonwealth Relations Office and Diplomatic Service 1963-66; Ministry of Defence 1966-69; Private Secretary to Secretary of State for Wales 1969-71; Assistant Sec. Welsh Office 1971-77; Under-Secretary and Principal Establishment Officer 1977-82; Civil Service Mbr. 1977-82; and External Mbr. 1982-86 of Civil Service Final Selection Bd; Consultant, Dept. of Educ. and Dir. China Studies Centre, Univ. College Cardiff 1984-87; Chrmn. Friends of Welsh College of Music and Drama 1990- ; and of Insole Court Action Group 1989- . *Recreation:* Swimming, tennis, watercolour painting. *Clubs:* Civil Service, Cardiff Lawn Tennis, Llandaff Institute. *Address:* Fairfields, Fairwater Road, Llandaff, Cardiff, CF5 2LF. Tel: 0222 562825.

KING, Mr Paul Lancaster, MBIM., MHCIMA. *Currently:* Director of Commercial Services, Clwyd County Council. *Born on* 28 Sept. 1950 at Ealing. *Son of* John King and Joan (nee Bailey). *Marriage:* to Fiona Jane (nee Humphreys) 1979. *Children:* Harriet and James. *Educated at* Monmouth School, Monmouth; Oxford Polytechnic. *Career:* Regional Manager-Wales, Hamard Catering 1978; Regional Manager-Wales, Grandmet Catering Services 1979; Area Manager-Arabian Gulf, Grandmet 1982; Managing Director, Heritage Leisure Ltd 1984; General Manager, Saudi Arabian Morrison Ltd., and Xenel Maintenance Ltd., Jeddah 1986; Director of

Commercial Services, Clwyd County Council 1988- ; Chairman of Forum of DSO Managers 1989-. *Publications:* Occasional articles on Competitive Tendering, Trout and Salmon Fishing in national press. *Recreation:* Fishing, wildlife, writing, photography, food and wine. *Clubs:* various Angling clubs, BASC, and British Deer Society. *Address:* Pendre Lodge, Pwllglas, Mold, Clwyd, CH7 6RA. Tel: 0352 700331.

KING, Mr Ronnie, Q.F.S.M., F.I.Fire E. *Currently:* CFO Dyfed 1983. *Born on* 21 Nov 1943 at Keighley (West Yorkshire). *Son of* the late Charles King and Evelyn King (nee Barrett). *Marriage:* to Carol King (nee Evans). *Children:* Beverley, Tracey, Catrin and Tristan *Educated at* Keighley Boys' Grammar School *Career:* DCO Dyfed 1979; SDO Fife, 3rd Officer, 1978; DC, Fife, 1977; Asst. Insp. Home Office, 1975; DO West Yorks, 1973; Stn. O. London, 1969; Joined Fm., West Riding, Yorks, 1961. *Recreation:* Cricket, music and theatre *Address:* 'Ucheldir', College Road, Carmarthen, Dyfed, SA31 3EF.

KINGHAM, His Honour John Frederick, MA;DL *Currently:* Lecturer - Broadcasting etc., Board Member Criminal Injuries Comp. Board. *Born on* 9 Aug 1925 at London. *Son of* Charles and Eileen Kingham. *Marriage:* to Valerie Vivienne Brown, J.P., 21 Mar 1958. *Children:* Sarah, Emma, Simon and Guy *Educated at* Blaenau Ffestiniog Grammar School; Wycliffe College, Lampeter. *Career:* R.N., 1943-47; Camb. Univ., 1947-49; BA, 1950; MA; Graz Univ., Called to Bar 1951 Grays Inn; Barrister 1951-73; Circuit Judge, 1973-90; Liason Judge Bedford, 1981-90; Dep. High Ct. Judge, 1985-90; Deputy L.Lieutenant Herts, 1989- ; Criminal Injuries Comp. Board member, 1990- ; Teacher Selwyn Col. Camb., 1990- ;Dept. Cty. Com., Herts Scouts, 1973-81; Venture Scout Leader. *Publications:* consultant Editor, Family Court Reports. *Recreation:* Squash; ski-ing; climbing; gardening and history. *Clubs:* Luton Town FC; Univ. Centre Camb; Western Club Glasgow. *Address:* Stone House, High Street, Kimpton, Hitchin Herts., SG4 8RJ.

KINNOCK M.P., Rt. Hon. Neil, BA. *Currently:* MP (Lab) Islwyn since 1983 (Bedwellty, 1970-83); Leader of the Labour Party, and Leader of the Opposition since 1983. *Born on* 28 March 1942 at Tredegar, S.Wales. *Son of* Gordon Kinnock, labourer and Mary Kinnock (nee Howells), nurse. *Marriage:* to Glenys Elizabeth Parry 1967. *Children:* one s one d. *Educated at* Lewis School, Pengam; University Coll., Cardiff. BA in Industrial Relations and History, UC, Cardiff (Chm Socialist Soc., 1963-66; Pres Students Union 1965-66; Hon Fellow 1982). *Career:* Tutor Organiser in Industrial and Trade Union Studies, WEA 1966-70; Member Welsh Hospital Board 1969-71; PPS to Sec. of State for Employment 1974-75; Member: Nat. Exec. Cttee, Labour Party, 1978- ; (Chm. 1987-88); Parly Cttee of PLP 1979- ; Chief Opposition spokesman on education 1979-83; Director (unpaid): Tribune Publications 1974-82; Fair Play for Children 1979- ; 7:84 Theatre Co. (England) Ltd 1979- ; Member: Socialist Educational Assoc., 1975- ; Pres. Assoc. of Liberal Education 1980-82. *Publications:* Wales and the Common Market 1971; Making Our Way 1986; contribs to Tribune, Guardian, New Statesman, etc. *Recreation:* male voice choral music, reading, children; Rugby Union and Association football. *Address:* House of Commons, London, SW1A OAA.

KIRK, Mr Malcolm Windsor, BA *Currently:* Controller of The Inland Revenue in Wales, 1989-. *Born on* 9 July 1943 at Cardiff. *Son of* Reginald Terrence and Phyllis Louise (nee Jenkins). *Marriage:* to Glenys Armytage, 1965. *Children:* Natalie Anne. *Educated at* Canton High School for Boys; University of Leicester, Cardiff. *Career:* Inland Revenue District Inspector, Newport, Gwent 1972-74; Inland Revenue Claims Branch Advisory Divn 1974-80; Inland Revenue, District inspector Soho 1980-81; Management Divn Personnel 1981-81; Group Controller Wales 1981-83; Head of the Llanishen Tax Complex 1983-87; District Inspector Bristol 1987-89. *Recreation:* Bonsai trees and averting my gaze from the Rugby field.

KNAPP, Mr Edward Ronald, CBE (1979) MA (Cantab). *Currently:* Retired. *Born on* 10 May 1919 at Cardiff. *Son of* Elsie Maria (nee Edwards) and Percival Charles Knapp. *Marriage:* Vera Mary Stephenson 1942. *Children:* Richard Ian, William Stephen, Vanessa Jane and Lucille Mary. *Educated at* Cardiff High School; St.Catharines College, Cambridge (MA 1940); Harvard Business School (AMP 1954): *Career:* RNVR Lt.Cdr. 1940-46; Joined British Timken, 1946; Managing Director, British Timken, 1969; Director Timken Co. (USA), 1976; Managing Director, Timken Europe, 1977-84; Technical and Management Educational Governor, Nene College, 1953- ; Regional Advisory Council for Organisation of Further Education, 1978- ; *Recreation:* Played Rugby for Wales 1940, Captain Cambridge Univ. 1940 and Northampton RFC, 1948; President Northampton RFC, 1988; Gardenning, Golf and World Travel. *Clubs:* Hawkes (Cambridge); East India; Northants County; *Address:* The Elms, 1 Millway, Duston, Northampton, NN5 6ER.

KNIGHT, Professor Bernard Henry, MD(Wales), BCh, MRCP, FRCPath, DMJ(Path), Barrister of Gray's Inn *Currently:* Professor of Forensic Pathology, University of Wales College of Medicine; Director, Wales Institute of Forensic Medicine; Consultant Pathologist, Cardiff Royal Infirmary; Home Office Pathologist; Visiting Professor, Universities of Hong Kong, Kuwait and Guangzhou (China). *Born on* 3 May 1931 at Cardiff. *Son of* the late Harold Ivor Knight and Doris Lawes. *Marriage:* to Jean Gwenllian Ogborne (Swansea). *Children:* Huw David Charles Knight. *Educated at* Herbert Thompson School, Ely, Cardiff; St.Illtyd's College, Cardiff; Dynevor Secondary School, Swansea; Welsh National School of Medicine; Gray's Inn, London. *Career:* Captain RAMC (Malaya) 1956-59; Lecturer, and Senior Lecturer in Forensic Medicine, Universities of London and Newcastle 1959-68; Senior Lecturer then Reader in Forensic Pathology, Welsh National School of Medicine 1968-80; President, British Association in Forensic Medicine; Vice-President, International Academy of Legal Medicine; President, Wales Medico-legal Society; Past-President, Forensic Science Society; Chairman of Forensic Committee and Board of Examiners of Royal College of Pathologists; Member, General Medical Council; Member, Home Office Policy Advisory Committee on Forensic Pathology; Hon Member, German Society of Forensic Medicine, Honorary Member, Finnish Society of Forensic Medicine; Member, Seville Working Group on EEC Forensic Medicine; Member Home Office Working Party on Forensic Pathology. *Publications:* seven medical textbooks; eight crime novels; two Welsh historical novels; a biography; history of medicine; radio and television drama and features; 150 articles in the medical press; Managing Editor of "Forensic Science International"; joint editor "Welsh Medical Gazette". *Recreation:* writing crime and historical novels and radio and TV scripts. *Address:* 26 Millwood, Llysfaen, Cardiff, CF4 5TL.

KNIGHT, Mr John (Roger), MBCS *Currently:* Managing Director, J.Computer Logic Ltd, since 1977, designed and developed unique method of Systems Configuration for Computer Systems for Plant Hire and Rental Industry, appointed the IBM Application Specialist 1991 and 1992 for this application. *Born on* 16 Aug 1946 at Merthyr Tydfil.

Son of the late Tom Knight and the late Friswyth (nee Raymond Jones). *Marriage:* to Wendy Laurena (nee May) 1980. *Children:* Thomas Roger (b.1983) and Lucy Jane (b.1985). *Educated at* Littleover, Derby. *Career:* Computer Systems Development and Troubleshooting. CIC Amsterdam 1970-72; Freelance Computer Consultant 1972-79. *Recreation:* Cycling, walking, food, restoration of ancient buildings. *Address:* J. Computer Logic Ltd, Golden Valley Software Factory, New Mills, Eaton Bishop, Hereford, HR2 9QE.

KNOWLES, Mr James Thomas Crawford, B.Sc. *Currently:* Mayor of Borough of Aberconwy 1991-92; Gwynedd County Councillor; Author, Consultant on Marine Biology. *Born on* 26 Sept. 1932 in Kent, England. *Son of* the late Herbert Norman Knowles MC & Bar and the late Marie Gwendoline (nee Hurst-Hodgson). *Marriage:* to Jennifer Tempest Durham 1965. *Children:* Philippa, Julia and Jane. *Educated at* Aldenham School 1946-51; London University 1953-56. *Career:* Paper Technologist, Wiggins Teape & Co., 1956-59; European Development Management, A.B.Dick Co., Chicago, USA 1959-64; Officer in Charge, Seed Oyster Unit, Conwy for White Fish Authority 1964-74; Manager, Seed Oysters (UK) Ltd., Brynsicyn, Anglesey 1974-76; Hotel Proprietor 1977-89; Consultant, Marine Biology 1977- ; Gwynedd County Councillor 1981- ; Vice Chairman of Economic Development Planning Committee; Aberconwy Borough Councillor 1983- ; Vice-Chairman Policy Committee; Chairman, Oriel Mostyn; Chairman, Llandudno Youth Club management committee; Director T.Q.S.Ltd; Director, North Wales Tourism Ltd; Member, North Wales Police Authority; Treasurer, Mayflower Foundation; Treasurer, Conwy Division Liberal Democratic Association; Governor, Ysgol John Bright, Ysgol Craig-y-Don, Ysgol Gogarth. *Publications:* Snowdonia-Northern Area; Walks for Motorists; Walker's Britian 1 North Wales section; Walker's Britain 2, North Wales and Mid Wales sections; Britain on Back Road, North Wales section. *Recreation:* Walking, Natural and Local History, opera, reading. *Clubs:* Member of Cambrian Ornithological Society; Member of Marine Conservation Society. *Address:* Sorrento, Nant-Y-Gamar Road, Craig y Don, Llandudno, Gwynedd, LL30 1YE.

KNOWLES, Mr Timothy (Tim), FCA *Currently:* Director - Welsh Water PLC. *Born on* 17 May 1938 at Cardiff. *Son of* the late Cyril William Knowles and the late Winifred Alice Knowles (nee Hood). *Marriage:* to Gaynor Hallett 1967. *Children:* Tracy. *Educated at* Bishop Gore Grammar School, Swansea. *Career:* Company Secretary & Accountant, Louis Marx & Co. Ltd., 1960-68; Controller, Modco Valenite, 1968-69; Company Secretary, HTV Ltd., 1969-78; Financial Director, 1975-81; Assistant Managing Director 1981-86; Financial Director, HTV Group p.l.c. 1976-86; Group Managing Director 1986-88; Finance Director - Exports Credits Guarantee Department - Insurance Services Group (for Privatisation), 1990-91; Financial Consultant - NCM (UK) Holdings Ltd., 1991-92. Member South Wales Electricity Board 1981-82; Member Welsh Water Authority 1982-89; Director Welsh Water PLC 1989- . Political: Conservative Candidate for Swansea East, 1966. *Recreation:* Travel; watching cricket; walking. *Clubs:* Cardiff & County. *Address:* Cae Ffynnon, 12 Ger-y-Llan, St. Nicholas, Cardiff., CF5 6SY.

KROLL, Revd Dr. Una Margaret Patricia, MB, B.Chir. *Currently:* Nun, Deacon, St.Mary's Monmouth, Writer, Broadcaster. *Born on* 15 Dec 1925 at London, England. *Daughter of* the late Brigadier George A.Hill, CB, DSO, DS and the late Hilda Evelyn (nee Pediani). *Marriage:* to Leopold Kroll, 1957. *Children:* Florence, Leo, Elisabeth and Una. *Educated at* Malvern Girls College, Girton; London Hospital, Whitechapel. *Career:* Retired General Practitioner; Deaconess in Church of England since 1970; Deacon, Church in Wales 1988; member, Provincial Validating Board CIW since 1989; Professor member of the Society of the Sacred Cross since 1991. *Publications:* A Sign post to the works 1974; Flesh of my Flesh 1975; Lament for a lost Enemy 1978; Sexual Counselling; A Spiritual Exercise Book, 1985; Growing Older, 1988; In Touch with Healing, 1991. *Address:* Tymawr Convent, Lydart, Monmouth, Gwent, NP5 4RN.

L

LAKER, Dr Michael Francis, MD, MB, BS, DipBiochem, FRCPath. *Currently:* Reader and Consultant in Clinical Biochemistry; Admissions sub-Dean, The Medical School, University of Newcastle-upon-Tyne. *Born on* 9 June 1945 at Newport, Gwent. *Son of* Walter John Laker and Joyce Laker (nee Ashill). *Marriage:* to Alison Jean Borland, 1969. *Children:* Hannah Mair, Bethan Jane, Christopher Philip and Jonathan Michael. *Educated at* Newport High School; St.Thomas's Hospital Medical School. *Career:* House Physician, St.Thomas's Hospital 1970; House Surgeon, Kingston Hospital 1970; Assistant Lecturer in Pathology, St.Thomas's Hospital Medical School 1971-73; Lecturer in Chemical Pathology, St.Thomas's Hospital Medical School 1973-80; Research Fellow, University of California Sandiego, USA 1979-80; Senior Lecturer and Consultant in Clinical Biochemistry, University of Newcastle-upon-Tyne and Royal Victoria Infirmary 1980-89. *Publications:* Short Cases in Clinical Biochemistry, 1984; published 130 research papers and reviews. *Recreation:* gardening, music, computing. *Clubs:* Royal Society of Medicine. *Address:* Department of Clinical Biochemistry, The Medical Sch, Framlington Place, Newcastle-Upon-Tyne, NE2 4HH. 9 Campus Martius, Heddon On The Wall, Northumberland, , NE15 0BP Tel: 0661 853798.

LAMFORD, Mr (Thomas) Gerald, OBE., LLB (London). *Born on* 3 April 1928 at Carmarthen. *Son of* the late Albert and Sarah Lamford. *Marriage:* to Eira Hale 1952. *Children:* one s and one d. *Educated at* Technical College, Swansea; London University (LLB (Hons), 1969); Police College (Intermed. Comd Course 1969; Sen. Comd. Course 1973). *Career:* Radio Officer, Merchant Navy 1945; Wireless Operator, RAF 1946-48; Aden. Carmarthenshire Constab. (now Dyfed Powys Police) 1949; reached rank of Chief Inspector, CID, Crime Squad; Force Training Officer Supt. Haverfordwest 1970; Chief Supt. Llanelli 1971-74; Asst. Chief Constable, Greater Manchester Police 1974-79; Investigating Officer, FCO 1981-84; ASVU Representative, Cyprus 1985-88; Commandant, Police Staff College 1976-79; Visiting Prof. of Police Science, John Jay Coll. of Criminal Justice, City Univ. of New York 1972; sometime visiting Lecturer: Southern Police Inst., Univ. of Louisville, Ky; N.Eastern Univ., Boston; NY Univ. Sch. of Law; Rutgers Univ., NJ; Mercy Coll., Detroit; County Comr. St. John Amb. Bde, Pembrokeshire, 1970; SBStJ. *Publications:* articles in Police Studies, Internat. Rev. of Police Develt; Police Rev; Bramshill Jl; *Recreation:* Genealogy, photography. *Clubs:* Rotary Club of Ammanford (President 1991-92). *Address:* 11 Llwyn y Bryn, Ammanford, Dyfed.

LANGFORD, 9th Baron: Colonel Geoffrey Alexander Rowley-Conwy, OBE., DL., Royal Artillery (retired) , Constable of Rhuddlan Castle and Lord of The Manor of Rhuddlan. *Born on* 8 March 1912 *Son of* the late Major Geoffrey Seymour Rowley-Conwy (killed in action, Gallipoli 1915) and of Bertha Gabrielle, d. of the late Lt. Alexander Cochran RN, Ashkirk, Selkirkshire. *Marriages:* 1st, 1938, to Ruth St.John (marr. dis.1956) (d.1991),da of late Albert St.John Murphy, The Island House, Little Island, County Cork; 2nd,1957, to Grete (d.1973) da of the late Col. E.T.C. von Freieselben formerly Chief of the King's Adjutant Staff to HM King of Denmark: three sons. 3rd 1975 Susan Winifred Denham d. of C.C.H. Denham, 1 son, 1 daughter. *Educated at* Marlborough College, RMA Woolwich. *Career:* Commissioned 2/Lt. RA 1932, Lieut. 1935,Capt. 1939, Major 1941, Lt.Col. 1945, served war of 1939-45 in Singapore (POW escaped) and with Indian Mountain Artillery in Burma 1941-45 (OBE 1943); Staff College,Quetta 1945, 4th Reg. RHA BAOR 1946,B erlin Air Lift, Fassberg 1948-49, GSO1 42nd Inf. Div. TA 1949-52, CO 31st Regt. RA Kinmel Park Camp 1954-57; Retired 1957 Col. (Hon.) 1967, DL Clwyd 1977,Freeman City of London 1986; *Recreation: Clubs:* Army and Navy *Address:* Bodrhyddan, Rhuddlan, Clwyd

LAURENCE, Professor Kurt Michael, MA(Cantab), MBChB (L'pool), DSc(Wales), FRCP(Ed), FRCPath *Currently:* Emeritus Professor of Paediatric Research, University College of Medicine; Hon. Consulting Clinical Geneticist,South Glamorgan Health Authority; Registry Leader for Wales of Eurocat (Malformations Registration and Surveillance for E.E.C.). *Born on* 7 Aug 1924 at Berlin. *Son of* the late Gustav Loebenstein and the late Greta Marks (nee Heyman). *Marriage:* 1949. *Children:* Stephen, Amanda and Elizabeth *Educated at* Newcastle under Lyme High School; Trinity Hall,Cambridge University; Liverpool University. *Career:* Senior House Officer in Pathology,Luton and Dunstable Hospital 1952; Registrar,Portsmouth Pathological Service 1953-55; Research Fellow in Hydrocephalus and Spina Bifida,Hospital for Sick Children,London 1955-58; Senior Lecturer in Paediatric Pathology Hon Consultant, University of Wales College of Medicine and Cardiff United Hospitals 1959-69; Reader in Applied Genetics,University of Wales College of Medicine and South Glamorgan Health Authority 1969-76; Professor / Co-Director of Regional Genetics Service for Wales/Hon Consultant in Medical Genetics 1976-89; President Paediatric Pathology Society 1974; Secretary and President of The Society for Research into Hydrocephalus and Spina Bifida 1970-82; Secretary and President of the Clinical Genetics Society 1975-88. *Publications:* Over 350 Scientific papers on Paediatric Pathology (mostly on Perinatal and Neurological Problems), Malformations (mostly on Hydrocephalus and Neural Tube Defects) and Genetics (mostly on prevention, diagnosis, prenatal detection and epidemiology of defects); Foetoscopy (written with I.Rocker), Elsiver 1981; chapters in multiauthor books on Neurological Diseases,Medical Genetics, Pediatric Pathology, Diseases in Wales, Hydrocephalus,Antenatal Care,Spina Bifida and Congenital Malformations etc. *Recreation:* music, gardening, antiquities and art. *Clubs:* Athenaeum. *Address:* Springside, Pen-Y-Turnpike, Dinas Powis, South Glamorgan, CF6 4HG. Department of Child Health, U.W.C.M., Heath Park, Cardiff, CF4 4XW Tel: 0222 513248.

LAURENCE, Professor Laurence, PhD *Currently:* Professor of Forestry, School of Agricultural and Forest Sciences, University of Wales, Bangor, Gwynedd, LL57 2UW, since 1975. *Born on* 20 Oct 1927 at Wexford, Ireland. *Son of* Bridget (nee Banville) and William Roche. *Marriage:* to Felicity Bawtree, 1962. *Children:* Nicola (28), Christopher (24) and Patricia (23). *Educated at* University of Dublin; Trinity College; University of British Columbia. *Career:* British Columbia Forest Service, Victoria, B.C., 1962-66; Canadian Forest Service, Quebec, /1966-72; Professor of Forestry, University of Badan, Nigeria, 1972-75. President of International Union of Forestry Societies 1976-81; Vice-Chiarman of Board of Trustees of International Council for Research in Agroforestry 1978-84. *Publications:* over 50 publications in forestry and agro forestry in the temperate zone and in the tropics. *Recreation:* sailing, fishing, reading. *Clubs:* Kildare St. University, Dublin. *Address:* 62 Upper Garth Road, Bangor, Gwynedd LL57 2SS. Madaboy, Murroe, Co. Limerick, Ireland.

LEACH, Ernest Terrance, LLB; FCIArb; Hon.FIQS; FInst; CES; FRICS; Barrister. *Currently:* retired. *Born on* 21 Jan 1933 at Wolverhampton. *Son of* the late Ernest Terrance Leach and Alice Maud (nee Hollyhead). *Marriage:* to Patricia (nee Cook), 1959. *Children:* Stephany Lorraine (b.1962) and Stella Therese (b.1965). *Educated at* Whitchurch Grammar School; University of Nottingham. *Career:* Partner: The Leach Partnership (formerly E.T.Leach & Partners), Quantity Surveyors 1963-83; Partner: Leach International (R.S.A.), Johannesburg, 1970-83; Partner: E.T.Leach and Associates (UK), Quantity Surveying and Construction claims Consultancy 1983; Freeman City of London, Liveryman, Worshipful Company of Arbitrators; former Governor Sir John Talbot's School and Whitchurch Shrops Branch Chairman RNLI and Save The Children Fund. *Publications:* various proceedural guides to Standard Forms and Conditions of Contract. *Recreation:* model making, painting *Address:* Trem-Y-Garn, Park Road, Barmouth, Gwynedd LL42 1PH.

LEACH, Mr Frank Edward Donald, Justice of the Peace, Chairman of Bench. *Currently:* retired Company Director. *Born on* 1 April 1911 at Newtown. *Son of* the late Andrew and Margretta Leach. *Marriage:* to Winifred M. George 1937. *Children:* Heather Jones, Neal Leach BA., Andrew Leach, FRICS., Susan Hughes, Perapetetic Violin Tutor *Educated at* Newtown High School. *Career:* Director, Leach & Son, after fathers death in 1942. Factory and machine shops were engaged during the two World Wars for the production of Service Equipment for the Airforce, Navy and Army. Turning attention to the development of Housing, Education and Commercial enterprises. Former Chairman of Scouting for Montgomeryshire and at present Life Vice President of the Boy Scouts Association for Montgomeryshire, in 1974 was elected to Powys County Council and in 1989 became Chairman. President of Hafren Tennis Club, Newtown. Former Chairman of Montgomeryshire Liberal Association during the time of the late Clement Davies, Q.C., M.P. *Recreation:* golf *Clubs:* President, Newtown Golf *Address:* The Pines, Llanidloes Road, Newtown, Powys, SY16 1EZ.

LEADBEATER, Mr Howell, BA degree History *Currently* retired. *Born on* 22 Oct 1919 at Ponthenri. *Son of* Thomas and Mary Ann Leadbeater. *Marriage:* to Mary Elizabeth Roberts, 1946. *Children:* Timothy Richard, Isobel Sarah and Edmund Owen. *Educated at* Pontardawe Secondary; Swansea University. *Career:* Army Service, Adjutant 11th East African Divisional Signals (1940-46); Successful in examination for Adminstrative Civil Service 1948; Promoted Principal (Ministry of Works) 1949; Assistant Secretary

1958; Under Secretary and Controller of Supplies (Min of Public Building and Works) 1968; Under Deputy Secretary (Dept. of Environment) 1973; Member of the Design Council 1967-76; Design Co-ordinator for the Investiture of the Prince of Wales at Caernarfon Castle 1969; Guest Lecturer for CBI Management courses at St.Catherine's College Oxford. Also at Manchester University, Civil Service Staff College et al. 1969; Member of the National Craft Council 1976-78. *Recreation:* Books, music, gardening, wine, travel. *Address:* Tides Reach, Llansteffan, Carmarthen, Dyfed, SA33 5EY.

LEAKER, Dudley Roberts, RIBA, FRIAS. *Currently:* retired. *Born on* 22 Dec 1920 at Swansea. *Son of* Charles and Mabel Leaker. *Marriage:* 12 June 1945, Swansea. *Children:* David, Margaret, Jane and Patricia. *Educated at* Dynevor School; Art School Swansea; Welsh School of Arch. *Career:* Architect on blitzed towns of Bristol, Plymouth, Coventry. Senior Architect Stevenage New Town then Chief Architect and Planner of Cumberland New Town. Chief Architect and Planner of Warrington New Town. Architect/adviser and Exec. Director, Milton Keynes Dev. Corp. Senior Independent Inspector, taking major public inquiries (retired 1991). Chairman of International Committee producing Technical books for 3rd world. Visiting Professor Pensylvannia. External Examiner at Universities. Hon Research Fellow of Open University. Recipient of Reynold Award. Former J.P., Board Member of two housing associations and Inter Action. *Publications:* various technical papers, also New Town in National Development etc. *Recreation:* travel, painting, music. *Address:* 'Anchorsholme', Heighway Lane, All Stretton, Shropshire, SY6 6HN.

LEE, Professor Mark Howard, BSc, PhD, CEng, MIEE, FRSA *Currently:* Professor of Computer Science, since 1987. *Born on* 9 April 1944. *Son of* C.H. Lee and P.A. Osbourne. *Marriage:* to Elizabeth Anne Wilmott, 1971. *Children:* Matthew, Joseph and Bethan. *Educated at* Noel Baker School Derby; University College Swansea. *Career:* Trainee Elect Eng., 1959-63; Lecturer, Leicester City Poly, 1969-74; Lecturer, UCW, 1974-85; Senior Lecturer, 1985-87. *Publications:* "Intelligent Robotics", Chapman & Hall, 1989. *Recreation:* mountaineering *Address:* Computer Science Dept, University College of Wales, Aberystwyth, Dyfed, SY23 3BZ.

LEGGE-BOURKE, Hon Mrs Elizabeth Shan Josephine, LVO *Born on* 10 Sept 1943 at Crickhowell. *Daughter of* the late Col Lord Glanusk DSO, and Margaret Shoubridge, (later married 1st Viscount De L'Isle, VC, KG). *Marriage:* to William N H Legge-Bourke, 1964. *Children:* Alexandra (b.1965), Zara (b.1966, m. Capt R.Plunkett-Ernle-Erle-Drax) and Harry (b.1972), page of honour to H.M.Queen 1984-87. *Career:* Lady in Waiting to HRH Princess Royal; Member, Brecon Beacons National Park Authority; Chief President for Wales, St.John's Ambulance Brigade; President of Council, Save The Children Fund for Wales; High Sheriff of Powys 1991-92. *Recreations:* country sports, gardening. *Address:* Penmyarth, Glanusk Park, Crickhowell, Powys, NP8 1LP.

LEGGE-BOURKE, Mr William Nigel Henry, *Currently:* Director, Kleinwort Benson Securities Ltd since 1986; Director, The London Stock Exchange. *Born on* 12 July 1939 .*Son of* the late Sir H.Legge-Bourke, KBE, DL, MP and Jean Grant of Monymusk. *Marriage:* to Hon Shan Bailey, 1964. *Children:* Alexandra (b.1965), Zara (b.1966, m.Capt R.Plunkett-Ernle-Erle-Drax) and Harry (b.1972, page of honour to H.M.Queen 1984-87). *Educated at* Eton; Magdalene Coll, Cambridge (MA). *Career:* Captain, sometime Adjutant, Royal Horse Guards, The Blues, retired

1968. Partner Grieveson Grant & Co., 1973-86;Kleinwort Benson Group Compliance Officer 1991; Member, Board of Stock Exchange since 1988; member, Representative Body of Church in Wales; Chairman, Finance Committee, Scout Association (past County Commissioner, Brecknock). F.R.S.A. *Recreation:* country sports, arboriculture. *Clubs:* White's *Address:* Penmyarth, Glanusk Park, Crickhowell, Powys, NP8 1LP. 8 Kensington Mansions, Trebovir Road, London, SW5 9TF.

LEONARD, Mr Colin William, IPFA *Currently:* Director, Power Marketing Division MANWEB plc. *Born on* 24 March 1940 at Chester, U.K. *Son of* the late Frederick William Leonard and Leah (nee Poole). *Marriage:* to Jean (nee Connah) 1963. *Children:* James Benjamin William and Victoria Jane. *Educated at* Chester City Grammar School 1951-56. *Career:* Bank Clerk, Martins Bank Ltd (now Barclays) 1956-59; Trainee Accountant, Shell Refining Co 1959-61; Computer Programmer, Cheshire County Council 1961-64; Systems Analyst, Leicestershire County Council 1964-66;Systems Analyst, Computer Manager, Director Management Services, Company Secretary, Director Power Marketing, MANWEB 1966- . *Recreation:* Golf, theatre (Trustee Chester Gateway Theatre). *Address:* C/o Manweb Plc, Head Office, Sealand Road, Chester, CH1 4LR.

LEVER, Professor Jeffrey Darcy, MA, MD, ScD (Cantab) *Currently:* Emeritus Professor, University of Wales. *Born on* 29 March 1923 at Johannesburg, S.A. *Son of* the late John Roger Lever and the late Dorothy May (nee Letts). *Marriage:* to Margaret Emily (nee Eastwood), 1950. *Children:* John (b.1952) and James (b.1954). *Educated at* Westminster; Trinity College Cambridge; St.Thomas's Hospital. *Career:* Surgeon Lt, RNVR 1947-50; University of Cambridge Demonstrator (Anatomy) 1950-54; Washington University St.Louis, USA, visiting teacher 1954-55; University of Cambridge Lecturer (Anatomy) 1955-61; Fellow of Trinity College Cambridge 1957-61; Professor of Anatomy, University of Wales Cardiff 1961-90. Deputy Principal University College Cardiff 1984-86; President Anatomical Society of Great Britain 1986-88. *Publications:* Author of > 170 Research publications in Medical journals; Author of Introducing Anatomy, 1980. *Recreation:* rowing, yachting, downhill skiing. *Clubs:* Leander, East India, London Rowing, Llandaff Rowing. *Address:* Troed Y Rhiw Farm, Ystrad Mynach, Mid Glamorgan, CF8 7EW. Tel: 0443 812175

LEWES, Captain R.N. (retired). John Hext, OBE, KStJ, FRAgSs. *Currently:* retired Farmer. Lieutenant of Dyfed, 1974-78 (Lord Lieutenant of Cardiganshire 1956-74. *Born on* 16 June 1903 at Devonport. *Son of* the late Colonel John Lewes, RA and of Mrs Lewes (nee Hext). *Marriage:* to Nesta Cecil, 1929, d of late Captain H.FitzroyTalbot, DSO, RN. *Children:* one s two d. *Educated at* RN Colleges Osborne and Dartmouth. *Career:* Sub-Lieut 1923, Lieut 1925; specialised in Torpedoes 1928; Commander 1939; commanded: HMS Shikari, Intrepid 1941-42 (despatches); Ameer 1944-45 (despatches); retired 1947, with war service rank of Captain RN. *Address:* Llanllyr, near Lampeter, Dyfed SA48 8QB.

LEWIN, Professor John, B.A., PhD. *Currently:* Professor of Physical Geography, University College of Wales, Aberystwyth. *Born on* 7 May 1940 at Bath, England. *Son of* Bernard and Ruth. *Marriage:* to Jane Elizabeth Sarah Cox. *Children:* Jenny Joy and Marianna. *Educated at* King Edward's School, Bath; University of Southampton. *Career:* Assistant Lecturer, University of Hull 1965-68; Lecturer, 1968- , Senior Lecturer 1979- , Reader 1982-86, University College of Wales, Aberystwyth, Dean of Science 1979-81. Visiting Associate Professor, Univ. of Colorado 1973-77. Distinguished visiting professor, Univ of Arizona 1988. Chairman, British Geomorphological Research Group 1989-90. *Publications:* Editor, British Rivers 1981; Timescales in Geomorphology 1980; Modern and Ancient Fluvial Systems 1983; Palaeohydrology in Practice 1987. *Recreation:* Reading, walking. *Address:* Institute of Earth Studies, University College of Wales, Aberystwyth, Dyfed, SY23 3DB.

LEWIS, County Councillor Alban Dewi, MA., DipEd. *Currently:* Retired. *Born on* 18 April 1914 at Treprior, Tremain, Cards. *Son of* Mr & Mrs John Lewis. *Marriage:* 1st to Rhiannon Moelwyn-Hughes 1940; to Katie Myanwy Thomas (nee Morgan) 1971. *Educated at* Cardigan Grammar School; University College of Wales, Aberystwyth. *Career:* English Master 1936-40; RAF (Flying Control Officer) 1940-46; Lecturer, Cartrefle Teachers Training College, Wrexham 1947; Dist. Educ. Officer, Hucknall, Notts 1949; Deputy and Acting Director of Education, Cardiganshire 1950; Headmaster Ardwyn Grammar School, Aberystwyth 1954-71; Member Cardiganshire Ed. Co; Chairman Mid Wales Hospital Management Committee 1970; Chairman S. West Wales Hospital Man. Co., 1972; (Founder) Chairman Dyfed Health Authority 1973-78; U.C.W. Coll. Council 1955-; Annan Commission (Future of Broadcasting) 1973-77; General Optical Council 1979; Dyfed County Council 1979- ; Chairman Dyfed Educ. Committee 1989-91; Moderator S. Wales Province Presbyterian Church of Wales 1987-88; Nat. Eisteddfod Gorsedd y Beirdd (White Robe). Urdd Chairman and Vice-President several years. *Recreation:* Sport (Coll. Rugby, Rowing, Boxing Colours - University Boxing Champion; Birkenhead Park and Bath 1st XV, Commodore Aberystwyth Yacht Club. *Clubs:* National Liberal Club and Farmers' Club (Whitehall). *Address:* Y Mans, Blaenannerch, Dyfed, SA43 2AL. Tel: 0239 810645.

LEWIS, Mr Alun Kynric, BSc; LLB; QC. *Currently:* Practising Barrister, Recorder of the Crown Court. *Born on* 23 May 1928 at Harlech. *Son of* Y Parch C.O. Lewis and Ursula Lewis. *Marriage:* to Bethan, elder daugher of Prof. Edgar Thomas CBE and Eurwen Thomas, 1955. *Children:* Emyr, Catrin and Sian. *Educated at* Ysgol Y Cyngor, Llanfairpwllgwyngyll; Ysgol Ramadeg, Beaumaris; Coleg Y Brifysgol, Bangor; London School of Economics. *Career:* After first graduation, taught science at Raine's Foundation Grammar School, London; called to the Bar, Middle Temple, 1954; elected member of Wales & Chester Circuit 1955; pupil of Mr Peter Thomas in Mr Vincent Lloyd-Jones QC's Chambers 1954-55; Barrister Grays Inn 1961; in practice in Chambers, specialising in Intellectual Property Matters 1955- ; Took Silk 1978; Recorder 1979; member Parole Board 1982-85; Committees of Investigation under Agricultural Marketing Act 1979-88; Welsh Arts Council 1985-92; with others, planted Gwinllan Pant Teg, 1986. First vintage, 1989. Assistant Boundary Commissioner 1976; Founder Trustee of Ymddiriedolaeth Ysgolion Cymraeg, Llundain 1961; QC Northern Ireland 1988; Bencher Middle Temple, 1988 Honorary Counsel; Welsh Book Council 1989. *Publications:* papers and short book on Intellectual Property Law and Common Market Law, Drama Fer, various ephemeral articles and a laymans Guide to Motoring Law. *Recreation:* walking, fishing, Gwinllana, wyron. *Clubs:* Reform. *Address:* Penrallt, Llys-faen, Caerdydd, CF4 5TG. Francis Taylor Building, Temple, Llundain, EC4.

LEWIS, Mr Anthony Robert, MA *Currently:* Writer - Broadcaster, BBC TV Presenter of cricket, Sunday Telegraph cricket correspondent. *Born on* 6 July 1938 at Swansea. *Son of* Wilfrid Llewellyn and Florence Marjorie (nee Flower). *Marriage:* to Joan (nee Pritchard). *Children:* Joanna Clare and Anabel Sophia. *Educated at* Neath G.S., Christ's

College, Cambridge. *Career:* Double Blue Cricket and rugby football, 1959; cricket, 1960-62; Captain of cricket, 1962; Cambridge University, Glamorgan CCC: cricketer, 1955-74; Captain, 1967-72; Chm., 1988- ; 9 Tests for England, 1972-73; Captained MCC to India, Ceylon and Pakistan, 1972-73. 1967-69; Member of Sports Council for Wales, 1970-81; Presenter of Sports Arena - HTV Wales, 1974-81; Presenter of HTV Wales Arts programmes, 1977-86; Inaugural presenter of Sport on 4 on Radio 4, 1987-90; Chairman (Wales) of the Association of Business Sponsorship of the Arts (ABSA). *Publications:* A Summer of Cricket, 1976; Playing Days, 1985; Double Century, 1987; Cricket In Many Lands, 1991. *Recreation:* Classical music and golf. *Clubs:* Honorary Life Member MCC; East India; Cardiff and County; Royal Porthcawl Golf; Royal Worlington and Newmarket Golf. *Address:* Castellau, Near Llantrisant, Mid Glamorgan, CF7 8LP.

LEWIS, The Hon Antony Thomas, JP, LLM. *Currently:* Chairman, Powys Family Health Services Authority, since 1990. *Born on* 4 June 1947. *Address:* The Skreen, Erwood, Builth Wells, Powys, LD2 3SJ.

LEWIS, Professor Clifford Thomas, MA(Cantab); PhD(London). *Currently:* Emeritus Professor, University London, since 1988. *Born on* 29 Aug 1923 at Newport, Mon. *Son of* Arthur Charles Lewis and Florence Lewis. *Marriage:* to Joan Willey, 1949. *Children:* Julian, Charles and Rosalind Jane. *Educated at* Newport High School; Queens' College, Cambridge. *Career:* Imperial College, London: Lecturer, Dept Zoology and Applied Entomology 1955-65; Senior Lecturer 1965-74; Reader in Insect Physiology 1974-78; Chm. Academic Staff Assembly 1972-75; Royal Holloway Coll., London (later Royal Holloway and Bedford New Coll.,): Prof. of Zoology 1978-88, Vice-Principal 1981-85; Visiting Prof: UCLA, California 1975, Ghana 1976, La Trobe, Australia 1986. *Publications:* many scientific papers, mostly on physiology of insects. *Recreation:* painting, sculpture, fell walking. *Clubs:* Athenaeum. *Address:* 9 Silwood Close, Ascot, Berkshire, SL5 7DX. Rhos Gwyn, Pengenffordd, Talgarth, Powys.

LEWIS, The Very Reverend David Gareth, MA., *Currently:* Dean of Monmouth. *Born on* 13 Aug 1931 at Dowlais. *Son of* the late Mordecai Lewis and the late Bronwen May (nee Evans). *Educated at* Cyfarthfa Castle Grammar School, Merthyr Tydfil; Univ. of Wales (Bangor); Univ. of Oxford (Oriel.) Curate of Neath 1960-63; Vice Principal of Salisbury Theological Coll., 1963-69; Dean of Belize 1969-78; Vicar of St.Mark, Newport 1978-82; Canon of Monmouth 1982-90; Clerical Secretary of the Governing Body of the Church in Wales. *Publications:* History of St. John's Cathedral Belize, Central America. *Recreation:* Swimming and travelling *Address:* The Deanery, Stow Hill, Newport, Gwent, NP9 4ED.

LEWIS, Mr David Gwynder, ACIB *Currently:* Exec. Director Hambros Bank Ltd., London; Jt. Deputy Chairman, Hambro Group Investments; Director of various Hambro Group Companies. *Born on* 31 Aug 1942 at Swansea, S.Wales. *Son of* the late Gwynder Eudaf Lewis and the late Gwyneth Jones. *Marriage:* to Susan Joyce Agnew, 1963, of Crowborough, Sussex. *Children:* Alexandra (b.1969) and George (b.1972). *Educated at* Rugby. *Career:* Warrant Officer TA C Battery Hon Artillery Co; Banker Hambros Bank Ltd 1961- (dir 1979, exec.dir 1991); MD Hambro Pacific Hong Kong 1974-82, pres Hambro America New York 1982-85, dir Hambro Countryside plc; ACIOB 1967. *Recreation:* fishing, classical music, shooting. *Clubs:* Turf, RAC, Madison Square Garden (NY), Royal Hong Kong Jockey, Hong Kong. *Address:* 57 Victoria Road, Kensington, London, , W8 5RH. Tel: 071 480 5000.

LEWIS, Dr C.B. David Thomas, CB; BSc(Wales) 1st Class Hons Chemistry; PhD(Wales); DSc. *Currently:* retired. *Born on* 27 March 1909 at Breconshire, Wales. *Son of* Emmanuel Lewis and Mary Lewis (nee Thomas). *Marriage:* 1st to Evelyn Smetham, 1934, one d; 2nd to Mary Sad 1959. *Children:* Sylvia Marilyn *Educated at* Brynmawr County School; University Coll. Aberystwyth. *Career:* Senior Chemistry Master, Quaker's Yard Secondary School 1934-38; Assistant Lecturer, University College Cardiff 1938-40; various scientific posts including Senior Superintendent of Chemistry Division, Atomic Weapons Establishment Aldermaston 1947-60; appointed Government Chemist to the United Kingdom 1960. *Publications:* Ultimate Particles of Matter 1959; Mountain Harvent (Poems) 1964; Analytical Research Investigations in learned journals; Scientific Articles in Encyclopaedias; Scientific Reviews etc. *Recreation:* writing, fishing. *Address:* Green Trees, 24 Highdown Hill Rd., Emmer Green, Reading Berks., RG4 8QP.

LEWIS, Mr Herbert John Whitfield, CB., FRIBA., FRTPI. *Currently:* Retired. *Born on* 9 April 1911 at Chepstow. *Son of* the late Herbert and the late Mary Lewis. *Marriage:* to Pamela Leadford, 1953. *Children:* David, Victoria and Polly. *Educated at* Monmouth School; Welsh School of Architecture. *Career:* Joseph Emberton, FRIBA - Assistant 1933; W.E. & Sydney Trent, FF.RIBA - Assistant 1934; Mendelsohn & Chermayeff, FF.RIBA - Chief Assistant 1935-38; Norman & Dawbarn - Senior Assistant 1938-40; Norman & Dawbarn - Associate 1945-50; Principal Housing Architect, London County Council 1950-59; County Architect, Middlx County Council 1959-64; Chief Architect, Ministry of Housing & Local Government (later DOE) 1964-71; Consultant and later partner (Planning) Clifford Culpin and Partners 1971-84. *Recreation:* Music and electronics *Address:* 8 St. John's Wood Rd, London, NW8 8RE.

LEWIS, Emeritus Professor Hywel David, MA, M.Phil, B.Litt, D.D.Hon. Professor of the History and Philosophy of Religion in the University of London, a Chair now attached to King's College, since 1955, after holding Chair of Philosophy 1947-55 at Bangor U.C.N.W., Fellow of King's College, since 1963. *Born on* 21 May 1910 at Llandudno. *Son of* Rev. D.J.Lewis and the late Mrs Rebecca Lewis (d.1962). *Marriage:* 1st to Megan Elias Jones 1943 (d.1962); 2nd to Megan Pritchard, 1965. *Educated at* UCNW Bangor; Jesus College, Oxford. *Career:* Prof. Philosophy, Univ.Coll., Bangor, 1947-55, previously Lecturer and Sub-Warden of Hall of Residence, 1936; Leverhulme Fellow, 1954-55, session being spent at Oxford; Visiting Prof, Bryn Mawr Coll., Pennsylvania, 1958-59; Vis.Lec., Harvard Divinity Sch, Spring 1963; Vis.Prof., Yale and Fellow of Jonathan Edwards Coll, 1964, one Semester. Miami 1968, Boston 1969; President: the Mind Assoc., 1948-49, the Aristotelian Soc., 1962-63, the Soc. for the Study of Theology, 1964-66; Chmn Council of Royal Inst. of Philosophy, elected 1964 on the resignation of Sir David Ross; mem. Central Advisory Council for Educ (Wales) 1963-66; Pres: Oxford Soc. for Historical Theology 1970, Inst. of Religion & Theology G.B. & Ireland, Int. Soc., for Metaphysics; Warden, Guild of Graduates of the Univ. of Wales; Dean of Faculty: Theology in the University of London 1964-68, Faculty of Arts, King's Coll., 1966-68, Faculty of Theology, King's Coll., 1970-72; H.Gifford Lectures Edinburgh 1966-68; Chmn Bd of Studs in Theology, Special Advisory Bd on Religious Studs; Representative Bd of Studs in Theology, General Bd of Faculty of Arts; mem., Univ. Scholarship Ctee and Research Grants Ctee, Central Research Ctee, the Athlone Press Bd; Chmn Univ of London Scholarships

Ctee; Lecture courses given at: Univs of Oxford, Birmingham, McMaster, Ontario; Belfast, Aberystwyth, Cardiff, Edinburgh, Nottingham, London, Massachusetts and Madras; Outside assessor for various Chairs in Philosophy and Theology; examining at Glasgow, Reading, Lampeter, Cambridge, Leeds, Sheffield, Wales, London and Colleges abroad; Editor, Muirhead Library of Philosophy, since 1947. *Publications:* Morals and the New Theology, 1947; Morals and Revelation, 1951; Contemporary British Philisophy, 1956; Our Experience of God, 1959, reprint p/back 1970; Freedom and History, Clarity is not Enough, 1962; Teach Yourself the Philisophy of Religion 1965; World Religions (jointly with R.L.Slater), 1966; Dreaming and Experience, 1968; The Elusive Mind 1969; The Self and Immortality, 1973; A Modern Introduction to Philosophy 1973; A volume of Welsh poems and Welsh books; Philosophy East and West (Ed), 1974; contribs to various anthologies and Collected Studies; a journal by the Cambridge University Press on Religious Studies; Persons and Life after Death, 1978; Jesus in the Faith of Christmas, 1981; The Elusive Self, 1982; Freedom and Alienation, 1985. *Address:* 1 Normandy Park, Near Guildford, Surrey, GU3 2AL.

LEWIS, Professor Emeritus Leonard John, C.M.G., B.Sc., Dip.Ed., F.C.P (Hon), F.R.S.A. *Currently:* Retired. *Born on* 28 Aug 1909 at Bedwas, Mon. *Son of* the late Thomas James and the late Rhoda (nee Gardiner). *Marriage:* to (1) Nora Brisdon 1940 (dissolved 1976) (2) Gwenda Black 1982 (d.1990). *Children:* David and John (deceased) *Educated at* Lewis School, Pengam; University College, Cardiff; Univ. of London. *Career:* Lecturer, Stn Andrew's Coll., Oyo, Nigeria, 1935-36; Headmaster, CMS Gram.Sch., Lagos, Nigeria, 1936-41; Education Sec., CMS Yoruba Mission, 1941-44; Lectr, University of London Institute of Education, 1944-48; Editorial staff, Oxford Univ. Press, 1948-49; Prof. of Educn and Dir of Institute of Educn, Univ. Coll. of Ghana, 1949-58; Professor of Education, Univ. of London, 1958-73; Principal and Vice-Chancellor, Univ. of Zimbabwe, 1980-81; Vice-Chancellor, PNG Univ. of Technology, 1982-83; Nuffield Visiting Prof., University of Ibadan, 1966; Hon. Professorial Fellow, Univ. Coll., Cardiff 1973. *Publications:* Equipping Africa, 1948; Henry Carr (Memoir), 1948; Education Policy and Practice in British Tropical Areas, 1954; (ed and Contrib.) Perspectives in Mass Education and Community Development, 1957; Days of Learning, 1961; Education and Political Independence in Africa, 1962; Schools, Society and Progress in Nigeria, 1965; The Management of Education (with A.J. Loveridge) 1965. *Recreation:* Music, reading and all sports, vicariously. *Address:* Flat 1, 6 Stanwell Road, Penarth, S. Glam., CF6 2EA.

LEWIS, Neville Julian Spencer, MA *Currently:* Barrister.*Born on* 17 March 1945 at Cardiff.*Son of* R.Malcolm Lewis and C.Margaret Lewis. *Marriage:* to Caroline Joy Holmes, 1967 (divorced). *Children:* Miranda Katharine and David Ilias. *Educated at* Radley College; Pembroke College Oxford. *Career:* Parliamentary Candidate, Liberal Party, Paddington 1974. *Publications:* Guide to Greece, 1977; Delphi and The Sacred Way, 1987. *Recreation:* sport, travel *Clubs:* National Liberal *Address:* 20 South Hill Park Gardens, London, NW3 2TG.

LEWIS, Mr Robert James Arthur, ACIB *Currently:* Regional Director (LBCS), Lloyds Bank plc, South Wales and Severnside Region. *Born on* 13 April 1939 at London. *Son of* Deceased. *Marriage:* to Janet. *Children:* Matthew, Sarah and Jacqueline *Educated at* Southend Grammar School *Career:* 3 Management appointments, London; Assistant Regional General Manager, Birmingham; Senior

Manager, Walsall Branch; Senior Manager, Newcastle Upon Tyne; Area Director, Newcastle Upon Tyne. *Recreation:* Sailing and walking *Clubs:* Penarth Yacht Club.

LEWIS, Hon Robin William, OBE (1988), MA. *Currently:* Chairman & Managing Director, The Magstim Company Limited. *Born on* 7 Feb 1941 at Hyssington, Powys. *Son of* the late 3rd Baron Merthyr and Lady Merthyr. *Marriage:* to Judith Ann Giardelli, 1967. *Children:* Christopher (b.1970) and Katharine (b.1972). *Educated at* Eton College; Magdalen College, Oxford. *Career:* Commonwealth Development Corporation 1964-66; Alcan Aluminium Ltd., 1967-68; Westminster Bank Ltd., 1968-72; Development Corporation for Wales 1972-83; Physiological Instrumentation/Novametrix Ltd., (Managing Director), 1983-89; High Sheriff of Dyfed 1987-88; Chairman, General Advisory Council of Independent Broadcasting Authority 1989-90, (memer 1985-90); member, National Trust Committee for Wales 1982-89 and 1992- ; chairman, Carms Branch, Council for Protection of Rural Wales 1984- ; president, RELATE, Dyfed Marriage Guidance 1987- . *Recreation:* sailing. *Clubs:* Leander. *Address:* Orchard House, Llanstephan, Carmarthen, Dyfed, SA33 5HA.

LEWIS, Professor Roland Wynne, BSc, PhD, DSc, CEng, FICE. *Currently:* Professor, Univ Coll of Swansea since 1984. *Born on* 20 Jan 1940 at Ammanford. *Son of* David and Mary Gladys. *Marriage:* to Celia Elizabeth (nee Morris). *Children:* Caroline, Andrew and Angharad. *Educated at* Amman Valley GS, University College of Swansea. *Career:* Research Eng with Imperial Oil, Calgary, Canada 1965-68; Standard Oil of California 1968-69; Lecturer U.C.Swansea 1969-79, Senior Lecturer 1979-82, Reader 1982-84; Managing Director 'Alpha Simulations Ltd 1991- ; Editor, ''Int Journal for Numerial Methods in Engineering'' 1972- ; Chief Editor 'Communications in Applied Numerial Methods' 1985- ; Editor 'Num Meth in Heat and Fluid Flow', 1991. *Publications:* 150 Research papers, Author and editor of 20 textbooks. *Recreation:* golf, photography, music, reading. *Clubs:* La Quinta at La Manga. *Address:* 'Oakridge', 331 Gower Road, Killay, Swansea, W.Glam, SA2 7AE. Civil Engineering Dept, Univ Coll Of Swansea, W.Glam, SA2 8PP.

LEWIS, Mr Trevor Oswin, CBE 1983; JP.*Born on* 29 Nov 1935. *Son of* 3rd Baron Merthyr, PC, KBE, TD and of Violet. *Marriage:* to Susan Jane, 1964. *Children:* one s three d. *Educated at* Downs School; Eton; Magdalen Coll, Oxford; Magdalene Coll., Cambridge. *Career:* Mem. Countryside Commn 1973-83 (Dep Chm., 1980-83); Chm., Countryside Commn's Cttee for Wales 1973-80. JP Dyfed, formerly Pembs 1969.*Address:* Hean Castle, Saundersfoot, Dyfed, SA69 9AL. Tel: 0834 812222.

LEWIS-JONES, Dr Margaret (Susan), MB, ChB, MRCP(UK). *Currently:* NHS Consultant Dermatologist, since November 1987. *Born* at St.Andrews, Scotland. *Daughter of* the late Ian Robert Munro Campbell and Jean Douglas Campbell. *Marriage:* to Dr. D.I. Lewis-Jones, MD, 1971. *Children:* Dafydd Sion and Shona Alys. *Educated at* Tudorgrange Girls Grammar School, Solihull; Liverpool University Medical School. *Career:* Qualified 1972 Liverpool Medical School; General Practitioner, Liverpool 1973-79; Senior Registrar and Registrar, Royal Liverpool Hospital 1982-87. *Publications:* in Immunology of dermatological disease. *Recreation:* golf, skiing, music. *Clubs:* Dolgellau Golf, Eaton Golf, Chester. *Address:* The Stable House, Huntington Hall, Aldford Road, Huntington, Chester, CH3 6EA. Wrexham Maelor Hospital, Wrexham, Clwyd, LL13 7TD.

LEYSHON, Mr Robert Lloyd, BSc, MB, BS, FRCS.

Currently: Consultant Orthopaedic Surgeon, Morriston Hospital, Swansea. *Born on* 12 Feb 1948 at Cardiff. *Son of* Squadron Leader Mervyn Leyshon and the late Joan (nee Lloyd). *Marriage:* to Catherine Edwards, 1977. *Children:* Aled Lloyd (b.1978) and Catherine Nia (b.1980). *Educated at* Ogmore Vale Grammar School 1958-66; St.Mary's Hospital, Paddington, London. *Career:* House Surgeon St.Mary's Hospital, London 1972; House Physician, Edgware General Hospital, London 1973;Rotating Registrar, Cardiff Hospitals 1974-77; Senior Orthopaedic Registrar, Cardiff & Swansea 1979-82; Senior Lecturer in Orthopaedic Surgery, Welsh National School of Medicine 1983-84. *Publications:* papers on Carbon Fibre for Ligament Reconstruction; papers on Bipopular Hip Prosthesis; papers on Treatment of Osteoporosis. *Recreation:* tennis, golf, skiing. *Clubs:* Clyne Golf, Honorary Surgeon, Llanelli Rugby. *Address:* 19 Westport Avenue, Mayals, Swansea, , SA3 5EA. St.Davids House, 1 Uplands Terrace, Swansea, SA2 OGU.

LIDDIARD, Captain Ronald, DMA, CSW, ATPL. *Currently:* Airline Pilot, Trislander Captain, Aurigny, Channel Isles since 1990. *Born on* 26 July 1932 at Cardiff. *Son of* the late Tom and the late Gladys Marion. *Marriage:* to June Alexandra (nee Ford) 1957. *Children:* Angela Jane and Clare Alexandra *Educated at* Canton High School, Cardiff; CWEB School, Cert & Matriculation; Welsh Coll. of Advanced Technology, Dip.Mun Admin; Coll. of Commerce, Cardiff, Cert Soc Work; Birmingham Univ, INLOGOV Adv. Man. Course; Airline Transport Pilots Licence, Oxford. *Career:* Jnr Trainee Accountant, City of Cardiff 1948-50; Nat. Service, RAF 1950-52; Trainee Accountant, City of Cardiff 1952-58; Admin. Officer, Public Health 1958-60; Social Worker, Welfare Dept., Cardiff 1960-61; Dist. Welfare Officer, Bournemouth 1961-64; Chf Admin Officer, Welfare Serv. Dept., Bournemouth 1964-70; Dir. of Social Serv., City of Bath 1971-74; Dir. of Social Serv., Birmingham 1974-85; Self emp. consultant and flying instructor 1985-86; Trislander Captain - Kondair 1987; J31 Jetstream and G.159 Gulfstream G.1 First Officer, Birmingham Executive Airways 1987-89; Jetstream Captain, Region Airways, Southend 1989. *Publications:* How to Become an Airline Pilot, 1989; Chapters in "Innovations in the care of the Elderly", 1984 and "Self-Care and Health in Old Age", 1986; articles on social work, public administration and management. *Recreation:* Free-lance journalism, travel and wines *Clubs:* Solihull Flying, Guernsey Aero. *Address:* Whitefriars, Portway, Worcs. B48 7HP.

LIGHTMAN, Mr Ivor Harry, CB *Currently:* Member Parole Board 1990- ; Chairman, all-Wales Advisory Panel on Services for Mentally Handicapped peope 1990- ; Chairman First Choice Housing Association 1989- ; Chairman Carmel Hsg. Assn. 1990- ; Public Affairs adviser . *Born on* 23 Aug 1928 at London. *Son of* Abraham Lightman OBE and Mary. *Marriage:* to Stella Blend 1950. *Children:* Brian Peter Leon. *Educated at* Abergele Grammar School N. Wales. *Career:* Clerical Officer Minoffood 1949; Officer Customs & Excise 1949-56; Asst. Principal & Principal, Min. of Works 1957-64 (Priv. Sec. to Successive Ministers); Prin. HM Treasury 1964-67; Asst. Sec. Dept. of Environment 1967-70; Civil Service Dept. 1971-73; Under Sec. Price Commision 1973-76; Dept. of Prices & Consumer Protection 1976-78; Dept. of Industry 1978-81; Deputy Secretary, Health & Social Policy, Welsh Office 1981-88; Retired 1988. *Publications:* Articles in Economic journals. *Recreation:* Walking; talking; making & listening to music. *Address:* 6 Clos Coedydafarn, Lisvane, Cardiff. CF4 5ER.

LINGARD, Brian Hallwood, DA(Manc), FRIBA *Currently:* Architect in Private Practice, offices in Llandudno (head office), Cardiff, Newtown, Caernarfon and London. *Born* at Melbourne, Australia. *Son of* Abel Keenan Lingard and Elsie May Lingard. *Marriage:* to Dorothy (nee Clay). *Children:* Christopher, Timothy and Rebecca. *Educated at* Stockport Grammar School; School of Architecture, Manchester. *Career:* Partner in: Brian Lingard and Partners, Architects; Lingard Styles Landscape, Landscape Architects; Gallery Lingard, Architectural Historians. Awards: RIBA Regional Award Wales; DOE/Welsh Office Housing Medals (7); Civic Trust (21 awards); Times RICS Conservation awards (2); Prince of Wales Conservation Awards (3). Chairman: Architects Benevolent Society. *Publications:* The Opportunities for The Conservation and Enhancement of our Historic Resports in Wales, 1983. *Recreation:* swimming, riding, tennis, old buildings. *Clubs:* Carlton, RAC *Address:* Plas Mor, Rhosneigr, Anglesey. 77 Cheyne Court, London, SW3.

LISBURNE, The Earl of John David Malet, MA *Currently:* retired. *Born on* 1 Sept 1918 at Watford, Herts. *Son of* The 7th Earl of Lisburne and Countess of Lisburne(nee Regina Bittencourt). *Marriage:* to Mary Shelagh Macauley, 1943. *Children:* Hon Viscount Vaughan, Hon Vaughan and Hon John Vaughan. *Educated at* Eton College; Magdalen Oxford. *Career:* served in H.M.Welsh Guards 1939-46, rank of Captain. Called to the Bar by Inner Temple 1947, retired 1969 Common Law, later at Parliamentary Bar. Founder director of Westward Television, Deputy Chairman 1966-81. Director, British Home Stores (late Stonehouse) 1963, retired 1987. Chairman, Council for Social Services in Wales, later Welsh Council for Voluntary Action, 1977, currently President. Director, South Wales Regional Board of Lloyds Bank 1978-88; Director, Nationwide Anglia Building, Divisional Board for Wales 1982-88. Member: National Executive Committee Automobile Association 1981-88. *Recreation:* fishing, shooting, all country sports. *Clubs:* Bucks, Beefsteak. *Address:* Cruglas, Ystrad Meurig, Dyfed, SY25 6AN.

LIVINGSTONE, Mr James, CMG; OBE *Currently:* Died during compilation. *Born on* 4th Apr 1912 at Bo'ness, West Lothian. *Son of* late Angus Cook Livingstone and Mrs Jean Fraser Aitken Wilson Livingstone. *Marriage:* to Dr Mair Eleri Morgan Thomas, 1945, e d of late John Thomas, DSc, Harlech, and Mrs O.M. Thomas, Lladewi Brefi and Wilmslow. *Children:* one daughter one son, deceased *Educated at* Bo'ness Academy; Edinburgh University; Moray House Training College, Edinburgh. *Career:* Adult Education and School Posts, Scotland and Egypt, 1936-42; British Council Service, Egypt and Iran, 1942-45; Middle East Dept., 1945-46; Asst Rep., Palestine, 1946-48; Dep. Dir, 1949, Dir, 1956, Personnel Dept; Controller: Establishments Div., 1962; Overseas A Div. (Middle East and Africa), 1962-72; Mem. Council, British Inst. of Persian Studies, 1977-88 (Hon. Treasurer 1977-82). *Recreation:* Photography, exploring the West Highlands and Islands. *Clubs:* Travellers, Royal Commonwealth. *Address:* Tan yr Allt, Llangeitho, Dyfed, SY25 6QH.

LIVSEY, Mr Richard Arthur Lloyd, MSc., NDA. *Currently:* Member of Parliament for Brecon & Radnor. *Born on* 2 May 1935. *Son of* Arthur Norman Livsey and Lilian Maisie Livsey (nee James). *Marriage:* to Irene Livsey (nee Earsman). *Children:* David, Jennifer and Douglas. *Educated at* Talgarth C.P. School; Bedales; Seale Hayne Agricultural College; Reading University. *Career:* ICI (a) dairy farming; (b) Commercial Representative; (c) Agricultural Development Officer giving farm cost advice 1961-67; Farm Manager, 1500 acre Blair Drummond Estate, Perthshire 1967-71; Senior Lecturer, Farm

Management at Welsh Agricultural College, Aberystwyth; Farm Manager of College farms for 3 years, 1971-85; also Sheep farming on 60 acres 1981-85; Elected MP, Brecon & Radnor By-Election 1985; Agricultural Spokesman for Liberal Democrats 1985-87; Water Bill Spokesman for Liberal Democrats 1988-90; Countryside Spokesman for Liberal Democrats 1987- ; Leader of the Welsh Liberal Democrats 1988- . *Publications:* Agricultural/Political/ Environmental articles, in various periodicals. *Recreation:* Angling, cricket, drama, music. *Address:* House of Commons, London, SW1A OAA.The Old Rectory, Llanfihangel Talyllyn, Brecon, Powys, LD3 7TG.

LLEWELLIN, Mr David William Norman, *Currently:* Rally Driver 1985-91. *Born on* 3 May 1960 at Haverfordwest. *Son of* Richard George Norman Llewellin and Janet Lewis. *Educated at* Haylett Grange Junior; Bush House, Pembroke Comp. *Career:* Farming 1976-84; Audi Sport UK - Driving Audi Quattro 1985; Austin Rover - driving Metro 6R4 1986; Audi Sport UK - Coupe Quattro, Audi 200 Quattro 1987-88; Team Toyota GB - Toyota Celica GT4 1989-90; British Rally Champion 1989-90. *Recreation:* Rugby - played schools and county level at youth, squash, shooting, water skiing. *Address:* Great Rudbaxton, Rudbaxton, Haverfordwest, Pembrokeshire, SA62 4DB.

LLEWELLIN, John Stephen, *Currently:* Director Coastal Cottages Ltd, since 1980; Director Little Haven Farms Ltd, since 1967; Director Dyfed Seeds Ltd, since 1982. *.Born on* 31 Oct 1938 at Milford Haven. *Son of* the late John Charles and the late Lilian (nee Jenkins). *Marriage:* to Christine Crewe, 1961. *Children:* Richard M and Peter C. *Educated at* Cheltenham College; Harper Adams Agricultural College. *Recreation:* sailing, swimming. *Clubs:* Lloyds of London. *Address:* Mill Race, Little Haven, Haverfordwest, Pembs, SA62 3UH. Fenton, Little Haven, Haverfordwest, Pembs, SA62 3TX.

LLEWELLIN DAVIES, Rev Dr Lawrence John David, *Born on* 26 June 1916 at Llangoedmor, nr Cardigan. *Son of* the late Rev Canon Llewellin Davies, of The Rectory, Narberth, Dyfed and the late Elizabeth Anne (nee Williams). *Marriage:* to Eileen May, da of late Harry Onion, 1949. *Children:* Elizabeth Anne (Mrs E A Kirby) b 1951). *Educated at* St.David's College School Lampeter, Dyfed; Jesus College Oxford (Schoolmaster Student 1967-68, BA, MA) Dip Ed (Oxon), University of Bonn (DTheol). *Career:* Ordained St.Davids Cathedral: deacon 1939, priest 1940; curate Narberth Dyfed 1939-48, officiating chaplain RAF 1942-44, chaplain Royal Marines School of Signalling 1944-46, chaplain RN Arms Depot Trecwn Dyfed 1947-48, TA CCF 1947-48, chaplain RAF (Extended Serv Commn) 1948-57, princ 2 Tactical Air Force Moral Leadership School Cologne, W.Germany 1953-57, Dean of Chapel and head Divinity Hall Herschel High School Slough 1959-80; secretary general: Schools Council for the Ordained Ministry 1970-80, BHS; FRSPB. *Publications:* The History of Early Hebrew Prohecy, 1958; The Rich History of Mounton's forgotten Sanctuary, 1971. *Recreation:* riding, gardening, protection of local environment. *Address:* Deans Lodge, Hollybush Hill, Stoke Poges, Slough, Berks, SL2 4PZ. Tel: 0753 4662495.

LLEWELLYN, Mr Daniel James Roy, Dyfed County Councillor (Plaid Cymru) *Currently:* County Councillor, Plaid Cymru, for the Whitland area on Dyfed County Council 1989- . *Born on* 28 June 1937 at Llanboidy. *Son of* the late Daniel John and Alice Mary (nee Williams). *Marriage:* to Rhoswen Mary Davies 1961. *Educated at* Whitland Grammar School *Career:* Clerk with British Railways 1954-56; 2 years National Service with Royal Army Pays Corps regiment at Devizes, Wilts., 1956-58;

Relief clerk with British Rail based at Swansea 1958-60; Station Master with British Rail at Dowlais Top and then at Johnston (Pembs) 1961-65; Movements Supervisor with B.R. at Llanelli 1966-67; Assist. County Sec. with Farmers Union of Wales, Carmarthen 1968; Sales Rep. with Bibby Agric 1969; Sales Rep. and S.Wales Area Adviser for UKF Ferts. Ltd 1970-89; Compered concerts in town and villages throughout Wales, also in London and Birmingham; Compered 35 concerts in Toronto, Canada, 1987; Compered 35 concerts in Toronto, Canada, 1990; Deacon and Financial Sec. of Ramoth Baptist Chapel, Cwmfelin Mynach 1974- ; played Rugby for Whitland RFC for 18 years. *Recreation:* Keen follower of Rugby, especially Wales *Address:* Bro Gronw, Cwmfelin Mynach, Hendygwyn-Ar-Daf, Dyfed, SA34 ODH. Tel: 0994 448283.

LLEWELLYN, Sir (2nd Bt) Michael Rowland Godfrey, K st J., JP. *Currently:* Lord-Lieutenant of West Glamorgan since 1987 (Deputy Lieutenant 1982, Vice Lord-Lieut.1986). *Born on* 15 June 1921 at Neath, West Glam. *Son of* the late Sir Godfrey Llewellyn Bt.C.B.CBE.MC.TD.JP, DL. *Marriage:* to Janet Prudence Edmondes 1956. *Children:* Sarah, Carolyn and Lucy. *Educated at* Harrow and Sandhurst. *Career:* Commissioned Grenadier Guards 1941; served in Italian Campaign 1943-44; retired 1949; Commanded 1st Bn. Glamorgan Army Cadet Force 1951-58; High Sheriff West Glamorgan 1980-81; J.P. 1984; President Swansea Business Club 1985-88; Pres. West Glam Scout Council 1987- ; Pres. West Glam SSAFA 1987-; Pres. Swanses branch Royal British Legion 1987- ; Pres. West Glam branch Magistrates Assn. 1988- ; Pres. W.Glam branch St. John Council 1988- ; (Chairman 1967-79, Vice Pres. 1979-88); Pres. TAVRA for Wales 1990- . *Recreation:* Shooting, gardening. *Clubs:* Cardiff & County, Bristol Channel Yacht. *Address:* Glebe House, Penmaen, Swansea, West Glam., SA3 2HH. Tel: 0792 371232.

LLEWELLYN, Major General. Richard Morgan, OBE., FBIM. *Currently:* Student at Salisbury and Wells Theological College. *Born on* 22 August 1937 at Princetown, Devon. *Son of* Griffith Robert Poyntz Llewellyn and Bridget Margaret Llewellyn (nee Karslake). *Marriage:* to Elizabeth (Polly) Lamond Llewellyn, daughter of Lieutenant Colonel F.T. Sobey, CBE, MC, of Ilkley, Yorkshire, 1964. *Children:* William Huw Griffith, Sally Frances, (d.1977), Glyn David Cledwyn, Robert Philip Francis and Katherine Lucy Bryony. *Educated at* Haileybury and Imperial Service College. *Career:* Commissioned into Royal Welch Fusiliers 1956; Active Service Malaya and Cyprus; Staff College 1970; Military Assistant to Chief of the General Staff 1971-72; Brigade Major 1974-76; Commanding Officer 1st Bn. The Royal Welch Fusiliers 1976-79; Directing staff Royal College of Defence studies 1979-81; Commander Gurkha field force 1981-84; Director of Army staff duties 1984-87; General officer commanding Wales 1987-90; Chief of staff HQ United Kingdom Land Forces 1990-91; Colonel The Gurkha transport regiment 1984- ; Colonel The Royal Welch Fusliliers 1990- ; Vice President Operation Raleigh; Council member Soldiers and Airmans Scripture Readers Association. *Publications:* Articles in Military journals. *Recreation:* Hill walking, gardening, painting. *Clubs:* Army and Navy Club. *Address:* C/o Lloyds Bank Ltd, Crickhowell, Powys.

LLEWELLYN-JONES, Professor Frank, CBE 1965; MA, DPhil, DSC (Oxon), Hon.LLD. (Wales). *Born on* 30 Sept 1907. *Son of* Alfred Morgan Jones, JP, Penrhiwceiber, Glamorgan. *Marriage:* 1st to Eileen, 1938 (d 1982); 2nd to Mrs Gwendolen Thomas, Rhossili, 1983. *Children:* one s (one d decd), from 1st marriage. *Educated at* West

Monmouth School; Merton College Oxford Science Exhibitioner 1925; 1st Cl Nat. Sci., physics, BA 1929; Research Scholar, Merton Coll., 1929, DPhil, MA, 1931; Senior Demy, Magdalen Coll., 1931, DSc 1955. *Career:* Demonstrator in Wykeham Dept of Physics, Oxford 1929-32; Lecturer in Physics, University Coll., of Swansea 1932-40; Senior Scientific Officer, Royal Aircraft Establishment 1940-45; Professor of Physics, University of Wales, and Head of Dept of Physics, University Coll. of Swansea 1945-65. Vice-Chancellor, Univ. of Wales 1969-71. Member: Radio Research Board DSIR 1951-54; Standing Conference on Telecommunication Research, DSIR 1952-55; Board of Institute of Physics 1947-50; Council of Physical Society 1951-58 (Vice President 1954-59). Visiting Professor to Univs in Australia 1956; Supernumerary Fellow, Jesus Coll., Oxford 1965-66, 1969-70; Hon. Professorial Res. Fellow, Univ of Wales 1974- ; Leverhulme Emeritus Fellow 1977-79; Fellow, UC of Swansea 1990. Regional Scientific Adviser for Home Defence, Wales 1952-59, Sen. and Chief Reg. Sci. Adv., 1959-77; Pres., Royal Institution of South Wales 1957-60; Member Council for Wales and Mon 1959-63, 1963-66; Dir (Part-time), S.Wales Group, BSC 1968-70; Chairman Central Adv. Council for Education (Wales) 1961-64. Sen. Consultant in Plasma Physics, Radio and Space Research Station of SRC 1964-65. Vice-Pres., Hon Soc of Cymmrodorian 1982. Hon LLD Wales 1975. C.V. Boys' Prizeman, The Physical Soc., 1960; Inaugural Ragnar Holm Scientific Achievement Award 6th Internat Conf. on Electric Contract Phenomena, Chicago 1972. Principal Univ Coll of Swansea 1965-74 (Vice-Principal 1954-56 and 1960-62; Acting Principal 1959-60); Professor Emeritus since 1974. Chairman Lower Swansea Valley Project 1965. Chairman, Gregynog Committee Univ. of Wales when restoring the Gregynog Press. *Publications:* Fundamental Processes of Electrical Contact Phenomena, 1953; The Physics of Electrical Contacts, 1957; Ionization and Breakdown in Gases, 1957, 2nd edition 1966; The Glow Discharge, 1966; Ionization, Avalanches and Breakdown, 1966; papers in scientific journals on ionization and discharge physics. *Recreation:* industrial archaeology. *Clubs:* Athenaeum. *Address:* Brynheulog, 24 Sketty Park Road, Swansea, SA2 9AS. Tel: 0792 202344.

LLEWELYN, Dr David Evan Huw (Huw), MBBCH Wales, MRCP (UK), MD *Currently:* Senior Lecturer in Medicine and consultant Physician at King's College School of Medicine and Dentistry, since 1979. *Born on* 1 Feb 1946 at Glanamman. *Son of* John Llewelyn and the late Catherine Jane (nee Jones). *Marriage:* to Angela Mary Williams, 1969. *Children:* Rhian, Bethan and Rhys *Educated at* Pontardawe Grammar School *Career:* House Officer, University Hospital of Wales 1971-75; Lecturer in Medicine, St.Bartholomew's Hospital Medical College 1975-79. *Publications:* M.D. thesis "Assessing the Validity of Diagnostic Tests and Clinical Decisions"; papers on Radioaminoassay; Statistics Book: "Personal Clinical Checklist".*Recreation:* music, theatre, reading, walking. *Clubs:* Royal Society of Medicine. *Address:* 73 Court Lane, Dulwich, London, SE21 7EF. 29 Abernant Road, Cwmgors, Ammanford, Dyfed. Tel: 081 693 5334.

LLOYD, Dr Brian Beynon, CBE, MA, DSc. *Currently:* Director, since 1990, and Company Secretary, International Nutrition Foundation, 41 High Street, Sutton Courtenay, Oxon, OX14 4AW. *Born on* 23 Sept 1920 at Port Talbot, Wales. *Son of* David J.Lloyd, MA and Olwen Lloyd (nee Beynon. *Marriage:* to Reinhild Johanna Engeroff, 1949. *Children:* Megan and Olwen (twins), Thomas, Martyn, Brian and Owen (twins) and Lucy. *Educated at* Newport High School; Winchester College; Balliol College Oxford.

Career: Registered as Conscientious Objector 1941; Technical, later Research Assistant, later Biochemist and Chemist in Oxford Nutrition Survey, Nutrition Survey Group (Netherlands and Germany), and Laboratory of Human Nutrition 1941-52; University Lecturer in Physiology, Oxford 1952-70; Senior Proctor 1960-61. Fellow of Magdalen College, Oxford 1948-70, Vice-President 1967 & 68, Emeritus Fellow 1970- . Chairman of Governors, Oxford College of Technology 1963-69; Director of Oxford Polytechnic 1970-80; Honorary Fellow 1991. Chairman of Health Education Council 1979-82. Chairman of Oxford Gallery 1967- . Chairman of Trumedia Ltd 1985- . of Oxford-Bonn Society 1973-81. *Publications:* Gas Analysis Apparatus (various patents), 1960; The Regulation of Human Respiration (jt ed), 1962; Cerebrospinal Fluid and the Regulation of Respiration (jt ed), 1965; Publications, since 1945, in various books and journals, on nutrition, vitamin C, respiration, and the limitations and trends in human athletic performance; 1990 Sinclair (jt.ed). *Recreation:* Correggio, Klavar, Sliderules, personal computers, tablemaking, athletic records. *Clubs:* Oxford Management, (Chairman 1979-80). *Address:* High Wall, Pullens Lane, Oxford, OX3 OBX. Tel: 0865 63353.

LLOYD, Professor David, PhD, DSc. *Currently:* Professor of Microbiology, University of Wales, College of Cardiff since 1988. *Born on* 26 Nov 1940 at Penygraig, Rhondda. *Son of* the late Frederick Lewis Lloyd and Annie Mary Wrentmore. *Marriage:* to Margaret Jones, 1969. *Children:* Alun Lewis and Sion Huw. *Educated at* Tai Boys; Porth County Grammar School; Univ of Sheffield. *Career:* Postgraduate Research Student, Dept Botany, Microbiology UCC 1961-64; ICI Research Fellow, Dept Microbiology Univ Coll, Cardiff 1964-67; Visiting Research Fellow Dept Biophysics, Univ of Pennsylvania; MRC Research Assistant, Cell Structure/Function Unit 1967-69;, Lecturer 1969-72, Reader 1972-78, Personal Chair 1978-82. Established Chair and Head of Department of Microbiology 1982-87, all at U.C.C. Visiting Professor, Rockefeller Univ, Harvard Univ. *Publications:* Mitochondria of Microorganisms, 1974; The Cell Division Cycle, 1982; Anaerobic Protozoa, 1989; Ultradian Rhythms, 1992. *Recreation:* cycling, tennis, music. *Clubs:* Icos. *Address:* 7 The Green, Radyr, S.Glam, CF4 8BR.(microbiology Group (PABIO)), Univ of Wales Coll of Cardiff, P.O. Box 915, Cardiff, CF1 3TL.

LLOYD, Dr Geoffrey Gower, MA, MD, FRCP, FRCPsych. *Currently:* Consultant Psychiatrist, Royal Free Hospital London. *Born on* 7 June 1942 at Carmarthen. *Son of* William Thomas Lloyd and Annie Lloyd (nee Davies). *Marriage:* to Dr. Margaret Hazel Rose, 1970. *Children:* Alison, Claire and Richard. *Educated at* Queen Elizabeth GS, Carmarthen; Emmanuel Coll Cambridge; Westminster Med. School. *Career:* Registrar and Senior Registrar, Maudsley Hospital, London 1970-76; Lecturer, Institute of Psychiatry and King's College Hospital Medical School 1976-79; Consultant Psychiatrist, Royal Infirmary Edinburgh 1979-85. *Publications:* Textbook of General Hospital Psychiatry 1991; editor, Journal of Psychosomatic Research 1986- . *Recreation:* watching rugby football, piano, golf. *Clubs:* Royal Society of Medicine. *Address:* 4 The Ridgeway, Mill Hill, London, , NW7 1RS.148 Harley Street, London, W1N 1AH.

LLOYD, Professor Howell Arnold, BA., D.Phil., FR.Hist.S. *Currently:* Professor of History, University of Hull, since 1985. *Born on* 15 Nov 1937 at Carmarthen. *Son of* the late John Lewis Lloyd and the late Elizabeth Mary (nee Arnold). *Marriage:* to Gaynor Ilid Jones, 1962. *Children:* Susanna, Rebecca, Jonathan, Timothy and Christian. *Educated at* Queen Elizabeth G.S., Carmarthen;

UCW Aberystwyth; Jesus Coll. Oxford. *Career:* Fellow, University of Wales 1961-62; Assistant Lecturer in History, University of Hull 1962-64; Lecturer, 1964-73; Senior Lecturer, 1973-82; Reader, 1982-85. *Publications:* The Gentry of South-West Wales, 1540-1640 (1968); The Relevance of History (with Gordon Connell-Smith) (1972); The Rouen Campaign, 1590-92: Politics, Warfare and the early-modern State (1973); The State, France and the Sixteenth Century (1983); The State and Education: University Reform in early-modern France (1987); contributions to various scholarly periodicals. *Recreation:* Theatre, swimming, walking. *Address:* Department Of History, The University Of Hull, Hull, HU6 7RX.

LLOYD, Mr Illtyd Rhys, BSc; MSc; Dip Stat; Dip Ed *Born on* 13th Aug 1929 at Cwmafan. *Son of* Melfina (nee Rees) and John Lloyd. *Marriage:* to Julia (nee Lewis) of Pontyberem. *Children:* Catrin Elinor and Huw Steffan. *Educated at* Cwmafan Primary School; Port Talbot (Glanafan) County School; University College Swansea. *Career:* RAF (Educ.Branch) Fl.Lt.; Second Maths Master, Howard School for Boys, Cardiff; Head Maths Dept., Pembroke Grammar School; Deputy Headmaster, Howardian High School 1959-63; Her Majesty's Inspectorate: HMI 1964-71, Staff Inspector 1972-82, Chief Inspector 1982-90; Member Family Health Services Ay, South Glamorgan 1990-; Member Educ Panel Indept Sch Tribunals; Member Governing Body Swansea Institute of Higher Education 1991-; Member Council Baptist Union of Wales 1990-; Hon. Treasurer Baptist Union of Wales 1992-; Member Council CEWC (Cymru) 1990-; Hon. Member Gorsedd of Bards; Hon. Fellow University of Wales, Swansea *Recreation:* Walking. *Address:* 134 Lake Road East, Roath Park, Cardiff. CF2 5NQ.

LLOYD, Mr Jeffrey Hywel, LL.B(Hons). *Currently:* Partner, James and Lloyd, Solicitors, 87 Holton Road, Barry and 6 Bradenham Place, Penarth, since 1979. *Born on* 9 June 1946 at Rhondda. *Son of* Gwillyn Hywel Lloyd and Olwen Menai Lloyd. *Marriage:* to Pauline Margaret Lloyd (nee Jones), 1975. *Children:* Adam Hywel Lloyd and Simon Jeffrey Lloyd. *Educated at* Barry Grammar; UWIST. *Career:* Articled at Leo Abse and Cohen Solicitors, Churchill Way 1970-72; Asst. at D.W.Harris Pontypridd and Caerphilly 1974-76; Asst. J.A.Hughes Barry 1976-79. *Recreation:* chess, walking, reading, golf. *Address:* 39 Porth-Y-Castell, Barry, S.Glamorgan. 87 Holton Road, Barry, S.Glam.

LLOYD, County Councillor John Henry, *Currently:* (was owner and Director of Powys Transport); Director of A.Lloyd Transport. *Born on* 9 Dec 1925 at Trewern (Welshpool). *Son of* John Henry Lloyd and Frances M.Lloyd (nee Leighton). *Marriage:* to Elsie Olive Lloyd (nee Edwards), 1949. *Children:* John Henry and Andrew William Lloyd. *Educated at* Trewern and Welshpool; Deythuer Private School. *Career:* ex-serviceman, served in Palestine as Staff Sargent with the R.A.O.C. Vicars Warden of Buttington/Trewern Churches for over 20 years. County Councillor, chairman Dyfed - Powys Police Authority 1986-88; Chairman Coleg Powys Governors, and many local committees; member of the Welsh Church acts; member of Legal Aid Board, Pepper House, Chester; was Chairman of Powys County Council 1984-85; he was involved in every sphere of council activity from education to highways and personnel management, holding many seats of office, he had a wealth of experience in local government matters and was active up to his death in July 1991. *Recreation:* Montgomeryshire Football, visiting Castles and Gardens in Wales. *Clubs:* British Legion. *Address:* Min-y-Nant, Trewern, Welshpool, Powys, SY21 8DU.

LLOYD, Dr John Walter, OBE, MA(Oxon), FFARCS (Eng). *Currently:* retired to follow research and private work in relief of chronic pain. *Born on* 26 Dec 1923 at London, England. *Son of* Dr. J.H. and Mrs K.M.Z. Lloyd. *Marriage:* to Mrs Mary Lloyd. *Children:* Tom, William, Sarah and John. *Educated at* Epsom College; London Hospital *Career:* House surgeon, London Hospital: Squadron Leader, RAF Medical Branch; Senior Medical Officer Air HQ, RAF Cyprus; Consultant Anaesthetist, Radcliffe Infirmary, Oxford; Founder Intensive Therapy Unit, Radcliffe Infirmary, opened the first Pain Relief in the NHS and was director from 1970-90; Chairman, Intractable Pain Society of Great Britain. *Publications:* Cryoanalgesia, A new approach to chronic pain relief, Lancet; Classification of Chest Injuries as an aid to Treatment, BMJ. *Recreation:* vintage cars, rugby football, squash. *Clubs:* RAF, Frewin (Oxford), Oxford Medical. *Address:* Gate House, Mill Street, Eynsham, Oxford, OX8 1JU. Bays Hill, Llandeilo, Dyfed, S.Wales.

LLOYD, Mr John Wilson, M.A. *Currently:* Deputy Secretary, Welsh Office, since 1988. *Born on* 24 Dec. 1940 . *Son of* the late Dr. Ellis Lloyd and Mrs Dorothy Lloyd. *Marriage:* to Buddug Roberts, 1967. *Children:* Sarah, Huw and Geraint. *Educated at* Swansea Grammar School; Clifton College, Bristol; Christ's College, Cambridge. *Career:* Assistant Principal, H.M. Treasury, 1962-67; Private Secretary to Financial Sec. 1965-67; Principal successively, H.M. Treasury, CSD and Welsh Office, 1967-75; Private Sec. to Secretary of State for Wales, 1974-75; Assistant Secretary, Welsh Office, 1975-82; Under Secretary, Welsh Office, 1982-88; Principal Establishment Officer, 1982-86; Head of Housing, Health and Social Services Policy Group, 1986-88. *Recreation:* Golf, squash and swimming. *Address:* c/o Welsh Office, Cathays Park, Cardiff. CF1 3NQ.

LLOYD, County Councillor Paul, *Currently:* Lecturer painting and decorating; TGWU Lay tutor. *Born on* 16 April 1953 at Porth, Rhondda. *Son of* Dilwyn John Lloyd and Hilda Lloyd. *Marriage:* to Linda Susan Lloyd. *Children:* Marie (b.4.2.92). *Educated at* Birchgrove Junior; Penlan Comprehensive Swansea; Swansea Art College; Gwent College of Higher Education. *Career:* South Wales Transport engineering dept., coachpainter, 1968-70. *Recreation:* DIY, football, cricket, travel, Trade Union activities, Labour Party, cycling, swimming. *Address:* 2 Hafnant, Winch Wen, Swansea, SA1 7LG.

LLOYD, Mr Robert Ian, *Currently:* Editor, Llanelli Star. *Born on* 21 Jan 1959 at Carmarthen. *Son of* the late Vincent Wales Lloyd and Mair Lloyd (nee Jenkins). *Marriage:* to Carol Ann Lloyd (nee Crowther). *Children:* Kathryn Mair and James Vincent. *Educated at* Queen Elizabeth Grammar School for Boys; *Career:* Reporter, Carmarthen Journal 1976-81; Reporter, South Wales Evening Post, Subsequently Sub-Editor, Deputy Sports Editor, 1981-89; Deputy Editor, Llanelli Star, 1989-91; *Recreation:* Horses, Golf, Reading and Music *Clubs:* Llanelli Rotary, Llanelli Wanderers Rugby Football; Loughor Boating; *Address:* C/o Llanelli Star, 10 Station Road, Llanelli, SA15 1BJ.

LLOYD, Mrs Shirley, *Currently:* Director, P.E. Thomas (Precision), joined company February 1952. *Born on* 7 Dec 1934 at Neath, West Glam. *Daughter of* the late Trevor Williams and the late Elsie Williams. *Marriage:* to R.D. Lloyd, 1968. *Educated at* Porthcawl Secondary Modern School *Career:* Brown Owl 1st Nottage (St.David's) Brownie Unit; Divisional Commissioner, Central Glamorgan Girl Guides; Secretary, Porthcawl Civic Festival Committee; President, Porthcawl Disabled Group; Vice-President,

South Wales Burma Star Choir (Cor-y-Seren); Vice-President, Porthcawl Rugby Club; Member: Glamorgan Business Women's Network. *Address:* 13 De Breos Drive, Porthcawl, Mid Glamorgan, CF36 3JP. P.E. Thomas (Precision) Ltd, Glan Road, Porthcawl, Mid Glamorgan, CF36 5DF.

LLOYD, Mr Thomas Owen Saunders, MA (Cantab), FSA. *Currently:* Writer and Architectural Historian. *Born on* 26 Feb 1955 at London. *Son of* Major and Mrs John Lloyd. *Marriage:* to Christabel Juliet Ann (nee Harrison-Allen), 1987. *Educated at* Radley College; Downing College, Cambridge. *Career:* Qualified as solicitor and in private practice for 10 years. Company Secretary Golden Grove Book Company, Carmarthen 1987-89; member, Historic Buildings Council for Wales 1985- ; Chairman, British Historic Buildings Trust 1987- ; Chairman, Pembrokeshire Historical Society 1991- ; member, Dyfed Family Health Service Authority 1990- ; National Trust Committee for Wales; Cardiff Castle Management Committee. *Publications:* The Lost Houses of Wales, 1986 (2nd ed 1989). *Address:* Freestone Hall, Cresselly, Kilgetty, Dyfed, SA68 OSX.

LLOYD (formerly Thomas), Mrs Constance Irene, *Currently:* retired. *Born on* 27 Feb 1905 at Haverfordwest. *Daughter of* Frederick & Emma Williams. *Marriage:* 1st marriage 1926; 2nd 1952. *Children:* two s two d. *Educated at* Taskes High School for Girls. *Career:* journalism, later becoming proprietor of ''Western Telegraph'', Haverfordwest since 1943. Justice of the Peace 1944-74; President, Pembrokeshire Blind Society; Award of Merit from Haverfordwest Town Council, 1989 ''for enriching the lives of successive generations of blind people''. currently chairman of the William Vawer Trust and United Charities. former chairman of the Sir John Perrot Trust and James Griffiths Trust. Burgess of the Guild of Freemen 1975. *Address:* Cherry Trees, Haven Road, Haverfordwest, Pembrokeshire, SA64 1DL.

LLOYD DAVIES, Mr Henri, (see also Davies, Mr Henri Lloyd). *Currently:* Managing Director, Bryneithin Estates Limited. *Born on* 12 Dec 1946 at Cardiff. *Son of* the late Henry George and the late Emmeline Mary (nee Thomas). *Marriage:* to Norma Yvonne (nee Davies), 1977. *Children:* Henry James, b.1981, William Meirion, b.1983 and Charlotte Emmeline, b.1987. *Educated at* Rugby, Bath University. *Career:* T I Group 1969-71; M.D.Cleglen Publishing Ltd., 1971-87; Governor University College Cardiff 1978-88; Life Vice-President Royal Welsh Agricultural Society; Chairman Wales Conservative Political Centre 1991- ; Conservative Parliamentary Candidate, Swansea East 1992. *Recreation:* Sailing. *Clubs:* Naval. *Address:* Bryneithin, New Inn, Llandeilo, Dyfed SA19 7LL 16 Dunraven House, Westgate Street, Cardiff CF1 1DL

LLOYD JONES, Sir Richard (Anthony), KCB 1988 (CB 1981) *Currently:* Permanent Secretary, Welsh Office since 1985. *Born on* 1 Aug 1933 at Hull. *Son of* Robert and Anne Lloyd Jones. *Marriage:* to Patricia Avril Mary Richmond, 1955. *Children:* two daughters *Educated at* Long Dene School, Edenbridge; Nottingham High School; Balliol College, Oxford. *Career:* Admiralty 1957; Assistant Private Secretary to First Lord of the Admiralty 1959-62; Private Secretary to Secretary of the Cabinet 1969-70; Assistant Secretary Ministry of Defence 1970-74; Welsh Office 1974- : Under Secretary 1974-78; Deputy Secretary 1978-85. Chairman, Civil Service Benevolent Fund 1987- ; Hon. Fellow University College of Wales, Aberystwyth 1990. *Recreation:* music, walking. *Clubs:* Oxford & Cambridge. *Address:* C/o Welsh Office, Cathays Park, Cardiff CF1 3NQ

LLOYD OF BLAEN-Y-GLYN, Gabriel Frederic

Garnons, OBE, JP, Hon.FRAM, Hon.RCM. *Currently:* retired. *Born on* 1 July 1918 at Oxford. *Son of* the late W.W.G.Lloyd and the late Minna L.M.Lloyd. *Marriage:* to Valerie, died 1945, da of Rev.John Buchanan Fraser of St.Cathartines, Nottingham. *Children:* William J.W.Lloyd and Hugh Vaughan Lloyd. *Educated* Privately and in France *Career:* regnl dir Arts Council (N.Midlands) 1943-50, dir Festival of GB Oxford 1950-51, gen manager D'Oyly Carte Opera and Trust. gen manager Savoy Theatre and dir Savoy Hotel Entertainments 1951-82, pres Theatre Managers Assoc 1967-70 (life vice-pres 1982); governor: Royal Academy of Music 1965 (chm 1980-84, vice pres 1984), Royal Gen Theatrical Fund 1960 (vice-pres 1986), Sadler's Wells Theatre; chairman Nottingham Co Music Ctee, warden Queens Chapel of the Savoy, convener Diocese of Moray Ross and Caithness; member: Royal Choral Soc, Royal Philharmonic Orch, Scottish Opera Council, Malcolm Sargent Cancer Fund for Children, Central City Opera Denver USA; Freeman City of London 1961, Liveryman Worshipful Co of Musicians 1960; hon citizen: Denver 1953, Texas 1973; hon FRAM 1970, hon member RCM 1976. *Publications:* The D'Oyly Carte Years (with Robin Wilson), 1984. *Recreation:* music, gardening, reading. *Clubs:* Garrick, MCC, Harvard (Boston USA). *Address:* West Park, Strathpeffer, Ross-Shire IV14 9BT. Tel: 0997 421429

LLOYD PARRY, Mr Eryl, MA, Diploma in Public and Social Administration. *Currently:* Barrister. Full-time Chairman of Industrial Tribunals, Manchester Region, since 1977. Book Reviewer. *Born on* 28 April 1939 at Crosby. *Son of* Capt Robert Parry and Megan (nee Lloyd). *Marriage:* to Nancy Kathleen Denby, 1967. *Children:* Richard Eryl, Robert Michael, Helen Nancy and Roland Denby. *Educated at* Caernarfon Grammar School; St.Peter's College Oxford; Barnet House Oxford. *Career:* called to the Bar, Lincoln's Inn, 1966; in practice on Northern Circuit 1966-92; part-time Chairman of Industrial Tribunals, 1977-92 (sitting in Liverpool, Manchester, Shrewsbury and North Wales); Vice-President, Merseyside and Cheshire Rent Assessment Panel, 1985-92; Lay Reader, Church of England 1991- . *Publications:* Poems, articles, book reviews variously published, one act plays variously performed. *Recreation:* reading, amateur dramatics, playwriting, cricket. *Clubs:* Southport Dramatic, Sussex Playwright, Liverpool Bar Cricket, Ainsdale Sports. *Address:* 6 Stanley Avenue, Birkdale, Southport, Merseyside, PR8 4RU. Office of The Industrial, Tribunals, Union Court, Cook Street, Liverpool L2 4UJ

LLOYD-EDWARDS, Captain Norman, K.St.J, RD*, JP, LL.B, RNR. *Currently:* Solicitor in private practice, partner with Cartwrights Adams and Black. *Born on* 13 June 1933 at Aberfan. *Son of* Evan Stanley Edwards and Mary Leah Edwards (nee Lloyd). *Educated at* Monmouth School for Boys; Quakers Yard Grammar School; Bristol University. *Career:* Joined RNVR 1952; National service in Royal Navy 1958-60; after which joined the South Wales Division of the Royal Navy Reserve; Awarded Reserve Decoration 1971 and Bar in 1980; Appointed Commanding Officer of H.M.S. Cambria 1981; promoted Captain 1982; appointed Naval ADC to H.M. The Queen 1984; President of the United Services Mess, Cardiff; Appointed Deputy Lieutenant for South Glamorgan 1978; Vice Lord Lieutenant 1986; Lord Lieutenant 1990; Chapter Clerk of Llandaff Cathedral 1975-90; Chairman of the Appeal for the Cathedral Bells and for the Parish Church of St. John Cardiff; Made Officer of the Order of St.John 1983, promoted Knight in 1988; Prior of Wales since 1989; as such he heads the Order which is responsible for running the St.John Ambulance in

Wales and for raising money for the Eye Hospital in Jerusalem; After many years is still Chairman of Wales Committee Duke of Edinburgh's Award; Chairman of Nat. Rescue Training Council; President of Cardiff Branch of Sail Training Assoc. Schooners and S.Glamorgan Scouts Council; formerly: Vice Pres. Cardiff Branch Royal Nat. Lifeboat Inst; served on the Board of Outward Bound in Aberdovey; formerly: Chairman of Cardiff Festival of Music and Glamorgan TAVRA and mbr of the Welsh Arts Council, and of BBC Wales Council; President of Cardiff Branch Nat. Trust, South Glamorgan Community Foundation and South Glamorgan Red Cross. Founder Chairman of Royal British Legion Housing Assn Wales; Chairman of Welsh Board of Rememberance. *Recreation:* Music, gardening and table talk. *Clubs:* Army & Navy, Cardiff and County. *Address:* Hafan Wen, Llantrisant Road, Llandaff, Cardiff, CF5 2PU.

LLOYD-HUGHES, Sir Trevor Denby, MA(Oxon). *Currently:* retired. *Born on* 31 March 1922 at Guiseley, Nr Leeds. *Son of* the late Elwyn and the late Lucy (nee Denby) Lloyd-Hughes. *Marriage:* 1st to Ethel Marguerite Durward Ritchie, 1950 (diss.1971) 2nd to Marie-Jeanne, 1971, d of Marcel and the late Helene Moreillon, Geneva, Switzerland. *Children:* (1st marriage) Katharine (b.1951) and Richard (b.1953); (2nd marriage) David (stillborn), Annabelle (b.1971), Marie-Nammon, Thai girl adopted 1975 (b.). *Educated at* Woodhouse Grove School, Yorks (school captain); Jesus College, Oxford, 1940-42 and 1945-47. *Career:* Army 1941-45; Commissioned, RA, Served with 75th (Shropshire Yeomanry) Medium Regt in Western Desert, Sicily and Italy. Chief Welfare Officer, Trieste, 6 AGRA; Assistant Inspector of Taxes, Manchester 1948; Free-lance journalist 1949; joined staff, Liverpool Daily Post 1949. Political Correspondent, "Liverpool Echo", 1950. Liverpool Daily Post 1951; Press Secretary to Prime Minister Harold Wilson 1964-69; Chief Information Adviser to Government and Deputy Secretary, Cabinet Office 1969-70; Chairman, Lloyd-Hughes Associates Ltd., International Consultants in Public Affairs 1971-89, advising major companies and Governments world wide. Also, member of Circle of Wine Writers, UK 1961-76, Chairman 1972-73. Director, Trinity International Holdings, plc (formerly Liverpool Daily Post and Echo Ltd) 1978-91. Former member of Institute of Directors, Reform Club, Fellow of British Institute of Management. *Publications:* Many political and wine articles in newspapers and specialist magazines. *Recreation:* golf, gardening, getting to know the Gers department in France, playing the guitar, walking, yoga, appreciating music, especially my wife playing the organ. *Clubs:* Mosimann's, London; Wellington, London; Guinlet, Eauze, France. *Address:* 'Au Carmail', Labarrere, 32250, Montreal-Du-Gers, France.

LLOYD-JONES, His Honour David Trevor, V.R.D. *Currently:* retired Circuit Judge. *Born on* 6 March 1917 at Birkenhead. *Son of* the late Trevor and Ann (nee Hughes Roberts) Lloyd-Jones. *Marriage:* 1st to Mary Anne Barnardo, 1942; 2nd to Elizabeth Perkins, 1958; 3rd to Mary Slinger, 1984. *Children:* Margaret Anne, Ceridwen Elizabeth and David Martyn. *Educated at* Holywell Grammar School. *Career:* Banking 1934, 4-, 1946-50; Called to the Bar, Gray's Inn 1951. Practised Northern Circuit and later, Wales and Chester Circuit 1952-71. Deputy Chairman Caernarvonshire Quarter Session 1966-70, Chairman 1970-72. Legal Member Mental Health Appeal Tribunal (Wales), Legal Member Agriculture Appeals Tribunal (Wales). Prosecuting Counsel to the Post Office, Wales and Chester Circuit. Appointed Circuit Judge, Wales and Chester Circuit 1972. World War II, Lt. Cdr., R.N.V.R., Atlantic,

Pacific V.R.D., 1952. *Recreation:* golf, music. *Clubs:* Army and Navy, Royal Dornoch Golf. *Address:* 29 Curzon Park, North, Chester CH4 8AP.

LLOYD-JONES, Mr Robert, MA (Hons), Cantab; FRSA. *Currently:* Director General, Brick Development Association, Woodside House, Winkfield, Berks, since 1983. *Born on* 30 Jan 1931 at Bangor, N.Wales. *Son of* the late Robert Lloyd-Jones and the late Edith May. *Marriage:* 1958, dissolved 1977. *Children:* Ashley Paul, Sarah Louise and Alasdair Guy. *Educated at* Wrekin College; Cambridge University; Harvard Business School. *Career:* Royal Navy 1956-59; Shell International 1959-62; Head of Legal/Licensing BTR 1962-64; Director (Woolmark) International Wool Secretariat 1964-71; PA Chairman/Export Director Schachenmayr, Germany 1971-77; Director General British Textile Employers 1977-78; Director General Retail Consortium 1981-83. *Recreation:* golf, tennis, squash, chess, reading, music, travel. *Clubs:* Lansdowne, Royal Birkdale Golf, Rye, Formby and Liphook Golf, Institute of Directors, Liveryman of City of London and member of The Tylers and Bricklayers Livery. *Address:* Mill Cottage, 10 High Street, Odiham, Hants, RG25 1LG. Woodside House, Winkfield, Berks SL4 2DX Tel: 0344 885651.

LOADES, Professor David Michael, M.A., Ph.D., Litt.D., F.R.HistS., F.S.A. *Currently:* Professor of History, University of Wales, Bangor. *Born on* 19th Jan 1934 at Cambridge. *Son of* late Reginald Ernest and Gladys Mary (nee Smith). *Marriage:* (1) to Ann Lomas Glover, 1965 (diss.1984) (2) to Judith Anne Atkins. *Educated at* Perse School, Cambridge (1945-53); Emmanuel College, Cambridge (1955-61) *Career:* Lecturer in Political Sciences, University of St Andrews (1961-63); Lecturer in History, University of Durham (1963-70); Senior Lecturer (1970-77); Reader (1977-80); Professor of History, University of Wales, Bangor (1980-). *Publications:* Two Tudor Conspiracies (1965, 1992); The Papers of George Wyatt (1968); The Oxford Martyrs (1970, 1992); Politics and the Nation, 1450-1650 (1974, 1979, 1986, 1992); The Reign of Mary Tudor (1979, 1991); (ed) The End of Strife (1984); The Tudor Court (1986); (ed) Law and Government under the Tudors: essays presented to Sir Geoffrey Elton (1988); Mary Tudor: a life (1989);(ed) Faith and Identity (1989); (ed) The Chronicles of the Tudor Kings (1990); Politics, Censorship and the English Reformation (1991); Thomas Cranmere and the English Reformation (1991); Scouting and the Open Society (1978); numerous articles and reviews in learned journals. *Recreation:* Scouting (Chief Commissioner for Wales 1985-) *Clubs:* Penn (London) *Address:* Department Of History, University College of N. Wales, Bangor, Gwynedd LL57 2DG. Plas Isaf, Upper Garth Road, Bangor, Gwynedd LL57 2SR

LOCK, Mr Thomas Graham, BSc., CEng., FIM., CBIM. *Currently:* Chief Executive, Amalgamated Metal Corporation plc 1983-. *Born on* 10 Oct 1931 at Cardiff. *Son of* Robert Henry Lock and Morfydd (nee Thomas). *Marriage:* to Janice Olive Baker (nee Jones). *Children:* Sian Kathrin and Sara Helen. *Educated at* Whitchurch Grammar School; University College S.Wales & Mon (Cardiff); Aston College of Advanced Technology; Harvard Business School. *Career:* Lieutenant Royal Navy 1953-56; Graduate Apprentice Lucas Industries 1956-57; Lucas Electrical Production Management 1958-61; Geschaeftsfuhrer Girling Bremsen GmbH, Koblenz, Germany 1961-65; Director Overseas Operation Girling Ltd and Director numerous Girling Overseas Companies 1966-72; Director and General Manager Lucas Service Overseas Ltd., and Director other Group companies overseas 1973-79; Managing Director, Industrial Division Amalgamated Metal Corporation plc 1979-82; Council

Member Australian British Trade Association 1976-79; Freeman City of London; Liveryman Gold & Silver Wyre Drawers. *Recreation:* Sailing, music, skiing. *Clubs:* City Livery, Royal Naval Sailing Assoc., Royal Southern Yacht club, Cruising Association. *Address:* The Cottage, Fulmer Way, Gerrards Cross, Bucks. SL9 8AJ.

LOCK - NECREWS, Mr John Ernest, Dip.Arch, ARIBA, ACI.Arb. *Currently:* Chief Executive, Hoggett Lock-Necrews plc. *Born on* 30 Aug 1939 at London. *Son of* the late William Ernest Necrews and the late May Constance (nee Lock). *Marriage:* to Daphne, 1978, da of Maj Stanley Dickin *Son of* Cardiff. *Children:* Christian (b.1979). *Educated at* Bridgend GS; University of Wales. *Career: Recreation:* golf, skiing, painting. *Clubs:* Carlton, Cardiff & County, Royal Porthcawl Golf. *Address:* Bishopsgate, Howells Crescent, Llandaff, Cardiff, CF5 2AJ. Westgate House, Womanby Street, Cardiff CF1 2UA.

LODWIG, Mr Luther, B.E.M. *Currently:* Retired (Ex miner) 45 years in industry. *Born on* 22 Dec 1924 at Clydach Vale, Rhondda Valley. *Son of* Margaret & Morgan Lodwig. *Marriage:* to Iris Doreen 1948. *Children:* Hilary, Diane and Kay. *Educated at* Secondary. *Career:* Started work in the Cambrian Colliery 1939 at age 15 years, retired at the Cwm Colliery Llantwit Fardre in 1984; past Vice-Chairman of Cambrian Colliery and Secretary of Cwm Colliery for 15 years prior to retirement; Awarded B.E.M. for services to the mining industry; past chairman of Old Llantwit Fardre Parish council and past chairman of Llantwit Fardre Community Council, of which still a member; Chairman Ysgol-Gymraeg Garth Olwyg; Chairman Ysgol-ty-Coch, special school Tonteg, Nr. Pontypridd; past member Board of Governors University of Wales; been in local government for 25 years, elected to Mid-Glam County Council in 1973; Vice Chairman of Public Protection for 10 years and for the last 3 years chairman; represented the Mid-Glam County Council on The Association of County Councils; Delegate to the Nuclear Free zones, county representative for 10 years; Being born in the Valleys has strong feelings for the working class communities with strong socialist views. *Recreation:* All sports. *Clubs:* Social. *Address:* 40 Heol Celyn, Church Village, Pontypridd CF38 1RU.

LOOSEMORE, Miss Sarah Jane, *Currently:* Student. *Born on* 15 June 1971 at Cardiff. *Daughter of* John and Pamela. *Educated at* New College, Cardiff; Oxford University, St.Hildas College *Career:* British National Senior Tennis Champion 1988, age 17; Runner-up, Singapore Open, 1990; Highest world ranking - 76 in April 1990-91; Reached 3rd Rd of Australian Open 1990; reached 2nd Rd of Wimbledon 1988 and 1990- beat 16th Seed in 1990 at Wimbledon; reached quarter finals Thailand open in 1991. *Recreation:* rowing, hockey, reading, theatre, good company! *Clubs:* Cardiff LTC; represent Oxford University at tennis. *Address:* High Trees, Druidstone Road, Old St.Mellons, S.Glam 31 Charleville Mansions, Charleville Road, London W14 9JA.

LOVEGROVE, Mr Ross, BA Hons, M.Des, RCA *Currently:* Own Design Studio, Lovegrove Studio X formed February 1990. Clients include BA, Carrera, Hermes, Louis Vuitton Paris, Cacharel, L'Oreal, Connolly Leathers, Knoll International, U.S., France, Italy, J.B.L., Harman Kardon, General, Wedgwood, Alfi Zitzmann, Atelier International, USA. *Born on* 16 Aug 1958 at Cardiff. *Son of* H.W.J. Lovegrove B.E.M., R.N.R, and Mary Eileen Lovegrove (b.Lovegrove). *Marriage:* to Miska Miller, Dip.Architect. *Children:* Son - Roman, Stormy, Andrzej. *Educated at* St.Cyres Comp, Penarth; Manchester Polytechnic; Royal College of Art. *Career:* Worked for various London Design Consultancies including Allied International Designers, 1980-83; Designer at Frog design, West Germany, responsible for Walkman and TV Monitors for Sony, Japan, Computers for Apple Computers, Car phone system and vacuum cleaner for AEG Telefunken, Soft Baggage for Louis Vuitton, 1983-84; Designer for Knoll International, Paris, 1984-86, responsible for the design of the 'Alessandri' office system; Member of the 'Atelier de Nimes', a group of five designers with: Gerard Barrau, Jean Nouvelle, Martine Bedin and Phillipe Stark, 1984; Cacharel Tableware, Baggage and Accessories, 1984; Co-founded Lovegrove and Brown Design studio, London 1986, dissolved January 1990. Laureat of 'Ogetti per Domus' pocket camera and film system 1985; member of the jury for "Les 25 Pbjets Temoins des Annes '80" for French Product Design 1985; "LEading Edge" New British Design Exhibition presented by Design Analysis Int at the Axis centre, Tokyo 1987; "Mondo Materialis" Exhibition. Pacific Design Centre, California. Curated by Jeffrey Osbourne for the Steelcase Design Partnership 1989-90; "Synthetic visions" plastics exhibition at the Victoria and Albert Museum, London 1990; Societe Des Artistes Decorateurs at the Grand Palais, Paris. Dining Room exhibited with- Martine Bedin, Shigeru Uchida, Michele de Lucchi, Piotr Sierakosky and Mathilde Bretillot 1990; Carbon Fibre Pen and 18 ct Gold Watch featured in "Image and Object, New Design in London" exhibition, Centre Pompidou, Paris, 1990; Winner of Creative Review Pantone Awards, Industrial Design Sections with "Erogenous Zones" neoprene dress 1991; "Projects Refusees" Villerbanne Lyon Exhibition of GE Plastic Door; 1991 Villerbane Lyon Exhibition of Disc Camera and Cassette System; 1991 "91 Objects by 91 Designers" Gallery 91, New York, disposable ceramic razor shown; 1991 Alfi Thermos Flask shortlisted for Minerva C.S.D. Awards; 1991 Contemporary Glasswork Exhibition, Rouen, Normandy with Champagne Bucket and Stand; visiting lecturer at the Royal College of Art, London, Ravensbourne and Kingston Colleges of Design; *Publications:* F.O.8 Chair featured in the Year Book of the London Design Museum 1990; Disc Camera and cassette system featured in the International Design Yearbook edited by Mario Bellini 1990; Included in Debrette's Who's Who of British Notaries in the first year that it included design as a listing 1991; Champagne Bucket and Metalarte Pendant lamp selected for the International Design Yearbook edited by Andre Putman 1991; work has been featured in Car Styling, Axis, Form, Intramuros, Designer's Journal, Design, Design Week, Blueprint, L'Architecture D'Aujourdhui, Architecture Cree, Creation, Domus, Brutus, Elle, Harpers and Queen, Interior Design, Vogue, Architectural Review, Sunday Times and Financial Times. *Recreation:* Design history, travel, fine art. *Clubs:* Chelsea Arts, Lampton Palace, Grouchos. *Address:* Studio X, 81 Southern Row, London W10 5AL. Hedgegate Court, 17 Powis Terrace, London W11.

LOVELUCK, Mr Paul Edward, JP., BA., FTS. *Currently:* Chief Executive, Wales Tourist Board, 1984- ; Director, Garden Festival Limited & Cardiff Marketing Ltd. *Born on* 3 Feb 1942 at Maesteg, Mid Glam. *Son of* Edward Henry Loveluck and Elizabeth Loveluck (nee Treharne). *Marriage:* to Lynne Loveluck (nee Gronow). *Children:* Christopher Paul and Stephanie Ruth *Educated at* Maesteg Grammar School and Univ.Coll. of Wales, Cardiff *Career:* Board of Trade, 1963-69; Welsh Office, 1969-84. *Recreation:* Walking hills, playing geriatric Squash and badminton, listening to classical music, viewing Rugby. *Clubs:* Vice-President, National Welsh-American Foundation *Address:*

Tudor Cottage, Rhiwbina Hill, Rhiwbina, Cardiff CF4 6UQ

LOXDALE, Peter Alasdair, ND, Agriculture. *Born on* 21 Nov 1959 at Bristol. *Son of* Hector Alasdair Robert Loxdale and Hilary Kathleen Ross Loxdale (nee Steen). *Educated at* Radley; Welsh Agricultural College. *Career:* Farmer and Land Proprietor. Vice-Chairman Dyfed Branch CLA 1990-. Member of Tax Committee CLA 1989-. Member of Welsh Committee CLA 1990-. President of Llanilar and North Cardiganshire Agricultural Soc., 1988-. President Llanilar Football Club 1991-. *Recreation:* shooting, music, wine. *Clubs:* Royal Overseas Legue; Farmers. *Address:* Castle Hill, Llanilar, Aberystwyth, Dyfed, SY23 4SB.

LOYN, Professor Emeritus Henry Royston, D.Litt., FBA., FSA., F.R.Hist.S. *Currently:* Professor Emeritus, Univ. of London, Historian. *Born on* 16 June 1922 at Cardiff. *Son of* the late Henry George Loyn and the late Violet Monica (nee Thomas). *Marriage:* to Patricia Beatrice (nee Haskew), 1950. *Children:* Richard Henry, John Andrew and Christopher Edward. *Educated at* Cardiff High School, University College, Cardiff. *Career:* Lecturer, Reader, Professor in the Department of History, Univ. College, Cardiff, 1946-77; Westfield College, Univ. of London, 1977-87; Professor, Head of Department History and History of Art, Vice Principal, 1980-86; Acting Principal, 1985-86; President, Historical Assoc., 1976-79; Society for Medieval Archeology, 1983-86; Vice President, Society of Antiquaries, 1983-87. *Publications:* Many books and articles on medieval history, including Anglo-Saxon England and the Norman Conquest (Longmans 1962: 2nd ed 1991) *Recreation:* Gardening, natural history. *Clubs:* Athenaeum *Address:* 25 Cunningham Hill Road, St. Albans, Herts. AL1 5BX.

LUDLAM, County Councillor Brian, *Currently:* Elected Member for Castle Ward in Swansea City Council 1970-74 then on West Glamorgan County Council, since 1974. *Marriage:* to Elizabeth. *Children:* Mark. *Career:* Member of Football Trust; Member Association of County Councils; Member Assembly of Welsh Counties; Member Welsh Joint Education Committee; Governor National Museum of Wales; Governor Swansea University; Labour Party Deputy Spokesman on ACC for Community Services; Labour Party Spokesman on ACC for the Arts and Sport and Recreation; Executive Member of the Football Forum; Local Authority Advisory Committee to the Arts Council; Local Authority Advisory Committee to the Sports Council; Local Authority Advisory Committee to the Theatre and Performing Arts; Member National Bureaux for Teachers Exchange; Former Chairman Community Services Committee County Council; Voce-Chairman County Council 1990-91; Chief Whip. Former Branch Chairman T.G.W.U; District Representative; Member National Committee. Served for two years Royal Air Force. *Recreation:* sport, music, good wine and holidays in Spain. *Clubs:* member Swansea Sportsmen's; Vice-President Swansea Harriers Athletic; Patron Swansea City A.F.C. *Address:* West Glamorgan County Council, County Hall, Swansea SA1 3SN.

LURVEY, Mr Roy, MSc; HND; FIOSH. *Currently:* Area Director, Wales Health & Safety Executive, 1987-. *Born on* 24 Jan 1939 at Oakdale. *Son of* the late Rudolph Lurvey and Lily (nee Roberts). *Marriage:* to Pearl Smith, 1960. *Children:* Claire Louise *Educated at* Pontllanfraith Secondary Technical; Polytecnic of Wales; Aston University. *Career:* Mining Engineer, NCB 1956-65; HM Inspector of Factories, 1966-75; HM District Inspector of Factories, 1975-79; Health & Safety Adviser to State of Bahrain, 1979-81; Head of Personel & Training, HSE, 1982-86. *Publications:* Guarding of Rolling Mills, 1972. *Recreation:* Boys Brigade, music, reading, walking.

Address: Welcome, 4 Blackbirds Close, Pentre Lane, Llantarnam, Cwmbran, Gwent, NP44 3AP.

LYON, Miss Polly Louise, *Currently:* British International Three Day Event Rider - Sponsored by TNT International Aviation Services, Windsor; Samuel Banner & Company Limited, Liverpool and Norco Signs, Denbigh, Clwyd. *Born on* 31 Jan 1969 at Wirral. *Daughter of* Christopher John Lyon and Susan Lyon (nee Aitken-Quack). *Educated at* Howells School, Denbigh. *Career:* European Junior 3 Day Event Champion. Winner of Team and Individual Gold Medals, riding "Highland Road" for Great Britain, Rome 1987; Young Rider British 3 Day Event Champion, riding "Highland Road", Bramham Park 1988; Young Rider European 3 Day Event Champion 1988. Winner of Team and Individual Gold Medals riding "Highland Road" for Great Britain, Zonhoven, Belgium; 3 Day Event Whitbread Championships, Ninth place, riding "Highland Road", Badminton International, 1989; Represented Great Britain at Senior European 3 Day Event Championships, riding "Highland Road", Burghley; Young Rider British 3 Day Event Champion, riding "Folly's Last", Bramham Park, 1990; Young Rider European 3 Day Event Champion. Winner of Team and Individual Gold Medals, riding "Folly's Last" for Great Britain, Rotherfield Park, Britain 1990. *Recreation:* National Hunt and Flat Racing and following sister Victoria's Point to Point Racing. *Clubs:* International Event Riders. *Address:* Pen Parc, Henllan, Denbigh, Clwyd, LL16 5DE. 35 Chipping Steps, Tetbury, Gloucestershire, GL8 8EU.

LYONS, Sir James Reginald, KCSG., OStJ., JP. *Currently:* Company Director. *Born on* 15 March 1910 at Cardiff. *Son of* the late James and the late Florence Hilda Lyons. *Marriage:* to Mary Doreen Fogg, 1937. *Children:* Colin Alfred Lyons *Educated at* Howard Gardens High School *Career:* Knighted, 1969; HM Forces, 1940-46, previously Airport Manager; Assist.Airport Dir., Glam (Rhoose) Airport; JP; City Councillor, from 1949; created Alderman, 1958; Deputy Lord Mayor, 1966-67; Lord Mayor of City of Cardiff, 1968-69; Ex mbr Council & Court of Governors, Univ.Coll., of S.Wales and Monmouthsire; Govnr.of St.Illtyds Coll., retired as Chairman; ex.Exec.Mbr. Council of the Nat.Playing Fields Assoc; Ex.mbr. S.East Glam. War Pensions Commt; Ex.mbr. S.Wales Sea Fisheries Dist.Commt; Ex.Trustee & mbr.of New Theatre Trust Co; mbr Welsh National Games Council, now President; Chrmn. (now President), Cardiff Horticultural Soc; Ex-Chrmn. Cardiff Small Holdings & Allotments Commt; Ex-Chrmn.Cardiff Sheep Dogs Trials Assoc; Ex-Vice-Pres. Schools Rugby Union; Ex.Vice-Pres. of Schools Cricket Assoc; Ex.Vice-Pres. Schools Swimming Assoc; Ex.Vice-Chrmn.S.Wales Sea Scouts Commt; mbr. Wales Tourist Brd; Trustee of S. Wales & Monmouth Trustee Savings Bank; mbr. Norfolk Commt; awarded Silver Acorn by Ch.Scout, Gold Medal by De La Salle Brothers for contribution to Education. *Recreation:* Rugby and all outdoor activities *Clubs:* Cardiff Athletic *Address:* 101 Minehead Avenue, Sully, S. Glam. CF6 2TL.

M

MABY, Mr Alfred Cedric, CBE., MA (Oxon). *Currently:* Retired. *Born on* 6 April 1915 at Prestbury, Glos. *Son of* Joseph Maby, Penrhos Raglan and Annie Leila Yates, Abergavenny, Gwent. *Marriage:* to Anne-Charlotte Modig, daughter of Envoyen EinarModig, Stockholm, 1944. *Children:* Timothy Dobyn, Alice Deborah and Catrin Myfanwy. *Educated at* Cheltenham College; Keble College Oxford. *Career:* mbr of H.M. Consular (later Diplomatic) Service, 1939-71; served in Peking 1939, Chungking 1940, Tsingtao 1941, Istanbul 1943, Ankara 1944, Buenos Aires 1946, Caracas 1949, Singapore 1954; Counsellor & Consul-General at Peking 1957-59, ; Charge d'affaires 1957 & 58; Deputy Consul-General, New York 1959-62; Counsellor (Commercial) and Consul-General, Vienna 1962-64; Asst.Sec. Min. of Overseas Development 1964-67; Consul-General Zurich and Liechtenstein 1968-71; Director Trade Promotion in Switzerland 1970-71; High Sheriff of Gwynedd 1976; Mbr. Governing Body Church of Wales 1975-78; Mbr.Church in Wales Advisory Comm. on Church & Society 1977-86. *Publications:* Venezuela (Overseas Economic Surveys) 1951; Dail Melyn o Tseina 1983; Y Cocatu Coch 1987. *Recreation:* Welsh history and literature, foreign languages, travel, music and gardening. *Clubs:* Fellow of Huguenot Society of Great Britain & Ireland, Mbr. of Cymmrodorion & Cymdeithas Cerdd Dant. *Address:* Cae Canol, Minffordd, Penrhyn-Deudraeth, Gwynedd LL48 6EN.

MacVE, Professor Richard Henry, MA (Oxon), MSc (London), FCA. *Currently:* Julian Hodge Professor of Accounting and Head of Department of Accounting, The University College of Wales, Aberystwyth. *Born on* 2 June 1946 at Folkestone, Kent. *Son of* Alfred Derek Macve and Betty Lilian (nee Simmons). *Marriage:* to Jennifer Jill Wort 1973. *Children:* Joanna Catherine, Thomas Charles and Arthur James. *Educated at* Chigwell School, Essex; New College, Oxford; LSE. *Career:* Peat, Marwick, Mitchell & Co., London 1968-74, articled clerk, senior accountant, assistant manager; internal auditor seconded to MoD 1973-74; Lecturer in Accounting, LSE 1974-78; Visiting Associate Professor of Accounting, Rice University, Houston, Texas 1982-83; member of Council ICAEW 1986- ; Chairman, Conference of Professors of Accounting 1990-. *Publications:* Books: A Conceptual Framework for Financial Accounting and Reporting (ICAEW 1981); A Survey of Lloyd's Syndicate Accounts (Prentice-Hall 1986, 2nd edn 1992); Marking to Market (ICAEW 1991). *Recreation:* sailing, mountain walking, Yr Iaith Cymraeg. *Clubs:* Royal Overseas League, Aberystwyth Sea Angling and Yacht. *Address:* Bronwydd, 3 Trefor Road, Aberystwyth SY23 2EH.

MacWILLIAM, Very Reverend Dr. Alexander Gordon, BA (Wales), BD, PhD (London) *Currently:* retired. *Born on* 22 Aug 1923 at Dolgarrog, Gwynedd. *Son of* Andrew and Margaret MacWilliam. *Marriage:* to Catherine Teresa (nee Bogue), 1951. *Children:* Andrew John (deceased). *Educated at* Llanrwst Grammar School; University of Wales; University of London. *Career:* Assistant Priest, Llanllyfni, Gwynedd 1946-49; Minor Canon, Bangor Cathedral 1950-55; Rector of Llanfaethlo, Anglesey 1955-58; Head of Dept. of Theology, Trinity College Carmarthen 1958-84; Visiting Professor of Philosophy, Central University of Iowa, USA 1983; Dean of St.Davids Cathedral 1984-90. *Publications:* articles: British Journal of Religious Education. *Recreation:* travel, classical music. *Address:* Pen Parc, Heol Smyrna, Llangain, Carmarthen, SA33 5AD.

MALCOLMSON, Mr Kenneth Forbes, MA, BMUS (Oxon), FRCO. *Currently:* retired. *Born on* 29 April 1911 at London. *Son of* the late Norman Malcolmson and the late Helen (nee Dubisson). *Marriage:* to Belle Dunhill. *Educated at* Eton College; Royal College of Music. *Career:* Organ Scholar, Exeter College, Oxford 1931-35; Commissioner, Royal School of Church Music 1935-36; Temporary Organist, St.Alban's Cathedral 1936-37; Organist, Halifax Parish Church 1937-38; Organist and Master of the Music, Newcastle Cathedral 1938-55; Precentor and Director of Music, Eton College 1956-71; Conductor of the Windsor & Eton Choral Society 1956-71. *Recreation:* tennis, cricket, reading. *Address:* Dixton House, Dixton Road, Monmouth, Gwent NP5 3PR.

MALONEY, Mr Michael John, JP., MA. *Currently:* Principal Moreton Hall since 1990. *Born on* 26 July 1932 at London. *Son of* John and Olive Maloney. *Marriage:* to Jancis Ann Ewing of Shrewsbury, 1960. *Children:* Patrick and Bridget. *Educated at* St Albans School; Trinity College, Oxford. *Career:* May & Baker Ltd., 1957-58; Shrewsbury School, 1958-66; Eastbourne College, 1966-72; Welbeck College (Headmaster), 1972-85; Kamuzu Academy, Malawi (Headmaster), 1986-89; Educational Consultant, 1989-90; National Service, 1955-57; Royal West Africa Frontier Force. *Publications:* Advanced Theoretical Chemistry (wtih D.E.P. Hughes); many articles, serious and humorous. *Recreation:* Restoring antique furniture, ornithology and hard crosswords. *Address:* Moreton Hall, Weston Rhyn, Oswestry, Shropshire SY11 3EW. Lower Lane Cottage, Chirbury, Montgomery, Powys, SY15 6UD Tel: 0691 773671

MALTHOUSE, Eric, *Currently:* retired - Self employed artist. *Born on* 20 Aug 1914 at Erdington, Birmingham. *Son of* the late James William Malthouse and the late Florence Dorothy (nee Alder). *Marriage:* to Anne May, 1942, daughter of late William Gascoigne of High Row, Haswell, Durham. *Children:* Jonathon Paul Gascoigne (b.1952), Penelope (b.1944) and Diana (b.1948). *Educated at* King Edward VI School, Aston, Birmingham; College of Arts and Crafts, Birmingham. *Career:* World War II service RAC 1940-42 (invalided out); artmaster Salt High School Saltaire Shipley 1938-43, assistant lecturer (later senior lecturer) Cardiff Coll of Art 1944-73; artist; exhibited first painting Royal Birmingham Soc of Artists 1931; mural paintings at: Wales Gas Helmont House, Penlyan Hostel Univ coll Cardiff, L G Harris & Co Ltd, Bromsgrove; exhibitions incl: Ten Year Retrospective 1959; Growth of Two Paintings 1963; New Vision Gallery (paintings) 1965; AIA (small paintings) 1969; Bangor Art Gallery (paintings and prints) 1970; Oxford Gallery 1971; Exeter Univ 1975; A Family Affair Sherman Theatre 1981; work in collections incl: Nat Museum of Wales, Welsh Art Council, Swansea Art Gallery, Newport Art Gallery, Bath Art Gallery, Bristol Art Gallery, V & A, Univ of Cardiff, Univ of Aberystwyth, Univ of Swansea, Univ of Exeter, Univ of Glasgow. Oxford CC, Glamorgan, Glamorgan CC, Someret CC; founder member: S Wales Group 1949, Watercolour Soc Wales 1959; founder 56 Group Wales 1956 (resigned 1970); Welsh Arts Council Prize for best designed book, Ancestor Worship by Emyr Humphreys 1971; member Print Makers Council 1971; RWA. *Recreation:* gardening, walking, jazz, chamber music. *Address:* 56 Porth Y Castell, Barry, S.Glam. CF6 8QE. Tel: 0446 749380

MANN, Mr Christopher John, *Currently:* Probation Officer, Merthyr Tydfil, in Probation Service since 1973. *Born on* 1 Oct 1950 at London. *Son of* John Peter Mann and June Elizabeth Finnis. *Marriage:* to Melanie Anne Sutton 1981. *Children:* Rebecca and Jennifer. *Educated at* Kingsbury High School, London, NW9; University of Dundee. *Career:* P.P.C. (Labour) Brecon and Radnor 1990-; County Councillor, Powys, Brecon (St.John's), 1985-; Governor, Coleg Powys; member University of Wales Court of Governors. *Recreation:* walking, bird watching, learning welsh. *Address:* 68 Pendre Gardens, Brecon, Powys, LD3 9EP.

MANSELL-JONES, Richard Mansell, MA (Oxon) (Literae Humaniories), FCA. *Currently:* Chairman J.Bibby & Sons PLC since 1988; member Stock Exchange; non-executive director Brown Shipley Holdings PLC, Barr & Wallace Arnold Trust PLC, Robert Bruce Fitzmaurice Ltd, Madison Trust Ltd,; Director Barlow Rand Ltd. *Born on* 14 April 1940 at Carmarthen. *Son of* the late Arnaud Milward Jones, of Carmarthen and the late Winifred Mabel (nee Foot). *Marriage:* to Penelope Marion Hawley, da of Sir David Henry Hawley 7Bt (d.1988). *Educated at* Queen Elizabeth's, Carmarthen; Private tuition; Worcester College Oxford. *Career:* articled to Price Waterhouse & Co; Manager N.M. Rothschild & Sons 1968-72; Brown Shipley & Co.Ltd, Director 1974-86; Dep Chairman 1986- 88; Director J.Bibby & Sons PLC 1979-87; Dep Chairman 1987-88. *Recreation:* art, music *Clubs:* Oriental. *Address:* 16 Stratford Place, London, W1A 9AF. 19 Astell Street, London, SW3 3RT

MANSEL LEWIS, Mr David Courtenay, JP; BA; KStJ *Born on* 25 Oct 1927 at London. *Son of* Charlie Ronald Mansel Lewis (d.1960) Lillian Georgina (d.1982) d. of Sir Courtenay Warner, 1st. Bt. *Marriage:* to Lady Mary Rosemary Marie-Gabrielle nee Montagu-Stuart-Wortley d. of 3rd Earl of Wharcliffe. *Children:* Patrick Charles Archibald, Catherine Maude Leucha and Annabel Lillian Elfrida *Educated at* Eton Keeble College Oxford *Career:* Welsh Guards 1946-49 tt 1948 RARO; High Sheriff Carmarthenshire 1965; JP 1969; DL 1971; HM Lt 1973-74; HM Lt of Dyfed 1974-79; Lord Lieutenant Dyfed 1979-; President W.Wales TAVRA 1979-90; President Mid & W.Wales TAVRA 1990-; Patron Carmarthen Royal British Legion 1974-; President Dyfed SSAFA 1986-; Founder President Llanelli Branch Welsh Guards Association 1974-; President Dyfed Branch Magistrates Association 1979-; President St. Johns Council for Dyfed; Patron Dyfed Branch British Red Cross Society; President Carmarthenshire Association Boy Scouts; President Carmarthen-Cardigan Branch Country Landowners ssociation 1977-91 & of Dyfed Branch CLA 1991-; Chairman South Western Division Royal Forestry Society 1963-; Chairman South Wales Woodlands 1969-85; President Dyfed Wildlife Trust 1978-; Patron Carmarthanshire Wildfowlers Association 1976-; Patron Carmarthenshire Federation of Young Farmers Clubs;

Member Ct of Governors UCW Aberystwyth 1974-; Member Council Nat. Museum of Wales 1987-91 & of Ct. 1974-91; Previously served on Music ct. of Wales Arts Council & on board of Welsh Nat. Opera; President Burry Port Operatic Society; President Llanelli Art Society 1956-; Founder Pres. Gwyl Llanelli Festival 1979-; Trustee of Llandovery College 1985-; Founder Chairman Carmarthen-Cardigan Cttee of the Sail Training Assoc., 1968-; Pres. Burry Port RNLI 1982-; Regional chrmn Sail Training Assoc., S Wales 1985-; Founder Commodore Burry Port Yacht club 1966, Pres., to 1990; Patron Tall Ships Council of Wales 1991-. *Recreation:* Music, sailing. *Clubs:* Royal Yacht Squadron. *Address:* Stadey Castle, Llanelli, Dyfed SA15 4PL.

MANSEL LEWIS, Lady Mary Rosemary Marie-Gabrielle, OBE, JP. *Currently:* Married woman and wife of Lord Lieutenant of Dyfed. *Born on* 11 June 1930 at London. *Daughter of* 3rd Earl of Whaincliffe and Countess of Whaincliffe. *Marriage:* 1953. *Children:* Patrick Mansel Lewis, Ms Catherine Mansel Lewis and Mrs Guy Herbert. *Educated at* Heathfield School, Ascot, Berks. *Career:* President Carmarthenshire Branch British Red Cross Society; President Dyfed Branch B.R.C.S. 1976-91. JP since 1974. *Recreation:* woodland gardening *Clubs:* Associate member R.Y.S. Cowes, Lansdown London. *Address:* Stradey Castle, Llanelli, Dyfed, SA15 4PL.

MANSFIELD, Professor Roger, MA, PhD. *Currently:* Director, Cardiff Business School. *Born on* 18 Jan 1942 at Buckinghamshire. *Son of* the late Arthur George Mansfield and the late Edith Mansfield. *Marriage:* to Helene Rica 1969. *Children:* Marie-Anne and Stephanie. *Educated at* Kingston Grammar School; Gonville & Caius College Cambridge; Wolfson College Cambridge. *Career:* Student Apprentice Stewarts & Lloyds Ltd., 1960-65; Research Engineer, Stewarts & Lloyds Ltd., 1965-66; Research Assistant, Cambridge Univ 1966-67; FME Teaching Fellow, Cambridge Univ 1967-68; Visiting Lecturer, Yale Univ 1968-69; Senior Research Officer, London Business School 1969-73; Lecturer, Imperial College 1973-76; Professor UWIST 1976-88; Deputy Principal UWIST 1985-88; Professor, Univ of Wales, Cardiff 1988-; Deputy Chairman Council of University Management Schools 1988-; Vice Chairman British Academy of Management 1990-; Director South Glam Tec 1989-; Council Member Institute of Welsh Affairs 1989-. *Publications:* (with D.S.Pugh and M.Warner) Research in Organisational Behaviour, 1975; (with M.J.F.Poole) (editors) Managerial Roles in Industrial Relations, 1980; (with M.J.F.Poole) (editors), International Perspectives on Management and Organization, 1981; (with M.J.F.Poole, P.Blyton and P.Frost), The British Manager in Profile, 1981; (with M.J.F.Poole), Managers in Focus: the British Manager in the early 1980s, 1981; (with M.J.F.Poole) (Editors), Managerial Roles in Industrial Relations (2nd ed), 1983; (with R.Zeffane), Organizational Structures and National Contingencies, 1983; Company Strategy and Organizational Design, 1986; (editor) Frontiers of Management Research and Practice, 1989; approximately 100 articles. *Recreation:* gardening. *Clubs:* Cardiff & County. *Address:* 64 Bishops Road, Whitchurch, Cardiff, CF4 1LW.

MAPLESON, Professor William Wellesley, DSc., FInst., FIPSM. *Currently:* Professor Emeritus of the Physics of Anaesthesia, Univesity of Wales College of Medicine (semi-retired). *Born on* 2 Aug 1926 at London, UK. *Son of* the late Francis Mapleson and the late Amy Kathleen (nee Parsons). *Marriage:* to Gwladys Doreen Wood, 1954. *Children:* Jennifer Margaret (b.1955) and Roger William (b.1963). *Educated at* Dr.Challoner's Grammar School,

Abersham, Bucks; University College, Durham (BSc, PhD, DSc). *Career:* RAF: National Service Instructor in radar, Flying Officer 1947-49; University of Wales College of Medicine: Lecturer 1952-65; Senior Lecturer 1965-69; Reader 1969-73; Professor 1973-91. Member of Health Care Committee 46 of the British Standards Institution. Member Editorial Board of the British Journal of Anaesthesia. Honours: Pask Certificate of Honour of the Association of Anaesthetists of Great Britain and Ireland 1972; Faculty Medal of the College of Anaesthetists 1981; Hon. member of the Brazilian Society of Anaesthesiology 1983; Hon. member of the Association of Anaesthetists of Great Britain and Ireland 1991. *Publications:* Automatic Ventilation of the Lungs (jointly) 3rd edn 1980; plus 160 scientific communications. *Recreation:* work, theatre-going, walking, collecting Wainwright peaks. *Clubs:* Royal Society of Medicine. *Address:* Department Of Anaesthetics, Univesity of Wales College of Medicine, Heath Park, Cardiff, CF4 4XN. Tel: 0222 742096.

MARCH, Professor Philip Vincent, *Currently:* Professor of Physics, Royal Holloway and Bedford New College, University of London, since 1984. *Born on* 16 Aug 1929 at Blackwood. *Son of* Arthur Philip March and Violet Ethel (nee Webb). *Marriage:* to Margaret Jean Lewis, 1955. *Children:* Peter Stephen, David Nicholas and Rosemary Margaret. *Educated at* University of Birmingham, BSc, PhD. *Career:* Lecturer in Physics, University of Glasgow 1956-61; Lecturer in Physics, Westfield College, London 1961-65; Reader in Physics, Westfield College, London 1965-71; Professor of Physics, Westfield College, London 1971-84; Professor of Physics, Royal Holloway and Bedford New College, London 1984-present; Dean of Science 1988-91. *Publications:* 100 research papers in nuclear and particle physics. *Recreation:* travel, music, art. *Address:* Fauns Wood, Queens Hill Rise, Ascot, Berks, SL5 7DP.

MAREK, Dr John, BSc., PhD. *Currently:* MP for Wrexham, 1983- . *Born on* 24 Dec 1940 at London. *Marriage:* to Anne (nee Pritchard). *Educated at* King's College, London. *Career:* Lecturer in Applied Mathematics; Univ. College of Wales, Aberystwyth 1966-83; Member of Ceredigion District Council 1979-83; Shadow health spokesman 1985-87; Shadow Treasury spokesman and shadow minister for the Civil Service 1987- . *Publications:* Various research papers. *Address:* House Of Commons, London, SW1A 0AA.

MARKS, Professor Ronald, MBBS, FRCP, FRCPath. *Currently:* Professor of Dermatology, Univ of Wales College of Medicine. *Born on* 26 March 1935 at London, England. *Son of* the late Isadore Marks and the late Jessie Marks. *Marriage:* 1st marriage dissolved 1978, 2nd to Hilary (nee Venmore). *Children:* Louise Anne (b.1962) and Naomi Suzanne (b.1965). *Educated at* St.Marylebone GS; Guy's Hospital Medical School (BSc Hons, MBBS Hons). *Career:* Nat Service MO short serv. cmmn 1960, med. div Queen Alexander Military Hospital 1961-63, specialist in dermatology Br. Mil Hospital Munster W.Germany 1963-65; Senior lecturer Inst of Dermatology and consultant dermatologist St.John's Hospital for Diseases of the Skin London 1971-73 Univ of Wales College of Medicine Cardiff: Senior lecturer in dermatology dept of med 1973, reader 1977, personal chair in dermatology 1980; hon consultant in dermatology Univ Hospital of Wales 1973; lit award Soc of Cosmetic Chemists NY USA 1985; hon chm Skin Charity to Advance Res, hon pres Int Soc for Bioengineering and the Skin; Freeman City of Besancon 1983; FRCP 1977 (mem 1964), FRCPath 1985 (mem 1980). Dowling Oration Lecturer 1984, Parkes Weber Lecturer 1985. *Publications:*

Author or co-editor of 23 books, over 300 papers published in scientific journals and over 85 chapters in books. *Recreation:* visual arts of the 19 and 20 centuries, squash. *Address:* 12 Penylan Place, Penylan, Cardiff.

MASCETTI, Mr Keith Peter, BA., MEd., AFBPsS., C.Psychol. *Currently:* Retired. *Born on* 6 June 1928 at Cardiff. *Son of* the late Umberto Mascetti and the late Amy (nee Owen). *Marriage:* to Nansi Hugh Thomas, 1956. *Children:* Hugh Peter Mascetti and David Hiram Mascetti (deceased). *Educated at* Howard Gardens High School, Cardiff; University College, Cardiff; University of Edinburgh. *Career:* Army 1945-48; School Teacher 1954-60; Educational Psychologist 1960-85; Chairman of Board of Directors, Gwili Railway Company 1974- ; Youth Hostels Assoc; Member National Countryside Commt 1965- ; Chairman South Wales Group 1961-86; National Vice Chairman 1966-73; President Wales Region 1986- ; Campaign for Protection of Rural Wales, Vice President; Vice President Bynea Cycling Club; Vice Chairman & Archivist, Gower Society 1979- ; Royal Inst. of S.Wales, Honorary Sec. 1990- ; Nominated Mbr Brecon Beacons Nat. Park Commt 1973-79; Nom. Mbr Countryside Commn. for Wales 1980-87; Nom. Mbr Gower Consumer Advisory Commt. 1982-89; Co-opted Mbr Glamorgan Land Drainage/ Flood Defence Commt. 1983- ; Vice Chairman Council for Nat. Parks. 1990- ; Chairman of Commt Cambrian Archaeological Assoc. 1981-83; Mbr of Court of Governors Univ. Coll. Swansea 1981- ; Mbr of Prince of Wales Environmental Study Group 1987- ; Nominated mbr of NRA Regional Rivers Commt 1989-91; Mbr of Ramblers Assoc. Wales Executive/Council 1988- . *Recreation:* Walking, Archaeology and Railways. *Address:* 34 Townhill Road, Cwmgwyn, Swansea, SA2 OUR. Royal Inst. Of S.Wales, Swansea Museum, Victoria Road, Swansea, SA1 1SN. Tel: 0792 202631.

MASON, Professor Haydn Trevor, BA, AM, DPhil, Officer dans L'Ordrc des Palmes Academ *Currently:* Professor of French, University of Bristol, since 1981. *Born on* 12 Jan 1929 at Saundersfoot. *Son of* the late Herbert and the late Margaret (nee Jones). *Marriage:* 2nd to Adrienne Barnes, 1982. *Children:* from first marriage, David and Gwyneth; stepdaughter Kate. *Educated at* Greenhill Grammar School, Tenby; U.C.W. Aberystwyth; Middlesbury College, Vermont, USA; Jesus College, Oxford. *Career:* National Service 1951-53 (commissioned 2nd Lt.RASC 1952); Instructor, Princeton University, USA 1954-57; Lecturer, University of Newcastle-upon-Tyne 1960-63; Lecturer 1964-67, Reader 1965-67 at University of Reading; Professor, University of East Anglia 1967-79; Professeur-Associe, Universite De Paris III (Sorbonne Nouvelle) 1979-81; Scholar in Residence, University of Maryland, USA 1986. President, Association of University Professors of French 1981-82; President, Society for French Studies 1982-84; President, British Society for Eighteenth-Century Studies 1984-86; Vice-President, International Society for Eighteenth-Century Studies 1987-91, and President 1991-95. Director, Voltaire Foundation, University of Oxford 1977- , and Chairman of Directors 1989- . *Publications:* Pierre Bayle and Voltaire, 1963; Voltaire, 1975; Voltaire: A Biography, 1981; French Writers and their Society, 1715-1800, Macmillan, 1982; Cyrano de Bergerac: L'Autre Monde, Grant & Cutler, 1984; Vita di Voltaire, Laterza 1984 (Italian translation of: Voltaire: A Biography); Voltaire, Salvat, 1985 (Spanish translation of Voltaire: A Biography); Ed. Marivaux: Les Fausses Confidences, OUP, 1964; Ed. and trans: Leibniz/Arnauld Correspondence (Introduction by G.H.R.Parkinson), Manchester Univ Press 1967; Ed.Voltaire: Zadig and Other

Tales, OUP, 1971; Ed(with R.J.Howells, A.Mason, D.Williams), Essays presented in honour of W.H.Barber, Oxford 1985; Ed.(with E.Freeman, M.O'Regan & S.W.Taylor), Myth and its Making in the French Theatre: Studies presented to W.D.Howarth, 1988; Ed(with W.Doyle), The Impact of the French Revolution on European Consciousness, 1989. *Recreation:* walking, music, theatre, gardening, crosswords, history *Address:* 11 Godlney Avenue, Bristol, BS8 4RA.

MASON, Prof. Sir Ronald, KCB., PhD., D.Sc., FRSC.Ceram, FRS., F.Inst.P *Currently:* Chairman, B.H.R. Group and B. Cevan Res. Ltd., Professor Univs., of Sussex and Wales (hon) U.K. rep UN Board Disarmament; Chair. DTI Engineering Technology. *Born on* 22 July 1930 at Merthyr Vale. *Son of* David James Mason and Olwen (nee James). *Marriage:* to E. Rosemary Grey-Edwards (previously E. Pauline Pattinson). *Children:* Carolyn Susan, Anne Fiona and Helen Sian. *Educated at* Quaker's Yard School, Universities of Wales and London. *Career:* Research Associate, Univ., Col., London, 1953-60; Lecturer Imperial College, 1960-63; Prof. Univ. Sheffield, 1963-71; Prof. Univ. of Sussex, 1971- ; Pro Vice Chancellor, Sussex, 1977-78; Chief Sci Adv. Min of Def., 1977-83; Chair Hunting Eng. Ltd., 1985-87; Chair Thomson (UK) Holdings, 1987-90; Vis. Prof in Univs. of Australia, France, Israel, Canada, New Zealand and U.S.A. *Publications:* Nearly 300 research papers in learned journals (molecular and surface sciences); many publications on international security; monographs on biological and chemical sciences. *Recreation:* Cooking, gardening, stirring. *Clubs:* Athenaeum *Address:* Chestnuts Farm, Weedon, Bucks., HP22 4NH.

MASTERMAN, Mr Crispin Grant, BA, FCI.Arb. *Currently:* Barrister. In Private Practice since 1971. *Born on* 1st June 1944 at Chalfont St.Peter. *Son of* the late Osmond Janson Masterman and Anne Masterman. *Marriage:* to Clare (nee Fletcher), 1976. *Children:* Claudia (b.1977), Kerrin (b.1979) and Laura (b.1982). *Educated at* St.Edward's School, Oxford; University of Southampton. *Career:* appointed Recorder, 1988; Elected Fellow of the Chartered Institute of Arbitrators 1991. *Recreation:* running, walking, sitting still. *Address:* 28 South Rise, Cardiff, CF4 5RH.

MATHIAS, Professor William (James), CBE; DMus; FRAM. *Currently:* Composer. *Born on* 1 Nov 1934 at Whitland, Dyfed. *Son of* James Hughes Mathias and Marian (nee Evans). *Marriage:* to Margaret Yvonne Collins 1959. *Children:* Rhiannon (b 1968). *Educated at* University Coll. of Wales, Aberystwyth (Robert Bryan School), Fellow 1990; Royal Academy of Music (Lyell-Taylor Schol.), DMus Wales, 1966; FRAM 1965 (LRAM 1958). *Career:* Lectr in Music, UC of N Wales, Bangor 1959-68; Sen.Lectr in Music, Univ of Edinburgh 1968-69; Professor & Head of Music Dept., U.C. of N.Wales, Bangor 1970-88. Mbr: Welsh Arts Council 1974-88 (Chm., Music Cttee. 1982-88); Music Adv. Cttee, British Council 1974-83; ISCM (British Section) 1976-80; BBC Central Music Adv.Cttee, 1979-86; Welsh Adv. Cttee, British Council 1979-91; Council, Composers' Guild of GB 1982- ; Bd of Governors Nat Museum of Wales, 1973-78; Artistic Dir, N Wales Music Festival 1972- ; Vice-Pres. British Arts Fests Assoc., 1988- ; (Vice-Chmn 1983-88); RCO 1985; Pres ISM 1989-90; Govrenor NYO of GB 1985- ; Hon.DMus Westminster Choir Coll. Princeton 1987; Arnold Bax Society Prize 1968; John Edwards Meml Award 1982; Fellow, Welsh College of Music and Drama, 1992. *Publications:* Piano Concerto No 2, 1964; Piano Concerto No 3, 1970; Harpsichord Concerto 1971; Harp Concerto 1973; Clarinet

Concerto 1976; Horn Concerto 1984; Organ Concerto 1984; Oboe Concerto 1990 Violin Concerto 1992; Flute Concerto 1992; Orchestral Compositions: Divertimento for string orch. 1961; Serenade for small orch. 1963; Prelude, Aria and Finale 1966; Symphony No 1 1969; Festival Overture 1973; Celtic Dances 1974; Vistas 1977; Laudi 1978; Vivat Regina (for brass band) 1978; Helios 1978; Requiescat 1979; Dance Variations 1979; Investiture Anniversary Fanfare 1979; Reflections on a theme by Tomkins 1981; Symphony No 2: Summer Music (commd by Royal Liverpool Philharmonic Soc.) 1983; Ceremonial Fanfare for 2 trumpets 1983; Anniversary Dances (for centenary of Univ. Coll. Bangor) 1985; Carnival of Wales 1987; Threnos, for string orch. 1990; Symphony No 3 1991; In Arcadia 1992; Chamber compositions: Sonata for violin and piano, 1963; Piano sonata, 1965; Divertimento for flute, oboe and piano, 1966; String Quartet 1970; Capriccio for flute and piano 1971; Wind Quintet 1976; Concertino 1977; Zodiac Trio 1977; Clarinet Sonatina 1978; String Quartet No 2 1981; Piano Sonata No 2 1984; Violin Sonata No 2 1984; Piano Trio 1986; Flute Sonatina 1986; String Quartet No 3 1986; Soundings for Brass Quintet 1988; Little Suite for Piano 1989; Santa Fe suite for harp 1989; Choral and Vocal Compositions: Wassail Carol 1965; Three Medieval Lyrics 1966; St. Teilo 1970; Ave Rex 1970; Sir Christemas 1970; Culhwch and Olwen 1971; A Babe is born 1971; A Vision of Time and Eternity (for contralto and piano) 1974; Ceremony after a fire raid 1975; This World's Joie 1975; Carmen Paschale 1976; Elegy for a Price (for baritone and orch.) 1976; The Fields of Praise (for tenor and piano) 1977; A Royal Garland 1978; Nativity Carol 1978; A May Magnificat 1980; Shakespeare Songs 1980; Songs of William Blake (for mezzo-soprano and orch.) 1980; Rex Gloriae (four Latin motets) 1981; Te Deum, for soli, chorus and orch. 1982; Salvator Mundi: a carol sequence, 1983; Angelus 1984; Four Welsh Folk Songs 1984; The Echoing Green 1985; O Aula Nobilis (for opening of Orangery at Westonbirt Sch. by TRH Prince and Princess of Wales), 1985; Veni Sancte Spiritus (Hereford Three Choirs Fest.) 1985; Gogoneddawg Argwlydd (for Nat. Youth Choir of Wales) 1985; Riddles 10987; Jonah (a musical morality) 1988; Sweet was the Song 1988; Learsongs 1989; World's Fire (poems of Gerald Manley Hopkins) for soprano and baritone soli, SATB chorus and orch. 1989; Bell Carol 1989; Yr Arglwydd yw fy Mugail (male voices and piano) 1989; Organ Compositions: Variations on a Hymn Tune 1963; Partita 1963; Postlude 1964; Processional 1965; Chorale 1967; Toccata giocosa 1968; Jubilate 1975; Fantasy 1978; Canzonetta 1978; Antiphonies 1982; Organ Concerto 1984; Berceuse 1985; Recessional 1986; A Mathias Organ Album 1986; Fanfare for Organ 1987; Fenestra 1989; Carillon 1989; anthems and church music: O sing unto the Lord 1965; Make a joyful noise 1965; Festival Te Deum 1965; Communion Service in C 1968; Psalm 150 1969; Lift up your heads 1970; O Salutaris Hostia 1972; Miss Brevis 1974; Communion Service (Series III) 1976; Arise, shine 1978; Let the people praise thee, O God (anthem composed for the wedding of the Prince and Princess of Wales) 1981; Praise ye the Lord 1982; All Wisdom is free from the Lord 1982; Except the Lord build the House 1983; A Grace 1984; Jubilate Deo, 1983; O How Amiable 1983; Tantum ergo 1984; Let us now praise famous men 1984; Alleluia! Christ is risen, 1984; Missa Aedis Christi - in memoriam William Walton, 1984; Salve Regina 1986; O clap you hands 1986; Let all the world in every corner sing 1987; Rejoice in the Lord 1987; I will lift up mine eyes unto the hills 1987; O Lord our Lord 1987; As truly as God is our Father 1987; The Heavens Declare 1988; I will Celebrate 1989; Praise is due to you, O God 1989; The Doctrine of Wisdom 1989; Lord, Thou hast been our dwelling place 1990; Magnificat of Nunc Dimittis (St. David's Service) 1992; Opera: The Servants (libretto by Iris Murdoch) 1980. *Clubs:* Athenaeum *Address:* Y Graigwen, Cadnant Road, Menai Bridge, Anglesey, Gwynedd, LL59 5NG. Tel: 0248 712392.

MATTHEW, Mr Chessor Lillie, JP; FRIBA; FRIAS; AMRTPI (Retired). *Currently:* retired. *Born on* 22 Jan 1913 at Tyrie, Scotland. *Son of* Willaim and Helen (nee Milne). *Marriage:* to Rita Ellis, 1939. *Children:* Stuart. *Educated at* Strichen Secondary School; Grays School of Art & Architecture. Anerdeen. *Career:* Lecturer/Senior Lecturer, Welsh School of Architecture 1937-58; RAF 1940-46, Flt/Lt.; Head of School of Architecture, Duncan of Jordanstow College of Art, Dundee 1958-64; Principal of Said College 1964-78; Member of the Royal fine Art Commission for Scotland 1966-78. *Recreation:* Hillwalking, music, reading, foreign travel. *Address:* 36 Albany Road, West Ferry, Dundee, DD5 1NW.

MATTHEWS, Mr Mervyn, *Currently:* retired 1979. *Born on* 19 March 1914. at Upper Cwmtwrch, Swansea Valley. *Son of* the late William and the late Margaret (nee Williams). *Marriage:* to Sarah Ealeanor Jones 1953. *Children:* Dr Sarah Helen Margaret Matthews, MBBch, MRCPhsych. *Educated at* Upper Cwmtwrch Elmm Sch; Llandovery Elmm. Sch; 1936 Final Further Ed. Cert., Maths (Dist), Science(Dist), English (Credit);1936 Deputy Coal Manager Cert;1956 BR Safeworking of Railway Cert(Merit);1959 BR Accountancy Cert. *Career:* Mining Trainee 1930-34; LMS/GWR/BR Porter/Signalman/Station Master/Goods Agent, Birmingham and Swansea Districts 1934-65, Inspector (Instructor) Lecturer in Rules on Safe Working of Railways (Excepting War Service 1940-46, serving as Gunner, NCO and latterly obtaining Commission Rank; left Railway Service 1965; Superindendent of Home for Eldery, and problem and homeless people, 1966, promoted to Senior Homes Officer (29 homes), Gwynedd Social Services; Submission to BR Bd plan "Matthew" - Reorganisation of BR 1969; Chmn, Welsh Railways Action Cttee 1971; Founder mbr and past President Rotary Club of Llanfairfechan and Penmaenmawr 1972; Chmn. N.Wales Transport 2000, 1973; Rotary Counsellor for Foreign Students at the Univ of Wales, Bangor, also mbr of 118 Rotary District Commn.Cttee 1979; Vice-Chmn Cowbridge Rotary Club Int.Cttee 1985; Elevated to the Gorsedd of Bards for Community Work, known as "Mervyn Cwmtwrch", 1986; Vice-Pres Cor Meibion Y Bontfaen 1987; The House of Commons Publish my submission to The Committee on Welsh Affairs on proposals: 1) North to South Wales Rail Link, 2) Rail Link Cardiff Wales Airport and Restoration of Passenger Services on the Vale of Glamorgan Line, 3) Re-opening of Neath and Brecon Branch line as A Tourist Attraction, 4) (Appendix 52) Proposals for Direct Electrified Rail System from Wales to The Euro-Tunnel, 1986-89; Submission to Secretary of State for Transport, re Privatisation of British Rail 1991. *Publications:* On The Move, 1914/89, At the request of the Cardiff and Swansea Maritime Museums and The National Library of Wales, Aberystwyth, where he has deposited a copy of his manuscript to their archives for the benefit of present and future researchers etc. *Recreation:* Rugby Union, reading, music, fishing. *Clubs:* Rotary and Probus. *Address:* 6 Mill Park, Cowbridge, South Glamorgan, CF7 7BG. Tel: 0446 772910.

MATTHEWS, Mr Neil Howard, BSc, B.Arch, RIBA. *Currently:* Consultant Architect, Neil H.Matthews Assoc, since 1982. *Born on* 2 Aug 1948 at Bridgend. *Son of* Howard and Gwyneth (nee Davies). *Marriage:* to Averil

Susan (nee Abbott), 1972. *Children:* Lydia Dee (b.1978) and Jack Timothy Rhys (b.1986). *Educated at* Dyffryn Grammar; W.S.A.(UWIST). *Career:* Architect, Percy Thomas Partnership 1972-78; Overseas manager P.T.P. International Saudi Arabia 1978-80; Consultant Architect Saudi Arabia, 1980-82. *Recreation:* swimming, reading *Address:* "Frongelli House", Llanedi, Pontardulais, W.Glam, SA4 1YR.

MAUNDER, Professor Leonard, OBE, BSc, ScD, PhD, FEng, FIMechE. *Currently:* Head of Department of Mechanical, Materials & Manufacturing Engineering, University of Newcastle upon Tyne. *Born on* 10 May 1927 at Swansea. *Son of* Thomas George, Engineer, and Elizabeth Ann Long. *Marriage:* to Moira Anne Hudson, Swansea 1958. *Children:* Joanna and David. *Educated at* Bishop Gore Grammar School; University of Wales; MIT; University of Edinburgh. *Career:* Instructor & Assistant Professor, MIT; Aeronautical Res. Lab., US Air Force 1954-56; Lecturer, Postgrad. School of App. Dynamics, Edinburgh University 1956-61; Christmas Lecturer Royal Institution 1983. Member: NRDC 1976-92, SERC Eng.Brd. 1976-80; Advisory Council on R & D, Dept. of Energy 1981- ; ACOST 1987- . Dep. Chairman, Newcastle Hospitals Management Cttee., 1971-73. President International Federation for the Theory of Machines & Mechanisms 1976-79. Vice-President I.Mech.E. 1975-80; Honorary Fellow Univ. College of Swansea, Honorary Foreign Member Polish Society for Theoretical & Applied Mechanics. *Publications:* (with R.N.Arnold) Gyrodynamics and Its Engineering Applications, 1961; Machines in Motion 1986; numerous papers in the field of Applied Mechanics. *Recreation:* gardening, music. *Address:* 46 Moorside South, Newcastle upon Tyne, NE4 9BB.

MAURICE, Mr Brian Dennison, MA (Lond). *Currently:* Project Organiser Workers Educational Association, Torfaen, since 1981. *Born on* 27 May 1939 at Newport, Gwent. *Son of* William Colin Maurice and Marion (nee Davies). *Marriage:* to Janice Constance McNab 1965. *Children:* David Ceri Maurice and Rachel Lynne Maurice. *Educated at* Jones' West Mon. G.S., Pontypool; Exeter Univ; London Univ. *Career:* Ast. Teacher, Hawkes Bay New Zealand 1963; P.T. Scriptwriter BBC External Services 1969; Hod. S.E. Asian Studies United World College Singapore 1972; P.T. Tutor WEA T.V. Studies 1977; County Councillor, Gwent 1981; Vice-Chair Educ. 1989. *Publications:* Articles International Politics - Health & Safety at Work - Adult Education. *Recreation:* Politics, rugby, travel. *Clubs:* Green Lawn Social; Griffin Pontypool. *Address:* 17 Coedygric Road, Griffithstown, Pontypool, Gwent, NP4 5HE.

MAY, Mr Phillip Stephen, BSc ECon (Hons) *Currently:* Gen and Comm Manager, Llanelli RFC. *Born on* 1 July 1956 at Llanelli. *Son of* Sidney and Maida. *Marriage:* to Ann. *Children:* Owen and David *Educated at* Llanelli Boys Grammar; Swansea University; Aberystwyth University. *Career:* Teacher. Brewery Representative: Crown Buckley, Harp. *Recreation:* horse racing, reading autobiographies. *Address:* C/o Llanelli R.F.C., Stradey Park, Llanelli, Dyfed.

MAYERS, William John, FHCIMA, MRSH. *Currently:* Domestic Bursar, Hereford Cathedral School. *Born on* 22 Oct 1935 at Pontypool. *Son of* William Henry and Irene Mary (nee Luxton). *Marriage:* to Audrey Whitcombe, 1960. *Children:* Sian Angharad and Simon John. *Educated at* Abersychan Grammar School; Welsh Coll of Advanced Technology, Cardiff. *Career:* National Service, RAF Bomber Command. Area Manager Gardner Merchant Ltd, 8 years; Group Catering Manager Sun Valley Poultry Ltd 16 years; Founder member: Welsh Federation of Coarse

Anglers (W.F.C.A.) 1974 ; Welsh Anglers Council 1975; Honorary Life member W.F.C.A., Newport AA, Cwmbran AA, Llay AA, Stratford on Avon AA. Member: Confederation Internationale Peche Sportif (World body); National River Authority; Hotel, Catering and Institutional Management Ass.; Royal Society of Health; Sports Council for Wales. Instigator of Home Countries International Angling competitions 1978; Wales entry into World Angling competition 1980. Captained Wales 1980-90. Bronze Medal-1980, Gold Medal-1989. *Recreation:* fishing, gardening, travel. *Address:* 6 Biddulph Rise, Tupsley, Hereford, HR1 1RA. Tel: 0432 358334.

MAYNARD, County / Town Councillor Kenneth Bryan, *Currently:* Retired. *Born on* 10 May 1932 at Carmarthen. *Son of* the late Frank Maynard and Doris Abra (nee Brown). *Marriage:* to Mary Sarah Lorraine (nee Thomas) District / Town Councillor, 1956, Mayor Elect 1992-93. *Children:* Micheal, Victoria, Christine, Anthony, Nicola, Francis and Davied. *Educated at* College Y Fro, Swansea University, British Rail Weeb House, Crewe; Faverdale Hall, Darlington (NEBBS) *Career:* Apprentice Mechanic 1947-49; Royal Air Force 1949-53; British Rail 1954-89; Swansea University Day Release 1976-78; 1978-86; 1986-89; Elected Carmarthen Town Council 1979-present; Elected Dyfed County Council 1985-present; Mayor, Carmarthen Town 1985-86; Chairman personnel 1991; Active member of NUR, Chairman of Carmarthen Branch and L.D.C. National Delegate. *Recreation:* Active boxing/rugby/swimming, interest in all sports *Clubs:* Active member Labour Party; President B.R.S.A., R.A.F.A; Vice President Carmarthen Athletic Rugby Club. *Address:* 21 Cadifor St., Carmarthen, Dyfed, SA31 1RY.

McCARTNEY, Mr Gordon Arthur, Solicitor *Currently:* Associate with Succession Planning Associates; Executive Search Consultants; Managing Director, Gordon McCartney Associates Ltd. *Born on* 29 April 1937 at Leicester. *Son of* Hannah and Arthur McCartney. *Marriage:* to Wendy. *Children:* Heather and Alison. *Educated at* Grove Park Grammar School, Wrexham; Law Soc. Finals. *Career:* Articles to Town Clerk, Wrexham 1953-59; admitted Solicitor 1959; Solicitor, Birkenhead & Bootle Corporations 1959-65; Deputy Clerk, Wrexham RDC 1965-73; Chief Executive, Delyn Borough Council, Clwyd 1974-81; Secretary, Association of District Councils 1981-91; Secretary, Council of Welsh Districts 1983-91. *Publications:* various through Council of Europe on the Management of Rural Areas. *Recreation:* cricket, music. *Clubs:* Northampton County Cricket. *Address:* 11 Raleigh Walk, Atlantic Wharf, Cardiff, CF1 5LN. 33 Duck Street, Elton, Peterborough, PE8 6RQ.

McGUFFIN, Professor Peter, MB, PhD, FRCP, FRC.Psych. *Currently:* Professor and Head of Dept of Psychological Medicine, Univ of Wales College of Medicine. *Born on* 4 Feb 1949 at Belfast. *Son of* Capt William B. and Melba (nee Burnison) McGuffin. *Marriage:* to Dr.Anne Farmer, 1972. *Children:* Catrina, Liam and Lucy. *Educated at* Sandown Grammar School; Leeds University; London University. *Career:* House Officer, then Registrar, St.James Hospital Leeds 1972-77; Registrar, then Senior Registrar, Maudsley Hospital London 1977-79; Research Fellow Institute of Psychiatry London, and Washington University, St.Louis, USA 1979-82. MRC Senior Fellow, Hon Consultant and Senior Lecturer Institute of Psychiatry, Kings College Hospital London 1982-87. *Publications:* 4 books, incl: 'The New Genetics of Mental Illness'; papers, articles on psychiatry, genetics. *Recreation:* music, jogging, tennis. *Clubs:* Lisvane Tennis. *Address:* University Of Wales College, of Medicine, Heath Park, Cardiff, CF4 4XN.

McINTYRE, Professor Neil, BSc, MD, FRCP *Currently:* Professor and Chairman, University Dept of Medicine, Royal Free Hospital School of Medicine, since 1983. *Born on* 1 May 1934 at Ferndale, Glam. *Son of* John Wiliam, and Catherine (nee Watkins). *Marriage:* to Wendy Ann (nee Kelsey). *Children:* Waveney; Hamish Rowan. *Educated at* Porth County School; Kings College; Kings College Hospital; University of London. *Career:* House Officer, King's College Hospital 1959; Hammersmith Hospital 1960. Flight Lieutenant, RAF Medical Branch 1960-63. MRC Junior Research Fellow, Registrar in Medicine, Lecturer in Medicine (all at Royal Free Hospital and Medical School, 1963-66); MRC Travelling Fellow, Harvard Medical School 1966-68; Senior Lecturer, Reader and Professor in Department of Medicine, RFHSM 1968-83; non-executive director, North Middlesex Hospital NHS Trust 1990- . *Publications:* Clinical Hepatology, 1991; Lipids and Lipoproteins in Clinical Practice, 1990; numerous papers on liver disease and medical education. *Recreation:* golf, photographing medical statues *Clubs:* Athenaeum *Address:* 20 Queenscourt, Wembley, Middx, HA9 7QU. University Dept of Medicine, Royal Free Hospital School of Medicine, London, NW3 2QG.

McKIBBIN, Professor Brian, MS, MD, FRCS(Eng). *Currently:* Professor of Traumatic and Orthopaedic Surgery, University of Wales College of Medicine; Honorary Consultant Surgeon South Glam A.H.A. *Born on* 9 Dec 1930 at Belfast. *Son of* the late William McKibbin and the late Elizabeth McKibbin (nee Wilson). *Marriage:* to Pamela Mary Pask, 1960. *Children:* Alexander John and Hugh James. *Educated at* Roundhay School, Leeds; Univ. Leeds; Univ. Oxford (University College). *Career:* former Senior Lecturer and Head of University Dept. of Orthopaedics, University of Sheffield. Appointments: Council member, Royal College of Surgeons of England; former President, British Orthopaedic Association; former President, Orthopaed Research Association; member, Standing Medical Advisory Committee, Dept. of Health *Publications:* various books and papers on Orthopaedic Surgery. *Recreation:* music, gardening. *Address:* The Orchard, Peterston-Super-Ely, Cardiff, CF5 6LH.

McLEOD - BAIKIE, Mr Ian, FRSM *Currently:* retired, 1984, Consultant Orthopaedic surgeon, Guilford & Epsom Grp Hospitals, etc. *Born on* 13 Dec 1921 at Edinburgh. *Son of* the late David Geo McLeod-Baikie and Winifred May. *Marriage:* to Dr. Sylvia Rosemary (nee Smith), 1949. *Educated at* Privately and Perth Academy; Glasgow University; Glasgow Royal Infirmary. *Career:* Hon Consultant Orthopaedic surgeon St. Anthonys Hospital. Member Medico-Legal Society; formerly Chairman Pembs Council for Protection of Rural Wales Coomb Cheshire Home. *Recreation:* gardening, sailing, history, music. *Clubs:* The Naval. *Address:* The Forge, Landshipping, Narberth, Pembs., SA67 8BG.

McLAREN (nee Paget), Lady Rose, *Currently:* retired. *Born on* 21 July 1919 at Anglesey. *Daughter of* Marquess and Marchioness of Anglesey. *Marriage:* to The Hon. John Mclaren, 1940. *Children:* Victoria Taylor and Harriet Geddes. *Educated at* mostly London and Ballet School. *Career:* Ballet Dancer, Sadlers' Wells and Florist, Flower Services London Ltd. *Recreation:* gardening, music, ballet. *Address:* Old Bodnod, Eglwysbach, Colwun Bay, North Wales, LL28 5RF.

MEARA, Dr Robert Harold, MA; MB; FRCP. *Currently:* retired, Emeritus Consultant, Middlesex Hospital, London; Hon.Senior Lecturer, Institute Dermatology, University of London. *Born on* 8 Dec 1917 at Abersychan. *Son of* the late Robert Meara and the late Anne (nee Davies). *Marriage:* to

Mair Jones, 1943. *Children:* Robert Jolyon, Jeniffer Anne and Jane Imogen. *Educated at* Jones' West Monmouth; Haberdashers School Pontypool; St.Catharines College Cambridge - Exhibitioner; University College Hospital Medical School, London. *Career:* Capt. RAMC 153 (Highland) Field Ambulance 1943-45; 15 Scottish Div. BAOR - Normandy to Lubeck, Germany; Consultant Dermatologist, Middlesex Hospital London 1955-83 and St.John's Hospital for Diseases of the Skin, London 1956-83; Dean, Institute Dermatology, Univ of London 1970-80; Honorary Consultant Dermatologist to British Army 1980-83; Hon.Dermatologist St.Lukes Hospital for Clergy 1956-86; Parkes-Weber Lecturer and Medal 1979, Royal College of Physicians. *Publications:* many publications on Dermatological subjects. *Recreation:* music, archaeology, Byzantime history, comparative religion, walking, travel. *Clubs:* Royal Society of Medicine, Wimpole St., W1. *Address:* 34 Channings Kingsway, Hove, East Sussex, BN3 4FT.

MEARS, The Right Reverend John Cledan, BA.Hons (2,I), Phil *Currently:* Bishop of Bangor, enthroned 1983. *Born on* 8 Sept 1922 at Ynyshir, Rhondda. *Son of* Joseph and Anna Lloyd Mears. *Marriage:* to Enid Margaret Williams 1949. *Children:* Wyn and Eleri. *Educated at* Ardwyn Grammar School, Aberystwyth; U.C.W. Aberystwyth & Wycliffe Hall, Oxford; Thomas Stephens and Gladstone research scholarships: UCW Aberystwyth 1945-46, S.Deiniol's Library, Hawarden 1946-47. M.A.(Wales) 1948-Blaise Pascal. *Career:* Curate - Mostyn 1947-49; Rhosllannerchrugog 1949-56; Vicar Cwm Dyserth 1956-59; Chaplain, St. Michael's College, Llandaff 1959-67; Sub warden 1967-73; Lecturer, University College Wales & Mon 1959-73; Readers' chaplain dioc. Llandaff 1962-71; Bp. of Llandaff Examining chaplain 1960-73; Vicar of Gabalfa, Cardiff 1973-82; Clerical Secretary of the Governing Body of the Church in Wales 1977-82; Hon. Canon of Llandaff Cathedral 1981; consecrated Bishop 1982. *Publications:* Y Cymun Bendigaid ac Offrwm Crist; Cais am athrawiaeth Cenhadaeth (Diwinyddiaeth); Gweddio dros y Meirw (Haul); Priodas ac Ysgariad (Efrydiau Athronyddol); Blaise Pascal (Barn); Gwasanaeth Bedydd Cyfamodol (Cristion). *Recreation:* Walking (mountains and long distance paths); music (choral & orchestral). *Address:* Ty'r Esgob, Bangor, Gwynedd, LL57 2SS.

MEARS, Mr Wyn, BA., MSc. *Currently:* Head of Corporate Affairs/Secretary Wales, BBC Wales. *Born on* 26 Dec 1950 at Rhos, Llannerchrugog, Clwyd. *Son of* John Cledan and Enid Margaret Mears. *Marriage:* to Ann Malvina Lloyd Lewis. *Children:* Rhodri, Catrin and Ceri *Educated at* Cathays High School for Boys; BA Hons Geography Univ. of London, MSc Tourism Univ. of Surrey. *Career:* Research Officer, Wales Tourist Board 1973-77; South Wales Tourism Manager, Wales Tourist Board 1977-84; UK Marketing Director, Wales Tourist Board 1984-91. *Recreation:* Golf, rugby, music, Welsh language education and other Welsh Community interests in Cardiff. *Address:* Room 3020, B.B.C. Wales Broadcasting House, Llandaff, Cardiff, CF5 2YQ.

MEEKE, Mr Ian Barrie, BSc.(Eng)., C.Eng., FICE., MConsE. *Currently:* Engineering Director of Wallace Evans Ltd., Engineering and Environment Consultants and Project Managers, formerly Snr Eng. Assoc., Partner, since 1970. *Born on* 8 July 1934 at Rushall, W.Mids. *Son of* Mr Henri & Mrs Evelyn Meeke of Handel Close, Penarth. *Marriage:* to Anne Mary Wakley, 1961. *Children:* Sarah, Katie and Daniel *Educated at* King Edward V1 School, Lichfield & Univ. of Southampton *Career:* Graduate Engineer with British Transport Docks Brd, 1957-59; Assist.Eng. with

Central Elec.Research Labs., 1959-63; Construction Eng. with Sydney Water Board, Australia, 1963-64; Snr Design Eng. with Geelong Harbour Trust, Victoria, Australia, 1964-66; Snr Eng. with Rendel Palmer & Tritton, London, 1966-70. *Publications:* Lecturing on Tourism and Waterside Dev., papers on Design of Ferry Terminals, Marinas and Barrages. *Recreation:* Family life, sailing, photography, restoration of canals, water transportation, ports and harbours and cottage restoration. *Clubs:* Inland Waterways Assoc., Dale Yacht Club, Flying Dutchman assoc. *Address:* Wallace Evans Ltd., Plymouth House, Plymouth Road, Penarth S.Glam., CF6 2YF.

MERCER, Professor Ian Dews, B.A. *Currently:* Chief Executive, Countryside Council for Wales. *Born on* 25 Jan 1933 at Wombourn. *Son of* Eric Baden Royds Mercer and Nellie Irene (nee Dews). *Marriage:* 1st to Valerie Jean Hodgson, d 1975; 2nd to Pamela Margaret Gillies Clarkson. *Children:* Jonathan, Ben, Tom and Dan from first marriage. *Educated at* King Edwards VI, Stourbridge; University of Birmingham. *Career:* Sub.Lt. RNR (National Service). Warden, Slapton Ley Field Centre 1959-68; Warden Malham Tarn Field Centre 1968-70; County Conservation Officer, Devon County Council 1970-73; Dartmoor National Park, Chief Officer 1973-90; President: Field Studies Council, Association Countryside Rangers, Devon Wildlife Trust; Governor Welsh Agricultural College. *Publications:* Nature Guide to South West England; Chapters in: Conservation in Practice 1973; Environmental Education 1974; National Parks in Britain 1987; Dartmoor Seasons 1987. *Recreation:* Landscape, birds, golf, watching sons play rugby, painting. *Address:* Victoria House, Llanddaniel, Ynys Mon, Gwynedd, LL60 6EB. Countryside Council For Wales, Plas Penrhos, Ffordd Penrhos, Bangor, Gwynedd., LL57 2LQ.

MERCER, Mr John Charles Kenneth, LL.B. *Currently:* Part-time Consultant, otherwise retired. *Born on* 19 Sept 1917 at Llanelli, Dyfed. *Son of* the late Charles Wilfrid Mercer and the late Cecil Maud Mercer. *Marriage:* to Barbara Joan, the elder daughter of the late A.S. Whitehead C.B., C.B.E., and the late Mrs E.M. Whitehead. *Children:* David Jeremy and Susan Jennifer. *Educated at* Ellesmere College and LL.B. London. *Career:* War Service - Rank Captain; Solicitor, Founder partner in the firm of Douglas-Jones & Mercer; Recorder of Crown Court, 1975-82; Member of the Royal Commission on Criminal Procedure, 1978-81; Member of River Authority for 15 years ending in 1974. *Recreation:* Fishing, Shooting, golf and sport generally. *Clubs:* Clyne Golf Club, Swansea; Swansea Amateur Anglers Assoc. Ltd., and White Springs Trout Fishing Club. *Address:* 334 Gower Road, Killay, Swansea, West Glam., SA2 7AW.

MEREDITH, David, *Currently:* Managing Director, David Meredith P.R., Penhill House, Penhill, Cardiff, formed on 1st October 1990, specialising in a personal service in Advertising, Public Relations and Design. David Meredith is the first company in this field to be based in North and South Wales. *Born on* 24 May 1941 at Aberystwyth, Dyfed. *Son of* the late Rev. J.E. Meredith, MA and Elizabeth Meredith BA. *Marriage:* to Luned Llywelyn Williams, 1967. *Children:* Owain Llywelyn, Elin Wynn and Gruffudd Seimon *Educated at* Ardwyn Grammar School, Aberystwyth; Bangor Normal College, University of Wales (Teaching Diploma). *Career:* Former Head of Press and Public Relations for HTV in Wales 1968-89. Former specialist teacher of Welsh, 1961-65. He joined The Wales Tourist Board in 1965, working in the five counties of mid Wales, later to become Advertising and Sales Executive for the Tourist Board, based in Cardiff. He was one of the founders and a former Director of Strata the Aberystwyth based public relations company and one of the founders and former Executive Director of Strata Matrix Advertising and Public Relations (Aberystwyth and Cardiff). At HTV he presented Pwy Fase'n Meddwl, a Quiz series, Gair o Wlad y Sais (for S4C) a series on well known literary figures of England, Thomas Hardy, George Borrow, John Bunyan, Emily Bronte, A.E.Houseman, William Wordsworth and Arlunwyr, an Art series on six well known current Welsh artists - a series shown later in English on HTV. He was the first person from Wales to present a television programme from inside the Sistine Chapel in Rome. He is a Fellow of the Public Relations Society of Wales (former chairman of the Society), a member of the Royal Welsh Show Publicity Cttee, member, Wales Cttee of Live Music Now, member, Welsh Cttee of ABSA (Business Sponsorship of the Arts), member, The National Eisteddfod of Wales Marketing Cttee. former member, Welsh Cttee of the Design Council and a member of the Publicity and Editorial Cttee of the Swansea Festival. *Publications:* written three books, on Michaelangelo, Rembrandt and a children's story book Congrinero (also published in Scottish Gaelic). *Address:* Ty'n Fedw, Llanuwchllyn, Bala, Gwynedd.   6 Fairleigh Road, Pontcanna, Cardiff.

METCALFE, Harold Arthur, DA (Leeds) ARIBA. *Currently:* retired from practice 30th April 1991. *Born on* 2 Jan 1926 at Yorks. *Son of* William and Marion Metcalfe. *Marriage:* to Margaret Doreen, 1953. *Educated at* Prince Henry's School, Otley; Dept of Architects, Leeds. *Career:* Architect: Building throughout U.K. In Wales, Tesco , Neath, Llanelli; BUPA Hospital Cardiff. Hotels: Inn on Avenue Cardiff; Stradey Park Hotel Llanelli; Ivy Bush Royal Carmarthen; Forge Hotel St. Clears; Fishguard Bay. Schools: Drefach Velindre; Llandovery and Llanelli. Library: Carmarthen. Prince of Wales Award 1991. Civic Society and Civic Trust Awards 1970, 1978, 1984, 1986 and 1989. *Recreation:* golf, swimming, painting. *Clubs:* Carmarthen Golf. *Address:* The Saltings, Llangain, Carmarthen, Dyfed.

MEYER, Sir Anthony, John Charles, Officer of the Legion'd', Honneur France *Currently:* Policy Director, European Movement, (British Section); Vice Chairman Franco- British Council (British Section);M.P. for Clwyd North West, 1983-92. *Born on* 27 Oct 1920 at London. *Son of* Sir Frank Cecil Meyer and Georgina Seeley. *Marriage:* to Barbadee Violet Knight. *Children:* Carolyn (Sands), Ashley, Tessa (Murdoch) and Sally(Vergette) *Educated at* Eton, Oxford New College. *Career:* Scots Guards, 1941-45; HM Foreign Service, 1945-62; (British Embassy Paris, 1951-56; Moscow, 1956-58) M.P. for Eton and Slough, 1963-64; M.P. for Flint West, 1970-83. *Publications:* 'Stand Up and Be Counted' (Heinemams, 1990) *Recreation:* Music, travel and ski-ing. *Clubs:* Beefsteak *Address:* 9 Cottage Place, London, SW3 Tel: 071 589 7416 Rhewl House, Axton, Llanasa, Holywell, Clwyd.

MEYRICK, Dr Roger Llewellyn, MBBS (Lond); FRCGP; JP. *Currently:* retired. *Born on* 31 March 1930 at London. *Son of* the late Thidal Francis and the late Helen (nee Jones). *Marriage:* to Barbara Treseder Coombs, 1954. *Children:* one s Huw, three d Olivia, Daryl and Clare. *Educated at* Dulwich College; King's College, London' K.C., Hospital (Lond). *Career:* Princ. General Medical Practice, Hospital Practitioner; Facilitator in G.P. Lewisham and N.Southwark; RCGP Chairman S.London Faculty; Provost S.London Fac; President West Kent Medico Chirurgical Society; Chairman, Magistrates Assoc., S.E.London; Freeman City of London, Liveryman Society of Apothecaries; Television & Radio Broadcaster BBC, ITV, local Radio (London). *Publications:*

Understanding Cancer (jointly); Principles of Practice Management Health Management; Patient Health Education; numerous articles in Medical & Health Journals. *Recreation:* Local history, gardening. *Clubs:* Royal Commonwealth Society *Address:* Boulters' Tor, Smeardon Down, Peter Tavy, Tavistock, Devon, PL19 9NX.

MILBURN, Mr Peter, *Currently:* Managing Director, Red Dragon Radio, Cardiff, since March 1991. *Born on* 28 Oct 1952 at Leeds, Yorkshire. *Son of* Edward Franklin and Joyce Milburn. *Marriage:* to Elizabeth, 1977 (dissolved 1986). *Children:* Benjamin Paul David (b.1981). *Educated at* Hanson Grammar School, Bradford, 1966-70. *Career:* Yorkshire Post, journalist 1970-75; Programme Controller, Pennine Radio, Bradford 1975-82; Presenter, Hereward Radio, Peterborough 1982-83; News Editor, Gwent Broadcasting 1983-85; Presenter, Programme Director, Red Dragon Radio 1985-91. *Recreation:* reading, travel, American politics. *Clubs:* Glamorgan C.C.C. *Address:* 6 Clwyd, Northcliffe, Penarth, S.Glamorgan, CF6 1DZ.Red Dragon Radio, West Canal Wharf, Cardiff, CF1 5XJ.

MILDRED, Mr Mark, BA(Cantab) *Currently:* Partner, Pannone Napier and Pannone March Pearson, Solicitors, since 1986. *Born on* 16 Sept 1948 at Chipperfield, Herts. *Son of* John Mildred, of Usk and the late Eileen Smith of Pontypool. *Marriage:* to Sarah Ruth Rackham, 1974. *Children:* Joe (b.1976) and Tom (b.1979). *Educated at* Lancing College; Clare College Cambridge. *Career:* Solicitor 1975; founder & partner Mildred and Beaumont Solicitors, London SW11, 1975-86. *Publications:* Group Actions, Learning from Opren 1988; Chapters in Butterworth's Medical Negligence Encyclopaedia 1990; Product Liability and Safety Encyclopaedia 1992; articles in New Law journal, New Society etc. *Recreation:* walking, singing, cooking, racquet games, politics. *Clubs:* Scorpions, Hawks, Battersea Labour. *Address:* Templar Cottage, Kemeys Commander, Usk, Gwent.

MILES, Alderman Dillwyn, FRGS *Currently:* Retired. *Born on* 25 May 1916 at Newport, Pembs. *Son of* Joshua Miles and Anne Mariah Miles (nee Lewis). *Marriage:* to the late Joyce Eileen Ord, Jerusalem 1944. *Children:* Anthony Ord and Marilyn Anne. *Educated at* Fishguard County School; University College of Wales, Aberystwyth. *Career:* Army Officer, Middle East, 1939-45; Nat Organiser, Palestine House, 1945; Extra-Mural Lec, Univ Of Wales, 1948; Community Centres Officer, Wales, 1951; Dir, Pembs Comm Council, 1954; Dir, Dyfed Rural Cncl, 1975-81; Mem, Pembs C.C., 1947-63; Mem, Cemaes R.D.C., 1947-52; Mem, Haverfordwest B.C., 1957-63; Mem, Pembs Coast Nat. Park Ctee., 1952-75; Mem, Exec.Ctee., CPRW, 1946-64; Mem, Nature Conservancy Ctee for Wales, 1966-73; Soc. for the Promotion of Nature Reserves, 1961-73; Countryside in 1970 Ctee for Wales, 1969-70; Prince of Wales Ctee, 1971-80; Sports Cncl for Wales, 1965-69; Mental Health Review Tribunal for Wales, 1959-71; Rent Tribunal for Wales, 1966-85; Pembs TA Assoc, 1956-59; Crt of Govnrs Univ of Wales, 1957-66; Crt of Govnrs Nat. Library of Wales, 1963-64; Cncl of Small Industries in Wales, 1968-72; Age Concern Wales, 1972-77; Exec ctee, Nat.Crícl of Soc Serv 1978-81; Exec.Ctee, Nat.Playing Fields Assn., 1977-81; Welsh Environment Foundation, 1971-80; Council, Royal Nat.Eisteddfod of Wales, 1957-; Brd of Gorsedd of Bards 1945; former chmn Further Educ Ctee, Pembroke C.C, Libraries & Museums Ctee, Pemb Jnr Chamber of Commerce, Pembs Cttee, Arthritis & Rheumatism Cncl; Pembs Commn Health Cncl, Pembs P.O. & Telecommnc Adv Ctee; Wales Playing Fields Assoc, Nat.Assoc of Local Cncls (now Vice-Pres); formerly: Hon Sec W.Wales Naturalists Assoc 1958-76;

Vice-Pres: Nat Assoc of Local Cncl, Dyfed Wildlife Trust; Mayor of Newport, Pembs: 1951, 66, 67, 79 & Alderman Mayor & Admiral of the Port of H'west 1961; Sheriff of Town & County of H'west 1963; Burgess Warden, Guild of Freemen of H'west 1974-; Grand Sword-bearer, Gorsedd of Bards 1959-66, Herald Bard 1966. *Publications:* Sheriffs of the County of Pembroke, 1974; The Royal National Eisteddfod of Wales, 1978; A Pembrokeshire Anthology, 1983; Portrait of Pembrokshire, 1984; The Pembrokeshire Coast National Park, 1987; and various pamphlets, articles etc. *Recreation:* Wildlife, Food and Wine. *Clubs:* Savile *Address:* Hendre, 9 St Anthony's Way, Haverfordwest, Pembs., SA61 1EL. Tel: 0437 765275.

MILES, Dame Margaret, DBE(1970). *Born on* 11 July 1911. *Daughter of* Rev E G Miles and Annie (nee Jones). *Educated at* Ipswich High School; Bedford Coll Univ of London (BA). *Career:* History teacher Westcliff High School 1935-39; Badminton School 1939-44; lecturer Dept of Educ Univ of Bristol 1944-46, Headmistress Pate's Grammar School Cheltenham 1946-52, headmistress Mayfield School Putney 1952-73; member Schools Broadcasting Council 1958-68, Educ Advisory Council ITA 1962-67, Nat Advisory Council on Trg and Supply of Teachers 1962-65, BBC Gen Advsy Council 1964-73, Campaign for Comprehensive Education 1966 (Chairman 1972, Pres 1979-) RSA, Council 1972-77; Chairman Central Bureau for Educational Visits and Exchanges 1978-82, Advisory Committee on Devpt Education ODM 1977-79; pres Br Assoc for Counselling 1980-; fell Bedford Coll 1983; Hon DCL Univ of Kent at Canterbury 1973; fell King's Coll London 1985. *Publications:* And Gladly Teach, 1965; Comprehensive Schooling, Problems and Perspectives, 1968. *Recreation:* opera, films, gardening, golf. *Clubs:* Univ Women's, Aberdovery Golf. *Address:* Tanycraig, Pennal, Machynlleth, Powys.

MILLWATER, Dennis Curtis, *Born on* 31 March 1934 *Son of* the late William Milson Millwater, of Rogerstone, Gwent and the late Kathleen Irene Millwater. *Marriage:* to Marlene Beatrice, 1957, da of Kenneth Collins, of Cliffs End, Ramsgate. *Children:* Christopher (b.1961), Grahame (b.1963), Jonathan (b.1967, d 1989) and Sara (b.1977). *Educated at* Bassaleg GS, Gwent; Univ of Bristol. *Career:* pensions superintendent Northern Assurance Co Ltd 1957-68, pensions controller Commercial Union Group 1968-69, director De Falbe Halsey Ltd 1969-71; group director H Clarkson (Insurance Holdings) Ltd 1971-81, Clarkson Puckle Group Ltd 1981-87, Bain Clarkson Ltd 1987; Chairman and Chief Exec Bain Clarkson Financial Services Ltd 1987-. gen cmmr of taxes; FPMI, ACII. *Recreation:* golf, music, cycling. *Clubs:* Royal St Georges Golf (Sandwich). *Address:* The Shieling, 32 Harkness Drive, Canterbury, Kent, CT2 7RW. Bain Dawes House, 15 Minories, London, EC3 Tel: 071 481 3232.

MOLLOY, The Rt Hon Lord William John, FRGS, FWASc *Currently:* ed. St Thomas's Council School., Swansea and Swansea College, University of Wales. *Born on* 26 Oct 1918 at Swansea. *Son of* Will Molloy and Annie Thomas. *Marriage:* to Eva Mary, 1945, da of Henry Lewis. *Children:* one d *Career:* TA served Field Company Royal Engineers 1939-46; Foreign Office, Whitley Council Departmental Staff-Side Chairman 1946-52; Trade Union Lecturer, Former Editor Civil Service Review; Leader Fulham Boro' Council 1956-66; MP (Lab) Ealing North 1964-79; Vice-Chairman and Founder Parl. Labour Party European Affairs Group. member Commons Estimates Committee 1968-70. PPS to PMG & Post & Telecommunications 1968-70. Member Assemblies Council of Europe (Chairman Health Services Ctee) and Western

European Union 1969-73. member European Parliament 1975-78. Pres. London Univ Society. President Stirling University Debating Society; Member Court of Reading University. Pres Metropolitan Area Royal British Legion. Member Exec Ctee IPU. member CPA. Education Lecturer COHSE and Parliamentary Adviser to COHSE. Vice Pres Health Assn 1984- . Vice-Pres. Greenford Branch Royal British Legion. Chairman, British/Tunisian Society; Chairman, British/Tunisian All Party Parliamentary Group; Fellow of the Royal Geographical Society. Fellow World Assn Arts and Sciences (elected 1985). Elected to RGS Council 1981. Vice Pres and Trustee Health Visitors Assoc 1985. Hon Fellow Univ Wales, Swansea College 1986. Hon Associate British Vetinerary Assoc 1988. Labour. Special Interest: NHS, Foreign and Commonwealth Affairs, Commerce, Industry. Raised to the peerage as Baron Molloy, of Ealing in Greater London 1981. *Recreation:* music, collecting diaries, horse-riding. *Clubs:* Victoria Westminster *Address:* 2a Uneeda Drive, Greenford, Middlesex, UB6 8QB. The House Of Lords, Westminster, London, SW1A OPW.

MOORE, Mr George, Dpl.Econ., MIMC., FBIM *Currently:* Chairman Grayne Marketing Co.Ltd. *Born on* 7 Oct 1923 at Glasgow. *Son of* G. Moore and N.B. Moore. *Marriage:* at Gilwern, 1945. *Children:* George, John and Thomas. *Educated at* Coatbridge Grammar School; Univ. Coll., Cardiff; Hull Univ. *Career:* Chartered Engineer, Anglo Iranian Oil Co., Abadam, Iran; Chief Electrical Engineer, Distillers Co., Chemical Div., Hull; Management Consultant, Main Assignment-Construction Llanwern Steel Works, (Also Ebbw Vale Steels); Development Director, Burton Group; Chief Executive, Spear & Jackson IN. Ltd., (Director severl overseas subsidiaries); Regional Director, Dept.of Ind., North West (Under Sec.); Chairman, Grayne Marketing Co.Ltd; Director, Cordel Corp.Dev., Ltd. *Recreation:* Sailing, golf, walking, gardening and writing *Clubs:* Reform Club *Address:* Leasgill House, Leasgill, near Milnthorpe, Cumbria., LA7 7ET.

MORETON, Mr Anthony John, MA(Oxon); BSc (Econ:Lond). *Currently:* Welsh Correspondent, Financial Times. *Born on* 8 July 1930 at Cardiff. *Son of* the late William and the late Clara Moreton (nee Jenkins). *Marriage:* to Ena Kendall, 1967. *Educated at* Penarth County School; Cardiff Technical College (now University of Wales College of Cardiff); Ruskin College, Oxford; Exeter College, Oxford. *Career:* Journalist, Financial Times 1963-, successively Home News Editor; Leader writer Western Mail 1956-58; emp.features sub-ed New Chronicle 1958-60; Daily Telegraph 1960-63, regional affairs editor; Commissioned in RAF on National Service 1954-56 Chairman of the Board, Welsh Economic Review 1991-; Councillor, London Borough of Wandsworth 1962-65 (chairman Libraries Cttee); Councillor, London Borough of Lambeth 1965-68 (chairman Finance and General Purposes Cttee); Chairman Lambeth Arts and Recreations Assoc., (LARA) 1966-72; Churchwarden and Treasurer, Holy Trinity, Clapham Common, London 1962-74; St.Gwynno's, Merthyr Tydfil 1985-90; Freeman, Worshipful Company of Glovers 1985- *Publications:* Articles in various magazines. *Recreation:* gardening, golf, cooking, wine. *Clubs:* Cardiff and County, Aberdare Golf. *Address:* Pandy Farm, Merthyr Tydfil, CF47 8PA. Tel: 0685 723003.

MORGAN, Mr (William) Geraint (Oliver), BA., LL.B. *Currently:* Now retired, save for occasional sittings as a Crown Court Recorder. *Born on* 2 Nov 1920 at Llanfihangel-Aberbythich, Llandeilo, Dyfed. *Son of* Morgan and Elizabeth Morgan (nee Oliver). *Marriage:* to J.S.M. Maxwell, 1957. *Children:* Frances, Bronwen, Owen and Llewelyn. *Educated* *at* U.C.W., Aberystwyth; Cambridge and London Universities and Gray's Inn, London. *Career:* Served in World War II in Royal Marines, demobilised as Major, 1946; Called to the Bar in 1947; Q.C., 1971; Recorder of the Crown Court, 1972; M.P. (Cons) for former Denbigh Division, 1959-83 (Left Conservative party in 1983), Chairman, Welsh Parliamentary Party, 1966-67; Member of Investiture Committee of H.R.H. The Prince of Wales, 1968-69; Member of Gorsedd of Royal National Eisteddfod of Wales, 1969; Member of Payne Committee on Recovery of Judgement Debts, 1965-69; Fellow of Institute of Arbitrators, 1986-87. *Recreation:* Reading and study of Celtic languages. *Address:* 13 Owen Road, Prescot, Merseyside. L35 OPJ.

MORGAN, Andrew Vladimir Rhydwen, *Currently:* Freelance Film and Television Director. *Born on* 20 Oct 1942 at Burnham-on-Sea. *Son of* Judge P.Hopkin Morgan and Josephine (nee Travers). *Marriage:* to Jacqueline (nee Webb) 1967. *Children:* Nicholas Hopkin and Zoe Olivia Lucy. *Educated at* Ysgol Abermad, Aberystwyth; Harrow School. *Career:* R.A.D.A.; Theatre Royal, York; BBC TV, Production Manager. *Recreation:* Inland waterways, rugby football, arts. *Clubs:* B.A.F.T.A. *Address:* 28 Wyndham St, London, W1H 1DD.

MORGAN, Reverend Chandros Clifford Hastings Mansel, CB, MA, RN. *Currently:* retired, 1989. *Born on* 12 Aug 1920 at Dublin, Eire. *Son of* Llewelyn Morgan and Elinor Clifford. *Marriage:* to Dorothy Mary (nee Oliver), 1946. *Children:* Evelyn Arden Chandros Mansel. *Educated at* Stowe School; Jesus College Cambridge; Ridley Hall Cambridge. *Career:* ordained 1944 to Holy Trinity Church, Tonbridge Wells 1944-47; Staff of Children's Special Service Mission 1947-51; Chaplain Royal Navy 1951-75; Archdeacon of The Royal Navy and Chaplain of the Fleet 1972-75; Q.A.C., 1972. C.B. 1973; Chaplain Dean Close School, Cheltenham 1976-78; Rector St.Margaret's Lothbury EC1 7HH, London. Chaplain to The Lord Major 1988-89. *Recreation:* riding, gardening, sailing. *Address:* Westwood Farmhouse, West Lydford, Somerton, Somerset, TAA11 7DL.

MORGAN, Mr Clifford Isaac, CVO, 1987; OBE, 1978. *Currently:* Freelance broadcaster. *Born on* 7 April 1930 at Trebanog, Rhondda. *Son of* Clifford Morgan and Edna May Morgan. *Marriage:* to Nuala Martin, 1955. *Children:* Nicholas Hywel Morgan and Catherine Jane Morgan. *Educated at* Tonyrefail Grammar School, 1942-49. *Career:* Rugby: Cardiff, Bective Rangers, Wales, British Lions, Barbarians, 1950-59; Broadcasting: Sports Organiser, BBC Wales, 1959-61; Editor "Sportsview" and "Grandstand", 1961-64; Editor, 'This Week', 1964-66; Head of Radio, sport and outside broadcast, 1973-76; Head of BBC TV Outside Broadcast, 1976-87; President, Welsh Sports Association for People with Mental Handicap, 1990- ; President, Wales Association for Disabled, 1989- ; Vice President, National Childrens Home, 1981- ; President, London Welsh Male Choir, 1990; President, London Glamorgan Society 1978- ; Hon. Doctorate of University of Keele, 1988; Hon. M.A. University of Wales, 1988; Hon. Fellowship, Polytechnic of Wales, 1989. *Recreation:* music, sport, sport for the disabled. *Clubs:* East India, London; Saints & Sinners, London. *Address:* 34 Kensington Mansions, Trebovir Road, London, SW5 9TQ.

MORGAN, His Honour Judge David Glyn, M.A. *Currently:* One of H.M.'s Circuit Judges, 1984- . *Born on* 31 March 1933 at Newport, Mon. *Son of* the late Dr. Glyn Morgan, MC and the late Nancy Morgan (nee Griffiths). *Marriage:* to Ailsa Murray Strang. *Children:* Sian, Catherine and Sara Elen Morgan. *Educated at* Newport High School; Mill Hill School; Merton College, Oxford. *Career:* Commissioned The Queen's Bays (2nd Dragoon Guards) 1955; Called to Bar (Middle Temple) 1958; Practised Oxford Circuit 1958-70; Wales and Chester Circuit 1970-84; Assist. Recorder City of Cardiff 1971; Recorder of the Crown Court 1974; Assist. Commissioner Local Government Boundary Commission for Wales 1976; Deputy Colonel 1st The Queen's Dragoon Guards 1976; Assist. Commissioner Parliamentary Boundary Commission for Wales 1983, (Gwent & Powys) and for Review of European Assembly Constituencies; An Hon. Pres. Royal National Eisteddfod (Casnewydd) 1988; County Court Judge, Newport & Gwent 1988; Designated Judge (Gwent) - Children and Family 1991. *Recreation:* Fishing, rugby football, gardening and opera. *Clubs:* Cavalry & Guards; Cardiff & County; Newport & County *Address:* C/o 30 Park Place, Cardiff. CF1 3BA.

MORGAN, Mr David Llewellyn, *Currently:* Partner, Richards Butler since 1965; non-executive chairman, since 1977, Deymel Investments Ltd. (holding company of David Morgan Ltd., Cardiff); Mem: Company Law sub-committee, City of London Law Society. *Born on* 5 Oct 1932 at Llandaff, Cardiff. *Eldest Son of* the late David Bernard Morgan and of Eleanor Mary (nee Walker). *Educated at* Charterhouse; Trinity College, Cambridge (MA). *Career:* Admitted Solicitor 1959; Assistant Solicitor Richards Butler 1959-63, Herbert Smith 1963-65; Director Deymel Investments Ltd., 1966- ; Liveryman, Worshipful Company of Clockmakers. *Publications:* contributions to the Journal of Business Law. *Recreation:* DIY in house and garden. *Clubs:* Travellers', United Oxford and Cambridge University, City University, Cardiff and County. *Address:* Flat 15, 52 Pont Street, London, SW1X OAE.

MORGAN, Professor David Rhys, MA(Oxon); PhD(Cantab); FRHist.S. *Currently:* Professor of Politics and Communication Studies and Director of The Centre for Media and Communication Studies Liverpool University 1965-91. *Born on* 22 May 1937 at Ammanford. *Son of* Philip Haydn Percival Morgan and Annie Irene Morgan. *Marriage:* to Sally May Lewis, 1963, of Binghamton, N.York. *Children:* Christopher (b.1968), Timothy (b.1970) and Sian (b.1973). *Educated at* Queen Elizabeth Grammar School, Carmarthen 1948-55; Jesus College, Oxford 1957-60; Emmanuel Coll., Cambridge 1961-65. *Career:* Visiting Professor, State University of N.York, Albany, NY 1974-75 and George Washington University, Washington DC 1980-81; Lecturer 1965-73; Senior Lecturer 1973-87; Reader 1987; Professor 1990, Liverpool University. Currently - Dean of Faculty of Social and Environmental Studies 1988- . *Publications:* Books: Suffragists and Democrats 1972; City Politics and The Press (with Harvey Cox) 1973; The Capitol Press Corps 1978; The Flacks of Washington 1986. *Recreation:* walking, travel, musical appreciation. *Address:* University Of Liverpool Centre, For Media And Public Commnctn, Roxby Bldg, The University, P.O. Box 137, Liverpool., L69 3BX.The Cottage, 54 Ashfield Road, Liverpool, L69 3BX.

MORGAN, Colonel David Richard, OBE, TD, DL. *Currently:* retired. *Born on* 27 Aug 1921 at Clyne, Vale of Neath. *Son of* the late Samuel Morgan and the late Elizabeth Morgan (nee Roberts). *Marriage:* to Gaynor Morgan (nee Roberts) (decd 1991). *Children:* Sian Morgan Hall (Mrs), Huw Morgan (Major) and John Morgan. *Educated at* Clyne School; Neath Technical; St.Luke's, Exeter University. *Career:* RAF 1941; Army, Royal Artillery 1942; Royal Welch Fusiliers; South Wales Borderers, Middle East, Palestine, Cyprus; Welch Regiment 4th Bn TA, King's Regiment, TA; School Master, Merchant Taylors' School,

Crosby; Commanding Officer, University of Liverpool Officers' Training Corps; Hon.Colonel Merseyside ACF 1979-86; Chairman ACF Sport and PA Committee 1981-86; Councillor, King's Regt; Chairman Army Benevolent Fund, Merseyside; Member, Military Education Committee, University of Liverpool; President, Old Comrades Royal Regt of Wales, Deeside and Merseyside Branch; High Sheriff of Merseyside 1989-90; President, Merchant Taylors' School Old Boys' Association 1992. *Recreation:* Rugby Football, music, tree husbandry *Clubs:* Waterloo, Artists (Liverpool). *Address:* 28 Hastings Road, Birkdale, Southport, PR8 2LW.

MORGAN, Professor David Vernon, BSc, PhD, DSc. *Currently:* Professor of Electronic Engineering, University of Wales, Cardiff. *Born on* 13 July 1941 at Llanelli. *Son of* David Grenville and Isobel Lovinia. *Marriage:* to Jean Morgan. *Children:* Suzanne Lisa and Grenville Dyfrig. *Educated at* Llanelli Boys Grammar School; University of Wales Aberystwyth; Gonville Caius College Cambridge. *Career:* Cavendish Laboratory Univ Cambridge, Fellow 1960-68; Atomic Energy Laboratory Harwell 1968-70; University of Leeds: Lecturer 1970-77, Senior Lecturer 1977-80, Reader 1980-84; Visiting Professor Cornell University 1978, 79 and 80. *Publications:* 18 books and 175 journal papers. *Recreation:* golf, walking. *Address:* University of Wales College of Cardiff, Cardiff.

MORGAN, Denys Malcolm, MSc, BEng, CEng, Dip.TP, FICE, FIHT, MBIM. *Currently:* Director of Environment and Highways, West Glamorgan County Council since 1991. *Born on* 18 March 1945. *Son of* Alfred John and Florence. *Marriage:* to Marilyn Joyce (nee Pearson), Walsall 1967. *Children:* Richard and Peter *Educated at* West Derby High School, Liverpool; Liverpool University; Bradford University. *Career:* Engineer with West Riding CC 1966-68; N.E.Road Construction Unit 1968-71; M62 Contracts 1971-73; South Yorkshire CC Traffic 1973-86; Sheffield City Traffic 1986-87; West Glamorgan CC Deputy C.Engineer 1987-91. *Recreation:* sailing, swimming, travel, walking, gardening. *Address:* County Hall, Oystermouth Road, Swansea, SA1 3JN.

MORGAN, Derek William Charles, B.A., F.I.M.C., F.B.I.M. *Currently:* Chairman, Abtrust Preferred Income Investment Trust PLC 1991-; Chairman, Ogwr Partnership Trust and Taff Ely Enterprise Partnership 1988-; Chairman Mid Glamorgan Education Business Partnership 1989-; Chairman t.Davids Hall Trust 1990-; Chairman RSNC Welsh Wildlife Trust 1989-; Vice Chairman Mid Glamorgan Health Authority 1990-; President Cardiff Chamber of Commerce and Industry 1990-91; Director, Mid Glamorgan Training and Enterprise Council 1989-; Director, Morganite Electrical Carbon Ltd 1981-; Director, Moulded Foams (Wales) Ltd 1991-; Member British Telecom Advisory Forum for Wales 1991-; Member Business in the Community Board for Wales 1991-; Member Welsh Office Higher Education Standing Working Group 1990-; Member CBI Wales Regional Council 1987-; Member of Institute of Welsh Affairs Council 1989-; Member of Council, University of Wales Swansea 1990-; High Sheriff of Mid Glamorgan 1988-89. *Born on* 28 Nov 1934 at Bargoed. *Son of* Thomas Brinley Morgan and Brenda Vanessa (nee Megraw). *Marriage:* to Anne Yvette Davies, 1963. *Children:* Two daughters Sian Elizabeth and Louise Rhiannon. *Educated at* Neath Grammar School; University of Nottingham. *Career:* Littlewoods Ltd 1958-62; Ilford Ltd 1961-67; Director P.A. Consulting Group 1967-90. *Recreation:* walking dogs, reading, seeking perfection in others. *Clubs:* Cardiff & County *Address:* Erw Graig, Merthyr Mawr, Bridgend, Mid Glam, CF32 ONU.

MORGAN, Rev. Prebendary Dewi Lewis, B.A. *Currently:* Retired. *Born on* 5 Feb. 1916 at Pengam, Mon. *Son of* David and Anne Morgan. *Marriage:* to Doris Povey. *Children:* Norna Ann Moses and Betty Nixon. *Educated at* University College, Cardiff; St. Michaels College, Llandaff. *Career:* Ordained in 1939, served in parishes in Cardiff, Aberdare and Aberavon; in 1947 he began writing; Moved to London as Press Officer of the Society for the Propagation of the Gospel, England's oldest missionary sending society, 1950; Society's Editorial and Press Secretary, 1952; Chaplain of the Guild of St. Bride, Fleet Street, 1953; Rector of St. Bride's Church 1962; On the site of this church can be seen remains of a Roman building, some 1800 years old, together with the remains of seven previous churches, the first belonging to the sixth century. When St. Bride's had already been a parish church for about 1,000 years, in the year 1500, Wynkyn de Worde brought Caxton's press from Westminster Abbey precincts to alongside St. Bride's churchyard. Consequently for nearly five centuries St. Bride's has had a unique link with printers, journalists and all the ancillary activities of the Press; Honorary Chaplain of many Fleet Street institutions such as the Press Club, the Inst. of Journalists, the British Fed. of Master Printers, the Nat. Advertising Benevolent Society, the Printers' Pensions Corp., the Publicity Club of London; For some 20 years was the U.K. Correspondent of Church papers in the United States, Canada and Australia; Travelled in the United States, Canada, Germany, Switzerland and Holland (lecturing and preaching) and Algeria, Iran, Korea and India (making documentary films and writing a book on refugees) Led several pilgrimages to the Holy Land; Became a Prebendary of St. Paul's Cathedral in 1976; Has broadcast and appeared on television. *Publications:* The author of a number of books and has contributed to periodicals in most English-speaking countries; Has been editor of periodicals including St. Martin-in-the-Fields Review; Edited the Quarterly Intercession Paper for over 20 years. *Recreation:* Travel. *Clubs:* Athenaeum. *Address:* 217 Rosendale Road, West Dulwich, London SE21 8LW.

MORGAN, Elizabeth Mary (Betty), *Currently:* Administrative Officer, Powys County Council, Estates Department. *Born on* 5 Sept 1942 at Brecon. *Daughter of* Margaret (nee Prothero) and Albert Bowen. *Marriage:* to Russell Morgan, Llanhamlach Church, 1962. *Children:* one daughter, Janine, two grandchildren, (Donna and Adam). *Educated at* Mount Street Primary; Brecon Girls Grammar. *Career:* Outdoor Achievements: in bowls (club and open tournaments not included), represented Wales: in World Bowls Series 1981, 85, 92. In Home Internationals 42 Games, won British Isles Fours 1978 and British Isles Triples 1990. Won National 2 wood singles 1978, 83, 86, 88, 89. 4 wood singles 1984, 86, 91, Pairs 1980. Triples 1989, Fours 1977, 83, Mixed pairs 1991. Mid Wales County results are: 2 wood singles 1974, 79, 81, 89, 91. 4 wood singles 1985, 87, 89, 91. Pairs 1981, 85, 86. 2 wood triples 1979, 81. 3 wood triples 1977, 78. fours 1985, 88, 89. Victrix Ludorum 1979, 81, 85, 86, 87, 88, 89, 91. Qualified Coach and Umpire and was Mid Wales President 1984. She is at present Secretary of Radnorshire Indoor Ladies Bowls Club, and sits on a further 4 local bowls committees. Past Captain and President of Ladies Outdoor Club. *Recreation: Clubs:* Llandrindod Wells Ladies Outdoor; Radnorshire Ladies Indoor. *Address:* 24 Pentrosfa Road, Llandrindod Wells, Powys, LD1 5NL.

MORGAN, Rev. Enid Morris (nee Roberts), MA(Oxon), BD. MA(Wales). *Currently:* Deacon in Charge of the Parishes of Llanafan y Trawsgoed and Gwnnws With Llanfihangel y Creuddyn and Ysbyty Ystwyth. *Born on* 9

Aug 1940 at Gorseinon. *Daughter of* Bryn Roberts and Irene (nee Morris). *Marriage:* to Gerald Rees Morgan, 1963. *Children:* Rhys, Geraint and Deiniol. *Educated at* Amman Valley Grammar School; St.Anne's College, Oxford; University College of North Wales, Bangor; United Theological. *Career:* Editorial staff, Western Mail 1961-62; Assistant at Welsh Books Council and Editor 'Llais Llyfrau', 1963-65; Councillor, Anglesey County Council 1969-73; Editor 'Y Llan' 1971-78; Reader, Diocese of St.David's 1974; Ordained Deacon 1984. *Publications:* "Emrys ap Iwan, Garddwr Geriau", 1973; Cyfoeth o'i Drysor, Casgliad o Weddiau (Gol), 1992. *Recreation:* Reading, music, craftwork, golf. *Address:* Y Ficerdy, Llanafan, Aberystwyth, Dyfed, SY23 4AX.

MORGAN, Mrs Fay, M.Des. RCA. *Currently:* Partner: Roger Oates Design Associates, since 1987. Production of Rugs, Carpets and other textiles and Design Consultancy. feature in the most prestigious interiors and design collections. Morgan & Oates Ltd., since 1986, company for design and manufacture of Interior and Fashion textiles, design for own label and clients i.e. Ralph Lauren, Christian Dior, Sonia Rykiel, Donna Karen, Laura Ashley. Presently a design consultant to the company. *Born on* 18 Dec 1946 at Fishguard, Dyfed. *Daughter of* Philip Hugh Morgan, of Goodwick Dyfed and Iris Friend (nee John). *Marriage:* to Roger Kendrew Oates, 1976. *Children:* Daniel Morgan Oates (b.1979). *Educated at* Bishopswood Secondary School; Hornsey College of Art, DipAD; Royal College of Art, M.Des.RCA. *Career:* Own studio in London for designing for the UK textile industry and hand woven textiles 1970-75; Director of Weavers Workshop, Edinburgh; Part time lecturer at Goldsmiths College, London 1975-79; Morgan Oates partnership with Roger Oates at The House in the Yard, Ledbury. Hand weaving studio, ranges of rugs and other textiles for UK and export 1975-86. Awards: Welsh Arts Council Bursary, to study production of hand & power woven textiles as related to a studio set up, 1975, USA Roscoe. Award for Diagonal Twill woven rugs 1984, British Design Award for Abstract/Fragments. Two tufted rug collections. Duke of Edinburgh's Certificate for services to design, 1988, British Design Award for Bordered Worsted, a collection of Throws for Morgan & Oates Ltd., 1988. TV: The Craft of the Weaver, 1981, The Clothes Show, finalist for BBC-TV Clothes Show Nomination, for Morgan & Oates Ltd., 1991. Main Exhibitions at: The Craftsmans Art, V & A Museum London 1973; The House in the Yard, Textiles from the Workshop of Fay Morgan & Roger Oates Welsh Arts Council Cardiff and tour 1978; Tufted Rugs, Environment London 1980; Texstyles, Crafts Council London and tour 1984-85; The Scarf Show, Liberty London 1987; Design Awards, Lloyds Building London 1988. *Publications:* Book: Clothes Without Patterns, 1977. *Address:* Church Lane, Ledbury, Herefordshire, HR8 1DW.

MORGAN, Mr Frank Leslie, CBE., BA.Hons (Econ) *Currently:* Joined family business 1956 - Morgan Bros (Mid Wales) Ltd at Llanfair Caereinion, now Chairman and Managing Director. *Born on* 7 Nov 1926 at Llanfair Caereinon, Mongomeryshire. *Son of* Mr E A Morgan and Mrs B Morgan. *Marriage:* to Victoria S. Morgan (nee Jeffery) 1962. *Children:* Amanada, Penelope and Christopher. *Educated at* Llanfair Primary; Llanfair High; UCW Aberystwyth. *Career:* Royal Army Ordnance Corps 1945-48; (and reserve until 1959) rank Captain; Chairman Warwick & Leamington Young Conservatives 1952-56; adopted Conservative Parliamentary Candidate for Montgomery Constituency and fought the 1959 General Election; Chairman, Mongomery Conservative Assoc.

1964-74; President, Mongomery Sonservative Assoc. 1974-80; Elected President, Mongomery Conservative Assoc. 1989; Mbr of Welsh Council 1970-79; Chairman, Welsh Council Infrastructure Commt 1976-79; Deputy Chairman Mid Wales new town development corp. 1973-77; Mbr Develop. Brd for Rural Wales (Mid Wales Dev) and Chairman of Newtown Commt. 1977-81; Chairman Mid Wales Dev. 1981-89; Mbr of Brd Welsh Dev. Agency 1981-89, Wales Toursit Brd 1982-89; Mbr Brtsh Tourist Auth. Dev.Commt 1982-89; Director Abbey National plc 1983-90; Awarded MBE for Public Service in Wales 1973; Awarded CBE in 1987 *Recreation:* Reading, travel jogging, cycling and swimming. *Address:* Wentworth House, Llangyniew, Welshpool, Powys, SY21 9EL.

MORGAN, Mr Gareth, *Currently:* Senior Partner, Milwyn Jenkins & Jenkins, Solicitors, Llanidloes, Newtown and Welshpool; President Rent Assessment Panel for Wales. *Born on* 9 Oct 1935 at Llandovery. *Son of* David and Leta Morgan (nee Jenkins). *Marriage:* to Gwen Helen Delves 1962. *Children:* Alison Anne (b.1965), David Gareth (b.1967) and Richard Huw (b.1972). *Educated at* Llandovery College; University of Wales, Aberystwyth. *Career:* Sometime Chairman, Welsh Liberty Party; Elected member Powys County Council, presently Vice Chairman Powys Education Committee; Chairman, Community Recreation and Leisure Committee; Sometime Member, Welsh Committee of Independent Broadcasting Authority. *Recreation:* Opera, reading, walking. *Clubs:* National Liberal. *Address:* Dolhafren, Llanidloes, Powys, SY18 6HZ. Mid Wales House, Great Oak Street, Llanidloes, Powys, SY18 6BN.

MORGAN, Mr Gerwyn John David, JP; BA. *Currently:* County Information Officer, Dyfed County Council. *Born* in Wales. *Marriage:* to Ann Eleri Morgan (nee Lloyd). *Children:* Rhodri Llwyd Morgan *Educated at* Llandysul G.S; Univ. of Reading; Univ. of N.Wales, Bangor. *Career:* Teacher, Cardiff 1961-64; Assistant Independent Broadcasting Authority, Officer for Wales, 1964-70; Public Relations Officer, IBA, London, 1970-73; Publicity Director, Development Corporation for Wales, 1973-74; Chairman D.C. Ceredigion Branch; Member of Dyfed Magistrates Courts Cttee; Represent Dyfed on Central Council of Magistrates County Cttee. *Publications:* Editor, 'Dyfed News' tabloid, Dyfed Handbook. *Recreation:* Golf, ski-ing, photography. *Address:* Muriau Gwyn, Beulah, Newcastle Emlyn, Dyfed, SA38 9QE.

MORGAN, Mr Handel Mason, MBE 1984/85 *Currently:* Retired. *Born on* 16 Feb 1922 at Cwmsymlog, Cardiganshire. *Son of* Morgan R. Morgan and Anne Maria Morgan (nee Mason). *Marriage:* to May (nee Thomas). *Children:* Gareth. *Educated at* Mountain Ash County School; Treforest School of Mines; Bangor Normal College. *Career:* Headteacher, Llanddona C.P.Sch., 1954-62; Rhosneigr CP.Sch., 1962-71; Llangefni CPS., 1972-84; Mbr. of Llangefni Town Council, Isle of Anglesey Borough Council and Gwynedd County Council; Llangefni Town Mayor, 1978-79; Chrmn.Gwynedd Educ. Commt; Deacon, Paran MC, Rhosneigr and Moriah MC, Llangefni; Mbr.Cor y Traeth and Lleisiau'r Frogwy; Sec. Anglesey & Gwynedd NUT Assoc., 1966-84; Mbr.Court and Council Nat. Eisteddfod, Wales; Gorsedd y Beirdd Board; Welsh Joint Educ.Commt; Court and Council, Univ. of Wales; Univ. Coll. North Wales; Univ. Coll. Aberystwyth; National Library, Wales; Court of Welsh Books Council; Court of Wales Nat. Museum; Chrmn Governing Bodies, Ysgol Corn Hir; Ysgol Y Graig; Ysgol Y Bont; Ysgol Gyfun, Llangefni; Mbr. Governing Body Coleg Pencraig, Llangefni; War Service 1941-47, Captain R.E. *Recreation:* Church, music, social activities and Eisteddfodau. *Clubs:* Llangefni & Dist., Probus Anglesey Antiquarian Soc., various choral and eisteddfodic activities. *Address:* Gogerddan, Lon Tudur, Llangefni, Ynys Mon, Gwynedd, LL77 7HP.

MORGAN, Mr Howard John, JP., BA., BSc. *Currently:* Farmer, (Company Director). *Born* at Swansea. *Son of* the late Griffith John and Ivy M. (nee Morgan). *Educated at* Gowerton Boy's Grammar; Reading Univ; Open University *Career:* Gower RDC Councillor 1970; Swansea City 1974- ; West Glam. County 1989- ; General Commissioner Inland Revenue 1971- ; Justice of the Peace 1975- ; Member IBA Welsh advisory Committee 1978-89; West Glam Probation Committee 1984- ; Director Welsh National Opera Co., 1990- ; Welsh Art Council Art Advisory Committee 1990- ; Ch Gower Festival of Music 1983- ; Ch. Swansea Festival of Music Art Committee 1978- ; Member University College Swansea Council and Ch. Taliesin Art Committee; Ch. Swansea City Council Art and Recreation Committee 1976-79; Ch. Gower Round Table 1975; Lord Mayor of Swansea 1988-89; President Swansea Philharmonic Choir 1991; Ch. Swansea & District NSPCC 1985- ; Honorary Member National Council NSPCC 1990- ; V.Ch. NSPCC Welsh Advisory Council 1991. *Recreation:* Music, art / antiques, breeding Budgerigars, reading, country pursuits, wine, people, horse racing / breeding. *Clubs:* Swansea St. Mary's Rotary. *Address:* Sunnyside Farm, Three Crosses, Swansea, SA4 3PU.

MORGAN, Mr Hugh Marsden, BCL (Oxon), MA (Oxon), Barrister-at-Law. *Currently:* Barrister-at-Law; Recorder of the Crown Court, since 1987. *Born on* 17 March 1940 at Llanelli. *Son of* the late Hugh Thomas Morgan and the late Irene Morgan (nee Rees). *Marriage:* to Amanda Jane (nee Tapley), 1967. *Children:* Richard, Charles and Zoe. *Educated at* Cardiff High School; Magdalen College, Oxford (Open Scholar). *Career:* Called to the Bar Gray's Inn 1964; Member: Matrimonial Causes Rule Committee 1989-91; Member: Family Proceedings Rule Committee 1991- ; Member: Fees & Legal Aid Committee of Senate and Bar Council 1976-82; Member: Committee of Family Law Bar Association 1976-89; Member: S.E.Circuit Wine Committee, (i.e. Executive Committee), 1986-88; Member: Disciplinary Tribunal of The Bar 1987- . *Recreation:* reading, listening, gardening, wining & dining, pottering through France. *Clubs:* Member of The Cymrodorrion. *Address:* 1 King's Bench Walk, Temple, London, EC4Y 7DB. Tel: 071 583 6266

MORGAN, John Christopher, BSc (Estate Management) *Currently:* Chairman, Morgan Lovell PLC, since 1977; Chairman, Overbury Group PLC, since 1985. *Born on* 31 Dec 1955 at Barnet, Herts. *Son of* Ieuan Gwyn Jones Morgan and Gwen Morgan (nee Littleshild). *Marriage:* to Rosalind Jane Kendrew, 1984. *Children:* James, Charles and Anna. *Educated at* Peter Symonds, Winchester; University of Reading. *Recreation:* sailing, reading. *Clubs:* RAC *Address:* 2 Fishermans Bank, Mudeford, Dorset, BH23 3NP.

MORGAN, John Gwynfryn, MA, DipEd. *Currently:* Head of E.C.Delegation to the State of Israel since 1987. *Born on* 16 Feb 1934 at Aberdare. *Son of* the late Arthur Morgan and the late Mary (nee Walters). *Marriage:* to Margery (nee Greenfield), 1990, previous marriage dissolved. *Children:* Sian, Gregory, Joanna and Eliot. *Educated at* Aberdare Grammar School; BA(Hons Latin), MA(Classics), DipEd, U.C.W. Aberystwyth. *Career:* Pres. Students Union, UCW Aberystwyth 1957-58; President National Union of Students 1960-62; Sec-Gen Int Student Conference 1962-65; International Secretary British Labour Party 1965-68; Deputy Gen Sec British Lab.Party 1968-72;

Chairman Finance Committee Socialist International 1968-72; Adviser to Council of Europe on Youth and Student Affairs 1962-66; Chef De Cabinet to E. C. Commissioner Rt.Hon George Thomson 1973-75; Head of E.C.Office Wales 1975-79; Head Press and Information Delegation, Canada 1979-83; Head E.C.Representation Turkey 1983-87; Assoc Professor Univ of Guelph Canada; Vice Pres London Welsh Rugby Club; Fellow, Royal Commonwealth Soc. *Publications:* Commandeur D'Hunneur, Chaine Des' Rotisseurs; numerous articles in press and political journals. *Recreation:* rugby, cricket, crosswords, reading, wine-tasting. *Clubs:* Reform, Cardiff and County, M.C.C. *Address:* 36 Hamessila St, Herzliya Bet, 46580 Israel E.C. Delegation, 3 Daniel Frisch St, Tel Aviv, 64731, Israel

MORGAN, Mr John Mansel, BSc, MI Chem E. *Currently:* Chairman, Porvair plc, since 1979. *Born on* 18 May 1939 at Swansea. *Son of* Sally and Jestyn Morgan. *Marriage:* to Janice Dennis Jones, 1963. *Children:* Julia Sian and Justine Fay. *Educated at* Dynevor Grammar School, Swansea; University College of Swansea, University of Wales. *Career:* Laporte Titanium, 1962-65; Griflex Products Ltd., 1965-67; Porvair plc, 1967-71; Flotex Ltd., 1971-75; Orr & Boss & Partners, 1976-79. *Recreation:* cricket, golf, skiing.

MORGAN, Prof. Kenneth Owen, D.Litt (Oxon)., F.B.A, 1983. *Currently:* Principal, University College of Wales, Aberystwyth, Pro-Vice Chancellor, University of Wales, since April 1989. *Born on* 16 May 1934 at London. *Son of* David James Morgan & Margaret (nee Owen). *Marriage:* to Jane Keeler, 1973. *Children:* David and Katherine Louise. *Educated at* University College School; Oriel College, Oxford. *Career:* Lecturer in History, University College of Swansea 1958-66; Senior Lecturer 1965-66; Fellow and Praelector, The Queen's College Oxford 1966-89; Hon Fellow, Univ. Coll., Swansea 1985; Amer. Council of Learned Socs Fellow, Columbia Univ 1962-63; Vis. Prof. Columbia Univ 1965; Member: Council, RHistS 1983-86; Bd of Celtic Studies 1972- ; Council, Univ Coll of Wales, Aberystwyth 1972-84. Editor, The Welsh History Review since 1965 (assistant editor 1961-65). *Publications:* Wales in British Politics 1963, (3rd edn 1980); David Lloyd George:Welsh radical as World Statseman 1963, (2nd edn 1982); Freedom or Sacrilege? 1966;Keir Hardie 1967;The Age of Lloyd George 1971, 3rd edn 1978; (ed)Lloyd George:Family Letters 1973;Lloyd George 1974;Keir Hardie:Radical and Socialist 1975, 2nd edn 1984 (Arts Council prize 1976);Consensus and Disunity 1979, 2nd edn 1986; (with Jane Morgan) Portrait of a Progressive 1980; Rebirth of a Nation:Wales 1880-1980, 1981, 2nd edn 1982(Arts Council prize 1982);David Lloyd George 1981;Labour in Power 1945-1951, 1984, 2nd edn 1985;(ed jtly) Welsh Society and Nationhood 1984;(ed) The Oxford Illustrated History of Britain 1984, new multi-volume edition, 1992; (ed) The Sphere Illustrated History of Britain 1985; Labour People 1987, 2nd ed., 1992;(ed) The Oxford History of Britain 1988; The Red Dragon and the Red Flag 1989; The People's Peace; British History 1945-89, 1990 new updated edition, 1992; Academic Leadership, 1991: *Recreation:* Music, Sport, Travel and Architecture. *Clubs:* Atheneum; Yr Academi Gymreig. *Address:* Plas Penglais, Aberystwyth, Dyfed., SY23 3DF. ''The Croft'', 63 Millwood End, Long Hanborough, Witney, Oxon, OX8 8BP

MORGAN, Mr Michael Albert Joseph, BSc. *Currently:* Personnel Director, Northern Foods plc, since 1967. *Born on* 22 April 1943 at Mosterton, Dorset. *Son of* Greta Morgan and Walter Morgan (step-father). *Marriage:* to Beryl Morgan, 1969. *Children:* Owen Nicholas and Kathryn Laura. *Educated at* Dyffryn G.S, Port Talbot; UCW

Aberystwyth. *Career:* English Electric Computers, Kidsgrove (Bureau Consultant) 1965-67. *Recreation:* Non executive director Yorkshire Health, books, food, classical music. *Address:* Northern Foods Plc, St.Stephens Square, Hull, East Yorkshire, HU1 3XG.

MORGAN, Mr Peter William Lloyd, MA *Currently:* Director-General, Institute of Directors since 1989. *Born on* 9 May 1936 at Neath, West Glamorgan. *Son of* Matthew Morgan and Margaret Gwynneth (nee Lloyd). *Marriage:* to Elisabeth Susanne Davis 1964. *Children:* Penelope, Gabrielle and Justine. *Educated at* Llandovery College; Trinity Hall, Cambridge. *Career:* Royal Signals 1954-56 (2nd Lieut); joined IBM UK Ltd., 1959; Director, IBM UK Rentals Ltd., 1973-75 and 1980-83; Gp. Dir. of Marketing, IBM Europe, Paris 1975-80; Director IBM UK Ltd., 1983-87; IBM UK Holdings Ltd., 1987-89; IBM Trust Ltd., 1987-89; Director: NCC 1981-89; South Wales Electricity PLC 1989; Director Publications Ltd., 1989- ; National Provident Instn 1990-; Member: Management Cttee, Action Resource Centre 1987-; Council, British Executive Service Overseas 1989- ; Council for Charitable Support 1990- ; Council Nat Forum for Management Educn and Develt 1990- ; Mem Worshipful Co. of Inf Technologists 1988- ; Trustee, Llandovery Coll., 1990- . *Recreation:* Music, history, gardening, skiing, exercising his dogs. *Clubs:* United Oxford & Cambridge University. *Address:* Institute of Directors, 116 Pall Mall, London SW1Y 5ED.

MORGAN, Richard Martin, MA *Currently:* Warden of Radley College. *Born on* 25 June 1940 at Weston-S-Mare. *Son of* the late His Honour Judge & the late Mrs Trevor Morgan. *Marriage:* to Margaret Kathryn (nee Agutter). *Children:* Pippa, Victoria and Rachel. *Educated at* Sherborne School; Cambridge University. *Career:* Assistant Master Radley College 1963; Housemaster 1969; Headmaster Cheltenham College 1978-90; member Adv. Council Understanding British Ind., 1977-79; JP.Glos, 1988-90 *Recreation:* reading, music, games. *Clubs:* Free Foresters, Jesters. *Address:* Radley College, Abingdon, Oxon, OX14 2HR.

MORGAN, Mr Robert, *Born on* 27 March 1967 at Cardiff. *Son of* James and Edith Morgan. *Educated at* Llaniltud Fawr Comprehensive School *Career:* Sport: represented Wales in Commonwealth Games in 1982/ 1986 (Bronze medal), 1990 Gold medal Highboard diving, Olympic Games 1984-88; World Championships 1991- 6th; European Championships 1991- 3rd. *Recreation:* sport, golf, interest in selling *Clubs:* Highgate Diving *Address:* 13 Windmill Close, Llantwit Major, S.Glam, CF6 9SW.

MORGAN, Reverend Robert Harman, BA *Currently:* Vicar of the Parish of Glanely, Cardiff, since 1961. *Born on* 28 Oct 1928 at Cardiff. *Son of* the late Leonard and Mary Morgan. *Children:* David, Eluned, Philip and Rhys. *Educated at* Aberdare Grammar School; University College, Cardiff. *Career:* R.A.F., 1947-49, National Service; University, 1952-55; Curate, Parish of Penarth 1957-61; member, Cardiff City Council 1974-80; Leader, South Glam C.C., 1981-86; Chairman, South Glam C.C., 1991-92; Fellow of the University College Cardiff; member, Assembly of Welsh Counties; member, Association of County Councils; Vice-Chairman, Welsh College of Music and Drama. *Publications:* Weekly columnist, South Wales Echo. *Recreation:* Formerly athletics, reading, politics and community. *Address:* Church House, Grand Avenue, Ely, Cardiff, CF5 4HX.

MORGAN, Mr Roger Hugh Vaughan Charles, CBE., FRSA., MA. *Currently:* Retired. *Born on* 8 July 1926 at Chelsea. *Son of* the late Charles Morgan and the late Hilda Vaughan, novelists. *Marriage:* to 1) Harriet Waterfield

1951; 2) to Susan Vogel Marrian 1965. *Children:* 2 s, 1 d (& one s dec'd) *Educated at* Downs School., Colwall; Phillips Acad., Andover USA; Eton Coll., Oxford Univ. *Career:* Grenadier Guards 1944-47 (Captain 1946); House of Commons Library 1951-63; House of Lords Library 1963-91; Librarian, House of Lords 1977-91. *Recreation:* Painting, photography, food *Clubs:* Garrick, Beefsteak, Saintsbury *Address:* Cliff Cottage, Laugharne, Dyfed., SA33 4SD.

MORGAN, Air Vice-Marshal William Gwyn, CB., CBE., FCCA., ACMA. Retired 1969. *Born on* 13 Aug 1914 at Crynant, Neath. *Son of* T.S. Morgan and Elizabeth Morgan (nee Jeffreys). *Marriage:* to Joan Russell. *Educated at* Pagefield Coll. Swansea; RAF Staff Coll; Joint Services Staff Coll. *Career:* Commissioned R.A.F. 1939; Group Captain 1958; Air Commodore 1965; DPS (2) RAF 1965-66; Air Officer in charge of Administration, RAF Technical Training Command 1966-68; Training Command 1968-69; Air Vice-Marshal 1967; Training Manager, Deloitte & Co. 1969-75. *Recreation:* Fell walking: *Clubs:* R.A.F: *Address:* c/o Lloyds Bank, 6 Pall Mall, London., SW1 5NA.

MORGAN-OWEN, Mr John Gethin, CB; MBE; QC. *Currently:* retired. *Born on* 22 Aug 1914 at Camberley, Surrey. *Son of* Major General Ll.I.G. Morgan-Owen and Mrs. E.B. Morgan-Owen. *Marriage:* to Mary (nee Rimington), 1950. *Children:* Margaret, Gethin and Huw. *Educated at* Shrewsbury School; Trinity College, Oxford. *Career:* Called to Bar, Inner Temple 1938; Wales & Chester Circuit 1939; practised at Cardiff 1939 and 1945-52; War Service, South Wales Borderers 1939-44 (North Norway 1940, 'D' Day Landing 1944); HQ 146 Infantry Brigade (North West Europe 1944-45); MBE 1945; Hon.Major, Deputy Judge Advocate 1952 (Germany 1953-56, Hong Kong 1958-60, Cyprus 1963-66); Assistant Judge Advocate General 1966, Deputy Judge Advocate General, Germany 1970-72; Vice Judge Advocate General 1972-79; Judge Advocate General of the Forces 1979-84. CB 1979, QC 1981. Joint Chairman, Disciplinary Appeals Cttee, Chartered Accountants (E&W) 1984-86 *Publications:* (in collaboration) article on Royal Forces, Halsbury's Laws of England, 4th edition. *Recreation:* beagling, inland waterways, antiquities. *Clubs:* Army & Navy *Address:* St. Nicholas House, Kingsley, Bordon, Hants, GU35 9NW.

MORGAN-OWEN, John Maddox, DL (Derbyshire 1986). *Currently:* Insurance Consultant. *Born on* 26 June 1931 at Donisthorpe, Leics. *Son of* the late Lt.Colonel Morgan Maddox Morgan-Owen, DSOTD, MA, JP and the late Doris Marjorie (nee Turner). *Marriage:* to Elsa Courtenay (Jill), 1958, daughter of the late Cdr Ronald Arthur Orlando Bridgeman, RD, RNR of Rockcliffe Hall Fintshire. *Children:* Timothy Maddox (b.1961), BA.Hons. *Educated at* Shrewsbury School. *Career:* Derbyshire Yeomanry 1949-52; South Wales Borderers 24th Regt. of Foot 1952-55; General Commissioner of Income Tax 1972- ; Member Derbyshire County Council 1967- (Deputy Leader Conservative Group 1977-); member South Derbyshire District Council 1973-79, (Leader of Soncervative Group 1973-79); member Cosira Derbyshire 1972-88; member TAVR Derbyshire Committee 1974- ; Governor Repton School 1972-81; member Derbyshire Historic Buildings Trust 1974- , Vice Chairman 1984- . Chairman East Midlands Museum Service 1988- . *Recreation:* shooting, music, opera, architecture. *Clubs:* M.C.C. *Address:* Pennfield House, Melbourne, Derby, DE7 1EQ.

MORRELL, John, FCA. *Born on* 10 Nov 1922 *Son of* the late John Morrell of Sunderland and Dorothy Ann (nee Thompson). *Marriage:* to Nora, 1947, da of John Edwards (d 1960), of Ripley, Derbys. *Children:* Nicholas John (b.1952) and Patricia Margaret (b.1957). *Educated at* Beds Collegiate Sunderland. *Career:* WWII RAF 1940-46, radar mechanic Lancaster Sqdn, radar teacher Cranwell; CA; ptnr W J James & Co Brecon, S Wales 1952- ; former pres Brecon Chamber of Trade, treas Brecon Rotary Club, founder and former Capt Penoyre GC; FCA 1951. *Recreation:* golf, sports. *Clubs:* Cradoc GC. *Address:* Brendon, 1 Sunnybank, Brecon, Powys, LD3 7RW. Bishop House, 10 Wheat St, Brecon, Powys LD3 7DG Tel: 0874 622381

MORRIS, Professor Alun Owen, BSc., PhD (Wales). *Currently:* Professor of Mathematics, University College of Wales, Aberystwyth, since 1969 *Born on* 17 Aug 1935 at Ruthin, Clwyd. *Son of* the late Arthur and Jennie Morris (nee Owen). *Marriage:* 1st to Margaret Erina Jones, 1960 (d.1987). 2nd to Mary Jones, 1992. *Children:* Lowri Clwyd, Iwan Rhys and Catrin Angharad. *Educated at* Brynhyfryd School, Ruthin; University College of North Wales, Bangor. *Career:* Assistant Lecturer 1959-60; Lecturer 1960-66; Senior Lecturer 1966-69 at University College of Wales Aberystwyth. Vice Principal, University College of Wales, Aberystwyth 1986-90; London Mathematical Society (Council 1974-78, Editor of Journal of the London Mathematical Society 1983-88); Y Gymdeithas Wyddonol Genedlaethol (Chairman 1980-82); Mathematics Committee of the University Grants Committee 1986-89; Mathematics Advisor to University Funding Council 1989- . *Publications:* Book: Linear Algebra - An Introduction (Van Nostrand-Reinhold) 1978, (second edition 1982); numerous articles in professional journals. *Recreation:* reading, music. *Address:* Hiraethog, Cae Melyn, Aberystwyth, Dyfed, SY23 2HA. Department of Mathematics, University College of Wales, Aberystwyth, Dyfed, SY23 3BZ

MORRIS, Andrew John, *Currently:* Gymnastic Development Officer, Swansea City Council. *Born on* 30 Nov 1961 at Swansea. *Son of* Robert John Morris and Dorothy (nee Prangle). *Marriage:* to Susan Cheesebrough, 1986 (divorced 1988). *Educated at* Penlan School, Swansea; West Glam Institute Higher Ed. *Career:* British Gymnastics Champion 1983, 84, 86 and 87; Welsh Champion 7 times. World Championships competed 1981, 83, 85, 87 and 89; European Championships competed 1983, 85 and 87; Olympic Games Los Angeles 1984, Seoul 1988; Commonwealth Games 90 Auckland (mens Team Captain); Welsh National Coach 1990-91. Life member WAGA. *Recreation:* surfing. *Address:* C/o Leisure Services Dept, Sport & Recreation Section, Guildhall, Swansea

MORRIS, David Griffiths, LL.B (Hons). *Currently:* Barrister. *Born on* 10 March 1940 at Newport, Gwent. *Son of* the late Thomas Griffiths Morris and Margaret Eileen (nee Osborne). *Marriage:* 1971. *Children:* Hannah Bethan and Owen Thomas. *Educated at* Abingdon School, Oxon; King's College, University of London. *Career:* Called to Bar, Lincoln's Inn 1965; London Chambers 1965-72; Cardiff Chambers 1972- ; Deputy Circuit Judge 1978; Recorder of Crown Court 1984; Head of Chambers 1984- ; Cardiff Local Juncor 1984-88. *Recreation:* Rugby Union football, cricket, swimming, reading, gardening, theatre. *Clubs:* Cardiff and County, United Services Mess, Cardiff. *Address:* Bryn Hafren, Newport Road, Castleton, Nr Cardiff, CF3 8NU. 30 Park Place, Cardiff.

MORRIS, Dr David William, BSc; PhD; FRAgS. *Currently:* Farmer, dairy and sheep since 1983. *Born on* 7 Dec 1937 at Aberystwyth. *Son of* the late David William Morris and the late Mary Olwen Anne Morris. *Marriage:* to Cynthia, 1966. *Children:* Sally and David. *Educated at* Ardwyn Grammar School, Aberystwyth; UCW, Aberystwth; University of Newcastle-upon-Tyne. *Career:* ICI Development Officer, Cumbria, 1968-69; University of Newcastle upon Tyne, Assistant Farm Director, 1966-69; Bowood Estates Manager 1969-70; Welsh Agricultural College, Aberystwyth 1970-83, Founder Principal, also UCW Aberystwth Professor of Agriculture 1980-83; Council member British Grassland Society; Council member British Charollais Sheep Society; Chairman Narberth Grassland Society; 1991 winner all Wales Grassland Farmer Award; 1974 Churchill Scholar; 1974 Treharne Trustee. *Publications:* Practical milk Production, Farming Press 1974; Grass Farming (co-author) Farming Press, 1975. *Recreation:* showing sheep. *Address:* Wern Berni Farm, Llanboidy, Whitland, Dyfed SA34 OEY.

MORRIS, Mr Edwin David, MD, FRCS, FRCOG. *Currently:* Consultant Obstetrician, Gynaecologist, Guys Hospital London; Consultant O & G Queen Charlottes and Chelsea Hospital London. *Born on* 31 July 1928 at Swansea. *Son of* Edwin Morris and Evelyn Amanda (nee Griffiths). *Marriage:* 1954. *Children:* Anne Elizabeth and Peter David. *Educated at* Brynhyfryd Briton Ferry; Bridgend Grammar; Welsh National School Medicine. *Career:* MB Bch 1950, Distinction and medals in Anatomy, Obstetrics and Gynaecology; House Surgeon Prof Units Cardiff; RAMC active service Malaya; Lecturer Anatomy Cardiff 1953-55, 3 years Surgery in Kings College Group London. FRCS 1958, 2 years Registrar Glossop Terrace and Royal Infirmary MRCOG 1960, Sen Lecturer Charing Cross 1 year resident obstetrician Queen Charlottes 4 years Consultant (O & G) Swansea 1966-67. MD 1969, FRCOG 1972. Regional Assessor Confidential enquiries into Mat. Mortality 1975-92; Former Council Member RCOG; Past-Pres and Council member Section Obstetrics and Gynae, Royal Soc Med. Examiner RCOG, Univ London Cent Midwives Board etc. Consultant Civ Advisor O & G to Army 1983- . *Publications:* papers on Obstetrics Gynaecology and chapters in Postgraduate text books. *Recreation:* reading, walking, music. *Clubs:* Past Pres Sect O & G Royal Soc Med; Fellow Roy.Soc Medicines; Former Council Mem RCOG *Address:* 22 Sheen Common Drive, Richmond TW10 5BN.

MORRIS, Ms Jan, FRSL; MA.Oxon. *Currently:* Writer. *Born on* 2 Oct 1926 *Career:* Member, Yr Academi Gymreig. Editorial Staff, The Times, 1951-56; Editorial Staff, The Guardian, 1957-62. *Publications:* (as James Morris until 1973, subseq. as Jan Morris): Coast to Coast. 1956, rev. edn. 1962; Sultan in Oman, 1957, rev. edn 1983; The Market of Seleukia, 1957; Coronation Everest, 1958; South African Winter, 1958; The Hashemite Kings, 1959; Venice, 1960, 2nd red. edn 1983; The Upstairs Donkey, 1962 (for children); The World Bank 1963; Cities, 1963; The Presence of Spain, 1964, rev.edns (as Spain), 1979, 1982, 1988; Oxford, 1965, 2nd edn 1986; Pax Britannica, 1968; The Great Port, 1970, rev. edn 1985; Places, 1972; Heaven's Command, 1973; Conundrum, 1974; Travels, 1976; Farewell the Trumpets, 1978; The Oxford Book of Oxford, 1978; Destinations, 1980; My Favourite Stories of Wales, 1980; The Venetian Empire, 1980, 2nd edn 1988; The Small Oxford Book of Wales, 1982; A Venetian Bestiary, 1982; The Spectacle of Empire, 1982; (with Paul Wakefield) Wales, The First Place, 1982; (with Simon Winchester) Stones of Empire, 1983; The Matter of Wales, 1984; Last Letters from Hav, 1985 (short listed for the Booker Prize); (with Paul Wakefield) Scotland, The Place of Visions, 1986; Manhattan '45, 1987; Hong Kong, 1988; Pleasures of a tangled life, 1989; (with Paul Wakefield) Ireland, Your Only Place, 1990; O Canada!, 1991; Sydney, 1992; Locations, 1992. *Address:* Trefan Morys, Llanystumdwy, Cricieth, Gwynedd LL52 OLP. Tel: 0766 522222. Fax: 0766 522426.

MORRIS, Rt. Hon. John, Q.C., M.P. *Currently:* Q.C., M.P. *Born on* 5 Nov 1931 at Aberystwyth. *Son of* David William Morris and Mary Olwen Ann Morris. *Marriage:* to Margaret Meinir Morris J.P. *Children:* Nia Cooke, Non Cross and Elinor Morris. *Educated at* Ardwyn, Aberystwyth; U.C.W., Aberystwyth; Gonville & Caius College, Cambridge. *Career:* M.P. Aberavon 1959- ; Parliamentary Sec., Min. of Power 1964-66; Parl. Sec., Min. of Defence Equipment 1968-70; Secretary of State for Wales 1976-79; Shadow Attorney General 1979-81; Recorder of Crown Court 1983- . *Recreation:* Fishing, shooting. *Address:* House of Commons, London SW1A OAA.

MORRIS, Prof John Gareth, D.Phil., FIBiol., FRS *Currently:* Professor of Microbiology, University College of Wales, Aberystwyth 1971- . *Born on* 25 Nov 1932 at Briton Ferry, Glam. *Son of* the late Edwin Morris and the late Evelyn Amanda (nee Griffiths). *Marriage:* to Aine Mary Kehoe 1962. *Children:* Martha Bronwen and Paul Gareth Edwin. *Educated at* Bridgend Grammar School; University of Leeds; Trinity College, Oxford. *Career:* Guiness Research Fellow, Univ. of Oxford 1957-61; Rockefeller Fellow Univ. of California, Berkeley 1959-60; Tutor in Biochemistry, Balliol College Oxford, 1960-61; Lecturer, then Snr. Lect., University of Leicester 1961-71; Visiting Associate Prof., Purdue University, USA 1965; Chm. SERC Biological Science Committee 1978-81; Member University Grants Committee 1981-86; Member Royal Commission for Environmental Pollution 1991- . *Publications:* A Biologist's Physical Chemistry 1968; numerous research papers and reviews on microbial physiology. *Recreation:* Gardening, walking. *Address:* Cilgwyn, 16 Lon Tyllwyd, Llanfarian, Aberystwyth SY23 4UH.

MORRIS, Professor John Llewellyn, BSc, FIMA, PhD, C.Math *Currently:* Professor of Computer Science, University of Dundee since 1986. *Born on* 19 Sept 1943 at Newtown, Powys. *Son of* John Noel and Myfanwy. *Marriage:* to Sylvia Eileen (nee Williams), 1965. *Children:* James Gavin, Rachel Nicole and Julian Lloyd. *Educated at* Tywyn Grammar School; Universities of Leicester and St.Andrew. *Career:* NCR Post Doctoral Fellow 1965-67; Lecturer, Dundee University 1967-75; Associate Professor 1975-83; Professor 1983-86, University of Waterloo. *Publications:* over 40 publications and numerous research reports. *Recreation:* squash, gardening, hill walking, music, reading. *Address:* 11 Whinfield Place, Newport On Tay, Fife, Scotland, DD6 8EF.

MORRIS, Professor John Llewelyn, BSc, PhD, FIMA, C.Math. *Currently:* Professor of Computer Science, Dundee University. *Born on* 19 Sept 1943 at Newtown, Mont. *Son of* John Noel and Myfanwy (nee Moss Davies). *Marriage:* to Sylvia Eileen Williams, 1965. *Children:* James Gavin, Rachel Nicole and Julian Lloyd. *Educated at* Tywyn Grammar School; Leicester University; St.Andrews University. *Career:* Post Doctorial Fellow, Lecturer, Dundee University 1967-75; Associate Professor, University of Waterloo, Canada 1975-83; Professor of Computer Science, University of Waterloo 1983-86. *Publications:* over 50 books plus research reports. *Recreation:* squash, hill walking, gardening, reading, music. *Address:* 11 Whinfield Place, Newport-on-Tay, Fife, Scotland, DD1 8EF. Mathematics & Computer Science Dept, Dundee University, Dundee, Scotland, DD1 4HN

MORRIS, Mr Peter Christopher West, MA., LL.B (Cantab). *Born on* 24 Dec 1937 at London. *Son of* Christopher Thomas Richard Morris, of Westbrook, Rottingdean, Sussex, and Lillian Beatrice (nee Briggs. *Marriage:* 1) to Joy Florence 1959, (m.diss). 2) to Terese Lindsay 1987.

Children: Mark, James and Amanda from 1st marriage; 1 step son Maxim, 2 step da Phillippa and Victoria. *Educated at* Seaford Coll, Christ's Cambridge (MA, LL.B). *Career:* Nat Serv 76 Co Lt RASC 1956-58 (cmmnd 2 Lt 1957); admitted slr 1965; partner Wild Hewitson and Shaw of Cambridge 1965; called to the Bar Middle temple 1982; recorder of the Crown Court 1980-84; voluntary removal from roll of slrs 1982, resigned recordership 1984; hockey player for Wales 1982-85; co dir 1985- . *Recreation:* Hockey, tennis, golf. *Clubs:* Hawks. *Address:* 1 Horse Pastures, Little Hawkwell Fm, Maidstone Road, Pembury. Kent TN2 4AQ.

MORRIS, Cllr. William, *Currently:* owner: Carreg Coch Opencast Coal mine; Organiser: Youth Action Group, Next Century Peace Foundation; Consultant: Minister of Education and Deputy Premier, Sultanate of Oman. *Born on* 7 May 1950 at London. *Son of* Claud Morris and Patricia Holton. *Marriage:* to Veronica Angela Harding 1978. *Children:* Joseph, Loveday and Samuel. *Educated at* Emmanuel Bible College, Swansea; London College of Printing; Royal Agricultural College. *Career:* Served as County Councillor, West Glamorgan, resigned Jan 1992; representing Upper Swansea Valley for Labour; previously Editor for Voice Newspapers (Middle East); Founder member: Families in the Wilderness (Environmental pressure group), 1979-87; previously Editor for Voice Newspapers (Swansea); Active interest in Environmental matters; member Glamorgan Wildlife Trust. *Publications:* Author/editor of numerous reports and articles on Middle East Affairs. *Recreation:* Egyptology, Lay Preacher, N.A.P.V. *Clubs:* Fabian Society, C.N.D. Cymru, Friends of the Earth, Survival International (Trade Union T&GWU). *Address:* Carreg Pentwyn Farm, Ystalyfera, Swansea, SA9 2BE. Tel: 0639 844704 University Administration, P.O. Box 32500, Al Khoud, Sultanate Of Oman 010968536579

MORRIS, Professor, Dr. William David, BSc (Eng), PhD., CEng., FIMechE., FIProdE. *Currently:* University College, Swansea, Prof. of Mechanical Engineering and Vice Principal. *Born on* 14 March 1936 at Gorseinon. *Son of* William Daniel and Elizabeth Jane. *Marriage:* to Pamela Eira. *Children:* Janet, Nigel and Ian *Educated at* London Univ. (Queen Mary College). *Career:* Lecturer, Univ. of Liverpool, 1963-67; Reader, Univ. of Sussex 1969-79; Professor, Univ. of Hull 1979-85. *Publications:* Numerous in Heat Transfer (incl 2 books) *Recreation:* Oil painting, walking *Address:* Dept of Mech Eng., University College Swansea, Singleton Park, Swansea SA2 8PP.

MORROW, Mr Herbert Stanley, B.Com; MIPR. *Currently:* retired. *Born on* 21 Feb 1915 at Willington, Co.Durham. *Son of* the late Revd J.W.Morrow and the late Isabel (nee vison). *Marriage:* to Marjorie Davison, SRN, SCM, 1942. *Educated at* Houghton Grammar School; University of Durham. *Career:* Senior Appointments with the Y.M.C.A. in Cambridge, Torquay, Swansea and London; Head of Fund Raising and Public Relations National Council of YMCAs England, Ireland & Wales, 1969-80. Independent Fund Raising and Public Relations Consultant 1980-85. District Governor Rotary International 1987-88; Chairman R.I.B.I. Public Relations Committee 1988-90; Vice-President and Chairman Finance Committee Durham University Society; Vice-President Methodist Sacramental Fellowship; Newport Community Association. *Recreation:* golf, travel, reading. *Clubs:* Wig & Pen, London. *Address:* "Dunelm", 27 Maes Y Cnwce, Newport, Dyfed, SA42 ORS.

MORTON, Professor Frank, CBE(1976), OBE(1968), DSc, PhD. *Currently:* retired, now Professor Emeritus, formerly Professor of Chemical Engineering, University of

Manchester 1956-73. *Born on* 11 Aug 1906 at Sheffield. *Son of* the late Joseph Morton, Manchester. *Marriage:* to Hilda May Seaston 1936 (d. 1991). *Children:* John Morton. *Educated at* Manchester University. *Career:* Superindendant of Research Development Trinidad Leaseholds Ltd 1936-45; Chief Chemist Trinidad Leaseholds UK 1945-49; Prof. of Chemical Engineering Univ. of Birmingham 1949-56; Deputy Principal Manchester College of Science and Technology 1964-65; Deputy Principal Manchester Inst. Science and Technology 1966-71; member of Council Manchester Business School 1964-72; Chemical & Allied Products Training Board 1968-71; European Federation of Chemical Engineering 1968-72; President Inst. of Chemical Engineers 1963-64; Society of Chemical Industry Vice President 1967; Jubilee Memorial Lecturer 1967 Medal, 1969. *Publications:* Report on Inquiry into the Safety of Natural Gas as a Fuel (Ministry of Technology) 1970; various papers on petroleum, organic chemistry, chemical engineering and allied subjects. *Recreation:* chess, walking. *Clubs:* Savage. *Address:* 47 Penrhyn Beach East, Llandudno, Gwynedd.

MOSELEY, Kevin, *Currently:* Printer, Severn Valley Press Ltd., *Born on* 2 July 1963 at Caerphilly. *Son of* Victor and Christine. *Marriage:* to Carol. *Children:* Cara-Lea *Educated at* Oakdale Comprehensive School *Career:* Blackwood 1979-83; Pontypool 1983-92; Newport 1990-92. Wales 10 caps; Wales B 6 caps; Monmouthshire Cap; Bay of Plenty (New Zealand), 12 provincial games. *Recreation:* family, walking my spaniels, most sports. *Clubs:* Pontypool, Newport, Blackwood. *Address:* Tredustan House, Springfield, Pontllanfraith, Blackwood, Gwent, NP2 2LX.

MOSTYN, The Lord Sir Roger Edward Lloyd, MC *Currently:* Peer of The Realm. *Born on* 17 April 1920 at London. *Son of* the late Lord Mostyn and the late Lady Mostyn. *Marriage:* 1st to Yvonne Margaret, 1943, da of A. Stuart Johnson; 2nd to Mrs Sheila Edmondson Shaw, DL (Clwyd 1982), da of Maj Reginald Fairweather. *Children:* Virginia and Llewellyn. *Educated at* Eton; RMC Sandhurst. *Career:* 2 Lt 9 Lancers 1939 (despatches 1940), temp Maj 1945. *Recreation:* hunting, racing, country *Clubs:* Cavalry. *Address:* Mostyn Hall, Mostyn, Clwyd, North Wales.

MOULAND, Mark Gary, *Currently:* Professional Golfer, turned pro 1981. *Born on* 23 April 1961 at St. Athan, S. Wales. *Son of* Sid and Shirley Mouland. *Marriage:* to Marianne. *Children:* Stephanie and Kimberley. *Educated at* Westbourne House Penarth; Millfield School Somerset. *Career:* Car Care Plan International 1986; Dunhill Cup 1986, 88, 89, 90; World Cup 1988, 89, 90; Kirin Cup 1988; Dutchg Open Champion 1988. Amateur 1976, British Boys Champion. *Recreation:* travel, TV, snooker. *Clubs:* Stonleigh Deer Park Golf. *Address:* Stoneleigh Deer Park Golf, The Clubhouse, The Old Deer Park, Coventry Rd, Stonleigh, CV8 3DR. C/o P.G.A. European Tour, Wentworth Club, Wentworth Dve, Virginia Water, Surrey, GU25 4LS

MOUNSEY, Dr John Patrick David, Hon. LLD (Wales), MA, MD (Cantab) FRCP (London). *Currently:* Retired. *Born on* 1 Feb 1914 in London. *Son of* the late John Edward Mounsey and the late Christine Frances Trail Robertson. *Marriage:* the late Vera Madeline Sara King, 1947. *Children:* Frances Sarah Ann Connell and John Christopher Hugh Mounsey. *Educated at* Eton College; Kings College, Cambridge; Kings College Hospital, London. *Career:* Sherbrook Research Fellow, Cardiac Dept., London Hospital, 1951; Royal Postgraduate Medical School, Lecturer, 1960; Senior Lecturer and Sub-Dean, 1962; Consultant Cardiologist, Hammersmith Hospital, 1960; Deputy Director, British Postgraduate Medical Federation,

1967; Provost, Welsh National School of Medicine, 1969-79; Member: GMC, 1970-79; GDC, 1973-79. *Publications:* Articles on Cardiology mainly in The British Heart Journal. *Recreation:* Gardening, music and painting. *Clubs:* The Athenaeum. *Address:* Esk House, Coombe Terrace, Wotton-under-Edge, Glos., GL12 7NA.

MOUNTBATTEN, The Most Honourable Janet Mercedes, *Born on* 29 Sept 1937 at Bermuda. *Daughter of* Major and Mrs Francis Bryce. *Marriage:* to David Michael Mountbatten, 3rd Marquis of Milford Haven. *Children:* George Ivar Louis Montbatten, 4th Marquis of Milford Haven and Ivar Alexander Michael Mountbatten. *Educated at* Gordounston. *Recreation:* Racehorse Breeder, charity committees.

MOURBY, Adrian Roy Bradshaw, BA *Currently:* Television Drama Producer. *Born on* 4 Dec 1955 *Son of* Roy Mourby of Montgomery, Powys and Peggy (nee Bradshaw). *Marriage:* to Dr. Katharine Nicholas, 1980. *Children:* Miranda Jane (b.1987) and John James (b.1990). *Educated at* St. David's University College, Lampeter; University of Bristol Film School. *Career:* Freelance local radio producer 1979, Local Radio Awards 1979; Regional Station Assistant, BBC TV North East, 1980; Attachment as radio feature producer, BBC Pebble Mill, 1982; MJA/SK&F Medical Journalism Award 1982; Radio drama producer, BBC Wales, 1983; Commendation in Sony Radio Awards 1985; Acting Editor "The Archers", 1988; Series Producer "Wales Playhouse", 1989; BAFTA/Cymru Award for Best English Language Drama 1991; Producer "The Old Devils", BBC2, 1991. *Publications:* regular contributions to "The Listener" magazine; 8 radio plays including "The Corsaint", "Other Men Do" and their sequels. *Recreation:* films of Woody Allen, fine wine, opera. *Address:* 55 Cardiff Road, Llandaf, Cardiff, CF5 2DQ.

MUIR, Miss Elizabeth Jean, MCInstM, MInstSM *Currently:* Founder and Managing Director of the European Marketing Consultancy, The Alternative Marketing Department Ltd, since 1982. Also training provider and guest speaker: European Marketing, Women's Personal Development, Women in Europe. Other Board Memberships and Appointments include: SHAW Homes, Co-op and Cost Sale, 1991- ; South Glamorgan Family Health Service Authority 1990- ; Member of Women & Training Group Committee, South Wales 1990-91; Secondary Housing Association for Wales 1988-91; Health Promotion Authority for Wales 1987-91; Welsh Water Authority 1986-89; Member of the Welsh Regional Council of CBI 1985-91; Member of Syllabus Advisory Groups for BTec 1985-87. *Born on* 20 Aug 1947 at Bridgend, Glamorgan. *Daughter of* Capt Kenneth Edward Muir MBE and Elsie (nee Harris). *Marriage:* single. *Educated at* Cowbridge Girls High School; Homerton College Cambridge; Cardiff Coll of Education (DipEd); currently studying part time at The University of Wales, Cardiff for MSc (Econ). *Career:* Sales & Marketing Controller, Memory Lane Cakes (Dalgety Spillers Co) 1978-82; Product Group Manager, Warner Lambert Animal Health 1976-78; Creative Executive, Parke-Davis Pharmaceuticals 1973-76; Mathematics and Physics Teacher, Cardiff Secondary Schools 1968-73. *Publications:* various articles in Business Magazines and short stories in Women's Magazines. *Recreation:* travelling in Europe, particularly Greece, writing, giving after dinner speeches and guest presentations, studying issues relating to women viz. currently examining the tensions which exist between career and personal lives of senior women executives who travel extensively or live abroad and whether the Single European market will increase the need for such career mobility. *Address:* Sunningdale House, 13 Ty Draw Road, Roath Park, Cardiff, CF2 5HA. Tel: 0222 499214. IBS, Michalakopoulou 29, 11528 Athens, Greece.

MULLENS, Peter Arthur Glanville, OBE, MA, FCA. *Currently:* Consultant, Mullens & Robinson, Chartered Accountants. *Born on* 16 March 1925 at Port Talbot. *Son of* the late G.Glanville Mullens and Mabel Mullens. *Marriage:* Edwina Mary Isaac. *Children:* William, Fiona and Lynette. *Educated at* Llandovery College; Sidney Sussex College, Cambridge. *Career:* Deloitte, Plender & Griffiths, articled clerk 1942-43, 1949-51; RAF Flight Lieutenant 1943-47; Unilever 1951-53; Partner, Mullens & Robinson Chartered Accountants 1953-90; Member: Welsh Development Advisory Board 1980-89; University College of Swansea: Member of Council, Treasurer 1980-89, Vice-President 1989- . Member of Court and Council of University of Wales. *Address:* 2 Stratford Drive, Porthcawl, Mid Glamorgan, CF36 3LG.

MULLIN, Professor John William, PhD(London), DSc(Wales), FEng, FRSC, FIChemE. *Currently:* Emeritus Professor, University of London. *Born on* 22 Aug 1925 at Rock Ferry, Cheshire. *Son of* the late Frederick and the late Kathleen Nellie (nee Oppy). *Marriage:* to Averil Margaret (nee Davies), 1952. *Children:* Jonathan Graeme and Susan Lisbeth. *Educated at* Hawarden Cnty Sch, Flintshire; Univ Coll Cardiff; Univ Coll London.Moulton Medal Inst.of Chemical Engineers 1970; Fellow,Univ.Coll.,Cardiff 1981; Fellow, Univ.Coll., London 1981; Dr.Honoris Causa, Inst.Nat.Polytechnique de Toulouse 1989. *Career:* Lecturer in Chemical Engineering, University College London ,1956-61; Reader, 1961-69; Professor, 1969-85. Ramsay Memorial Professor and Head of Dept., 1985-90. Visiting Prof.University of New Brunswick, Canada, 1967. Vice-Provost, University College London 1980-89/. Dean Faculty of Engineering University of London 1979-85. Chairman British and International Standards Cttees on Particle Sizing 1970- ; Mem.Cttee of Management, Institute of Child Health, Univ of London 1970-83; Mem. of Court of Governors, University College Cardiff 1982- ; Vice-Chmn of Council School of Pharmacy, Univ. of London 1983- . N.S.Kurnakov Memorial Medal,USSR Academy of Sciences 1991. *Publications:* ''Crystallization'', 1st ed. 1961, 2nd ed. 1972, 3rd ed. 1992; ''Industrial Crystallization'' (Editor) 1976. *Recreation:* gardening. *Clubs:* Athenaeum. *Address:* 4 Milton Road, Ickenham, Uxbridge, Middlx, UB10 8NQ. University College London, Gower Street, London, WC1E 6BT. Tel: 071 387 7050.

MULLINS, Rt. Rev. Daniel Joseph, B.A. *Currently:* Bishop of Menevia. *Born on* 10 July 1929 at Kilfinane, Co. Limerick. *Son of* Mary and Thomas Mullins. *Educated at* Kilfinane National School; Mount Melleray College; St. Mary's College, Aberystwyth 1944-47; Oscott College, Sutton Coldfield 1947-53; University College of Wales (B.A.). *Career:* Curate, St. Helen's, Barry 1953-55; Ordained priest 1953; Curate, Barry 1953-56, Newbridge 1956, Bargoed 1956-57, Maesteg 1957-60; Asst. Chaplain to University College, Cardiff 1964-68; Vicar General Archidocese of Cardiff 1968; Auxiliary Bishop 1970-87; Chairman Ctee for Catechetics; Mbr. Court of University College Swansea; President Catholic Record Society; Fellow University College Cardiff; Hon. Fellow St. David's University College Lampeter. *Recreation:* Golf, walking, *Address:* Bryn Rhos, 79 Walter Road, Swansea, West Glam., SA1 4PS.

MUNKLEY, James, qualified table tennis coach *Born on* 8 Jan 1949 at Merthyr Tydfil. *Son of* James William Munkley and Nancy Munkley (nee Thomas). *Marriage:* to Christine Williams, 1976. *Educated at* Aberfan Secondary Modern.

Career: Have been involved in Sport for the Disabled since 1968, after a driving accident left him paralysed (quadraplegic). Competed at both National and International levels winning many medals. He has travelled throughout Europe, New Zealand (Commonwealth Games 1974), Australia; World Wheelchair Table Tennis Championships 1987; World Wheelchair Bowls Championships 1990; Paralympic Games, Seoul, Korea 1988. Chairman (and founder member) Welsh Paraplegic and Tetraplegic Sports Assoc 1987- ; Chairman Rookwood Paraplegic and Tetraplegic Sports Club (based at Rookwood Hospital, Cardiff), since 1975; Committee member British Wheelchair Table Tennis Association; Team Captain, 1991-92, Great Britain Wheelchair Table Tennis Squad; 1984 Paralympic Games held at Stoke Mandeville; 1970 Commonwealth Games, Edinburgh. *Recreation:* travel, reading, table tennis, bowls. *Clubs:* Rookwood Para & Tetra Sports, Welsh Para & Tetra Sports Assoc. *Address:* 43 Penhill Close, Llandaff, Cardiff, CF5 1EA. Tel: 0222 565117

MURPHY, Mr Ian Patrick, LLB *Currently:* Barrister. *Born on* 1 July 1949 at Cardiff. *Son of* Patrick Murphy and Irene Grace (nee Hooper). *Marriage:* to Penelope Gay, 1974. *Children:* Anna (b.1982) and Charlotte (b.1984). *Educated at* St.Illtyd's College, Cardiff; L.S.E. *Career:* Chartering Clerk, Baltic Exchange 1970-71; Called to Bar 1972; Recorder 1990, Wales & Chester Circuit. *Recreation:* golf, skiing, travel. *Clubs:* Royal Porthcawl Golf; Cardiff County. *Address:* 3 Llandaff Chase, Llandaff, Cardiff, CF5 2NA.

MURPHY, Mr Paul Peter, MA., MP. *Currently:* M.P. *Born on* 25 Nov 1948 at Usk, Gwent. *Educated at* St. Francis School, Abersychan; Jones West Monmouth School;Pontypool; Oriel College, Oxford. *Career:* Management Trainee, CWS, 1070-71; Lecturer in Government, Eddw Vale College of Further Education, 1971-87; Member, Torfaen Borough Council, 1973-87; M.P. for Torfaen, 1981- ; Opposition Spokesman on Welsh Affairs, 1988- . *Recreation:* Classical music. *Address:* 42 Wiston Path, Fairwater, Cwmbran, Gwent. NP44 4PY. House Of Commons, Westminster, London, SW1A OAA.

MURPHY, Mrs Penelope Gay, LL.B/Solicitor. *Currently:* Partner with Edwards Geldard Solicitors, Dumfries House, Dumfries Place, Cardiff, CF1 4YF, since 1977. *Born on* 28 Oct 1949 at Brighton, Sussex. *Daughter of* the late Gerald Hugh-Smith and Pamela Daphne Edwards (nee Miller). *Marriage:* to Ian Murphy, 1974. *Children:* Anna Louise (b.1982) and Charlotte Clare (b.1984). *Educated at* Brighton & Hove High School, GPDST; London School of Economics; College of Law, Lancaster Gate London. *Career:* Court Clerk Director of Public Prosecutions Central Criminal Court London 1971-73; qualified as a Solicitor 1976; Treasurer of Association of Women Solicitors, S E Wales Branch 1984- ; member of the Law Society 1974- . *Recreation:* family life, skiing, swimming, tennis. *Address:* 3 Llandaff Chase, Llandaff, Cardiff, CF5 2NA. Dumfries House, Dumfries Place, Cardiff, CF1 4YF.

MUSHIN, Professor William Woolf, CBE, DSc (Wales), FRCS, FCAnaes, MA(Oxon), FFARCSI, FFARACS, FFA(SA) *Currently:* Emeritus Professor of Anaesthetics, University of Wales College of Medicine. *Born on* 29 Sept 1910 at London,England. *Son of* the late Moses Mushin and Jessie (nee Kalmenson). *Marriage:* to Betty Hannah Goldberg 1939. *Children:* Jeremy Dillwyn, Susan Esther, Dilys Jessica and Elizabeth Sian. *Educated at* Davenant Foundation School 1922-27; London Hospital Medical College 1927-32. *Career:* Professor of Anaesthetics University of Wales College of Medicine 1947-75; formerly 1st Asst. Nuffield Dept. of Anaesthetics University of

Oxford; Dean, Faculty of Anaesthetics, Royal College Surgeons; Member: Central Health Services Commission; Medicine Commission; Commonwealth Scholarships Commission; Safety of Medicines Committee; Welsh Hospital Board (Chair. Planning Comm) Court Univ. of Wales; Senate, Coll. of Medicine; Honorary Fellow, Royal Soc. Medicine, England; numerous eponymous lectures and visiting Professor to many foreign universities. *Publications:* Numerous papers and several books on Anaesthesia and related subjects. *Address:* 30 Bettws-Y-Coed Road, Cardiff. CF2 6PL.

MYDDELTON, Lady Mary Margaret Elizabeth., *Currently:* Water colour painter. *Born on* 6 Feb 1910 at London. *Daughter of* the late Major Lord Charles Mercer Nairne, 2nd son of the 5th Marquis of Lansdowne killed in the 1914-1918 War, and Lady Violet Elliot, daughter of the 4th Earl of Minto, later married Lord Astor of Hever.

Marriage: to the late Lt.Col Ririd Myddelton, 1931, Coldstream Guards, LVO, JP, DL (d.1988). *Children:* David Foulk (b.1932), Hugh Robert (b.1938) and Fiona Violet (now Lady Aird), (b.1934). *Educated at* Queens College, Harley Street, London and privately; Attended Art Schools in London, Paris and Rome. *Career:* Mostly housewife. Warwork draftswoman, Parachute factory - After the 2nd World War and moving to Wales, Girl Guides, one time Chief Commissioner for Wales; previously County Commissioner for Denbighshire, subsequently Clwyd. *Publications:* Prints of a large number of Water Colour paintings of flowers, available in National Trust Shops. *Recreation:* Gardening, breeding Welsh ponies, fishing. *Address:* Chirk Castle, Chirk, Clwyd, LL14 5AF.

N

NAPIER, Major-General (Retd) Lennox Alexander Hawkins, CB; OBE; MC; OStJ; DL. *Currently:* Chairman, Central Transport Consultative Committee and Inspector on Lord Chancellors' Panel of Independent Inspectors of Public Enquiries. *Born on* 28 June 1928 at Broadway. *Son of* Major and Mrs C.M. Napier. *Marriage:* to Miss J.D. Wilson, 1959. *Children:* Joanna Aitken, Philip Napier and Sally Napier *Educated at* Radley and RMA Sandhurst. *Career:* Joined Army 1946; commnd into South Wales Borderers, 1948; commanded 1st Bn S Wales Borderers and 1st Bn Royal Regt of Wales, 1967-70; Instructor, JSSC, 1970-72; served Min. of Defence, 1972-74; Brigade Commander, Berlin Infantry Bde, 1974-76; Prince of Wales's Division: Divisional Brigadier, 1976-80; Col. Commandant, 1980-83; General Officer Commanding Wales 1980-83; Col, The Royal Regt of Wales, 1983-89; Hon. Col, Cardiff Univ. OTC, 1985-92; Gwent: DL 1983; High Sheriff 1988. *Publications:* Armed Services Year Book. *Recreation:* riding, shooting, bees. *Clubs:* Lansdowne. *Address:* c/o Barclays Bank, 17/18 Agincourt Square, Monmouth, Gwent.

NASH, Professor William Frederick, BSc; MSc; PhD; CBE, 1987; CPhys; FInstP; FRAS; FRSA; Jubilee Medal *Currently:* Emeritus Professor of Physics, University of Nottingham. *Born on* 28 Jan 1925 at Ammanford, Carmarthenshire. *Son of* the late William Henry Nash and Doris (nee Jenkins). *Marriage:* to (Gladys) Christabel (nee Williams), 1951. *Children:* Sian Christabel (Mrs Crosby) and Dr.Dylan Llywelyn. *Educated at* Amman Valley G.S; Univ. Coll. Wales, Swansea (BSc, MSc); University of Manchester (PhD). *Career:* Research Phsicist, Metropolitan

Vickers Manchester 1945-48; Head of Dept. of Physics, University of Nottingham 1981-84, (Assistant Lecturer, Lecturer, Senior Lecturer 1950-64, Reader 1964-74, Professor of Physics 1974-90, Pro-Vice Chancellor 1974-80); Chm. East Midlands Universities Military Education Cttee 1973-90; Member, Court, Council, Senate, Finance Cttee, Chairman Home Defence Scientific Advisory Cttee., Chief Regional Scientific Advisor for No. 3 Home Defence Region; member, SERC Astronomy and Space Board 1980-84. Visiting Physics Departments in overseas countries. Acted as Examiner and assessor for several overseas Physics Dept; Currently act as assessor for Hire Overseas Research Grant Governing Bodies. *Publications:* More than 100 articles on Cosmic Rays and Astro Physics. *Recreation:* rugby (played when young), operatic singing, walking. *Address:* 6 Spean Drive, Aspley Hall, Nottingham NG8 3NQ. Tel: 0602 296607.

NAYLOR, Professor Ernest, BSc., Ph.D., D.Sc., F.I.Biol. *Currently:* Lloyd Roberts Professor of Marine Zoology, UCNW, Bangor since 1982. *Born on* 19 May 1931 at Derbyshire. *Son of* Joseph and Evelyn (nee Keeton). *Marriage:* to Carol Gillian (nee Bruce). *Children:* Sally Elizabeth and Helen Ruth *Educated at* Swanwick Hall Grammar, Swanwick, Derby; University of Sheffield; University of Liverpool. *Career:* Lecturer, Senior Lecturer, Reader in Zoology, Univ. Coll., Swansea, 1956-71; Professor of Marine Biology, Univ. of Liverpool; Director, Port Erin Marine Laboratory, Isle of Man, 1971-82; Dean, Faculty of Science, UCNW, Bangor, 1989-91. *Publications:* Over 100 papers in scientific journals, including one book and one jointly edited book. *Recreation:* Gardening *Address:* School of Ocean Sciences, Univ. of Wales, Menai Bridge, Anglesey, Gwynedd. LL57 5EY.

NAYLOR-LEYLAND, Sir. Philip Vyvian, (4th)Bart; MFH. *Currently:* Landowner, farmer; Master of Foxhounds 1987- ; President, National Coursing Club, 1988- ; Vice Chairman, Peterborough Royal Foxhound Show Society, 1990- ; Director, BMSS plc et al. *Born on* 9 Aug 1953 at Oxford. *Son of* the late Sir Vivyan Edward N-L, Bt., and The Hon. Lady Hastings. *Marriage:* to Lady Isabella Lambton, 1980. *Children:* Thomas Philip, Violet Mary and George Antony. *Educated at* Eton; Sandhurst; NYU Business School; RAC Cirencester. *Career:* Lt. L.G. *Recreation:* hunting, coursing, shooting, conservation, aviation, gardening. *Clubs:* White's, Daniel's. *Address:* Nantclwyd Hall, Ruthin, Clwyd. LL15 2PR. The Ferry House, Milton Park, Peterborough PE6 7AB.

NEAL, Mr Nicholas Geoffrey, LL.B.(Hons) *Currently:* Chief Solicitor, South Glamorgan C.C.1988- . *Born on* 6 June 1949 at Cardiff. *Son of* Frank Neal and Sheila Neal (nee Bennett). *Educated at* Cardiff High School; UWIST *Career:* Articles to the Clerk to the Justices Cardiff 1971-73; Assist. Clerk to the Justices 1973-74; Assist. Solicitor S.Glam C.C., 1974-80; Assist. County Solisitor S.Glam C.C., 1980-85; Deputy County Solicitor 1985-88; Board of Visitors H.M.Prison, Cardiff 1984- . *Recreation:* Badminton, French, music and reading *Address:* 1 Westville Road, Penylan, Cardiff. CF1 5UW. County Hall, Atlantic Wharf, Cardiff.

NEALE, Mr Gareth John Jarvis, CBE., BA., LLB. Barrister at Law. *Currently:* Head of Business Studies, Crosskeys College, Gwent, 1974- . *Born on* 12 April 1935 at Bristol. *Son of* the late Stanley Charles Jarvis Neale and Gwellian Margaret (nee Jones). *Marriage:* to Anne Jarvis (nee Bryant). *Children:* Rhys Goronwy Jarvis and Allyson Llunos Jarvis *Educated at* Barry Grammar School; Univ. Coll., of Wales, Aberystwyth; London Univ. (External); Grays Inn. *Career:* Research Economic Dev.Corp. for Wales, 1959; Management Serv. Off. Rolls Royce, 1961; Data Processing Man. Mettoy, Swansea, 1963; Lecturer, Llandaff Tech. Coll., 1965; Head of Management Serv., Assoc., British Foods, 1971; County Councillor, S.Glam, 1973- ; Leader of the Opposition, 1985-91; Cardiff City Councillor, 1979- ; Deputy Lord Mayor of Cardiff, 1991-92; Chrmn. of Wales Area Cons. Local Govrn. Advisory Commt, 1986- . *Recreation:* Territorial Army - Major, music, reading and jogging. *Address:* Durlston,105 Heol Y Deri, Rhiwbina, Cardiff, CF4 6HE. Tel: 0222 620113.

NELSON, Countess Mary Winifred, *Born on* 22 May 1916 at Swansea. *Daughter of* the late William and the late Gladys Bevan. *Marriage:* to The Rt. Hon. Earl Nelson, 1945 (decd). *Children:* Lady Sarah Nelson-Roberts. *Educated at* Glanmor Girls School *Recreation:* watching sport, particularly golf. *Address:* 9 Pwll Du Lane, Bishopston, Swansea, SA3 3HA.

NEWTON, Mr Ian Stenhouse, MA(Oxon), FCIS, ACIArb, FBIM, Solicitor *Currently:* Partner, Percy Thomas Partnership. *Born on* 6 Sept 1951 at Cardiff. *Son of* the late Peter Newton and Esme (nee Jones). *Marriage:* to Elizabeth Vanessa Wilson, 1973. *Children:* Kate and Ailsa. *Educated at* Cardiff HS for Boys; New College Oxford. *Career:* Art Clerk & Solicitor, Biddle & Co 1974-77; Legal Adviser, Percy Thomas Partnership 1978-81; Dir & Sec Insight Computer Systems Ltd 1981-92; Dir PTP Seward Ltd 1991-92; Dir.Wren Insurance Association Ltd 1987-92; Partner, PTP Design Group 1990-92; Partner PTP Landscape 1985-92; Past Member, Partnership Panel ICSA 1985-89; Past Chairman Cardiff & S.E.Wales Branch ICSA 1986; Hon Sec. Chartered Secretaries G.S., 1989- . *Recreation:* golf, eastern philosophy, creative management. *Clubs:* Cardiff &

County, Wig & Pen, Royal Porthcawl Golf, Llanishen Golf. *Address:* The Old Mill, Llancarfan, Barry, South Glamorgan, CF6 9AD.

NICHOLAS, Sir David, Hon LLD.,Univ of Wales. CBE. *Currently:* Chairman I.T.News 1989-91. *Born on* 25 Jan 1930 at Tregaron. *Son of* the late Bernice and the late Daniel Nicholas. *Marriage:* to Juliet Powell Davies 1952. *Children:* Helen and James. *Educated at* Neath Grammar School; University College of Wales, Aberystwyth. *Career:* National Service 1951-53; Journalist with Yorkshire Post, Daily Telegraph, Observer; joined ITN 1960; Deputy Editor 1963-77; Editor & Chief Executive 1977-89; Produced ITN General Election Results, Apollo coverage, and ITN special programmes; Fellow Royal Television Society 1980; CBE 1982; Producer's Guild Award 1967; on return of Sir Francis Chichester; Cyril Bennett Award, RTS, 1985; Kt 1989; RTS Judges' Award 1991. *Recreation:* Riding, sailing, walking, reading. *Clubs:* Reform *Address:* Lodge Stables, 2f Kidbrooke Park Road, Blackheath, SE3 OLW. Tel: 081 319 2823. Fax: 081 319 2417.

NICHOLAS, Lilian, *Currently:* retired. *Born on* 24 Nov 1907 at Ebbw Vale *Marriage:* 1934. *Children:* Martyn *Educated at* left school at 14. *Career:* After leaving school learned to be a dressmaker. Started bowling at 40 years of age and have continued to play up to the present days, hope to continue for the rest of his life. *Recreation:* bowls. *Address:* Ebbw Vale, Gwent, NP3 6JX.

NICHOLSON, Mavis, Finals English, Hon Fell. Swansea Univ. *Currently:* Freelance Journalist and Radio and T.V. Broadcaster. *Born on* 19 Oct 1930 at Briton Ferry, Glamorgan. *Daughter of* Olive Irene (nee Davies) and Richard John Mainwaring. *Marriage:* to Geoffrey Nicholson, Freelance Journalist and Author. *Children:* Steve, Lewis and Harry (Grand Children: Ben, Tess and Samantha). *Educated at* Cwrt Sart Mixed Infants; Neath County School for Girls; Swansea University. *Career:* Copy writer London Agencies to 1958; Full-time mother 1958-70; Freelance Writer, 1965- : Nova Magazine, Sunday Times, Observer, Evening Standard, Family Circle, South Wales Echo. TV presenter 1970- : including Good Afternoon, Afternoon, Afternoon Plus, Afternoon Plus 4, Mavis on 4, Mavis Meets, Mavis Wanting to Know, Mavis Catches up With, 3rd Wave with Mavis Nicholson, Garden Party, Relative Speaking, BBC Radio 2, Arts Programme. *Publications:* Help Yourself, 1974; Martha Jane and Me, A Girlhood in South Wales. *Recreation:* talking, reading, gardening, photography, table tennis. *Clubs:* Llanrhaeadr Table Tennis, member of Amnesty, Alzheimer's, National Trust, Montgomery Conservation, Royal Society Protection of Birds, Carer's Association. *Address:* C/o John Thurley, 213 Linen Hall, 156 Regent Street, London, W1R 5TA.

NICOLLE, Geoffrey Reginald, BA *Currently:* retired. *Born on* 5 June 1934 at Caerleon. *Son of* the late Reginald Francis Nicolle and the late Hilda Alice Nicolle (nee Shepherd). *Marriage:* to Sonia Aileen Bain, 1959. *Children:* Mary Olwen McSparron and Philip David Nicolle. *Educated at* Caerleon Endowed School; West Mon Grammar School; Pontypool; UCW Aberystwyth. *Career:* Assistant teacher, Hawkwell Holt School, Essex, Markham's Chase School Basildon, Janet Duke School Basildon. Head teacher, Rosemarket V.C.School, Pembs., 1965-89; Sec. Pembs. N.U.T., 1981-87; President Dyfed N.U.T., 1988; Vice Chairman University of the Third Age Pembrokeshire 1991- . Holder of the National Collection of Garden Auriculas (Nation Council for The Conservation of Plants and Gardens). *Publications:* Rosemarket: A Village Beyond Wales (Dyfed Cultural Services Department - 1982); A History of Rosemarket Church, 1983. *Recreation:* gardening, plant breeding, local history. *Address:* Rising Sun Cottage, Nolton Haven, Haverfordwest, Pembs, SA62 3NN.

NORRIS, Professor Christopher Charles, PhD. *Currently:* Professor of English, University of Wales, Cardiff. *Born on* 6th Nov 1947 at London. *Son of* Charles Frederick Norris and Edith Norris (nee Ward). *Marriage:* to Alison (nee Newton), 1971. *Children:* Clare Tamsin and Jennifer Mary. *Educated at* East Ham Grammar School; London University. *Career:* Lecturer, University of Dvisburg (W.Germany), 1974-76; Assistant Editor, 'Books & Bookmen', 1976-77; Lecturer, Reader and Professor of English University of Wales, Cardiff, since 1978. *Publications:* William Empson and the Philosophy of Literary Criticism, 1978; Deconstruction: theory and practice, 1982, (trans into Japanese, Hebrew, Korean, Serbo-Croat), second ed. expanded and revised, 1991; The Deconstructive Turn: essays in the rhetoric of philosophy, 1983 (Japanese trans forthcoming); The Contest of Faculties: philosophy and theory after deconstruction, 1985; Jacques Derrida, 1987 (Japanese, Russian and Portuguese trans forthcoming); Paul de Man: deconstruction and the critique of aesthetic ideology, 1988; Deconstruction and the Interests of Theory, 1988; What's Wrong with Postmodernism: critical theory and the ends of philosophy, 1990; Spinoza and the Origins of Modern Critical Theory, 1990; Uncritical Theory: postmodernism, intellectuals and the Gulf War, 1992; (with Andrew Benjamin) What Is Deconstruction?, 1989 (ed.); Shostakovitch: the man and his music 1982; (ed.) Inside the Myth: George Orwell - views from the left 1984; (ed.) Music and the Politics of Culture 1989; (ed. with Richard Machin) Post-Structuralist Readings of English Poetry 1987. *Recreation:* music (especially singing: member Cor Cochion Caerdydd). *Address:* 14 Belle Vue Terrace, Penarth, South Glamorgan, CF6 1DB. Dept of English, University Of Wales, P.O. Box 94, Cardiff, CF1 3XE

NORSTER, Mr Robert Leonard, BA (Hons) Fine Art; Post Grad Teaching Certificate *Currently:* Marketing Manager, Standard Chartered Group, since 1990. *Born on* 23 June 1957 at Ebbw Vale, Gwent. *Son of* Mr L.G.Norster and Mrs. E.M. Norster (nee King). *Marriage:* to Catherine Halina Price, 1986. *Educated at* Hafod y Ddol Grammar; Nantyglo Comprehensive; Gwent College of Higher Ed; Cardiff University. *Career:* Schoolmaster 1980-82; Rank Xerox (U.K.) Ltd 1983-90. Rugby: Cardiff 1977-89, Capt 1987-88, 1988-89, Wales 34 Caps; British Lions Tours to New Zealand 1983, Australia 1989, Barbarians, World XV etc. Hon. Wales Team Manager 1991- . *Recreation:* golf, country life. *Address:* C/o Welsh Rugby Union, P.O. Box 22, Cardiff, CF1 1JL.

NORTON, Mr Tom, TD, JP, DL. *Currently:* retired. *Born on* 15 April 1920 at Llandrindod Wells. *Son of* the late Tom Norton, JP and the late Elsie Norton (nee Cummins). *Marriage:* to Pauline Fane, dau of the late A.L.F. Evans, DIG Indian Police, 1948. *Children:* three s one d. *Educated at* Hanley Castle; University of Birmingham. *Career:* Joined TA(RA) 1939, served in World War II (despatches 1946), demobilised as Hon.Capt. 1946. Commnd TA (REME) 1947. Man.Director The Automobile Palace (Holdings) Ltd., 1955-85; High Sheriff (Radnorshire) 1966; Queen's Silver Jubilee Medal 1977. *Recreation:* gardening, collecting old cycles. *Address:* Sargodha, Brookfields, Cefnllys Lane, Llandrindod Wells, Powys. LD1 5LF.

NUNN, Dr John Francis, MD, DSc, FRCS, FCAnaes, FFARACS (Hon), FFARCSI (Hon). *Currently:* retired 1991. *Born on* 7 Nov 1925 at Colwyn Bay. *Son of* Francis Nunn and Lilian (nee Davies). *Marriage:* to Sheila Ernestine Doubleday, 1949. *Children:* Geoffrey, Carolyn and Shelley. *Educated at* Wrekin College; University of Birmingham. *Career:* Univ of Birmingham Spitzbergen Expedition 1948; Malayan Medical Service 1949-53; Leverhulme Research Fellow, Royal College Surgeons 1957-64; Professor of Anaesthesia, University of Leeds 1964-68; Head of Division of Anaesthesia, Clinical Research Centre (of Medical Research Council) 1968-91; Dean of Faculty of Anaesthetists 1979-82; Pres. Sect. of Anaesth. Royal Society of Medicine 1984-85. *Publications:* Applied Respiratory Physiology (3 editions); General Anaesthesia (joint editor, 3rd, 4th, 5th editions); 230 papers in scientific journals. *Recreation:* Egyptology, geology. *Clubs:* Royal Society of Medicine. *Address:* 3 Russell Road, Moor Park, Northwood, Middlesex HA6 2LJ.

O`BRIEN, Professor (Patrick Michael) Shaughn, MB, Bch, MD. *Currently:* Professor, Obstetrics and Gynaecology, Keele University; Consultant Obstetrician and Gynaecologist, North Staffordshire Hospital Centre. *Born on* 1 April 1948 *Son of* the late Patrick Michael O'Brien, of Treforest, Glamorgan and Joan (nee Edelston). *Marriage:* to Sandra Louise, 1985, da of Edward Arthur Norman (d 1979), of Henley-on-Thames. *Children:* James (b. 1986) and Louise (b. 1988). *Educated at* Pontypridd Boys' GS, University of Wales, Welsh Nat School of Medicine. *Career:* lecturer and hon senior registrar University of Nottingham 1979-84, senior lecturer and hon consultant in obstetrics and gynaecology Royal Free Hospital School of Medicine London 1984-89. foundation professor of Obstetrics and Gynaecology University of Keele 1989-, consultant obstetrician and gynaecologist North Staffordshire Hospital 1989- ; MRCOG, member RSM. *Publications:* Premenstrual Syndrome, 1987. *Recreation:* classical music, jazz, clarinet/saxophone, skiing, windsurfing. *Clubs:* Royal Society of Medicine, Ronnie Scott's. *Address:* Upper Farm House, Field Aston, Newport, Shropshire, TF10 9LE. University of Keele, Academic Dept of Obstetrics and Gynaecology, North Staffordshire Maternity Hospital, Thornburrow Drive, Hartshill, Stoke-on-Trent, ST4 7QB Tel: 0952 811510.

O`LEARY, Mr Edmund (Eamon), OBE, BE, CEng, FICE, FIStructE, FIEI, MIHT, MConsE. *Currently:* Senior Partner, Veryard & Partners, Consulting Engineers, since 1971. *Born on* 14 Aug 1933 at Waterford. *Son of* James O'Leary and Margaret (nee Cullinane). *Marriage:* to Denise Coffey, 1958. *Children:* Michele Ann and Clodagh Denise. *Educated at* St. Kieran's College, Kilkenny; University College, Cork. *Career:* Assistant Engineer Waterford CC 1954; Resident Engineer Waterford CC 1955; Assistant Engineer Rendel Palmer & Tritton 1958; Partner Veryard & Partners 1959; Chairman Concrete Society Wales 1970 and 1976; Chairman I. C. E South Wales 1978; President South Wales Institute of Engineers 1987; President Concrete Society 1989; Hon. Associate, Polytechnic of Wales 1991 *Publications:* Radar Aerial Towers 1972; Prestressed Concrete Buildings 1974; Crown Offices Cardiff 1980; Supervision of Construction 1985; Joints in Concrete 1988. *Recreation:* reading, golf, painting. *Clubs:* Royal Porthcawl Golf, Radyr Golf. *Address:* 39 Heol Don, Whitchurch, Cardiff, CF4 2AS. Veryard & Partners, Crwys House, Crwys Road, Cardiff, CF2 4NB.

O`NEILL, Dennis, FTCL, FWC, MD, ARCM *Currently:* Opera Singer. *Born on* 25 Feb 1948 at Pontardulais, W. Glam. *Son of* the late Dr. W. P. O'Neill and E. A. O'Neill. *Marriage:* to Ellen Folkestad, da of Hans Einar Folkestad, Norway. *Children:* Sean and Clare. *Educated at* Gowerton Grammar and studied singing London, Mantora and Tome. *Career:* Debuts: Royal Opera House Covent Garden 1979, (thereafter annually), Metropolitan N. Y. , 1986, Vienna State 1981, Hamburg State 1981, San Francisco 1984, Chicago Lyric 1985, Paris 1986 and thereafter at all leading Operas of the world. Speciality - roles of Verdi, many recordings and broadcasts. *Recreation:* cookery *Clubs:* *Address:* C/o Ingpen & Williams, 14 Kensington Court, London, W8.

O`REILLY, Professor John James, B. Tech, PhD, CEng, FIEE, CPhys, FInstP, FRSA. *Currently:* Head of School of Electronic Engineering Sceince, University of Wales, Bangor since 1985; Chief Executive IDB Ltd. , since 1986. Director, Communications and Information Systems Engineering Centre (WDA Centre of Excellence); Chaiman: DTI / SERC Communications and Distributed Systems committee 1991- ; member, DTI / SERC Information Technology Advisory Bd 1991- ; member, former SERC Communications Sub-committee 1987-91; Chairman, IEE Telecommunications Network Systems Committee 1990- , and formerly member on several occasions. *Born on* 1 Dec 1946 at Bromsgrove, Worcs, UK. *Son of* Patrick William and Dorothy Ann (nee Lewis). *Marriage:* to Margaret Brooke, 1968. *Children:* Jenny Ann and Edward James. *Educated at* Sacred Heart College, Droitwich; College of Electronics, Malvern; Brunel University. *Career:* Lecturer 1972, then Senior Lecturer, Department of Electrical Engineering Science, University of Essex. Industrial experience includes periods of employment with: Royal Radar Establishment, Ultra Electronics Ltd. , Post Office Research Centre, now BT Labs. *Publications:* Telecommunication Principles 1984, 1990; Problems of Randomness in Communications Engineering (with K. W. Cattermole) 1984; Optimisation Methods in Electronics and Communications 1984; author/co author of some 80 papers in research journals and a similar number of conference papers in the field of digital and optical fibre telecommunications. *Recreation:* reading, theatre, music, family. *Clubs:* Athenaeum. *Address:* University Of Wales, Dean Street, Bangor, Gwynedd, LL57 1UT.

O`RIORDAN, Professor Jeffrey Lima Hayes, DM, FRCP. *Currently:* Professor of Metabolic Medicine, University College and Middlesex School of Medicine and Physician, Middlesex Hospital, London. *Born on* 27 March 1931 at Newport, Gwent. *Son of* Dr. Michael O'Riordan and Mrs Milwen O'Riordan (nee Lima Jones). *Marriage:* to Sarah Berridge, 1963. *Children:* five children and one deceased. *Educated at* Newport High School; Pembroke College Oxford. *Career:* Nuffield Medical Scholar, Pembroke College, Oxford; House Physician and Registrar, The Middlesex Hospital; Senior Lecturer, UCMSM and University College London; Honorary Physician, The Middlesex Hospital. *Publications:* in the field of endocrinology and mineral metabolism. *Recreation:* sailing *Clubs:* Royal Cruising. *Address:* The Middlesex Hospital, Mortimer Street, London, W1N 8AA. Tel: 071 380 9373.

OAKSEY, Lord John Godfffrey Tristram, OBE *Currently:* Journalist and T. V. Commentator, commentated for ITV since 1970, and Channel 4. *Born on* 21 March 1929 at London. *Son of* Godfffrey and Marjorie Laurence (later Lord & Lady Trevethin and Oaksey). *Marriage:* 1st to

Victoria Dennistoln; 2nd to Rachel Crocker. *Children:* Patrick Lawrence and Sara Bradstock. *Educated at* Horris Hill; Eton, Oxford; Yale Law School. *Career:* Racing Correspondent for Daily Telegraph 1957- ; Sunday Telegraph 1959-89; Horse & Hound 1959-89. *Publications:* Millreef 1973; History of Steeplechasing (1/4), 1969; Oaksey on Racing 1991. *Recreation:* Riding, skiing, reading. *Clubs:* Brooks's. *Address:* Hill Farm, Oaksey, Malmesbury, Wilts. SN16 9HS.

ODLING, Mr Christopher, M. B. I. M. *Currently:* retired. *Born on* 1 Dec 1929 at Warrington. *Son of* Harold Odling FCA and Myrtle Odling (nee Huband). *Marriage:* Bangkok, Thailand, 1963. *Children:* Philippa, Claire and Richard. *Educated at* Boxgrove School, Radley College, St. Mary's Hospital London, Exeter College Oxford. *Career:* National Service 1948-50; The Hongkong and Shanghai Banking Corporation 1952-81; District Commissioner North Pembrokeshire Scout Association; Member, Governing Body of Church in Wales; Governor, Sir Thomas Picton School, Haverfordwest. *Recreation:* scouting, walking. *Clubs:* The Royal Hong Kong Jockey. *Address:* Manor House, Wiston, Haverfordwest, Pembs, SA62 4PN.

OLIVER, Dennis Stanley, CBE 1981; PhD, FEng, FIM, FInstP. *Currently:* Director, Pilkington Brothers plc, 1977-86. *Born on* 19 Sept 1926 *Son of* the late James Thomas Oliver and Lilian Mabel Oliver (nee Bunn). *Marriage:* 1st to Enid Jessie Newcombe, 1952 (marr diss 1984); 2nd to Elizabeth Emery, 1988. *Educated at* Deacon's School, Peterborough; Birmingham Univ. BSc, PhD. *Career:* Research Fellowship, Univ of Bristol 1949-52; Senior Scientific Officer, UKAEA, Culcheth 1952-55; Head of Metallurgy Division, UKAEA, Dounreay 1955-63; Chief R & D Officer, Richard Thomas & Baldwin Ltd 1963-68; Group R & D Dir, Pilkington Brothers plc 1968-77. Member: Board, British Technology Group; Member: NEB, 1981- ; NRDC 1981- ; Court and Council, Cranfield Inst. of Technology 1976-88. Visiting Professor Cranfield Inst of Technology 1984-88. Director: Anglo-American Venture Fund Ltd 1980-84; Monotype Corp 1985-90. Chairman Industrial Experience Projects Ltd 1981-86; Pres. , European Industrial Res. Management Assoc. , 1977-81. Patron, Science and Technology Education on Merseyside 1982- (Pres 1978-81); Governor: Liverpool Inst. of Higher Education 1979-85; Christ's and Notre Dame Coll. , Liverpool 1979-87; Royal Nat. Coll for the Blind 1981-85; Director L'Ecole Superieure du Verre, Belgium 1971-86; Governor, Community of St. Helens Trust Ltd 1978-86; Founder Trustee, Anfield Foundation 1983-88. Freeman of City of London; Liveryman: Spectaclemakers Co (Court of Assts 1985-88); Co. of Engrs 1984. FBIM. KSG 1980. *Publications:* The Use of Glass in Engineering, 1975; Glass for Construction Purposes, 1977; various publications on technical subjects and technology transfer. *Recreation:* music, poetry, travel. *Clubs:* Institute of Directors. *Address:* Castell Bach, Bodfari, Denbigh, Clwyd, LL16 4HT.

OLSEN, Roy, Architect RIBA *Currently:* Principal in Private Architects practise, Arran Buildings, Dolgellau, Gwynedd, LL40 1HE. *Born on* 20 April 1945 at Liverpool. *Son of* the late John Sigmund and the late Florence Mary. *Marriage:* to Francesca Carey Olsen. *Children:* Luke Joen Olsen and Alexander Hall Olsen. *Educated at* St. Margarets; Art High School; College of Building All Liverpool. *Career:* various architectural practises in Liverpool, incl: Lord Holfords Office, 1961-69; Architect with Merionydd County Council 1969-72; Principal with Olsen Associates, Architects and Conservation Consultants 1972- . Awards: Architectural - Snowdonia National Park, Montgomeryshire Planning

Design Award, National Stone Federation Award. *Recreation:* golf, photography. *Clubs:* Royal St. David's Golf. *Address:* Trem Yr Eglwys, Dolgellau, Gwynedd, LL40 2YW

ORMEROD, Dr Stephen James, BSc (Class 1); MSc; PhD; MIEEM. *Currently:* Head, Catchment Research Group, School of Pure and Applied Biology, University of Wales College of Cardiff, 1984- . *Born on* 24 Jan 1958 at Burnley, Lancs. *Son of* Harry Ormerod and Marjorie (nee Crossley). *Educated at* Huddersfield Polytechnic; UWIST. *Career:* Winston Churchill Memorial Trust - awarded travelling fellowship for work on the ecological impact of acid deposition in N. America 1987; Invited Assessor of the Review of the aquatic effects of long range air pollutants in Canada by Environment Canada 1990; Research/teaching assistant, Juniper Hall Field Centre 1978-79; Committee membership: DoE UK Acid Waters Review Group 1987-88; DoE UK Critical Loads Advisory Gp 1989- ; CEC Expert Gp on Catchments 1988- ; Editorial Bd, Environmental Pollution 1988- ; Editorial Bd, Ringing and Migration 1989- ; DoE Gp 'INDITE' (Impact of Nitrogen Deposition on Terrestrial Ecosystems) 1991- ; Countryside Council for Wales 1991- ; British Trust for Ornithology Research and Surveys Committee 1992- ; British Trust for Ornithology Research and Surveys Committee 1992- . Admitted as a member of IEEM 1991- ; Research Interest: The impact of acidification, climatic change and catchment land use on the ecology of streams; Ecosystem experimentation; The ecology of river and wetland birds; Modelling freshwater ecosystems; Air pollution and terrestrial birds; Referee to 11 scientific journals and book reviewer to 3. *Publications:* Author of over 90 scientific papers on the ecology and ornithology of rivers, wetlands and their catchments. *Recreation:* Music (guitar), poetry, travel, ornithology. *Clubs:* Freshwater Biological assoc; British Ecological Soc; Ecological Soc. of America; British Ornithologists Union; Oriental Bird club (founder mbr); Soc. of Conservation Biologists; RSPB; Nth American Benthological Soc; CPRW; British Trust for Ornithology; Wildfowl and Wetlands Trust; Dyfed and Glamorgan Wildlife Trusts. *Address:* University Of Wales, P. O. Box 915, Cardiff, CF1 3TL.

ORMROD, The Hon. Mrs. Barbara Helen, *Currently:* Housewife. *Born on* 19 Dec 1928 at London. *Son of* Captain The Viscount Daventry and Viscountess Daventry. *Marriage:* to Colonel Peter Charles Ormrod, MC, JP, DL. *Children:* Mrs Emma Holloway and Mrs Alice St. George Hedley. *Educated at* home. *Recreation:* sailing, gundogs. *Clubs:* Lloyds Yacht, Cruising Association. *Address:* Pen-Y-Lan, Ruabon, Wrexham, Clwyd, LL14 6HS.

ORMROD, Colonel Peter Charles, MC, JP, DL, M.I.C.For. *Currently:* Independant Consultant Forester, Company Director, Farmer, Landowner. *Born on* 31 Aug 1922 at Ruabon, nr. Wrexham. *Son of* Major James Ormrod and Mrs Ormrod. *Marriage:* to The Honourable Barbara Fitzroy. Children: Emma Holloway and Alice Hedley. *Educated at* Harrow School and RMA, Sandhurst. *Recreation:* Shooting, Sailing. *Clubs:* Army and Navy. *Address:* Pen-Y-Lan, Ruabon, Wrexham, Clwyd, LL14 6HS.

ORWIG, Mr Dafydd, B. A. *Currently:* Wedi ymddeol. *Born on* 17 Medi 1928 at Neiniolen. *Son of* a Mr & Mrs D. A. Jones. *Marriage:* Beryl Griffith, 1956. *Children:* Huw, Guto ac Owain. *Educated at* ysgolion cynradd Carnew (Wicklow) a Deiniolen, Ysgol Sir Brynrefail, Coleg Prifysgol Cymru, Aberystwyth. *Career:* Athro Daearyddiaeth Ysgol Sir Ffestiniog 1950-51, 1953-6; Trefnydd Plaid Cymru yn y Canolbarth 1951-53; Athro Daearyddiaeth Ysgol Dyffryn Ogwen 1956-62; Darlithydd Daearyddiath yn y Coleg Normal 1962-81; Aelod o Gyngor Sir Gwynedd o 1973 ymlaen: Cadeirydd Addysg a Chadeirydd yr Isbwyllgor Polisi Dwyieithog. Aelod o'r Cyd-bwyllgor Addysg a Chyngor y Brifysgol. Cadeirydd Pwllgor y Deyrnas Gyfunol o Fiwro Ewropeaidd yr Ieithoedd Llai. *Publications:* addasiadau i'r Gymraeg o Fy Atlas Cyntaf; Edrychwch ar y Map; Tirlun Prydain, golygydd Yr Atlas Cymraeg; Medrau Map 1-3 ac Atlas Medrau Map. *Recreation:* Darllen a theithio. *Address:* Cil Cacafan, Braichmelyn, Bethesda, Bangor, Gwynedd, LL57 3RD. Tel: 0248 600423.

OSMAN, Mr Louis, BA (Arch); FRIBA. *Currently:* artist, architect, goldsmith, medallist. *Born on* 30 Jan 1914. *Son of* Charles Osman, Exeter. *Marriage:* to Dilys Roberts, 1940, d of Richard Roberts, Rotherfield, Sussex. *Children:* one d. *Educated at* Hele's School, Exeter; London University (Fellow, UCL, 1984-). *Career:* Open exhibition at Bartlett School of Architecture, University Coll. London, 1931, and at Slade School; Donaldson Medallist of RIBA, 1935. With British Museum and British School of Archaeology Expeditions to Syria, 1936, 1937; designed private and public buildings, 1937-39. Served War of 1939-45, Major in Intelligence Corps: Combined Ops HQ and Special Air Service as specialist in Air Photography, Beach Reconnaissance Cttee, prior to invasion of Europe. Resumed practice in London, 1945, designed buildings, furniture, tapestries, glass, etc; work in Westminster Abbey, Lincoln, Ely and Exeter Cathedrals; Staunton Harold for National Trust; Bridge, Cavendish Square, with Jacob Epstein; Newnham Coll. , Cambridge; factory buildings for Cambridge Instrument Co. , aluminium Big Top for Billy Smart's Circus, two villages on Dartmoor, etc; consultant architect to British Aluminium Co. ; executed commissions as goldsmith and jeweller, 1956-; commissioned by De Beers for 1st Internat. Jewellery Exhibition, 1961; designed and made Prince of Wales' crown for investiture, 1969; British Bicentennial Gift to America housing Magna Carta, 1976; Verulam Medal for Metals Soc. , 1975; EAHY Medal, 1975; Olympic Medal, 1976; works in art galleries, museums and private collections in GB, Europe, Canada, USA, S Africa, Australia, Japan, etc; one-man retrospective exhibition, Goldsmiths' Hall, 1971. Member Exec. Cttee: The Georgian Group, 1952-56; City Music Soc. , 1960-70. *Publications:* reviews and contributions to learned journals. *Recreation:* music. *Clubs: Address:* Harpton Court, near New Radnor, Presteigne, Powys, LD8 2RE. Tel: 054421 380.

OWEN, Mr Albert, MBE *Currently:* Joiner and funeral Director. *Born on* 28 Sept 1922 at L'annerch-y-medd. *Son of* the late William Owen and Kate (nee Jones). *Marriage:* April 16, 1948. *Educated at* Llannerchymedd Primary; Llangefni County School. *Career:* District Councillor 1957-74; Chairman of Twrcelyn District Council; served on Amlwch Bench as chairman of the Council; Anglesey County Councillor 1966-74; Gwynedd County Councillor 1974- ; Chairman of Gwynedd County Council Property Committee; member: North Wales Police Authority; member Eryri National Park Committee; Chairman of the Anglesey Smallholdings Farms. *Recreation:* Play acting. *Address:* Coedlys, Llanerch-y-Medd, Gwynedd, LL71 8EB.

OWEN, Mr Alun Davies, *Currently:* Playwright. *Born on* 24 Nov 1925 at Liverpool. *Son of* Sidney Owen and Ruth Owen (nee Davies). *Marriage:* to Theodora Mary O'Keefe 1942. *Children:* Teifion Davies Davies Owen and Gareth Robert Owen. *Educated at* Oulton High School; Cardigan County School. *Career:* Actor 1942-57; Writer 1957-1991; After leaving school he went to Perth Repertory Company as an assistant stage manager, then joined Southport Rep where his acting career was interrupted by war service as a 'Bevin Boy' in the pits in South Wales. After two trips as a seaman in the Merchant Navy he resumed his profession at Birmingham Rep when the war ended in 1945; First London appearance was at the Old Vic; Under contract to Associated Rediffusion in 1956; Since the late 50's right through to 1981 Alun Owen was associated with the Dublin Theatre Festival; he has written prolifically for the stage and the cinema, and is generally recognised as one of the major pioneers of the television play. Awards: Screenwriters and Producers Guild, Script of The Year 1960; Screenwriters Guild 1961; Daily Mirror Award 1961; Golden Star Award, Ass. Rediffusion 1967; Oscar Nomination, A Hard Day's Night, USA 1964; Emmy Award, USA Male Of The Species 1969. *Publications:* The Rough and Ready Lot 1960; Progress To The Park 1962; No Trams, Lena and After The Funeral 1961, three television plays, 1961; The Rose Affair Anatomy of a Television Play 1962; Dare To Be A Daniel, 8 plays 1965; A Little Winter Love 1965; The Wake, collection of modern short plays, 1972; George's Room, Shelter 1971; Norma 1971; Doreen, The Best short plays 1971; The Male Of The Species 1972; George's Room 1969; A Hard Day's Night (Title, film script four) edited by George P Garrett, O B Hardison, Jane R Gelfman, 1972; Passing Through 1977. *Recreation:* History and languages. *Clubs:* Chelsea Arts, Dramatist. *Address:* 5 Upham Park Road, Chiswick, London W4 1PG.

OWEN, His Honour Judge. Aron, BA (Hons); PhD (Wales). *Currently:* Circuit Judge. *Born on* 16 Feb 1919 at Tredegar, Gwent. *Marriage:* to Rose (nee Fishman) J. P. 1946. *Children:* Barbara, Verity and Robert. *Educated at* Tredegar County Grammar School; University College Cardiff. *Career:* Called to the Bar by Inner Temple 1948; Appointed Circuit Judge 1980; Resident Judge at Clerkenwell County Court since 1986; Also sits as a High Court Judge in the Family Division at the Royal Courts of Justice, Strand, London; Freeman City of London 1963. *Recreation:* Travel, gardening. *Address:* 44 Brampton Grove, Hendon, London, NW4 4AQ. Clerkenwell County Court, 33 Duncan Terrace, Islington, London, N1 8AN.

OWEN, Dr Gareth, CBE, BSc (Wales), DSc (Glasgow), MRIA, FIBiol. *Currently:* retired 1989 as Principal, University College of Wales, Aberystwyth. *Born on* 4 Oct 1922 at Cilfynydd, Pontypridd. *Son of* the late John Richard Owen and the late Bronwen May (nee Davies). *Marriage:* to Beti Jones, 1953. *Children:* Shan, Gwyneth and Huw Geraint. *Educated at* Pontypridd Grammar School; University College Cardiff (1st Class Hons Zool.) *Career:* Pilot, RAF 1942-47; Lecturer, Univ of Glasgow 1950-64; Prof. of Zoology and Head of Dept Queen's Univ. , Belfast 1964-79; Pro-Vice-Chancellor Queen's Univ., 1974-78; Principal Univ. College of Wales, Aberystwyth 1979-89; Vice-Chancellor Univ. of Wales 1985-87; Elected Member of the Royal Irish Academy 1976; Welsh Supernumerary, Jesus College Oxford 1981-82, 1986-87; Honorary D. Sc. Queen's University Belfast 1982; Honorary Fellow, University College Cardiff 1982; Honorary Member of the Gorsedd 1983; Member of the Nature Conservancy Council 1983-91; Chairman, Nature Conservancy Committee for Wales 1985-91; CBE 1988. Hon. LL. D. , University of Wales 1989; President, Welsh Centre for International Affiars 1989- ; Honorary Fellow AFRC Institute of Grassland and Environmental Research 1991; Member RSPB Advisory Committee for Wales 1991; Chairman, Management Committee, University of London Marine Biology Laboratory, Millport 1991. *Publications:* Scientific papers on Marine Biology, Electron Microscopy and Morphology and Physiology of Mollusca and Brachiopoda. *Recreation:*

photography, travel *Clubs:* Commonwealth. *Address:* 6 A St Margaret's Place, Whitchurch, Cardiff, CF4 7AD.

OWEN, Mr Glyn, OBE (1973), BSc (Wales), MSc (London). *Born on* 20 April 1926 at Borthygest. *Son of* the late William and Sally (nee Jones). *Marriage:* to Laura Diana Davies 1952. *Children:* Susan Jane and Peter Davies. *Educated at* Portmadoc County School; University College of North Wales, Bangor; Chelsea Polytechnic. *Career:* Assistant Examiner, Patent Office 1946-48; Scientific Officer-Senior Principal Scientific Officer, Royal Naval Scientific Service, Admiralty, 1948-65; Staff of Superintendent of Scientific Personnel, Ministry of Defence (Navy) 1965-66; Private Secretary to Chief Scientific Adviser, Cabinet Office 1966-71; Senior Principal Scientific Officer, Cabinet Office 1971-73; Member of U.K. Delegation to the United Nations Conference on the International Law of the Sea 1973-76; Assistant Secretary, Welsh Office, 1976-86; Secretary of the Local Government Boundary Commission for Wales 1989-91. *Recreation:* Watching and reading about soccer and cricket, chapel and social activities. *Address:* 5 Maes yr Awel, Radyr, Cardiff, CF4 8AN.

OWEN, Councillor Glyn, *Currently:* Retired Primary School Headmaster. *Born on* 20 July 1926 at Bethesda, Caerns. *Son of* the late John Lewis Owen and the late Catherine Owen (nee Hughes). *Educated at* Bethesda Grammar School; Normal College, Bangor & Faculty of Educ. Aberystwyth. *Career:* Headmaster, Llanllyfni C. P. Schl, 1962-73; Headmaster, Hendre C. P. Schl, Caernarfon, 1974-84; Mbr. of the Bethesda Urban D. C., 1952-64; Mbr. of the Gwyrfai R. D. C., 1964-74; Mbr. of the Arfon B. C. since 1974 and former Mayor of the Borough, 1989-90; Mbr. of the Gwynedd C. C. since 1989; Former mbr. of the Council for the Principality and the Council of the Assoc. of Dist. Councils; Mbr. of the Industrial Appeals Tribunal. *Recreation:* Local Government, classical music and reading. *Address:* Crud yr Awel, Dinas, Llanwnda, Caernarfon, Gwynedd, LL54 7YL.

OWEN, Major-General Harry, C. B. *Currently:* retired from Army 1971; Was Chairman of Medical Appeal Tribunal 1972-1984. *Born on* 17 July 1911 at Beaumaris. *Son of* John Lewis and Susan Owen. *Marriage:* to Maureen (nee Summers), 1952. *Children:* Elspeth Susan and Julian Summers. *Educated at* University College, Bangor, BA Hons Philisophy. Admitted Solicitor 1939. *Career:* Joined Army 1939, Cameron Highlanders, J. A. G's (Judge Advocate General), Office; Served in West Indies, West Africa, Middle East, Austria, Far East and Germany. M. O. D. as Director of Army Legal Services 1969-71. *Recreation:* swimming, walking, reading, Philosophy. *Address:* 1 The Beeches, Slab Lane, West Wellow, Romsey, Hants, SO51 6RN. Tel: 0794 23562.

OWEN, John (Graham), BDS (Lond), LDS, RCS (Eng). *Currently:* Self employed Dental Surgeon. *Born on* 30 Aug 1952 at Bridgend. *Son of* John (Hugh) Owen and Mair Eluned (nee Evans). *Marriage:* to Belle Steadman (Monney), 1977. *Children:* Robert, Annabelle and Jonathan Martin. *Educated at* Epsom College; Guys Hospital. *Career:* Former lecturer in Maxillo-Facial & Oral Surgery, Guys Hospital; Hon. Sec. Dental Society of London 1990-91-92. *Recreation:* Light Aircraft pilot, rugby, cricket, athletics. *Clubs:* Rugby Club of London *Address:* High View, 339 Main Road, Westerham Hill, Kent, TN16 2HP. 84 Harley Street, London, W1.

OWEN, Professor John Bryn, BSc, PhD (Wales), MA (Cantab), FIBiol, FRAgS. *Currently:* Professor of Agriculture, since 1978, and Head of School of Agricultural and Forest Sciences. *Born on* 23 May 1931 at Cerrig Y

Drudion. *Son of* O. W. Owen and J. Owen. *Marriage:* to Margaret Helen, 1955. *Children:* Gareth Wyn, David Huw and Helen Rachel. *Educated at* Ysgol Sir Ffestiniog; UCNW Bangor *Career:* Farm Manager 1955-58; Lecturer UCW Aberystwyth 1958-62; University lecturer Cambridge 1962-72; Professor of Animal Production and Health University of Aberdeen 1972-78. *Publications:* Breeding for disease resistance in Farm Animals; Weight Control and Appetite: Nature over Nature etc. *Recreation:* choral singing (Penrhyn Male Voice Choir). *Clubs:* Farmers, London. *Address:* School of Agricultural & Forest Sciences, Univ of Wales, Bangor, Gwynedd, LL57 2UW.

OWEN, Mr John Wyn, MA (Cantab)., MHSM, Dip. HSM, Hon FFPHM; Hon. Fellow Univ. of Wales. *Currently:* Director, NHS Wales since 1985. *Born on* 15 May 1942 at Bangor, N. Wales. *Son of* the late Idwal Wyn Owen and Myfi Hughes. *Marriage:* to Elizabeth Ann Lacfarlane 1967. *Children:* Dafydd Wyn and Sian Wyn *Educated at* Friars School Bangor; St. John's Coll., Cambridge; King Edward VIII's Hospital Fund for London, Hospital Admin. Staff College. *Career:* Trainee, King Edward VIII's Hospital Fund for London 1964-66; Deputy Hospital Sec., W. Wales General Hospital, Carmarthen 1966-67; Hospital Sec. Glantawe HMC, Swansea 1967-70; Staff Training Officer, Welsh Hospital Bd., Cardiff 1968-70; Div. Administrator, Univ. of Wales, Cardiff HMC 1970-72; St. Thomas' Hospital: Asst. Clerk and King's Fund Fellow 1972-74; Dist. Administrator, St. Thomas' Health Dist. Teaching 1974-79; Trustee, Refresh 1976-78; Hon. Tutor, Medical School 1974-79; Praeceptor, School of Health Admin., Univ. of Minnesota 1974-79; Visiting Fellow, Univ. of New South Wales, Australia 1979; Executive Dir., United Medical Enterprises, London 1979-85; Trustee, Florence Nightingale Museum Trust 1983-90; Trustee, Management Advisory Service 1987-90; Chrmn., Health Building Educ. Group, British Consultants' Bureau 1983-85; Chairman, Welsh Health Common Services Authority since 1985. *Publications:* Contributions to professional journals *Recreation:* Organ, opera *Clubs:* Athenaeum *Address:* Welsh Office, Cathays Park, Cardiff CF1 3NQ.

OWEN, Mrs Molly Eileen, MBE, 1992, FSAE. *Currently:* Director, Cardiff Chamber of Commerce and Industry. *Born on* 13 Oct 1934 in London. *Daughter of* the late Ernest James and Anne Timpson. *Marriage:* to Alan David Charles Owen, 1954. *Children:* Graham Thomas and Judith Anne. *Educated at* Streatham House School, Crosby, Liverpool; Waterloo College of Secretarial and Business Studies, Liverpool. *Career:* Finance, Liverpool University 1951; ICI Liverpool, Exports, 1952-57; Rover British Leyland, Cardiff 1970; CBI Wales 1970-71; Secretary, Cardiff Chamber of Commerce and Industry 1971; Deputy Director Cardiff Chamber of Commerce and Industry 1978; Board member, South Glamorgan Compact. *Publications:* Chamber of Commerce - Welsh Business Contact. *Recreation:* music, antiques, overseas travel, gardening. *Clubs:* Society of Association Executives; Association British Chamber of Commerce Executives. *Address:* Cardiff Chamber of Commerce & Industry, 101-108 The Exchange, Mount Stuart Sq, Cardiff, CF1 6RD. ''Glan-Yr-Eigion'', Cog Road, Sully, S Glam, CF6 2TD.

OWEN, Chairman Federation Sports Associations for the Disabled Wales, Patricia, M. S. C. P. *Currently:* Partner in Husband's Engineering Business, Est. 1970. *Born on* 24th Apr 1940 at Leigh, Lancs. *Daughter of* Hugh and Dilys H. Williams of Holyhead. *Marriage:* to Islwyn Frazer Owen (second marriage). *Children:* Anthony Kevin, Sharon Yovonn, Robert Paul, Andrew Mark. *Educated at* Leigh Grammar School, Lancs. *Career:*

Chairman Federation Sports Associations for the Didsabled Wales. Welsh Amputee's Les Autres Sports Association Disabled. Wales, Treasurer, British Les Autres's Sports Assoc Great Britain. *Recreation:* Sports: swimming, athletics, walking, Music Classics, enjoy reading & gardening. *Address:* Tal-Y-Llyn, Lon Dryll, Llanfairpwll, Gwynedd, LL61 6MX. Ffingar Auto Repairs, Llanedwen, Gwynedd, LL61 6EQ.

OWEN, Mr Philip Loscombe Wintringham, TD; QC; MA (Oxon). Assumed surname of Owen by Deed Poll dated February 21st 1942. *Currently:* One of Her Majesty's Counsel. *Born on* 10 Jan 1920 at London. *Son of* The Rt. Hon. Sir Wintringham Norton Stable and Lady Lucie Haden Stable. (nee Freeman). *Marriage:* to Elizabeth Jane (nee Widdicombe). *Children:* James Wintringham, Michael Lewis; Teresa Catherine; Philip Anthony and Sophie Jane. *Educated at* Winchester College; Christ Church College, Oxford. *Career:* Served War of 1939-45, Royal Welch Fusiliers: W. Africa, India, Ceylon, Burma, 1939-47; Major TARO. Received into Roman Catholic Church 1943; Called to Bar, Middle Temple 1949; Bencher 1969; Mem., Gen. Council of the Bar of England and Wales 1971-77; a Deputy Chairman of Quarter Sessions: Montgomeryshire 1959-71; Cheshire 1961-71; Recorder of Merthyr Tydfil 1971; a Recorder of the Crown Court 1972-82; Leader Wales and Chester Circuit 1975-77; Chm., Adv. Bd. constituted under Misuse of Drugs Act 1974- ; Legal Assessor to: Gen. Med. Council, 1970- ; Gen. Dental Council 1970-; RICS 1970-; Contested (C) Montgomeryshire Parliamentary Constituency: 1945. Pres. Montgomeryshire Soc., 1974-75; Dir, Swansea City AFC Ltd 1976-87; Trustee of and on the Committee of Management of Young Musicians Symphony Orchestra, London. *Recreation:* Music (plays Bassoon), shooting, fishing, forestry, Association football. *Clubs:* Carlton, Pratt's Cardiff & County, Bristol Channel Yacht Club (Mumbles); Welshpool & District Conservative. *Address:* Plas Llwyn Owen, Llanbrynmair, Powys SY19 7BE. Tel: 0650 521542. 15-19 Devezeux Court, Brick Court Chambers, Strand, London, WC2R 3JJ Tel: 071 583 0777.

OWEN, Miss Sheila Yorke, FIL *Currently:* retired. *Born on* 13 March 1912 at Butterworth, South Africa. *Daughter of* the late Captain William Owen, SAMR and Ethel Lucy Yorke (nee Weedon), descended from Baron Lewis Owen, murdered in 1555 by the Gwylltiaid Cochion Mawddwy. *Educated at* Berkhamsted Grammar School for Girls; Queen Anne's School, Caversham, Freiburg im Breisgau; Lycee Francais London, University of Geneva, Mrs Hoster's Secretarial Training College, London. *Career:* Secretary/translator Unilever Ltd., London and Paris 1932-68; Secretary to Mr. V. Cavendish-Bentinck (Duke of Portland) 1947-68 and of Cttee of British Industrial Interests in Germany 1950-68. Hon. Sec. Cons Assn Branch Hernhill, Kent 1968-70; Dolgellau 1985-87; Meirionnydd Nant Conwy 1986-87; Vice-Chm Aberaeron Branch, Dyfed. Languages: Dutch, French German, Norwegian, smattering Polish and Russian, Welsh. Fellow of Institute of Linguists. *Recreation:* mountain walking, gardening. *Clubs:* Royal Over-seas League. *Address:* Clawdd Dewi, Aberarth, Dyfed, SA46 OJX.

OWEN, Mr Thomas Arfon, MA (Oxon and Wales); FRSA. *Currently:* Director, Welsh Arts Council 1984- . *Born on* 7 June 1933 at St. Davids. *Son of* the late Hywel Peris Owen and Jenny (nee Jones). *Marriage:* to Mary Joyce Phillips 1955. *Children:* Huw, Marc, Sian and Philip. *Educated at* Ystalyfera Grammar School; Magdalen College, Oxford; University of Wales. *Career:* Master at New College, Oxford 1954-55; County Treasurer's Dept., Gloucestershire County Council 1955-58; Deputy Registrar, The University

of Wales, Aberystwyth 1959-66; Registrar, The University of Wales, Aberystwyth 1966-84; High Sheriff of the County of Dyfed 1976-77; Appointed by Sec. of State for Wales to the following bodies: Mid Wales Hospital Management Cttee, Chairman 1972-74; Cardiganshire Nat. Health Serv. Exec. Cttee; Dyfed Family Practitioner Cttee; Dyfed Health Auth. and its successor, East Dyfed Health Auth, to 1984; S. Glam Health Auth. 1984-88; Vice Chairman 1986-88; Chairman, Educ. Cttee; Chairman Medical Ethics Cttee; Mbr of Whitley Council, Admin and Clerical; Former mbr of Whitley Council (doctors and dentists); Dyfed Council on Alcoholism; Appoint. by Minister of Agrig. as member of the Consumers Cttee for G. B. 1975-91; Served as governor of the proposed Nat. Arts Centre for Wales; as a mbr and Chairman of various Nat. Savings cttees; as a mbr of the Finance Cttee of Urdd Gobaith Cymru; mbr of other charitable Cttees; Gvnr, Welsh Coll. of Music and Drama (sole co-opted governor); Nat. Library of Wales; Univ. Coll of Wales, Abersytwyth; Univ. Coll of N. Wales, Bangor; Mbr. of Cncl, Univ. of Wales Coll of Cardiff; Univ. Coll of Wales, Abersytwyth; Nat. Library of Wales; Vice-Pres. Llangollen Int. Eisteddfod; Vice-Chmn, Management Ctee (Chairman), Coleg Harlech, a College for adult student; former mbr: Court of Governors & Cncl of the Univ of Wales Central Council, Fed. Superannuation System for Universities; Standing Conference on Univ. Entrance; Univs. Cttee for Non-Teaching Staffs; trustee of Davies Charities (personal capacity). *Publications:* Various articles in Educational Journals *Recreation:* The Arts and crosswords *Clubs:* Cardiff and County *Address:* Argoed, Ffordd Y Fulfran, Borth, Dyfed, SY24 5NN.

OWEN, Tudor Wyn, LLB (Hons) (Lond), Barrister. *Currently:* Barrister. *Born on* 16 May 1951 at Aberdare. *Son of* the late Abel Rhys Owen and Mair Owen (nee Jenkins). *Educated at* Aberdare Boys' Grammar; King's College, London University. *Career:* Called to the Bar, Gray's Inn 1974; Asst. Recorder of the Crown Court, since 1990. DTI Inspector, since 1989. Member of General Council of the Bar of England and Wales 1988- . member of Bar Professional Conduct Committee 1988-90; Bar Committee 1989-91 (Vice Chairman 1991); General Management Committee 1992- . Professional Standards Committee 1992- . *Publications:* Co-author of "Quality of Justice: The Way Forward", the Response of the Bar Council to the Lord Chancellor's Advisory Committee on Legal Education and Conduct, 1991; Co-author of the Bar Council's Submissions to the Royal Commission on Criminal Justice, 1992. *Recreation:* flying vintage aircraft, motor racing, shooting, skiing, riding the Cresta Run. *Clubs:* Carlton, St. Moritz Tobogganing, Royal Aero. *Address:* 4 Paper Buildings, Temple, London, EC4Y 7EX. 25 Dancer Road, Fulham, London, SW6 4DU. Tel: 071 583 7765.

OWEN, Professor Walter Shepherd, Ph. D. , D. Eng. *Currently:* Professor Emeritus, Massachusetts, Inst. of Technology, Cambridge, Massachusetts, U. S. A. since 1985. *Born on* 13 March 1920 at Liverpool. *Son of* Walter Lloyd and Dorothea Owen. *Marriage:* to Geraldine Feinstein, 1980. *Children:* Ruth Ann *Educated at* Alsop High School, Liverpool; Univ. of Liverpool. *Career:* Prof. of Metallurgy, Univ. of Liverpool, 1957-65; Dean of Engineering, Univ. of Liverpool, 1963-65; Prof. of Materials Science, Cornell Univ. Ithaca, N. Y. , 1965-70; Dean of Eng. & Vice-Pres. , Northwestern Univ. Illinois, 1970-73; Prof. of Materials Science and Eng. , Massachusetts, Inst. of Technology (MIT), Cambridge, Massachusetts, 1973-85. *Publications:* Numerous papers in scientific research journals *Recreation:* Walking *Clubs:* Madog Yacht club, Porthmadog; St.

Botolph, Boston, Massachusetts. *Address:* "Winstay", 1 Marine Terrace, Porthmadog, Gwynedd, LL49 9BL. 199 Commonwealth Avenue, Boston, Massachusetts 02116, U.S.A.

OWEN-JONES, Mr David Roderic, LLB 1970; LL. H 1971 *Currently:* Barrister-at-Law, acting Metropolitan Stipendiary Magistrate. *Born on* 16 March 1949 at Bangor. *Son of* John Eryl Owen-Jones, CBE, JP, DL and Mabel Clara (nee McIlvride). *Educated at* Llandovery College, Dyfed; University College London. *Career:* Called to the Bar Inner Temple 1972; Parliamentary Candidate (Lib) Carmarthen Div Feb and Oct 1974 (Lib. Alliance) Rugby and Kenilworth, 1983 and 1987. Memb. Lord Chancellors Advisory Cttee on the Appointment of J. P's for Inner London 1984-90; Trustee International Students Trust, FRSA. *Publications:* The Prosecutorial Process in England and Wales. *Recreation:* theatre, political biography. *Clubs:* National Liberal (chairman 1988-91), Reform. *Address:* 17 Albert Bridge Road, London SW11 4PX. 3 Temple Gardens, Temple, London, EC4Y 9AU.

OWEN-JONES, Mr John Eryl, CBE; MA; LL. B; Solicitor Adm. 1938. *Currently:* Retired (Clerk of Caernarvonshire County Council, 1956-74) and Clerk of Lieutenancy. *Born on* 19 Jan 1912 at Dolgellau. *Son of* the late John Owen-Jones, Hon. FTSC and Jane Griffith (Old Colwyn). *Marriage:* to Mabel Clara McIlvride, S. R. N. (b. Bombay, India). *Children:* (Mrs) Jennifer Ann Davies; David Roderic, LL. M. *Educated at* Portmadoc Grammar School; Univ. College of Wales, Aberystwyth (LL.B.); Gonville & Caius Coll. Cambridge (M.A.) *Career:* Assistant Solicitor, Chester Corporation 1939; Squadron Leader RAFVR 1945; Legal Staff Officer Judge Advocate General's Dept. Mediterranean; Dep. Clerk Caernarvonshire County Council 1946; Clerk of the County Council and Clerk of the Peace, Caernarvonshire 1956; Secretary, North Wales Probation & After-Care Committee; Clerk Gwynedd Police Authority 1956-67; Sec. North Wales Ccl. for County Council Roadmen; Dep. Clerk Snowdonia Park Joint Advisory Cttee; Memb. Central Ccl. for Magistrates' Courts Committees 1980-82; Sec. Caernarvonshire Historical Soc; Board Memb. of Civic Trust for Wales (N. Wales Vice Chmn); Board Memb. Gwynedd Archaelogical Trust; Chmn. Caernarvon Civic Soc. 1980-89; Fellow of Royal Soc. of Arts (FRSA); Memb. of Druidic Order, Gorsedd of Bards 1990; Deputy Lieutenant, Caernarvonshire 1971, Gwynedd 1974; Justice of the Peace 1974. *Publications:* Articles to journals. *Recreation:* Music (Organ), gardening, photography. *Clubs:* No London clubs (formerly National Liberal). *Address:* Rhiw Dafnau, Caernarfon, Gwynedd LL55 1LF.

OWENS, Mr Bernard Charles, FLS; FRGS; FRSA; FZS *Currently:* Deputy Chairman, Hamdden Ltd; member, Monopolies & Mergers Commission; President, British Jewellery & Giftware Federation. *Born on* 20 March 1928 at Birmingham. *Son of* Charles Owens and the late Sheila (nee O'Higgins). *Marriage:* to Barbara Madeline Murphy, 1954. *Children:* Michael, Jacqueline, Jennifer, Peter, Teresa and Susan. *Educated at* Solihull School; London School of Economics. *Career:* Councillor, Solihull U. D. , and B. C. , 1954-64; Cons. Parliamentary Candidate, Small Heath, Birmingham, 1959 and 1961; Chairman and Managing Director, Undchrome International PLC, 1964-80; member, Order of Malta; member, Honourable Artillery Company; member of Lloyd's; Freeman of City of London; Liveryman, Worshipful Company of Gardeners; Life Governor, RNLI. *Clubs:* Carlton, MCC, City Livery Yacht (Hon. Sec), Stroud RFC, City Livery. *Address:* The Vatch House, Stroud, Gloucestershire, GL6 7JY.

P

PACKENHAM-WALSH, Mabel, *Currently:* Artist. *Born on* 2 Sept 1937 at Lancaster. *Daughter of* Dr. R. Pakenham-Walsh and Joyce Braithwaite Savory. *Educated at* Lancaster & Wimbledon Colleges of Art; Pinewood & Shepperton Film Studies. *Career:* Exhibited painted wood carving in "The Craftsmans Art", Victoria & Albert Museum 1973; National Museum of Wales 1978; Mappin Museum Sheffield 1980; St. Davids Hall, Cardiff 1982; National Eisteddfod 1983; Aberystwyth Art Centre 1984; International Exhibition of Applied Arts in Bratislava 1986; Sothebys Decorative Art Exhibition 1988; Studio at Barn Community Centre Aberystwyth 1984-86. Painted carvings permanently at Craft Council Collection London, Ulster Museum and Grizedale, Cumbria *Recreation:* planting trees, bird wrecking, colour, swimming, public transport *Clubs: Address:* "Archnoa", Tanyfynwent, Llanbadarn Fawr, Aberystwyth, Dyfed, SY23 3RA.

PAGINTON, County Councellor Eilleen Dorothy, *Currently:* Councellor since May 1985. *Born on* 24 July 1941 at Runcorn, Cheshire. *Daughter of* the late Leonard & Vera (nee Carter) Hallett. *Marriage:* to David Paginton, 1961. *Children:* Alison, Margaret and Anthony. *Educated at* Westover GirlsSchool, Bridgwater, Bridgwater Art & Technical College. *Career:* Housewife until 1978; Full time Secretarial course, Crosskeys College 1978-79; Joined Labour Party 1978; Ward Secretary L. P. 1979-84; County Councellor for Risca South Ward 1985; County Councellor Risca East Ward 1989; Secretary Islwyn Labour Party Women's Council since 1984; Vice/Chairperson Residential Services 1989-91; Chairperson appointment panel - Social Services, Gwent County Council 1991. *Recreation:* Dressmaking, Music, Reading and Gardening. *Address:* 175 Elm Drive, Ty Sign, Risca. Gwent, NP1 6PN.

PALIA, Dr Satnam Singh, MBBS, MRCPsych, DPM, FRSH *Currently:* Consultant Psychiatrist and Hon. Postgraduate Organiser and clinical tutor in Psychiatry. *Born on* 5 Oct 1952 at Punjab, India. *Son of* Mr. Daljit Singh and Mrs Pritam Kaur. *Marriage:* 3rd July 1976 (Indian Ceremony 21 August 1976).*Children:* Satwinder, Navjinder and Rajinder. *Educated at* Medical College Amritsar, India. *Career:* Senior Registrar in Psychiatry, Cardiff 1983; Registrar in Psychiatry, 1981; Senior House Officer/ Registrar in Psychiatry 1977. *Publications:* Water Intoxication in Psychiatric patients; Mood disorders in Epilepsy and Psychopharmacological Studies. *Recreation:* badminton, music, reading *Address:* Glanrhyd / Penyfai Hospitals, Tondu Road, Bridgend, Mid Glam, CF31 4LN. 35 Herbert March Close, Radyr Vale, Llandaff, Cardiff, CF5 2TD.

PALIN, Mr Hugh Mair, MBE, TD. *Currently:* retired, but currently Chairman National Motor Museum, Beaulieu. *Born on* 31 May 1912 at Wallington, Surrey. *Son of* V. C. Palin (member of Treasury, Bank of England). *Marriage:* 1st to Margery Free, 1938 (dissolved); 2nd to Peggy Bailey, 1962. *Children:* Michael John (b. 1944), Rosemary Grace (b. 1950) and Jonathan Hugh (b. 1963). *Educated at* Brighton College. *Career:* Member Committee Royal Automobile Club (RAC); Director (non executive) Auto Cycle Union (ACU), (governing body motorcycle sport); Previously: Director, RAC; Chairman, Motor Cycle Industry Assoc of G. B; President, British Motorcyclists Federation; Director, Norton Motors Ltd; Past President: International Motorcycle Manufacturers Assoc; served in Royal Tank Regiment in Europe and N. Africa 1939-45; Attended War Staff Course, Staff College, Camberley; Demobbed, rank of Major. *Recreation:* Motorcycle sport, motor sport, vintage cars and motorcycles. *Clubs:* RAC, Cavalry & Guards. *Address:* Bay View, Freshwater East, Pembroke, SA71 5LE.

PALMER, Dr Keith Francis, PhD *Currently:* Director, N. M. Rothschild & Sons Ltd, since 1984, also NMR Wales. *Born on* 26 July 1947 at Cardiff, Wales. *Son of* the late Frank and Gwenda (nee Merick). *Marriage:* to Penelope Anne McDough, 1974. *Children:* Alexandra, Georgia, Katherine and Megan. *Educated at* University of Birmingham (BSc(Hons), Geology 1968, PhD 1971); University of Cambridge (DDE 1974). *Career:* World Bank Energy Dept, Senior Economist, 1979-84; International Monetary Fund, Fiscal Economist, 1978-79; Finance Ministry, Papua New Guinea, 1974-78; Post-doctoral fellow University of Columbia, NY, 1971-73. *Publications:* numerous books and articles. *Recreation:* Geology, running, classical music. *Clubs:* Institute of Directors.

PARAVICINI, Nicolas Vincent Somerset, *Currently:* Chief Executive, Ely Place Investments Ltd; Consultant, Bank Sarasin & Co. *Born on* 19 Oct 1937 at London. *Son of* the late Colonel Vincent Paravicini and Baroness Glendevon (nee Maugham). *Marriage:* to Susan Rose Phipps. *Children:* Charles V. S. , Elizabeth Ann and Derek N. S. *Educated at* Eton and RMA Sandhurst. *Career:* Army (The Life Guards), retd Major 1969; Member, London Stock Exchange 1972-80; Director, Joseph Sebag & Co. , 1972-80; Chairman and Chief Executive, Bank Sarasin (UK) Ltd. 1980-90; Freeman City of London. *Recreation:* shooting, skiing, wine. *Clubs:* Whites, Pratts, City Livery, Institute of Directors. *Address:* Glyn Celyn House, Brecon, Powys, LD3 OTY. 62 Marsham Court, Marsham St, London, SW1

PARKER, Emeritus Professor Clifford Frederick, JP. MA., LL.M. (Cantab) *Currently:* Retired. *Born on* 6 March 1920 at Cardiff. *Son of* the late Frederick James and Bertha Isabella Parker (nee Kemp). *Marriage:* to Christine Alice (nee Knowles) 1945. *Children:* Vivien Frances Parker and Denise Christine Parker. *Educated at* Cardiff High School; Gonville & Caius College, Cambridge. *Career:* Solicitor of the Supreme Court 1947; Lectr. in Common Law, Univ. of Birmingham 1951-57; Bracton Professor of Law, Univ. of Exeter 1957-85; Deputy Vice-Chancellor 1963-65; Public Orator 1977-81; Pres. Society of Public Teachers of Law 1974-75; Justice of the Peace for the County of Devon 1969- Chairman of Exeter Social Security Appeal Tribunal 1978- *Publications:* Contributions to Legal Journals *Interests:* Touring, music *Address:* Lynwood, Exton, Exeter EX3 OPR. Tel: 0392 874051.

PARKER, Miss Malinda Florence Muriel (known as Linda), *Currently:* Private Secretary, C. C. Harley Esq. Estate Office, Brampton Bryan, Bucknell, Shropshire (part-time). *Born on* 11 Dec 1925 at Beckjay, nr. Clungunford. *Daughter of* the late Florence (nee Hughes) Parker and John Rich Parker. *Educated at* Bucknell Primary School; Llandrindod Wells Grammar School; Hampstead Secretarial College. *Career:* Private Secretary to Managing Director, The Radnorshire Co. Ltd. , Knighton, Powys, 1944-82 (Radnorshire Co. was taken over by RHM (Agriculture) in 1966, so was employed by RHM Agriculture from 1966-82); Secretary in Kolynos Toothpaste, Chenies St (Off Tottenham Court Rd), London 1943-44; Secretary to Territorial Army in Knighton fron Jan 1944-June 1944, but when they moved their offices to Hay went to work for The Radnorshire Company. Secretary, Welsh Women's Bowling Assoc 1980- ; Founder Secretary, Mid Wales Women's Bowling Assoc 1975-; President, Welsh Women's Bowling Assoc 1980. Member: Commonwealth Games Council for Wales Executive Committee. Welsh Singles Champion 1972 and won Welsh Triples (Skip) 1982. Winner of many Mid Wales County & Open Tournaments. Manageress of the Welsh Ladies' Bowls Team at the Commonwealth Games in Brisbane 1982 and Manageress of the Welsh Ladies' Bowls Team at the Commonwealth Games in Auckland, New Zealand 1990. Skipped Wales to Commonwealth Games Fours Gold Medal in 1986 Games in Edinburgh; skipped Wales to Triples Bronze Medal in World Bowls Championships, Melbourne 1985; skipped Wales to Fours Bronze Medal in World Bowls Championships, Auckland, N. Z. , 1988. Was Secretary of Knighton Cricket Club 1956-66; Founder Secretary, Knighton Ladies' Bowling Club 1961-82. Qualified Umpire & Coach. *Recreation:* playing bowls and in bowls administration. *Address:* Ffrydd Cottage, 2 Ffrydd Road, Knighton, Powys, LD7 1DB. Tel: 0547 528331.

PARKER, Professor Ralph, DSc, CEng, FIMechE, MRAeS, FIOA. *Currently:* Professor and Head of Department of Mechanical Engineering, University College of Swansea, since 1964. *Born on* 3 Dec 1926 at Porth, Glamorgan. *Son of* the late Harry Parker and the late Elizabeth Parker. *Marriage:* to Betty Frank, 1951. *Children:* three d. *Educated at* Glanmor Boys School, Swansea; University College Swansea. *Career:* Junior engineer, Brush Electrical Engineering Co. Ltd. , Loughborough, Leics 1947-49; Scientific Officer/Senior Scientific Officer, Ministry of Supply. (Marine Aircraft Experimental Establishment, Felixstowe, M of S. Headquarters and National Gas Turbine Establishment, Farnborough Hants), 1950-57; Rolls-Royce Ltd., Derby 1957-58; English Electric Co. Ltd., Gas Turbine Division, Whetstone, Leics 1958-64; Chairman of South Wales Branch of Institution of Mechanical Engineers 1989-90. *Publications:* various papers in 'Journal of Sound and Vibration' and 'Proceedings of the Institution of Mechanical Engineers', etc. *Recreation:* *Address:* Department of Mechanical Eng, University College of Swansea, Singleton Park, Swansea, SA2 8PP.

PARKINSON, Mr Ewart West, O St J; BSc(Eng); DPA; C. Eng; FICE; PPRTPI. *Currently:* Development Adviser; Associate Director W. S. Atkins Wales Consultants. *Born on* 9 July 1926 at Leicester. *Son of* Thomas Edward and Esther Lilian West Parkinson. *Marriage:* to Patrician Joan Wood 1948. *Children:* Mark Nigel, Michael John and Veronica Ruth. *Educated at* Wyggeston School Leicester; College of Technology, Leicester. *Career:* Miller Prize (bridge design), Instn CE, 1953; After working with Leicester, Wakefield, Bristol and Dover Councils, he became Dep. Borough Engr. Chelmsford 1957-60; Dep.

City Surveyor Plymouth 1960-64; City Planning Officer, Cardiff 1964-73; Director of Environment South Glamorgan County Council 1973-85; specialising in Central Area Regeneration. Mem Cncl, RTPI 1971-83 (Vice-Pres. , 1973-75, Pres. , 1975-76, Chm. Internat Affairs Bd, 1975-80); Mbr. Sports Council for Wales 1966-78 (Chm. Facilities Cttee); Internat. Soc. of City and Regional Planners 1972; Govt. Deleg. to UN Conf. on Human Settlements, 1976; Watt Cttee for Energy 1977-83 (Chm. Working Gp on Energy and Envt 1980-83); UK mem. Internat Wkg Party on Urban Land Policy, Internat. Fedn for Housing and Planning 1979-85; Chmn: Internat Wkg Party on Energy and the Environment, Internat. Fedn for Housing and Planning 1982-85 (Life Mbr. 1986); Wkg Party on Land Policy, Royal Town Planning Inst. 1983-85; led Study Tours to Soviet Union 1977, India and Bangladesh 1979, China 1980, Kenya, Zimbabwe and Tanzania 1981; lecture visits to People's Republic of China at invitation of Ministry of Construction 1982, 1986, 1989, 1990, 1991; Director: Moving Being Theatre Co. , 1986-91; W. S. Atkins and Partners (Wales 1988- ; Chmn: STAR Community Trusdt Ltd 1979- ; Intervol 1985-89; Wales Sports Centre for the Disabled Trust 1986- ; Vice-Pres. Wales Council for the Disabled 1982- ; Managing Trustee, Norwegian Church Preservation Trust 1988- ; Diamond Jubilee Silver Medal, Nat. Housing and Town Planning Council 1978, OStJ 1980 (S. Glamorgan Council 1975-). *Publications:* The Land Question 1974; And Who is my Neighbour? 1976; articles in prof. journals on land policy, energy and the environment, and public participation. *Recreation:* Working, travelling, being with family, talking with friends. *Address:* 42 South Rise, Llanishen, Cardiff, CF4 5RH. Tel: 0222 756394

PARROTT, Professor-Emeritus Ian, MA, DMus (Oxon), FTCL, ARCO, Hon. FLCM. *Currently:* retired. *Born on* 5 March 1916 at London. *Son of* Horace Bailey Parrott and Muriel Annie Blackford. *Marriage:* to Elizabeth Olga Cox, 1940. *Children:* Michael and Richard. *Educated at* Harrow School 1929; Royal Coll of Music 1932; New College Oxford 1934. *Career:* Lecturer, Univ. of Birmingham 1946-50; Gregynog Prof. of Music, Univ College of Wales, Aberystwyth 1950-83; Examiner, Trinity College of Music, London from 1949. First Prize of R. Phil Soc. for symphonic impression Luxor, 1949; Harriet Cohen Musicology Award 1966. *Publications:* Many musical compositions and the following books: Pathways to Modern Music, A. Unwin, 1947; A Guide to Musical Thought, Dobson, 1955; Method in Orchestration, Dobson, 1957; The Music of 'An Adventure', Regency, 1966; The Spiritual Pilgrims, Christopher Davies, 1969; Elgar (Master Musicians), Dent, 1971; The Music of Rosemary Brown, Regency, 1978; The Story of the Guild for the Prom of Welsh Music, 1980; also a large number of articles and chapters in books. Forthcoming: Cyril Scott and His Piano Music, Thames, 1992. *Recreation:* Psychical Research. *Clubs:* New Cavendish (I.S.M. member). *Address:* Henblas Abermad, Aberystwyth, Dyfed, SY23 4ES.

PARRY, Mr Dennis Roy, *Currently:* British Steel plc, Shotton Works, Deeside, N. Wales. *Born on* 6 Dec 1947 at St. Asaph. *Son of* Thomas Gilbert Parry and Marion (nee Carrington). *Marriage:* to Liana Lamb. *Children:* two s, Christopher and Russell, two d, Melanie and Karen. *Educated at* Holywell High School; Kelserton College. *Career:* Trade Union A. E. U. W. , 1967- ; Labour Party 1969- ; Holywell Town Councillor 1983- ; Mayor 1985-86; Delyn District Councillor 1983- ; Housing spokesperson, Labour; Clwyd County Councillor 1980- ; Chair of Labour Group 1988-90; Leader of Clwyd County Council 1991- ; Vice Chair of Clwyd County Council 1991; Ass. of Welsh County

Council's; Vice Chair of European Committee 1991-. *Clubs:* Crown Green Bowls. *Address:* 6 Providence Court, Greenfield, Holywell, Clwyd. CH8 7EW.

PARRY, Mr Glyn David, *Currently:* Advertising and Direct Marketing Manager, Rank Xerox (UK) Ltd., Uxbridge, England, since 1990. *Born on* 29 June 1955 in Liverpool. *Son of* Albert George Parry of Rhyl, North Wales and the late Drina Margaret Elizabeth (nee Eveson). *Marriage:* to Jane Catherine Roberts, 1984. *Children:* David John (b. 1985) and Laura Eve (b. 1988). *Educated at* Alsop GS for Boys, Liverpool; University of Manchester. *Career:* Auditor Inland Revenue 1977-78; Advertising Manager Corgi-Bantam Books 1978-81; Account Director Barneys Advertising Bristol 1982-85; Group Head Ogilvy & Mather Direct London 1985-87; Direct Marketing Manager Rank Xerox 1987-90. *Recreation:* yoga, swimming, happy families. *Address:* 36 Salisbury Road, Carshalton Beeches, Surrey, SM5 3HD. Tel: 081 669 5265.

PARRY, The Lord Gordon Samuel David, Life Baron, UK. *Born on* Nov 30 1925 at Molleston, nr Narberth, Pembrokeshire. *Son of* the late Rev. Thomas Lewis Parry. *Marriage:* to Glenys Catherine, d. of Jack Leslie Incledon. (1d). *Children:* Catherine. *Educated at* Trinity Coll Carmarthen; University of Liverpool. *Career:* Asst Teacher at Coronation Sch, Pembroke Dock 1945-46; Llanstadwell Voluntary Sch. 1946-47; Haverfordwest Voluntary Sch 1947; Neyland Board Sch. 1946-52; Housemaster, County Sec. Sch. Haverfordwest 1952-62; Inst. of Education, Liverpool Univ 1962-63; Housemaster, Haverfordwest 1963-67; Warden, Pembrokeshire Teachers' Centre 1967-76; Mbr of Neyland (Dyfed) UDC 1948-65; Mbr Welsh Ind. TV Auth: Welsh Ind. Broadcasting Auth: General Advisory Cncl. IBA: Welsh Dev. Agency: Welsh Arts Cncl: Schools Cncl for Wales; Chrmn The Wales Tourist Bd; Mbr British Tourist Auth 1978-84; Pres. Wales Spastics Soc; Pres. Pembrokeshire Spastics Society; Pres. Pembrokeshire Multiple Sclerosis Society; Mbr Council until end 1972, Open Univ. and Chrmn of its Educ. Cttee; Vice-Pres. Mentally Handicapped Soc. for Wales; Chrmn Keep Wales Tidy Campaign's Consultative Cttee; Chrmn Commonwealth Games 1982 Appeal Ctee for Wales; Pres. British Inst. of Cleaning Science; Chrmn British Cleaning Cncl; Mbr Brd of BR, Western Region 1982-83; Mbr BBC Advisory Cncl and of its Cncl for Wales; Pres. Milford Docks Co; chrmn Milford Docks group of companies and of Milford Leisure Co. 1984; Chairman Tidy Britain Group until 1991 and the Beautiful Britain Campaign 1985; Pres. Tidy Britain Group 1992. Dir. Guidehouse 1988; Chrmn Taylor Plan Services 1988; Hon. Fell. of James Cook University, Australia; Fell. of the Tourism Soc; Fell. of the Royal Society of Arts; Fell. of the British Inst. of Cleaning Science; Fell. of the Hotel and Catering and Institutional Management Assoc; Hon. Fell. Inst. of Wastes Mgmnt; Hon Fell. of Trinity Coll, Carmarthen; Hon. Fell. Polytechnic of Wales; *Publications:* many articles in newspapers and periodicals. *Recreation:* Tourism, Welsh Matters; N. American Matters; Australian Matters; Watching the Welsh Rugby XV win, travelling, reading, writing. *Address:* Willowmead, 52 Port Lion, Llangwm, Haverfordwest, SA62 4JT.

PARRY, Mr John Alderson, CBE (1985); NA; VET MB; MRCVS; FRAgS. *Currently:* Veterinarian. *Born on* 3 Jan 1934 at Aberystwyth. *Son of* Albert Parry and Mary (nee Alderson). *Marriage:* to Joan (nee Rathbone). *Children:* Shan and Richard. *Educated at* Leighton Park, Reading; Christ's College, Cambridge. *Career:* BBC National Governor for Wales 1987- ; Member of S4C Authority; Chairman of BBC Children in Need Trust; Member of

Secretary of State Wales Agricultural Advisory Committee 1981- ; Member of Agricultural & Food Research Council 1983-89; Chiarman AFRC Animals Research Div. , 1984-89; Chairman Governing Body AFRC Institute of Grassland & Environmental Research 1987- ; Chairman Hill Farming Research Organisation (Edinburgh) 1980-87; Board Member Maccauley Institute of Land Use 1987- ; Director Animal Disease Research Association (Edinburgh) 1986- ; President British Veterinary Association 1976-77; President Royal College of Veterinary Surgeons 1986-87. *Publications:* Keith Entwhistle Lecturer, Cambridge University 1980. *Recreation:* Field sports. *Clubs:* United Oxford & Cambridge, Farmers, Cardiff & County, Hawks (Cambridge). *Address:* Watergate Mill, Brecon, Powys. LD3 9AN.

PARRY, Mrs Margaret Joan, BA, Class I, Hons. Eng, Univ. of Wales. *Currently:* Retired Headmistress. *Born on* 27 Nov 1919 at Llantrisant, Glam. *Daughter of* W. J. & C. M. Tamplin, Llantrisant. *Marriage:* to Raymond Howard Parry, 1946. *Children:* Richard William, Alison Margaret and Simon David. *Educated at* Scholar of Howell's School, Llandaff, Cardiff; Graduate of University College of S. Wales & Mon. *Career:* Married to Housemaster at Eton College; Examiner for Civil Service, L. C. C. School Examinations Boards; Headmistress of Heathfield School, Ascot, Berks 1973-82; Member of House of Laity for Oxford Diocese; Member of Council for University of Buckingham, later Patron. *Recreation:* Books; music; embroidery. *Address:* Carreg Gwaun, 23a Murray Court, Ascot, Berks SL5 9BP.

PARRY, County Councillor Meurig Wyn, *Currently:* Chef, part-time. *Born on* 18 Sept 1961 at Llandudno. *Son of* Councillor Robert Hugh and Mary Louisa Parry. *Marriage:* divorced. *Children:* Sean and Sophie. *Educated at* Aberconwy Comp. School; Llandrillo Tech. College; Obtained cooking qualifications 706/1. 706/2, RIPHH. , HCITB. *Career:* Left school at 16, at 20 became Head Chef of 3 Star Hotel; at 21 became Head Chef at 4 Star Hotel; aged 25 entered into politics and at 27 became a County Councillor representing Llandudno; representing Gwynedd on statutory committees as well as outside bodies including: Aberconwy Mind, Aberconwy Homestart, Board of Governors of John Bright secondary school, Ysgol Morfa Rhianedd, Ysgol Wyddfyd, Ysgol Saint Sior (primary schools) and Court of University Bangor. *Recreation:* Football and the music of John Barry. *Address:* c/o The Secretary, 33 Maes y Castell, Llanrhos, Llandudno, Gwynedd.

PARRY, Mr Robert Griffith, *Currently:* farmer. *Born on* 25 Oct 1944 at Anglesey. *Son of* the late Richard and the late Mary. *Marriage:* to Margaret. *Children:* Michael, Judith, Gary, Dylan and Gethin. *Educated at* Llanddeusant Primary School; Sir Thomas Jones Secondary School, Amlwch; Bangor Technical College. *Career:* Elected President of the Farmers' Union of Wales 1991; elected Deputy President of the Farmers' Union of Wales 1990; Chairman of the Union's Livestock, Wool and Marts Committee 1985-90; member of MLC's Regional Liaison Committee and Beef Promotion Council. Mayor of Ynys Mon Council 1989-90. member Ynys Mon Borough Council since 1981; former chairman of planning committee. *Recreation:* reading *Clubs:* former member of Rhosybol YFC. *Address:* Treban Meurig, Bryngwran, Holyhead, Gwynedd, LL65 3YN. Tel: 0407 720437.

PARRY, County Councillor Thomas Maurice, *Currently:* Retired. *Born on* 7 June 1928 at Mostyn. *Son of* Edward and Miriam. *Marriage:* to Brenda 1955. *Children:* Nigel, Gareth, Trefor and Helen. *Educated at* Holywell G. S; Bangor Normal College. *Career:* Headmaster, Ysgol Bodnant, Prestatyn 1960-88; Deputy Head, Ysgol Melyd

1949-60; International Soccer Referee 1952-76; Governor Theatr Clwyd; Member of Court University of Wales; Member of Court UCNW; President Rotary Club of Prestatyn 1991-92; Executive Committee Wales Council for the Blind, Liverpool FC, N. Wales "Scout". *Recreation:* Golf, snooker, football, theatre. *Clubs:* St. Melyd G. C. *Address:* 103 Meliden Road, Prestatyn, Clwyd LL19 8LU.

PARRY, Mr Victor Thomas Henry, MA (Oxon); FLA; FRSA. *Currently:* retired. Previously Director, Central Library Services and Goldsmiths' Librarian, University of London Library 1983-88. *Born on* 20 Nov 1927 at Newport, Mon. *Son of* the late Thomas and the late Daisy Parry. *Marriage:* to Mavis Russull 1959. *Children:* Richard, Matthew and Katharine. *Educated at* St. Julians High School, Newport, Mon; St. Edmund Hall, Oxford University. *Career:* Librarian, School of Oriental & African Studies, University of London 1978-83; Chief Librarian & Archivist, R. B. G., Kew 1974-78; Chairman, Government Libraries Group 1977-78; Editor, Society for the Bibliography of Natural History 1975-78; British Museum (Natural History) 1964-74; Chairman, Circle of State Librarians 1966-68; Librarian, The Nature Conservancy 1960-64; Senior Examiner, Library Association 1959-68; Colonial & Commonwealth Relations Offices Library 1956-60; Manchester Public Libraries 1950-56. *Publications:* (ed) Conservation of Threatened Plants 1976; contributions to professional books and journals. *Recreation:* books, ball games, railways, bridge. *Clubs:* Commonwealth Trust. *Address:* 69 Redway Drive, Twickenham TW2 7NN.

PARSONS, Professor (John) David, BSc., MSc. (Eng)., DSc. (Eng)., F.Eng. *Currently:* David Jardine Professor of Electrical Engineering and Pro-Vice-Chancellor (since 1990), University of Liverpool. *Born on* 8 July 1935 at Ebbw Vale. *Son of* Oswald Parsons and Doris Anita (nee Roberts). *Marriage:* to Mary Winifred Stella Tate, 1969. *Educated at* University College Cardiff; King's College London. *Career:* GEC Applied Electronics Laboratories 1959-62; The Polytechnic, Regent Street, London 1962-66; City of Birmingham Polytechnic 1966-68; University of Birmingham, 1969-82: (Lecturer 1969-76; Senior Lecturer 1977-82; Reader 1982); University of Liverpool, 1982- ; Head of Department 1983-86; Dean, Faculty of Engineering 1986-89; Royal Signals and Radar Establishment Malvern 1978-82 - Honorary; UN Expert in India 1977; Visiting Professor, University of Auckland, N. Z. , 1982; Visiting Research Engineer, NTT, Japan 1987. *Publications:* Electronic and Switching Circuits (with Bozic Cheng), 1975; Mobile Communications Systems (with Gardiner), 1989; The Mobile Radio Propagation Channel, 1992; approximately 100 papers in Learned Journals. *Recreation:* golf, bridge, skiing. *Address:* Department of Electrical Eng. and Electronics, The University of Liverpool, P.O. Box 147, Liverpool L69 3BX.

PATERSON, Mr Martin James Mower, BSc Eng Prod (Birmingham), MBA CEng; MCIM; DipM. *Currently:* Chairman: Manufacturing Investments Ltd since 1991; Chairman and Chief Executive: Gallery Home Fashions Ltd. *Born on* 14 March 1951 at Aylesbury, Bucks. *Marriage:* to Anne Vivien Bowyer, 1977. *Children:* Andrew, David and Victoria. *Educated at* Dunbdle School; Birmingham University; Cranfield Institute of Technology. *Career:* Metal Box 1973-81: graduate trainee 1973-74, development technician 1974-76, manufacturing manager 1975-78, works manager (Thailand) 1978-81; Betec plc 1981-84; director and general manager Black and Luff Ltd 1981-82 (divisional manufacturing director 1982-84); Cranfield Institute of Technology 1984-85; special assignments exec TI Group plc 1985-86; MD: Seals Div Aeroquip Ltd 1986-

88, STS Ltd 1988-91. *Recreation:* sailing. *Clubs:* Royal Ocean Racing, Royal Lymington Yacht. *Address:* Crossways House, Cowbridge, South Glamorgan, CF7 7LJ.

PATERSON, Mr Owen William, M. A. Cantab. *Currently:* from 1980 Family Business - British Leather Co. Ltd. , Sales Director since 1985. *Born on* 24 June 1956 at Whitchurch. *Son of* Alfred Dobell and Cynthia Marian (nee Owen). *Marriage:* Rose Emily Ridley 1980. *Children:* Felix Charles, Edward Owen (Ned) and Evelyn Rose. *Educated at* Radley College; Corpus Christi, Cambridge. *Career:* Adopted Conservative Prospective Parliamentary Candidate, Wrexham, March 1990; U. K. Representative, Cotance; Liveryman, The Leathersellers' Company, 1990. *Recreation:* riding, gardening, Deputy Chairman of Ellesmere Community Care Centre Trust. *Address:* Shellbrook Hill, Ellesmere, Shropshire, SY12 9EW.

PATHY, Prof. John, OBE, FRCP (Lond), FRCP (Edin). *Currently:* Director, Health Care Research Unit, Newport; Emeritus Professor, University of Wales. *Born on* 26 April 1923 at London, England. *Son of* the late Dr. Pathy and Agnes (nee Purchell). *Marriage:* to Norma Mary (nee Gallwey), 1949. *Children:* Damian, Aidan, Anne, Sarah and Helen. *Educated at* Kings College, Univ of London, Kings College Hospital, London. *Career:* Junior Hospital medical posts in London and Essex. Assistant Physician Oxford Regional Hospital Board; Consultant Physician, Geriatric Medicine, South Glamorgan Health Authority 1960-79; Professor, Geriatric Medicine, University of Wales College of Medicine 1979-90. *Publications:* ed. Principles and Practice of Geriatric Medicine 1985, 1991; Author: 120 scientific publications in cardiology, neurology, dementia. *Recreation:* music, creative gardening. *Address:* Mathern Lodge, 3 Cefn Coed Crescent, Cyncoed, Cardiff, CF2 6AT

PAVORD, Anna, *Currently:* Journalist/Writer/Broadcaster. *Born on* 20 Sept 1940 at Abergavenny. *Daughter of* the late Arthur Pavord and Christabel (nee Lewis). *Marriage:* to Trevor David Oliver Ware, 1966. *Children:* Oenone, Vanessa, Tilly. *Educated at* Abergavenny Girls' High School; University of Leicester. *Career:* Lintas Ltd. Advertising Agency (copywriter), 1962-63; BBC Television, Researcher/Director, 1963-69; Journalist and writer, The Observer etc 1970- ; Flowering Passions, 10 part TV series (wrote and presented), 1991; Gardening correspondent, The Independent 1986- . *Publications:* Foliage (Pavilion) 1990; The Flowering Year (Chatto & Windus), 1991. *Recreation:* sailing, walking, gardening, black & white films. *Address:* C/o The Independent, 40 City Road, London, EC1Y 2DB.

PEARCE, Mr David John, BScTech; CEng; FIStructE; MICE; MConsE. *Currently:* Independent Structural Engineering Consultant. *Born on* 25 March 1928 at Halifax, England. *Son of* Dr Raymond Maplesden Pearce and Ivy (nee Shingler). *Marriage:* 1st to Doreen, 1954 (d. 1977); 2nd to Eileen, 1986. *Children:* Andrew and Sheila. *Educated at* Manchester Grammar School; Manchester University. *Career:* Graduate Engr. Oscar Faber & Partners (Consulting Engineers), 1949-51; National Service, Lance Corporal HQ RE BAOR, 1951-53; Assistant Engineer, Merz & McLlelan, 1953-54; Sr. Development Engineer, Matthews & Mumby Ltd. , 1954-71; partner, Denis Matthews & Partners, 1972-79; partner, Pearce Matthews Partnership, 1979-88; Resident partner, Wallace Evans and Partners, North Western office, 1988-90; chairman, Lancs. & Cheshire Brance I Struct E, 1983. Divisional Director (Managing), Wallace Evans Ltd, North Western Office, Cheadle, 1990 to retirement 31st January 1992. *Publications:* Shear Walls - An Appraisal of their design &

construction in Box-frame structures, HMSO DoE. *Recreation:* travel, walking, swimming, crafts. *Clubs:* Rotary of Worsley. *Address:* The Chimes, 19 Bellpit Close, Ellenbrook Grange, Worsley, Manchester.

PEARCE, George Malcolm, MBE 1987, JP, FCA. *Currently:* Self-employed Chartered Accountant. *Born on* 3 Feb 1926 at Cardiff. *Son of* the late Edward Ewart Pearce, MBE, JP, FCA, Lord Mayor of Cardiff 1961-62 and Winifred Constance. *Marriage:* to Thelma Mavis Jones, 1949. *Children:* Patricia, Christine, Lester, Carol and Mark. *Educated at* Howard Gardens High School, Cardiff. *Career:* Chartered Accountant qualified 1949; Partner, Deloitte Haskins Sells (now Coopers Lybrand Deloitte), retired 1985. Army: Lieut. Paymaster RAPC, Palestine 1945-47; President: Cardiff Battalion The Boys Brigade 1960-87, now Honorary President; Hon. Vice President, The Boys Brigade 1987- ; Magistrate, Cardiff 1973- ; Treasurer, Wales Festival of Rememberance 1980- ; President, Cardiff East Rotary Club 1974; Captain, Cardiff Golf Club 1982. *Recreation:* golf, bridge. *Clubs:* Cardiff & County, Cardiff Golf, Cardiff East Rotary. *Address:* 'Whitefriars', 22 Westminster Crescent, Cyncoed, Cardiff, CF2 6SE.

PEARSON, Sir James Denning, WhSc Scholar; BSc Eng. *Currently:* retired. *Born on* 8 Aug 1908 at Bootle. *Son of* James and Elizabeth. *Marriage:* to Eluned Henry, 1932. *Children:* Jill and Anne. *Educated at* Canton Secondary School, Cardiff; Cardiff Technical College. *Career:* Joined Rolls-Royce as a junior engineer in 1932 and progressed to Chief Executive in 1961, Chairman 1970. *Publications:* various *Recreation:* gardening *Address:* Green Acres, Holbrook, Derbys, DE5 OTF.

PEGINGTON, Mrs Anne, RGN; FBIM *Currently:* Chief Officer, Wales and Secretary to the RCN Welsh Board, Royal College of Nursing since 1978; Chairman of the Staff Side of the Joint Staff Consultative Council for the Welsh Health Service; Chairman of the full Council; member of the Management Board of Children in Wales. *Born* at Swansea, West Glam. *Daughter of* Reuben Stanley Liddiard and Elsie May Solloway. *Marriage:* 1959. *Children:* One s, Ian Richard, b. 1965. *Educated at* Pontypool Grammar School for Girls. *Career:* Numerous posts within the Health Service prior to taking up present post. *Recreation:* Golf, Theatre, and Travel abroad visiting nurses in under-developed countries. *Clubs:* Monmouthshire Golf. *Address:* Royal College Of Nursing, Welsh Board, Ty Maeth, King George V Drive East, Cardiff, CF4 4XZ. Treetops, 100 Allt-yr-yn View, Newport, Gwent, NP9 5EH

PEMBROKE, Mary Countess of Pembroke Mary Dorothea, CVO; DL *Born on* 31st Dec 1903 at Edinburgh. *Daughter of* The Marquis and Marchioness of Linlithgow. *Marriage:* July 27th 1936. *Children:* Diana Herbert, The Earl of Pembroke *Career:* Hon First OFFR WRNS; Lady-in-Waiting to H. R. H. The Duchess of Kent 1934-49; Extra Lady-in-Waiting 1949-68 *Address:* Old Rectory, Wilton, Salisbury, Wiltshire, SP2 0HT.

PENGELLY, Mr Richard Anthony, B.Sc.(Econ) *Currently:* Retired. *Born on* 18 Aug 1925 at Plymouth, Devon. *Son of* the late Richard Francis and Ivy Mildred Pengelly (nee Warren). *Marriage:* (1) to Phyllis Mary Rippon (nee Stinson) (2) to Margaret Ruth Crossley. *Children:* Michael Anthony, James Francis, Thomas Richard, Sarah Darnton. *Educated at* Plymouth College, School of Oriental & African Studies, London School of Economics & Political Science. *Career:* Monmouthshire Regt. & Intelligence Corps 1943-47; Civil Servant, London 1950-77; Nato Defence College 1960-61; Royal College of Defence Studies 1971; Under Secretary, Health & Social Work Department, The Welsh Office 1977-85. *Recreation:*

Golf and Skiing. *Clubs:* Cardiff Golf Club *Address:* Byways, Wern Goch Road, Cyncoed, Cardiff CF2 6SD.

PENHALIGAN, County Councillor. Leslie George, OBE *Currently:* retired County Councillor. *Born on* 18 April 1913 at Morriston, Swansea. *Son of* deceased. *Marriage:* widower. *Children:* Alan, Brian and Terrence. *Educated at* Elimentary School; Technical College. *Career:* Building Trade worker, bricklayer, mason, stone dresser. Trade Union Secretary, Chairman, Shopsteward. Politics: President Swansea Labour Association, Labour Member West Glamorgan County Council; Chairman West Glamorgan Water Board, when the Llyn Brianne Dam was built; Member Welsh Water Authority 1973-83; Chairman West Glamorgan County Council 1977-78; Present Chairman Transport Committee embraces Road Safety Traffic Management. *Recreation:* bowls, (used to be draughts). *Clubs:* Bonymaen Rugby. *Address:* 271 Bonymaen Road, Bonymaen, Swansea, West Glamorgan County Hall, Swansea, SA1 7AT.

PENN, Mr Richard, BSc Econ; DipEd; FBIM; MBPS. *Currently:* Chief Executive, City of Bradford Council. *Born on* 4 Oct 1945 at Southsea, Hants. *Son of* George Stanley Penn and the late Sylvia Doris Land. *Marriage:* to Jillian Mary Elias. *Children:* Nathan, Jessica, Mathew and Daniel. *Grandchild:* Joel Thomas. *Educated at* Canton HS Cardiff; University College, Cardiff; University College, Swansea. *Career:* Director, Upper Afan Community Development Project (working for Glamorgan, the West Glamorgan County Council), 1970-76; Assistant Chief Executive, Cleveland County Council 1976-78; Deputy Chief Executive, West Midlands County Council 1978-80; Chief Executive, Knowsley Metropolitan Borough Council 1980-89; Deputy Chair, Bradford & District Training & Enterprise Council; Director, Bradford Breakthrough; Director, Public Finance Foundation; Member of Morgan Committee on Crime Prevention; Member of National Museum of Film, Photography and Television Advisory Committee; Principal Advisor, Bradford City Challenge Trust; Adviser to Howe inquiry into Residential Social Work. *Recreation:* good food, foreign travel, Rugby Union. *Clubs:* Royal Overseas. *Address:* (Home) 25 Westwood Drive, Ilkley, West Yorks. LS29 9QX. (Work) City Hall, Bradford. Tel: 0274 752002. Fax: 0274 392718.

PENNEY, Beverley Jane, *Currently:* Ramblers' Association, Welsh Officer; Hon. Sec. Wales Wildlife and Countryside Link. *Born on* 4 Feb 1957 at Bourneville. *Educated at* Exeter University; UCW, Swansea. *Career:* *Recreation:* learning Welsh, walking. *Address:* Pantwood, Pant Lane, Marford, Wrexham, Clwyd, LL12 8SG. Tel: 0978 855 148.

PERCIVAL, Prof. John, M. A., D.Phil (Oxon), F.S.A. *Currently:* Prof. of Ancient History and Head of School of History & Archaeology, Univ. of Wales College of Cardiff. *Born on* 11 July 1937 at Great Tey, Essex. *Son of* Walter William Percival and Eva Percival (nee Bowers). *Marriage:* (1) Carole Ann Labrum (d. 1977) (2) Jaqueline Anne Gibson (nee Donovan). *Children:* Alice Mary Ann and Jessica Jane. *Educated at* Colchester Royal Grammar School, Hertford College Oxford, Merton College Oxford. *Career:* Asst. Lecturer, Ancient History, Univ. College Cardiff 1962; Lecturer Ancient History, Univ. College Cardiff 1964; Senior Lecturer in Classics, Univ. College Cardiff 1972; Reader in Classic, Univ. College Cardiff 1979; Professor of Ancient History, Univ. College Cardiff 1985; Deputy Principal, Univ. of Wales College of Cardiff 1987-90. *Publications:* The Reign of Charlemagne 1975 (with H. R. Loyn) The Roman Villa 1976 (new paperback edition 1988) *Recreation:* Music *Address:* 26 Church Road,

Whitchurch, Cardiff CF4 2EA.

PEREGRINE, Mr Gwilym Rhys, D.L. *Currently:* Retired. *Born on* 30 Oct 1924 at Ystradowen. *Son of* Rev and Mrs T. J. Peregrine. *Marriage:* to Gwyneth Rosemary Williams, 1958. *Children:* John Christopher and Jane Elizabeth. *Educated at* Caterham School, Surrey and Gwendraeth Valley Grammar School. *Career:* Assistant Solicitor, Carmarthenshire County Council, 1949- ; Deputy Clerk, Carms C.C., and Deputy Clerk of the Peace, 1956-72; Clerk and Chief Executive, Carmarthenshire County Council, 1972-74; Chief Executive, Dyfed County Council, 1974-81; Member of Welsh Fourth Channel Authority (S4C), 1982-89; Welsh National Member of Independent Broadcasting Authority (IBA) & Chairman of Welsh advisory committee, 1982-89. *Recreation:* Reading, music, cricket and golf *Clubs:* Glamorgan County Cricket (V.P.) and Fairwood Golf. *Address:* 1 Newnham Crescent, Sketty, Swansea, SA2 0RZ

PERKINS, Air Vice-Marshal RAF Irwyn Morse, MBE; MRCS; LRCP; MFCM. *Currently:* Retired 1985, but occasional part time general practice RMCS and Honorary Consultant in Medical computing Royal Military College of Science, Shrivenham. *Born on* 15 Dec 1920 at Ystalyfera, Swansea. *Son of* the late William Lewis Perkins and the late Gwenllian (nee Morse). *Marriage:* to Miss Royce Villiers Thompson, The Mountain, Tangier, Morocco, 1948. *Children:* Alison Villiers Perkins and Geoffrey John Perkins. *Educated at* Pontardawe School; Swansea Technical College; St. Mary's Hospital, Paddington. *Career:* MRCS LRCP - St. Mary's Hospital, Paddington, London 1945; MFCM 1973; Commissioned RAF 1946; SMO: RAF Gibraltar followed by SMO several flying stations in the UK 1946-49; DSMO 61 Group RAF Kenley 1953-55; DGMS Dept MOD 1955-57; SMO - RAF Laarbruch Germany 1958-61; SMO - RAF VALLEY Anglesey 1961-64; SMO - RAF KHORMAKSER Aden 1964-66; DPMO Bomber and Strike Commands during which period promoted to Group Captain 1966-69; CO RAF Hospital Ely Cambs 1969-72; PMO RAF Germany as Air Commodore 1972-75; CO RAF Hospital Halton 1975-77; PMO Support Command as Air Vice-Marshal 1977-80; Retired from RAF and took up duties as Medical Officer to Royal Military College of Science Shrivenham 1980-85. *Publications:* Shephard-Perkins Injury Classification (with Professor R. W. Shephard, Royal Ordnance, Shrivenham) 1990. *Recreation:* Woodworking, bodging, computing, scientific reading. *Clubs:* Royal Air Force. *Address:* 5 Redlands Close, Highworth, Swindon, Wilts SN6 7SN. Royal Military College of Science, Shrivenham, Nr Swindon, SN6 8LA.

PERKINS, Mr Peter George, Dip in Social Studs; BSc Hons (Econ); CQSW. *Currently:* Operations Manager, STAR Centre, Splott. Chairman, South Glamorgan County Council, 1992-93. *Born on* 8 April 1937. *Marriage:* to Iris Elizabeth, 1960. *Children:* one s one d. *Educated at* Radnor Road Secondary Modern; Llandaff Technical Coll; Univ. Coll., Cardiff; Gwent Coll. of Education. *Career:* Edward Curran Ltd., Assistant Toolsetter, 1952-58; National Service, Royal Artillery, 1956-58; Cardiff City Transport, Driver, 1958-64; British Steel Corp., Transport Controller, 1964-78, when works closure became imminent, was seconded to the Counselling Service to advise and help members of the work force develop strategies on how best to face their future; Elected South Glamorgan County Councillor for Grangetown, 1981; Deputy Chairman of the Education Committee 1982; Chairman, Education Committee; Deputy Leader of the County Council; Chairman of Governors, Cardiff Inst. of Higher Education; Governor, National Staff College; Director, Welsh National Opera Company; Member, Cardiff New Theatre St. Davids Concert Hall & Sherman Theatre Management Boards; Director, South Glamorgan Compact Ltd; Secretary, Channel View Trust; Honorary Fellow, Cardiff Inst. of Higher Education. *Recreation:* music, reading, theatre. *Address:* 77 Pentrebane Street, Grangetown, Cardiff. CF1 7LP. Tel: 0222 372673.

PERRY, Mr Christopher James, MA; CSW; MBASW; MISW. *Currently:* Director of Social Services, South Glamorgan County Council. *Born on* 22 March 1942 at Wakefield, Yorks. *Son of* the late Leslie John Horrace Perry (headmaster) and Freda Phyllis (nee Wigmore). *Marriage:* to Josephine (nee Booth), 1965. *Children:* Ian Anthony Neil (b. 1972) and Donna Elizabeth Clare (b. 1974). *Educated at* Ecclesfield Grammar School; Manchester College of Commerce; Brunel University. *Career:* Self Employed Manager of Rock Groups, Agent and Promoter of Rock n' Roll Show, 1957-64, raised considerable sums for charity; member Grenoside Community Association Committee and Cub Master; qualified in Social work 1965; worked for Sheffield C. B. C., until 1971; Council Member: Association of Social Workers and Branch Secretary of the Association of Social Workers and the Association of Family Case Workers; first convenor of the Sheffield S. C. O. S. W. group and Sheffield branch of the British Association of Social Workers; Area Social Services Officer, Reading C. B. C., 1971-74; seconded Brunel University, 1972-73, Masters Degree (Public and Social Administration), Vice Chair Salaries Conditions of Service Cttee of B. A. S. W; Assistant Div. Director of Social Services, Berkshire C. C., 1974-75; Deputy Dir., of Social Services, Bolton Metropolitan B.C., 1975-82; Chairman West Pennine branch B.A.S.W., Council member B.A.S.W., Vice-Chairman Professional Practice Div. Cttee of B.A.S.W; moved to South Glamorgan C.C. in 1983 as Deputy Director; completed Senior Management Dev. course, 1983-84 and attented Skunk Camp with Tom Peters 1989; member children and families cttee and Community Care Steering Group of the Assoc. of Directors of Social Services; Mbr. NACRO Young Offenders Cttee; Vice Pres. S. Wales RELATE; Chmn Nat. Childrens Bureau Welsh Early Years Unit; Vice-Chmn Children in Wales; Advisor to the Assoc. of County Councils; Nominee Welsh Cttee NSPCC. *Publications:* many articles in professional journals. *Recreation:* cricket, chess, gardening, travel. *Clubs:* *Address:* County Hall, Atlantic Wharf, Cardiff. CF1 5UW.

PERRY, Mr Martin Roger, *Currently:* Conservative Central Office, Agent for Wales July 1989. *Born on* 9 Nov 1944 at Stratford Upon Avon. *Son of* Jim Perry and Jessie (nee Smith). *Marriage:* to Jane Mary Vivian, 1969. *Children:* Emma Claire, Oliver Miles and David Howard Thomas. *Educated at* Sir James Smiths Grammar School, Camelford, Cornwall; Bristol University. *Career:* Conservative Agent - Bristol South, (Conservative candidate - David Hunt - now Secretary of State for Wales), 1967-69; Agent for Durham Group of Constituencies - Blaydon, Chester Le Street, Durham, Easington, Houghton Le Spring, 1969-71; Agent North Cornwall, Chm. Agents Society (Western), 1971-80; Deputy Central Office Agent West Midlands Area, 1981-90; Chm Princethorpe R. C. College, Rugby Parents Assoc., 1989-90. *Recreation:* Antiques, photography, gardening, opera, Mbr. various charitable bodies, Lions Int., RNLI., Life., Catholic Charities. *Clubs:* St. Stephens, Cardiff and County. *Address:* Conservative Party of Wales, 4 Penlline Rd. Whitchurch, Cardiff CF4 2XZ. 7 Beauchamp Hill, Leamington Spa, Warwickshire, CV32 5NH.

PERRY, Mr Roy James, BA Hons *Currently:* Senior Lecturer in Politics since 1966; Leader of Test Valley

Borough Council, Hants. *Born on* 12 Feb 1943 at London. *Son of* the late G C Perry and Mrs D E Perry. *Marriage:* to Veronica G W Perry (nee Haswell) 1968. *Children:* Elizabeth Helen Veronica and Caroline Fiona Helen. *Educated at* Grammar School; Exeter University. *Career:* Executive, Marks & Spencer Limited 1964-66. *Recreation:* Local Government, travelling in France. *Clubs: Address:* Tarrants Farmhouse, Maurys Lane, West Wellow, Romsey, SO51 6DA.

PETHIG, Professor Ronald, PhD, DSc, CEng, FIEE. *Currently:* Professor, School of Electronics, University of Wales, Bangor, since 1986. *Born on* 10 May 1942 at Ripley, Surrey. *Son of* Charles Edward Pethig and Edith Jane (nee Jones). *Marriage:* to Angela Jane Sampson, 1968. *Children:* Richard John (b. 1971) and Helen Jane (b. 1971). *Educated at* Purley G. School; University of Southampton. *Career:* ICI Fellow, University of Nottingham 1968-71; Corpn member Marine Biological Laboratory, Woods Hole (USA) 1982- ; Adj. Professor of Physiology, Med. University, S. Carolina, Charleston 1984- ; University of Wales: Reader 1982-86, Personal chair 1986. Director, Inst of Molecular & Biomolecular Electronics 1986- ; Member: Molecular Electronics Committee SERC 1991- ; Exec. Committee Snowdonia Nat. Park Society 1991- . *Publications:* book: 'Dielectric' and Electronic Properties of Biological Materials, 1979. *Recreation:* mountain walking, old scientific instruments. *Address:* Lleyn, Telford Road, Menai Bridge, Gwynedd, LL59 5DT. Institute of Molecular and Biomolecular Electronics, Univ of Wales, Bangor, Gwynedd, LL57 1UT

PETHYBRIDGE, Research Professor Roger William, MA (Oxon), D.Phil (Geneva). *Currently:* Research Professor, University College, Swansea. *Born on* 28 March 1934 at Skipton, Yorks. *Son of* Arthur and Sadie Pethybridge. *Educated at* Worcester College, Oxford; Institute of International Studies, Geneva. *Career:* Rockefeller Foundation fellowship at Harvard University 1963; Appointed lecturer in the Centre for Russian Studies, University College, Swansea, 1963; Director of the Centre 1972, Personal Chair 1975; Visiting Professor, Australian National University, Canberra 1976; Visiting Fellow, Kennan Institute Washington DC., 1982; Member of Council for National Academic Awards 1975-81; British Council Culture Exchange with Russia 1975-79; Economic and Social Research Council 1976-83; National Association for Soviet and East European Studies 1974-80. *Publications:* Books: A Key to Soviet Politics - The Crisis of the Anti-Party Group, (Allen and Unwin, London; Frederick Praeger, New York, 1962); Chinese translation, Peking 1964; (editor) Witnesses to the Russian Revolution, (Allen and Unwin, London 1964; Stafleu, Leiden 1964; Soderstrom, Helsinki 1967; Longanesi, Milan 1967; Citadel Press, New York, 1967; (editor) The Development of the Communist Bloc, (Harraps, London; D. C. Heath, Boston, USA, 1965); A History of Postwar Russia, (Allen and Unwin, London 1966; New American Library, New York; Gredos, Buenos Aires and Madrid, 1968); The Spread of the Russian Revolution: Essays on 1917, 1972; The Social Prelude to Stalinism, 1974, p/back ed 1977; One Step Backwards, Two Steps Forward: Society Society and Politics under the New Economic Policy, Oxford Univ Press, 1990. *Recreation:* Welsh National Opera, languages. *Clubs:* Athenaeum. *Address:* 113 Dunvant Road, Swansea SA7 NN.

PHILLIPS, Mr (Peter) Anthony, *Currently:* Designer/ Design Manager, Resources, BBC Wales since 1991. *Born on* 21 June 1938 at Cardiff. *Son of* Thomas George Phillips and Hilda Maud Connolly. *Educated at* Howardian High School, Cardiff; Cardiff College of Art; Welsh College

Advanced Technology. *Career:* Trainee Designer, Company Design Studio, 1955-60; National Service, Gunner R. A. 1960-62; Designer, International Company, 1962-63; Designer, BBC Wales, 1963-80; Senior Designer, BBC Wales, 1980-82; Manager TV Production Services BBC Wales 1982-91. Awarded Royal Television Society Award for the design of a television Opera: 'The Rajah's Diamond'. TV Design Credits include: Design of "Hawkmoor", "Dylan, a life of Dylan Thomas", "Enigma Files". Theatre Design Credits include: 'My People' and 'Solidarity', for Theatre Clwyd, 'War Music and Pity of War', for Peter Florence, Productions at the Lyric, Hammersmith. Chartered Society of Designers, elected to membership 1970, National Council Member 1989-91. *Recreation:* gardening, travel. *Clubs: Address:* 'Telynfa', Gwaelod-y-Garth, Nr Cardiff, CF4 8HJ. Tel: 0222 810791

PHILLIPS, Professor Dewi Zephania, BA., MA., B. Litt. *Currently:* Professor of Philosophy, Dept. of Philosophy, Univ. Coll., Swansea, 1971- . *Born on* 24 Nov 1934 at Swansea, Wales. *Son of* David Oakley Phillips and Alice Frances Phillips (nee Davies). *Marriage:* to Margaret Monica Hanford, 1959. *Children:* Aled Huw, Steffan John and Rhys David. *Educated at* Univ. Coll. Swansea; Oxford Univ. *Career:* Assist. Lec. in Philosophy, Queen's Coll. Dundee 1961-62; Lec. in Philosophy, Queen's Coll., 1962-63; Lec. in Philosophy, Univ. Coll., of N. Wales, Bangor 1963-65; Lec. in Philosophy, Univ. Coll., Swansea 1965-67; Senior Lec. Univ. Coll., Swansea 1967-70; Dean of the Faculty of Arts 1982-85; Vice Principal 1989-92. *Publications:* The Concept of Prayer, 1965 (rep. 1981); Faith & Philosophical Enquiry, 1970; Death and Immortality, 1970; Moral Practices 1970; Sense and Delusion, 1971; Athronyddu Am Grefydd, 1974; Religion Without Explanation, 1976; Through a Darkening Glass: Philosophy, Literature and Cultural Change, 1982; Dramau Gwenlyn Parry, 1982; Belief, Change and Forms of Life, 1986; R. S. Thomas: Poet of the Hidden God, 1986; Faith After Foundationalism, 1988; From Fantasy to Faith, 1991; Intervention in Ethics, 1991; Wittgenstein and Religion forthcoming, 1992. *Recreation:* Tennis *Address:* Dept. of philosophy, Unit. Coll. of Swansea, Singleton Park, Swansea, W. Glam SA2 8PP. 45 Queen's Road, Sketty, Swansea, W. Glam. SA2 OSB

PHILLIPS, Professor Glyn Owen, PhD; DSc (Wales), Hon D. Sc (Benin, Nigeria), C.Chem; FRSC. *Currently:* Chairman, Newtech Innovation Centre. *Born on* 6 Nov 1927 at Rhosllanerchrugog, N. Wales. *Son of* the late Samuel and the late Laura Ann Phillips. *Marriage:* to Rhiain Margaret Phillips. *Children:* Elen Angharad Phillips and Aled Owain Phillips. *Educated at* University College of North Wales, Bangor, Gwynedd. *Career:* Until April 1991, Executive Principal, The North East Wales Institute of Higher Education; Until April 1975, Professor of Chemistry and Chairman, Dept of Chem & Applied Chem. University of Salford. Foundation Vice-Chancellor, University of Benin, Bendel State, Nigeria 197- & 1971 subsequently Advisor and External Examiner in Chemistry. Lecturer and Senior Lecturer in Chemistry, University College Cardiff 1954-67. Visiting Professor University of Alabama Medical School, Birmingham, Alabama, USA and Univesity of Gunma, Japan. Consultant and Research Associate, Boston Biomedical Research Institute, Boston, USA; subsequently Biomatrix Inc. New York. Visitor on behalf of the President of CNR 9 National Research Council of Italy) to the Board of the CNR Laboratory for Biomolecules, Pisa. Warden, University of Wales Guild of Graduates and Member of Council, University of Wales. Director, HTV Group plc. Hon. Member, Japan Society of Fiber Science and Technology. *Publications:* 25 books and over 400 scientific papers. Editor of Welsh Science Journal Y Gwyddonydd (University of Wales Press), since 1963. *Recreation:* music, reading, running. *Address:* Newtech Innovation Centre, Newtech Square, Deeside Industrial Park, Deeside, Clwyd CH5 2NT

PHILLIPS, Lady Hazel Bradbury, JP, LLB, Barrister-at-Law. *Currently:* Lawyer member (Chairmans Panel) London Rent Assessment Panel, 1966- , Vice President 1972, President 1973-79. *Born on* 26 Nov 1924 at Cardiff. *Daughter of* the late Thomas John Evans OBE, and the late Elsie Rosina Evans (nee Bradbury). *Marriage:* to Hon. Mr Justice (Raymond) Phillips, MC, 1951 (d. 1982). *Children:* David John (b. 1953) and Richard Anthony Rupert (b. 1955). *Educated at* Howells School Llandaff; Roedean School Brighton; Kings College London. *Career:* Barrister, Inner Temple 1948; Member of the Wales and Chester Circuit 1948- ; JP 1961- ; Member Parole Board 1979-82; Chairman Richmond and Thomas P.S.D., 1985-89. *Recreation:* walking, reading, gardening. *Clubs:* United Oxford and Cambridge. *Address:* The Elms, 22 Park Road, Teddington, TW11 OAQ.

PHILLIPS, Mr Mervyn Hugh, CBE; MA; LL. B. *Currently:* Chief Executive Clwyd County Council. *Born on* 7 Sept 1931 at Barry, S. Wales. *Son of* the late Thomas and Margaret Phillips. *Marriage:* to Joyce Taylor 1956. *Children:* Stephen, Catherine and Christopher. *Educated at* Liverpool University. *Career:* Started career in South Wales as an Assistant Solicitor with Cardiff City Council. He has taken a lead in such economic network as Newtech on Deeside, Clwydfro, Deeside Enterprise Trust and Medtech in Wrexham. He is a member of the North East Wales Training and Enterprise Council. Economic recovery has been a priority but along with, and seen as part of it, tourist and cultural developments in the country. He is also Clerk to the North Wales Police Authority and Clerk to the Clwyd Lieutenancy; was Secretary of the Welsh Counties Committee 1980-85, and is currently secretary of the successor body, the Assembly of Welsh Counties; has been a member or officer of the Regional Planning Committee for Children's Services in Wales, the Welsh Arts Council and the Institute of Welsh Affairs; took a leading part in the involvement of the Welsh Counties in Europe and is an Executive Delegate to the Conference of Peripheral Maritime Regions; is chairman of the European Centre for Traditional and Regional Cultures in Llangollen; involved in a Presbyterian Church, of which he is an elder. *Recreation:* Reading, gardening. *Address:* Newlands, Gwernaffield Road, Mold, Clwyd, CH7 1RE. Clwyd County Council, Shire Hall, Mold, CH7 6NB.

PHILLIPS, Sian, Hon D. Litt; BA *Currently:* Actress. *Born* at Betws, Wales. *Daughter of* D. Phillips and Sally Phillips. *Marriage:* to 1). Peter O;Toole 1959 (diss. 1979); 2). to Robin Sachs 1979, (diss. 1992). *Children:* Kate and Pat. *Educated at* Pontardawe Grammar School; Cardiff College, Univ. of Wales; Royal Academy of Dramatic Art, London. *Career:* As a child she worked on Stage and for the BBC, Wales; at eighteen she became a BBC TV Announcer and News Reader; she has also acted in French; won a scholarship to the Royal Academy of Dramatic Art, where she was awarded the Bancroft Gold Medal; during the early part of her career, Sian specialised in the 'classics' and roles included: 'Desdemona' in OTHELLO, 'Queen Katherine' in HENRY VIII, 'Helena' in A MIDSUMMER NIGHT'S DREAM, 'Candida' in CANADA, 'Elena' UNCLE VANYA, 'Viola', TWELTH NIGHT, 'Kate', TAMING OF THE SHREW, 'St Joan', Shaw's ST JOAN, 'Masha', THE THREE SISTERS; these plays encompassed both

Theatre and Television; many leading roles including: Macbeth, The Bear, The Proposal, Platonov, The Man of Destiny, You Never Can Tell, A Woman of No Importance, Lady Windermere's Fan; London Theatre Credits: 'Hedda', HEDDA GABLER, THE LIZARD ON THE ROCK, The Phoenix Theatre; GENTLE JACK, The Queens Theatre MAXIBULE, The Queens Theatre and many many more; extensive Television career and films including: Becket, Murphy's War, Goodbye Mr Chips, Under Milk Wood, Dune (David Lynch), Valmont (Milos Forman), 1992 - The Age of Innocence (Scorcese). Awards: New York Critics', Goodbye Mr Chips; Critics Circle, Goodbye Mr Chips; Royal Television Society, I Cladius 'Livia'; British Academy of Film & TV, I Cladiuis 'Livia' and How Green Was My Valley 'Beth Morgan'; Award Nominations: 'Vera' in PAL JOEY, 'Emmeline Pankhurst' in SHOULDER TO SHOULDER, 'Anne' in MAN AND SUPERMAN, 'Hannah Jelkes' in NIGHT OF THE IGUANA, Sian is an Honorary Fellow, Cardiff Univ; Hon Doctor of Literature, Univ of Wales; Member of the Gorsedd of Bards, G. B; Fellow Polytechnic of Wales, Governor Welsh College of Music & Drama. *Publications:* General Journalism, 'Sian Phillips' Needle Point, Elm Tree. *Recreation:* Gardening, painting, needlepoint. *Address:* c/o Saraband Ltd., 265 Liverpool Road, Barnsbury, London, N1 1HS.

PHILLIPS, Mr William John, MA., LL.B. *Currently:* Chief Executive, Dyfed County Council. *Born on* 29 Aug 1932 at Gwauncaegurwen. *Son of* Philip and Caroline Anne. *Marriage:* to Bethan (nee Richards). *Children:* Geraint and Catrin *Educated at* Pontardawe Grammar School; U.C.W., Aberystwyth; Univ. of London *Career:* Teaching London, Merthyr Tydfil; Further Education Officer, Glamorgan C.C., 1962-65; Deputy, then Director of Education, Cardiganshire, 1965-74; Deputy then Director of Education, Dyfed C. C., 1974-90; former Chrmn. Soc. of Educ., Officers (Wales); Educ. broadcasting council (Wales); current chrmn. Christian Educ. Movement (Wales); mbr. Gorsedd. *Publications:* Articles in various journals on literary, historical and educational topics *Recreation:* Travelling, local history and rugby *Address:* 2 Maesyllan, Lampeter, Dyfed, SA48 7EN.

PHILP, (Dennis Alfred) Peter, *Currently:* Writer, self-employed, since 1990. *Born on* 10 Nov 1920 at Cardiff. *Son of* Alfred Thomas Philp and Elsie May (nee Whitt). *Marriage:* to Pamela Mary Coxon-Ayton, 1940. *Children:* Paul (b. 1941) and Richard (b. 1943). *Educated at* Penarth County School. *Career:* Trained as furniture designer 1936-40; Served with RAF 1940-42; Combined freelance writing with dealing in antiques, broadcasting and lecturing, writing includes plays for stage, television and radio. Plays produced but not published: Elizabeth Or Lola, Zodiac, A Quiet Clap of Thunder, King Of The Wood, Never Stop To Wonder (BBC Radio), Valuation For Purposes of. . (BBC TV), Zeticula (BBC TV). *Publications:* numerous articles for newspapers and magazines, books and contributions to encyclopedias. Beyond Tomorrow (Play in three acts), Samuel French 1947; The Castle of Deception (Play in three acts, Arts Council Award, Foyle Award, 1951), J. Garnet Miller 1952; Love and Lunacy (Play in three acts, Ustinov Award, 1954), J. Garnet Miller 1955; Antiques Today, J. Garnet Miller 1960; Antique Furniture for the Smaller Home, Arco Publications 1962; Furniture of The World, Octopus 1974; Antique Furniture Expert (with Gillian Walkling), Century 1991, American title The Field Guide To Antique Furniture, Houghton Mifflin 1992. *Recreation:* Literature, theatre, music, history. *Clubs:* East India. *Address:* 77 Kimberley Road, Cardiff CF2 5DP.

PICKEN, Ralph Alistair, LL. B. (Univ of Birmingham).

Currently: Solicitor, Partner, Trowers & Hamlins, London. *Born on* 23 May 1955 at Cardiff. *Son of* Dr. David Kennedy Watt Picken, TD, JP, DL, of Cardiff and Liselotte Lore Inge (nee Regensteiner). *Educated at* Shrewsbury School; University of Birmingham. *Career:* Slaughter & May, articles clerk, assistant solicitor, 1978-81; Trowers & Hamlins 1981- (Partner since 1984). Resident in Muscat, Sultandate of Oman, 1981-86. Member of the Law Society, International Bar Association and The Anglo-Omani Society. *Recreation:* Bridge and the Baroque, Bordeaux and Bangkok. *Clubs:* M.C.C. *Address:* 6 New Square, Lincoln's Inn, London, WC2A 3RP. 3 Gloucester Crescent, London, NW1 7DS

PICKETT, Hon. Mr Justice Thomas, C.B.E. 1972 *Currently:* Retired. *Born on* 22 Nov 1912 at Glossop, Derbyshire. *Son of* John Joseph and Caroline Pickett (nee Brunt). *Marriage:* to Winifred Irene Buckley, d of late Benjamin Buckley, 1940. *Educated at* Glossop Grammar School; London University LL. B. (Hons) *Career:* Barrister at Law, Lincoln's Inn, called to Bar 1948; served in Army 1939-50, returning with permanent rank of Major; Dep. Asst. Dire., of Army Legal Services, 1948; District Magistrate Gold Coast, 1950; Resident Magistrate Northern Rhodesia, 1955; Senior Res. Magistrate, 1956; Acting Puisne Judge, 1960; Puisne Judge, High Courts of Northern Rhodesia, 1961-64; Zambia, 1964-69; Justice of Appeal, 1969-70; Acting Chief Justice, 1970; Judge President, of Appeal, 1971; Chairman Tribunal on Detainees, 1967; Electoral Commission (Supervisory) Delimitation Commission for Zambia, 1968; Referendum Commn, 1969; Local Government Commn, 1970; Senior Regional Chairman North West Area Industrial Tribunals, (England & Wales) 1975-84; Chairman for Manchester, 1972. *Recreation:* Walking and swimming. *Clubs:* County Club, Llandudno; Victoria Club, Craig-y-Don, Llandudno. *Address:* Bryn Awelon, Aber Place, Craigside, Llandudno, LL30 3AR.

PICKLES, Mr Roger Albert, BA(Econ); ACA; ATII *Currently:* Managing Tax Consultant at Price Waterhouse. *Born on* 29 Oct 1960 at Cheshire (Nantwich). *Son of* the late Albert Pickles and June Pickles. *Educated at* Larkfield Grammar; Durham University. *Career:* Commenced in 1982; Qualified as a Chartered Accountant 1985, specialised in corporate tax since 1985 (with Arthur Andersen and then Price Waterhouse). *Recreation:* Golf, walking. *Clubs:* Past President of Cardiff Junior Chamber; Treasurer of Dewstow Golf Club. *Address:* 34 Bigstone Grove, Tutshill, Nr Chepstow, Gwent, NP6 7EN.

PICTON, Mr Jacob Glyndwr (Glyn), CBE 1972. Senior Lecturer in Industrial Economics, University of Birmingham 1947-79; Harpist, City of Birmingham Symphony orchestra. *Born on* 28 Feb 1912 at Aberdare. *Son of* David Picton. *Marriage:* to Rhiannon Mary James (Merch Megan Glantawe), LRAM, ARCM, 1939 (d 1978). *Children:* one s one d. *Educated at* Aberdare Boys' County School; Birmingham University (MCom). *Career:* Chance Bros Ltd, 1933-47, Assistant Secretary 1945-47, President W Midland Rent Assessment Panel 1965-72 (chairman Committee 1973-81); Governor, United Birmingham Hospitals 1953-74; Chairman, Children's Hospital 1956-66; Teaching Hospitals Rep. Professional and Techn. Whitley Council 1955-61; member Birmingham Regional Hospital Board 1958-74 (Vice-chairman 1971-74); member NHS Nat. Staff Committee 1964-73 (Vice-chairman 1968-73); chairman Birmingham Hospital Region Staff Committee 1964-74; Vice-chairman W. Midlands RHA 1973-79 (member 1979-82); Vice-chairman NHS Nat. Staff Committee (Admin & Clerical) 1973-82; NHS Nat. Assessor (Admin) 1973. chairman Birmingham Industrial Therapy

Assoc Ltd 1965-79 and W Bromwich Industrial Therapy Assoc Ltd 1969-79; Indep. member Estate Agents Council 1967-69; chairman of Wages Councils 1953-82; Dep chairman Commn of Inquiry concerning Sugar Confectionery and Food Preserving Wages Council 1961; chairman Commn of Inquiry concerning Licensed Residential Estabts and Restaurants Wages Council 1963-64; sole Comr of Inquiry into S Wales Coalfield Dispute 1965, report published by H. M. S. O. ; Dep chairman Commn of Inquiry concerning Industrial and Staff Canteens Wages Council 1975; Independent Arbitrator, Lock Industry 1976-81. *Publications:* Has donated working papers: on Picton family to Nat. Library of Wales; on academic and public service to University of Birmingham; various articles and official reports. *Recreation:* music, gardening, Pembrokeshire history. *Address:* Maes Y Tannaud Road, 54 Chesterwood Road, Kings Heath, Birmingham, B13 0QE. Tel: 021 444 3959.

PICTON-TURBERVILL, Mr Richard Charles Quentin, JP (Glamorgan 1959), DL (Mid Glamorgan 1982); *Born on* 6 July 1924 *Son of* Col Charles Thomas Edmondes, of Old Hall, Cowbridge, Glam, by his w Eleanor, o child of Charles Grenville Turbervill, JP, Lord of the Manor of Ewenny (whose maternal gf was Sir Grenville Temple, 10 Bt, of the family which at one time enjoyed the Dukedom of Buckingham and a branch of which still has the Earldom of Temple of Stowe). *Marriage:* 1, 1950 (m dis 1971), Catherine Vivian Lindsay, da of Col E D Corkery; 3 s; m 2, 1972, Ann Elizabeth, da of Geoffrey Field Arthur (d 1960), of Ranskill, Notts. *Educated at* Radley, RAC Cirencester. *Career:* WWII mobile radar RA 1942-46; Cncllr 1951-82, High Sheriff Glam 1965, chm: Gen Cmmrs of Income Tax, petty sessional div of Newcastle and Ogmore 1982-87, Political Pty Assoc; pres Bridgend Show Soc 1965-86; memb: Indust Cncl for Wales, Agric Land Trbnl (Wales); former memb Welsh Water Authy. *Recreation:* shooting, gardening, reading, music. *Clubs:* Royal Overseas, Farmers' County (Cardiff). *Address:* Ewenny Priory, Bridgend, Mid Glamorgan, CF35 5BW. Tel: 0656 2913.

PIERCE, Ms Ann Elen, BSc; MTS *Currently:* Managing Director, Tourism South Wales, 1991- . *Born on* 8 July 1950 at Bangor. *Daughter of* Gwilym and Haulwen (nee Whiteside-Lloyd). *Educated at* Sir Hugh Owen Grammar School Caernarfon; UNIC Wales Aberystwyth. *Career:* Deputy President, UCW Aberystwyth Students Union, 1972; Wales Tourist Board, Projects Dept., 1973-83; Tourism Adviser/Consultant (self-emoloyed), 1983-87; Neath Development Partnership; Chairman Vale of Neath Tourist Association, Member South Wales Tourism Council. Regional Manager, Wales Tourist Board, 1987-91. *Recreation:* Golf, Bridge. *Address:* 5 Abernethy Quay, The Marina, Swansea, SA1 1UF.

PIERCE, Mr Hugh Humphrey, LLB; MIPM; Barrister-at-Law. *Born on* 13 Oct 1931. *Son of* Dr Gwilym Pierce, Abercynon, Glam. *Marriage:* to Rachel Margaret Procter, 1958. *Children:* two s. *Educated at* Clifton; King's Coll. Univ of London. LLB Hons 1954. *Career:* Pres. Faculty of Laws Soc; Pres. Union; Called to Bar, Lincoln's Inn 1955; Diploma Personnel Management 1962; MIPM 1963; Army Service, 2nd Lieut Intell. Corps (Cyprus) 1955-57; Kodak Ltd, legal and personnel work 1957-63; joined BBC 1963, personnel and industrial relations; Admin. Officer, Local Radio 1967-68; Local Radio Develt Manager 1968-69; General Manager, Local Radio 1970-74; Asst Controller, Staff Admin. 1974-78; Asst. Controller, Employment Policy and Appts, 1978-80; Chm., First Framework Ltd 1988- ; Member: Indep. Cttee for Supervision of Telephone

Information Standards 1987- ; Indep. Manpower Commn, Coll. of Occupational Therapists 1988-89; Exec. Cttee Howard League 1979-91; Treas., Prisoners' Advice and Law Service 1986-89; Member: Justice; Amnesty; Trustee: Community Develt. Trust; Nat. Council for the Welfare of Prisoners Abroad. *Recreation:* chamber music. *Clubs: Address:* 11 Wood Lane, Highgate, London N6 5UE. Tel: 081 444 6001. Pantybryn, Llanwnog, Caersws, Powys SY17 5NZ. Tel: 0686 688229.

PIERCY, Professor Nigel Francis, BA, MA, PhD, Dip. M, FCIM. *Currently:* Professor of Marketing and Strategy, Cardiff Business School, University of Wales since 1988; Free-lance Management Consultant. *Born on* 13 Jan 1949 at Hounslow, Middlesex. *Son of* Helena Gladys (nee Sargent) and the late Gilbert. *Marriage:* 1st, 1970 (divorced 1983); 2nd 1985. *Children:* Niall Christopher. *Educated at* Cambridge Grammar School; Heriot-Watt University; Durham University; University of Wales. *Career:* Lecturer, Newcastle Polytechnic 1972; Planner, Amersham International 1974; Senior Lecturer, Newcastle Polytechnic 1977; Lecturer, UWIST 1981; Senior Lecturer, UWIST 1983; Reader, UWIST 1986. *Publications:* approximately 200 articles and papers on management and marketing and eight books - most recently Market-Led Strategic Change (Thorsons/Harper Collins 1991). *Recreation:* badminton, food. *Address:* Cardiff Business School, University of Wales College Cardiff, Column Drive, Cardiff, CF1 3EU. 9 The Green, Radyr, Cardiff, CF4 8BR

PILL, Hon. Sir Malcolm (Thomas), KT 1988 *Currently:* a Judge of the High Court of Justice, Queen's Bench Division, since 1988; Presiding Judge, Wales and Chester Circuit, since 1989. Member Employment Appeal Tribunal, 1992. *Born on* 11 March 1938. *Son of* the late Reginald Thomas Pill, MBE and Anne Pill (nee Wright). *Marriage:* to Roisin Pill (nee Riordan), 1966. *Children:* two s one d. *Educated at* Whitchurch Grammar School; Trinity College, Cambridge, MA, LLM, Dip Hague of Internat Law. *Career:* Served RA, 1956-58; Glamorgan Yeomanry (TA), 1958-67. Called to Bar, Gray's Inn, 1962, Bencher, 1987; Wales and Chester Circuit, 1963 (Treas., 1985-87); a Recorder, 1976-87; QC 1978. 3rd Sec., Foreign Office, 1963-64. Chm., UNA (Welsh Centre) Trust, 1969-77, 1980-87; Chm., Welsh Centre for Internat. Affairs, 1973-76. Chm. UK Cttee, Freedom from Hunger Campaign, 1978-87. *Clubs:* Cardiff and County. *Address:* Royal Courts Of Justice, Strand, London, WC2A 2LL.

PINNINGTON, Mr Roger Adrian, TD, MA(Oxon). *Currently:* Chairman, Aqualisa Products Ltd; Chairman, Telfos Holdings PLC. *Born on* 27 Aug 1932 at Salford, Lancs. *Son of* Willian Austin and Elsie Amy. *Marriage:* to Marjorie Ann Russell. *Children:* Andrew, Sally, Suzanne and Nichola. *Educated at* Rydal School, Colwyn Bay; Lincoln College, Oxford. *Recreation:* Rugby, collecting Sad Irons and Wine Funnels. *Clubs:* Vincent's *Address:* 46 Willoughby Road, Hamptead, London. NW3 1RU.

PITCHFORD, His Honour Charles Neville, *Currently:* Circuit Judge, Wales & Chester Circuit 1972-87. *Career:* Called to the Bar, Middle Temple 1948. *Address:* Llanynant, Kennel Lane, Coed Morgan, Abergavenny.

PITCHFORD, Christopher John, Q. C. *Currently:* Barrister. *Born on* 28 March 1947 at Keighley, Yorks. *Son of* Charles and Shirley. *Marriage:* 1st in 1970; 2nd in 1991. *Children:* Anna and Samantha from 1st marriage. *Educated at* Dyffryn Comprehensive Newport Gwent; Queens College Taunton; Queen Mary College Univ of London. *Career:* Called to Bar 1969; Wales and Chester Circuit 1972; Silk 1987; Recorder 1987. *Recreation:* fishing, turf *Clubs:* Bedlinog Racing, Cardiff & County, Sloane. *Address:*

Garth Gynydd, Bedlinog, Mid Glamorgan, CF46 6TH

POLLARD, Mrs Vivien Mary, FHCIMA *Currently:* Non-Exec. Director, South Wales Electricity PLC; Director Dramah Investments Ltd. *Born on* 1 March 1940 at Rochdale, Lancs. *Daughter of* Edwin and Alice Hornby. *Marriage:* 1963. *Children:* Rebecca Sarah. *Educated at* Haberdasher's Askes School, London; Ealing Hotel and Catering School. *Career:* Hotel and Catering Industry - Leisure Industry, 1963-86; Management Services in U. K. and Middle East; Personal Interest in Development Companies and non exec directorship, South Wales Electricity PLC, 1986- . *Recreation:* Travel, antiques, food, wine and entertaining. *Address:* Penarth House, Cliff Parade, Penarth, S. Glam CF6 2BP.

POLLOCK, Admiral of the Fleet Sir Michael Patrick, GCB; LVO; DSC. *Currently:* Retired. *Born on* 10 Oct 1916 at Altringham, Cheshire. *Son of* the late C. A. Pollock and G. J. Pollock (nee Mason). *Marriage:* 1). Margaret Steacy of Bermuda, died 1951; 2). Marjory Reece (nee Bisset) married 1954. *Children:* David, Vanessa, William and Janet. *Educated at* Royal Naval College, Dartmouth and various specialist Service Colleges, eg Naval Staff College. *Career:* Entered Royal Navy 1930, served War of 1939-45 in H. M. S. Warspite, Vanessa, Arethusa and Norfolk taking part in operations in North Atlantic, Arctic, Mediterranean and Indian Oceans. 3 times mentioned in despatches D. S. C. 1944, Commander 1950, Captain 1955, Rear Admiral 1964, Vice Admiral 1969, Admiral 1970, Admiral of The Fleet 1974, Commanded HMS Vigo & Portsmouth Squadron 1959; HMS Ark Royal 1963; Assist. Chief of Naval Staff 1964; Flag Office Second in Command Home Fleet 1967-68; Flag Officer Submarines and NATO Commander, Submarines Eastern Atlantic 1968-69; Controller of the Navy 1970; First Sea Lord and Chief of Naval Staff 1971-74; First and Principal ADC to The Queen 1972-74; Bath King of Arms 1976-85; Chairman Naval Insurance Trust 1976-84. *Recreation:* Sailing, shooting, travel. *Clubs:* Royal Thames. *Address:* C/o National Westminster Bank, Mardol Head, Shrewsbury, SY1 1HE

POMEROY, Margaret, *Currently:* Housewife. *Born on* 20 Oct 1922 at Treorchy, Rhondda. *Daughter of* Helen and George Lewis. *Marriage:* to William Ronald Pomeroy. *Children:* Anthony and Susan. *Educated at* Pentre Grammar School. *Career:* Started bowling 1963, represented Wales at International level 129 times to date. Winner of 19 National titles, similar record at County level and winner of many Open Tournaments (British Isles (Indoor)); winner of singles, pairs and triples B. I. (Outdoor), pairs (twice), Fours (twice). World titles Gold in triples, fours (two bronze). represented Wales Womens World Bowls Worthing 1977, Toronto 1981, Auckland 1988. represented Wales in Commonwealth Games Brisbane 1982 (team vice captain), Edinburgh 1986. *Recreation:* bowls, crosswords, knitting, cooking, gardening. *Clubs:* Sophia Gardens Ladies Bowls, Cardiff Indoor Bowls. *Address:* 106 Ty Glas Road, Llanishen, Cardiff, CF4 5EG.

PORTER, Mr Richard James, MA, MSc, BM, BCh, MRCOG *Currently:* Consultant Obstetrician/Gynaecologist, Bath District Health Authority since 1988. *Born on* 28 Nov 1951 at London. *Son of* James Graham Porter and Ann Wharry. *Marriage:* to Diana Isabel Austin, 1974. *Children:* Charlotte (b. 1977) and Alice (b. 1980). *Educated at* Eton College, Oxford University. *Career: Currently:* Medical Director, Wiltshire Health Care, N. H. S. Trust 1992- ; Chairman, 1989, Division of Obstetrics and Gynaecology; Hon Cellarer, Royal College of Obstetrics & Gynaecology 1990. *Publications:* various medical journals. *Recreation:* wine, theatre. *Clubs:* Royal Society of Medicine. *Address:*

Weston Lea, Weston Park, Bath, BA1 4AL.

POUNDER, Prof Derrick John, MB, ChB, FRCPA, FFPathRCPI, FCAP, MRCPath. *Currently:* Professor of Forensic Medicine, University of Dundee, since 1987. *Born on* 25 Feb 1949 at Pontypridd. *Son of* Wilfred Pounder and Lilian (nee Jones). *Marriage:* to Georgina Kelly, 1975. *Children:* Sibeal (b. 1985), Emlyn (b. 1989) and Sinead (b. 1991). *Educated at* Pontypridd Boys Grammar School; Univ. of Birmingham. *Career:* Lecturer then Senior Lecturer, Forensic Pathology, Univ., of Adelaide, South Australia; Dep. Chief Medical Examiner, Edmonton, Alberta, Canada; Assoc. Professor Univs of Alberta and Calgary 1985-87; Freeman of Llantrisant. *Recreation:* Photography, medieval architecture, almost-lost causes. *Clubs:* Roy Tay Yacht. *Address:* Dept of Forensic Medicine, The Royal Infirmary, Dundee, DD1 9ND. 12 Hill Street, Broughty Ferry, Dundee, DD5 2JL.

POWELL, Dr Bryan Llewelyn, B.Sc., M.A., Ph.D. *Currently:* Director of the Open University in Wales. *Born on* 5 Feb 1936 at Alltwen, Pontardawe. *Son of* the late Clifford Powell and the late Phoebe (nee Lewis). *Marriage:* to Beti Lyn Edwards, 1958. *Children:* Alison Jane and David Gareth. *Educated at* Ystalyfera Grammar School and University College, Swansea. *Career:* Lecturer in Zoology, Trinity College, Dublin, 1960-67; Senior Lecturer and Registrar, School of Education, Trinity College, Dublin, 1967-76; Visiting Science Curriculum Consultant, University of West Indies, St. Augustine, Trinidad, 1969-70; Senior Assistant Director of Education, Gwynedd County Council, 1976-82; Secretary, Wales Advisory Body for Local Authority Higher Education, 1982-90. *Publications:* "Intermediate Biology", 1967; "Practical Biology", 1970. *Recreation:* Music (former Conductor Cor y Traeth, Anglesey and Caernarfon Male Voice Choir), Cricket and Rugby. *Address:* 15 Brynderwen Close, Cyncoed, Cardiff., CF2 6BR. The Open University In Wales, 24 Cathedral Road, Cardiff, CF1 9SA.

POWELL, David Beynon, *Currently:* Group Legal Director, Midland Bank plc since 1984. *Born on* 9 Feb 1934 at Loughor, W. Glam. *Son of* the late David Eynon Powell and Catherine Ada Powell. *Marriage:* to Pamela Susan Turnbull (divorced). *Educated at* Gowerton GS; Christ's College, Cambridge (MA, LL. B); Yale Law School (Graduate Fellow) (LL. M); Harvard Business School (SMP18). *Career:* National Service, RAF 1952-54. Flg Officer. Solicitor of The Supreme Court 1962; Deputy Legal Adviser, BLMC 1969-72; Director of Legal Services, BL plc (British Leyland) 1973-83. *Recreation:* reading, music, social bridge *Associations:* Member, Friends of Templeton College, Oxford. *Address:* 20c Randolph Crescent, London, W9 1DR. Midland Bank Plc, Poultry, London, EC2 2BX.

POWELL, His Honour Judge Dewi Watkin, JP, MA. *Currently:* Circuit Judge and Official Referee, Wales and Chester Circuit. *Born on* 29 July 1920 at Trecynon, Aberdar. *Son of* William H and Mary A Powell. *Marriage:* to Alice Williams, Garddllygardydydd, Nantmor, 1951. *Children:* Nia Mair Watkin. *Educated at* Ysgol Sir Penarth; Jesus College, Oxford. *Career:* Yarborough Anderson Scholar, Inner Temple; called to the Bar 1949; Junior Wales and Chester Circuit 1968-69; Deputy Chairman Merioneth Quarter Sessions 1966-71, and Cardiganshire Quarter Sessions 1967-71; designated Judge Merthyr Tydfil Crown Court 1988-91; Member of the Council 1968- , Chairman of the Council 1977-84, Vice President 1984- ;Hon. Soc. of Cymmrodorion: President Cymdeithas Theatr Cymru 1982-89; Mbr. of The Court 1972- ; and Council 1990- ; Univ. of Wales: Court and Council, Univ. Coll. of Wales,

Aberystwyth 1972-91; Court and Council Univ. Coll., Cardiff 1977-88; Vice Pres. 1980-88; Chairman of Council 1987-88; Mbr. of Court and Council (Vice Chairman) and Vice President, Univ. of Wales, Coll. of Cardiff 1988- ; Mbr. of Council Univ. of Wales Coll. of Medicine 1989- ; Vice Pres., Magistrates Assoc., Mid and South Glamorgan 1974- ; and Gwynedd 1990- . Honorary arwid Gorsedd of Bards. Religion: Welsh Baptist. *Publications:* Ymadroddion Llys Barn (Forensic Phraseology), Aberystwyth 1974; Iaith Cenedl a Deddfwriaeth, National Eisteddfod Lecture 1990; Contributor to: Lawyers and Laymen, Cardiff Univ. of Wales Press 1986; and Y Gair a'r Genedl, Swansea: Gwasg John Penry 1986. *Recreation:* engaging in matters relating to The Church and to Wales and the Welsh language; gardening; theology; history; travel (seasonally) and Psephology (spasmodically). *Address:* Llysoedd Barn, Parc Cathays, Caerdydd.

POWELL, Mr Graham, *Currently:* retired railwayman. *Born on* 16 July 1925 at Aberdare, Mid Glam. *Son of* Charles and Kathleen Powell. *Marriage:* divorced and re-married. *Children:* David John and Gillian. *Educated at* Secondary. *Career:* 45 years as an elected representative on Parish Council Rural District and 30 years a County Councillor; Trade Union representative as member of National Union of Railwaymen; Partliamentary Labour Candidate, Exeter 1974; Served as Board member on Cwmbran Development Corp; member of assoc. County Councils, assembly of Welsh Counties; Leader of Gwent C. C. on two occasions, Chairman 1980-81 of County Council; Chairman of Ed. Com., 14 years, served on all committees of C.C; Chairman Local Com. Muir Group Housing Association. *Recreation:* sport, priority cricket. *Address:* 75B Sandy Lane, Caldicot, Newport, Gwent, NP6 4NR. County Hall, Cwmbran, Gwent, NP44 2XG

POWELL, John Lewis, QC; MA; LL.B (Cantab). *Currently:* Barrister. *Born on* 14 Sept 1950 at Carmarthen. *Son of* the late Gwyn Powell and Lilian Mary Powell (nee Griffiths). *Marriage:* Eva Zufia Powell (nee Lomnicka), 1973. *Children:* Sophie Anna, Catrin Eva and David John. *Educated at* Christ College, Brecon 1961-64; Amman Valley Grammar School 1964-68; Trinity Hall, Cambridge 1969-73 (MA,1972, LL.B.,1973). *Career:* Practising Barrister 1974; Q.C., 1990; President, Society of Contruction Law 1991. General Election: Labour Candidate, Cardigan Constituency 1979. *Publications:* Jackson & Powell, "Professional Negligence"; Lomnicka & Powell, "Encyclopedia of Financial Services Law"; Palmer's Company Law (contrib ed.); Issues & Offers of Company Securities. *Recreation:* travel, sheep farming, mountains, international politics. *Clubs: Address:* 2 Crown Office Row, Temple, London, EC4Y. Rhandir, Trap, Llandeilo, Dyfed, SA19 6UD. Tel: 071 797 8000.

POWELL, Professor Percival Hugh, MA; D.Litt; PhD. *Currently:* Emeritus Professor of Germanic Studies, Indiana University. *Born on* 4 Sept 1912 at Cardiff. *Son of* Thomas James Powell and Marie Sophia Roeser. *Marriage:* 1st to Mavis Pattison, 1944, div. 1964; 2nd to Mary Wilson, 1966. *Children:* Anton and Nicholas (1st marriage) Dominic (2nd marriage). *Educated at* Howard Gardens High School, Cardiff; University College, Cardiff; Universities of Rostock, Zurich and Bonn. *Career:* Modern Languages Master, Towyn School, Towyn, 1934-36; Fellow of University of Wales, 1936-38; Lektor in English, Univ. of Bonn, 1938-39; Assistant Lecturer in German, Univ. Coll. Cardiff, 1939-40; War Service, 1940-46; Lecturer and Professor of German, University of Leicester, 1946-69; Dean of Faculty of Arts, Univ. of Leicester 1959-63; Barclay Acheson Professor of International Studies, Macalester College,

Minnesota, USA, 1965-66; Professor of German, Indiana University, 1969-83. Fellow of University of Wales College of Cardiff, 1981. *Publications:* 12 volumes on literature and culture of Germany; numerous articles. *Recreation:* music and travel. *Address:* Germanic Studies, Indiana University, Ballantine Hall, Bloomington, Indiana 47405, U. S. A. 904 South Rose Avenue, Bloomington, Indiana 47401, U.S.A.

POWELL, Mr William Rhys, MA, MP. *Currently:* Member of Parliament, Corby 1983-. *Born on* 3 Aug 1948 at Colchester. *Son of* The Reverence Canon Edward and Mrs Powell. *Marriage:* to Elizabeth Vaudin, 1973. *Children:* Sophie, Victoria and Natasha. Educated at Lancing; Emmanuel College Cambridge. *Career:* Barrister (south East Circuit), 1972-87; PPS Minister for Overseas Development 1985-86; PPS Sec. of State Environment (Rt. Hon Michael Heseltine), 1990-. *Address:* C/o House Of Commons, London.

PREECE, Mr Michael John Stewart, MA *Currently:* Senior Partner, Messrs Carter, Vincent, Preece Brown & Co., Bangor (Solicitors); Diocesan Registrar Bangor; Clerk to Dean and Chapter of Bangor Cathedral; Under Sheriff of Anglesey. *Born on* 29 Dec 1934 at Hartshill. *Son of* the late Lieutenant Colonel James Preece, OBE andMargaret Stewart (nee Paterson) of Jersey. *Marriage:* to Tessa Gillian Rosamond Williams, 1958, 2nd da of Sir Francis Williams, Bt, QC. *Children:* James Francis Stewart (b.1964), Hugh Michael Stewart (b. 1969) Emily Margaret(b. 1961) and RosamondAlice (b.1963). Educated at Rugby School; Emmanuel College, Cambridge. *Career:* 2nd Lieut (Nat.Service), Korea, Hong Kong 1954-55; Capt.TA, Cheshire Yeomanry 1963-70; Solicitor since 1962. *Recreation:* golf, squash, shooting, Roman history. *Clubs:* Lansdowne *Address:* Plas Llanddyfnan, Talwrn, Llangefni, Anglesey, Gwynedd, LL77 7TH. Tel: 0248 750659.

PRESCOTT THOMAS, John Desmond, RD, MA. *Currently:* Managing Director, Westcountry Television, since 1991. *Born on* 28 May 1942 at Prestatyn, Clwyd. *Son of* the late William Prescott Thomas and Beatrice Isobel (nee Jones). *Marriage:* to Bridget Margaret Somerset-Ward, 1967. *Children:* Viveka Ruth and Bronwen Jane. Educated at Rhyl Grammar School, Clwyd; Whitchurch Grammar School, Glamorgan; Jesus College Oxford (Modern Languages). *Career:* BBC General Trainee 1963-65; Assistant Producer, School Television 1965-68, Producer 1968-76; Senior Producer Modern Languages and European Studies 1976-81; Head of School Broadcasting, Television 1981-84; Head of Network Production Centre, Bristol 1984-86; Head of Broadcasting, South & West 1986-91. Governor, Bristol Polytechnic; Deputy Chairman Bath International Festival; Trustee St George's Music Trust, The Exploratory, Bristol Cathedral Trust; Member Policy Advisory Ctee, Univ of Bristol Veterinary School; Commander Royal Naval Reserve. Formerly: Trustee Television Trust for the Environment; Vice-President, Bristol Operato Association; Member of Court Univ of Bath; Member Management ctee South West Arts, Friends Ctee Arnolfini Gallery, Publicity ctee Royal Bath & West of England Show, Communications Group Diocese of Bath & Wells. *Publications:* Who's That Out There?-The Relationship between Broadcasters and their Audiences, 1984; Des Le Debut, Dicho Y Hecho, Alles Vlar, 1982-83; Encounter: France, 1980; Two Efl stories for Children; articles in Tes, British Language Teaching Journal, Le Francais Dans Le Monde. *Recreation:* languages, sailing, photography, industrial archaeology & model engineering, heraldry, playing the alto saxophone. *Clubs:* Naval *Address:* Earl's Pool, Ladymead Lane,

Lower Langford, Avon, BS18 7EQ. Westcountry Television, Plymouth, PL1 3EW.

PRICE, Mr (John) Maurice, Q.C., M.A. (Cantab), FCI.Arb. *Currently:* Barrister. *Born on* 4 May 1942 at Wrexham, Denbighshire. *Son of* Edward Samuel Price and Hilda Myfanwy Price (nee Davies) J.P. *Marriage:* to Mary Gibson, daughter of Dr.Horace Gibson DSO and bar of Fremantle, Western Australia, 1945. *Children:* Toby (b.1952) and Barnaby (b 1956). Educated at Grove Park School, Wrexham; Trinity College, Cambridge. *Career:* Royal Navy 1941-46, (submarines 1943-46) Lieut.RNVR; Called to Bar by Gray's Inn 1949 (Holt Scholar, Holker Senior Scholar), Lincoln's Inn (Adieundem) 1976; Called to Singapore Bar 1976; Appointed Queen's Counsel 1976; Member Senate of Inns of Court and Bar 1975-78; Member Supreme Court Rules Committee 1975-79; Bencher of Gray's Inn 1981- ; Chairman of Management Committee of Gray's Inn 1989; Master of the Estate of Gray's Inn 1988. Admitted Fellow of Chartered Institute of Arbitrators, 1991. *Recreation:* fishing, reading, D.I.Y. *Clubs:* Flyfishers. *Address:* Bowzell Place, Weald, Sevenoaks, Kent., TN14 6NF. 2 New Square, Lincoln's Inn, London, WC2A 3RU Tel: 071 242 6201.

PRICE, Mr Alan Edward, *Currently:* Proprietor 'Sportsflair' (sports retail business, 5 shops), since 1980. *Born on* 11 June 1953 at Caerphilly, Mid Glam. *Son of* Leonard and Pamela Price. *Marriage:* to Jan Price, 1973. *Children:* James Edward and Richard Alan. *Educated at* Caerphilly Grammar School, Mid Glam. *Career:* Chairman Wales Squash Racketts Federation, since 1989. *Recreation:* squash, golf, cricket, music. *Clubs:* Cardiff SRC; Radyr Golf; Lisvane Cricket; Cardiff L. T. C. *Address:* Waterways, Lisvane Road, Lisvane, Cardiff, CF4 5SF.

PRICE, Cyril, F. InstD: *Currently:* semi-retired. *Born on* 26 Feb 1924 at Porth, Glam. *Son of* the late Ieuan Penry Price and the late Elsie Price. *Marriage:* to Nancy Joy, da of Frederic Seaton, JP, of Australia (d 1966). *Children:* David Seaton Price and Susan Joy Price (Heath) *Educated at* Cathays, Cardiff 1936-42. *Career:* Fleet Air Arm, Lt RNVR (A) 828 Sqdn: HMS Formidable and Implacable, 1942-46; Export Executive C. Tennant Sons & Co 1946; Director Tennant Guaranty Ltd (renamed The Royal Bank of Canada Trade & Finance Ltd 1982), 1964-83; Director Orford Trading Co. Ltd 1964-83; Director Tennant Guaranty Trust 1969-83; Director Tennant Guaranty International 1976-83; Snr Executive AMCA Netherlands B.V., 1983-84; International Business Consultant 1984- ; Chairman High Wycombe Centre Institute of Directors 1988-90; Dep. Chairman Probus Club of Beaconsfield 1987- ; Volunteer VSS Club 1987-. *Publications:* various newspaper features on International Trade and Finance *Recreation:* golf, music, walking *Clubs:* Hazelmere Golf and Country *Address:* Cooinda, Hubert Day Close, Beaconsfield, Bucks, HP9 1TL

PRICE, Mr Gareth, *Currently:* Controller, Broadcasting Division, The Thomson Foundation. *Born on* 30 August 1939 at Corby, Northants. *Son of* the late Mr Morgan Price and Mrs Rowena Price (nee Jones). *Marriage:* to Mari Griffiths, 1962. *Children:* Hywel, Aled and Menna *Educated at* Aberaeron & Ardwyn G. S., Aberystwyth; UCW Aberystwyth. *Career:* Lecturer in Economics, Queen's Univ., Belfast 1962-64; Current Affairs Radio Producer, BBC Wales 1964-66; TV Features and Documentary Producer, BBC Wales 1966-74; Assistant Head of Programmes, BBC Wales 1974-81; Head of Programmes, BBC Wales 1981-86; Controller, BBC Wales 1986-90; Advisory Commt - British Council Welsh Advisory Commt 1990- ; President, GEWC Cymru, Welsh Centre for International Affairs 1989- ; Chairman, LIP

Wales, National Library of Wales, Aberystwyth; Member, Welsh Political Archive Committee. *Publications:* Lloyd George - A Photographic Memoir (with Emyr Price and Bryn Parry) *Address:* 98 Pencisely Road, Llandaff, Cardiff, CF5 1DQ.

PRICE, Mr Hugh Maxwell, *Currently:* Partner, Morgan Bruce, Solicitors, Cardiff. *Born on* 25 April 1950 at Bridgend. *Son of* Denis Lewin Price and Patricia Rosemary Price. *Marriage:* to Sarah Anne (nee Snape), 1965. *Children:* Andrew and Emma. *Educated at* Haileybury College, Herfford. *Career:* Coutts & Co., Bankers 1969-70; joined Messrs Hardwickes, Solicitors, Cardiff 1970; Partner: Hardwickes 1978-87, then Morgan Bruce & Hardwickes, now Morgan Bruce; appointed Deputy Registrar/District Judge of High Court in 1988. *Recreation:* gardening, squash, running, DIY. *Clubs:* Cardiff & County, Cardiff Athletic, Cowbridge Squash. *Address:* Orchard House, Llanblethian, Nr Cowbridge, S. Glam., CF7 7EY. Bradley Court, Park Place, Cardiff, CF1 3DP.

PRICE, Margaret Berenice, CBE *Currently:* British opera singer. *Born on* 13 April 1941 at Tredegar, Wales. *Daughter of* the late Thomas Glyn Price and Lilian Myfanwy Richards. *Educated at* Pontllanfraith Grammar School; Trinity College of Music, London. *Career:* operatic debut with Welsh Nat. Opera in Marriage of Figaro; renowned for Mozart operatic roles; has sung in world's leading opera houses and festivals; has made many recordings of opera, oratorio, concert work and recitals, many radio broadcasts and television appearances; Hon. Fellow, Trinity Coll. of Music; Elisabeth Schumann Prize for Lieder, Ricordi Prize for Opera, Silver Medal of the Worshipful Co. of Musicians; Hon. D. Mus. (Wales) 1983. Major roles include: Countess in Marriage of Figaro, Fiordiligi in Cosi fan Tutte, Amelia in Simone Boccanegra, Desdemona in Otello, Elisabetta in Don Carlo, Aida and Norma. Hon. Fellow University of Aberystwyth; Hon. RAM. *Recreation:* cookery, reading, walking, swimming, driving. *Clubs:* *Address:* c/o Bayerische, Staatsoper Munchen, Max Josef Platz 2, 8000 Munchen 22. Germany,

PRICE, Richard Henry, BSc (Econ). *Currently:* Deputy Director-General, Confederation of British Industry since 1990. *Born on* 13 July 1944 at Lydney, Glos. *Son of* Henry George Price and the late Nesta Suzanne (nee Jones). *Marriage:* to Sally Josephine McCowen. *Children:* Guy, Toby and Tom. *Educated at* Monmouth School; University College, London; University of Cambridge. *Career:* Head of Economics, Queens College, Taunton 1968-70; Confederation of British Industry: Economic Adviser 1970-79, Director of Regions to 1983, Employment Affairs Director to 1987, Executive Director for Government Relations to 1990. Member, Council of ACAS 1984- ; Manpower Services Commissioner/Training Commissioner 1987-89. *Publications:* various articles on economic forecasting; business surveys and industrial relations. *Recreation:* bridge, skiing, cricket, rugby football. *Clubs:* United Oxford and Cambidge University. *Address:* Kingscot, The Parade, Monmouth, Gwent, NP5 3PA. 10 Beechwood Grove, East Acton Lane, London, N3

PRICE, Mr Richard Stephen, LLb (Hons). *Currently:* Partner, McKenna & Co., Solicitors since 1988. *Born on* 27 May 1953 at Bridgend, Wales. *Son of* Dr David Brian Price and the late Menna Myles Price. *Marriage:* to Nicola Mary Griffin, 1980. *Children:* Roseanna Holly Price and Nicholas William Price. *Educated at* Cowbridge Grammar School; Leeds University. *Career:* Articles Clerk McKenna & Co., 1975-77; Solicitor, McKenna & Co., 1977-84; Partner, McKenna & Co based in the Arabian Gulf 1984-88. *Recreation:* golf, gardening. *Clubs:* City of London

Solicitors, Institute of Welsh Affairs. *Address:* Mitre House, 160 Aldersgate Street, London, EC1A 4DD.

PRICE, Robert Thomas, LL. B. *Currently:* Solicitor and H. M. Coroner. *Born on* 10 Oct 1932 at Criccieth. *Son of* the late Richard James Price and the late Laura Price. *Marriage:* to Ann Wyn Hughes, 1978. *Children:* Anna Eluned Price. *Educated at* Criccieth Primary School; Porthmadoc Grammar School; University College Aberystwyth. *Career:* qualified as solicitor in 1957; RAF 1958-60; practised as solicitor in partnership, Messrs William George & Son, Porthmadog 1960- ; appointed H. M. Coroner for Lleyn and Eifionydd District of Gwynedd 1984. Chairman Dwyfor District Council 1980-81; Capt. Criccieth Golf Club 1968; President Gwynedd Law Society 1991-92. Chairman Criccieth Town Council 1967, 1973, 1980 and 1989. *Recreation:* yachting, golf, angling *Clubs:* *Address:* Monfa Beach Bank, Criccieth, Gwynedd.

PRICE, Professor (Emeritus) William Charles, FRS *Currently:* retired since 1967. *Born on* 1 April 1909 at Swansea. *Son of* the late Richard Price and the late Margaret Florence (nee Charles). *Marriage:* to Nest Myra (nee Davies), 1939. *Children:* David Richard and Elizabeth Helen. *Educated at* Swansea Grammar; University College Swansea; John Hopkins Univ, Baltimore; Trinity Coll., Cambridge; Commonwealth Fellow 1932; PhD(John Hopkins) 1934; Cambridge: Senior 1851 Exhibitioner 1935. *Career:* University Demonstrator 1927-43, PhD (Cantab) 1937. Prize Fellow, Trinity Coll., 1938; ScD(Cantab) 1949; Meldola Medal of Inst of Chem 1938; Senior Spectroscopist, ICI (Billingham Div) 1943-48; Research Associate, University of Chicago 1946-47; Reader in Physics, University of London (Kings Coll) 1948. FKC 1970. FRIC 1944; FIP 1950; Co-editor, British Bulletin of Spectroscopy 1950- ; Hon. DSc Wales 1970. *Publications:* research and review articles on physics and chemistry in scientific journals. *Recreation:* gardening *Address:* 38 Cross Way, Orpington, Kent, BR5 1PE. Kings College, Strand, London, WC2R 2LS.

PRICE, Mr William Leslie, (current) Med-University of Cardiff. *Currently:* Director, Welsh Association of Youth Clubs, 1987- . *Born on* 26 Sept 1945 at Wrexham. *Son of* the late William Horace Price and Annie Price (nee Duffy). *Marriage:* to Julie Ann Thomas, 1989. *Children:* Angela Jane and Robert Clive. *Educated at* Grove Park Grammar School, Wrexham. *Career:* Diploma in Youth Work, NCTYL Leicester, 1969; Warden, Netteswell Y.C. Harlow, Essex, 1970-72; Regional Officer, North Wales A.Y.C., 1972-76; Warden, Wrexham-Victoria Y.C., 1976-87; Royal Jubliee & Prince's Trust, North Wales panel, 1982-87; Vice Chair, British and Irish Confederation of Youth Clubs; 1987- ; Executive Member, Council for Wales of Voluntary Youth Services, 1987- ; Executive member, Youth Clubs U.K. Management Council, 1987- *Publications:* Proprietor /Managing Director - Nightshift Publications, P. O. Box 23, Abergavenny, Gwent, NP7 7YE. *Recreation:* Reading, working and writing. *Clubs:* *Address:* Welsh Assoc. Youth, Clubs, Sachville Avenue, Heath Cardiff., CF4 3NY. 26 Dingle Road, Abergavenny, Gwent, NP7 7AR .

PRICE-THOMAS, Mr D. Geraint, BA., Solicitor *Currently:* Under Secretary (Wales); Association of District Councils, since 1983. *Born on* 14 Nov 1943 at Aberystwyth. *Son of* the late John Price Thomas and Eirian Price Thomas(nee Pearson). *Marriage:* to Marian Elizabeth Morgan, 1982. *Children:* Simon, Katherine and Gareth. *Educated at* Ardwyn Grammar School, Aberystwyth; UCW Aberystwyth; Manchester University & Law Society, College of Law. *Career:* Manchester City Council, 1966-77; Solicitor Preseli District Council, 1977-81; Deputy

Town Clerk, Ellesmere Port and Neston Borough Council, 1981-83. *Recreation:* Music, all sports and reading. *Clubs:* Stow Park Lawn Tennis Club, Newport. *Address:* 10/11 Raleigh Walk, Atlantic Wharf, Cardiff CF1 5LN.

PRICHARD, Francis Anthony, LLB *Born on* 10th June 1949 at Liverpool. *Son of* Francis Leo Prichard and Dorothy Joanne Prichard. *Marriage:* to Elizabeth Ann Prescott on 21st December 1974. *Children:* Mark, (b. 10. 8. 79); Paul, (b. 6. 4. 81) and James (b. 28. 12. 83). *Educated at* Ratcliffe College, Leicester; Liverpool University *Career:* Admitted Solicitor 1974; partner Weightman Rutherfords 1976-; Notary Public *Recreation:* tennis, Bridge, skiing *Clubs:* Racquet Club; Blundellsands Lawn Tennis Club. *Address:* Merrywood, Downhills Road, Blundellsands, Liverpool, L23 8SP. Tel: 051 931 2315.

PRICHARD, Mr Mathew Caradoc Thomas, BA (PPE). *Currently:* Chairman, Booker Entertainment and Agatha Christie Ltd; Chairman Welsh Arts Council, 1986- . *Born on* 21 Sept 1943 at Cheadle, Cheshire. *Son of* the late Major H. de B. Prichard and Rosalind Hicks. *Marriage:* to Angela Caroline (nee Maples), 1967. *Children:* Alexandra (23), James (21) and Jo (19). *Educated at* Eton College; New College, Oxford. *Career:* Penguin Books 1965-69; Advisory Local Dir, Barclays Bank plc, 1977- ; Pres., Welsh Group of Artists 1974-; Member: Court of Governors and Council, Nat. Museum of Wales 1975- ; Welsh Arts Council, 1980-; (Vice-Chm., 1983-86); Arts Council of GB 1983- ; High Sheriff, Glamorgan 1972-73. *Recreation:* golf, cricket, arts generally. *Clubs:* Royal Porthcawl Golf; Cardiff and County; RLA Golf; MCC. *Address:* Pwllywrach, Cowbridge, South Glam., CF7 7NJ

PRITCHARD, Mr Austin Leslie, *Currently:* Garage Director of two businesses. *Born on* 21 Sept 1913 at The Ystrad, Llandrindod Wells. *Son of* Mr & Mrs Thomas Pritchard. *Marriage:* to Katie Williams. *Educated at* County Primary School, Llandrindod Wells; County Secondary School; Pagefields College, Swansea, Glamorgan. *Career:* past chairman Powys County Council 1977-78; past chairman of Llandrindod Wells Urban District Council, year 1954 and 1962; chairman Dyfed Powys Police Authority 1991-92; chairman Radnorshire Disabled; president Llandrindod Wells Royal British Legion; president Llandrindod Wells Tennis Club; member Llandrindod Wells Rotary club. *Recreation:* public life. *Address:* Ystrad House, Dyffryn Road, Llandrindod Wells, Powys, LD1 6AN.

PRITCHARD, Mr Iorwerth Gwynn, MA, Chevalier De L'Ordre Des Arts Et Des Lettres. *Currently:* Pennaeth Rhaglenni Cymraeg, BBC Cymru, since 1992. *Born on* 1 Feb 1946 at Ffynnongroyw, Clwyd. *Son of* the late Rev. Robert Islwyn Pritchard and Megan Mair Pritchard (nee Lloyd). *Marriage:* to Marilyn Patricia (nee Bartholomew), 1970. *Children:* Matthew Osian (b. 1975), Nia Sian (b. 1977) and Dafydd Islwyn (b. 1989). *Educated at* King's College Cambridge; University of London. *Career:* Senior Commissioning Editor, Channel 4 Television, 1985-92; BBC Television 1969-82; HTV Wales 1982-85; Trustee Welsh Writers Trust; Trustee Broadcast Support Services; Governor National Institute for Adult and continuing education. *Recreation:* swimming, walking, reading. *Address:* B.B.C. Cymru/Wales, Llandaf, Caerdydd,

PRITCHARD, Mr Kenneth John, CB, MA, FInstPS *Currently:* Director of Greenwich Hospital. *Born on* 18 March 1926 at Newport, Gwent. *Son of* William Edward Pritchard and Ethel Mary Cornfield. *Marriage:* 1st to Elizabeth Margaret Bradshaw 1949)d. 1978);2nd to Angela Madeiline Palmer 1979. *Children:* Elizabeth Anne and Barbara Jane, from 1st marriage; Jonathan Robin, Lucy Geridwen and Emma Louise from 2nd marriage. *Educated*

at Newport High School; St. Catherines College Oxford. *Career:* Army 1944-48, Indian Military Academy Dehra Dun, served 8/12th Frontier Force Regiment, Assistant Principal Admiralty 1951; Private Secretary to Secretary of State for Wales 1964-65; Asst. Secretary Ministry of Aviation 1966; Principal Supply and Transport Officer (Naval), Portsmouth 1978; Director General, Supplies and Transport (Naval) MOD 1981-86, retd F. Inst. PS 1986. *Recreation:* squash, tennis, theatre. *Clubs:* Bath & County (Bath). *Address:* Pickford House, Bath Road, Beckington, Somerset, BA3 6SJ Tel: 0373 830329.

PRITCHARD, Professor Thomas Owen (Tom), JP; BSc; PhD; FRSA. *Currently:* Environmental Consultant specialising in policy studies and training. *Born on* 13 May 1932 at Pwllheli. *Son of* Owen and Mary Elizabeth Pritchard. *Marriage:* to Enyd Ashton, 1957. *Children:* Rhianand Iwan. *Educated at* Botwnnog Grammar School; University of Wales; University of Leeds. *Career:* Director for Wales, Nature Conservancy Council, 1973-91; Hon. Professor, Institute of Earth Studies, University of Wales, Aberystwyth; Chairman, Ce Cynefin Environmental Ltd; Member: Genetical Society; British Ecological Society; Gorsedd of Bards, Royal National Eisteddfod; Hon. Soc. of Cymmrodorion; Prince of Wales' Ctee; JP Bangor, 1978- ; FRSA; Vice-Chmn Int. Union for Conservation (IUCN) and mem. Exec. Bd. 1966-73; Convenor, Int. Biological Programme, 1967-72; Consultant, Cncl of Europe 1968; Chmn, Welsh office Land Use Study Gp 1969; Sec. Welsh Cttee, European Conservation, Year, 1968-71; Mem. Committee for Wales, Nat. Trust 1968- ; Chmn. Exec. Prince of Wales' Cttee 1971-73; British Council advisor to Israel 1973; Chmn. Govrn working party on conservation in the marine environment 1974-79; Sec. Cttee of Chmn of Chief Officers of Stat. Bodies in Wales 1977-80; Dep. Chmn. Anglo-Soviet Environmental Protection Agreement 1977-80; Mem. Crt of Governors & Council, Nat. Museum of Wales 1978-91; Mem. Government's Interdepartmental Cttee on the marine environment 1979-81; Visiting Prof. Univ. of California 1981-87; Mem. Crt of Govns & Council, University of Wales, Bangor 1981; Mem. Bd of Dir. CTF Training Ltd 1982- ; Chmn. Bardsey Island Trust Ltd 1987- ; Mem. External Review Cttee, Univ of California 1988; Trustee, Caernarfon Harbour Trust 1989- ; Chmn. Steering Cttee on UK Policies for Environmental Education & Training 1991-; Chmn. Gwynedd, Welsh Historic Gardens Trust 1991- ; Chmn. Richard Wilson Arts Trust 1991- ; Mem. TSB Environmental Investor Fund Cttee 1991- . *Publications:* Cynefin Y Cymro, 1989; numerous contributions to scientific and educational journals, and policy publications. *Recreation:* sailing *Address:* Graig Llwyd, 134 Penrhos Road, Bangor, Gwynedd, LL57 2BX.

PROBERT, Mr Gordon Spencer, BA(Hons), FRTPI *Currently:* County Planning Officer, Gwent County Council 1974-92. *Born on* 19 March 1930 at Whitland, Dyfed. *Son of* Cecil George Probert and Hannah Maria Probert. *Marriage:* to Carol Ann Probert, 1977. *Children:* Susan Davey, John Probert, Steven Probert and Andrew Probert. *Educated at* Port Talbot County Grammar School; University of Manchester; University College, London. *Career:* Senior Planning Officer, Gloucestershire, Glamorgan, Somerset and Hertfordshire County Councils, 1955-62; Assistant County Planning Officer, Surrey County Council, 1962-65; Deputy City Planning Officer, Cardiff City Council, 1965-73; County Planning Officer, South Glamorgan County Council, 1973-74. *Publications:* Gwent Structure Plan, 1981; Revised Gwent Structure Plan 1992. *Recreation:* reading, landscape gardening. *Clubs:* Gwent NALGO. *Address:* 30 Rannoch Drive, Cyncoed, Cardiff,

CF2 6LQ. Tel: 0222 756102. Gwent County Planning Dept, County Hall, Cwmbran, Gwent, NP44 2XF. Tel: 0633 838838.

PROTHERO, Dr William Bernard Francis, MB, MRCPsych *Currently:* Consultant Psychiatrist, Hounslow and Specthorne Mental Health Unit. *Born on* 12 July 1953 at Carmarthen. *Son of* the late Huw Prothero and Falmai Prothero. *Educated at* Ysgol Sir, Aberaeron; University of Wales College of Medicine, Cardiff. *Career:* Senior House Officer, Registrar, Guys Hospital 1979-83; Senior Registrar, Westminster Hospital, Charing Cross Hospital 1983-88. *Publications:* medical publications in psychopharmacology. *Recreation:* theatre, opera, travel. *Address:* 13 Seymour Road, Chiswick, London, W4 5ES.

PROTHEROE, Colonel Alan Hackford, CBE; TD; FBIM; MIPR. *Currently:* Managing Director, The Services Sound and Vision Corporation, since 1987. *Born on* 10 Jan 1934 at St. Davids, Pembs. *Son of* the late Rev. B. P. Protheroe and Mrs R. C. M. Protheroe. *Marriage:* to Anne (nee Miller), 1956. *Children:* Christopher and Michael. *Educated at* Maesteg Grammar School, Glamorgan. *Career:* National Service, 2nd Lieutenant The Welch Regt, 1954-56; Lieutenant-Colonel Royal Regiment of Wales (TA) 1979-84; Colonel 1984-90. Honorary Colonel, Territorial Army Pool of Information Officers 1991- ; Deputy Chairman, Eastern Wessex Reserve Forces Association. Reporter, Glamorgan Gazette 1951-53; BBC Wales: Reporter, 1957-59; Industrial Correspondent 1959-64; Editor, News and Current Affairs 1964-70; BBC London: Assistant Editor BBC-TV News 1970-72; Deputy Editor 1972-77; Editor 1977-80; Assist. Dir, BBC News and Current Affairs 1980-82; Assist. Dir Gen, BBC 1982-87. (During BBC career wrote, produced, directed and presented films, radio and television programmes, reported wars, and travelled extensively, particularly in the Middle East and South Africa: seconded to Greek Government to assist in reorganisation of Greek TV, 1973). Mem. Steering Cttee, European Broadcasting Union News Group 1977-87; Chairman, Chaltec Ltd., 1987- ; Chairman, Europac Group Ltd., 1991- ; Director Defence Public Affairs Consultants (DPAC) 1987- ; Director: Visnews Ltd., 1982-87; Member of Council, Royal United Services Inst. for Defence Studies (RUSI) 1984-87. Association of British Editors: Founder Member and Deputy Chairman 1984-87; Chairman 1987. Honorary Consultant, The Royal British Legion. Fellow, British Institute of Management; Member, Institute of Public Relations; Territorial Decoration (and bar). *Publications:* contributions to newspapers and specialist journals on media and defence affairs. *Recreation:* photography, pistol and rifle shooting. *Clubs:* Savile *Address:* Amberleigh House, Chapman Lane, Flackwell Heath, Bucks, HP10 9BD. SSVC, Chalfont St Peter, Gerrards Cross, Bucks, SL9 8TN.

PRYCE, Dr. William Thomas Rees, BSc, MSc Wales, PhD CNAA, DipEd Wales. *Currently:* Senior Lecturer & Staff Tutor in Social Sciences, The Open University in Wales, Cardiff, since 1971. *Born on* 5 May 1935 at Wern, Pool Quay, Powys. *Son of* James William and Edith Maud Pryce, Llanfair Caereinion, Powys. *Marriage:* to Mary Hughes Jones, 1963, of Pentre Celyn, Clwyd. *Children:* Iwan Rhys Pryce and Guto Dafydd Pryce. *Educated at* Ysgol Uwchradd Caerieinion, Llanfair Caereinion; private study at Oxford; University College of Wales, Aberystwyth. *Career:* Lecturer Geography, Denbighshire Technical College, Wrexham, 1960-62; Lecturer in Geography & Education, Flintshire Technical Coll., 1962-65; Tutor (part time), N. Wales Workers' Educational Assoc., 1963-65; Lecturer/Acting Head of Geography, Coventry (Lanchester)

Polytechnic 1965-70; Correspondence Tutor, National Extension College, Cambridge 1969-72; Hon. Lecturer in Sociology, University College, Cardiff 1975- ; Hon., Research Assoc., Welsh Folk Museum (Nat. Mus. Wales), 1981- ; member, Court of Governors, Univ. of Wales, 1985- ; Co-opted member, Board of Celtic Studies, Univ. of Wales, 1985- ; member, Court of Governors, Univ. College of Wales, Aberystwyth, 1990- ; External Examiner, Trinity College, Carmarthen 1990- ; External Examiner, Polytechnic Central London 1992- ; External Examiner, Univ. of Wales PhD 1984, 1987, 1991; External Examiner, Univ. of Salford MPhil 1989. Holder of research grants and awards from the British Academy, the Open University and the European Community. *Publications:* author of over fifty publications, mainly in historical and cultural geography; books include W. T. R. Pryce and T. Alun Davies, Samuel Roberts Clock Maker: an eighteenth-century craftsman in a Welsh rural community (National Museum of Wales, 1985); Ian Hume and W. T. R. Pryce (eds) The Welsh and their Country: Selected Readings in the Social Sciences (Gomer Press, Llandysul, 1986); W. T. R. Pryce The Photographer in Rural Wales: A Photographic Archive of Llanfair Caereinion and its Region, c. 1865-1986 (The Powysland Club, 1991). *Recreation:* Geo-linguistics, Antiquarian Horology, music for the pipe organ, family history, travel in Europe, applied photography, baking of bread. *Address:* The Open University in Wales, 24 Cathedral Road, Cardiff., CF1 9SA. 26 Charlotte Square, Rhiwbina, Cardiff, CF4 6NE. Tel: 0222 397911.

PRYCE THOMAS, Mr David Hamilton, CBE, 1977. *Currently:* Retired. *Born on* 3 July 1922 at Abercarn, Gwent. *Son of* Trevor John Thomas and Eleanor Maud Thomas. *Marriage:* to Eluned Mair Morgan 1948. *Children:* Michael Christopher, Patrick David and Hilary Margaret. *Educated at* Barry Boys County School; Univ. Coll. Cardiff *Career:* Military Service, terminal rank T/Capt. 1941-47; Qualified as Solicitor with Hons. 1948; Partner in J. A. Hughes & Co., Barry 1950-75; Chrmn. E. Glam Rent Tribunal 1967-70; District Commissioner Barry Scout District 1963-70. Pres. Rent Asst. Panel for Wales 1970-88; Chrmn. Barry Mutual Bldg. Soc. 1971-78; Chrmn. Glamorgan Bldg. Soc., 1982-84; Chrmn. Wales Bd., Bradford & Bingley Bldg. Soc., 1984-87; Deputy Chrmn. Land Authority for Wales 1975-80; Chrmn. 1980-86. *Recreation:* Books, music. *Address:* 34 Camden Road, Brecon, Powys, LD3 7RT.

PUGH, Mr Dennis, OBE, JP. *Currently:* Special Adviser Welsh Development International; Director Kronospan Ltd. *Born on* 27 July 1930 at Blaenau Ffestiniog. *Son of* the late Rees and Elizabeth Pugh. *Marriage:* to Annie Lloyd Rees, 1952. *Children:* Carolyn and Judith. *Educated at* Ysgol Sir Ffestiniog. *Career:* Entered Civil Service 1947; Ministry of Pensions 1947-66 (RAF Berlin 1948-50); Board of Trade 1966; Customs and Excise 1972-76; Welsh Office 1976; Director Industry Dept North Wales 1981-90. *Recreation:* hill walking, Justice of Peace. *Address:* Moelwyn, Tyn Y Groes, Conwy, Gwynedd, LL32 8SZ.

PUGH, Sir Idwal Vaughan, KCB; MA(Oxon); Hon. LLD(Wales). *Currently:* Chairman, Royal Northern College of Music; Vice President University College of Swansea; President Coleg Harlech. President Cardiff Business Club. *Born on* 10 Feb 1918 at Ton Pentre, Rhondda. *Son of* Rhys Thomas Pugh and Elizabeth Vaughan Pugh. *Marriage:* to the late Mair Airona Lewis 1946 (died 1985). *Children:* David Vaughan Pugh and Elinor Vaughan Driver. *Educated at* Cowbridge Grammar School; St. John's College Oxford. *Career:* Civil Service 1946-76 (permanent secretary, Welsh Office 1969-71: 2nd permanent secretary,

Dept. of the Environment 1971-76); Parliamentary Commissioner for Administration and Health Service Commissioner 1976-79; Director Standard Chartered Bank: Chairman Chartered Trust 1979-88; Director Halifax Building Society 1979-88; Chairman Development Corporation for Wales 1980-83. *Clubs:* Brooks's; Cardiff and County; Royal Porthcawl Golf Club. *Address:* Flat 1, The Old House, Cathedral Green, Llandaff, Cardiff, CF5 2EB.

PUGH, John Arthur, OBE *Currently:* retired. *Born on* 17 July 1920 at Hay, Brecon. *Son of* Thomas Arthur Pugh and Dorothy Roberts Baker. *Children:* Jakawan. *Educated at* Brecon Grammar School; Bristol University. *Career:* RN 1941-45. Home CS 1950-54; Gold Coast Admin. Service 1955-58; Adviser to Ghana Government 1958-60; First Sec., British High Commission, Lagos 1962-65; First Sec (Economic), Bangkok and British Perm. Rep. to Economic Commission for Asia and Far East 1965-68; British Dep. High Comr, Ibadan 1971-73; Diplomatic Service Inspector 1973-76; British High Commisioner, Seychelles 1976-80. *Publications:* "The Friday Man", editorial and other contributions to journals etc., on political affairs, travel and history. *Recreation:* Oriental ceramics, anthropology, travel. *Clubs:* Commonwealth Trust. *Address:* Boatside Lane, Hay-On-Wye, Hereford, HR3 5RS.

PULESTON JONES, Mr Haydn, LL.B; A.K.C. *Currently:* Partner of Linklaters & Paines, City Solicitors, since 1979. *Born on* 16 Sept 1948 at Welshpool, Powys. *Son of* the late Mr Iago Oliver Puleston Jones and Elizabeth Ann (nee Morris). *Marriage:* to Susan Elizabeth (nee Karn), 1973. *Children:* Simon and Nicholas. *Educated at* Welshpool High School; King's College, London. *Career:* All with Linklaters & Paines: Articled Clerk 1971-73; Assistant Solicitor 1973-79; Member, Banking Law Sub-Committee, City of London Solicitors Company 1980- ; Secretary, Montgomeryshire Society 1972-74; Member, Committee, Montgomeryshire Society 1974-91; Trustee, Montgomeryshire Society Charitable Trusts 1983- . *Recreation:* gardening, classical music, genealogy. *Address:* Ducks Farm, Dux Lane, Plaxtol, Nr Sevenoaks, Kent., TN15 ORB. Linklaters & Paines, Barrington House, 59-67 Gresham St, London, EC2V 7JA. Tel: 071 606 7080.

PULVERMACHER, Francis Michael, LL. M. *Currently:* Partner, Alms Young Solicitors, Taunton, since 1966. *Born on* 26 July 1938 at Gloucester. *Son of* the late F. H. Pulvermacher and M. C. D. Pulvermacher, (formerly of Pentyrch, Mid Glamorgan). *Marriage:* to D. Penrose, 1966. *Children:* three d one s. *Educated at* Framlingham College, Suffolk. *Career:* Solicitor and Notary 1961; Assistant solicitor Edward Horley & Sons, Cardiff 1961-65; Assistant solicitor, F. J. Suter, Tiverton 1965-66. President Association of South Western Law Societies (includes Gwent), 1977-78; Member, Lord Chancellors' Legal Aid Advisory Committee 1986- ; Council member, The Notaries Society 1990- ; Hon. Secretary, Somerset Law Society 1971-84. *Publications:* Land Use Survey second edition - Mountain Ash and Rhondda Fach. *Recreation:* hill walking, bee-keeping, sailing, campanology. *Address:* Causeway Cottages, West Buckland, Wellington, Somerset.

PURCELL, Henry, OBE *Currently:* Deputy Central Office Agent, Conservative Party in Wales. *Born on* 25 Oct 1934 at Warrington. *Son of* the late William and the late Winifred Mary (nee McDonald). *Marriage:* to Marcia Wright, 1960. *Children:* Jonathan and Jennifer Mary. *Educated at* Boteler Grammar School. *Career:* Trainee Manager, Wholesale Meat Supply Co., 1951-53; National Service, 3rd Regt. R. H. A., 1953-55; Spectrographical Analyst British Aluminium 1955-57; Conservative Party Agent, Manchester, Bury,

Fylde Coast 1957-77; Deputy Conservative Central Office Agent North West 1977-89 *Recreation:* cricket, music, reading. *Clubs:* Lancashire Cricket, Creigiau Golf. *Address:* 19 Woodland Crescent, Creigiau, Cardiff, CF4 8SF. Tel: 0222 892167.

PURNELL, Professor John Howard, BSc, PhD(Wales), MA, PhD, ScD. (Cantab), FRSC. *Currently:* Professor of Chemistry, U. C. Swansea, since 1965. *Born on* 17 Aug 1925 at Rhondda. *Son of* the late Walter John Purnell and Sarah Ceridwen (nee Davies). *Marriage:* to Elizabeth Mary Edwards, 1954. *Children:* Rachel Elizabeth Sullivan and Nicholas Howard Purnell. *Educated at* Maesydderwen C. S; Pentre S. S; University College, Cardiff; University of Cambridge. *Career:* Lecturer U. C. Cardiff 1947-52; U. W. Fellow Univ Cambridge 1952-55; University Demonstrator 1955-60; and lecturer 1960-65, University of Cambridge; Fellow and Director of Studies, Trinity Hall 1958-65. Vice President, The Chemical Society 1976-80 and Royal Institute of Chemistry 1978-80. Hon Treasurer, Royal Society of Chemistry 1985-90. Chairman, Heads of University Chemistry Departments 1976-77. Chairman Physical Chemistry Committee, Science Research Council 1974-78; Chairman Working Party on The University/Industrial Interface in Wales 1988; Chairman Swansea Rugby Patrons 1987-91. *Publications:* 200 research papers in learned journals. *Recreation:* gardening, rugby football, music. *Clubs:* Savage, Swansea Rotary, Swansea C & F. *Address:* 1 Bishopston Road, Bishopston, Swansea, SA3 3EH. Department of Chemistry, University College of Swansea, Singleton Park, Swansea, SA2 8PP.

PUXLEY, Mr Charles John Lavallin, *Currently:* Estate Agent. *Born on* 20th Aug 1950 in London. *Second son of* J.P.L. Puxley, Esq., and A.C. Puxley (nee Wilson), Newbury, Berks. *Marriage:* to Saran Eleanor Gamon, on 7th Feb 1981. *Children:* Alexander 6, Charlotte 4 and John 2. *Educated* Eton; Mons Officer Cadet School; RMA Sandhurst. *Career:* Commissioned Royal Green Jackets 1970; ADC to Deputy Supreme Allied Commander Europe 1973-75; Adjutant 3rd Battalion 1976-78; C.T. Bowring Insurance Brokers 1978-80; Career in property since 1980-. Currently Residential Associate Partner Haslams, Chartered Surveyors, Reading; Mentioned in despatches for gallantry, Nothern Ireland 1972; UN Medal Cyprus 1970; Queens Jubilee Medal 1977 *Recreation:* Shooting, Cricket, Collecting wine. *Clubs:* Whites; MCC; Royal Green Jackets. *Address:* Easton Farm House, Newbury, Berks., RG16 8EE. Llethr Llestri, Llanddarog, Carmarthenshire.

QUARREN EVANS, His Honour Judge John Kerry,
MA., LL. M(Cantab). *Currently:* Circuit Judge. *Born on* 4 July 1926 at Pentre, Mid Glam. *Son of* the late Hubert Royston Quarren Evans M.C. and Violet Soule Quarren Evans. *Marriage:* to Janet Shaw Lawson 1958. *Children:* Sian Alison and Andrew John. *Educated at* King Henry VIII School, Coventry; Cardiff High School; Trinity Hall, Cambridge. *Career:* 21 Glam (Cardiff) Bn Home Guard 1943-44; Enlisted Grenadier Guards 1944; Commissioned Royal Welch Fusiliers from O.T.S. Bangalore 1946; Attached 2nd Bn. The Welch Regt., Burma 1946-47; Captain 1947; Trinity Hall Cambridge 1948-51; Admitted Solicitor 1953; Partner Lyndon Moore & Co., Newport 1954-71; Partner T. S. Edwards & Son, Newport 1971-80; Recorder Wales & Chester Circuit 1974-80; Clerk to Gen. Comrs. of Income Tax, Dinas Powis Division 1960-80; Circuit Judge South Eastern Division 1980. *Recreation:* Golf, rugby football, oenology, staurologosophy, old things. *Clubs:* The Arkaves, Newport Golf, Royal Porthcawl Golf, Denham Golf, Cardiff High School Old Boys RFC, Glamorgan Wanderers RFC, Crawshays Welsh RFC. *Address:* 2 Mount Park Cres., Ealing, London, W5 2RN.

QUICK, Miss Dorothy, LLB(London). *Currently:*
Metropolitan Stipendiary Magistrate, appointed 1986. *Born on* 10 Dec 1944 at Neath, Glamorgan. *Daughter of* Frederick and Doris Quick of Laleston, Bridgend. *Marriage:* to Charles Dcanlan, 1971. *Children:* Christopher, b 1977 and Stephen, b 1980. *Educated at* Glanafan Grammar School, Port Talbot; Read Law at University College, London. *Career:* Called to Bar by Inner Temple, 1969; practised from 5 Essex Court, EC4 until 1986. *Recreation:* music, books, gardening, theatre. *Clubs:* *Address:* Highbury Corner Magistrates, Court, Holloway Road, London, N5.

RAFFAN, Mr Keith William Twort, MA *Currently:*
Member of Parliament for Delyn. *Born on* 21 June 1949 at Aberdeen. *Son of* Dr Alfred William Raffan TD MB ChB FFARCS and the late Jean Crampton Raffan (nee Twort) MB ChB. *Educated at* Robert Gordon's College, Aberdeen; Trinity College, Glenalmond; Corpus Christi College, Cambridge University. *Career:* Editorial Writer Daily Express 1979-81; Political Correspondent, Daily Express 1981-83; member National Union of Journalists. Contested Dulwich Feb 1974 and East Aberdeenshire Oct 1974. Member for Delyn since June 1983. Member, Select Committee on Welsh Affairs 1983-91. Introduced Controlled Drugs (Penalties) Act, 1985, Tourism (Overseas Promotion) (Wales) Bill 1991. President Wales Conservative Trade Unionists 1984-87. President Wales Young Conservatives 1987-90. Special Interest: Wales; Europe; British-American relations; regional development; tourism; drug abuse.

Clubs: Carlton, Royal Automobile, Chelsea Arts, Flint and Prestatyn Conservative. *Address:* House of Commons, London, SW1A OAA.

RAIKES, Vice Admiral Sir Iwan (Geoffrey), KCB,
CBE, DSC, DL. *Currently:* retired. *Born on* 21 April 1921 at Weymouth, Dorset. *Son of* Admiral Sir Robert H. T. Raikes, KCB, CVO, DSO & bar, and Lady Ida Guinivere Raikes (nee Evans). *Marriage:* to Cecilia Primrose Hunt, 1947. *Children:* Rowland Gerard Taunton and June Marguerite. *Educated at* Royal Naval College, Dartmouth. *Career:* Royal Navy 1935, HMS Sussex 1939-40, HMS Repulse 1940, HMS Beagle Atlantic Convoys 1941, Submarines Atlantic, Mediterranean and North Sea 1942-45, Command of HM Submarines H43, 1943-44, Varne 1944-45, Virtue 1945-46, Talent 1948-49, Aeneas 1951-52. Commander 1952. Staff of C in C Allied Forces Mediterranean 1953-55, Executive Officer HMS Newcastle

(Far East) 1955-57, JSSC 1957, Captain 1960, Command HMS Loch Insh (Persian Gulf) 1961-62, Deputy Director Undersurface Warfare MoD 1962-64, Director Plans and Operations (Singapore) on Staff of C in C Far East 1965-66, IDC 1967, Command HMS Kent 1968-69, ADC to HM The Queen 1969, Rear Admiral 1970, Naval Secretary MoD 1970-72, Flag Officer First Flotilla 1973-74, Flag Officer Submarines and Nato Commander Submarines Eastern Atlantic 1974-76, Vice-Admiral 1973, retired 1977. Member Governing Body and Representative Body of Church in Wales 1980- , Chairman United Usk Fishermens Association 1978- . *Recreation:* country pursuits, gardening. *Clubs:* Naval and Military. *Address:* Aberyscir Court, Brecon, Powys, LD3 9NW.

RALPH, EUR.ING Prof. Dr. Brian, MA, PhD, ScD(Cantab), FIM, CEng, FInstP, CPhys, Hon. FRMS. *Currently:* Head of Department of Materials Technology, since 1987; Dean of Technology, since 1991, Brunel University, Uxbridge. *Born on* 4 Aug 1939 at Norwich. *Son of* the late Reginald James Ralph and the late Gwen Annie Ralph (nee Thomas). *Marriage:* to Anne Mary Perry, 1961. *Children:* Zoanna. *Educated at* City of Norwich School; Jesus College Cambridge. *Career:* Fellow and Tutor Jesus College Cambridge, 1964-83, and Demonstrator/ Lecturer in Dept of Metallurgy and Materials Science, Cambridge University. Head of Department of Metallurgy and Materials Science, University College Cardiff 1984- 87; Director of Institute of Materials, U. C. Cardiff 1986- 87; Visiting Professor: Georgia Tech, 1967; Vanderbilt Univ, 1969; Technical Univ of Twente, 1975; External Director The Royal Mint 1986-89. *Publications:* over 300 papers in the Academic Literature and editor of over 30 technical books from 1970-80; Editor of Physics of Metals and Metallography since 1990. *Recreation:* sailing, windsurfing, music, building furniture. *Clubs:* Cardiff & County. *Address:* Ty Carrog, St. Brides Super Ely, Cardiff, CF5 6EY. Flat 2, Oak Lane Cottage, Priest Hill, Egham, Surrey, TW20 0YU. Tel: 0446 760469.

RANFURLY, Countess of The Rt. Hon Hermione, OBE. *Currently:* retired. *Born on* 13 Nov 1913 at Winchcombe, Glos. *Daughter of* Mr & Mrs G. R. P. Llewellyn of Baglan Hall, Briton Ferry. *Marriage:* 1939. *Children:* Lady Caroline Simmonds. *Educated at* Southover Manor School, Lewes, Sussex. *Career:* Secretary War Office. Secretary to Lord Wakehurst, 1937, Governor of New South Wales. Secretary to Sir Harold MacMichael, High Commissioner Palestine 1941. P.A. to Gen. Sir Henry Maitland Wilson, Persia/Iraq Command 1942 and later when he was Field Marshal, Supreme Allied Commander Mediterranean Theatre. P.A. to Air Chief Marshall Sir John Slessor C-in-C Air Mediterranean. Creator of Ranfurly Homes for Children, Bahamas. Creator of the Ranfurly Library Service (Round the World) 1954. *Recreation:* Gardening, reading, collecting things, children, travelling. *Clubs:* Commonwealth Societies. *Address:* Great Pednor, Chesham, Bucks, HP5 2SU. Tel: 02406 2155.

RANKIN-HUNT, Major David, TD *Currently:* Specialist in Military History and Artefacts in The Royal Collection. *Born on* 26 Aug 1956 in Wales (Glamorgan). *Son of* Mr and Mrs James Rankin-Hunt. *Educated at* Christ College; St. Martin's School. *Career:* Welsh Office 1976-78; Regular Army 1978-81; Lieutenant Scots Guards; Entered Lord Chamberlain's Office in 1981; Registrar 1987-89; transferred to The Royal Collection in 1989; Major in The London Scottish Regt TA; Deputy Director of Ceremonies, Order of St. John, Priory for Wales; A Divisional President St. John Ambulance; Lay Steward, St. George's Chapel, Windsor Castle. *Publications:* contributed to various

magazines and journals on Military and Associated subjects. *Recreation:* Military history, Heraldry, conservation issues, Welsh Affairs. *Clubs:* Army & Navy. *Address:* 7 Cumberland Lodge Mews, The Great Park, Windsor, Berkshire, SL4 2JD. The Royal Collection, Stable Yard House, St. James's Palace, London, SW1A 1JR

RAPPORT, Mr Cecil Herbert, MBE, KStJ, JP, DL. *Born on* 12 Oct 1915 *Son of* the late Maurice Aaron Rapport and the late Phoebe Annie (nee Jacobs). *Marriage:* to Audrey Rachel Fligelstone, 1942. *Children:* Derek Ivor Rapport, Valerie Avery Gee (nee Rapport) and Heather Hockley (nee Rapport). *Educated at* Monkton House Coll Cardiff; City of Cardiff Tech Coll. *Career:* Welch Regt 1939-45; Pres: Cardiff Inst for the Blind, Royal British Legion Cardiff, Friends of Cardiff Royal Infirmary, Cardiff Central Cons Assoc; Chm Wales Festival of Rememberance; High Sheriff S. Glamorgan 1984-85, former Dep Lord Mayor City of Cardiff; former Alderman City Cardiff, Freeman City of London 1959; mem: Worshipful Co of Horners 1958. Guild of Freemen of the City of London 1969; mem IOD; KStJ. Past President Cardiff & District Chamber of Trade. *Recreation:* swimming, sailing, music. *Clubs:* City Livery, RAC. *Address:* Cefn Coed House, 37 Cefn Coed Road, Cyncoed, Cardiff, CF2 6AP.

RAYNER, County Councillor Bryan Joseph, B. A. Hons (Wales) *Currently:* Funeral Director, Thomas Morgan, Llanelli. *Born on* 28 July 1936 at Eastbourne. *Son of* Norman Rayner and Eiluned Rayner (nee Jones). *Marriage:* to Nora Mary (nee McCutcheon). *Children:* Robert Thomas Ludwig *Educated at* Eastbourne Technical School; Open University and University College, Swansea (single honours History) *Career:* Formerly Detective Sergant, Metropolitan Police; Power Worker; Part time W.E.A., Lecturer; Member Burry Port now Cefn Sidan Community Council since 1974; County Council, Burry Port since 1981; Labour Parliamentary candidate for Pembroke 1987 election; Deputy leader Labour Group, Dyfed C. C. since 1985; Member University of Wales Court and Trinity College Carmarthen Council. *Recreation:* Welsh History, politics, music (member of Elgar Society and Historical Association) *Clubs:* British Legion, Burry Port. *Address:* 130 Elkington Road, Burry Port, Dyfed, SA16 0AD. Tel: 0554 62445.

REDMAN-BROWN, Geoffrey Michael, MA (Oxon) *Currently:* Non-executive Director, Wadlow Grosvenor; Director, UBS Phillips & Drew (retired). *Born on* 30 March 1937 at Newport, Gwent. *Son of* Arthur Henry Brown and the late Marjorie Frances (nee Redman). *Marriage:* to Mrs Jean Wadlow, 1988. *Educated at* Newport H. S., 1948-56; Balliol College Oxford 1958-61. *Career:* National Service, RAF 1956-58; Member of Stock Exchange, London 1967- ; Partner, Phillips & Drew 1970-85 (joined 1961); Director, Phillips & Drew Stockbrokers 1985-88; Director, UBS Phillips & Drew 1988-90; Director, Wadlow Grosvenor 1990- ; Endowment Fund Trustee, Balliol College 1987- ; Chairman Old Members Committee, Balliol College 1991- ; Provincial Grand Master for Oxfordshire, United Grand Lodge of England 1985- . Freeman, City of London 1977- ; Liveryman Worshipful Company of Borderers 1977- . *Recreation:* gardening, theatre, travel, swimming. *Clubs:* City of London, Royal Automobile *Address:* 5 Three Kings Yard, Mayfair, London, W1Y 1FL. Priestfield, Hook Norton, Banbury, Oxon, OX15 5NH.

REED, Mr Paul, *Currently:* Executive Chef, Grosvenor Hotel, Eastgate Street, Chester, since 1986. *Born on* 18 Aug 1956 at Exeter, Devon. *Son of* Donald Henry Reed and Mrs Irene Reed. *Marriage:* to Sheridan Elizabeth Woodman, 1977. *Children:* Harriet and Emily. *Educated at* Ladysmith School, Exeter; Exeter College of Further Education.

Career: Buckerell Lodge Hotel, Exeter, Devon 1974-79; Hilton Hotel, Park Lane, London 1979-81; Dorchester Hotel, Park Lane, London 1981-82; London House Restaurant, Exeter 1982-83; Copper Inn, Pangbourne, Berkshire 1983-85; Dorchester Hotel, Park Lane, London 1985-86. *Recreation:* golf. *Clubs:* Academie Culinaire de France, North West Chefs, Circle, Upton-by-Chester Golf. *Address:* 4 West Way, Trevalyn Park, Rossett, Clwyd, LL12 ODX.

REES, Emeritus Professor (Florence) Gwendolen, B. Sc; PhD; DSc; FRS; FI. Biol. *Currently:* Retired, 1973 - Now Emeritus Professor in The University of Wales. *Born on* 3 July 1906 at Abercynon, Glam. *Daughter of* the late E and E. A. Rees. *Educated at* Aberdare Girls' Grammar School; University College, Cardiff. *Career:* Lecturer in Zoology, Univ College of Wales, Aberystwyth 1930-46; Senior Lecturer in Zoology 1946-66; Reader in Zoology, Univ Coll of Wales, Aberystwyth 1966-71; Professor of Zoology in the University of Wales (personal chair) 1971; Emeritus Professor in the Univ of Wales 1974, after retirement; Fellow of the Royal Society, London 1971; Fellow of the Institute of Biology 1971; Honorary member of the American Society of Parasitologists 1976; Fellow of University College, Cardiff 1981; Founder member and later Honorary member of the British Society for Parasitology; Gold medal of the Linnean Society of London (Zoology) 1990; Research Grant: The Royal Society, London; Shell Grant Committee; Nat. Science Research Council USA; Univ. of Accra, Ghana and others; teaching at all undergraduate levels and in many aspects of Zoology; Direction of Research: many post graduate students (MSc & PhD) over the years; Research interests: Parasitology: Research Award: Univ of Accra, Ghana, 3 months 1961; Marine Biological Station, Bermuda, 6 weeks 1966; Scientific visits abroad: conferences etc., Denmark, Spain, Portugal, Berlin, Rome, Leningrad and Moscow, New York & Washington etc. *Publications:* Numerous papers on parasitology (helminthology) in scientific journals. scientific journals;Parasitology; International Journal of Parasitology; Journal of Helminthology and others, 1931-88. *Recreation:* Riding, amateur dramatics, 'the arts'. *Address:* Grey Mist, North Road, Aberystwyth., SY23 2EE. Department of Biological, Sciences, Univ Coll of Wales, Penglais, Aberystwyth, SY23 3DA.

REES, Mr (Thomas Morgan) Haydn, CBE *Born on* 22 May 1915 at Gorseinon, Swansea. *Son of* the late Thomas Rees and Mary Rees. *Marriage:* to Marion 1941. *Children:* one d. *Educated at* Swansea Business Co. *Career:* Served War 1939-45; Admitted solicitor 1946; Sen. Asst. Solicitor, Caernarvonshire CC 1947; Flints C. C. 1948-65; Dep. Clerk Dep. Clerk of the Peace, Police Authority, Magistrated Courts Commt and of Probation Commt. 1966-74; Chief Exec., Clerk of Peace (until office abolished 1967); Clerk Flints Police Auth., (until merger with N. Wales Police Auth.) 1967; Clerk of Probation Magistrates Courts and of Justices Adv. Commt: Clerk to Lieutenancy; Chief Exec., Clwyd CC and Clerk Magistrates Courts Commt. 1974-77; Clerk to Lieutenancy and of Justices Ad. Commt, Clwyd 1974-77; Clerk N. Wales Police Auth. 1967-77; Sec: Welsh Counties Commt, 1968-77; (Corresp) Rep. Body (Ombudsman) Cmmt. for Wales, 1974-77; Mbr. Severn Barrage Commt. 1978-81; Asst. Comr. Royal Commn on Constitution 1969-73; Chm., New Jobs Team Shotton Steekworks 1977-82; p/t Mbr Bd., BSC (Industry) Ltd, 1979-83; Chm. N. Wales Arts Assoc., 1981- ; Mbr. Lord Chancellor's Circuit Commt. for Wales and Chester Circuit 1972-77; Welsh Council 1968-79; Welsh Arts Council 1968-77; (Mbr. Regional Commt. 1981- ; Gorsedd Royal National Eisteddfod for Wales; Prince of Wales Commt 1976-79; Clerk 1974-77; Mbr. 1983- ; Theatr Clwyd Governors. Chariman; Govt. Quality of Life Experiment in Clwyd 1974-76; Deeside Enterprise Trust Ltd., 1982-88; DL Flints 1969; Clwyd 1974; JP Mold 1977 (Dep. Chm., 1978-84; Chm., 1985); Pres. Clwyd Vol. Services Council 1977- ; Pres. Clwyd _re-retirement Assn., 1988- ; Mbr. N. Wales Music Fest. 1982- . Pres. Mold Cancer Research Committee 1980- . *Recreation:* the arts, golf. *Clubs:* Mold Golf. *Address:* Cefn Bryn, Gwernaffield Road, Mold, Clwyd., CH7 1RQ.

REES, Lord -, QC., PC. *Born* 1926 at Camberley. *Son of* late Maj-Gen T.W. Rees, Indian Army. *Educated at* Stowe and Christ Church, Oxford. *Career:* Called to the Bar 1953; QC, 1969; Parliamentary career began in 1970 as MP for Dover (and Deal), a seat he held until he stood down at the General Election in 1987; Parliamentary Private Secretary to Solicitor General 1972; Minister of State, HM Treasury, 1979-81; Minister for Trade 1981-83; and Chief Secretary to HM Treasury 1983-85; Member of Lloyds since 1971; appointed Chairman of LASMO PLC, 1988, having been a non-executive Director since 1985; other directorships are: EFG plc (Economic Forestry Group - Chairman); James Finlay; Fleming Mercantile Investment Trust; Leopold Joseph Holdings (Deputy Chairman); Duty Free Confederation (Chairman); General Cable Limited (Chairman); Bradford General Cable Limited; The Cable Corporation Limited; Talkland International Limited; Quadrant Group; Westminster Industrial Brief (Chairman); Member of the Court and Council of the Museum of Wales, and a Member of the Museum and Galleries Commission; Lord Rees became Privy Councillor in 1983 and was created a Baron in 1987. *Clubs:* Boodles, Beefsteak, White's. *Address:* 100 Liverpool Street, London, EC2M 2BB.

REES, Mr Allen Brynmor, LL.B (Solicitor). *Currently:* Senior Partner, Rees Page (incorporating Darbey-Scott-Rees, Pages and Skidmore Hares & Co) - Solicitors of Bilston, Dudley, Perton and Wolverhampton (incl Internal Legal Dept of Midland News Association). *Born on* 11 May 1936 at Penarth, Glamorgan. *Son of* Allen Brynmor Rees and Elsie Louise Rees. *Marriage:* to Nerys Eleanor Rees 1961. *Children:* Meriel Anne Brynmor Rees and Eleanor Haf Brynmor Rees. *Educated at* Monmouth School; University College of Wales, Aberystwyth. *Career:* Chairman, West Midlands Rent Assessment Panel 1968- ; firm Head office, Solicitors of Birmingham Midshires Building Society 1976- ; Chairman, Social Security/Medical Appeals/Disability Tribunals 1980- ; Part-time Chairman, Industrial Tribunals 1982-; Negligence Panel Representative for Wolverhampton area of Law Society 1982- ; Committee member, Legal Aid Board. *Publications:* Author of Solicitors Notebook for Solicitors Journal 1968-; *Recreation:* Member, Bilston Rotary since 1974 (President 1984), squash, shooting, skiing, gardening. *Clubs:* The Old Monmothians. *Address:* Rossleigh, Shaw Lane, Albrighton, Wolverhampton, WV7 3DS. Yr Hen Ystabl, Meifod, Powys, SY22 6BP.

REES, Mr Arthur Morgan, CBE; KStJ; QPM; MA; DL *Currently:* retired. *Born on* 20 Nov 1912 at Llangadog. *Son of* Thomas and Jane Rees. *Marriage:* to Dorothy Webb, 1943 (d. 1988). *Children:* Rosemary. *Educated at* Llandovery College; St. Catherine;s College, Cambridge. *Career:* RAF Pilot, 1941-46, Wing Cdr; Chief Constable Denbighshire Constabulary, 1956-64; Staffordshire and Stoke on Trent Police, 1964-77; Consult. dir: Wedgwood, 1977-80, Royal Daulton, 1980-83, Armitage Shanks, 1980-83, Wales Britannia Building Soc., 1983-87; Inter Globe Security Servs. Ltd., 1985- ; chm: Crawshays RFC

1962- ; Midlands Sports Cncl, 1967-77; Queens Silver Jubilee Appeal, Prince's Trust, 1974-88; Br. Karate Bd; Dep. pres. Staffs Boys Club 1970- ; Founder Ex Police in Industry and Commerce; Pres. Eccleshall RFC 1979- . *Recreation:* sport in general, especially Rugby, former WRU International, past referee for London Soc. *Clubs:* RAF, Hawks (Cambridge). *Address:* 18 Broom Hall, Oxshott, Surrey, KT22 OJZ.

REES, Cllr Bernard Hugh, *Currently:* Senior Partner of Bernard Rees, Luxton Solicitors, 60 Merthyr Road, Whitchurch, Cardiff CF4 1XL and Ravenscourt, 9A Tynewydd Road, Barry, S. Glam CF6 1AY. *Born on* 30 May 1934 at Neath. *Son of* the late David Henry Rees and the late Mary Doris Rees (nee Jarman). *Marriage:* 1) to Janet Catherine Williams 1957, 2) to ValeriePowell (nee Jones). *Children:* 1st marriage Ashley Paul Myrddin Rees, Victoria Jayne Nolan and Helen Frances Anne Rees-Bidder; 2nd marriage 2 step d. *Educated at* Cardiff High School; Cardiff University College. *Career:* South Glamorgan County Councillor 1977- ; Vice-Chairman Libraries Committee 1979-81; South Glamorgan County Council Conservative Group Whip 1985-91; Leader 1991- ; Cardiff North West Conservative Association Treasurer 1980-83; Cardiff North Conservative Association Treasurer 1983-86; Chairman 1986-89; President 1989- ; Member Court of Governors University College of Cardiff 1977-81; Council Member 1979-81; Governor Welsh College of Music and Drama 1977-81; Chairman of Governors Llanishen High School 1977-89. *Recreation:* Music, reading, cooking. *Address:* Yr Hen Sgubor, The Old Barn, Flemingston, S Glam, CF6 9QJ.

REES, Professor Emeritus Brinley Roderick, MA; PhD; Hon. LLD. *Currently:* Retired. *Born on* 27 Dec 1919 at Tondu. *Son of* the late John David and the late Mary Ann (nee Roderick). *Marriage:* to Zena Muriel Stella Mayall 1951. *Children:* Idris John Mark and Alan Hugh. *Educated at* Christ College, Brecon; Merton College, Oxford. *Career:* Welch Regiment 1940-45; Assistant Master, Cardiff HS for Boys 1947-48; Lecturer in Classics, UCW, Aberystwyth 1948-56; Senior Lecturer in Greek, Manchester Univ., 1956-58; Professor of Greek, UC Cardiff 1958-70; Dean of Arts 1963-65; Dean of Students 1967-68; Professor of Greek, Birmingham Univ., 1970-75; Dean of Arts 1973-75; Principal, St David's Univ Coll, Lampeter 1975-80; President of the Classical Association 1978-79; Vice-President 1970- ; Vice-President, UC Cardiff 1986-88. *Publications:* The Merton Papyri, Vol 2, 1959; The Use of Greek 1959; Papyri from Hermopolis 1964; Lampas, 1970; Classics for The Intending Student 1970; Aristotle's Theory and Milton's Practice 1971; Strength in What Remains 1979; Pelagius, A Reluctant Heretic 1988; The Letters of Pelagius and His Followers 1991; articles and reviews in various journals and periodicals. *Recreation:* Reading, writing. *Address:* 31 Stephenson Court, Wordsworth Avenue, Cardiff, CF2 1AX. Tel: 0222 472058.

REES, Christopher Neil, *Currently:* Petrol Station Manager 1991-. *Born on* 30th June 1965 at Bridgend. *Son of* Wyndham and Lydia Rees. *Educated at* Pencoed Comprehensive 1976-82 *Career:* Badminton player 1974- ; Notable Achievements include: European Junior Mens Doubles Champion 1983, first medal of any sort for a Welsh player; Tour of Far East, Last 16 Mens Singles Malaysian Open 1987; European Mens Doubles Bronze Medal Senior 1988; Represented Wales at the last two Commonwealth Games, Scotland and New Zealand; Represented Wales on 78 occasions; 9 mens doubles, 2 mixed doubles, 4 singles National Titles. *Clubs:* Texaco Penarth Badminton Club *Address:* 8 Woodland Avenue, Pencoed, Nr Bridgend, Mid

Glamorgan, CF35 6UP.

REES, Dr Gareth Mervyn, MS(Lond), FRCP(Lond), FRCS(Eng). *Currently:* Consultant Heart and Chest Surgeon, St. Bartholomew's Hospital, EC1. *Born on* 30 Sept 1935 at Llangadog. *Son of* Joseph Rees and Gwen Rees. *Marriage:* to Lesley David-Dawson. *Children:* Joseph Philip Mervyn. *Educated at* Llandovery Highschool. *Career:* MB, BS (Hons) London 1960, St. Mary's Hospital Medical School; Senior Registrar National Heart and Chest Hospitals, Brompton, 1971-73; International Research Fellow, Univ Oregon Medical School, Portland USA 1970. *Publications:* numerous articles in specialist medical journals. *Recreation:* rugby football, skiing, fishing. *Clubs:* Garrick, RAC. *Address:* 10 Upper Wimpole Street, London, W1.

REES, Prof. Hubert, D.F.C., B.Sc., Ph.D., D.Sc., F.R.S. *Currently:* Retired. *Born on* 2 Oct 1923 at Llangennech. *Son of* Owen and Tugela Rees. *Marriage:* to Mavis Rosalind. *Children:* Wynne (deceased), Hubert, Gwyneth and Judith. *Educated at* Llandovery and Llanelli Grammer Schools, UCW Aberystwyth. *Career:* RAFVR 1942-46; Student at UCW Aberystwyth, 1946-50; Lecturer, Genetics Dept., Univ. of Birminham 1950-59; Senior Lecturer, subsequently Reader and Professor, Dept. of Agricultural Botany 1960-91; Elected Fellow of the Royal Society in 1976. *Publications:* Books: Chromosome Genetics, B Chromosomes. Papers on chromosome evolution and behaviour. *Recreation:* Fishing and painting. *Clubs:* St. David's, Aberystywth. *Address:* Irfon, Llanbadarn Road, Aberystwyth, Dyfed. SY23 1EY.

REES, Mr Ioan Bowen, MA (Oxon); Solicitor *Currently:* Author. *Born on* 13 Jan 1929 at Dolgellau. *Son of* the late A. M. Rees and the late K. Olwen (nee Parry). *Marriage:* to Margaret Wynn Meredith 1959. *Children:* Dayfydd, Non and Gruffudd (two s one d). *Educated at* Dolgellau; Bootham School; The Queen's College, Oxford. *Career:* Assistant Solicitor, Lancashire County Council 1956-58; Cardiff City Council, Prosecuting Solicitor 1958-62; City Prosecutor 1962-65; Pembrokeshire County Council, Assistant Clerk 1965-67; Deputy Clerk 1967-73; County Secretary, Dyfed County Council 1973; Gwynedd County Council, County Secretary 1974-80; Chief Executive 1980-91; Secretary, North Wales Probation Ctee 1980-91; Haldane Medal (Royal Inst. of Public Administration) 1968; Council, UCW Aberystwyth 1977-85; President, Clwb Rygbi Bethesda 1974- ; Hon. Druid, Gorsedd y Beirdd 1980; Chairman, Welsh Mountain Leader Training Bd 1980-90; UK Mbr. European Bureau for Lesser Used Languages 1982-88; President, Gwynedd Law Society 1984-85; Chief Exec. Advisor on National Parks, Assoc. of County Councils 1984-90; Council, Welsh Sculpture Trust 1985-90; Chmn, Soc. of Local Authority Chief Executives, Wales 1986-87; Welsh Advisory Bd for Higher Education 1986-89; UGC/WAB Ctee on Teacher Training in Wales 1987; Chief Executive Exchange with Zimbabwe 1988; Council of Inst. for Welsh Affairs 1989-91; Director, North West Wales Training and Enterprise Council 1989-91; A Vice-president, Coleg Harlech 1990- . Literature Selection Panel, Arts 2000 (Arts Council of G. B.) 1991-92; Hon. Fellow, University College of N. Wales, Bangor 1991; Executive Cttee, N. Wales Arts Association 1991- ; Council, Oriel Mostyn/Mostyn Art Gallery, Llandudno 1980-. *Publications:* Galwad Y Mynydd 1961; Dringo Mynyddoedd Cymru 1965; Government by Community 1971; Mynyddoedd 1975; The Mountains of Wales 1987; Contributions to many journals and symposia. *Recreation:* mountaineering, The Arts, Swiss Affairs. *Clubs:* Clwb Rygbi Bethesda (President); Clwb Mynydda Cymru; Swiss

Alpine Club (Veteran 1986); National Liberal, London(non-political). *Address:* Tal-Sarn, Llanllechd, Bangor, Gwynedd, LL57 3AJ.

REES, Right Reverand John Ivor, B.A., O.St.J. *Currently:* Bishop of St. David's. *Born on* 19 Feb 1926 at Llanelli. *Son of* the late David Morgan and Cecilia Maria Perrott Rees (nee Evans). *Marriage:* to Beverley (nee Richards), 1954. *Children:* Meirion, Mark and Stephen. *Educated at* Llanelli Grammar; UCW Aberystwyth; Westcott House, Cambridge. *Career:* Served Royal Navy, 1943-47; Ordained, 1952; Fishguard w. Llanychar, 1952-55; Llangathen (Cwrt Henri) 1955-57; P in C. Uzmaston 1957-59; V. Slebech, Uzmaston and Boulston 1959-65; V. Llangollen and Trevor (St. Asaph) 1965-74; R. D. Llangollen 1970-74; R. Wrexham 1974-76; Canon of St. Asaph 1975-76; Dean of Bangor 1976-88; V. Cathedral Parish of Bangor 1979-88; Officer and serving Chaplain of the Order of St. John 1981; Chairman of the Provincial Working Group on Parochial Administration 1976-79; Chairman of the Archbishop's Commission on Churchyards 1981-83; Consecrated Assistant Bishop of St. Davids in the Metropolitical Cathedral St. Davids, 1988; Assistant Bishop and Archdeacon of St. Davids, 1988-91; Enthroned as Bishop of St. Davids, 1991. *Publications:* The Churches of Llangollen 1871-1971 (1971); Keeping Forty Days (Lenten Addresses (1988) *Recreation:* Music and good light reading. *Address:* Llys Esgob, Abergwili, Carmarthen, Dyfed, SA31 2JG. Tel: 0267 236597.

REES, Mr John Samuel, *Currently:* Lecturer, Centre for Journalism Studies, University of Wales College of Cardiff 1988- . *Born on* 23 Oct 1931 at Merthyr Tydfil. *Son of* the late John Richard and the late Mary Jane (nee Thomas). *Marriage:* to Ruth Jewell Shepherd. *Children:* Jonathan Paul and Diane Mary. *Educated at* Cyfarthfa Castle Grammar School, Merthyr Tydfil. *Career:* Reporter, Merthyr Express 1948-50; Sports Editor 1952-54; National Service, Welch Regiment & Royal Army Education Corps 1950-52; Reporter, The Star, Sheffield 1954; Sub-Editor 1956; Deputy Chief Sub Editor 1958; Deputy Sports Editor 1960; Assistant Editor 1962-66 (All on The Star); Deputy Editor Evening Echo, Watford 1966-69; Editor Evening Mail, Slough and Hounslow 1969-72; Editor The Journal, Newcastle 1972-76; Editor Evening Post-Echo, Hemel Hempstead 1976-79; Assistant Managing Director, Evening Post-Echo 1979-81; Editor, Western Mail 1981-88; President, South Wales Region, Guild of British Newspaper Editors 1985. *Publications:* Edited and designed "20 Questions on Cardiff Bay"; Edited and designed first Mid Glamorgan County Guide. *Recreation:* Watching sport, particularly Rugby and cricket, walking, reading. *Address:* Timbertops, St. Andrews Road, Dinas Powys, S. Glam., CF6 4HB.

REES, Rt. Rev. Leslie Lloyd, *Currently:* Assistant Bishop, Diocese of Winchester. *Born on* 14 April 1919 at Clydach-on-Tawe. *Son of* the late Rees Thomas and Elizabeth Rees. *Marriage:* to Rosamond Smith (d 1990), 1944. *Children:* Christopher Michael and Gerald Hugh. *Educated at* Pontardawe Secondary School, Kelham Theological College. *Career:* Asst. Curate, Roath St. Saviour, Asst. Chaplain H. M. Prison, Cardiff, 1942-45; Chaplain H. M. Prison, Durham, 1945-48; Dartmoor, 1948-55; Winchester, 1955-62; Chaplain General of Prisons, 1962-80; Hon. Canon of Canterbury, 1966-80; Chaplain to H. M. The Queen, 1971-80; Bishop of Shrewsbury, 1980-86; Hon. Canon of Lichfield, 1980-86. *Recreation:* Music and watching rugby. *Address:* Kingfisher Lodge, 20 Arle Gardens, Alresford, Hants., SO24 9BA.

REES, Rt Hon Merlyn, M. P. *Currently:* M. P. *Born on* 18 Dec 1920 at Cilfynydd, S. Wales. *Son of* Lev Daniel Rees and Edith May Rees (nee Williams). *Marriage:* to Colleen Cleveley, 1949. *Children:* Patrick Merlyn, Gareth David and Glyndwr Robert. *Educated at* Primary Sch, Cilfynydd; Sec. Sch. Harrow Weald Grammar School, Middx; Goldsmiths' Coll, Pres. of Student's Union; London Sch of Economics, B. Sc. (Econ); London Sch. of Economics, M. Sc. (Econ), ; Inst. of Education, London. *Career:* Nottingham Univ. Air Squadron, 1941; In RAF, demobilised with rank of Squadron Leader, 1941-46; Head of Econ. Dept. Harrow Weald Grammar Sch, 1949-60; Organised Festival of Labour for Labour Party, 1960-62; Lectr in Management Dept., Luton College of Tech., 1962-63; Parliamentary Labour Candidate for Harrow East Const., 1955; Parl. Lab. Cand. inby-elec. & gen. elec. for Harrow East Const., 1959; Elected mbr of Parliament for S. Leeds Const. following death of Rt. Hon. Hugh Gaitskell, Leader of Labour party, 1963; Appnt Parliamentary Pvt Sec. to Chancellor of Exchequer, Rt. Hon. James Callaghan, MP, 1964; Minist. for Army, Minst, for Royal Air Force & Under-Sec. of State at Home Office, 1964-70; elected to Shadow Cabinet, 1972; Sec. of State for N. Ireland, 1974; Home Sec., 1976; Shadow Home Sec., 1979; Co-ordinator Econ. Affairs, 1982; Appnt. Franks Select Commt. on Official Secrets Act, 1972; Appnt. to Franks Select Commt. on the Origins of the Falklands War, 1982; Appnt. Hon. Fellow of Goldsmith's Coll. Univ. of London, 1984; Asked by Neil Kinnock MP, to write report on legal & policing aspects of the Miners' Strike, 1985; Invited by P. M. to become mbr of Privy Cncl. Commt., which oversees the appointments of senior Civil Servants and mbrs of the Armed Forces; Hon LLD University of Wales; 1992 to be awarded Hon. LLD University of Leeds. *Publications:* The Public Sector in the mixed Economy; Northern Ireland: A Personal Perspective; Thesis (not published) The Economic & Social Development of Extra-Metropolitan Middlx during the Nineteenth Century (1800-1914) for M. Sc. (Econ) degree. *Recreation:* Reading, drama and grandchildren.

REES, Mr Owen, CB *Currently:* Head of Agriculture Department, Welsh Office, 1990- . *Born on* 26 Dec 1934 at Trimsaran, Dyfed. *Son of* John Trevor Rees and Esther Rees (nee Phillips). *Marriage:* to Elizabeth Gosby, 1958, (d. 1991). *Children:* Philippa, Helen and David *Educated at* Llanelli Grammar School and Manchester University *Career:* Bank of London and South America, 1957-59; Board of Trade, 1959-69; Cabinet Office, 1969-71; Welsh Office, 1971- ; Head of Education Department 1977-80; Director of Industry Department, 1980-85; Head of Economic and Regional Policy Group, 1985-90. *Address:* 4 Llandennis Green, Cyncoed, Cardiff, CF2 6JX.

REES, Lord Peter Wynford Innes, PC, QC. *Currently:* Chairman, Lasmo plc; Deputh chairman Leopold Joseph plc; director of various companies; member Council of Museum of Wales. *Born on* 9 Dec 1926 at Camberley, Surrey. *Son of* Major General T. W. Rees Indian Army, and Mrs A. R. Rees. *Marriage:* to Anthea, 1969, daughter of Major Maxwell Hyslop. *Educated at* Stowe; Christchurch, Oxford. *Career:* Scots Guards (Lieut), 1945-47; Barrister, Oxford Circuit, QC 1969; contested Abertillery 1964 and 1965; MP Dover 1970-87; Minister of State Treasury 1979-81; Minister of Trade 1981-83; Chief Secretary of Treasury 1983-85; Privy Councillor 1983, Life Peer 1987. *Recreation:* *Clubs:* Boodle's, Beefsteak, White's. *Address:* Goytre Hall, Abergavenny, Gwent, NP7 9DL.

REES, Mr Peter Wynne, BSc., BArch., BTP., RIBA., FRTPI., FRSA *Currently:* City Planning Officer, Corporation of London (from 1987). *Born on* 26 Sept 1948 at Swansea. *Son of* Gwynne Rees and the late Elizabeth Rodda (nee Hynam). *Educated at* Pontardawe Grammar Sch; Whitchurch Grammar Sch, Cardiff; Bartlett School of Architecture, UCL; Welsh Sch of Architecture, Univ. of Wales; Polytechnic of the South Bank. *Career:* Architectural Asst, Historic Building Div, GLC, 1971-72; Asst to Gordon Cullen CBE, RDI, FSIA, 1973-75; Architect, Historic Areas Conservation Div, DOE, 1975-79; UK Rep Council of Europe Working Parties Studying "New uses for Historic

Buildings'' and ''The Economics of Building Conservation'', 1977-78; Asst Chief Planning Officer, London Borough of Lambeth, 1979-85; Controller of Planning, Corpn of London, 1985-87; Trustee, Building Conservation Trust, 1985-91; Board Member, British Council for Offices, 1990- . *Publications:* City of London Local Plan, 1989; City of London Unitary Development Plan, 1991; Contributions to Professional studies and journals. *Recreation:* Swimming, playing the viola, music and tidying. *Clubs:* Guildhall, Cottons. *Address:* City Planning Officer, Guildhall, London EC2P 2EJ.

REES, Mr Philip, Ll. B. (Bristol) *Currently:* Barrister (Head of Chambers). *Born on* 1 Dec 1941 at Bangor, North Wales. *Son of* John Trevor Rees and the late Olwen Muriel Rees (nee Jones). *Marriage:* to Catherine Good, 1969. *Children:* David Stephen and Sian Catrin. *Educated at* Monmouth School; Bristol University. *Career:* Called to Bar 1965; Recorder of the Crown Court 1983. *Recreation:* Music and sport. *Clubs:* Cardiff and County Club *Address:* 34 Park Place, Cardiff, CF1 3BA.

REES, Dr Robert Simon Owen, MA; MB; FRCP; FRCR. *Currently:* Consultant Radiologist, Medical Director and Director of Imaging, Royal Brompton Hospital, London SW3. *Born on* 24 May 1933 at Carmarthen. *Son of* Edward Bertram Rees and Dorothy Rees (nee Owen). *Marriage:* to Dr. Jacqueline Jane (nee Layton) 1958. *Children:* Rupert, Jasper and Sheridan. *Educated at* Harrow, Gonville and Caius College, Cambridge (Choral Exhibitioner); Westminster Hospital. *Career:* Consultant Radiologist National Heart and St. Bartholomew's Hospitals, London 1966-89; Dean, Institute of Cardiology 1971-73; Director and Chairman Scientific Advisory Committee, CORDA charity. *Publications:* Clinical Cardiac Radiology, Butterworths, London 1973, 2nd ed. 1980 and 200 other publications in same field. *Recreation:* hunting, driving, choral singing. *Clubs:* Boodle's *Address:* Rubbin Cottage, Treyford, Midhurst, West Sussex, GU29 OLD.

REES, Mr Roger Thomas, MB, BS, BDS, LRCP, MRCS, FDSRCS *Currently:* Consultant Oral and Maxillofacial Surgeon to United Norwich Hospitals and James Paget Hospital Gorleston, since 1979. *Born on* 16 Oct 1943 at Pen-y-Groes, Dyfed. *Son of* Mr & Mrs A. H. Rees. *Marriage:* to Sandra Jones Williams. *Children:* Richard Hywel and Sara Jane. *Educated at* Mercer's School; Colfe's Grammar School; Royal Dental Hospital, St. Bartholomews London Medical College; Univ London. *Career:* House Officer, St. Thomas, St. Bartholomews Hospital; Registrar Oral Surgery, Guys Hospital & Queen Mary Roehampton, 1972-74; Senior Registrar, Oral Surgery, 1974-79: Queen Victoria Hospital, East Grinstead, King College Hospital London, Ammadu Bello Univ Kaduna Nigeria - Technical Adviser (overseas development Ministry) in Max-Fac Surgery to Nigerian Military Government in 1976, *Publications:* papers on oral surgery and oral medicine topics. *Recreation:* restoring furniture *Clubs: Address:* 9 The Street, Brooke, Norwich, Norfolk, NR15 1JW.

REES, Dr. Ruth Mary, BSc (Wales), Cert Ed. (London), MSc (Calgary), Ph.D (Brunel), F.I.M.A., C.Math, F.Inst.P., C.Phys. *Currently:* Freelance Consultant in Physics and Mathematics Education, specializing in assessment of Numeracy and Mathematical ability. *Born on* 23 Sept 1929 at Swansea. *Daughter of* Ethelbert Wilfred Godsall and Doris Annie Godsall (nee Shepherd). *Marriage:* to David John Rees 1951, Divorced 1978. *Children:* Diane Eluned Rees, Stephen John Rees, Michael David Rees. *Educated at* Swansea High School for Girls 1941-47; State Scholar at Department of Physics, University College of Swansea 1947-50. *Career:* 1951-69, taught Physics and Mathematics at Schools, Further Education Colleges and Universities in Canada and U.K. 1970-87, British Petroleum Senior Research Fellow and Senior Lecturer in Faculty of Education of

Brunel University of West London. Director of BRUMATE (Brunel Research Unit for Mathematical and Technological Education) at Brunel University. Warden of Runnymede Campus of Brunel University. Consultant to and Honorary Member of City and Guilds, London. Freelance Broadcaster - B.B.C. Radio 4 Series on Maths with Meaning. 1988-90 Visiting Professor and Consultant in Mathematics Education in Faculty of Science Education at Universiti Brunei Darussalam. Visiting Professor at Johore Baru campus of Universiti Teknologi Malaysia. *Recreation:* Walking, music, globetrotting. *Clubs:* Royal Overseas League, St. James London. *Address:* 1 Dale Close, St. Ebbes, Oxford, OX1 1TU.

REES, Professor William Linford Llewelyn, CBE; LLD (Hon); DSC; MD; FRCP; FRCPsych (Hon); FACPsych (Hon); DPM *Currently:* Emeritus Pofessor of Psychiatry, University of London 1980; Consulting Physician, St. Bartholemew's Hospital London since 1981; Lecturer in Psychological Medicine, St. Bartholomew's Medical College since 1958; Recognised Clinical Teacher in Mental Diseases, Institute of Psychiatry, University of London, since 1956; Chairman: University of London Teachers of Psychiatry Committee; Armed Services Consultant Advisory Board in Psychiatry since 1979. *Born on* 24 Oct 1914 at Burry Port. *Son of* the late Edward Parry Rees and Mary Rees (nee John. *Marriage:* to Catherine Magdalen Thomas 1940. *Children:* David, Angharad, Vaughan and Catrin. *Educated at* Llanelli Grammar School; Univ. College, Cardiff; Welsh National School of Medicine; University of London. *Career:* David Hepburn Medal and Alfred Hughes Medal in Antatomy 1935; John Maclean Medal and Prize in Obstetrics and Gynaecology 1937 etc. Specialist, EMS; Dep. Med. Supt. Mill Hill Emergency Hosp., 1945; Asst Physician and Postgrad. Teacher in Clinical Psychiatry, The Maudsley Hosp., 1946; Dep. Physician Supt, Whitchurch Hosp., 1947; Regional Psychiatrist for Wales and Mon 1948; Consultant Physician, The Bethlem Royal Hosp, and The Maudsley Hosp., 1954-66; Med. Dir. Charter Clinic, London 1980- ; Chief Psychiatrist and Exec. Med. Dir. Charter Medical 1984- ; Dir. and Med. Advr, Huntercombe Manor Hosp. and Rehabilitation Gp. Ltd 1989. Consultant in Psychiatry to RAF; WHO Consultant to Sri Lanka 1973; Hon. Consultant, Royal Sch for Deaf Children, Lectures to Univs and Learned Socs in Europe, USA, Asia, Australia and S. America. Examiner: Dip. Psychological Med, RCP 1964-69; MRCP, RCP, RCPE and RCPGlas 1969- ; MB and DPM, Univ of Leeds 1969- . Pres: Soc for Psychosomatic Research, 1957-58; Royal Coll of Psychiatrists 1975-78 (Vice-Pres. 1972-75; Chm. E. Anglian Region); Section of Psychiatry, RSM 1971-72 (Vice-Pres. 1968; Hon. Mem 1982); BMA 1978- ; (Fellow 1981); Vice-Pres: Stress Foundn 1984- ; Psychiatric Rehabilitation Assoc 1988- ; Chm. Medico-Pharmaceutical Forum 1982 (Vice-Chmn. 1981); Treasurer, World Psychiatric Assoc. 1966- (Hon. Mem 1982); Mem: Clinical Psychiatry Cttee, MRC 1959- ; Cnl Royal Medico-Psychological Assoc. (Chm. Research and Clinical Section 1957-63); Soc. for Study of Human Biology; Asthma Research Cncl; Cttee on Safety of Medicines (also Toxicity and Clinical Trials Sub-Cttee) 1971- ; Psychological Medicine Gp, BMA 1967- ; Bd of Advanced Med. Studs, *Publications:* (with Eysenck and Himmelweit) Dimensions of Personality 1947; Short Textbook of Psychiatry 1967. Chapters in: Modern Treatment in General Practice 1947; Recent Progress in Psychiatry 1950; Schizophrenia: Somatic Aspects 1957; Psychoendocrinology 1958; Recent Progress in Psychosomatic Research 1960; Stress and Psychiatric Disorders 1960. Papers in: Nature, BMJ, Jl of Mental Sci., Jl of Psychosomatic Research, Eugenics Review etc. Contribs to Med. Annual 1958-68. *Recreation:* fishing, photography, swimming, entertaining grandchildren. *Clubs:* Athenaeum, Apothecaries, Barfer Surgeon, Livery Companies. *Address:* Penbryn, 62 Oakwood Avenue,

Purley, Surrey CR2 1AQ. 14 Devonshire Place, London, W1N 1PB

RENOWDEN, The Very Revd. Dean Charles Raymond, BA (Lampeter) MA (Cantab) *Currently:* Dean of Asaph, 1971- . *Born on* 27 Oct 1923 at Trealaw, Glam. *Son of* The Canon Charles Renowden and Mary Elizabeth (nee Williams). *Marriage:* to Ruth Cecil Mary Collis 1951. *Children:* Alison Mary, Anne Elizabeth and Anthony Charles *Educated at* Llandysul Grammar School; St. David's Univ. Coll., Lampeter; Selwyn Coll., Cambridge. *Career:* Deacon 1951; priest 1952; lectr. in Philosophy and Theology St. David's Univ. Coll., Lampeter 1955-57; Head of Dept. of Philosophy 1957-69; sr. Lectr. Philosophy and Theology 1969-71. *Publications:* Contribution to: Theology, The Modern Christian, Church Quarterly Review, Trivium, Province and author of The Idea of Unity 1965, and New Patterns of Ministry 1973 *Recreation:* Music, ornithology *Address:* The Deanery, St. Asaph, Clwyd LL17 ORL. The Cathedral Office, High Street, St. Asaph.

RENTON, Mr Gordon Pearson, *Currently:* Chairman, R & D Communications Ltd. *Born on* 12 Dec 1928 at Sheffield, U.K. *Son of* Herbert Renton and Annie (nee Pearson). *Marriage:* 1). to Joan Mary Lucas 1952, divorced 1971; 2). to Sylvia Jones 1978. *Children:* two sons by 1st marriage, Nigel Miles and Paul Marcus. *Educated at* King Edward VIII School, Sheffield 1940-47; Lincoln College, Oxford 1947-51. *Career:* 2nd. Lt. R. Sigs. 1951-53; Asst. Classics master, Bridlington School 1953-54; Asst. Principal Home Office 1954-58; Asst. Private Secretary to Home Secretary and Lord Privy Seal 1958-59; Principal 1959-67; Asst. Secretary of State 1967-78; Under Secretary of State 1978-83; Head of Radio Regulatory Dept., Dept. of Trade & Industry 1983-85; Member of Parole Board 1985-88; Director, Mediajet Ltd., 1987- . *Recreation:* DIY, computers, snooker. *Clubs:* Reform and Bristol Channel Yacht club. *Address:* Ship Cottage, Pwll Du, Bishopston, Swansea., SA3 2AU.

REYNOLDS, Mr Leighton Durham, FBA (1987) *Currently:* Fellow and Tutor in Classics, Brasense College, Oxford, 1957- . *Born on* 11 Feb. 1930 at Abercanaid. *Son of* Edgar James and Hester Anne Reynolds (nee Hale). *Marriage:* to Susan Mary (nee Buchanan) 1962. *Children:* Lucy, Elizabeth and William. *Educated at* Caerphilly Grammar School; University College Cardiff; St. John's College, Cambridge. *Career:* Junior Research Fellow, The Queen's College, Oxford 1954-57; Visiting Professor, Cornell University, 1960 and 1971; Institute for Advanced Study, Princeton, 1965 and 1987; University of Texas at Austin, 1967. *Publications:* Oxford Classical Texts of Seneca (Letters, 1965; Dialogues 1977) and Sallust (1991); Scribes and Scholars (with N. G. Wilson), 1968, ed. 3 1991; Texts and Transmission. A Survey of the Latin Classics (ed). 1983. *Recreation:* Walking, camping, gardening, plant hunting. *Address:* Winterslow Cottage, Lincombe Lane, Boars Hill, Oxford OX1 5DZ.

RHYS, Professor David Garel, O. B. E. *Currently:* Head of Economics Section, Cardiff Business School, University of Wales; Director of Centre of Automotive Industry Research (C. A. I. R.), Cardiff Business School. *Born on* 28th Feb 1940 at Swansea. *Son of* Emyr(d) Phyllis. *Marriage:* Charlotte Mavis (nee Walters). *Children:* Angela Gillian Jeremy. *Educated at* Ystalyfera Grammar School University College Swansea University of Birmingham *Career:* Lecturer, University of Hull (1965-70); Lecturer, University College Cardiff (1971-77); Senior Lecturer, University College Cardiff (1977-84); Professor of Motor Industry Economics, U. C. C. (1984-88); Head of Economics Dept., U. C. C. 1988; Head of Economics Section, Cardiff Business School, U. W. C. C. *Publications:* The Motor Industry: an Economic Survey; The Motor Industry in the European Community *Recreation:* Walking

RHYS, Colonel David Lewellin, OBE;MC; KStJ; DL.

Currently: retired. *Born on* 2 April 1910 at Cardiff. *Son of* Owen Lewellin Rhys MD, FFR. *Marriage:* to Doreen Rowley of San Francisco. *Children:* Michael, Mark, Linda and Janice. *Educated at* Epsom College; R. M. College, Sandhurst. *Career:* Regular Officer, S. Wales Bord., Served Palestine 1936, N. W. Frontie, India, wounded 1937-39; Burma 1942-43; Italy 1944-45; Malaya 1955-56; Mil. Attache Java 1947-49; Sec. MON TAFA 1957-69; Sec. Wales TAVRA 1969-75; Chief Comissioner St. John Ambulance Brigade (Wales) 1975-79. *Recreation:* rugby, cricket, golf, fishing, shooting. *Clubs:* Army & Navy, London, Cardiff & County, Royal Porthcawl Golf. *Address:* Paradwys, Aberthin, Cowbridge, S. Glam, CF7 7HB.

RHYS, Hon. Mrs. Sheila Mary, *Currently:* retired. *Born on* 21 Dec 1925 at Basingstoke, Hants. *Daughter of* Douglas James Phillips and Winifred Mary Phillips. *Marriage:* to the late The Hon David Reginald Rhys, 21st October, 1963. *Children:* George Dafydd. *Educated* Privately. *Career:* Farming - Equestrian. *Recreation:* Horse Events, golf, travel. *Clubs:* Farmers, Sham Castle Golf. *Address:* Southwick Court Chapel, Southwick, Nr. Trowbridge, Wilts., BA14 9QB. Tel: (0225) 752469.

RHYS WILLIAMS, Sir Gareth Bart, BSc, CEng, MIEE, MBPICS, MBIM. *Currently:* Managing Director, NFI Electronics, since 1990. *Born on* 9 Nov 1961 at London. *Son of* the late Sir Brandon Rhys Williams, MP and Caroline (nee Foster). *Educated at* Eton; Durham University; Insead. *Career:* Manufacturing Analyst, STC 1983-85; Materials Manager, Lucas CAV 1985-88. *Recreation:* shooting, Territorial Army, travel. *Clubs:* Brooks's. *Address:* Gadairwen, Groes Faen, Pontyclun, Mid Glamorgan, CF7 8NU. 32 Rawlings Street, London, SW3 2LT.

RICHARD, Lord Ivor Seward, MA QC *Currently:* Baron cr 1990 (Life Peer), of Ammanford in the County of Dyfed; Barrister. *Born on* 30 May 1932 at Cardiff. *Son of* Seward Thomas and Isabella Richard. *Marriage:* Janet Jones 1989 (Previous marriage dissolved). *Children:* David, Alun, Isobel and William. *Educated at* St. Michael's School, Bryn, Llanelly; Cheltenham College, Pembroke College, Oxford; *Career:* BA Oxon (Jurisprudence) 1953; MA 1970: Called to Bar, inner Temple, 1955; Bencher, 1985; Practised in Chambers, London 1955-74; UK Perm. Representative to UN, 1974-79; Member Commn. of EEC, 1981-84; Chmn. Rhodesia Conf., Geneva, 1976; Parliamentary Candidate, South Kensington, 1959; MP (Lab) Barons Court, 1964-74; Delegate: Assembly, Councilof Europe, 1965-68; Western European Union, 1965-68; Vice Chmn., Legal Cttee., Council of Europe, 1966-67; PPS, Sec of State for Defence, 1966-69; Parliamentary Under Sec. (Army), Min. of Defence, 1969-70; Opposition Spokesman, Broadcasting, Posts & Telecommunications, 1970-71; Deputy Spokesman, Foreign Affairs, 1971-74; Chmn. World Trade Centre Wales Ltd. (Cardiff), 1985- ; Member Fabian Society; Society of Labour Lawyers; Institute of Strategic Studies; Royal Institute of International Affairs; *Publications:* (jt) Europe or the Open Sea, 1971; We, the British, 1983 (USA); Articles in various Political Journals. *Recreation:* Music and walking. *Address:* 11 South Square, Gray's Inn, London WC2. House Of Lords, Westminster, London, SW1

RICHARDS, Mr (David) Wyn, MA, LLB. *Currently:* Barrister-at-Law. *Born on* 22 Sept 1943 at Carmarthen. *Son of* the late Evan Gwylfa Richards and the late Florence Margretta (nee Evans). *Marriage:* to Thelma Frances (nee Hall), 1972. *Children:* Gareth Mark (b. 1974), David Cennydd (b. 1976), Andrew Hywel (b. 1977), Daniel Owen (b. 1981) and Evan Aled Wyn (b. 1988). *Educated at* Gwendraeth GS; Llanelli GS; Trinity Hall, Cambridge. *Career:* Called to the Bar, Inner Temple 1968; Appointed Recorder 1985. *Address:* 2 Queens Road, Sketty, Swansea, W. Glam, SA2 0SD. Iscoed Chambers, 86 St. Helen's Road,

Swansea, W. Glam, SA1 4BQ.

RICHARDS, Dr. Brian Mansel, CBE., BSc., PhD., (CBE in 1990) *Currently:* Chairman - British Bio-technology Group plc, Oxford 1989- . *Born on* 19 Sept 1932 at Abertridwr, Glam. *Son of* Cyril Mansel Richards and Gwendolyn Hyde Richards. *Marriage:* to Joan Lambert Breese 1952. *Children:* Amanda Deborah and Jonathan Nicholas. *Educated at* The Lewis School, Pengam, Glam 1943-49; Univ. Coll. of Wales, Aberystwyth (BSc) 1949-52; Kings Coll. London (PhD) 1952-55. *Career:* Btsh Empire Cancer Campaign Fellowship 1955-57; Nuffield Fellowship 1957; Medical Research Council Biophysics Research Unit 1957-64; Reader in Biology, Univ. of London 1964-66; G. D. Searle & Co. Ltd., Research Div. 1966-86; Vice Pres. UK Preclinical Research & Development 1980-86; Chairman, British Bio-technology plc, 1986-present; CBI. Chairman, Bio-technology Working Party 1988; Research and Mfg Commt 1988; SERC: Science Board 1987; Chairman, Bio-technology Joint Advisory Board (AFRC, NERC, SERC, DTI) 1989; HSE: Advisory Commt for Genetic Modification (previously Manipulation) 1984; OECD: Consultant on Biotechnology 1987. *Publications:* Papers in Scientific Journals *Recreation:* Collecting Jaguar cars, photography and deprecating ball games. *Address:* British Bio-Technology Group, Watlington Road, Cowley, Oxford, OX4 5LY.

RICHARDS, Catherine Margaret, BSc., C.Math.L, FIMA. *Currently:* Secretary and Registrar, Institute of Mathematics and its Applications *Born on* 12 May 1940 at Newport, Gwent. *Daughter of* John Phillips Richards and Edna Vivian Richards (nee Thomas). *Educated at* Newport High School for Girls; Bedford College, Univ. of London. *Career:* Information Officer, British Oxygen Co., 1962-63; Chemistry Teacher, St. Joseph's Convent Grammar School, Abbeywood 1963-65; Assist., Ed., "Analyst", Society for Analytical Chemistry 1965-70; Deputy Sec., Inst. of Mathematics and its Applications (IMA) 1970-87. *Clubs:* University Women's, Wig and Pen. *Address:* Inst of Mathematics, 16 Nelson Street, Southend-on-Sea, Essex. SS1 1EF.

RICHARDS, Mr David Stuart, Cert. of Educ. *Currently:* Director, County Leasing & Finance Ltd. *Born on* 23 May 1954 at Cwmgwrach. *Son of* the late Glyn and Nina. *Marriage:* to Pamela Davies, 1979. *Children:* Gareth and Marianne *Educated at* Neath Boys Grammar; Cardiff Co. of Ed. *Career:* Teacher, Cefn Hengoed Comp., Swansea, 1976-77; County Credit Finance (Representative), 1978-81; Charter House Japhet Finance (Branch Manager), 1981-83; County Leasing & Finance (Director), 1983-91. *Publications:* Featured in "Focus on Rugby" and "Giants of Post War Welsh Rugby. *Recreation:* Golf, rugby, music and reading *Clubs:* Swansea Cricket & Football; Royal Porthcawl Golf; RIGS; The Rugby Club of London; Crawshays RFC. *Address:* 64 Anglesey Way, Porthcawl, Mid Glam., CF36 3QP.

RICHARDS, Emeritus Professor Elfyn John, OBE; FEng; Hon. FRAeS; FIMechE. *Currently:* Vice-Chancellor, Loughborough University 1967-75; Research Professor, Southampton University and Acoustical Consultant 1975-84; Research Assistant, Bristol Aeroplane Co., 1938-39; Scientific Officer, National Physical Laboratory, eddington 1939-45, and Secretary, various Aeronautical Research Council sub-cttees; Chief Aerodynamicist and Asst Chief-Designer, Vickers Armstrong Ltd, Weybridge, 1945-50; Prof. of Aeronautical Engineering 1950-64, and Founder Dir. Inst of Sound and Vibration Research 1963-67, Univ. of Southampton. *Born on* 28 Dec 1914 at Barry, South Wales. *Son of* Edwards James Richards, Barry, schoolmaster and Catherine Richards. *Marriage:* 1). to Eluned Gwynddydd Jones 1941, (d 1978), Aberh, Cardigan; 2) to Olive Meakin 1986, (d 1989), Romsey, Hants. 3). to Miriam Davidson 1990, Romsey, Hants. *Children:* three d. (1st marr).

Educated at Barry County School; Univ. Coll. of Wales, Aberystwyth (DSc); St. John's Coll., Cambridge (MA), DSc (Wales). *Career:* Vice-Chancellor, Loughborough University 1967-75; Research Professor, Southampton University and Acoustical Consultant 1975-84; Research Assistant, Bristol Aeroplane Co., 1938-39; Scientific Officer, National Physical Laboratory, Teddington 1939-45, and Secretary various Aeronautical Research Council sub-cttees; Chief Aerodynamicist and Asst Chief-Designer, Vickers Armstrong, Weybridge 1945-50; Prof. of Aeronautical Engineering 1950-64, and Founder Dir. Inst. of Sound and Vibration Research 1963-67, Univ., of Southampton, also Aeronautical Engineering Consultant; Res. Prof. Florida Atlantic Univ 1983-86; Member: SRC 1970-74; Noise Council; Noise Research Council, ARC 1968-71; Construction Research and Adv. Council 1968-71; Inland Transport and Devel Council 1968-71; Gen. Adv. Council of BBC (Chm Midlands Adv. Council 1968-71); Cttee of Scientific Advisory Council; Wilson Cttee on Problems of Noise; Planning and Transport Res. Adv. Council 1971- ; Chm. Univs. Council for Adult Educn; President: British Acoustical Soc., 1968-70; Soc. of Environmental Engrs 1971-73; Mem. Leics CC; Hon LLD Wales 1973; Hon. DSc: Southampton 1973; Herriot-Watt 1983; Hon. DTech Loughborough 1975, Hon FIOA 1978; Hon. Fellow Acoustical Soc. of America 1980; Hon. Fellow RAeS 1991; Taylor Gold Medal, RAeS, 1949; James Watt Medal, ICE 1963; Silver Medal, RSA 1971; Hon. Member of Welsh Bardic Circle (Gorsedd), 1970. *Publications:* books and research papers (250) in acoustics, aviation, education. *Recreation:* music, travel. *Address:* 53 The Harrage, Romsey, Hants.

RICHARDS, Mr Hywel Francis, J.P., F.R.Ag.S. *Currently:* Farmer. *Born on* 18 April 1926 at Llanbrynmair. *Son of* Sylfanus and Gwladus Richards. *Marriage:* to Elizabeth, 1957. *Children:* Lowri Ann and Norfudd. *Educated at* Machynlleth Grammar School. *Career:* High Sheriff, Gwynedd 1989-90; Justice of The Peace since 1974; Member Council National Farmers Union 1981-91; Member Council Royal Welsh Agricultural Society; Member Farmers Club Management Committee. *Recreation:* shooting, fishing. *Clubs:* Farmers, Whitehall Court, London. *Address:* Ro-Wen, Lon Merllyn, Criccieth, Gwynedd, LL52 OHNY.

RICHARDS, Professor Ivor James, MA(Wales), Dip. Arch(Dist) ARIBA. *Currently:* Professor of Architecture, University of Wales, Cardiff since 1986; Principal, Ivor Richards Architects & Designers, Cambridge, established 1980. *Born on* 1 May 1943 at Chelmsford, Essex. *Son of* the late Philip James, of Maes-y-Cwmer, S. Wales and Ivy Gwenllian (nee Kimber) of Aber-Bargoed. *Marriage:* to Anne Rostas, 1976. *Children:* Sarah Elizabeth and Owen James. *Educated at* Newmarket Grammar School; Cambridgeshire Art School (CCAT); Southend School of Architecture, Essex. *Career:* Associated with Sir Leslie Martin, Cambridge (private practice), 1969-87; collaborated as a principal architect in the practice: Sir Leslie Martin in association with Ivor Richards, 1977-87. The King's Mill, Gt. Shelford, Cambridge; Hyde Chair for Excellence in Architecture, Univ. of Nebraska, USA, 1991. *Awards:* Richards House, RIBA Commendation Award 1986; Sindall plc Company Headquarters RIBA Award (Eastern): Craftsmanship. Major International Architectural Competitions: Amsterdam City Hall, Amersterdam 1968; Pahlavi National Library, Tehran 1978; International Communication Centre, Paris 1983; Museum of the Acropolis: Athens (with students from WSA / UWCC), Athens 1990; Many Building and Projects, including Richards House; Courtyard Houses, Cambridge; Ecumenical Church Centre Cambridge 1991;. Building and Projects (with Sir Leslie Martin), include: Music School (Faculty of Music) Univ of Cambidge 1978-85; Mecca Hotel, Mecca,

Saudi Arabia; Arts Faculty, Univ of Bristol; Glasgow City Halls & Commercial Centre, Royal Concert Hall, City of Glasgow Scotland 1978-90; Glasgow Academy, Royal Scottish Academy of Music and Drama, 1982-88; Gulbenkian Foundation: Centre for Contemporary Art, Lisbon, Portugal 1979-84 (awarded RIBA Trustees Medal 1991);. *Publications:* Projects by Sir Leslie Martin in association with Ivor Richards featured in numerous publications incl: The Architectural Review, July 1978; The Architects Journal, Oct 1983; Ideias & Edificios (1933-86), May 1986; The Times Higher Educational, 1988. Many articles and projects by Ivor Richards incl: Ivor Richards Courtyard Houses in Cambridge AJ.7/85, Architect & Building News, Final Thesis Project - Housing 1967; Cambridge Perimeters (Courtyard Houses), The Architectural Review Feb 1986; Ediciones Atrium S.A. (Barcelona 1987/88) European Masters; A.J. Review features: The Meier Way, 1990; History and Legacy: Case Study Houses, 1990; Ralph Erskin, 1991; Berlage Tectonic Master; Organic Aalto; Meier Modernism, 1990; Pei: Commerce and Culture, 1991. AD Reviews and features; Two Collections, Two Competitions, 1989; The New Moderns: Arguments and Facts, 1990; The New Modern Aesthetic: Modernism Symposium, extract, 1990; UIA Congress 1990, with Dr. C. Cooke; An Educational Framework to Transmit the Positive Legacy of Modernism; Writing Architecture, 1990; Richard Meier: Barcelona Museum, 1991; World Architecture. *Recreation:* travel and cities, mountain walking, the Arts. *Address:* School of Architecture, University of Wales, P.O. Box 25, Cardiff, CF1 3XE. Ivor Richards - Architects & Designers, 10 The Fairway, Bar Hill, Cambridge, CB3 8SR

RICHARDS, Revd. Peter Dewi, D. Theol. *Currently:* General Secretary, Baptist Union of Wales, since 1992. *Born on* 7 April 1945 at Llanelli. *Son of* Harry and Elsie Richards. *Marriage:* to Wendy. *Children:* Dylan Wyn Richards and Bethan Wyn Richards. *Educated at* University College Bangor; Bangor Bapt. College. *Career:* Jabes and Caersalem Baptist Churches, Minister 1966-70; Bethesda Baptist Church Glanaman, Minister 1970-80; Assistant Secretary Bible Society 1980-81; Secretary for Wales Bible Society 1981-88; Assistant Secretary Baptist Union of Wales 1988-91; General Secretary Designate Baptist Union of Wales 1991. *Publications:* Gair yn ei bryd; Daily meditation notes; various articles for Seren Cymru, Welsh Religians Newspaper. *Recreation:* rugby, athletics, reading. *Clubs:* Clwb Cinio Cymraeg, Rhydaman. *Address:* Penmaen, 15 Lon Ger-Y-Coed, Ammanford, Dyfed, SA18 2JA. (office) Ilston House, 94 Mansel Street, Swansea, SA1 5TZ.

RICHARDS, Mr Peter John Roland, FIPM *Currently:* Deputy Director, ACAS Wales, since 1988. *Born on* 26 August 1944 at Cardiff. *Son of* Thomas Gwyn Richards BEM and Elizabeth Mary Richards BEM. *Marriage:* to Barbara Hilary (nee Lloyd) 1969. *Children:* Suzanne and Melanie. *Educated at* Cathays High School, Cardiff. *Career:* Tax Officer, Board of Inland Revenue 1962; Clerical Officer, Dept. of Employment 1967; Executive Officer, Dept. of Employment 1970; Manager (HEO), Professional and Executive Recruitment 1973; Industrial Relations Officer, ACAS Wales 1975; Senior Industrial Relations Officer, ACAS Wales 1982. *Publications:* 'Successful Industrial Relations - The Experience of Overseas Companies in Wales' (co-author). *Recreation:* reading, rugby, music. *Address:* 10 The Paddocks, Upper Church Village, Mid Glamorgan, CF38 1TL.

RICHARDS, Mr Philip Brian, LL. B. *Currently:* Barrister. *Born on* 3 Aug 1946 at Nottingham. *Son of* Glyn and Nancy Richards. *Marriage:* to Dorothy 1971 (dissolved 1988). *Children:* Rhuanedd and Lowri. *Educated at* Cardiff High School; Bristol University. *Career:* Called Inner Temple 1969; Part-time Chairman, S.S.A.T., 1987- ; Plaid Cymru Parliamentary Candidate, Cardiff North 1974, Aberdare

1979; Editor, Welsh Nation 1980-84; Trustee, Welsh Writers' Trust; Chairman, Governors, Ysgol Gyfun Rhydfelin 1988- . *Recreation:* music, writing, walking, sport. *Clubs:* Mountain Ash R.F.C. (Vice President), Neyland R.F.C. (Vice President). *Address:* Cwm Pandy, Llanwynno Road, Cwmaman, Aberdare, CF44 6PG. 30 Park Place, Cardiff, , CF1 3BA

RICHARDS, Mr Richard Alun, BVSc., MRCSVS. *Currently:* retired. *Born on* 2 Jan 1920 at Llanbrynmair. *Son of* Sylvanus and Gwladys Richards. *Marriage:* to Ann Elonwy (Nansi) Price of Morriston, Swansea, 1944. *Children:* Hugh and Stephen. *Educated at* Machynlleth County School and Liverpool University. *Career:* Veterinary Officer with State Veterinary Service, Caernarfon & Glamorgan 1943-57; Divisional Veterinary Officer, Headquarters (Tolworth) & Warwick 1957-65; Deputy Regional Veterinary Officer, Wales 1965-67; Seconded to New Zealand Govt. to advise on control of Foot & Mouth Disease 1967-68; Regional Veterinary Officer HQ Tolworth 1968-71; Assist. Chief Veterinary Officer 1971-77; Assist. Sec. Welsh Dept. Maff 1977-78; Under Secretary in charge of Welsh Office Agriculture Dept 1978-81. *Publications:* Contributions to Veterinary publications *Recreation:* Bee-keeping, fishing and shooting. *Address:* Isfryn, Llandre, Aberystwyth., Dyfed SY24 5BS.

RICHARDS, Mr Roderick, BSc(Hon) *Currently:* Businessman. *Born on* 12 March 1947 at Llanelli. *Son of* Ivor George and Jenny (nee Evans). *Marriage:* to Elizabeth Knight 1975. *Children:* Rhodri Huw, Trystan Rhys and Elen Mair *Educated at* Llandovery College; Univ. of Wales. *Career:* Government Service; Broadcaster/Journalist; Special Adviser Sec. of State for Wales; Mbr Welsh Consumer Council; Mbr Development Board for Rural Wales; Con. Party Candidate, Carmarthen 1987 Gen. El; Con. Party Candidate, Vale of Glamorgan 1989 By. El; Con Party PPC Clwyd N. W. *Recreation:* Rugby, cricket and family *Clubs:* Special Forces *Address:* c/o 3 Llewelyn Road, Colwyn Bay, Clwyd LL29 7AP.

RICHARDS, Mr Stephen Price, MA *Currently:* Barrister; First Junior Treasury Counsel, Common Law. *Born on* 8 Dec 1950 at Bangor, Caernarvonshire. *Son of* Richard Alun Richards and Ann Elonwy Mary Richards (of Llandre, Aberystwyth). *Marriage:* to Lucy Elizabeth Stubbings, 1976. *Children:* Matthew (b. 1979), Thomas (b. 1981) and Emily (b. 1984). *Educated at* King's College School, Wimbledon; St. John's College Oxford. *Career:* Called to the Bar, Gray's Inn, 1974 (Arden Scholar and Bacon Scholar of Gray's Inn). Standing Counsel to Director General of Fair Trading 1989-91 (second Junior Counsel 1987-89). A Junior Counsel to the Crown, Common Law 1990-91. Specialist Adviser to the European Communities Committee of the House of Lords 1988-89. *Publications:* Co-ed. Chitty on Contracts (25th and 26th eds); contrib to other legal publications. *Recreation:* The Welsh hills. *Address:* 4 Raymond Buildings, Gray's Inn, London, WC1R 5BP.

RICHARDS, Professor Thomas Harford Evans, DSc, MSc, BSc, FIMechE, FIMA. *Currently:* Senior Pro-Vice Chancellor, Aston University, since 1990. *Born on* 21 Feb 1931 at Crosshands, Dyfed. *Son of* David Brinley Richards and the late Lizzie Mary Richards. *Marriage:* to Frances Jean Holden, 1957. *Children:* Julian Mark, Frances Louise and David Alan. *Educated at* Jones West Monmouth School; Birmingham University. *Career:* University of Birmingham: R. A. 1955-57; Lecturer 1957-61. Lucas GTE, Mech. Design Consultant 1961-62; Birmingham Cat, 1962-66; Aston University Senior Lecturer 1966-78; Reader 1978-89; Professor 1989- ; Dean of Engineering 1986-90. *Publications:* 3 books and numerous publications in learned journals in the field of stress/vibration analysis. *Recreation:* family, gardening, DIY. *Address:* Aston University, Aston Triangle, Birmingham, B4 7ET.

RICHARDSON, Mr Horace Vincent, OBE., LL.B. *Currently:* Retired. *Born on* 28 Oct. 1913 at Mold. *Son of* Arthur John Alfred Richardson and Margaret Helena Jane (nee Hooson). *Marriage:* to Margery Tebbutt 1942. *Children:* Diana Margaret Kincaid, Ian Glyn Richardson and Keith Richardson. *Educated at* Abergele County School 1924-31; Kings College, London 1934-47. *Career:* London County Council 1931-35; Royal Courts of Justice 1935-47; Army 1940-45; Diplomatic Service 1947-73; Lord Chancellors Office 1973-78. *Recreation:* Gardening, golf, cricket. *Clubs:* M. C. C., Highgate Golf club, Civil Service club. *Address:* 34 Friern Barnet Lane, Friern Barnet, London, N11 3LX.

RIGBY, Mr John Derek, MHCI *Currently:* Secretary, Newport & Gwent Chamber of Commerce. *Born on* 25 Aug 1930 at Southport, Lancs. *Son of* the late John F. H. Rigby and Harriet (nee Terry). *Marriage:* 1st to Doreen Mary, 1955 (d. 1979); 2nd to Bridget Mary, 1981. *Children:* John Adrian (b. 1957). two stepdaughters Virginia and Deidre. *Educated at* Christ Church School Southport; Southport Technical College. *Career:* Cadet, Elder Dempster Lines - West African Royal Mail 1947-51; Assistant Purser to Chief Purser, Canadian Pacific Steamships 1952-69; Superindendant, Cargo Fleet Canadian Pacific 1970-72; Manager Budgets and Purchasing, Canadian Pacific 1972-75; Manager Administration and Purchasing, Canadian Pacific 1976-85. Governor Liverpool Catering College (Nautical) 1965; Member, Catering Panel, General Council of British Shipping 1972-75; retired March 1985. Started own Consultancy Company 1987. *Recreation:* reading, horses and dogs, DIY. *Clubs:* Fulcorn. *Address:* Barecroft House, Barecroft Common, Magor, Gwent, NP6 3EB.

ROACHE, William Patrick, *Currently:* Coronation Street. *Born on* 25 April 1932 at Ilkeston, Derbyshire. *Son of* Dr. William Vincent & Hester Vera Roache. *Marriage:* to Sara Mottrami, 1979. *Children:* Verity Elizabeth and William James. *Educated at* Rydal School 1939-50. *Career:* Commissioned into Royal Welch Fusiliers 1952, served with the Trucial Oman Scouts 1955-56, rank of Captain. Theatre, films and television until December 1960, when appeared with first episode of Coronation Street. *Recreation:* golf, tennis, riding. *Address:* Granada T.V., Quay Street, Manchester, M60 9EA.

ROBERTS, Mr (David) Peter, *Currently:* Editor, The Cambrian News since July 1991. *Born on* 24 Aug 1948 at Ferryside, Dyfed. *Son of* the late Douglas William Roberts and the late Mair (nee Marks). *Marriage:* Elaine Williams. *Children:* Nicola and Claire. *Educated at* Queen Elizabeth Grammar School, Carmarthen. *Career:* Junior Reporter with Carmarthen Journal 1965-68; Junior Reporter, Carmarthen with South Wales Evening Post 1970-73; District Reporter, Western Mail, Aberystwyth 1973-94; Deputy Editor, The Cambrian News, July 1984 - July 1991. *Recreation:* rugby, weekend reading of council minutes and annual reports of Welsh "Quangos". *Clubs:* Aberystwyth Rugby (Press Officer and Committee member); team manager of Cardigan County RFC. Member of Court of Governors of University of Wales, Aberystwyth. *Address:* 12 Gwarfelin, Llanilar, Dyfed, SY23 4PE. Cambrian News, 18-22 Queen Street, Aberystwyth, SY23 1PX.

ROBERTS, County Councillor Alan, Diploma in Youth & Community. *Currently:* House husband. *Born on* 1 Dec 1954 at Wrexham. *Son of* the late Idris Roberts and Violet Roberts (nee Davies). *Marriage:* to Vicky Pritt Roberts. *Children:* Tomos Aaron Roberts. *Educated at* Ruabon Comprehensive; Newi/HE *Career:* Self-Emoloyed, 1977-84; Community Programme, 1985-86; College (Newi), 1986-88; County Councillor (Clwyd), 1989- ; Member of the Welsh Joint Education Committee; Chairman Education Development & Resources Sub-Committee; Member of the Labour; Party Community Councillor, 1986- . *Recreation:* Golf, politics. *Address:* 30 Hall Street, Penycae, Wrexham,

Clwyd, LL14 2RY.

ROBERTS, Dr. Alun Wyn, BA Leeds; PhD Leeds. *Currently:* Registrar and Secretary, University of Wales College of Medicine since 1984. *Born on* 26 May 1944 at Eccles, Lancs. *Son of* the late Rev. William John Roberts and the late Beryl (nee Evans). *Marriage:* to Cynthia Ellen Waterhouse. *Educated at* King's School, Chester; University of Leeds. *Career:* Assistant Lecturer in History, University of Leeds, 1968-69; Administrative Assistant, then Assistant Registrar Faculty of Medicine and Dentistry, University of Birmingham, 1969-84; Member U.C.C.A. Executive committee, 1987-89; member Court of the University of Wales, 1984- ; member Management/Executive Boards South Glamorgan Health Authority, 1984- ; member Information Task Group and Information Development Working Group of the Steering Group on Undergraduate Medical and Dental Education and Research, 1988- ; member Committee of Vice-Chancellors and Principals Working Group on Health and Safety 1991- . *Publications:* articles and reviews on Historical and Higher Education themes in Northern History, Aesculapius and the C. U. A. Newsletter. *Recreation:* photography, travel, history. *Clubs:* Llantwit Fardre Sports and Social. *Address:* University of Wales, College of Medicine, Heath Park, Cardiff, CF4 4XN.

ROBERTS, Mr Alwyn, MA (Cantab) BA., LL.B (Wales) *Currently:* Vice Principal and Director Extra Mural Studies, University College of N. Wales, Bangor. *Born on* 26 Aug 1933 at Llanrwst. *Son of* the late Rev. Howell and Buddug Roberts. *Marriage:* to Mair Rowlands Williams, 1960. *Children:* Hywel Glyn. *Educated at* Penygroes Grammar School; UCW, Aberystwyth; UCNW, Bangor; Cambridge University. *Career:* Principal P.M. Govt. College, Aizawl, Assam, India, 1960-67; University College Swansea, Lecturer in Social Administration, 1967-70; Univ. College of N. Wales, Bangor, Lecturer and Senior Lecturer, 1970-79; Director Extra Mural Studies, UCNW, 19790 ; Vice Principal UCNW, 1985- ; Member Gwynedd County Council (Chairman Social Services Comm), 1973-81; Member Gwynedd Health Authority, 1973-80; Member Royal Comm. on Legal Services, 1976-79; Member Broadcasting Council Wales, 1974-79; National Govnr of the BBC in Wales, 1979-86; Member S4C Authority, 1981-86; Member Council of the National Eisteddfod of Wales, 1979- ; Chairman of the National Eisteddfod Council, 1989- ; Member Parole Board, 1987-90; Chairman ACEN, 1989- . *Address:* Brithdir, 43 Talycae, Tregarth, Bangor Gwynedd.

ROBERTS, Anthony Mark, *Currently:* Professional Footballer, goalkeeper with Queens Park Rangers F. C, since 1987. *Born on* 4 Aug 1969 at Holyhead. *Son of* Edward and Ruth Roberts. *Educated at* Thomas Ellis Primary School; Holyhead Secondary School; Coleg Pencraig. *Career:* Holyhead United Juniors 1982-87; Wales Youth Team, 6 caps; Wales under 21 Team, 2 caps and 1 sub; Wales Full Team, 1 sub. *Recreation:* golf, snooker. *Address:* Rangers Stadium, Loftus Road, Shepherds Bush, London The Lodge, Ucheldre Avenue, Holyhead, Anglesey.

ROBERTS, Mr Bernard, F.R.C.M. ; Hon.D. Univ. Brunel *Currently:* Concert Pianist; Piano Professor at the Royal College of Music, London. *Born on* 23rd July 1933 at Manchester. *Son of* William Wright Roberts and Elsie Alberta (nee Ingham). *Marriage:* to Patricia May Russell, 27th Aug 1955, dissolved 1988. *Children:* Andrew 1958, Nicholas 1960. *Educated at* William Hulme's Grammar School, Manchester 1943-49; Royal College of Music 1949-55. *Career:* Debut as Concert Pianist, Wigmore Hall 1957; many concerto and broadcasts in this country and abroad as recitalist, chamber player and concerto player, including BBC Promenade Concerts 1979; recorded the complete Beethoven Piano Sonatas for Nimbus Records,

1984-85; appointed piano professor at Royal College of Music 1962. *Recreation:* Philosophy, Reading, Railways. *Address:* Uwchlaw'r Coed, Llanbedr, Gwynedd, LL45 2NA. Tel: 0341 23532.

ROBERTS, Mr Bertie, *Currently:* retired Civil Servant, 1979. *Born on* 4 June 1919 at Blaengarw, Mid Glam. *Son of* Thomas and Louisa Roberts. *Marriage:* 1st to Dr Peggy Clark, MD, 1946; 2nd to Catherine Matthew, 1962. *Children:* Andrew Mark Roberts (b 1951). *Educated at* Garw Secondary School, Mid Glamorgan. *Career:* HM Forces, 1942-46, Captain RAOC, active service Normandy, France and Belgium. Director, Dept. of Environment 1971-79; Leader of study on feasibility of introducing computers in Ministry of Public Building and Works, 1958; formed and directed computer organisation 1962; Comptroller of Accounts 1963; Director of Computer Services 1967; Head of Organisation and Methods 1969; Director of Estate Management Overseas (with FCO), Dept of Environment 1971; Regional Director DOE (Maj-Gen equiv), British Forces Germany 1976-79; Lay member Ethical Committee and member Community Health Council (Hastings Health District) 1982-89. *Recreation:* Music, foreign travel, watching rugby, community work. *Clubs:* Rotary, St Leonards-on-Sea; Dickens Pickwick. *Address:* Fairmount, 41 Hollington Pk Rd, St.Leonards on Sea, E.Sussex TN38 OSE.

ROBERTS, Brian Reginald, M.A. (Cantab.) *Currently:* Stockbroker; Senior Executive, Hargreave Hale, Bangor. *Born on* 3rd Jan 1927 at Wanstead, Essex. *Son of* the late Reginald Howard Roberts and Eileen Mary. *Marriage:* 1st to Beryl Nesta (dissolved) 2nd to Marianne. *Children:* Alison, Louise, and Samantha. *Educated at* Royal Liberty School, Romford 1938-45; Pembroke College Cambridge 1950-54. *Career:* Schoolmaster 1954-56; Industrial Administration D. C. L. Hull 1956-62; Town Clerk, Hedon, Yorkshire 1960-62; Member of the Stock Exchange 1965-; Senior Partner, R. A. Coleman & Co. Bangor 1966-87; Member Bangor City Council 1967-70; Member of Council of the Stock Exchange 1981-86 *Recreation:* Gardening, Snooker, Crosswords *Clubs:* Bangor Cricket Club; Churchill Club *Address:* Walnut Cottage, Llandegai, Bangor, Gwynedd, LL57 4HU.

ROBERTS, Dr. Brynley Francis, MA; PhD; FSA; FRSA. *Currently:* Librarian, National Library of Wales since 1985. *Born on* 3 Feb 1931 at Aberdare, Glam. *Son of* Robert F. Roberts and Laura Jane Roberts (nee Williams). *Marriage:* to Rhiannon (nee Campbell), 1957. *Children:* Rolant Ll, O. Maredudd. *Educated at* Grammar School, Aberdare; University College of Wales, Aberystwyth. *Career:* Lecturer/Reader, Dept. of Welsh, UCW, Aberystwyth 1957-78; Professor of Welsh, Univ. College of Swansea 1978-85; Intellegence Corps 1954-56; A Fellow, University of Wales, 1956-57; Sir John Rhys Fellow, Jesus College, Oxford 1973-74; Chairman Welsh Books Council 1989-; Vice-Chairman 1986-89; Pres. Welsh Library Ass., 1985-. *Publications:* Gwassanaeth Meir, 1961; Brut y Brenhinedd, 1971; Cytranc Lludd a Llyfelys, 1975; Brut Tysilio, 1980; Edward Llwyd, 1980; Gerald of Wales, 1982; Studies on Middle Welsh Literature, 1992; numerous articles. *Recreation:* music *Address:* Hengwrt, Ffordd Llanbadarn, Aberystwyth, Dyfed, SY23 1HB.

ROBERTS, His Honour Judge Eifion, QC., DL of Clwyd, LL. B. (Wales)., BCL(Oxon) *Currently:* Circuit Judge on Wales and Chester Circuit; Liaison Judge for Clywd; Designated Family Judge for Gwynedd. *Born on* 22 Nov 1927 at Isle of Anglesey. *Son of* Revd. E. P. Roberts and Margaret Roberts (nee Jones). *Marriage:* to Buddug (nee Williams), 1958. *Children:* Sian, Rhian and Huw. *Educated at* Beaumaris Grammar School; UCW Aberystwyth; Exeter College, Oxford and Grays Inn. *Career:* Called to Bar, 1953; practised from Chester 1953-71; appointed Q.C. 1971 and practised from London 1971-77; Deputy Chairman

of Anglesey Quarter Sessions 1966-71, and of Denbighshire Quarter Sessions 1970-71; Assist. Parliamentary Boundary Commissioner for Wales 1967-69; Mbr. for Wales of the Crawford Commt. on Broadcasting Coverage 1972-74; Recorder of the Crown Court 1971-77; Vice-President of the Univ. of Wales, Bangor. *Recreation:* Gardening and walking *Address:* Maes-y-Rhedyn, Gresford Road, Llay, Wrexham, LL12 ONN. Tel: 0978 85 2292.

ROBERTS, Professor Gareth Gwyn, BSc, PhD, DSc, MA Oxon 1987. *Currently:* Vice Chancellor, University of Sheffield, since 1991; Visiting Professor of Electronic Engineering, Department of Engineering Science and Fellow, Brasenose College, Oxford University, since 1985. *Born on* 16 May 1940 at Bangor, N. Wales. *Son of* Edwin and Meri Roberts. *Marriage:* to Charlotte (nee Standen). *Children:* Peris, Bronwen and Daron. *Educated at* University College of N. Wales (Bangor). *Career:* Lecturer in Physics, University of Wales 1963-66; Res. Physicist Xerox Corp., USA 1966-68; Senior Lecturer, Reader, and Professor of Physics, NUU 1968-76; Prof. of Applied Physics and Head, Dept of Applied Physics and Electronics, Univ of Durham 1976-85; Director of Research 1986-90, Thorn EMI plc (Chief Scientist 1985). BBC/ Royal Institution Christmas Lectures 1988. Member UFC 1989-. Holweck Gold Medal and Prize, Inst. of Physics 1986. *Publications:* Insulating Films on Semiconductors, 1979; Langmuir-Blodgett Films, 1990; many publications and patents on physics of semiconductor devices and molecular electronics. *Recreation:* soccer, duplicate bridge, classical music. *Address:* Vice Chancellor's Office, University of Sheffield, P. O. Box 594, Sheffield, S10 2UH.

ROBERTS, Dr Gwilym Edffrwd, BSc., PhD., FIS. *Currently:* Statistical and economic analyst; Univ. and Polytechnic Consultant. *Born on* 7 Aug 1928 at Clwt-y-Bont, Gwynedd. *Son of* William Roberts and Jane Ann Roberts. *Marriage:* to Mair Griffiths 1954. *Educated at* Brynefai County; Univs. Wales and London. *Career:* Business Manager, 1952-57; Polytechnic & Univ., Lecturer, 1957-; Executive Dir. Aids to Management Serv., 1960-; Mbr. of Parliament for fourteen years, representing South Beds., 1966-70, and Cannock, 1974-83; Four years Parliamentary Private Sec. at the Dept. of Ind; Vice Pres. of the Parliamentary and Scientific Commt., Chairman of the Parliamentary Information Technology Commt; Local government leader of two major councils; Chairman of Finance and Resources, Economic Development, etc; Vice Pres., of the Inst. of Statisticians. *Publications:* Regular contributor on economic, business matters and gambling to a corp. of national and local newspapers and professional journals; Author of several books on gambling statistics; Editor of the Institute of Statisticians publications from 1967-78. *Recreation:* Table tennis and writing. *Address:* 60 Swasedale Road, Luton, Beds., LU3 2UD. 8 Main Road, Brereton, Rugeley, Staffs., WS15 1DT. Tel: 0582 573893

ROBERTS, Mr Hilary Llewelyn Arthur, LLB, *Currently:* Barrister. *Born on* 30 Sept 1953 at Cardiff. *Son of* Michael Roberts and Eileen Roberts. *Marriage:* to Shirley, 1986. *Children:* Thomas. *Educated at* Whitchurch Grammar School; UCW Aberystwyth. *Career:* Called to Bar 1978; Practise as Barrister at Newport Chambers. *Recreation:* sport, music. *Clubs:* United Services Mess, Cardiff. *Address:* 12 Clytha Park Road, Newport, Gwent, NP9 4SL.

ROBERTS, Hywel Heulyn, JP: *Currently:* retired. *Born on* 16 March 1919 at Liverpool. *Son of* John and Lily Roberts. *Marriage:* to Margaret Eluned Davies of Llanarth, 1944. *Children:* Gyln Heulyn, Meinir Heulyn, Rhian Heulyn and Mair Heulyn. *Educated at* Liverpool Institute. *Career:* Member, Cardiganshire County Council 1952-74 (Chairman 1971-72); member, Dyfed County Council 1973-89 (Chairman 1973-76); Chairman Superanuation Investment Panel 1964-89; member, Nat. Museum Court 1961-74 (Council 1964-74); member, A.C.C. 1964-89; Leader of

Independents A.C.C. 1973-89; Vice Chairman A.C.C. 1985-89; member, S. W. Wales H.M.C. 1961-73 (Vice chairman 1967-73); Bd Cwmni Theatr Cymru 1961-84; Bd Welsh Theatre Co 1961-69; member, Welsh Tourist Board 1961-72; member, Welsh Counties Committee 1964-89 (Chairman 1972-74); member, Dyfed Powys Police Authority 1967-89 (chairman 1980-82); member, Sports Council for Wales 1972-84; Chairman Welsh Folk Museum St. Fagans 1971-74; Trustee S. W. Wales T. S. B. 1973-80; member, Police Council and PNB (UK) 1974-89; Chairman JNC Coroners (Wales & England) 1974-88; member, Exec Bd W.N.O. 1974-88; High Sheriff of Dyfed 1982-83; member, Univ of Wales Court and Council 1974- ; member, Land Authority for Wales 1975-86; admitted Order Druidic Gorsedd of Bards 1976; Plaid Cymru Candidate Carmarthen 1959; Plaid Cymru Exec 1951-71. Welsh Water Authority 1974-80. *Recreation:* reading, walking, gardening, writing (a little). *Clubs:* Farmers *Address:* Synod Parc, Synod, Llandysul, Dyfed, SA44 6JE.

ROBERTS, Right Honourable Sir Ieuan Wyn Pritchard, MA (Oxon). *Currently:* M.P. (C) Conwy, since 1970 and Minister of State, Welsh Office, since 1987. *Born on* 10 July 1930 at Anglesey. *Son of* the late Rev E. P. Roberts and M. A. Roberts. *Marriage:* to Enid Grace (nee Williams). *Children:* Rhys, Geraint and Huw. *Educated at* Harrow; University College, Oxford. *Career:* Sub-editor, Liverpool Daily Post 1952-54; News Asst. BBC 1954-57; TWW Ltd: News, Special Events and Welsh Language Programmes Producer 1957-59; Production Controller 1959-60; Exec. Producer 1960-68; Welsh Controller 1964-68; Programme Exec., Harlech TV 1969; Opposition Front-Bench Spokesman on Welsh Affairs 1974-79; PPS to Sec. of State for Wales 1970-74; Parly Under Sec of State, Welsh Office 1979-87; Vice-Pres., Assoc. of District Councils, 1975-79; Mbr. of Gòrsedd, Royal National Eisteddfod of Wales 1966; Mbr. Court of Governors: Nat. Library of Wales; Nat. Museum of Wales; University Coll. of Wales, Aberystwyth 1970- . *Recreation:* gardening. *Clubs:* Savile; Cardiff and County (Cardiff). *Address:* Tan y Gwalia, Rowen, Conwy, LL32 8TY.

ROBERTS, Mr John Edward, BEng., CEng., FIEE., FCCA., DMS. *Currently:* Managing Director, MANWEB plc., appointed 1991. *Born on* 2 March 1946 at Wallasey. *Son of* the late Arthur and the late Dora Roberts (nee Watkin). *Marriage:* to Pamela Baxter, 1970. *Children:* Richard and Gemma *Educated at* Oldershaw Grammar School, Wallasey; University of Liverpool. *Career:* Joined Manweb 1967; Appointed Chief Accountant, 1984; Finance Director, 1989. *Recreation:* Squash, gardening and walking *Address:* Whitehouse Farm, Village Road, Northop Hall, Clwyd, CH7 6HT.

ROBERTS, John Frederick, OBE, CB, CBE. *Currently:* retired. *Born on* 24 Feb 1913 at Pontardawe. *Son of* Catherine and John Roberts. *Marriage:* 1st to Mary Wyn, 1942 (d. 1942); 2nd to Pam Joy Roberts. *Children:* John *Educated at* Pontardawe Grammar School. *Career:* RAF, Air Vice Marshal. *Recreation:* member of MCC *Clubs:* MCC *Address:* 1 Lon Cadog, Sketty, Swansea.

ROBERTS, John Griffith, *Currently:* Solicitor. *Born on* 10 June 1912 at Llangybi, Chwilog, Gwynedd. *Son of* the late Griffith Roberts and the late Mary Ann Roberts (nee Jones). *Marriage:* to Betty (nee Thomas) BA, 1948, da of David Thomas, MA (d. 1963) of Pontardawe. *Children:* Rhiannon Vaughan Griffiths (nee Roberts), M. A. *Educated at* Penygroes County School. *Career:* Admitted Solicitor 1934; In practice since 1935. Member of Law Society since 1955. Chairman, Rent Tribunal for North West Wales till 1982. Member of Pwllheli Town Council since 1974 (former Mayor of Pwllheli); member Caernarvonshire County Council 1946-74, (chairman 1955-56); Gwynedd County Council 1974-89. Member Association of County Councils and Welsh Counties Committee until 1989. Former member

of Court and Council of University of Wales and Court and Council of University College of North Wales. Former Chairman of Gwynedd Education Committee and Policy and Resources Committee of Gwynedd County Council. Former member of Wales Advisory Body for Local Authority Higher Education. *Recreation:* motoring, travelling, billiards, bowls, reading. *Clubs:* Snooker, Pwllheli; Clwb y Bont, Pwllheli. *Address:* Maesywern, Glancymerau, Pwllheli, Gwynedd, LL53 5PU. 26 Stryd Penlan, Pwllheli, Gwynedd, LL53 5DE. Tel: (0758) 612362.

ROBERTS, Rev. John Stuart, *Currently:* Head of Television, BBC Wales since 1986. *Born on* 3 June 1939 *Son of* the late Alec Roberts and Bronwen (nee Thomas). *Marriage:* to Verina Gravelle, 1961. *Children:* Iona and Bethan. *Educated at* Dunvant Secondary School; Swansea Technical College; Presbyterian College, Carmarthen; Memorial College, Swansea. *Career:* Ordained - Ford and Letterson, Pembs 1961; Minister - Soar, Lampeter 1966; Producer, Religious Programmes, BBC Wales 1969; Head of Religious Programmes, BBC Wales 1976; Editor 'Everyman & 'Heart of the Matter', BBC London 1980; Head of Religious Programmes & Community Affairs, BBC Wales 1982. *Address:* c/o BBC Cymru Wales, Broadcasting House, Llandaff, Cardiff, CF5 2YQ.

ROBERTS, Professor Lewis Edward John, CBE; D. Phil; FRSC; FRS. *Currently:* Independent Consultant. *Born on* 31 Jan 1922 at Cardiff, Glam. *Son of* Revd. William Edward Roberts and Mrs Lilian Lewis Roberts (nee John). *Marriage:* to Eleanor Mary Luscombe, 1949. *Children:* Matthew William Lewis. *Educated at* Swansea Grammar School, 1932-39; Jesus College, Oxford, 1939-45. *Career:* Scientific Officer, Chalk River Laboratories, Ontario, 1946-48; A. E. R. E., Harwell, 1948-58; Commonwealth Fund Fellow, Univ. California, Berkeley, 1954-55; Group Leader, A. E. R. E., Harwell, 1958-68; Assistant Director 1968-74, and Director, A. E. R. E., 1975-86; member, Board of Atomic Energy Authority, 1979-86; Wolfson Professor of Environmental Risk Assessment, University of East Anglia, Norwich, 1986-90; Emeritus Professor, 1990; Governor, Abingdon School, 1978-86; Spec. Adviser House of Lords Select Committee on the European Communities, 1987; Adviser, Secretary of State for Wales, 1990. *Publications:* Nuclear Power and Public Responsibility, Cambridge U.P., 1984; Power Generation and the Environment (with P. S. Liss and P. A. H. Saunders), Oxford U.P., 1990; articles in scientific and technical journals. *Recreation:* music, history, gardening. *Address:* Penfold Wick, Church Hill, Chilton, Didcot, Oxfordshire, OX11 OSH.

ROBERTS, Professor Meirion Wyn, PhD, DSc, CChem, FRSC. *Currently:* Professor of Physical Chemistry and Head of the School of Chemistry & Applied Chemistry since 1979; Deputy Principal, University of Wales College of Cardiff, since 1988. *Born on* 1 Feb 1931 at Ammanford, Dyfed. *Son of* Tom Roberts, OBE and Mary (nee Willliams). *Marriage:* to Catherine Angharad, 1957. *Children:* Karen and Mark. *Educated at* Amman Valley Grammar School, Dyfed; University College, Swansea. *Career:* Post-doctoral fellow, Imperial College, London 1955-57; Senior Scientific Officer, National Chem Laboratory, Teddington 1957-59; Lecturer, Queen's University, Belfast, N. Ireland 1959-66; First Chair of Physical Chemistry, University of Bradford 1966-79; SERC Chemistry Committee 1973-76; UGC & UFC Physical Sciences Committee 1984-89; CNAA Physical Sciences Comm., 1988-91; Governor of Cardiff Inst of Higher Education 1992- ; Council of University of Wales 1988- . *Publications:* 200 publications, author and co-author of 11 books. *Recreation:* watching rugby. *Address:* School of Chemistry & Applied Chemistry, Univ of Wales Coll of Cardiff, P.O. Box 912, Cardiff, CF1 3TB. 37 Heol-Y-Delyn, Lisvane, Cardiff, CF4 5SR.

ROBERTS, Professor Paul Harry, MA; PhD; ScD; FRAS; FRS. *Currently:* Professor of Mathematics and Geophysical Scinces, University of California, Los Angeles since 1986. *Born on* 13 Sept 1929 at Aberystwyth. *Son of* the late Percy Harry Roberts and the late Ethel Francis Roberts (nee Mann). *Marriage:* to Mary Francis Tabrett, 1989. *Educated at* Ardwyn Grammar School, Aberystwyth; UCW, Aberystwyth; Gonville & Caius College, Cambridge. *Career:* Research Associate, University of Chicago, 1954-55; Scientific Officer, AWRE, 1955-56; I.C.I. Fellow, Durham University, 1956-59; Lecturer in Physics, Armstrong College, Durham Univ., 1959-61; Associate Professor of Astronomy, University of Chicago, 1961-63; Professor of Applied Mathematics, Univ. of Newcastle upon Tyne, 1963-85. *Publications:* Introduction to Magnetohydrodynamics, Longmans, 1965; also approx. 190 scientific papers. *Recreation:* music, chess, reading. *Address:* 2642 Cordelia Road, Los Angeles, Calif. 90049, USA,. 1 Coupland Beck Cottages, Appleby In Westmorland, Cumbria, CA16 6LN.

ROBERTS, Archdeacon Raymond Harcourt, CB., MA. *Currently:* Chairman, Customer Service Commt. for Wales, Office of Water Services 1990; Hon. Chaplain of Llandaff Cathedral 1991. *Born on* 14 April 1931 at Maesycwmmer, Mon. *Son of* Thomas and Caroline Maud Roberts. *Educated at* Pontywaun Grammar School, Risca; St. Edmund Hall, Oxford; St. Michael's Coll., Llandaff. *Career:* National Service (Royal Navy) 1949-51; Parish of Bassaleg Diocese of Monmouth 1956-59; Chaplain RNVR 1957; Chaplain Royal Navy 1959; Appointed: Destroyers & Frigates, Far East Fleet 1959; RN Supply Training Sch, Chatham 1961; Dartmouth Training Squadron 1963; Royal Marines Commando Course 1965; 45 Commando, Royal Marines (in Aden & S. Arabia) 1965; R.N. Eng. Coll., 1966; HMS Bulwark (Commando Helicopter Carrier) 1968; Britannia R. N. Coll.,1970; HMS Ark Royal 1973; Commando Training Centre, Royal Marines, Chaplain of Fleet's Co-ordinating Chaplain for the Royal Marines (Area Dean) 1975; H. M. Naval Base, (Snr Chaplain responsible for H. M. Ships, H. M. Dockyard, Fleet Accomodation Centre and Married Quarters in Plymouth: Chaplain of Fleet's Co-ordinating Chaplain (Area Dean) for Plymouth Command; Staff Chaplain to the Admiral; Chaplain of the Fleet and Archdeacon for the R. N. 1980; Hon. Chaplain to HM the Queen 1980; Canon of Gibraltar Cathedral, Diocese of Europe 1980; Mbr. of C of E General Synod 1980; Appointed Companion of the Order of the Bath 1985; Gen. Sec. of the Jerusalem and the Middle East Church Assoc. 1986. *Recreation:* Cooking, driving and listening to Mozart, not necessarily simultaneously. *Address:* c/o Room 140, Caradog House, 1-6 St. Andrew's Plce, Cardiff CF1 3DE.

ROBERTS, Dame Shelagh Marjorie, DBE *Currently:* Chairman of London Tourist Board. *Born on* 13 Oct 1924 at Port Talbot. *Daughter of* Ivor Glyn and Cecelia May Roberts. *Educated at* St. Wyburn, Southport. *Career:* Member, Greater London Council 1970-81; member, European Parliament 1979-89; Chairman, National Union of Conservative Party 1976-77; President National Union of Conservative Party 1988-89; former member, Basildon Development Corporation Race Relations Board, part of London Authority Occupational Pensions Board and Panel of Industrial Tribunals. *Publications:* part author "Fair Share for the Fair Sex"; "More Help for the Cities". *Recreation:* enjoying the sun and fresh air. *Clubs:* Hurlingham, St. Stephens, United and Cecil. *Address:* 47 Shrewsbury House, Cheyne Walk, London, SW3 5LW.

ROBERTS, Mr Thomas Somerville, JP; FCIT. *Born on* 10 Dec 1911 at Ruabon, N. Wales. *Son of* Joseph Richard Robert, Rhosllanerchrugog and Lily Agnes (nee Caldwell). *Marriage:* to 1st. Ruth Moira Teasdale, 1938; 2nd to Margaret Peggy Anderson, Sunderland, 1950. *Children:* 1st marr. two s. *Educated at* Roath Park Elem School,

Cardiff; Cardiff High School; Balliol Coll., Oxford (Domus Exhibnr). *Career:* Traffic Apprentice, LNER 1933; Docks Manager, Middlesbrough and Hartlepool 1949; Chief Docks Manager, Hull 1959; S. Wales 1962; Port Dir. S. Wales Ports 1970-75; Chm., S Wales Port Employers 1962-75; Member: Nat. Jt Council for Port Transport Industry, 1962-75; Nat. Dock Labour Bd 1970-75; Race Relations Bd 1968-76; Dir. Develt Corp. for Wales 1965-80, Vice-Pres 1979-83; Chairman, Milford Haven Conservancy Bd 1976-82;Dep. Chm., Welsh Develt Agency. 1976-80; Member: Court, Univ. of Wales; Pwyllgor Tywysog Cymru (Prince of Wales' Cttee), 1977-81; Hon. Fellow and Life Governor, Univ. of Wales Coll. Cardiff (formerly University Coll., Cardiff and UWIST); JP City of Cardiff 1966. *Recreation:* TV *Clubs:* Cardiff Business. *Address:* Marcross Lodge, 9 Ely Road, Llandaff, Cardiff CF5 2JE. Tel: 0222 561153.

ROBERTS, Councillor William Gavin, *Currently:* Councillor. *Born on* 14 Jan 1941 at Manchester. *Son of* Gwilym Carrington Roberts and the late Freda Roberts. *Marriage:* to Hilary Davies, 1966. *Children:* one son and one daughter, one grandaughter and one grandson *Educated at* Brymbo Secondary Modern School 1952-56 *Career:* Politics: Member of Labour party Wales 1964; Member Executive Committee Clwyd County Labour Party 1987-93; Member Brymbo Community Council 1983; Chairman 1990-91; Member Clwyd County Council 1989-93;Member Education & Policy Finance & Resources; Social Services Committees Vice Chairman; Adult Services Sub-Committee; Chairman Residential Care Homes panel; Member Executive Committee Age Concern Wrexham Maelor 1989; Management Committee Tanyfron Youth Club 1978; Chairman Brymbo Labour Party 1984-89; School Governor Tanyfron School 1983; School Governors St. David's High School Wrexham; The Groves High School Wrexham; Alexandra Junior & Infants School Wrexham; Member Caia Park Community Liaison; Group Member Management Committee Queen Park Youth Centre 1989, Wrexham 1989; Member T.G.W.U. Vice-Chairman Greystones House Management Committee. *Recreation:* Music, reading, Politics and youth work. *Address:* 15 Meadow View, Tanyfron, Wrexham, Clwyd LL11 5TP. Tel: (0978) 750685.

ROBERTS, Mr William Morys, M. A.; F. C. A. *Currently:* Partner, Head of Corporate Advisory Services 1989-, Ernst & Young, Becket House, 1 Lambeth Palace Road, London, SE1 7EU. *Born on* 8th Dec 1934 at Harrow. *Son of* the late Gwilym James Roberts M. D. Eileen Burford. *Marriage:* 1967 to Patricia Anne Bettinson (nee Chivers). *Children:* Sarah Amelia, Simon William, Alice Mary Patricia *Educated at* Kingswood School, Bath; Gonville and Caius College, Cambridge *Career:* National Service, Royal Artillery 1953-54, Intelligence Corps 1954-55, 2nd Lieutenant (later Lt. RARO); Turquand Youngs & Co. 1958-61; Wm Brandt's Sons & Co. Limited 1961-73: Chief Accountant 1965, Secretary 1970, Director 1971; Edward Bates & Sons Ltd 1973-75, Director; Ernst & Young, Partner 1976- (Head of London Insolvency 1987-89); Public Appointment - Practising Accountant Member of Insolvency Rules Advisory Committee 1984- *Publications:* Insolvency Law and Practice (with J. S. H. Gillies) 1988 *Recreation:* Gardening, Churchwarden All Saints Gt. Chesterford 1976- *Clubs:* Institute of Directors *Address:* Brock House, Manor Lane, Great Chesterford, Saffron Walden, Essex, CB10 1PJ.

ROBERTSON, Professor Norman Robert Ean, CBE., MDS., DDS. *Currently:* Dean of the Dental School 1985-, and Head of the Department of Child Dental Health 1985- *Born on* 13 March 1931. at Glasgow. *Son of* the late Robert Robertson (d 1980) and Jean Thompson Robertson. *Marriage:* to Morag Wyllie 1954. *Children:* Stephen, Peter, Nigel, Lois and Mary. *Educated at* Hamilton Acad., Univ. of Glasgow (BDS), Univ. of Manchester (MDS DDS). *Career:* Nat. Serv. RAF 1954-56; Sen. Lectr.

Orthodontics Univ. of Manchester 1963-70; Prof. and Head of Dept. Orthodontics Univ. Wales Coll. Med. 1970-85; Hon. consultant in Orthodontics S. Glam and Gwent Health Authority 1970- ; member UGC Dental Review Working Party (co-author of its report 1988); Cncl Univ. of Wales Coll. Med. 1985- ; Consultant Orthodontists Gp. 1988- ; S. Glam Health Authority 1976- ; Gen. Dental Council, and Dental Education Advisory Council 1985- ; Standing Dent Advisory Committee 1988- ; Welsh Council Postgrad. Med & Dent. Education 1989- ; Member: BDA, COG, BSSO, BAO. *Publications:* Oral Orthopaedics and Orthodontics for Cleft Lip and Palate. A Structured Approach. *Recreation:* Sailing. *Clubs:* RYA, Cruising Association. *Address:* 51 Heol y Coed, Rhiwbina, Cardiff CF4 6HQ.

ROBERTSON, Sholto David Maurice (known as Toby), OBE *Currently:* Artistic Director, Theatr Clwyd, 1985-92. *Born on* 29 Nov 1928 at Chelsea. *Son of* David Lambert Robertson and Felicity Douglas Tomlin. *Marriage:* to Jane McCulloch, 1964 (dissolved 1981). *Children:* Sebastian, Francesca, Sasha and Joshua. *Educated at* Stowe; Trinity College, Cambridge, BA(Hons) MA. *Career:* Actor, Theatre and TV Director, Freelance 1954-66; Director Prospect Theatre Company 1966-80; Director Old Vic 1977-80; Opera productions in USA with Pavorotty, Jenze, Norman 1981-84; Professor Brooklyn College NY 1981-83; Hon Professor University College N. Wales 1988-97. *Recreation:* painting. *Clubs:* Garrick. *Address:* Theatr Clwyd, Clwyd, N Wales, CH7 1YA. 210 Brixton Road, London, SW9 6AP.

ROGERS, Mr Allan, BSc., FGS., MP. *Currently:* Member of Parliament - Rhondda 1983- . *Born on* 24 Oct 1932 at Gelligaer, Glam. *Son of* John Henry and Madeleine. *Marriage:* to Ceridwen, daughter of Cynonfryn James. *Children:* Cerilan, Richard, Alison and Catherine. *Educated at* Gelligaer Primary; Bargoed Sec., Univ. Coll., Swansea. *Career:* Army, Welch Regt. & Royal Welsh Fusiliers 1951-53; National Coal Bd., Surveyor/Geologist, U. S. A. & Canada, Petroleum Geologist, Australia & Africa, Geologist, 1956-62; Graddfa School, Ystrad Mynach, History Teacher 1962-65; (WEA) Workers Educational Assoc., Tutor Organiser 1965-70; District Sec., WEA, 1970-79; Mbr. European Parliament S. E. Wales 1979-84; Vice-Pres., European Parliament 1979-82; Sec/Whip, British Labour, European Parliament 1979-84; Gelligaer Dist., Councillor 1965-71, Chrmn. Transport Commt; Glamorgan County Councillor 1969-74; Mid-Glamorgan County Councillor 1973-79; Vice Chairman, Education Commt, 1973-79; Chrmn. Polytechnic of Wales 1973-79; Mbr. Welsh Joint Educ. Commt; Mbr. Assoc. of Adult and Continuing Educ. *Recreation:* All sports, gardening *Clubs:* Penygraig Labour, Treorchy Workmens. *Address:* 70 Cemetery Road, Porth, Rhondda, Mid Glam., CF39 OBL. House Of Commons, London, SW1A OAA.

ROLLES, Mr Keith, MA, MS, FRCS. *Currently:* Consultant Surgeon and Director of the Liver Transplant Unit, The Royal Free Hospital, London, NW3 2QG, since 1988. *Born on* 25 Oct 1947 at Merthyr Tydfil. *Son of* Betty and Trevor Rolles. *Marriage:* to Sharon (nee McGrath). *Children:* David and Thomas. *Educated at* Quakers Yard Grammar School; London Hospital Medical College. *Career:* University Lecturer in Surgery and Honorary Consultant Surgeon, University of Cambridge and Addenbrookes Hospital Cambridge 1984-88. *Publications:* numerous relating to various aspects of organ transplantation. *Recreation:* squash, wine, theatre. *Address:* University Dept of Surgery, The Royal Free Hospital, London, NW3 2QG.

ROSE, Mrs Eda Mary Bernice, NDD; RSA(TEFL). *Currently:* Self employed Society Milliner: Designer and producer of Bespoke Model Hats. *Born on* 22 July 1941 at Merthyr Tydfil. *Daughter of* the late Llywela Mair (nee Jones) and the late John Daniel Thomas. *Marriage:* divorced.

Educated at Cyfartha Castle Grammar School, Merthyr Tydfil; Goldsmiths College School of Art, London; International House, Piccadilly, London. *Career:* Teacher of Art 1964; Teacher of English as a foreign language 1969; Designer and producer of Model Hats 1980; Founder of Eda Rose Millinery 1984; Radio commentator/fashion reporter at Henley Royal Regatta, Royal Ascot etc. *Recreation:* fashion, antiques, theatre, interior design. *Clubs:* Royal Overseas League, London; member of Royal Enclosure, Ascot. *Address:* 3 Upton Close, Henley-On-Thames, Oxon, RG9 1BT.

ROSEN, Professor Michael, CBE., FRCA., FRCOG *Currently:* Consultant Anaesthetist, Hon Professor, Univ. of Wales, College of Medicine. *Born on* 17 Oct 1927 at Dundee. *Son of* Israel and Lily Rosen. *Marriage:* to Sally (nee Cohen) 1955. *Children:* Timothy, Amanda and Mark. *Educated at* Dundee High School, St. Andrews University *Career:* President, Coll. of Anaesthetists 1988-91; President, Assoc. of Anaesthestists, Great Britain and Ireland 1985-88; Founder Academic European Academy of Anaesthesiology 1985-91; Mbr General Medical Council 1989-91; Mbr Clinical Standards Advisory Group 1991- . *Publications:* Percutaneous Cannulation of Great Veins 1981; Obstetric Anaesthesia and Analgesia: safer practice 1982; Patient-Controlled Analgesia 1984; Tracheal Intubation 1985; Awareness and Pain in General Anaesthesia 1987. *Recreation:* Family, reading and opera *Clubs:* Royal Society of Medicine *Address:* 45 Hollybush Road, Cardiff CF2 6SZ. Dept. of Anaesthetics, Univ. Hospital of Wales, Cardiff, CF4 4XW.

ROSIER, Air Chief Marshal Sir Frederick Ernest, GCB, CBE, DSO. *Currently:* retired. *Born on* 13 Oct 1915 at Wrexham. *Son of* the late Ernest George and Frances Elizabeth Rosier. *Marriage:* to Hettie Denise (nee Blackwell, 1939. *Children:* Elisabeth, David, Nicholas and John. *Educated at* Grove Park School, Wrexham. *Career:* Commissioned R.A.F. 1935, served World War II in France, UK, Western Desert and Europe; postwar appointments included: O.C. Horsham St. Faith; Exchange duties with U.S.A.F; Group Captain Plans Fighter Cd; Chairman Directors of Plans M.O.D; A.D.C. Middle East Air Force; Senior Air Staff Officer Transport Command; Air Officer C in C Fighter Cd; Deputy C in C Allied Forces Central Europe. A.D.C. to the Queen 1956-58; Air A.D.C. to the Queen 1972-73; After retirement from the R.A.F, 1978, became Air Advisor to B.A.C. 1973-77, and Director, 1977-80, in charge B.A.C., in Saudi Arabia. Commander Order of Orange Nassau and Order of Polania Restituta. *Clubs:* R.A.F, Polish Air Force, Victory Services. *Address:* Ty Haul, Sunbank, Llangollen, Clwyd, LL20 7UH. 286 Latymer Court, London, W6 7LD.

ROWLANDS, Mr Alan Paul, M. A. (Econ) B. Sc. (Econ) MCIT, MBIM, MILDM *Currently:* Coal Business Manager (Wales). *Born on* 12 April 1951 at Caerphilly. *Son of* Alan and Patricia (nee Coughlan). *Marriage:* to Mary Helena Corcoran, 1978. *Children:* Matthew and Peter *Educated at* Caerphilly G.T.S., De La Salle College, Salford; University College, Cardiff; Manchester Univ. *Career:* BR Management Trainee, London/Midland region, 1974; BR Divisional Movements Inspector, Nottingham, 1976; BR Traffic Assistant, Seven Tunnel Junction, 1978; BR Traffic Assistant, Garston, Liverpool, 1979; BR Parcels Salesman, Liverpool, 1980; BR Head of Marketing Development, Parcels Business, Crew, 1982; BR Speedlink Salesman, North Wales & Merseyside, 1983; BR Marketing Manager, Railfreight Chemicals, Liverpool, 1985; BR Railfreight Officer, Construction Industries, BRHQ, London, 1987; BR Marketing Officer, Construction Industries, BRHG, London. 1988; BR Coal Business Manager, Wales, Cardiff, 1989. *Recreation:* Flying, Rugby and reading. *Address:* Trainload Coal, British Railways Board, Brunel House, 2 Fitzalan Road, Cardiff,

CF2 1SA.

ROWLANDS, Mr Gwynn Price, LL. B., Barrister (1985) Solicitor (1976) *Currently:* Barrister in Private Practice (Liverpool and North Wales). *Born on* 18 Jan 1951 at Bangor, Gwynedd. *Son of* Emyr Price and Aileen Mair Rowlands. *Marriage:* to Dr Catherine Elizabeth Jane (nee Evans) 1991. *Educated at* Friars School Bangor; Univ. of Liverpool and London School of Economics (Plus Coll. of Law) *Career:* Solicitor 1976; Partner, Knapp-Fishers, Westminster 1976-80; Partner, D. J. Freeman & Co., London 1980-85; Called to the Bar by Inner Temple 1985; Mbr George Carman Q. C's Chambers, London until 1988; now mbr of R. J. Livesey Q. C's Chambers, Liverpool; Prospective candidate (Cons) for Anglesey/Ynys Mon since 1989. *Recreation:* Public speaking (N. Wales Youth Champion 1969); tennis (N. Wales Junior Champion 1968 and 1969); rugby, cricket, golf and reading. *Address:* Peel House, 5/7 Harrington Street, Liverpool, L2 9QAPN. 49 Bridge Street, Llangefni, Anglesey/ynys Mon, Gwynedd, LL77 7PN.

ROWLANDS, The Reverend Canon John Henry Lewis, MA., M. Litt. *Currently:* Warden of Saint Michael & All Angels' Theological College, Llandaff, Cardiff. Honorary Canon of Llandaff Cathedral. *Born on* 16 Nov 1947 at Carmarthen. *Son of* the late William Lewis and Elizabeth Mary Rowlands (nee Lewis). *Marriage:* to Catryn Meryl Parry Edwards 1976. *Children:* William Parri Llewelyn (b 1977), Sara Kate Llea (b 1979) and Elena Angharad Lisa (b 1981) *Educated at* Queen Elizabeth Grammar School, Carmarthen; Saint David's Univ. Coll., Lampeter; Magdalene College, Cambridge; Univ of Durham; Westcott House, Cambridge. *Career:* Ordained deacon 1972 (St. Peter's, Carmarthen); priest 1973 (St. Davids Cathedral); Curate in the Rectorial Benefice of Aberystwyth 1972-76; Chaplain, St. David's Univ Coll, Lampeter 1976-79; diocesan Youth Chaplain, diocese of St. Davids, 1976-79; Director of Academic Studies, Saint Michael's College, Llandaff, 1979-84; Sub-Warden, 1984-88; Lecturer, Faculty of Theology, Univ. Coll., Cardiff, now University College of Wales, Cardiff), from 1979; Assistant Dean, 1981-83; Diocesan Director of Ordinandsn for the diocese of Llandaff, 1985-88; Examining Chaplain to the Bishop of Saint Davids, 1977-86 and 1991; to the Archbishop of Wales, 1987-91; Member, Working Party of the Council of Churches for Wales Report, 'Towards A Theology of Work', 1979-81; Governing Body of the Church in Wales, 1988- ; Court of the University of Wales, 1988-; Court of the Univ. of Wales Coll of Cardiff, 1988- ; Academic Board of the University of Wales 1991- ; Secretary of the Standing Doctrinal Commission of the Church in Wales, 1986- ; President of Diwinyddiaeth (Guild of Theology Graduates of the University of Wales), 1989-91; Dean of Divinity of the Univ of Wales, 1991- ; Member of Council, Llandaff Cathedral School, 1991-. *Publications:* Editor, Essays on the Kingdom of God (Koda Press, Cardiff, 1986); Church, State and Society, The Attitudes of John Keble, Richard Hurrell Froude and John Henry Newman, 1827-45 (Churchman 1989); Doing Theology, A Study Guide (Hallmark, 1992). Contributor to Diwinyddiaeth, Insight. *Recreation:* Beachcombing, racket games, auctioneering, antique markets, breeding of Siamese sealpoint cats. *Clubs:* Captain Scott. *Address:* The Old Registry, Cardiff Road, Llandaff, Cardiff CF5 2DQ. Saint Michael's College, Llandaff, Cardiff CF5 2YJ.

ROWLANDS, Mr Ken, CEng, MIMinE *Currently:* Director of Refereeing, Welsh Rugby Union. *Born on* 7 June 1936 at Ynysybwl. *Son of* Thomas and Jane. *Marriage:* to Catherine (nee Rees), 1957. *Children:* Haydn Rees, James Huw and Gareth Wyn. *Educated at* Pontypridd Boys' Grammar School; Polytechnic of Wales; Keele University. *Career:* 2 years National Service, Malaya; National Coalboard, Under Manager Trelewis Drift mine; S. Wales Area Engineer, Explosives and Chemical Products; Chief Engineer, U. K. Opencast Coal Explosives; holder of the Royal Humane Society Award; Welsh Rugby Union International Referee 1980-86. *Publications:* The Middleman; The Thirty-First Man. *Recreation:* all sports, reading. *Address:* 24 Crawshaw Street, Ynysybwl, Mid Glam, S. Wales, CF37 3EF. Welsh Rugby Union, Cardiff Arms Park, Cardiff.

RUBENS, Dr. (Honorary) Bernice Ruth, BA, D. Litt (Hon Univ of Wales). *Currently:* Full-time writer. *Born on* 26 July 1928 at Cardiff. *Daughter of* Dorothy Cohen and Eli Rubens. *Marriage:* to Rudi Nassauer (dissolved). *Children:* Sharon and Rebecca. *Educated at* University College, Cardiff. *Career:* Teacher of English and French. Writer/Director Documentary films for T.V., United Nations Sponsorship. *Publications:* Set on Edge; Madame Sousatzka; Mate in Three; The Elected Member (Booker Prize 1970); Sunday Best; I Sent A Letter To My Love; The Ponsonby Post; Go Tell The Lemming; Spring Sonata; A Five Year Sentence; Birds of Passage; Brothers; Mr. Wakefield's Crusade; Our Father; Kingdom Come; A Solitary Grief; Mother Russia. *Recreation:* playing cello. *Address:* 16a Belsize Park Gardens, London, NW3 4LD.

RUMBELOW, Mr (Roger) Martin, B.Sc; M.Sc; C.Eng. *Currently:* Under Secretary, Department of Trade & Industry. *Born on* 3 June 1937 at Cardiff, Wales. *Son of* Leonard Rumbelow and Phyllis (nee Perkins). *Marriage:* to Elizabeth (nee Glover) of Macclesfield, 1965. *Children:* none *Educated at* Cardiff High School; Bristol University; Cranfield Institute of Technology. *Career:* RAF Pilot 1955-57; British Aircraft Corporation 1958-74; Deputy Production Controller 1967-73; Concorde Manufacturing Project Manager 1973-74; DTI 1974- ; Principal 1974-78; Assnt Sec. 1978-86. *Recreation:* Singing, opera, theatre, tennis, computing and electronics. *Clubs:* RAF *Address:* D. T. I., Kingsgate House, 66-74 Victoria Street, London., SW1E 6SW.

RUMBELOW, Howard (Clive), *Currently:* Director, The Law Debenture Corporation plc. *Born on* 13 June 1933 at Cardiff. *Son of* Leonard Douglas Rumbelow and Phyllis Mary Rumbelow (nee Perkins). *Marriage:* to Carolyn Sandra MacGregor, 1968. *Children:* Michael William, Jane Harriet and Helen Clare. *Educated at* Cardiff High; Cambridge University. *Career:* Royal Air Force, Pilot Transport Command, 1951-53; Partner, Slaughter and May, 1968-89. *Recreation:* golf, languages, electronics. *Address:* 79 Princes Way, London, SW19 6HY.

RUSSELL, Lord Hugh Hastings, ARICS *Currently:* Farmer, since 1959. *Born on* 29 March 1923 at Havant, Hants. *Son of* 12th Duke and Duchess of Bedford. *Marriage:* to Rosemary Markby, 1957. *Children:* Mark Hugh and Karen Diana Russell. *Educated at* privately and Christ's College, Cambridge, associate member Royal Institution of Chartered Surveyors. *Career:* General Practice as Chartered Surveyor 1947-59; British Horse Society Horse Trials Committee 1960-85; 12 years Training and Examinations Committee; Chairman, International Selection Committee 1972-76; British Horse Society Steward 1960-85. *Recreation:* fishing, shooting, horse trials, carriage driving. *Address:* The Bell House, Dolau, Llandrindod Wells, Powys, LD1 5UN.

RUTTER, His Hon. Judge John Cleverdon, MA., LL.B. *Currently:* Senior Circuit Judge, 1990- . *Born on* 18 Sept 1919 at Cardiff. *Son of* the late Edgar John Rutter and the late Nellie Rutter (nee Parker). *Marriage:* to Jill McIntosh, 1951. *Children:* Jeremy John Rutter and Philippa Jane James. *Educated at* Cardiff High School; University College of South West, Exeter; Keble College, Oxford. *Career:* Called to Bar, Lincoln's Inn, 1948; Practised Wales & Chester Circuit, 1948-66; Stipendiary Magistrated for City of Cardiff, 1966-71; A legal member Mental Health Review Tribunal for Wales Region, 1960-66; An assistant

Recorder of Cardiff, 1962-66; Merthyr Tydfil, 1962-66; Swansea 1965-66; Deputy Chairman Glamorgan Quarter Sessions, 1969-71; Circuit Judge, 1972-90. *Recreation:* Golf and reading. *Address:* Law Courts, Cardiff CF1 3ND.

RUTTER, Mr Trevor, CBE *Currently:* retired 1991, British Council. *Born on* 26 Jan 1934 at Bournemouth. *Son of* the late Alfred and Agnes Rutter. *Marriage:* to Jo Henson. *Children:* one s Orlando. *Educated at* Monmouth School; Brasenose College, Oxford. *Career:* British Council 1959-66 and 1968-91. Foreign Office, First Secretary 1967; British Council: Assistant Director General 1981-85 and 1990-91; Director for Germany 1986-90; Thailand 1971-75; Singapore 1968-71. various posts in London HQ 1975-85 (incl Head, Home Division), posts in Indonesia, Germany and London 1959-66. *Address:* West House, West Street, Wivenhoe, Essex, CO7 9DE

RYAN, Mr John Michael, *Currently:* Surveyor of Customs and Excise, Newport, Gwent. *Born on* 29 Sept 1939 at Newport, Gwent. *Son of* the late John Ryan and Evelyn Mildred (nee Bull). *Marriage:* to Joan Evelyn Smith, 1967. *Children:* Caroline, Katharine and Michael John. *Educated at* St. Michaels R. C. Junior School; Father Hill Memorial School, Newport; Newport High School; Nottingham University. *Career:* As a player - Welsh Secondary Schools 1958, Newport RFC 1959-61, London Welsh RFC 1961-65, Universities Athletic Union 1960, Middlesex County 1963-65, Civil Service 1961-65; Coach: to Newport HSOB RFC 1970-74, Newport RFC 1974-78 (winners of WRU Cup 1977, runners up 1978, merit table winners 1977), East Wales v Argentina 1976, Cardiff RFC 1979-81 (winners WRU Cup 1981), Wales under 21's 1986-88, Welsh National Coach 1988-90; WRU Coaching Advisory Committee 1976-91; WRU staff coach, WRU National representative 1991- .*Recreation:* all sports, reading, keeping fit. *Clubs:* Newport High School Old Boys. *Address:* 29 Allt-Yr-Yn- Crescent, Newport, Gwent, NP9 5GE.

RYAN, Mr John Patrick, MA, FIA, ACAS, MAAA, FIRM, ASMIA *Currently:* Vice President and Principal, Tillinghast, Consulting Actuary. *Born on* 19 Aug 1943 at Cheshire. *Son of* James Patrick Ryan and Marie Elsie Ryan. *Marriage:* to Verna Marguerite Ryan. *Children:* Nicholas, Annabel and Alastair. *Educated at* St. Mary's College, Rhos-on-Sea, N. Wales; Queens College Cambridge. *Career:* Partner, James Capel Stockbrokers 1968-76. Vice Principal & Principal Tillinghast/Towers Perrin 1976- . Member Council of Institute of Actuaries 1987-91. *Publications:* Appraisal Value of General Insurance Companies (jointly with K. Larner). *Recreation:* travel, golf, racing. *Address:* 15 Priory Gardens, Highgate, London, N6 5QY. The Mill House, Engine Drove, West Row Fen, Mildenhall, Suffolk

RYLEY, Professor Alan, B.Sc., M.Sc., Ph.D., C.Math., CEng., FIMA, MIEE, *Currently:* Head of Department of Mathematics and Computing, Polytechnic of Wales, 1989- *Born on* 9 Oct 1940 at Weybridge. *Son of* Michael and Judy Mary (nee Robinson). *Marriage:* to Hilary Alison (nee Ripley). *Children:* Siobhan and Martin. *Educated at* Lymm Grammar School; Battersea C.A.T; Salford University. *Career:* Engineer, Research Division Marconi Company, 1964-70; Lecturer, Mid Essex Technical College, 1970-72; Senior then Principal Lecturer, Department of Mathematics and Physics, Manchester Polytechnic, 1972-88 *Publications:* Various Journal Publications *Recreation:* Sailing, walking, listening to music. *Clubs:* Sully Sailing Club *Address:* 13 St. Michaels Road, Llandaff, Cardiff, CF5 2ALL.

S

SAGAR, Prof. Geoffrey Roger, CBE; MA; DPhil. *Currently:* Vice-Principal, University College of North Wales and Prof. of Agricultural Botany, University College of North Wales. *Born on* 6 March 1933 at Rishton, Lancs. *Son of* the late Eric Arthur Sagar and the late Phyllis Margaret Sagar (nee Rogers). *Marriage:* to Margaret Ann (nee Beyer), 1955. *Children:* Jill Mary, Stephen John and Ruth Helen. *Educated at* Kirkham G. S; Univ., Oxford. *Career:* National Service, RAF Flying Officer 1954-56; Lecturer 1960-65; Senior Lecturer 1965-77; Professor 1977-; Vice-Principal 1981- ; Deputy Chairman Advisory Committee on Pesticides 1989- ; member, Advisory Committee on Pesticides 1976- ; Independent member, Governing Body Coleg Normal 1992- ; CBE 1990; Editor J. appl Ecol 1979-81. *Publications:* 85 papers in scientific journals. *Recreation:* gardening, books, music. *Clubs:* Farmers. *Address:* Tan-Y-Graig, Llandegfan, Menai Bridge, Gwynedd, LL59 5PL.

SAINSBURY, Mr Edward Hardwicke, *Currently:* Solicitor and Partner, Dawson Hart & Co., Uckfield, since 1963; District Notary Public, Uckfield, since 1965. *Born on* 17 Sept 1912 *Elder son of* of Henry Morgan Sainsbury, and g s of C. Hardwicke. *Marriage:* to Ann 1946. *Children:* Timothy Hardwicke Sainsbury and Mrs Catherine Annhnson-Hill. *Educated at* Cardiff High School; University of S. Wales and Monmouth. *Career:* Solicitor in private practice, 1935; commissioned (TA) 1936; Prosecuting Solicitor, Cardiff 1938; Sen. Pros. Solicitor 1939; Served War of 1939-45; Adjutant, 77th HAA Regt, 1940; comd 240 HAA Battery Gibraltar 1944; demobilised Nov. 1945, Hong Kong: Asst. Crown Solicitor, 1946; commissioner for revision of the laws of Hong Kong 1947, magistrate 1948; registrar, High Court 1949; sen. magistrate Kowloon 1951; Barrister, Inner Temple 1951; Land Officer and crown counsel, Hong Kong 1952; legal draftsman, Nigeria, 1953; Principal Legal Draftsman, Fed of Nigeria 1958; President, Commonwealth Parliamentary Assoc., Southern Cameroons 1959-63; Judge, High Court of Lagos 1960-63 and of Southern Cameroons 1961-63 Speaker, House of Assembly, 1958-63, Chm., Public Service Commn, 1961-63, Southern Cameroons). *Publications:* (jointly) Revised Laws of Hong Kong 1948. *Recreation:* squash (a memory) golf. *Address:* Little Gassons, Fairwarp, Uckfield, East Sussex, TN22 3BG.

SAINSBURY, Councillor Jeffrey Paul, FCA *Currently:* Partner, Pannell Kerr Forster, Chartered Accountants. *Born on* 27 June 1943 at Cardiff. *Son of* Walter Ronald and Joan Margaret Sainsbury (nee Slamin). *Marriage:* to Janet Elizabeth (nee Hughes), 1967. *Children:* Mark and Emma. *Educated at* Cardiff H.S. *Career:* Member, Cardiff City Council, since 1969; Deputy Lord Mayor 1977-78; Lord Mayor 1991-92; Member Board of Cardiff Bay Development Corporation 1991- ; Trustee South Glamorgan Community Foundation; Trustee Bobath Cymru; Leader City Council Conservative Group. *Recreation:* Theatre, music, sport, cookery. *Clubs:* Cardiff and County *Address:* 34 Heol Iscoed, Rhiwbina, Cardiff, CF4 6PA. 18 Park Place, Cardiff, CF1 3PD.

SALAMAN, Professor John Redcliffe, MChir, FRCS.

Currently: Consultant Surgeon and Professor of Transplant Surgery, South Glamorgan Health Authority and University of Wales College of Medicine. *Born on* 14 Oct 1937 at Wenden, Essex. *Son of* the late Dr Arthur G Salaman and Mrs Nancy A Salaman. *Marriage:* to Dr Patricia Burkett, 1961. *Children:* Robert, Janet, Mary and Paul. *Educated at* Bedales School; Cambridge University; London Hospital. *Career:* House Officer at the London Hospital 1963-64; Surgical Trainee at Adenbrooke's Hospital, Cambridge 1964-68; Research Assistant to Professor R Y Calne at Cambridge 1968-69; Lecturer in Surgery at the London Hospital 1969-70; Consultant Surgeon and Senior Lecturer in Surgery, Cardiff 1970- , Reader in Transplant Surgery 1977. Professor of Transplant Surgery 1983. *Publications:* more than 150 publications on Transplantation, 3 books on Transplantation and General Surgery. *Recreation:* Silversmithing and cabinet making, sailing and cruising (summer), cross country skiing (winter). *Address:* 25 Heol Don, Whitchurch, Cardiff, CF4 2AR. Department of Surgery, Cardiff Royal Infirmary, Newport Road, Cardiff, CF2 1SZ Tel: 0222 492233.

SALISBURY, Mark Pryce, LL.B (Hons). *Currently:* Solicitor in private practice, Senior Partner in firm of Galmins Solicitors Llandudno. *Born on* 15 Oct 1955 at Hawarden, Clwyd. *Son of* Andrew Salisbury and Iris Helen Salisbury (nee Roberts). *Marriage:* to Christine Anne Morris, 1981. *Children:* Adam (b. 1986) and Emma (b. 1991). *Educated at* Caernarfon Grammar School; Liverpool University. *Recreation:* shooting, sailing, golf. *Clubs:* Maesdu Golf, Llandudno. *Address:* Bryn Teg, 23 Vicarage Road, Llandudno, Gwynedd, LL30 1PT. Gamlins Solicitors, 14/15 Trinity Square, Llandudno, Gwynedd, LL30 2RB

SALTER, Mr Michael Anthony John, FCA *Currently:* Managing Director Crown Brewery plc, since 1990; Managing Director Buckleys Properties Ltd., since 1990. *Born on* 21 May 1943 at Harrow on the Hill. *Son of* James Joseph Salter and Grace Elizabeth Salter. *Marriage:* to Mary Elizabeth Feeny, 1968. *Children:* Mark Andrew (b. 1969), Helen Jane (b. 1971) and Jennifer Ann (b. 1974). *Educated at* Malvern College. *Career:* Chief Financial Executive Nashua Corporation (UK) 1977-79; Fin. Controller, subsequently Financial Director and Company Secretary, Coral Racing Ltd., 1979-85; Financial Director Bass Wales & West Ltd., 1985-89; Director Welsh Brewers Ltd; Managing Director, Bass & Welsh Brewers Inns., 1989-90; Managing Director Charrington Inns, 1990- . Chairman, Lisvane T. C; Chairman, Diversions Dance Co; Chairman, ABSA Wales. *Recreation:* tennis, music, opera. *Clubs:* Rugby, of London. *Address:* 6 The Paddock, Lisvane, Cardiff, CF4 5UE.

SAMPLES, Mr Reginald McCartney, CMG., DSO., OBE., B. Com. *Currently:* Retired, British Diplomatic Service. Volunteer work recording books for blind (CNIB); Director Canadian-Scottish Philharmonic Foundation. *Born on* 11 Aug 1918 at Liverpool. *Son of* Jessie and William Samples. *Marriage:* to Elsie R. Hide 1947. *Children:* Murcia Valentine Mears (step-daughter), Graeme McCartney and William Paul McCartney. *Educated at* Rhyl County School; Liverpool University. *Career:* RNVR

(Fleet Air Arm) Lieut (A) 1940-46, shot down and wounded Feb. 1942 in torpedo action against German battleships Scharnhorst and Gneisenau in Channel; DSO; C. O. I. Economic Editor, Overseas Newspapers 1946-48; British Diplomatic Services 1948-78; Bombay 1948-52; New Delhi 1952-56; Counsellor, Information, UK High Commission, Karachi, Pakistan 1956-59; Counsellor, Information, UK HC Ottawa 1959-65; CounsellorsInformation, UK. HC. New Delhi, India 1965-68; Assistant Under Sec. of State 1968-69; CRO, Senior Trade Commission, then British Consul-General, Toronto, Canada 1969-78; In 1978 joined Royal Ontario Museum, Toronto, as Director of Development, then Assistant Director. *Recreation:* Watching Ballet, music, tennis, volunteer recording for the blind. *Clubs:* Naval (London), Queens (Toronto). *Address:* 44 Jackes Ave # 1105, Toronto, Canada, M4T 1E5.

SAMUEL, Mr David Byron, J.P., CEng., M.I.E.E. *Currently:* Operations Director, South Wales Electricity PLC. *Born on* 8 March 1934 at Llanelli. *Son of* the late David Benjamin and Mary Anne. *Marriage:* to Gwyneth, 1957. *Children:* Lisa Jayne Samuel *Educated at* Llanelli Grammar School; Swansea Technical College. *Career:* Electrical Engineer, SWEB, Llanelli, 1959; Electrical Engineer, SWEB, Bridgend, 1967; Commercial Manager, Carmarthen SWEB, 1975; Commercial Manager, Swansea SWEB, 1977; Deputy Chief Commercial Officer, St. Mellons, SWEB, 1980; District Manager, Swansea SWEB, 1983; Commercial Director, St. Mellons SWEB, 1988. *Recreation:* Golf, rugby and theatre *Clubs:* Cardiff Business Club *Address:* 8 Harries Avenue, Llanelli, Dyfed, SA15 3LF. 4 Marlborough Terrace, Cardiff CF1 3DW.

SANDERS, Dr Eric, BSc, FRCP *Currently:* Consultant Physician, West Wales Hospital. *Born on* 22 Oct 1946 at Bishop Auckland. *Son of* Albert Sanders and Caroline (nee Johnson). *Marriage:* to Dianne Marilyn (nee Thomas). *Children:* Gareth Wyn, Gethyn Huw, Angharad Jane. *Educated at* Grammar School, Stanley, Co. Durham; Welsh National School of Medicine. *Career:* House Physician, Registrar, Lecturer-Institute of Renal Disease, Cardiff Royal Infirmary 1971-81. Trustee Kidney Research Unit for Wales Foundation 1985; Medical Director West Wales Dialysis Centre 1985. Postgrad Tutor, West Wales Hospital 1983-89; Tutor, Royal College of Physicians 1986-91; President, Lions Club of Carmarthen 1987. *Publications:* Clinical Atlas of the Kidney; Slide Atlas of the Kidney. *Recreation:* music, theatre. *Address:* Dunelm, Ael Y Bryn, Carmarthen, Dyfed, SA31 2HB. West Wales Hospital, Carmarthen, Dyfed, SA31 2AF. Tel: 0267 235151.

SANDERSON, Dr John Elsby, MA, MD, FRCP *Currently:* Consultant physician and cardiologist since 1983; University clinical tutor, University of Bristol. *Born on* 1 May 1949 at Kirkuk. *Son of* Arthur John Sanderson and Ruth Megan (nee Griffiths). *Marriage:* to Dr. Julia Billingham, 1980. *Children:* Vanessa and Henry. *Educated at* Llandaff Cathedral School; Blundells School; Cambridge University; St. Bartholomews Hospital, London. *Career:* House physician and Home surgeon, St. Bartholomews Hospital 1973-74; House physician and Home surgeon Brompton Hospital, London 1974; House physician, Home surgeon and Registrar Hammersmith Hospital, London 1975-78; University lecturer in Cardiovascular medicine, University of Oxford 1978-81; Wellcome Tropical lecturer St. Mary's Hospital London and University of Nairobi 1981-83. *Publications:* 45 publications on various cardiological and medical subjects. *Recreation:* music (playing the violin), tennis, reading novels. *Clubs:* Presidents. *Address:* Oaks House, Hatch Beauchamp, Taunton, Somerset, TA3 6TH. Taunton & Somerset Hospital, Musgrove Park, Taunton. TA1 5DA.

SAUNDERS, Mr Peter, BSc, FInstD. *Currently:* Chairman & Managing Director, Holgates Ltd, since 1976, acquired by Rowntree in 1983; Rowntree was acquired by Nestle in 1988; Chairman, The Original Welsh Pantry Company Ltd;

Board Member, Development Board for Rural Wales. *Born on* 10 April 1951 at Sale, Cheshire. *Son of* Thomas Saunders and the late Mary (nee Smith). *Marriage:* to Judith Margaret George of Clydach, 1972. *Children:* Richard, Paul and Nigel. *Educated at* Sale Grammar School 1962-69; Polytechnic of Wales 1969-73. *Career:* BP 1969-75; Holgates Honey Farm, 1975-76. *Recreation:* long distance running. *Address:* Holgates Ltd, Tywyn, Gwynedd, LL36 9LW.

SCHOFIELD, Mr Peter, MA (Cantab). *Currently:* Vice-President Eurosite. *Born on* 4 July 1933 at Leeds. *Son of* D.H. Schofield and Betty Wynne Parry. *Marriage:* to Jacqueline Mary Boocock 1957. *Children:* Richard, Deborah, Sally and Emma. *Educated at* King Edward School, Lytham; Emmanuel College, Cambridge. *Career:* Recently retired from Countryside Council for Wales, Administration and Resources Director. Royal Air Force. Imperial Chemical Industries. Nature Conservancy, Bangor; Regional Officer, South, Nature Conservancy Council, RSPB Committee for Wales; Council Cheshire Conservation Trust; President Cambrian Ornithological Society; Council Bardsey Island Trust; Member OECD Environmental Mission to Finland; Churchill Fellow 1991. *Publications:* Exploring Woods; British Birds; contributions to several books on British Countryside; a number of papers in journals, inc. Puffins on St. Kilda 1972; The Birds of The Monarch Isles 1977. *Recreation:* Ornithology, painting, Islands, Eastern Europe. *Address:* Llwyn Onn, Tal-y-Bonte, Bangorirfechan, Gwynedd, LL57 3YH.

SCHUTZ, Professor Bernard Frederick, PhD, FInstP, CPhys, FRAS. *Currently:* Professor of Physics & Astronomy, University of Wales College of Cardiff, since 1984. *Born on* 11 Aug 1946 at Paterson, NJ, USA. *Son of* Bernard F. Schutz and Virginia M. Schutz (nee Lefebure). *Marriage:* to Sian Lynette (nee Pouncy), 1983. *Children:* Rachel Grace, Catherine Virginia and Annalie Eileen. *Educated at* Bethpage High School, NY; Clarkson College, NY, BSc(1967); California Inst. of Technology, Pasadena, Calif, PhD(1972). *Career:* National Science Found. Res. Fellow, Cambridge UK 1971-72; Postdoctoral Research Asst., Yale University 1972-74; Lecturer, University College Cardiff 1974-76; Reader University College Cardiff 1976-84. *Publications:* 3 books: Geometrical Methods of Mathematical Physics, (Cambridge Univ. Press 1980); A First Course in General Relativity, (Cambridge Univ. Press 1985); Gravitational Wave Data Analysis, (Kluner 1989); more than 60 articles. *Recreation:* choral singing, skiing. *Clubs:* Icosahedron *Address:* Dept of Physics & Astronomy, University of Wales College of Cardiff, P.O. Box 913, Cardiff, CF1 3TH. Tel: 0222 874203.

SEABROOK, Mr Graeme, *Currently:* Managing Director and Chief Executive Kwik Save Group PLC, appointed 1989. *Born on* 1 May 1939 at Australia. *Son of* Mr Norman Seabrook and Mrs Amy Winifred Seabrook. *Marriage:* to Lorraine Ellen (nee Ludlow) 1967. *Children:* Kym and Mark. *Educated at* Australia, plus Advanced Management Program Harvard Business School. *Career:* Employment with G. J. Coles & Coy Limited, 1955, in Australia (later Coles Myer Ltd); Appointed Chief General Manager of G. J. Coles 1982; prior to acquisition of Myer in 1985; Managing Director of Discount Stores Group 1985; Appointed one of two joint Managing Directors of Coles Myer Ltd., 1987; Resignation from Coles Myer Ltd., 1988; Joined Dairy Farm International Hong Kong and immediately seconded to Kwik Save Group plc as Managing Director 1988. *Recreation:* Tennis *Address:* Warren Drive, Prestatyn, Clwyd, LL19 7HU.

SEAGER, Gerald Elliot, *Born on* 29 June 1924 at Cardiff, Wales. *Son of* the late Capt. John Elliot, MC (d. 1955), and the late Dorothy Irene Seager (nee Jones), (d. 1986). *Marriage:* to Margaret Elizabeth, 1948, (d. 1988), da of William Jones Morgan (d. 1971), of Aberbran Fawr, Brecon. *Educated at* Charterhouse. *Career:* WWII Lt Welsh Guards

1943-46, served Italy, POW 1944; dir: Stalco Aden 1966-67, Newport Stevedoring Co Ltd and Newport Screw Towing Co Ltd 1967-69, Cory Bros Shipping Ltd 1968-77, Stephenson Clarke Shipping Ltd 1970-77, Newport Stevedoring Co Ltd 1970-77, Transcontinental Air Ltd, Powell Duffryn Shipping Services Ltd 1976-77; chief exec: Rais Hassan Saadi & Co Dubai (UAE) 1977-78, Rais Shipping Co Dubai (UAE) 1977-78; dir Thabet Int Ltd 1987- (chief exec 1978-86); vice chairman Aden Shipping Conf 1967, life govr Royal Hosp and Home for Incurables Putney 1967; chm: Newport Shipowners Assoc 1972-77, Newport Harbour Cmmrs 1974-75, S Wales Coal Exporters Assoc 1970-71; memb Baltic Exchange 1964. *Recreation:* antiques, football, Welsh affairs. *Address:* Rudhall Barns, Rudhall, Ross-On-Wye, Hereford, HR9 7TL. Casa De La Paz, 9 Baladrar, Buzon 18, E03720 Benissa, Alicante, Spain.

SEAGER, Lord Leighton of St. Mellons, John Leighton, *Currently:* Retired. *Born on* 11 Jan 1922 at Cardiff. *Son of* Marjorie and the late Leighton. *Marriage:* to Ruth Hopwood (second). *Children:* Robert, Simon, Carole. *Educated at* Leys School Cambridge. *Career:* Past Director W. H. Seager & Co. Ltd; Past Chairman Bristol Channel Shipowners; Past Director Principality Building Society; Chairman Willie Seager Memorial Trust; Director Watkin Williams & Co. *Recreation:* Photography, gardening. *Address:* 346 Caerphilly Road, Birchgrove, Cardiff, CF4 4NT.

SECOMBE, Sir Harry Donald, CBE *Currently:* Entertainer. Since October 1984 he has presented the networked Tyne Tees TV programme 'Highway'. *Born on* 8 Sept. 1921 at Swansea. *Son of* Frederick (Ernest) Secombe and (Nellie Jane) Gladys Davies. *Marriage:* to Myra Joan Atherton in Swansea 1948. *Children:* Jennifer, Andrew, David and Katherine. *Educated at* Dynevor School, Swansea. *Career:* After serving in the Royal Artillery during World War II he was demobbed in 1946 and auditioned for The Windmill Theatre, London. BBC radio work followed, notably 'The Goon Show', special performance for 50th Anniversary of BBC, 1972; starred in the West End in the musicals 'Pickwick' (which also toured the USA), and 'The Four Musketeers' and the satirical play 'The Plumber's Progress'; films include 'Oliver' and 'Song of Norway'. *Publications:* Twice Brightly 1974; Goon for Lunch 1975; Katy & the Nurgla 1978; Welsh Fargo 1981; Goon Abroad 1982; The Harry Secombe Diet Book 1983; Harry Secombe's Highway 1984; The Highway Companion 1987; Arias & Raspberries (autobiog) 1989; The Nurgla's Magic Tear, 1991. *Recreation:* Photography, golf, cricket. *Clubs:* Savage, Royal Automobile, Lord's Taverners, Variety Club of Great Britain, (founder member). *Address:* 46 St. James's Place, London, SW1.

SENIOR, Dr Michael, DL; PhD. *Born on* 14 April 1940 at Llandudno. *Son of* the late Geoffrey Senior and the late Julia (nee Cotterell). *Educated at* Uppingham; Open University. *Career:* Writer. *Publications:* Play: The Coffee Table, BBC Third Programme. Canadian B. C. New Zealand B. C. Stage production: Toronto Playhouse. Books: Portrait of North Wales, 1973; Portrait of South Wales, 1974; Greece and Its Myths, 1978; Myths of Britain, 1979; Sir Thomas Malory's Tales of King Arthur, 1980; The Age of Myth and Legend in Heroes and Heroines, 1980; The Life and Times of Richard II, 1981; Who's Who in Mythology, 1985. Poetry: Anglo-Welsh Review, BBC, Tribune; Anthologised: New Poetry 2. The Green Horse. Articles: Folklore. The Ecologist; local papers. Local history booklets etc: paperback ed. Portrait of North Wales, 1987; Bartholomew's pictorial map, North Wales, 1979; Conwy, The Town's Story, 1977; Caernarfon, The Town's Story, 1982; The Conwy Valley, Its long history, 1984; Llandudno's Story, 1986; Anglesey, The Island's Story, 1987; Harlech and Lleyn, The history of south-west Gwynedd!, 1988;

Disputed Border - the history of the North Wales Marches from Chester to Shrewsbury, 1989; The Story of the Dee in Wales - from Bala to Llangollen, 1990; The Crossing of the Conwy, and its role in the story of North Wales, 1991. *Recreation:* painting, hill walking, croquet. *Clubs: Address:* Bryn Eisteddfod, Glan Conwy, Colwyn Bay, N. Wales, LL28 5LF. C/o David Higham Associates, 5-8 Lower John Street, London, W1R 4HA.

SETTERFIELD, County Councillor Edward George, *Currently:* retired 1984. Now Town, District and County Councillor "IND". *Born on* 27 March 1941 at Milford Haven. *Son of* George Frederick William Setterfield and Phyllis Gwendolain (nee Roach). *Educated at* Milford Haven schools. *Career:* with late father ran one of Pembrokeshires best private car hire and contract hire firms to Esso, Gulf, power station etc; father started business in 1948. Then went into Public Service, elected to Milford Town and Preceli District Councils which I still remain on. *Recreation:* sailing, motor boating, fishing, swimming. *Clubs:* Pembrokeshire Yacht. *Address:* High View, Cromwell Road, Milford Haven, SA73 2EG.

SEYS-LLEWELLYN, His Honour Judge John Desmond, MA; JP. *Born on* 3 May 1912 at Cardiff. *Son of* Charles Ernest Llewellyn, FAI and Hannah Margaretta Llewellyn of Cardiff. *Marriage:* 1st to Elaine, 1939 (d 1984), d of H. Leonard Porcher, solicitor and Mrs Hilda Porcher, JP of Pontyprdd, 2nd to Mrs Joan Banfield James, 1986, d of R. H. Cumming JP, of Plymouth. *Children:* three s from 1st marriage. *Educated at* Cardiff High School; Jesus College, Oxford; Exhibitioner, MA. *Career:* Joined Inner Temple 1936; War Service, RTR 1940-46 (Captain); Called to Bar, Inner Temple, in Absentia OAS, 1945; Profumo Prizeman, 1947; practised on Wales and Chester Circuit 1947-71; a Circuit Judge 1971-85; Local Insurance Appeal Tribunal 1958-71; Dep. Chm., Cheshire QS 1968-71; joined Gray's Inn, ad eundem, same day as youngest son 1967. Contested Chester Constituency (L), 1955 and 1956. *Recreation:* languages, travel, archaeology, art galleries, music, swimming, English Setter. *Clubs:* Athenaeum (Liverpool). *Address:* Little Chetwyn, Gresford, Clwyd., LL12 8RT. Tel: 0978 852419.

SHANNON, Professor Richard Thomas, MA, PhD. *Currently:* Professor of Modern History, University College of Swansea, since 1979. *Born on* 10 June 1931 at Fiji Islands. *Son of* Edward Arthur Shannon and Grace (nee McLeod). *Educated at* M. T. Albert Grammar School, Auckland, N. Z; University of Auckland; Caius Coll., Cambridge. *Career:* Lecturer in History, University of Auckland, 1955-57, 1960-62; Lecturer and Reader in History, University of East Anglia, 1963-79; Visiting Fellow, Peterhouse, Cambridge, 1988-89. *Publications:* Gladstone and The Bulgarian Agitation 1876, 1963; The Crisis of Imperialism, 1974; Gladstone, 1809-1865, 1982; articles and reviews. *Recreation:* books, gardens, wine, travel. *Clubs:* Athenaeum. *Address:* Dept. of History, University College Of Swansea, Swansea, SA2 8PP.

SHELLEY, Mr Charles William Evans, M. A. (Cantab) Barrister at Law *Currently:* Retired Charity Commissioner. *Born on* 15 Aug 1912 at London. *Son of* George Shelley and Frances Mary Anne (nee Dain). *Marriage:* to Patricia May Dolby, 1939. *Children:* Anne, Moyra Helen (d 1954), Elizabeth Jane and Monica Patricia. *Educated at* Alleyn's School, Dulwich, Fitzwilliam House, Cambridge. *Career:* Called to Bar, Inner Temple, 1937; Served in Army during war, first RAPC, later Department of Judge Advocate - General, rank Major; Joined Charity Commission in 1947 as Legal Assistant; Senior Legal Assistant, 1958; Deputy Commissioner, 1964; Commissioner, 1968. *Recreation:* Literature, music and mountaineering. *Address:* Pen y Bryn, Llansilin, Oswestry, Shropshire, SY10 7QG.

SHEPHERD, Professor Emeritus Michael, CBE(1989), MA, DM, FRCP, FRCPsych (Hon). *Currently:* Editor,

'Psychological Medicine' (Cambridge University Press). *Born on* 30 July 1923 at Bournemouth. *Son of* Solomon Shepherd and Cecilia (nee Wayne). *Marriage:* to Margaret Helen Rock, 1947. *Children:* two d Catherine and Lucy; two s Simon and Daniel. *Educated at* Cardiff High School for Boys; University of Wales; Oxford University. *Career:* Training posts in medicine and psychiatry 1946-52; military service, R. A. F., 1952-54; Nuffield postgraduate fellowship (Johns Hopkins' University), 1955-56; senior lecturer and reader in psychiatry, Institute of Psychiatry, University of London, 1956-67; professor of epidemiological psychiatry, Institute of Psychiatry, 1967-88. *Publications:* Circa 30 books and 200 scientific papers on various aspects of psychological medicine. *Recreation:* literature, walking, travel, music. *Clubs:* Athenaeum. *Address:* 73 Alleyn Park, London, SE21 8AT. Tel: 081 670 0718.

SHERIDAN, Dr Lionel Astor, LLB, Barrister at Law, PhD, LLD(Hon), LLD. *Currently:* retired. *Born on* 21 July 1927 at Croydon. *Son of* the late Stanley Frederic Sheridan and the late Anne Agnes (nee Quednau). *Marriage:* to Margaret Helen Beghin, 1948. *Children:* Linda Anne (deceased) and Peter Louis. *Educated at* Whitgift School; London University, Fellow of University College, London 1979; Queen's University of Belfast. *Career:* Part-time lecturer, Nottingham University 1949; lecturer, Queen's Univ. of Belfast 1949-56; Professor of Law, University of Malaya, Singapore 1956-63; Professor of Comparative Law, Queen's Univ. of Belfast 1963-71; Professor of Law, University College, Cardiff 1971-88; Acting Principal, Univ. Coll., Cardiff 1980 and 1987. *Publications:* many, many books and articles on law. *Recreation:* theatre, reading, travel. *Clubs:* Athenaeum. *Address:* Cherry Trees, Broadway Green, St. Nicholas, S. Glamorgan, CF5 6SR.

SHORT, Christopher Albert, LL.B. (Honours), London. *Currently:* Solicitor and Managing Director: Cromford Properties Ltd. *Born on* 15 April 1947 at Derby, England. *Son of* Helen May Short (nee Jones) and Albert Edgar Short. *Marriage:* to Cherry Rose Pamelia Lewis. 1987. *Children:* Oliver Edgar Short and Soyinka Harris Joshua. *Educated at* Bemrose Grammar School, Derby; Univ. of Wales Institute of Science and Technology; Univiversity College, London and the Institute of Advanced Legal Studies. *Career:* Qualified as Solicitor 1972; Partner at Brian Thompson and Partners, Solicitors 1974-83; sole Practitioner and Principal, Christopher Short Solicitors, 1983-date; Parliamentary Candidate (Labour) Monmouth 1983 General Election; Parliamentary Candidate (Labour) Hereford, Worcester and West Gloucestershire, 1989 European Election; Labour Councillor, Vale of Glamorgan Borough Council 1987 to date; Chairman of Finance and Policy Committee, 1991; Served in RAAF; Former Chairman Stonham Housing Association (South Glamorgan) and Treasurer and Vice President of Cardiff Trades Union Council; Treasurer Miners Support Fund, South Glamorgan 1984-85; Chairman Conference and Elections Committee National Council for Civil Liberties 1981-82; and former Governor South Glamorgan Institute of Higher Education and Chairman Trade Union Studies Unit, Llandaff; Chairman of Wales Anti-Apartheid Movement 1981-89; Chairman of Friends of the Earth Cymru 1991. *Recreation:* Shooting, Cycling, Fine Art and Politics. *Clubs:* United Services Mess, Cardiff; West End Labour Club, Barry. *Address:* 56 Redbrink Cres., Jackson's Bay, Barry Island, Barry, CF6 8TU. 3rd Floor, Usdaw Building, 42 Charles Street, Cardiff, CF1 4EE. Tel: 0446 742402.

SHUTE, Mr Kenneth, MB; BS; MS; FRCS. *Currently:* Consultant Surgeon (General and Vascular), Royal Gwent Hospital, Newport, Gwent. *Born on* 22 Dec 1945 at Pontypool, Gwent. *Son of* Stanley and Elizabeth Shute. *Marriage:* to Jennifer Catherine (nee Burchfield), 1975. *Children:* Daniel (b. 1980) and Susannah (b. 1982).

Educated at Jones West Mon School, Pontypool; St. Thomas' Hospital Medical School, London. *Recreation:* squash, skiing, rugby. *Clubs:* Patron, Pontypool Rugby Club. *Address:* Llangybi House, Llangybi, Usk, Gwent, NP5 1NP.

SHUTTE, Gaynor, BA. Hons. *Currently:* Editor, Radio Wales. *Born on* 18 Oct 1951 at Warwickshire. *Daughter of* David Emlyn Jones and Leah Jones. *Educated at* Hodge Hill Girls Grammar School; Univ. of East Anglia. *Career:* Floor Manager, BBC Norwich; Researcher continuing Education; Writer/presenter Radio 4 Presentation; Producer - Features, Arts Radio; Editor Radio 5. *Recreation:* Tennis, walking, reading and anything French! *Address:* B. B. C. Broadcasting House, Llantrisant Road, Llandaff, Cardiff, CF5 2YQ.

SIBERRY, Mr John William Morgan, *Currently:* Retired. *Born on* 26 Feb 1913. *Son of* the late John William and Martha (nee Morgan) Siberry. *Marriage:* to Florence Jane Davies, 1949. *Children:* one s one d. *Educated at* Porth County School, Rhondda; Univ. Coll. Cardiff. *Career:* Entered Civil Service as Asst Principal, Unemployment Assistance Board (later Nat. Assistance Board), 1935; Principal 1941; Asst. Sec., 1947; transferred to Min. of Housing and Local Govt as Under-sec., 1963 Welsh Secretary, Welsh Office and Office for Wales of the Ministry of Housing and Local Goverment 1963-64; Under-Secretary, Welsh office, 1964-73; Secretary to Local Government Staff Commission for Wales, and NHS Staff Commission for Wales, 1973-75; Chm., Working Party on Fourth Television Service in Wales, 1975. *Recreation:* golf. *Clubs:* Cardiff and County. *Address:* Northgates, Pwllmelin Road, Llandaff, Cardiff, CF5 2NG. Tel: 0222 564666.

SIBLEY, Edward, LL.B. *Currently:* Solicitor in private practice. *Born on* 21 July 1935 at Rhymney, Gwent. *Son of* the late William Sibley and the late Myfanwy Williams. *Marriage:* to Sonia Beynon, 1957. *Children:* Deborah Jane, Stephen and Neil Edward. *Educated at* Rhymney Grammar School; University College of Wales, Aberystwyth; College of Law, Lancaster Gate. *Career:* First Class Honours Degree (LL. B), 1961; Qualified as Solicitor (Second Class Honours), 1965; Partner in Berwin Leighton, Solicitors, 1968. Member International Bar Association, 1980; member Litigation sub-committee of City of London Solicitors Company 1982; member National Committee of Union International Des Avocats; member New York State Bar and American Bar Association 1985. *Publications:* 1992 and Beyond. *Recreation:* opera, theatre, literature, golf, skiing, running. *Clubs:* Reform. *Address:* The Outer Lodge, Beach Hill Park, Waltham Abbey, Essex, EN9 3QL. Flat 511 Butler's Wharf, 36 Shad Thames, London, SE1 2YE

SILVER, Max Joseph, BSc(Hons); CEng; FIEE; FIERE; FIProdE; FSCA; FBIM. *Currently:* Acquisitions and Mergers Consultant, since 1980. *Born on* 14 April 1925 at Cardiff. *Son of* the late Benjamin Silver and the late Rose Silver (nee Spira). *Marriage:* 1964. *Children:* one d, Rochelle and one s, Jonathan. *Educated at* City of Cardiff High School; Univ. of Wales (BSc); Croydon 'Poly (DipTelecoms). *Career:* Electronics Research work GEC Wembley 1947-50; Research & Production Management with Assoc. Co. of GEC on airborne defence projects 1950-59, with Elliot Automation & Associated Automation Ltd., (later part of GEC) 1960-70; "Co. Doctor", Philips Group & Pye of Cambridge 1971-80; Adviser on Education Ctee, Brent Council, Vice-Chairman Governors, Kilburn Poly 1982-86. *Recreation:* Reading, gardening, travel, interior design. *Address:* 34 Pangbourne Drive, Stanmore, Middx, HA7 4QT.

SILVERMAN, Professor Hugh Richard, MSc; Dip.Arch; ARIBA; FRSA. *Currently:* Professor of Architecture in the University of Wales and Head of the Welsh School of

Architecture since 1986. *Born on* 23 Sept 1940 at Brighton, Sussex. *Marriage:* to Kay Aase (nee Sonderskov Madsen) 1963. *Children:* Jennifer and Sophie. *Educated at* University of Edinburgh. *Career:* Lecturer/Senior lecturer, University of Bristol 1971-82; Director, Alex Franch Partnership, Architects, Bristol 1982-86; Board Member, Cardiff Bay Development Corporation 1990- ; Chairman, CBDC Design and Architecture Review Panel; Member RIBA Visiting Board 1991- . *Publications:* Building: 1, Bridewell St, Bristol. *Recreation:* Opera, walking. *Address:* Welsh School of Architecture, Bute Buildings, King Edward VII Avenue, Cardiff, CF1 3AP

SIMON, Mr Robin John Hughes, MA *Currently:* Editor, Apollo, since 1990; Art Critic, Daily Mail since 1990. *Born on* 23 July 1947 at Llandaff. *Son of* the late Most Revd Dr William Glyn Hughes Simon, Archbishop of Wales and the late Sarah Sheila Ellen. *Marriage:* 1st to Margaret (nee Brooke), 1971; 2nd to Joanna (nee Ross 1979.) *Children:* Benet Glyn Hughes (b. 1974), Alice Emily Hughes (b. 1976) and Poppy Candida Hughes (b. 1991). *Educated at* Cardiff HS; University of Exeter (BA; Courtauld Institute of Art (MA). *Career:* Lecturer in History of Art and in English Lit., Univ. of Nottingham 1972-78; Delmas Foundation Fellow, Venice, Autumn 1978; Historic Buildings Representative, National Trust 1979-80; Director, Institute of European Studies, London 1980-90; Arts Correspondent, Daily Mail 1987-90; visiting Professor in the History of Art and Architecture, Westminster College, Fulton, Missouri 1989. *Publications:* Books: The Art of Cricket (with Alastair Smart), 1983; The Portrait in Britain and America, 1987; Scholarly articles and journalism in various journals, newspapers and magazines. *Recreation:* cricket (captain, Poor Fred's XI), music. *Clubs:* Athenaeum, Academy. *Address:* Apollo, 3 St James's Place, London, SW1A 1NP. Tel: 071 629 4331

SIMPSON, The Very Reverend John Arthur, M. A. *Currently:* Dean of Canterbury since 1986. *Born on* 7 June 1933 at Cardiff. *Son of* the late Arthur Simpson and the late Mary Esther (nee Price). *Marriage:* to Ruth Marian (nee Dibbens), 1968. *Children:* Rebecca (b. 1970), Damian (b. 1972) and Helen (b. 1974). *Educated at* Cathays High School, Cardiff; Keble College, Oxford; Clifton Theological College. *Career:* Curate: Leyton 1958-59, Christ Church Orpington 1959-62; Tutor, Oak Hill College, London 1962-72; Vicar of Ridge, Herts 1972-79; Director of Ordinands and Post Ordination Training, Diocese of St. Albans 1975-81; Honorary Canon, St. Albans Cathedral 1977-79; Residentiary Canon, St.Albans and Priest-in-Charge of Ridge 1979-81; Archdeacon of Canterbury and Residentiary Canon of Canterbury Cathedral 1981-86. *Recreation:* travel, theatre, opera. *Clubs:* Athenaeum. *Address:* The Deanery, Canterbury, Kent, CT1 2EP. Cathedral House, 11 The Precincts, Canterbury, Kent, CT1 2EH

SIMPSON, Professor John Harold, BA (Oxon), PhD, DSc (Liverpool). *Currently:* Professor of Oceanography, University of Wales Bangor. *Born on* 21 May 1940 at York. *Son of* the late Frederick Harold Simpson and Margaret Morrison Lees. *Marriage:* to Frances Mary (nee Peacock), 1964. *Children:* Amanda, Rachel and Joanna. *Educated at* Bootham School York; Exeter College Oxford; Liverpool University. *Career:* Assistant Lecturer UCNW 1965; NERC Research Fellow, National Institute of Oceanography 1969-70; Reader in Physical Oceanography 1977; Personal Chair in Physical Oceanography 1982; Council Member NERC; Established Chair in Physical Oceanography 1986. *Publications:* some 70 papers in the scientific literature. *Recreation:* Windsurfing, hill-walking, gardening. *Clubs:* Penn. *Address:* Adare, Holyhead Road, Menai Bridge, Gwynedd, LL59 5RH. School of Ocean Sciences, University of Wales, Bangor Tel: 0248 712610

SIMPSON, Dr Judith Caroline, M.A., D.Phil. *Currently:* Private Secretary to Secretary of State for Wales. *Born on* 31 Jan 1952 at Carshalton. *Daughter of* Anthony John Simpson and Mabel Eleanor Drummond Simpson. *Educated at* Abbey School, Reading;Lady Margaret Hall; St. Hilda's College Oxford. *Career:* H. M. Customs and Excise, 1979-83; H. M. Treasury, 1983-90; (Assistant Private Secretary to Chancellor of the Exchequer, 1983-84; Deputy Press Secretary, 1989-90). *Recreation:* Reading, music and walking. *Address:* Welsh Office, Gwydyr House, Whitehall, London, SW1A 2ER.

SIMS, Neville William, MBE, FCA, MAAT. *Currently:* Chartered Accountant (self-employed). *Born on* 15 June 1933 at Cardiff. *Son of* William Ellis Sims and Ethel Stacey Colley (nee Inman). *Marriage:* to Jennifer Ann (nee Warwick), 1964. *Children:* Jeremy Warwick Sims, Heather Jane Sims, Caroline Louise Sims and Matthew William Sims. *Educated at* Penarth County School. *Career:* articles to T. H. Trump (decd) and qualified as a Chartered Accountant 1957. Partner Ernst & Young 1960-85 and Managing Partner Cardiff Office 1974-84. Retired 1985 and now consultant with Watts Gregory & Daniel. Council member ICAEW 1981- ; Council member Association of Accounting Technicians 1989- ; Chairman Governors Howell's School Llandaff Cardiff 1981- ; Hon Treasurer Cardiff Central Conservative Association 1987- ; President S. Wales Society of Chartered Accountants 1977-78; Deputy Chairman CABW (Chartered Accountants for Business in Wales); member: Welsh Regional Board Homeowners Friendly Society 1984-88; member: Welsh National Board for Nursing Midwifery and Health Visiting Standing Finance Committee 1989- ; member: CG90, Chairman Wales Area Young Conservatives 1960-63, Chairman Barry (now Vale of Glamorgan) Conservative Association 1962-72, Hon Treasurer YMCA Cardiff Centre 1963-70. *Recreation:* theatre, music, gardening, walking. *Clubs:* Vice-President Cardiff Business, Cardiff & County, Chartered Accountants Dining, Old Penarthians RFC. *Address:* 'The Chimes', 15 Westminster Crescent, Cyncoed, Cardiff, CF2 6SE.

SINNOTT, Mr Kevin Fergus, M. A. (RCA); Dip. ; A. D. *Currently:* Professional Artist (Painter). *Born on* 4th Dec 1947 at Sarn, Bridgend, Glamorgan. *Son of* Myles Vincent Sinnott and Honora Burke. *Marriage:* to Susan Margaret Forward. *Children:* Mathew, Gavin, Thomas, Lucy *Educated at* Sc. Roberts R. C., Aberkenfig, Mid Glam. ; Cardiff College of Art and Design 1967-68; Gloucester College of Art and Design 1968-71; Royal College of Art, London 1971-74 *Career:* Visiting lecturer, Canterbury College of Art and Epsom College of Art 1981-88; Part-time teacher, St. Martin's School of Art, London 1981-; Exhibitions include: John Moores, Liverpool 1978, 1980 (prizewinner), 1991; California 1986, 1987; Chicago 1988; New York 1987, 1988; Chapter Art Centre, Cardiff 1984; London 1980, 1981, 1982, 1983, 1984, 1986, 1990 at Blond Fine Art, House Gallery, Riverside Studios, Bernard Jacobson respectively; Group Exhibitions include: Whitechapel Open, London 1978; Open Studio Show, London 1979; Whitechapel Open, London 1980; Ruskin School of Art, Oxford 1981; Second International Drawing Triennial, Nurenburg 1982; Self Portrait, Art Site Gallery, Bath 1987; British Art Now, The Contemporary Arts Centre, Cincinnati 1988; Museum and Public Collections include: British Council; Arts Council of Great Britain; Royal College of Art; British Museum *Recreation:* Reading; Travel; Television *Clubs:* Chelsea Arts Club *Address:* 43 Capel Road, East Barnet, Hertfordshire, EN4 8JF.

SIZER, County Councillor Geoffrey, Justice of the Peace *Currently:* Tugmaster, Cory Towage, Milford Haven, Auxillary Coastguard, Milford Haven 1981-. *Born on* 19 July 1954 at Haverfordwest. *Son of* Edmond and Lillian (nee Adams) Sizer. *Marriage:* to Marion Brooks. *Children:* Nicola and Michelle. *Educated at* Milford Secondary Modern, Plymouth College of Maritime Studies, Warsash Nautical College. *Career:* Deck Cadet, 3rd Officer, 2nd

Officer Reardon Smith Line 1970-81; Cory Towace Milford Haven 1981-; Chairman, Milford Liberals 1983-91; County Councillor 1985- ; Secretary TGWU 4/148 Branch 1988- ; Appointed Justice of the Peace, Chairman Dyfed County Council Public Protection Committee 1990- ; Member South Wales Sea Fisheries Committee 1985- ; Member Saundersfoot Harbour Commission 1989- ; Member St. Katharine's and St. Peter's Parochial Church Council 1986- ; Member Board of Management Torch Theatre, Milford Haven 1985-; Trustee Milford Haven Heritage and Maritime Museum 1989- ; Vice Chairman Pembrokeshire Liberal Democrat Association 1990-91; Governor of Milford School, Milford C. P. School, Meads Infant and Mount Infants Schools, Overdale Special School 1985- . *Recreation:* Reading, Crosswords and Family. *Address:* Hillcrest, Great North Road, Milford Haven. SA73 2LE.

SKEWIS, Mr William Iain, BSc., Ph.D., MCIT., FTS. *Currently:* Consultant; Currently Chairman, Regional Studies Association; Director, The Ian Rush International Soccer Tournament. *Born on* 1 May 1936 at Glasgow. *Son of* John Jamieson and Margaret Skewis. *Marriage:* to Jessie Frame Skewis (nee Weir). *Children:* Jan, Alan and Guy David *Educated at* Hamilton Academy, University of Glasgow. *Career:* Chief Executive, Development Board for Rural Wales to 1990; Director, Yorkshire and Humberside Dev. Association; Director of Tourism; Director of Industrial Development and Marketing: Highlands and Islands Development Board; Assistant Economist, Transport Holding Co. ; Traffic Survey Officer, British Railways. *Publications:* Transport in the Highlands and Islands of Scotland, etc. *Recreation:* Soccer: Director Ian Rush Soccer Tournament, Chairman Mid Wales Soccer Development Project, and travel. *Address:* Rock House, The Square, Montgomery, Powys. SY15 6PA.

SKINNER, The Honourable Mrs Rose Marian, *Currently:* Pensioner. *Born on* 6 June 1915 at Farnborough, Hants. *Daughter of* Major G. S. Rowley Conwy and Mrs. *Marriage:* to Mr. Ralph B. Skinner, 1938. *Children:* David, Meriel and Rosalind. *Educated at* Howell's School. *Career:* One years nursing in London before marriage, to a mechanical engineer; after marriage living in Portugal for three years, then in various places during war while husband served with Roya Engineers, then lived in Buxton, South Wales and Cumbria, until husband retired. Served on Cowbridge District Council for three years while in Glamorgan; Worked with WRVS and Red Cross. *Recreation:* Money raising for Church and Conservatives, gardening, embroidery *Address:* The Fold, Cwm, Nr. Rhyl, Clwyd, LL18 5SG

SLATER, Professor (James) Howard, BSc, PhD, DSc. *Currently:* Professor of Applied Microbiology, University of Wales, Cardiff since 1982. *Born on* 16 Dec 1947 at Tamale, Northn Territories Ghana (form)Gold Coast. *Son of* Arthur Robert Frank Slater, of Arundel Sussex and Mildred Dorothy Slater (nee White). *Marriage:* to Georgette Eloise Edwina Baldwin, da of Cecil Edwin Baldwin of Worthing Surrey. *Children:* Elisabeth Joy (b. 1977) and Catherine Helen (b. 1979). *Educated at* Worthing Technical High School; University College, London, BSc. Microbiology, First Class honours (1969); University College, London, PhD. Microbiol Physiology and Biochemistry (1972). *Career:* Lecturer in Microbiology, Univ of Kent at Canterbury 1972-75; Lecturer in Environmental Sciences, Univ of Warwick 1975-79; Senior Lecturer in Environmental Sciences, Univ of Warwick 1979-82; Visiting Prof. of Microbiology, Univ of Connecticut 1982; Professor of Applied Microbiology, Univ of Wales, Inst of Science and Technology 1982-88; Senior Research Consultant, BioTechnica International Inc., 1982-84; Research Director, BioTechnica Ltd., 1984-88; Director International Inst of Biotechnology 1990- , (a charity); Director Biodiversity Ltd., 1990- (trading arm of ITB); Director Carbury Herne

Ltd., 1991-; Director Cardiff Waste Ltd. Fellow, Institute of Biology 1984; Fellow, International Institute of Biotechnology 1988; Fellow, Royal Society of Arts, Manufacture and Commerce 1991. *Publications:* Author many scientific publications and patents; Editor 5 books. *Recreation:* photography, sailing, travelling, sports watching. *Address:* School of Pure & Applied Biol, University of Wales, Cardiff, P. O. Box 915, Cardiff, CF1 3TL. Tel: 0222 874771 Fax: 0222 874305

SLAY, Professor Desmond, MA (Oxon), PhD (Wales). *Currently:* retired. *Born on* 30 Dec 1927 at Thame, Oxon. *Son of* the late Wilfred Charles Slay and the late Doris Elizabeth Slay (nee Walker). *Marriage:* to Leontia Mary Cecilia McCartan, 1958. *Children:* Gregory (b. 1959), Deborah (b. 1960), Benet (b. 1961), Jonathan (b. 1965) and Matthew (b. 1965). *Educated at* Lord Williams's Grammar School Thame; University of Oxford. *Career:* Department of English, University College of Wales, Aberystwyth: Assistant Lecturer 1948-50; Lecturer 1950-62; Senior Lecturer 1962-72; Reader 1972-78; Acting Head of Department 1976-78; Rendel Professor of English and Head of Department 1978-90; Research Professor 1990- . *Publications:* Books: Codex Scardensis, 1960; The Manuscripts of Hrolfs Saga Kraka, 1960; Hrolfs Saga Kraka (ed 1960); Romances, 1972; Proceedings of First International Saga Conference (jointly), 1973; articles in learned journals. *Recreation:* Supporting Scouting. *Clubs:* Viking Society for Northern Research, Aberystwyth 41. *Address:* 52 Maeshendre, Waunfawr, Aberystwyth, Dyfed, SY23 3PS. Department of English, University College of Wales, Aberystwyth

SMAIL, Dr Simon Andrew, MA, FRCGP, DCH, DRCOG *Currently:* Senior Lecturer in General Practice, University of Wales College of Medicine, since 1979. *Born on* 24 Jan 1946 at Harrow, Middlx. *Son of* the late Andrew Charles Smail and Freda Smail (nee Moule). *Marriage:* to June Elizabeth Bird, 1970. *Children:* Joanna Kathryn Smail and Wendy Elizabeth Smail. *Educated at* Univ. College School, London; Worcester College Oxford; University of Oxford Medical School. *Career:* Principal in General Practice, Oxford 1975-77; Lecturer in General Practice, Welsh National School of Medicine 1977-79; Member of Council, Royal College of General Practitioners 1978-85; member of Health Education Council 1981-87; member of Health Education Adv. Committee for Wales 1984-86, Chairman 1986-87; member Community Nursing Review for Wales 1985-87; chairman, Health Promotion Authority for Wales 1987-92; Presenter and Medical Editor "Wellbeing", Channel 4 TV/S4C. *Publications:* Medical Editor "Advice" partwork, 1989-90; Medical Editor "Mediquest" partwork; publications on health promotion and general practice. *Recreation:* choral singing, medical journalism. *Address:* 46 Dan-y-Bryn Ave, Radyr, Cardiff, CF4 8DD. Dept of General Practice, Univ of Wales Coll of Medicine, Health Centre, Maelfa, Llanedyrn, Cardiff, CF3 7PN

SMART, Mr Richard Anthony, FCA, FIPA, MSPI, MICM *Currently:* Partner, Coopers & Lybrand Deloitte, since 1990; Partner, Cork Gully, since 1990. *Born on* 8 March 1942 at Neath, West Glam. *Son of* the late James Clifford and the late Rose Beryl (nee Penn). *Marriage:* to Gaynor (nee Isaac), 1968. *Children:* Matthew James (b. 1974) and Jonathan Anthony (b. 1974). *Educated at* Neath Grammar School. *Career:* ACA 1966; FCA 1977. Joined Deloitte Plender Griffiths & Co, 1959; Partner in Deloitte Haskins & Sells 1976-90. *Recreation:* sport, music. *Clubs:* Cardiff & County. *Address:* 2 Fox Hollows, Maendy, Cowbridge, S. Glam, CF7 7TS

SMITH, Mr Andrew Mark, *Currently:* Conservative Prospective Parliamentary candidate for the Cynon Valley; Deputy Managing Director, Ian Greer Associates Ltd 1982- *Born on* 5 July 1962 at Guildford, Surrey. *Son of* Mr & Mrs George Smith. *Educated at* St. Columbia RC Boys School,

Kent. *Career:* Civil Servant, Ministry of Agriculture, Fisheries and Food 1978-82. *Recreation:* Sailing, aviation, defence. *Clubs:* RAC, Travellers. *Address:* 56 Cavell Street, London E1 2JA. 1 Elm Grove, Aberdare, Mid Glamorgan, CF44 8DN

SMITH, Sir (Knight Bachelor 1979) James Alfred, CBE (1964); TD *Currently:* retired, 1980. *Born on* 11 May 1913 at Llandyssul. *Son of* Charles Silas Smith and Elizabeth S. (nee Williams). *Educated at* Lampeter Central School; Christ College, Brecon; Solicitor of Supreme Court; Barrister (Lincoln's Inn) *Career:* War Service: various staff appointments, 1939-46: I. O. R. A. 38 WDN (Lt): GSO III 47DN (Capt): GSO 2 (V) GH4 W. Africa (Major): Special duties HW Sacsea (Ceylon), demolilised Feb. 1946; appointed to Colonial Legal Service, 1946, posted to Nigeria; Resident Magistrate, Nigeria 1946; Chief Magistrate, Nigeria 1951; Chief Registrar Supreme Court 1953; Puisne Judge, N. Nigeria 1955; Senior Puisne Judge, N. Nigeria 1960-65; Puisne Judge S. C. T. Bahamas 1965; Senior Puisne Judge, Bahamas 1975; Chief Justice, Bahamas 1978; Justice of Appeal, Bermuda 1980-84; Justice of Appeal, Bahamas 1981-83; Justice of Appeal, Turks & Caicos Islands 1981-89; Justice of Appeal, Belize 1981-84; President Belize Court of Appeal 1984-89; President of Royal Commission of inquiry into the transhipment of narcotic drugs through Bahamas to U.S.A., report of commission published Dec. 1984, 1983-84. *Recreation:* gardening, Bridge. *Clubs:* Naval & Military (Picadilly); Lyford Cay (Bahamas, to 1991). *Address:* Berry Cottage, W. Bay Street, Nassau, P.O. Box Cb 11508, Bahamas

SMITH, Mr John Patrick, BSc. Econ (Honours), Wales; Dip. IRTU. *Currently:* MP, Vale of Glamorgan. *Born on* 17 March 1951 at Cardiff. *Son of* John Henry Smith and Mary Margaret Smith. *Marriage:* to Kathleen Mulvaney. *Children:* Nathan, Melanie and Theo. *Educated at* Fairfield School; Penarth Grammar School; University of Wales. *Career:* Construction Worker, Senior Lecturer in R. A. F., Higher Education. *Recreation:* Swimming, reading, camping. *Clubs:* Sea View Labour Club, Barry. *Address:* 60 Wyndham St, Barry, S. Glam. CF6 6EL.

SMITH, Sir Joseph William Grenville, MD FRCP FRCPath FFPHM FIBiol Dip. Bact. *Currently:* Director, Public Health Laboratory Service of England and Wales since 1985. *Born on* 14 Nov 1930 at Cardiff. *Son of* Douglas Ralph and Hannah Margaret Smith. *Marriage:* to Nira Jean (nee Davies), Burry Port. *Children:* one son Jonathan. *Educated at* Cathays High School for Boys, Cardiff; Welsh National School of Medicine. *Career:* Director, National Institute for Biological Standards and Control 1976-85; Deputy Director, Epidemiological Research Laboratory, PHLS Central Public Health Lab., Colindale, London 1971-76; Consultant Bacteriologist, Oxford 1965-68; Senior Lecturer, Dept. of Bacteriology and Immunology, London School of Hygiene & Tropical Medicine 1963-65; *Publications:* Papers on Tetanus, Influenza Immunization. *Recreation:* The Arts. *Clubs:* Athenaeum. *Address:* Public Health Laboratory Service, 61 Colindale Avenue, London, NW9 5DF

SMITH, Mr Karl Wingett, C. Eng., M. R. Ae. S. *Currently:* Managing Partner, Design and Furnishings, Consultant on Aviation and High Temperature Plastics; Designer of Protective Breathing Equipment; Design of Mobility Aids for elderly and disabled. *Born on* 16th Dec 1932 at Carshalton, Surrey. *Son of* Muriel Mary Smith (nee Wingett) and Ernest Walter Smith. *Marriage:* to Patricia Grace (nee Franklin), 15th Sept 1962. *Children:* Andrew, 1965; Ian, 1969; Gavin, 1972; Neil, 1974; Alastair, 1975; Duncan, 1977 *Educated at* Pontypridd Intermediate School; John Ruskin Grammar, Croydon; Battersea College of Technology *Career:* Aircraft Systems Design - Handley Page Ltd (1952-60), Hawker Aircraft Ltd (1960-62), Teddington Aircraft Controls Ltd, Cefn Coed (1962-68),

Hawker Siddeley Dynamics Ltd (1968-73), Hawker Siddeley Aviation Ltd (1974-75); Self-employed Aviation Consultant (1975-78); Lecturer R. A. F. School of Technical Training, Halton (1978-82); Lecturer/Senior Lecturer, R.A.F. College Cranwell (1982-91); Member of CAA Committees preparing specifications for:- (1) Protective breathing equipment for cabin crew members (2) Protective breathing equipment for passengers; Member of EUROCAE Working Group preparing specification for passenger protective breathing equipment *Publications:* Technical papers on approximate methods of calculating aircraft cabin heat loads; AGARD and Aero-Tech papers on heat resistance testing of composite materials *Recreation:* Aviation *Address:* Heckington House, Heckington, Sleaford, Lincolnshire, NG34 9JD

SMITH, Michael John, FIPR *Currently:* Managing Director, Golley Slater Public Relations Ltd, established in Cardiff 1969; Director Golley Slater Group. *Born on* 23 Sept 1939 at Edgware, Middx. *Son of* the late Frank and Margorie Smith. *Marriage:* to Diane White, 1966. *Children:* Jeremy and Philip. *Educated at* City of London School. *Career:* Journalist in London and North Carolina, USA 1960-65; PR Consultant in London 1965-69. *Recreation:* Chairman, Inst of Public Relations, Wales Group, reading. *Address:* Golley Slater Public, Relations Ltd, 9 / 11 The Hayes, Cardiff, CF1 1NU

SMITH, Dr Peter, BA; Hon. D. Litt (Wales); FSA. *Currently:* Retired 1991 as Secretary Royal Commission on Ancinet Monuments in Wales, since 1973. *Born on* 15 June 1926 at Winlaton, Co. Durham. *Son of* L. W. Smith, HMI and the late Hilda Smith (nee Halsted). *Marriage:* to Joyce Evelyn Abbot 1954. *Children:* Stephen Lloyd, Charles Kenyon and Sarah Caroline. *Educated at* Peter Symonds', Winchester; Oriel & Lincoln Coll., Oxford; Hammersmith School of Building Arts & Crafts. *Career:* Junior Investigator RCAM 1949; Senior Investigator 1954; Investigator in charge of National Monuments Record 1963; President Cambrian Archaelogical Association 1979; President Vernacular Arch. Group 1983-86. *Publications:* House of the Welsh Countryside, 1975, 2nd ed. 1988; contributor to Cambridge Agrarian History etc. *Recreation:* Sketching, studying languages, especially Welsh. *Address:* Ty-coch, Lluest, Llanbadrn Fawr, Aberystwyth SY23 3AU

SMITH, Peter James Mead, Solicitor (Hons) *Currently:* Senior Partner, Smith Llewellyn Partnership, 18 Princess Way, Swansea, formed in 1975. *Born on* 25 Aug 1948 at Hornchurch, Essex. *Son of* Douglas William Mead Smith and Doris Maud Smith. *Marriage:* to Sarah Madeline Anita Richards, 1972. *Children:* Richard William Mead Smith. *Educated at* St. Clares Convent, Porthcawl; Dyffryn Grammar Port Talbot; College of Law Guildford. *Career:* Qualified 1972, (Hons). *Recreation:* Rugby Union, sport, antiques. *Clubs:* Hon. Secretary Aberavon Green Stars RFC, since 1975. *Address:* "Hendre", 1 Westernmoor Road, Neath, W. Glam, SA11 1BJ

SNAPE, Mr Royden Eric, *Currently:* Recorder in Crown Court; Chairman Medical Appeal Tribunal; Consultant Solicitor. *Born on* 20 April 1922 at Maesteg, Glamorgan. *Son of* John Robert Snape and Gwladys Constance Snape. *Marriage:* to Unity Frances (Jo) Money 1949. *Children:* Peter John Snape and Sarah Anne Price. *Educated at* Bromsgrove School. *Career:* Royal Artillery 1940-47; Commission 1941, Major (D. A. A. G.) 1945-47; Solicitor 1949- ; Deputy Circuit Judge 1975-79; Recorder 1979- ; Chairman Medical Appeal Tribunal 1985- ; Governor St. Johns School, Porthcawl 1971-89. *Recreation:* Golf, Rugby Union Football, cricket, swimming. *Clubs:* Royal Porthcawl golf, Glamorgan County Cricket, Cardiff Athletic, Cowbridge Athletic, The Ogmore. *Address:* West Winds, Love Lane, Llanblethian, Cowbridge CF7 7JQ

SNOWDON, 1st Earl Of, Cr 1961, Antony Charles Robert Armstrong-Jones, GCVO 1969; RDI 1978; FCSD; Viscount Linley, 1961. *Currently:* Photographer,

Telegraph Magazine, since 1990; Constable of Caernarvon Castle, since 1963. *Born on* 7 March 1930 *Son of* the late Ronald Owen Lloyd Armstrong-Jones, MBE, QC, DL and Anne, o d of Lt. Col Leonard Messel, OBE (later Countess of Rosse) *Marriage:* 1st to HRH The Princess Margaret, 1960 (marr diss1978); 2nd to Lucy Lindsay-Hogg, d of Donald Davies, 1978. *Children:* one s one d, from 1st marriage; one d fron 2nd marriage. *Educated at* Eton; Jesus College Cambridge (coxed winning Univ. crew 1950) *Career:* Joined Staff of Council of Industrial Design 1961, continued on a consultative basis 1962-87, also an Editorial Adviser of Design Magazine 1961-87; an Artistic Adviser to the Sunday Times and Sunday Times Publications Ltd., 1962-90. *Designed:* Snowdon Aviary, London Zoo, 1965; Chairmobile 1972. Member Council, National Fund for Research for Crippling Diseases; Patron, Circle of Guide Dog Owners; Chairman, Working Party on Integrating the Disabled (Report 1976); President for England, Cttee, International Year for Disabled People, 1981. Hon. Fellow: Institute of British Photographers; Royal Photographic Soc; Manchester College of Art and Design; Hon. Member: North Wales Society of Architects; South Wales Institute of Architects; Royal Welsh Yacht Club; Patron: Welsh Nat. Rowing Club; Metropolitan Union of YMCAs; British Water Ski Federation. President: Contemp. Art Society for Wales; Civic Trust for Wales; Welsh Theatre Company; Member Council, English Stage Co., 1978-82. Senior Fellow, RCA 1986. FRSA. Dr hc Bradford 1989; Hon. LLD Bath 1989. Silver Progress Medal, RPS 1985. *Television films:* Don't Count the Candles, 1968 (2 Hollywood Emmy Awards; St. George Prize, Venice; awards at Prague and Barcelona film festivals); Love of a Kind, 1969; Born to be Small, 1971 (Chicago Hugo Award); Happy being Happy, 1973; Mary Kingsley, 1975; Burke and Wills, 1975; Peter, Tina and Steve, 1977; Snowdon on Camera, BBC (presenter), 1981. *Exhibitions include:* Photocall, London, 1958; Assignments, Cologne, London, Brussels, USA, 1972, Japan, Canada, Denmark, Holland, 1975, Australia, 1976, France, 1977; Serendipity, Brighton, Bradford, 1989, Bath, 1990. *Publications:* London, 1958; Malta (in collaboration), 1958; Private View (in collaboration), 1965; A View of Venice, 1972; Assignments, 1972; Inchcape Review, 1977; (jtly) Pride of the Shires, 1979; Personal View, 1979; Sittings, 1983; Israel: a first view, 1986; (with Viscount Tonypandy) My Wales, 1986; Stills 1983-1987, 1987; Public Appearances, 1991. *Clubs:* Buck's, United Oxford & Cambridge University; Leander (Henley-on-Thames); Hawks (Cambridge). *Address:* 22 Launceston Place, London, W8 5RL

SPACKMAN, Brigadier. John William Charles, PhD; C. Eng; FBCS. *Currently:* Director, European Telecommunications Information Services; Director John Spackman Associates Ltd; Director Act Logsys Ltd; Director Intelligent Networks Ltd. *Born on* 12 May 1932 at Merthyr Tydfil. *Son of* Lt. Col Robert Thomas Spackman MBE and Ann (nee Rees). *Marriage:* to Jeanette Vera (nee Samuel) 1955. *Children:* Michael, Sarah (Lamb) and David. *Educated at* Cyfarthfa Castle Grammar School, Merthyr Tydfil; Wellington Grammar School; RMCS BSc 1st. cl Hons London (external) 1960, PhD 1964; MSc (Management Science UMIST 1968. *Career:* Nat. Service 1950-52; Regular Commission RAOC 1952; Regtl Appts 1952-72; Project Wayell 1969-72; RARDE 1972-75; Senior Mil Officer Chem. Defence and Microbiological Defence Estb. Porton Down 1975-78; Branch Chief Inf. Systems Div Shape 1978-80; Dir. Supply Computer Service 1980-83; Retired from Army 1983 (Brig); Under Secretary and Dir. Social Security Operational Strategy DHSS 1983-87; Director Computing and Information Services BT 1987-90; FBCS 1987; MBCS 1970; M.Inst.D. 1983. Liveryman and Assistant to the Court, Company of Information

Technologists *Recreation:* Mountaineering, gardening, opera. *Clubs:* Naval and Military. *Address:* 4 The Green, Evenley, Brackley, Northants. Plas Newydd, Sint Pauluslaan 9, 3080 Vossem, Belgium

SPEED, Gary Andrew, *Currently:* Professional Footballer, Leeds United AFC. *Born on* 8 Sept 1969 at Mancot, N. Wales. *Son of* Roger and Carol (nee Huxley). *Educated at* Hawarden High School *Career:* joined Leeds at 16. 6 Welsh Youth Caps, 3 under "21" caps. First team debut v Oldham 1989. Second Division Championship Medal season 1990-91. over 150 appearances and 25 goals to date. Ten Full International Caps to date. *Recreation:* golf, tennis, socialising *Address:* 8 Courtland Drive, Aston Park, Deeside, Clwyd, N. Wales, CH5 1UQ. 98 Dolk House, Victoria Quays, Navigation Walk, Leeds LS10 1JJ

SQUIRRELL, Dr Hew Crawford, MSc; PhD. *Currently:* Deputy Director, The Golf Foundation, since 1986. *Born on* 15 Aug 1932 at Cardiff. *Son of* William Crawford Squirrell and the late Katherine May (nee Gill). *Marriage:* to Gwendoline Ann Samuel, 1965. *Children:* Katherine Louise, Daniel Hew and Camilla Jane. *Educated at* Howardian Grammar School, Cardiff; Birmingham University. *Career:* Principal Geologist, British Geological Survey 1956-86. *Golf Career:* Welsh Amateur Champion 1958, 59, 60, 64 and 65; Represented Wales 1955-75, Captain 1969-71. *Publications:* New Occurances of Fish Remains in the Silurian of the Welsh Borderland, Geol Mag., 1958; (with E. V. Tucker), The Geology of the Woolhope Inlier, Herefordshire, Quart. J. Geol. Soc., 1960; (with R. A. Downing) On the attenuation of the Coal Measures in the south-east part of the South Wales Coalfield, Bull Geol. Surv. Gt. Brit., 1964; (with R. A. Downing) On the red and green beds in the Upper Coal Measures of the South Wales Coalfield, Bull. Geol. Surv. G. B., 1965; (with M. L. K. Curtis, J. D. Lawson, E. V. Tucker and V. G. Walmsley, The Silurian Inliers of the South-Eastern Welsh Borderland, Geol. Assoc Guide, 1967; (with C. R. Bristow), A letter concerning the use of air photographs in site investigations. Road and Road Construction, 1968; (with R. A. Downing), The Geology of the South Wales Coalfield, Part 1. The Country around Newport (Mon), 3rd ed. Mem. Geol. Surv. U. K., 1969; (with T.N. George) Excursion guide for east crop of South Wales Coalfield, 1971; Old Red Sandstone, Carboniferous Limestone and Coal Measures sections around Newport and Risca, Mon. 43-55, in Geol. Assoc. publication Geological Excursions in South Wales and the Forest of Dean, 1971; (with I.H.S. Hall) New sections in the basal Westphalian and uppermost Namurian strata at Risca and Abersychan, Mon., Bull. Geol. Surv. Bt. Brit., No. 38, 15-41 1972; The Downtonian- Dittonian junction, Quart.J.Geol.Soc. 129, 205-6, 1973; The Sand and Gravel resources of the Thames and Kennet valleys, the country around Pangbourne, Berkshire: Description of 1:25,000 resource sheet 67, Miner. Assess. Rep. Inst. Geol. Sci., No. 21, 97 pp., 1975; The Sand and Gravel resources of the country around Aldermaston, Berkshire: Description of parts of 1:25,000 resource sheets SU 56 and SU 66, Miner. Assess. Rep. Inst. Geol. Sci., No.24, 83 pp., 1976; (with D.E. White) Stratigraphy of the Silurian and Old Red Sandstone of the Cennen Valley and adjacent areas, south-east Dyfed, Wales., Rep. Inst. Geol. Sci., No. 78/6 45 pp., 1978; The Sand and Gravel resources of the country around Sonning and Henley, Berkshire, Oxfordshire and Buckinghamshire., Miner. Assess. Rep. Inst. Geol. Sci., No. 32, 98 pp., 1978; Pricipal compiler and editor, of "United Kingdom Mineral Statistics" for 1977, 78, 79, 80, 81, 82, 83, 84 and 1985, Geol. Surv. Gt. Brit. *Recreation:* golf, walking, theatre. *Address:* 'The Nut House', 8 Hill Rise, Rickmansworth, Herts, WD3 2NZ

ST DAVIDS, Rt. Hon. Viscount. (Philipps, Colwyn Jestyn John), *Born on* 30 Jan 1939 *Marriage:* December 1965. *Children:* two s, aged 25 and 21. *Educated at*

Dulwich Coll. Prep. Sch; Haverfordwest Gram. Sch; Sevenoaks Sch; George Taylor and Staff, Melbourne, Australia; Guildhall Sch of Music; Kings College, London, Cert. of Advanced Musical Studies. *Career:* Trainee Securities Agency Ltd (known as the 117 Old Broad Street Group, later M.I.M.), 1957-58; National Service, commissioned Second Lieutenant in the Welsh Guards 1958-60; Securities Agency Ltd 1960-65; became a member of the Stock Exchange and joined Maguire Kingsmill and Co., as investment analyst, 1965; joined Kemp-Gee and Co., as institutional equity salesman, 1968. Became a partner March 1971. In March 1980 the firm took over J and A Scrimgeour and Co., and became Scrimgeour Kemp-Gee and Co. During the period 1975-85 the firm was rated in the top three U. K. stockbrokers being the recognized specialists in a number of areas. In April 1985 the partners sold the firm to Citicorp and became directors of Citicorp Scrimgeour Vickers (Securities) Ltd., October 1985. I started the European equity sales department, left the company in 1988 on removal of "golden handcuffs"; appointed a director of Greig Middleton & Co. Ltd, 1989, resigned directorship 1991 but remain as consultant; Interests in The Scout Association, family connected with the Association since its inception; Member of the board of The Roland House Scout Settlement 1975-77; District Commissioner, Islington Dist. Scout Cncl 1976-78; member Baden-Powell Fellowship 1983- ; trustee of The Docklands Scout Trust 1990- ; liveryman, Worshipful Co. of Musicians 1971- ; Associated with the Fondazione Rossini, Pesaro 1983-; the Purcell Society 1988; The Handel Inst. 1990- ; built up a very substantial collection of manuscrip, autograph and first and early printed editions of the music of major composers. The Rossini collection is said to be the largest extant collection of the composer's work printed. *Recreation:* The Scout Association, English literature, The Natural Sciences. *Clubs:* The City of London, elected to membership 1979. *Address:* House of Lords, London SW1A OPW

STABLE, His Hon Judge (Rondle) Owen (Charles), QC (1963). *Born on* 28 Jan 1923 *Son of* the late Rt Hon Sir Wintringham Stable, MC, of Plas Llwyn Owen, Llanbrynmair, Powis and Lucie Haden. *Marriage:* to Yvonne Brook, 1949, da of Lionel Brook Holliday, OBE (d 1965), of Copgrove Hall, Boroughbridge, Yorkshire. *Children:* Emma (Mrs Hay) and Victoria. *Educated at* Winchester. *Career:* World War II Capt RB 1940-46; barrister Middle Temple 1948; Bencher 1969, dep chairman Herts Quarter Sessions 1963-71, recorder of Crown Courts 1972-79, circuit judge 1979; res judge: Wood Green Crown Court 1980-81, Snaresbrook Crown Court 1982- ; senior circuit judge 1982- ; board of trade inspector: Cadco Group of Cos 1963-64, HS Whiteside and Co Ltd 1965-67, Int Learning Systems Corporation Ltd 1969-71, Pergamon Press 1969-73; member: General Council of the Bar 1962-64, Senate of 4 Inss of Court 1971-74, Senate of Inns of Court and the Bar 1974-75; chllr Dio of Bangor 1959-88, member Governing Body of Church in Wales 1960-88, layreader Dio of St. Albans 1961- ; chairman Horserace Betting Levy Appeal Tribunal 1969-74. *Publications:* A Review of Coursing (with R M Studdard), 1971. *Recreation:* shooting, listening to music. *Clubs:* Boodles. *Address:* The Crown Court At Snaresbrook, Hollybush Hill, London, E11 1QW

STANLEY OF ALDERLEY, 8th Lord Stanley of Alderley Thomas Henry Oliver, Bart., D. L. *Currently:* Farmer, Trysglwyn since 1972. *Born on* 28 Sept 1927 at London. *Son of* Lt. Col The Hon O. H. Stanley DSO and The Lady Kathleen Stanley (nee Thynne). *Marriage:* to Jane Barrett Hartley, 1955. *Children:* Richard Oliver, Charles Ernest, Harry John and Lucinda Maria. *Educated at* Wellington College, Berks; Northamptonshire Institute of Agriculture. *Career:* Served Coldstream Guards and Guards Independent Parachute Company 1945-51, retired Captain.

Tenant farmer, New College Oxford 1955-88, Rectory Farm Stanton St. John, Oxford; Governor St. Edward's School, Oxford; Member Committee Management RNLI 1981- , Chairman of its Fund Raising Committee 1985- ; Trustee of UCNW Development Trust 1989- ; President, Anglesey Antiquarian Society 1991, Conservative back bench peer. *Recreation:* fishing, sailing, skiing. *Clubs:* Farmers *Address:* Trysglwyn Fawr, Amlwch, Ynys Mon, LL68 9RF

STEANE (nee Glenwright), Dr. Patricia Ann, MBBS, DA, FFARCS *Currently:* Consultant Anaesthetist, West Glamorgan Health Authority, since 1977; Clinical Manager Singleton Hospital Theatres, since 1991. *Born on* 3 April 1938 at Middlesex. *Daughter of* the late Louie and George Glenwright. *Marriage:* to Henry Alfred Steane, 1960. *Children:* Katherine and Robert. *Educated at* Hitchin Girls Grammar School; Royal Free Hospital; London University. *Career:* House Surgeon Royal Free Hospital London 1962; House Physician Bedford General Hospital 1963; Senior House Officer Anaesthetics, Royal Free Hospital London 1963-64; Registrar Anaesthetics, West Herts Hospital Hemel Hempstead 1964-65; Senior Registrar Anaesthetics, Swansea Hospitals 1971-77. *Recreation:* music, reading, tennis, skiing. *Clubs:* Royal Overseas League, St. James, London. *Address:* White Lodge, 279 Gower Road, Sketty, Swansea, SA2 7AA. Anaesthetic Dept, Singleton Hospital, Sketty, Swansea, SA2 8QA

STEEL, Emeritus Professor Robert Walter, CBE;Hon. D. Sc; Hon. LLD (Wales & Liverpool) HonD. Univ (Open) *Currently:* Retired from Principalship of the University College of Swansea in 1982. *Born on* 31 July 1915 at Theale, Berks. *Son of* the late Rev. Frederick G. Steel and the late Winifred B (nee Harrison). *Marriage:* to Eileen Margaret Page, 1940. *Children:* Alison Margaret, Elizabeth Mary and David Robert *Educated at* Gt. Yarmouth Grammar Sch; Cambridge High Sch for Boys; Jesus Coll., Oxford. *Career:* Research in Sierra Leone, 1938;Lctr. in Commonwealth Geography, Univ. of Oxford, 1939-56; Geographer, Ashanti Social Survey, Gold Coast, 1945-46; Fellow of Jesus Coll., Oxford, 1954-56; John Rankin Prof. of Geography, Univ. of Liverpool, 1957-74; (Pro-Vice-Chancellor, 1971-73); Principal, Univ. Coll. of Swansea, 1974-82; Vice-Chnclr, Univ. of Wales, 1979-81; Dir., Commonwealth Geographical Bureau, 1972-81; Chrmn, Brd of the Welsh Advisory Body on Local Authority Higher Educ., 1982-86; Chrmn, Governor of Westhill Coll., Birmingham, 1981- ; Chrmn, Swansea Festival of Music and the Arts, 1982- ; Hon. Fellow, Swansea. *Publications:* ed. (with A. F. Martin) and contributor to The Oxford Region: a Scientific & Historical Survey, 1954; ed (with C. A. Fisher), and cont. to Geographical Essays on Btsh Tropical Lands, 1956; ed. (with R. M. Prothero), and cont. to Geographers and the Tropics: Liverpool Essays, 1964; ed. (with R. Lawton), and cont. to Liverpool Essays on Geography: a Jubilee Collection, 1967; (with Eileen M. Steel) Africa, 1974, 3rd ed. 1982; ed. Human Ecology and Hong Kong. report for the Commonwealth Human Ecology Cncl, 1975; The Institute of British Geographers, the First Fifty Years, 1984; ed. British Geography, 1918-19, 1986; articles, mainly on tropical Africa, in Geographical Journal and other geographical journals *Recreation:* Walking, gardening, reading and music. *Clubs:* Royal Commonwealth Society, London. *Address:* 12 Cambridge Road, Langland, Swansea SA3 4PE Tel: 0792 369087

STEPHENS, Mr Meic, BA. *Born on* 23 July 1938 at Treforest, nr Pontypridd, Glam. *Son of* Alma (nee Symes) and the late Herbert Arthur Lloyd. *Marriage:* to Ruth Wynn Meredith, 1965. *Children:* Lowri, Heledd, Brengain and Huw. *Educated at* Pontypridd Boys' Grammar School; U. C. W. Aberystwyth; Univ of Rennes; U. C. N. W. Bangor. *Career:* French teacher, Ebbw Vale Grammar School 1962-66; Journalist, Western Mail 1966-67; Literature Director,

Welsh Arts Council 1967-90; Freelance Editor, Journalist and Consultant 1990- . White Robe of the Gorsedd of Bards 1978; Honorary Fellow of St. David's Univ College Lampeter 1986; Life member of the Welsh Academy 1990; member: Literature Panel of the British Council 1990; Centre for the study of Welsh Writing in English, the Polytechnic of Wales 1990; Chairman The Rhys Davies Trust 1990; Visiting Professor of English, Brigham Young University, Utah, USA 1991; member: The Radnorshire Society; The Kilvert Society; Trustee of The Paolo Pistoi Memorial Fund. *Publications:* Poetry Wales (ed) 1965-73; The Lilting House (ed) 1969; Writers of Wales (ed) 1970, 76 vols to date: Artists in Wales (ed) 3 vols 1971, 73, 77; The Welsh Language Today (ed) 1973; A Reader's Guide to Wales (ed) 1973; Linguistic Minorities in Western Europe 1976; Green Horse (ed) 1978; The Arts in Wales 1950-75, (ed) 1979; Y Celfyddydau yng Nghymru 1950-75, (ed) 1979; The Curate of Clyro (ed) 1983; The Oxford Companian to the Literature of Wales 1986; Cydymaith i Lenyddiaeth Cymru 1986; A Book of Wales (ed) 1987; A Cardiff Anthology (ed) 1987; The White Stone, trans 1987; a Dictionary of Literary Quotations 1989; The Gregynog Poets (ed) 12 vols, 1989-90; The Bright Field (ed) 1991; The Oxford Illustrated Literary Guide to Great Britain and Ireland (ed) 1992. *Recreation:* The world of Wales. *Address:* 10 Heol Don, Whitchurch, Cardiff CF4 2AU Tel: 0222 623359

STEPHENS, His Honour Judge Stephen Martin, M.A. (Oxon), Q.C. *Currently:* Circuit Judge since 1986. *Born on* 26 June 1939 at Swansea. *Son of* the late Abraham Stephens and of Freda Stephens. *Marriage:* to Patricia (nee Morris). *Children:* Richard and Marianne (and one son deceased) *Educated at* Swansea Grammar School; Wadham College, Oxford. *Career:* Barrister on Wales & Chester Circuit 1964-82; QC 1982; Recorder, Wales & Chester Circuit 1979-86. *Recreations:* Cricket and theatre. *Address:* C/o The Law Courts, Glebeland Place, Merthyr Tydfil, Mid Glamorgan, CF47 8BH.

STEVENS, Mr R. Jack, *Currently:* Newspaper Columnist; Clwyd County Councillor. *Born on* 29 Nov 1925 at Torpoint, Cornwall. *Son of* the late Ernest and Christina. *Marriage:* 1st to Eileen Bull, 1946 (deceased); 2nd to Enis Griffiths, 1991. *Children:* Richard, Ann, Roy, Elain, Rex, Kay, Paul, Christina and Sarah. *Educated at* Grammar School, Plymouth, Devon. *Career:* Merchant Navy 1942-46; Liverpool City Police 1948-58; Insurance Agent 1958-60; Managing Director, Contract Cleaning Co., 1961-74; Greetings Card Retailer 1974-91; Chairman, Theatr Clwyd, Board of Governors 1991- ; member of many Council Committees. *Recreation:* music hall theatre, Plymouth Argyle F. C., public speaking. *Clubs:* Chester & Wrexham Cornish Society. *Address:* The Pilgrims, 2 Clarendon Ave., Stansty, Wrexham Clwyd., LL11 2DF Tel: 0978 354565

STIRK, Mr James Richard, MA (Cantab). *Currently:* Company Secretary and Solicitor, Tarmac Quarry Products Limited, Wolverhampton, since 1989; Company Director, Samuel Parkes & Co. Limited. *Born on* 29 Oct 1959 at Birmingham. *Son of* Edward Thomas Stirk, TD and Peggy Isobel Phyllis (nee Soper). *Educated at* Shrewsbury School; Trinity College, Cambridge. *Career:* Articled Clerk and Solicitor with Coward Chance, London 1982-85; Solicitor, Wragge & Co., Birmingham 1985-87. *Publications:* Historical and Legal articles in the "Montgomeryshire Collections" and the "Radnorshire Transactions". *Recreation:* history, horology, the countryside. *Clubs:* Powysland, Welshpool (Hon. Solicitor). *Address:* Drover's Cottage, 53 Upper Cound, Cound, Nr Shrewsbury, Shropshire, SY5 6AS. Clochfaen, Llangurig, Nr Llanidloes, Powys SY18 6RP

STODDART, Professor John Little, BSc, PhD, DSc, FIBiol, ARPS. *Currently:* Research Director, AFRC Institute of Grassland and Environmental Research. *Born on* 1 Oct 1933 at South Shields. *Son of* John Little Stoddart and Margaret Pickering Dye. *Marriage:* to Wendy Dalton Leardie. *Children:* daughter Janet, son (decd). *Educated at* South Shields High School for Boys; Univ. Coll. Durham (BSc Botany); Univ. of Wales, Aberystwyth (PhD); Durham Univ. (DSc); (FIBiol). *Career:* Welsh Plant Breeding Station, Aberystwyth 1966, Dep. Dir 1985-87; Dir 1987-88; Vis., Prof. Reading Univ; Hon. Prof. Sch of Agric and Biol. Scis Univ of Wales 1966-67 Fulbright-Hays Sen. Fellow. Res. Assoc. Mich. State Univ/Atomic Energy Commn Plant Research Lab. 1966-67. *Publications:* Scientific articles, reviews and contributions to scientific books. *Recreation:* Pictorial photography, golf, swimming, gardening. *Clubs:* St. Davids. *Address:* AFRC Inst of Grassland and Environmental Research, Plas Gogerddan, Nr Aberystwyth, SY23 3EB

STONE, Mr. Martin, MD., FRCOG. *Currently:* Consultant Obstetrician and Gynaecologist, Gwent A.H.A. since 1980. *Born on* 8 Feb 1945 at Cardiff. *Son of* the late Abraham Stone and the late Eva Priscilla (nee Anstee). *Marriage:* to Jane, 1970, da of Tudor Lloyd-Williams (d. 1978) of Mold. *Children:* Andrew Martin, Robert Charles and Louise Jane. *Educated at* The Cathedral School, Llandaff; Canton H. S., Cardiff; Liverpool University. *Career:* Junior Doctor, Liverpool Hospitals 1968-72; S.H.O., Torquay Hospital 1972-73; Registrar, Charing Cross Hospital 1973-75; Medical Research Council 1975-76; Senior Registrar, St. George's Hospital, London 1976-77; Senior Registrar, Southampton Hospital 1977-80. *Publications:* Obstetrics, Gynaecology and Hydratidiform Mole. *Recreation:* Claret, golf, skiing, theatre. *Clubs:* Caerleon Rotary (president 1991-92), St. Pierre Golf & Country. *Address:* Ye Olde Forge, Llanmartin, Newport, Gwent NP6 2EB. St. Joseph's Private Hospital, Harding Avenue, Malpas, Newport, Gwent NPT 6QS Tel: 0633-413073 (Home)

STOWELL, Dr Michael James, BSc, PhD, FInstP, CPhys, FIM, CEng, FRS. *Currently:* Research Director, Alcan International, Banbury. *Born on* 10 July 1935 at Swansea. *Son of* the late Albert James and Kathleen Maud Stowell. *Marriage:* to Rosemary B. Allen 1962 (dissolved 1990). *Children:* George Vernon and Heather Joanne. *Educated at* St. Julians H. S. for Boys, Newport; Bristol University. *Career:* T.I. Research 1961-88; Research Fellow, Ohio State University, USA 1962-63; University of Minnesota, USA 1970. *Publications:* numerous scientific publications on epitaxy, nucleation theory, superplasticity and physical metallurgy. *Recreation:* music, amateur operatics *Address:* Alcan International Ltd, Banbury Laboratory, Southam Road, Banbury, Oxon, OX16 7SP

STRONG, Air Commodore RAF David Malcolm, CB, AFC *Currently:* Retired RAF Officer. *Born on* 30 Sept 1913 at Cardiff. *Son of* the late Theo & Margaret Strong. *Marriage:* to Daphne Warren Brown, 1941. *Children:* Simon, Christopher and Carolyn *Educated at* Cardiff High School 1924-31 *Career:* Pilot under training 1936; No. 166(B) Squadron Leconfield 1937-39; Instructing at No. 10 Operational training unit Abingdon on Whitley aircraft 1940-41; Flight Commander No. 104 (B) Squadron Driffield July-Sept 1941; Wellington Mk 2 Aircraft on night of 10/11 Sept 1941 Forced landing in North Sea on returning from bombing raid. All six crew members rescued from dinghy by Danish fishing boat. Taken to Ebsjerg and handed over to Germans. POW Stalagluft III until released May 1945; Commanding Officer No. 5 Air Navigation School Jurby 10M 194546; Commanding No. 10 ANS Driffield 1946-47; Air Ministry, Personnel Staff Officer 1947-48; RAF Staff College student (PSa) 1948-49; Wing Commander Air Training officer Rhodesian Air Training Group, Bulawayo 1949-51; Directing staff, RAF Staff college 1952-55; Student RAF Flying college (pfc) 1956; Commanding RAF Coningsby, bomber station 1957058; Director of Personnel (Air) at Air Ministry (Air Commodore) 1959-61; Senior Air Staff Officer RAF Germany 1961-63; Commandant RAF

Halton 1964-66. *Recreation:* Golf, walking and reading. *Clubs:* RAF, Ashridge Golf club. *Address:* Old Coach House, Wendover, Bucks HP22 6EB Tel: 0296 624724

STROUD, Prof Sir (Charles) Eric, MB; Bch; BSc; FRCP; DCH; FKC. *Currently:* Hon. Medical Director, Children Nationwide Research Fund; Hans Sloane Fellow, Royal College of Physicians; Director Overseas Dept., Royal College of Physicians. *Born on* 15 May 1924 at Cardiff. *Son of* Frank Edmund Stroud and Lavinia May Stroud (nee Noakes). *Marriage:* to June Mary Neep, 1950. *Children:* Diana Rosemary, Amanda Caroline and Charles David. *Educated at* Splott Road School; Cardiff High School; Welsh Nat. School of Medicine. *Career:* RAF Med. Br, Flying Officer 1950-51, Sqdn Ldr 1951-52; sr registrar Hosp for Sick Children Gr. Ormond Street 1956-61, paediatrician Uganda Govt 1958-60, asst to dir Paediatric Dept Guys Hospital 1961-62, consultant paediatrician King's College Hospital 1962-68, prof and dir Paediatric Dept King's 1968-88; dir Variety Club Children's Hospital King's 1984-88, emeritus prof of paediatrics Univ of London and King's Coll Hospital 1989; chm Standing Medical Advsy Ctee to sec of State 1986-89; civil consultant in paediatrics RAF; chm Overseas Ctee, trustee Save the Children Fund; second vice pres Royal Coll of Physicians, London 1989-90; MRCP 1955, FRCP 1968, FKC 1989; kt 1988. *Recreation:* fishing, golf, cricket. *Address:* 84 Copse Hill, Wimbledon, London., SW20 OEF. Royal College of Physicians, 11 St Andrews Place, Regents Park, London, NW1 4LE

STYLES, Mr Showell, FRGS *Currently:* Retired, but writing one novel a year. *Born on* 14 March 1908 at Four Oaks, Warwickshire. *Son of* the late Frank Styles and the late Edith (nee Showell). *Marriage:* to Kathleen Jane Humphreys 1954. *Children:* Glynda Jane, Elizabeth Ann and David Showell (all bilingual). *Educated at* Bishop Vesey's Grammar School, Sutton Coldfield. *Career:* Bank Clerk 1924-34; Tramp 1934-36; Freelance journalist 1936-39; Royal Navy 1939-46, Lieutenant Commander; Author 1946- ; Led two Arctic expeditions 1952 and 1953; led Himalayan expedition (to Baudha, Nepal) 1954. *Publications:* 121 books - novels, biography, children's books, detective stories; many of these have Wales and Welsh mountains as setting. *Recreation:* Mountaineering, music, gardening. *Clubs:* Clwb Dringo Porthmadog; Midland Association of Mountaineers. *Address:* Trwyn Cae Iago, Borth-y-Gest, Porthmadog, Gwynedd LL49 9TW

SULLIVAN, Mr Terence Alistair, *Currently:* Bowls Coach. *Born on* 6 Nov 1935 at Swansea. *Son of* the late Cecil Christopher Sullivan and the late Violet Ann Sullivan (nee Green). *Marriage:* to Valerie May Williams, 1957. *Children:* Carole Sullivan, Linda Sullivan and Martin Sullivan. *Educated at* Hafod Boys School; Swansea Technical College. *Career:* Bowls Player: Champion: Welsh Singles (indoor) 1983 and 1986. UK Singles 1984 (indoor). World Singles (indoor) 1985. Welsh Triples (indoor) 1985. Welsh Champion of Champions (outdoor) 1985 and 1986. Welsh and British Isles Fours (indoor). Australian Mazda Int. Singles (outdoor) 1988. Represented Wales in 29 (indoor) and 9 (outdoor) Championships. Welsh Team Captain for British Indoor Championships 1990. Welsh Pairs (Outdoor), 1990. Welsh Singles (Indoor), 1992. *Recreation:* gardening, walking, reading. *Clubs:* Swansea Indoor Bowls, Old Landorians Bowls. *Address:* 6 Ocean View Close, Derwen Fawr, Swansea, W. Glam, SA2 8EP

SUNDERLAND, Professor Eric, BA MA Phd F. Inst Biol. *Currently:* Principal, Univ. of Wales, Bangor. *Born on* 18 Mar 1930 at Ammanford, Dyfed. *Son of* the late Leonard Sunderland and Agnes Sunderland. *Marriage:* to Jean Patricia (nee Watson). *Children:* Rowena and Frances. *Educated at* Amman Valley Grammar School; Univ. of Wales, Aberystwyth; Univ. College London *Career:* Research Assistant in Anthropology, Univ. College, London

1953-54; National Service. Commissioned Officer, Royal Artillery. 1954-56; Research Scientist, National Coal Board 1957-58; Lecturer in Anthropology, Univ. of Durham 1958-66; Senior Lecturer in Anthropology, Univ. of Durham 1966-71; Professor of Anthropology, Univ. of Durham 1971-84; Pro Vice Chancellor, Univ. of Durham 1979-84; Director, Centre for Middle Eastern and Islamic Studies, Univ. of Durham. 1980-82; Chairman of NUMAC (Northern Univs. Multiple Access Computer Ctee.) involving Univs. of Durham, Newcastle and Newcastle Polytechnic. 1980-82; Vice-Chancellor, Univ. of Wales 1989-91; President, Royal Anthropological Institute of Great Britain and Ireland 1989-91; Secretary-General, International Union of Anthropological and Ethrological Sciences 1978- . *Publications:* Elements of Human and Social Geography: some Anthropological Perspectives 1973; Genetic Variation in Britain 1973 (ed jtly); The Operations of Intelligence; Biological Preconditions for the Operation of Intelligence 1980 (ed jtly); Genetic and Population Studies in Wales 1986 (ed jtly); further 80 or so articles published in journals dealing with human biology, demography and biological anthropology. *Recreation:* Travelling, Book Collecting, Gardening and Watercolours. *Clubs:* Athenaeum *Address:* University College, of North Wales, Bangor, Gwynedd LL57 2DG. Bryn, Ffriddoedd Road, Bangor, Gwynedd LL57 2EH

SUTTON, Mr Philip Colin, MILAM *Currently:* Manager, Fitness Consultant, since 1991, Health & Fitness Suite, Gosling Sports Park, Welwyn Garden City, Herts. *Born on* 4 May 1960 at Ebbw Vale. *Son of* Anne Sutton (nee Williams) and the late Eric Sutton. *Marriage:* to Jane Anne Webster, 1984. *Children:* Matthew Gordon Sutton and Robert Brian Sutton. *Educated at* Glyn Coed Secondary Modern; Ebbw Vale Comprehensive. *Career:* Sports Assistant, Surrey University 1978-81; Full time Badminton player (self-employed) 1981-87, 1st player in Wales to become licensed (Professional); most capped player in Wales at present, 86 Internationals; won 6 Welsh Singles titles 1979-86; won 1 Welsh National Mens Doubles title 1980; won 3 Welsh National Mixed Doubles titles 1987, 88, 90; took part in 2 Commonwealth Games, Australia and Edinburgh; took part in 6 European Championships 1978, 80, 82, 84, 86 and 1988; took part in 2 Thomas Cups (World Team Championships, men only, 1986, 90; International Titles Won: Oslo Open, Norway '84 mens singles, mens doubles, mixed doubles, Peru Open, Lima '82 mens singles, mens doubles, Swiss Open, Switzerland '86 mens singles; Major Open Tournaments won: Ulster Open N. Ireland, Poona Open Belgium, Northern Open, England, Lancashire Open, Wimbledon Open, Staffordshire Open, Leicestershire Open; best ever result, reached quarter final of All-England mens singles 1983, lost to Morton Frost (world No. 1); highest world ranking No. 22 Grand Prix rating 8. Golf: played for Wales in Ford Home Internationals at Belfry 1987, Wales won tournament. Racket Ball: played for Great Britain twice, 1980. Assistant Manager, Harpenden Sports Centre, St. Albans D. C., 1987-89; Operations Manager, Livingwell Health & Leisure Ltd., promoted to General Manager, Health Club, Hilton National Hotel, Watford, 1989-91. *Recreation:* golf (hcp 2), reading, collecting books. *Clubs:* Whipsnade Golf, A. C. Delco Badminton. *Address:* 2 Bowland Crescent, Dunstable, Beds, LU6 3QD Tel: 0582 666351

SWANN, Mr Benjamin Colin Lewis, C. A. *Currently:* Retired. *Born* 9 Mat 1922 at Pyle, Glam. *Son of* Henry Basil Swann and Olivia Ophelia Lewis. *Married:* to Phyllis Julia Sybil Lewis, 1946. *Children:* Jane, Nigel, Clive and Simon. *Educated at* Bridgend County School. *Career:* RAFVR, 1941; Transatlantic Ferry, 1942; Flt. Lt. Transport Command, 1944; Flight Supervisor BOAC, 1946; Apprentice chartered accountant, 1950; Audit asst., George A. Touche & Co., 1953; Treasury acct., Malaya, 1954;

Financial adviser, Petaling Jaya, 1956; Partner, Milligan Swann & Co., Chartered Accountants, Exeter, 1957; British Council, 1960, Regional Acct SE Asia 1961; Dep. Dir. Audit, 1965; Asst. representative Delhi, 1970; Director Budget, 1972; Deputy Controller Finance, 1972; Controller Finance, British Council, 1975-79. *Recreation:* Cuisine, Lepidoptery. *Address:* Malardeau, St. Sernin, 47120 Duras, France.

SWANSEA, The Rt Hon Lord (4th baron) John Hussey Hamilton, D. L. (Powys). *Born on* 1 Jan 1925 at Builth Wells, Powys. *Son of* the late 3rd Baron Swansea and the late Hon Winifred Hamilton daughter of 1st Baron HolmPatrick. *Marriage:* 1st to Miriam Antoinette Caccia-Birch, 1956, d. of A. W. F. Caccia-Birch MC of Marton N. Z. marr diss. 1973 (she died 1975); 2nd to Lucy Temple-Richard (nee Gough), 1982, d. of Rt. Rev. H. R. Gough. *Children:* Hon Richard Anthony Hussey, b. 1957, Hon Amanda Ursula Georgina, b. 1958. m. 1985 Hugh Lowther (2d), on Louisa Caroline Sarah, b. 1963, m. 1990 Paul Vincent. *Educated at* Eton and Trinity College, Cambridge. *Career:* Member of Council National Rifle Association from 1955, now Vice-Chairman, ; Member of British Shooting Sports Council from its inception in 1964, Chairman 1986-90 (now President); President Shooting Sports Trust, Welsh Rifle Association; Represented Wales (Rifle Shooting) in Commonwealth Games 1966, 1974, 1978, 1982, 1986 - Gold medal 1966, Silver Medal 1982. *Recreation:* Shooting, fishing, rifle shooting, Welsh Affairs, road safety. *Clubs:* Carlton. *Address:* House Of Lords, London, SW1A OPW.

SWANSEA & BRECON, The Bishop of-, BA (Lampeter), MA (Cantab) *Currently:* (see also Bridges, The Right Reverend Dewi Morris) Elected on Tuesday, 26th January, 1988, by the Electoral College of The Church in Wales assembled in the Cathedral Church at Brecon; Election confirmed by the Synod of Bishops of The Church in Wales at Bangor Cathedral on 8th March, 1988. Consecrated in the Metropolitical Cathedral of St. Davids on Lady Day, 25th March, 1988, by the Archbishop of Wales and the Bishops of St. Asaph, Bangor, Llandaff, Monmouth, Aberdeen and Orkeny, Wyoming, Bishop Eric M. Roberts, Bishop J. J. A. Thomas, Bishop Mark Wood and Bishop R. W. Woods. Enthroned in Brecon Cathedral on 23rd April, 1988. *Born on* 18 Nov 1933 at Beaufort. *Son of* Harold Davies Bridges and Elsie Margaret Bridges. *Marriage:* to Rhiannon (nee Williams). *Children:* (Mrs) Sian Rhian Cammack and Jonathan Huw Bridges *Educated at* S.D.C., Lampeter 1951-54; Traherne Schol. BA (Hist. Hons. 1), 1954; Corpus Christi Coll, Cambridge 1954-56; Purvis Prize & Exhib. BA (Theol. Hons 2. 1) 1956; M. A., 1960. Westcott Hse., Cambridge 1957. *Career:* D: 1957. P: 1958. Mon. Crawley Prize, 1958. C: Rhymney 1957-60. C: Chepstow 1960-63. V: Tredegar, St. James 1963-65. Lecturer, Summerfield Coll of Education, Kidderminster 1965-68: Senior Lecturer, 1968-69. Gen. Lic. Dio, Worcester 1965-69. V: Kempsey (Dio. Worcester), 1969-79. R. D. of Upton on Severn 1974-79. R: Tenby W. Gumfreston 1979-85. R: Rectorial Benef. of Tenby W. Penally & Gumfreston 1985-88. R. D. of Narberth 1980-82. Archdeacon of St. Davids 1982-88. *Recreation:* music, walking, gardening. *Address:* Ely Tower, Brecon, Powys, LD3 PDE. The Bishop's Flat, Church & House of The Good Shepherd, Eastmoor, Clyne Common, Swansea, SA3 3JA

SWEENEY, Mr Walter Edward, BA; M. Phil (Cantab); Cert.Ed. *Currently:* Consultant Solicitor with Gordon Kemp & Co., 42 Holton Road, Barry, CF6 6HD. *Born on* 23 April 1949 at Dublin. *Son of* Patrick Anthony Sweeney (Veterinary Surgeon) and Jane Yerbury Sweeney. *Educated at* Lawrence Sheriff School, Rugby; Universities of Cambridge, Hull and Aix-Marseille. *Career:* Admitted as Solicitor 1976; formed own practice in 1986; part time teacher and lecturer in Law 1981-91; Parish Councillor 1971-74; Borough Councillor 1974-76; County Councillor 1981-89; contested Stretford in 1983 general election; in November 1989, selected as Conservative prospective Parliamentary candidate for The Vale of Glamorgan; May 1991, appointed to South Glamorgan Community Health Council. *Recreation:* Walking, swimming, theatre, travel. *Clubs:* Bedford, Old Laurentian R.F.C. *Address:* 30 Teifi Drive, Barry, S.Glamorgan CF6 8TL

T

TAMLIN, Mr Keith Maxwell, LL. B. *Currently:* Senior Partner, Cuff Roberts, Solicitors, Old Hall Street, Liverpool; Director General of The Mail Traders' Association. *Born on* 19 July 1928 at Dartmouth, Devon. *Son of* Madeline Isabel Tamlin (nee Prowse) and the late Sidney Thomas Tamlin. *Marriage:* to Marian Roberts, 1954. *Children:* Helen and Michele. *Educated at* Ruthin School, Ruthin, Clwyd; University College of Wales, Aberystwyth. *Career:* Chairman, Liverpool Junior Chamber of Commerce 1960; President, Liverpool Round Table 1966; President, Liverpool Law Society 1983; Member, Distributive Industry Training Board; Mail Order Training Committee 1980; Member, Economic and Social Committee in Brussels 1984-90; member, Council of the CBI; member, Council of The Retail Consortium; member, Council of the Advertising Association; member, Post Officer Users National Council 1970-90; member, European Commission's Committee for Commerce and Distribution; Deputy Chairman H. Samuel Group of Companies 1985 and Main Board Director; Director Everton Football Club. *Recreation:* Professional football, golf, walking, swimming. *Clubs:* Athenaeum, Liverpool and East India, London. *Address:* 100 Old Hall Street, Liverpool L3 9TD Tel: 051 227 4181

TARUSCHIO, Mr Franco Vittorio, *Currently:* Chef / Patron. *Born on* 29 March 1938 at Montefano (MC) Italy. *Son of* Giuseppe and Apina Taruschio. *Marriage:* to Ann Dunant Taruschio (nee Forester). *Children:* Pavinee. *Educated at* G.S. (Osimo) Hotel School Bellagio (Como) Italy. *Career:* Restauranteur for 28 years at Walnut Tree Inn. *Publications:* contributed to various publications; personal cookery book in process of being written! *Recreation:* swimming, walking, travel, gardening. *Clubs: Address:* Walnut Tree Inn, Llandewi Skirrid, Abergavenny, Gwent NP7 8AW

TASKER WATKINS, Rt Hon Sir -, VC 1944; GBE 1990; Kt 1971; PC 1980; DL. *Currently:* Rt. Hon Lord Justice Watkins: a Lord Justice of Appeal since 1980; Senior Presiding Judge for England and Wales, since 1983-91; Deputy Chief Justice of England, since 1988. *Born on* 18 Nov 1918 *Son of* the late Bertram and Jane Watkins, Nelson, Glam. *Marriage:* to Eirwen Evans, 1941. *Children:* one d (one s decd). *Educated at* Pontypridd Grammar Sch. *Career:* Served War, 1939-45 (Major, the Welch Regiment); Called to Bar, Middle Temple, 1948; Bencher 1970; QC 1965; Deputy Chairman: Radnor QS, 1962-71; Carmarthenshire QS, 1966-71; Recorder: Merthyr Tydfil 1968-70, Swansea 1970-71; Leader, Wales and Chester Circuit 1970-71; Judge of the High Court of Justice, Family Div., 1971-74, QBD, 1974-80; Presiding Judge, Wales and Chester Circuit, 1975-80; Counsel (as Deputy to Attorney-General) to Inquiry into Aberfan Disaster, 1966; Chairman: Mental Health Review Tribunal, Wales Region, 1960-71; Judicial Studies Bd, 1979-80, Pres., Univ. of Wales Coll. of Medicine 1987- ; Pres., British Legion, Wales 1947-68, Patron 1991- ; TA Assoc., Glamorgan and Wales, 1947- ; Chm., Welsh RU Charitable Trust 1975- ; Hon. LLD Wales, 1979; DL Glamorgan, 1956- . *Clubs:* Army and Navy; Cardiff and County (Cardiff); Glamorgan Wanderers Rugby Football (Pres., 1968-). *Address:* Royal Courts of Justice, Strand, London, WC2A 2LL. Fairwater Lodge, Fairwater Road, Llandaff, Glamorgan, Tel: 0222 563558

TATE, Mr David Read, MA, MSc, ACA. *Currently:* Director, Chartered West LB Limited, Merchant Bankers, since 1990. *Born on* 10 Feb 1955 at Penarth, S. Glam. *Son of* Mr & Mrs Maurice Tate. *Educated at* Jesus College, Oxford, 1973-76 (Meyricke Exhibition); University College, London, 1977. *Career:* Deloitte Haskins & Sells 1977-80; Deloitte Haskins & Sells Management Consultants 1980-83; Barclays de Zoete Wedd 1983-90, Director 1987-90. *Recreation:* golf, opera, music, hillwalking. *Clubs:* Oxford & Cambridge, Royal Porthcawl Golf, Glamorganshire Golf. *Address:* 33-36 Gracechurch St, London EC3V OAX Tel: 071 220 8434

TATTERSALL, John Hartley, MA, FCA *Currently:* Partner, Coopers & Lybrand Deloitte (formerly Coopers & Lybrand) since 1975. *Born on* 5 April 1952 at Colwyn Bay, Clwyd. *Son of* Robert Herman Tattersall and Jean Tattersall (nee Stevens). *Marriage:* to Madeleine Virginia (nee Coles). *Children:* Robert Hartley, Luke Richard and Clare Elizabeth. *Educated at* Shrewsbury School; Christ's College University of Cambridge; Univesity of Besancon. *Career:* Kleinwort, Benson Limited 1973-75. Director, London City Ballet Trust Limited 1987- ; Churchwarden, St. Jude's Church, London SW5, 1984- . *Publications:* The Investment Business: Compliance with the Rules, 1990; (contrib) Current Issues in Auditing, 1991. *Recreation:* opera, ballet, walking. *Address:* 3 St Ann's Villas, London W11 4RU. Plumtree Court, London EC4A 4HT

TAYLOR, Professor Emeritus James Allan, MA, DipEd, FRGS. *Currently:* retired, Self-employed as founder Director of Environmental Consultants Ltd., Aberystwyth. *Born on* 20 June 1925 at St. Helens, Lancs. *Son of* the late John William and Ethel Taylor (nee Middlehurst). *Marriage:* to Sylvia Brenda Parr, 1962. *Children:* Amanda Jayne and Marcus Jonathan. *Educated at* Prescot Grammar School; Liverpool University. *Career:* Grammar School teacher of Geography, Pudsey (Yorks) and Farnworth Lancs, 1946-50; Lecturer and Reader in Geography, 1950-85, Professor of Geography, Personal Chair both at the University College of Wales, Aberystwyth, 1985-91; Moderator for 'A' level geography at U.L.E.A.C., London 1977-92; Chairman, International Bracken Group 1985-91. *Publications:* over 100 papers and 20 books (edited with contributions) in the fields of biogeography, ecology and climatology. *Recreation:* golf, jazz piano, countryside, environmental management. *Address:* Glyn Ceiro, Dole, Bow Street, Aberystwyth, SY24 5AE

TAYLOR, Mr William Bernard, M.A., I.P.F.A., F.R.S.A. *Currently:* Public Sector Consultant - Specialist Adviser to Invesco Mim. DLC, Sedgwick James (National) Ltd., Lombard North Central PLC., Member & Chairman of Finance and Review Commitee, Medway Health Authority, Governor and Chairman of Finance & Audit Commitee, Kent Institute of Art & Design, Director Interlake DRC Ltd. *Born on* 13 Dec 1930 at London. *Son of* the late Francis Augustus and the late Mary Elizabeth Taylor (nee George). *Marriage:* to Rachel May (nee Davies) 1956. *Children:* Simon, Kim and Deborah. *Educated at* Dynevor Grammer School, Swansea, University of Kent, Canterbury. *Career:*

Nat. Service 1949-51; Commnd RNVR 1950; Sub Lt. RNVR 1951-53; District Audit Service 1951-61; Treasurer Llwchwr UDC 1967-68; (Dep. Treasurer 1961-67); Asst. Educ. Officer Fin. & Management Manchester Corp 1969-72; County Treasurer Kent 1980-87 (Asst. Ct. Treas. 1972-73-Dep Ct. Treas 1973-80); Treasurer Dartford Tunnel Committee 1980-86; Hon. Treasurer South East England Tourist Board 1980-86; Financial Adviser to the Social Services Comm. Assoc. of City Councils 1984-86; MBR of Professional Committee Soc of City Treasurers 1982-84; MBR of Executive Comm. of Soc. of City Treasurers 1984-86; Financial Adviser to Standing conference of Planning Authorities in the S.E. of England 1983-86; Chairman of Working party of Council of Europe on Borrowing by Municipalities in Europe 1982-84; Honorary examiner in Accountancy for IPFA 1964-67; Member of D of I Working party on Terotechnology 1976-80. Underwriting member at Lloyds 1988- . *Publications:* Terotechnology and the Pursuit of Life Cycle Costs 1980; Author of numerous articles for Learned Magazines. *Recreation:* Public Speaking, Tennis, Golf, Cricket and watching Rugby. *Clubs:* Maidstone Rotary, Maidstone Club, Tudor Park Golf Club. *Address:* Selby Shaw, Heath Road, Boughton Monchelsea, near Maidstone, Kent ME17 4JE

TEDDY, Mr Peter Julian, BSc, MA, DPhil, BM, BCh, FRCS. *Currently:* Consultant Neurosurgeon, Radcliffe Infirmary Oxford; Consultant Neurosurgeon, National Spinal Injuries Centre Stoke Manderville Hospital. *Born on* 2 Nov 1944 at Rhyl. *Son of* Francis Gerald Teddy and Beryl Dorothy Teddy. *Marriage:* 2nd to Rosalee Margaret (nee Elliott). *Children:* Alexander, William and Timothy. *Educated at* Rhyl Grammar School; University Wales Cardiff; University of Oxford Medical School. *Career:* Medical Research Council Scholar 1968-70;.University of Oxford Medical School Scholar 1970-72; Neurosurgical training in Oxford, Bristol, Cape Town, Birmingham and Zurich; Director of Clinical Studies, University of Oxford Clinical School 1988-91; Senior Research Fellow, St. Peter's College Oxford 1984- ; Assistant Editor, British Journal of Neurosurgery. *Publications:* on Microneurosurgery, Intractable pain, Spinal Neurosurgery, Head injuries. *Recreation:* foreign travel, tennis, sailing. *Clubs:* Norham Gardens L.T.C., Oxford. *Address:* Dept of Neurological Surgery, The Radcliffe Infirmary, Oxford, OX2 6HE. St. Peter's College, Oxford OX1 2DL

TEMPLETON, Mr Richard, BA Hons, MSc. *Currently:* Director, Robert Fleming & Co. Limited, since 1978, Corporate Finance. *Born on* 11 April 1945 at Radyr, Cardiff. *Son of* Capt John Templeton and Mrs Janet Templeton (nee Morgan). *Marriage:* to Belinda (nee Timlin), 1986. *Educated at* Clifton College; Reading University (BA.Hons); Bradford University (MSc). *Career:* Barclays Bank, Clerical 1964-65; J.Henry Schroder Wagg, Clerical, 1965-66; Phillips & Drew, Analyst 1969-70; Robert Fleming, Analyst, 1971-75; Save-Prosper, Fund Manager, 1975-78. Director, West of England Trust Ltd; Director, Fleming Fledgeling Investment; Director, Trust plc. *Recreation:* beagling, reading. *Clubs:* Turf, MCC. *Address:* C/o Robert Fleming & 'Co. Ltd., 25 Copthall Avenue, London, EC2R 7DR

TERLEZKI, Mr Stefan, *Marriage:* to Mary Bumford 1955. *Children:* Helena and Caryl. *Educated at* High School in Ukraine and Coll. of Food Tech and Commerce Cardiff. *Career:* Conservative MP for Cardiff West 1983-87; Member of Parliament Select Cttee on Welsh affairs 1983-87; made radio Political Broadcast on behalf of the Conservative Party in 1987. Gen. Election; Chmn of the Bd of Governors of Cardiff High School 1974-83; Chmn Cons. Gp for European Movement 1973; Chmn of Licensing Cttee 1975-80; Chmn of Environment Serv. Cttee 1978-80; Chmn Joint Consultative Cttee S. Glam Health Auth 1978-79; Chmn Cardiff City Football Club 1975-77; Mbr Cardiff City

Cncl 1968-83; Mbr S. Glam C. C. 1973-84; Political Press Officer 1970-83; Mbr Chamber of Trade 1976-80; Mbr Hotel and Catering Inst 1965-80; Mbr Catering & Food Assoc 1980- ; Mbr S. Wales Tourist Cncl 1972-83; Mbr Welsh Joint Cttee 1975-80; Mbr Educ Auth, Cardiff City and S. Glam C. C. 1969-; Mbr Finance, Planning and Policy Cttees 1965-83; Mbr of Welsh Games Cncl 1974-80; Mbr S. Wales Police Auth 1979-83; Mbr United Nations Organisation-Temple of Peace Cardiff 1979-87; Mbr Foreign Affairs Forum; Mbr Cardiff Wales Airport Auth 1979-83; Mbr Cons. Political Central Cncl 1979-83; Mbr Official Nat & European Speaking panels of Cons. Party; Hotel Consultant; Pres of Wales Arean Young Cons. 1975-85; Mbr of UK Delegation to the Council of Europe and Western European Union 1985-87; Rapporteur to Assembly of Western European Union Cttee, for Parliament and Public Relations; 6th May 1987, Presented to the Parliamentary Assembly of the Council of Europe in Stratsbourg, a motion for a Resolution on - The Right of Ukranian peoples' to self determination and the situation in Ukraine. Member of the Council of European Convention Cttee., for Prevention of Torture, 1989; mbr Commonwealth Parliamentary Assoc UK Branch; mbr Industry and Parlt. Trust Inter-Parlt. Union, British Group; Radio and TV Broadcasts and occasional journalism; audience with Pope John II at the Vatican in Rome; met members of the Royal Family; Pres. Reagan and Mrs Reagan; Mr Mrs Gorbachev; Mr Mrs Schewernadze; Gen Haig - Supreme Commander Allied Forces NATO; Mr. Henry Kissinger and other State leaders*Recreation:* European Community; Economic Relations and International Trade; Law & Order; Environment; Tourism; Food and Catering Organisations; Senior Citizens; Human Rights; Foreign Affairs, East-West Relations, Defence, Debates, Sport and travel. Languages: Ukranian, Polish, Russian and German (basic)*Address:* 16 Bryngwyn Road, Cyncoed, Cardiff CF2 6PQ

TETTENBORN, Mr Richard Garstin, MA; IPFA. *Currently:* County Treasurer, South Glamorgan C.C., and Treasurer, S. Wales Police Authority. *Born on* 23 Sept 1940 at Camelsdale, Sussex. *Son of* Philip A. De G Tettenborn and Helena (nee Sharp). *Marriage:* to Susan Margaret Wrigley (nee Crew) 1983. *Children:* Matthew and Mark. *Educated at* Paisley Grammar School; Herbert Strutt School, Belper & Brasenose College, Oxford. *Career:* Deputy Treasurer, Mid Glamorgan 1976-79; Assistant Treasurer, West Sussex CC 1970-76; Vice President, Society of County Treasurers 1991; Commissioner, Public Works Loan Board 1991- ; Financial Adviser Assembly of Welsh Counties 1984-90. *Publications:* Various articles in Professional journals. *Recreation:* Family, gardening, golf, theatre. *Clubs:* United Oxford and Cambridge University Club. *Address:* County Hall, Atlantic Wharf, Cardiff CF1 5UW

THATCHER, Grant Ashley, *Currently:* Actor. *Born on* 24th Nov 1962 at Bristol. *Son of* Steven Thatcher and Doreen nee Lambton. *Educated at* Rodway Tech Comp. ; Filton Tech.; R.A.D.A. *Career:* Recent theatre: RSC 1990-92 season - Diomedes in ''Troilus & Cressida'', Anfriso in ''The Last Days of Don Juan'', Gaveston in ''Edward II''; televison work includes Hannay, Lovejoy, Aliens In The Family, The Diary Of Anne Frank, Strapless *Recreation:* Gardening *Address:* C/o JM Associates, 12 Flitcroft Street, London, WC2H 8DJ

THE LORD OGMORE, Gwilym Rees, *Currently:* Peer. *Born on* 5 May 1931 at Penang. *Son of* David Rees 1st Baron and Constance Lady Ogmore. *Marriage:* to Gillian Mavis, The Lady Ogmore. *Children:* Christine and Jennet Rees-Williams. *Educated at* Mill Hill School. *Address:* The House of Lords, London SW1A OPW

THOMAS, Mr (John) Alan, BSc(Hons), C. Eng., MIEE., FCMA (Prizewinner) *Currently:* Head of Defence Export Services Organisation, Ministry of Defence. *Born on* 4 Jan

1943 at Swansea. *Son of* Idris Thomas and Ellen Constance Thomas. *Marriage:* to Angela Taylor 1966. *Children:* Andrew James, b 1971 and Alexander Michael, b 1974. *Educated at* Dynevor School, Swansea; Univ. of Nottingham. *Career:* Chief Executive, Data Logic 1972-85; President & Chief Executive Officer, Raytheon Europe 1987-89; Vice President, Raytheon Company (US) 1985-89; Director, various European Raytheon Companies 1977-89; President, Computing Services Association 1980-81; Visiting Professor, Polytechnic of Central London 1981-; Member of Court, Polytechnic of Central London 1989-; Freeman, City of London 1988-. *Recreation:* Music, sport. *Clubs:* Athenaeum, Annabels. *Address:* 0217, Ministry of Defence, Main Building, Whitehall London., SW1A 2HB

THOMAS, Sir (John) Maldwyn, Fellow-Chartered Inst. of Secretaries & Administ; Barrister *Currently:* Retired; Non-Exec Director, Westland Group PLC 1985-. *Born on* 17 June 1918 at Nantgarw, Glam. *Son of* Daniel and Gwladys Thomas. *Marriage:* to Maureen (Elizabeth) 1975. *Educated at* Grammar School, Porth, Glam. *Career:* Lewis & Taylor Ltd, Cardiff, Director/Co. Sec 1940-56; Signode Ltd, Swansea, Asst. Co. Sec / Accountant 1956-59; UK Atomic Energy Auth. Commercial Agreements Manager 1959-64; Rank Xerox Ltd., Co. Sec 1964, Dir. 1969, Man. Dir 1970, Chairman/Chief Exec. 1972, retired 1980; Director, Xerox Corporation USA 1974-79; Non-Exec Dir. Intl. Military Services Ltd 1978-85; Non-Exec. Dir. Thomas Cook Inc USA 1980-84; Non-Exec. Dir & Dep. Chairman John Brown PLC 1984-86. President Welsh Liberal Party 1985-86. *Recreation:* London Welsh Societies; Politics (Lib.Dem); Rugby; Cricket. *Clubs:* Reform. *Address:* 9 Chester Terrace, Regent's Park, London NW1 4ND

THOMAS, (Roger) John Laugharne, Q. C. *Currently:* Barrister. *Born on* 22 Oct 1947 at Carmarthen. *Son of* Roger E.L. Thomas of Ystradgynlais and Dinah A. Thomas. *Marriage:* to Elizabeth Ann Buchanan of Ohio, U.S.A., 1973. *Children:* David M. L and Alison Sian B. *Educated at* Cambridge Univesity (Trinity Hall); University of Chicago. *Career:* Teaching Assistant, Mayo College, India 1965; Commonwealth Fellow, University of Chicago Law School 1970; Commenced practice as a Barrister 1972; Queen's Counsel 1984; Recorder, Wales and Chester Circuit 1987; Faculty Fellow, University of Southampton Law School 1990-92. *Publications:* Papers on insurance, reinsurance and Maritime Law. *Recreation:* Gardens, walking, travel. *Address:* Four Essex Court, Temple, London, EC4Y 9AJ.

THOMAS, Mr Andrew Crawford, FCA *Currently:* Assistant Director (Financial Affairs), Polytechnic of Wales. *Born on* 3 Jan 1947 at Cwmbran. *Son of* Edgar and Andrewina (nee Grieve). *Marriage:* to June Platt, 1971. *Children:* Sarah Louise and Rachel Elizabeth. *Educated at* Croesyceiliog GS and Garw GS *Career:* Articles to H. B. Singer, Bridgend 1965-70; British Gas 1972-85; Post Office (Royal Mail), 1985-89; Former District Councillor with Bridgend Urban District Council and Ogwr Borough Council. *Recreation:* Squash, gardening. *Address:* Poly technic of Wales, Pontypridd, Mid Glamorgan, CF37 1DL

THOMAS, Mr. Aneurin Morgan, *Currently:* retired, Director, Welsh Arts Council 1967-84. *Born on* 3 April 1921 *Son of* Philip Hopkins Thomas and Olwen Amy Thomas (nee Davies). *Marriage:* to Mary Ida Dineen, 1947. *Children:* Josephine Shan and David Christopher *Educated at* Ystalyfera Intermediate School; Swansea School of Art, U. C. Swansea. *Career:* British & Indian Armies 1941-46 (Major); Lecturer, later Vice-Principal, Somerset College of Art 1947-60; Vice-Principal, Hornsey College of Art, 1960-67; member, Board of Governors: Loughborough Coll. of Art and Design 1980-89; S. Glamorgan Inst of Higher Educn 1985-89 (Chm., Faculty of Art and Design Adv. Cttee 1985-); Carmarthenshire Coll., of Tech and Art 1985-89 (Chm Faculty of Art and

Design Adv Cttee 1985); Vice-Pres Nat. Soc. for Art Educn 1967-68. Chm Assoc. of Art Instns 1977-78. *Publications:* periodic contribs to books and professional journals. *Recreation:* reading, walking, gardening, observing with interest and humour. *Address:* Netherwood, 8 Lower Cwrt-y-Vil Road, Penarth, S. Glam CF6 2HQ Tel: 0222 702239

THOMAS, Mr Angus Arnold, MA, FIMechE, CEng. *Currently:* retired 1990. *Born on* 7 Sept 1927 at Cardiff. *Son of* David Arnold Thomas and Dorothy Mabel Thomas (nee Angus). *Marriage:* to Margaret Ruth Bird, 1953. *Children:* Charles David Arnold Thomas, Sarah Catherine Jones and Victoria Mary Jaques. *Educated at* Bryanston School; Clare College Cambridge. *Career:* National Service 1946-48; Cambridge Univ 1948-51; Joined Davy & United Engineering Co (presently Davy Corporation) as a Graduate Apprentice 1951; Sales Dept, Davy-United, as Sales Engr: became Engrg Sales Manager 1957; Director of Sales 1961; General Mangr 1970; dir Davy Ashmore Benson Pease & Co, dep chm Davy Ashmore Int, dir Loewy Robertson Engrg Co, joined Head Wrightson & Co Ltd, MD, BS Massey Ltd 1972, chm Head Wrightson Machine Co Ltd 1974, dir Head Wrightson Process Engrg 1976, dir of marketing Davy McKee Sheffield (following Head Wrightson merger with Davy) 1978, chief exec Process Engrg and Non Ferrous Div Davy McKee Stockton 1982, dir Davy McKee in HK 1986-87, dir Davy McKee Int 1990; chm Br Metalworking Plantmakers Assoc 1976-77; memb Capital Goods Ctee BOTB, European Trade Ctee BOTB, Br and South Asian Trade Assoc BOTB 1979-85; Freeman: Worshipful Co of Cutlers in Hallamshire, City of London, Court Assistant, Worshipful Co of Tin Plate Workers alias Wire Workers; memb, Joint Government Commissions for Trade and Co-operation with (severally) Romania and Poland and USSR. *Publications:* two papers on Rolling Mills in The Iron and Steel Institute Journal. *Recreation:* photography, music, field sports. *Clubs:* United Oxford and Cambridge University. *Address:* The Old Rectory, Oswaldkirk, York, YO6 5XT Tel: Ampleforth 209

THOMAS, Emeritus Professor Brinley, CBE., FBA. *Currently:* Retired. *Born on* 6 Jan 1906 at Port Talbot, Glamorgan. *Son of* Thomas Thomas and Annie Walters. *Marriage:* to Cynthia, d of the late Dr. & Mrs C. T. Loram. *Children:* Patricia *Educated at* University College, Aberystwyth and the London School of Economics. *Career:* Lecturer in Economics, London School of Economics, 1935-39; Director, Northern Section, Political Intelligence Department of the Foreign Office, 1941-45; Professor, University of Wales at Cardiff, 1946-73; Visiting Professor, University of California, Berkeley, 1980-86. *Publications:* Monetary Policy and Crises, 1936, reprinted 1983; The Welsh Economy: Studies in Expansion (ed 1962); Migration and Econonimc Growth (2nd ed. 1973) *Recreation:* Travel *Address:* 44a Church Road, Whitchurch, Cardif CF4 2EA. 2550 Dana Street, Apt 5g, Berkeley, California, 94704 U.S.A.

THOMAS, Professor David, *Currently:* Head of School of Geography 1991- . *Born on* 16 Feb 1931 at Bridgend, Mid Glam. *Son of* William and Florence Grace Thomas. *Marriage:* to Daphne Elizabeth Berry, 1955. *Children:* one s one d. *Educated at* Bridgend Grammar School; University College of Wales, Aberystwyth (BA, MA); PhD London. *Career:* Asst. Lecturer, Lecturer, Reader, University College London 1957-70; Prof. and Head of Dept, St David's University College, Lampeter, 1970-78; Head of Department of Geography 1978-87; Pro Vice-Chancellor, University of Birmingham, 1984-89. *Publications:* Agriculture in Wales during the Napoleonic Wars, 1963; London's Green Belt, 1970; (ed) An Advanced Geography of the British Isles, 1974; (with J. A. Dawson) Man and his world, 1975; (ed) Wales: a new study, 1977; (with P. T. J. Morgan) Wales: the shaping of a nation, 1984; articles in learned journals. *Recreation:* music, wine, dedicated spectator. *Address:* 6 Plymouth Drive, Barnt Green, Birmingham B45 8JB. School of Geography, The University of Birmingham, Edgbaston, Birmingham, B15 2TT Tel: 021 445 3295

THOMAS, Dr. David Albert Terence, BA; MA; M.Th; PhD. *Currently:* Senior Lecturer (Staff Tutor) The Open University. *Born on* 26 May 1931 at Drefach, Felindre. *Son of* the late Albert John Thomas and Olwen (nee Evans). *Marriage:* to Rosemary Carole Davies 1956. *Children:* Steffan, Gethin and Huw. *Educated at* Aberbanc V. P; Llandysul County Grammar; St. David's College, Lampeter; St. Catherine's College, Oxford. *Career:* St. David's Diocese, Church in Wales 1958; Church Missionary Society 1961; The Open University in Wales 1971; Secretary: British Association for the Study of Religions 1987; Director, North American Paul Tillich Society 1988-91; Fellow Royal Asiatic Society, London. *Publications:* The British: Their Religious Beliefs and Practices 1988; The Encounter of Religions and Quasi-Religions 1989. *Recreation:* Angling, classical music, Spain. *Address:* 29 Lakeside Drive, Lakeside, Cardiff CF2 6DD

THOMAS, Mr David Hugh, O.St.J. (1986); Cross of the Order of Merit of the Federal Republic of Germany *Currently:* Chief Executive, Mid Glamorgan County Council. *Born on* 1st Apr 1937 at Clydach, Nr. Swansea. *Son of* the late David Rogers Thomas and the late Mary (nee Jones). *Marriage:* to Beryl Dorothy Williams on 22nd August 1963. *Children:* Nia Prys *Educated at* Amman Valley Grammar School; Law School of Wales, University College Swansea *Career:* Solicitor to Carmarthenshire County Council 1961-64 and Llanelli R.D.C. 1964-65; Deputy Town Clerk, Port Talbot 1965-74; Deputy County Clerk, West Glamorgan County Council 1974-1980; County Clerk and Co-ordinator, Mid Glamorgan County Council, 1980-91; Chief Executive Mid Glamorgan County Council 1991-; Public and Honorary Appointments: Hon. Secretary of the Court of the Royal National Eisteddfod 1975-; Hon. Membership Secretary of the Gorsedd 1971-; Chairman of the Order of St. John Council, Mid Glamorgan 1984-; Hon. Secretary of the Welsh Counties Committee 1985-90; Member of the Welsh Arts Council and Chairman of the Arts Committee 1986-92; Director and Member of the Board of Management, Welsh National Opera 1986-91; Deputy Clerk, South Wales Police Authority 1980-90; Clerk to the South Wales Police Authority, 1990-; Chairman of the Association of County Chief Executives, England and Wales 1992-93; Member of the Council of University of Wales College, Cardiff 1990-; Director of Cardiff (Wales) Airport and of the Mid Glamorgan Training and Enterprise Council (TEC); Trustee of Bridgend R. F. C. 1991-; Founder Member of the St. Davids Forum; Member of the Institute of Welsh Affairs and Chairman of the Steering Committee which produced on behalf of the Institute the report on "Wales: The Arts of The Possible". *Recreation:* Rugby, Bowls and the Arts *Address:* Llys Gwyn, 70 Brynteg Avenue, Bridgend, Mid Glamorgan, CF31 3EL

THOMAS, County Councillor Edward John, *Currently:* retired miner and County Councillor. *Born on* 4 Sept 1923 at Newbridge, Mon. *Son of* William and Elsie Thomas. *Marriage:* 1947. *Children:* Gaynor Anne Thomas. *Educated at* Elementary, Trade Union courses and postal courses. *Career:* worked in the mining industry 45 years; Trade Union Official 30 years, still a voluntary worker for the N. U. M; member of Supplementary Appeals Tribunal for 20 years; Chairman of Valuation Appeals Panel for Taff Ely District; past member of East Glamorgan Community Health Council for 16 years, and was Chairman and Vice Chairman of that council; Freeman of Llantrisant and a member of the Town Trust. *Recreation:* gardening, local politics, looking after the interests of retired miners and their widows. *Clubs:* Llantrisant Workingmen's, Llantrisant Rugby, Mid Glamorgan County Members. *Address:* 1 Heol Gwynno, Llantrisant, Mid Glamorgan, CF7 8DD. Mid Glamorgan County Hall, Cardiff CF1 3NE

THOMAS, Rev. Edward Walter Dennis, *Currently:* Vicar St. Mark & St. Luke, Dukinfield; Officiating Chap. to H.M. Forces; Divisional Police Chap; Chap; of Grt. Manchester Special Constabulary. *Born on* 16 June 1932 at Waunarlwydd. *Son of* Roseline Jane (nee Matthias) and Edward John Thomas. *Marriage:* to Phyllis Evelyn (nee Japp), 1955. *Children:* Christopher Dennis, Andrew David, Simon Paul and Sian Maria. *Educated at* Bible Coll. of Wales; Neath Tech. Coll; St. Michael's Theol. Coll. Cardiff. *Career:* R.A.F. (air-wireless), 1951-54; Int. Nickel (Mond) Ltd, 1954-61; curate Loughor, 1963-69; Vicar, Ystradfellte, 1969-74; Vicar, St. Mark's & St. Luke's 1974- ; Chap. to Mayor of Tameside, 1977-79 and 1990-91; High Sheriff of Grtr. Manchester, 1986-87; Officiating Chap. to H. M. Forces 1988- ; Cty Cllr. Breconshire 1970-74; Chm. Ystradfellte Parish Cncl, 1972 and Community Cncl, 1973-74; Co-founder Tameside Play Council; Community Prog. Unit; Y.T.S; Age Concern; Crime Prevention Panel 1978- ; Comm. Health Cncl 1985-91; Chm. Vol. Bodies (Tameside) 1978-85, Govr. High School 1975- . Pres. Ashton Canals Festival 1992. Asst. Grand Chaplain United Grande Lodge 1989-90, Deputy Grand Chaplain, 1992 - : *Recreation:* Police, education, sport, charity, Free-Masons, helping unemployed. *Clubs:* Gtr Manchester Police Senior Officers' Mess; Army. *Address:* The Vicarage, 2 Church Square, Dukinfield, Cheshire, SK16 4PX Tel: 061 330 2783

THOMAS, The Right Reverend Eryl Stephen, M.A., Oxford 2nd Class Theology *Currently:* Retired. *Born on* 20 Oct 1910 at Bodorgan, Anglesey. *Son of* Edward Stephen and Margaret Susannah (nee Williams). *Marriage:* to Jean Mary Alice (nee Wilson), 1939. *Children:* Stephen, Clare, Michael and Patrick. *Educated at* Rossall School (Fleetwood), St. John's College, Oxford, Wells Theological College. *Career:* Curate Colwyn Bay 1933; Curate Hawarden 1938-43; Vicar of Risca 1943-48; Warden St. Michael's College, Llandaff 1948-54; Dean & Vicar of Llandaff 1954-68; Bishop of Monmouth 1968-71; Bishop of Llandaff 1971-75; Hon. Assistant Bishop Swansea & Brecon 1989; Chairman Church in Wales Liturgical Commission 1954-68. *Recreation:* Music, Reading, Gardening and Travelling. *Address:* 17 Orchard Close, Gilwern, Abergavenny, Gwent NP7 OEN

THOMAS, County Councillor Eunydd, BSc (Econ) Hons; JP. *Born on* 24 May 1940 at Llanelli. *Son of* Catherine Helena and Brinley Thomas. *Marriage:* 1975. *Children:* Michael and Matthew Ashley. *Educated at* Coleshill Secondary Modern. *Recreation:* Local politics, fishing. *Address:* 52 Tir Einon, Llwynhendy, Llanelli, Dyfed, SA14 9DF Tel: 0554 759111

THOMAS, Sir (11th Baronet of Wenvoe) Godfrey Michael David, Bt *Currently:* retired. *Born on* 10 Oct 1925 at London. *Son of* Rt Hon Sir Godfrey Thomas, BT, PC, GCVO, KCB, CSI and Lady Diana Thomas (nee Hoskyns). *Marriage:* to Margaret Cleland, 1956. *Children:* David John Godfrey, Anne Margaret and Diana Elizabeth. *Educated at* Harrow. *Career:* Army, The Rifle Brigade, Major, 1944-56; Member of the London Stock Exchange, 1956-88. *Recreation:* golf, bowls, drawing, reading. *Clubs:* MCC, Hurlingham. *Address:* 2 Napier Avenue, London SW6 3PS

THOMAS, Mr Graham Phillip, *Currently:* Instrument Maker, Comrad Electronics A/F3 Hirwaun Industrial Estate. *Born on* 2 March 1951 at Penywaun. *Son of* the late Doreen May Thomas (nee Condon) and the late Alfred Thomas. *Marriage:* divorced. *Educated at* Abertaf Selective Sec; Mountain Ash Comp; Aberdare College F. E. *Career:* Time served Toolmaker 1967-78; Engineering Apprentice instructor 1978-89; Instrument maker 1989-91; Mid Glam County Councillor 1985-91; Labour Party Member 1981-91; Member of Labour Party Parliamentary 'A' list 1988-

91; Member of A. E. U. Parliamentary Panel 1988-91; Chairman of Direct Services Cttee; Chairman of Hirwaun, Rhigos and Penderyn School Governors. *Recreation:* Music, badminton, gymnasium, reading. *Address:* 10 Greenwood Drive, Hirwaun, Aberdare, Mid Glam, CF44 9QZ

THOMAS, Gwilym Lloyd, *Currently:* Public Relations Officer, Farmers' Union of Wales. *Born on* 27 April 1932 at Aberystwyth. *Son of* the late Mabel and Evan James Thomas. *Marriage:* to Edith Doreen (nee Lewis). *Children:* Rhian Lyn Thomas and Alan Lloyd Thomas. *Educated at* Ardwyn Grammar School, Aberystwyth. *Career:* Reporter 'Welsh Gazette', Aberystwyth; Chief Reporter and Sports Editor 'Cambrian News', Aberystwyth; Freelance Reporter (Wales; Editor 'Y Tir and Welsh Farmer') *Publications:* Numerous articles for Welsh and Agricultural media. *Recreation:* photography, writing, DIY. *Clubs:* Brynamlwg SS; Aberystwyth Golf. *Address:* 43 Brynglas, Llanbadarn, Aberystwyth, Dyfed, SY23 3QR.

THOMAS, Mr Huw Owen, MB, B.Ch (Wales), MCh. Orth, FRCS(Eng), FRCS(Ed). *Currently:* Senior Consultant Orthopaedic Surgeon, Wirral Hospital Trust, since 1978. *Born on* 11 May 1941 at Holywell. *Son of* the late Goronwy Evan and Morfydd (nee Jones). *Marriage:* to Judith Audrey Classey, 1975. *Children:* Tom Owen(b. 1977) and Tristan Goronwy (b. 1979). *Educated at* Liverpool College; Welsh National School of Medicine. *Career:* Capt, TA RAMC 1970-73; House Surgeon Cardiff Royal Infirmary 1966; Prosecutor RCS 1967; Senior Registrar Wrightington Hospital For Hip Surgery 1974; Member Medical Appeals Tribunal, Fellow Royal Soc. Medicine, Member Low Friction Society. *Publications:* Metallic Implants from Crematorim; Isolated Dislocation of Scaphoid; Recurrant Dislocation of Patella. *Recreation:* Fishing, shooting, music, family. *Address:* "Pinwydden", 18 Pine Walks, Prenton, Wirral, L42 8NE. Arrowe Park Hospital, Upten, Wirral

THOMAS, Mr Huw Vaughan, BA., MSc., FBIM., MIPM. *Currently:* Chief Executive, Gwynedd County Council; Deputy Clerk, North Wales Police Authority; Director, North West Wales, Training & Enterprise Council. *Born on* 23 Nov 1948 at Wanstead, Essex. *Son of* Idris Thomas & Winifred Thomas (nee Lewis). *Marriage:* seperated. *Children:* David Vaughan Thomas *Educated at* Chigwell School, Essex; Durham University; City University, London. *Career:* London Manager, Professional & Executive Recruitment, 1973-75; Private Secretary Parliamentary Under Secretary of State for Employment, 1975-77; Principal Employment Rehabilitation Service, 1978-81; Industrial Relations Manager, Manpower Services Commission, 1982-84; Regional Director Dept of Employment, South West England, 1984-88; Director for Wales, Department of Employment, 1988-91. Finance Committee, National Eisteddfod of Wales; Council Member, Inst. of Welsh Affairs. *Publications:* Various articles on Employment & Training in UK. *Recreation:* mountain walking; cultural and historical studies. *Address:* Gwynedd County Council, County Offices, Caernarfon, Gwynedd, LL55 1SH Tel: 0286 679002

THOMAS, Mr Ian David, *Currently:* Director General and Chief Executive of IFPI, since 1982. *Born on* 16 March 1932 at Maesteg, Glam. *Son of* the late Evan Morgan Thomas and the late Nancy nee Watkin). *Educated at* Haverfordwest Grammar School; Cathays High School; Trinity College Dublin (M. A.) *Career:* Legal Assistant, South Wales Electricity Board 1961-63; Principal Assistant, The Electricity Council 1963-66; Senior Officer, The Gas Council (British Gas) 1966-68; Legal Adviser, IFPI 1968-74; Deputy Director General, IFPI 1974-82. *Publications:* various articles on Intellectual Property Law. *Recreation:* music, travel. *Clubs:* Oriental, London, Kildare Street and University, Dublin. *Address:* IFPI (International Fed. of

The Phonographic Industry), 54 Regent Street, London, W1R 5PJ.

THOMAS, Councillor Jack Frederick, *Currently:* Full time Councillor. *Born on* 10 May 1920 at Caernarfon. *Son of* John and Catherine Thomas. *Marriage:* to Elsie Thomas. *Children:* Eirian, now Mrs Eirian Griffiths. *Educated at* Caernarfon Boys School; Caernarfon Higher Grade School. *Career:* Served over 35 years in Local Government, on Caernarfon Borough Council, Caernarfon Royal Town Council, still serving on Arfon Borough Council. On Gwynedd County Council, honoured by Caernarfon Royal Town Council by being elected Mayor 1983 and 1988, also honoured by Arfon Borough Council by being elected Mayor 1991-92. Served on 32 committees, Chairman and Life member of Caernarfon Town Football Club with 35 years service, Life President of Caernarfon Swimming Club, 30 years service; President of Caernarfon branch of the St. Johns Ambulance Brigade; member of Arfon/Dwyfor health council; member, Welsh Home Safety Council; North Wales Town Council Association, Caernarfon Civic Society, Caernarfon Harbour Trust, North Wales and Lancashire Fishery Board; Vice Chairman Arthritis Care Committee Caernarfon & Dist. branch, Guide Dogs for the Blind Committee, Caernarfon Kidney Research Committee; Governor of four schools inc. one Special school for the Disabled; serving on Citizens Advice Bureau, and many other Charitable Committees. *Publications:* I am in the process of writing a book about my life; having given over 50 talks to various organisations, clubs, societies, etc. *Recreation:* football and serving the People. *Address:* Pen Y Bryn, 24 Llys y Foel, Caernarfon, Gwynedd, LL55 2LU.

THOMAS, Mr James, CBE; FRASC. *Currently:* Agricultural Business; Chairman East Dyfed Health Authority; Vice Chairman Health Promotion Authority Wales. *Born on* 3 Jan 1933 at Llanfihangel-ar-arth. *Son of* the late David and the late Hannah. *Marriage:* to Ann (nee Roberts). *Children:* David Richard, Dorothy Anna and Catrin Margaret. Chairman of Royal Agricultural Society of the Commonwealth, to 1990; Deputy Chairman 1990-; Hon Treasurer since 1977. Member: Board of Management Royal Welsh Agricultural Society. Vice Chairman of Council of R.W.A.S. Member: Council U.C. W. College of Medicine; Governor, Coleg Ceredigion; Governor, Llanwenog V.P. School; Chairman, Welsh Health Authorities; Chairmen's Com., Chairman of Joint Staff Consultative Cttee for Wales. Member: National Whitley Council for British Isles. *Address:* Tyngrug, Llanwenog, Llanybydder, Dyfed, SA40 9XL. Starling Park House, Johnstown, Carmarthen, Dyfed, SA31 3HL.

THOMAS, Mr James Raymond, B.Sc; C.Chem; MRIC. *Currently:* Retired schoolmaster. *Born on* 18 Feb 1935 at Kidwelly. *Son of* the late Trevor and Sarah Ann (nee Davies). *Marriage:* to Nesta Ann Roberts 1964. *Children:* James Robert Hywel and John Rhys Wyn. *Educated at* Carmarthen Boys Grammar School; Cardiff University College. *Career:* Welsh Schools XV 1950; Welsh A.T.C. XV 1951; Chemistry master at Llanelli Boys Grammar School 1958-66; Carmarthen Boys Grammar School, Head of Chemistry 1966-73; Carmarthen Girls Grammar School, Head of Chemistry 1973-78; Carmarthen Queen Elizabeth CAMBRIA School, Head of Science 1978-88. Treasurer Kidwelly Rugby Club 1959-90; Treasurer Kidwelly Rugby Club and Kidwelly Rugby Social Club 1964-91; Cttee West Wales Rugby Union 1972-present; Treasurer, Life Member Kidwelly Rugby Club, Life Member West Wales Rugby Union 1974-91; Welsh Rugby Union Cttee 1989-present; Governor, Glan-y-Mor Comprehensive School 1989; Examiner CSE Chemistry W.J.E.C., 1972-75; Joint Chief Examiner CSE Chemistry W.J.E.C. 1975; Chief Examiner CSE Chemistry W.J.E.C., 1976-88; Chief Examiner, GCSE Chemistry W.J.E.C., 1988-present. *Recreation:* Rugby, golf, music. *Clubs:* Kidwelly RFC; Kidwelly RFC Social;

Ashburnham Golf. *Address:* 'Roselawn', 68 Station Road, Kidwelly, Dyfed, SA17 4UR.

THOMAS, Professor Jean Olwen, FRS; BSc; PhD; MA; ScD; C.Chem; MRSC *Currently:* Professor of Macromolecular Biochemistry, University of Cambridge since 1991; Fellow, New Hall, Cambridge, since 1969. *Born on* 1 Oct 1942 at Swansea. *Daughter of* Lorna Prunella Thomas (nee Harris) and John Robert Thomas. *Educated at* Llwyn-y-Bryn High School for Girls, Swansea; University College, Swansea. *Career:* Beit Memorial Fellow, MRC Laboratory of Molecular Biology, Cambridge, 1967-69; Demonstrator in Biochemistry 1969-73; Lecturer in Biochemistry, 1973-87; Reader in the Biochemistry of Macromolecules, 1987-91, University of Cambridge; College Lecturer, 1969-91; Tutor, 1970-76; Vice-President, 1983-87, New Hall, Cambridge 1983-87; Elected member of European Molecular Biology Organization 1982; member of Academia Europea 1991; SERC, Biophysics and Biochemistry Sub-committee, 1983-86; Molecular Recognition Panel 1986-89; Council 1990- ; Royal Society Council 1990- .Elected Honorary Fellow, University College, Swansea. *Publications:* Companion to Biochemistry Vol. 1, 1974, vol. 2, 1979 (edited jointly and contributed); papers in scientific journals, especially on histones, chromatin structure and protein-DNA interactions. *Recreation:* reading, music, walking. *Address:* Department of Biochemistry, University of Cambridge, Tennis Court Road, Cambridge, CB2 1QW. 26 Eachard Road, Cambridge, CB3 OHY.

THOMAS, Mr Jenkin, BA (Hons) Lond; MA (Michigan). Deputy Permanent Representative, United Kingdom Delegation to the Organisation for Economic Co-operation and Development, Paris, since 1990. *Born on* 2 Jan 1938 at Cwmgeidd, nr Ystradgynlais. *Son of* the late William John Thomas and the late Annie Muriel (nee Thomas). *Educated at* Maesydderwen Comp. School, Ystradgynlais; University College, London; University of Michigan, Ann Arbor. Joined HM Foreign (later Diplomatic) Service in 1960; Foreign Office (Arabian Department and American Department) 1960-63; Third, later Second, Secretary and Private Secretary to HM Ambassador Pretoria Cape Town 1963; Second Secretary Saigon 1966; Centre for Administrative Studies 1968; First Secretary FCO (Defence Policy Department) 1968; First Secretary (Trade Policy) Washington 1973; First Secretary FCO (European Integration Department) 1977; on loan to Cabinet Office 1978; Counsellor (Economic), Tokyo 1980; Counsellor (Economic and Commercial) Athens 1983; Head of Claims Department FCO, 1987. *Recreation:* reading, music, theatre. *Address:* C/o Foreign & Commonwealth Office, King Charles Street, London, SW1A 2AH.

THOMAS, John Alan, BSc(Hons), C Eng, MIEE, FCMA (Prizewinner). *Currently:* Head of Defence Export Services. *Born on* 4 Jan 1943 at Swansea. *Son of* Idris Thomas and Ellen Constance Thomas. *Marriage:* Angela Thomas. *Children:* Andrew James Thomas and Alexander Michael Thomas. *Educated at* Dynevor School, Swansea; Nottingham University. *Career:* Chief Executive, Data Logic 1972-85; President & Chief Executive Officer, Raytheon Europe 1985-89; Vice President, Raytheon Company (US) 1985-89; Director, various European Raytheon Companies 1977-89; President, Computing Services Association 1980-81; Visiting Professor, Polytechnic of Central London 1981- ; Member of Court, Polytechnic of Central London 1989- ; Freeman, City of London 1988-. *Recreation:* music, sport. *Clubs:* Athenaeum, Annabel's *Address:* Room 0219, Ministry of Defence, Main Building, Whitehall, London, SW1A 2HB.

THOMAS, Mr John Richard, BSc (Hons.) *Currently:* Retired. *Born on* 11 Feb 1928 at Barmouth, Gwynedd. *Son of* the late Richard Thomas and the late Katie Thomas (nee Roberts). *Marriage:* to Mair Miles Jones, 1956. *Educated at* Barmouth Grammar School; Univ. College Wales Aberystwyth 1946-50; *Career:* School Teacher Ysgol y Grango, Rhosllannerchrugog 1951-65; Deputy Headteacher, Ysgol Morgan Llwyd, Wrexham 1965-85; President U. C. A. C. 1976-7; Chairman Local Executive Ctee. National Eisteddfod of Wales, Wrexham 1977; Member Wrexham Maelor Borough Council 1974- ; Mayor of Borough 1981-2; Member Clwyd County Council 1987- ; Former Parliamentary Candidate (Plaid Cymru); Lay Preacher (Presbyterian Church of Wales); *Publications:* Crist a'i Deyrnas Handbook for Sunday School Scholars; *Recreation:* Photography, Crossword Puzzles, Reading and Travel. *Address:* 53 Stryt y Farchnad, Rhos, Wrexham, Clwyd, LL14 2LA. Tel: 0978 841467.

THOMAS, Sir Keith Vivian, Hon. D.Litt; Hon. LL.D; FBA 1979. *Currently:* President of Corpus Christi College, Oxford. *Born on* 2 Jan 1933 at Wick, South Glamorgan. *Son of* the late Vivian Jones Thomas and the late Hilda Janet Eirene Thomas (nee Davies). *Marriage:* to Valerie June Little 1961. *Children:* Emily Joanna (now Dr. Gowers) and Edmund Vivian. *Educated at* Barry County G. S., Balliol College, Oxford. (Hon. Fellow 1984). *Career:* Fellow of All Souls College, Oxford 1955-57; Fellow of St. John's College, Oxford 1957-86 (Tutor 1957-85; Hon. Fellow 1986); Reader in Modern History, University of Oxford 1978-85; Professor of Modern History, Univ. of Oxford 1986; Pro-Vice-Chancellor 1988- ; Mbr., Hebdomadal Council 1988- ; Vis. Prof. Louisiana State Univ., 1970; Vis. Fellow, Princeton Univ., 1978; Joint Literary Dir. Royal Historical Soc., 1970-74; Mbr. Council 1975-78, Vice-Pres., 1980-84; Mbr: ESRC 1985-89; Reviewing Cttee on Export of Works of Art 1989- ; Delegate, OUP 1980- ; Trustee, National Gallery 1991- ; Lectures: Stenton Univ. of Reading 1975; Raleigh, British Acad., 1976; Neale, Univ. Coll. London 1976; G. M. Trevelyan, Univ. of Cambridge 1978-79; Sir D. Owen Evans, Univ. Coll. of Wales, Aberystwyth 1980; Kaplan, Univ. of Pennsylvania 1983; Creighton, Univ. of London 1983; Ena H. Thompson, Pomona Coll. 1986; Prothero, RHistS, 1986; Merle Curtis Univ. of Wisconsin-Madison, 1989; For Hon. Mbr. Amer. Acad. of Arts and Scis 1983; Hon. DLitt: Kent 1983; Wales 1987; Hon LLD Williams Coll., Mass, 1988; Cavaliere Officiale, Ordine al Merito della Repubblica Italiana, 1991; Gen. Editor, Past Masters Series, OUP, 1979- . *Publications:* Religion and the Decline of Magic 1971 (Wolfson Lit. Award for History 1972); Rule and Misrule in the Schools of Early Modern England 1976; Age and Authority in Early Modern England 1977; ed (with Donald Pennington), Puritans and Revolutionaries, 1978; Man and the Natural World 1983; contribs to historical books and journals. *Recreation:* visiting secondhand bookshops. *Address:* President's Lodgings, Corpus Christi College, Oxford, OX1 4JF.

THOMAS, Mr Leslie John, *Currently:* Author. *Born on* 22 Mar 1931 at Newport, Gwent. *Son of* David James and Dorothy Thomas. *Marriage:* to (1) Maureen Crawe (disolved) (2) Diana Miles, 1970. *Children:* Lois, Mark, Gareth and Matthew. *Educated at* Dr. Barnardo's Homes. *Career:* Journalist; Author; Travel Writer since 1951. *Publications:* Many inc. 'The Virgin Soldiers' *Recreation:* Music, books, philately and cricket. *Clubs:* The Lords Taverners; Saints & Sinners; Wig and Pen. *Address:* The Walton Canonry, The Close, Salisbury, Wilts. 2a Campdon Hill Court, Kensington, London, W8.

THOMAS, Mr Mark, B.Mus. Hons. Univ of Wales. *Currently:* Music Associate for S4C, Producer, musical director and composer. *Born on* 12 Dec 1956 at Swansea. *Son of* Olive Mary Thomas and Ambrose Thomas. *Marriage:* to Mary-Jane Westlake of Lymouth, Devon, 1982. *Children:* Imogen Holly, Rosanna Natalie and Tristam Ambrose. *Educated at* Gowerton Grammar School; University of Wales (Cardiff). *Career:* Co-leader Royal Ballet Orchestra

1980-82; Freelance Session violinist with LSO, RPO, National Philharmonic Orchestra, 1982-88, member of original orchestra for "Phantom of The Opera", prolific composer for film and television. Musical Director and composer for HTV, working in Light Entertainment and Drama. Producer of The Swansea Festival 1991 and composer of film scores: "Y Llyffant", Richard Burton's "A Christmas Story", HTV's "Jazz Detective", BBC2 "Trauma", Yorkshire TV's "Mind to Kill", "Yn Nos Olaleuad" (One Full Moon) Ffilm Cymru. Commissions for 1992 include: Ballet score for "The Magic of The Dream", for S4C, composed "Introduction and Allegro", to be performed at Swansea Festival (The Adagio movement was inspired by Dylan Thomas' "Return Journey. Composed the music for numerous light entertainment productions for both S4C and HTV, including "Elinor", "Merched Lazarus", "Lliean Byd, Gora'n Byd", "Mewn Glan Briodas". Compact discs on release to date include, the ballet score, "Three Men in a Boat", "The Grand Design", "String Quartet Authology", "Seven Ages of Man", "Landscapes", "Presentation and Sport", "User Friendly", "Rock of Ages", Horror and Suspense", "Classics III". In January 1990, composed the score for the WDA promotional video, "Wales in Europe", which is to be the centrepiece of the WDA display at Garden Festival Wales-Ebbw Vale 1992. Formed his own music production company, "Pirot Music Ltd", in 1987. Nominated for BAFTA Cymru Award (For Christmas Story), 1991. *Publications:* numerous compact discs of original music for various publishers. *Recreation:* music, my family. *Address:* Tavistock House, Queens Road, Sketty, Swansea, SA2 OSB.

THOMAS, Mark David Clement, BA (Hons), MA (Cantab). *Currently:* Commercial Property Surveyor, Richard Ellis International Property Consultants 1988-92. *Born on* 23 June 1964 at Swansea. *Son of* Clem Thomas and Ann Barter. *Educated at* Gowerton CS; Loughborough University; Magdalene College, Cambridge University. *Career:* Rugby *Career:* Loughborough University 1982-85; Cambridge Univesity 1985-88, 2 rugby blues; Vail RFC (USA) 1985-87; Swansea RFC 1982-88; Durban H.S.O.B. 1988; Harlequins RFC 1988-89; London Welsh RFC 1989-90; Rosslyn Park RFC 1990-92; Welsh Students 1985; Crawshays Welsh 1983-90; Middlesex 1989-90; Public School Wanderers 1989; Swiss Barbarians 1990; Bahrain Warblers 1991; Anglo Welsh 1991-92. *Recreation:* rugby, water skiing, skiing, travelling, wine tasting *Clubs:* Hawks Club, Cambridge; *Address:* 33 Hambalt Road, London, SW4 9EA. C/o Heatherslade, Blackhills Road, Fairwood, Swansea.

THOMAS, County Councillor, (Gwent), Marlene, LL.B, Barrister-at-Law. *Currently:* W.E.A. Tutor. *Born on* 15 Sept 1932 at Garnant, Dyfed. *Daughter of* William Meurig Jones and Sarah Henrietta Jones. *Marriage:* to Alan Rees Thomas, 1958. *Children:* Mair, Rhys and Thomas. *Educated at* Amman Valley Grammar School, Ammanford; UCW Aberystwyth; Grays Inn London. *Career:* Prudential Assurance Company Head Office, London; Law Lecturer Pontypool College; member of Board of Cwmbran Development Corporation 1975-87; member of the Medicines Commission 1975-80; member of Wales Broadcasting Council; member of Gwent Health Authority 1974-77; Chair of Social Services 1985-89; Deputy Leader Gwent C.C., 1989-90; Welsh Representative on the European Women's Lobby 1990-91. *Recreation:* music, walking, travel, reading. *Address:* 26 Plantation Drive, Croesyceiliog, Cwmbran, Gwent, NP44 2AN.

THOMAS, Meyric Leslie, OBE 1987, MA(Oxon). *Currently:* Solicitor. *Born on* 17 Nov 1928 at Neath. *Son of* the late Charles Leslie Thomas and the late Edith Annie Thomas (nee Turnock). *Marriage:* to Jillian Hamilton Armstrong, 1956. *Children:* Peter Leslie, Charles Leslie

and Clare Leslie. *Educated at* Oxford University; Clifton College. *Career:* National Service 2nd Lieut, Gloucestershire Regiment. Rowed for Oxford 1952-53, President OUBC; qualified as Solicitor 1956; Partner L. C. Thomas & Son, Neath 1956-90; Consultant L. C. Thomas 1990- ; Neath Borough Council 1957-72, Mayor 1967; Clerk, Neath Harbour Commissioners; Clerk, Commissioners Income Tax Neath Division; member, Post Office Users Council for Wales, Wales Advisory Committee for Telecommunications. *Recreation:* ex-president and chairman Neath RFC. *Clubs:* Vincents, Neath Constitutional. *Address:* 13 Westernmoor Road, Neath, SA11 1BJ.

THOMAS, Professor Peter David Garner, MA (Wales), PhD (London), FRHistS. *Currently:* Professor of History, University College of Wales, Aberystwyth, since 1976. *Born on* 1 May 1930 at Bangor. *Son of* the late David Thomas and the late Doris (nee Davies). *Marriage:* to Sheila Scott, 1963. *Children:* Alan, Michael (d. 1983) and Sally. *Educated at* St. Bees School, Cumberland; UCNW, Bangor; UCL, London *Career:* Lecturer, University of Glasgow 1956-65; Lecturer 1965-68, Senior Lecturer 1968-71, Reader 1971-75, UCW Aberystwyth. Chairman, Dyfed LTA since 1981; Chairman Aberystwyth Liberal Democrats since 1988. *Publications:* Books: House of Commons in the Eighteenth Century, 1971; British Politics and the Stampact Crisis, 1975; Lord North, 1976; The American Revolution, 1986; The Townshend Duties Crisis, 1987; Tea Party to Independence, 1991. *Recreation:* Lawn tennis. *Address:* 16 Penygraig, Aberystwyth, Dyfed, SY23 2JA.

THOMAS, Professor Phillip Charles, BSc; PhD; FIBiol; CBiol. *Currently:* Principal and Chief Executive of The Scottish Agricultural College since 1990; Professor of Agriculture of the University of Glasgow; Honorary Professor of the University of Edinburgh. *Born on* 17 June 1942 at Abersychan, Gwent. *Son of* the late William Charles Thomas and Gwendolen Thomas (nee Emery). *Marriage:* to Pamela Mary (nee Hirst) 1967. *Children:* Rachel Louise and Adam James. *Educated at* Pontnewynydd Primary School; Abersychan Grammar School; University Coll. of N. Wales, Bangor, B.Sc., with Honours; Min. of Agriculture, Fisheries and Food Postgraduate Scholar; Univ. of Wales, PhD. *Career:* University of Leeds: Lecturer in Animal Nutrition and Physiology, 1966-71; Hannah Research Institute: Research Scientist, 1971-87; Principal of the West of Scotland College and Professor of Agriculture University of Glasgow, 1987-90. *Publications:* Silage for Milk Production, 1982 Ed. J. A. F. Rook and P. C. Thomas, National Institute for Research in Dairying, Reading; Nutrition Phsyiology of Farm Animals, 1983 Ed. J. A. F. Rook and P. C. Thomas, Longman, London. *Recreation:* Rugby - waiting for a Welsh revival. *Clubs:* Farmers. *Address:* Scottish Agricultural College, Central Office, West Mains Road, Edinburgh, EH9 3JG.

THOMAS, Mr Richard Stephen, MIHSM; MIPM *Currently:* General Manager, Carmarthen / Dinefwr Health, East Dyfed Health Authority. *Born on* 13 June 1943 at London. *Son of* Richard Thomas and Leah Mary Bowen. *Marriage:* to Sandra Bishop. *Children:* Christopher Richard Thomas and Sarah Elizabeth Thomas *Educated at* Pentre Grammar School; University of Wales Science & Technology. *Career:* Assistant Hospital Administrator, University Hospital of Wales Cardiff; Commissioning Officer Merthyr and Aberdare Hospital Management Committee; Personnel Manager West Glam Health Authority; Assistant General Manager East Dyfed Health. *Recreation:* music, sport, walking, family *Clubs:* past chairman Carmarthen Round Table; chairman Carmarthen ex-Tablers; member Carmarthen Tywi Rotary *Address:* 7 Llygad-Yr-Haul, Llangunnor, Carmarthen, Dyfed, SA31 2LB. West Wales General Hospital, Glangwili, Carmarthen, Dyfed.

THOMAS, Mr County Councillor Robert Gwyn, A.C.I. *Currently:* Farmer. *Born* at Colwinston. *Son of* Mr Emlyn Thomas and Mrs Gwen Thomas. *Educated at* Colwinston School & Bridgend Prep. & Comm. *Career:* Pres. Bridgend & Dist. Young Farmers Club, 1965-; Chrm Glam. Fed. YFC, 1965; Vice-Pres. Glam. Fed. YFC, 1970-; Mbr. CLA, 1965-; Mbr. CLA Exec. Cmmt, 1977-; Mbr. Joint Cmmt. Welsh Coll. of Agric., 1974-; Mbr. Glam. Farmers Club, 1965- ; Mbr. W. W. A. Land Drainage Cmmt, 1977-80; Mbr. W. W. A. Consumer Advisory Commt, 1982-85; Mbr. Meat & Lvstck Commsn S. W. Region, 1978-84; Mbr. A. C. C. Agric Cmmt., 1975-80; Mbr. Forestry Commsn. S. Wales Region, 1977-85; Mbr. Cowbridge R. D. C., 1961-73; Chrmn. Cowbridge R. D. C., 1971-72; Mbr. Vale of Glam. Borough Council, 1973- ; Mbr. S. Glam. C. C., 1973- ; Chrmn, Planning Commt. VGBC., 1977-78; Chrmn. Agric. Commt. SGCC., 1977-81; Deputy Major Vale of Glam. B. C., 1977-78; Major, Vale of Glam. B. C., 1978-79; Chrmn. S. Glam. C. C., 1979-80; Mbr. Planning Commt. Leisure Cmmt., Public Health Commt., Finance & Policy Commt., VGBC, 1973- ; Mbr. Educ. Commt., Property Serv. Commt., Agric Commt., Pub. Protection Commt., Economic Dev. Commt., SGCC., 1973- ; Chrmn, Colwinston Parish Meeting, 1963-82; Chrmn, Colwinston Comm. Council, 1982; Mbr. Glam. Archives Commt, 1974; Mbr Court of Governors, Univ. of Wales, 1974- ; Mbr. and Past Chrmn, Cowbridge Comp. Govnrs., 1973- ; Govrn. Ysgol Iolo Sch., Colwinston C/W Sch., Llansannor C/W Sch; Mbr S. W. Police Auth., 1985- ; Mbr S. W. Police Auth. Bldg Commt., 1985- ; Dir. St. Donats Arts Centre, 1978- ; Mbr. Citizens Advice Bureau Commt. 1974- ; Chrmn Cowbridge Youth Centre Commt., 1974- ; Chrmn. Area Youth & Commn. Advis. Commt., 1974- ; Mbr. S. Glam. Valuation Panel,· 1988- ; Pres: Colwinston Comm. Assoc., Cowbridge Branch Cons. Assoc., Assoc. Mbr of the Inst. of Commerce *Address:* Golygfa, Colwinston, Nr. Cowbridge, CF7 7NL.

THOMAS, Mr Robert Neville, QC, MA, BCL. *Currently:* Practising Queen's Counsel, Commercial Law. *Born on* 31 March 1936 at Denbigh, Clwyd. *Son of* the late Robert Derfel Thomas and the late Enid Ann Thomas. *Marriage:* to Jennifer Anne (nee Brownrigg), 1970. *Children:* Gerran Emlyn Philip (b.1973) and Meriel Bronwen Camilla (b. 1975). *Educated at* Ruthin School; Oxford University. *Career:* Lieutenant, Intelligence Corps 1957; BA/MA Oxon 1960; BCL Oxon 1961; Called to Bar 1962; Queen's Counsel 1975; Master of the Bench, Inner Temple 1984. *Recreation:* gardening, fishing, reading. *Clubs:* Garrick *Address:* Glansevern, Berriew, Welshpool, Powys, SY21 8AH. 3 Gray's Inn Place, London, WC1R 5EA. Tel: 071 831 8441.

THOMAS, Roger Geraint, LL.B. (1966). *Currently:* Partner, Phillips & Buck Solicitors, since 1969, Head of Company Commercial Department, Member of Board. *Born on* 22 July 1945 at Cardiff, Wales. *Son of* Geraint Philips and Doreen Augusta (nee Cooke). *Marriage:* to Rhian Elisabeth Kenyon Thomas, 1971. *Educated at* Penarth County School; Leighton Park School Reading; University of Birmingham. *Career:* Vice Chairman Techniquest, Cardiff; Member of Court & Council, Nat Museum of Wales 1983; Welsh Council CBI 1987; Member of Cardiff branch BIM (Chairman 1988-90); Member Law Society 1969- ; FBIM 1984. *Recreation:* sailboarding, hill walking. *Clubs:* Cardiff & County, Penarth Yacht. *Address:* Fitzalan House, Fitzalan Road, Cardiff, CF2 1XZ.

THOMAS, Mr. Roger Lloyd, MA (Oxon). *Currently:* Retired. *Born on* 7 Feb 1919 at Abercarn. *Son of* Trefor John Thomas and Eleanor Maud (nee Jones). *Marriage:* to Stella Mary Willmett 1945. *Children:* Julian, Andrew, Ursula and Rupert. *Educated at* Barry County School, Magdalen College, Oxford; Doncaster Scholar 1936-39; Heath Harrison Travelling Scholar 1937; President O. U.

Italian Soc. 1938-39. *Career:* War Service with Royal Artillery and General Staff-Major G. S. O. 2. 1939-46; Civil Service: Ministry of Fuel 1948; Home Office 1950; Private Secretary to Permanent Secretary and successive Parliamentary Secretaries 1950-53; Treasury 1960-62; Assistant Secretary Home Office 1962-65; Welsh Office 1965-68; (Secretary, Aberfan inquiry tribunal 1967-68); Ministry of Housing and Local Govt. 1968-70; General Manager, The Housing Corporation 1970-73; Dept. of The Environment 1974-79; Adviser, Cabinet Office 1979; Senior Clerk, House of Commons 1979-84; (Clerk, Select Cttee on Welsh Affairs 1982-84). *Publications:* Sundry reports. *Recreation:* Travel, music, gardening. *Clubs:* Union (Oxford). *Address:* 5 Park Avenue, Caterham, Surrey., CR3 6AH.

THOMAS, Mrs Rosalind Mary, *Born on* 28 May 1921 at Northampton. *Daughter of* the late John Wyndham Pain and the late Nina Owena(nee Lankester). *Marriage:* 1st to John Stuart Hallam, Lieut. K. R. R. C., killed in action 1943; 2nd to Edward Llewellyn Thomas d. 1963. *Children:* Nina Munoz de Laborde (nee Hallam), Evan David Thomas and Celia M. Thomas. *Educated at* Royal College of Music 1938-39. *Career:* High Sheriff of Powys 1987-88; Chairman Powys C.C. 1987-88; Mbr. Brecon & Radnor Hospital Management Cttee 1956- ; Powys Health Authority 1973-90; Radnorshire C.C. 1964-73; Chairman Children's Regional Planning Cttee for Wales: Radnorshire L.E.A. 1964-73; Pres. Howey Young Farmers Club 1964- ; Former Pres. Radnorshire Federation of Young Farmer's *Clubs:* Former Pres. Brecon & Radnor Country Landowners Assoc., member of Executive, former member of CLA Council; Holder of Queen's Silver Jubilee Medal 1977; member of BBC General Advisory Council 1988-91; Chairman of S. East Wales Arts Assoc; Vice Pres. Radnor Council of St. John's Ambulance Brigade; Pres. Builth Wells League of Hospital Friends 1965- ; Former President of Llanelwedd Women's Institute; member of Royal Welsh Agricultural Society; Council member: Chairman Llandrindod Wells High School 1980- . *Recreation:* reading, swimming, riding, music, Church-in-Wales, community/ working with elderly people. *Address:* Pengraig, Cefndyrys, Builth Wells, Powys, LD2 3TF.

THOMAS, Professor Trevor, B.A. (Wales). *Currently:* Retired. *Born on* 8 June 1907 at Ynysddu, Gwent. *Son of* the late Mary Jane (nee Richards) and the late William Jenkin Thomas. *Marriage:* to Sheila Margaret Pilkington, 1947. *Children:* Giles and Joshua. *Educated at* Governor's Scholar at Pontywaun County School, Risca, Gwent; Sir Alfred Jones Scholar, Univ. Coll. of Wales, Aberystwyth. *Career:* Demonstrator, Dept. of Geography and Anthropology, Univ Coll. of Wales, Aberystwyth 1929-30; Secretary and Lecturer-Assistant to Prof. H. J. Fleurre, Dept. of Geography, Victoria Univ. Manchester 1930-31; Cartographer to Geographical Assoc., Manchester 1930-31; Keeper, Departments of Ethnology and Shipping, Liverpool Public Museums 1931-40; Rockefeller Foundation Museums Fellow, USA 1938-39; Director, Museums and Art Gallery, Leicester 1940-46; Surveyor, Regional Guide to Works of Art, Arts Council of Great Britain 1946-48; Designer of Exhibitions for the British Institute of Adult Education 1946-48; Director-Designate, Crafts Centre of Great Britain 1947-48; Programme Specialist for Education through the Arts, UNESCO, Paris 1949-56; Visiting Prof. of Art Education, Teachers' Coll., Columbia Univ., NY, USA 1956; Prof. of Art, State Univ. of New York, College for Teachers, Buffalo 1957-58; Prof. of Art Hist., University of Buffalo, and Art Critic, Buffalo Evening News 1959-60; Art Editor, Gordon Fraser Gall. Ltd, 1960-72; Mbr. Exec Cttee, Campaign for Homosexual Equality 1976-78, 1979-82; Hon. Sec, Gaydaid, 1980-89; Hon. Mbr. United Soc. of Artists 1980- ; Hon. Member, Bedford Society of Artits 1986; Exhibitions of paintings and theatre designs held over the years in Buffalo, Bedford, Paris, London. *Publications:* Penny Plain Twopence Coloured: the Aesthetics of Museum Display (Museum Jl, April 1939); Education and Art: a Symposium (jt Editor with Edwin Ziegfeld), Unesco, 1953; Creating with Paper: basic forms and variations (Foreward and associate writer with Pauline Johnson), 1958; contribs to: Museums Journal, Dec. 1933, April 1935, April 1939, Oct 1941; Parnassus, Jan and April 1940; Unesco Educn Abstracts, Feb 1953; Sylvia Plath: Last Encounters, Bedford 1989. *Recreation:* art, music, theatre, gardening. *Address:* 36 Pembroke Street, Bedford MK40 3RH Tel: 0234 358879

THOMAS, Professor William John, DSc., PhD., FIChemE. *Currently:* Professor of Chemical Engineering, since 1986 and Pro-Vice-Chancellor at Bath University. *Born on* 13 July 1929 at Swansea. *Son of* the late Trevor Roylance Thomas and the late Gwendoline Novello Thomas. *Marriage:* to Pamela Heather (nee Rees), 1955. *Children:* Mark Gareth and Clare Heather. *Educated at* Dynevor GS Swansea; University College Swansea; Imperial College London. *Career:* Mond Nickel Co., Clydach Swansea 1954-55; University College Swansea 1955-58 (Dept Chemistry); Atomic Energy Research Establishment, Harwell 1958-60; Univesity College Swansea, Dept Chemical Engineering, 1960-68; Professor of Chemical Engineering and Head of School of Chemical Engineering, Bath University 1968-86. *Publications:* Introduction to Principles of Heterogeneous Catalysis (with J. M. Thomas); contribution to 4 other books; over 50 original publications in scientific journals. *Recreation:* Ex WRU referee, deputy organist at Bathampton Parish Church. *Address:* University of Bath, Claverton Down, Bath, BA2 7AY. 5 Kennet Park, Bathampton, Bath, BA2 6SS

THOMAS, Mr Wyndham, C.B.E., awarded in 1982. *Currently:* Chairman, Inner City Enterprises PLC. *Born on* 1 Feb 1924 at Maesteg. *Son of* the late Robert John and Hannah Mary Thomas. *Marriage:* to Elizabeth Terry Hopkin 1947. *Children:* Sally, Jenny, Tessa and Gareth. *Educated at* Maesteg Secondary Grammar; Carnegie College; London School of Economics. *Career:* Served Army (Lieut, Royal Welch Fusiliers), 1943-47; Schoolmaster 1950-53; Director, Town and Country Planning Association 1955-67; Gen. Manager, Peterborough New Town Development Corp., 1968-83; Member: Land Commission 1967-68; Commission for the New Towns 1964-68; Property Adv. Group DoE 1975-90; London Docklands Development Corp., 1981-88; Chairman, House Builders' Federation Commn of Inquiry into Housebuilding and the Inner Cities, 1986-87 (report published 1987); Mayor of Hemel Hempstead 1958-59; Hon. MRTPI 1979 (Mem. Council, 1989-); Officer of the Order of Orange-Nassau (Netherlands) 1982. *Publications:* many articles on town planning, housing etc, in learned journals. *Recreation:* collecting old furniture, work, golf. *Clubs:* Royal Over-Seas League. *Address:* 8 Westwood Park Rd., Peterborough PE3 6JL

THOMAS OF GWYDIR, The Rt. Hon Lord Peter John Mitchell, PC, QC, MA. *Currently:* retired. *Born on* 31 July 1920 at Llanrwst. *Son of* David Thomas (Solicitor) and Anne Gwendoline (nee Mitchell). *Marriage:* to Frances Elizabeth Tessa (nee Dean), 1947 (died 1985). *Children:* Nigel, Huw, Jane and Clare. *Educated at* Llanrwst Council School; Epworth College, Rhyl; Jesus College, Oxford. *Career:* RAF 1939-45, Pilot in Bomber Command; Prisoner of War in Germany 1941-45; Barrister At Law, Middle Temple, Member of Wales and Chester Circuit 1947; Member of Parliament, Conway Division of Caernarvonshire 1951-66; Parliamentary Private Secretary to Solicitor General 1954-59; Parliamentary Secretary Ministry of Labour and National Service 1959; Under Secretary of State for Foreign Affairs 1961; Minister of State for Foreign Affairs 1963-64; Privy Councillor 1964; Queen's Counsel 1965; Opposition Front Bench Spokesman

on Foreign Affairs and Law 1964-66; Deputy Chairman Cheshire Quarter Sessions 1966-70; Deputy Chairman Denbighshire Quarter Sessions 1968-70; Deputy Recorder Cardiff, Swansea, Birkenhead, Merthyr Tydfil, Portsmouth, Oxford and Birmingham 1964-70; M.P. for Hendon South 1970-87; Secretary of State for Wales 1970-74; Chairman of the Conservative Party 1970-72; President of the National Union of Conservative and Unionist Associations 1974-76; Master of the Bench, Middle Temple 1971-91 (Master Emeritus 1991); Deputy Chairman House of Commons Select Committee on Foreign Affairs 1983-87; Arbitrator of ICC Court of Arbitration, Paris 1974-88; A Recorder of the Crown Court 1974-88. Baron (Life Peer UK) 1987. *Clubs:* Carlton *Address:* 37 Chester Way, London SE11 4UR. Millicent Cottage, Elstead, Surrey, GU8 6HD

THOMASON, Professor George Frederick, CBE, BA, MA, PhD, CIPM. *Currently:* Consultant in Personnel Management and Industrial Relations (Director: Enterprise Development and Training Ltd). *Born on* 27 Nov 1927 at Hawkshead, Lancs. *Son of* George Frederick Thomason and Eva Elizabeth (nee Walker). *Marriage:* to Jean Elizabeth Horsley 1953. *Children:* Sian Elizabeth and Geraint Richard George. *Educated at* Kelsick Grammar School, Ambleside, 1939-46; College of the Rhine Army (University of Gottingen), 1947; University of Sheffield, (Economics), 1948-52; University of Toronto, (Business Administration), 1952-53. *Career:* Royal Army Service Corps, 1946-48; Research Assistant, Dept. of Industrial Relations, Univ. Coll, Cardiff 1953-54; Assistant Lecturer, Dept. of Industrial Relations, Univ. Coll, Cardiff 1954-56; Research Associate, Dept. of Industrial Relations, Univ. Coll, Cardiff 1956-59; Lecturer, Dept. of Industrial Relations, Univ. Coll, Cardiff 1959-60; Assistant to the Managing Director of Flex Fasteners Ltd and Porth Textiles Ltd, 1960-62; Lecturer, Dept. of Industrial Relations, Univ. Coll, Cardiff 1962-63; Senior Lecturer, Dept. of Industrial Relations, Univ. Coll, Cardiff 1963-69; Acting Head of Department, Dept. of Industrial Relations, Univ. Coll, Cardiff 1966-69; Reader, Dept of Industrial Relations, Univ. Coll, Cardiff 1969; Montague Burton Professor of Industrial Relations and Head of the Department of Industrial Relations and Management Studies 1969-84; Dean of the Faculty of Economic and Social Studies 1971-73; Deputy Principal for the Humanities 1974-77. *Publications:* A Textbook of Human Resource Management (IPM, 1988); A Textbook of Industrial Relations Management (IPM, 1984); Job Evaluation: Objectives and Methods (IPM, 1980); Improving the Quality of Organisation (IPM, 1973); Experiments in Participation (IPM, 1971); The Managment of Research and Development (Batsford, 1970); The Professional Approach to Community Work (Sands, 1968) etc. *Recreation:* Gardening. *Clubs:* Cardiff & County; Athenaeum. *Address:* 149 Lake Road West, Cardiff CF2 5PJ

THOMPSON, Esq Charles Arthur Jonathan, M. I. *Currently:* Director, Historic House Hotels Ltd. *Born on* 27 May 1954 at Liverpool. *Son of* William Arthur Lisle Thompson of Anglesey. *Marriage:* to Caroline Jane Howard. *Children:* Elizabeth Jane (b. 1989) and Emily Louise (b. 1990). *Educated at* Liverpool College. *Recreation:* History and Heritage *Address:* Awelfor, Ffordd Llechi, Rhosneigr, Isle of Anglesey, LL64 5JY. Bodysgaccen Hall, Llandudno, N. Wales, Gwynedd, LL30 1RS

THOMPSON, Mr Donald Henry, MA, JP (suppl). *Currently:* Retired. Lay-Reader, Churchwarden, Council Member Somerset Trust for Nature Conservation. *Born on* 29 Aug 1911 at Swansea. *Son of* the late Henry Thompson and Irene (nee Gage). *Marriage:* to Helen Mary Wray 1942. *Children:* 4 sons. *Educated at* Shrewsbury School and Merton College, Oxford. *Career:* Assistant Master, Haileybury College 1934-46; Served R.A. 1940-45; Headmaster, Chigwell School 1947-71. *Recreation:*

Conservation, bird-watching. *Address:* Glasses Farm, Brewery Lane, Holcombe, Somerset BA3 5EQ

THOMPSON, Mr Frank Robert, BA, Dip, Ed. *Currently:* County Councillor since 1981. Leader of the Labour Group on Gloucestershire County Council, since 1985. *Born on* 1 Jan 1938 at Newark, Notts. *Son of* Mr & Mrs Arthur Robert Thompson. *Marriage:* to Janet Deirdre Skinner, 1963. *Children:* Virginia and Alastair. *Educated at* Magnus Grammar School, Newark; Hull University. *Career:* Took early retirement from career as an F. E. Lecturer on 30th April 1990. Prior to that worked for almost seventeen and a half years at Pontypool College as the lecturer in charge of General Studies, (from 1975-82 he was Head of the General Studies Dept). Have three times stood for Parliament as a Labour Candidate, in South Norfolk constituency 1964, Wells 1970 and Monmouth 1974. Staunton Parish Councillor 1979-87 (chairman of the council 1981-87 and Vice-chairman 1979-81). Elected to Gloucestershire County Council in 1981, became Deputy Leader in 1982 of the County Council Labour Group. Was chosen to be a representative of Gloucestershire County Council in 1985, on The Association of County Councils (A. C. C.) and has been a representative ever since. Member of the A. C. C. Executive Council and the A. C. C. Environment Committee. Has been the A. C. C. Labour Groups Deputy Spokesman on the A. C. C. Environment Committee since 1990 and a member of that Committees Strategic Member Group and he is frequently involved in meetings with Government Ministers. He became Vice-Chairman of the Strategy and Resource Committee of Gloucestershire County Council and Chairman of its Support Services Sub-Committee in 1991. *Publications:* some newspaper articles on political subjects. *Recreation:* long-distance walking, swimming, chess, listening to music. *Address:* Steep Meadow, Staunton, Coleford, Gloucestershire GL16 8PD Tel: Dean 833873

THOMPSON, Mr John Michael Anthony, BA, MA, FMA. *Currently:* Museums Consultant. *Born on* 3 Feb 1941 at Colwyn Bay. *Son of* the late George Edward Thompson and Joan Thompson (nee Smith). *Marriage:* to Alison Sara Bowers. *Children:* Hannah Jane and Harriet Mary. *Educated at* William Hulme's Grammar School, Manchester; University of Manchester. *Career:* Research Assistant, Whitworth Art Gallery, University of Manchester 1965-66; Keeper, Rutherston Collection, City Art Galleries, Manchester 1966-68; Director, North West Museum and Art Gallery Service 1968-70; Director, Arts and Museums, City of Bradford 1970-75; Director, Tyne and Wear Museums Service, Newcastle upon Tyne 1975-91. President, Museums North 1991-92; Museums Assoc, Fellowship Committee 1990-; Standards Development cttee, Museums Training Institute 1990- ; Adviser to Association & Metropolitan Authorities 1981-91; Councillor, Museums Association and Chair of Accredition cttee and deputy-chair of Education, during the 1970's and 80's. Arts Council of Great Britain, Art Panel member 1973-75. Chairman of Board, The Manual of Curatorship 1981- ; Founder member and first Hon. Sec. The Group of Directors of Museums in the British Isles (GODS). Directorships: North of England Museums Service 1991-92; The Museums and Galleries Consultancy Ltd 1992- . *Publications:* The Manual of Curatorship (editor) 1st ed 1984, 2nd ed 1992; articles in Museum journal, Connoisseur etc. *Recreation:* running, travel, visiting exhibitions, cinema. *Clubs:* Museums Association, ICOM, AIM *Address:* 21 Linden Road, Gosforth, Newcastle Upon Tyne NE3 4EY. 30 Llwyn Estyn, Deganwy, Gwynedd

THORBURN, Mr Paul Huw, BSc.Hon Microbiology *Currently:* Regional Executive, Welsh Development International, WDA. *Born on* 24 Nov 1962 at Wegberg, W. Germany. *Son of* Geoff Thorburn and Pauline. *Marriage:* to Sharon Elizabeth Ann 1987. *Children:* Kelly Elizabeth

Ann, born 1990, son, Rory George Thomas, born 15.3.92 *Educated at* Hereford Cathedral School; Univ. College, Swansea. *Career:* South Gower RFC; Swansea University RFC; Ebbw Vale RFC; Neath 1984-91/2; Wales 1985-91, 37 caps, Captain 1991. *Recreation:* numerous sports. *Clubs:* South Gower RFC; Swansea Univ RFC; Ebbw Vale RFC. *Address:* 15 Heol-y-Waun, Pontlliw, Swansea, W Glam SA4 1EL

THURSBY-PELHAM, Brig Mervyn Christopher, OBE (1986). *Born on* 23 March 1921 at London. *Son of* the late Nevill Cressett Thursby-Pelham, Danyrallt, Dyfed and the late Yseulte (nee Peel). *Marriage:* to Rachel Mary Latimer, 1943 da of Sir Walter Willson (d. 1952), of Tonbridge, Kent. *Children:* David Thomas Cressett (b. 1948) and Philippa Rachel Mary (b. 1943). *Educated at* Wellington; Merton College Oxford. *Career:* cmmnd Welsh Guards 1941; serv 3 Bn: N. Africa, Italy, Austria 1943-45, 1 Bn serv Palestine and Egypt, graduate Staff Coll Camberley 1950, GS02 (Ops) 6 Armd Div BAOR 1951-53, Regtl Adjt Staff Welsh Guards 1956-57, DS Coll Camberley 1957-60, Cmdt Guards Depot Pirbright 1960-63, GS01 (Ops) Allied Staff Berlin 1963-64, Regtl Lt-Col cmdg WG 1964-67, COS British Forces Gulf 1967-69, COS London Dist 1969-72, Dep Fortress Cdr Gibraltar 1972-74, Dep Cdr Midwest Dist UK 1974-76; ADC to The Queen 1972-76; dir general British Heart Foundation 1976-86 and 1988-90, co pres Royal British Legion Berks 1985-91; pres Welsh Guards Assoc Monmouthshire branch 1987-; Guards Assoc Reading branch 1991- . *Publications:* various articles in regimental publications *Recreation:* fishing, sailing, travel, reading. *Clubs:* Royal Yacht Squadron, Cavalry & Guards. *Address:* Ridgeland House, Finchampstead, Berkshire, RG11 3TA. King's Quay, Whippingham, Isle Of Wight, PO32 6NU

THYNNE, Dr John Corelli James, CB 1990; PhD; DSc. *Currently:* Director General, Electronics Component Industry Federation; Director, Camrose Consultancy Services; Governor, Polytechnic of Wales; Senior Adviser, Inter Matrix Consultancy Group; Consultant, Ensigma plc; Deputy Chairman, Museum of Science & Industry; Member, Japan Electronic Business Association Steering Committee; Member, Management Board, Royal Society / Fellowship of Engineering Science & Engineering Policy Studies Research Unit. *Born on* 27 Nov 1931 at Milford Haven. *Son of* the late Corelli James and Isabel Ann Thynne. *Educated at* Nottingham University. *Career:* Research Chemist, English Electric Co., Luton, 1955-58; Research Fellow, National Research Council, Ottawa, Canada, 1958-59; Research Fellow, University of California, Los Angeles, USA, 1959-60; Research Fellow, University of Leeds, 1960-63; Lecturer in Chemistry and Director of Studies, University of Edinburgh, 1963-70; Visiting Professor, University of Toronto, Canada, 1965; Direct entry Principal, Ministry of Technology, April 1970; Finance and Economic Appraisal Division, DTI, 1970-72; Civil Aviation Policy Division, DTI, 1972-73; Seconded to Foreign & Commonwealth Office, Sept. 1973; Army School of Foreign Languages (Russian Language Course), 1973-74; Counsellor (Science & Technology), British Embassy, Moscow, 1974-78; Assistant Secretary, Information Technology (IT) Division, DTI, 1978-83; Regional Director (Under-Secretary), North-West Region, DTI, 1983-86; Under-Secretary and Head of Information Technology Division, DTI, 1986-90. *Publications:* contributions on physical chemistry and information technology to scientific and learned journals. *Recreation:* watching cricket *Clubs:* Athenaeum, MCC. *Address:* 5 Eldon Grove, Hampstead, London, NW3 5PS. 'Hoch', Roch, Nr Haverfordwest, Dyfed

TIBBELLS, Mr John Terence, FCA, ATII *Currently:* Chartered Accountant. Principal, J. T. Tibbells & Co., Chartered Accountants, Dyserth, since 1968. *Born on* 5 May 1931 at Liverpool. *Son of* the late William Shearer Tibbells and the late Martha Tibbells (nee Fox). *Marriage:*

to Sheila Myfanwy Roberts, 1964, of Dyserth Hall. *Children:* Sally Fox Tibbells (b. 1967) and Nicola Shearer Tibbells (b. 1970). *Educated at* Liverpool College. *Career:* Subaltern, S. Lancs Regt (Prince of Wales Volunteers) 1955-57, 24 Brigade Barnard Castle & Berlin Independent Brigade. Chartered Accountant: Glass & Edwards Liverpool 1949-58, other professional firms 1962-67. Secretary Liverpool Companies in Seagram Group 1958-61. Accountant of Wine Companies in John Holt Group 1961-62. *Recreation:* country life, travel, rugby. *Clubs:* Liverpool St. Helens FC (RU), Old Lerpoolian Society. *Address:* Clarence House, Bryniau, Dyserth, Rhyl, Clwyd, LL18 6BY

TOMS, Dr Rhinedd Margaret, MB, BChir. 1967, MA 1968, MRCPsych 1981. *Currently:* Consultant Psychiatrist, North East Essex Mental Health Trust, since 1984. *Born on* 18 June 1942 at Gorseinon, Glamorgan. *Daughter of* the late David Peregrine Jones and Margaret Edith (nee Davies). *Marriage:* to Brian Frank Toms, 1968 (died 1985). *Children:* Eleanor Clare (b. 1969) and David Frank (b. 1971). *Educated at* Howell's School, Denbigh; Girton College, Cambridge; Westminster Medical School, London. *Career:* Medical Officer, London Borough of Southwark, 1968-73; Senior Medical Officer Lambeth, Lewisham and Southwark Area Health Authority, 1973-75; Training Posts in Psychiatry 1976-84; Hon Consultant St. Luke's Hospital for the Clergy 1990-; Hon. Consultant Colchester Branch RELATE 1987-; Hon. Consultant Colchester Branch MIND 1991-. *Publications:* papers on Rehabilitation and part-time training in Psychiatry. *Recreation:* gardening, music, choral singing. *Address:* 45 Oaks Drive, Colchester, Essex, CO3 3PS Tel: 0206 549547

TONYPANDY, The Right Honourable George, Viscount, Hon. DCL; DD; LL. D. *Currently:* Retired. *Born on* 29 Jan 1909 at Port Talbot. *Son of* Zacharia and Emma Jane Thomas. *Educated at* Tonypandy Grammar School; University of Southampton. *Career:* Member of Parliament 1945-83; Member of House of Lords 1983-. *Publications:* Christian Heritage in Politics; Memoirs of Mr Speaker; My Wales. *Recreation:* Charity work. *Clubs:* Cardiff & County; Travellers; Reform; Oxford & Cambridge. *Address:* Tilbury, 173 King George V Drive, Cardiff, CF4 4EP. House Of Lords, Westminster, London, SW1A OPW

TOOMEY, Mr Ralph, *Currently:* Retired. *Born on* 26 Dec 1918 at Merthyr Tydfil. *Son of* the late James and Theresa Toomey. *Marriage:* to Patricia Tizard 1951. *Children:* Anne and Frances. *Educated at* Cyfarthfa Grammar School, Merthyr Tydfil; University College, London; University of Caen. *Career:* Served British and Indian Army 1940-46; Lecturer, University of London School of Oriental and African Studies 1948; Department of Education and Science 1948-78; Under-Secretary 1969-78; Seconded to Government of Mauritius 1960-63; Principal Assistant Secretary in Colonial Secretary's Office. UK representative High Council, European University Institute, Florence 1974-78; Honorary D. Univ. (Open University) 1979. *Recreation:* Archaeology, golf. *Clubs:* Knole Park Golf club, Sevenoaks. *Address:* 8 The Close, Montreal Park, Sevenoaks, Kent TN13 2HE

TOUHIG, Mr James Donnelly (Don), *Currently:* General Manager Group of Newspapers. *Born on* 5 Dec 1947 at Abersychan. *Son of* Michael Touhig and Agnes Catherine (nee Corten). *Marriage:* to Jeniffer Hughes 1968. *Children:* Matthew, Charlotte, James and Katie. *Educated at* St. Francis School, East Mon College. *Career:* Apprentice Engineer 1963-66; Factory worker 1966-68; Trainee Journalist 1968-71; Chief Reporter 1971-77; Editor 1977-90; Gwent County Councillor 1973-; Chairman Estates Cttee 1985-89; Vice Chairman Finance Cttee 1989-91; Chairman Finance Cttee 1991-; Labour Party PPC Richmond and Barnes 1991-; Founder Director Radio Gwent; Chairman Torfaen Museum Trust; President South Wales Newspaper

Society 1990-91; Member Guild of Newspaper Editors, T & GWU. Made Papal Knight (order of St. Sylvester) December 1991. *Recreation:* cooking, reading, music, visiting France. *Clubs:* NALGO, Panteg House. *Address:* The Mount, Greenhill Road, Griffithstown, Pontypool., NP4 5BE. Bailey Group, Long Street, Dursley, Glos. GL11 4LS

TOWILL, Professor Denis Royston, DSc, FEng. *Born on* 28 April 1933 *Marriage:* to Christine Ann Forrester, 1961. *Children:* Rachel, Jonathan and Edwin. *Educated at* BSc (Eng), Bristol University; MSc, Birmingham University; DSc, Birmingham University. *Career:* Apprenticeship with Newman Industries, Yate; Dynamic Analyst with British Aerospace; Senior Lecturer, RMCS Shrivenham; Head of School of Electrical, Electronics and Systems Engineering, University of Wales College of Cardiff. *Publications:* books: Transfer Function Techniques for Control Engineers; Coefficient Plane Models for Control Systems; Analysis and Design. *Recreation:* music, sport. *Clubs:* Bristol Rovers President, Radyr C.C. *Address:* 77 Heol Isaf, Radyr, Cardiff, CF4 8DW

TOWNSEND, Mrs Joan, MA (Oxon), MSc (Wales). *Currently:* Headmistress, Oxford High School, G.P.D.S.T., since 1981. *Born on* 7 Dec 1936 at Holywell, Flint (now Clwyd). *Daughter of* Mr & Mrs Emlyn Davies (Emlyn and Amelia Mary Tyrer). *Marriage:* to William Godfrey Townsend, (now Professor W.G. Townsend), 1960. *Children:* Frances Mary Walker (nee Townsend) (b. 1965) and Helen Louise Townsend (b. 1967). *Educated at* Wigan High School 1946-53; Somerville College, Oxford 1955-58, Beilby Scholar, BA Class I, Maths 1958, MA 1959; University College of Swansea, MSc 1964. *Career:* Teaching career began at Hawarden Grammar School, N. Wales and Llwyn-y-Bryn Girls' Grammar School, Swansea. Head of Maths, School of SS Helen & Katharine, Abingdon 1976-81; Head of Maths, Cefn Hengoed Comprehensive School, Swansea 1975-76. various part-time teaching / tutoring positions with: Oxford Polytechnic, Open University, Swansea Technical College, Swansea University etc. *Publications:* paper in Quarterly Journal of Mechanics and Applied Mathematics, 1964. *Recreation:* singing and other musical activities, reading, walking, sewing, skiing. *Address:* Silver Howe, 62 Iffley Turn, Oxford, OX4 4HN

TOWNSHEND, Prof. Alan, BSc; PhD; DSc; C.Chem; FRSC. *Currently:* Dean, School of Chemistry, University of Hull, since 1989. *Born on* 20 June 1939 at Clydach, Swansea. *Son of* Stanley Charles Townshend and Betsy Townshend (nee Roberts). *Marriage:* to Enid Horton, 1962. *Children:* Robert Michael, Peter Charles and Gareth Richard. *Educated at* Pontardawe Grammar School; University of Birmingham. *Career:* Res. Fellow, Case Institute of Technology, Cleveland, Ohio 1963-64; Lecturer in Chemistry, University of Birmingham 1964-80; Senior Lecturer, then Reader in Analytical Chemistry, Univ., of Hull 1980-84; Professor of Analytical Chemistry, 1984-. *Publications:* Inorganic Reaction Chemistry, 3 vols, 1980-82; 250 research publications. *Recreation:* gardening, books, wine and food, walking. *Clubs:* Savage *Address:* School of Chemistry, University of Hull, Hull, HU6 7RX Tel: 0482 465027

TRAHERNE, Sir Cennydd George, KG, TD. *Currently:* Landowner and farmer. *Born on* 14 Dec 1910 at Coedarhydyglyn, Nr Cardiff. *Son of* the late Crd. Llewellyn Edmund Traherne RN and Dorothy (nee Sinclair). *Marriage:* to the late Olivera Rowena 1934, d of James Binney & Lady Marjory (nee Brudenell Bruce). *Educated at* Wellington, Brasenose College, Oxford. *Career:* Capt. RA & CMP Home & NW Europe (despatches) 1939-45; Barrister-at-Law, Inner Temple 1938; HM Lord Lieutenant of Glamorgan 1952-74 and of Mid, South and West Glamorgan 1974-85; Director Cardiff Building Society 1953-80; Director Wales Gas Board 1958-71; Chairman Wales Gas Consultative Council 1958-71; President Welsh National School &

University of Wales College of Medicine 1970-87; Director Commercial Bank of Wales 1972-89; Fellow University of Wales College of Medicine 1989; President Cambrian Archaelogical Association 1983-84; Hon Colonel Glamorgan Army Caded Force 1983-85; KT 1964, KG 1970. Member of Gorsedd of the Bards of Wales; Hon Master of the Bench Inner Temple. *Recreation:* fishing, walking. *Clubs:* Atheaeum, Cardiff & County. *Address:* Coedarhydyglyn, near Cardiff, S. Wales CF5 6SF

TREASURE, Professor John Albert Penberthy, BA, PhD. *Currently:* Non-Executive Director of 1). Household Mortgage Corp, 2). Afia Ltd, 3). Addison Consulting Group. *Born on* 20 June 1924 at Usk, Gwent. *Son of* Harold Paul Treasure and Constance Shapland. *Marriage:* to M. Valerie Bell 1954. *Children:* Jonathan, Julian and Simon. *Educated at* University College, Cardiff; Cambridge University. *Career:* 1st class Hons, Degree in Economics, Cardiff Univ, 1946; Joined J. Walton Thompson Co 1952; Ph. D. degree, Cambridge Univ, 1956; Chairman of J. Walton Thompson Co. Ltd, 1965; Dean of Cardiff University Business Studies 1978; Vice-Chairman of Sartchi & Sartchi - retired 1988. *Publications:* numerous articles in journals on advertising, marketing and economics. *Recreation:* golf, opera. *Clubs:* Queens, Royal Mid Surrey, Hurlingham. *Address:* 1 Cholmundeley Walk, Richmond, Surrey, TW9 1NS

TREFGARNE, Lord David Garro, Privy Councellor, 1989. *Currently:* Director of various companies; Hon. President of Metcom, 1990. *Born on* 31 March 1941 at Llandrindod Wells. *Son of* the late George Morgan, First Baron Trefgarne and Elizabeth (nee Churchill). *Marriage:* to Rosalie (nee Lane, 1968 (daughter of Lord Lane of Horsell). *Children:* George, Justin and Rebecca *Educated at* Haileybury, Princeton University. *Career:* Aviation Industry until 1979; Lord in waiting (Govt Whip), 1979-81; Parl. Sec. DoT, 1981; FCO, 1981-82; DHSS, 1982-83; Under Sec. of State (Armed Forces), 1983-85; Minister for Defence Support, 1985-86; Minister for Defence Procurement, 1986-89; Minister for Trade (DTI), 1989-90. *Recreation:* Aviation, Photography and walking. *Address:* House of Lords, London SW1A OPW

TREHARNE, Miss Jennet Mary Lloyd, LLB (Hons), Barrister-at-Law. *Currently:* Barrister, 33 Park Place, Cardiff, since July 1991. *Born on* 6 Sept 1953 at Hertford. *Daughter of* William Alan and Janet Treharne. *Marriage:* to Dr. S.W. Warren, 1980. *Children:* Huw and Sian Warren. *Educated at* Welwyn High School; London University. *Career:* called to Bar 1975; Tenant in Chambers in London, moved to Abergavenny 1982; Barrister Chambers Newport 1987-91. *Recreation:* walking, family. *Clubs:* Dale Yacht *Address:* Glaslyn, 4 Avenue Road, Abergavenny, Gwent, NP7 7DA. 73 Blue Anchor Way, Dale, Pembrokeshire

TREVERTON-JONES, Ronald, BSc. *Currently:* Senior partner, Harris Allday Lea & Brooks, Stockbroker, Birmingham. *Born on* 1 Aug 1949 at Newport, Gwent. *Son of* the late Dennis Ford Treverton-Jones and Mrs Alison Joy Bielski. *Marriage:* 1, 1971 (dissolved 1985), 2 to Jacqueline Diane, 1987, da of James Leslie Beckingham Welch. *Children:* Peter James and Michael Stuart. *Educated at* Hillstone School, Malvern; University of Wales, Swansea. *Career:* graduate trainee National Westminster Bank 1970-72, trainee N Lea Barham & Brooks 1970-74, partner Harris Allday Lea & Brooks 1976- , (assoc member 1974-76); vice chairman The Bow Group London 1979-80, chairman Birmingham Bow Group 1979-90, sec Round Table Nat Conference Birmingham, trustee Avoncroft Museum Development Trust 1989; member Stock Exchange 1975. *Publications:* Financing our Cities (with Edwina Currie and Peter McGauley), 1976; Right Wheel - A Conservative Policy for the Motor Industry, 1977. *Recreation:* country pursuits, travel. *Clubs:* Birmingham. *Address:* Ravenhill Court, Lulsley, Knightwick, Worcs.,

WR6 5QW. Harris Allday Lea & Brooks, 33 Great Charles Street, Birmingham, B3 3JN

TRICE, Mr John Edward, MA, LL.M. *Currently:* Honorary Lecturer in Law, UCW, Aberystwyth since 1989. *Born on* 29 Jan 1941 at Pembroke, Dyfed. *Son of* the late Edward Victor Trice and the late Denise Mary (nee Bray). *Educated at* Pembroke G.S., Gonville and Caius College, Cambridge (BA, LLM, MA). *Career:* Legal Dept., Manchester Corp, 1963-66; Joint founder Cambrian Law Review 1970; Lecturer in Law, UCW Aberystwyth 1966-89, emeritus ed Cambrian Law Review 1989; Sec. UCW Music Club 1973-88; member, World Congress of Legal Editors 1982; external examiner to Univs of Dundee, Birmingham and London; Hon. Mem. Soc. Public Teachers of Law; Law Legal Adviser to C.A.B., Aberystwyth. *Publications:* author of numerous articles and reviews in legal periodicals; English and Continental Systems of Administrative Law (jointly), 1978. *Recreation:* music, cats, victoriana, travel. *Clubs:* U.C.W., Staff Sports and Social. *Address:* Ty Penfro, Lluest Mews, Llanbadarn Fawr, Aberystwyth, SY23 3AU. Law Faculty U.C.W., Aberystwyth Tel: 0970 623111

TRIGGER, Mr Ian James Campbell, MA (Cantab); LLM (Cantab); LLB (Wales). *Currently:* Barrister, practising since 1971. *Born on* 16 Nov 1943 at Ruthin. *Son of* the late Walter James Trigger and the late Mary Elizabeth Trigger. *Marriage:* to Jennifer Ann Trigger (nee Downs), 1971. *Children:* Ieuan Mungo Campbell and Simon Huw Campbell. *Educated at* Ruthin School; UCW Aberystwyth; Downing College, Cambridge. *Career:* Major Scholar Inner Temple 1967; Lecturer in Law, UWIST (Cardiff) 1967-70; Part-time Chairman Social Security Appeal Tribunal 1983- ; Assistant Recorder 1986-90; Part-time Chairman Medical Appeal Tribunal 1988-; Recorder 1990-; Part-time Chairman Disability Appeal Tribunal 1992- . *Recreation:* maintaining the use of the Book of Common Prayer, gardening, walking, supporting Wrexham F. C. *Clubs:* Royal Over-seas League. *Address:* Alyn Bank, Llanarmon-Yn-Ial, Mold, Clwyd CH7 4QX. Oriel Chambers, 5 Covent Garden, Liverpool L2 8UD

TRIPP, Mr John Peter, CMG *Currently:* retired. *Born on* 27 March 1921 at Teddington. *Son of* Charles Howard Tripp and Constance Tripp. *Marriage:* to Rosemary Rees-Jones, 1948. *Children:* Charles and Shan. *Educated at* Bedford School; Sutton Valence School; L'Institut de Touraine. *Career:* Royal Marines (war service) 1940-46; Sudan Political Service 1946-54; Foreign (subsequently Diplomatic) Service 1954-81; Chairman PICA (London) 1981-86; Director, Gray Mackenzie Ltd., 1981-86; Powys County Councillor 1983-86; Chairman Montgomeryshire Branch CPRW 1990- . *Recreation:* gardening, politics *Clubs:* Special Forces, London. *Address:* Tanyffridd, Llanfechain, Powys, SY22 6UE

TROTMAN-DICKENSON, Sir Aubrey (Fiennes), PhD, DSc. *Currently:* Principal, University of Wales College of Cardiff since 1988 (University of Wales Institute of Science and Technology, 1968-88; University College Cardiff, 1987-88) and Vice-Chancellor, University of Wales since 1991. *Born on* 12 Feb 1926 at Wilmslow, Cheshire. *Son of* the late Edward Newton Trotman-Dickenson and Violet Murray Nicoll. *Marriage:* to Danusia Irena Hewell 1953. *Children:* Casimir, Beatrice and Dominic. *Educated at* Winchester Coll. ; Balliol Coll., Oxford, MA Oxon, BSc Oxon; PhD Manchester; DSc Edinburgh. *Career:* Fellow, National Research Council, Ottawa 1948-50; Asst Lecturer, ICI Fellow, Manchester Univ., 1950-53; E. I. du Pont de Nemours, Wilmington, USA 1953-54; Lecturer, Edinburgh Univ., 1954-60; Professor, University College of Wales, Aberystwyth 1960-68; Vice-Chancellor, Univ. of Wales 1975-77 and 1983-85; Chm., Job Creation Programme, Wales 1975-78; Member: Welsh Council 1971-79; Planning and Transport Res. Adv. Council, DoE

1975-79; Tilden Lecturer Chem. Soc., 1963. *Publications:* Gas Kinetics 1955; Free Radicals 1959; Tables of Bimolecular Gas Reactions 1967; (ed) Comprehensive Inorganic Chemistry 1973; contrib. to learned journals. *Address:* University of Wales Cardiff, P.O. Box 920, Cardiff CF1 3XP

TRUBSHAW, Mr (Ernest) Brian, CBE; MVO; FRAeS (Hon. Doc (Tech). *Currently:* Aviation Consultant. *Born on* 29 Jan 1924 at Liverpool. *Son of* Harold E. Trubshaw and Victoria (nee Carter). *Marriage:* to Yvonne Patricia Edmondson (widow), 1973. *Educated at* Winchester College, RAF. *Career:* RAF 1942-50. Bomber Command 1944; Transport 1945-46; Kings Flight 1946-48; RAF Flying College 1948-50; Joined Vickers-Armstrongs as Experimental Test Pilot 1950; Deputy Chief Pilor 1953; Chief Test Pilot 1960 (British Aircraft Corp); Director of Flight Test and Chief Test Pilot 1966-80; Director, British Aerospace (Filton 1980-86); Board member CAA 1986- ; Warden, Guild of Air pilots 1958-61; Director, A. J. Walter Aviation; Hon Doc. Technology (Loughborough) 1986; Derry and Richards Memorial Medal 1961 and 1964; Richard Hansford Burroughs Award (USA) 1964; R. P. Alston Memorial Medal 1964; Segrave Trophy 1970; Air League Founders Medal 1971; Iven C. Kincheloe Award (USA) 1971; Harmon Trophy (USA) 1971; Bluebird Trophy 1973; French Aeronautical Medal 1976. *Publications:* various technical papers. *Recreation:* cricket, golf, gardening, horses and ponies. *Clubs:* MCC, RAF. *Address:* The Garden House, Dodington, Nr Chipping Sodbury, Avon, BS17 6SG

TRUSWELL, Professor Arthur Stewart, MB., ChB., MD., FRCP., FFPHM. *Currently:* Boden Professor of Human Nutrition, University of Sydney 1978- . *Born on* 18 Aug 1928 at Wallasey, Wirral. *Son of* George Truswell and Molly Truswell (nee Stewart-Hess). *Marriage:* to 1). Sheila McGregor (diss. 1983) 2). to Catherine Hull 1986. *Children:* 1st Marr. Graham, John, Peter and Andrew; 2nd Marr Emma and Alice. *Educated at* Ruthin School, Ruthin, Clwyd; Liverpool University; Cape Town University. *Career:* Medical registrar Groote Schuur Hospital 1954-57; Research Fellow, Clinical Nutrition, University of Cape Town 1958-59 and 1962; Postgraduate training and research London and New Orleans 1960 and 1961; Scientific Staff MRC Atheroma Research Unit, Western Infirmary, Glasgow 1963-64; Full time Lecturer then Senior Lecturer in Medicine and Consultant Physician, University of Cape Town and Groote Schuur Hospital 1965-71; Warden Medical Students Residence, Cape Town University 1967-69; Professor of Nutrition and Dietetics, Queen Elizabeth College, London University 1971-78. *Publications:* 350 Scientific papers; Author or co-author of several books, including 'ABC of Nutrition' 1986, 1992. *Recreation:* Gardening, walking (especially on mountains). *Clubs:* Vice President International Union of Nutritional Sciences. *Address:* Human Nutrition Unit, The University Of Sydney, New South Wales 2006, Australia 23 Woonona Road, Northbridge, New South Wales 2063, Australia

TUCKER, Mr Clifford Lewis, JP, BA. *Currently:* Industrial Relations Advisor, BP plc (retired); Consultant Industrial Relations BP plc. *Born on* 18 Dec 1912 at Redditch, UK. *Son of* the late Rev. F.C. Tucker of Monmouth and the late Phebe (nee Thomas). *Educated at* Monmouth School; St. David's Univ., College, Lampeter. *Career:* Industrial Relations Staff I. C. I. plc., 1936-46; Manager, Industrial Relations Overseas B. P. plc., 1946-51; Manager, Industrial Relations UK and overseas B. P. plc., 1951-72; member: Arbitration Panel, ACAS 1972-82; member: I.L.O. Petroleum Cttee, Geneva, 1948-50; Tutor, I.L.O., Summer School for Trade Union Officers, Geneva 1955; Ford Foundation int. Conference on Industrial Relations 1965; Trustee, Toynbee Hall University Settlement 1952- ; J. P., Inner London, Chairman Thames Magistrates 1975-81; Former Alderman of Stepney, St. Pancras and of

Camden; Deputy Charter Mayor of Camden 1964-66. *Publications:* articles on Parliamentary Representation of Monmouthshire and on Chartism, in Gwent local history journal. *Clubs:* Reform; RAC. *Address:* 2 Streatley Place, Hampstead, London, NW3 1HP

TUDOR JOHN, William, MA (Cantab). *Currently:* Managing Partner, Allen & Overy, since 1992; International Finance; Financial Services. *Born on* 26 April 1944 at Cardiff. *Son of* Tudor and Gwen John. *Marriage:* to Jane Clark, 1967. *Children:* Rebecca, Katherine and Elizabeth. *Educated at* Cowbridge Grammar School; Downing College, Cambridge. *Career:* Allen & Overy Articled Clerk 1967-69; Assoc Lawyer 1969-70; Orion Bank Ltd Banker 1970-72; Allen & Overy Partner 1972 to present day. Directorships: Suttons Seeds Ltd 1978 Chm (non-exec); Horticultural & Botanical Holdings Ltd 1985 Chm (non-exec). Associate Fellow Downing College, Cambridge; Steward of Appeal, British Boxing Board of Control, City of London Solicitors' Co. Professional Organisations: The Law Society, International Bar Association. *Publications:* Chapters on Law relating to Sovereign Immunity in Euromoney's International Financial Law. *Recreation:* shooting, rugby football, music, books. *Clubs:* The Justinians, Cardiff & County. *Address:* Willian Bury, Willian, Herts, SG6 2AF. 34 Son Parc, Mercadal, Menorca, Spain

TUDOR-WILLIAMS, Dr Robert, BDS (Lond) LDS, RCS (Eng), MGDS RCS (Edin) *Currently:* Dental Surgeon, Harley Street London, since 1988, with special interest in cosmetic dentistry, headaches, migraine and TMJ dysfunction. Also Radio Dentist, LBC Radio. *Born on* 4 Nov 1945 at Haverfordwest, Wales. *Son of* the late David Tudor-Williams, LDS RCS (Eng) and Nanette Llewellin. *Marriage:* to Margaret Ann Morris of Pembridge, Herefordshire, 1971. *Children:* Laurence (b. 1973), Dylan (b. 1974) and Rebecca (b. 1979). *Educated at* Haverfordwest Grammar School; Guys Hospital London. *Career:* Assistant house surgeon Guy's Hospital 1970, house surgeon King's College Hospital 1970-71, senior hospital dental officer Eastman Dental Hospital 1972, general practice in City and West End 1970-72, princ of group practice Fulham 1972-80, clinical assistant in oral surgery Charing Cross Hospital 1974-87; in private practice: Fulham and Esher Surrey 1980-88. Lecturer Hammersmith and W London College: to med secs 1978-87, to dental surgery assts 1977-88; lecturer and course director to dental surgery assts BDA 1988- ; member Panel of Examiners: RCS (Edinburgh) 1988- , Examining Board for Dental Surgery Assts 1982- ; member: BDA 1970- (chairman Kingston and Dist Section 1983-84), Br Soc of Periodontology 1985- , L D Pankey Assoc 1985- , Br Dental Migraine Study Group 1985- , Br Soc of Gen Dental Surgery 1986- , Br Dental Health Foundation 1988- , Federation Dentair Int 1990- . Member Esher Round Table 1974-86 (Master of Ceremonies May Fayre 1976-). *Recreation:* sailing, shooting, fishing, gardening, theatre. *Clubs:* Royal Society of Medicine, Esher 41. *Address:* 73 Harley Street, London W1N 1DE. The Birches, 50 Grove Way, Esher, Surrey, KT10 8HL

TUNE, Mr Laurence Kenneth, BSc *Currently:* Chairman, Coopers & Lybrand Deloitte Executive Resourcing Ltd. *Born on* 30 Sept 1939 at Holywell, Clwyd. *Son of* Elijah Thomas Tune and Catherine Tune. *Marriage:* to Ann Bridget, 1964. *Children:* Christopher and Helen. *Educated at* Holywell Grammar School; University of Wales. *Career:* Procter & Gamble 1962-67; PA Management Consultants 1967-83; Coopers & Lybrand Deloitte as a Partner since 1983. Member of the Launch Committee for the Newtech Inovation Centre in 1987. *Recreation:* theatre, cinema. *Clubs:* Portico Library. *Address:* 8 Danebank Road, Lymm, Cheshire, WA13 9DH. Flat 1, 11 Cosway Street, London, NW1 5NR Tel: 071 402 2679

TURNER, Mrs Dorothy Marianne, *Currently:* Housewife and elected member of South Glamorgan County Council.

Born on 6 Oct 1945 at West Bromwich. *Daughter of* the late James William Jones and the late Gladys Mary Jones (nee Morris). *Marriage:* to Dr.Martin James Turner 1968. *Children:* Kathryn Frances (1972) and Ewan Michael James (1982). *Educated at* Oldbury Grammar School; City of Birmingham Teachers Training College. *Career:* Teacher in primary and special schools in West Midlands; Deputy Head Teacher, Brandhall Infants school, Sandwell; Chairman of Cardiff South and Penarth Conservative Assn; Conservative spokesman on education committee of S.G.C.C. *Recreation:* Music, reading, embroidery. *Address:* 28 Whitcliffe Drive, Penarth South Glamorgan, CF6 2RY

TURNER, John Warren, CBE, FCIOB, CBIM *Currently:* Construction Consultant; Dir. Principality Building Society 1985- ; Dir. Peter Alan Ltd 1991- ; Chairman Principality Property Sales Ltd 1991- . *Born on* 12 Oct 1935 at Cardiff. *3rd Son of* Thomas Henry Huxley Turner, CBE of Cardiff and Phebe Elvira (nee Evans). *Marriage:* to Jillian Fiona Geraldine, da of Thomas Ouchterlony Turton Hart, 1966. *Children:* 1s. Gavin Huxley (b. 1972). *Educated at* Shrewsbury, St. Johns College Cambridge. *Career:* National Service, 2 Lt. RE Middle East. former Chmn and MD, E. Turner & Sons Ltd (Dir 1964-89); Chairman Building Regulations Advisory Ctee (BRAC) 1985-91 (member 1972-91); Member Cncl British Board of Agreement (BBA) 1980- ; Chmn Cncl for Building and Civil Engineering, BSI 1985-91; Chmn Technical Sector Bd for Building and Civil Engineering, BSI 1991- ; UK Permanent Representative Technical Sector Bd for Building and Civil Engineering, European Committee for Standardisation (CEN) 1990- ; President, Building Employers Confederation 1985-86 (Chmn Building Practice Committee 1977-81 and 1986- ; Chmn Wages & Conditions Committee 1981-84; President South Wales Region 1978, Member, National Joint Council for The Building Industry 1980- (Leader, Employers Side 1981-84); President, Concrete Society 1976-77 (Chmn Wales Committee 1972); Member, Employment Committee, Inst of Directors 1982- (Chairman Wales Ctee 1979-81; President Wales Division 1981-86); Member Wales Council CBI, 1980-86 (Chairman South Glamorgan Group 1984-86); Member TAVR Association for Wales 1974-91; Member South Glamorgan Crime Prevention Panel 1971-84 (Chairman Cardiff Panel 1979-84); JP for South Glamorgan 1979-85; Governor Christ College, Brecon 1981-84; Member, Building & Civil Engineering Joint Advisory Ctee for Wales 1976-80; Member Medium & Small Firms Advisory Group for 1992 (DTI), 1988-91; UK Employer Delegate XII Construction Industry Conference 1LO Geneva 1983; UK Employer Delegate XIII Construction Industry Conference ILO Geneva 1987; Deputy Leader Concrete Society Delegation to Peoples Republic of China 1975. Member Housing Mission from Great Britain and Ireland to Canada 1967. Award: I.A.A.S. Peter Stone Award for his contribution to the development of Building Regulations. *Recreation:* golf. *Clubs:* Cardiff & County; Leander; Royal Porthcawl Golf; Royal & Ancient Golf. *Address:* 38 Victoria Road, Penarth, S.Glam, CF6 2HX

TYRRELL, Dr Jean Margaret, OBE, LLD, LD *Currently:* Chairman Sirdar PLC, since 1960. *Born on* 1 July 1918 at Wakefield. *Daughter of* Frederick and Bertha Harrap. *Marriage:* 15 July 1944. *Children:* Susan, Maureen and Carolyn. *Educated at* St. Leonards School, St. Andrews Fife; Geneve University. *Career:* joined Sirdar September 1939, Director 1953, Joint Managing Director 1959, Chairman & Joint Managing Director 1960. *Recreation:* golf, sailing, bridge *Clubs:* Wakefield Golf *Address:* 23 Woodthorpe Lane, Sandal, Wakefield, West Yorkshire, WF2 6JG. Keewaydin, Golf Road, Abersoch

U

UNDERHILL, Professor Allan Edward, BSc, PhD, DSc, FRCS, CChem. *Currently:* Professor, Dept. of Chemistry, Univ. of Wales, Bangor, since 1983. *Born on* 13 Dec 1935 at Derby. *Son of* the late Albert Underhill and the late Winifred (nee Bailey). *Marriage:* to Audrey Jean, 1960. *Children:* Ann Caroline and David Edward. *Educated at* Derby Grammar School; Univ. of Hull. *Career:* Research Chemist ICI Ltd., 1961-62; Lecturer, Univ of Loughborough 1962-65; Lecturer, Univ of Wales, Bangor 1965-74, Senior Lecturer 1974-83; SERC Co-ordinator Initiative in 21st Century Materials 1988- . *Publications:* over 180 papers in journals related to chemistry and materials. *Recreation:* photography, badminton, theatre. *Address:* Dept. of Chemistry, Univ. of Wales, Bangor, Gwynedd, LL57 2UW Tel: 0248 351151

UNWIN, Cllr David Alan, *Currently:* Manager, ʳed Dragon Sport Mail Order Company, Bridgend since 1987. *Born on* 21 Jan 1947 at London. *Son of* the late William Henry and Doris Edna (nee Fisk). *Educated at* Southgate County Grammar, London. *Career:* UK Distribution and Export Shipping Manager, H.M. Royal Mint 1964-83; Political Agent Bridgend 1983-87; Political Career-Member Ogwr Borough Council 1976- ; Opposition Leader since 1983; Member Mid Glamorgan County Council 1977-85; Member St. Brides Major Community Council 1979- ; Chairman three successive years 1981-84; member Bridgend Town Council 1984- ; Mayor of Bridgend 1990-91; Selected as Conservative prospective Parliamentary candidate for Bridgend in 1989. *Recreation:* Amateur Drama, Philately, travel. *Clubs:* Active member Bridgend Chamber of Trade. *Address:* 4 West Farm Road, Ogmore-By-Sea, Bridgend, Mid Glam, CF32 OPU

URSELL, The Revd Philip Elliott, MA *Born on* 3 Dec 1942 at Cardiff. *Son of* the late Clifford Edwin Ursell and the late Hilda Jane Ursell (nee Tucker). *Educated at* Cathays HS, Cardiff; Univ College Cardiff (BA); St.Stephen's House Oxford (MA). *Career:* ordained Llandaff Cathedral: deacon 1968. priest 1969; asst. curate Newton Nottage 1968-71; asst. chaplain Univ Coll Cardiff 1971-77; chaplain The Poly of Wales 1974-77; fell chaplain and dir of studies in music Emmanuel Coll Cambridge 1977-82; princ Pusey House Oxford 1982- ; fell St. Cross Coll Oxford 1982- ; warden Soc of the Holy and Undivided Trinity Ascot Priory 1986- ; examining chaplain to the Bishop of London 1986- . *Address:* Pusey House, Oxford OX1 3LZ Tel: 0865 278415

VALLANCE - OWEN, Professor John, MA., MD., (Cantab), FRCP, FRCPI, FRCPath. *Currently:* visiting Professor, The Royal Postgraduate Medical School, Hammersmith Hospital since 1988; Consultant Physician, London Independent Hospital E1, since 1988. *Born on* 31 Oct 1920 at Ealing. *Son of* Edwin Owen and Julia (nee Vallance). *Marriage:* to Renee Thornton, 1950. *Children:* two s two d. *Educated at* Friars School Bangor; Epsom College; St. Johns College Cambridge; The London Hospital. *Career:* At the London Hospital: various appointments including pathology assistant and medical first assistant to Sir Horace Evans - later Lord Evans of Merthyr Tydfil, 1946-51; at the Royal Postgraduate Medical School of London, Hammersmith Hospital: various appointments including liaison physician with the obstetric department and senior medical registrar to Professor Russell Fraser, 1951-55 and 1956-58; Rockerfeller Travelling Fellowhsip, University of Pennsylvania, Philadelphia, USA, 1955-56; At the Royal Victoria Infirmary, Newcastle-upon-Tyne: Consultant Physician and Lecturer in Medicine, Durham University, 1958-64; Consultant Physician and Reader in Medicine, Univ of Newcastle-upon-Tyne, 1964-66; Consultant Physician and Professor of Medicine, The Queen's University of Belfast at the Royal Victoria Hospital, Belfast, N. Ireland, 1966-82; Director of Mechanical Services, the Maltese Islands 1981-82; Foundation Professor and Chairman of the Department of Medicine, The Chinese Univ of Hong Kong, at the Prince of Wales Hospital, Shatin, NT, Hong Kong, 1983-88; Associate Dean of the Faculty of Medicine, The Chinese University of Hong Kong, 1984-88; Honorary Consultant in Medicine to the Hong Kong Government and to the Prince of Wales Hospital, 1984-88; Honorary Consultant in Medicine to the British Army in Hong Kong, 1985-88 *Publications:* Essentials of Cardiology, 1961 2nd ed. 1968, Lloyd Luke Ltd; Diabetes: Its Physiological and Biochemical Basis, 1975 MTP Press Ltd; numerous original papers in medical and scientific journals. *Recreation:* music, golf, tennis. *Clubs:* East India, Gog/magog (golf), United Services Recreation (Hong Kong). *Address:* 10 Spinney Drive, Great Shelford, Cambridge, CB2 5LY. 17 St Matthews Lodge, Oakley Square, London, NW1 1NB

VAUGHAN, Rt. Rev. Benjamin Noel Young, *Currently:* retired, Hon. Assistant Bishop, Swansea and Brecon. *Born on* 25 Dec 1917 *Son of* the late Aldermann and Mrs J. O. Vaughan, Newport, Pembs. *Marriage:* to Nesta Lewis, 1945 (d 1980); to Magdalene Reynolds 1987. *Educated at* St. David's Coll., Lampeter (BA; Hon. Fellow 1990); St. Edmund Hall, Oxford (MA); *Career:* Westcott House, Cambridge, Deacon 1943; Priest 1944; Curate of Llanon 1943-45; St. David's, Carmarthen 1945-48; Tutor, Codrington Coll., Barbados 1948-52; Lecturer in Theology, St. David's Coll., Lampeter, and Public Preacher, Diocese of St. David's 1952-55; Rector, Holy Trinity Cathedral, Port of Spain, and Dean of Trinidad 1955-61; Bishop Suffragan of Mandeville 1961-67; Bishop of British Honduras 1967-71; Assistant Bishop and Dean of Bangor 1971-76; Bishop of Swansea and Brecon 1976-87; Examining Chaplain to Bishop of Barbados 1951-52; to Bishop of Trinidad 1955-61; Commissary for Barbados 1952-55;

Formerly Chairman: Nat. Council for Educn in British Honduras; Govt Junior Secondary Sch; Provincial Commn on Theological Educn in WI; Provincial Cttee on Reunion of Churches, Christian Social Council of British Honduras; Ecumerical Commn of British Honduras; Agric. Commn of Churches of British Honduras. Chairman: Provincial Cttee on Missions, Church in Wales; Church and Soc. Dept, Council of Churches for Wales; Adv. Cttee on Church and Society, Churches in Wales 1977; Judge of Provincial Court, Church in Wales, Pres., Council of Churches for WQales 1980-82. Member: St. David's Univ. Coll., Lampeter 1976-89 (Sub-visitor 1987-); Council and Ct, Swansea Univ. Coll., 1976-89; Ct, Univ. of Wales 1986-89. Sub-Prelate, OStJ 1977; Order of Druids, Gorsedd y Beirdd; Chairman Christ College; Hon Fellow UC Lampeter. *Publications:* Structures for Renewal 1967; Wealth, Peace and Godliness 1968; The Expectation of the Poor 1972. *Address:* 4 Caswell Drive, Caswell, Swansea, West Glam., SA3 4RJ Tel: 0792 360646

VAUGHAN, Professor David John, D.Phil; DSc; FIMM. *Currently:* Professor of Mineralogy, University of Manchester (and Chairman, Manchester University Geoscience Research Institute), since 1988. *Born on* 10 April 1946 at Newport, Gwent, Wales. *Son of* the late Samuel John Vaughan and the late Esther (nee Edwards). *Marriage:* to Heather Elizabeth Ross, 1971. *Children:* one s, Emlyn James. *Educated at* Newport High School (Newport, Gwent); London Univ. ; Oxford Univ. *Career:* Visiting Scientist, Canada Centre for Minerals and Energy Technology, Ottawa 1970; Research Associate, Massachusetts Institute of Technology (Cambridge Mass, USA) 1971-74; Lecturer, Geological Sciences, Aston University (Birmingham) 1974-79; Reader in Mineralogy, Aston University 1979-88; Visiting Professor, Virginia Polytechnic Inst & State University 1980; President, Mineralogical Society (of Gt. Britain) 1988-89. *Publications:* Mineral Chemistry of Metal Sulfides (with J. Craig), Cambridge U. P., 1978; Ore Microscopy and Ore Petrography (with J. Craig) Wiley, 1981; Resources of the Earth (with J. Craig and B. Skinner) Prentice-Hall 1987; Theoretical Geochemistry (with J. Tossell) Oxford U. P., 1992; plus over 100 scientific papers. *Recreation:* painting, walking, aerobics, music. *Address:* Department of Geology, The University, Manchester, M13 9PL

VAUGHAN, Doctor Elizabeth, LRAM; ARAM; FRAM; Hon. D. Mus. *Currently:* Professor of singing, Guildhall School of Music and Drama and W.C.M.D. *Born on* 12 March 1937 at Llanfyllin. *Daughter of* Mr & Mrs Wm. Jones. *Marriage:* to Ray Brown. *Children:* Mark and Sarah. *Educated at* Llanfyllin Grammar School; Royal Academy of Music. *Career:* Debut W.N.O; Royal Opera House, roles - Butterfly, Traviata, Leonora, Gilda, Abigaille, Elettra, Donna Elvira, Teresa, Llu, Musetta, Alice; E.N.O. guest Aida, Butterfly, Fidelio; S.N.O., W.N.O., Opera North, Lady Macbeth, Abigaille, Butterfly, Traviata; worldwide - Metropolitan, New York, Paris, Vienna, Florence, Berlin, Hamberg, Japan, S. America, Canada, Australia; T.V., Radio Symphony concerts. *Recreation:* Antique Fairs, cooking, needlepoint. *Address:* 19 Battersea Square, London SW11 3RA

VAUGHAN, Sir Edgar George Edgar, KBE; MA; FRHS. *Currently:* retired University Professor and British diplomat. *Born on* 24 Feb 1907 at Cardiff. *Son of* William John Vaughan and Emma Kate Vaughan (nee Caudle). *Marriage:* 1). to Elsie Winifred Deubert 1933, dies 1982; 2). to Mrs Caroleen Mary Sayers 1987. *Children:* Doreen Elizabeth, Pauline Winifred and John David. *Educated at* Cheltenham Grammar School; Jesus College, Oxford; Laming Travelling Fellow, The Queen's College, Oxford 1929-31. *Career:* Member of H.M. Consular and Diplomatic Services 1931-66, serving in Consular and Diplomatic posts in Europe, Africa, the United States of America and Latin America; Ambassador to Panama 1960-64 and to Colombia 1964-66; In 1966 joined University of Saskatchewan as Special Lecturer in History at its Regina Campus, Professor of History there 1967-74; Dean of the Faculty of Arts and Science 1969-73; Honorary Fellow of Jesus College, Oxford since 1966; awarded the Venezuelan Order of Andres Bello in the First Class, 1990. *Publications:* Joseph Lancaster en Caracas 1824-1827 y sus relaciones con el Libertador Simon Bolivar, 2 volumes, Caracas 1987 and 1989; various historical articles in Colombian and Canadian journals. *Recreation:* Reading, watching sport on the television. *Clubs:* Travellers; Royal Automobile Club, London. *Address:* 9 The Glade, Sandy Lane, Cheam, Sutton, Surrey., SM2 7NZ

VAUGHAN, County Councillor Morgan Lewis, *Currently:* Farmer and County Councillor. *Born on* 21 April 1929 at Tywyn. *Son of* the late Richard Vaughan and Elizabeth Jane Vaughan (nee Lewis). *Marriage:* to Catherine Jane Williams, 1963. *Children:* Richard Maurice Vaughan and Elizabeth Mary Jarvis (nee Vaughan) *Educated at* Tywyn Primary School; Tywyn Secondary School. *Career:* Member TyWyn Urban District Council, 1959-69; 1970-74; Chairman U.D.C. 1970-71; Mbr Merioneth D.C. 1973-77; Mbr Gwyneth C.C. 1977- ; Chairman Gwynedd C.C. 1990-91; Chairman Gwynedd CC. Social Services Commtt, 1987- ; Chairman Glynllifon Argricultural College, 1988- ; Mbr Tywyn Community Council, 1974-91; Mbr Gwynedd Area Health Authority, 1987-90; Mbr Wales Flood Prevention Commt of National River Authority, 1988- ; Governor Welsh College of Aberystwyth, 1977- . *Clubs:* Former Treasurer Brynlong Young Farmers Club. *Address:* Pall Mall Farm, Tywyn Gwynedd, LL36 9RU

VAUGHAN DAVIES, Geoffrey, MA (Cantab), Barrister-at-Law. *Currently:* retired Barrister. *Born on* 21 July 1928 at Swansea. *Son of* the late Hubert Vaughan Davies and the late Elsie Fielding (nee Turner). *Marriage:* to Esther Lockie Menzies (nee Anderson), 1956. *Children:* Angela Lockie (b. 1960), Elizabeth Louisa (b. 1962) and Andrew Hubert Menzies (b. 1966). *Educated at* Bishop Veseys Grammar School; Carlisle Grammar School; Fitzwilliam House, Cambridge; Inner Temple. *Career:* Served in Royal Navy 1947-49 (HMS Wizard 1948-49); Barrister in private practice on Northern Circuit (Manchester) 1953-70; Deputy Assistant Registrar Criminal Appeal Office 1970-74; Assistant Director Office of Fair Trading (Legal Division) 1974-88; a Legal Advisor Consumer Affairs Division, Department of Trade and Industry 1988-90. Liberal Candidate Withington Division, Manchester 1955, 1959, 1964 and 1966. Chairman Unifield Appeal Committee United Reformed Church 1972-79. Elder St. Pauls United Reformed Church, South Croydon 1970- . *Recreation:* cricket, chess, walking, political history, biblical studies. *Address:* "Ardmore", 13 Norfolk Avenue, Sanderstead, South Croydon, CR2 8BT

VELLACOTT, Keith David, DM, FRCS, DCH *Currently:* Consultant, General Surgeon. *Born on* 25 Feb 1948 at Tavistock. *Son of* the late Douglas Vellacott and Lorraine (nee Tibbs). *Marriage:* to Jinette Gibbs 1973. *Children:* Darren (decd), Guy and Adele. *Educated at* Kelly College; The London Hospital Medical College. *Career:* Research Fellow, Nottingham University 1979-81; Sen. Reg. United Bristol Hospitals 1981-86; Mem: British Society of Gastroenterology; mem: Association of Surgeons of Great Britain and Ireland; mem: Society of Minimally Invasive General Surgeons. *Publications:* Thesis: Easier detection of colorectal cancer; medical papers on gastroenterology and endoscopy. *Recreation:* gardening, reading. *Clubs:* Rotary. *Address:* Glasllwch House, 4 Glasllwch Crescent, Newport, Gwent, NP9 3SE. Royal Gwent Hospital, Cardiff Road, Newport, Gwent

VENABLES, Cyril James Newton, *Currently:* retired, Group Secretary National Farmers Union, branches Steynton and St. Ishmaels Pembrokeshire. *Born on* 20 March 1928 at Burton, Milford Haven, Pembs. *Son of* the late James Henry Venables and Annie Jane Venables (nee Newton). *Marriage:* 1st to Elizabeth Mary Lavis, 1950 (decd 1990); 2nd to Julia Rose Hoyle, 1991. *Children:* Cyril Graham Venables, B. ED. Oxon Assistant Head teacher, Ashfold Preparatory Sch, Bucks and Colin Stephen Venables, A.I.B. Business Sector Manager, Barclays Bank, Newport and step children, Rosemary Johnstone B.A. and Thomas Edwin Hoyle B.A., M.I.C.E., Civil Engineer. *Educated at* Burton Primary; Haverfordwest Grammar School. *Career:* Bank Clerk, Lloyds Bank, Milford Haven 1944-46; Farmer, Brompton Park, Burton, Milford Haven 1946-66, National Farmers Union Group Secretary 1966-87; Council member, National Association of Group Secretaries (known as NAGS) 1973-81; Vice Chairman of Insurance Committee of NAGS 1977-80; Chairman Insurance Committee of NAGS 1980-81; Vice Chairman of National Ass of Group Secs 1981-83; National Chairman, National Association of Group Secs 1983-85; Chairman, Pembrokeshire Association of Cricket Umpires 1985-90; President, Pembroke Assoc of Cricket Umpires 1990- ; Assistant Secretary, Pembroke County Cricket Club 1960-77, Vice Chairman 1990- ; Made Life member of Pembroke County Cricket Club 1977; Made Life member of Pembroke Assoc of Cricket Umpires 1990. Registration Officer of National Assoc of Cricket Umpires 1970's; Regional Examiner for Nat. Assoc of Cricket Umpires 1986-90. In the early 70's umpired two first class cricket matches at St. Helens, Glamorgan v Jamaica 1970, and Glamorgan v Cambridge University, 1975. Umpired Welsh Cup Final 1985. *Recreation:* sport, gardening. *Clubs:* Burton. *Address:* The Glen, Burton, Milford Haven, Pembs., SA73 1NT

VERMA, County Councillor Mehar, MA, MED, AFBPsS *Currently:* Retired Educational Psychologist. *Born on* 15 Aug 1931 at Punjab, India. *Son of* the late Murli Dhar Verma and Mrs Ganeshi Bai Verma. *Marriage:* to Mrs. Lajwanti. *Children:* two s. Mohinder Verma and Dhirender Verma. *Educated at* Punjab State Schools; University of Punjab, India. *Career:* Vice-Chairman Dynevor School Governing Body; School Governor BishopGore and Parkland; member Court of Governors, Univ. College, Swansea; Vice-Chairman special needs working party, West Glam County Council; Chairman West Glam Community Relations Council 1986-87; Founder Chairman Indian Society of South West Wales; member, Swansea & Lliw Valley Community Health Council; member, West Glam Council of Voluntary Societies; County Councillor, West Glamorgan County Council. *Publications:* co-author 'School Psychological Service', hand book. *Recreation:* Yoga, literary pursuits, voluntary work. *Address:* 22 Glynderwen Close, Derwen Fawr, Swansea, SA2 8EQ. County Hall, Swansea, SA1 3SN

VERNEY, Sir Ralph Bruce, Bt, KBE, JP, DL. *Currently:* *Born on* 18 Jan 1915 *Son of* the late Sir Harry Calvert Williams Verney, 4 bt, DSO (d 1974). *Marriage:* to Mary, 1948, da of late Percy Charles Vestey (3 sir Edmund Vestey, 1 BT) and 2 cous of the present Lord Vestey. *Children:* 1 s, 3 da; Heir s, Edmund Ralph Verney. *Educated at* Canford, Balliol Coll Oxford (BA). *Career:* Maj RA Java 1945; Vice Lord-Lt for Bucks 1965-85; High

Sheriff 1957; Co cncllr 1952-73; Co alderman 1961-73; chm Nat Cttee for England of Forestry Cmmn 1968-80 (produced plan for Chiltern Hills 1971); pres CLA 1961-63; memb Royal Cmmn on Environmental Pollution 1973-79; tstee: Radcliffe, Ernest Cook and Chequers Tsts; chm Nature Conservancy Council 1980-83; Hon Doctorate Univ of Buckingham; Hon FRIBA 1977, hon fellow Green Coll Oxford. *Clubs:* Cavalry & Guards. *Address:* Claydon House, Middle Claydon, Buckingham, MK18 2EX. Plas Rhoscolyn, Holyhead LL65 2AZ Tel: 0296 730297 or 0407 860288

VICKERS, Professor Michael Douglas, MB, BS, FC. Anaes. *Currently:* Professor of Anaesthetics, University of Wales, College of Medicine. *Born on* 11 May 1929 at London. *Son of* George Alexander and Freda Kathleen. *Marriage:* to Ann Hazel, 1961. *Children:* Charlotte and Guy. *Educated at* Abingdon School; Guys Hospital. *Career:* 1st assistant, University of Newcastle, 1963-65; Lecturer, Royal Postgraduate Medical School, 1965-68; Consultant in Clinical Investigation, Birmingham, 1968-75. Editor:

European Journal of Anaesthesiology; Secretary-General, World Federation of Societies of Anaesthesiologists. *Publications:* Drugs in Anaesthetic practice; Medicine for Anaesthetists;. Principles of Measurement for Anaesthetitsts. *Recreation:* music. *Clubs:* Royal Society of Medicine. *Address:* 2 Windsor Close, Radyr, Cardiff, CF4 8BZ. Les Treilles Haute, 24250, Grolejac, France

VOYLE, Mr Dilwyn Davies, BA (Hons) *Currently:* Company Chairman, J. W. Hammond & Co. *Born on* 11 Aug 1934 at Haverfordwest. *Son of* the late Emrys and Florence Voyle. *Marriage:* to Jane Rosemary Voyle (nee Wilkins). *Children:* Susanna, Katherine, Miranda and Laura. *Educated at* Haverfordwest Grammar School; University of Wales. *Career:* Former executive director of Charterhouse Industries Group and of Grand Metropolitan Associate of Booz-Allen and Hamilton, N. V. *Recreation:* golf, skiing, music. *Clubs:* Naval and Military, Piccadilly, W. 1., various sporting clubs *Address:* Cleeve House, 11 Goat Street, Haverfordwest., Pembs, SA61 1NH. Broadway Farm, Haycastle Cross, Pembs

WADE, Professor Owen Lyndon, CBE; MD; FRCP; FFPM; MD Hon; QU. Belf; FRCPI Hon. *Currently:* retired. *Born on* 17 May 1921 at Penarth, Glam. *Son of* James Owen David Wade, FRCS and Katie Wade (nee Jones). *Marriage:* to Margaret Burton, 1948. *Children:* Robin Elizabeth, Josephine Margaret and Sian Mary. *Educated at* Repton, Cambridge; University College Hospital, London. *Career:* Resident Medical Officer, Univ. Coll., Hospital, London 1946; Clinical Assistant Pneumokoniosis Research Unit, MRC, Cardiff 1948-51; Lecturer Dept of Medicine, University of Birmingham 1951-56; Senior Lecturer Dept of Medicine, and Consultant Physician to United Birmingham Hospital 1956-57. Whitla Professor of Therapeutics, Queen's University of Belfast and Consultant physician Northern Ireland Hospitals Authority 1957-71; Deputy Dean, Faculty of Medicine Queen's University 1968-71; Professor of Therapeutics and Clinical Pharmacology University of Birmingham and Consultant Physician, Queen Elizabeth Hospital, Birmingham 1971-85; Dean Faculty of Medicine and Dentistry 1978-85; Vice Principal and Pro-Chancellor, Birmingham University 1984-85; Member Northern Ireland General Health Servi. Bd., 1957-71; mem. Standing Med. Advis. Cttee Min of Health and Soc. Security, Northern Ireland 1968-71 (Chmn Subcttees on Community Med. and Psychogeriatric Care 1969); mem. Joint Formulary Cttee for the British Nat. Formulary 1963-85, Chmn 1978-85; mem. Dunlop Cttee on Safety of Drugs, Min of Health, London 1963-70; Chmn Subcttee on Adverse Reactions to drugs 1967-80; mem. Medicines Commission, DHSS, London 1969-77;Chmn Cttee on Review of Medicines, DHSS, London 1977-83; mem. Clinical Research Bd, Medical Research Council 1969-74; mem. Gen. Med. Council, London 1979-83; Consultant Advisor World Health Org: Med. educn 1960, 63 and 65, drug monitoring 1964, intensive hospital drug

monitoring 1968, drug monitoring 1968, drug consumption in Europe 1969, Drug Utilisation Research Group 1968-91; Trustee Arthur Thomson Charitable Trust 1978, Chairman 1984- . *Publications:* Cardiac Output and Regional Bloodflow 1962; Adverse Reaction to Drugs, 1st ed 1970, 2nd ed 1976. ; papers to: Jnl. Physiology, Clinical Science, Jnl Clin. Invest. *Recreation:* sailing, woodwork. *Clubs:* Athenaeum. *Address:* 26 West Street, Stratford On Avon, CV37 6DN

WALCOT, Professor Peter, PhD (London); MA (Yale); BA (London). *Currently:* Professor, School of History and Archaelogy, University of Wales College of Cardiff since 1988. *Born on* 10 May 1931 at London. *Son of* Cedric Ernest William Walcot and Harriet Walcot (nee Reed). *Marriage:* to Jean Margaret Ellen Day, 1956. *Children:* two s one d, Timothy James, Alison Susan and Christopher John. *Educated at* Wilson's Grammar School, London; University College London; Yale University. *Career:* Pilot Officer, Flying Officer, Royal Air Force 1955-57; Assistant Lecturer, lecturer, Senior lecturer, Professor, University College, Cardiff 1957-88; Visiting Lecturer/Professor, University of California, Los Angeles 1982; University of Florida 1983; Stanford University, California 1991. *Publications:* Hesiod and the Near East, (Cardiff) 1966; Greek Peasants, Ancient and Modern (Manchester) 1970; Greek Drama in its Theatrical and Social Context (Cardiff) 1976; Envy and the Greeks (Warminster) 1978. *Recreation:* walking, watching TV, cricket. *Address:* 28 Rowan Way, Lisvane, Cardiff, S. Glam CF4 5TD. University of Wales College of Cardiff, Cardiff, S. Glam, CF1 3XU

WALDRON, Mr Ron, *Currently:* James Scott Electrical Contractors. Welsh Rugby Union National Representative. *Marriage:* to Eunice Waldron. *Children:* six children *Career:* First played Rugby for Neath Schoolboys aged 12 years. Joined Neath Y. M. C. A, R. F. C., played youth and under "21" rugby. Joined Neath R. F. C., aged 18 years, left Neath aged 21 for two years National Service, played for Royal Navy and Combined Services. Returned to Neath for a further 11 seasons playing for Babarians, Crawshays, Wolfhounds and Wales in the championship season of 1964. Coached Neath R. F. C. Coached Neath Cotte, Neath District Youth and Welsh Youth. Team Manager at Neath and coach in their club championship and Schweppes Cup winners season. Joined the W. R. U., National Representative, Team Manager and Coach seasons 1990 / 91 / 92. Past employment with British Steel Corporation. *Recreation:* walking, reading, theatre *Address:* C/o Welsh Rugby Union, P.O. Box 22, Cardiff, CF1 1JL

WALFORD, Mr John Thomas, OBE; DL *Currently:* Chief Executive (General Secretary), The Multiple Sclerosis Society of Great Britain and Northern Ireland since 1977. *Born on* 6 Feb 1933 at London. *Son of* Frederick Thomas Walford and Rose Elizabeth Walford. *Marriage:* 1955, divorced 1970. *Children:* Martin, David and Susan. *Educated at* Richmond & East Sheen County Grammar School. *Career:* Deputy General Secretary M. S. Soc 1965-77; Moo Cow Milk Bars Ltd 1960-64; Stanley Eades & Co., 1955-60; C. C. Wakefield & Co. Ltd., 1953-55; National Service, RAF 1951-53; C. C. Wakefield & Co. Ltd., 1949-51. *Publications:* Editor: The MS News; Editor: The Messenger. *Recreation:* Collecting Victorian fairings and all things Welsh. *Clubs:* Royal Society of Medicine. *Address:* Rhoslyn, Talley, Llandeilo, Dyfed SA19 7AX. 109b Holland Road, London W14 8AS

WALKER, The Rt. Hon. Peter Edward, MBE (1960); MP. *Currently:* Member of Parliament. *Born on* 25 March 1932 at London. *Son of* Sydney and Rose Walker. *Marriage:* to Tessa Joan (nee Pout), 1969. *Children:* 3 sons, 2 daughters. *Educated at* Latymer Upper School. *Career:* Member, National Executive of Conservative Party, 1956- ; National Chairman, Young Conservatives, 1958-60; Parliamentary Candidate (Conservative) for Dartford, 1955 and 1959; PPS to Leader of House of Commons, 1963-64; Opposition Front Bench Spokesman on Finance and Economics, 1964-66; Opposition Front Bench Spokesman on Transport, 1966-68; Opposition Front Bench Spokesman on Local Government, Housing and Land, 1968-70; Minister of Housing and Local Government, June-Oct 1970; Secretary of State for the Environment, 1970-72; Secretary of State for Trade and Industry, 1972-74; Opposition Spokesman on Trade, Industry and Consumer Affairs, Feb-June 1974; Opposition Spokesman on Defence, June 1974-Feb 1975; Minister of Agriculture, Fisheries and Food, 1979-83; Secretary of State for Energy, 1983-87; Secretary of State for Wales, 1987-90. *Publications:* The Scent of Britain, 1977; Trust The People, 1987; Staying Power, 1991. *Recreation:* music, reading, tennis. *Clubs:* Worcestershire County Cricket, Buck's.

WALKER, Peter Michael, *Currently:* Managing Director, Merlin Film and Video Ltd, founded 1985. *Born on* 17 Feb 1936 at Bristol, UK. *Son of* the late Oliver and Freda. *Marriage:* to Susan Mary. *Children:* Sarah, Justin and Daniel *Educated at* Highlands North High School, Johannesburg, South Africa. *Career:* Professional cricketer Glamorgan C.C.C., 1954-72, played 3 times for England v S.A., 1960. Tours: Pakistan, East Africa, West Indies. BBC reporter/presenter/producer 1964; sporting columnist for "Mail on Sunday" newspaper, also other Fleet St papers and magazines. *Publications:* 3 books: "Winning Cricket"; "Cricket Conversations"; "The All Rounder". *Recreation:* golf, classical music, modern jazz. *Clubs:* Radyr Golf, Cardiff County. *Address:* 14 Chargot Road, Llandaff, Cardiff, CF5 1EW

WALL, Mr. Brian Owen, BSc (Eng), ACGI, CEng, FRINA, RCNC *Currently:* Formerly Chief Naval Architect, Ministry of Defence; now independent consultant.

Born on 17 June 1933 at Newport, Mon. *Son of* Maurice Stanley Wall and Ruby Wall (nee Holmes). *Marriage:* to Patricia Thora, da of Percival Spencer Hughes (d 1965) of Langstone, Monmouthshire, 4 Aug 1960. *Children:* one s Andrew (b 1969). *Educated at* Newport High School; Imperial College London; Royal Naval College Greenwich. *Career:* M.O.D. : Ship Vulnerability 1958-61; Submarine Design 1961-66; Head of Propeller Design 1966-71; Staff of C in C Fleet 1971-73; Royal College of Defence Studies 1977; Ship Production Division 1978-79; Project Director Vanguard Class 1979-84; Director Cost Estimating 1985; Chief Naval Architect 1985-90; member Royal Corps of Naval Constructors. C. Eng 1969; FRINA 1986. *Publications:* non for public release. *Recreations:* photography, walking, music, golf *Address:* "Wychwood", 39 High Bannerdown, Batheaston, Bath, BA1 7JZ 0225 858694

WALLER, Major Patrick John Ronald, MBE; JP; DL. *Currently:* Director, A.R. Mountain & Son (Lloyds Agents); Landowner, Farmer. *Born on* 24 Nov 1923 in India. *Son of* Brigadier R.P. Waller, DSO, MC, DL and Olave de Robeck. *Marriage:* to Mary Joyce Frewen, 1952. *Children:* Richard Patrick and Olivia Louise (Mrs Stirling). *Educated at* St. Aubyns, Rottingdean; Wellington College, Berkshire. *Career:* Army 1941-68, 12th Royal Lancers and 9/12th Royal Lancers (Prince of Wales) Staff College 1952; MBE (1959), Served N. Africa, Italy, Palestine and Malaya. Chairman Welsh Cttee County Landowners Assoc., 1985-90; Herefordshire County Councillor 1970-74; member, Agricultural Land Tribunal (Wales) 1977- ; High Sheriff Gwent 1982; Chairman Monmouth School Cttee 1979-89; Chairman South Herefordshire Bench 1990-. *Publications:* Special operations on the Pahang Johore border, June-July 1958. *Recreation:* country sports. *Clubs:* Cavalry & Guards, La Societe des Cincinatti de France *Address:* Hadnock Court, Monmouth, Gwent, NP5 3NJ

WALTERS, Mr Geraint Gwynn, CBE *Currently:* Retired. *Born on* 6 June 1910 at Gaiman, Argentina. *Son of* Rev. D.D. Walters and Mrs R.G. Walters. *Marriage:* 1). to Doreena Owen 1942, died 1959; 2). to Sarah Ann Ruth Price 1968. *Educated at* various schools in Argentina and Wales; University College Bangor 1928-33. *Career:* Schoolmaster 1933-34; Political Organiser under Rt. Hon. David Lloyd George (Council for Action) 1935-40; Ministry of Information - Dep. Reg. Information Officer for Bristol and Plymouth 1940-45; Ministry of Public Building and Works H. Q. London - Director of Training 1945-48; M. P. B. W. - Director for Wales 1948-63; Director Far East Region 1963-66; Director for Wales 1966-70; Director for Wales Department of Environment 1970-72; Parliamentary Commissioner for Merthyr Tydfil (Housing) 1972-73; Member Welsh Bd for Industry 1948-62; Housing Production Bd for Wales; Cttee of Enquiry on Welsh Television 1963; Member Council, Univ. of Wales Inst of Science and Technology 1970-87 (Vice-Chm., 1980-83); Member Court, Univ. of Wales 1982-88; Life Member Court, Univ.of Wales Coll. of Cardiff 1989-. *Recreation:* Reading, sport, politics. *Clubs:* Cardiff & County, Cardiff; Civil Service Club, London. *Address:* 1 The Mount, Cardiff Road, Llandaff, Cardiff CF5 2AR.

WALTERS, Mr Geraint Wyn, LL.B (Hons), Wales; Barrister *Currently:* Barrister at Law since 1981, Angel Chambers, Walter Road, Swansea. *Born on* 31 Dec 1957 at Glanamman, Dyfed. *Son of* Mr Thomas Eifion Walters and Mrs Dilys Walters (nee Deer). *Marriage:* to Kathryn Ann Walters (nee Jenkins), 1986. *Children:* Lowri Angharad Walters (b. 1987) and Catrin Wyn Walters (b. 1989). *Educated at* Ysgol Gyfun Ystalyfera 1969-76; University College of Wales, Aberystwyth 1977-80; President of Aberystwyth Law Students 1979-80; Inns of Court School of Law 1980-81. *Career:* Called to the Bar of Grays Inn London in 1981. Member of the Gorsedd of Bards of the Isle of Britain since 1975; Director and Executive Committee Member of the Swansea Festival of Music and Art; Hon. Secretary of the Guild for the Promotion of Welsh Music; Member of the Press and Publicity sub-committee of the Aberystwyth University Old Student Association; Member of the Arts Committee of the Institute of Welsh Affairs. *Address:* Cwmdwr House, Ynystawe, Swansea, SA6 5BE. Angel Chambers, 94 Walter Road, Swansea, SA1 5QA Tel: 0792 464623

WARD, Most Reverend John Aloysius, O.F.M., Cap. *Currently:* Archbishop and Metropolitan of Cardiff Province. Appointed 1983. *Born on* 24 Jan 1929 at Leeds (Domicile in Wrexham). *Son of* Eugene Owen and Hannah Josephine Ward (nee Cheetham). *Educated at* St. Mary's Wrexham, Grove Park Wrexham, Prior Park Bath, Philisophy Olton, Theology Crawley. *Career:* as Franciscan Capuchin (OFM. Cap) 1945-80; formation 1945-53; travelling Missioner for Menevia Diocese 1954-60; Guardian of Peckham & Parish Priest 1960-66; Provincial Definitor (Councillor) 1963-69; Minister Provincial (GB) 1969-70; General Definitor in Rome 1970-80; Coadjutor Bishop of Menevia 1980- ; Bishop of Menevia 1981-83; Archbishop of Cardiff 1983- *Address:* Archibishop's House, 41-43 Cathedral Road, Cardiff, S. Glamorgan CF1 9HD

WARDELL, Mr Gareth Lodwig, BSc (Econ), MSc, FRGS *Currently:* Member of Parliament (Gower); Chairman, Select Committee on Welsh Affairs. *Born on* 29 Nov 1944 at Carmarthen. *Son of* John T. Wardell and Jenny C. Wardell. *Marriage:* to Mrs. Jennifer Wardell. *Children:* Alistair *Educated at* Gwendraeth Grammar School; L.S.E. *Career:* Geography teacher, Chislehurst & Sidcup Technical High School 1967-68; Head of Economics Dept., St. Clement Danes Grammar School 1968-70; Economics Master, Haberdashers' Aske's School Elstree 1970-72; Sociology Lecturer, Bedford College of Physical Education 1972-73; Senior Geography Lecturer, Trinity College Carmarthen 1973-82. Vice-President, National Society for Clean Air; Welsh Vice-President, National Association of Local Councils; Trustee & Fellow, Industry and Parliament Trust; Fellow of Armed Forces Parliamentary Scheme (Royal Navy); President, Mumbles/Kinsale Twinning Association. *Publications:* many articles in Regional Economics in "British Economy Survey (O.U.P.). *Recreation:* coin collecting, photography, swimming, cycling, running. *Address:* House Of Commons, London SW1A OAA

WAREING, Emeritus Professor Philip Frank, OBE., DSc., FRS; Member Akad. Leopoldina. *Currently:* Retired. *Born on* 27 April 1914 at Leigh-on-Sea, Essex. *Son of* the late Frank Wareing and the late Mrs Gladys Wareing. *Marriage:* to Helen Clark 1939. *Children:* Margaret Linda, David Peter (and one d. deceased). *Educated at* Watford Boys Grammar School; Birbeck College, University of London. *Career:* Executive Officer, Inland Revenue 1931-41; Captain REME 1942-46; Lecturer, Bedford College, University of London 1947-50; Senior Lecturer, University of Manchester 1950-58; Professor of Botany, University College of Wales, Aberystwyth 1958-81; Vice-Principal, Univ. College of Wales 1977-79; Former member of various committees of Science Research Council, Forestry Commission, Environmental Research Council, Nature Conservancy and Water Resources Board. *Publications:* P.F. Wareing & I.D.J. Phillips: Growth & Development in Plants, 3rd ed. 1981; C.F. Graham & P.F. Wareing: Development Control in Animals & Plants, 2nd ed. 1984; 240 scientific papers on plant growth regulators and tree physiology. *Recreation:* gardening, music. *Address:* Brynrhedyn, Cae Melyn, Abersytwyth, Dyfed. SY23 2HA

WATERS, Mr Roger Michael, FRICS *Currently:* Director Wales, Country Landowners' Association. *Born on* 23 Apr 1935 at Bristol. *Children:* Mark, Tanya and Deborah. *Educated at* St. Brendan's Collage, Clifton, Bristol; College

of Estate Management; *Career:* County Valuer and Land Agent with Clwyd and Denbighshire County Councils 1968-80; Regional Secretary North Wales CLA 1980-91; Past Chairman N. Wales Royal Institution of Chartered Surveyors *Recreation:* Walking and swimming. *Clubs:* Farmers, London. *Address:* Berthen Gron, Llanfwrog, Ruthin, Clwyd, LL15 2AH

WATERS, Professor Ronald Thomas, PhD, CEng, FIEE *Currently:* Professor of Electrical Engineering, UWCC. *Born on* 20 June 1930 at Caerphilly, Glam. *Son of* David Waters and Mary (nee Rees). *Marriage:* to Catherine Margaret Cullen, 1956. *Children:* Janet and Deborah. *Educated at* Caerphilly Grammar; U.C., Swansea. *Career:* Research Officer, A.E.I., Aldermaston 1954-63; University of Wales 1963- ; Member Science, Education & Technology Board IEE 1982-86; Member Welsh Joint Education Committee 1986-90. *Publications:* over 200 research reports and papers including IEE Review on High Voltage Engineering, 1986. *Recreation:* golf, reading. *Clubs:* Cardiff Golf. *Address:* University of Wales College of Cardiff, Cardiff, CF2 1XH. 7 South Rise, Cardiff CF4 5RF

WATERS, Professor William Estlin, MB, BS, FFPHM, DIH. *Currently:* Professorial Fellow, Community Medicine, University of Southampton. *Born on* 6 Nov 1934 at Toronto, Canada. *Son of* the late Edward Thomas Waters and the late Cicely (nee Weatherall). *Marriage:* to Judith Isabel Lloyd, 1964. *Children:* Robert Miles and David Karl. *Educated at* Cardiff High School; University of London; St. Andrews University. *Career:* S.H.O. M.R.C. Pneumoconiosis Research Unit, Llandough Hospital, Penarth 1959-60; Scientific Staff M.R.C. Epidemiology Research Unit, Cardiff 1965-70; Secretary International Epidemiological Association 1974-77. *Publications:* Series in Clinical Epidemiology Headache Croom Helem 1986; Community Medicine (with K.S. Cliff) Croom Helm 1987; jointly: Public Health in Europe (W.H.O. Copenhagen) No. 21, 1983 and No. 29, 1989; Visible Autumn Migration at St. David's Head, Nature in Wales II, 20-7, 1968. *Recreation:* Birdwatching, visiting small islands. *Clubs:* Welsh Ornithological Society, British Ornithologists Union. *Address:* Community Medicine, South Academic Block, Southampton General Hospital, Southampton, SO9 4XY. Orchards, Broxmore Park, Sherfield English, Romsey, Hampshire, SO51 6FT

WATERSTONE, Mr David George Stuart, CBE; MA *Currently:* Chief Executive, Energy & Technical Services Group plc. *Born on* 9 Aug 1935 at Bearsden. *Son of* Malcolm Waterstone and Sylvia Sawday. *Marriage:* 1st to Dominique Viriot; 2nd to Sandra Packer. *Children:* Caroline, Isabel and Mark. *Educated at* Tonbridge; St. Catherines College, Cambridge. *Career:* HM Diplomatic Service 1959-70; Sen. Exec. I.R.C. 1970-71; BSC 1971-81; Board Member 1976-81; M.D. Commercial 1972-77; subsequently Chairman BSC Chemicals 1977-81 and Redpath Dorman Long 1977-81; Chief Exec. Roth International 1981-83; Chief Exec. WDA 1983-90. *Recreation:* painting, design and making furniture. *Clubs:* Reform *Address:* 1 Prior Park Buildings, Prior Park Road, Bath, BA2 4NP

WATKINS, Mr Alan (Rhun), *Currently:* journalist; Political Columnist, Observer, since 1976. *Born on* 3 April 1933 *Son of* the late D.J. Watkins, schoolmaster, Tycroes, Dyfed and Violet Harris. *Marriage:* to Ruth Howard 1955 (d 1982). *Children:* one s one d (and one d decd). *Educated at* Amman Valley Grammar School, Ammanford; Queens' Coll., Cambridge. *Career:* Chm., Cambridge Univ. Labour Club 1954; National Service, FO, Education Br., RAF 1955-57; Called to Bar, Lincoln's Inn 1957; Research Asst, Dept. of Govt, LSE 1958-59; Editorial Staff, Sunday Express 1959-64; (New York Corresp., 1961; Actg. Political Corresp., 1963; Cross-Bencher Columnist 1963-64); Political

Correspondent: Spectator 1964-67; New Statesman 1967-76; Political Columnist, Sunday Mirror 1968-69; Columnist, Evening Standard 1974-75; Rugby Columnist: Field 1984-86; Independent 1986- ; Mem. (Lab) Fulham Bor. Council 1959-62; Dir. The Statesman and Nation Publishing Co. Ltd 1973-76; Chm., Political Adv. Gp. British Youth Council 1978-81; Awards: Granada, Political Columnist 1973; British Press, Columnist 1982, commended 1984. *Publications:* The Liberal Dilemma 1966; (contrib) The Left 1966; (with A. Alexander) The Making of the Prime Minister 1970, 1970; Brief Lives 1982; (contrib) The Queen Observed 1986; Sportswriter's Eye 1989l A Slight Case of Libel 1990; A Conservative Coup, 1991. *Recreation:* reading, walking. *Clubs:* Garrick, Beefsteak. *Address:* 54 Barnsbury St., London N1 1ER Tel: 071 607 0812

WATKINS, Brian, *Currently:* British High Commissioner to The Kingdom of Swaziland, since May 1990. *Born on* 26 July 1933 at Newport, Gwent. *Son of* James Edward Watkins and Gladys Ann (nee Fletcher). *Marriage:* to Elisabeth Arfon (nee Arfon-Jones). *Children:* Mark Gareth and Caroline Ann Arfon *Educated at* LSE; Worcester College Oxford. *Career:* RAF 1954-58; HMOCS (Sierra Leone) 1959-63; Articles, Deal, Kent 1963-66 (Solicitor 1971); Administrator, Tristan Da Cunha 1966-69; Tutor and Lecturer, University Manchester 1969-71; HM Diplomatic Service 1971: FCO 1971-73, New York 1973-76, N. I. O. 1976-78, FCO 1978-81, Deputy Governor Bermuda 1981-83, B. E. Pakistan 1983-86; Consul General Vancouver 1986-90. *Recreation:* theatre, dancing, music. *Clubs:* Royal Bermuda Yacht. *Address:* C/o Foreign & Commonwealth Office (mbabane), King Charles St, London SW1A 2AH

WATKINS, John Kerswell, *Currently:* retired. *Born on* 8 Sept 1920 at Aberdare. *Son of* Thomas and Muriel Watkins. *Children:* Susan Hiatt. *Educated at* Cathays High School, Cardiff. *Career:* Principal Insurance Clerk Royal Liver Insurance Society. Ex-navigator Royal Air Force 1941-46. (Founder) member of the British Amateur Boxing Association. Official Recorder at 1958 British Empire & Commonwealth Games. *Recreation:* varied, main sport no Hon. Gen Secretary Welsh Amateur Boxing Association, since 1951. *Clubs:* United Service Mess Cardiff, the Royal Air Force Association, Cathedral Road Cardiff. *Address:* 8 Erw Wen, Rhiwbina, Cardiff, CF4 6JW

WATKINS, Mr. Mark Christopher, BSc Econ. *Currently:* Management Consultant, Alexander Proudfoot PLC since 1987. *Born on* 27 July 1961 at Griffithstown. *Son of* Christopher Rhys Watkins and Constance Moira Jones. *Marriage:* to Nicola Wigfield 1989. *Educated at* Jones West Monmouth Boys Grammar; Universi*;' College, Cardiff. *Career:* Freightliner Ltd 1981-85; Hoyer GMBH 1985-87; adopted Conservative candidate Torfaen 1989- . *Recreation:* shooting, Rugby Union, politics. *Clubs:* Vice Pres. West Mon. Old Boys RFC; Member Game Conservancy. *Address:* 28 Stafford Road, Griffithstown, Pontypool, Gwent, NP4 5LQ

WATKINS, Mr Thomas Frederick, BSc Hons (Wales) 1935, MSc(Wales) 1936. *Currently:* retired. *Born on* 19 Feb 1914 at Caerphilly. *Son of* the late Edward and the late Louisa Watkins (nee Talbot). *Marriage:* to Jeanie Blodwen Roberts, 1939. *Children:* Dilys (Jerman) and Gwyneth (Sommerlad). *Educated at* Cowbridge Grammar School 1925-32; University of Wales, Cardiff 1932-36. *Career:* Joined Chemical Defence Research Establishment, Porton 1936; Seconded to Government of India 1939; rejoined C.D.R.E., Porton 1944; seconded to Department of National Defence, Canada to establish a research group for Organic Chemistry 1947; Head of Research Section, Chemical Defence Establishment, Sutton Oak, Lancashire 1949, later moved to Nance Kuke, Cornwall; Superintendent Chemistry Research Division, C.D.R.E., Porton 1956; Assistant Director, in charge of Chemical Research and Development at C.D.R.E., Porton and C.D.R.E., Nancekuke 1963; Deputy Director, C.D.R.E., 1966; Under Secretary, Director C.D.R.E. Porton 1972-74; member Chemical Defence Advisory Board 1975-78; Chairman, Civil Service Commission Selection Boards 1974-83. *Publications:* miscellaneous papers inscientific journals. *Recreation:* gardening, reading, cooking. *Address:* 34 Harnwood Road, Salisbury, Wilts., SP2 9DB. 'Dolfor', Moelfre, Anglesey, LL72 8HD

WATTLEY, Mr Graham Richard, Pilot Officer RAF 1949-50; Civil Service 1950-90; Director, Driver and Vehicle Licensing Centre Swansea 1985-90. *Born on* 12 Mar 1930 at Plymouth. *Son of* R.C.H. Wattley and Sylvia (nee Orman). *Marriage:* to Yvonne, 1953 (d. 1990). *Children:* Lesley, Gillian and Jeffrey. *Educated at* Devonport High School *Recreation:* Walking, Churchwarden St. Pauls, Sketty, Hon. Treasurer Dewi Saint Housing Assn. *Clubs:* Civil Service *Address:* Caradoc, 36 The Ridge, Derwen Fawr, Swansea SA2 8AG

WEBB, Professor Adrian Leonard, B. SOC. SCI., MSC. *Currently:* Senior Pro-Vice-Chancellor & Professor of Social Policy and Administration, Loughborough University, since 1990. *Born on* 19 July 1943 at Gwent. *Son of* Rosina (nee Staines) and Leonard Webb. *Marriage:* to Caroline Frances. *Children:* Rhicert and Geraint. *Educated at* St. Julian's High School, Newport, Gwent; Birmingham University. *Career:* Lecturer, London School of Economics 1966-74; Research Director, Personal Social Service Council 1974-76; All at Loughborough University: Professor of Social Policy and Administration 1976- ; Head of Department of Social Sciences 1981-86; Director of the Centre for Research in Social Policy 1982-90; Dean of the School of Human and Environmental Studies 1986-88; Pro-Vice-Chancellor 1988-90. *Publications:* Books: with J.E.B. Sieve) Income Distribution and the Welfare State, 1971; (with R.D. Hadley and C. Farrell) Across The Generations: Old People and Young Volunteers, 1975; (with Hall, Land & Parker) Change, Choice and Conflict in Social Policy, 1975; (joint ed. and contrib) Teamwork in the Personal Social Services and Health Care, 1980; (with G. Wistow) Whither State Welfare: Issues of Policy and Implementation, 1982; (with G. Wistow) Planning, Need and Scarcity: Essays on the Personal Social Services, 1986; (with Susan Charles) The Economic Approach to Social Policy, 1986; (with G. Wistow) Social Work, Social Care and Social Planning: The Personal Social Services Since Seebohm, 1987; (with Challis, Fuller, Henwood, Klein, Plowden, Whittingham, Wistow) Joint Approaches to Social Policy: Rationality and Practice, 1988. many papers and chapters in books. *Recreation:* Ornithology, music, walking, painting (water colour). *Address:* Loughborough University, Loughborough, Leics, LE11 3TU

WEBSTER, Mr Alec, FCCA; CIGasE. *Currently:* retired. *Born on* 22 March 1934 *Son of* Clifford Webster and Rose Webster (nee Proctor). *Marriage:* to Jean Thompson 1958. *Children:* one 2 two d. *Educated at* Hull Univ (BScEcon Hons). *Career:* Chief Accountant, British Gas Southern 1974; Controller of Audit and Investigation, British Gas 1979; Treas., British Gas 1981; Reg. Dep. Chm., British Gas Southern 1984; Regional Chairman, British Gas Wales, 1989. Pres., Chartered Assoc. of Certified Accountants 1989-90. FRSA 1990. *Recreation:* sailing, mountaineering, wood carving. *Address:* Ty Carreg, 2 Maillards Haven, Penarth, S. Glam. CF6 2RF

WEBSTER, Professor Emeritus John Roger, OBE., MA., PhD. *Currently:* Professor Emeritus *Born on* 24 June 1926 at Anglesey. *Son of* Samuel and Jessie Webster. *Marriage:* to Ivy Mary Garlick MBE. *Children:* Matthew, Catrin and Paul (foster son). *Educated at* Llangefni County School; UCW Aberystwyth. *Career:* Lecturer Trinity College Carmarthen 1948; Lecturer in Education, University College Swansea 1951; Director for Wales, Arts Council of

Great Britain 1961; Professor of Education and Dean of Faculty of Education, UCNW, Bangor 1966; Professor of Education and Dean of the Faculty of Education UCW, Aberystwyth 1978-91; Committee Membership: WJEC 1967-91; Executive Ctee N Wales Arts Trust 1965-78; Lord Lloyd Ctee on National Film School 1965-66; Council Open University (Chairman Educational Studies Advisory Ctee) 1969-78; Lord James Ctee on Teacher Education and Training 1971; Chairman Standing Conference on Studies in Education 1972-76; Chairman Teacher Training Ctee, University Council for the Education of Teachers 1972-76; Sir Peter Venebles Ctee on Continuing Education 1974-76; CNAA 1976-79; Post Office Users Council (Chairman Welsh Advisory Ctee) 1981-88; British Council Welsh Advisory Ctee 1982-91; Chairman Wales Telecomunications Advisory Ctee 1984-88; Governor Commonwealth Institute 1984-91. *Publications:* Ceri Richards 1961; Joseph Herman 1962; The Arts and Education in Wales 1978; School and Community in Rural Wales 1992; Contributions on Education and the Arts to collective works and learned journals. *Address:* Bron y Glyn, Rhydyfelin, Aberystwyth, Dyfed, SY23 4QD

WEBSTER, Mr Patrick, BA Barrister-at-Law; a Recorder of the Crown Court since 1972; Chairman, Industrial Tribunals, Cardiff Region since 1976 (a part-time Chairman, 1965-75). *Born on* 6 Jan 1928 *Son of* Francis Glyn Webster and the late Ann Webster. *Marriage:* to Elizabeth Knight 1955. *Children:* two s, four d. *Educated at* Swansea Grammar School; Rockwell Coll., Eire; St. Edmund's Coll., Ware; Downing Coll., Cambridge (BA). *Career:* Called to Bar, Gray's Inn 1950; Practised at bar, in Swansea 1950-75; Chairman Medical Appeals Tribunal (part-time) 1971-75. *Recreation:* listening to music, watching rowing and sailing. *Clubs:* Penarth Yacht; Beechwood (Swansea). *Address:* 103 Plymouth Road, Penarth, S. Glam. CF6 2DE Tel: 0222 704758

WEBSTER, Mr Richard Edward, *Currently:* Sales Representative. *Born on* 19 July 1967 at Swansea. *Son of* June Elizabeth and William Graham. *Children:* Kelly Joanne. *Career:* Capped 4 Wales' Senior; Capped 6 Wales' under 19's; Capped 1 Wales' under 21's. *Recreation:* horse riding, rugby. *Clubs:* Swansea and Bonymaen. *Address:* 24 Yr Waun Fach, Llangyfelach, Morriston, Swansea

WEEKES, Mr Philip Gordon, OBE, BSc Hons (Wales), FIMinE, CE. *Currently:* Chairman, Garden Festival Wales Ltd; Chairman, Flectalon Ltd. *Born on* 12 June 1920 at Nantybwch, Gwent. *Son of* the late Albert and Mattie Weekes. *Marriage:* to Branwen Mair Jones 1944. *Children:* Gareth, Carolyn, Jane and Huw. *Educated at* Tredegar County School; University College, Cardiff. *Career:* RAF 1942-44; Colliery Manager 1946-50; various coalfield management posts 1950-70; Chief Mining Engineer NCB 1970-71; Director General of mining NCB 1971-73; Director, S. Wales coalfield 1973-85; part-time member NCB from 1977-84. *Publications:* various technical. *Recreation: Clubs:* Cardiff Aero; Cardiff & County. *Address:* Hillbrow, Llantwit Major, S. Glam. CF6 9RE

WESTON, Mr Bryan H., CEng., MIEE., CBIM *Currently:* Chairman, Manweb since 1985. *Born on* 9 April 1930 at . *Marriage:* to Heather (nee West). *Children:* two d two s. *Educated at* St. George Grammar School, Bristol; Rutherford & Oxford Technical Colleges. *Career:* South Western Electricity Board, Apprentice Engineer 1949-53 followed by various engineering and commercial posts; National Service, Captain, Royal Engineers. SWEB Commercial Director and Executive Director; Yorkshire Electricity Board Deputy Chairman, 1977; Directorship Chloride Silent Power. *Recreation:* Gardening, walking, caravanning and DIY *Address:* Chairman, Manweb plc, Sealand Road, Chester, CH1 4LR. Tel: 0244 377111

WESTON, Mr John Pix, SBStJ, BSc (Eng). (Hons). BSc (Econ) (Hons), CEng, FIEE, FRIM, MIES, MAPLE., FSS., FREcons. *Currently:* retired Chartered Engineer and Economist. *Born on* 3 Jan 1920 at Harborne, Staffs. *Son of* the late John Pix Weston and the late Margaret Elizabeth (nee Cox). *Marriage:* to Ivy Glover, 1948. *Children:* John Pix, David Maxwell and Ian Christopher. *Educated at* King Edward VI, Birmingham; University of Aston and London School of Economics; University of Atlanta, Georgia. *Career:* City of Birmingham Police Dept., 1936-39; City of Birmingham Elec. Supply Dept., 1939-48; Midlands Elec Bd (Third Eng), 1948-50; Tech Eng., E. E. Co. Ltd., 1950-51; North Western Elec. Bd. (Second Eng. (Tech))., 1951-58; Eastern Elec. Bd (Senior Asst. Eng (Comm))., 1958-60; Jamaica Public Service Co. (Deputy Op. Man.), 1960-61; Midlands Elec. Bd. Principal Asst. Eng (Tech and Comm), 1961-64; South of Scotland Elec. Bd. (Asst. Ch. Comm Officer), 1964-67; Senior Econ. Adviser to Mrs. Barbara Castle (Min of Transport), 1967-69; World Bank, Washington (Senior Eng and Economist), 1968-70; Michelin Tyre Co., France, 1970-72; Director, Open University 1972-75; Director-General, Royal Soc. for the Prevention of Accidents 1974-78; Ind. Dev. Officer, Argyll and Bute D. C., 1977-79 Health and Safety Adv., Newcastle-on-Tyne Poly and Northants C.C., 1979; Ch. Admin Officer, Westbromwich College of Comm. and Tech 1979-85; Cons. Eng. and Econ 1985- . Lecturer, Allen Technical Institute, Kendal 1951-58; Ipswich Civic College 1958-60; Halesowen and Bromsgrove Colleges of Further Education 1961-64; Senior Lecturer, University of Aston 1961-64. *Publications:* numerous papers on edn., eng., transport and health. *Recreation:* fell walking, cine and still photography, swimming, hi-fi, gardening. Programme, Outings and Compn Sec., Birmingham Photographic Soc., Council member and Council member of Birmingham Photographic Fedn., 1982-5., Chairman of Marlbrook Residents Assoc. 1982-87., Member of Probus Clubs - Narberth 1988- . St. Clears 1989- . (President 1990-91., Tenby 1990- . *Clubs:* Farmers, St. John's House. *Address:* Brook Mill & Woodside, Brook, Pendine, Dyfed, SA33 4NX

WESTWOOD, The Right Reverend William John, MA; LL. D. *Currently:* Bishop of Peterborough. *Born on* 28 Dec 1925 at Gloucestershire. *Son of* Ernest and Charlotte Westwood. *Marriage:* to Shirley Ann Jennings, 1954. *Children:* Alison and Timothy. *Educated at* Grove Park Grammar School, Wrexham; Emmanuel College, Cambridge; Westcott House, Cambridge. *Career:* Assistant Curate, Hull, 1952-57; Rector of Lowestoft, 1957-65; RD Lothingland, 1959-65; Vicar St. Peter Mancroft, Norwich, 1965-75; RD Norwich, 1966-70; City Dean Norwich, 1970-73; Hon. Canon Norwich Cathedral, 1969-75; Bishop of Edmonton, 1975-84; member, Archbishop's Commission on Church and State, 1966-70; Chairman, Governing Body College of All Saints Tottenham, 1976-78; member, Press Council 1975-81; chairman, Church of England Committee for Communications, 1978-86; member, IBA Panel of Religious Advisers, 1983-87; member, BBFC Video Consultative Council, 1985-89; member, Broadcasting Standards Council, 1988-; Church Commissioner; President, English Churches Housing Group; President, National Deaf-Blind League; Hon. Fellow, Emmanuel College, Cambridge; member of the House of Lords. *Recreation:* Art Galleries, the countryside, wine bars. *Address:* The Palace, Peterborough, Cambs., PE1 1YA

WHARTON, Mr Peter, Dip. Arch; RIBA; FRSA. *Currently:* Director of Architecture and Planning, Powys C. C. *Born on* 25 May 1932 at Derbyshire. *Son of* William Hugh and Lily May Wharton. *Marriage:* to Shirley (nee Spencer). *Children:* Andrea Gaye and Mark Anthony Spencer. *Educated at* Herbert Strutt Grammar; Nottingham & Leicester Schools of Architecture. *Career:* District Architect, West Norfolk B.C; Principal Asst. Borough Architect, Doncaster M.B.C; Chief Asst. Architect, Corby D.C. *Recreation:* Piano and classical organ. *Address:* The Green

Dell, Cefnllys Lane, Llandrindod Wells, Powys, LD1 5LE

WHITE, Captain Colin Philip Woodruff, M.N.I. *Currently:* Partner Retail outlet also County Councillor of Gwent. *Born on* 31 Aug 1930 at Bedwas. *Son of* the late Fred White and Advice Elizabeth (nee Woodruff). *Marriage:* to Patricia Ann Michael, 1957. *Children:* Sarah Louise Woodruff *Educated at* Monmouth School for Boys; Cardiff Technical College *Career:* Started sea going career as apprentice deck officer with Moller Line (U.K.) Ltd., 1947; promoted Captain, with Denholm Ship Management, 1968; retired 1981; elected County Councillor for Chepstow (North), 1989. *Recreation:* Golf, tennis, motoring holidays abroad. *Address:* Penrhiw, Mynyddbach, Shirenewton, Chepstow NP6 6RN

WHITE, The Rt. Hon. Baroness White Eirene Lloyd, Honourary LL.D. *Currently:* Life Peer since 1970; a Deputy Speaker 1979-89. *Born on* 7 Nov 1909 at Belfast. *Daughter of* Dr. Thomas Jones C.H., and Eireen Theodora Lloyd. *Marriage to* John Cameron White, 1948 (d. 1968). *Educated at* St. Paul's Girls' School; Somerville College, Oxford (Hon. Fellow); (University of Wales; Bath & Queen's University, Belfast). *Career:* M.P. (Labour) East Flintshire, 1950-70; Parliamentary Secretary, Colonial Office, 1964-66; Minister of State Foreign Office 1966-67; Welsh Office, 1966-70; Chairman, Labour Party 1968-69; Chairman / President UWIST 1983-88; Vice President UWCC 1989- (Hon. Fellow); Chairman, Land Authority Wales 1975-80; President, Council for Protection of Rural Wales 1974-89. *Publications:* The Ladies for Gregynog. *Address:* House of Lords, London SW1A 0PW Tel: 071 219 5435

WHITE-JONES, John Dale, *Currently:* Resource and Marketing Director, Studios Division, Thames Television plc. *Born on* 3 Oct 1934 at Maesteg. *Son of* the late George David White-Jones, of Llangollen and Vera (nee Dale). *Marriage:* to Hilary Ann (nee Porter), 1972. *Children:* Gemma (b. 1975) and Kate (b. 1977). *Educated at* Llandovery College. *Career:* National Service RA, 1953-55; Production Director, Thames Television plc, 1986-99; Director, Kingston Training and Education Council 1988-89. *Recreation:* gardening. *Address:* 6 St. Nicholas Drive, Shepperton, Middlesex, TW17 9LD

WHITEHEAD, Dr Neville Nick, OBE, PhD, MEd. *Currently:* Deputy Chief Executive, Sports Council for Wales, since 1985. *Born on* 29 May 1933 at Brymbo, nr Wrexham. *Son of* the late John Whitehead and Margaret (nee Williams). *Marriage:* divorced. *Children:* Simon, Jane and Rachel. *Educated at* Grove Park GS, Wrexham; Universities of Loughborough, Leeds, Leicester and Aston, Birmingham. *Career:* Teacher, Hertford & Birmingham 1958-61; Lecturer, St.John's, York 1961-67; Principal Lecturer, Carnegie College, Leeds 1967-83. First Director, National Coaching Foundation 1983-85. Honorary Gt. Britain Overall Athletics Manager 1978-84 (including Moscow and Los Angeles Olympics); Founder Chairman, Fed Sports Association for Disabled (Wales). Bronze Medal Athletics, Rome Olympics 1960; Bronze Medal, Commonwealth Games 1962; Vice President Brymbo Male Choir. *Publications:* Conditioning for Sport: Track Athletics; PE in England; Soccer Training; Teaching PE; Weight-Training etc. articles in International Journals. *Address:* Sports Council For Wales, Cardiff CF1 9SW

WICKRAMASINGHE, Prof. Nalin Chandra, MA., PhD., ScD. *Currently:* Profesor of Applied Mathematics and Astronomy, School of Mathematics, University of Wales College of Cardiff. *Born on* 20 Jan 1939 at Colombo, Sri Lanka. *Son of* Percival Herbert & Theresa Elizabeth Wickramasinghe. *Marriage:* to Nelum Priyadarshini Pereira, 1966. *Children:* Anil Nissanka, Kamala Chandrika and Janaki Tara. *Educated at* Royal College, Colombo; University of Ceylon; University of Cambridge. *Career:* Fellow of Jesus College Cambridge 1963-73; Staff Member of the Inst. of Theoretical Astronomy, Univ. of Cambridge 1968-73; UNDP Consultant/Advisor to President of Sri Lanka 1980-81; Director of Institute of Fundamental Studies, Sri Lanka 1982-83; Professor and Head of Department of Applied Mathematics and Astronomy 1973-88. Powell Prize for English Verse, Trinity College, Cambridge 1961; Dag Hammarskjold Gold Medal for Science, Academic Diplimatique de la Paix 1986; Scholarly Achievement Award of the Institute of Oriental Philisophy Japan, 1989. *Publications:* Interstellar Grains 1967; Interstellar Matter (with F. D. Kahn & P. G. Mezger) 1972; Light Scattering Functions for Small Particles with Applications in Astronomy 1973; Cosmic Laboratory 1975; Solid State Astrophysics (ed with D. J. Morgan) 1976; Fundamental Studies and the Future of Science (ed) 1984; with F. Hoyle: Lifecloud 1978; Diseases from Space 1979; Evolution from Space 1981; Space Travellers the Bringers of Life 1981; From Grains to Bacteria 1984; Living Comets 1985; Archaeopteryx, the Primordial Bird: a case of Fossil Forgery 1986; Cosmic Life Force 1987; The Theory of Cosmic Grains 1991. *Recreation:* Photography, poetry, gardening and walking. *Clubs:* Icosahedron Dining Club, Cardiff Univ. *Address:* School of Mathematics, University of Wales College of Cardiff, Senghenydd Road, Lisvane, Cardiff CF24AG. 24 Llwynypia Road, Lisvane, Cardiff, CF4 5SY

WIEGOLD, Professor James, MSc, PhD, DSc, FIMA. *Currently:* Professor, School of Mathematics, UWCC, since 1974. *Born on* 15 April 1934 at Trecenydd, Caerphilly. *Son of* Walter John Wiegold and Elizabeth (nee Roberts). *Marriage:* to Edna Christine Dale, 1958. *Children:* Helen Elizabeth (Mrs Fish), Alison Ruth (Mrs Sharrock) and Richard John. *Educated at* Caerphilly Boys' Grammar; University of Manchester. *Career:* Assistant Lecturer, Univ Coll. North Staffs, 1957-60; Lecturer, Faculty of Technology, Univ Manchester 1960-63; Lecturer, Univ Coll Cardiff 1963-66; Senior Lecturer, Univ Coll Cardiff 1966-69; Reader, Univ Coll, Cardiff 1969-74; Professor UCC and UWCC; Visiting Prof. U of Adelaide 1973; Dean of Science, UCC 1982-85; Member Math Science Sub-committee, UGC 1981-86; Joint Editor-in-Chief, Proc. London Math Soc. 1986-92; Distinguished visiting Scholar, U of W Michigan 1982. *Publications:* articles in Pure Math. Journals; (with J. C. Lennox) The Burnside problem and identities in groups (Springer 1979); translation from the Russian of S. I. Adian; Around Burnside (Springer 1990); translation of A. I. Kostrikin. *Recreation:* walking, music (choral singing) language. *Address:* 131 Heol-y-Deri, Rhiwbina, Cardiff, CF4 6UH

WIGLEY, Mr Dafydd, BSc; MP *Currently:* Member of Parliament for Caernarfon since 1974; President, Plaid Cymru. *Born on* 1 April 1943 at Derby. *Son of* Elfyn Edward Wigley and Myfanwy Wigley (nee Batterbee). *Marriage:* to Elinor Bennett Owen 1967. *Children:* Alun (decd), Geraint (decd), Eluned and Hywel. *Educated at* Ysgol Syr Hugh Owen, Caernarfon; Rydal, Colwyn Bay; Manchester University. *Career:* Economic Analyst, Ford Motor Company 1964-67; Chief Cost Accountant, Mars Ltd, 1967-71; Financial Controller, Hoover Ltd, 1971-74; Former Councillor, Merthyr Tydfil County Borough Council, 1972-74; President, Plaid Cymru 1981-84; Member, Select Cttee on Welsh Affairs 1983-87; Hon. Member (Wisg Wen), Gorsedd of Brds 1981; Vice-President, Federation of Industrial Development Authorities 1983- ; Sponsor: Disabled Persons Act 1981 (Private Members Bill); Recipient of Grimshaw Memorial Award 1981, by Nat. Federation of The Blind; Vice-President: Wales Council for the Disabled; Chairman: All Party House of Commons Reform Group 1983-87; Secretary: Parliamentary Friends of the Welsh National Opera; Treasurer: British-Yugoslav Parliamentary Group; Chairman: Alpha Dyffryn Cyf 1980-91, manufacturers of electronic equipment. *Publications:* An Economic Plan For Wales 1970; Tourism in Wales: an Alternative Report 1987. *Recreation:* Football, tennis, swimming, chess. *Address:* Hen Efail, Bontnewydd, Caernarvon, Gwynedd, LL54 7YH. Swyddfa's Blaid, 21 Penllyn, Caernarvon, Gwynedd, LL55 1NW

WILIAMS-WYNNE, Mr William Robert Charles, JP; FRICS. *Currently:* Williams Wynne Farms; Mount Pleasant Bakeries; W.W. Fine Arts; Wynne Holdings. *Born on* 7 Feb 1947 *Son of* Col. John and the late Margaret (nee Roper). *Marriage:* to The Hon Veronica Frances Buxton, 1975. *Children:* three d. *Educated at* Parkwood Haugh; Eton College. *Career:* Articles to Berry Bros, Ch Surveyors (Northants), 1969-82; elected Board and F&GP Committee Royal Welsh Agric Soc., 1971-82; qualified ARICS (converted FRICS 1977), 1972; Prospective Conservative Candidate Montgomery 1972; President Wales Young Conservatives 1973; appointed JP in 1974; contested both General Elections for Montgomery 1974; Executive Cttee CLA (Merioneth) 1974-84; Chairman Merioneth Conservative Association 1977-79; N. Wales member of Council Royal Agric Soc., of England 1978-85; RICS Member Agricultural Lands Tribunal (Wales) 1978-85; Chairman of Council Welsh Agric Sales & Export Council 1979-85; Council and Founder member Welsh Mule Society 1980-86; National Parks Commission (Snowdonia Nat Park) 1982-85; Member Prince of Wales Committee 1983-85; President Welsh Agric Sales & Export Council 1985-87; Chairman Mt Pleasant Bakery Ltd., 1983-92. *Publications:* The Rural Crisis, 1974; Housing The Young, 1975. *Recreation:* windsurfing, I.T., Art. *Clubs:* The Rag, Pratts. *Address:* Williams Wynne Farms, Tywyn, Gwynedd, LL36 9LG. Mount Pleasant Bakery, Bilston, West Midlands, WV14 7NE

WILKINS, Professor Malcolm Barrett, BSc PhD DSc AKC FRSE *Currently:* Regius Professor of Botany, Glasgow University since 1970. *Born on* 27 Feb 1933 at Cardiff. *Son of* Barrett Charles Wilkins and Eleanor Mary Wilkins (nee Jenkins). *Marriage:* to Mary Patricia Maltby 1959. *Children:* Nigel Edward Barrett Wilkins and Fiona Louise Emma Barrett Wilkins (decd). *Educated at* Monkton House School, Cardiff and King's College, London BSc 1955; PhD London 1958; AKC 1958; DSc 1972; *Career:* Lecturer in Botany King's College London 1958-64; Professor of Biology, Univ. of East Anglia 1965-67; Professor of Plant Physiology, Univ. of Nottingham 1967-70; Rockefeller Fellow, Yale Univ. 1961-62; Research Fellow, Harvard Univ. 1962-63; Lecturer in Biology, Univ. of East Anglia 1964-65; Darwin Lecturer, British Association for Advancement of Science 1967; Member Biological Science Cttee. of SRC 1971-74; Governing Body Hill Farming Res. Orgn, 1971-81; Scottish Crops Research Inst. 1974-90; Glasshouse Crops Res. Inst. 1979-89; Exec. Cttee. Scottish Field Studies Assoc 1972-86; British National Cttee for Biology 1977-82; Life Science Working Group ESA 1983-89 , Chairman, 1987-89; Director West of Scotland Sch. Co. ; Chmn., Laurel Bank Sch. Co. Ltd 1980-87; Cons. Editor in Plant Biology McGraw-Hill Publishing Co., 1968-80; Managing Editor Planta, 1977- ; Trustee, Royal Botanic Gardens, Edinburgh 1990- ; Council Member, Royal Society of Edinburgh 1988- . *Publications:* (ed) The Physiology of Plant Growth and Development 1969; (ed) Advanced Plant Physiology 1984; (ed) Plant Biology (series) 1981-;Plantwatching; 100 Scientific Papers on Experimental Botany, Plant Physiology, Planta, Nature; *Recreation:* Sailing, fishing, and model engineering *Clubs:* Caledonian, London. *Address:* 5 Hughenden Drive, Glasgow G12 9XS. Botany Department, Glasgow University, Glasgow, G12 8QQ

WILKINSON, Revd. Canon Alan Bassindale, M. A. ; Ph. D. *Currently:* Writer, Lecturer, Tutor, Open University; Hon. Priest, Portsmouth Cathedral. *Born on* 26th Jan 1931 at Cradley Heath. *Son of* late Revd. Dr John Thomas Wilkinson and Mrs Marion Wilkinson (nee Elliot). *Marriage:* to Fenella Ruth Holland, 1975. *Children:*

Sarah, John, and Conrad by 1st marriage, 1 d 2 s. *Educated at* William Hulme's Grammar School, Manchester; St Catharine's College, Cambridge; College of the Resurrection, Mirfield. *Career:* Curate St Augustine's, Kilburn 1959-61; Chaplain St Catharine's College, Cambridge 1961-67; Vicar Barrow Gurney; Chaplain and Lecturer College of St Mathias, Bristol 1967-70; Principal Chichester Theological College 1970-74; Director Auxiliary Ministry and Warden Verulam House 1974-75; Senior Lecturer Crewe and Alsager College of Higher Education 1975-78; Director of Training Diocese of Ripon 1978-84; Priest in charge of Thornthwaite, Thruscross, Darley 1984-88; Hon. Priest Portsmouth Cathedral 1988-; Hon. Canon Chichester 1970; Hon. Canon Ripon 1984 *Publications:* The Church of England and The First World War (1978); Dissent or Conform? War, Peace and the English Churches 1900-1945 (1986); The Community of the Resurrection: A Centenary History (1992) *Recreation:* Walking, Cinema, Victorian Architecture. *Address:* 27 Great Southsea St, Portsmouth, PO5 3BY.

WILLDIG, Mrs Mildred, *Currently:* retired. *Born on* 14 Sept 1927 at Manchester. *Daughter of* the late James and the late Agnes Appleton. *Marriage:* to Edward Willdig, 1949. *Children:* Carl, Robin, Mark and Peter. *Educated at* Manchester and Durham. *Career:* Nursery teacher; Post Mistress; Gwynedd County Councillor; Town Councillor, Conwy; past Mayor of Conwy 1986-87; past Constable of Conwy Castle 1986-87. *Recreation:* reading, social work, Amature dramatics, painting. *Clubs:* Endeavour (C.H.A.Ps Founder, Deganwy), Mothers Union. *Address:* ''Angorfa'', Station Road, Deganwy, Conwy, Gwynedd, LL31 9DB.

WILLIAMS, Mr (James) Vaughan, DSO 1942; OBE 1959; K. StJ; TD 1947; JP *Currently:* Lord-Lieutenant for the County of West Glamorgan, 1985-87. *Born on* 25 Oct 1912. *Son of* James Vaughan Williams, Merthyr Tydfil. *Marriage:* to Mary Edith Jones 1938 (d. 1972), d of G. Bryn Jones, OBE, JP, Merthyr Tydfil. *Children:* two d. *Career:* Local Government Service 1930-39. Commnd RE (TA) 1934; served War of 1939-45, BEF, France, Egypt, Italy Berlin (despatches 1942 and 1943); psc 1946; Lt-Col TA 1947-59; Hon. Col 53rd (W) Div. RE, 1959-67. Mem. Wales TA&VRA 1968; Vice-Chm. Glam TA&VR Cttee 1968; Pres., Dunkirk Veteran Assoc., Pat President, Swansea Branch, Royal British Legion; Scout Council West Glamorgan; West Glam Council St John of Jerusalem; West Glam SSAFA; Royal Engrs Assoc. Past Chm., S Wales Assoc. ICE DL Glam 1959; H. M. Lieut, W. Glam 1974; JP Glamorgan 1975. KTStJ 1979. *Address:* 5 The Grove, Mumbles, Swansea, W. Glam. Tel: 0792 368551.

WILLIAMS, Professor Adrian Charles, MD, FRCP *Currently:* Bloomer Professor, since 1988 and Head of Department of Neurology, since 1991, University of Birmingham. *Born on* 15 June 1949 at Solihull. *Marriage:* to Linnea (nee Olsen). *Children:* Sarah, Alec and Henry. *Educated at* Epsom College *Career:* Registrar, National Hospital 1979; NIH Research Fellow 1976; Consultant Neurologist, Birmingham 1981; Medical Patron Motor Neurone Disease Association 1991- ; Medical Advisory Panel Parkinson's Disease Society 1991- . *Publications:* on Parkinson's disease; Motor neurone disease; Multiple sclerosis. *Recreation:* skiing, France *Address:* 53 Weoley Hill, Selly Oak, Birmingham, B29 4AB. Tel: 021 472 0218.

WILLIAMS, Professor Alan, BSc, PhD, CChem, FRSC, CEng, FInstE, FInst. Pet, FIGasE. *Currently:* Livesey Professor and Head of Department, since 1973 of Fuel and Energy; Director of the Centre for Combustion and Energy Studies, 1988-92; Dean of Engineering, 1991-93. *Born on* 26 June 1935 at Merthyr Tydfil. *Son of* the late Ralph Williams and Muriel Williams (nee Lewis). *Marriage:* to Maureen Mary Williams (nee Baywall). *Children:* Christopher, Nicholas and Simon. *Educated at* Cyfarthfa Grammar School, Merthyr Tydfil; Leeds University, BSc (1955) PhD. (1959). *Career:* Research Fellow, Leeds

University 1959; Lecturer Leeds University 1964, Senior Lecturer 1972. member SERC Process Engineering Committee 1984-87; Technical Adviser to the Parliamentary Select Committee of the House of Commons (on acid rain), 1984-87; Fellowship of Engineering Task Group (acidic emissions from gas-fired systems) 1987-88; ACARD sub-committee on Government Funded R & D (ANREV) 1987-88; Engineering Professors' Conference Committee 1987-90; Council member British Flame Research Committee 1986-91; Council member Institute of Energy 1980-91; President Institute of Energy 1982-83; Honorary Secretary Institute of Energy 1985-91; Chairman Watt Committee Working Group on Methane Emissions. Member of Department of Energy Coal Task Force. *Publications:* 190 research publications and two books. The Combustion of Sprays of Liquid Fuels and Combustion of Liquid Fuel Sprays. *Recreation:* photography. *Address:* Department of Fuel & Energy, University of Leeds, Leeds, Yorkshire, LS2 9JT.

WILLIAMS, Alan Harding, MIME (1963), MIWSOM (1965), CEng(1968). *Currently:* retired. *Born on* 24 July 1925 at Tredegar. *Son of* the late Edward Todd and Anne Williams. *Marriage:* 1946. *Children:* Sandra. *Educated at* Elementary; Grammar; Mining Colleges. *Career:* Coal Mining Engineer. Bowls Administrative Experience: Past Treasurer and Secretary, Management Committee 1969- ; President 1978- ; Secretary 1987-90; Life Member 1990, Bedwellty Park B.C. Officer and/or Management Committee 1969- ; Chairman 1971; Life Member 1990, Rhymney & Sirhowy Valley B. A. Management Committee since 1989; President 1977; Hon Secretary 1974-87; Executive Member 1974- ; Life Member 1991, Monmouthshire B. A. Executive Member 1974-85; Hon. Asst. Secretary 1985-87; Hon. Sec 1987- ; President 1981, Welsh B. A. W. B. A Delegate 1982-84; President 1983; Delegate 1987- , British Isles Bowling Council. Management Ctee 1976- ; Chairman 1979-81; Umpires Panel 1987-89; Officiated at Outdoor and Indoor International Events, Welsh Bowls Umpires Association. Panel Member 1979-89, Welsh Bowls Coaching Panel. W. B. A. Representative 1985-86; Executive Member 1987- , Commonwealth Games Council for Wales. Member 1981, Executive member 1987- ; Senior Vice President 1991-92, International Bowling Board. Management Committee 1981-87; Hon Sec/Treasurer 1984-88; President 1990, Barbarians Bowls Association. *Recreation:* Lawn bowls. *Clubs:* Bedwellty Park B. C., Tredegar 1965, Merthyr Tydfil Indoor B. C., 1975 (Founder Member). *Address:* 48 Pochin Crescent, Tredegar, Gwent, NP2 4JS. Tel: 0495 253836

WILLIAMS, Dr. Alan Wynne, PhD Member of Parliament for Carmarthen 1987- ; *Born on* 21 Dec 1945 at Carmarthen. *Son of* the late Tom Williams and Mary Hannah Williams. *Marriage:* to Marian 1973. *Educated at* Carmarthen Grammar School; Jesus College Oxford. *Career:* Lecturer in Environmental Science, Trinity College, Carmarthen 1971-87. *Recreation:* Reading & Watching Sport. Political Interest:- Education, Energy, Environment, Welsh Affairs. *Address:* Cwmaber, Alltycnap Road, Carmarthen; Dyfed, SA33 5BL. House Of Commons, London, SW1A OAA.

WILLIAMS, Sir Alwyn, PhD; FRS; FRSE; Hon FRCPS; FDS RCPS; Hon. LLD; Hon. DCL. *Currently:* Honorary Research Fellow, Dept. of Geology and Applied Geology, University of Glasgow. *Born on* 8 June 1921. at Aberdare, Wales. *Son of* David Daniel and Emily May (nee Rogers). *Marriage:* to E.Joan Bevan 1949. *Children:* Gareth and Sian. *Educated at* Aberdare Boys Grammar School; Univ. Coll. of Wales; Hon. FRCPS; Hon. FDS RCPS; Hon. DSC. Wales, 1974; Belfast 1975; Edinburgh 1979; Hon. LLD: Strathclyde 1982; Glasgow 1988, Hon. DCL Oxford 1987; Fell. Univ Coll of Wales, Aberystwyth, 1990 *Career:* Research, Sedgwick Museum, Cambridge 1947-48; Amer.

Museum of Nat. Hist., Washington DC., 1948-50; Lecturer in Geology, Univ. of Glasgow 1950-54; Prof. Geology, Queen's Univ., Belfast 1954-74; Bigsby Medal, 1961, Murchison Medal 1973, Geol. Soc., Clough Medal Edinb. Geol. Soc., 1976; Pro-Vice Chancellor, Queen's Univ., Belfast 1967-74; Lapworth Prof., Univ. of Birmingham 1974-76; Principal and Vice-Chancellor, University of Glasgow 1976-88; T. Neville George Medal, Glasgow Geol. Soc., 1984. Pres. Palaeontological Assoc., 1968-70. Trustee, British Museum (Nat. History) 1971-79; Chmn. Trustees 1974-79. Member: Equip. & Phys. Sci sub-cttees, UGC 1974-76; NERC 1974-76; Adv. Council, British Library 1975-77; Scottish Tertiary Educn. Adv. Council 1983-87; Adv. Bd for the Res. Councils 1985-88; Chmn: Cttee on Nat. Museums and Galleries in Scotland 1979-81; Cttee on Scottish Agricultural Colleges 1989; Scottish Hospital Endowments Research Trust 1989- ; Vice-Chmn., Cttee of Vice-Chancellors and Principals 1979-81; Non-Exec. Dir., Scottish Daily Record & Sunday Mail Ltd., 1984-90; Pres., Royal Society of Edinburgh 1985-88. FRSAMD 1988; Hon. Fellow, Geol. Soc. of America 1970- ; Foreign. Mem., Polish Academy of Sciences 1979- . *Publications:* contribs to: Trans. Roy Socs., of London & Edinburgh; Journal of Geological Soc. ; Geological Mag. ; Washington Acad of Sciences; Geolog. Socs. of London & America; Paleontology; Journal of Paleontology; etc. *Recreation:* music, art. *Address:* 25 Sutherland Avenue, Pollokshields, Glasgow G41 4HG. University of Glasgow, Dept. of Geology & Applied, Geology, 8 Lilybank Gardens, Glasgow, G12 8QQ Tel: 041 339 8855 Ext 5650 / 1

WILLIAMS, Catrin Mary, BSc; MB; BCh; FRCS (Ed). *Currently:* retired, Ear, Nose and Throat Surgeon, Clwyd North 1956-86. *Born on* 19 May 1922 at Caerphilly. *Daughter of* the late Ald. Richard Williams, J. P. and the late Margaret (nee Jones). *Educated at* Pwllheli Grammar School; Welsh National School of Medicine. *Career:* Pres. Med Women's Fed, 1973-74, Past pres. of N. Wales Assoc., N. Wales Career Advisor & mem. of Post-Grad. Dean's Review Cttee, Mem. various working parties and Careers Cttee; Mem. of Int. sub-cttee; MWF. rep. on Women's Nat. Cmmsn and U. N. Women's Advis. Cttee; Elected UK Council member, Med. Womens Int. Assoc., past-chairman, Resolutions Cttee, mem. Ethics & Resol Cttee, Procedure Advisor & ex-official mem., Management & Exec. Ctees, Chmn organising cttee for MWIA Congress, Birmingham; Elected mem. Exec. Cttee three times, Women's Nat. Cmmsn, mem. Int. Cttee., mem. working parties on reform of prostitution laws, abortion, abuse, children in hospital etc., elected Co-Chmn 1981-83; Chmn, East Denbigh & Flintshire div of British Med Assoc., Sec. of N. Wales branch, former mem. Welsh Council, former N. Clwyd rep. to A. R. M; Sec. & Chmn Clwyd & Deeside Hospital Medical Staff cttee; chmn Colwyn Bay and also St. Asaph Hosp Med. Staff cttees; past chmn Surgical Div. & Private Practice cttees; mem. Hosp. Mngmnt cttee; chmn Dist Med. Cttee, Consultant mem. Denbigh & Flint Local Med. cttee, mem. Post-grad. cttee; former mem. Court Univ. Coll. N. Wales; former mem. Gen. Advis. Cttee BBC; Past pres, local Save the Children Fund, Royal Coll. of Nursing & Royal British Legion; past chmn Wales Cncl for the Deaf; elec. mem. Exec. Cttee Wales Cncl for Disabled elec. mem. of Cncl & Exec. Cttee, Royal Nat. Inst. for Deaf, Chmn Commnc. Cttee, mem. of its Med & Scientific sub-cttee; Pres. Meniere's SocUK; Past Chmn N. Wales Meniere's & Tinnitus Self-help gp; Pres Clwyd Laryngectomee club; mem Finance & Gen Purposes Cttee, Nat. Assoc Laryngectomee clubs; mem Exec Cttee Wales Assemb of Women; Chmn Wales Women's *Recreation:* embroidery, reading. *Address:* Gwrych House, Abergele, Clwyd, LL22 8EU.

WILLIAMS, His Honour Judge David Barry, TD., QC., MA. *Currently:* Circuit Judge since 1979. *Born on*

20 Feb 1931 at Garndiffaith. *Son of* Dr. William Barry Williams and Gwyneth Williams. *Marriage:* to Angela Joy Davies, 1961. *Children:* Rhodri, Crisyn, Rhidian and Catrin. *Educated at* Cardiff High School for Boys'; Wellington School, Somerset; Exeter College, Oxford; Grays Inn. *Career:* Served South Wales Borderers, 1949-51; 2nd Bn the Monmouthshire Regt (T. A.)., 1951-67; T. D., 1964, Retired as Major; Called to the Bar, Gray's Inn, 1955; joined Wales and Chester Circuit, 1957; Assistant Recorder of Merthyr Tydfil, 1970-71; Recorder of the Crown Court, 1972-79; Q. C., 1975; Asst. Commissioner Local Govt Boundary Commsn for Wales, 1976-79; Commissioner for Trial of Local Govt. Election Petitions, 1978-79; A President Mental Health Review Tribunal, 1983- ; Deputy Sen. Judge (non-res.) Sovereign Base Areas, Cyprus, 1983-; Designated/Resident Judge Swansea Crown Court, 1983- ; Liaison Judge for W. Glam, 1983-87; Mbr Parole Board, England & Wales, 1988-91; Chairman Legal Affairs Commt., Welsh Centre for International Affairs, 1980-88; Mbr of Court of Univ. Coll. Cardiff, 1980-88; Vice Pres., UWIST, 1985-88; Mbr of Court & Council, UWIST, 1981-88; Vice-Chairman of Council, 1983-88; Mbr of Court & of Council of Univ. Coll., of Wales, Cardiff, 1988- . *Recreation:* Mountain walking; rugby football. *Clubs:* Army & Navy; Cardiff & County; Glam. Wanderers RFC. *Address:* 52 Cyncoed Road, Cardiff, CF2 6BH.

WILLIAMS, Sir David Glyndwr Tudor, M. A., LL. M., Kt 1991. *Currently:* Vice-Chancellor, University of Cambridge, since 1989; President, Wolfson College, Cambridge, since 1980; Rouse Ball Professor of English Law, University of Cambridge, since 1983. *Born on* 22 Oct 1930 at Carmarthen. *Son of* the late Tudor Williams OBE, (Headmaster, Q. E. G. S., Carmarthen 1929-55) and Anne Williams (nee Rees). *Marriage:* to Sally Gilliam Mary (Cole), 1959. *Children:* Rhiannon, Rhys and Sian. *Educated at* Q. E. G. S., Carmarthen; Emmanuel College, Cambridge. *Career:* Called to the Bar, Lincoln's Inn, 1956 (now Hon Bencher of Inn); Harkness Fellowship U. S. A., 1956-58; Taught at Nottingham University and Oxford University (Keble College) before coming to Cambridge in 1967. Member of Council on Tribunals, 1972-82; Member of the Royal Commission on Environmental Pollution, 1976-83; Member of the Commission on Energy and the Environment 1978-81; Member of the Clean Air Council, 1971-79; Member of the Justice-All Souls Committee on Administrative Law, 1978-88; Members of the Berrill Committee of Investigation, SSRC, 1982-83; Member of the Marre Committee on the Future of the Legal Profession, 1986-88; Member of the Nuffield Council on Bioethics, 1991- ; Chairman of the Animal Procedures Committee 1987-90; President of the National Society for Clean Air, 1983-85. Sabbatical periods abroad: University of Adelaide, 1967; the Australian National University in Canberra, 1975; and the University of Sydney, 1985. Honorary Degrees: Loughborough University. of Technology, 1988; University of Hull, 1989; University of Sydney, 1990, University of Nottingham, 1991. Hon. Fellow of Emmanuel College, 1984. *Publications:* "Not in the Public Interest", 1965; "Keeping the Peace", 1967; Numerous articles and papers. *Address:* The Old Schools, Cambridge, CB2 1TN.

WILLIAMS, David John, FIFireE, FBIM. *Currently:* Chief Fire Officer, Mid Glamorgan County Council, since 1987. *Born on* 25 March 1945. *Marriage:* to Diane. *Children:* Katherine and Jayne. *Educated at* Ross-on-Wye Grammar School. *Career:* Joined Hereford County Fire Service 1965; Staffordshire Fire Brigade 1968; Powys Fire Service, Senior Fire Prevention Officer 1977; Dyfed County Fire Brigade, Senior Fire Prevention Officer 1979; Senior Staff Officer 1982; Deputy Chief Fire Officer 1983. Vice President Institution of Fire Engineers; Past Chairman Cardiff Branch British Institute of Management; Member

Chief and Assistant Chief Fire Officers' Association; Secretary CACFOA Appliances, Equipment & Uniform Technical Committee; Member of Appliances, Equipment & Uniform, Fire Research and Training Committees of CFBAC; ACC advisor on Training; Chairman British Standards Committee on Fire Pumps; U. K. delegate on CEN Standards Committee on Fire Pumps; Chairman Fire Services Sports and Athletics Association, Walking and Mountaineering Section; Member of Child Accident Prevention Trust 1984-91. *Recreation:* music, reading, sports - particularly walking, DIY, bell-ringing. *Clubs:* Rotary. *Address:* Mid Glamorgan Fire Service, Headquarters, Laneley Hall, Pontyclun, Mid Glamorgan, CF7 9XA.

WILLIAMS, Mr David Lincoln, *Currently:* Costa Rica Coffee Co. Ltd., Chairman; Allied Profiles Ltd., Chairman; Cox (Penarth) Ltd., Chairman. *Born on* 10 Feb 1937 at Cardiff. *Son of* the late Lewis Bernard Williams and the late Eileen Elizabeth Williams (nee Cadogan). *Marriage:* to Gillian Elisabeth Phillips, 1959. *Children:* Jonathan (b. 1961) and Sophia (b. 1964). *Educated at* Cheltenham College. *Career:* Served RA Gibralter 1955-57; Chairman: Allied Windows (S. Wales) Ltd, 1971-85; Cardiff Broadcasting PLC 1979-84; Chm. and Man. Dir. John Williams of Cardiff PLC 1983-88 (Dir 1968-88). President Aluminium Window Assoc., 1971-72; Member: CBI Welsh Council 1986-89; Welsh Arts Council 1987- (Chm Music Cttee 1988-). Chm. Vale of Glamorgan Festival 1978- ; Nat. Chm. Friends of Welsh National Opera 1980-; FInstD; Freeman, City of London 1986; Liveryman, Founders' Co., 1986. *Recreation:* opera, sailing, gardening. *Clubs:* Liveryman-Worshipful Company of Founders, Cardiff and County, Cardiff. *Address:* Rose Revived, Llantrithyd, Cowbridge, S.Glam., CF7 7UB.

WILLIAMS, Mr David Oliver, RMN. *Born on* 12 March 1926. *Marriage:* to Kathleen Eleanor Jones, Dinorwic, 1949. *Children:* two s five d (and one s decd). *Educated at* Brynrefail Grammar School; North Wales Hospital, Denibgh (RMN 1951). *Career:* General Secretary, Confederation of Health Service Employees, 1983-87. COHSE full time officer, Regional Secretary, Yorkshire Region 1955; National Officer, Head Office 1962; Sen. National Officer, 1969; Asst General Secretary, 1964; Chairman: Nurses and Midwives Whitely Council Staff Side 1977-87; General Whitely Council Staff Side 1974-87. Jubilee Medal 1977. *Recreation:* walking, birdwatching, swimming, music. *Address:* 1 Pen Cilan, Cilgwyn, Carmel, Gwynedd.

WILLIAMS, Professor David Raymond, B. Sc., PhD., D. Sc., C. Chem., FRSC., FRSA. *Currently:* Prof. of Applied Chemistry UWCC, 1977- ; Honorary Chairman of British Council Science Advisory Committee, 1986-. *Born on* 20 March 1941 at Wrexham, Clwyd. *Son of* Mr & Mrs Eric T. Williams. *Marriage:* to Gillian K. Williams (nee Murray). *Children:* Caroline Susan and Kerstin Jane Williams. *Educated at* Grove Park Grammar School, Wrexham and UCNW, Bangor. *Career:* Univ. of Lund, 1965-66; (Nato Fellow), Univ. of St. Andrews, 1966-77, (Lecturer), *Publications:* 300 on Trace Elements in Man, 6 books on Bioinorganic Chemistry. *Recreation:* Swimming, after dinner speaking and cycling. *Clubs:* Roy. Soc. Chemistry and Royal Society of Arts. *Address:* Cerrig Llwydion, 12 St. Fagans Drive, St. Fagans, Cardiff., CF5 6EF. School of Chemistry & Applied Chemistry, U.W.C.C., P.O. Box 912, Cardiff, CF1 3TB. Tel: 0222 874779.

WILLIAMS, Dr David Wakelin (Lyn), M. Sc., Ph. D., F. I. Biol. *Currently:* Retired - writer. *Born on* 2 Oct 1913 at Llwynypia, Rhondda. *Son of* John Thomas Williams and Ethel Williams (nee Lock). *Marriage:* to Margaret Mary Wills, B. Sc. *Children:* John Richard Williams. *Educated at* Porth County School, Univ. Coll., S. Wales & Monmouthshire. *Career:* University Demonstrator

(Zoology)., P/Time teaching at Crumlin Technical College (Pharmacy & Pre-nursing students) Biochemist at Treforest Industrial Estate; Inspector-Senior Inspector Infestation Control, Ministry of Food, Scotland & N. Ireland; Principal Scientific Officer, Dept. Ag. & Fish Scotland, Senior Principal S. O; Deputy Chief Scientific Officer-Director Agricultural Scientific Services, 1963-73; Member British Institute of Management, 1970-76; Chairman Potato Trials Advisory Committee, 1963-68; Council Member Scottish branch, Institute of Biology, 1966-69; As Director of Agricultural Scientific Services he was on the Board of the Scottish Society for Plant Breeding and of the D. S. I. R. Pest Infestation Laboratories. Also on the Pesticides Safety Precautions Committee. *Publications:* Some thirty or so articles in various journals and magazines, mainly for the intellectual layman. *Recreation:* Natural history, photography, music and Nicolson Sq. Methodist Church, Edinburgh. *Address:* 8 Hillview Road, Edinburgh, EH12 8QN. Tel: 031 334 1108.

WILLIAMS, Lt. Col. David William Bulkeley, MA., MInstP., MIEE., MIWES., psc. *Currently:* retired in 1982. *Born on* 22 Jan 1922 at Tientsin, N. China. *Son of* the late Robert Arthur Williams, of Porth yr Aur, Caernarfon and the late Winifred Baker Brown. *Marriage:* to Frances Felicity Latham, 1947. *Children:* Marion Dilys, Kenneth David and Christine Frances. *Educated at* Dover College; Birmingham University, 6 months war course; Cambridge Univ, Mechanical Sciences Tripos First class Hons. *Career:* Commissioned into Royal Engineers, October 1941; War service in UK and N. W. Europe with Gds Armd Div 1941-45; army Service in Middle East, Greece, Egypt, Palestine 1945-46; Cambridge University 1947-50; Staff College, Camberley 1951; Army Service in UK and Malaya 1952-72; retired from Army 1972; Senior Planning Officer at Thames Conservancy 1972-82. *Publications:* àll classified. *Recreation:* gardening, carpentry, badminton, geology. *Clubs:* Geologists Association. *Address:* Maen Melin, Peasemore, Nr Newbury, Berks, RG16 OJF. Tel: 0635 248415.

WILLIAMS, Mr Edward Thomas, MA, LL. M. (Cantab). *Currently:* Consultant Solicitor to R.L. Edwards & Partners; Appointed part-time Chairman National Insurance (now Social Security) Appeals Tribunals, appointed 1965; Part-time Chairman Medical Appeals Tribunal (Wales), appointed 1985; or General Commissioners, appointed 1986. *Born on* 21 Feb 1927 at Trealaw, Rhondda. *Son of* the late Thomas and the late Mabel Elvira (nee Thomas). *Marriage:* to Marjorie (Jane) Stanley Evans, 1955. *Children:* Anne Judith (Morgan), Rhodri Clive Edward and Susan Jane (Lowis). *Educated at* Porth County; Kingswood School; Trinity Hall, Cambridge. *Career:* National Service, Royal Navy 1945-48; Qualified Solicitor January 1954; Past President of Pontypridd & District Law Society 1968-69; Past President of Associated Law Societies of Wales 1976-77; Past President of Bridgend Law Society 1977-78. Appointed part-time Chairman Nat Ins Appeals Tribunals 1965. President of Porthcawl Rotary Club 1987-88. Chairman South Wales Autistic Society. *Recreation:* golf. *Clubs:* Royal Porthcawl, Law Society. *Address:* 2 Mallard Way, Porthcawl, CF36 3TS. 65 Mary Street, Porthcawl CF36 3YZ Tel: 065 671 784151

WILLIAMS, Mr Eirian, BA, LLB. *Currently:* Partner with Ungoed-Thomas & King, Solicitors, Llandysul. *Born on* 15 May 1952 at Carmarthen. *Son of* Reverend Professor C.G. Williams and Irene Williams. *Marriage:* to Glesni Evans. *Children:* Iwan and Dylan. *Educated at* Carleton University, Ottawa; University College of Wales, Aberystwyth. *Career:* Barrister and Solicitor, Supreme Court of Alberta, Canada; Solicitor, Supreme Court England and Wales. *Address:* Rhosawel, Heol Llynyfran, Llandysul, Dyfed

WILLIAMS, Emrys, BA in Fine Art, Slade School of Art.

Currently: Artist. *Born on* 18 Jan 1958 at Liverpool. *Son of* Robert Williams and Thelma Williams (nee Friess). *Educated at* Eirias High School, Colwyn Bay; Slade School of Art; Univ College London. *Career:* Awards, Solo Exhibitions: Andrew Knight Gallery, Cardiff, "Pastimes Past", Wrexham Arts Centre, 1984; "The Welsh Mountain Zoo", South Hill Part Arts Centre & Wilde Theatre, Bracknell, "Off Season-Winter Paintings", Oldham Art Gallery 1985; Lanchester Polytechnic Gallery, London, Benjamin Rhodes Gallery, London, 1986; Benjamin Rhodes Gallery, London, 1989; Wrexham Library Arts Centre, Wrexham, 1990; Benjamin Rhodes Gallery, London, 1991. Group exhibitions: "Clwyd Ten", Wrexham Arts Centre 1981; "Through The Artist's Eyes", Mostyn Art Gallery Llandudno, John Moores Liverpool Exhibition XIII, Walker Art Gallery, Liverpool, 1982; Serpentine Summer Show II, Serpentine Gallery, London. "Heritages", Oriel Gallery, Cardiff, 1983; "Pauline Carter & Emrys Williams", Chapter Gallery, Cardiff, 1984; John Moores Liverpool Exhibition XIV, Walker Gallery Liverpool. Royal National Eisteddfod of Wales, Fine Art Section Rhyl-with tour to Llanbedrog & Swansea. "Life & Landscape from Scotland & Wales", Newport Museum & Art Gallery. "Stephen Dunn, Sylvia Guirey & Emrys Williams", Benjamin Rhodes Gallery London, 1985; "Group 75", Wrexham Arts Centre & London Inst. of Educ. "New Members of Group 56", Univ Coll of Wales. "Some Famous Sons & Daughters", Rhyl Centre N. Wales Open, Mostyn Art Gallery, Llandudno. "Group 56", Bratislava, Czechoslovakia, 1986; "David Hepher & Emrys Williams", Castlefield Gallery Manchester. "The Other Landscape", John Keane, Ed Whittaker & Emrys Williams, Southampton City Art Gallery. "56 Group Wales", Worcester City Art Gallery. "Group 75", Rhyl Art Centre. "Correspondences"m Theatre Clwyd Mold, 1987; "56 Group Wales", Oriel Mostyn Llandudno. *Address:* C/o Benjamin Rhodes Gallery, 4 New Burlington Place, London, W1X 1SB

WILLIAMS, Sir Francis (John Watkin), 8th Bt cr 1798; QC 1952. *Born on* 24 Jan 1905 at Anglesey. *Son of* the late Col Lawrence Williams, OBE, DL, JP. *Marriage:* to Brenda, 1932, d of Sir John Jarvis, 1st Bt. *Children:* four d *Educated at* Malvern College; Trinity Hall, Cambridge. *Career:* Barrister of Middle Temple 1928. Served War of 1939-45; Wing Comdr, RAFVR. Recorder of Birkenhead 1950-58; Recorder of Chester 1958-71; Chm Anglesey QS 1960-71 (Dep. Chm 1949-60); Chm Flint QS 1961-71 (Dep Chm 1953-61); Dep Chm Cheshire QS 1952-71; a Recorder of the Crown Court 1972-74; Hon Mem Wales and Chester Circuit 1986. JP Denbighshire 1951-74; Chm Medical Appeal Tribunal for N Wales Areas 1954-57; High Sheriff: of Denbighshire 1957, of Anglesey 1963. Chancellor, Diocese of St. Asaph 1966-83. Freeman of City of Chester 1960. *Clubs:* United Oxford and Cambridge University. *Address:* Llys, Middle Lane, Denbigh, Clwyd Tel: 0745 712984

WILLIAMS, Professor Frederic (Fred) Ward, MA, PhD, ScD, CEng, FICE, FIStructE, FRAeS *Currently:* Head of Division of Structural Engineering, School of Engineering, University of Wales College of Cardiff since 1975. *Born on* 4 March 1940 at Romiley, Cheshire. *Son of* Sir Frederic Calland Williams and Gladys Williams (nee Ward). *Marriage:* to Jessie Anne Hope Williams (nee Wilson). *Children:* Frederic John Wilson Williams and David Ward Williams. *Educated at* Shrewsbury School; St Johns College Cambridge; Bristol University. *Career:* Freeman, Fox & Partners 1964; Lecturer, Ahmadu Bello Univ., N. Nigeria 1964-67; Lecturer, Univ of Birmingham 1967-75; Consultant to NASA 1981- . *Publications:* over 100 technical papers. *Recreation:* Christian Anglican, hill walking, jogging. *Address:* Brandelhow, 12 Ridgeway, Lisvane, Cardiff, CF4 5RS

WILLIAMS, County Councillor Gareth, *Currently:* County Councillor, represented Pontardulais on West Glamorgan Council since 1977, and non-executive director Cardiff Airport. *Born on* 13 June 1938 at Llangennech. *Son of* T.M. Williams and the late G. Williams. *Marriage:* 1960. *Children:* Mark, Paul and Claire. *Educated at* Llanelli Grammar School. *Career:* Mining, N.C.B. for 34 years; worked at Morlais, Brynlliw and Bettws collieries; Lodge Secretary at Morlais colliery for 12 years District Councillor for Lliw Valley for 4 years; Vice-Chairman Community Services, West Glamorgan 1981-85; Chairman, Finance, Staffing G.P. 1985-90; Chairman, Resources Management 1990- ; all positions within education section of West Glamorgan; Chairman, Local Authorities cttee, Welsh Joint Education Cttee 1989- ; Member, Welsh Books Council and Welsh language development cttee (W.J.E.C.). *Recreation:* Walking, reading, football, cricket. *Clubs:* Pontardulais Cricket and Rugby, patron. *Address:* 32 Heol-y-Maes, Pontardulais, Swansea, SA4 1PQ

WILLIAMS, Prof. Gareth Howel, JP., PhD., DSc., FRSC. *Currently:* Retired. *Born on* 17 June 1925 at Treherbert. *Son of* the late Morgan John and the late Miriam Williams. *Marriage:* to Marie Jessie Thomson Mitchell, 1955. *Children:* John Morgan Howel and Barbara Ann. *Educated at* Pentre Secondary School, 1935-42; University College, London, 1942-47. *Career:* Assistant Lecturer then Lecturer, King's College, University of London, 1947-60; Research Fellow, Univ. of Chicago, 1953-54; Reader in Organic Chemistry, Birkbeck College, Univ. of London, 1960-67; Visiting Lecturer, Univ. of Ife, Nigeria, 1965; Professor of Chemistry and Head of Dept. of Chemistry, Bedford College, Univ. of London, 1967-84; Rose Morgan Visiting Professor, Univ, of Kansas, USA, 1969-70; visiting Professor Univ. of Auckland, New Zealand, 1977. *Publications:* Homolytic Aromatic Substitution, 1960; Organic Chemistry: A Conceptual Approach, 1977; (Editor) Advances in Fre-Radical Chemistry, Vo. 1, 1965; Vol II, 1967; Vol. III, 1969; Vol IV, 1972; Vol V, 1975; Vol VI, 1980; Numerous papers in journal of the Chemical Society and other Scientific Journals; Justice of the Peace, Brent PSA, 1979- ; Deputy Chairman, Brent PSA, 1989-91; Chairman London Welsh Trust and London Welsh Assoc., 1987-90; Member of the Honourable Society of Cymmrodorion. *Recreation:* Music, travel. *Clubs:* Athenaeum. *Address:* Hillside, 22 Watford Road, Northwood, Middx., HA6 3NT

WILLIAMS, Gareth James, *Currently:* Divisional Director, Marks and Spencer. *Born on* 22 Dec 1944 at Cardiff. *Son of* Daniel James Williams and Elizabeth Beatrice Walters. *Marriage:* to Ruth Elizabeth Laugharne, 1969. *Children:* Rhian Margaret, Catherine Haf and Geraint David. *Educated at* Cardiff High School; Exeter University. *Career:* Store Management 1967-71; Buying Executive 1971-81; Distribution and Budgeting and Strategic Planning 1981-87; Acquisition Team in U. S. A. 1987-88; Div Director for Logistics, Information Technology and Physical Distribution 1988- . Non-executive of British Academy; member of the Council of Logisics; member of Information Systems Committee of St. Bartholomews Hospital. *Publications:* Private papers, Marks and Spencer and interviews, e.g., Financial Times. *Recreation:* education; health; music, especially opera; sport, especially rugby. *Clubs:* The Rugby, London, Friends of Covent Garden, Cardiff HSOB *Address:* Talgarth House, Hervines Road, Amersham on the Hill, Bucks, HP6 5HS Tel: 0494 432168

WILLIAMS, Q.C. Gareth Wyn, MA, LLM (Cantab), QC. *Currently:* Queens Counsel. *Born on* 5 Feb 1941 at Prestatyn. *Son of* Albert Thomas Williams and Selina Williams. *Marriage:* to Pauline Clarke, 1962. *Children:* Martha, Emma and Daniel. *Educated at* Mostyn CP; Christ Church Rhyl; Rhyl Grammar; Queens College, Cambridge. *Career:* Open Scholarship Queen's Cambridge 1958, MA,

LLM (Cantab) 1st class honours. Called to Bar Gray's Inn 1965. Q.C. 1978. Leader, Wales and Chester Circuit 1986-89; Member, Bar Council 1985- ; Chairman Professional Conduct Committee 1988, 1989; Vice Chairman of Bar 1991; Chairman of Bar 1992. Chairman Committee of Inquiry into Tymawr Childrens Home 1991. *Recreation:* making bread, collecting antiques. *Address:* 36 Great Tew, Oxon, OX7 4AL. Farrars Building, Temple, London, EC4Y 7BD

WILLIAMS, Mr George Alun, *Currently:* Consultant S.D. Dew Prothero Williams. *Born on* 29 Aug 1925 at Rhoscolyn. *Son of* Thomas and Catherine Ellen. *Marriage:* to Gwenno Puleston, 1953. *Children:* Stephen Puleston and David Puleston. *Educated at* Holyhead County School; Wigan Mining Tech; Law Society, College of Law. *Career:* Royal Engineers; Assistant, David Thomas & Co., Llanrwst, 1953-56; practised as solicitor on own account as S.R. Dew Prothero Williams and in partnership, 1957- ; Anglesey County Council, 1961-74, chairman 1969-71; Welsh Council member from 1970; Gwynedd County Council 1974- , Chairman 1991; Hon. Sec. Tabor Presbyterian Church Valley, 1984- ; Former president Holyhead Rotary Club. *Recreation:* opera, classical music, playing the piano (very badly), gardening. *Address:* Rhianfa, Trearddur, Gwynedd, LL65 2BJ

WILLIAMS, Mr George Mervyn, CBE (1977); MC (1944); TD *Currently:* Vice Lord Lieutenant Mid Glamorgan; Directors of Kitagawa Europe Limited & Williams & Morgan Limited. *Born on* 30 Oct 1918 at London. *Youngest son of* the late Owain and Maude Williams and grandson of Morgan Stuart Williams. *Marriage:* to Grizel Cochrane Stewart DstJ, 1950. *Children:* Owain Williams *Educated at* Radley *Career:* Royal Fusiliers (Major) 1939-46; Gus 1946-49; Christie-Tyler Plc, Chairman, 1949-85; Formerly a director of Lloyds Bank Plc. & Chairman South Wales Regional Board; High Sheriff of Glamorgan 1966. *Recreation:* Gardening *Clubs:* Brooks's; Cardiff and County *Address:* Craig Y Bwla, Crickhowell, Powys, NP8 1SU. Llanharan House, Llanharan, Mid Glamorgan, CF7 9NR

WILLIAMS, Professor Glanmor, CBE, FBA, MA, DLitt, FRHistS, FSA. *Currently:* Retired. *Born on* 5 May 1920 at Dowlais. *Son of* the late Daniel and Ceinwen Williams. *Marriage:* 1946. *Children:* Margaret Nest and Jonathan Huw. *Educated at* Cyfarthfa Castle Grammar School 1931-37; University College of Wales 1937-42. *Career:* Lecturer in History, University College of Swansea 1945-52; Senior Lecturer 1952-57; Professor of History 1957-82; Vice-Principal 1975-78; Chairman BBC Wales 1965-71; British Library Bd 1973-80; Historic Buildings Council Wales 1962-89; Royal Commission Ancient Monuments Wales 1962-90; Chairman, Ancient Monuments Bd 1983- ; Chairman, Board of Celtic Studies 1970-90; President Cambrian Archaeological Assoc., 1980; Chairman, Welsh Folk Museum 1987-90; Chairman, Pantyfedwen Trusts 1973-79. Cymmrodorion Society Medal 1991. Vice-President, University College of Wales, Aberystwyth, 1986- ; Cadw Advisory Committee, 1991- . *Publications:* Yr Esgob Richard Davies 1953; The Welsh Church 1962; Owen Glendower 1966; Welsh Reformation Essays 1967; Reformation Views of History 1971; Language, Religion and Nationality in Wales 1979; Grym Tafodau Tan 1984; Wales, c1415-1642, 1987; (ed) Swansea: An Illustrated History 1990; The Celts and The Renaissance 1990; The Welsh and Their Religion 1991; The Reformation in Wales, 1991; Editor, Glamorgan County History 1971-88; editor Oxford History of Wales 1980- ; many historical articles in English and Welsh. *Address:* 11 Grosvenor Road, Sketty, Swansea, SA2 0SP.

WILLIAMS, Rev. Dr. Glen Garfield, BA., BD., (Wales), BD(London) D.Th(Tubingen), HonD.Th; Hon.DD *Currently:* Retired. *Born on* 14 Sept 1923 at Caerleon, Mon. *Son of* John Archibald Douglas and Violet May (nee

Tucker). *Marriage:* to Velia Cristina (nee Baglio), 1945. *Children:* none. *Educated at* Newport High School; University of Wales; University of London; University of Tubingen (F. R. G.) *Career:* Active Service North Africa and Italy, RAC, 1943-45; RAEC, 1945-47; Theological Student, 1947-55; Ordained Baptist Minister, 1955; Minister Dagnall Street Baptist Church, St Albans, 1955-59; European Secretary, Inter-Church Aid Div., World Council of Churches, Geneva, 1959-68; Executive Secretary, Conference of European Churches, Geneva, 1961-68; General Secretary, Conference of European Churches, Geneva, 1968-87; Visiting Professor of Church History and Ecumenics, Austin Presbyterian Theological Seminary, Texas, USA, 1987. *Publications:* Numerous articles on European Ecumenical subjects mainly in Continental learned or specialised journals and books. *Recreation:* Reading, travel and religious affairs. *Clubs:* Athenaeum, London. *Address:* 139 Rue De Lausanne, 1202 Geneva, Switzerland.

WILLIAMS, The Venerable Henry Leslie, B. A. *Currently:* Retired. *Born on* 26 Dec 1919 at Tregarth, Nr. Bangor. *Son of* Henry and Catherine Anne Williams. *Marriage:* to Elsie Marie Evans 1949. *Children:* David Wyn *Educated at* Bethesda County School; SDC Lampeter; St. Michael's Llandaff. *Career:* Curate of Aberdovey 1943-45; St. Mary's Bangor 1945-47; Chaplain HMS Conway 1947-49; Curate St. Mary's Handbridge Chester 1949-53; Vicar of Christ Church, Barnston 1953-84; Part time Chaplain, Clatterbridge Hospital 1955-75; C. F. (T. A.) 1953-62; R. D. Wirral North 1967-75; Canon of Chester Cathedral 1972-75; Archdeacon of Chester 1975-88. *Recreation:* Bee-keeping, fly-fishing. *Address:* 1 Bartholomew Way, Westminster Park, Chester, CH4 7RJ. Tel: 0244 675296

WILLIAMS, Huw Rhys Charles, MA(Oxon), Solicitor. *Currently:* Partner and Partner in Charge of Public Law, Edwards Geldad, Cardiff, since 1988. *Born on* 4 Jan 1954 at Llanelli, Dyfed. *Son of* the late David Charles Williams MSc and Glenys Margaret Williams (nee Williams). *Educated at* Llanelli Grammar School; Jesus College, Oxford. *Career:* Mid Glamorgan County Council 1978-87, (Principal Assistant Solicitor Environment from 1984); Edwards Geldard from 1987. *Recreation:* skiing, swimming, architecture, art, history. *Clubs:* United Oxford and Cambridge. *Address:* Dumfries House, Dumfries Place, Cardiff, CF1 4YF.

WILLIAMS, Mr Huw Tregelles, M. A., B. Mus., F.R.C.O. *Currently:* Head of Music, BBC Wales since 1986. *Born on* 13 March 1949 at Gowerton, Swansea. *Son of* the late Rev. Tregelles Williams and the late Bettie (nee Davies). *Educated at* Llanelli Boys' Grammar School; University College Cardiff. *Career:* Music Producer, BBC Wales 1973-78; Senior Producer 1978-86. Director, Llandaff Festival 1982-85. Member Welsh Arts Council 1988- ; Adjudicator Llangollen International Eisteddfod 1988- ; Organ recitalist: performances on Radio 3, S4C and BBC 2, inaugural recital at St. David's Hall, performances at Royal Northern College of Music and Royal Festival Hall etc. Many recordings with Welsh artists and Choirs. Broadcaster on radio and television. Executive Producer, Cardiff Singer of the World Competition. *Address:* C/o B.B.C. Wales, Broadcasting House, Llandaff, Cardiff, CF5 2YQ.

WILLIAMS, Councillor Ieuan, *Currently:* Local authority direct services organisation, Borough of Brecknock. *Born on* 25 Oct 1946 in Brecon, Wales. *Son of* the late Richard Thomas Williams and Sarah Jane Williams (nee Griffiths). *Marriage:* to Olga Catherine, 1988. *Educated at* Mount Street C. P., Brecon Secondary Modern Technical School. *Career:* RAF 1962-68; W. B. F. A. Ltd., 1968-71; Vice-Chair Brecon branch GMW Trade Union 1981; branch Secretary Brecon branch GMW Trade Union 1983; first elected Labour Councillor to Brecon Town Council since

1974, 1983; elected as a Labour Councillor onto Powys C. C., 1985; Regional Council Mem. South Western Region, GMB Trade Union 1985-87; elected Shop Steward and Safety Rep. GMW Trade Union 1981; Regional Cncl mem. S. Western Region, GMB Trade Union 1987-89; re-elected to Brecon Town Council 1987; re-elected to Powys C. C., 1989; delegate to Nat Congress, GMB Trade Union 1989; confirmed as Bch Sec Brecon branch GMB-APEX Partnership Trade Union 1989; Deputy Mayor, Brecon Town Council 1989-90; delegate to Nat Congress, GMB Trade Union 1990; First Labour Mayor since 1974, of Brecon Town Council 1990-91; re-elected to Brecon Town Council 1991; reg cncl mem. S. Western Region, GMB Trade Union 1991-93; Sch Gov., Penmaes, Mount Street Jnr and Mount Street Infants; Vice-Chair Mount Street Jnr and Mount Street Infants Schools and on 27th November 1987 opened the new Mount Street Jnr sch; Brecon and Radnor Const. Labour Party Secretary 1988-90; presently their Trade Union Liaison officer; Vice-Chair of Brecon Group of Powys Drug and Alcohol Abuse Management Body; Management ctteee of Brecon C. A. B; Chair of Central Gp of the Town & Comm Councils within the Brecon Beacons Nat Park; mem. Brecon Dist of the Powys Assoc., of Town and Community Councils and from this body was elected on to the Exec Cttee Powys Assoc of Town and Community Councils; mbr Brecon Guildhall Theatre Ltd Mangmnt Cttee; Brecon Sports Hall Local Mngmnt Cttee. *Recreation:* sit on Management Bd of Lion's Den Alcohol Free Bar in Brecon, collecting picture post cards, walking, eating out, travel, photography, crossword puzzles. *Clubs:* Life member Brecon RAFA Branch, Brecon Lion's International. *Address:* 7 Charles Street, The Watton, Brecon, Powys, LD3 7HF.

WILLIAMS, Mr John Albert Norman, *Currently:* Professional Flat Jockey, 1983-91. *Born on* 14 Jan 1948 at Swansea. *Son of* Mr Albert Williams and Mrs Norma Williams. *Marriage:* to Susan Mary Davies, 1971. *Children:* Emma Jayne, Claire Louise and Katie Victoria. *Educated at* Oystermouth Secondary Modern. *Career:* Professional Jump Jockey 1968-83. *Recreation:* golf, foreign travel.

WILLIAMS, The Venerable Archdeacon John Charles, *Currently:* retired. *Born on* 17 July 1912 at Cardiff. *Son of* William & Edith Williams. *Marriage:* to Agnes Mildred Hutchings, MA, 1940. *Children:* Mrs Edith Elizabeth J Cox BA and Peter Martin Williams MA, MSc, D. Phil. *Educated at* Cowbridge Sch; St. David's University Coll., Lampeter; University College, Oxford. *Career:* Asst. Curate, Christ Church, Summerfield, Birmingham, 1937-39; Asst Curate, Hales Owen, in charge of St. Margaret's Hasbury, 1939-43; Vicar: Cradley Heath, Staffs, 1943-48; Redditch, Worcs, 1948-59. Surrogate, 1951-71; Rural Dean of Bromsgrove, 1958-59; Rector, Hales Owen, 1959-70; Archdeacon of Dudley, 1968-75; Vicar of Dodderhill, 1970-75. Hon. Canon, Worcester Cathedral, 1965-75; Examng Chaplain to Bishop of Worcester, 1969-80; Dir. Worcester Diocesan Central Services, 1974-75; Dir. of Ordination Candidates, 1975-79. Archdeacon of Worcester 1975-80; Canon Residentiary Worcester Cathedral 1975-80. Substitute Chaplain, HM Prison Long Lartin, Evesham, 1982-87; Chairman, Redditch District Education Cttee, 1951-59; Chmn, Redditch County High School Governors, 1954-59; Chmn, Halesowen Grammar School Governors, 1963-70; Chmn, Halesowen Girl's High School Governors, 1963-70; Mem. Finance Committee of C of E General Synod, 1975-80; Chmn, Ecumenical Church's Cttee, Redditch Development Corporation, 1968-75. *Publications:* One Hundred Years, 1847-1947; A History of Cradley Heath Parish. *Recreation:* history of architecture, sailing. *Clubs:* Oxford University Occasionals, United Oxford & Cambridge University. *Address:* The Old Vicarage, Norton With Lenchwick, Evesham, Worcs., WR11 4TL.

WILLIAMS, Professor John Ellis Caerwyn, *Currently:*

retired. *Born on* 17 Jan 1912. *Son of* John R. and Maria Williams. *Marriage:* to Gwen Watkins, Gwauncaegurwen, 1946. *Children:* None. *Educated at* Ystalyfera Int. County School 1924-30; University Coll. of North Wales, Bangor 1930-39; National Univ. of Ireland, Dublin 1939-40; Trinity Coll. Dublin 1940-41; United Teological Coll. Aberystwyth 1941-44; Theo. Coll. Bala 1944-45. *Career:* Lecturer 1945-51, Senior Lecturer 1951-53, Professor of Welsh 1953-1965 at Univ. Coll. of North Wales, Bangor; Professor of Irish, Univ. Coll. of Wales, Aberystwyth, 1965-79; Director Centre for Advanced Welsh and Celtic Studies, Aberystwyth, 1979-85; Visiting Professor Univ. of California, Los Angeles 1968, Summer School Harvard 1968; Lectures: O'Donnell in Celtic Studies, Oxford Univ. 1979-80; Dr. Daniel Williams, Aberystwyth 1983; Sir John Morris Jones, Oxford 1983; R. T. Jenkins, Bangor 1983. Pres., Welsh Acad., 1989- (Chm., 1965-75); Mem., Council for Name Studies in GB and Ireland 1965- ; Cons. Editor, Univ. of Wales Welsh Dict. Fasc. xxiii-; Cons. Ed. Cyfres Beirdd y Tywysogion; Chm., Editorial Cttee, Welsh Acad. Dict., 1976-; Editor: Y Traethodydd 1965- ;Ysgrifau Beirniadol, i-xvii; Studia Celtica, i-xxiii; Llen y Llenor 1983- ; Llyfryddiaeth yr Iaith Gymraeg 1988. FSA 1975; FBA 1978; Hon. MRIA 1990; Hon. DLitt: Celt., Univ. of Ireland, 1967; Univ. of Wales 1983. Derek Allen Prize, British Acad., 1985. *Publications:* trans., Ystoriau ac Ysgrifau Padraic O Conaire 1947; trans., Yr Ebol Glas 1954; Traddodiad Llenyddol Iwerddon 1958; trans., Aderyn y Gwirionedd 1961; Edward Jones, Maes-y-Plwm 1963; ed. Llen a Llafar Mon 1963; trans., I. Williams, Canu Taliesin (Poems of Taliesin), 1968; The Court Poet in Medieval Ireland 1972; Y Storiwr Gwyddeleg a'i Chwedlau 1972; Beirdd y Tywysogion - Arolwg 1970, in Llen Cymru, and seperately 1972; ed. Literature in Celtic Countries 1971 trans. Jakez Riou, An Ti Satanazet (Diawl yn y Ty), 1972;Canu Crefyddol y Gogynfeirdd (Darlith Goffa Henry Lewis) 1976; The Poets of the Welsh Princes 1978;Cerddi'r Gogynfeirdd i Wragedd a Merched 1979; (with Mairin Ni Mhuiriosa) Traidisiun Liteartha Na nGael 1979; Geiriadurwyr y Gymraeg yng nghyfnod y Dadeni 1983; contribs to Encyclopaedia Britannica, Princeton Encyclopedia of Poetry and Poetics, Bull Bd of Celt. Studies, Celtica, Etudes Celt., Llen Cymru, etc. *Recreation:* Walking *Address:* Iwerydd, 6 Pant-y-Rhos, Aberystwyth, Dyfed., SY23 3QE. Centre For Advanced Welsh and Celtic Studies, Univ. Coll. of Wales, Aberystwyth, SY23 2AX.

WILLIAMS, John Godfrey, *Currently:* retired Solicitor. *Born on* 15 May 1922 at Abergavenny. *Son of* Godfrey Williams and Clara Ellen Williams. *Marriage:* to Margaret Jean David, 1966. *Children:* Richard John Williams. *Educated at* King Henry VIII Grammar School, Abergavenny. *Career:* Served H. M. Navy 1941-46; qualified as Solicitor, July 1950, Clerk to Justices Hay and Talgarth Divisions 1957-66; Superintendent Registrar Hay Division 1957-74; Pres. Herefordshire Breconshire and Radnorshire Incorporated Law Soc., 1977, Life member Cambrian Archaeological Soc 1955; Member British Dowsers Soc 1963; member Research into Lost Knowledge Organisation, London 1960. *Publications:* (with Chris Barber) The Ancient Stones of Wales 1989; articles in Stonehenge Viewpoint (Los Angeles) and Rilko journal, London. *Recreation:* country life, prehistory. *Clubs:* Abergavenny and Hay-on-Wye Conservative. *Address:* Aurora, 129 Chapel Road, Abergavenny, Gwent, NP7 7BL.

WILLIAMS, Professor John Gwynn, MA *Currently:* Emeritus Professor. *Born on* 19 June 1924 at Llanfechain, Powys. *Son of* The Rev John Ellis Williams and Annie Maude (nee Rowlands). *Marriage:* to Beryl Stafford, 1954, dau of the Rev. Stafford Henry Morgan Thomas (d. 1968) and of Blodwen (nee Griffiths (d. 1978). *Children:* William Gwynn (b. 1965), Gruffudd Rowland (b. 1969)and Thomas Ellis (b. 1972). *Educated at* Holywell Grammar School,

Clwyd; University College of North Wales, Bangor. *Career:* Royal Navy 1943-46; Staff Tutor, Department of Extra Mural Studies, Univesity of Liverpool 1951-54, University College of North Wales: Assistant Lecturer 1955, Professor of Welsh History 1963-83; Vice-Principal 1974-75; University of Wales: member of Council and Court 1973-85; Chairman, Press Board 1979-92; Director, Gregynog Press 1979-92; member, Daniel Committee 1987-89. National Library of Wales: President, 1986- (Vice President 1984-86). Cambrian Archaeological Association: President 1987-88. Hon. Soc. of Cymmrodorion: Vice President 1988- . Hon. member, Gorsedd of Bards 1984; member Royal Commission Ancient and Historical Monuments in Wales 1967-91. *Publications:* The University College of North Wales: Foundations, 1985; The Founding of the University College of North Wales (gwasg Gregynog, 1985); contributions to learned journals on seventeenth-century Wales. *Recreation:* Travelling, walking. *Address:* Llywenan, Siliwen, Bangor, Gwynedd, 2BS LL57.

WILLIAMS, Mr John Isgoed, LICW *Currently:* Consultant, Clerk of Works. *Born on* 14 Dec 1925 at Trawsfynydd, Gwynedd. *Son of* the late Hywel and Margaret Elizabeth Williams. *Marriage:* to Alice Eleanor (nee Rowlands). *Children:* Ieuan, Llion and Ynyr. *Educated at* Trawsfynydd Primary and Ffestiniog Central School. *Career:* Elected member of Trawsfynydd Community Council 1956; appointed sec. and treasurer, Dr. John Humphreys Charity, Trawsfynydd 1961; Transport Users Consultative Cttee for Wales 1968-73; Founder member Wales Association of Community and Town Councils 1975, Chairman 1976-79; Member of Cyngor Dosbarth Meirionnydd (Plaid Cymru) 1976-91; Member Welsh Centre for International Affairs Standing Cttee 1980; appointed member Gas Consumers Council for Wales 1980; Chairman North Wales Region National Housing and Town Planning Council 1985-87; executive member N. H. T. P. C., Britain 1985; Elected member Gwynedd County Council (Plaid Cymru) 1986; member Snowdonia Nat. Park Planning Cttee; Life member National Eisteddfod Court; Chairman Building Cttee, Cyfeillion Ellis Wynne, Las Ynys; Chairman Appeal Cttee Access for the Disabled, Theatr Ardudwy, Harlech; deacon and secretary Salem Baptist Church, Trawsfynydd. *Recreation:* Local Government, travelling. *Address:* Bryn Eglwys, Trawsfynydd., Gwynedd, LL41 4UB.

WILLIAMS, The Reverend Canon John James, TD, MA(Oxon) *Currently:* retired 1985. Now part-time Chaplain Worcester Royal Infirmary. *Born on* 4 May 1920 at Brymbo, Wrexham. *Son of* John Ifor Williams and Marie Williams. *Marriage:* to Kaye Law, 1953. *Children:* John Kelby, David Michael and Karen Jane. *Educated at* Grove Park School Wrexham; Lincoln College Oxford; St. Michael's Llandaff *Career:* Deacon 1944; Priest 1945 by Bishop of Saint Asaph; Curate of Rhosymedre 1944; Curate of Flint 1947; Curate of Eglwysrhos, Llandudno 1950; Vicar of Whixall, Salop 1953; Vicar of Prees, Salop 1957; Vicar of Powyke, Worcester 1964; Chaplain of Powick Psychiatric Hospital 1967-85. Chaplain Flint & Denbigh Yeomanry 1949; Chaplain 4KSLI(TA) 1954; Senior Chaplain 48 Div (TA) 1962, retired 1967. *Recreation:* reading, gardening. *Address:* 9 Saint Nicholas Road, Peopleton, Pershore, WR10 2EN.

WILLIAMS, Mr John Kyffin, OBE, RA, MA, DL. *Currently:* Artist (painter); Book Illustrator; Writer. *Born on* 9 May 1918 at Llangefni. *Son of* Henry Inglis Wynne Williams and Essyllt Mary (nee Williams). *Educated at* Shrewsbury School; Slade School of Fine Art; Univ Coll London. *Career:* Senior Art Master Highgate School 1944-73; Painter of Portraits and Landscape, mainly of Wales; Winston Churchill Fellow to Record Welsh in Patagonia, 1968; elected Associate of Royal Academy 1970; Royal Academician 1974; Hon MA University of Wales 1980;

Deputy Lieutenant for Gwynedd 1985; Hon Fellow Univ College of Wales Swansea 1989; Hon Fellow Univ Coll N. Wales Bangor 1991; Medal of Honorary Society of Cymmrodorion 1991; Order of The British Empire 1982; President of Royal Cambrian Academy 1969-75. Member of Art Committee Nat Museum of Wales 1965- . Retrospective Exhibition National Museum of Wales, Mostyn Gallery Llandudno, Glynn Vivian Art Gallery Swansea 1987. Fifteen one-man shows in London, Colnaghi, Leicester Galleries, Thackeray Gallery since 1948. *Publications:* Autobiography "Across The Straits", Duckworth 1973; Autobiography "A Wider Sky", Gomer 1991. *Recreation:* sport, history of Art, countryside. *Address:* Pwllfanogl, Llanfairpwll, Anglesey, Gwynedd, LL61 6PD.

WILLIAMS, Mr John Lasarus, MA *Currently:* retired Lecturer (Normal College, Bangor); Gwynedd County Councillor since 1974. *Born on* 29 Oct 1924 at Llangoed (Ynys Mon). *Son of* the late Lazarus Williams and the late Mary (nee Thomas). *Marriage:* to Beti (nee Jones) 1956. *Children:* Gwen, Rhiannon and Olwen. *Educated at* Llangoed Primary; Beaumaris Grammar; UCNW Bangor. *Career:* CWB, Higher: Maths, Chem, Physics 1943; BA Hons Welsh 1951; MA Educ 1954; Royal Navy 1943-46; Head of Welsh, Beaumaris Grammar 1955-61; Head of Welsh, Penygroes 1961-63; Co. founder 'UNDEB Y Gymraeg' 1965, and 'Sioe Gymraeg Porthaethwy'; Lecturer Normal 1963-81; Plaid Cymru Parliamentary Candidate 1970 and 1979 (Ynys Mon); Chairman Policy & Resources Gwynedd C. C., 1988; past Chair Educ; member of W. J. E. C., Assembly of Welsh Counties and Assoc of County Councils England and Wales. *Publications:* 'Ysgrifau Llenorion ed; articles in 'Y Faner' etc., 'Cofiant Emrys Ap Iwan' T. Gwynn Jones (Adargraffiad). *Recreation:* gardening, art appreciation, reading, radio. *Address:* Bodafon, Llanfair Pwllgwyngyll, Ynys Mon, Gwynedd, LL61 5YN.

WILLIAMS, Mr John Peter Rhys, MBE, MB, BS (London), LRCP, MRCS, FRCS (Edinburgh). *Currently:* Consultant Orthopaedic surgeon, Princess of Wales Hospital, Bridgend. *Born on* 2 March 1949 at Cardiff. *Son of* Peter and Margaret Williams. *Marriage:* to Pricilla. *Children:* Lauren, Anneliese, Francine and Peter. *Educated at* Bridgend G. S., Millfield, St. Mary's Hospital Medical School. *Career:* Reg. Orthopaedics, Cardiff 1980-82; Senior Reg. Orthopaedics, St. Mary's, London 1982-85; 55 Welsh Rugby Caps 1969-81; Captain 1978-79; British Lions, N. Z. 1971, SA 1974; British Junior Tennis Champion 1966. *Publications:* "JPR" autobiography, 1979; Trans Oral Fusion of the Cervical Spine, J. B. J. S. 1985. *Recreation:* Sport, music. *Clubs:* Wig & Pen; Lord's Taverners; Crawshay's Welsh RFC; Bridgend RFC; London Welsh RFC; Tondu RFC. *Address:* Llansannor Lodge, Llansannor, near Cowbridge, S. Glam., CF7 7RX.

WILLIAMS, Mr John Roland, BSc (Hons), OND, NCA. *Currently:* Chief Executive, Farmers' Union of Wales, since 1989. *Born on* 14 Feb 1952 at Chirk. *Son of* Aneurin and Catherine Williams. *Marriage:* to Eirlys Noela, 1980. *Children:* Mared (d), Ilan (s) and Buddug (d). *Educated at* Pontfadog CP School, Llangollen 1956-62; Oswestry School 1962-69; Llysfasi College of Agriculture Ruthin 1969-70; Welsh Agricultural College Aberystywth 1971-74; University College of North Wales Bangor 1976-79. *Career:* Lecturer, Welsh Agricultural College 1979-89; Courier, Enterprise Recording and Relief Farm Services in UK and abroad 1969-79. YFC Activities/representative positions 1971-78. CMA Board member 1984; member, Welsh Mountain Sheep Society Committee 1984-88; member, British Friesland Sheep Society Committee 1988; Secretary, Wales Farm Management Association 1985-89; Founder member of the Wales Farm Management Association. Member, The Rhoserchan Alcohol and Drug

Rehabilitation Centre's Management Committee. Member, NAC Sheep Club. *Publications:* regular contributor to the National Press, 1979-89. *Recreation:* travel: New Zealand, Canada and European countries, School Governor, Urdd activities, music, drama, Pedigree Suffolk sheep flock. *Address:* Llys Amaeth, Queen's Square, Aberystwyth, Dyfed, SY23 2EA. Tel: 0970 612755.

WILLIAMS, Mr Karl, LLB *Currently:* Barrister-at-Law, 34 Park Place, Cardiff, CF1 3TN. *Born on* 29 May 1959 at Tredegar. *Son of* Mr Joseph Bernard Williams and Mrs Maria Williams. *Marriage:* to Margaret McCann, 1991. *Educated at* De La Salle School; Saint Illtyd's College Cardiff; London School of Economics. *Address:* 34 Park Place, Cardiff, CF1 3TN. Tel: 0222 382731.

WILLIAMS, Lawrence Hugh, *Born on* 25 Aug 1929. *Son of* Col Lawrence Williams, OBE, JP, DL, by his 2 w and 1cous once removed, Elinor, da of Sir William. *Marriage:* to Sara, 1952, da of Prof Sir Harry Platt, 1 Bt, MD, MS, FRCS. *Children:* Emma (b. 1961 and Antonia (b. 1963). *Educated at* RNC Dartmouth. *Career:* cmmnd RM 1947; served in: Korea 1951, Cyprus 1955, Near East 1956; Capt 1959, ret. 1964; Lt Cdr RNXS 1965-87; farmer; chm Parciau Caravans Ltd 1964- ; underwriting mem Lloyd's; High Sheriff Anglesey 1970. *Clubs:* Army and Navy. *Address:* Parciau, Marianglas, Anglesey, LL73 8PH.

WILLIAMS, Professor Lawrence John, BA, MA *Currently:* Professor of Economic and Social History, U. C. W., Aberystwyth. *Born on* 12 June 1927 at Cardiff. *Son of* the late Elizabeth Jeanetta and the late Arthur John Williams. *Marriage:* to Mair Eluned (nee Hussey). *Children:* Stephen Richard, Katherine Sian and Roger John. *Educated at* Howard Gardens HS; University College Cardiff *Career:* Research Officer, Cabinet Office 1951-52, then successively Research Assistant. Lecturer, Senior Lecturer and Professor, UCW Aberystwyth. *Publications:* numerous articles plus thirteen books including: Welsh Historical Statistics; The South Wales Coal Industry, 1846-75; Why Are the British Bad at Manufacturing; The Struggle for Europe, 1992. *Recreation:* walking, reading, music. *Address:* 22 Danycoed, Aberystwyth, Dyfed, SY23 2HD.

WILLIAMS, Mr Lyndon John, BTEC HND Des *Currently:* Coaching/Development Officer W. B. U. (Welsh Badminton Union). *Born on* 24 Oct 1964 at Cardiff. *Son of* Eileen Doris Williams and Victor Garfield Williams. *Marriage:* to Sarah Williams. *Educated at* Eglwys Newydd Junior School; Whitchurch High School; South Glam Institute of H. E. Howard Gardens Art College. *Career:* Started Badminton at 6 years at Celyn Badminton Club. Member of only Welsh Junior side to win British Junior Championships 1982; First Senior cap v Ireland 1981; 62 Senior caps; undefeated in 3 Thomas Cup (World Team) championships; Junior European Doubles champion, Finland, 1983; Senior European doubles Bronze Medal, Norway, 1988; a record 7 consecutive National doubles partnered by Chris Rees 1982-88; 12 senior National titles in all. Current senior National doubles champion. Retired from International play in 1988 through back injury (still uncured). spent 3 years training in Redbridge, London before injury with Top English. 1 year part-time assistant W. B. U., 8 months full-time assistant; 18 months Development Officer. *Recreation:* design, bikes (motor), music concerts. *Clubs:* Cardiff Badminton, British Institute of Sports Coaches. *Address:* 6 Cantref Close, Thornhill, Cardiff, CF4 9HF. 20 Glan-Y-Nant Road, Whitchurch, Cardiff, CF4 1AP

WILLIAMS, Rev. Morgan John, BA, BD(Wales). *Currently:* retired. *Born on* 30 Aug 1910 at Aberdare, Mid Glamorgan. *Son of* Benjamin L. Williams and Elizabeth Williams (nee Watkins). *Marriage:* to Barbara (nee John), dau of Rev. D. R. John, Minister of Rhyduslyn Baplist Church, nr Clunderwen. *Children:* Rhys Watcyn Williams and Sian (Jones). *Educated at* Aberdare Boys Grammar School; Baptist College Cardiff; University College Cardiff.

Career: Minister of Zion, Ebbw Vale 1934-37, Abercarn 1937-49, North Road, Milford Haven 1949-58. General Secretary Baptist Union of Wales 1958-77; President of the Baptist Union of Wales 1977-78; Moderator of the Free Church Federal Council of England and Wales 1977. *Publications:* 'Thomas Lewis, Missionary', 1978. *Address:* 76 Dunraven Road, Sketty, Swansea, SA2 9LQ.

WILLIAMS, Owain Llewelyn, BA(Hons), Ph(dip). *Currently:* Art Director for film and television. *Born on* 10 Oct 1964 at Bridgend. *Son of* Maelgwyn Williams and Ann (nee Board). *Educated at* Brynteg Comprehensive, Bridge; South Glamorgan Inst; Kingston Polytechnic. *Career:* Rugby: Welsh Schools 1983, student 1984, 85, 86, Barbarians, Crawshays, Wolfhounds, Saltaires, Welsh Academicals, Penguins. Began playing with Glamorgan Wanderers 1983 - transferred to Bridgend 1987, represented Queensland, Australia 1988. Toured and played for Wales in Nanibia 1990, one cap, one try, also played for Wales B. *Recreation:* mainly keeping fit, work, cinema. *Clubs:* Bridgend Rugby Football, B & T's. *Address:* Ogmore Farm, Ogmore-By-Sea, Nr Bridgend, Mid Glamorgan, CF35 5BT. Tel: 0656 653650

WILLIAMS, Mr Owen John, MA (Oxon); Barrister-at-Law. *Currently:* Barrister; Company Chairman. *Born on* 17 May 1950 at Carmarthen. *Son of* Owen John Williams and Dilys Williams (nee Evans). *Marriage:* to Mary Elizabeth Evans. *Children:* Olivia Jane Williams. *Educated at* Ysgol Abermad; Harrow; University College, Oxford. *Career:* Graduated Modern History, Hons, Oxford 1972; Called to Bar, Middle Temple, Member of Wales & Chester Circuit 1974; Chairman, O. J. Williams & Son Ltd., O. J. Williams & Son (merchants) Ltd., O. J. Williams & Son (Transport) Ltd., 1975; Chairman, O. J. Williams & Son (Engineers) Ltd., 1981; Chairman, O. J. Williams Ltd., 1991; Director, St. Clears Market Co., 1975; Conservative Candidate, Ceredigion & Pembroke North 1987; Cons. Candidate, Mid & West Wales (European Elections), 1989; Conservative candidate, Ceredigion & Pembroke North 1992 general election. Non-Executive Director, East Dyfed Health Authority 1990-. *Recreation:* Racing, rugby, country and western music. *Clubs:* Aberystwyth Conservative; St. Stephen's Constitutional. *Address:* The Beeches, St. Clears, Dyfed, SA33 4BP. 4 Brick Court, Temple, London, EC4Y 9AD Tel: 0994 230355

WILLIAMS, Peter John Frederick, *Born on* 20 Aug 1935 at . *Son of* Clifford Thomas Williams, of Westwinds, Nash, Newport, Gwent and Ethel (nee Holmes). *Marriage:* to Gladys Bronwen, da of Albert Colbourne, 1958 (d. 1966). *Children:* Simon Nicholas Alexander (b. 1960) and Andrew John (b. 1961). *Educated at* Bassaleg GS; Newport Tech Coll; Newport Coll of Art; Welsh School of Architecture Cardiff (DipArch). *Career:* principal: Stowfield Ltd Newport, OLP/Y & H London, OLP/Peter Williams Ltd London, Shoredene Ltd Newport; director Detention Corp Ltd London; sncllr Magor & Mellons RDC 1966-67; member: Westminster C of C, Br Consultants Bureau, CLAWSA, Inst of Welsh Affairs; Freeman: City of London 1984, Worshipful Co of Chartered Architects; member ARIBA 1960, FRIBA 1970, fell Faculty of Building 1983. *Recreation:* sailing, golf, shooting, fishing. *Clubs:* St. Pierre Golf & Country, Chepstow, City Livery. *Address:* Bali Hai, Whitson, Newport, Gwent. 310 Nelson House, Dolphin Square, London, SW1 Tel: 0222 100283

WILLIAMS, Professor Rhys Watcyn, MA, DPhil(Oxon). *Currently:* Professor of German, University College of Swansea, since 1984. *Born on* 24 May 1946 at Caerleon, Gwent. *Son of* Morgan John Williams and Barbara Williams (nee John). *Marriage:* to Kathleen Gould, 1971. *Children:* Daniel and Thomas. *Educated at* Milford Haven Grammar; Bishop Gore School, Swansea; Jesus College, Oxford. *Career:* Tutorial Research Scholar, Bedford College, University of London 1972-74; Lecturer in German,

University of Manchester 1974-84; Dean of Faculty of Arts 1988-91; Chairman of School of European Languages 1989- ; President of International Carl Einstein Society 1987- . *Publications:* Carl Sternheim, A Critical Study, 1980; numerous articles on Twentieth-Century German Literature. *Address:* 48 Derwen Fawr Road, Derwen Fawr, Swansea, SA2 8AQ.

WILLIAMS, Mr Richard Derrick, MA (Cantab). *Currently:* Principal of Gloucestershire College of Arts and Technology until 1989 (since retired). *Born on* 30 March 1926 at Whitchurch, Shropshire. *Son of* the late Richard Leslie and the late Lizzie (nee Paddington). *Marriage:* to Beryl Newbury Stonebanks 1949. *Children:* Richard Keith, Clive David, Glynn Nicholas and Martin Guy. *Educated at* Whitchurch Grammar School and St. John's College, Cambridge. *Career:* Assistant Education Officer Suffolk 1960-65; Deputy Education Officer Bristol 1965-73; Chief Education Officer County of Avon 1973-77; President Educational Centres Association 1977-88. *Recreation:* Music; photography; cricket. *Address:* Swn Y Nant, Bontnewydd, Dolgellau, Gwynedd, LL40 2DF.

WILLIAMS, Mr Richard Hall, BSc, Wales. *Currently:* Wedi ymddeol. Dirprwy Gadeirydd Comisiwn Ffiniau Llywodaeth Leol Cymru, 1989-92. *Born on* 21 Oct 1921 at Caerdydd. *Son of* Edward Hall Williams a Kitty (nee Hughes). *Marriage:* i Nia Wynn Jones 1949. *Children:* Beti Wyn, Carys, Huw and Gareth. *Educated at* Ysgol Sir Y Barri a Rhifysgol Cymru, Aberystwyth. *Career:* Wedi gyrfa mewn llywodraeth leol, busnes ac addysg dechnegol, ymuno a'r Swyddfa Gymreig yn 1967. Wedi swyddi ym meysydd polisi economaidd, iechyd, materion Europeaidd, ymeddeol wedi sawl blwyddyn fel pennaeth Adran Amaethyddol y Swyddfa *Recreation:* Popeth Cymraeg a Chymreig *Address:* Argoed, 17 West Orchard Cres, Llandaff, Caerdydd, CF5 1AR

WILLIAMS, Mr Richard Wayne, LLB (Wales), LLM (London). *Currently:* Partner of Ince & Co., since 1978, firm of marine lawyers with offices in London, Hong Kong and Singapore and a representative office in Beijing. *Born on* 13 June 1948 at Glanamman. *Son of* the late David Victor and Sarah Irene Williams (nee Jones). *Marriage:* to Linda Pauline (nee Elvins), 1974. *Children:* Rhodri Christopher Wynn (b. 1982) and Robin Owen Wyn (b. 1985). *Educated at* Ystalyfera GS 1959-66; U. C. W., Aberystwyth 1966-69; U. C., London 1970-71. *Career:* Joined Ince & Co after leaving U. C., London, specializes in the field of carriage of goods by sea and chartering. Speaks regularly on these and related topics at conferences in the U. K., and abroad and publishes articles and papers in the U. K., and abroad. *Publications:* Limitation of Liability for Maritime Claims (1st edition 1986, 2nd edition 1992); numerous articles and papers on maritime law matters. *Recreation:* archaeology, travel, trying to keep up with my boys, playing the guitar badly. *Clubs:* Baltic Exchange, Supporting Member of London Maritime Arbitrators Association. *Address:* Ince & Co, Knollys House, 11 Byward Street, London, EC2R 5EN.

WILLIAMS, Reverend Canon Robert, QSJM OBE BA *Currently:* Clerk in Holy Orders. *Born on* 4 Jul 1920 at Talysarn, Caernarfon. *Son of* the late David Williams and the late Margaret Williams. *Marriage:* to Edith Myfanwy Jones 1949. *Children:* Mair Gwenllian. *Educated at* Penygroes Grammar School; Univ. of Wales; St. Michael's College, Llandaff; *Career:* Curate of Holyhead, Diocese of Bangor, 1945-55; Rector of Llangwnadl with Penllech with Bryncroes, 1955; Vicar of Aberdaron with Llanfaelrhys, 1989-90 (Retired); Member of Cyngor Dosbarth Dwyfor 1974-86; Member of Caernarfonshire County Council 1970-74; Gwynedd County Council, 1974- ; Member Welsh Water Authority, 1974-83; Member Gwynedd Health Authority, 1975-90, and Vice-Chairman 1982-90; Chairman Gwynedd County Council, 1986-87; *Recreation:* Country Life, Politics, Books and St. Francis of Assisi; *Address:*

Hendre Bach, Aberdaron, Pwllheli, Gwynedd, LL53 8BL.

WILLIAMS, Professor Robert Hughes, BSc; PhD; DSc; FInstP; C. Phys; FRS *Currently:* Head of The Dept. of Physics and Astronomy; University of Wales, Cardiff, 1984-. *Born on* 22 Dec 1941 at Bala, Wales. *Son of* Emrys and Catherine. *Marriage:* to Gillian Mary. *Children:* Sian Hughes and Alun Hughes. *Educated at* Bala Grammar; University College of N. Wales, Bangor. *Career:* Lecturer and Professor, Univ. of Ulster 1968-84; visiting Professor, Max-Plank Inst., Stuttgart 1976-77; visiting Professor, Xerox Research Labs., Palo-Alto, USA 1979-80; Chairman, SERC Synchron Radiation Cttee, UK 1982-85; Chairman, SERC Electronic Materials Cttee, UK 1990-; Chairman, S. Wales branch of Institute of Physics. *Publications:* over 250 papers in learned journals; "Metal Semiconductor Contacts", with E. H. Rhoderick. *Recreation:* football, walking, fishing. *Address:* Dolwerdd, Trerhyngyll, Cowbridge, S. Glam., CF7 7TN. Dept. of Physics and Astronomy, University of Wales, P.O. Box 913, Cardiff, CF1 3TH

WILLIAMS, Robert James, BA(Econ), FCA. *Currently:* Managing Director, Mills & Boon Ltd. *Born on* 12 Nov 1943 at Newport, Gwent. *Son of* Wyndham James and Minnie Williams. *Marriage:* to Janice Williams (nee Evans). *Children:* Ian James Williams. *Educated at* Newport High School; Sheffield University; Cooper & Lybrands Accountants. *Career:* Articles with Cooper Brothers 1966-69, qualified as Chartered Accountant 1969; Unilever 1970-77; various positions United Gas Industries 1977-79, Deputy Group Chief Accountant. Joined Mills & Boon 1979, Financial Controller, Director of Direct Marketing. *Recreation:* Sport- playing tennis, squash, skiing, rugby (watching). *Clubs:* Leatherhead LTC, Institute of Directors. *Address:* Mills & Boon Ltd, Eton House, 18-24 Paradise Road, Richmond, Surrey, TW9 1SR. Tel: 081 948 0444

WILLIAMS, Revd. Canon Professor Rowan Douglas, MA., DPhil., DD., FBA(1990) *Currently:* Lady Margaret Professor of Divinity, Oxford. Elected Bishop of Monmouth, Dec. 1991. *Born on* 14 June 1950 at Swansea. *Son of* Aneurin and Delphine Williams. *Marriage:* to Hilary Jane Paul 1981. *Children:* Rhiannon Mary. *Educated at* Dynevor School, Swansea; Christ's College, Cambridge; Christ Church & Wadham Coll. Oxford. *Career:* Lecturer, Coll. of the Resurrection, Mirfield, 1975-77; Chaplain, Westcott House, Cambridge, 1977-80; Assist. Priest, St. George's, Chesterton, 1980-83; Lecturer in Divinity, Cambridge Univ., 1980-86; Dean, Clare Coll., Cambridge, 1984-86; Mbr of Advisory Council for the Church's Ministry & Chairman of General Synod Commt for Theological Education, 1986-91; Mbr Doctrinal Commission of Church in Wales, 1987-. *Publications:* include, Arius: Heresy & Tradition, 1987; The Making of Orthodoxy (ed) 1989; Teresa of Avila, 1991 *Recreation:* Gardening, music and fiction *Address:* Priory House, Christ Church, Oxford., OX1 1DP.

WILLIAMS, Mr Steven Michael, *Currently:* Trainee Surveyor, James Scott Ltd. *Born on* 3 Oct 1970 at Neath. *Son of* Michael and Margaret Williams. *Educated at* Glanafon Comp School; Neath Tertiary College. *Career:* Athletics: Captained Wales under 20's and Welsh Schools. Basketball: under 15's 6 caps, Team Captain. Rugby: Welsh Schools under U18's 6 caps. Welsh Tertiary College -2 caps (captain). Wales under 19's- 1 cap. Welsh Students Wales under 21's, 4 caps (current Captain), Wales 'B', 1 cap. Wales 7 a side in Hong Kong 1990, toured Namibia 1990. Member Welsh Senior Squad 1989-90, 1990-91, World Cup Squad 1991, under 21's 1989-90, 1990-91, 1991-92. Crawshays Welsh. *Recreation:* music, films. *Clubs:* Neath, Swansea, Bryncoch Youth, Neath Tertiary, Baglan Juniors. *Address:* 109 Maes Ty Canol, Baglan, Port Talbot, West Glamorgan, SA12 8UR.

WILLIAMS, Mrs. Susan Eva, MBE *Currently:* Widow. *Born on* 17 Aug 1915. at Llantwit Major, S. Glamorgan. *Daughter of* Robert Henry Williams and Dorothy Marie Williams (nee Poole). *Marriage:* to Charles Crofts Llewellyn Williams, 1950 (decd). *Educated at* St. James's, West Malvern. *Career:* WAAF 1939-45; Magistrate 1961-85; High Sheriff, Glamorgan 1968; H. M. Lieutenant, S. Glamorgan 1981-85; H. M. Lord Lieutenant, S. Glamorgan 1985-90. *Recreation:* National Hunt racing. *Clubs:* Royal Air Force, Piccadilly. *Address:* Caercady, Welsh St. Donats, Cowbridge, S. Glam., CF7 7ST.

WILLIAMS, Professor Thomas Eifion Hopkins, CBE., PhD., CEng., FICE., FIHT., FCIT. *Currently:* Research Professor, Civil Engineering, Univ. of Southampton. *Born on* 14 June 1923 at Cwmtwrch, Swansea. *Son of* D. G. & A. M. Williams. *Marriage:* to Elizabeth Lois Davies 1947. *Children:* Maelor, Amanda and Huw. *Educated at* Ystradgynlais Grammar School; Univ. Coll. Swansea; Univ: Durham & California, Berkeley. *Career:* Research Stressman, Sir W. G. Armstrong-Whitworth Aircraft 1945; Ass Engr, Trunk Roads, Glam CC, 1946; Asst. Lectr Civil Engrg, UC Swansea 1947; Lectr. in Civil Engrg, King's College Univ. of Durham 1948; Resident Site Engr, R. T. James & Partners 1952; Vis. Prof. Civil Engrg, Northwestern Univ. 1957; Sen. Lectr, Reader and Prof. of Civil & Transport Engrg, King's Coll. Univ. of Durham (syseq. Univ. of Newcastle upon Tyne) 1958-67; Chrmn: Civil Engrg EDC, NEDO 1976-80; Chrmn: Standing Adv. Commt. on Trunk Rd Assessment, Dept of Transport 1980-87; Transport Commt, SRC. Roads Engrg Bd, ICE; British Nat. Commt. PIARC; Council and Transport Engrg Bd, Inst. Highway Engrs. (Pres. 1979-80); Specialist Adviser, Select Commts. 1989-90; House of Commons (Transport); House of Lords (European Communities). *Publications:* (Ed) Urban Survival and Traffic 1961; Capacity, in Traffic Eng. Practice 1963; Prediction of Traffic in Industrial Areas 1966; Autostrade: Strategia, di sviluppo industriale e la vitalita delle nostre citta 1965; Inter-City VTOL: Potential Traffic and Sites, 1969; Mobility and the Environment 1971 (ed) Transportation and Environment: policies, plans and practice 1973; Integrated Transport: developments and trends 1976; Air, Rail and Road Inter-City Transport Systems 1976; Land Use, Highways & Traffic 1977; Motor Vehicles in a Changing World 1978; Traffic Engineering 1960-81, 1981; Transport Policy: facts, frameworks: econometrics 1983; Assessment of Urban Roads 1986; contribs. to Proc. ICE, Highway Engrs, IMunE, Road International, Traffic Engrg and Control, Segnalazioni Stradali, OTA/PIARC Confs. *Recreation:* music. *Clubs:* Royal Automobile. *Address:* Willowdale, Woodlea Way, Ampfield, Romsey Hants., SO51 9DA.

WILLIAMS, Dr Trevor Illtyd, MA; BSc; D. Phil; C. Chem. FRSC; FRHistS *Currently:* Self employed writer and editor, especially History of Science and Technology. *Born on* 16 July 1921 at Bristol. *Son of* Illtyd Williams and Alma Mathilde (nee Sohlberg). *Marriage:* to Sylvia Irene Armstead, 1952. *Children:* Darryl, Lloyd, Clare, Adam and Benjamin. *Educated at* Clifton College; The Queen's College, Oxford. *Career:* Editor Endeavour, 1954- ; Academic relations advsr ICI, 1962-74; Chm. World list of Scientific Periodicals, 1966-88; Chm. Soc. for History of Alchemy & Chemistry, 1957-84; Mbr. Council Univ. Coll. Swansea, 1965-83; Mbr. Adv. Council Science Museum, 1972-84; Dexter award for contributions to History of Chemistry, American Chemical Soc., 1976; Visiting Fellow Australian Nat. Univ., 1981; Leverhulme Fellow, 1985. *Publications:* Drugs from Plants, 1943; The Chemical Industry, 1953; Jt. Ed. A History of Technology (8 vols.) 1954-84; (with T. K. Derry), A Short History of Technology, 1960; A Biographical Dictionary of Scientists (3rd Ed.) 1982; A History of the British Gas Industry, 1981; A Short History of 20th Century Technology, 1982; Florey:

Penicillin and After, 1984; The Triumph of Invention, 1987; Robert Robinson:Chemist Extraordinary, 1990; Science - Invention and Discovery in the 20th Century, 1990. *Recreation:* Gardening and hill walking *Clubs:* Athenaeum *Address:* 20 Blenheim Drive, Oxford. OX2 8DG. Pen-Y-Cwm, Corris Uchaf, Machynlleth, Powys, SY20 7HN. Tel: 0865 58591.

WILLIAMS, Professor William Elwyn, PhD; DSc. *Currently:* Professor of Mathematics, University of Surrey, since 1965. *Born on* 6 July 1931 at Llangefni, Anglesey. *Son of* Owen and Maggie Williams (nee Jones). *Marriage:* 1st to Judith Davies, 1956 (d. 1976); 2nd to Janet Adams, 1984. *Children:* Richard Aled. *Educated at* Holyhead C. S. School; Manchester University. *Career:* Research Associate, New York University 1954-55; Mathematician, English Electric 1955-57; Lecturer/Senior Lecturer, Applied Mathematics, University of Liverpool 1957-65. *Publications:* Numerous papers in mathematical journals; Partial Differential Equations OUP, 1980; Dynamics (van Nostrand), 1975; Applied Mathematics for Advanced Level (with A. R. Waltham) 1985, Hodder & Stoughton. *Recreation:* golf, walking, reading. *Address:* The Limes, Lime Grove, West Clandon, Guildford, Surrey.

WILLIAMS, County Concillor William Gwyn, BSc., 1982 *Currently:* Farmer. *Born on* 30 Oct 1960 at Denbigh. *Son of* Gwilym Clwyd Williams and Olwen (nee Jones). *Educated at* Ruthin School; Reading University. *Career:* Clwyd S. W. Liberal Assoc., Vice-Chairman, 1986-88; Elected Clwyd County Council, 1986- ; Bangor Univ. Court of Governors, 1986-89; Member Clwyd Health Authority, 1989-90; Liberal Democrat County Group Leader, 1990- ; Welsh Liberal Democrat Executive Ctee, 1989- ; Chairman, 1990- ; Member Welsh Agric. Coll., Joint Education Ctee, 1989- ; Member from 1987- ; Vice-Chairman Llysfasi Agric. Coll., Governors, 1989-; Liberal Democrat Prospective Parliamentary candidate, Clwyd S. West, President Clwyd S. W. Liberal Democrats, 1991- ; Member National Farmers Union; Farmers Union of Wales. *Recreation:* Gardening, music and reading. *Address:* Wern, Llanbedr Dyffryn, Clwyd, Ruthin Clwyd, LL15 1SW.

WILLIAMS, Mr William Hywel, M. A. (Cantab). *Currently:* VIth Form Master, Rugby School and Tutor of School House, Rugby School. *Born on* 3 June 1954 at Bangor. *Son of* Revd. & Mrs W. Raymond Williams. *Educated at* Ysgol Gymraeg Llandeilo; Bishop Gore School, Swansea; St. John's College, Cambridge (Exhibitioner and Senior Scholar). *Career:* 1st Class Pt. II, English Tripos 1977;IInd. Cl. Div. I, Pts. I, II, Historical Tripos 1975, 1976; Master's Prizeman; College Prizeman, Pendlebury Student in the History of Ideas 1977-80; Steel Student in Ecclesiastical History 1980-81; College Supervisor in History and English, St. John's College, Cambridge 1978-82; Chairman of Arnold Revisited, A National Colloquium on the future of Education in Britain 1988; Chairman of Educating Europe: Prospects and Realities, A National & International Colloquium on Secondary and Higher education in the Europe of the 1990's; Prospective Conservative Parliamentary Candidate, Aberavon 1990. *Publications:* Articles, essays, reviews (Daily Telegraph, Sunday Telegraph, Times Literary Supplement, Times Higher Education Supplement), Old School Ties: Education and Success in Britain (with Tim Devlin). *Recreation:* Languages, travel. *Clubs:* United Oxford & Cambridge, University Club. *Address:* 12 Hillmorton Road, Rugby, Warwickshire, CV22 5DQ. 55 Cherry Grove, Derwen Fawr, Swansea, SA2 8AU

WILLIAMS, Sir William Maxwell Harries (Max), *Currently:* Director: Royal Ins. plc 1985- ; Royal Ins. Holding plc 1988- ; Royal Ins. Co. of Canada 1991- ; 3i Group plc 1988- ; Garden Pension Trustees Ltd 1990- ; Waterloo Trustee Co. Ltd 1991- ; 3i Trustee Co. Ltd 1991- *Born on* 18 Feb 1926 at Fishguard. *Son of* Llwyd and Hilary

Williams. *Married:* to Jenifer Burgin. *Children:* Julia and Miranda. *Educated at* Nautical College, Pangbourne. *Career:* Served 178 Assault Field Regt. R. A. Far East (Captain) 1943-47; Admitted Solicitor 1950; Snr Partner Clifford-Turner 1984-87, Joint Senior Partner of (the merged firm of Coward Chance and Clifford Turner) Clifford Chance 1987-90; Law Society: Mbr of Council 1962-85, Pres. 1982-83; Mbr Crown Agents for Overseas Govrn and Admin. 1982-86; Lay mbr of Stock Exchange Council 1984-91; Chrmn of Review Board for Government Contracts 1986- ; Mbr Royal Commsn on Legal Services 1976-79; Commt of Management of Inst. of Advanced Legal Studies 1980-86; Council Wildfowl Trust (Hon Tresurer 1974-80; Pres City of London Law Soc. 1986-87; Mbr American Law Inst. 1985- ; Hon. mbr American Bar Assoc, Canadian Bar Assoc; Master Solicitor' Co 1986-87; Hon. Lld Birmingham 1983. *Recreation:* Golf, fishing and ornithology *Clubs:* Garrick; Marks; Flyfisher, Mid-Herts Golf. *Address:* Orinda, Holly Lane, Harpenden, Herts., AL5 5DY.

WILLIAMS, Colonel William Trevor, MA, FCIS, FBIM, MCIT. *Currently:* Director General, Engineering Industries Association. *Born on* 16 Oct 1925 at Cardiff. *Son of* Francis Harold Williams and Ellen Mabel (Gwyther) Newton Manorbier. *Marriage:* to Elizabeth, 1951, daughter of late Brigadier Arthur Goldie. *Children:* Alistair Stephen Boy Gwyther, Richard John Goldie, Diane Amanda and Mary Elizabeth. *Educated at* Whitchurch Grammar School; Staff College Camberley; Joint Staff College Latimer; Darwin College, University of Kent (MA). *Career:* Commissioned Infantry 1945. Regimental Service India. Malaya to 1949. Seconded to Guyanese Government 1964-65. Commander Maritime Air Regiment, Far East 1967-69. Project Officer National Defence College 1970-71. Advisor Ethiopian Government 1971-72. Colonel Rhine Army 1973-76. Chairman Berlin Committee. Head of Secretariat MoD 1976-77. Director Satra 1979-80. *Publications:* Military. *Recreation:* golf, photography. *Clubs:* Institute of Directors. *Address:* 15 Mill Lane, Lower Harble Down, Canterbury, Kent, CT2 8NE. Tel: 0227 768170. Engineering Industries Assoc., 16 Dartmouth Street, Westminster, London, SW1H 9BL. Tel: 071 222 2367.

WILLIAMS OF ELVEL, Lord Charles Cuthbert Powell, CBE., MA Oxon. *Currently:* Deputy Leader of the Opposition since 1989, opposition spokesman on Trade and Industry, since 1986 and on Energy, since 1988. *Born on* 9 Feb 1933 at Oxford. *Son of* the late Dr. H. P. Williams and Muriel De L. Williaazenove). *Marriage:* to Jane Gillian Portal 1975. *Children:* stepson: Justin Welby. *Educated at* Westminster School; Christ Church, Oxford (MA); LSE. *Career:* British Petroleum Co. Ltd., 1958-64; Bank of London and Montreal, 1964-66; Eurofinance SA, Paris 1966-70; Baring Brothers and Co. Ltd., 1970-77 (Man. Dir, 1971-77); Chm., Price Commn, 1977-79; Man. Dir 1980-82, Chm. 1982-85, Henry Ansbacher & Co. Ltd; Chief Exec., Henry Ansbacher Holdings PLC, 1982-85. Parly Candidate (Lab), Colchester, 1964. Founder Mem, Labour Econ. Finance and Taxation Assoc. (Vice-Chm., 1975-77, 1979-83). Director, Pergamon Holdings Ltd, 1985- ; Mirror Group Newspapers Ltd, 1985- . Chm. Acad. of St. Martins in the Fields, 1988- ; Pres., Council for Protection of Rural Wales, 1989 - . FRSA. *Recreation:* cricket (Oxford Univ. CC, 1953-55, Captain 1955; Essex CCC, 1953-59); music, real tennis. *Clubs:* Reform, MCC. *Address:* Pant-y-Rhiw, Llansantffraed-In-Elvel, Powys, LD1 5RH. 48 Thurloe Square, London, SW7 2SX

WILLIAMS-ELLIS, Mrs Elizabeth Ann, J. P. *Born on* 10 Nov 1935 at Lincoln. *Daughter of* Evan Christopher Lewis and Madge Constance Pilkington. *Marriage:* May, 1958. *Children:* Jonathan Clough, Christopher Rupert and Mark Roger. *Educated at* Rosemead. *Career:* Christies 1972-74; Winchester Bowring 1977-80; Committee member N. Wales Family Planning Assoc., 1963-72; Vice Pres

Caernarvonshire Red Cross 1964-72; Member Arts Purchasing Committee National Gallery and Museum of Wales 1966-74; Member Nat. Health Executive Committee 1970-72; Home Office Bail Project 1975-77; member Com. Westminster Soc., 1987- ; Selection panel for most outstanding new panel in City of Westminster 1990, 1989. Chairman Westminster DFAS. Deputy NAR Greater London 1992. *Recreation:* history, sailing, walking, fine arts. *Clubs:* The Berkley. *Address:* 18 Wilton Street, London, , SW1X 7AX.

WILLIAMS-WYNN, Sir (David) Watkin Bt., DL *Currently:* Landowner. *Born on* 18 Feb 1940 at London. *Son of* Sir Owen Watkin Williams-Wynn Bt. *Marriage:* 1st to Harriet V. Elspeth Tailyour; 2nd to Victoria Jane De'Ath. *Children:* Charles Edward Watkin, Alexandra June, Lucinda Jean and Robert Ewan Watkin from 1st marriage; Nicholas Watkin and Harry Watkin from 2nd marriage. *Educated at* Eton *Career:* Lt. Royal Dragoons, 1958-63; Major, Queens Own Yeomanry, 1967-78; Deputy Lieutenant Clwyd 1969; member, Agricultural Lands Tribunal (Wales), 1975; High Sherrif, Clwyd, 1990. *Publications:* Director of magazine 'Countryweek'. *Recreation:* fieldsports *Clubs:* Cavalry and Guards. *Address:* Plas-yn-Cefn, St. Asaph, Clwyd., LL17 OEY. Tel: 0745 582200

WILLIAMS-WYNNE, The Honourable Veronica Frances, *Currently:* Farmer. *Born on* 24 Mar 1953 at Epping, Essex. *Son of* Lord Buxton of Alsa and The late Lady Buxton. *Marriage:* to William Williams-Wynne, 1975. *Children:* Chloe, Leonora and Rose. *Educated at* St. Mary's School, Ascot. *Career:* Governor, Outward Bound Aberdovey, local WRVS Organiser 1975-92. President, Tywyn Girl Guides 1990- . *Recreation:* horses, tennis, wildlife, art. *Address:* Talybont Farm, Tywyn, Gwynedd, LL36 9LG. 25 Langham Mansions, Earls Court Square, London, SW5

WILSON, Sir (Robert) Donald, DL *Currently:* Chairman, Mersey Regional Health Authority since 1982. *Born on* 6 June 1922 at Wrexham. *Son of* John and Kate Wilson. *Marriage:* to E. Elizabeth Ellis, 1946. *Educated at* Grove Park School, Wrexham, Clwyd. *Career:* Served RAF, 1940-46; Tyre Industry 1946-60; Farming 1954- ; Member of Lloyd's 1970- ; Board member (part-time) NORWEB 1981-87; Chairman, Ayrshire Cattle Soc., 1966-67; Cheshire Branch C. L. A., 1980-82; Nat. Staff Committee, Admin, Catering & other Services 1983-85; Vice Chairman, Governors, Cheshire Coll. of Agric. 1980-84; High Sheriff, Cheshire 1985-86; D. L., 1987; FRSA 1986; Director of various farming and property companies. Member Teachers Review Body 1991- . *Recreation:* fishing, shooting. *Clubs:* Farmers, City (Chester). *Address:* The Oldfields, Pulford, Chester, Cheshire, CH4 9EJ.

WILSON, Mr Anthony Joseph, B. Ed (Hons); D.L.C. *Currently:* Member of European Parliament. *Born on* 6 July 1937 at Birkenhead. *Son of* the late Joseph Samuel and Eleanor Annie Wilson (nee Jones). *Marriage:* to June Mary (nee Sockett) 1960, divorced 1988. *Children:* Joseph Glen, Carla Jane and Jessica Lee. *Educated at* Birkenhead School; Loughborough College; University of Wales. *Career:* Teacher Guernsey 1960-66; Manager, St. Mary's Bay School Journey Centre, Kent 1966-69; Lecturer, North East Wales Institute (previously Denbighshire Tech. College), 1969-89; Wrexham Maelor Councillor 1970-73 and 1979-89; Vice-Chair Committee of Welsh District Councils 1987-89. *Recreation:* Camping, basketball. *Address:* 79 Ruabon Road, Wrexham, Clwyd, LL13 7PU.

WILSON, Professor David, M. Agr. Sc., PhD. *Currently:* Director, Welsh Plant Breeding Station, Head of IGER Plant Science Division. *Born on* 6 Oct 1935 at Edinburgh. *Son of* the late Thomas Wilson and the late Mary (nee Miller). *Marriage:* to Wendy Henderson 1958. *Children:* Rory James and Fiona Caroline. *Educated at* George Watson's College, Edin; HMS Conway School Ship; Univ.

Canterbury, N. Z. *Career:* MN Officer 1952-58; Lecturer, Linc. Coll., N. Z., 1962-63; Res. Scientist Dsir., N. Z., 1963-72; N. Z. Nat. Res. Fellow 1965-68; Res. Scientist WPBS Aberystwyth 1972; Head Dev. Genetics Dept. WPBS 1975-85; Head Crop Improvement Dept. 1985-89; Director WPBS and Head of Plant Science Division of IGER 1989- ; Hon. Prof. Dept. Agric Sci. Board Rur. Sci., Faculty of Rur. Sci., School Life Sciences; Member NIAB Herb Trials Adv. Committee. *Publications:* 56 Scientific publications, including 36 refereed papers and 20 scientific reviews and contributions to conference proceedings and text books. *Recreation:* Golf, gardening, walking, reading. *Clubs:* Conway. *Address:* AFRC Inst. of Grassland &, Environmental Research, Welsh Plant Breeding Station, Plas Gogerddan, Aberystwyth, SY23 3EB.

WILSON, Mr Francis Amcotts, O. St. J. *Currently:* retired Farmer ; Member of Lloyds. *Born on* 3 April 1922 at Builth Wells. *Son of* the late Commander A. T. L. Wilson RN and the late Mrs Margaret Wilson (nee Hirsch). *Marriage:* to Katherine Mary Scott (nee Bruce), 1968. *Children:* Robert Mathew (b. 1970) and Jane Mary (b. 1972). *Educated at* Shrewsbury School. *Career:* H. O. rating R. N. 1941, sub Lieut. RNVR served: Atlantic, Home waters and Med. 1942-45; member Builth RDC 1960-67; Breconshire C. C. 1967-74; Chairman, St. John Council for Brecknock 1980; High Sheriff Powys 1974-75. *Recreation:* shooting, fishing. *Clubs:* Army and Navy. *Address:* Garth House, Llangammarch Wells, Powys, LD4 4AL.

WILSON, Professor Herbert Rees, BSc, PhD, CPhys, FInstP, FRSA, FRSE. *Currently:* Professor Emeritus of Physics, University of Stirling. *Born on* 28 Jan 1929 at Nefyn, N. Wales. *Son of* the late Thomas Rees Wilson and the late Jane (nee Humphreys). *Marriage:* to Elizabeth Turner, 1952. *Children:* Iola, Neil and Helen. *Educated at* Twllheli Grammar School; University Coll of North Wales, Bangor. *Career:* Research Scientist, Wheatstone Physics Laboratory, King's College London 1952-57; Lecturer in Physics, Queen's College Dundee 1957-64; Research Associate, Harvard Medical School, Boston 1962; Senior Lecturer and Reader in Physics, Dundee Univ 1964-83; Prof of Physics, Univ of Stirling 1983-90; Head of Physics Dept 1983-88; Head, Division of Physics and Chemistry 1988-89. *Publications:* 'Diffraction of X-Rays by Proteins, Nucleic Acids and Viruses'(book); numerous research papers on biomolecular structures. *Recreation:* literature, theatre, travel. *Address:* Lower Bryanston, St Margaret's Drive, Dunblane, FK15 ODP. Dept of Biological and Molecular Sciences, University of Stirling, Stirling, FK9 4LA Tel: 0786 823105

WILSON, Mr Peter John Edgar Malyan, MB, BS, LRCP, FRCS(Eng), FRCS(Edin). *Currently:* Consultant neurosurgeon, West Glamorgan Health Authority. *Born on* 8 April 1933 at Portsmouth, Hants. *Son of* the late Herbert Edgar and the late Kathleen Phyllis Wilson. *Marriage:* to Patience Mary (nee Wood). *Children:* Mark Richard, James Alexander and Felicity Jane. *Educated at* Surbiton County Grammar School; Guy's Hospital, London. *Publications:* papers to various scientific journals on head injury; cervical spondylosis; pituitary tumours; surgical treatment of epilepsy; criteria for brain-death. *Address:* 40 West Cross Lane, Swansea, SA3 5LS.

WINCH, Hon. Mrs. Jean Rosemary Vera, *Currently:* Managing Castle Barn and two dogs. *Born on* 30 Oct 1928 in London. *Daughter of* 14th Viscount Falkland and Mrs Astley-Rushton. *Marriage:* to the late Capt. Henry Herman Evelyn Montague Winch, late Scots Guards and Former High Sheriff Merioneth. *Educated at* Lady Walsinghams, Norfolk. *Recreation:* flat racing, watching T.V., horse breeding. *Clubs:* Turf. *Address:* Castle Barn, Portmeirion, Penrhyndeudraeth, Gwynedd, LL48 6EN.

WINTER, Revd. David Brian, BA *Currently:* Priest in

charge, Ducklington and Bishop's Officer for Evangelism, Diocese of Oxford. *Born on* 19 Nov 1929 at London. *Son of* Walter George Winter and Winifred Ella Oughton. *Marriage:* to Christine Ellen Martin. *Children:* Philip David, Rebecca Ann and Adrian Luke. *Educated at* Machynlleth County School; Kings College, London; Oak Hill Theological College. *Career:* School Teacher 1954-59; Editor 'Crusade' 1959-70; Producer, BBC Religious Broadcasting 1970-84; Head of Religious Programmes, Radio 1984-87; Head of Religious Broadcasting, BBC 1987-89. *Publications:* 20 books, most recent titles: Truth in the Son 1987; Battered Bride 1989. *Recreation:* Watching and writing about cricket, golf. *Clubs:* member, Radio Academy. *Address:* The Rectory, 6 Standlake Road, Ducklington, Witney Oxon., OX8 7XG. 1 Hendy Ffaldybrenin, Llanwrda, Dyfed, SA19 8QE

WINTERBONE, Professor Desmond Edward, BSc., PhD., DSc., FIMechE., FEng. *Currently:* Professor of Mechanical Engineering, University of Manchester, Institute of Science and Technology, since 1980. *Born on* 15 Jan 1943 at Carmarthen. *Son of* the late Edward Frederick Winterbone and Hilda Phoebe (nee Lane). *Marriage:* to Veronica Mary (nee Cope), 1966. *Children:* Anne Caroline and Edward Joseph. *Educated at* Greenhill Grammar Tenby; Rugby College of Engineering and Technology; Univsity of Bath. *Career:* Student Apprentice - English Electric Co. Ltd Rugby, sandwich course with 6 months industry/6 months college, 1960-65; Awarded English Electric Student Apprentice Prize 1965; Design Engineer, Diesel Engine Division, English Electric Co. Ltd 1965-67; Research Fellow, University of Bath 1967-70; Lecturer, Department of Mechanical Engineering, UMIST, Manchester 1970-78; Senior Lecturer, Department of Mechanical Engineering, UMIST, Manchester 1978-80; Head of Mechanical Engineering, UMIST 1981-83; Vice Principal of External Affairs, UMIST 1986-88; Deputy Principal 1987-88; Head of Thermodynamics and Fluid Mechanics Division, Department of Mechanical Engineering 1990- ; Head of Mechanical Engineering Department 1991-. *Publications:* over 80 papers relating to mechanical engineering. *Recreation:* running, cycling (time trials), wind surfing, travel. *Address:* Dept of Mechanical Engineering, UMIST, P.O. Box 88, Manchester, M60 1QD.

WINTERS, Wyndham David, MBE *Currently:* retired. *Born on* 14 May 1919 at Port Talbot. *Son of* the late Alex and Mary Winters. *Educated at* Mountain School, Port Talbot. *Career:* Vice-Chairman Wales Council for Disabled, Ex Sport's Council for Wales member 1972-90; President Welsh Sports Association for the Disabled; President Federation Sports for the Disabled; Vice President The Welsh Paraplegic and Tetraplegic Association; Secretary The Welsh Paraplegic and Tetraplegic Association. Paul Harries Fellow, Rotary Foundation of Rotary International 1990. Taken part in 3 Paraplegic Olympic Games-Rome 1960, Tokyo 1964 and Israel 1968; taken part in 4 Paraplegic Commonwealth Games-Australia 1962, Jamaica 1966, Edinburgh 1974 and New Zealand 1974, captain of all 4; European Games France 1961, Awarded the MBE in 1974. Worked with the disabled sports for over 30 years and still doing so. *Recreation:* painting, "Disabled Sport's". *Clubs:* The Welsh Paraplegic and Tetraplegic Association. *Address:* C/o Rookwood Hospital, Llandaff, Cardiff, CF5 2YN.

WINTLE, Dr Richard Vivian, MBBS. *Currently:* Surgical H. O., Singleton Hospital Swansea. *Born on* 11 Dec 1967. at Kenfig Hill, Bridgend. *Son of* Vivian Wintle and Glenys (nee Mills). *Educated at* Cynffig Comprehensive School 1979-86; St. Marys Hospital Medical School, London, 1986-91. *Career:* Rugby: 2 Welsh schools under 15 caps (1983), 12 Welsh schools under 18 caps (1984-86); 1 Wales under 21 cap (1988); 2 Wales student caps (1989-90); 1 Wales 'B' cap (1988); 1 senior cap (1988). Athletics: Welsh Schools 100m Champion (15 group) 1983; Welsh Schools 100m and 200m champion (18 group), 1985; Wales junior men, 200m and 400m hurdles champion, 1985; Welsh senior mens 200m champion, 1985; senior International Vest 200m and 4 x 100m relay 1986. *Recreation:* diving, music, travelling, other sports. *Clubs:* Cardiff RFC, St. Mary's Hospital RFC. *Address:* 17 Picton Street, Kenfig Hill, Nr Bridgend, Mid Glam, CF33 6EF. St. Marys Hospital Medical, School, Norfolk Place, Paddington, London, W2

WITTON-DAVIES, The Venerable Carlyle, *Currently:* retired. *Born on* 10 June 1913 at Bangor, Gwynedd. *Son of* Thomas and Hilda Witton-Davies. *Marriage:* to Mary Rees, 1941. *Children:* Bridget, Cathlene, Anne, David, Edward, Frances and Giles. *Educated at* Friars School, Bangor; University of Bangor, BA; Oxford MA. *Career:* Sub-warden St. Michaels College, Llandaff; Canon of St. George's, Jerusalem; Dean of St. David's; Archdeacon of Oxford and Canon of Christ Church Oxford. Professor of Hebrew, University of Wales, Bangor. *Publications:* Journey of a Lifetime 1962; (part translated) Martin Buber's Hasidism 1948; (translated) Martin Buber's The Prophetic Faith 1949; contrib to Oxford Divtionary of the Christian Church 1957; contrib to The Mission of Israel 1963. *Address:* Hill Rise, 199 Divinity Road, Oxford, OX4 1LS.

WOOD, Gareth Haydn, A. R. A. M. *Currently:* Chairman of The Royal Philharmonic Orchestra. *Born on* 7 June 1950 at Cilfynydd. *Son of* Joyce Jenkins and Haydn W. G. Wood. *Educated at* Pontypridd Boys Grammar; Royal Academy of Music. *Career:* joined R. P. O. as a Double Bass Player 1972, 'Tomstone Arizona', performed at Royal Albert Hall by Massed Bands 1975, Butlins Youth Brass Band Test piece 1977, Suffolk Punch overture commissioned and performed by R. P. O., 1980, also 3 Sinfoniettas for the National Youth Orchestra of Wales, and Fantasy of Welsh Song for the Welsh Proms. *Publications:* works published by Boosey and Markes, Concord Partnership, R. Smith & Co., Rosehill Music. *Recreation:* golf, tennis, sunshine, travel. *Address:* 57 Marischal Road, London, SE13 5LE.

WOOD, Professor Graham Allan, MBChB, BDS, FDS, FRCS *Currently:* Consultant Oral & Maxillofacial Surgeon, N. Wales; Clinical Professor in Oral and Maxillofacial Surgery, University of Texas, Houston; Post-Graduate Tutor in Dentistry, N. Wales. *Born on* 15 Aug 1946 at Glasgow. *Son of* William Wales Wood and Ann Fleming Wood (nee Blackwood). *Marriage:* to Lindsay Balfour, 1970. *Children:* Nicola and Alexander *Educated at* Hillhead High School, Glasgow; University of Glasgow Dental School; University of Dundee Medical School. *Career:* General Dental Practice, Glasgow 1968-70; Glasgow Dental Hospital and School, HO Oral Surgery (6 months), SHO Conservative Dentistry (6 months), 1970-72; Registrar Oral & Maxillofacial Surgery (6 months), Canniesburn Hospital; Registrar Oral & Maxillofacial Surgery (6 months), Glasgow Dental Hospital and Victoria Infirmary; Dental Surgeon. Int Grenfell Assoc, Canada 1972-73; Registrar Oral & Maxillofacial Surgery Queen Elizabeth and Birmingham Accident Hospitals 1973-74; Part-time (Medical Undergraduate), General Dental Practice 1974-78; HO General Medicine (6 months), Stracathro Hospital, Angus 1978-79; HO General Surgery (6 months), HO Plastic Surgery (6 months) Ninewells Hospital and Dundee Royal Infirmary; Senr Registrar Oral & Maxillofacial Surgery, Glan Clwyd, Maelor and Caernarfon and Anglesey Hospital 1979-83; Clinical Tutor to Dental Students, Glasgow Dental Hospital and School 1970-72; Clinical Tutor to Medical and Dental Students, Queen Elizabeth Hospital, Birmingham 1973-74; Asst. Prof in Oral & Maxillofacial Surgery Jackson Memorial Hospital, Univ of Miami, Florida 1981; Clinical Tutor in Maxillofacial Oncology to Final Year Med Students, The Cancer Inst, Sri Lanka 1982; Consultant in charge of Senr Registrar, Registrar and Senr House Officer training as well as training of two Honorary Clinical Assistants in posts recognised for Fellowship training by the Royal Coll of Surgeons of England 1983- ; Hon Prof to the Univ of Texas, Houston, Dept of Oral & Maxillofacial Surgery 1988- ; Member Panel of Examiners for the Fellowship Examination in Dental Surgery, Royal Coll of Physycians & Surgeons, Glasgow. *Publications:* 'Cervical Oesophagostomy and the Use of a Fine Bore Tube', 1983; 'Nutritional Support for the Oral Surgery Patient', 1984; 'Anterior Midline Neck Webbing with Microgenia and Symphyseal Exostosis', 1983; 'The Uses of Lyophilised Bone in the Maxillofacial Regions', 1985; 'Cervical Paragangliomas: Report of Four Cases', 1986; 'The Chondroid Syringoma: Report of a Case in the Upper Lip', 1986; 'Eosinophilic Granuloma of the Mandibular Condyle', 1988; 'A Cheek Splitting Approach to the Posterior Oral Cavity: A Case Report', 1988; 'Small Plate Oseosynthesis for Mandibular Reconstruction Following Osteotomy for Tumour Resection', 1989; Reconstruction in a Case of Malignant Melanoma of the Palate', 1990; 'A Drape for Temporomandibular Joint Surgery', 1991; 'The Management of a Plastic Bullet Injury to the Mandible', 1992. *Recreation:* golfing, skiing, mountaineering, sailing, squash, music. *Clubs:* Rotary of St. Asap, Llyn Aled Sailing, Denbigh Golf, Oral Surgery of G. B. *Address:* Dept Of Oral & Maxillofacial, Surgery, Glan Clwyd Hospital, Bodelwynnan, Clwyd, LL18 5UJ. 'Northcote', Mount Road, St. Asaph, Clwyd, LL17 ODE

WOOD, John Peter, NDH, FIHort. *Currently:* Freelance Horticultural Journalist, since 1989. *Born on* 27 March 1925 at Mold, Clwyd. *Son of* the late Walter Ralph Wood and the late Henrietta Wood (nee Martin). *Marriage:* to Susan Maye White, 1956. *Children:* David Andrew and Victoria Catherine. *Educated at* Grove Park Grammar School, Wrexham; Seale-Hayne Agricultural College, Devon; Royal Horticultural Society's Gardens, Wisley, Surrey. *Career:* Assistant editor, Amateur Gardening 1952-67; Deputy editor, Amateur Gardening 1967-71; Editor, Amateur Gardening 1971-85; Consultant editor, Amateur Gardening 1985-89. *Publications:* contributions to Amateur Gardening and Channel 4's programme "Garden Club". *Recreation:* gardening, choral singing. *Address:* 1 Charlton House Court, Charlton Marshall, Blandford, Dorset, DT11 9NT.

WOOD, Bishop Stanley Mark, BA *Currently:* retired, 1987. *Born on* 21 May 1919 at Cardiff. *Son of* the late Arthur Mark Wood and Jane Wood (nee Thomas). *Marriage:* to Winifred Ruth Toase, 1947. *Children:* Felicity, Cecilia, Austin (deceased), Paul and David. *Educated at* Pontypridd Grammar; University College, Cardiff; College of the Resurrection Mirfield. *Career:* Deacon, 1942; Priest, 1942; Curate, St. Mary's Cardiff, 1942-45; Mission Priest S. Africa 1945-55; Rhodesia 1955-77; Rector Marandellas 1955-65; Dean of Salisbury 1965-70; Bishop of Matableland 1971-77; Assistant Bishop of Hereford 1977-81; Bishop of Ludlow 1981-87. *Address:* Glen Cottage, The Norton, Tenby, Dyfed., SA70 8AG. Tel: 0834 843463

WOODCOCK, Sir John, CBE, QPM, CBIM. *Currently:* H. M. Chief Inspector of Constabulary. *Born on* 14 Jan 1932 at Preston, Lancs. *Son of* Joseph and Elizabeth May Woodcock. *Marriage:* to Kathleen Margaret Abbot, 1953. *Children:* Clive John, Aidan Edward and Karen Belinda. *Educated at* Preston Technical College. *Career:* Lancashire Constabulary, Police Cadet, 1947, and served for three years at Force Headquarters, Hutton, being conscripted to the Army on National Service in May 1950, served in Army Special Investigation Branch in Japan and Korea, returning to the Force in 1952; Promoted to Sgnt, 1959, then to Inspector in charge of Accident Prevention Bch, 1963, later appointed as Personel Assist to the Chief Constable; Took command of the Westhoughton Sub-Division, 1965, then as Chief Insp of the Swinton Sub-Div; Promoted to

Superindendent in charge of the Dunstable, of the Bedford and Luton Constabulary being further promoted to Chief Superintendent later the same year, Div, 1967; appointed Assist Chief Constable 1968, of the Gwent Constabulary becoming the Deputy Chief Constable in 1970; Deputy Chief Constable of the Devon and Cornwall Constabulary, 1974; Chief Constable of North Yorks Police 1978 and of the South Wales Constabulary in 1979; Was appointed Her Majesty's Inspector of Constabulary for the Midlands and Wales on 1st July 1983, became Chief Insp of Constabulary on 1st April 1990. Awarded the Honour of Knight Batchelor in Birthday Honours of June 1989; Awarded The Queen's Police Medal for Distinguished Service, 1976; was made a Commander of the Most Excellent Order of the British Empire, 1983. Appointed Officer of the Most Venerable Order of St. John of Jerusalem, 1981; Formerly a Fellow of British Inst of Mgmnt he was elected a Companion of the Inst in 1980; Conferred a Papal Knighthood by His Holiness, Pope John Paul II in July 1984, in connection with his work regarding the Papal Visit to Wales, 1983. Mem. Governing Body for the United World College of the Atlantic; mem. of the Admin. Council of the Royal Jubilee Trusts, and Chairman of the South Wales Committee of The Royal Jubilee and Prince's Trusts. *Recreation:* golf, walking. *Clubs:* Hon., Member Swansea Lions. *Address:* Home Office, Queen Anne's Gate, London, SW1H 9AT.

WOODFORD, Dr F(rederick) Peter, MA Phd FRCPath CChem FRSC MBES *Currently:* Chief Scientific Officer to the Department of Health, London since 1984. *Born on* 8 Nov 1930 at Portland, Oregon USA. *Son of* Wilfrid Charles Woodford and Mabel Rose Woodford (nee Scarff). *Marriage:* Susan Silberman, 1964. *Children:* Julia. *Educated at* The Lewis School, Pengam, Glamorgan (Head Boy 1947-48); *Career:* Dosmus Exhibitioner, Balliol College, Oxford, 1948-52; Phd Leeds Univ., 1955; FRCPath 1984; CChem, FRSC 1990; MBES 1991; Waverley Gold Medal 1955; RAF 1956-57; Res. Fellow, Leiden Univ. Netherlands 1958-63; Visiting Lecturer, University of Tennesee, National Heart Institute, Bethesda, Maryland 1962-63; Guest Investigator Rockefeller University, New York, 1963-71; Scientific Historia, Ciba Foundation, & Scientific Associate, Wellcome Trust, 1971-74; Chmn. Council of Biology Editors 1969-70 (Meritorious Award 1984); Managing Editor, Journal of Atherosclerosis Research 1960-62; Journal of Lipid Research, 1964-69; Procs. of Nat. Acad. of Sciences (USA) 1970-71; Exec. Director Institute for Research into Mental and Multiple Handicap, 1974-77; Principal Scientific Officer, DHSS 1977-84; *Publications:* Scientific Articles on lipid and atherosclerosis research, scientific publication, organisation and ethics of scientific clinical services; Books on scientific writing, prevention and treatment of mental and physical handicap, training of medical technicians, etc. ; *Recreation:* Playing chamber music (pianist). *Clubs:* Athenaevm *Address:* 1 Akenside Road, London, NW3 5BS.

WORLEY, Mr Edward Michael, MA(Cantab), JP. *Currently:* Chairman/ Managing Director, William King Ltd since 1962; Vice Chairman, Wesleyan Assurance Society. *Born on* 29 March 1936 at Birmingham. *Son of* the late Clifford Worley and the late Hilda Worley(nee Johnson). *Marriage:* to Ann Patricia Bailey, 1966. *Children:* Andrew, Thomas and Rachel. *Educated at* Uppingham School; Downing College, Cambridge. *Career:* Steel Company of Wales Ltd., Port Talbot 1957-62; President, National Association of Steel Stockholders 1988-90. *Recreation:* gardening, sailing, reading, working. *Clubs:* *Address:* Parc Canol, St. Dogmaels, Cardigan, Dyfed, SA43 3JN. 50 Somerset Road, Edgbaston, Birmingham, B15 2PD

WORMALD, Dame Ethel (May), DBE; JP; DL; BA. *Currently:* retired. *Born on* 19 Nov 1901 at Blyth, Tyneside. *Daughter of* John Robert Robinson and Alice Fulbeck. *Marriage:* to Stanley Wormald, 1923. *Children:* Derek

Z

ZAMBONI, Mr Richard Frederick Charles, FCA, CBIM. *Currently:* Managing Director, Sun Life Assurance Society plc 1979-89. *Born on* 28 July 1930 at Richmond, Surrey. *Son of* the late Alfred Charles Zamboni and the late Frances (nee Hosler). *Marriage:* to Pamela Joan (nee Marshall), 1960. *Children:* Edward, Rupert and Charlotte. *Educated at* Monkton House School, Cardiff. *Career:* articled to Gordon Thomas & Pickard, Chartered Accountants; Chief Accountant, British Egg Marketing Board 1965-71; Chief Accountant, Sun Life Assurance Society plc 1972-76; General Manager 1976-79; Director 1975-89; Vice Chairman 1986-89; Director, Worldtech Ventures Ltd., 1981-87; Member, Management Committee, Life Offices Assoc., 1981-86; Deputy Chairman 1985-86; Chairman, Life Insurance Council of Association of British Insurers 1986-88; Member: Council, Chartered Insurance Institute 1983-85; Member: Life Assurance and Unit Trust Regulatory Organisation's steering group 1985-86; Director, Avon Enterprise Fund PLC 1984- , Chairman 1990- ; Chairman, Council of Management, Grange Training Centre for Handicapped 1991- ; President, Insurance Offices RFU 1985-87; President, Old Monktonians Association 1990- ; Liveryman, Worshipful Company of Insurers. *Recreation:* ornithology, gardening. *Address:* Long Meadow, Beech Avenue, Effingham, Surrey, KT24 5PH.

ZEHETMAYR, Mr John Walter Lloyd, OBE, VRD, BA, FIFor. *Currently:* Retired. *Born on* 24 Dec 1921. at Twickenham. *Son of* the late Walter Zehetmayr and the late Gladys (neePembroke). *Marriage:* to Isabell (Betty) Neill Kennedy 1945. *Children:* Brian, Peter and Susan. *Educated at* St. Paul's Hammersmith; Keble College, Oxford. *Career:* RNVR/RNR 1942-66 (despatches), now Lieut. Cdr. RNR (rtd); Forestry Commission: Silviculturist 1948, Chief Work Study Officer 1956, Conservator West Scotland 1964, Senior Officer Wales and Conservator South Wales 1966-81; Prince of Wales Cttee, member 1970-89, chaired various groups; member, Brecon Beacons National Park Cttee 1982-91; Chairman, Forestry Safety Council 1986-92. *Publications:* Experiments in Tree Planting on Peat, 1954; Afforestation of Upland Heaths, 1960; The Gwent Small Woods Project 1979-84, 1985; Forestry in Wales 1985; Effectiveness of Health & Safety Measures in Forestry (un-published). *Recreation:* Nature Conservation, gardening, skiing. *Address:* The Haven, 13 Augusta Road, Penarth, S. Glam., CF6 2RH. Tel: 0222 701694

ZIENKIEWICZ, Professor Olgierd Cecil, CBE; FRS; F. Eng; D. Sc. *Currently:* Director, Inst. Num. Meth. Engineering, and Professor Emeritus, University College, Swansea; Unesco Professor, University of Catalunya, Barcelona; Royal Society Kan Tong Po Professor Univ. of Hong Kong. *Born on* 18 May 1921 at Caterham, Surrey. *Son of* Casimir Raphael and Edith Violet (nee Penny). *Marriage:* to Helen Jean (nee Fleming). *Children:* Andrew Olgierd, David John and Krystyna Helen. *Educated at* Imperial College London. *Career:* B. Sc; Ph. D. at Imperial College London 1945; Civil Engineer, Sir William Halcrow & Partners 1945-49; Lecturer, University of Edinburgh 1949-57; Professor, Northwestern University USA 1957-61; Head of Civil Engineering Dept, 1961-88, and Director Inst. Numcilcol Methods, Univ. College, Swansea 1961- ; He has received many honorary degrees including ones from Portugal, Ireland, Belgium, Norway, Sweden, China, Poland, Scotland, Hungary, Italy, Hong Kong and the United States; he has also received many special honors and medals including the title of Commander of the British Empire and the Royal Medal from H. M. Queen Elizabeth 11, the "Carl Friedrich Gauss" medal of The West German Academy of Science, the Nathan Newmark Medal of the American Society of Civil Engineers, the James Alfred Ewing Medal of the Institution of Civil Eng (UK), the Worcester Warner Reed Medal of the American Society of Mechanical Engineers, the Gold medal of the Institution of Structural Engineers (UK) and was elected as Foreign Member of the United States National Academy of Engineering and of the Polish Academy of Science; he is one of the early pioneers of the finite element method and the first to realize its general potential for solution of problems outside the area of solid mechanics; he is a founder member of the French Association of GAMNI and of the International Association of Institutional Computational Mechanics; Professor Zienkiewicz has, with his team of researchers, contributed many fundamental developments of the method which today make it the widely applicable tool of computational mechanics. *Publications:* He founded the first journal dealing with computational mechanics in 1968 (int. J. Numerical Methods in Engineering); The books: Finite Element Method; The Finite Element Method in Structural Mechanics, McGraw Hill, 1967; The Finite Element in Engineering Science, McGraw Hill, 1971; the later editions of the book The Finite Element Method 111, McGraw Hill, 1977 (787 pp) and The Finite Element Method 1V, with R. L. Taylor (2 vols. pp 1400) McGraw Hill, 1989/91, remain today the standard reference texts. *Recreation:* Sailing, swimming, antique collecting. *Clubs:* Athenaeum *Address:* 29 Somerset Road, Langland, Swansea SA3 4PG. Institute Numerical Methods In Engineering, University College, Swansea SA2 8PP Tel: 0792 295250

STOP PRESS

The publishers would like to point out that following a general election in April 1992, a number of details in some entries may have changed. Some are listed below. V.I.P. WALES 1993 will, of course, reflect all such changes.

Monday 13th April 1992: **Rt. Hon. Neil Kinnock, M.P.,** resigns as Leader of the Labour Party. In a cabinet reshuffle after the Conservative Government is re-elected, **Rt. Hon. Michael Heseltine, M.P.,** becomes Secretary of State for Trade and Industry. **Rt. Hon. David Hunt, M.P.,** continues as Secretary of State for Wales. **Cynog Dafis** is elected M.P. for Ceredigion and Pembroke North, replacing the Liberal M.P. Geraint Howells. A biography of Cynog Dafis appears below.

EDITORIAL NOTE:
The entry for **Gilli Davies** is unfortunately inaccurate; an amended version appears here. V.I.P. WALES would like to apologise for any inconvenience this may have caused.

DAFIS, Cynog, *Currently:* Plaid Cymru - Green M.P., Ceredigion and Pembroke North. *Born* 1938 at Treboeth, Swansea. *Educated at* Aberaeron County Secondary School, Neath Boys' Grammar School (A-level in English, Welsh, History), UCW Aberystwyth (1956-60 Honours Degree English; Teacher's Certificate), UCW Aberystwyth (1978-79 MEd) *Career:* Pontardawe College of Further Education 1960-62; Newcastle Emlyn Secondary School 1962-80: Head of English; Aberaeron Comprehensive School 1980-84; Dyffryn Teifi Comprehensive School 1984-91: Head of English; Department of Adult Continuing Education University of Wales Swansea 1991-92: Research Officer; 1992 Elected Member of Parliament for Constituency of Ceredigion and Pembroke North. Founder Member of Cantref Housing Association and Chairperson for the last three years. Member of Bwlch y Fadfa Unitarian Chapel. Member of Plaid Cymru National Executive over several years; formerly editor of monthly Y Ddraig Goch, Vice-chair Publications and Publicity. Influential in creating links with Green Party Wales. *Publications:* Author of numerous articles on Welsh political life, bilingualism etc. *Address:* Plaid Cymru Offices, Pier Street, Aberystwyth, Dyfed.

DAVIES, Gilli, cordon blue certificate *Currently:* FOOD Editor, Thomson Regional Newspapers, Freelance journalist, author, broadcaster, TV presenter and cook, specialist in Welsh food. *Born on* 18 Oct 1950 at Sleaford, Lincs. *Daughter of* Douglas Arthur & Barbara Peacock. *Marriage:* to Alun James Davies, 1973. *Children:* Max, Augusta and Bonnie. *Educated at* Winceby House School, Bexhill; Secretarial and Cookery Diplomas. *Career:* 1970 Opened a Bistro in the Buttery Bar of St.Anthony's College for Graduates in Oxford. 1972 Chalet girl in Switzerland. Head Cook at the Open Air Theatre in Regent's Park. 1973 Ran courses of Cookery Demonstrations for the Royal Army Education Corps in Osnabruck, West Germany. 1974

Appointed Catering Manager in a country hotel in Northern Ireland. 1978 Managed two restaurants for the Army in Berlin. Broadcast on British Forces Broadcasting Services in Berlin and Cologne with a 'live' cookery spot. Produced an accompanying cook book. Wrote cookery columns for the Forces magazines The Berlin Bulletin and Sixth Sense. Took part in the Ski Leaders Course with the Ski Club of Great Britain, and subsequently lead annual parties in the Alps for members of the Ski Club. Set up a Directors Dining Room for Alan Mann's Aviation Company in Surrey. 1985 Returned to Cardiff after 10 years abroad. Broadcast on Red Dragon Radio. Wrote for Western Mail and had weekly page in Echo about food in Wales. Took a business course. Appeared as guest on BBC Wales and HTV in various chat shows. Broadcast regularly on 'The Food Show' on BBC Wales, Radio. Gave 'microwave' cookery demonstrations. Became 'Welsh' correspondant for TASTE magazine. Contributed to various national magazines and travel and ski books. Commissioned by Grafton (Collins) to write cook book on Welsh food, LAMB LEEKS and LAVERBREAD, published Spring 1989. 1987 Moved to Cyprus with British Forces, broadcast and wrote regularly for British and Cypriot media. Wrote and published 'A TASTE OF CYPRUS' by Interworld Publications in 1990. Wrote GOOD FOOD GUIDE TO CYPRUS for Cyprus Consumer Council. 1989 Returned to Wales. Submitted entry for TASTE OF WALES guides to hotels and restaurants. Researched/presented BBC Wales TV series TASTES OF WALES. Broadcast nationally. Wrote accompanying cook book for TV series. Contributed to South Wales Evening Post, Western Mail and Evening Echo. Worked with the Media to highlight and promote quality food in Wales by means of TV, freelance journalism and public appearances. *Recreation:* sport - skiing, swimming, food. *Clubs:* Guild of Food Writers. *Address:* Glebe Farm, St.Andrew's Major, S.Glamorgan CF6 4HD. Tel: 0222 514141.